Sociology

Wes. 11

Sociology:
A Down-to-Earth Approach

FOURTH EDITION

▼

James M. Henslin

Southern Illinois University, Edwardsville

Allyn and Bacon

Boston   London   Toronto   Sydney   Tokyo   Singapore

Executive Editor-in-Chief, Social Sciences: Karen Hanson
Editorial Assistant: Heather Ahlstrom
Cover Administrator: Linda Knowles
Composition and Prepress Buyer: Linda Cox
Manufacturing Buyer: Megan Cochran
Marketing Manager: Suzy Spivey
Signing Representative: Ward Moore
Photo Researcher: Stephen Forsling
Fine Art Researcher: Laurie Frankenthaler
Editorial-Production Service: The Book Company
Text Designer: Carol Somberg, Omegatype Typography, Inc.
Electronic Composition: Omegatype Typography, Inc.
Cover Designer: Susan Paradise

Copyright © 1999, 1997, 1995, 1993 by James M. Henslin
Allyn and Bacon
A Viacom Company
Needham Heights, Massachusetts 02194

Internet: www.abacon.com

Library of Congress Cataloging-in-Publication Data

Henslin, James M.
   Sociology : a down-to-earth approach / James M. Henslin. — 4th
ed.
      p.   cm.
   Includes bibliographical references and index.
   ISBN 0-205-28653-4
   1. Sociology.   I. Title.
   HM51.H398   1999
301—dc21   96-17397
                                                      CIP

Chapter Opener Art Credits:

Chapter 1: *Crowd with Happy Faces* by Margaret Cusack, 1983. Machine stitch appliqué. © Margaret Cusack/SIS.

Chapter 2: *Clan Songs* by Tony Abeyta, 1995. Collagraph, 18" x 24". Courtesy of El Cerro Graphics.

Chapter 3: *Man Reading to Child* by Cynthia Fitting, 1992. Gouache, water color opaque. © Cynthia Fitting/SIS.

Chapter 4: *Patria B* by Alejandro Xul Solar, 1925. Water color, crayon, and pencil. Christie's Images/SuperStock.

Chapter 5: *Untitled* by Diana Ong, 1995. Diana Ong/SuperStock.

Chapter 6: *Chief Robes* by Helen Hardin, 1968. © Helen Hardin 1968. Photograph © Cradoc Bagshaw 1998.

Chapter 7: *Conference in Color* by Diana Ong, 1997. Computer graphics. Diana Ong/SuperStock.

Chapter 8: *Judgement After the War* by Tsing-Fang Chen, 1977. Acrylic on canvas. Lucia Gallery, New York City/TF Chen/SuperStock.

Chapter 9: *Farm in Haiti* by Roosevelt. Oil on canvas, 100 x 76 cm. Private Collection/Van Hoorick Fine Art/SuperStock.

Chapter 10: *City Gleaners* by Tsing-Fang Chen. Paul Lee Collection/TF Chen/SuperStock.

Chapter 11: *Dissension* by Wendy Seller, 1993. Oil on canvas, 34" x 30". © 1993 Wendy Seller. In the collection of Robert and Elayne Simandl.

Chapter 12: *Revolt On the Amistad* by Jacob Lawrence, 1989. Gouache/paper, 29 $\frac{3}{4}$" x 33". Photo by Chris Eden. Courtesy of the artist and Francine Seders Gallery, Seattle, WA.

Chapter 13: *Fragments* by Deidre Scherer, 1987. Fabric and thread, 26" x 22". © 1987 by Deidre Scherer. Photo by Jeff Baird.

Chapter 14: *Workers Walking in a City Landscape* by Harvey Chan, 1996. Acrylic on board. © Harvey/Chan/SIS.

Chapter 15: *Hail to the Statue of Liberty* by Tsing-Fang Chen, circa 1986. Acrylic on canvas, 72" x 50". Lucia Gallery, New York City/TF Chen/SuperStock.

Chapter Opener Art Credits and Photo Credits continue on page 719, which is a continuation of this copyright page.

Printed in the United States of America
10 9 8 7 6 5 6 5 4 3 2   VHP 02 01 00 99 98

To my fellow sociologists, who do such creative research on social life and who communicate the sociological imagination to generations of students.

With my sincere admiration and appreciation

Brief Contents

Contents

PART II   Social Groups and Social Control

PART III   *Social Inequality*

PART IV   *Social Institutions*

PART V Social Change

Boxes

▼ Perspectives

▼ Thinking Critically About Social Controversy

To the Student from the Author

If you like to watch people and try to figure out why they do what they do, you will like sociology. Sociology pries open the doors of society, so you can see what goes on behind them.

In this venture into sociology, you will see especially how social class sets us on different paths in life, and how in one direction these paths lead to better health, more education, higher income, even better marriages—and in the other to more illness and disease, higher school dropout rates, lower income, and greater chances of having a failed marriage. These paths even affect your chances of making it to your first birthday, as well as of getting in trouble with the police—and of reading this book in the first place.

When I took my first course in sociology, I was "hooked." Seeing how marvelously my life had been affected by these larger group influences opened my eyes to a new world, one that has been fascinating to explore. I hope that this will be your experience also.

From how people become homeless to how they become presidents, from why women are treated as second-class citizens around the world to why people commit suicide—all are part of sociology. This breadth, in fact, is what makes sociology so intriguing. We can place the sociological lens on broad features of society, such as social class, gender, and race, and then immediately turn our focus to the small-scale aspects of everyday life. If we look at two people interacting—whether quarreling or kissing—we see how these broad features of society are being played out in their lives.

We aren't born with instincts. We don't come into this world with preconceived notions of what life should be like. At birth, we have no ideas of race, gender, age, social class, of how people "ought" to be. Yet we all learn such things as part of growing up in our society. Uncovering the "hows" and the "whys" of this process is also part of sociology's fascination.

One of sociology's many pleasures is that as we study life in groups (an apt definition of sociology), whether those groups be in some far-off part of the world (if there still are far-off places) or in some nearby corner of our own society, we constantly gain insights into our own selves. As we see how other people's customs influence their lives, the effects of our own society on ourselves become more visible.

You can look forward to reading this book, then, for it can be the path to a new way of looking at the social world—and in the process, it can help you to better understand both society and yourself.

I would count it a privilege if you would share with me your experiences with this book. If there are sections of this text that you especially enjoy, or that you wish to comment on for whatever reason, don't hesitate to write me. I enjoy communicating with students.

I wish you the very best in college—and in your career afterward. It is my sincere hope that *Sociology: A Down-to-Earth Approach* contributes to that success.

James M. Henslin
Department of Sociology
Southern Illinois University
Edwardsville, IL 62026
henslin@aol.com

Preface

To study sociology is to embark on a fascinating journey into a new world of perception and understanding. It is an exploration of other worlds and ideas far from your own—as well as a quest to understand your own world and ideas. Since this book is designed to help you on this journey, I'd like to show you how it is organized, and then review its themes and features. After this, I'll summarize its learning aids and supplements.

THE ORGANIZATION OF THIS TEXT

I have organized your text into five parts. Each has a broad focus and is designed to help you acquire the sociological perspective. This will enable you to better analyze social relations—and the particular corner of life in which you find yourself.

Part I focuses on the sociological perspective, an essential concept that I introduce in the first chapter. In the following chapters, I contrast macrosociology and microsociology, present an overview of culture, introduce socialization, and then look at how sociologists do research.

Part II builds on these ideas as we continue our exploration of the significant influence social groups have on our lives. We first present an overview of groups—from society, which encompasses us, to the smaller networks in which we are immersed. Then we examine the impact of bureaucracy and formal organizations. We close this section by examining how groups exert social control on those who violate their norms.

Part III focuses on social inequality, which has such a tremendous impact on our lives. Because social stratification is so significant—and to understand social life we need to know that it penetrates every crevice of our existence—I have written two chapters on this topic. The first has a global focus. In it, I present an overview of the principles of stratification. These principles serve as background for the next chapter, in which I turn the sociological spotlight on social class. After establishing this broader context, we then focus on gender, the most global of the social inequalities. Following this, we examine the inequalities of race, ethnicity, and age.

In Part IV, we turn to those engulfing social arrangements called social institutions. Social institutions are so significant that without understanding them we cannot understand life in society. We begin our analysis with the economy and politics, currently our overarching institutions, which exert such an incredible amount of control over our lives. Following this, I devote separate chapters to four other social institutions that also play a significant role in our lives—the family, education, religion, and medicine.

In Part V, you will gain insight into why your world is changing so rapidly, as well as catch a glimpse of what is yet to come. I open this concluding part by examining population and urbanization, which have such an impact on us all. Then we look at the fascinating topics of collective behavior and social movements, which students often find to be among their favorite topics in sociology. We close this journey into sociology by exploring the "cutting edge" of the changes that engulf us all—technology and the environment.

THEMES AND FEATURES

Perhaps the single greatest goal of the introductory sociology course is to see the connection between the individual and society, to understand how social forces shape our behavior. To help students reach this goal, I use four central themes. Two of these themes, down-to-earth sociology and diversity, have been in the text since the first edition. The third edition introduced the timely and fascinating theme of technology and society. Because of the enthusiastic response that this theme generated, as well as the major impact that technology has on our lives, I maintain technology as a central theme in this edition. With controversy so sharp in our society, I have added a new theme, a contrast of liberal and conservative perspectives on social issues.

Let's look at these themes in more detail.

Down-to-Earth Sociology

Why shouldn't sociology be presented in a manner that conveys its inherent excitement? Without any doubt in my mind, sociology is the most enticing of all the social sciences. Yet textbooks often make sociology seem dull, and thereby fail to reach students.

My choice of subtitle for this book, *A Down-to-Earth Approach*, is deliberate, for my goal is to share sociology's excitement as we embark on our fascinating journey. To note how the basic substance of sociology penetrates our everyday lives is to make visible the influence of the *social* on who we are. I know that you already have an awareness of the influence of the social on your life, and we are going to build on this awareness. Gradually, as we continue our journey, you should become aware of how the social plays a central role in even your innermost being.

This down-to-earth approach is present in the vignettes that open each chapter. Many of these lively vignettes are based on my own sociological experiences. In order to stimulate your sociological imagination, within each chapter I also use examples that you can relate to. Threaded through these examples are the central insights provided by sociology's major perspectives. As we apply symbolic interactionism, for example, you will see how symbols create social life. As we examine functionalism, you will see how people's actions are riddled with both manifest and latent consequences. And you will have no difficulty seeing the far-reaching implications for your own life of the conflict perspective's stress that groups compete for scarce resources.

To underscore this approach, I have written "Down-to-Earth Sociology" boxes. They focus on such topics as Du Bois and race relations (Chapter 1), how college football helps to explain social structure (Chapter 4), strategies women use to survive in the male-dominated business world, a real-life example written by one of my students (Chapter 7), how society is being "McDonaldized" (Chapter 7), how welfare ravages the self-concept, also written by one of my introductory students (Chapter 10)—and in the same chapter an account of my own personal journey out of poverty. I also include Down-to-Earth boxes on the alarming aspects of the racist mind (Chapter 12), and how urban fear is stimulating gated fortresses (Chapter 20). Pages xix–xx contain a complete listing of these Down-to-Earth boxes.

A "Down-to-Earth" Writing Style. I have attempted to reinforce this down-to-earth theme through a writing style that is also "down-to-earth," that is, one that is accessible and inviting. Textbooks, in my opinion, often are written to appeal to the adopters of texts, rather than to the students who study them. As I strive to share with you the excitement and insights of sociology, a constant goal is to maintain and improve this down-to-earth style. The title of my introductory reader, *Down-to-Earth Sociology*, which has now reached its tenth edition (Free Press, 1999), also reflects this approach.

I have tried, then, to avoid unnecessary jargon so you won't have to wade through a linguistic torture path in order to grasp basic ideas. These ideas are of utmost importance in your sociological journey, and to introduce them I attempt to use concise explanations, clear (but not reductive) language, and relevant examples. In addition, I include "In Sum" sections at various places, to help you review important points before going on to new materials. At the end of each chapter, I have written a "user-friendly" summary, which presents the major chapter topics in a question-and-answer format designed to enhance your learning.

Cultural Diversity and Globalization

Any attempt to explain U.S. society must pay keen attention to its diverse populations, for ours is truly a multicultural society. It also must explore the many implications of the globalization of the world's societies. Consequently, this feature is again stressed in this edition.

Cultural Diversity in the United States. Each year about one million people from around the world legally move to the United States. The number of illegal entrants is at least as large. Currently, about one American in four defines himself or herself as Latino or nonwhite. In the next few years, the population of Asian Americans and Latinos is expected to increase by about 22 percent, that of African Americans by 12 percent. In contrast, whites are expected to increase by a mere 2 percent. In some places the future has already arrived. In New York, for example, 40 percent of all primary and secondary students belong to an ethnic minority, while in California that figure stands at 51 percent.

A sociology textbook that does not explore the implications of this century's second great demographic shift (the first took place in the early 1900s), simply cannot serve as an adequate introduction to the realities of life in a multicultural society. Thus, in each chapter, Perspectives boxes headed "Cultural Diversity in the United States" explore issues such as the conflict over the use of English versus Spanish (Chapter 2), why Native Americans like Westerns (Chapter 2), a Latino's reaction to his socialization into Anglo culture (Chapter 3), how the Amish resist social change (Chapter 4), how to define deviance among newly arrived immigrants who come from cultures with different norms (Chapter 8), Tiger Woods and the emerging multiracial identity (Chapter 12), the immigrants' path to political participation (Chapter 15), the new neighbor, Islam in the United States (Chapter 18), and the Million-Man March as an indicator of an unfinished social movement (Chapter 21). (See page xx for a complete listing of the Perspectives boxes.)

These cultural diversity boxes, as well as the many discussions of diversity throughout the text, help you apply your growing sociological imagination to fundamental changes occurring in U.S. society. They also will help you see connections among key sociological concepts such as culture, socialization, norms, race, gender, and social class. As your sociological imagination grows, you will better understand the social structure of U.S. society—and your own place in it.

Cultural Diversity Around the World. A primary goal as I wrote and revised this text was to increase your awareness of how global interconnections profoundly affect your life. The dawn of a global economy—new to world history—influences the kinds of skills and knowledge you need in order to make a living, the types of work that will be available to you, and the variety and costs of the goods and services you consume. This new global economy, which has married our fate with that of other nations, also determines other essential aspects of your life, such as whether you will experience war or peace, which can be a matter of life and death for you and your children.

Consequently, I stress globalization throughout this text. I have written a separate chapter on global stratification, given extensive coverage of global matters in the chapters on social institutions, and provided a global focus in the final chapter on technology, social change, and the environment. In addition, I have written Perspectives boxes entitled "Cultural Diversity Around the World." They address such issues as female circumcision (Chapter 11), ethnic conflict among nations and states (Chapter 15), health care in other countries (Chapter 19), urbanization in the Least Industrialized Nations (Chapter

20), and threats posed to the world's remaining preliterate groups (Chapter 22). (See page xx for a complete listing of this feature.)

Sociology and the New Technology

One of the most profound social forces that you face is the accelerated rate of technological change. In just a single generation, computers have become integrated in our daily lives; alternative, or niched, media outlets have proliferated, including online services and the Internet; "sci-fi"-like technologies are being used to aid reproduction; distance learning is becoming common. Each of these topics is the subject of a boxed feature, "Sociology and the New Technology." Other topics, selected both for their relevance and timeliness, include changing images of women in the mass media (Chapter 3), cyber-communications and the creation of electronic communities (Chapter 6), how pornography has gone high tech (Chapter 8), the adverse impact of technology on African Americans (Chapter 12), how technology affects democracy (Chapter 15), Internet University (Chapter 17); the dilemma of medical rationing (Chapter 19), and opposition to technology (Chapter 22).

I introduce this theme in Chapter 2, where I present technology as a major aspect of culture. The box that I wrote for this chapter—"Technology and Culture—Is Technology the Cart or the Horse?"—harkens back to the French sociologist Jacques Ellul's fear that technology was destroying civilization and to Marshall McLuhan's celebration of "the global village"; it concludes by introducing the emerging sociological theory of technology called the "social construction of technology." Rather than regarding technology as an out-of-control force that drives culture and on which all social change depends, the social construction of technology theorists emphasize that individuals and groups—with all their values and special interests—shape technology. (For a complete listing of the technology boxes, see page xix.)

Because technology is so vital to our well being, I also discuss technology throughout the text. I stress how technology is used to control workers in order to produce the "maximum security" workplace (Chapter 7), how technology helps to maintain global stratification (Chapter 9), how the consequences of technology differ by social class (Chapter 10), how technology often outpaces norms (Chapter 13), and how the new technology stimulates downsizing and the restructuring of work (Chapter 14). In the final chapter, "Technology, Social Change, and the Environment," I again stress technology as I conclude this introduction to your sociological adventure.

Thinking Critically

Thinking Critically About Social Controversy sections are another important feature of this text. These sections, which address pressing and often controversial social issues, underscore the significance of sociology for understanding the events that are challenging our ideas and changing our lives. They consider the Milgram experiment and conformity to evil authority (Chapter 6), bounties paid to kill homeless children in Brazil (Chapter 9), the welfare debate (Chapter 10), racial and ethnic self-segregation on campus (Chapter 12), the restructuring of work (Chapter 14), marital tensions caused by "the second shift" (Chapter 16), how to get single teen mothers back in school (Chapter 17), a conflict interpretation of the destruction of the Branch Davidians (Chapter 18), and abortion as a social movement (Chapter 21). (For a full listing of these sections, see page xx.)

These Thinking Critically sections make excellent points of departure for class discussions, for they contrast several points of view or theoretical interpretations about areas of social controversy. After presenting these multiple perspectives, you are asked to evaluate the issue. In "Self-Segregation on Campus" (Chapter 12), for instance, you are asked to consider the controversy over students living in segregated housing on campus, along with the many unresolved questions this practice has raised.

A New Theme: Contrasting Liberal and Conservative Views

With our society increasingly divided in its perspectives on social issues, I have written a series of boxes that reflect these contrasting perspectives. This new theme also provides an excellent opportunity for in-class discussions of controversial topics. Using the title "Liberal and Conservative Views on Social Issues," we examine diversity training in corporations (Chapter 7), our growing dependence on imprisonment as a response to crime (Chapter 8), sexual harassment and training women in the military (Chapter 11), and rolling back no-fault divorce, the controversial "covenant" form of marriage passed by the Louisiana legislature (Chapter 16).

New Topics

Since sociology is about social life, as society changes the topics in an introductory text reflect those changes. Among the numerous new topics of this edition are culture wars (Chapter 2), myths about the poor (Chapter 10), the dynamics of poverty (Chapter 10), barter in the former Soviet Union (Chapter 14), nuclear, biological, and chemical terrorism (Chapter 15), and intentional families (Chapter 16). I have also made spouse abuse the explanatory theme for research methods in Chapter 5.

IN-TEXT LEARNING AIDS

Sociology: A Down-to-Earth Approach includes a number of other pedagogical aids to help your learning. These include:

Down-to-Earth Chapter Opening Vignettes. In order to pique your interest and alert you to key topics, I wrote opening vignettes for each chapter. To make these vignettes down-to-earth, I have based many of them on my own experiences—from my stay with the homeless (Chapters 1 and 10) to my travels in Africa (Chapters 2 and 11) and Mexico (Chapter 20). I also wrote an opening vignette on the night I spent with street people at Du Pont Circle in Washington, D.C. (Chapter 4). For other opening vignettes, I chose current and historical events (Chapters 12, 19, 21, and 22), classic studies in the social sciences (Chapters 3, 8, and 13), and even a scene from a classic novel (Chapter 15). Many students have reported that these vignettes are compelling, that they stimulate interest in the chapter. I hope that this is your experience as well.

Social Maps. New to this edition is a series of fascinating social maps that help make sociology come alive. Portraying either the United States or the world, they illustrate how geographical areas differ on social conditions. For example, at a glance you will be able to see which states are the safest, and which are the most dangerous (Chapter 8); which states have the highest and lowest divorce rates (Chapter 16); and which areas of the world AIDS has hit the hardest (Chapter 19).

Key Terms. I know that learning new terms is difficult. To help you, I have introduced each key term within a context that explains or illustrates it. I also highlight each term when I introduce it, and then define it again in the margin. To learn sociology, it is necessary to learn the sociologists' basic vocabulary, and these terms provide a working definition of the most important sociological concepts.

Interactive Chapter Summaries. At the end of each chapter I summarize and review the main points of the chapter. To enhance your learning, I use a question-and-answer format that asks you to think along with me. Organized by major chapter headings, this interactive format highlights and reinforces the important concepts and issues discussed in the chapter.

Using the Internet. Because the Internet has become such a significant aspect of our culture, and because it contains such a vast amount of sociological information, at the end of each chapter is a set of projects and exercises to help you use the Internet to explore ideas from the chapter. You may wish to check my Web site at http://www.abacon.com/henslin

Suggested Readings. At the end of the book (page 659), I recommend readings for each chapter, including relevant sociology journals. To help you further investigate topics and to write papers, I include a brief description of these sources.

Comprehensive Glossary. An instructor wrote me about how useful she finds the glossary in her teaching. She pointed out how complete it is and how clear the definitions are. I hope that you, too, find it useful. It is designed to bring together the important concepts and terms that I introduce in the text, organizing them into a single, accessible format.

SUPPLEMENTS FOR THE STUDENT

Study Guide Plus. Prepared by Professor Gwendolyn E. Nyden of Oakton Community College this guide provides learning objectives, key terms, self-tests, and glossaries. Students who need special language assistance will find a glossary for potentially confusing idioms and colloquialisms.

Practice Tests. Consisting of approximately fifteen questions per chapter, these self-tests help students gain mastery of the material covered in the text, above and beyond their reading in the text and the study guide.

Careers in Sociology, 2nd ed. Written by Professor W. Richard Stephens, Jr. of Greenville College this supplement goes beyond the academic career path to explore careers in applied sociology. It examines how people working as sociologists entered the field, and how a degree in sociology can be a preparation for careers in areas such as law, gerontology, social work, and the computer industry.

Breaking the Ice: A Guide to Understanding People From Other Cultures, 2nd ed. This guide helps students better understand and interact with people from other cultures, encouraging them to react and draw upon their experiences. Drawing upon her own personal experience as a Ugandan-born woman living in the United States, Professor Daisy Kabagarama of Wichita State University uses examples to illustrate behavior in different cultures. Numerous exercises are included to help the reader discover and deal with his or her own biases.

Thinking Sociologically: A Critical Thinking Activities Manual, 2nd ed. Written by Professor Josephine Ruggiero of Providence College, this book contains a series of twelve related exercises that focus on helping students to improve their critical thinking skills. Through these exercises, they will learn how to identify and challenge commonly held assumptions, and to better understand and use the sociological perspective. The exercises are arranged to allow students to build increasingly more complex skills and a better understanding of how to think sociologically.

The Essential Sociology Reader. Edited by Professor Robert Thompson of Minot State University, this "essential" anthology consists of sixteen readings in sociology. An introduction to each reading provides a context for the selection, and discussion questions appear at the end of each article.

SUPPLEMENTS FOR THE INSTRUCTOR

Annotated Instructor's Manual

This unique teaching aid provides instructor's annotations keyed to reduced versions of actual text pages. Annotations include learning objectives, suggestions for introducing the chapter, discussion questions, guest speaker suggestions, class activities, student projects, and internet activities. Annotations also tie the text to numerous elements of the supplementary package, including the Test Bank, PowerPoint lectures, Digital Image Archive, Blockbuster Video Guide, the Allyn and Bacon Interactive Video, Learning by Doing Sociology, and the book-specific Web site. Annotations are also provided for several other Allyn and Bacon saleable supplements including Stephens *Careers in Sociology*, 2nd ed. Carter *Doing Sociology with Student CHIP*, 2nd ed. Carter *Analyzing Contemporary Social Issues*, and Thompson *The Essential Sociology Reader*.

In addition to the extensive annotations program, this manual contains a section for the instructor that consists of chapter summaries, outlines a list of "what's new" in each chapter, learning objectives, and a detailed lecture outline, chapter-at-a-glance grids, and a list of key terms page referenced to the text.

This manual also contains a video guide in the accompanying interactive video for this text. They are also available on disk, which allows instructors to customize lectures by adding their own notes. (Available for Windows and Macintosh.)

Learning by Doing Sociology: In-Class Experiential Exercises. This manual offers step-by-step procedures for numerous in-class activities, general suggestions for managing experiential learning, and trouble-shooting tips. It contains twenty-two exercises on a broad range of topics covered in the introductory sociology course.

PowerPoint Presentation. This PowerPoint presentation provides approximately 500 graphic and text images for complete multimedia presentations in the classroom. The presentation is available on a cross-platform CD-ROM. PowerPoint software is not required to use this program; a PowerPoint viewer is included to access the images.

Test Banks. Thoroughly revised for this edition and prepared by Professor Jacqueline Fellows of Riverland Community College, the test bank contains approximately 2,200 questions in multiple choice, true-false, short answer, and essay formats. An alternative test bank, prepared by Professor Kanwal Prasher of Rock Valley Community College, contains approximately 1,500 questions in the same format. Computerized versions in both Windows and Macintosh are available for both test banks.

Transparencies. Thoroughly revised for this edition, this package includes 100 color acetates featuring illustrations both from the text and from other sources.

Allyn and Bacon Interactive Video. This custom video features both national and global topics. The up-to-the-minute video segments are great to launch lectures, spark classroom discussion, and encourage critical thinking. The accompanying video user's guide provides detailed descriptions of each video segment, specific tie-ins to the text, and suggested discussion questions and projects.

The Blockbuster Approach: A Guide to Teaching Sociology with Video. Written by Casey Jordan of Western Connecticut State University, this manual provides extensive lists, with descriptions, of hundreds of commercially available videos, and shows how they can be incorporated in the classroom.

A&B Video Library. Qualified adopters may select from a wide variety of high quality videos from such sources as Films for the Humanities and Sciences and Annenberg/CPB.

CD-ROM Library. Qualified adopters may select from several exciting CD-ROMs made available by Allyn & Bacon, including: Material World: A Global Family Portrait, and Our Times: Multimedia Encyclopedia of the 20th Century.

Digital Image Archive for Sociology. This exciting new CD-ROM contains hundreds of images you can incorporate in your multimedia presentations in the classroom. The CD-ROM includes original images, as well as selected art from many Allyn and Bacon sociology texts, providing instructors with a broad selection of graphs, charts, and tables to use to illustrate key sociological concepts.

Web site. An extensive Web site has been developed for this text at http://www.abacon.com/henslin Features of the Web site include learning objectives; practice tests (interactive multiple choice, true-false, fill-in and essay questions); Web destinations; exploring the Internet; and an interactive video site.

Allyn and Bacon Quick Guide to the Internet for Henslin: Sociology, 4th ed. This reference guide, which introduces users to the basics of the Internet and the World Wide Web, provides a multitude of sociology-specific references and exercises designed especially for users of this text.

Doing Sociology with Student CHIP: Data Happy!, 2nd ed, and *Analyzing Contemporary Social Issues: A Workbook with Student CHIP Software.* Written by Gregg Lee Carter of Bryant College, these workbooks provide students with the opportunity to explore sociological issues using real data. Exercises explore major subfields of sociology.

ACKNOWLEDGMENTS

The highly gratifying response to the first three editions indicates that my efforts at making sociology down to earth have succeeded. The years that have gone into writing this text are a culmination of the many more years that preceded its writing—from graduate school to that equally demanding endeavor known as classroom teaching. But no text comes solely from its author. Although I am responsible for the final words on the printed page, I have received invaluable feedback from instructors who have used this book. I especially want to thank the following reviewers:

Reviewers of previous editions:
Sandra L. Albrecht, *The University of Kansas*
Kenneth Ambrose, *Marshall University*
Alberto Arroyo, *Baldwin-Wallace College*
Karren Baird-Olsen, *Kansas State University*
Linda Barbera-Stein, *The University of Illinois*
John K. Cochran, *The University of Oklahoma*
Russell L. Curtis, *University of Houston*
John Darling, *University of Pittsburgh-Johnstown*
Ray Darville, *Stephen F. Austin State University*
Nanette J. Davis, *Portland State University*
Lynda Dodgen, *North Harris Community College*
Terry Dougherty, *Portland State University*
Helen R. Ebaugh, *University of Houston*
Obi N. Ebbe, *State University of New York-Brockport*
Cy Edwards, Chair *Cypress Community College, Long Beach, CA*
David O. Friedrichs, *University of Scranton*
Norman Goodman, *State University of New York-Stony Brook*
Donald W. Hastings, *The University of Tennessee-Knoxville*
Michael Hoover, *Missouri Western State College*
Erwin Hummel, *Portland State University*
Charles E. Hurst, *The College of Wooster*
Mark Kassop, *Bergen Community College*
Myles Kelleher, *Bucks County Community College*
Alice Abel Kemp, *University of New Orleans*
Diana Kendall, *Austin Community College*
Gary Kiger, *Utah State University*
Abraham Levine, *El Camino Community College*
Ron Matson, *Wichita State University*
Armaund L. Mauss, *Washington State University*
Evelyn Mercer, *Southwest Baptist University*
Robert Meyer, *Arkansas State University*
W. Lawrence Neuman, *University of Wisconsin-Whitewater*
Charles Norman, *Indiana State University*
Laura O'Toole, *University of Delaware*
Phil Piket, *Joliet Junior College*

Trevor Pinch, *Cornell University*
Daniel Polak, *Hudson Valley Community College*
Adrian Rapp, *North Harris Community College*
Howard Robboy, *Trenton State College*
Walt Shirley, *Sinclair Community College*
Marc Silver, *Hofstra University*
Roberto E. Socas, *Essex County College*
Susan Sprecher, *Illinois State University*
Randolph G. Ston, *Oakland Community College*
Gary Tiederman, *Oregon State University*
Kathleen Tiemann, *University of North Dakota*
Judy Turchetta, *Johnson & Wales University, Providence, RI*
Larry Weiss, *University of Alaska*
Douglas White, *Henry Ford Community College*
Stephen R. Wilson, *Temple University*
Anthony T. Woart, *Middlesex Community College*
Stuart Wright, *Lamar University*

Reviewers of this edition:
Francis O. Adeola, *University of New Orleans*
Richard Alman, *Sierra College*
Ronnie J. Booxbaum, *Greenfield Community College*
Cecil D. Bradfield, *James Madison University*
Francis Broouer, *Worcester State College*
Sandi Brunette-Hill, *Carroll College*
Karen Bullock, *Salem State College*
Joan Cook-Zimmern, *College of Saint Mary*
Ray Darville, *Stephen T. Austin State University*
Vincent Davis, *Mt. Hood Community College*
Marlese Durr, *Wright State University*
Cy Edwards, *Cypress College*
Louis J. Finkle, *Horry-Georgetown Technical College*
Ramon Guerra, *University of Texas-Pan American*
Kathleen R. Johnson, *Keene State College*
Irwin Kantor, *Middlesex County College*
Myles Kelleher, *Bucks County Community College*
Gene W. Kilpatrick, *University of Maine-Presque Isle*
Michele Lee Kozimor-King, *Pennsylvania State University*

David Maines, *Oakland University*
John Mitrano, *Central Connecticut State University*
Charles Norman, *Indiana State University*
Patricia H. O'Brien, *Elgin Community College*
Ruth Pigott, *University of Nebraska-Kearney*
Deedy Ramo, *Del Mar College*
Ray Rich, *Community College of Southern Nevada*

Barbara Richardson, *Eastern Michigan University*
Michael L. Sanow, *Catonsville Community College*
Steven Vassar, *Mankato State University*
Jay Weinstein, *Eastern Michigan University*
Mary Lou Wylie, *James Madison University*
Diane Kholos Wysocki, *University of Nebraska-Kearney*

I especially appreciate the herculean efforts of Hannah Rubenstein, development editor. Her energy, creativity, insightful questioning, and acute perception of the relevance of social events have left an indelible mark on this text. It is difficult for me to adequately express my appreciation for her fine contributions to this book.

I also am indebted to the capable staff of Allyn and Bacon. I wish to thank Karen Hanson, who saw the promise of the early manuscript and has strongly supported this project from the beginning to the present. Heather Ahlstrom at Allyn and Bacon ably coordinated the project as it moved from one person to another. Stephen Forsling did an excellent job researching photos. Dusty Davidson of The Book Company deserves special mention for her cheerful, energetic, and capable handling of both the routine and the urgent.

To all these people, I owe a debt of gratitude. From the bottom of my heart, a sincere thank you—and my best wishes for your many endeavors in life.

About the Author

JAMES M. HENSLIN, who was born in Minnesota, graduated from high school and junior college in California and from college in Indiana. He earned his master's and doctorate in sociology at Washington University in St. Louis, Missouri. He then spent a year as a post-graduate fellow for the National Institutes on Mental Health. His primary interests in sociology are the sociology of everyday life, deviance, social psychology, and the homeless. Among his more than a dozen books is *Down to Earth Sociology* (Free Press), now in its tenth edition, a book of readings that reflects these sociological interests. He also has published widely in sociology journals, including *Social Problems* and *American Journal of Sociology*.

While a graduate student, Jim Henslin taught at the University of Missouri at St. Louis. After completing his doctorate, he joined the faculty at Southern Illinois University, Edwardsville, where he is Emeritus Professor of Sociology. He says, "I've always found the introductory course enjoyable to teach. I love to see students' faces light up when they first glimpse the sociological perspective and begin to see how society has become an essential part of how they view the world."

During his research on the homeless, Jim learned first hand of the plight of street children. As a result, he is working with and on behalf of the street children of South America. He currently is focusing his efforts on the street children of Medellín and Cúcuta, Colombia.

Henslin enjoys spending time with his family, reading, and fishing. His two favorite activities are writing and traveling. He especially enjoys living in other cultures, for this brings him face to face with behaviors that he cannot take for granted, experiences that "make sociological principles come alive."

Sociology

Margaret Cusack, Crowd with Happy Faces, 1983

C H A P T E R 1

The Sociological Perspective

VEN FROM THE DIM GLOW of the faded red-and-white exit sign, its light barely reaching the upper bunk, I could see that the sheet was filthy. Resigned to another night of fitful sleep, I reluctantly crawled into bed—tucking my clothes firmly around my body, like a protective cocoon.

The next morning, I joined the long line of disheveled men leaning against the chain-link fence. Their faces were as downcast as their clothes were dirty. Not a glimmer of hope among them.

No one spoke as the line slowly inched forward. When my turn came, I was handed a styrofoam cup of coffee, some utensils, and a bowl of semiliquid that I couldn't identify. It didn't look like any food I had seen before. Nor did it taste like anything I had ever eaten.

My stomach fought the foul taste, every spoonful a battle. But I was determined. "I will experience what they experience," I kept telling myself. My stomach reluctantly gave in and accepted its morning nourishment.

The room was strangely silent. Hundreds of men were eating, but each was sunk deeply into his own private hell, his head aswim with disappointment, remorse, bitterness.

As I stared at the styrofoam cup holding my solitary postbreakfast pleasure, I noticed what looked like teeth marks. I shrugged off the thought, telling myself that my long weeks as a sociological observer of the homeless were finally getting to me. "That must be some sort of crease from handling," I concluded.

I joined the silent ranks of men turning in their bowls and cups. When I saw the man behind the counter swishing out styrofoam cups in a washtub of water, I began to feel sick at my stomach. I knew then that the jagged marks on my cup really had come from a previous mouth.

How much longer did this research have to last? I felt a deep longing to return to my family—to a welcome world of clean sheets, healthy food, and "normal" conversations.

The Sociological Perspective

Why were these men so silent? Why did they receive such despicable treatment? What was I doing in that homeless shelter? (After all, I hold a respectable, secure professional position, and I have a home and family.)

Sociology offers a perspective, a view of the world. The **sociological perspective** (or imagination) opens a window onto unfamiliar worlds, and offers a fresh look at familiar worlds. In this text you will find yourself in the midst of Nazis in Germany, chimpanzees in Africa, and warriors in South America. But you will also find yourself looking at your own world in a different light. As you look at other worlds, or your own, the sociological perspective casts a light that enables you to gain a new vision of social life. In fact, this is what many find appealing about sociology.

The sociological perspective has been a motivating force in my own life. Ever since I took my first introductory course in sociology, I have been enchanted by the perspective that sociology offers. I have thoroughly enjoyed both observing other groups and questioning my own assumptions about life. I sincerely hope that the same happens to you.

Seeing the Broader Social Context

The **sociological perspective** stresses the social contexts in which people live. It examines how these contexts influence their lives. At the center of the sociological perspective is the question of how people are influenced by their **society**—a group of people who share a culture and a territory.

sociological perspective: an approach to understanding human behavior by placing it within its broader social context

society: a term used by sociologists to refer to a group of people who share a culture and a territory

4

Examining the broad social context in which people live is essential to the sociological perspective, *for this context shapes our beliefs and attitudes and sets guidelines for what we do. From this photo, you can see how distinctive those guidelines are for the Yanomamo Indians who live on the border of Brazil and Venezuela. How have these Yanomamo youths been influenced by their group? How has your behavior been influenced by your groups?*

To find out why people do what they do, sociologists look at **social location**, where people are located in a particular society. Sociologists consider their jobs, income, education, gender, age, and race. Take, for example, how growing up identified with a group called females or a group called males affects our ideas of what we should attain in life. Growing up as a male or a female influences not only our aspirations, but also how we feel about ourselves and how we relate to others in dating and marriage and at work.

Sociologist C. Wright Mills (1959) put it this way: "The sociological perspective enables us to grasp the connection between history and biography." Because of its history, each society has certain broad characteristics—such as its ideas of the proper roles of men and women. By biography, Mills referred to the individual's specific experiences in society. In short, people don't do what they do because of inherited internal mechanisms, such as instincts. Rather, *external* influences—our experiences—become part of our thinking and motivations. The society in which we grow up, and our particular corners in that society, then, lie at the center of our behavior.

Consider a newborn baby. If we were to take the baby away from its U.S. parents and place that infant with a Yanomamo Indian tribe in the jungles of South America, you know that when that child begins to speak, his or her sounds will not be in English. You also know that the child will not think like an American. He or she will not grow up wanting credit cards, for example, or designer jeans, a new car, and the latest video game. Equally, the child will unquestioningly take his or her place in Yanomamo society—perhaps as a food gatherer, a hunter, or a warrior—and will not even know about the world left behind at birth. And, whether male or female, that child will grow up, not debating whether to have one, two, or three children, but assuming that it is natural to want many children.

People around the globe take their particular world for granted. Something inside us Americans tells us that hamburgers are delicious, small families attractive, and designer clothing desirable. Yet something inside some of the Sinai Desert Arab tribes used to tell them that warm, fresh camel's blood makes a fine drink and that everyone should have a large family and wear flowing robes (Murray 1935; McCabe and Ellis 1990). And that something certainly isn't an instinct. As sociologist Peter Berger (1963) phrased it, that "something" is "society within us."

Although obvious, this point frequently eludes us. We often think and talk about people's behavior as though it were caused by their sex, their race, or some other factor transmitted by their genes. The sociological perspective helps us escape from this cramped

social location: the group memberships that people have because of their location in history and society

personal view by exposing the broader social context that underlies human behavior. It helps us see the links between what people do and the social settings that shape their behavior.

The Growing Global Context

As is evident to all of us—from the labels on our clothing to the components in our cars—our world is becoming a global village. We used to live isolated on farms and in small towns, where beyond the borders of our community lay a world only dimly perceived. Communications used to be so slow that in the War of 1812 the Battle of New Orleans was fought two weeks after the adversaries, the United States and Great Britain, had signed a peace treaty. The armed forces there had not yet heard that the war was over (Volti 1995).

Today, in contrast, instantaneous communications connect us with remote areas of the globe, and a vast economic system connects us not only with Canada and Mexico but also with Belgium, Taiwan, and Indonesia. At the same time that we are immersed in such global interconnections, however, we continue to occupy little corners of life, marked by differences in family background, religion, job, gender, race, and social class. In these corners, we learn distinctive ways of viewing the world.

One of the beautiful—and fascinating—aspects of sociology is that it is able to analyze both parts of our current reality, the changes that incorporate us into a global network and our unique experiences in our smaller corners of life. In this text, we shall examine both of these vital aspects of the contemporary experience.

Sociology and the Other Sciences

Just as humans today have an intense desire to unravel the mysteries around them, people in ancient times also attempted to understand their world. Their explanations, however, were not based only on observations, but were also mixed with magic and superstition.

To satisfy their basic curiosities about the world around them, humans gradually developed **science,** systematic methods used to study the social and natural worlds, as well as the knowledge obtained by those methods. **Sociology,** the scientific study of society and human behavior, is one of the sciences that modern civilization has developed.

A useful way of comparing these sciences—and of gaining a better understanding of sociology's place—is to first divide them into the natural and the social sciences.

The Natural Sciences

The **natural sciences** are the intellectual and academic disciplines designed to comprehend, explain, and predict the events in our natural environment. The natural sciences are divided into specialized fields of research according to subject matter, such as biology, geology, chemistry, and physics. These are further subdivided into even more highly specialized areas, with a further narrowing of content. Biology is divided into botany and zoology, geology into mineralogy and geomorphology, chemistry into its inorganic and organic branches, and physics into biophysics and quantum mechanics. Each area of investigation examines a particular "slice" of nature (Henslin 1997b).

The Social Sciences

People have not limited themselves to investigating nature. In the pursuit of a more adequate understanding of life, people have also developed fields of science that focus on the social world. These, the **social sciences,** examine human relationships. Just as the natural sciences attempt to objectively understand the world of nature, the social sciences attempt to objectively understand the social world. Just as the world of nature contains ordered (or lawful) relationships that are not obvious but must be discovered through

science: the application of systematic methods to obtain knowledge and the knowledge obtained by those methods

sociology: the scientific study of society and human behavior

natural sciences: the intellectual and academic disciplines designed to comprehend, explain, and predict events in our natural environment

social sciences: the intellectual and academic disciplines designed to understand the social world objectively by means of controlled and repeated observations

controlled observation, so the ordered relationships of the human or social world are not obvious, and must be revealed by means of controlled and repeated observations.

Like the natural sciences, the social sciences are divided into specialized fields based on their subject matter. These divisions are anthropology, economics, political science, psychology, and sociology. And the social sciences, too, are subdivided into further specialized fields. Thus, anthropology is divided into cultural and physical anthropology; economics has macro (large-scale) and micro (small-scale) specialties; political science has theoretical and applied branches; psychology may be clinical or experimental; and sociology has its quantitative and qualitative branches. Since our focus is sociology, let us contrast sociology with each of the other social sciences.

Political Science.   *Political science* focuses on politics and government. Political scientists study how people govern themselves: the various forms of government, their structures, and their relationships to other institutions of society. Political scientists are especially interested in how people attain ruling positions in their society, how they maintain those positions, and the consequences of their activities for those who are governed. In studying a constitutional government, such as that of the United States, political scientists also analyze voting behavior.

Economics.   *Economics* also concentrates on a single social institution. Economists study the production and distribution of the material goods and services of a society. They want to know what goods are being produced at what rate and at what cost, and how those goods are distributed. They also are interested in the choices that determine production and consumption; for example, why a society produces a certain item instead of another.

Anthropology.   *Anthropology*, in which the primary focus has been preliterate or tribal peoples, is the sister discipline of sociology. The chief concern of anthropologists is to understand *culture*, a people's total way of life. Culture includes (1) the group's artifacts such as its tools, art, and weapons; (2) the group's structure, that is, the hierarchy and other patterns that determine how its members interact with one another; (3) a group's ideas and values, especially how its belief system affects people's lives; and (4) the group's forms of communication, especially language. The anthropologists' traditional focus on tribal groups is now giving way to the study of groups in industrialized settings.

Psychology.   The focus of *psychology* is on processes that occur *within* the individual, within the "skin-bound organism." Psychologists are primarily concerned with mental processes: intelligence, emotions, perception, and memory. Some concentrate on attitudes and values; others focus on personality, mental aberration (psychopathology, or mental illness), and how individuals cope with the problems they face.

Sociology.   *Sociology* has many similarities to the other social sciences. Like political scientists, sociologists also study how people govern one another, especially the impact of various forms of government on people's lives. Like economists, sociologists are concerned with what happens to the goods and services of a society—but sociologists place their focus on the social consequences of production and distribution. Like anthropologists, sociologists study culture; they have a particular interest in the social consequences of material goods, group structure, and belief systems, as well as in how people communicate with one another. Like psychologists, sociologists are also concerned with how people adjust to the difficulties of life.

Given these overall similarities, then, what distinguishes sociology from the other social sciences? Unlike political scientists and economists, sociologists do not concentrate on a single social institution. Unlike anthropologists, sociologists focus primarily on industrialized societies. And unlike psychologists, sociologists stress factors *external* to the individual to determine what influences people. The Down-to-Earth Sociology box on the next page revisits an old fable about how members of different disciplines perceive the same subject matter.

Down-to-Earth Sociology

An Updated Version of the Old Elephant Story

It is said that in the recent past five wise men and women, all blindfolded, were led to an elephant and asked to explain what they "saw." The first, a psychologist, feeling the top of the head, said, "This is the only thing that counts. All feeling and thinking take place inside here. To understand this beast, we need study only this."

The second, an anthropologist, tenderly touching the trunk and the tusks, said, "This is really primitive. I feel very comfortable here. Concentrate on these."

The third, a political scientist, feeling the gigantic ears, said, "This is the power center. What goes in here controls the entire beast. Concentrate your studies here."

The fourth, an economist, feeling the mouth, said, "This is what counts. What goes in here is distributed throughout the body. Concentrate your studies on this."

Then came the sociologist (of course!), who, after feeling the entire body, said, "You can't understand the beast by concentrating on only one part. Each is but part of the whole. The head, the trunk and tusks, the ears, the mouth—all are important. But so are the parts of the beast that you haven't even mentioned. We must remove our blindfolds so we can see the larger picture. We have to see how everything works together to form the entire animal."

Pausing for emphasis, the sociologist added, "And we also need to understand how this creature interacts with similar creatures. How does their life in groups influence their behaviors?"

I wish I could conclude this fable by saying that the psychologist, the anthropologist, the political scientist, and the economist, dazzled on hearing the wisdom of the sociologist, amid gasps of wonderment threw away their blindfolds and, joining together, began to examine the larger picture. But, alas and alack! On hearing this sage advice, each stubbornly bound their blindfolds even tighter to concentrate all the more on the single part. And if you listened very, very carefully you could even hear them mutter, "The top of the head is mine—stay away from it." "Don't touch the tusks." "Take your hand off the ears." "Stay away from the mouth— that's my area."

The Goals of Science

The first goal of each science is to *explain* why something happens. The second goal is to make **generalizations,** that is, to go beyond the individual case and make statements that apply to a broader group or situation. For example, a sociologist wants to explain not only why Mary went to college or became an armed robber but also why people with her characteristics are more likely than others to go to college or to become armed robbers. To achieve generalizations, sociologists look for **patterns,** recurring characteristics or events. The third scientific goal is to *predict,* to specify what will happen in the future in the light of current knowledge.

To attain these goals, scientists must rely not on magic, superstition, or common beliefs but on conclusions based on systematic studies. They need to examine evidence with an open mind, in such a way that it can be checked by others. Secrecy, prejudice, and other biases, with their inherent closures, go against the grain of science.

Sociologists and other scientists also move beyond **common sense,** those ideas that prevail in a society that "everyone knows" are true. Just because "everyone" knows something is true does not make it so. "Everyone" can be mistaken, today just as easily as when common sense dictated that the world was flat or that no human could ever walk on the moon. As sociologists examine people's assumptions about the world, their findings may contradict commonsense notions about social life. To test your own "common sense," read the Down-to-Earth Sociology box on the next page.

Sometimes the explorations of sociologists take them into nooks and crannies that people would prefer remain unexplored. For example, a sociologist might study how people make decisions to commit a crime or to cheat on their spouses. Because sociologists want above all to understand social life, they cannot cease their studies because people feel uncomfortable. With all realms of human life considered legitimate avenues of exploration by sociologists, their findings sometimes challenge even cherished ideas.

As they examine how groups operate, sociologists often confront prejudice and attempts to keep things secret. It seems that every organization, every group, nourishes a pet image that it presents to the public. Sociologists are interested in knowing what is re-

generalization: a statement that goes beyond the individual case and is applied to a broader group or situation

patterns: recurring characteristics or events

common sense: those things that "everyone knows" are true

Down-to-Earth Sociology

Enjoying a Sociology Quiz—
Sociological Findings Versus Common Sense

Some findings of sociology support commonsense understandings of social life, while others contradict them. Can you tell the difference? If you want to enjoy this quiz fully, before turning the page to check your answers complete *all* the questions.

1. True/False The earnings of U.S. women have just about caught up with those of U.S. men.
2. True/False When faced with natural disasters such as floods and earthquakes, people panic and social organization disintegrates.
3. True/False Revolutions are more likely to occur when conditions remain bad than when they are improving.
4. True/False Most people on welfare are lazy and looking for a handout. They could work if they wanted to.
5. True/False Compared with men, women touch each other more while they are talking to one another.

6. True/False Compared with women, men maintain more eye contact while they are conversing.
7. True/False The more available alcohol is (as measured by the number of places to purchase alcohol per one hundred people), the more alcohol-related injuries and fatalities occur on U.S. highways.
8. True/False Couples who live together before they marry usually report higher satisfaction with their marriages than couples who do not live together before they marry.
9. True/False The reason that people discriminate against minorities is prejudice; unprejudiced people don't discriminate.
10. True/False Students in Japan are under such intense pressure to do well in school that their suicide rate is about double that of U.S. students.

ally going on behind the scenes, however, so they peer beneath the surface to get past that sugarcoated image (Berger 1963). This approach sometimes brings sociologists into conflict with people who feel threatened by that information—which is all part of the adventure, and risk, of being a sociologist.

The Development of Sociology

Just how did sociology begin? In some ways it is difficult to answer this question. By the time Jesus Christ was born, the Greeks and Romans had already developed intricate systems of philosophy about human behavior. Even preliterate peoples tried to figure out social life. They, too, asked questions about why there was war, why some people became more powerful, or why some were richer. They often based their answers on superstition, myths, or even the positions of the stars, however, and did not *test* their assumptions.

Simple assertions of truth—or observations mixed with magic or superstition or the stars—are not adequate. *All science requires the development of theories that can be proved or disproved by systematic research.*

This standard simplifies the question of the origin of sociology. Measured by this standard, sociology is clearly a recent discipline. It emerged about the middle of the nineteenth century when European social observers began to use scientific methods to test their ideas. Three factors combined to lead to the development of sociology.

The first was the Industrial Revolution. By the middle of the nineteenth century, Europe was changing from agriculture to factory production. This brought social upheaval, violently changing people's lives. Masses of people were forced off the land. They moved to the cities in search of work where they were met with anonymity, crowding, filth, and poverty. Their ties to the land, to the generations that had lived there before them, and to their way of life were abruptly broken. The city greeted them with horrible working conditions: low pay; long, exhausting hours; dangerous work; foul smoke; and much noise. To survive, families had to permit their children to work in these same conditions, some of them even chained to factory machines to make certain they did not run away.

Down-to-Earth Sociology

Sociological Findings Versus Common Sense—
Answers to the Sociology Quiz

1. False. Over the years, the income gap has narrowed, but only slightly. On average, full-time working women earn only about 65 percent of what full-time working men earn; this low figure is actually an improvement, for in the 1970s women's incomes averaged about 60 percent of men's.

2. False. Following such disasters, people develop *greater* cohesion, cooperation, and social organization to deal with the catastrophe.

3. False. Just the opposite is true. When conditions are consistently bad, people are more likely to be resigned to their fate. Rapid improvement causes their aspirations to outrace their circumstances, which can increase frustrations and foment revolution.

4. False. Most people on welfare are children, the old, the sick, the mentally and physically handicapped, or young mothers with few skills. Less than 2 percent meet the common stereotype of an able-bodied male. See also "Exploring Myths about the Poor" on page 270.

5. False. Men touch each other more during conversations (Whyte 1989).

6. False. Female speakers maintain considerably more eye contact (Henley et al. 1985).

7. False. In California, researchers compared the number of alcohol outlets per population with the alcohol-related highway injuries and fatalities. They found that counties in which alcohol is more readily available do not have more alcohol-related injuries and fatalities (Kohfeld and Leip 1991).

8. False. The opposite is true. The reason, researchers suggest, is that many couples who marry after cohabiting are less committed to marriage in the first place—and a key to marital success is firm commitment to one another (Larson 1988).

9. False. When racial discrimination was legal in the United States, sociologists found that due to business reasons and peer pressure some unprejudiced people did discriminate (LaPiere 1934). For these same reasons, some prejudiced people do not discriminate, although they want to.

10. False. The suicide rate of Japanese students is about one-half that of U.S. students (Haynes and Chalker 1997).

With the successes of the American and French revolutions, in which the idea that individuals possess inalienable rights caught fire, the political systems in Western countries slowly began to give way to more democratic forms. As the traditional order was challenged, religion lost much of its force as the unfailing source of answers to life's perplexing questions. Each fundamental social change further undermined traditional explanations of human existence.

When tradition reigns supreme, it provides a ready answer: "We do this because it has always been done this way." Such societies discourage original thinking. Since the answers are already provided, why search for explanations? Sweeping change, however, does the opposite: By upsetting the existing order, it encourages questioning and demands answers.

The second factor that stimulated the development of sociology was imperialism. The Europeans had been successful in conquering many parts of the world. Their new colonial empires, stretching from Asia through Africa to North America, exposed them to radically different cultures. Startled by these contrasting ways of life, they began to ask why cultures differed.

The third impetus for the development of sociology was the success of the natural sciences. Just at the time when the Industrial Revolution and imperialism moved people to question fundamental aspects of their social worlds, **the scientific method**—objective, systematic observations to test theories—used in chemistry and physics had begun to transform the world. Given these successes, it seemed logical to apply this method to the questions now being raised about the social world.

the scientific method: the use of objective, systematic observations to test theories

positivism: the application of the scientific approach to the social world

Auguste Comte

This idea of applying the scientific method to the social world, known as **positivism,** was apparently first proposed by Auguste Comte (1798–1857). With the French Revolution still fresh in his mind, Comte left the small, conservative town in which he had grown up and moved to Paris. The changes he himself experienced, combined with those France underwent in the revolution, led Comte to become interested in the twin problems of social order and social change (which he called "social statics" and "social dynamics"). What holds society together? he wondered. Why is there social order instead of anarchy or chaos? And once society becomes set on a particular course, what causes it to change? Why doesn't it always continue in the direction it began?

As he pondered these questions, Comte concluded that the right way to answer them was to apply the scientific method to social life. Just as it had revealed the law of gravity, so, too, it would uncover the laws that underlie society. This new science, based on positivism, not only would discover social principles but it would also apply them to social reform. Comte called this new science *sociology*—"the study of society" (from the Greek *logos*, "study of," and the Latin *socius*, companion, "being with others").

Comte had some ideas that today's sociologists find humorous. For example, as Comte saw matters, there were only six sciences—mathematics, physics, chemistry, biology, astronomy, and sociology—with sociology far superior to the others (Bogardus 1929). To Comte, applying the scientific method to social life apparently referred to "armchair philosophy"—drawing conclusions from informal observations of social life. He did not do what today's sociologists would call research, and his conclusions have been abandoned.

Nevertheless, Comte's insistence that we cannot be dogmatic about social life, but that we must observe and classify human activities in order to uncover society's fundamental laws, is well taken. Because he developed this idea and coined the term *sociology*, Comte is often credited with being the founder of sociology.

Auguste Comte (1798–1857), who is identified as the founder of sociology, began to analyze the bases of the social order. Although he stressed that the scientific method should be applied to the study of society, he did not apply it himself.

Herbert Spencer

Herbert Spencer (1820–1903), who grew up in England, is sometimes called the second founder of sociology. He, too, believed that society operates according to fixed laws. Spencer became convinced that societies evolve from lower ("barbarian") to higher ("civilized") forms. As generations pass, he said, the most capable and intelligent ("the fittest") members of a society survive, while the less capable die out. Thus, over time, societies steadily improve.

Spencer called this principle "the survival of the fittest." Although Spencer coined this phrase, it is usually attributed to his contemporary, Charles Darwin, who proposed

This eighteenth-century painting (artist unknown) depicts the execution of Louis XVI on January 21, 1793. The French Revolution of 1789 overthrew not only the aristocracy but upset the entire social order. With change so extensive, and the past no longer a sure guide to the present, Auguste Comte began to analyze how societies change, thus ushering in the science of sociology.

Karl Marx (1818–1883) believed that the roots of human misery lay in the exploitation of the proletariat, or propertyless working classes, by the capitalist class, those who own the means of production. Social change, in the form of the overthrow of the capitalists by the proleteriat, was inevitable from Marx's perspective. Although Marx did not consider himself a sociologist, his ideas have profoundly influenced many in the discipline, particularly conflict theorists.

class conflict: Marx's term for the struggle between the proletariat and the bourgeoisie

The French sociologist Emile Durkheim (1858–1917) contributed many important concepts to sociology. When he compared the suicide rates of several countries, he discovered an underlying social factor: People are more likely to commit suicide if their ties to others in their communities are weak. Durkheim's identification of the key role of social integration in social life remains central to sociology today.

that living organisms evolve over time as they survive the conditions of their environment. Because of their similarities, Spencer's views of the evolution of societies became known as *social Darwinism*.

Unlike Comte, Spencer did not think sociology should guide social reform. In fact, he was convinced that no one should intervene in the evolution of society. The fittest members didn't need any help. They would always survive on their own and produce a more advanced society unless misguided do-gooders got in the way and helped the less fit survive. Consequently, Spencer's ideas—that charity and helping the poor were wrong, whether carried out by individuals or by the government—appalled many. Not surprisingly, wealthy industrialists, who saw themselves as "the fittest" (superior), found Spencer's ideas attractive. And not coincidentally, his views also helped them avoid feelings of guilt for living like royalty while people around them starved.

Like Comte, Spencer was more of a social philosopher than a sociologist. Also like Comte, Spencer did not conduct scientific studies, but simply developed ideas about society. Eventually, after gaining a wide following in England and the United States, Spencer's ideas about social Darwinism were discredited.

Karl Marx

Karl Marx (1818–1883), not only influenced sociology but also left his mark on world history. Marx's influence has been so great that even that staunch advocate of capitalism the *Wall Street Journal* has called him one of the three greatest modern thinkers (the other two being Sigmund Freud and Albert Einstein).

Like Comte, Marx thought that people should take active steps to change society. Marx, who came to England after being exiled from his native Germany for proposing revolution, believed that the engine of human history is **class conflict**. He said that the *bourgeoisie* (the controlling class of *capitalists*, those who own the means to produce wealth—capital, land, factories, and machines) are locked in inevitable conflict with the *proletariat* (the exploited class, the mass of workers who do not own the means of production). This bitter struggle can end only when members of the working class unite in revolution and throw off their chains of bondage. The result will be a classless society, one free of exploitation in which all individuals will work according to their abilities and receive according to their needs (Marx and Engels 1848/1967).

Marxism is not the same as communism. Although Marx stood firmly behind revolution as the only way for the workers to gain control of society, he did not develop the political system called *communism*, which was a later application of his ideas (and rapidly changing ones at that). Indeed, Marx himself felt disgusted when he heard debates about his insights into social life. After listening to some of the positions attributed to him, he even declared, "I am not a Marxist" (Dobriner 1969b:222; Gitlin 1997:89).

Unlike Comte and Spencer, Marx did not think of himself as a sociologist. He spent years studying in the library of the British Museum in London, where he wrote widely on history, philosophy, and, of course, economics and political science. Because of his insights into the relationship between the social classes, especially the class struggle between the "haves" and the "have-nots," many sociologists today claim Marx as a significant early sociologist. He also introduced one of the major perspectives in sociology, conflict theory, which is discussed on pages 26–27.

Emile Durkheim

Emile Durkheim (1858–1917) had a primary goal of getting sociology recognized as a separate academic discipline. Up to this time, sociology was viewed within the university as an offshoot of history and economics. Durkheim, who grew up in eastern France and was educated in both Germany and France, achieved this goal when he received the first academic appointment in sociology (the University of Bordeaux, in 1887) (Coser 1977).

Durkheim also had two other major goals (Giddens 1978). One was to study how individual behavior is shaped by social forces. In one of his most enduring studies, he compared the suicide rates of several European countries. He (1897/1966) found that each country's suicide rate was different, and that it remained remarkably stable year after year. He also found that different groups within a country had different suicide rates. For example, Protestants, males, and the unmarried killed themselves at a higher rate than did Catholics, Jews, females, and the married. From this, Durkheim drew the highly insightful conclusion that suicide is not simply a matter of individuals here and there deciding to take their lives for personal reasons. Instead, *social factors underlie suicide,* and this is what keeps those rates fairly constant year after year.

Durkheim identified **social integration,** the degree to which people are tied to their social group, as a key social factor in suicide. He concluded that people with weaker social ties are more likely to commit suicide. This factor, he said, explained why Protestants, males, and the unmarried have higher suicide rates. It works this way, Durkheim argued: Protestantism encourages greater freedom of thought and action; males are more independent than females; and the unmarried lack the ties and responsibilities of marriage. In other words, because their social integration is weaker, people in these groups have fewer social ties that keep them from committing suicide.

Although strong social bonds help protect people from suicide, Durkheim noted that in some instances strong bonds encourage suicide. To illustrate this type of suicide, which Durkheim termed *altruistic suicide,* he used the example of people, torn apart by grief, who kill themselves following the death of a spouse. Their own feelings are so integrated with those of their spouse that they prefer death rather than life without the one who gave meaning to life.

A hundred years later, Durkheim's study is still quoted because of its scientific rigor and excellent theoretical interpretations. His research was so thorough that the principle he uncovered still applies: People who are less socially integrated have higher rates of suicide. Even today, those same categories that Durkheim identified—Protestants, males, and the unmarried—are still more likely to kill themselves.

Durkheim's third concern was that social research be practical. He thought of sociologists as similar to physicians. Where physicians apply scientific findings to determine

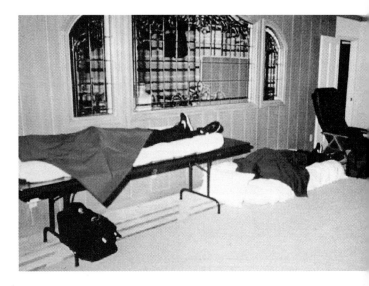

Sociologists analyze almost all aspects of human behavior, from the joys of marriage and college graduation to the despair that leads to suicide—or, in some instances, the hope that leads to suicide. Hope was the unusual motivation for suicide for thirty-nine members of the Heaven's Gate cult, who thought they would be beamed aboard a spaceship. Emile Durkheim was the first sociologist to study suicide, and his 1897 study remains a classic in sociology.

social integration: the degree to which people feel a part of social groups

Emile Durkheim used the term anomie *to refer to feeling rootless and normless, lacking a sense of intimate belonging—the opposite of what sociologists mean by* community. *Durkheim believed that modern societies produce feelings of isolation, much of which comes from the division of labor. In contrast, members of traditional societies, who work alongside family and neighbors and participate in similar activities, experience a high degree of* social integration—*the opposite of anomie.*

Max Weber (1864–1920) was another early sociologist who left a profound impression on sociology. He used cross-cultural and historical materials to determine how extensively social groups affect people's orientations to life.

the sickness and health of the body, sociologists should do the same for society (Giddens 1978). They should diagnose causes of social ills and develop remedies for them. For example, as today, in Durkheim's time people were concerned that there was too much individualism. Durkheim concluded that the new individualism was not pathological, but a normal, healthy expression of a changing society. Individualism can go too far, however. It then poses the danger of what Durkheim called **anomie,** a breaking down of the controlling influences of society. Under these conditions, people become detached from society and are left with too little moral guidance. This is dangerous, for their desires are no longer regulated by social norms (Coser 1977). Durkheim suggested that sociologists intervene: To prevent anomie, they should create new social groups to stand between the state and the family. These groups, he said, would help meet the need for a sense of belonging that the new, impersonal industrial society was eroding.

In sum, perhaps Durkheim's major contribution was his thorough sociological approach to understanding human behavior. Suicide, for example, appears to be such an intensely individual act that psychologists should examine it, not sociologists. Yet, as Durkheim illustrated, if we look at suicide only in individualistic terms, we miss its *social* basis.

Max Weber

Max Weber (1864–1920) (Mahx VÁY-ber), a German sociologist and a contemporary of Durkheim's, also held professorships in the new academic discipline of sociology. With Durkheim and Marx, Weber is one of the most influential of all sociologists, and you shall come across his writings and theories in the coming chapters.

One of Weber's most important contributions to sociology was his study of the rise of capitalism. How, he asked, did capitalism come about—and why did some countries adopt it with enthusiasm, while others lagged behind? Weber suspected that religion might be the key. As background, we need to understand that the typical approach to life at this time was not to strive "to get ahead," but to work only enough to maintain one's usual way of life. Weber (1904/1958) theorized that the Roman Catholic belief system encouraged Catholics to cling to this traditional way of life, while the Protestant belief system, especially Calvinism, encouraged people to embrace change. For Catholics, the accumulation of material objects was taken as a sign of greed and discontent. Protestantism, in contrast, while also denouncing greed, pushed people to work hard, to save money, and to invest it. Thus, Weber theorized, Protestantism, which overtook Catholicism as the dominant religion in some European countries after the Reformation of the 1500s, led to the development of capitalism.

To test his theory, Weber compared Roman Catholic and Protestant countries. In line with his theory, he found that the Protestant countries were much more likely to have embraced the new economic system called capitalism. This theory was controversial when Weber developed it, and it continues to be debated today (Dickson and McLachlan 1989; Zou 1994). We will review this theory in greater depth in Chapter 7.

The Role of Values in Social Research

anomie: Durkheim's term for a condition of society in which people become detached, cut loose from the norms that usually guide their behavior

value free: the view that a sociologist's personal values or biases should not influence social research

values: ideas about what is good or worthwhile in life; attitudes about the way the world ought to be

objectivity: total neutrality

Weber also raised another issue that remains controversial among sociologists when he declared that sociology should be **value free.** By this, he meant that a sociologist's **values,** personal beliefs about what is good or worthwhile in life and the way the world ought to be, should not affect his or her social research. Weber wanted **objectivity,** total neutrality, to be the hallmark of sociological research. If values influence research, he said, sociological findings will be biased.

Objectivity as an ideal is not a matter of debate in sociology. On the one hand, all sociologists agree that objectivity is a proper goal, in the sense that sociologists should not distort data to make them fit preconceived ideas or personal values, and that research reports must accurately reflect actual, not desired findings. On the other hand, it is equally clear that no sociologist can escape values. Like everyone else, sociologists are members of a particular society at a given point in history and are therefore infused with values of

Figure 1.1

The Debate over Values

The Purposes of Social Research

To advance understanding of human behavior *versus* To investigate harmful social arrangements

The Uses of Social Research

Can be used by anyone for any purpose *versus* Should be used to reform society

all sorts, and these inevitably play a role in their research. For example, values are part of the reason that one sociologist chooses to do research on the Mafia, while another turns a sociological eye on kindergarten students. To overcome the distortions that values can cause, sociologists stress **replication,** that is, the repetition of a study by other researchers to see how the results compare. If values have unwittingly influenced research findings, replication by other sociologists should uncover this problem and correct it.

Despite this consensus, however, the proper role of values in sociology is still hotly debated (Seubert 1991; Hewa 1993). The problem centers on the proper purposes and uses of sociological research. Regarding the *purpose* of sociology, some sociologists take the position that sociology's proper role is to advance understanding. Sociologists should gather data on any aspect of social life in which they are interested and then use the best theory available to interpret their findings. Others are convinced that it is the responsibility of sociologists to explore harmful social arrangements of society—to investigate what causes poverty, crime, war, and other forms of human exploitation. (See Figure 1.1)

Regarding the *uses* of sociology, those who say that understanding is sociology's proper goal take the position that the knowledge gained by social research belongs to the scientific community and to the world. Accordingly, it can be used by anyone for any purpose. In contrast, those who say that the goal of sociology should be to reform society take the position that sociologists should explore harmful social arrangements. They say that sociologists should use their studies to alleviate human suffering and make society a better place to live.

Although the debate about the proper role of values in social research is infinitely more complicated than the argument summarized here—few sociologists take such one-sided views—the preceding sketch does identify its major issues. Perhaps sociologist John Galliher (1991) best expresses the majority position:

> Some argue that social scientists, unlike politicians and religious leaders, should merely attempt to describe and explain the events of the world but should never make value judgments based on those observations. Yet a value-free and nonjudgmental social science has no place in a world that has experienced the Holocaust, in a world having had slavery, in a world with the ever-present threat of rape and other sexual assault, in a world with frequent, unpunished crimes in high places, including the production of products known by their manufacturers to cause death and injury as has been true of asbestos products and continues to be true of the cigarette industry, and in a world dying from environmental pollution by these same large multinational corporations.

Verstehen and Social Facts

Weber and *Verstehen*

Weber also stressed that one cannot understand human behavior simply by looking at statistics. Those cold numbers may represent people's activities, he said, but they must be interpreted. To understand people, he said that we should use ***Verstehen*** (a German word meaning "to understand"). Perhaps the best translation of this term is "to grasp by insight." By emphasizing *Verstehen,* Weber meant that the best interpreter of human action is someone who "has been there," someone who can understand the feelings and motivations of the people they are studying. In short, we must pay attention to what are called

replication: repeating a study in order to check the findings of a previous study

Verstehen: a German word used by Weber that is perhaps best understood as "to have insight into someone's situation"

subjective meanings, the ways in which people interpret their own behavior. We can't understand what people do, Weber insisted, unless we look at how people themselves view and explain their own behavior.

To better understand this term, let's return to the homeless in the opening vignette. Why were the men so silent? Why were they so unlike the noisy, sometimes boisterous college students in their dorms and cafeterias?

Verstehen can help explain this. When I interviewed men in the shelters (and in other settings, homeless women), they revealed their despair. As someone who knows—at least on some level—what the human emotion of despair is, you are immediately able to apply it to their situation. You know that people in despair feel a sense of hopelessness. The future looks bleak, hardly worth plodding toward. Consequently, what is there worth talking about anyway? Who wants to hear another hard-luck story?

By applying *Verstehen*—your own understanding of what it means to be human and to face various situations in life—you gain an understanding of people's behavior, in this case the silence, the lack of communication, among the homeless.

Durkheim and Social Facts

In contrast to Weber's use of *Verstehen*, or subjective meanings, Durkheim stressed what he called **social facts.** By this term, he meant the patterns of behavior that characterize a social group. (Note however that Weber did not disagree about the significance of social facts, for they are the basis of his conclusions about Protestantism and capitalism.) Examples of social facts in the United States include June being the most popular month for weddings, suicide being higher among people 65 and over, and more births occurring on Tuesdays than any other day of the week.

Durkheim said that we must use social facts to interpret social facts. In other words, each pattern reflects some underlying condition of society. People all over the country don't just coincidentally decide to do similar things, whether getting married or committing suicide. If that were the case, in some years middle-aged people would be the most likely to kill themselves, in other years, young people, and so on. Patterns that hold true year after year, however, indicate that as thousands and even millions of people make their individual decisions, they are responding to conditions in their society. It is the job of the sociologist, then, to uncover social facts and then to explain them through other social facts. In the following section, we shall see how these particular social facts are explained by the school year, conditions of the aged, and the social organization of medicine, respectively.

How Social Facts and *Verstehen* Fit Together

Social facts and *Verstehen* go hand in hand. As a member of U.S. society, you know how June weddings are related to the end of the school year and how this month, now locked in tradition, common sentiment, and advertising, carries its own momentum. As for suicide among the elderly (see Chapter 13), you probably already have a sense of the greater despair that many Americans of this age feel.

But do you know why more Americans are born on Tuesday than any other day of the week? One would expect Tuesday to be no more common than any other day, and that is how it used to be. But no longer. To understand this change, we need a combination of social facts and *Verstehen*. Four social facts are relevant: First, technological developments have made the hospital a dominating force in the U.S. medical system. Second, current technology has made delivery by cesarean section safer. Third, as discussed in Chapter 19, men took over the delivery of babies. Fourth, profit is a top goal of medicine in the United States. As a result, an operation that used to be reserved for emergencies has become so routine that one-fifth (21 percent) of all U.S. babies are now delivered in this manner (*Statistical Abstract* 1997:Table 100), the highest rate of such births in the world (Wolff et al. 1992). To these social facts, then, we add *Verstehen*. In this instance, it is understanding the preferences of mothers-to-be to give birth in a hospital, and their perceived lack of alternatives. Consequently, physicians schedule large numbers of deliveries for their own convenience, with most finding that Tuesdays fit their week best.

subjective meanings: the meanings that people give their own behavior

social facts: Durkheim's term for the patterns of behavior that characterize a social group

Sexism in Early Sociology

Attitudes of the Time

As you may have noticed, all the sociologists we have discussed are males. In the 1800s, sex roles were rigidly defined, with women assigned the roles of wife and mother. In the classic German phrase, women were expected to devote themselves to the four K's: *Kirche, Küchen, Kinder,* und *Kleider* (church, cooking, children, and clothes). To dare to break out of this mold risked severe social disapproval.

Most women received no education beyond basic reading and writing, and many not even that. A few women from wealthy families, however, insisted on pursuing higher education, which at that time was reserved almost exclusively for men. A few even managed to study sociology, although deeply entrenched sexism in the university stopped them from obtaining advanced degrees or becoming professors. In line with the times, their own research was almost entirely ignored.

Harriet Martineau

A classic example is Harriet Martineau (1802–1876), who was born into a wealthy English family. When Martineau first began to analyze social life, she would hide her writing beneath her sewing when visitors arrived, for *writing was "masculine" and sewing "feminine"* (Gilman 1911:88). Martineau persisted in her interests, however, and she eventually studied social life in both Great Britain and the United States. In 1837, two or three decades before Durkheim and Weber were born, Martineau published *Society in America*, in which she reported on this new nation's family customs, race and gender relations, politics, and religion. In spite of her insightful examination of U.S. life, which is still worth reading today, Martineau's research met the fate of other early women sociologists and, until recently, has been ignored. Instead, she is primarily known for translating Comte's ideas into English.

Interested in social reform, Harriet Martineau (1802–1876) turned to sociology, where she discovered the writings of Comte. An active advocate for the abolition of slavery, she traveled widely and wrote extensively.

Sociology in North America

The Beginnings.   Transplanted to U.S. soil in the late nineteenth century, sociology first took root at the University of Chicago and at Atlanta University, then an all-black school. From there, academic specialties in sociology spread throughout U.S. higher education. The growth was gradual, however. Although the first departments of sociology in North America opened in 1892 at the University of Chicago and in 1889 at the University of Kansas, it was not until 1922 that McGill University gave Canada its first department of sociology. Harvard University did not open its department of sociology until 1930, and the University of California at Berkeley did not follow until the 1950s.

At first, sociology in the United States was dominated by the department at the University of Chicago, founded by Albion Small (1854–1926), who also founded the *American Journal of Sociology* and was its editor from 1895 to 1925. Members of this first sociology department whose ideas continue to influence today's sociologists include Robert E. Park (1864–1944), Ernest Burgess (1886–1966), and George Herbert Mead (1863–1931), who developed the symbolic interactionist perspective examined later.

Early Women Sociologists.   The situation of women in North America was similar to that of European women, and their contributions to sociology met a similar fate. Among the early women sociologists were Jane Addams, Emily Greene Balch, Isabel Eaton, Sophie Germain, Charlotte Perkins Gilman, Alice Hamilton, Florence Kelley, Elsie Clews Parsons, and Alice Paul. Denied faculty appointments in sociology, many turned to social activism (Young 1995). Because some worked with the poor rather than as professors of sociology, until recently they were regarded as social workers.

Jane Addams.   Jane Addams (1860–1935), who like Harriet Martineau also came from a background of wealth and privilege, is the most outstanding example. Addams attended

Jane Addams, 1860–1935, a recipient of the Nobel Peace Prize, tirelessly worked on behalf of poor immigrants. With Ellen G. Starr, she founded Hull-House, a center to help immigrants in Chicago. She was also a leader in women's rights (women's suffrage) and in the peace movement.

The Women's Medical College of Philadelphia, but dropped out because of illness (Addams 1910/1981). On one of her many trips to Europe, she was impressed with work being done to help London's poor. From then on, Addams tirelessly worked for social justice. She founded Hull-House in Chicago's notorious slums, which was open to people who needed refuge—to immigrants, the sick, the aged, the poor. With her piercing insights into the social classes, especially how workers were exploited and how peasant immigrants adjusted to industrializing cities, Addams strived to bridge the gap between the powerful and the powerless. At her invitation, sociologists from nearby University of Chicago were frequently visitors at Hull-House. Her efforts at social reform were so outstanding and so effective, that in 1931 she was a co-winner of the Nobel Peace Prize, the only sociologist to win this coveted award.

W.E.B. Du Bois.   With the racism of this period, African American professionals also found life difficult. The most notable example is provided by W.E.B. Du Bois (1868–1963), who, after earning a bachelor's degree from Fisk University, became the first African American to earn a doctorate at Harvard (Lemert 1994). Awarded a fellowship, he also studied in Germany (including lectures by Max Weber), then taught Greek and Latin at Wilberforce University, as well as sociology at Atlanta University, where he spent most of his career (Du Bois 1935).

Du Bois, whose passionate concern was to eliminate social injustice (he once saw the fingers of a lynching victim displayed in a Georgia butcher shop [Aptheker 1990]) published a book on relations between African Americans and whites *each* year between 1896 and 1914. Du Bois's writings, numbering almost 2,000, preserve a picture of race relations of that period. In addition to his classic, *The Philadelphia Negro* (1899), I highly recommend his elegantly written *The Souls of Black Folks*, which reviews race relations immediately after the Civil War. The box on the facing page is taken from this book.

Du Bois's life was marked by continual frustration. Despite his education, faculty position, and accomplishments, he could not afford to attend the 1909 meeting of the American Sociological Society, where he was scheduled to present a paper. When Du Bois did manage to attend such meetings, due to the discrimination of this period he was unable to eat or stay at the same hotels as the white sociologists. Later in life, when he had money and wanted to travel, for nine years the U.S. State Department, fearing he would criticize the United States, refused to give him a visa (Du Bois 1968).

At first Du Bois was content simply to collect and interpret objective data. Later, frustrated at the lack of improvement in race relations, he turned to social action. Along with Jane Addams, Florence Kelley, and others from Hull-House, he founded the National Association for the Advancement of Colored People, or NAACP (Deegan 1988). Continuing to battle racism both as a sociologist and as a journalist, Du Bois eventually embraced revolutionary Marxism. Dismayed that so little improvement had been made in race relations, at the age of 93 he moved to Ghana, where he is buried (Stark 1989).

Until recently, W.E.B. Du Bois was sadly neglected in sociology, his many contributions going unrecognized. As a personal example, during my entire graduate program at Washington University, I was never introduced to Du Bois's books and thought. Today, however, sociologists are rediscovering Du Bois, and he is beginning to receive a long-deserved appreciation.

W(illiam) E(dward) B(urghardt) Du Bois (1868–1963) spent his lifetime studying relations between African Americans and whites. Like many early North American sociologists, Du Bois combined the role of academic sociologist with that of social reformer. He was also the editor of Crisis, *an influential journal of the time.*

Social Reform Versus Social Theory.   Like Du Bois, and following the advice of Comte, many early North American sociologists combined the role of sociologist with that of social reformer. They saw society, or parts of it, as corrupt and in need of serious reform. During the 1920s and 1930s, for example, Park and Burgess not only studied prostitution, crime, drug addiction and juvenile delinquency, but they also offered suggestions for how to alleviate these social problems.

Then during the 1940s, sociology took a different direction. As greater emphasis was given to gaining the academic respectability of sociology, the focus shifted from social reform to social theory. Talcott Parsons (1902–1979), for example, developed abstract models of society that exerted great influence on sociology. These models of how the parts of society harmoniously work together did nothing to stimulate social activism.

 *Down-to-Earth Sociology*

Early North American Sociology: Du Bois and Race Relations

The works of W.E.B. Du Bois, who expressed sociological thought more like an accomplished novelist than a sociologist, have been neglected in sociology. To help remedy this omission, I reprint the following excerpts from pages 66–68 of *The Souls of Black Folk* (1903). In this book, Du Bois analyzes changes that occurred in the social and economic conditions of African Americans during the thirty years following the Civil War. For two summers, while he was a student at Fisk, Du Bois taught in a log-hut, segregated school "way back in the hills" of rural Tennessee. The following excerpts help us understand conditions at the turn of the last century.

It was a hot morning late in July when the school opened. I trembled when I heard the patter of little feet down the dusty road, and saw the growing row of dark solemn faces and bright eager eyes facing me. . . . There they sat, nearly thirty of them, on the rough benches, their faces shading from a pale cream to deep brown, the little feet bare and swinging, the eyes full of expectation, with here and there a twinkle of mischief, and the hands grasping Webster's blue-black spelling-book. I loved my school, and the fine faith the children had in the wisdom of their teacher was truly marvelous. We read and spelled together, wrote a little, picked flowers, sang, and listened to stories of the world beyond the hill. . . .

On Friday nights I often went home with some of the children,— sometimes to Doc Burke's farm. He was a great, loud, thin Black, ever working, and trying to buy the seventy-five acres of hill and dale where he lived; but people said that he would surely fail and the "white folks would get it all." His wife was a magnificent Amazon, with saffron face and shiny hair, uncorseted and barefooted, and the children were strong and barefooted. They lived in a one-and-a-half-room cabin in the hollow of the farm near the spring. . . .

I liked to stay with the Dowells, for they had four rooms and plenty of good country fare. Uncle Bird had a small, rough farm, all woods and hills, miles from the big road; but he was full of tales,—he preached now and then,—and with his children, berries, horses, and wheat he was happy and prosperous. Often, to keep the peace, I

must go where life was less lovely; for instance, 'Tildy's mother was incorrigibly dirty, Reuben's larder was limited seriously, and herds of untamed insects wandered over the Eddingses' beds. Best of all I loved to go to Josie's, and sit on the porch, eating peaches, while the mother bustled and talked: how Josie had bought the sewing-machine; how Josie worked at service in winter, but that four dollars a month was "mighty little" wages; how Josie longed to go away to school, but that it "looked like" they never could get far enough ahead to let her; how the crops failed and the well was yet unfinished; and, finally, how "mean" some of the white folks were.

For two summers I lived in this little world. . . . I have called my tiny community a world, and so its isolation made it; and yet there was among us but a half-awakened common consciousness, sprung from common joy and grief, at burial, birth, or wedding; from common hardship in poverty, poor land, and low wages, and, above all, from the sight of the Veil* that hung between us and Opportunity. All this caused us to think some thoughts together; but these, when ripe for speech, were spoken in various languages. Those whose eyes twenty-five and more years had seen "the glory of the coming of the Lord," saw in every present hindrance or help a dark fatalism bound to bring all things right in His own good time. The mass of those to whom slavery was a dim recollection of childhood found the world a puzzling thing: it asked little of them, and they answered with little, and yet it ridiculed their offering. Such a paradox they could not understand, and therefore sank into listless indifference, or shiftlessness, or reckless bravado. There were, however, some— such as Josie, Jim, and Ben—to whom War, Hell, and Slavery were but childhood tales, whose young appetites had been whetted to an edge by school and story and half-awakened thought. Ill could they be content, born without and beyond the World. And their weak wings beat against their barriers,—barriers of caste, of youth, of life; at last, in dangerous moments, against everything that opposed even a whim.

*"The Veil" is shorthand for the Veil of Race, referring to how race colors all human relations. Du Bois's hope was that "sometime, somewhere, men will judge men by their souls and not by their skins" (p. 261).

Robert Merton (b. 1910) stressed the need for sociologists to develop **middle-range theories,** explanations that tie together many research findings but avoid sweeping generalizations that attempt to account for everything. Such theories, he claimed, are preferable because they can be tested. Grand theories, in contrast, while attractive because they seem to account for so much of social life, are of little value because they cannot be tested. Merton (1968) developed a middle-range theory of crime and deviant behavior (discussed on pages 203–204) that explains how U.S. society's emphasis on attaining material wealth encourages crime.

C. Wright Mills (1916–1962), however, deplored the theoretical abstractions of this period, which he said were accompanied by empty research methods. Mills (1956) urged sociologists to get back to social reform, seeing imminent danger to freedom in the coalescing of interests of the power elite—the wealthy, the politicians, and the military. After his death, the turbulence in U.S. society in the 1960s and 1970s, fueled by the Vietnam War, also disturbed U.S. sociology. As interest in social activism revived, Mills's ideas became popular among a new generation of sociologists.

middle-range theories: explanations of human behavior that go beyond a particular observation or research but avoid sweeping generalizations that attempt to account for everything

The Present.   Since the 1970s, U.S. sociology has not been dominated by any one theoretical orientation or by any single concern. Three theoretical frameworks are most commonly used, as we shall see later, and social activism remains an option for sociologists. Some sociologists are content to study various aspects of social life, interpret their findings, and publish these findings in sociology journals. Others direct their research and publications toward social change and actively participate in community affairs to help bring about their vision of a more just society.

During the past two decades, the activities of sociologists have broadened. Once just about the only occupation open to a graduate in sociology was teaching. Although most sociologists still enter teaching, the government has now become their second-largest source of employment. Many other sociologists work for private firms in management and planning positions. Still others work in criminology and demography, in social work, and as counselors. Sociologists put their training to use in such diverse efforts as tracking the spread of AIDS and helping teenage prostitutes escape from pimps. Later we shall look more closely at some of these applications of sociology.

At this point, however, let's concentrate on a better understanding of sociological theory.

Theoretical Perspectives in Sociology

Facts never interpret themselves. In everyday life, we interpret what we observe by using common sense, placing any particular observation or "fact" into a framework of more-or-less related ideas. Sociologists place their observations into a conceptual framework called a theory. A **theory** is a general statement about how some parts of the world fit together and how they work. It is an explanation of how two or more facts are related to one another. By providing a framework in which to fit observations, each theory interprets reality in a distinct way.

Sociologists use three major theories: symbolic interactionism, functional analysis, and conflict theory. Let's first examine the main elements of these theories. (See Table 1.1.) Then let's see how each theory provides a different understanding of social life. To do so, we'll use each theory to explain why the U.S. divorce rate is so high.

Symbolic Interactionism

We can trace the origins of **symbolic interactionism** to the Scottish moral philosophers of the eighteenth century, who noted that people evaluate their own conduct by comparing themselves with others (Stryker 1990). In the United States, a long line of thinkers added to this analysis, including the pioneering psychologist William James (1842–1910) and the educator John Dewey (1859–1952), who analyzed how people use symbols to encapsulate their experiences. This theoretical perspective was brought into sociology by sociologists Charles Horton Cooley (1864–1929), William I. Thomas (1863–1947), and George Herbert Mead (1863–1931). Cooley's and Mead's analyses of how symbols lie at the basis of the self-concept are discussed on pages 66–69.

Symbolic interactionists view *symbols*—things to which we attach meaning—as the basis of social life. First, without symbols our social relations would be limited to the animal level, for we would have no mechanism for perceiving others in terms of relationships (aunts and uncles, employers and teachers, and so on). Strange as it may seem, only because we have symbols can we have aunts and uncles, for it is these symbols that define for us what such relationships entail. Second, without symbols we could not coordinate our actions with others; we would be unable to make plans for a future date, time, and place. Unable to specify times, materials, sizes, or goals, we could not build bridges and highways. Without symbols, there would be no books, movies, or musical instruments. We would have no schools or hospitals, no government, no religion. In short, as symbolic interactionists point out, symbols make social life possible. Third, even the self is a sym-

George Herbert Mead (1863–1931) is one of the founders of symbolic interactionism, a major theoretical perspective in sociology. He taught at the University of Chicago, where his lectures were very popular. Though he wrote very little, after his death his students compiled his lectures into an influential book, Mind, Self, and Society.

theory: a general statement about how some parts of the world fit together and how they work; an explanation of how two or more facts are related to one another

symbolic interactionism: a theoretical perspective in which society is viewed as composed of symbols that people use to establish meaning, develop their views of the world, and communicate with one another

		TABLE 1.1		

Major Theoretical Perspectives in Sociology

Perspective	Usual Level of Analysis	Focus of Analysis	Key Terms	Applying the Perspectives to the U.S. Divorce Rate
Symbolic Interactionism	Microsociological—examines small-scale patterns of social interaction	Face-to-face interaction; how people use symbols to create social life	Symbols Interaction Meanings Definitions	Industrialization and urbanization change marital roles and lead to a redefinition of love, marriage, children, and divorce.
Functional Analysis (also called *functionalism and structural functionalism*)	Macrosociological—examines large-scale patterns of society	Relationships among the parts of society; how these parts are *functional* (have beneficial consequences) or *dysfunctional* (have negative consequences)	Structure Functions (manifest and latent) Dysfunctions Equilibrium	As social change erodes the traditional functions of the family, family ties are weakened and the divorce rate increases.
Conflict Theory	Macrosociological—examines large-scale patterns of society	The struggle for scarce resources by groups in a society; how dominant elites use power to control the less powerful	Inequality Power Conflict Competition Exploitation	When men control economic life, the divorce rate is low because women find few alternatives to a bad marriage; the rising divorce rate reflects a shift in the balance of power between men and women.

bol, for it consists of the ideas that we have about who we are. And it is a changing symbol, for as we interact with others, we constantly adjust our views of the self based on how we interpret the reactions of others.

Symbolic interactionists analyze how our behaviors depend on how we define ourselves and others. For example, if you think of someone as an aunt or uncle, you behave in certain ways, but if you think of that person as a boyfriend or girlfriend, you behave quite differently. It is as though everyday life is a stage on which we perform, switching roles to suit our changing audiences. Symbolic interactionists primarily examine face-to-face interaction, looking at how people work out their relationships and make sense out of life and their place in it.

Applying Symbolic Interactionism.   To better understand symbolic interactionism, let us see how changing symbols (meanings) help to explain the high U.S. divorce rate. For background, understand that marriage used to be seen as a sacred, lifelong commitment, and divorce as evil, a flagrant abandoning of adult responsibilities.

1. *Emotional satisfaction.* In the earlier part of this century, symbolic interactionists observed that the basis for family solidarity was changing. As early as 1933, sociologist William Ogburn noted that personality was becoming more important in mate selection. Then in 1945, sociologists Ernest Burgess and Harvey Locke found that family solidarity was coming to depend more and more on mutual affection, understanding, and compatibility. What these sociologists had observed was a fundamental shift in U.S. marriage: Husbands and wives were coming to expect—and demand—greater emotional satisfaction from one another.

    As this trend intensified, intimacy became the core of marriage. At the same time, as society grew more complex and impersonal, Americans came to see marriage as a solution to the tensions that society produced (Lasch 1977). This new form, "companionate marriage," contributed to divorce, for it encouraged people to expect that their spouse would satisfy "each and every need." Consequently, sociologists say, marriage became an "overloaded institution."

2. *The love symbol.* Our symbol of love also helps to "overload" marriage. Unrealistic expectations that "true love" will be a constant source of emotional satisfaction set people up for crushed hopes, for when dissatisfactions enter marriage, as they inevitably do, spouses tend to blame one another for what they see as the other's failure. Their engulfment in the symbol of love at the time of marriage blinds them to the basic unreality of their expectations.

3. *The meaning of children.* Ideas about childhood have undergone a deep historical shift with far-reaching consequences for the contemporary U.S. family (Henslin 1992a). In medieval European society children were seen as miniature adults, and there was no sharp separation between the worlds of adults and children (Ariès 1962). Boys were apprenticed at about age 7, while girls at the same age learned the homemaking duties associated with the wifely role. In the United States, just three generations ago children "became adults" when they graduated from eighth grade and took employment. The contrast is amazing: From miniature adults, children have been culturally fashioned into impressionable, vulnerable, and innocent beings.

4. *The meaning of parenthood.* These changed notions of childhood have had a corresponding impact on our ideas of good parenting. Today's parents are expected not only to provide unending amounts of affection, love, and tender care but also to take responsibility for ensuring that their children "reach their potential." Today's child rearing lasts longer and is more demanding, pushing the family into even greater "emotional overload" (Lasch 1977).

5. *Marital roles.* In earlier generations, newlyweds knew what they could legitimately expect from each other, for the responsibilities and privileges of husbands and wives were clearly defined. In contrast, today's much vaguer guidelines leave couples to work out more aspects of their respective roles on their own. Many find it difficult to figure out how to divide up responsibilites for work, home, and children.

6. *Perception of alternatives.* While the above changes in marriage expectations were taking place, another significant social change was under way: More and more women began taking jobs outside the home. As they earned paychecks of their own, many wives began for the first time to see alternatives to remaining in unhappy marriages. Symbolic interactionists consider the perception of an alternative an essential first step to making divorce possible.

7. *The meaning of divorce.* As these various factors coalesced—greater expectations of emotional satisfaction and changed marital and parental roles, accompanied by a new perception of alternatives to an unhappy marriage—divorce steadily increased. (Figure 1.2 shows the increase in divorce in the United States, from practically zero in 1890 to the current 1.2 million divorces a year. The plateau for both marriage and divorce since 1980 is probably due to increased cohabitation.)

    As divorce became more common, its meaning changed. Once a symbol of almost everything negative—failure, irresponsibility, even immorality—divorce became infused with new meanings—personal change, opportunity, even liberation. This symbolic change from failure to self-fulfillment reduced the stigma of divorce, setting the stage for divorce on an even larger scale.

8. *Changes in the law.* The law, itself a powerful symbol, began to reflect these changed ideas about divorce—and to encourage divorce. Where previously divorce was granted only when the most rigorous criteria, such as adultery, were met, legislators now made "incompatibility" legitimate grounds for divorce. Eventually, states pioneered "no-fault" divorce, in which couples could dissolve their marriage without accusations of wrongdoing. Some even provide do-it-yourself divorce kits.

In Sum Symbolic interactionists explain an increasing divorce rate in terms of the changing symbols (or meanings) associated with both marriage and divorce. Changes in people's ideas—about divorce, marital satisfaction, love, the nature of children and parenting, and the roles of husband and wife—have put extreme pressure on today's married couples. No single change is *the* cause, but taken together, these changes provide a strong "push" toward divorce.

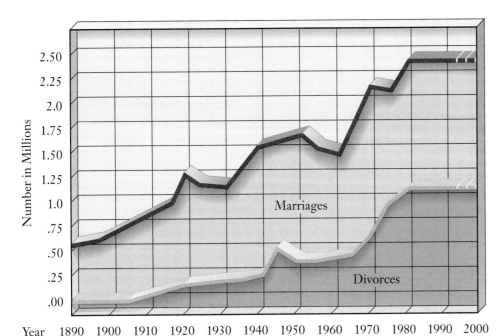

Figure 1.2

U.S. Marriage, U.S. Divorce

Sources: For 1996, "Population Update" 1997; for 1950–1990, *Statistical Abstract* 1994: Table 146; and 1995: Table 142; earlier editions for earlier years. The broken lines indicate the author's estimates.

Are these changes good or bad? Central to symbolic interactionism is the position that to make a value judgment about change (or anything else) requires a value framework from which to view the change. Symbolic interactionism provides no such value framework. In short, symbolic interactionists, like other sociologists, can analyze social change, but they cannot pass judgment on that change.

Functional Analysis

The central idea of **functional analysis** is that society is a whole unit, made up of interrelated parts that work together. Functional analysis, also known as *functionalism* and *structural functionalism*, is rooted in the origins of sociology (Turner 1978). Auguste Comte and Herbert Spencer viewed society as a kind of living organism. Just as a biological organism has interrelated tissues and organs that function together, they wrote, so does society. Like an organism, if society is to function smoothly, its various parts must work together in harmony.

Emile Durkheim also saw society as composed of many parts, each with its own function. When all the parts of society fulfill their functions, society is in a "normal" state. If they do not fulfill their functions, society is in an "abnormal" or "pathological" state. To understand society, then, functionalists say that we need to look at both *structure* (how the parts of a society fit together to make the whole) and *function* (what each part does, how it contributes to society).

Although Robert Merton dismissed the organic analogy, he continued the essence of functionalism—the image of society as a whole composed of interrelated parts. Merton used the term *functions* to refer to the beneficial consequences of people's actions that help keep a group (society, social system) in equilibrium. In contrast, *dysfunctions* are consequences that undermine a system's equilibrium.

Functions can be either manifest or latent. If an action is intended to help some part of a system, it is a *manifest function*. For example, suppose the tuition at your college is doubled. The intention, or manifest function, of such a sharp increase may be to raise faculty salaries and thus recruit better faculty. Merton pointed out that people's actions can also have *latent functions*, unintended consequences that help a system adapt. Let us suppose that the tuition increase worked, that the quality of the faculty improved so greatly that your college gained a national reputation overnight. As a result, it was flooded with new applicants

functional analysis: a theoretical framework in which society is viewed as composed of various parts, each with a function that, when fulfilled, contributes to society's equilibrium; also known as functionalism and structural functionalism

Sociologists who use the functionalist perspective stress how industrialization and urbanization undermined the traditional functions of the family. Before industrialization, members of the family worked together as an economic unit. As production moved away from the home, it took with it first the father, and more recently the mother. One consequence is a major dysfunction, the weakening of family ties.

and was able to expand both its programs and its campus. The expansion contributed to the stability of your college, but it was unintended. Therefore, it is a *latent* function of the tuition increase.

Sometimes human actions have the opposite effect, of course, and hurt the system. Because such consequences are usually unintended, Merton called them *latent dysfunctions*. Let's assume that doubling the tuition backfired, that half the student body couldn't afford the increase and dropped out. With this loss of income, the college had to reduce salaries. They managed to get through one year this way, but then folded. Because these results were not intended and actually harmed the social system (in this case the college), they represent a *latent* dysfunction of the tuition increase.

▼   **In Sum** From the perspective of functional analysis, then, the group is a functioning whole, with each part related to the whole. Whenever we examine a smaller part, we need to look for its functions and dysfunctions to see how it is related to the larger unit. This basic approach can be applied to any social group, whether an entire society, a college, or even a group as small as a family.

Applying Functional Analysis. Now let's apply functional analysis to the U.S. divorce rate. Functionalists stress that industrialization and urbanization undermined the traditional functions of the family. Let us see how each of these basic functions has changed.

1. *Economic production.* Prior to industrialization, the family constituted an economic team. Most families found the availability of food uncertain, and family members had to cooperate in producing what they needed to survive. When industrialization moved production from home to factory, it disrupted this family team and weakened the bonds that tied family members together. Especially significant was the transfer of the husband/father to the factory, for this move separated him from the family's daily routine. In addition, the wife/mother and children now contributed less to the family's economic survival.

2. *Socialization of children.* As these sweeping economic changes occurred, the government, growing larger and more powerful, usurped many family functions. To name just one example, local schools took away from the family the responsibility of educating children. In so doing, they assumed much of the responsibility for socializing children. To make certain that families went along with this change, states passed laws requiring that children attend school and threatened parents with jail if they did not send their children.

3. *Care of the sick and elderly.* With new laws governing medical schools and hospitals, institutionalized medicine grew more powerful, and care of the sick gradually shifted from the family to outside medical specialists. As the central government expanded and its agencies multiplied, care of the aged changed from a family concern to a government obligation.

4. *Recreation.* As more disposable income became available to Americans, business enterprises sprang up to compete for that income. This cost the family much of its recreational function, for much entertainment and "fun" changed from home-based, family-centered activities to attendance at paid events.

5. *Sexual control of members.* Even the control of sexuality was not left untouched by the vast social changes that swept the country. Traditionally, only sexual relations within marriage were considered legitimate. Although this sexual control was always more ideal than real, for even among the Puritans matrimony never did enjoy a monopoly over sexual relations (Smith and Hindus 1975), it is now considerably weaker than it used to be. The "sexual revolution" of the past few decades has opened many alternatives to marital sex.

6. *Reproduction.* On the surface, the only family function that seems to have been left untouched is reproduction. Yet even this vital and seemingly inviolable function has not gone unchallenged. A prime example is the greater number of single women who are having children. Figure 1.3 shows that in the United States unmarried women now account for about one-third of all births—and that the same upward trend is common throughout the industrialized world. (Japan is the only exception.) Even schools and private agencies have taken over some of the family's control over reproduction. A married woman, for example, can get an abortion without informing her husband, and some high schools distribute condoms.

A Glimpse of the Past. To see how sharply family functions have changed, it may be useful to take a glimpse of family life in the 1800s.

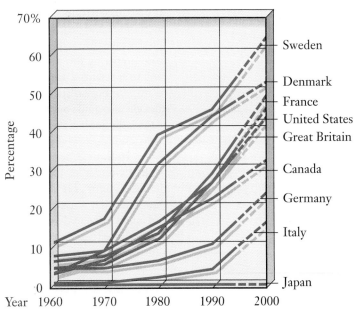

Source: *Statistical Abstract* 1994:1358 and 1997:1338.
Dotted lines indicate the author's projections.

Figure 1.3

Global Trends: Percentage of Births to Unmarried Mothers

When Phil became sick, he was nursed by Ann, his wife. She cooked for him, fed him, changed the bed linen, bathed him, read to him from the Bible, and gave him his medicine. (She did this in addition to doing the housework and taking care of their six children.) Phil was also surrounded by the children, who shouldered some of his chores while their father was sick.

When Phil died, the male neighbors and relatives made the casket while Ann, her mother, and female friends washed and dressed the body. Phil was then "laid out" in the front parlor (the formal living room), where friends, neighbors, and relatives viewed him, paying their last respects. From there friends moved his body to the church for the final message, and then to the grave they had dug.

In the 1800s, poverty was widespread in the United States. Most people were so poor that they expended their life energies on just getting enough food, fuel, and clothing to survive. Formal education beyond the first several grades was a luxury. This photo depicts the conditions of the people Du Bois worked with. (See the Down–to–Earth Sociology box on page 19.)

As you can see from this event, the functions of the family were diverse, covering many aspects of life and death that are now handled by outside agencies. Not only did the care of the sick take place almost exclusively within the family, but death was also a family affair—from preparing the body to burying it. Today we assume that such functions *properly* belong to specialized agencies, and few of us can even imagine preparing the body of a close relative for burial. Such an act may even seem grotesque, almost barbarous, for our current customs also guide our feelings, another fascinating aspect of social life, but one, regrettably, that we do not have time to pursue. (On pages 71–73, I return to the topic of emotions.)

▼ **In Sum** The family has lost many of its traditional functions, while others are presently under assault. From a functionalist perspective, these changes have weakened the family unit. The fewer functions that family members have in common, the fewer their "ties that bind." This erosion of family functions has made the family more fragile and an increase in divorce inevitable. Thus, functionalists attribute the high divorce rate in the United States to a weakening or loss of family functions, which previously had held a husband and wife together in spite of the problems they experienced.

Conflict Theory

Conflict theory provides a third perspective on social life. Karl Marx, who developed conflict theory, witnessed the Industrial Revolution that transformed Europe. He saw that peasants who had left the land to seek work in urbanizing areas had to work at wages that barely provided enough to eat. (The average worker died at age 30, the wealthy at age 50 [Edgerton 1992:87]). Shocked by this suffering and exploitation, Marx began to analyze society and history. As he did so, he developed **conflict theory,** concluding that the key to all human history is class struggle. In each society, some small group controls the means of production and exploits those who do not. In industrialized societies the struggle is between the **bourgeoisie,** the small group of capitalists who own the means to produce wealth, and the **proletariat,** the mass of workers exploited by the bourgeoisie. The capitalists also control politics, so that when workers rebel the capitalists are able to call on the power of the state to control them (Angell 1965).

When Marx made his observations, capitalism was in its infancy and workers were at the mercy of their employers. Workers had none of what we take for granted today—the right to strike, minimum wages, eight-hour days, coffee breaks, five-day work weeks, paid vacations and holidays, medical benefits, sick leave, unemployment compensation, Social Security. His analysis reminds us that these benefits came not from generous hearts, but from workers who forced concessions from their employers.

Some current conflict sociologists use conflict theory in a much broader sense. Ralf Dahrendorf (b. 1929) sees conflict as inherent in all relations that have authority. He points out that **authority,** or power that people consider legitimate, runs through all layers of society—whether small groups, a community, or the entire society. People in positions of authority try to enforce conformity, which in turn creates resentment and resistance. The result is a constant struggle throughout society to determine who has authority over what (Turner 1978).

Another sociologist, Lewis Coser (b. 1913), pointed out that conflict is especially likely to develop among people who are in close relationships. Such people are connected by a network of responsibilities, power, and rewards and to change something can easily upset arrangements that they have so carefully worked out. Consequently, we can think even of close relationships as a balancing act—of maintaining and reworking a particular distribution of responsibilities, power, and rewards.

▼ **In Sum** Unlike the functionalists who view society as a harmonious whole, with its parts working together, conflict theorists see society as composed of groups fiercely competing for scarce resources. Although alliances or cooperation may prevail on the surface, beneath that surface is a struggle for power. Marx focused on struggles between the bourgeoisie and proletariat, but today's conflict theorists have expanded this perspective to include smaller groups and even basic relationships.

conflict theory: a theoretical framework in which society is viewed as composed of groups competing for scarce resources

bourgeoisie: Karl Marx's term for capitalists, those who own the means to produce wealth

proletariat: Marx's term for the exploited class, the mass of workers who do not own the means of production

authority: power that people consider legitimate

Applying Conflict Theory.   To explain the current high rate of divorce, conflict theorists look at men's and women's relationships in terms of basic inequalities—men dominate and exploit, while women are dominated and exploited. They also point out that marriage reflects the basic male–female relationship of society and is one of the means by which men maintain their domination and exploitation of women.

Conflict theorists stress that women have traditionally been regarded as property and passed by one male, the father, to another, the husband (Dobash and Dobash 1981). In society after society, women have been assigned the role of satisfying the needs of men—their fathers, husbands, and brothers. Although marriage still reflects these millennia-old patterns of female subordination, the relationship between men and women is undergoing fundamental change. Because today's females increasingly participate in social worlds beyond the home, women refuse to bear burdens previously accepted as inevitable and are much more likely to dissolve a marriage that has become intolerable. Changing relationships of power and inequality, then, are the keys to understanding the current divorce rate (Bernard 1992). Increases in the number of women who work outside the home and in women's organizations advocating changes in male–female relationships have upset traditional imbalances of rights and obligations. Conflict in marriage is primarily due to husbands' resentment of their decreasing power and wives' resentment of their husbands' reluctance to share marital power.

▼   **In Sum** Conflict theorists see marriage as reflecting society's basic inequalities between males and females. Higher divorce rates result from changed male–female power relationships, especially as wives attempt to resolve basic inequalities and husbands resist those efforts. From the conflict perspective, then, the increase in divorce is not a sign that marriage has weakened but, rather, a sign that women are making headway in their historical struggle with men.

Levels of Analysis: Macro and Micro

A major difference between the theoretical orientations described above is their level of analysis. Functionalists and conflict theorists focus on **macro-level analysis;** that is, they examine large-scale patterns of society. In contrast, symbolic interactionists usually focus on **micro-level analysis;** that is, they analyze **social interaction,** or what people do when they are in one another's presence. (See Table 1.1, p. 21).

Let's return to the example of homelessness to make this distinction between micro and macro levels clearer. In studying the homeless, symbolic interactionists would focus on what they say and what they do. They would analyze what homeless people do when they are in shelters and on the streets, focusing especially on their communications, both their talk and their **nonverbal interaction** (how they communicate by gestures, silence, use of space, and so on). The observations I made earlier about the despair and silence of the homeless, for example, would be areas of interest to symbolic interactionists.

This micro level, however, would not interest functionalists and conflict theorists. They would focus instead on the macro level. Functionalists would examine how changes in the parts of society are related to homelessness. They might look at how changing relationships in the family (smaller, more divorce) and economic conditions (higher rents, inflation, fewer unskilled jobs, loss of jobs overseas) cause homelessness among people who are unable to find jobs and do not have a family to fall back on. For their part, conflict theorists would stress the struggle between social classes, especially how the policies of the wealthy push certain groups into unemployment and homelessness. That, they would point out, accounts for the disproportionate number of African Americans who are homeless. Chapter 4 focuses on the distinctions between macro and micro levels of analysis.

Putting the Theoretical Perspectives Together

Which theoretical perspective should we use to study human behavior? Which level of analysis is the correct one? As you have seen, these theoretical perspectives provide different and often sharply contrasting pictures of our world. No theory or level of analysis

macro-level analysis: an examination of large-scale patterns of society

micro-level analysis: an examination of small-scale patterns of society

social interaction: what people do when they are in one another's presence

nonverbal interaction: communication without words through gestures, space, silence, and so on

Down-to-Earth Sociology

Sociologists at Work: What Applied Sociologists Do

Applied sociologists work in a wide variety of settings—from counseling children to improving work relationships. To give you an idea of that variety, let's look over the shoulders of four sociologists.

Leslie Green, who does marketing research at Vanderveer Group in Philadelphia, Pennsylvania, earned her bachelor's degree in sociology at Shippensburg University. To develop marketing strategies so doctors will choose to prescribe a particular drug, her company has physicians meet in groups to discuss prescription drugs. Green sets up the meetings, locates moderators for the discussion groups, and arranges payments to the physicians who participate in the research. "My training in sociology," she says, "helps me in 'people skills.' It helps me to understand the needs of different groups, and to interact with them."

Stanley Capela, whose master's degree is from Fordham University, works as an applied sociologist at HeartShare Human Services in New York. He evaluates how children's programs—such as housing, AIDS, care in group homes, and preschool programs for developmentally disabled children—actually work, compared with what they are supposed to do. He spots problems and suggests solutions. One of his projects was to find out why adoption was taking so long, why there was a backlog of unadopted children although there was a list of eager adoptive parents. He identified the problem as an inefficient information system; that is, the paperwork got bogged down as it was routed through the system. The solution was to improve the flow of paperwork.

Laurie Banks, who received her master's degree in sociology from Fordham University, works for the New York City Health Department, where she analyzes vital statistics.

By examining data on death certificates, she identified high- and low-cancer areas in the city. She found that a Polish neighborhood had high rates of stomach cancer. Follow-up interviews by the Centers for Disease Control traced the cause to eating large amounts of sausage. In another case, she compared birth certificates and school records and found that problems at birth—low birth weight, lack of prenatal care, and birth complications—were linked to low reading skills and behavior problems in school.

Ross Cappell, whose doctorate is from Temple University, runs his own research company, Social Research Corporation, in Philadelphia. His work, too, is filled with variety—from surveying the customers of a credit card company so the company can understand its market to analyzing the impact of fare increases in public transportation. In one case, Cappell was asked to evaluate the services that unemployed workers received when a steel mill closed down. He found that the services and training were not particularly helpful. Too many workers were retrained in a single field, such as air conditioner repair, and the local market was flooded with more specialists than it could use. When Cappell testified before Congress, he stressed how the training given to displaced workers must match the needs of the local labor market.

From just this small sample, you can catch a glimpse of the amazing variety of work that applied sociologists do. You can see that some applied sociologists work for corporations, some for government and private agencies, and others operate their own firms. You can also see that a doctorate is not necessary to work as an applied sociologist. For another example of an applied sociologist at work, see the Down-to-Earth Sociology box on page 134.

encompasses all of reality. Rather, by focusing on different features of social life, each provides a distinctive interpretation. Consequently, it is necessary to use all three theoretical lenses to analyze human behavior. By putting the contributions of each perspective and level of analysis together, we gain a more comprehensive picture of social life.

As you can see, the sociological perspective leads to an entirely different understanding of divorce than the commonsense understanding of "They were simply incompatible." To take this larger view of human events, which is the sociological perspective, gives us a different way of viewing social life. This will become even more apparent in the following chapters as we explore topics as broad as sexism and as highly focused as a kindergarten classroom.

Applied and Clinical Sociology

Sociologists Paul Lazarsfeld and Jeffrey Reitz (1989) divide sociology in the United States into three phases. First, as we have already seen, when sociology began it was indistinguishable from attempts to reform society. The primary concern of early sociologists was to make the world a better place. The purpose of analyzing social conditions was to use the information to improve social life. Albion Small, one of the first presidents of the American Sociological Society (1912–1913), said that the primary reason for the existence of sociology was its "practical application to the improvement of social life." Sociologists, he said, should use science to gain knowledge and then use that knowledge to "realize visions" (Fritz 1989). This first phase of sociology lasted until the 1920s.

During the second phase, it became the goal of sociologists to establish sociology as a respected field of knowledge. To this end, sociologists sought to develop **pure** or **basic sociology,** that is, research and theory aimed at making discoveries about life in human groups, but not at making changes in those groups. This goal was soon achieved, and within a generation sociology was incorporated into almost every college and university curriculum in the United States. World War II marked the end of this phase.

During the third and current phase, there has been an attempt to merge sociological knowledge and practical work. Dissatisfied with "knowledge for the sake of knowledge," many sociologists use their sociological skills to bring about social change, to make a difference in social life. The final results of this phase are not yet known, but the emphasis on applying sociology has gained much momentum in just the past few years.

Efforts to blend sociological knowledge and practical results are known as **applied sociology.** This term refers to the use of sociology to solve problems. One of the first attempts at applied sociology—and one of the most successful—was the founding of the NAACP by W.E.B. Du Bois and sociologists Jane Addams and Florence Kelley of Hull-House (Deegan 1988). Today's applied sociologists work in a variety of settings, recommending practical changes that can be implemented. A business firm may hire a sociologist to solve a problem in the workplace; sociologists may do research for government commissions or agencies investigating social problems such as pornography, crime, violence, or environmental pollution. The Down-to-Earth Sociology box on the preceding page features sociologists who do applied sociology.

Some applied sociologists not only make recommendations for change based on their findings but they themselves become directly involved in solving problems. This type of applied sociology is called **clinical sociology.** Clinical sociologists who work in industrial settings may try to change work conditions to reduce job turnover. Others work with drug addicts and ex-convicts, while still others are family counselors who try to change basic relationships between a husband and wife or between children and their parents. Figure 1.4 contrasts basic and applied sociology.

The Future. Sociology is now swinging full circle. From an initial concern with improving society, sociologists switched their focus to developing abstract knowledge. Currently sociologists are again seeking ways to apply their findings. These efforts have gained momentum in recent years, and the future is likely to see much more applied sociology. Many departments of sociology now offer courses in applied sociology, and some offer specialties, and even internships, in applied sociology at both the graduate and undergraduate levels.

pure or basic sociology: sociological research whose only purpose is to make discoveries about life in human groups, not to make changes in those groups

applied sociology: the use of sociology to solve problems—from the micro level of family relationships to the macro level of crime and pollution

clinical sociology: the direct involvement of sociologists in bringing about social change

Figure 1.4

Comparing Basic and Applied Sociology

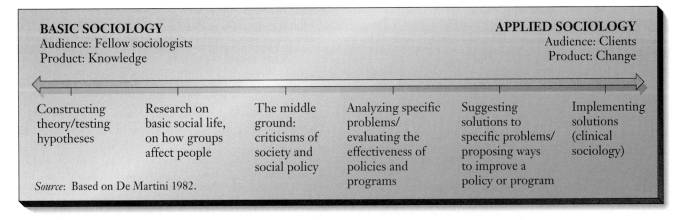

BASIC SOCIOLOGY					APPLIED SOCIOLOGY
Audience: Fellow sociologists					Audience: Clients
Product: Knowledge					Product: Change
Constructing theory/testing hypotheses	Research on basic social life, on how groups affect people	The middle ground: criticisms of society and social policy	Analyzing specific problems/ evaluating the effectiveness of policies and programs	Suggesting solutions to specific problems/ proposing ways to improve a policy or program	Implementing solutions (clinical sociology)

Source: Based on De Martini 1982.

These changes are taking sociology closer to its starting point. They provide renewed contact with the discipline's roots, promising to invigorate sociology as they challenge us to grasp a vision of what society can become—and what sociology's role can be in that process of change.

Summary and Review

The Sociological Perspective

What is the sociological perspective?

The **sociological perspective** stresses that people's social experiences—the groups to which they belong and their particular experiences within these groups—underlie their behavior. C. Wright Mills referred to this as the intersection of biography (the individual) and history (social factors acting on the individual). Pp. 4–6.

Sociology and the Other Sciences

What is science, and where does sociology fit in?

Science is the application of systematic methods to obtain knowledge and the knowledge obtained by those methods. The sciences are divided into the **natural sciences,** which seek to comprehend, explain, and predict events in the natural environment; and the **social sciences,** which seek to understand the social world objectively by means of controlled and repeated observations. **Sociology** is the scientific study of society and human behavior. Pp. 6–9.

The Development of Sociology

When did sociology first appear as a separate discipline, and what factors contributed to its emergence?

Sociology emerged as a separate discipline in the mid-1800s in western Europe, during the onset of the Industrial Revolution. Industrialization brought social changes so sweeping they affected all aspects of human existence—where people lived, the nature of their work, and interpersonal relationships. Early sociologists who focused on these social changes include Auguste Comte, Herbert Spencer, Karl Marx, Harriet Martineau, Emile Durkheim, and Max Weber. Pp. 9–14.

The Role of Values in Social Research

Should the purpose of social research be only to advance human understanding or also to reform society?

All sociologists concur that social research should be **value free:** the researcher's personal beliefs should be set aside in order to permit objective findings. But sociologists do not agree on the uses and purposes of social research. Some believe its purpose should be only to advance understanding of human behavior; others, that its goal should be to reform harmful social arrangements. Pp. 14–15.

Verstehen and Social Facts

How do sociologists use Verstehen **and social facts to investigate human behavior?**

According to Weber, to understand why people act as they do, sociologists must try to put themselves in their shoes. He used the German term *Verstehen,* "to grasp by insight," to describe this essentially subjective approach. Although not denying the importance of *Verstehen,* Emile Durkheim emphasized the importance of uncovering "social facts" that influence human actions. **Social facts** are objective social conditions that influence how people behave. Contemporary sociology uses both approaches to understand human behavior. Pp. 15–16.

Sexism and Early Sociology

What was the position of women in early sociology?

Only a few wealthy women received advanced education, and their writings were largely ignored. Harriet Martineau is an example. P. 17.

Sociology in North America

How recently were academic departments of sociology established in the United States?

The earliest departments of sociology were established around the turn of the twentieth century at the universities of Chicago, Kansas, and Atlanta. During the 1940s sociology was dominated by the University of Chicago. Today, no single university or theoretical perspective dominates. In sociology's early years, the contributions of women and minorities were largely ignored. Pp. 17–20.

Theoretical Perspectives in Sociology

What is a theory?

A **theory** is a general statement about how sets of facts are related to one another. A theory provides a conceptual framework within which facts are interpreted. P. 20.

What are the major theoretical perspectives?

Sociologists make use of three primary theoretical frameworks to interpret social life. **Symbolic interactionism** examines how people use symbols to develop and share their views of the world. Symbolic interactionists usually focus at the micro level—on small-scale patterns of human interaction. **Functional analysis,** in contrast, focuses on the macro level—on large-scale patterns of society. Functional theorists stress that a social system is made up of various parts. When working properly, each part contributes to the stability of the whole, fulfilling a function that contributes to a system's equilibrium. **Conflict theory** also focuses on large-scale patterns of society. Conflict theorists stress that society is composed of competing groups struggling for scarce resources.

Because no single theory encompasses all of reality, at different times sociologists may use any or all of the three theoretical lenses. With each perspective focusing on certain features of social life and each providing its own interpretation, their combined insights yield a more comprehensive picture of social life. Pp. 20–28.

Applied and Clinical Sociology

What is the difference between pure (or basic) and applied sociology?

Pure (or basic) **sociology** is sociological research whose only purpose is to make discoveries. In contrast, **applied sociology** is the use of sociology to solve problems. Pp. 28–30.

Where can I read more on this topic?

Suggested readings for this chapter are listed on page 659.

 Sociology and the Internet

All URLs listed are current as of the printing of this book. URLs are often changed. Please check our Web site http://www.abacon.com/henslin for updates.

1. To learn more about sociology's founders, including Comte, Durkheim, Marx, and many others, go to the Dead Sociologists Society site *http://www.runet.edu/~lridener/DSS/DEADSOC.HTML* and select one of the sociologists discussed in the text. Gather material for a report on the sociologist's personal background, ideas, and writing. Present your findings to the class as part of a panel discussion on early sociologists.

If you can't access the site (it may have moved), go to one of the following search engines and enter the words "dead sociologists" (without the quotation marks). Some search engine addresses are:

http://www.lycos.com/
http://www.excite.com/
http://webcrawler.com/

2. After reading the section "Applied and Clinical Sociology" and the Box "Sociologists at Work: What Applied Sociologists Do," browse the National Coalition for the Homeless' home page *http://nch.ari.net* Write a one-page paper addressing the following: If you were a sociologist working for the coalition, what specific concerns might you consider? What kinds of uniquely sociological perspectives might you have to offer? What facts about homelessness surprised you? Why is homelessness viewed as a social problem instead of as a uniquely individual matter?

3. The Beanie Baby Craze caught the United States, Canada, and Europe by storm. If you are unfamiliar with this social phenomenon, go to the following sites:

http://beaniemom.com
http://www.ty.com
http://beaniex.com
http://beaniemania.com

Many people have tried to explain how small beanbag animals that cost between five and seven dollars retail could have caused people to stand in line for hours, spend days on the Internet, and pay hundreds of dollars to acquire them. Many have used economic terms such as *supply and demand* to explain it. Using the information from the above links, as well as what you have learned about the sociological perspective in the text, describe why both adults and children went crazy for this toy. How would Emile Durkheim explain this event? What about Karl Marx? How would Herbert Spencer describe what he sees? What would Max Weber say?

4. Examine the Beanie Baby Sites listed in item 3, and use the symbolic interactionist perspective to examine this craze. How are Beanie Babies a symbol of social life? Why were some people crazy about Beanie Babies while others were unmoved? How do changing meanings of Beanie Babies help to explain the popularity of these tiny creatures? Next, apply functional analysis to the Beanie Baby Craze. What functions do Beanie Babies serve in our society, and how has their function changed since their introduction in 1993? Finally, use conflict theory to examine this Beaniemania. How is the craze a result of basic inequalities in society? Did everyone have the same chance of obtaining Beanie Babies?

Tony Abeyta, Clan Songs, 1995

CHAPTER

2

Culture

I HAD NEVER FELT HEAT LIKE this before. If this was northern Africa, I wondered what it must be like closer to the equator. The sweat poured off me as the temperature soared past 110 degrees Fahrenheit.

As we were herded into the building—without air conditioning—hundreds of people lunged toward the counter at the rear of the building. With body crushed against body, we waited as the uniformed officials behind the windows leisurely examined each passport. It was at times like this that I wondered what I was doing in Africa.

When I had arrived in Morocco, I found the sights that greeted me exotic—not far removed from my memories of Casablanca, Raiders of the Lost Ark, *and other movies that over the years had become part of my collective memory. The men, women, and even the children did wear those white robes that reached down to their feet. What was especially striking was the fact that the women were almost totally covered. In spite of the heat, every woman wore not only a full-length gown, but also a head covering that reached down over the forehead and a veil that covered her face from the nose down. All you could make out were their eyes—and every eye the same shade of brown.*

And how short everyone was! The Arab women looked to be on average 5 feet, and the men only about three or four inches more. As the only blue-eyed, blonde 6-foot-plus person around, wearing jeans and a pullover shirt, in a world of white-robed short people, I stood out like a sore thumb. Everyone stared. No matter where I went, they stared. Wherever I looked, I found brown eyes watching intensely. Even staring back at those many dark brown eyes had no effect. It was so different from home, where, if you caught someone staring at you, the person would immediately look embarrassed and glance away.

And lines? The concept apparently didn't even exist. Buying a ticket for a bus or train meant pushing and shoving toward the ticket man (always a man—no women were visible in any public position), who just took the money from whichever outstretched hand he decided on.

And germs? That notion didn't seem to exist here either. Flies swarmed over the food in the restaurants and the unwrapped loaves of bread in the stores. Shopkeepers would considerately shoo off the flies before handing me a loaf. They also had home delivery of bread. I still remember a bread vendor delivering an unwrapped loaf to a woman standing on a second-floor balcony. She first threw her money to the bread vendor, and he then threw the unwrapped bread up to her. Only, his throw was off. The bread bounced off the wrought-iron balcony railing and landed in the street filled with people, wandering dogs, and the ever-present burros. The vendor simply picked up the loaf and threw it again. This certainly wasn't his day, for again he missed. But the man made it on his third attempt. And the woman smiled, satisfied, as she turned back into her apartment, apparently to prepare the noon meal for her hungry family.

As I stood in the oppressive heat of the Moroccan–Algerian border, the crowd had once again become unruly. Another fight had broken out. And once again, the little man in uniform appeared, shouting and knocking people aside as he forced his way to the little wooden box nailed onto the floor. Climbing onto this makeshift platform, he would shout at the crowd, his arms flailing about him. The people would grow silent. But just as soon as the man would leave, the shoving and shouting would begin again as the people clamored to get their passports stamped.

The situation had become unbearable. Pressed body to body, the man behind me had decided that this was a good time to take a nap. Determining that I made a good support, he placed his arm against my back and leaned his head against his arm. Sweat streamed from my back at the point that his arm and head touched me.

Finally, I realized that I had to abandon U.S. customs. I pushed my way forward, forcing my frame into every space I could make. At the counter, I shouted in English. The official looked up at the sound of this strange tongue, and, thrusting my long arms over the heads of three people, I shoved my passport into his hand.

Technology is central to social life. From these two forms of transportation, it becomes evident how technology limits or expands human activities—and, ultimately, how it plays a significant role in the types of societies we develop. The photo on the left is of a Tajik man in China, near Tashkurgan.

What Is Culture?

What is culture? The concept is sometimes easier to grasp by description than by definition. For example, suppose you meet a young woman who has just arrived in the United States from India. That her culture is different from yours is immediately evident. You first see it in her clothing, jewelry, makeup, and hairstyle. Next you hear it in her language. It then becomes apparent by her gestures. Later, you may hear her express unfamiliar beliefs about the world and opinions about what is valuable in life. All these characteristics are indicative of **culture,** the language, beliefs, values, norms, behaviors, and even material objects that are passed from one generation to the next.

In northern Africa, I was surrounded by a culture quite alien to my own. It was evident in everything I saw and heard. The **material culture**—such things as jewelry, art, buildings, weapons, machines, and even eating utensils, hairstyles, and clothing—provided a sharp contrast to what I was used to seeing. There is nothing inherently "natural" about material culture. That is, it is no more natural (or unnatural) to wear gowns on the street than it is to wear jeans.

I also found myself immersed in a contrasting **nonmaterial culture,** that is, a group's ways of thinking (its beliefs, values, and other assumptions about the world) and doing (its common patterns of behavior, including language, gestures, and other forms of interaction). North African assumptions about crowding to buy a ticket and staring in public are examples of nonmaterial culture. So are U.S. assumptions about not doing either of these things. Like material culture, neither custom is "right." People simply become comfortable with the customs they learn during childhood, and—as in the case of my visit to northern Africa—uncomfortable when their basic assumptions about life are challenged.

Culture and Taken-for-Granted Orientations to Life

To develop a sociological imagination, it is essential to understand how culture affects people's lives. While meeting someone from a different culture may make us aware of culture's pervasive influence, attaining the same level of awareness regarding our own culture is quite another matter. *Our* speech, *our* gestures, *our* beliefs, and *our* customs are

culture: the language, beliefs, values, norms, behaviors, and even material objects that are passed from one generation to the next

material culture: the material objects that distinguish a group of people, such as their art, buildings, weapons, utensils, machines, hairstyles, clothing, and jewelry

nonmaterial culture: a group's ways of thinking (including its beliefs, values, and other assumptions about the world) and doing (its common patterns of behavior, including language and other forms of interaction) usually taken for granted. We assume that they are "normal" or "natural," and we almost always follow them without question. As anthropologist Ralph Linton (1936) said, "The last thing a fish would ever notice would be water." So it is with people: Except in unusual circumstances, the effects of our own culture generally remain imperceptible to us.

Yet culture's significance is profound; it touches almost every aspect of who and what we are. We came into this life without a language, without values and morality, with no ideas about religion, war, money, love, use of space, and so on. We possessed none of these fundamental orientations that we take for granted and that are so essential in determining the type of people we are. Yet at this point in our lives we all have them. Sociologists call this culture *within* us. These learned and shared ways of believing and of doing (another definition of culture) penetrate our beings at an early age and quickly become part of our taken-for-granted assumptions concerning normal behavior. *Culture becomes the lens through which we perceive and evaluate what is going on around us.* Seldom do we question these assumptions, for, like water to a fish, the framework from which we view life remains largely beyond our ordinary perception.

The rare instances in which these assumptions are challenged, however, can be upsetting. Although as a sociologist I should be able to look at my own culture "from the outside," my trip to Africa quickly revealed how fully I had internalized my own culture. My upbringing in Western industrialized society had given me strong assumptions about aspects of social life that had become deeply rooted in my being—staring, hygiene, and the use of space. But in this part of Africa these assumptions were useless for helping me get through daily life. No longer could I count on people to stare only surreptitiously, to take precautions against invisible microbes, or to stand in an orderly way one behind the other on the basis of time of arrival to obtain a service.

As you can tell from the opening vignette, I personally found these different assumptions upsetting, for they violated my basic expectations of "the way people *ought* to be"—although I did not even know I held these expectations until they were so abruptly challenged. When my nonmaterial culture failed me—when it no longer enabled me to make sense out of the world—I experienced a disorientation known as **culture shock.** In the case of buying tickets, the fact that I was several inches taller than most Moroccans and thus able to outreach almost everyone helped me to adjust partially to their different ways of doing things. But I never did get used to the idea that pushing ahead of others was "right," and I always felt guilty when I used my size to receive preferential treatment.

An important consequence of culture within us is **ethnocentrism,** a tendency to use our own group's ways of doing things as the yardstick for judging others. All of us learn that the ways of our own group are good, right, proper, and even superior to other ways of life. As sociologist William Sumner (1906), who developed this concept, said, "One's own group is the center of everything, and all others are scaled and rated with reference to it." Ethnocentrism has both positive and negative consequences. On the positive side, it creates in-group loyalties. On the negative side, ethnocentrism can lead to harmful discrimination against people whose ways differ from ours.

The effects of culture on our lives fascinate sociologists. By examining more explicitly just how profoundly culture affects everything we are, this chapter will serve as a basis from which you can start to analyze your previously unquestioned assumptions of reality and thus help you gain a different perspective on social life and your role in it.

▼ **In Sum** To avoid losing track of the ideas under discussion, let's pause for a moment to summarize, and in some instances clarify, the principles we have covered.

1. There is nothing "natural" about material culture. Arabs wear gowns on the street and feel that it is natural to do so; Americans do the same with jeans.

2. There is nothing "natural" about nonmaterial culture; it is just as arbitrary to stand in line as it is to push and shove.

3. Culture penetrates deep into the recesses of our spirits, becoming a taken-for-granted aspect of our lives.

culture shock: the disorientation that people experience when they come in contact with a fundamentally different culture and can no longer depend on their taken-for-granted assumptions about life

ethnocentrism: the use of one's own culture as a yardstick for judging the ways of other individuals or societies, generally leading to a negative evaluation of their values, norms, and behaviors

4. Culture provides the lens through which we see the world and obtain our perception of reality.

5. Culture provides implicit instructions that tell us what we ought to do in various situations. It provides a fundamental basis for our decision making.

6. Culture also provides a "moral imperative"; that is, by internalizing a culture, people learn ideas of right and wrong. (I, for example, deeply believed that it was unacceptable to push and shove to get ahead of others.)

7. Coming into contact with a radically different culture challenges our basic assumptions of life. (I experienced culture shock when I discovered that my deeply ingrained cultural ideas about the use of space and hygiene no longer applied.)

8. Although the particulars of culture differ from one group of people to another, culture itself is universal. That is, all people have culture. There are no exceptions. A society cannot exist without developing shared, learned ways of dealing with the demands of life.

9. All people are ethnocentric, which has both functional and dysfunctional consequences.

cultural relativism: understanding a people from the framework of its own culture

Practicing Cultural Relativism

To counter our tendency to use our own culture as a standard to judge other cultures, we can practice **cultural relativism;** that is, we can try to understand a culture on its own terms. Cultural relativism is to look at how the elements of a culture fit together, without judging those elements as superior or inferior to one's own way of life.

Because we tend to use our own culture to judge others, cultural relativism presents a challenge to ordinary thinking. For example, most U.S. citizens appear to have strong feelings against raising bulls for the sole purpose of stabbing them to death in front of crowds shouting "Olé!" According to cultural relativism, however, bullfighting must be viewed strictly within the context of the culture in which it takes place—*its* history, *its* folklore, *its* ideas of bravery, and *its* ideas of sex roles.

You may still regard bullfighting as wrong, of course, if your culture, which lies deep within you, has no history of bullfighting. We all possess culturally specific ideas about cruelty to animals, ideas that have evolved slowly and match other elements of our culture. In the United States, for example, practices that once were common in some areas—cock fighting, dog fighting, bear–dog fighting, and so on—have been gradually weeded out (Bryant 1993).

None of us can be entirely successful at practicing cultural relativism; we simply cannot help viewing a contrasting way of life through the lens that our own culture provides. Cultural relativism, however, is an attempt to mute that lens and thereby appreciate other ways of life rather than simply asserting, "Our way is right."

Although cultural relativism is a worthwhile goal and helps us to avoid cultural smugness, this view has come under attack. In a provocative book, *Sick Societies* (1992), anthropologist Robert Edgerton points out that some cultures endanger their people's health, happiness, or survival. He suggests that we should develop a scale to evaluate cultures on their "quality of life," much as we do for U.S. cities. He also asks why we should consider cultures that practice female genital mutilation, gang

Many Americans perceive bullfighting, which is illegal in the United States, as a cruel activity that should be abolished everywhere in the world. To Spaniards and those who have inherited Spanish culture, however, bullfighting is a beautiful, artistic sport in which matador and bull blend into a unifying image of power, courage, and glory. Cultural relativism requires the suspension of our own perspectives in order to grasp the perspectives of others, much easier described than attained.

The material culture in which we are reared becomes a taken-for-granted part of our lives. It is no more natural, or unnatural, for the Arab women in the photo above to wear gowns, veils, and head coverings in public than it is for the U.S. women in the photo on the right to appear on the beach in scanty attire. For Americans, the scene above appears strange, and for some, distressful, for they see this clothing as a sign of female subservience in a male-dominated society. For many Moroccans, the scene on the right is not only strange, but distressful, as they consider it a sign of moral depravity.

rape, wife beating, or that sell daughters into prostitution as morally equivalent to those that do not. Cultural values that result in exploitation, he says, are inferior to those that enhance people's lives.

Edgerton's sharp questions and incisive examples bring us to a point that will come up repeatedly in this text—disagreements that arise among scholars as they confront changing views of reality. It is such questioning of assumptions that keeps sociology interesting.

Components of Symbolic Culture

Sociologists sometimes refer to nonmaterial culture as **symbolic culture** because a central component is the symbols that people use to communicate. A **symbol** is something to which people attach meaning and which they then use to communicate. Symbols are the basis of culture. They include gestures, language, values, norms, sanctions, folkways, and mores. Let's look at each of these components of symbolic culture.

Gestures

Gestures, the use of one's body to communicate with others, are useful shorthand ways to give messages without using words. While people in every culture of the world use gestures, their meaning may change completely from one culture to another. North Americans, for example, communicate a succinct message by raising the middle finger in a short, upward stabbing motion. I wish to stress "North Americans," for that gesture does not convey the same message in South America or most other parts of the world.

I was once surprised to find that this particular gesture was not universal, having internalized it to such an extent that I thought everyone knew what it meant. When I was comparing gestures in Mexico, however, this gesture drew a blank look from friends. After I explained its intended meaning, they laughed and showed me their rudest gesture—placing the hand under the armpit and moving the upper arm up and down. To me, they simply looked as if they were imitating a monkey, but to them the gesture meant "Your mother is a whore," absolutely the worst possible insult in that culture.

symbolic culture: another term for nonmaterial culture

symbol: something to which people attach meanings and then use to communicate with others

gestures: the ways in which people use their bodies to communicate with one another

Indicates animal height   Indicates plant height   Indicates human height

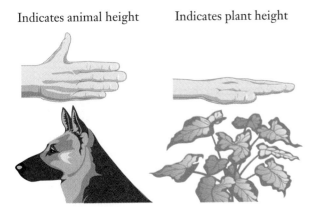

Figure 2.1

Gestures to Indicate Height, Southern Mexico

Gestures thus not only facilitate communication but, since they differ around the world, can also lead to misunderstandings, embarrassment, or worse. Once in Mexico, for example, I raised my hand to a certain height to indicate how tall a child was. My hosts began to laugh. It turned out that Mexicans use several hand gestures to indicate height: separate ones for people, animals, and plants. (See Figure 2.1.) What had amused them was that I had ignorantly used the plant gesture to indicate the child's height.

To get along in another culture, then, it is important to learn the gestures of that culture. If you don't, you will not only fail to achieve the simplicity of communication that gestures allow but you will also miss much of what is happening, run the risk of appearing foolish, and possibly offend people. In many cultures, for example, you would provoke deep offense if you were to offer food or a gift with your left hand, because the left hand is reserved for dirty tasks, such as wiping after going to the bathroom. Left-handed Americans visiting Arabs, please note!

Now suppose for a moment that you are visiting southern Italy. After eating one of the best meals in your life you are so pleased that when you catch the waiter's eye, you smile broadly and use the standard U.S. "A-OK" gesture of putting your thumb and forefinger together and making a large "O." The waiter looks horrified, and you are struck speechless when the manager asks you to leave. What have you done? Nothing on purpose, of course, but in that culture that gesture refers to a part of the human body that is not mentioned in polite company (Ekman et al. 1984).

Is it really true that there are no universal gestures? There is some disagreement on this point. Some anthropologists claim that no gestures are universal. They point out that even nodding the head up and down to indicate "yes" is not universal, since in some parts of the world, such as areas of Turkey, nodding the head up and down means "no" (Ekman et al. 1984). Ethologists, researchers who study biological bases of behavior, however, claim that expressions of anger, pouting, fear, and sadness are built into our biology and are universal (Eibl-Eibesfeldt 1970:404). They point out that even infants who are born blind and deaf, who have had no chance to learn these gestures, express themselves in the same way.

Although this matter is not yet settled, we can note that gestures tend to vary remarkably around the world. It is also significant that gestures can create emotions. Some gestures are so associated with emotional messages that the gesture itself summons up an emotion. For example, my introduction to Mexican gestures took place at a dinner table. It was evident that my husband-and-wife hosts were trying to hide their embarrassment at actually using this obscene gesture at their dinner table. And I felt the same way—not about *their* gesture, of course, which meant absolutely nothing to me—but about the one I was teaching them.

Although most gestures are learned, and therefore vary from culture to culture, some gestures that represent fundamental emotions such as sadness, anger, and fear appear to be inborn. This crying Masai child in Kenya differs little from a crying child in China or the United States or anywhere else on the globe. In a few years, however, this child will demonstrate a variety of gestures highly specific to Masai culture.

Language

The primary way in which people communicate with one another is through **language**—a system of symbols that can be strung together in an infinite number of ways for the purpose of communicating abstract thought. Each word is actually a symbol, a sound to which we have attached a particular meaning so that we can then use it to communicate with one another. Language itself is universal in the sense that all human groups have language, but there is nothing universal about the meanings given to particular sounds. Thus, like gestures, in different cultures the same sound may mean something entirely different—or may have no meaning at all. As the Down–to–Earth Sociology box below illustrates, such differences can create difficulties in communicating across cultural boundaries.

The significance of language for human life is difficult to overstate, as will become apparent from the following discussion of the primary ways that language allows culture to exist.

language: a system of symbols that can be combined in an infinite number of ways and can represent not only objects but also abstract thought

culture contact: encounter between people from different cultures, or coming in contact with some parts of a different culture

Language Allows Human Experience to Be Cumulative.   By means of language one generation is able to pass significant experiences on to the next, allowing that next generation to build on experiences it may not itself undergo. This building process enables humans to modify their behavior in the light of what previous generations have learned.

Down-to-Earth Sociology

Communicating Across Cultural Boundaries

When viewed from afar, cultural differences among human groups may be only a matter of interest. But when there is **culture contact**—that is, when we come into contact with people from different cultures—those differences can lead to problems in communication.

Not only travelers face this problem. Increasingly, business has become international, making cultural differences a practical problem for businesspeople. And at times, even highly knowledgeable and experienced firms don't quite manage to break through those cultural barriers. General Motors, for example, was very successful in marketing its automobile, the Nova, in the United States. When they decided to export that success south of the border, they were perplexed when people snickered and the car sold very, very slowly. Finally, someone let them in on the secret: In Spanish, *"No va"* is an entire sentence that means "It does not go."

Not all results are negative, of course, and businesspeople are also able to capitalize on cultural differences. In Korea, Green Giant tested local tastes and now advertises its sweet corn as a topping for ice cream sundaes. In Vantage Point, a subdivision in California, not a single street address ends in 4. Most buyers are from China, and "four" sounds like a Chinese word for death (Wysocki 1996).

A U.S. entrepreneur found out that Japanese women are embarrassed by the sounds they make in public toilets. To drown out the offensive sounds, they flush the toilet an average of 2.7 times a visit (Iori 1988). This wastes water, however, and that creates its own problems. The entrepreneur developed a battery-powered device that is mounted next to the toilet. When a woman activates the device, it emits a 25-second flushing sound. Although a toilet-sound duplicator may seem useless for our culture, the Japanese government and private companies are buying about three thousand of these devices a month.

Let's suppose that you were publishing a magazine about sports heroes in Japan. It wouldn't surprise you to know that your readers expect you to chronicle their idol's height and hobbies. But they also expect to read about their hero's blood type, for it is viewed as a sort of zodiac birth sign (Ono 1993). And if you could get hold of the idol's umbilical cord (Japanese mothers save that last little bit of a baby's umbilical cord in a wooden box), you could make a small fortune (Shirouzu 1995).

If you ran a golf course, you would have to understand why Japanese golfers are alarmed if they are so unlucky as to shoot a hole-in-one: it obligates them to buy expensive gifts for their fellow players, to throw a drinking party, and to plant a commemorative tree near the tee to mark their "joy." Of course, to ward off such a catastrophe, for $100 golfers can buy $5,000 hole-in-one insurance before a game (Hardy 1993a).

Japanese trying to get along in the United States, of course, also face cultural hurdles, but at least they have a plain-talking phrase book to guide them, called *New York English* (Hardy 1993b). There they will learn how "real" Americans talk, memorizing such phrases as "suck face" and "chill out." But what about the subtle differences, such as when *not* to say the phrase (which this book teaches) "Get outta my face, you lying bag of scum!"? (Probably at this point the Japanese value of learning martial arts comes in handy.)

Hence the central sociological significance of language: *Language allows culture to develop by freeing people to move beyond their immediate experiences.*

Without language, human culture would be little more advanced than that of the lower primates. People would be limited to communicating by some system of grunts and gestures, which would greatly shorten the temporal dimension of human life and limit communication to a small time zone surrounding the immediate present: events now taking place, those which have just taken place, or those which will immediately take place—a sort of "slightly extended present." You can grunt and gesture, for example, that you want a drink of water, but in the absence of language how could you share ideas concerning past or future events? There would be little or no way to communicate to others what event you had in mind, much less the greater complexities that humans communicate—ideas and feelings about events.

Language Provides a Social or Shared Past.   Even without language, an individual would still have memories of experiences. Those memories, however, would be extremely limited, for people associate experiences with words and then use words to recall the experience. Such memories as would exist in the absence of language would also be highly individualized, for they could be but rarely and incompletely communicated to others, much less discussed and agreed on. With language, however, events can be codified, that is, attached to words and then recalled so they can be discussed in the present.

Language Provides a Social or Shared Future.   Language also extends our time horizons forward. When people talk about past events, they share meanings that allow them to decide how they will or should act in similar circumstances in the future. Because language enables people to agree with one another concerning times, dates, and places, it also allows them to plan activities with one another.

Think about it for a moment. Without language how could people ever plan future events? How could they possibly communicate goals, purposes, times, and plans? Whatever planning could exist would have to be limited to extremely rudimentary communications, perhaps to an agreement to meet at a certain place when the sun is in a certain position. But think of the difficulty, perhaps impossibility, of conveying just a slight change in this simple arrangement, such as "I can't make it tomorrow."

Language Allows Shared Perspectives or Understandings.   Our ability to speak, then, allows us a social past and future. These two vital aspects of our humanity represent a watershed that distinguishes us from animals. But speech does much more than this. When humans talk with one another, they are exchanging ideas about events, that is, exchanging perspectives. Their words are the embodiment of their experiences, distilled and codified into a readily exchangeable form, mutually intelligible for people who have learned that language. Talking about events allows people to arrive at the shared understandings that form the essence of social life.

Language Allows Complex, Shared, Goal-Directed Behavior.   Common understandings further enable people to establish a *purpose* for getting together. Let us suppose that you want to go on a picnic. You use speech not only to plan the picnic but also to decide on reasons for the picnic—which may be anything from "because it's a nice day and it shouldn't be wasted studying" to "because it's my birthday." Language permits you to blend individual activities into an integrated sequence. In other words, through discussion you decide where you will go; who will drive; who will bring the hamburgers, the potato chips, the soda; where you will meet; and so on. Only because of language can you participate in such a common yet complex event.

Language and Perception: The Sapir–Whorf Hypothesis.   In the 1930s, two anthropologists, Edward Sapir and Benjamin Whorf, became intrigued when they noted that the Hopi Indians of the southwestern United States had no words to distinguish among the past, the present, and the future. English, in contrast, as well as German,

French, Spanish, and so on, distinguish carefully just when something takes place. From this observation, Sapir and Whorf concluded that the commonsense idea that words are merely labels that people attach to things was wrong. Language, they concluded, has embedded in it ways of looking at the world. Thus thinking and perception are not only expressed through language, but are also shaped by language. When we learn a language, we learn not only words, but also a particular way of thinking and perceiving (Sapir 1949; Whorf 1956).

The implications of the **Sapir–Whorf hypothesis,** which alerts us to how extensively language affects us, are far-reaching. *The Sapir–Whorf hypothesis reverses common sense:* It indicates that rather than objects and events forcing themselves onto our consciousness, it is our very language that determines our consciousness, and hence our perception, of objects and events. Eskimos, for example, have many words for snow. As Eskimo children learn their language, they learn distinctions between types of snowfalls that are imperceptible to non-Eskimo speakers. Others might learn to see heavy and light snowfalls, wet and dry snowfalls, and so on; but not having words for "fine powdery," "thicker powdery," and "more granual" snowfalls actually prevents them from perceiving snow in the same way as Eskimos do.

Although Sapir's and Whorf's observation that the Hopi do not have tenses was incorrect (Edgerton 1992:27), we still need to take their conclusion seriously, for the classifications that we humans develop as we try to make sense of our worlds do influence our perception. Sociologist Eviatar Zerubavel (1991) gives a good example. Hebrew, his native language, does not differentiate between jam and jelly. Only when Zerubavel learned English could he "see" this difference, which is "obvious" to native English speakers. Similarly, if you learn to classify students as "dweebs," "dorks," "nerds," "brains," and so on, you will perceive a student who asks several questions during class in an entirely different way from someone who does not know these classifications.

▼ **In Sum** The sociological significance of language is that it takes us beyond the world of apes and allows culture to develop. Language frees us from the present by providing a past and a future, giving us the capacity to share understandings about the past and to develop common perceptions about the future, as well as to establish underlying purposes for our activities. Consequently, as in the case of the picnic, each individual is able to perform a small part of a larger activity, aware that others are carrying out related parts. In this way a series of separate activities become united into a larger whole.

Language also allows us to expand our connections far beyond our immediate, face-to-face groups, so that our *individual* biological and social needs are met by extended networks of people. This development, in turn, leads to far-flung connections with our fellow humans—extending outward from our family and local community to worldwide networks of production and distribution. Although language by no means *guarantees* cooperation among people, language is an *essential* precondition of collaboration. Without language, the extended cooperative human endeavors on which society is based simply could not exist (Malinowski 1945; Hertzler 1965; Blumer 1966).

Learning a language means not just learning words but also acquiring the perceptions embedded in that language. In other words, language both reflects and shapes cultural experiences. Precisely because language is such a primary shaper of experience and culture, difficulties arise among people who live among each other but do not share a language as illustrated in the Perspectives box on the next page.

In short, our entire way of life is based on language, although, like most aspects of culture, its *linguistic base* is usually invisible to us.

Values, Norms, and Sanctions

To learn a culture is to learn people's **values,** their ideas of what is desirable in life. When we uncover people's values, we learn a great deal about them, for values are the standards by which people define good and bad, beautiful and ugly. Values underlie our preferences, guide our choices, and indicate what we hold worthwhile in life.

Sapir–Whorf hypothesis: Edward Sapir and Benjamin Whorf's hypothesis that language creates ways of thinking and perceiving

values: the standards by which people define what is desirable or undesirable, good or bad, beautiful or ugly

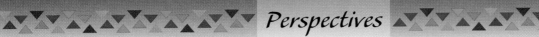

Perspectives

Miami—Language in a Changing City

In the years since Castro seized power in Cuba, the city of Miami has been transformed from a quiet southern city to a Latin-American mecca. Few things better capture Miami today than its ethnic divisions, especially its long-simmering feud over English versus Spanish. Half of the city's 360,000 residents have trouble speaking English. Only 25 percent of Miami residents speak English at home.

As this chapter stresses, language is a primary means by which people learn—and communicate—their social worlds. Consequently, Miami's language differences reflect not just cultural diversity but people who live in separate worlds. Although the ethnic stew makes Miami culturally one of the richest cities in the United States, the language gap sometimes creates anger and misunderstanding. The aggravation felt by Anglos—tinged with hostility—is seen in the bumper stickers reading, "Will the Last American Out Please Bring the Flag?"

But Latinos, now a majority in Miami, feel equally frustrated. Many feel Anglos should be able to speak at least some Spanish. Nicaraguan immigrant Pedro Falcon, for example, is studying English and wonders why more people don't try to learn his language. "Miami is the capital of Latin America," he says. "The population speaks Spanish."

Language and cultural flare-ups sometimes make headlines in the city. Latinos were outraged when an employee at the Coral Gables Board of Realtors lost her job for speaking Spanish at the office. And protesters swarmed a Publix supermarket after a cashier was fired for chatting with a friend in Spanish.

What's happening in Miami, says University of Chicago sociologist Douglas Massey, is what happened in cities such as Chicago at the beginning of the century. Then, as now, the rate of immigration exceeded the speed with which new residents learned English, creating a pile-up effect in the proportion of non-English speakers. "Becoming comfortable with English is a slow process," he points out, "whereas immigration is fast."

Massey expects the city's proportion of non-English speakers to rise with continuing immigration. But he says that this "doesn't mean in the long run that Miami is going to end up being a Spanish-speaking city." Instead, Massey believes that bilingualism will prevail. "Miami is the first truly bilingual city," he says. "The people who get ahead are not monolingual English speakers or monolingual Spanish speakers. They're people who speak both languages."

Based on Sharp 1992; Usdansky 1992.

Every group develops expectations concerning the right way to reflect its values. Sociologists use the term **norms** to describe those expectations, or rules of behavior, that develop out of a group's values. They use the term **sanctions** to refer to positive or negative reactions to the ways in which people follow norms. **Positive sanction** refers to an expression of approval given for following a norm, while **negative sanction** denotes disapproval for breaking a norm. Positive sanctions can be material, such as a money reward, a prize, or a trophy, but in everyday life they usually consist of hugs, smiles, a clap on the back, soothing words, or even handshakes. Negative sanctions can also be material—a fine is one example—but they, too, are more likely to consist of gestures, such as frowns, stares, harsh words, or raised fists. Being awarded a raise at work is a positive sanction, indicating that the norms clustering around work values have been followed, while being fired is a negative sanction, indicating the opposite. The North American finger gesture discussed earlier is, of course, a negative sanction.

Folkways and Mores

Norms that are not strictly enforced are called **folkways.** We expect people to comply with folkways, but we are likely to shrug our shoulders and not make a big deal about it if they don't. If someone insists on passing you on the left side of the sidewalk, for example, you are unlikely to take corrective action—although if the sidewalk is crowded and you must move out of the way, you might give the person a dirty look.

norms: the expectations, or rules of behavior, that develop out of values

sanctions: expressions of approval or disapproval given to people for upholding or violating norms

positive sanction: a reward given for following norms, ranging from a smile to a prize

negative sanction: an expression of disapproval for breaking a norm, ranging from a mild, informal reaction such as a frown to a formal prison sentence or an execution

folkways: norms that are not strictly enforced

The violation of mores is usually a very serious matter. In this case, it is serious enough that the police at this international rugby tournament have swung into action to protect the public from seeing a "disgraceful" sight—at least as designated by this group. Yet, unlike the reactions to most violations of mores, this scene also shows barely suppressed laughter.

Other norms, however, are taken much more seriously. We think of them as essential to our core values, and we insist on conformity. These are called **mores** (MORE-rays). A person who steals, rapes, and kills has violated some of society's most important mores. As sociologist Ian Robertson (1987:62) put it,

> A man who walks down a street wearing nothing on the upper half of his body is violating a folkway; a man who walks down the street wearing nothing on the lower half of his body is violating one of our most important mores, the requirement that people cover their genitals and buttocks in public.

It should also be noted that one group's folkways may be another group's mores. Although a man walking down the street with the upper half of his body uncovered is deviating from a folkway, a woman doing the same thing is violating a more. In addition, the folkways and mores of a subculture (the topic of the next section) may be the opposite of mainstream culture. For example, to walk down the sidewalk in a nudist camp with the entire body uncovered would conform to that subculture's folkways.

A **taboo** refers to a norm so strongly ingrained that even the thought of its violation is greeted with revulsion. Eating human flesh and having sex with one's parents are examples of such behaviors (Benales 1973; Read 1974; Henslin 1997c).

Many Cultural Worlds: Subcultures and Countercultures

> We can make epistemically subjective statements about entities that are ontologically objective, and similarly, we can make epistemically objective statements about entities that are ontologically subjective. . . . Mental phenomena are ontologically subjective; and the observer-relative features inherit that ontological subjectivity. (Searle 1995:8, 12–13)

My best guess is that you are unable to decipher the meaning of these statements. They might as well be written in Greek for all they mean to most of us. Philosophers, however, write like this, and—to them—the author's intent is clear. Philosophers form a **subculture,** *a world within the larger world of the dominant culture.* Each subculture has some distinctive way of looking at life. Even if we cannot understand the preceding quote, it makes us aware that the philosopher's view of life is not quite the same as ours.

U.S. society contains tens of thousands of subcultures. Some are as broad as the way of life we associate with teenagers, others as narrow as those we associate with body builders—or with philosophers. Some U.S. ethnic groups also form subcultures: Their values, norms, and foods set them apart. So might their religion, language, and clothing. Occupational groups also form subcultures, as anyone who has hung out with cab drivers (Davis 1959; Henslin 1993), artists (McCall 1980), or construction workers (Haas 1972) can attest. Even sociologists form a subculture, who, as you are learning, use a unique language for carving up the world.

Consider this quote from another subculture:

> If everyone applying for welfare had to supply a doctor's certificate of sterilization, if everyone who had committed a felony were sterilized, if anyone who had mental illness to any degree were sterilized—then our economy could easily take care of these people for the rest of their lives, giving them a decent living standard—but getting them out of the way. That way there would be no children abused, no surplus population, and, after a while, no pollution. . . .

> Now let's talk about stupidity. The level of intellect in this country is going down, generation after generation. The average IQ is always 100 because that is the ac-

mores: (MORE-rays) norms that are strictly enforced because they are thought essential to core values

taboo: a norm so strong that it brings revulsion if violated

subculture: the values and related behaviors of a group that distinguish its members from the larger culture; a world within a world

cepted average. However, the kid with a 100 IQ today would have tested out at 70 when I was a lad. You get the concept . . . the marching morons. . . .

When the . . . present world system collapses, it'll be good people like you who will be shooting people in the streets to feed their families. (Zellner 1995:58, 65)

Welcome to the world of the Survivalists—where the message is much clearer than that of the philosophers, and much more disturbing.

The values and norms of most subcultures are compatible with the larger society to which they belong. In some cases, however, such as these survivalists, the group's values and norms place it in opposition to the dominant culture. Sociologists use the term **counterculture** to refer to groups whose values and norms place them in opposition to mainstream culture. Heavy metal adherents who glorify satanism, hatred, cruelty, sexism, violence, and death are an example of a counterculture. Note that motorcycle enthusiasts—who emphasize personal freedom and speed *and* affirm cultural values of success—are members of a subculture. In contrast, the members of an outlaw motorcycle gang—who also stress freedom and speed, but add the values of dirtiness and despising women and work—form part of a counterculture (Watson 1988). Countercultures do not have to be negative. The Mormons, for example, were originally a counterculture when its members challenged the culture's core value of monogamy in the 1800s.

Often, members of the broader culture feel threatened by a counterculture, and they sometimes move against it in the attempt to affirm their own values. The Mormons, for example, were driven out of several states before they finally settled in Utah, what was then a wilderness. Even there the federal government would not let them practice polygyny (one man having more than one wife) and Utah's statehood was made conditional on its acceptance of monogamy (Anderson 1942/1966).

Each subculture provides its members with sets of values and distinctive ways of viewing the world. Subcultures can form around almost any topic, including, as shown here, the human body itself.

Values in U.S. Society ▶

An Overview of U.S. Values

As you well know, the United States is a **pluralistic society,** made up of many different groups. The United States has numerous religious, racial, and ethnic groups, as well as countless interest groups centering on such divergent activities as collecting Barbie dolls and hunting deer. This state of affairs makes the job of specifying U.S. values difficult. Nonetheless, sociologists have tried to identify the underlying core values that are shared by the many groups that make up U.S. society. Sociologist Robin Williams (1965) identified the following:

1. *Achievement and success.* Americans place a high value on personal achievement, especially outdoing others. This value includes getting ahead at work and school, and the goal of attaining wealth, power, and prestige.

2. *Individualism.* Americans have traditionally prized success through individual efforts and initiative. They cherish the ideal that an individual can rise from the bottom to the very top of society. If someone does not "make it" or fails to "get ahead" to the degree that others expect, Americans generally find fault with

counterculture: a group whose values, beliefs, and related behaviors place its members in opposition to the broader culture

pluralistic society: a society made up of many different groups

...where you can listen to your radio in your living room – – not in a hideout. Where you are free to hear both sides of a question and form your own opinion • *This is your America* ... *Keep it Free!*

Freedom, a major U.S. value, has different meanings for different people. By freedom, *Americans usually mean a freedom of individual action, of individual choice. People in some other cultures find this meaning of freedom excessive and willingly give up some individual freedom of choice in exchange for greater security and freedom from criminal violence. This issue of choice versus security is becoming a matter of controversy in U.S. society. The poster depicted here, distributed by the U.S. government in 1942, refers to a meaning of freedom to which almost everyone agrees —freedom from totalitarianism.*

that individual, rather than with the social system for placing roadblocks in his or her path.

3. *Activity and work.* Americans expect people to work hard and to be busily engaged in some activity even when not at work. This value is becoming less important.

4. *Efficiency and practicality.* Americans award high marks for getting things done efficiently. Even in everyday life, Americans consider it important to do things as fast or as well as possible, and constantly seek changes to increase efficiency.

5. *Science and technology.* Americans have a passion for applied science, for using science to control nature—to tame rivers and harness winds—and to develop new technology, from improved carburetors to talking computers.

6. *Progress.* Americans expect rapid technological change. They believe that they should constantly build "more and better" gadgets that will help them move toward some vague goal called "progress."

7. *Material comfort.* Americans expect a high level of material comfort. This comfort includes not only nutrition, medical care, and housing, but also late-model cars and recreational playthings—from boats to computer games.

8. *Humanitarianism.* Americans emphasize helpfulness, personal kindness, aid in mass disasters, and organized philanthropy.

9. *Freedom.* This core value pervades U.S. life. It underscored the American Revolution, and Americans today bristle at the suggestion of any limitation on personal freedom. The Perspectives box on the next page highlights some interesting research on how this core value applies to Native Americans.

10. *Democracy.* By this term, Americans refer to majority rule, to the right of everyone to express an opinion, and to representative government.

11. *Equality.* It is impossible to understand Americans without being aware of the central role that the value of equality plays in their lives. Equality of opportunity, an important concept in the ideal culture discussed later, has significantly influenced U.S. history and continues to mark relations between the groups that make up U.S. society.

12. *Racism and group superiority.* Although it sharply contradicts freedom, democracy, and equality, Americans value some groups more than others and have done so throughout their history. The institution of slavery in earlier U.S. society is the most notorious example.

In an earlier publication, I updated Williams's analysis by adding the following three values (Henslin 1975).

13. *Education.* Americans are expected to go as far in school as their abilities and finances allow. Over the years, the definition of an "adequate" education has changed sharply, and today the expectation of a college education is held as an appropriate goal for most Americans. Some even view people who have an opportunity for higher education and who do not take it as doing something "wrong," not merely making a bad choice, but somehow involved in an immoral act.

14. *Religiosity.* There is a feeling that "every true American ought to be religious." This does not mean that everyone is expected to join a church or synagogue, but that everyone ought to acknowledge a belief in a Supreme Being and follow some set of matching precepts. This value is so pervasive that Americans stamp "In God We Trust" on their money and declare in their national pledge of allegiance that they are "one nation under God."

15. *Romantic love and monogamy.* Americans feel that the only proper basis for marriage is romantic love. Songs, literature, mass media, and "folk beliefs" all stress this value, and sometimes include the theme that "love conquers all."

Perspectives

Why Do Native Americans Like Westerns?

U.S. audiences (and even German, French, and Japanese) devour westerns. In the United States, it is easy to see why Anglos might like westerns, for it is they who seemingly defy odds and emerge victorious. It is they who are portrayed as heroically taming a savage wilderness, who fend themselves from cruel, barbaric Indians intent on their destruction. But why would Indians like westerns?

Sociologist JoEllen Shively, a Chippewa who grew up on Indian reservations in Montana and North Dakota, found that westerns are so popular that Native Americans bring bags of paperbacks into taverns to trade with one another. They even call one another "cowboy."

Intrigued, Shively decided to investigate the matter by showing a western movie to adult Native Americans and Anglos in a reservation town. To select the move, Shively (1991, 1992) previewed over seventy westerns and then chose a John Wayne movie, *The Searchers*, because it focuses not only on conflict between Indians and cowboys but also shows the cowboys defeating the Indians. The Native Americans and Anglos were matched on education, age, income, and percentage of unemployment. After the movie, she had the viewers fill out questionnaires and interviewed them.

Shively found something surprising: *all* Native Americans and Anglos identified with the cowboys; *none* identified with the Indians.

The ways in which Anglos and Native Americans identified with the cowboys, however, were quite different, for each projected a different fantasy onto the story. While Anglos saw the movie as an accurate portrayal of the Old West

and a justification of their own status in the social system, Native Americans saw it as embodying a free, natural way of life. In fact, Native Americans said that they were the "real cowboys." They said, "Westerns relate to the way I wish I could live"; "He's not tied down to an eight-to-five job, day after day"; "He's his own man."

Shively adds,

What appears to make Westerns meaningful to Indians is the fantasy of being free and independent like the cowboy. . . . Indians . . . find a fantasy in the cowboy story in which the important parts of their ways of life triumph and are morally good, validating their own cultural group in the context of a dramatically satisfying story. (1992)

To express their real identity—a combination of marginality on the one hand, with a set of values which are about the land, autonomy, and being free—they (use) a cultural vehicle (that is) written for Anglos about Anglos, but it is one in which Indians invest a distinctive set of meanings that speak to their own experience, which they can read in a manner that affirms a way of life they value, or a fantasy they hold to. (1991)

In other words, values, not ethnicity, are the central issue. If a Native American film industry were to portray Native Americans with the same values as the Anglo movie industry projects onto cowboys, then Native Americans would identify with their own group. Thus, says Shively, Native American viewers make cowboys "honorary Indians," for the cowboys express their values of bravery, autonomy, and toughness.

Value Contradictions and Social Change

As you can see, not all values fall into neat, integrated packages. Some may even contradict one another. The **value contradiction** of group superiority violates freedom, democracy, and equality. There simply cannot be full expressions of freedom, democracy, and equality along with racism and sexism. Something has to give. One way in which Americans sidestepped this contradiction in the past was to say that the values of freedom, democracy, and equality applied only to certain groups. The contradiction was bound to surface, however, and so it did, as is evident from the Civil War and the women's liberation movement.

As society changes, then, some values are challenged and undergo modification. Such change may be gradual, with people slowly adjusting their behaviors and ideas, or it may come suddenly and be extremely disrupting. *It is precisely at the point of value contradictions that one can see a major force for social change in a society.*

value contradictions: values that contradict one another; to follow the one means to come into conflict with the other

Value Clusters

As is also apparent from the overview of U.S. values, values are not independent units. Instead, some cluster together to form a larger whole. In the **value cluster** surrounding

value cluster: a series of interrelated values that together form a larger whole

success, for example, we find hard work, education, efficiency, material comfort, and individualism all bound up together. Americans are expected to go far in school, to work hard afterward, to be efficient, and then to attain a high level of material comfort, which, in turn, demonstrates success. Success is attributed to the individual's own efforts, the lack of success to his or her own faults.

An Emerging Value Cluster.   A value cluster of four interrelated core values—leisure, self-fulfillment, physical fitness, and youngness—appears to be emerging in the United States.

16. *Leisure*. The emergence of leisure as a value is reflected in the rapid growth of a huge recreation industry—from computer games, boats, and motor homes, to sports arenas, vacation homes, and a gigantic travel and vacation industry.

17. *Self-fulfillment*. This value is reflected in the "human potential" movement, a concern with becoming "all one can be," "self-help," "relating," and "personal development."

18. *Physical fitness*. Physical fitness is not a new U.S. value, but the much greater emphasis being placed on it is moving it into this new value cluster. This trend can be seen in the "natural" foods craze; brew bars; obsessive concerns about weight and diet; the many joggers, cyclists, and backpackers; and the mushrooming of health clubs and physical fitness centers.

19. *Youngness*. While valuing youth and disparaging old age is not new, some note a new sense of urgency. They attribute this to aging baby boomers, who, aghast at their physical changes, attempt to deny their biological fate. An extreme view is represented by a physician who claims that "aging is not a normal life event, but a disease" (Cowley 1996). It is not surprising, then, that techniques of youth enhancement—from cosmetics to surgery—have become popular.

This emerging value cluster is a response to the needs and interests resulting from fundamental changes in U.S. society. Americans used to be preoccupied with forging a nation and fighting for economic survival. They now have come to a point in their economic development where millions of people are freed from long hours of work, and millions more are able to retire from work when they can still expect decades of life ahead of them. This value cluster centers around enabling them to enjoy those years of retirement, or to maintaining their health and vigor during their younger years while they look forward to a life of leisure.

A Value in Search of a Cluster.   Related to, but not an essential part of this emerging value cluster, is environmental concern, which is still in the process of emerging.

20. *Concern for the environment*. During most of U.S. history, the environment was seen as a challenge—a wilderness to be settled, forests to be chopped down, rivers and lakes to be fished, and animals to be hunted. The lack of concern for the environment that characterized earlier Americans is illustrated by the near extinction of the bison and the extinction in 1915 of the passenger pigeon, a bird previously so numerous that its annual migration would darken the skies for days. Today, Americans have developed a genuine, and (we can hope) long-term concern for the environment.

This emergent value of environmental concern is also related to the current stage of U.S. economic development, a point that becomes clearer when we note that people act on environmental concerns only after basic needs are met. At this point in their development, for example, the world's poor nations have a difficult time "affording" this value.

Values, though firmly held, are changeable, both those held by individuals and those representing a nation or people. It is difficult for many of us today to grasp the pride with which earlier Americans destroyed trees that took thousands of years to grow, are located only in one tiny speck of the globe, and are part of the nation's and world's heritage. But this is a value statement, representing current views. The evident satisfaction and pride at a job well done depicted here by both lumberjacks and managers of the timber company represent another set of values entirely.

Culture Wars: When Values Clash

Core values do not change without meeting strong resistance from traditionalists, those who hold them dear. Consequently, many people are upset at the changes swirling around them, seeing their way of life challenged and their future growing insecure. Efforts to change gender roles, for example, arouse intense controversy, as does support of alternative family forms and changes in sexual behavior. Alarmed at such onslaughts to their values, traditionalists fiercely defend historical family relationships and the gender roles they grew up with. Also at the center of controversy are socialist economic principles versus profit and private property. Today's clash in values is so severe that the term "culture wars" has been coined to refer to it.

Values as Blinders

Values and their supporting beliefs paint a unique picture of reality, as well as forming a view of what life *ought* to be like. Because Americans value individualism so highly, for example, they tend to see people as free to pursue whatever legitimate goals they desire. This value blinds them to the many social circumstances that impede people's efforts. The dire consequences of family poverty, parents' low education, and dead-end jobs tend to drop from sight. Instead, Americans cling to the notion that anyone can make it—with the right amount of effort. And to prove it, dangling before their eyes are success stories of individuals who have succeeded in spite of huge handicaps.

"Ideal" Versus "Real" Culture

Many of the norms that surround cultural values are only partially followed. Differences always exist between a group's ideals and what its members actually do. Consequently, sociologists use the term **ideal culture** to refer to a group's ideal values, and *norms* to the goals they hold out for themselves. The idea of success, for example, is part of ideal culture. Americans glorify academic progress, hard work, and the display of material goods as signs of individual achievement. What people actually do, however, usually falls short

ideal culture: the ideal values and norms of a people, the goals held out for them

49

of this cultural ideal. Compared with their capacities, for example, most people don't go as far as they could in school or work as hard as they can. Sociologists call the norms and values that people actually follow **real culture.**

Cultural Universals

With the amazing variety of human cultures around the world, are there any **cultural universals**—values, norms, or other cultural traits that are found everywhere?

Anthropologist George Murdock (1945) sought to answer this question. After combing through data gathered by anthropologists on hundreds of groups around the world, he drew up a list of customs concerning courtship, cooking, marriage, funerals, games, laws, music, myths, incest taboos, and even toilet training. He found that although such activities are present in all cultures, *the specific customs differ from one group to another.* There is no universal form of the family, no universal way of disposing of the dead. Similarly, specific games, rules, songs, stories, and methods of toilet training differ from one culture to another.

Even incest is defined differently from group to group. For example, the Mundugumors of New Guinea extend the incest taboo so far that for each man seven of every eight women are ineligible marriage partners (Mead 1935/1950). Other groups go in the opposite direction and allow some men to marry their own daughters (La Barre 1954). In certain circumstances, some groups require that brothers and sisters marry one another (Beals and Hoijer 1965). The Burundi of Africa even insist that, to remove a certain curse, a son have sexual relations with his mother (Albert 1963). Such sexual relations were allowed only for special people (royalty) or in a special situation (such as that of a lion hunter before a dangerous hunt), and no society permits generalized incest for its members.

In short, although there are universal human activities (speech, music, storytelling, marrying, disposing of the dead, preparing food, and so on), there is no universally accepted way of doing any of them. Humans have no biological imperative that results in one particular form of behavior throughout the world. As indicated in the following Thinking Critically section, a few sociologists do take the position that genes significantly influence human behavior, although almost all sociologists reject this view.

Thinking Critically About Social Controversy

Are We Prisoners of Our Genes?
Sociobiology and Human Behavior

▼ A controversial view of human behavior, called **sociobiology**, provides a sharp contrast to the perspective of this chapter, that human behavior is primarily due to culture. Sociobiologists hold that due to natural selection the basic cause of human behavior is biology.

According to Charles Darwin (1859), natural selection is based on four principles. First, reproduction occurs within a natural environment. Second, the genes of a species, the basic units of life that contain the individual's traits, are passed on to offspring. These genes have a degree of random variability; that is, different characteristics are distributed among the members of a species. Third, because the members of a species possess different characteristics, some members have a better chance of surviving in the natural environment than do others—and of passing their particular genetic traits to the next generation. Fourth, over thousands of generations, those genetic traits that aid survival in the natural environment tend to become common in a species, while those that do not tend to disappear.

Natural selection not only explains the physical characteristics of animals, but also their behavior, for over countless generations instincts emerged. Edward Wilson (1975), an insect specialist, claims that human behavior is also the result of natural selection. Human behavior,

real culture: the norms and values that people actually follow

cultural universal: a value, norm, or other cultural trait that is found in every group

sociobiology: a framework of thought that views human behavior as the result of natural selection and considers biological characteristics to be the fundamental cause of human behavior

he said, is no different from the behavior of cats, dogs, rats, bees, or mosquitoes—it has been bred into *Homo sapiens* through evolutionary principles.

Wilson deliberately set out to create a storm of protest, and he succeeded. He claims that religion, competition and cooperation, slavery and genocide, war and peace, envy and altruism—all can be explained through sociobiology. He provocatively adds that because human behavior can be explained in terms of genetic programming, the new discipline of sociobiology will eventually absorb sociology—as well as anthropology and psychology.

Obviously, most sociologists find Wilson's position unacceptable. Not only is it a direct attack on their discipline, but it also bypasses the essence of what sociologists focus on: humans designing their own cultures, their own unique ways of life. Sociologists do not deny that biology underlies human behavior, at least not in the sense that it takes a highly developed brain to develop human culture, that there would be no speech if humans had no tongue or larynx, that abstract thought could not exist if we did not have a highly developed cerebral cortex.

But sociologists find the claim that human behavior is due to genetic programming to be quite another matter (Howe et al. 1992). Pigs act like pigs because they don't have a cerebral cortex, and instincts control their behavior. So it is for spiders, elephants, and so on. But humans possess a self and have abstract thought. They discuss principles that underlie what they do. They decide on rational courses of action. They develop purposes and goals. They consider, reflect, and make choices.

This controversy has turned into much more than simply an academic debate among scientists. Homosexuals, for example, have found its outcome to be of high personal interest. If homosexuality is due to a choice of lifestyle, then those who consider that lifestyle immoral will use this as a basis to exclude homosexuals from full social participation. If, however, homosexuality is due to genetic traits, then that reason for social exclusion is removed. Sociologist Peter Conrad (1997) expresses the dominant sociological position when he points out that not all homosexuals have Xq28, the so-called "gay gene," and some people who have this gene are not homosexual. This gene, then, does not determine behavior. Instead, we must look for *social* causes.

In short, sociobiologists and sociologists stand on opposite sides, the one looking at human behavior as determined by genetics, the other as determined by social learning, by experiences in the human group. Sociologists point out that if humans were prisoners of their genes, we would not have developed such a variety of fascinating ways of life around the world—we would live in a monoculture of some sort. ▲

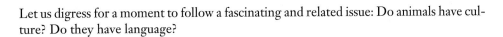

Animals and Culture ▲

Let us digress for a moment to follow a fascinating and related issue: Do animals have culture? Do they have language?

Do Animals Have Culture?

According to our definition of culture as a learned way of life that is passed on to others, it would seem that animals could not have culture. They certainly could not possess culture if their behavior is entirely under the control of *instincts*, inherited patterns of behavior common to all normal members of a species, such as the distinctive nest building of a Baltimore oriole. The basic sociological question is this: Are there any behaviors that animals learn, and then pass on to others?

The answer begins with an observation by Japanese anthropologists. In 1953, they saw a young monkey pick up a sweet potato covered with sand, dip it in water, and wash off the sand with her hands. A month later, her playmates began to wash their sweet potatoes. Several months later, her mother followed suit. In ten years, 75 percent of the troop were doing this (Hanson 1973). At a minimum, then, animals do learn from one another, and a learned behavior can be adopted by other animals.

The solution to our question continues with a chance meeting in 1957 between Louis Leakey, a world-renowned anthropologist and paleontologist, and Jane Goodall, a secretary from London. Leakey, who had been collecting fossils in an area of Tanzania called

Jane Goodall's research demonstrated that animals have a primitive culture; that is, they teach one another behavior that is transmitted across generations. Such culture is very limited, however, because, unlike humans, animals do not have language.

the Olduvai Gorge, asked Goodall if she would like to study some chimpanzees living on the shores of a lake. Leakey explained that because the remains of early humans were often found on lake shores an understanding of chimpanzee behavior might shed light on the behavior of our Stone Age ancestors (Van Lawick-Goodall 1971).

Goodall accepted the invitation. The first six months in the jungle were very discouraging, for the chimps fled whenever she approached. When the chimps became accustomed to her and allowed her to join them, Goodall slowly figured out how they communicate. Eventually she was even able to participate in their gestures, hoots, and facial expressions. For the next thirty years, Goodall lived in the remote jungle in a house made of concrete blocks with a roof of thatch and corrugated tin, no running water, and windows covered in mesh to keep out the baboons (Walters 1990). Today she is on a globe-spanning crusade to promote conservation and improve conditions for captive chimps (Miller 1995).

The exotic nature of this fieldwork apart, what did Goodall learn that might help us decide whether animals have culture? She observed that these wild chimps made and used **tools;** that is, they modified objects and used them for specific purposes. Until this observation, it was assumed that only humans used tools. The chimps' tool was very simple, but tool it was. The chimps would first pick a blade of grass, then strip off its leaves and lick one end. Next they would poke the sticky end into a nest of termites. After waiting a bit, they would pull it out covered with termites, then savor the taste as they licked off the stick.

Stimulated by Goodall's discovery, scientists began trying to determine the extent of **animal culture**—learned, shared behavior among animals. They separated infant animals from their parents and others of their species, and then observed their behaviors. The surprise, of course, was not the behaviors that these animals continued to share with their species—these were to be expected. And, indeed, squirrels raised in isolation still bury nuts, and spiders still spin distinctive webs. The surprise was the behaviors that did *not* continue. For example, although many birds raised in soundproof chambers sing the songs unique to their species, a bullfinch raised with canaries sings like a canary (Eibl-Eibesfeldt 1970).

From one of the more humorous footnotes to these scientific endeavors, we learn that even the mating behavior of some animals is learned. Zookeepers around the world have been dismayed that their gorillas will not mate, and they have had to replenish their supply of these animals from the wild. Then zookeepers in Sacramento, California, noticing that the gorillas appeared to want to mate, concluded that maybe they just didn't know how (Stark 1989). Taking a long shot, they showed the animals a movie of two adult gorillas mating. The lesson turned out to be a success.

Goodall's research and subsequent experiments answer our question: on a rudimentary level, animal culture exists. Although this principle has been established, we do not yet know the particulars. What animals? What specific behaviors? The initial answers, enticing though they may be, only point to further provocative questions.

Do Animals Have Language?

A related question that has intrigued scientists and nonscientists alike is whether animals have language. Do those barks and meows your pets make constitute language?

Social scientists think of language as more complex than mere sounds. They view language as symbols that can be infinitely strung together to communicate abstract thought. Animal sounds, however, appear to be closer to a baby's cries. Although a baby will cry when in pain, this cry of distress, even though it brings a parent running, is not language. The cry is merely a biological response to pain, similar to reflexes.

tool: an object that is created or modified for a specific purpose

animal culture: learned, shared behavior among animals

Social scientists also point out that animals do not even have the vocal apparatus necessary to utter the complex sounds that make up language. Do animals lack speech, then, because they lack intelligence (the inability to learn speech), or because they are unable to make the sounds of speech? When Allen and Beatrice Gardner (1969), psychologists at the University of Nevada, learned from Goodall's research that chimps in the wild use many more hand signals than vocal signals, they decided to teach chimps gestures instead of words (Fleming 1974). Their first pupil was Washoe, a female chimpanzee who was born in the wild. In 1966, when Washoe was 1 year old, her language training began. Washoe was like a human baby. She slept a lot, had just begun to crawl, and her daily routine centered on diapers and bottles.

The Gardners tried to teach Washoe American Sign Language, in which hand gestures correspond to individual words. They were encouraged when Washoe began to learn some of the signs, and they were elated when she began to *generalize*, to apply a sign learned in one situation to other situations. For example, they taught her the sign for "open," using three doors in the house trailer she lived in. After learning that gesture, Washoe transferred it to all the trailer's doors and drawers—then to containers, the refrigerator, and even to the water faucet.

Within a year, Washoe had become inventive and was putting signs together in the equivalent of simple sentences. She even made up combinations, such as joining the sign for "give me" with "tickle" to indicate that she wanted to be tickled. At the end of four years, Washoe could use 160 signs.

Another experiment is taking place at Northwestern University. Irene Pepperberg has taught Alex, an African Gray parrot, to name eighty objects, such as wool, walnut, and shower; to identify colors; and to tell how many objects there are in groups up to six. Skeptics reply that the only thing that distinguishes Alex from pigeons taught to peck buttons for food is that his responses sound like English (Stipp 1990).

Do animals have the capacity for language? Such experiments have persuaded some scientists that they do. Others, however, remain unconvinced. For the answer to this question, then, we must await further evidence.

Technology in the Global Village ▲

New Technologies

The gestures, language, values, folkways, and mores that we have discussed—these all are part of symbolic or nonmaterial culture. Culture, as you recall, also has a material aspect, a group's *things*, from its houses to its toys. Central to a group's material culture is its technology. In its simplest sense, **technology** can be equated with tools. In its broader sense, technology also includes the skills or procedures necessary to make and to use those tools.

We can use the term **new technology** to refer to the emerging technologies of an era that have a significant impact on social life. Many minor technologies appear from time to time, but most are slight modifications of existing technologies. Occasionally, however, there appear on the human scene technologies that make a major impact on human life. It is primarily to these that the term new technologies refers. For people 500 years ago, the new technology was the printing press. For us, these new technologies are computers, satellites, and various forms of the electronic media.

The sociological significance of technology is that its importance goes far beyond the tool itself. *The type of technology a group has sets the framework for its nonmaterial culture.* Technology influences the way people think and how they relate to one another, a focus of the box on Sociology and the New Technology on the next page. Consider gender relations. Through the centuries and throughout the world, it has been the custom (a group's nonmaterial culture) for men to dominate women. Today, with instantaneous communications (the material culture), this custom has become much more difficult to maintain.

technology: in its narrow sense, tools; its broader sense includes the skills or procedures necessary to make and use those tools

new technology: the emerging technologies of an era that have a significant impact on social life

 *Sociology and the New Technology*

Is Technology the Cart or the Horse?

WARNING! This machine is subject to breakdowns during periods of critical need. A special circuit in the machine called a "critical detector" senses the operator's emotional state, in terms of how desperate he or she is to use the machine. The "critical detector" then creates a malfunction proportional to the desperation of the operator. Threatening the machine with violence only aggravates the situation. Keep cool and say nice things to the machine. Nothing else seems to work. Never let the machine know you are in a hurry.

All over the country, users of copiers have laughed at some version of this attempt to turn frustration into humor. This sign comes close to a point of view called **technological determinism,** the idea that technology is the single greatest force in shaping our lives. Like the preceding warning, some technological determinists believe that machines have become an independent force that is out of human control (Chandler 1995). For them, technology is more important than anything else—politics, economics, religion, or any other social factor—in creating the kind of society we live in.

In 1954, long before the personal computer and most other forms of modern communications appeared on the scene, the French sociologist, Jacques Ellul, wrote an influential book, *The Technological Society.* In it, he (1964) claimed that technology had begun to dominate civilization. Technology, he said, is rapidly taking charge, and we humans are in danger of losing our freedom to the machines we have built.

Neil Postman has echoed this negative sentiment. He (1992) argues that television's emphasis on immediate gratification and quick responses has ruined children's attention spans. Countless hours in front of television's "short bursts" of imagery have made it difficult for children to "organize their thought into logical structure, even in a simple paragraph."

Not all technological determinists are pessimists. While maintaining the emphasis on technology as the driving force in social change, the late media guru Marshall McLuhan (1911–1980) was optimistic about our technological future. McLuhan sought to understand the impact of the electronic media on symbolic culture—on people's ideas, values, and

ways of life. Coining a term that has become part of our common vocabulary, McLuhan (1964) noted that electronic communications are transforming the world into a "global village." By allowing people around the world to share experiences, the media shrink geographical boundaries and bring diverse peoples and ideas together.

Instead of stressing how technology shapes culture, other analysts stress that culture shapes technology. This view, called **the social construction of technology,** emphasizes how values and special interests shape the development and use of technology (Bijker et al. 1987). For example, in the 1500s guns were imported to Japan (Volti 1995). The Japanese copied them, modified their design, and manufactured them. The use of guns, however, threatened the Samurai, the warrior class that used swords and followed ancient rituals in hand-to-hand combat. Suddenly, from a distance, anyone with a gun, even cowards and social inferiors, could kill the best-trained and bravest Samurai. The Japanese government then centralized the production of guns and sold them only by license, which they refused to grant. Eventually the skills to make guns were lost, and guns disappeared from Japan. People and culture—in this case the Samurai and adherence to Japanese rituals of bravery—dominated technology.

In short, the *social constructionists* emphasize how people control, influence, or use technology. People, or culture, are "the horse" that drives technology. The *technological determinists*, in contrast, emphasize how technology affects people's customs, lifestyles, relationships, and even ideas. They see technology as "the horse" and culture as "the cart."

For Your Consideration

The technological determinists and the social constructionists bring us to a significant issue: Does technology free us, or is it yet another force of society that programs us? In other words, are we in control of technology, or is technology in control of us? Which is the cart, and which the horse?

Perhaps the truth consists of a combination of these views; perhaps technology both liberates and constrains. If so, can you provide examples from your own experience of how people mold technology, and how it, in turn, molds us?

technological determinism: the view that technology determines culture, that technology takes on a life of its own and forces human behavior to follow

social construction of technology: the view (opposed to *technological determinism*) that culture (people's values and special interests) shapes the use and development of technology

For example, when women from many nations gathered in Beijing for a U.N. conference in 1995, satellites instantly transmitted their grievances around the globe. Such communications create discontent, sometimes a feeling of sisterhood, and women agitate for social change.

In today's world, the long-accepted idea that it is proper to withhold rights on the basis of someone's sex can no longer hold. What is usually invisible in this revolutionary change is the role of technology, which joins the world's nations into a global communication network. Until recent technological advances, this was impossible.

Cultural Lag and Cultural Change

A couple of generations ago, sociologist William Ogburn (1922), a functional analyst, coined the term **cultural lag.** By this, Ogburn meant that not all parts of a culture change at the same pace. When some part of a culture changes, other parts lag behind.

Ogburn pointed out that *a group's material culture usually changes first, with the nonmaterial culture lagging behind,* playing a game of catch up. For example, when we get sick, we could type our symptoms into a computer and get an immediate printout of our diagnosis and best course of treatment. In fact, in some tests computers outperform physicians (Waldholz 1991). Yet our customs have not caught up with the technology, and we continue to visit doctors' offices.

Sometimes nonmaterial culture never does catch up. Instead, we rigorously hold onto some outmoded form, one that once was firmly needed, but long ago has been bypassed by new technology. A striking example is our nine-month school year. Have you ever wondered why it is nine months long, and why we take off the summers? For most of us, this is "just the way it's always been," and we've never questioned it. But there is more to this custom than meets the eye, for it is an example of cultural lag.

In the nineteenth century, when universal schooling came about, the school year matched the technology of the time, which was labor intensive. For survival, parents needed their children's help at the critical times of planting and harvesting. Although the invention of highly productive farm machinery eliminated the need for the school year to be so short, generations later we live with this cultural lag.

Technology and Cultural Leveling

For most of human history, communication was limited and travel slow. Consequently, in their relative isolation, groups of people developed highly distinctive ways of life as they responded to the particular situations they faced. The characteristics they developed that distinguished one culture from another tended to change little over time. The Tasmanians, who lived on an inaccessible island off the coast of Australia, provide an extreme

The new technology of electronic communications did not develop overnight. Only gradually, as one modification after another was added, did this technology become more efficient. Microchips, fiber optics, and satellites are only the latest in a long series of developments that have brought us to our current state of communications. In the late 1800s, as shown here, a telephone operator had to connect each caller to the person called, a labor-intensive process that now is "handled" electronically.

COCHRAN!

"COOL! A KEYBOARD THAT WRITES WITHOUT A PRINTER."

Technological advances are now so rapid that the technology of one generation is practically unrecognizable by the next generation.

cultural lag: William Ogburn's term for a situation in which nonmaterial culture lags behind changes in the material culture

Shown here is a Masai Barbie Doll. Mattel Toys, the U.S. manufacturer, has modified Barbie to match Masai (Kenya) culture by dressing her in a traditional "shuka" dress, beads, shawl, headdress, and anklets. As objects diffuse from one culture to another, they are modified to meet the tastes and specific needs of the adoptive culture. In this instance, the modification has been done intentionally as part of the globalization of capitalism. Now that Barbie is a Masai, can a Masai Ken be far behind?

example. For thousands of years, they had no contact with any other culture. They were so isolated that they did not even know how to make clothing or fire (Edgerton 1992).

Except in such rare instances, humans always had *some* contact with other groups. During these contacts, people learned from one another, adapting some part of the other's way of life. In this process, called **cultural diffusion,** groups are most open to a change in their technology or material culture. They usually are eager, for example, to adopt superior weapons and tools. In remote jungles in South America one can find metal cooking pots, steel axes, and even bits of clothing spun in mills in South Carolina. Although the direction of cultural diffusion today is primarily from the West to other parts of the world, cultural diffusion is not a one-way street, as bagels, woks, and hammocks in the United States show.

With today's technology in travel and communications, cultural diffusion is occurring rapidly. Air travel has made it possible to journey around the globe in a matter of hours. In the not-so-distant past, a trip from the United States to Africa was so unusual that only a few hardy people made it, and newspapers would herald their feat. Today, hundreds of thousands make the trip each year.

The changes in communication are no less vast. Communication used to be limited to face-to-face speech and to visual signals such as smoke, light reflected from mirrors, and written messages passed from hand to hand. In spite of newspapers, people in some parts of the United States did not hear about the end of the Civil War until weeks and even months after it was over. Today's electronic communications transmit messages across the globe in a matter of seconds, and we learn almost instantaneously what is happening on the other side of the world.

cultural diffusion: the spread of cultural characteristics from one group to another

In fact, travel and communication unite us to such an extent that there almost is no "other side of the world" anymore. One result is **cultural leveling,** a process in which cultures become similar to one another as expanding industrialization brings not only technology but also Western culture to the rest of the world. Japan, for example, has adapted not only Western economic production but also Western forms of dress and music. These changes, superimposed on Japanese culture, have turned Japan into a blend of Western and Eastern cultures.

Cultural leveling, occurring rapidly around the world, is apparent to any traveler. The Golden Arches of McDonald's welcome today's visitors to Tokyo, Paris, London, Madrid, and even Moscow, Beijing, and Hong Kong. In Mexico, the most popular piñatas are no longer of donkeys but of Mickey Mouse and Fred Flintstone (Beckett 1996). In the Indian Himalayan town of Dharmsala, a Buddhist monk and two Indian boys, sitting on benches in a shack with a dirt floor waiting for a videotaped U.S. movie to begin, watch a Levis commercial on MTV. "Thanks to MTV," says an Indian girl in Calcutta, "I can wear a miniskirt to a disco" (Brauchli 1993b).

Although the bridging of geography and culture by electronic signals does not in itself mark the end of traditional cultures, it inevitably results in some degree of *cultural leveling,* some less bland, less distinctive way of life—U.S. culture with French, Japanese, and Bulgarian accents, so to speak. Although the "cultural accent" remains, something vital is lost forever.

> **cultural leveling:** the process by which cultures become similar to one another, and especially by which Western industrial culture is imported and diffused into developing nations

Summary and Review

What Is Culture?

All human groups possess **culture**—language, beliefs, values, norms, and material objects passed from one generation to the next. **Material culture** consists of objects (art, buildings, clothing, tools). **Nonmaterial** (or **symbolic**) **culture** is a group's ways of thinking and patterns of behavior. **Ideal culture** is a group's ideal values and norms, and their goals. **Real culture,** people's actual behavior, often falls short of their cultural ideals. Pp. 34–37.

What are cultural relativism and ethnocentrism?

People are naturally **ethnocentric;** that is, they use their own culture as a yardstick for judging the ways of others. In contrast, those who embrace **cultural relativism** try to understand other cultures on those cultures' own terms. Pp. 37–38.

Components of Symbolic Culture

What are the components of nonmaterial culture?

The central component is **symbols,** anything to which people attach meaning and use to communicate with others. Universally, the symbols of nonmaterial culture are **gestures, language, values, norms, sanctions, folkways,** and **mores.** Pp. 38–39.

Why is language so significant to culture?

Language allows human experience to be goal directed, cooperative, and cumulative. It also lets humans move beyond the present and share a past, future, and other common perspectives. According to the **Sapir–Whorf hypothesis,** language even shapes our thoughts and perceptions. Pp. 39–42.

How do values, norms, folkways, mores, and sanctions reflect culture?

All groups have **values,** standards by which they define what is desirable or undesirable, and **norms,** rules or expectations about behavior. Groups use **positive sanctions** to show approval of those who follow their norms, and **negative sanctions** to show disapproval of those who do not. Norms that are not strictly enforced are called **folkways,** while **mores** are norms to which groups demand conformity because they reflect core values. Pp. 42–44.

How do subcultures and countercultures differ?

A **subculture** is a group whose values and related behaviors distinguish its members from the general culture. A **counterculture** holds values that at least in some ways stand in opposition to those of the dominant culture. Pp. 44–45.

Values in U.S. Society

What are the core U.S. values?

Although the United States is a **pluralistic society,** made up of many groups, each with its own set of values, certain values dominate; chiefly achievement and success, individualism, activity and work, efficiency and practicality, science and technology, progress, material comfort, equality, freedom, democracy, humanitarianism, racism and group superiority, education, religiosity, romantic love and monogamy. Some values cluster together (**value clusters**) to form a larger whole. **Value contradictions** (such as equality and racism) indicate areas of social tension, which are likely points of social change. Changes in a society's fundamental values are opposed by people who hold strongly to traditional values. Leisure, physical fitness, self-fulfillment, and concern for the environment are emerging core values. Pp. 45–50.

Cultural Universals

Do cultural universals exist?

Cultural universals are values, norms, or other cultural traits that are found in all cultures. Although all human groups have customs concerning cooking, funerals, weddings, and so on, because the specific forms these customs take vary from one culture to another there are no cultural universals. Pp. 50–51.

Animals and Culture

Do animals have culture?

To the extent that some animals teach their young certain behaviors, animals also have a rudimentary culture. No animals have language in the sociological sense of the term, although some experiments indicate that some animals may have a limited capacity to learn language. Pp. 51–53.

Technology in the Global Village

How is technology changing culture?

Ogburn coined the term **cultural lag** to refer to a group's nonmaterial culture lagging behind its changing technology. With today's technological advances in travel and communications, **cultural diffusion** is occurring rapidly. This leads to **cultural leveling,** whereby many groups are adopting Western culture in place of their own customs. Much of the richness of the world's diverse cultures is being lost in the process. Pp. 53–57.

Where can I read more on this topic?

Suggested readings for this chapter are listed on page 659.

 Sociology and the Internet

All URLs listed are current as of the printing of this book. URLs are often changed. Please check our Web site http://www.abacon.com/henslin for updates.

1. Freedom is a core value in U.S. society. Examine the material concerning religious freedom at the religious freedom site *http://www.religious-freedom.org/* What does religious freedom mean? How is our religious freedom protected? Click on "RFRA." What is the Religious Freedom Restoration Act? What are some of the arguments in support of such an act? Do people in our society agree on what religious freedom means? Do all people support the RFRA? Who may object to the RFRA?

2. Search the Internet for information on a value conflict by accessing the following search engines and entering the word "abortion" in the search term blank.

http://www.lycos.com/
http://www.excite.com/
http://webcrawler.com/

What are the major arguments put forth by the prolife and prochoice sides? Prepare a written or oral report on your find-

ings. To what extent does this disagreement indicate changes in core values in our society?

3. What do you think of when you hear the word *Amish?* Do you think of horses and buggies? What about their clothing? Maybe you think about farms, quilts, and wood crafts. There is much more to the Amish, however, than their material culture. Examine the following sites:

www.amish-heartland.com/amish/
www.800padutch.com/amishexp.html/
www.poopets.com

Discuss both the material and nonmaterial cultures of the Amish. Compare the material and nonmaterial cultures of the Amish to the larger U.S. culture. Are most of the differences in the material or the nonmaterial culture? In what ways is the nonmaterial culture of the Amish similar to the larger U.S. culture? Why do we usually think of nonmaterial culture when we visualize the Amish?

4. Are the Internet and the cyber community a culture? Explore this possibility by going to Yahoo!: *http://www.yahoo.*

com/society_and_culture Click on "Cultures and Groups." You should now see the category "Cybercultures." Choose "Cybercultures" and examine some of its links. Is cyberspace a culture? Does it contain all the components of a symbolic culture as discussed in the text? Do you think the Internet and Web are cultures? Is cyber culture a culture, a subculture, or a counterculture? Use examples from your text and from the links to support your answer to these questions.

5. Every culture develops expectations about the behavior of its members. There are "right" and "wrong" ways to reflect the values of each culture. Cyber culture is no different. In cyberspace, there are norms that govern the behavior of those "residing" there. These rules of conduct have become known as netiquette. Use Yahoo! *http://www.yahoo.com/society_and_culture* to examine the norms of the cyber culture. Click on "Etiquette." You should now see the category "Netiquette." Examine some of the links that are listed. What are some of the norms governing your behavior in cyberspace? What kind of sanctions can you expect to receive if you do not follow the norms? Were you surprised about how many norms there are? Were you familiar with the norms? Which norms are mores and which are folkways? How can you tell?

Cynthia Fitting, Man Reading to Child, 1992

CHAPTER 3

Socialization

*T*HE OLD MAN WAS HORRIFIED *when he found out. Life never had been good since his daughter had lost her hearing when she was just 2 years old. She couldn't even talk—just fluttered her hands around trying to tell him things. Over the years, he had gotten used to that. But now . . . he shuddered at the thought of her being pregnant. No one would be willing to marry her; he knew that. And the neighbors, their tongues would never stop wagging. Everywhere he went, he could hear people talking behind his back.*

If only his wife were still alive, maybe she could come up with something. What should he do? He couldn't just kick his daughter out into the street.

After the baby was born, the old man tried to shake his feelings, but they wouldn't let loose. Isabelle was a pretty name, but every time he looked at the baby he felt sick to his stomach.

He hated doing it, but there was no way out. His daughter and her baby would have to live in the attic.

. . .

Unfortunately, this is a true story. Isabelle was discovered in Ohio in 1938 when she was about 6½ years old, living in a dark room with her deaf-mute mother. Isabelle couldn't talk, but she did use gestures to communicate with her mother. An inadequate diet and lack of sunshine had given Isabelle a disease called rickets. Her legs

> *were so bowed that as she stood erect the soles of her shoes came nearly flat together, and she got about with a skittering gait. Her behavior toward strangers, especially men, was almost that of a wild animal, manifesting much fear and hostility. In lieu of speech she made only a strange croaking sound. (Davis 1940/1997:121–129)*

When the newspapers reported this case, sociologist Kingsley Davis decided to find out what happened to Isabelle after her discovery. We'll come back to that later, but first let's use the case of Isabelle to give us some insight into what human nature is.

What Is Human Nature?

For centuries, people have been intrigued with the question of what is human about human nature. How much of people's characteristics comes from "nature" (heredity) and how much from "nurture" (the **social environment,** contact with others)? One way to answer this question is to study identical twins who have been reared apart, such as those discussed in the Down-to-Earth Sociology box on the next page. Another way would be to examine people who have been reared without human contact. Let us begin by looking at such children.

Feral Children

Over the centuries, the discovery of **feral** (wild) **children** has been reported from time to time. Supposedly, these children were abandoned or lost by their parents at a very early age and then raised by animals. In one instance, a feral child, known as the wild boy of Aveyron, was studied by the scientists of his day (Itard 1962). This boy, who was found in the forests of France in 1798, walked on all fours, and pounced on small animals, devouring them uncooked. He could not speak, and he gave no indication of feeling the cold. Other reports of feral children have claimed that on discovery, these children acted like wild animals: they could not speak; they bit, scratched, growled, and walked on all fours; they ate grass, tore ravenously at meat, drank by lapping water; and showed an insensitivity to pain and cold (Malson 1972).

Most social scientists today dismiss the significance of feral children, taking the position that children cannot be raised by animals and that children found in the woods were reared by their parents as infants but abandoned, probably because they were retarded.

social environment: the entire human environment, including direct contact with others

feral children: children assumed to have been raised by animals, in the wilderness isolated from other humans

Down-to-Earth Sociology

Heredity or Environment?
The Case of Oskar and Jack, Identical Twins

Identical twins share exact genetic heredity. One fertilized egg divides to produce two embryos. If heredity is the cause of personality (or of people's attitudes, temperament, and basic skills), then identical twins should be identical not only in their looks but also in these characteristics.

The fascinating case of Jack and Oskar helps us unravel this mystery. From their experience, we can see the far-reaching effects of the environment—how social experiences override biology.

Jack Yufe and Oskar Stohr are identical twins born in 1932 to a Jewish father and a Catholic mother. They were separated as babies after their parents divorced. Oskar was reared in Czechoslovakia by his mother's mother, who was a strict Catholic. When Oskar was a toddler, Hitler annexed this area of Czechoslovakia, and Oskar learned to love Hitler and to hate Jews. He became involved with the Hitler Youth (a sort of Boy Scout organization designed to instill the "virtues" of patriotism, loyalty, obedience,—and hatred).

Jack's upbringing provides an almost total contrast. Reared in Trinidad by his father, he learned loyalty to Jews and hatred of Hitler and the Nazis. After the war, Jack emigrated to Israel, where, at the age of 17, he joined a kibbutz. Later, Jack served in the Israeli army.

In 1954, the two brothers met. It was a short meeting, and Jack had been warned not to tell Oskar that they were Jews. Twenty-five years later, in 1979, when they were 47 years old, social scientists at the University of Minnesota brought them together again. These researchers figured that since Jack and Oskar had the same genes, whatever dif-

The question of the relative influence of heredity and the environment on human behavior has fascinated and plagued researchers. Identical twins reared apart provide an opportunity to examine this relationship. Almost all identical twins, however, as is the case with these girls, are reared together, frustrating efforts to separate heredity and environment.

ferences they showed would have to be due to the environment—to their different social experiences.

Not only were Oskar's and Jack's attitudes toward the war, Hitler, and Jews different, so, too, were their other basic orientations to life. In their politics, Oskar is quite conservative, while Jack is more liberal. Oskar enjoys leisure, while Jack is a workaholic. And, as you can predict, Jack is very proud of being a Jew. Oskar, however, won't even mention it.

That would seem to settle the matter. But there is another side to the findings. The researchers also found that Oskar and Jack both like sweet liqueur and spicy foods, excelled at sports as children but had difficulty with math, and have the same rate of speech. Each even flushes the toilet both before and after using it, and enjoys startling people by sneezing in crowded places.

For Your Consideration

Heredity or environment? How much influence does *each* have? The question is not yet settled, but at this point it seems fair to conclude that the *limits* of certain physical and mental abilities are established by heredity (such as ability at sports and mathematics), while such basic orientations to life as attitudes are the result of the environment. We can put it this way: For some parts of life, the blueprint is drawn by heredity; but even here the environment can redraw those lines. For other parts, the individual is a blank slate, and it is entirely up to the environment to determine what is written on that slate.

Sources: Based on Begley 1979, Chen 1979, Wright 1995.

But what if this were not the case? (See photo on page 64.) Could it be that by nature, if untouched by society, we would all be like feral children?

Isolated Children

Cases like Isabelle's surface from time to time. Because they are well documented, what can they tell us about human nature? We can first conclude that humans have no natural language, for Isabelle, and others like her, are unable to speak.

Most scientists dismiss the possibility that human children could be adopted by animals. When Binti Jua, a female gorilla at Brookfield Zoo in Brookfield, Illinois, rescued a 3-year-old boy who fell into the gorilla pit, and protected him from harm from the other gorillas, it opened the possibility that feral children may be more than mere myth. Shown here is Binti Jua with her baby, Koola.

Most human traits

But maybe Isabelle was retarded, as most scientists claim feral children are, and could not go through the usual stages of development. When given an intelligence test, she scored practically zero. But when Isabelle was given intensive language training, a surprising thing happened. In only two months, she was able to speak in short sentences. In about a year, she could write a few words, do simple addition, and retell stories after hearing them. Seven months later, she had a vocabulary of almost 2,000 words. It took only two years for Isabelle to reach the intellectual level normal for her age. She then went on to school, where she was "bright, cheerful, energetic . . . and participated in all school activities as normally as other children" (Davis 1940/1997:127).

As discussed in the last chapter, language is the key to human behavior. Without language, people have no mechanism for developing thought. Unlike animals, humans have no instincts that take the place of language. If an individual lacks language, he or she lives in an isolated world, a world of internal silence, without shared ideas, without connections to others.

Without language, there can be no culture—no shared way of life—and culture is the key to what people become. Each of us possesses a biological heritage, but this heritage does not determine specific behaviors, attitudes, or values. It is our culture that superimposes the specifics of what we become onto our biological heritage.

Institutionalized Children

But what besides language is required if a child is to develop into what we consider a healthy, balanced, intelligent human being? The key is stimulating interaction.

Two or three generations ago, when we had a much higher death rate, orphanages dotted the United States. Children reared in orphanages tended to be smaller than other children, to have difficulty establishing close bonds with others, and to have lower IQs—if they survived, that is, for their death rates were much higher than average (Spitz 1945). These orphanages were not Dickensian institutions where ragged children were beaten and denied food. The children were kept clean and given simple but nutritious food. Nevertheless, the contrast with today's standards is remarkable. Here is an account of a good orphanage in Iowa during the 1930s.

> Until about six months, they were cared for in the infant nursery. The babies were kept in standard hospital cribs that often had protective sheeting on the sides, thus effectively limiting visual stimulation; no toys or other objects were hung in the infants' line of vision. Human interactions were limited to busy nurses who, with the speed born of practice and necessity, changed diapers or bedding, bathed and medicated the infants, and fed them efficiently with propped bottles. (Skeels 1966)

Although everyone "knew" that the cause of mental retardation was biological ("They're just born that way"), two psychologists who consulted in this Iowa orphanage, H. M. Skeels and H. B. Dye (1939), began to suspect that the absence of stimulating social interaction was the basic problem, not some biological incapacity on the part of the children. To test their controversial idea, they placed thirteen infants whose mental retardation was so obvious that no one wanted to adopt them, in Glenwood State School, an institution for the mentally retarded. Each infant, then about 19 months old, was assigned to a separate ward of women ranging in mental age from 5 to 12 and in chronological age from 18 to 50. The women were pleased with this arrangement. They not only did a good job taking care of the infants' basic physical needs—diapering, feeding, and so on—but they also loved to play with the children, to cuddle them, and to shower them with attention. They even competed to see which ward would have "its baby" walking or talking first. One woman would become

particularly attached to him (or her) and figuratively "adopted" him (or her). As a consequence, an intense one-to-one adult–child relationship developed, which was supplemented by the less intense but frequent interactions with the other adults in the environment. Each child had some one person with whom he (or she) was identified and who was particularly interested in him (or her) and his (or her) achievements. (Skeels 1966)

The researchers left a control group of twelve infants, also retarded but higher in intelligence, at the orphanage, where they received the usual care. Two and a half years later, Skeels and Dye tested all the children's intelligence. Their findings were startling: Those assigned to the retarded women had gained an average of twenty-eight IQ points while those who remained in the orphanage had lost thirty points.

What happened after these children were grown? Did these initial differences matter? Twenty-one years later, Skeels and Dye did a follow-up study. Those in the control group who had remained in the orphanage averaged less than third grade in education. Four still lived in state institutions, while the others held low-level jobs. Only two had married. In contrast, the average level of education for the thirteen individuals in the experimental group was twelve grades (about normal for that period). Five had completed one or more years of college. One had not only earned a B.A. but had gone on to graduate school. Eleven had married. All thirteen were self-supporting and had higher-status jobs or were homemakers (Skeels 1966). Apparently, then, one characteristic that we take for granted as being a basic "human" trait, high intelligence, depends on early, intimate relations with other humans.

Let's consider one other case, the story of Genie:

In 1970, California authorities found Genie, a 13½-year-old girl who had been kept locked in a small room since she was 20 months old. Apparently her father (70 years old when Genie was discovered) hated children, and probably had caused the death of two of Genie's siblings. Her 50-year-old mother was partially blind and frightened of her husband. Genie could not speak, did not know how to chew, was unable to stand upright, and could not straighten her hands and legs. On intelligence tests, she scored at the level of a 1-year-old. After intensive training, Genie learned to walk and use simple sentences (although they were garbled). As she grew up, her language remained primitive, she took anyone's property if it appealed to her, and she went to the bathroom wherever she wanted. At the age of 21, Genie went to live in a home for adults who cannot live alone. (Pines 1981)

From this pathetic story, we can conclude that not only intelligence but also the ability to establish close bonds with others depends on early interaction. In addition, apparently there is a period prior to age 13 in which language and human bonding must occur for humans to develop high intelligence and the ability to be sociable and follow social norms.

Deprived Animals

A final lesson can be gained by looking at animals that have been deprived of normal interaction. In a series of experiments with rhesus monkeys, psychologists Harry and Margaret Harlow demonstrated the importance of early learning. The Harlows (1962) raised baby monkeys in isolation. They gave each monkey two artificial mothers. One "mother" was only a wire frame with a wooden head, but it did have a nipple from which the baby could nurse. The frame of the other "mother," which had no bottle, was covered with soft terrycloth. For their food, the baby monkeys nursed at the wire frame. But when the Harlows (1965) frightened the babies with a large mechanical bear or dog, the babies did not run to the wire frame "mother"; instead, they would cling pathetically to their terrycloth "mother." The Harlows drew the significant conclusion that infant–mother bonding is due not to feeding but rather to what they termed "intimate physical contact." To most of us, this phrase means cuddling.

It is also significant that the monkeys raised in isolation were never able to adjust to monkey life. Placed with other monkeys when they were grown, they didn't know how to enter into "monkey interaction"—to play and to engage in pretend fights—and the other

Like humans, monkeys need interaction to thrive. Those raised in isolation are unable to interact satisfactorily with others. In this photograph, we see one of the monkeys described in the text. Purposefully frightened by the experimenter, the monkey has taken refuge in the soft terrycloth draped over an artificial "mother."

monkeys rejected them. Neither did they know how to engage in sexual intercourse, in spite of futile attempts to do so. The experimenters designed a special device, which allowed some females to become pregnant. After giving birth, however, these monkeys were "ineffective, inadequate, and brutal mothers . . . [who] . . . struck their babies, kicked them, or crushed the babies against the cage floor."

In one of their many other experiments, the Harlows isolated baby monkeys for different lengths of time. They found that monkeys isolated for short periods (about three months) were able to overcome the effects of their isolation. Those isolated for six months or more, however, were unable to adjust to normal monkey life. They could not play or engage in pretend fights, and the other monkeys rejected them. In other words, the longer the isolation, the more difficult it is to overcome. There also may be a critical learning stage that, if missed, may be impossible to overcome. That may have been the case with Genie.

Because humans are not monkeys, we must be careful about extrapolating from animal studies to human behavior. The Harlow experiments, however, support what we know about the effects of isolation on children.

▼ **In Sum: Society Makes Us Human** Apparently, babies do not "naturally" develop into human adults. Although their bodies certainly get bigger, if raised in isolation they become little more than big animals. Without the concepts that language provides, they can't experience or even grasp relations between people (the "connections" we call brother, sister, parent, friend, teacher, and so on). And without warm, friendly interaction, they aren't "friendly" in the accepted sense of the term; nor do they cooperate with others. They do not think in terms of a past and a future. Indeed, they do not appear to think in any meaningful way.

In short, to develop into adults with the characteristics that we take for granted as "human," children need to be surrounded by people who care for them. Only then do they develop into social adults within the limits set by their biology. This process by which we learn the ways of society (or of particular groups), called **socialization,** is what sociologists have in mind when they say, "Society makes us human."

socialization: the process by which people learn the characteristics of their group—the attitudes, values, and actions thought appropriate for them

self: the unique human capacity of being able to see ourselves "from the outside"; the picture we gain of how others see us

looking-glass self: a term coined by Charles Horton Cooley to refer to the process by which our self develops through internalizing others' reactions to us

The Social Development of the Self, Mind, and Emotions

At birth, we have no idea that we are separate beings, no idea even that we are he or she. How do we develop a **self,** the picture we have of how others see us, our view of who we are?

Cooley and the Looking-Glass Self

Back in the 1800s, Charles Horton Cooley (1864–1929), a symbolic interactionist who taught at the University of Michigan, concluded that this unique aspect of "humanness" called the self is *socially created;* that is, our sense of self develops from interaction with others. He coined the term **looking-glass self** (1902) to describe the process by which a sense of self develops, which he summarized in the following couplet:

Each to each a looking-glass
Reflects the other that doth pass.

The looking-glass self contains three elements:

1. *We imagine how we appear to those around us.* For example, we may think that others see us as witty or dull.

2. *We interpret others' reactions.* We come to conclusions about how others evaluate us. Do they like us being witty? Do they dislike us for being dull?

3. *We develop a self-concept.* Based on our interpretations of the reactions of others, we develop feelings and ideas about ourselves. A favorable reflection in this "social mirror" leads to a positive self-concept, a negative reflection to a negative self-concept.

Note that the development of the self does *not* depend on accurate evaluations. Even if we grossly misinterpret how others think about us, those misjudgments become part of our self-concept. Note also that although the self-concept begins in childhood, *its development is an ongoing, lifelong process.* The three steps of the looking-glass self are a part of our everyday lives, and as we monitor how other people react to us, we continually modify the self. The self, then, is never a finished product, but is always in process, even into old age.

Mead and Role Taking

Another symbolic interactionist, George Herbert Mead (1863–1931), who taught at the University of Chicago, added that play is critical to the development of a self. In play, children learn to **take the role of the other,** that is, to put themselves in someone else's shoes—to understand how someone else feels and thinks and to anticipate how that person will act.

Young children attain this ability only gradually (Mead 1934; Coser 1977). In a simple experiment, psychologist J. Flavel (1968) asked 14-year-olds and 8-year-olds to explain a board game to some children who were blindfolded and to others who were not. The 8-year-olds gave the same instructions to everyone, while the 14-year-olds gave more detailed instructions to those who were blindfolded. The younger children could not yet take the role of the other, while the older children could.

taking the role of the other: putting oneself in someone else's shoes; understanding how someone else feels and thinks and thus anticipating how that person will act

Mead analyzed taking the role of the other *as an essential part of learning to be a full-fledged member of society. At first, we are able to take the role only of* significant others, *as these children are doing. Later we develop the capacity to take the role of* the generalized other, *which is essential not only for extended cooperation but also for the control of antisocial desires.*

To help his students understand what the term generalized other *means, Mead used baseball as an illustration. The text explains why team sports and organized games are excellent examples to explain this concept.*

As they develop this ability, at first children are able to take only the role of **significant others,** individuals who significantly influence their lives, such as parents or siblings. By assuming their roles during play, such as dressing up in their parents' clothing, children cultivate the ability to put themselves in the place of significant others.

As the self gradually develops, children internalize the expectations of larger numbers of people. The ability to take on roles eventually extends to being able to take the role of an abstract entity, "the group as a whole." To this, our perception of how people in general think of us, Mead gave the term **generalized other.**

Taking the role of the other is essential if we are to become cooperative members of human groups—whether the family, peers, or work. This ability allows us to modify our behavior by anticipating the reactions of others—something Genie never learned.

Learning to take the role of the other goes through three stages:

1. *Imitation*. Children under 3 can only mimic others. They do not yet have a sense of self separate from others, and they can only imitate people's gestures and words. (This stage is actually not role taking, but it prepares the child for it.)

2. *Play*. During the second stage, from the age of about 3 to 5 or 6, children pretend to take the roles of specific people. They might pretend that they are a firefighter, a wrestler, the Lone Ranger, Supergirl, Batman, and so on. They also like costumes at this stage and enjoy dressing up in their parents' clothing, or tying a towel around their necks to "become" Superman or Wonder Woman.

3. *Games*. This third stage, organized play, or team games, begins roughly with the early school years. The significance for the self is that to play these games the individual must be able to take multiple roles. One of Mead's favorite examples was that of a baseball game, in which each player must be able to take the role of all the other players. To play baseball, the child must know not only his or her own role but must also be able to anticipate who will do what when the ball is hit or thrown.

Mead also distinguished between the "I" and the "me" in the development of the self. The "*I*" is *the self as subject*, the active, spontaneous, creative part of the self. In contrast, the "*me*" is *the self as object*, made up of attitudes internalized from our interactions with others. Mead chose pronouns to indicate these two aspects of the self because in our language "I" is the active agent, as in "I shoved him," while "me" is the object of action, as in "He shoved me." Mead stressed that the individual is not only a "me"—like a com-

significant other: an individual who significantly influences someone else's life

generalized other: the norms, values, attitudes, and expectations of people "in general"; the child's ability to take the role of the generalized other is a significant step in the development of a self

puterized robot passively absorbing the responses of others. Rather, the "I" actively makes sense of those responses. By this, Mead meant that we (our "I") react to our social environments: We evaluate the reactions of others and organize them into a unified whole. Mead added that the "I" even monitors the "me," fine-tuning our actions to help us better match what others expect of us.

Mead also drew a conclusion that some find startling—that *not only the self but also the human mind is a social product.* Mead stressed that we cannot think without symbols. But where do these symbols come from? Only from society, which gives us our symbols by giving us language. If society did not provide the symbols, we would not be able to think, and thus would not possess what we call the mind. Mind, then, like language, is a product of society.

Vygotsky and the Development of Thinking

In Russia, Lev Vygotsky (1896–1934) did research that supported Mead's position. In the 1930s, he set up a laboratory where he observed children at play. He noticed that preschool children often talk to themselves (the child development specialists call this "self-directed speech"). When Vygotsky (1995) set up an obstacle, such as not providing paper or a pencil for a child who was getting ready to draw, the child's self-directed speech increased: "Where's the pencil. I need a blue pencil. Never mind, I'll draw with a red one."

Children of school age, in contrast, when confronted with similar problems, would pause in their activities. After silently scrutinizing the matter, they would find a solution. When asked what they had been thinking during their pause, these children gave answers that paralleled what the younger children had spoken out loud.

For Vygotsky, these simple observations were highly significant. Vygotsky concluded that the younger children were using self-directed speech to talk themselves through the problem. Their self-directed speech reflected how others had talked them through problems in the past. Since the older children did not talk aloud about the problem, Vygotsky concluded that self-directed speech is a transitional stage on our way to internalizing society's ideas. Thinking, which he called soundless inner speech, is our individual use of the symbols we learn from society. Vygotsky, then, came to the same conclusion as Mead: Because thinking (or mind) depends on language, our mind is a product of society.

Piaget and the Development of Reasoning Skills

Essential to the human mind is the ability to reason. How do we learn this skill?

This question intrigued Jean Piaget (1896–1980), a Swiss psychologist, who noticed that younger children would give *consistent* wrong answers on intelligence tests. This might mean, he thought, that younger children follow some sort of incorrect rule in figuring out answers.

To find out, Piaget set up a laboratory where he could give children of different ages problems to solve (Piaget 1950, 1954; Phillips 1969). After years of research, Piaget concluded that children go through four stages as they develop their ability to reason. At each stage, children develop new reasoning skills. (As we review these stages, it may be helpful to mentally substitute reasoning skills for Piaget's term *operational*.)

1. *The sensorimotor stage* (from birth to about age 2)

   During this early stage, the infant's understanding is limited to direct contact with the environment. It is based on sucking, touching, listening, seeing. Infants do not think in any sense that we understand. During the first part of this stage, they do not even know that their bodies are separate from the environment. Indeed, they have yet to discover that they have toes. Neither can infants recognize cause and effect. That is, they do not know that their actions cause something to happen.

2. *The preoperational stage* (from about age 2 to age 7)

   During this stage, children *develop the ability to use symbols.* They do not yet understand common concepts, however, such as size, speed, or causation. Although they can count, they do not really understand what numbers mean. Nor do they yet have the ability to take the role of the other. Piaget asked preoperational children to describe a clay mountain range and found that they could do so. But when he asked them to describe how the mountain range looked from where another child was sitting, they could not do so. They could only repeat what they saw from their view.

3. *The concrete operational stage* (from the age of about 7 to 12)

Although reasoning abilities are more developed, they remain *concrete*. Children can now understand numbers, causation, and speed, and they are able to take the role of the other and to participate in team games. Without concrete examples, however, they are unable to talk about such concepts as truth, honesty, or justice. They can explain why Jane's answer was a lie, but they cannot describe what truth itself is.

4. *The formal operational stage* (after the age of about 12)

Children are now capable of abstract thinking. Without concrete examples, they can talk about concepts, come to conclusions based on general principles, and use rules to solve abstract problems. During this stage, they are likely to become young philosophers (Kagan 1984). For example, if shown a photo of a slave, a child at the concrete operational stage might have said, "That's wrong!" Now, however, he or she is more likely to ask, "If our country was founded on equality, how could people have owned slaves?"

Global Considerations: Developmental Sequences

Cooley's conclusions about the looking-glass self and Mead's conclusions about role taking and mind as a social product appear to be universal. There is less agreement, however, that Piaget's four stages are globally true. Some researchers, for example, suggest that the stages are exaggerated, that children develop reasoning skills much more gradually than Piaget concluded (Berk 1994; Diver-Stamnes and Thomas 1995).

In addition, some adults apparently get stuck in the concreteness of the third stage and never reach the fourth stage (Kohlberg and Gilligan 1971). College, for example, is a social experience that carefully nurtures the fourth stage, and most people without this experience apparently have less ability for abstract thought. If so, social experiences modify these stages, and the stages may differ from one culture to another.

Certainly the *content* of what we learn varies from one culture to another. This, in turn, has remarkable influence on our thinking. For example, Brazilian street children have little or no schooling. Yet through selling candy they develop sophisticated mathematical and bargaining abilities (Saxe 1988). With such abilities so unlike those learned by children in our culture, and with thinking processes that revolve around these activities, we cannot assume that the developmental sequences observed in our children are true of children around the globe (Berk 1994).

Freud and the Development of Personality

Along with the development of the mind and the self comes the development of personality. Let's look at a theory that has influenced the Western world.

In Vienna at the turn of the century, Sigmund Freud (1856–1939), a physician, founded psychoanalysis, a technique for treating emotional problems through long-term, intensive exploration of the subconscious mind. We shall look at that part of his thought that applies to the development of personality.

Freud believed that personality consists of three elements. Each child is born with the first, an **id**, Freud's term for inborn drives for self-gratification. The id of the newborn is evident in cries of hunger or pain. The pleasure-seeking id operates throughout life, demanding the immediate fulfillment of basic needs: attention, safety, food, sex, aggression, and so on.

But the id's drive for immediate and complete satisfaction runs directly against the needs of other people. As the child comes up against norms and other constraints (usu-

id: Freud's term for our inborn basic drives

ally represented by parents), he or she must adapt to survive. To help adapt to these constraints that block his or her desires, a second component of the personality emerges, which Freud called the **ego.** The ego is the balancing force between the id and the demands of society that suppress it. The ego also serves to balance the id and the **superego,** the third component of the personality, more commonly called the conscience.

The superego represents *culture within us,* the norms and values that we have internalized from our social groups. As the *moral* component of the personality, the superego gives us feelings of guilt or shame when we break social rules, or pride and self-satisfaction when we follow them.

According to Freud, when the id gets out of hand, we follow our desires for pleasure and break society's norms. When the superego gets out of hand, we become overly rigid in following those norms, finding ourselves bound in a straitjacket of rules that inhibit our lives. The ego, the balancing force, tries to prevent either the superego or the id from dominating. In the emotionally healthy individual, the ego succeeds in balancing these conflicting demands of the id and the superego. In the maladjusted individual, however, the ego cannot control the inherent conflict between the id and the superego, and the result is internal confusion and problem behaviors.

ego: Freud's term for a balancing force between the id and the demands of society

superego: Freud's term for the conscience, the internalized norms and values of our social groups

Sociological Evaluation.   What sociologists appreciate about Freud is his emphasis on socialization—that the social group into which we are born transmits norms and values that restrain our biological drives. Sociologists, however, object to the view that inborn and unconscious motivations are the primary reasons for human behavior, for this denies *the central principle of sociology:* that social factors such as social class, religion, and education underlie people's behaviors (Epstein 1988; Bush and Simmons 1990). Feminist sociologists have been especially critical of Freud. Although what we just summarized applies to both females and males, Freud assumed that what is "male" is "normal." He even analyzed females as inferior, castrated males (Gilligan 1982; Chodorow 1990).

Global Considerations: Socialization into Emotions

As we have seen, the mind is a social product, and through socialization we acquire the particulars that go into human reasoning. Now we shall examine how emotions, too, are not simply the result of biology, but how they also depend on socialization (Hochschild 1975; Pollak and Thoits 1989; Johnson 1992; Wouters 1992).

This conclusion may sound strange. Don't all people get angry? Doesn't everyone cry? Don't we all feel guilt, shame, sadness, remorse, happiness, fear? What has socialization to do with emotions?

Let's start with the obvious. Certainly people around the world all feel these particular emotions, but the way in which they express them varies from one culture to another. Let's consider, for example, close adult male friends who are reunited after a long separation. Americans might shake hands vigorously or even pat each other on the back. Japanese might bow, while Arabs will kiss. A good part of childhood socialization centers on learning how to express emotions, for each culture has "norms of emotion" that demand conformity (Clark 1991).

How we express emotions depends not only on culture but also on our social location. Consider gender. When two U.S. female friends are reunited after a long separation, they are much more likely than men to hug instead of merely shaking hands or patting each other on the back. But gender (and racial/ethnic) differences in expressing emotions are modified by social class. Upon seeing a friend after a long absence, lower-class women, men, African Americans, and so on are likely to express emotions of delight differently from upper-class women, men, African Americans, and so on.

Although males are socialized to express less emotion than are females, such socialization goes against their nature. In certain settings, especially sports, males are allowed to be openly emotional, even demonstrative, with one another. Shown here is Scottie Pippen embracing an exhausted Michael Jordan after a Chicago Bulls victory against the Utah Jazz.

But the matter goes deeper than this. People in some cultures learn to experience emotions quite unlike our own. For example, the Ifaluk, who live on the Western Caroline Islands of Micronesia, use the word *fago* to refer to feelings evoked by seeing someone suffer or in need of help, something close to what we refer to as sympathy or compassion. But they also use this term to describe their feelings when they are around someone who has high status, someone who is highly admired or respected (Kagan 1984). To us, these are two distinct emotions, and they require distinct terms.

▼   **In Sum** As we are socialized into a culture, we learn not only how to express our emotions, but also what emotions to feel. Because feelings influence behavior, to understand emotions is to broaden our understanding of human behavior. For a glimpse of a culture in which emotions, values, and behaviors are shockingly different from those we expect, see the Down-to-Earth Sociology box below.

Down-to-Earth Sociology

Signs of the Times: Are We Becoming Ik?

Anthropologist Colin Turnbull (1972/1995) studied the Ik, a formerly proud nomadic people in northern Uganda whose traditional hunting lands were taken from them by the government. Devastated by drought, hunger, and starvation, the Ik turned to a form of extreme individualism in which selfishness, emotional numbness, and lack of concern for others reign supreme. The pursuit of food has become the only good, with society replaced by a passionless, numbed association of individuals.

Imagine, for a moment, that you were born into the Ik tribe. After your first three or four years of life, you are pushed out of the hut. From then on, you are on your own. You can sleep in the village courtyard or take shelter, such as you can, against the stockade. With permission, you can sit in the doorway of your parents' house, but you may not lie down or sleep there.

There is no school. No church. Nothing from this point in your life that even comes close to what we call family. You join a group of children aged 3 to 7. The weakest are soon thinned out, for only the strongest survive. Later, you join a band of 8- to 12-year olds. At 12 or 13, you split off by yourself.

Socialization usually involves learning some aspect of life by what you see going on around you. But here you see coldness at the center of life. The men hunt, but game is scarce. If they get anything, they refuse to bring it back to their families, saying, "Each one of them is out seeing what he can get for himself. Do you think they will bring any back for me?"

You also see cruelty at the center of life. When blind Lo'ono trips and rolls to the bottom of the ravine, the adults laugh as she lies on her back, her arms and legs thrashing feebly. When Lolim begs his son to let him in, pleading that he is going to die in a few hours, Longoli drives him away. Lolim dies alone.

The children learn their lesson well: Selfishness is good, the survival of the individual paramount. But the children add a childish glee to the adults' dispassionate coldness. When blind Lolim took ill, the children would dance and tease him, kneeling in front of him and laughing as he fell. His grandson would creep up and with a pair of sticks drum a beat on the old man's bald head.

Then there was Adupa, who managed, for a while, to keep a sense of awe of life. When Adupa found food, she would hold it in her hand, looking at it with wonder and delight. As she would raise her hand to her mouth, the other children would jump on her, laughing as they beat her.

For Your Consideration

From the Ik, we learn that the values we take to be uniquely human are not inherent in humanity. Rather, they arise from society, and, as such, can be lost when the sense of mutuality that lies at the basis of society breaks down.

It is easy to criticize a society and not have to walk in their shoes, so let's turn the critical lens on our own society. Just as the Ik are obsessed with food, we have become obsessed with achievement and material goods. Money is becoming more important than values, and we may be rushing headlong toward the day that we, too, lose our sense of mutuality and purpose. Then, like the Ik, no longer will we be able to perceive truth, beauty, and goodness.

Even people are treated like things—discarded when no longer needed. Corporations fire older workers because they can pay younger ones less—or move an entire factory to a land of cheaper labor. As they leave hundreds and even thousands of workers stranded, managers and owners shrug their shoulders and say, "That's business." For the sake of higher salaries, people sever themselves from kin and community. Successful executives discard same-age mates, the co-parent of their own children, in exchange for younger "trophy" mates—who are more photogenic. Isolation and alienation become common.

Finally, the humane values, those we would wish for in friends and family—kindness, generosity, patience, tolerance, cooperation, compassion—are undervalued: Any job that requires such talents is low in pay and prestige (Maybury-Lewis 1995).

The Self and Emotions as Social Control: Society Within Us

Much of our socialization is intended to turn us into conforming members of society. Socialization into self and emotions is essential to this process, for both the self and our emotions mold our behavior. Although we like to think we are "free," consider for a moment just some of the factors that influence how we act: the expectations of friends and parents; neighbors and teachers; classroom norms and college rules; and federal and state laws. For example, if for some reason, such as a moment of intense frustration or a devilish desire to shock people, you wanted to tear off your clothes and run naked down the street, what would stop you?

The answer is your socialization—*society within you.* Your experiences in society have resulted in a self that thinks along certain lines and feels particular emotions. This keeps you in line. Thoughts such as "Would I be kicked out of school?" "What would my friends (parents) think if they found out?" represent an awareness of the self in relationship to others. So does the desire to avoid feelings of shame and embarrassment. Our *social mirror,* then—the result of being socialized into a self and emotions—sets up effective controls over our behavior. In fact, socialization into self and emotions is so effective that some people experience embarrassment just thinking about running nude in public!

Socialization into Gender

Society also channels our behavior through **gender socialization.** By expecting different attitudes and behaviors from us *because* we are male or female, the social group nudges boys and girls in separate directions in life. This foundation of contrasting attitudes and behaviors is so thorough that, as adults, most of us act, think, and even feel according to the guidelines laid down by our culture as appropriate for our sex.

How do we learn gender messages? Because the significance of gender is emphasized throughout this book, with a special focus in Chapter 11, for now let's briefly consider the influence of just the family and the mass media.

Gender Messages in the Family

Our parents are the first significant others who teach us our part in this symbolic division of the world. Sometimes they do so self-consciously, perhaps by bringing into play pink and blue, colors that have no meaning in themselves but have social associations with gender. But our parents' own gender orientations are so firmly established that they also teach us **gender roles,** the behaviors and attitudes considered appropriate for our sex, without being aware of what they are doing.

A classic study illustrates how deeply ingrained these orientations are. Psychologists Susan Goldberg and Michael Lewis (1969) asked mothers to bring their 6-month-old infants into their laboratory, supposedly to observe the infants' development. Secretly, however, the researchers also observed the mothers. They found that the mothers kept their female children closer to them. They also touched and spoke more to their daughters. By the time the children were 13 months old, the girls stayed closer to their mothers during play. When Goldberg and Lewis set up a barrier to separate the children from their mothers, who were holding toys, the girls were more likely to cry and motion for help; the boys, to try to climb over the barrier. Goldberg and Lewis concluded that in our society mothers unconsciously reward daughters for being passive and dependent, but their sons for being active and independent.

These lessons continue throughout childhood. On the basis of sex, children are given different kinds of toys. Preschool boys are allowed to roam farther from home than their preschool sisters, and they are subtly encouraged to participate in more rough-and-tumble play—even to get dirtier and to be more defiant (Gilman 1911/1971; Henslin 1997a). This process that begins in the family is completed as the child is exposed to other aspects

gender socialization: the ways in which society sets children onto different courses in life *because* they are male or female

gender role: the behaviors and attitudes considered appropriate because one is a female or a male

of society (Thorne 1990). Teachers, for example, expect male and female students to be different. They then nurture the "natural" differences they find, with the result that boys and girls develop different aspirations in life.

Gender Messages in the Mass Media

The **mass media,** forms of communication directed to large audiences, reinforce cultural expectations of gender. Of the many ways they do this, let's examine advertising, television, and video games.

Advertising. Although advertising uses a mix of gender images, it continues to perpetuate stereotypes by portraying males as dominant and rugged and females as sexy and submissive. The Marlboro man with his cowboy hat, lariat, horse, and rugged looks, smoking a cigarette in mountainous settings, comes to mind. Semi-clad female bodies whose assets are intended to sell a variety of products, from automobiles to hamburgers, are at the other end of the spectrum of stereotypical, culturally molded images

Television. Television reinforces stereotypes of the sexes. On prime-time television, male characters outnumber female characters two to one. They also are more likely to be portrayed in higher-status positions (Vande Berg and Streckfuss 1992). Viewers get the message, for the more television people watch, the more they tend to have restrictive ideas about women's role in society (Signorielli 1989, 1990).

The exceptions to the stereotypes are notable—and a sign of changing times. One program, perhaps the most stereotype-breaking of all, is *Xena, Warrior Princess,* a popular television series imported from Australia. Portrayed as dominant and possessing magical powers, Xena overcomes all obstacles and easily defeats all foes—whether male or female.

Video Games. Some youths spend countless hours playing video games in arcades and at home. Even college students, especially males, relieve stress by escaping into video games. Unfortunately, we have no studies of how these games affect their players' ideas of gender. Because these games are on the cutting edge of society, they sometime also reflect cutting-edge changes in sex roles, as examined in the Sociology and the New Technology box on the next page.

mass media: forms of communication, such as radio, newspapers, and television, that are directed to mass audiences

Absorbing Gender Messages: The Peer Group. When sociologist Melissa Milkie (1994) studied a group of junior high school boys, she found that much of their talk cen-

The mass media not only reflect gender stereotypes, but they also play a role in changing them. Sometimes they do both simultaneously. The images of Lara and of Xena, Warrior Princess, reflect women's changing role in society and, by exaggerating the change, also mold new stereotypes.

 *Sociology and the New Technology*

From Xena, Warrior Princess, to Lara Croft, Tomb Raider: Changing Images of Women in the Mass Media

As women change their roles in society, the mass media reflect those changes. Although media images of women as passive, subordinate, or as mere background objects remain and still predominate, a new image has broken through. Exaggerating changes in society, this new image nonetheless reflects a changing role of women—from passive to active in life outside the home, from acquiescent to dominant in social relations. As mentioned in the text, Xena, the Warrior Princess, is an outstanding example of this change.

Though it is unusual to call video games a form of the mass media, I think it is appropriate to do so. Like books and magazines, video games are made available to a mass audience. And with digital advances, they have crossed the line from what we traditionally think of as games to something that more closely resembles interactive movies.

Sociologically, what is significant is that the *content* of video games socializes their users. Gamers, as they are known, are exposed not only to action, but also to ideas as they play. Especially significant are gender images that communicate powerful messages, just as they do in other forms of the mass media.

Lara Croft, an adventure-seeking archeologist and star of *Tomb Raider* and *Tomb Raider 2*, is the essence of the new gender image. Lara is smart, strong, and able to utterly vanquish foes. With both guns blazing, she is the cowboy of the twenty-first century, the term *cowboy* being purposefully chosen, as Lara breaks gender roles and assumes what previously was the domain of men.

Yet, the old remains powerfully encapsulated in the new. As the photo on the opposite page makes evident, Lara is a fantasy girl for young men of the digital generation. No matter her foe, no matter her predicament, Lara always is dressed in form-fitting outfits—which reflect the mental images of the men who created this digital character. So successful has their effort been that boys and young men have bombarded corporate headquarters with questions about Lara's personal life. Lara has caught young men's fancy to such an extent that more than 100 Web sites are devoted to her (Croal and Hughes 1997).

When the final reward of the game is to see Lara in a nightie, one can legitimately question—regardless of tough-girl images—just how far stereotypes have been left behind.

---

tered on the latest movies, videos, and TV programs. Of the many images presented in these media, the boys would single out sex and violence. They would joke and laugh about what they had seen, repeat lines, and act out parts for the amusement of one another.

If you know boys in their early teens, you've probably seen something like this yourself. You may have been amused, or even shaken your head in disapproval. Like a good sociologist, however, Milkie peers beneath the surface. She concludes that the boys were using media images to discover who they are as males. In the experience of these boys, and so many like them throughout our society, to be male is to be obsessed with sex and violence. Not to joke and laugh about murder and promiscuous sex would have marked a boy as a "weenie," a label to be avoided at all costs. I should add that this was a normal group of young teenagers, who were in the process of learning what it is to be a male in our society.

▼ **In Sum** All of us are born into a society in which "male" and "female" are significant symbols. Sorted into separate groups from childhood, we come to have shared ideas of what to expect of ourselves and of one another based on our sex. These images become integrated into our view of the world, forming a picture that forces an interpretation of the world in terms of gender. We are not simply passive consumers of these images. Rather, we select those images that are significant to our situation in life and use them to help construct our worlds.

Gender images, then, no matter their source, shape our ideas about the world. Lying mostly beneath our level of awareness, the messages they send affect the ways in which we view females and males, and how we ourselves fit into that picture. Images can break down or perpetuate myths and stereotypes. They can promote equality or inequality. Because gender serves as a primary basis for **social inequality**, giving privileges and obligations to one group of people while denying them to another, the role of the media and

social inequality: a social condition in which privileges and obligations are given to some but denied to others peers is worth exploring. For example, we have no studies of how girls use media images to construct their ideas of feminity, and precious few of how boys do so. Perhaps you will become the sociologist to do such research.

Agents of Socialization

People and groups that influence our self-concept, emotions, attitudes, and behavior are called **agents of socialization.** Of the many agents of socialization that prepare us to take our place in society, we shall examine the family, religion, day care, school, peers, sports, mass media, and workplace.

The Family

Around the world, the first group to have a major impact on humans is the family. Unlike some animals, we cannot survive by ourselves, and as babies we are utterly dependent on our family. Our experiences in the family are so intense that they have a lifelong impact on us. They lay down our basic sense of self, establishing our initial motivations, values, and beliefs (Gecas 1990). The family gives us ideas about who we are and what we deserve out of life. It is in the family that we begin to think of ourselves as strong or weak, smart or dumb, good-looking or ugly—or somewhere in between. And as already noted, here we begin the lifelong process of defining ourselves as female or male.

To study this process, sociologists have observed parents and young children in public settings, where their act of observing does not interfere with the natural interaction. Researchers using this unobtrusive technique have noted what they call the "stroller effect" (Mitchell et al. 1992). Fathers are more likely to push the stroller when the child is in it, the mother when the stroller is empty. In addition, the father is more likely to carry the child. From these observations, the researchers conclude that parents send their children subtle gender messages, teaching them about expected differences between men and women. Indeed, probably most of the ways by which parents teach their children gender roles is not by specific instruction, but by such nonverbal cues.

The Family and Social Class.   To see how far-reaching, yet subtle, social class is, consider how working-class and middle-class parents rear their children. Sociologist Melvin Kohn (1959, 1963, 1976, 1977, 1983; Kohn et al. 1986) found that the main concern of working-class parents is their children's outward conformity. They want their children to be obedient, neat, and clean, to follow the rules, and to stay out of trouble. They are likely to use physical punishment to make their children obey. In contrast, middle-class parents focus on developing their children's curiosity, self-expression, and self-control. They stress the motivations for their children's behavior and are more likely to reason with their children than to use physical punishment.

These findings were a sociological puzzle. Just *why* should working-class and middle-class parents rear their children so differently? From his sociological imagination, Kohn knew that life experiences of some sort held the key. Kohn found this key in the world of work. Blue-collar workers are usually supervised very closely. Their bosses expect them to do exactly as they are told. Since blue-collar parents expect their children's lives to be similar to their own, they draw on these experiences as they rear their children. Consequently, they stress obedience and conformity. Middle-class parents, in contrast, especially those in management and the professions, experience a much freer workplace. They have greater independence, are encouraged to be imaginative, and advance by taking the initiative. Expecting their children to work at similar jobs, they, in turn, socialize them into these qualities—which they assume will be essential to their well-being.

What still puzzled Kohn was that these class differences were only tendencies. Not all working-class or middle-class parents treat their children alike. Instead, some work-

agents of socialization: people or groups that affect our self-concept, attitudes, or other orientations toward life

ing-class parents act more like middle-class parents, and vice versa. As Kohn probed this puzzle, the pieces fell into place. He found that the parents' type of job was more important than their social class. Many middle-class office workers, for example, are closely supervised. Kohn found that such workers follow the working-class pattern of child rearing, for they stress outward conformity. In contrast, some blue-collar workers, such as those who do home repairs, have a good deal of freedom. These workers follow the middle-class model in rearing their children (Pearlin and Kohn 1966; Kohn and Schooler 1969).

Religion

Religion plays a significant role in the socialization of most Americans. It especially influences morality, becoming a key component in people's ideas of right and wrong. Religion is so important to Americans that 69 percent belong to a local congregation, and during a typical week two of every five Americans attend a religious service (*Statistical Abstract* 1997:Table 86). Religion is significant even for persons reared in nonreligious homes, for religious ideas pervade U.S. society, providing basic ideas of morality that become significant for us all.

The influence of religion extends to many areas of our lives. For example, participation in religious services teaches us not only beliefs about the hereafter but also ideas about the dress, speech, and manners appropriate for formal occasions. Religion is so significant that we shall treat this social institution in a separate chapter.

Day Care

With more mothers working for wages today than ever before, day care has become a significant agent of socialization in Western, industrialized societies. Concerns about its effects have propelled day care into the center of controversy. Researchers find that the effects of day care, at least in the United States, largely depend on the child's background (Scarr and Eisenberg 1993). Children from poverty-stricken backgrounds, as well as those from dysfunctional families (such as alcoholic, inept, or abusive parents), appear to benefit from day care. For example, the language skills of children from low-income homes increase. In contrast, day care may slow these skills in middle-class children, who would have received more intellectual stimulation at home. As you would expect, much depends on the quality of day care: high-quality day care (safe, small numbers, warm interaction, with low turnover of a trained staff) benefits children, while low-quality care has negative effects.

At this point, however, findings are preliminary, many even contradictory. For example, some studies show that children in day care are more cooperative and secure, while others show that they are more aggressive and insecure. Perhaps the fairest summary of current knowledge is that children from stable families receive no clear benefit or detriment from day care, and that children in poverty and from dysfunctional families benefit from quality day care.

Obviously, we need better studies. We need to match children by age and family background and compare those in day care with those who stay home or who are cared for by relatives and friends. And in order to compare results, we also need solid measures of the "quality" of day care—as well as the "quality" of home care.

The School

If asked how schools socialize students, you might stress the formal knowledge and skills they transmit, such as reading, writing, and arithmetic. As part of the **manifest function,** or intended purpose, of formal education, transmitting such skills is certainly part of socialization. Our schools' **latent functions,** the unintended consequences that help the social system, are also significant. Let's look at this less visible aspect of education.

manifest function: the intended consequences of people's actions designed to help some part of a social system

latent functions: the unintended consequences of people's actions that help to keep a social system in equilibrium

Schools are one of the primary agents of socialization. One of their chief functions is to sort young people into the adult roles thought appropriate for them, as well as to teach them the attitudes and skills that match those roles. What sorts of attitudes and adult roles do you think these junior high school girls are being socialized into? Is this a manifest or a latent function? Is it a dysfunction?

At home, children learn attitudes and values that match their family's situation in life. At school, they learn a broader perspective that helps prepare them to take a role in the world beyond the family. At home, for example, a child may have been the almost exclusive focus of doting parents, but in school the child learns *universality*—that the same rules apply to everyone, regardless of who their parents are or how special they may be at home. The Perspectives box on the next page explores how these new values and ways of looking at the world sometimes even replace those they learned at home.

Sociologists have also identified a *hidden curriculum* in our schools. This term refers to values that, though not explicitly taught, form an inherent part of a school's "message." For example, the stories and examples used to teach math and English grammar may bring with them lessons in patriotism, democracy, justice, and honesty. As conflict theorists point out, as schools teach their students to take their place in the work force, they also teach "correct" attitudes toward the economic system (Marger 1987). To learn that the economic system is basically just, for example, is to simultaneously learn that social problems such as poverty and homelessness have nothing to do with economic power, oppression, and exploitation. In short, in schools around the world students learn to support their nation's economic and political system.

Peer Groups

As a child's experiences with agents of socialization broaden, the influence of the family lessens. Entry into school marks only one of many steps in this transfer of allegiance. One of the most significant aspects of education is that it exposes children to **peer groups,** individuals of roughly the same age who are linked by common interests. Examples of peer groups are friends, clubs, gangs, and "the kids in the neighborhood."

Sociologists Patricia Adler, Steven Kless, and Peter Adler (1992) document how the peer group provides an enclave in which boys and girls resist the efforts of parents and schools to socialize them their way. Observing children at two elementary schools in Colorado, they saw children separate themselves by sex and develop their own worlds with unique norms. The norms that make boys popular were athletic ability, coolness, and toughness. For girls, they were family background, physical appearance (clothing and ability to use makeup), and the ability to attract popular boys. In this children's subculture,

peer group: a group of individuals roughly the same age linked by common interests

CULTURAL DIVERSITY IN THE UNITED STATES

Caught Between Two Worlds

Just as an individual is socialized into becoming a member of a culture, so a person can lose a culture through socialization. If you are exposed to a new culture as an adult, as older immigrants are, you can selectively adopt aspects of the new culture without entirely relinquishing your native culture. If the immersion occurs as a child, however, the second culture will vie for dominance with your native heritage. This, in turn, can lead to inner turmoil. To cut ties with your first culture—one way of handling the conflict—can create a sense of loss that is recognized only later in life.

Richard Rodriguez, a literature professor and essayist, was born in the 1950s to working-class Mexican immigrants. Wanting their son to be successful in their adopted land, his parents named him Richard instead of Ricardo. While his Spanish-English hybrid name indicated the parents' aspirations for their son, it was also a portent of the conflict Richard would experience.

Like other children of Mexican immigrants, Richard's first language was Spanish—a rich mother tongue that provided his orientation to the world. Until the age of 5 when he began school, he knew but fifty words in English. He described what happened when he began school:

The change came gradually but early. When I was beginning grade school, I noted to myself the fact that the classroom environment was so different in its styles and assumptions from my own family environment that survival would essentially entail a choice between both worlds. When I became a student, I was literally "remade"; neither I nor my teachers considered anything I had known before as relevant. I had to forget most of what my culture had provided, because to remember it was a disadvantage. The past and its cultural values became detachable, like a piece of clothing grown heavy on a warm day and finally put away.

Like millions of immigrants before him, whose parents spoke German, Polish, Italian, and so on, learning English eroded family and class ties and ate away at his ethnic roots. For him, they were not simply devices that eased the transition to the dominant culture. Instead, they transformed Richard into a *pocho,* "a Mexican with gringo aspirations." They slashed at the roots that had given him life.

To face such inner turmoil is to confront a fork in the road. Some turn one way and withdraw from the new culture—a clue that helps explain the high dropout rate of Latinos from U.S. schools. Others go in the opposite direction and, cutting ties with their family and cultural roots, wholeheartedly adopt the new culture.

Rodriguez took the second road. He excelled in his new language—so well, in fact, that he went to Stanford University and then became a graduate student in English at the University of California at Berkeley. He was even awarded a prestigious Fulbright fellowship to study English Renaissance literature at the British Museum.

But the past wouldn't let Rodriguez alone. Prospective employers were impressed with his knowledge of Renaissance literature. Yet at job interviews, they would ask if he would teach the Mexican novel in translation and be an adviser to Latino students. Rodriguez was haunted by the image of his grandmother, the warmth of the culture he had left behind, the language to which he was now a stranger.

Richard Rodriguez represents millions of immigrants—not just those of Latino origin but millions from other cultures, too—who want to be a part of the United States without betraying their past. They fear that to integrate into U.S. culture is to lose their roots. They are caught between two cultures, each beckoning, each offering rich rewards.

Sources: Based on Richard Rodriguez 1975, 1982, 1990, 1991.

academic achievement pulled in opposite directions: for boys, to do well academically hurt popularity, while among her peers getting good grades increased a girl's standing.

You know from personal experience how compelling peer groups are. With the cardinal rule seeming to be "conformity or rejection," anyone who doesn't do what the others want becomes an "outsider," a "nonmember," an "outcast." For preteens and teens just learning their way around in the world, it is not surprising that the peer group is king.

As a result, the standards of our peer groups tend to dominate our lives. If your peers, for example, listen to rap, heavy metal, rock and roll, country, folk, gospel, classical, hip hop, or any other kind of music, it is almost inevitable that you also prefer that kind of music. It is the same for clothing styles and dating standards. Peer influences also extend to behaviors that violate social norms. If your peers are college bound and upwardly striving, that is most likely what you will be; but if they use drugs, cheat, and steal, you are likely to do so, too.

 *Down-to-Earth Sociology*

Of Boys and Sports

In some sports the "male values" of competition and rough physical contact, akin to violence, are exalted, and those who play these sports learn to be "real men." Even if they don't play a sport, boys and men who intensely follow sports are openly affirming male cultural values and displaying their own masculinity.

Sociologist Michael Messner (1990) interviewed former male professional athletes and other men for whom sports provided a central identity during and after high school. Usually the father, an older brother, or an uncle had encouraged the boy to develop his athletic abilities, or had served as a role model for the boy's later success. A former professional football player, whose two older brothers had gained wide reputations for sports, said:

My brothers were role models. I wanted to prove—especially to my brothers—that I had heart, you know, that I was a man. . . . And . . . as I got older, I got better and I began to look around me and see, well hey! I'm competitive with these guys, even though I'm younger, you know?

Success at sports, then, brings recognition from others—and to the self—that one has achieved manly characteristics. This same football player also said,

And then of course all the compliments come—and I began to notice a change, even in my parents—especially in my father—he was proud of that, and that was very important to me. He was extremely important . . . he showed me more affection, now that I think of it.

In other words, success at sports brought recognition, not only from a community of peers, but as Messner found, sometimes from an emotionally distant father, who warmed up at his son's success.

The boost in the boy's self-esteem, however, can come at a high cost to others. Messner recounts a haunting scene during his visit to a summer basketball camp headed by a professional basketball coach:

The youngest boys, about eight years old (who could barely reach the basket with their shots) played a brief scrimmage. Afterwards, the coaches lined them up in a row in front of the older boys who were sitting in the grandstands. One by one, the coach would stand behind each boy, put his hand on the boy's head (much in the manner of a priestly benediction), and the older boys in the stands would applaud and cheer, louder or softer, depending on how well or poorly the young boy was judged to have performed. The two or three boys who were clearly the exceptional players looked confident that they would receive the praise they were due. Most of the boys, though, had expressions ranging from puzzlement to thinly disguised terror on their faces as they awaited the judgments of the older boys.

Messner also noted that the *meaning* of sports success differs by social class. As is well known, many poor people see sports as a way out of poverty. For middle-class boys, in contrast, sports are only one of many options open to success in life. Consequently, middle-class boys are more easily able to discard sports and to invest energy and self-identity in a future career.

For Your Consideration

Messner concludes that the implications of sports go far beyond the game itself—even into intimate relationships. It works like this. In the intensely competitive world of sports, being accepted by others depends on being a "winner." Following the notion of Cooley's *looking-glass self*, with their acceptance depending on success the boys begin to see themselves in those same terms—if they win, they are better people than if they lose. Accomplishments, then, become the key to relationships. In turn, they tend to develop *instrumental* (useful, goal-directed, not emotional) relationships. This brings built-in problems, for they try to relate instrumentally to females—who have been socialized to construct identities on meaningful relationships, not competitive success.

Sports

Sports are also a powerful socializing agent. Everyone recognizes that sports teach not only physical skills but also values. In fact, "teaching youngsters to be team players" is often given as the justification for financing organized sports. How effective sports are in socializing boys is the topic of the Down-to-Earth Sociology box above.

The Workplace

Another agent of socialization that comes into play somewhat later in life is the workplace. Those initial jobs that we take—part-time work after school and in college—are much more than a way to earn a few dollars. From the people we rub shoulders with at work, we learn not only a set of skills but also a perspective on the world.

Most of us eventually become committed to some particular line of work, which often involves trying out various jobs. It also may involve **anticipatory socialization**, learning

anticipatory socialization: because one anticipates a future role, one learns parts of it now

Many adults who wish to reduce gender distinctions prefer that grade schoolers of both sexes participate in the same playground activities. In spite of the sometimes not-so-subtle suggestions of teachers, however, grade school children insist on separating by sex, where they pursue different interests and activities and develop contrasting norms.

to play a role before entering it, a sort of mental rehearsal for some future activity. We may read novels about people who work in a career, talk to them, or take a summer internship. This allows us to gradually identify with the role, to become aware of some of its expectations and rewards. Sometimes this saves people fruitless years, as with some of my students who tried student teaching, found they couldn't stand it, and moved on to another major more to their liking.

An interesting aspect of work as a socializing agent is that the more you participate in a line of work, the more the work becomes a part of your self-concept. Eventually you come to think of yourself so much in terms of the job that if someone asks you to describe yourself, you are likely to include the job in your self-description, saying, "I am a teacher, accountant, nurse" or whatever.

Resocialization

What does a woman who has just become a nun have in common with a man who has just divorced? The answer is that they both are undergoing **resocialization**; that is, they are learning new norms, values, attitudes, and behaviors to match their new situation. In its most common form, resocialization occurs each time we learn something contrary to our previous experiences. A new boss who insists on a different way of doing things is resocializing you. Most resocialization is mild, only a slight modification of things already learned.

Resocialization can be intense, however. People who join Alcoholics Anonymous (AA), for example, expose themselves to a barrage of testimony about the destructive effects of excessive drinking. Some students also find the process of leaving high school and entering college to be an intense period of resocialization—especially during those initially scary, floundering days before becoming comfortable and fitting in. Even more so is psychotherapy or joining a cult, for these events expose people to ideas that conflict with their previous ways of looking at the world. If these ideas "take," not only does the individual's behavior change, but he or she also learns a fundamentally different way of looking at life.

The Case of Total Institutions

Relatively few of us experience the powerful agent of socialization Erving Goffman (1961) called the **total institution.** He coined this term to refer to a place in which people are cut off from the rest of society and where they come under almost total control of the officials who run the place. Boot camp, prisons, concentration camps, convents, some religious cults, and some boarding schools, such as West Point, are total institutions.

resocialization: the process of learning new norms, values, attitudes, and behaviors

total institution: a place in which people are cut off from the rest of society and are almost totally controlled by the officials who run the place

Resocialization often is a gentle process, as we gradually are exposed to different ways of thinking and doing. Sometimes, however, resocialization can be swift and brutal, as it is for this unwilling inductee to prison boot camp, an alternative to prison for nonviolent offenders.

A person entering a total institution is greeted with a **degradation ceremony** (Garfinkel 1956), an attempt to remake the self by stripping away the individual's current identity and stamping a new one in its place. This unwelcome greeting may involve fingerprinting, photographing, shaving the head, and banning the person's **personal identity kit** (items such as jewelry, hairstyles, clothing, and other body decorations used to express individuality). Newcomers may be ordered to strip, be examined (often in humiliating, semi-public settings), and then be given a uniform to designate their new status. (For prisoners, the public reading of the verdict and being led away in handcuffs by armed police also form part of the degradation ceremony.)

Total institutions are extremely effective in stripping away people's personal freedom. They are isolated from the public (the walls, bars, or other barriers not only keep the inmates in but also keep outsiders from interfering). They suppress preexisting statuses (inmates learn that their previous roles such as spouse, parent, worker, or student mean nothing, and that the only thing that counts is their current role). Total institutions suppress the norms of "the outside world," replacing them with their own rules, values, and interpretation of life. They also closely supervise the entire lives of the residents—eating, sleeping, showering, recreation are all standardized. They also control information, which helps the institution shape the inmates' ideas and "picture" of the world. Finally, they control the rewards and punishments. (Under conditions of deprivation, simple rewards for compliance such as sleep, a television program, a letter from home, extra food, or even a cigarette, are powerful incentives in controlling behavior.) The institution also holds the power to punish rule breaking—often severely, such as by solitary confinement.

No one leaves a total institution unscathed, for the experience leaves an indelible mark on the individual's self that colors the way he or she sees the world. Boot camp, as described in the Down-to-Earth Sociology box on the next page, is brutal, but swift. Prison, in contrast, is brutal and prolonged. Neither recruit nor prisoner, however, has difficulty in pinpointing how the institution affected the self.

degradation ceremony: a term coined by Harold Garfinkel to describe an attempt to remake the self by stripping away an individual's self-identity and stamping a new identity in its place

personal identity kit: items people use to decorate their bodies

life course: the sequence of events that we experience as we journey from birth to death

Socialization Through the Life Course

Some compare our lives to an empty canvas on which a series of portraits are painted, others to the seasons of the year. Each analogy depicts an image of personal change as we touch, and are touched by, events in which we are immersed. That series of major events, the stages of our lives from birth to death, is called the **life course** (Elder 1975).

 *Down-to-Earth Sociology*

Boot Camp as a Total Institution

The bus arrives at Parris Island, South Carolina, at 3 A.M. This is no accident. The recruits are groggy, confused. Up to a few hours ago, the boys had been civilians. Now, as a sergeant sneeringly calls them "maggots" and their heads are buzzed (25 seconds per recruit), they are quickly and deeply thrust into the heart of marine life.

After eleven weeks here, the Beavises and Butt-heads emerge self-disciplined, physically fit, and even courteous to their elders. Each time they see a superior, they automatically respond with "Good day, sir." Even skinheads and black separatists have been known to lay aside antagonistic identities and to live and work together as a team.

Every intense moment of those eleven weeks reminds them that they are joining a subculture of self-discipline. Here pleasure is suspect and sacrifice is good. As they learn the Marine way of talking, walking, and thinking, they are denied the diversions they knew: television, cigarettes, cars, candy, soft drinks, video games, music, alcohol, drugs, and sex.

Buzzing their hair is just the first step in stripping away their previous identities so a new one can be stamped in its place. The uniform serves the same purpose. There is a ban on using the first person, and even simple requests must be made in precise Marine style or they will not be acknowledged. ("Sir, Recruit Jones requests permission to make a head call, sir.")

Lessons are given with utter intensity. When Sgt. Carey checks brass belt buckles, Recruit Robert Shelton nervously blurts, "I don't have one." Sgt. Carey's face grows red as his neck cords bulge. "I?" he says, his face just inches from the recruit. With spittle flying from his mouth, he screams, " 'I' is gone!"

"Nobody's an individual, understand?" is the lesson that is driven home again and again. "You are a team, a Marine. Not a civilian. Not black or white, but a Marine. You will live like a Marine, fight like a Marine, and, if necessary, die like a Marine."

Each day begins before dawn with close order formations. The rest of the day is filled with training in hand-to-hand combat, marching, running, calisthenics, and Marine history.

The pressure to conform is intense. Those sent packing for insubordination or suicidal tendencies are mocked in cadence during drills. ("Hope you like the sights you see / Parris Island casualty.") Exhausted, as lights go out at 9 P.M. the recruits perform the day's last task: the entire platoon, in unison, shouts the virtues of the Marines.

Recruits are constantly scrutinized. Subperformance is not accepted, whether it be a dirty rifle or a loose thread on a uniform. The subperformer is shouted at, derided, humiliated.

The group suffers for the individual. If a recruit is slow, the entire platoon is punished with additional exercise.

The system works.

"Pick your nose!" Simultaneously 59 index fingers shoot into nostrils.

"An M-16 can blow someone's head off at 500 meters," Sgt. Norman says. "That's beautiful, isn't it?"

"Yes, sir!" shout the platoon's fifty-nine voices.

In the Marine vocabulary, the highest praise is "intense" and "motivated." Their opposites are "undisciplined" and "civilian."

At the end of the eleven weeks, one Marine (until graduation, they are recruits, not Marines) says, "I feel like I've joined a new society or religion."

For Your Consideration

Of what significance is the recruits' degradation ceremony? Why are recruits not allowed video games, cigarettes, or calls home? Why are the Marines so unfair as to punish an entire platoon for the failure of an individual? Use concepts in this chapter to explain why the system works.

Source: Based on Garfinkel 1956; Goffman 1961; "Anybody's Son Will Do," 1983; Ricks 1995.

Analysts have tried to depict the typical stages through which we go, but they have not been able to agree on a standard division of the life course (Levinson 1978; Schlossberg 1990; Carr et al. 1995). In the following sketch, a composite of the stages they have proposed, I shall stress the *historical* setting of people's lives in order to emphasize the sociological significance of the life course.

Childhood (from birth to about age 12)

It may strike you as strange to say this, but what a child "is" differs from one culture to another. To understand this point, consider how different your childhood would have been if you had grown up during the Middle Ages.

When historian Philippe Ariès (1962) examined European paintings from this period, such as the one on the next page, he noticed that children were always dressed up in

In contemporary Western societies such as the United States, children are viewed as innocent and in need of protection from adult demands such as work and self-support. Historically and cross-culturally, however, ideas of childhood vary. For instance, as illustrated by this painting of Sir Walter Raleigh and son (artist unknown), in fifteenth-century Europe children were viewed as miniature adults who assumed adult roles at the earliest opportunity.

adult clothing. If children were not stiffly posed for a family portrait, they were depicted as engaging in adult activities. Ariès concluded that at that time and in that place childhood was not regarded as a special time of life. Rather, the Europeans considered children miniature adults. Ariès also pointed out that boys were apprenticed at very early ages. At the age of 7, for example, a boy might leave home for good to learn to be a jeweler or a stonecutter. A girl, in contrast, stayed home until she married, but by the age of 7 she had to do her daily share of household tasks.

Childhood also used to be harsh. Another historian, Lloyd DeMause (1975), documented the nightmare of childhood in ages past. To beat children used to be *the norm*. Parents who did not beat their children were considered neglectful of their social duty to keep them off the road to hell. Even teachers were expected to beat their students, and one nineteenth-century German schoolteacher methodically recorded every beating he administered. His record shows 124,000 lashes with a whip, 911,527 hits with a stick, 136,715 slaps with his hand, and 1,115,800 cuffs across the ears. Beating children was so general that even future kings didn't escape brutal punishment. Louis XIII, for example, "was whipped every morning, starting at the age of two, simply for being 'obstinate.' " He was even whipped on the day of his coronation at the age of 9 (McCoy 1985:392).

To keep children in line, parents and teachers also felt it their moral duty to use psychological terror. They would lock children in dark closets for an entire day and frighten them with tales of death and hellfire. It was also common to terrify children into submission by forcing them to witness gruesome events.

A common moral lesson involved taking children to visit the gibbet [an upraised post on which executed bodies were left hanging from chains], where they were forced to inspect rotting corpses hanging there as an example of what happens to bad children when they grow up. Whole classes were taken out of school to witness hangings, and parents would often whip their children afterwards to make them remember what they had seen. (DeMause 1975)

To see children as adults seems strange to us. In some of today's Least Industrialized Nations, however, this view persists. Vivid in my memory from a visit to Africa is a Moroccan blacksmith. Standing next to an open furnace, nude from the waist up and sweating profusely in the insufferable heat, he beat his hammer rhythmically on some glowing, red-hot metal. The blacksmith was about 12 years old.

Industrialization's economic surplus brought fundamental change to the role of children. When children had the leisure to go to school, they came to be thought of as tender and innocent, as needing more adult care, comfort, and protection. Such attitudes of dependency continued to develop, and today we view children as needing gentle guidance if they are to develop emotionally, intellectually, morally, socially, even physically. We take our view for granted—after all, it is only "common sense." Yet, as you can see, our view is not "natural," but historically rooted.

Childhood, then, is much more than biology. The point in history in which we live, as well as our social location, create a framework that is laid on top of our biological foundation. Although a child's *biological* characteristics (such as small and dependent) are universal, the child's *social* experiences (what others expect of the child) are not.

Adolescence (about ages 13–17)

In earlier centuries, societies did not mark out adolescence as a distinct time of life. People simply moved from childhood into young adulthood, with no stopover in between.

The Industrial Revolution brought such an abundance of material surpluses, however, that for the first time millions of teenagers were able to remain outside the labor force. At the same time, the demand for education grew. The convergence of these two forces in industrialized societies created a gap between childhood and adulthood. In the early part of this century, the term *adolescence* was coined to indicate this new stage in life (Hall 1904), one that has become renowned for inner turmoil.

Preliterate societies hold initiation rites to ground the self-identity and mark the passage of children into adulthood (Gilmore 1990), but adolescents in the industrialized world must "find" themselves on their own. As they attempt to carve out an identity distinct from both the "younger" world being left behind and the "older" world still out of range, adolescents develop a subculture with distinctive clothing, hairstyles, language, gestures, and music. Although these outward patterns are readily visible, we usually fail to realize that adolescence is a social creation: It is contemporary society, not biological age, that makes these years a period of turmoil.

In many societies, manhood is not bestowed upon males simply because they reach a certain age. Manhood, rather, is a standing in the community that must be achieved. Shown here is an initiation ceremony in Indonesia, where boys, to lay claim to the status of manhood, must jump over this barrier.

Young Adulthood (about ages 18–29)

If society invented adolescence as a special period in life, can it also invent other periods? Historian Kenneth Keniston suggested it could. He noted that industrialized societies seem to be adding a period of prolonged youth to the life course, in which postadolescents postpone adult responsibilities and are "neither psychological adolescents nor sociological adults" (Keniston 1971). From the end of high school through extended education, including vocational schools, college, and even graduate school, many young adults remain free from adult responsibilities, such as a full-time job, marriage, and home ownership.

Somewhere during this period of extended youth, young adults gradually ease into adult responsibilities. They finish school, take a full-time job, engage in courtship rituals, get married—and go into debt. The self is considerably more stable during the latter part of this period than it was during adolescence.

The Middle Years (about ages 30–65)

The Early Middle Years. During the next period, the early middle years (ages 30–49), most people are much surer of themselves and of their goals in life. As with any point in the life course, however, the self can receive severe jolts—in this case from such circumstances as divorce or being fired (Dannefer 1984). It may take years for the self to stabilize after such ruptures.

Because of recent social change, the early middle years pose a special challenge for U.S. women, who increasingly have been given the message, especially by the media, that they can "have it all." They can be superworkers, superwives, and supermoms—all at the same time. The reality, however, often consists of too many conflicting pressures, of too little time and too many demands. Something has to give. Attempts to resolve this dilemma are often compounded by another hard reality—that during gender socialization their husbands learned that child care and housework are not "masculine." In short, adjustments continue in this and all phases of life.

The Later Middle Years. During this period (ages 50–65), people attempt to evaluate the past and to come to terms with what lies ahead. They compare what they have accomplished with how far they had hoped to get. Although many do not like the gap they see between where they now are and where they had planned to be, most adjust fairly well (Carr 1995). Looking at the years ahead, most people conclude that they are not likely to get much farther, that their job or career is likely to consist of "more of the same." During this time of life, many people find themselves caring not only for their own children but also their aging parents. Because of this often crushing set of twin burdens, people in the later middle years are sometimes referred to as the "sandwich generation."

Health and mortality also begin to loom large. People feel physical changes in their bodies, and they may watch their parents become frail, ill, and die. This brings about a fundamental reorientation in thinking—*from time since birth to time left to live* (Neugarten 1976). This combination of concerns, centering on attainment and mortality, often results in behavior commonly termed the "mid-life crisis."

In spite of such concerns, many people find the later middle years to be the most comfortable period of their entire lives. They may enjoy job security and a higher standard of living than ever before, a bigger house (perhaps paid for), newer cars, and more exotic vacations. The children are grown, the self is firmly planted, and fewer upheavals are likely to occur.

As they anticipate the next stage of life, however, few people like what they see.

The Older Years (about 66 on)

The Early Older Years   In industrialized societies, the older years begin around the mid-60s. This, too, is recent, for in preindustrial societies, when most people died early, old age was thought to begin around age 40. The improved nutrition, public health, and medical care that industrialization brought, however, delayed the onset of old age. For those in good health, being over 65 is often experienced not as old age, but as an extension of the middle years. People who continue to work or to be active in rewarding social activities are especially unlikely to see themselves as old (Neugarten 1977). Although frequency of sex declines, most men and women in their 60s and 70s are sexually active (Denney and Quadagno 1992).

Because we have a self and can reason abstractly, we can contemplate death. Initially death is something vaguely "out there," but as people see their friends die and their own bodies no longer functioning as before, death becomes less abstract. Increasingly, people feel that "time is closing in" on them.

The Later Older Years.   As with the preceding periods of life except the first one, there is no precise beginning point to this last stage. For some, the 75th birthday may

This January 1937 photo from Sneedville, Tennessee, shows Eunice Johns, age 9, and her husband, Charlie Johns, age 22. The groom gave his wife a doll as a wedding gift. The new husband and wife planned to build a cabin, and, as Charlie Johns phrased it, "go to housekeeping." This photo illustrates the cultural relativity of life stages, which we sometimes mistake as fixed. It also is interesting from a symbolic interactionist perspective—that of changing definitions—for while our sensibilities are shocked by such marriages, though not common they once were taken for granted.

mark entry into this period of life. For others, that marker may be the 80th or even the 85th birthday. For most, this stage is marked by growing frailty and illness; for all who reach this stage, by death. For some, the physical decline is slow, and a rare few manage to see their 100th birthday mentally alert and in good physical health.

The Sociological Significance of the Life Course

The sociological significance of the life course is that it does not merely represent biology, things that naturally occur to all of us as we add years to our lives. Rather, *social* factors influence our life course. As you just saw, *when* you live makes a huge difference for the course that your life takes. And the difference does not have to be vast. Being born just ten years earlier or later may mean that you experience war or peace, an expanding economy or a depression—which vitally affects what happens to you not just during childhood but throughout your life.

Your *social location*, such as social class, gender, and race, is also highly significant. Because of it, your experience of society's events will be similar to people who share your location, but different from people who do not. If you are poor, for example, you likely will feel older faster than most wealthy people for whom life is much less demanding. The life course is also influenced by individual factors, such as your health, or marrying early or entering college late, that may make your life course "out of sequence" or atypical.

For all these reasons, this sketch of the life course may not adequately reflect your own past, present, and future. As sociologist C. Wright Mills (1959) would say, because college recruiters are beating down the door of your school, or failing to do so, you are more inclined to marry, to buy a house, and to start a family—or to postpone these life course events, perhaps indefinitely. In short, changing times change lives, steering the life course into different directions.

Are We Prisoners of Socialization? ▲

From our discussion of socialization, you might conclude that sociologists think of people as little robots: The socialization goes in, and the behavior comes out. People cannot help what they do, think, or feel, for everything is simply a result of their exposure to socializing agents.

Sociologists do *not* think of people in this way. Although socialization is powerful, and profoundly affects us all, we have a self. Laid down in childhood and continually modified by later experience, the self is dynamic. It is not a sponge that passively absorbs influences from the environment but a vigorous, essential part of our being that allows us to act on our environment (Wrong 1961; Meltzer et al. 1975; Couch 1989).

Indeed, it is precisely because individuals are not little robots that their behavior is so hard to predict. The countless reactions of the many people important to us merge in each person—as discussed earlier, even twins do not receive identical reactions from others. As the self develops, we internalize or "put together" these innumerable reactions, producing a unique whole that we call the individual. And, each unique individual uses his or her own mind to reason and to make choices in life.

In this way, *each of us is actively involved in the social construction of the self.* For example, although our experiences in the family lay down the basic elements of our personality, including fundamental orientations to life, we are not doomed to keep those orientations if we do not like them. We can purposely expose ourselves to groups and ideas that we prefer. Those experiences, in turn, will have their own effects on our self. In short, although socialization is powerful, within the limitations of the framework laid down by our social location we can change even the self. And that self—along with the options available within society—is the key to our behavior.

Summary and Review

What Is Human Nature?

How much of our human characteristics come from "nature" (heredity) and how much from "nurture" (the social environment)?

Observations of isolated, institutionalized, and **feral children** help answer this question, as do experiments with monkeys that have been raised in isolation. Language and intimate social interaction—functions of "nurture"—appear to be essential to the development of what we consider to be human characteristics. Pp. 62–66.

The Social Development of the Self, Mind, and Emotions

How do we acquire a self?

Humans are born with the *capacity* to develop a **self,** but the self must be socially constructed; that is, its contents depend on social interaction. According to Charles Horton Cooley's concept of the **looking-glass self,** our self develops as we internalize others' reactions to us. George Herbert Mead identified the ability to **take the role of the other** as essential to the development of the self. Mead concluded that even the mind is a social product. Vygotsky's observations of "self-directed speech" support Mead's conclusions. Pp. 66–69.

How do children's thinking processes develop?

Jean Piaget identified four stages that children go through as they develop the ability to reason: (1) *sensorimotor,* in which understanding is limited to sensory stimuli such as touching, seeing, and listening; (2) *preoperational,* the ability to use symbols; (3) *concrete operational,* in which reasoning ability is more complex but not yet capable of complex abstractions; and (4) *formal operational,* abstract thinking. Researchers have also found that emotions develop in an orderly sequence. Pp. 69–70.

How do sociologists evaluate Freud's psychoanalytic theory of personality development?

Freud viewed personality development as the result of self-centered inborn desires, the **id,** clashing with social constraints. The **ego** develops to balance the id as well as the **superego,** the conscience. In contrast, sociologists do not examine inborn and unconscious motivations, but, rather, how social factors—social class, gender, religion, education, and so forth—underlie personality development. Pp. 70–71.

How does socialization influence emotions?

Socialization influences not only *how* we express our emotions, but also *what* emotions we feel. Socialization into emotions is a major means by which society produces conformity. Pp. 71–73.

Socialization into Gender

How does gender socialization affect our sense of self?

Gender socialization—sorting males and females into different roles—is a primary means of controlling human behavior. We learn **gender roles** beginning in infancy. A society's ideals of sex-linked behaviors are reinforced by its social institutions. Pp. 73–76.

Agents of Socialization

What are the main agents of socialization?

The main **agents of socialization** are family, religion, day care, school, **peer groups,** the **mass media,** sports, and the workplace. Each has its particular influences in socializing us into becoming full-fledged members of society. Pp. 76–81.

Resocialization

What is resocialization?

Resocialization is the process of learning new norms, values, attitudes, and behaviors. Intense resocialization occurs in **total institutions.** Most resocialization is voluntary, but some, as with prisoners, is involuntary. Pp. 81–82.

Socialization Through the Life Course

Does socialization end when we enter adulthood?

Socialization occurs throughout the life course. In industrialized societies, the **life course** can be divided into childhood, adolescence, young adulthood, the early middle years, the later middle years, the early older years, and the older older years. Typical patterns include obtaining education, becoming independent from parents, building a career, finding a mate, rearing children, and confronting aging. Life course patterns vary by history, culture, and by social location such as gender, ethnicity, and social class, as well as by individual experiences such as health and age at marriage. Pp. 82–87.

Are We Prisoners of Socialization?

Although socialization is powerful, we are not merely the sum of our socialization experiences. Just as socialization influences human behavior, so humans act on their environment and influence it. P. 87.

Where can I read more on this topic?

Suggested readings for this chapter are listed on page 660.

Sociology and the Internet

All URLs listed are current as of the printing of this book. URLs are often changed. Please check our Web site http://www.abacon.com/henslin for updates.

1. As we've seen in this chapter, child rearing and child care practices vary widely around the world and also within industrial societies. To explore some of these differences on the Internet, use one of the following search engines:

> *http://www.lycos.com/*
> *http://www.excite.com/*
> *http://webcrawler.com/*

After conducting your search, what does "child rearing" mean? Does everyone use the same definition? What kinds of sites are included under "child rearing" and "child care?" What are some of the opposing views of child care? Is there a gender difference in the definition of "child care?" What about a difference due to social class?

2. What can you discover about childhood socialization by examining children's games and pastimes? Explore this question by looking at children's pages on the Internet. Some starting places are:

> *http://db.cochran.com/li_toc:theoPage.db*
> *http://www.kids-space.org/*
> *http://www.geocities.com/Heartland/5127/tvlinks.html*

(Note that Internet sites often disappear. If you have trouble accessing the above addresses, use one of the search engines to look for "kids' pages.")

What is the relationship between childhood socialization and play? What are the children learning? What do they want to learn? Are the answers to these questions what you expected? Do they conform to what you think traditional wisdom in our society says about children? Write a brief report on your conclusions, and compare them with others in your class.

3. Gender socialization is an important aspect of our lives. How do the Internet and the Web reinforce cultural expectations of gender? Use Yahoo! *http://www.yahoo.com/society_and_culture* to examine some of the gender expectations as portrayed on the Web. Once again, click on "Gender." You can examine the following categories, their subcategories, and links: "Humor," "Men," and "Women." What are the images of men/women on the Internet? Compare these images with those of the mass media as discussed in your text. Does the Web reinforce common stereotypes of men and women?

4. You have read about resocialization in your text. Take a look at the Gamblers Anonymous International home page *http://www.gamblersanonymous.org* and use it to discuss how resocialization takes place. Why is it necessary to resocialize gamblers? How does this organization attempt to resocialize its members? Is it a mild resocialization or a more intense experience?

Alejandro Xul Solar, Patria B, 1925

Social Structure and Social Interaction

MY CURIOSITY HAD GOTTEN THE *better of me. When the sociology convention finished, I climbed aboard the first city bus that came along. I didn't know where the bus was going, and I didn't even know where I was going to spend the night.*

"Maybe I overdid it this time," I thought as the bus began winding down streets I had never seen before. Actually, since this was my first visit to Washington, D.C., I hadn't seen any of the streets before. I had no direction, no plans, not even a map. I carried no billfold, just a driver's license shoved into my jeans for emergency identification, some pocket change, and a $10 bill tucked into my socks. My goal was simple: If I see something interesting, I'll get off and check it out.

"Nothing but the usual things," I mused, as we passed row after row of apartment buildings and stores. I could see myself riding buses the entire night. Then something caught my eye. Nothing spectacular—just groups of people clustered around a large circular area where several streets intersected.

I climbed off the bus and made my way to what turned out to be Dupont Circle. I took a seat on a sidewalk bench and began to observe. As the scene came into focus, I noted several street corner men drinking and joking with one another. One of the men broke from his companions and sat down next to me. As we talked, I mostly listened.

As night fell, the men said that they wanted to get another bottle of wine. I contributed. They counted their money and asked if I wanted to go with them.

Although I felt a churning inside—emotions combining hesitation and fear—I heard a confident "Sure!" coming out of my mouth. As we left the circle, the three men began to cut through an alley. "Oh, no," I thought. "That's not what I had in mind."

I had but a split second to make a decision. I found myself continuing to walk with the men, but holding back half a step so that none of the three was behind me. As we walked, they passed around the remnants of their bottle. When my turn came, I didn't know what to do. I shuddered to think about the diseases lurking within that bottle. I made another decision. In the semidarkness I faked it, letting only my thumb and forefinger touch my lips and nothing enter my mouth.

When we returned to Dupont Circle, the men finished their new bottle of Thunderbird. I couldn't fake it in the light, so I passed, pointing at my stomach to indicate that I was having problems.

Suddenly one of the men jumped up, smashed the emptied bottle against the sidewalk, and thrust the jagged neck in a menacing gesture. He stared straight ahead at another bench, where he had spotted someone with whom he had some sort of unfinished business. As the other men told him to cool it, I moved slightly to one side of the group—ready to flee, just in case.

Levels of Sociological Analysis

On this sociological adventure, I almost got myself in over my head. Fortunately, it turned out all right. The man's "enemy" didn't look our way, the broken bottle was set down next to the bench "just in case he needed it," and until dawn I was introduced to a life that up to then I had only read about.

Sociologists Elliot Liebow (1997) and Elijah Anderson (1978, 1990, 1997) have written fascinating accounts about men like these. Although street corner men may appear to be disorganized, simply coming and going as they please and doing whatever feels good at the moment, these sociologists have analyzed how, like us, these men are also influenced by the norms and beliefs of our society. This will become more apparent as we examine the two levels of analysis that sociologists use.

Macrosociology and Microsociology

The first level, **macrosociology,** places the focus on broad features of society. Sociologists who use this approach, especially conflict theorists and functionalists, analyze such things as social class and how groups are related to one another. If macrosociologists were to analyze street corner men, for example, they would stress that these men are located at the bottom of the U.S. social class system. Their low status means that many opportunities are closed to them: the men have few skills, little education, hardly anything to offer an employer. As "able-bodied" men, however, they are not eligible for welfare, so they hustle to survive. As a consequence, they spend their lives on the streets.

Conflict theory and functionalism, both of which focus on the broader picture, are examples of this macrosociological approach. In these theories, the goal is to examine the large-scale social forces that influence people.

The second approach sociologists use is **microsociology.** Here the emphasis is placed on **social interaction,** what people do when they come together. Sociologists who use this approach are likely to focus on the men's survival strategies ("hustles"); their rules for dividing up money, wine, or whatever other resources they have; their relationships with girlfriends, family, and friends; where they spend their time and what they do there; their language; their pecking order; and so on. With its focus on face-to-face interaction, symbolic interactionism is an example of microsociology.

With their different emphases, macrosociology and microsociology yield distinctive perspectives, and both are needed to gain a more complete understanding of social life. We cannot adequately understand street corner men, for example, without using *macrosociology*. It is essential that we place the men within the broad context of how groups in U.S. society are related to one another—for, as with ourselves, the social class of these men helps to shape their attitudes and behavior. Nor can we adequately understand these men without *microsociology*, for their everyday situations also form a significant part of their lives.

To see how these two approaches help us to understand social life, let's look at each. As we do so, you may find yourself feeling more comfortable with one approach than the other. That is what happens with sociologists. For reasons of personal background and professional training, sociologists find themselves more comfortable with one approach and tend to use it in their research. Both approaches, however, are necessary for a full understanding of life in society.

macrosociology: analysis of social life focusing on broad features of social structure, such as social class and the relationships of groups to one another; an approach usually used by functionalist and conflict theorists

microsociology: analysis of social life focusing on social interaction; an approach usually used by symbolic interactionists

social interaction: what people do when they are in the presence of one another

Sociologists use both macro and micro levels of analysis to study social life. Those who use macrosociology to analyze the homeless— or any human behavior—focus on broad social forces, such as the economy and social classes. Sociologists who use the microsociological approach analyze how people interact with one another. Note how this scene invites both levels of analyses: Here you have both social interaction and social classes (power and powerlessness).

The Macrosociological Perspective: Social Structure

Why did the street people in the opening vignette act as they did, staying up all night drinking wine and ready to use a lethal weapon? Why don't *we* act like this? Social structure helps us answer such questions.

The Sociological Significance of Social Structure

To better understand human behavior, we need to see how social structure *establishes limits on our behavior.* **Social structure** is the framework of society that was already laid out before you were born; it is the patterns of a society, such as the relationships between men and women or students and teachers that characterize a particular society.

Because the term *social structure* may seem vague, consider first how you personally experience social structure in your own life. As I write this, I do not know if you are African American, white, Latino, Native American, Asian American. I do not know your religion. I do not know if you are young or old, tall or short, male or female. I do not know if you were reared on a farm, in the suburbs, or in the inner city. I do not know if you went to a public high school or an exclusive prep school. But I do know that you are in college. And that, alone, tells me a great deal about you.

From this one piece of information, I can assume that the social structure of your college is now shaping what you do. For example, let us suppose that today you felt euphoric over some great news. I can be fairly certain (not absolutely, mind you, but relatively certain) that when you entered the classroom, social structure overrode your mood. That is, instead of shouting at the top of your lungs and joyously throwing this book into the air, you entered the classroom fairly subdued and took your seat.

The same social structure influences your instructor, even if, on the one hand, he or she is facing a divorce or has a child dying of cancer, or, on the other, has just been awarded a promotion or a million-dollar grant. The instructor may feel like either retreating into seclusion or celebrating wildly, but it is most likely that he or she will conduct class. In short, personal feelings and desires tend to be overridden by social structure.

Just as social structure influences you and your instructor, so it also establishes limits for street people. They, too, find themselves in a specific social location in the U.S. social structure—although it is quite different from yours or your instructor's. Consequently, they are affected differently—and nothing about their social location leads them to take notes or to lecture. Their behaviors are as logical an outcome of where they find themselves in the social structure, however, as are your own. It is just as "natural" in their position in the social structure to drink wine all night as it is for you to stay up studying all night for a crucial examination. It is just as "natural" for you to nod and say, "Excuse me," when you enter a crowded classroom late and have to claim a desk on which someone has already placed books or a coat as it is for them to break off the head of a wine bottle and glare at an enemy.

In short, people learn certain behaviors and attitudes because of their location in the social structure (whether privileged, deprived, or in between), and they act accordingly. This is equally true of street people. *The differences in behavior and attitudes are not due to biology (race, sex, or any other supposed genetic factors), but to people's location in the social structure.* Switch places with street people and watch your behaviors and attitudes change!

To better understand social structure, read the Down-to-Earth Sociology box on the next page. Because social structure so critically affects who we are and what we are like, let us look in more detail at its major components: culture, social class, social status, roles, groups, and institutions.

Culture

In Chapter 2, we looked in detail at how culture affects us. At this point, let's simply review the main impact of culture, the largest envelope that surrounds us. Sociologists use

social structure: the framework that surrounds us, consisting of the relationship of people and groups to one another, which give direction to and set limits on behavior

Down-to-Earth Sociology

College Football as Social Structure

To gain a better idea of what social structure is, think of college football (see Dobriner 1969a). You know the various positions on the team: center, guards, tackles, ends, quarterback, and running backs. Each is a *status*; that is, each is a recognized social position. For each of these statuses, there is a *role*; that is, each of these positions has particular expectations attached to it. The center is expected to snap the ball, the quarterback to pass it, the guards to block, the tackles to tackle or block, the ends to receive passes, and so on. Those *role expectations* guide each player's actions; that is, the players try to do what their particular role requires.

Let's suppose that football is your favorite sport and you never miss a home game at your college. Let's also suppose that you graduate and move across the country. Five years later you return to your campus for a nostalgic visit. The climax of your visit is the biggest football game of the season. When you get to the game, you might be surprised to see a different coach, but you are not surprised that each of the playing positions is occupied by people you don't know, for all the players you knew have graduated, and their places have been filled by others.

This scenario mirrors *social structure*, which is the framework around which a group exists. In this football example, that framework consists of the coaching staff and the eleven playing positions. The game does not depend on any particular individual, but rather on statuses, the positions that the individuals occupy. When someone leaves a position, the game can go on because someone else takes over the position and plays the role. The game will continue even though not a single individual remains the same from one period of time to the next. Notre Dame's football team endures today even though Knute Rockne, the Gipper, and his teammates are long dead.

Even though you may not play football, you nevertheless live your life within a clearly established social structure. The statuses you occupy and the roles you play were already in place before you were born. You take your particular positions in life, others do the same, and society goes about its business. Although the specifics change with time, the game—whether of life or of football—goes on.

the term *culture* to refer to a group's language, beliefs, values, behaviors, and even gestures. Culture also includes the material objects used by a group. In short, culture is our social inheritance, what we learn from the people around us. Culture is the broadest framework that determines what kind of people we become. If we are reared in Eskimo, Japanese, Russian, or U.S. culture, we will grow up to be like most Eskimos, Japanese, Russians, or Americans. On the outside, we will look and act like them; and on the inside, we will think and feel like them.

Social Class

To understand people, we must examine the particular social locations that they hold in life. Especially significant is social class, which is based on income, education, and occupational prestige. Large numbers of people who have similar amounts of income and education and who work at jobs that are roughly comparable in prestige make up a **social class.** It is hard to overemphasize this aspect of social structure, for our social class heavily influences not only our behaviors but even our ideas and attitudes. We have this in common, then, with the street people described in the opening vignette—both they and we are influenced by our location in the social class structure. Theirs may be a considerably less privileged position, but it has no less influence on their lives. Social class is so significant that we shall spend an entire chapter (Chapter 10) on this topic.

Social Status

When you hear the word *status*, you are likely to think of prestige. These two words are welded together in common thinking. Sociologists, however, use **status** in a different way: to refer to the position that an individual occupies. That position may have a great deal of prestige, as in the case of a judge or an astronaut, or it may carry very little prestige, as in the case of a gas station attendant or a hamburger flipper at a fast-food

social class: a large number of people with similar amounts of income and education who work at jobs that are roughly comparable in prestige

status: the position that someone occupies in society or a social group

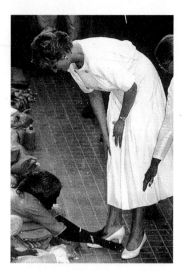

Each of us occupies several statuses. Among the statuses of Diana Spencer were wife, mother, and Princess of Wales. Because she married into the Royal Family, her status as Princess of Wales was an achieved rather than an ascribed status. Upon her divorce from Prince Charles, she lost this achieved status and added others, among them those of divorcee, former Princess, and former wife. The woman touching Princess Diana's feet is a member of the Untouchable caste in India. Her caste status is ascribed, or involuntary.

restaurant. The status may also be looked down on, as in the case of a street corner man, an ex-convict, or a bag lady.

All of us occupy several positions at the same time. You may be simultaneously a son or daughter, a worker, a date, and a student. Sociologists use the term **status set** to refer to all the statuses or positions that you occupy. Obviously your status set changes as your particular statuses change; for example, if you graduate from college and take a full-time job, get married, buy a home, have children, and so on, your status set changes to include the positions of worker, spouse, homeowner, and parent.

Statuses, like other aspects of social structure, are part of our basic framework of living in society. The example given earlier of students and teachers doing what others expect of them in spite of their temporary moods is an illustration of how statuses affect our actions—and those of the people around us. Our statuses—whether daughter or son, worker or date—serve as guides for our behavior.

Ascribed Statuses and Achieved Statuses. The first type, **ascribed statuses,** is involuntary. You do not ask for them, nor can you choose them. Some you inherit at birth such as your race, sex, and the social class of your parents, as well as your statuses as female or male, daughter or son, niece or nephew, and granddaughter or grandson. Others, such as teenager and senior citizen, are related to the life course discussed in Chapter 3, and are given to you later in life.

The second type, **achieved statuses,** is voluntary. These you earn or accomplish. As a result of your efforts you become a student, a friend, a spouse, a rabbi, minister, priest, or nun. Or, for lack of effort (or efforts that others fail to appreciate), you become a school dropout, a former friend, an ex-spouse, or a defrocked rabbi, priest, or nun. In other words, achieved statuses can be either positive or negative; both college president and bank robber represent achieved statuses.

The significance of social statuses for understanding human behavior is that each status provides guidelines for how people are to act and feel. Like other aspects of social structure, they set limits on what people can and cannot do. Because social statuses are an essential part of the social structure, they are found in all human groups.

Status Symbols. People who are pleased with their particular social status may want others to recognize that they occupy that status. To gain this recognition, they use **status symbols,** signs that identify a status. For example, people wear wedding rings to announce their marital status; uniforms, guns, and badges to proclaim that they are police officers (and to not so subtly let you know that their status gives them authority over you); and "backward" collars to declare that they are Lutheran ministers or Roman Catholic or Episcopal priests.

Some social statuses are negative, and so, therefore, are their status symbols. The scarlet letter in Nathaniel Hawthorne's book by the same title is one example. Another is the CONVICTED DUI bumper sticker that some U.S. counties require convicted drunk drivers to display if they wish to avoid a jail sentence.

All of us use status symbols to announce our statuses to others and to help smooth our interactions in everyday life. You might consider your own status symbols. For example, how does your clothing announce your statuses of sex, age, and college student?

Master Statuses. A **master status** is one that cuts across the other statuses that you hold. Some master statuses are ascribed. An example is your sex. Whatever you do, people perceive you as a male or as a female. If you are working your way through college by flipping burgers, people see you not only as a burger flipper and a student but as a *male* or *female* burger flipper and a *male* or *female* college student. Other master statuses are race and age.

Some master statuses are achieved. If you become very, very wealthy (and it does not matter if your wealth comes from an invention or the lottery—it is still *achieved* as far as sociologists are concerned), your wealth is likely to become a master status. No matter what else, people are likely to say, "She is a very rich burger flipper." (Or more likely, "She's very rich, and she used to flip burgers!")

status set: all the statuses or positions that an individual occupies

ascribed statuses: positions an individual either inherits at birth or receives involuntarily later in life

achieved statuses: positions that are earned, accomplished, or involve at least some effort or activity on the individual's part

status symbols: items used to identify a status

master status: a status that cuts across the other statuses that an individual occupies

Master statuses are those that over-shadow our other statuses. Shown here is Stephen Hawking, who is severely disabled by Lou Gehrig's disease. For many, his master status is that of a disabled person. Because Hawking is one of the greatest physicists who has ever lived, his astounding accomplishments have given him another status, that of world-class physicist in the ranking of Einstein. Thus, Hawking occupies two master statuses simultaneously, the one ascribed and the other achieved.

Similarly, people who become disabled or disfigured find, to their dismay, that their condition becomes a master status. For example, a person whose face is extremely scarred will be viewed through this unwelcome master status no matter what the individual's occupation or accomplishments. People confined to wheelchairs can attest to how "disabled" overrides all their other statuses and determines others' perceptions of everything they do.

Although our statuses usually fit together fairly well, sometimes a contradiction or mismatch between statuses occurs; this is known as **status inconsistency** (or discrepancy). A 14-year-old college student is an example. So is a 40-year-old married woman on a date with a 19-year-old college sophomore.

From these examples, you can understand an essential aspect of social statuses: Like other components of social structure, they come with a set of built-in *norms* (that is, expectations) that provide guidelines for behavior. When statuses mesh well, as they usually do, we know what to expect of people. Status inconsistency, however, upsets our expectations. In the preceding examples, how are you supposed to act? Are you supposed to treat the 14-year-old as you would a teenager or as you would your college classmate? The married woman as the mother of your friend or as a classmate's date?

Roles

All the world's a stage
And all the men and women merely players.
They have their exits and their entrances;
And one man in his time plays many parts . . .
William Shakespeare, *As You Like It*, Act II, Scene 7

Like Shakespeare, sociologists, too, see roles as essential to social life. When you were born, **roles**—the behaviors, obligations, and privileges attached to a status—were already set up for you. Society was waiting with outstretched arms to teach you how it expected you to act as a boy or a girl. And whether you were born poor, rich, or somewhere in between, certain behaviors, obligations, and privileges were attached to your statuses.

The difference between role and status is that you *occupy* a status, but you *play* a role (Linton 1936). For example, being a son or daughter is your status, but your expectations of receiving food and shelter from your parents—as well as their expectations that you show respect to them—is your role.

Our roles are a sort of fence that helps keep us doing what society wants us to do. That fence leaves a certain amount of freedom, but for most of us that freedom doesn't

status inconsistency (or discrepancy): a contradiction or mismatch between statuses

role: the behaviors, obligations, and privileges attached to a status

go very far. Suppose a female decides that she is not going to wear dresses—or a male that he will not wear suits and ties—regardless of what anyone says. In most situations they won't. When a formal occasion comes along, however, such as a family wedding or a funeral, they are likely to cave in to norms that they find overwhelming. Almost all of us stay within the fences that mark out what is "appropriate" for our roles. Most of us are little troubled by such constraints, for our socialization is so thorough that we usually *want* to do what our roles indicate is appropriate.

The sociological significance of roles is that they lay out what is expected of people. As individuals throughout society perform their roles, those roles mesh together to form this thing called society. As Shakespeare put it, people's roles provide "their exits and their entrances" on the stage of life. In short, roles are remarkably effective at keeping people in line—telling them when they should "enter" and when they should "exit," as well as what to do in between.

Groups

A **group** consists of people who regularly and consciously interact with one another. Ordinarily, the members of a group share similar values, norms, and expectations. Just as our actions are influenced by our social class, statuses, and roles, so, too, the groups to which we belong represent powerful forces in our lives. In fact, *to belong to a group is to yield to others the right to make certain decisions about our behavior.* If we belong to a group, we assume an obligation to act according to the expectations of other members of that group.

Although this principle holds true for all groups, some groups wield influence only over small segments of our behavior. If you belong to a stamp club, for example, the group's influence may center around your attendance at meetings and display of knowledge about stamps. Other groups, however, control many aspects of our behavior. The family is an example. When parents say to their 15-year-old daughter, "As long as you are living under my roof, you had better be home by midnight," they show their expectation that their children, as members of the family, will conform to their ideas about many aspects of life, including their views on curfew. They are saying that so long as the daughter wants to remain a member of the household her behavior must conform to their expectations.

To belong to any group is to relinquish to others at least *some* control over our lives. Those social groups that provide little option to belong are called **involuntary memberships** (or involuntary associations). These include our family and the sexual, ethnic, and racial groups into which we are born. Groups to which we choose to belong are called **voluntary memberships** (or voluntary associations). These include the scouts, professional associations, church groups, clubs, and work groups. If we want to remain members in good standing, we must conform to what people in those groups expect of us. Both voluntary and involuntary memberships are vital in affecting who we are, for our participation in them shapes our ideas and orientations to life.

group: people who regularly and consciously interact with one another

involuntary memberships: (or involuntary associations) groups in which people are assigned membership rather than choosing to join

voluntary memberships: (or voluntary associations) groups that people choose to join

social institutions: the organized, usual, or standard ways by which society meets its basic needs

Social Institutions

At first glance, the term *social institution* may appear far removed from our personal lives. The term seems so cold and abstract, something remotely "out there." In fact, however, **social institutions**—the organized means that each society develops to meet its basic needs—involve concrete and highly relevant aspects of our lives.

Sociologists have identified nine social institutions: the family, religion, law, politics, economics, education, medicine, science, and military. In industrialized societies, these are highly developed separate institutions, while in preliterate societies they are less developed and more informal. In industrialized societies, for example, the social institution of education is highly structured, while in preliterate societies education may consist of informally learning expected roles. Figure 4.1 on the next page summarizes the basic social institutions. Note that each institution has its own set of roles, values, and norms. Part IV of this text focuses on social institutions.

Social Institution	Basic Needs	Some Groups or Organizations	Some Values	Some Roles	Some Norms
Family	Regulate reproduction, socialize and protect children	Relatives, kinship groups	Sexual fidelity, providing for your family, keeping a clean house, respect for parents	Daughter, son, father, mother, brother, sister, aunt, uncle, grandparent	Have only as many children as you can afford, be faithful to your spouse
Religion	Concerns about life after death, the meaning of suffering and loss; desire to connect with the Creator	Congregation, synagogue, denomination, charitable association	Reading and adhering to holy texts such as the Bible, the Koran, and the Torah; honoring God	Priest, minister, rabbi, worshipper, teacher, disciple, missionary, prophet, convert	Attend worship services, contribute money, follow the teachings
Law	Maintain social order	Police, courts, prisons	Trial by one's peers, innocence until proven guilty	Police officer, lawyer, judge, defendant, prison guard	Give true testimony, follow the rules of evidence
Politics	Establish a hierarchy of power and authority	Political parties, congresses, parliaments, monarchies	Majority rule, the right to vote as a sacred trust	President, senator, lobbyist, voter, candidate, spin doctor	One vote per person, voting as privilege and right
Economics	Produce and distribute goods and services	Credit unions, banks, credit bureaus, credit card companies	Making money, paying bills on time, producing efficiently	Worker, boss, buyer, seller, creditor, debtor, advertiser	Maximize profits, "the customer is always right," work hard
Education	Transmit knowledge and skills across the generations	School, college, student senate, sports team, PTA, teachers' union	Academic honesty, good grades, being "cool"	Teacher, student, dean, principal, football player, cheerleader	Do homework, prepare lectures, don't snitch on classmates
Science	Master the environment	Local, state, regional, national, and international associations	Unbiased research, open dissemination of research findings	Scientist, researcher, technician, administrator	Follow scientific method, fully disclose research findings
Medicine	Heal the sick and injured, care for the dying	AMA, hospitals, pharmacies, insurance companies, HMOs	Hippocratic oath, staying in good health, following doctor's orders	Doctor, nurse, patient, pharmacist, medical insurer	Don't exploit patients, give best medical care available
Military	Protection from enemies, support of national interests	Army, navy, air force, marines, coast guard, national guard	To die for one's country is an honor, obedience unto death	Soldier, recruit, enlisted person, officer, prisoner, spy	Be ready to go to war, obey superior officers, don't question orders
Mass Media (an emerging institution)	Disseminate information, mold public opinion, report events	Television networks, radio stations, publishers	Timeliness, accuracy, large audiences, freedom of the press	Journalist, newscaster, author, editor, publisher	Be accurate, fair, timely, and profitable

Figure 4.1

Social Institutions in Industrialized Societies

The Sociological Significance of Social Institutions

To understand social institutions is to realize how profoundly social structure affects our lives. Much of their influence lies beyond our ordinary awareness. For example, because of our economic institution, we consider it normal to work 8 hours a day for five days every week. There is nothing natural about this pattern, however. Its regularity is only an

Johann Gutenberg's invention of movable type in 1436 or 1437 was destined to influence the course of world history. Among its many consequences were the wide dissemination of news and religious and political views and the stimulation of the need to learn to read. Although this new technology is now old, its many new forms deeply influence our lives, for rapid communication has become part of the taken-for-granted foundation of our society and of our everyday lives. Shown here is the linotype machine, which automated the setting of type. Invented in 1884 by Ottomar Mergenthaler, the linotype machine was the industry standard for newspapers and magazines until about 1960.

arbitrary arrangement for dividing work and leisure. Yet this one aspect of a single social institution has far-reaching effects not only on how we structure our time and activities but also on how we deal with family and friends, and how we meet our personal needs and nonwork obligations.

Each of the other social institutions also has far-reaching effects on our lives. By weaving the fabric of society, our social institutions establish the context in which we live, shaping almost everything that is of concern to us. Social institutions are so significant that if they were different, we would be different people. We certainly could not remain the same, for social institutions influence our orientations to the social world, and even to life itself.

An Example: The Mass Media as an Emerging Social Institution

Although not all sociologists agree, the mass media can be considered a social institution. Far beyond serving simply as sources of information, the media influence our attitudes toward social issues, other people, and even our self-concept. Because the media significantly shape public opinion, all totalitarian governments attempt to maintain tight control over them.

The mass media are a relatively recent historical development, owing their origins to the invention of the printing press in the 1400s. This invention had immediate and profound consequences on virtually all other social institutions. The printing of the Bible altered religion, for instance, while the publication of political broadsides and newspapers altered politics. From these beginnings, a series of inventions—from radio and movies to television and, more recently, the microchip—have made the media an increasingly powerful force.

Indeed, one of the most significant questions we can ask about this new social institution is, Who controls it? That control, which in totalitarian countries is obvious, is much less visible in democratic nations. From a functionalist perspective, we might conclude that the media in a democratic nation represent the varied interests of the many groups that make up that nation. Conflict theorists, however, would see a different scenario: The mass media—at least a country's most influential newspapers and television stations—represent the interests of the political elite, the wealthy and powerful who use the media to mold public opinion.

Since the mass media are so influential, the answer to this question of control is of more than passing interest, and further sociological research on it can contribute to our better understanding of contemporary society.

Comparing Functionalist and Conflict Perspectives

Just as the functionalist and conflict perspectives of the mass media differ, so do their perspectives of the very nature of social institutions. Let's compare these views.

The Functionalist Perspective.   Functionalists stress that social institutions exist because they perform vital functions for society. No society, they point out, is without social institutions. A group may be too small to have people specializing in education or the military, but it will have its own established ways of teaching skills and ideas to the young, and it will have some mechanism of self-defense. Every society must meet its basic needs (or **functional requisites**) to survive; and according to functionalists, that is the purpose of social institutions.

functional requisites: the major tasks that a society must fulfill if it is to survive

What are those basic needs? Functionalists identify five functional requisites that each society must fulfill if it is to survive (Aberle et al. 1950; Mack and Bradford 1979).

1. *Replacing members.* If a society does not replace its members, it cannot continue to exist. Because reproduction is so fundamental to a society's existence, then, and there is such a vital need to protect infants and children, all groups have developed some version of the family. The family gives the newcomer to society a sense of belonging by providing a "lineage," an account of how he or she is related to others. The family also functions to control people's sex drive and to maintain orderly reproduction.

2. *Socializing new members.* People who are born into a human group must be taught what it means to be a full-fledged member. To accomplish this, each human group develops devices to ensure that its newcomers learn the group's basic expectations. As the primary "bearer of culture," the family is essential to this process, but other social institutions, such as religion and education, also help meet this basic need.

3. *Producing and distributing goods and services.* Every society must produce and distribute basic resources, from food and clothing to shelter and education. Consequently, every society establishes an *economic* institution, a means of producing such resources along with routine ways to distribute them.

4. *Preserving order.* Societies face two threats of disorder: one internal, the potential of chaos, and the other external, the possibility of being conquered. To defend themselves against external conquest, they develop some means of defense, some form of the military. To protect themselves from internal threat, they develop some system of policing themselves, ranging from formal organizations of armed groups to informal systems of gossip.

5. *Providing a sense of purpose.* For people to cooperate with one another and willingly give up self-centered, short-term gains in favor of working with and for others, they need a sense of purpose. They need to be convinced that it is worth sacrificing for the common good. Human groups develop various ways to instill such beliefs, but a primary one is religion, which attempts to answer questions about ultimate meaning. All of a society's institutions are actually involved in meeting this functional requisite, for the family provides one part of an interrelated set of answers about the sense of purpose, the school another, and so on.

Functionalist theorists have identified five key functional requisites for the survival of a society. One, providing a sense of purpose, is often met through religion. To most people, snake handling, as in this church service in Jolo, West Virginia, is nonsensical. From a functional perspective, however, it makes a great deal of sense. Can you identify its sociological meanings?

The Conflict Perspective.   Although conflict theorists agree that social institutions were originally designed to meet basic survival needs, they do not see social institutions as working harmoniously for the common good. On the contrary, conflict theorists stress that a society's institutions are controlled by an elite that manipulates them in order to maintain its own privileged position of wealth and power (Useem 1984; Domhoff 1983, 1990, 1997).

As evidence of their position, conflict theorists point out that a fairly small group of people has garnered the lion's share of the nation's wealth. Members of this elite sit on the boards of major corporations and of the country's most prestigious universities. They make strategic campaign contributions to control the nation's lawmakers, and it is they who make the major decisions in this society: to go to war or to refrain from war, to raise or to lower taxes, to raise or to lower interest rates, to pass laws that favor or impede moving capital, technology, and jobs out of the country.

Feminist sociologists (both women and men) have used conflict theory to gain a better understanding of how social institutions affect gender relations. Their basic insight is that gender, too, is an element of social structure, not simply a characteristic of individuals.

In other words, throughout the world social institutions separate males and females into separate groups that have unequal access to their society's resources.

▼ **In Sum** Conflict theorists regard our social institutions as having a single primary purpose—to preserve the social order—which they interpret as preserving the wealthy and powerful in their privileged positions. Functionalists, in contrast, view social institutions as working together to meet universal human needs.

Changes in Social Structure

This enveloping system that we call social structure, which so powerfully affects our lives, is not static. Our culture changes as it responds to new technology, to innovative ideas from home and abroad, and to evolving values. In our new era of "globalization," we come into contact with the customs of many other people. This exerts profound changes in our basic orientations to life. Nor do social classes remain immune to the winds of change, for growth and contraction in the economy move people in and out of positions of relative privilege, while shifting relationships between racial and ethnic groups also bring with them changes in relative power and prestige. Similarly, groups that did not exist, such as the IRS, come into being, and afterward wield extraordinary power over our lives.

What Holds Society Together?

With its many different groups and its extensive social change, how does society manage to hold together? Let us examine two answers to this question.

Mechanical and Organic Solidarity. Sociologist Emile Durkheim (1893/1933) found the key to **social cohesion**—the degree to which members of a society feel united by shared values and other social bonds—in what he called **mechanical solidarity.** By this term Durkheim meant that people who perform similar tasks develop a shared consciousness, a sense of similarity that unites them into a common whole. Think of an agricultural society in which everyone is involved in planting, cultivating, and harvesting. Members of this group have so much in common that they know what most others feel about life.

As societies increase in size, their **division of labor** (how they divide up work) becomes more specialized. Instead of almost everyone doing the same jobs, some become jewelers, while others become artists, authors, shopkeepers, soldiers, and so on. Rather than splitting society apart, however, the division of labor makes people depend on one another—for the activities of each contribute to the welfare of the whole. Durkheim called this new form of solidarity based on interdependence **organic solidarity.** To see why he used this term, think about how you depend on your teacher to guide you through this introductory course in sociology. At the same time, your teacher needs you and other students in order to have a job. The two of you are like organs in the same body. Although each of you performs different tasks, your dependence on one another creates a form of unity.

Due to the change from mechanical to organic solidarity, people no longer cooperate with one another because they *feel* alike (mechanical solidarity), but because they *depend* on one another's activities for their own survival (organic solidarity). In the past, societies tolerated little diversity in thinking and attitudes, for their unity depended on similar thinking. With this change to organic solidarity, modern societies can tolerate many differences among people and still manage to work as a whole. Note that both past and present societies are based on social solidarity but that the types of solidarity are remarkably different in each case.

Gemeinschaft* and *Gesellschaft. Ferdinand Tönnies (1887/1988) also saw a new type of society emerging. Tönnies used the term ***Gemeinschaft*** (Guh-MINE-shoft), "intimate community," to describe the traditional type of society in which everyone knows everyone else and people share a sense of shared fate. In such a society people toe the line because they are acutely sensitive to the opinions of others and know that if they deviate, others will gossip and damage their reputation. Although their lives are sharply controlled by the opinions of others, they draw comfort from being part of an intimate group.

social cohesion: the degree to which members of a group or a society feel united by shared values and other social bonds

mechanical solidarity: a shared consciousness that people experience as a result of performing the same or similar tasks

division of labor: the splitting of a group's or a society's tasks into specialties

organic solidarity: solidarity based on the interdependence brought about by the division of labor

Gemeinschaft: a type of society in which life is intimate; a community in which everyone knows everyone else and people share a sense of togetherness

The text contrasts Gesellschaft *and* Gemeinschaft *societies. The French café represents a* Gemeinschaft *approach to life, while the cybernet café, where people ignore one another in favor of concentrating on electronic interactions via the Internet, represents a* Gesellschaft *orientation. Internet interactions do not easily fit standard sociological models—another instance of cultural lag.*

Tönnies saw that industrialization was tearing at this intimate fabric of village life. He noted that in this emerging society personal ties, family connections, and lifelong friendships were growing less important. Instead, short-term relationships, individual accomplishments, and self-interests were being emphasized. Tönnies called this new type of society **Gesellschaft** (Guh-ZELL-shoft), or "impersonal association." As much as anyone might hate it, in *Gemeinschaft* society informal mechanisms such as gossip had been effective in controlling people. In this new world of *Gesellschaft*, however, gossip was of little use, and to keep people in line society had to depend on more *formal* agencies, such as the police and courts.

How Relevant Are These Concepts Today?   I know that *Gemeinschaft*, *Gesellschaft*, and *mechanical* and *organic solidarity* are strange terms and that Durkheim's and Tönnies's observations must seem like a dead issue with no connection to life today. The concern these sociologists expressed, however—that their world was changing from a community in which people are united by shared ideas and feelings to an anonymous association built around impersonal, short-term contacts—are still very real. In large part, this same concern explains why our world is witnessing the rise of Islamic fundamentalism (Volti 1995). Islamic leaders fear that their traditional culture will be uprooted by Western values, that

organic

Gesellschaft: a type of society dominated by impersonal relationships, individual accomplishments, and self-interest

Gemeinschaft societies do not give in to the encroachments and seductions of industrialization without a struggle. That is, people resist having the intimate bases of their lives transformed into more formal arrangements. Shown here is a school in Tehran, Iran, part of the means by which Iranian leaders attempt to maintain traditional Gemeinschaft *society.*

cold rationality will replace relationships built on long-term associations between families and clans. Although the terms may sound strange, even obscure, the ideas remain a vital part of today's world.

▼ **In Sum** The sociological point, again, is that social structure sets the context for what we do, feel, and think. In short, social structure lies at the basis of what kind of people we become. This becomes even more evident in the Perspectives box on the next page, in which we examine one of the few remaining *Gemeinschaft* societies in the United States.

The Microsociological Perspective: Social Interaction in Everyday Life

While the macrosociological approach stresses the broad features of society, the microsociological approach has a narrower focus, placing its emphasis on *face-to-face social interaction*, or what people do when they are in the presence of one another.

Symbolic Interaction

For symbolic interactionists, the most significant part of life in society is social interaction. Symbolic interactionists are especially interested in the symbols that people use to define their worlds. They want to know how people look at things and how that, in turn, affects their behavior. Of the many areas of social life that microsociologists study, let's look at stereotyping, personal space, and touching.

Stereotypes in Everyday Life. You are familiar with how first impressions "set the tone" for interaction. When you first meet someone, you cannot help but notice certain highly visible and distinctive features, such as the person's sex, race, age, and physical appearance. Despite your best intentions, your first impressions are shaped by the assumptions you make about such characteristics. You probably also know that these assumptions affect not only your ideas about the person, but also how you act toward that person.

Mark Snyder, a psychologist, wondered if **stereotypes**—the assumptions we make of what people are like—might be self-fulfilling. Knowing that our reactions to people are shaped by our stereotypes, he began to wonder if those reactions might actually produce behaviors that match the stereotype. Snyder (1993) came up with an ingenious way to test this idea. He gave college men a Polaroid snapshot of a woman, supposedly taken just moments before, and told them that they would be introduced to her after they talked with her on the telephone. Actually, the photograph, which showed either a physically attractive or unattractive woman, had been prepared before the experiment began. The one given to the subject had been chosen at random.

Stereotypes of physical attractiveness came into play even before the men spoke to the women they were going to meet. As Snyder gave each man the photograph, he asked him what he thought the woman would be like. The men who had been given the photograph of an attractive woman said they expected to meet a poised, humorous, outgoing woman. The men who had been given a photo of an unattractive woman described the person they were going to meet as awkward, serious, and unsociable.

These stereotypes then influenced the men's behavior. As each man talked on the telephone to the woman he was expecting to meet, the stereotype affected his style of getting acquainted. Men who had seen the photograph of an attractive woman were warm, friendly, humorous, and highly animated. Those who had seen the photograph of an unattractive woman were cold, reserved, and humorless.

These differences, in turn, affected the women's behavior. Although the women did not know about the man's evaluation of their looks, those who were believed to be attractive responded to the men in a warm, friendly, outgoing manner, while those who were perceived as homely became cool, reserved, and humorless. In short, *stereotypes tend to bring out the very kinds of behavior that fit the stereotype.*

stereotype: assumptions of what people are like, based on previous associations with them or with people who have similar characteristics, or based on information, whether true or false

Perspectives

The Amish—*Gemeinschaft* Community in a *Gesellschaft* Society

U.S. society exhibits the characteristics Ferdinand Tönnies identified as those of a *Gesellschaft* society. Impersonal associations pervade everyday life. Local, state, and federal governments regulate many activities. Impersonal corporations hire and fire people not on the basis of long-term, personal relationships, but on their value to the bottom line. And, perhaps even more significantly, millions of Americans do not even know their neighbors.

Within the United States, a handful of small communities exhibits characteristics that depart from those of the larger society. One such community is the Old Order Amish, followers of a sect that broke away from the Swiss-German Mennonite church in the late 1600s, settling in Pennsylvania around 1727. Today, about 150,000 Amish live in the United States. The largest concentration, about 14,000, reside in Lancaster County, Pennsylvania. The Amish can also be found in about twenty other states and in Ontario, Canada, but 75 percent live in just three states: Pennsylvania, Ohio, and Indiana. The Amish, who believe that birth control is wrong, have doubled in size in just the past two decades.

To the nearly five million tourists who pass through Lancaster County each year, the quiet pastures and almost identical white farmhouses, simple barns, horse- or mule-drawn carts, and clothes flapping on lines to dry convey a sense of peace and wholeness reminiscent of another era. Although just sixty-five miles from Philadelphia, "Amish country" is a world away.

The Amish faith rests on separation from the world, taking Christ's Sermon on the Mount literally, and obedience to the church's teachings and leaders. This rejection of worldly concerns, writes Donald Kraybill in *The Riddle of Amish Culture*, "provides the foundation of such Amish values as humility, faithfulness, thrift, tradition, communal goals, joy of work, a slow-paced life, and trust in divine providence."

The village life that Tönnies identified as fostering *Gemeinschaft* communities—and which he correctly predicted was fast being lost to industrialization—is very much alive among the Amish. The Amish make their decisions in weekly meetings, where, by consensus, they follow a set of rules, or *Ordnung*, to guide their behavior. Religion and the discipline that it calls for are the glue that holds these communities together. Brotherly love and the welfare of the community are paramount values. Most Amish farm plots of one hundred acres or less, keeping their farms small so that horses can be used instead of tractors and neighbors can pitch in with the chores. In these ways, intimacy—a sense of community—is maintained.

The Amish are bound by many other communal ties, including language (a dialect of German known as Pennsylvania Dutch), a distinctive style of plain dress that has remained unchanged for almost three hundred years, and church-sponsored schools. Nearly all Amish marry, and divorce is forbidden. The family is a vital ingredient in Amish life; all major events take place in the home, including weddings and worship services, even births and funerals. Most Amish children attend church schools only until the age of 13. To go to school beyond the eighth grade would expose them to "worldly concerns" and give them information considered of no value to farm life. They believe that all violence is bad, even in personal self-defense, and register as conscientious objectors during times of war.

As urban sprawl has made the cost of farmland soar, it also has forced slow social change. No longer can parents easily help their children buy their own farms. Consequently, almost a third of Amish men work at jobs other than farming, most in farm-related businesses or in woodworking. Some Amish women have opened up their own businesses, such as greenhouses and gift shops that specialize in craft items. Some women make several hundred thousand dollars a year in these businesses.

Nonfarmwork challenges the Amish way of life—especially their traditional husband–wife roles. Recognizing this, Amish men go to great lengths to avoid leaving the home, for they believe that when a husband works away from the home all aspects of life change—certainly an excellent sociological insight. Similarly, some successful businesswomen list their husbands' names first on their business cards. Others build a kitchen at the business so that they can continue to pack their husbands' lunches, as Amish wives have done for three centuries.

Economic success also challenges the Amish's traditional values. They frown on showy possessions, viewing them as worldly, so they invest their profits. This, in turn, stimulates further economic success, resulting in even greater pressures to spend the growing profits. (This process, called "The Protestant Ethic and the Spirit of Capitalism," is discussed later; see pages 169–170.)

Sources: Hostetler 1980; Kraybill 1989; Bender 1990; Raymond 1990; Kephart and Zellner 1994; Aeppel 1996.

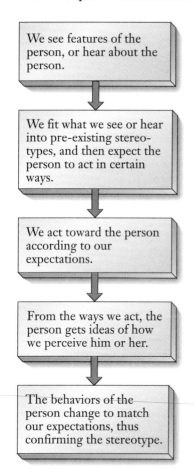

We see features of the person, or hear about the person.

We fit what we see or hear into pre-existing stereo-types, and then expect the person to act in certain ways.

We act toward the person according to our expectations.

From the ways we act, the person gets ideas of how we perceive him or her.

The behaviors of the person change to match our expectations, thus confirming the stereotype.

Figure 4.2

Self–Fulfilling Stereotypes

Social space is one of the many as-pects of social life studied by sociolo-gists who have a microsociological focus. What do you see in common in these two photos?

A number of experiments have been conducted to see how stereotypes of gender, race, ability, and intelligence influence people (Snyder 1993). In one, a welding instruc-tor in a vocational training center was told that five men in his training program had an unusually high aptitude for welding. Although the five had actually been chosen at ran-dom and knew nothing about the experiment, the effects were dramatic. These men were absent less often than other trainees, learned the basics of welding in about half the usual time, and scored ten points higher than the other men on their final welding test. The dif-ference was noted even by the other trainees, who singled these five out as their preferred co-workers. The men were no different in their initial abilities, but the instructor's stereo-type of their abilities changed his behavior, which brought about a change in the men's performance. This principle is illustrated in Figure 4.2.

Personal Space. Each of us surrounds his or her self with a "personal bubble" that we go to great lengths to protect. We open the bubble to intimates—to close friends, chil-dren, parents, and so on—but are careful to keep most people out of this space. In the hall, we might walk with books clasped in front of us (a strategy often chosen by females); we carefully line up at the drinking fountain, making certain there is space between us so we don't touch the person in front of us and we aren't touched by the person behind us.

At times we extend our personal space. In the library, for example, you may place your coat on the chair next to you—claiming that space for yourself even though you are not using it. If you want to really extend your space, you might even spread books in front of the other chairs, keeping the whole table to yourself by giving the impression that oth-ers have just stepped away.

The amount of space people prefer varies from one culture to another. South Amer-icans, for example, like to be closer when they speak to others than do people reared in the United States. Anthropologist Edward Hall (1959) recounts a conversation with a man from South America who had attended one of his lectures.

> He came to the front of the class at the end of the lecture. . . . We started out fac-ing each other, and as he talked I became dimly aware that he was standing a little too close and that I was beginning to back up. Fortunately I was able to suppress my first impulse and remain stationary because there was nothing to communicate aggression in his behavior except the conversational distance. . . .

> By experimenting I was able to observe that as I moved away slightly, there was an associated shift in the pattern of interaction. He had more trouble expressing himself. If I shifted to where I felt comfortable (about twenty-one inches), he looked somewhat puzzled and hurt, almost as though he were saying, "Why is he acting that way? Here I am doing everything I can to talk to him in a friendly man-ner and he suddenly withdraws. Have I done anything wrong? Said something I shouldn't?" Having ascertained that distance had a direct effect on his conversa-tion, I stood my ground, letting him set the distance.

As you can see, in spite of Hall's extensive knowledge of other cultures, he still felt un-comfortable in this conversation. He first interpreted the invasion of his personal space

as possible aggression, for people get close (and jut out their chins and chests) when they are hostile. But when he realized that was not the case, Hall resisted his impulse to move.

After Hall (1969/1997) analyzed situations like this, he observed that North Americans use four different "distance zones."

1. *Intimate distance.* This is the zone that the South American unwittingly invaded. It extends to about 18 inches from our bodies. We reserve this space for lovemaking, comforting, protecting, wrestling, hugging, and intimate touching.
2. *Personal distance.* This zone extends from 18 inches to 4 feet. We reserve it for friends and acquaintances and ordinary conversations. This is the zone in which Hall would have preferred speaking with the South American.
3. *Social distance.* This zone, extending out from us about 4 to 12 feet, marks impersonal or formal relationships. We use this zone for such things as job interviews.
4. *Public distance.* This zone, extending beyond 12 feet, marks an even more formal relationship. It is used to separate dignitaries and public speakers from the general public.

Norms of touching, including kissing, vary widely around the world. Shown here are Palestinian President Yasser Arafat and Monsignor Capucci of the Greek Orthodox Church kissing one another. In North America, in constrast, men shake hands. At most, two male friends, even after a long absence, will hug or clap one another on the back.

Touching.   Do you get uncomfortable if a stranger touches you? Many of us do. Just as we observe unwritten rules about speaking distance, so from our culture we learn rules about touching—and only the "cultural boor" dares to break them. Researchers who observed couples in coffee shops around the world concluded that the United States is a "low-touch" culture (Thayer 1988). In Gainesville, Florida, couples averaged only two touches an hour, while in Paris they touched 110 times an hour. The touching record, however, was made in San Juan, Puerto Rico, where couples touched 180 times an hour. The lowest-touch city, however, was not Gainesville, but London, where couples averaged zero touches per hour.

Not only does frequency of touching differ across cultures, but so does the meaning of touching within a culture. In general, higher-status individuals do more touching. Thus you are much more likely to see teachers touch students and bosses touch secretaries than the other way around. Apparently it is considered unseemly for lower-status individuals to put their hands on superiors. An interesting experiment with surgery patients illustrates how touching can have different meanings. When the nurse came in to tell patients about their coming surgery and after-care, she touched the patients twice, once briefly on the arm when she introduced herself, and then for a full minute on the arm during the instruction period. When she left, she shook the patient's hand.

Men and women reacted very differently. Touching lowered the blood pressure and anxiety of women, both before the surgery and for more than an hour afterward. The touching upset the men, however. Their blood pressure and anxiety rose. Apparently men in the United States find it harder to acknowledge dependency and fear than women do. For men, then, instead of a comfort, a well-intentioned touch may be a threatening reminder of their vulnerability (Thayer 1988).

Let us now turn to dramaturgy, a special area of symbolic interactionism.

Dramaturgy: The Presentation of Self in Everyday Life

It was their big day, two years in the making. Jennifer Mackey wore a white wedding gown adorned with an 11-foot train and 24,000 seed pearls that she and her mother had sewn onto the dress. Next to her at the altar in Lexington, Kentucky, stood her intended, Jeffrey Degler, in black tie. They said their vows, then turned to gaze for a moment at the four hundred guests.

That's when groomsman Daniel Mackey collapsed. As the shocked organist struggled to play Mendelssohn's "Wedding March," Mr. Mackey's unconscious body was dragged away, his feet striking—loudly—every step of the altar stairs.

"I couldn't believe he would die at my wedding," the bride said. (Hughes 1990)

Sociologist Erving Goffman (1922–1982) added a new twist to symbolic interactionism when he developed **dramaturgy** (or dramaturgical analysis). By this term he meant that

dramaturgy: an approach, pioneered by Erving Goffman, analyzing social life in terms of drama or the stage; also called dramaturgical analysis

social life is like a drama or the stage: birth ushers us onto the stage of everyday life, and our socialization consists of learning to perform on that stage.

Everyday life, Goffman (1997) said, involves playing our assigned roles. We have **front stages** on which to perform them, as did Jennifer and Jeffrey. (By the way, Daniel Mackey didn't really die—he had just passed out from the excitement of it all.) But we don't have to look at weddings to find front stages. Everyday life is filled with them. Where your teacher lectures is a front stage. And if you make an announcement at the dinner table, you are using a front stage. In fact, you spend most of your time on front stages, for a front stage is wherever you deliver your lines. We also have **back stages,** places where we can retreat and let our hair down. When you close the bathroom or bedroom door for privacy, for example, you are entering a back stage.

The same setting can serve as both a back and a front stage. For example, when you get into your car by yourself and look over your hair in the mirror or check your makeup, you are using the car as a back stage. But when you wave at friends or give that familiar gesture to someone who has just cut in front of you in traffic, you are using your car as a front stage.

Everyday life brings with it many roles. The same person may be a student, a teenager, a shopper, a worker, a date, as well as a daughter or a son. While a role lays down the basic outline for a performance, it also allows a great deal of freedom. The particular emphasis or interpretation that an individual gives a role, the person's "style," is known as **role performance.** Take your role as son or daughter as an example. You may play the role of ideal daughter or son, being very respectful, coming home at the hours your parents set, and so forth. Or that description may not even come close to your particular role performance.

Ordinarily our roles are sufficiently separated that conflict between them is minimized. Occasionally, however, what is expected of us in one role is incompatible with what is expected of us in another role. This problem, known as **role conflict,** makes us very uncomfortable, as illustrated in Figure 4.3, in which family, friendship, student, and work roles come clashing together. Usually, however, we manage to avoid role conflict by segregating our roles, which in some instances may require an intense juggling act.

Sometimes the *same* role presents inherent conflict, a problem known as **role strain.** Suppose that you are exceptionally prepared for a particular class assignment. Although the instructor asks an unusually difficult question, you find yourself knowing the answer when no one else does. If you want to raise your hand, yet don't want to make your fel-

front stage: where performances are given

back stage: where people rest from their performances, discuss their presentations, and plan future performances

role performance: the ways in which someone performs a role within the limits that the role provides; showing a particular "style" or "personality"

role conflict: conflicts that someone feels *between* roles because the expectations attached to one role are incompatible with the expectations of another role

role strain: conflicts that someone feels *within* a role

Figure 4.3

Role Strain and Role Conflict

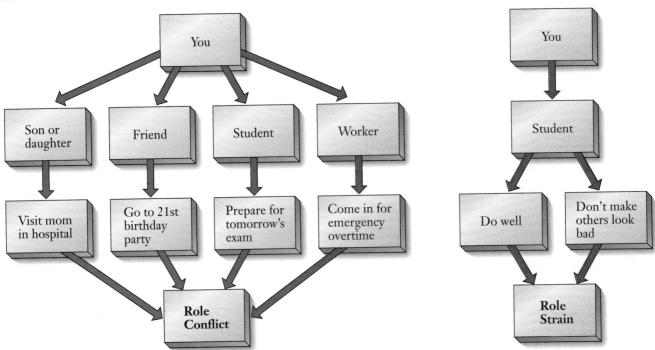

low students look bad, you will experience role strain. As illustrated in Figure 4.3, the difference between role conflict and role strain is that role conflict is conflict *between* roles, while role strain is conflict *within* a role.

A fascinating characteristic of roles is that *we tend to become the roles we play.* That is, roles become incorporated into the self-concept, especially those for which we prepare long and hard and which become part of our everyday lives. When sociologist Helen Ebaugh (1988) interviewed people who had left marriages, police work, and military, medical, and religious vocations, she found these roles had become so intertwined with the subjects' self-concepts that leaving them threatened their very identity. The question over which they struggled was "Who am I, now that I am not a nun (or physician, wife, colonel, etc.)?" Even years after leaving these roles, in their dreams many continued to perform them.

How these roles, having become such a part of the person, linger on after the individual has left them is illustrated by one of my own respondents, who said,

> After I left the (Protestant) ministry, I felt like a fish out of water. *Wearing that turned-back collar had become a part of me.* It was especially strange on Sunday mornings when I'd listen to someone else give the sermon. I knew that I should be up there preaching. I felt as though I had left God.

At the center of our performances in everyday life is the self and how we want others to think of us. We use our roles to communicate ideas that we want others to form about us. Goffman calls these efforts to manage the impressions that others receive of us **impression management.**

To communicate information about the self, we use three types of **sign-vehicles:** the social setting, our appearance, and our manner. The **social setting** is the place where the action unfolds. This is where the curtain goes up on your personal performances, where you find yourself on stage playing parts and delivering lines. A social setting might be an office, dorm, living room, church, gym, or bar. It is wherever you interact with others. Your social setting includes *scenery*, the furnishings you use to communicate messages, such as desks, blackboards, scoreboards, couches, and so on.

The second sign-vehicle is **appearance,** or how we look when we play our roles. Appearance includes *props*, which are like scenery, but they decorate the person rather than

impression management: the term used by Erving Goffman to describe people's efforts to control the impressions that others receive of them

sign-vehicles: the term used by Goffman to refer to how people use social setting, appearance, and manner to communicate information about the self

social setting: the place where the action of everyday life unfolds

appearance: how an individual looks when playing a role

All of us contrast the reality we see when we look in the mirror with our culture's ideal body types. Cindy Crawford, a top U.S. model represents an ideal body type that has developed in some parts of Western culture. Partly because of such cultural images, large women sometimes find themselves social outcasts. Consequently, as in the photo on the left, some now band together in support groups to help overcome the emotional impact of their unwelcome status.

the setting. The teacher has books, lecture notes, and chalk, while the football player wears a special costume called a uniform. Although few of us carry around a football, we all use makeup, hairstyles, and clothing to communicate messages about ourselves. Props and other aspects of appearance serve as a sort of grease for everyday life: by letting us know what to expect from others, they tell us how we should react. Think of the messages that props communicate. Some people use clothing to say that they are college students, others that they are old; some that they are clergy, others that they are prostitutes. Similarly, people use different brands of cigarettes, liquor, and automobiles to convey messages about the self. The Down-to-Earth Sociology box below focuses on a situation in which body size overwhelms other messages about the self.

Down-to-Earth Sociology

Disgusting, Pathetic, and Bizarrely Beautiful: Mass Media and the Presentation of the Body in Everyday Life

When you stand before a mirror, do you like what you see? To make your body more attractive, do you watch your weight? Where do you get your ideas of "proper" weight?

A common message of advertisers is that there is something wrong with our bodies, something needs to be improved. Although we may shrug off many of these messages, knowing that they are clear attempts to sell a particular product, they still penetrate our thinking, affecting our images of the way we "ought" to look. Such advertising is not limited to the United States or even the West. In both Japan and China, for example, advertisers push a soap that supposedly slims the body by "sucking up fat through the skin's pores" (Marshall 1995).

Today, television programs rank high among the mass media's influences on how we feel about our bodies. In her study of television talk shows that feature women and weight, sociologist Karen Honeycutt (1995) identified four recurring patterns of how obese women feel about themselves and how audiences react to them:

- *Disgusting.* In this, the most prevalent category, disgust about fat people prevails. As one guest said, "What really offends me about obese people is that they take up way too much room in buses and at concerts—and they smell." The overweight people sometimes cry as they are confronted by rude stares and nasty personal remarks. The host may play the role of the sympathizer, sometimes even with a closeup of her or him wiping away a tear.
- *Pathetic.* Although this category is sometimes difficult to separate from disgusting, it contains an element of compassion. When obese children are featured, for example, the guests express sympathy, even a bit of hope for change.
- *Bizarrely beautiful.* These shows feature obese people and guests who find them sexually attractive. The women, who often say they are happy with their weight, may strike provocative poses. The audience still views them as freaks, however. In one show, for example, one of the male guests asked the 300-pound women if their

boyfriends and lovers were sick. The audience roared in laughter.
- *Transformed.* These shows feature women who have lost weight, such as a guest who had gone from 621 pounds to just over 200 pounds. These shows often feature "makeovers" of the now socially acceptable women— new hairstyles and makeup to go with their transformed bodies. The implicit message, says Honeycutt, is that only *now* are they good enough to care about their hair, makeup, and other elements of their appearance.

It is almost as though the obese are sinners who need repentance and a life change—indicated by the applause given to those who have lost weight, the sympathy to those who are trying to lose weight, and the general disgust shown to most others. For obese people who have the confidence to consider themselves beautiful and for those who find them sexually attractive, the audience expresses revulsion.

Always, there is the matter of judgment. Even programs that are presented as neutral ("the issue is health") contain hidden assumptions and moral judgments that women's bodies need to be remolded. Even the term "overweight" is not neutral, for it implies that certain people have too much weight, while most of us are the "right" weight from which we measure their "over" weightness.

For Your Consideration

How do cultural expectations of the body's appearance underlie these television shows? Are common stereotypes of obese people (unattractive, sexless, lazy, poor workers) self-fulfilling? (Studies indicate that obese people generally have lower self-concepts.)

Most advertising and television shows focusing on weight are directed at women. Is this because women are more concerned than men about weight, more likely to have eating disorders, and more likely to express dissatisfaction with their bodies (Honeycutt 1995)? Or does this targeting of women create these attitudes and behaviors? Or is it a bit of both; that is, does one feed the other?

The third sign-vehicle is **manner,** the attitudes we demonstrate as we play our roles. We use manner to communicate information about our feelings and moods. By communicating anger or indifference, sincerity or good humor, for example, we indicate to others what they can expect of us as we play our roles.

We become so used to our roles in everyday life that we tend to think of ourselves as "just doing" things, not preparing for impression management. Yet every time we dress for school, or for any other activity, impression management is exactly what we are doing. Have you ever noticed how your very casually dressed classmates tend to change their appearance on the day they are scheduled to make a report to the class? No one asks them to do so, but their role has changed, and they dress for their slightly modified part. Similarly, you may have noticed that when teenagers begin to date they take several showers a day, stand before a mirror for hours as they comb and recomb their hair, and then change and rechange their clothing until they "get it just right."

In spite of our best efforts to manage the impressions that others receive of us, however, we sometimes fail. One of my favorite television scenes is of the character Molly Dodd trying to impress a date. She went to the "powder room," a backstage fix-up place reserved for women, where she did the usual things. Satisfied that she looked good, she made a grand entrance, with exaggerated movements and an expectant smile on her face—all the while trailing a long piece of toilet paper from her shoe. The scene is humorous because it highlights the fact that an incongruity of elements creates *embarrassment*, which in dramaturgical terms is a feeling that results when a performance fails.

To show ourselves as adept role players brings positive recognition from others, something that we all covet. To accomplish this, said Goffman, we often use **teamwork,** whereby two or more people work together to make certain that a performance goes off as planned. When a performance doesn't come off quite right, however, it may require **face-saving behavior.** We may, for example, ignore someone's flaws in performance, which Goffman defines as *tact*. Suppose your teacher is about to make an important point. Suppose also that her lecturing has been outstanding and the class is hanging on every word. Just as she pauses for emphasis, her stomach lets out a loud growl. She might then use a face-saving technique by remarking, "I was so busy preparing for class that I didn't get breakfast this morning." It is more likely, however, that both class and teacher will simply ignore the sound, both giving the impression that no one heard a thing—a face-saving technique called *studied nonobservance*. This allows the teacher to make the point, or as Goffman would say, it allows the performance to go on.

Before closing this section, we should note that impression management is not limited to individuals. Families, corporations, colleges, sports teams, in fact probably all groups, try to manage impressions. So do nations. An interesting example occurred when the International Olympic Committee was looking for a nation to host the Olympic 2000 games. Because hosting these games is so prestigious, the committee had a long list of candidates from which to choose. To impress the committee, China tried to put on a different face, to show that it was no longer repressive. With fanfare, China released a political prisoner a generous six months before he had finished serving his fifteen-year sentence (Brauchli 1993a). That this was impression management only, not a fundamental change, soon became apparent. After China lost its bid for the games, repression of political dissenters resumed in earnest.

Ethnomethodology: Uncovering Background Assumptions

As discussed in Chapter 1, symbolic interactionists stress that the events of life do not come with built-in meanings. Rather, we give meaning to things by classifying them. When we place objects and events into the classifications provided by our culture, we are doing more than naming things—we are interpreting our world.

Ethnomethodologists study how people make sense of life. They try to uncover people's basic assumptions as they interpret their everyday worlds. To better understand **ethnomethodology,** consider the word's three basic components. "Ethno" means folk or

manner: the attitudes that people show as they play their roles

teamwork: the collaboration of two or more persons interested in the success of a performance to manage impressions jointly

face-saving behavior: techniques used to salvage a performance that is going sour

ethnomethodology: the study of how people use background assumptions to make sense out of life

people; "method" means how people do something; "ology" means "the study of." Putting them together, then, *ethno/method/ology* means "the study of how people do things." Specifically, ethnomethodologists study how people use commonsense understandings to get through everyday life.

Let us suppose that you go to a doctor and she says that she doesn't feel like "doing doctoring" today. She then comments on how long your hair is, takes out a pair of scissors, and tries to give you a haircut. This would violate basic assumptions about what doctors are supposed to do. At the very least, we expect our doctor to listen to our medical problems and prescribe medicines. Haircuts, however, are simply not part of our expectations.

These assumptions about the way life is and the way things ought to work (what ethnomethodologists call **background assumptions**) lie at the root of social life. Exactly how these background assumptions work is what ethnomethodologists try to discover. They are so deeply embedded in our consciousness that we are seldom aware of them, for almost everyone fulfills them unquestioningly. Thus, your doctor does not offer you a haircut, even if he or she is good at cutting hair and you need one!

The founder of ethnomethodology, sociologist Harold Garfinkel, conducted some interesting exercises to uncover our background assumptions. Garfinkel (1967) asked his students to act as though they did not understand the basic rules of social life. Some tried to bargain with supermarket clerks; others would inch closer to people and stare directly at them. They were met with surprise, bewilderment, even anger. One of the more interesting exercises that Garfinkel's students conducted was to act as though they were boarders in their own homes. When they returned from class they addressed their parents as "Mr." and "Mrs.," asked permission to use the bathroom, sat stiffly, were extremely courteous, and spoke only when spoken to. The other family members were stupefied (Garfinkel 1967):

> They vigorously sought to make the strange actions intelligible and to restore the situation to normal appearances. Reports (by the students) were filled with accounts of astonishment, bewilderment, shock, anxiety, embarrassment, and anger, and with charges by various family members that the student was mean, inconsiderate, selfish, nasty, or impolite. Family members demanded explanations: What's the matter? What's gotten into you? . . . Are you sick? . . . Are you out of your mind or are you just stupid?

In another exercise Garfinkel asked students to take words and phrases literally. This is what happened when one student asked his girlfriend what she meant when she said that she had a flat tire:

> What do you mean, "What do you mean?"? A flat tire is a flat tire. That is what I meant. Nothing special. What a crazy question!

Another conversation went like this.

> *Acquaintance:* How are you?
>
> *Student:* How am I in regard to what? My health, my finances, my schoolwork, my peace of mind, my . . .?
>
> *Acquaintance* (red in the face): Look! I was just trying to be polite. Frankly, I don't give a damn how you are.

Students who are given the assignment to break background assumptions can be highly creative. The young children of one of my students were surprised one morning when they came down for breakfast to find a sheet spread across the living room floor. On it were dishes, silverware, burning candles—and ice cream. They, too, wondered what was going on—but they dug eagerly into the ice cream before their mother could change her mind.

▼ **In Sum** Ethnomethodologists explore background assumptions, our taken-for-granted ideas about the world, which underlie our behavior and are violated only with risk. These basic rules of social life are an essential part of the social structure. Deeply

background assumptions: deeply embedded common understandings, or basic rules, concerning our view of the world and of how people ought to act

embedded in our minds, they give us basic directions for living everyday life. Although often below our awareness, we depend on our background assumptions to guide us through our daily lives.

The Social Construction of Reality

On a visit to Morocco, in Northern Africa, I decided to buy a watermelon. When I indicated to the street vendor that the knife he was going to use to cut the watermelon was dirty ("encrusted with filth" would be more apt), he was very obliging. He immediately bent down and began to swish the knife in a puddle on the street. I shuddered as I looked at the passing burros, freely defecating and urinating as they went. Quickly, I indicated by gesture that I preferred my melon uncut after all.

For that vendor, germs did not exist. For me, they did. And each of us acted according to the way we saw matters. Our behavior did not result from the existence or nonexistence of germs, but, rather, *from our definitions, from our growing up in a group that teaches that germs are real or does not teach this.*

Microbes *objectively* exist, of course, and whether or not germs are part of our thinking makes no difference in our getting infected by them. Our behavior, however, depends on the way we define reality—on our **definition of the situation**—not on the *objective* existence of something.

Let's consider another example. Do you remember the identical twins, Oskar and Jack, who grew up so differently? As discussed on page 63, Jack was reared in Trinidad and learned to hate Hitler, while Oskar was reared in Germany and learned to love Hitler. Thus what Hitler means to Oskar and Jack (and to us) does not depend on Hitler's acts, but, rather, on the way we view his acts, that is, on our definition of the situation.

This is what **the social construction of reality** is. Our society, or the social groups to which we belong, have their particular views of life. From our groups (the *social* part of this process), we learn specific ways of looking at life—whether that be our view of Hitler (he's good, he's bad), germs (they exist, they don't exist), or of *anything else in life*. In short, through our interaction with others, we *construct reality*; that is, we learn ways of looking at our experiences in life.

definition of the situation: the way we look at matters in life; the way we define reality or some particular situation

the social construction of reality: the process by which people use their background assumptions and life experiences to define what is real for them

Gynecological Examinations.   To better understand the social construction of reality, let's consider an extended example.

A gynecological nurse, Mae Biggs, and I did research on pelvic examinations. Reviewing about 14,000 cases, we looked at how the medical profession constructs social reality in order to define this examination as nonsexual (Henslin and Biggs 1997). This desexualization is accomplished by painstakingly controlling the sign-vehicles—the setting, appearance, and manner.

The pelvic examination unfolds much as a stage play does. I will use "he" to refer to the physician because only male physicians participated in this study. Perhaps the results would be different with female gynecologists.

Pelvic examinations provide an excellent illustration of the social construction of reality. *As the text explains, this term refers to how people jointly agree that a particular situation has some certain meaning rather than another.*

Scene 1 (the patient as person) In this scene, the doctor maintains eye contact with his patient, calls her by name, and discusses her problems in a professional manner. If he decides that a vaginal examination is necessary, he tells a nurse, "Pelvic in room 1." By this statement, he is announcing that a major change will occur in the next scene.

Scene 2 (from person to pelvic) This scene is the depersonalizing stage. In line with the doctor's announcement, the patient begins the transition from a "person" to a "pelvic." The doctor leaves the room, and a female nurse enters to help the patient make the transition. The nurse prepares the "props" for the coming examination and answers any questions the woman might have.

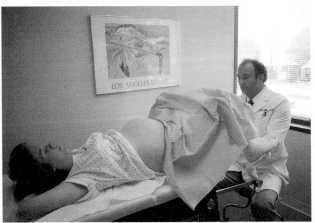

What occurs at this point is essential for the social construction of reality, for *the doctor's absence at this point removes even the suggestion of sexuality*. The act of undressing in front of him could suggest either a striptease or intimacy, thus undermining the reality so carefully being defined, that of nonsexuality.

The patient also wants to remove any hint of sexuality in the coming interaction, and during this scene she may express concern about what to do with her panties, perhaps muttering to the nurse, "I don't want him to see these." Most women solve the problem by either slipping their panties under their clothes or placing them in their purse.

Scene 3 (the person as pelvic) This scene opens with the doctor entering the room. Before him is a woman lying on a table, her feet in stirrups, her knees tightly together, and her body covered by a drape sheet. The doctor seats himself on a low stool before the woman, tells her, "Let your knees fall apart" (rather than the sexually loaded "Spread your legs"), and begins the examination.

The drape sheet is critical in this process of desexualization, for it *dissociates the pelvic area from the person:* Bending forward and with the drape sheet above his head, the physician can see only the vagina, not the patient's face. Thus dissociated from the individual, the vagina is dramaturgically transformed into an object of analysis. If the doctor examines the patient's breasts, he also dissociates them from her person by examining them one at a time, with a towel covering the unexamined breast. Like the vagina, each breast becomes an isolated unit dissociated from the person.

In this critical scene, the patient cooperates in being an object, becoming for all practical purposes a pelvis to be examined. She withdraws eye contact, from the doctor for certain but usually from the nurse as well, is likely to stare at the wall or at the ceiling, and avoids initiating conversation.

Scene 4 (from pelvic to person) In this scene the patient becomes "repersonalized." The doctor has left the examining room; the patient dresses and takes care of any problems with her hair and makeup. Her reemergence as person is indicated by such statements as "My dress isn't too wrinkled, is it?" indicating a need for reassurance from the nurse that the metamorphosis from "pelvic" back to "person" has been completed satisfactorily.

Scene 5 (the patient as person) In this scene, the patient is once again treated as a person rather than an object. The doctor makes eye contact with her and addresses her by name. She, too, makes eye contact with the doctor, and the usual middle-class interaction patterns are followed. She has been fully restored.

▼ **In Sum** To an outsider to our culture, the custom of women going to a male stranger for a vaginal examination might seem bizarre. But not to us. We assume that such behavior is normal, and females in our society are encouraged to participate in this process because they have learned that pelvic examinations are nonsexual. To sustain this definition requires teamwork—patients, doctors, and nurses working together to jointly produce this definition of reality. Thus, sociologists say that we *socially construct reality*.

Although pelvic examinations are socially constructed as nonsexual, many women still cannot rid themselves of uncomfortable feelings during this procedure, especially if their physician is a man. As the second wave of feminism gathered force in the 1960s and 1970s, women revealed this discomfort to one another. At this time, when less than 10 percent of obstetricians and gynecologists were female, some women decided to "take back control" of their reproductive health. Meeting in "consciousness raising" groups, they taught themselves how to examine their own bodies.

Since then, the situation has changed radically, and today 30 percent of obstetricians and gynecologists are women. Even more startling, 60 percent of first year ob/gyn residents are women (Council on Resident Education in Obstetrics and Gynecology, 1994). How this changed sex ratio may affect the ways that pelvic examinations—and medicine itself—are socially constructed is yet to unfold. Whatever the particulars may be, the same principles will apply: team players working to maintain agreed-on definitions of the situation.

The social construction of reality is not limited to small segments of social life, such as to medical procedures or watermelons in Africa. Rather, it is an essential part of our everyday lives. Our definitions of reality, stress symbolic interactionists, underlie our behavior. Or, as sociologist W. I. Thomas put it, in a classic statement that has become known as the **Thomas theorem**, "If people define situations as real, they are real in their consequences." To understand human behavior, then, whether that be how people react to microbes, to a photo of Hitler or the swastika, to pelvic examinations, or to anything else in life, we need to know how people define reality.

The Need for Both Macrosociology and Microsociology

As noted earlier in this chapter, to understand social life adequately, we need both microsociology and macrosociology. Each makes a vital contribution to our understanding of human behavior, and our understanding would be vastly incomplete without one or the other.

To illustrate this point, consider the research on two groups of high school boys conducted by sociologist William Chambliss (1973/1997). Both groups attended Hanibal High School. One group was composed of eight promising young students, boys who came from "good" families and were perceived by the community as "going somewhere." Chambliss calls this group the "Saints." The other group consisted of six lower-class boys who were seen as going down a dead-end road. Chambliss calls this group the "Roughnecks."

Both groups were seriously delinquent. Both skipped school, drank a lot, and committed criminal acts, especially fighting and vandalism. The Saints were actually somewhat more delinquent. They were truant more often, and they committed more acts of vandalism. Yet it was the Saints who had the good reputation, while the Roughnecks were seen by teachers, the police, and the general community as no good and heading for trouble.

These reputations followed the boys throughout life. Seven of the eight Saints went on to graduate from college. Three studied for advanced degrees: One finished law school and became active in state politics, one finished medical school and set up a practice near Hanibal, and one went on to earn a Ph.D. The four other college graduates entered managerial or executive training with large firms. After his parents divorced, one Saint failed to graduate from high school on time and had to repeat his senior year. Although this boy tried to go to college by attending night school, he never finished. He was unemployed the last time Chambliss saw him.

In contrast, only four of the Roughnecks even finished high school. Two of these boys did exceptionally well in sports and received athletic scholarships to college. They both graduated from college and became high school coaches. Of the two others who graduated from high school, one became a small-time gambler and the other disappeared "up north" where he was last reported to be driving a truck. Of the two who did not complete high school, each was last heard of serving time in state penitentiaries for separate murders.

To understand what happened to the Saints and the Roughnecks, we need to grasp *both* social structure and social interaction. That is, we need both macrosociology and microsociology. Using *macrosociology*, we can place these boys within the larger framework of the U.S. social class system. This context reveals how opportunities open or close to people depending on their membership in the middle or lower social class, and how different goals are instilled in youngsters as they grow up in vastly different groups. We can then use *microsociology* to follow their everyday lives. We can see how the Saints used their "good" reputations to skip classes repeatedly and how their access to automobiles allowed them to transfer their troublemaking to different communities and thus prevent damage to their local reputations. In contrast, lacking access to automobiles, the Roughnecks were highly visible. Their lawbreaking activities, limited to a small area, readily came to the attention of the community. Microsociology also reveals how their respective reputations opened doors of opportunity to the first group of boys while closing them to the other.

Thus we need both kinds of sociology, and both will be stressed in the following chapters.

Thomas theorem: William I. Thomas's classic formulation of the definition of the situation: "If people define situations as real, they are real in their consequences."

Summary and Review

Levels of Sociological Analysis

What are the two levels of analysis that sociologists use?

Sociologists use macro- and microsociological levels of analysis. In **macrosociology,** the focus is placed on large-scale features of social life, while in **microsociology,** the focus is on **social interaction.** Functionalists and conflict theorists tend to use a macrosociological approach, while symbolic interactionists are more likely to use a microsociological approach. Pp. 92–93.

The Macrosociological Perspective: Social Structure

How does social structure influence our behavior?

The term **social structure** refers to a society's framework, which forms an envelope around us and establishes limits on our behavior. Social structure consists of culture, social class, social statuses, roles, groups, and social institutions; together these serve as foundations for how we view the world.

Our location in the social structure underlies our perceptions, attitudes, and behaviors. Culture lays the broadest framework, while **social class** divides people according to income, education, and occupational prestige. Each of us receives **ascribed statuses** at birth; later we add various **achieved statuses.** Our behaviors and orientations are further influenced by the **roles** we play, the groups to which we belong, and our experiences with the institutions of our society. These components of society work together to help maintain social order. Pp. 94–98.

Social Institutions

What are social institutions?

Social institutions are the organized and standard means that a society develops to meet its basic needs. As summarized in Figure 4.1, industrialized societies have ten social institutions—the family, religion, law, politics, economics, education, medicine, science, the military, and the mass media. From the functionalist perspective, social institutions meet universal group needs, or **functional requisites.** From the conflict perspective, the elite use social institutions to maintain its privileged position. Pp. 98–102.

When societies are transformed by social change, how do they manage to hold together?

In agricultural societies, said Emile Durkheim, people are united by **mechanical solidarity** (similar views and feelings). With industrialization comes **organic solidarity** (peo-ple depend on one another to do their jobs). Ferdinand Tönnies pointed out that the informal means of control of **Gemeinschaft** (small, intimate) societies are replaced by formal mechanisms in **Gesellschaft** (larger, more impersonal) societies. Pp. 102–105.

The Microsociological Perspective: Social Interaction in Everyday Life

What is the focus of symbolic interactionism?

In contrast to functionalists and conflict theorists, who as macrosociologists focus on the "big picture," symbolic interactionists tend to be microsociologists who focus on face-to-face social interaction. Symbolic interactionists analyze how people define their worlds, and how their definitions, in turn, influence their behavior. P. 104.

How do stereotypes affect social interaction?

Stereotypes are assumptions of what people are like. When we first meet people, we classify them according to our perceptions of their visible characteristics and our ideas about those characteristics. These assumptions guide our behavior toward them, which, in turn, influences them to behave in ways that reinforce our stereotypes. Pp. 104–106.

Do all human groups share a similar sense of personal space?

In examining how people use physical space, symbolic interactionists stress that each of us is surrounded by a "personal bubble" that we carefully protect. People from different cultures have "personal bubbles" of varying sizes, so the answer to the question is no. Americans typically use four different "distance zones": intimate, personal, social, and public. Pp. 106–107.

What is dramaturgy?

Erving Goffman developed **dramaturgy** (or dramaturgical analysis), which analyzes everyday life in terms of the stage. At the core of this analysis are the impressions we attempt to make on others. For that, we use the **sign-vehicles** of setting, appearance, and manner. Our performances often call for **teamwork** and **face-saving behavior.** Pp. 107–111.

What is the social construction of reality?

Ethnomethodology is the study of how people make sense of everyday life. Ethnomethodologists try to uncover our **background assumptions,** our basic ideas about the way life is. The phrase **the social construction of reality** refers to how we construct our views of the world. Pp. 111–115.

The Need for Both Macrosociology and Microsociology

Why are both levels of analysis important?

Because each focuses on different aspects of the human experience, both microsociology and macrosociology are necessary for us to understand social life. P. 115.

Where can I read more on this topic?
Suggested readings for this chapter are listed on page 660.

 Sociology and the Internet

All URLs listed are current as of the printing of this book. URLs are often changed. Please check our Web site http://www.abacon.com/henslin for updates.

1. The power of the media, including the Internet, is raising new questions about who controls the flow of information. Since the 1996 telecommunications bill became law, the debate over censorship issues has exploded. Use the Lycos search engine *http://www.lycos.com* to explore this issue, entering the search words, "censorship Internet." What are the main issues? The main arguments? What do you think about what you read at this site? Prepare a written or oral report on your findings and opinions.

2. The creation of "intentional communities" represents an attempt to restore *Gemeinschaft* to modern living. Access the list of Intentional Communities of the Web by going to *http://www.well.com/user/cmty/index.html* Browse several of the sites. What are main characteristics of intentional communities? Look for *Gemeinschaft* elements featured in the descriptions, as well as any *Gesellschaft* components that may be there. Write a report comparing the particular *Gesellschaft* emphases of the communities you explored. What characteristics of postindustrial societies draw people to intentional communities?

3. After reading the Perspectives box on page 105 of your text, examine the following Web links:

> *www.amish-heartland.com/amish*
> *www.800padutch.com/amishexp./html*
> *www.poopets.com/*

Your author discusses ways in which the Amish form a *Gemeinschaft* community in a *Gesellschaft* society. We can see how the Amish way of life is different from the larger U.S. *Gesellschaft* society, but it takes a more sociological eye to see the similarities, of which there are many. Focus on and discuss the similarities in the social institutions of Amish and U.S. society. Does Amish society contain all nine social institutions? How are the institutions of family, religion, law, education, and medicine similar in the two societies?

4. According to your text, politics is a social institution that fulfills certain basic needs of a society. Use Yahoo *http://www.yahoo.com* to examine the basic needs that politics fulfills. Click on "Government" and then "Politics." Examine some of the current political headlines and a few of the subcategories to determine what specific needs politics fulfills. Do any of the other social institutions also fulfill these same needs?

Diana Ong, Untitled, 1995

How Sociologists Do Research

*C*INDY *HUDO, A 21-YEAR-OLD MOTHER of two in Charleston, South Carolina, who was charged with the murder of her husband, Buba, said:*

I start in the car, and I get down the road, and I see Buba walking, and he's real mad. . . . I pull over, you know, and [I said] "I didn't know to pick you up. You know, I'm sorry." And he didn't even say nothing to me. He just started hitting on me. And that's all I wanted to do, was just get home, because I was just self-conscious. I don't want nobody to see him hitting me, because I didn't want him to look bad.

I had to go to work in a half-hour, because I was working a double-shift. And he told me I had forty minutes to get all my furniture out of the house and get my clothes and be out or he was going to throw them out. And I was sitting there, because I could talk him down. You know, because I didn't want to leave him. I just talked to him. I said, "Buba, I don't want to leave." I said, "This is my house." And then he told me . . . (unclear) . . . "my kids." And I said, "No, you're not taking my kids from me. That's too much." And so I said, "Just let me leave. Just let me take the kids. And, you know I'll go, and you know, I won't keep the kids from you or nothing like that." And he said, "I'm going to take them, and you're getting out."

[After they went inside their trailer, Buba threatened to shoot Cindy. He loaded a shotgun, pointed it at her, and said]: "The only way you're going to get out of this is if you kill me, and I'll—I'll kill you." [Buba gave me the shotgun and] turned around and walked right down the hall, because he knew I wouldn't do nothing. And I just sat there a minute. And I don't know what happened. I just, you know, I went to the bedroom, and I seen him laying there, and I just shot him. He moved. I shot him again because I thought he was going to get up again. . . .

I loved him too much. And I just wanted to help him. (20/20, October 18, 1979)

Source: *ABC Television, 20/20, October 18, 1979*

What Is a Valid Sociological Topic?

Sociologists do research on just about every area of human behavior. On the macro level, they study such broad matters as the military (Moscos and Butler 1997), race relations (Wilson 1996), and multinational corporations (Kanter et al. 1997). On the micro level, they study such individualistic matters as pelvic examinations (Henslin and Biggs 1997), how people interact on street corners (Whyte 1989, 1997), and even how people decorate their homes at Christmas (Caplow 1991). In fact, no human behavior is ineligible for sociological scrutiny—whether that behavior is routine or unusual, respectable or reprehensible.

What happened to Cindy and Buba, then, is also a valid topic of sociological research. But exactly *how* would you research spouse abuse? As we look at how sociologists conduct their research, we shall try to answer this question.

Common Sense and the Need for Sociological Research

First, why do we need sociological research? Why can't we simply depend on common sense, on "what everyone knows"? As noted in Chapter 1 (pages 8–10), commonsense ideas may or may not be true. Common sense, for example, tells us that spouse abuse has a significant impact on the lives of the people who are abused.

Although this particular idea is accurate, we need research to test commonsense ideas, because not all such ideas are true. After all, common sense also tells us that if a woman is abused she will pack up and leave her husband. Research, however, shows that the reality of abuse is much more complicated than this. Some women do leave right away, some

120

even after the first incident of abuse. For a variety of reasons, however—the main one being that they feel trapped and don't see viable alternatives—some women put up with abuse for years.

This brings us to the need for sociological research, for we may want to know why some women put up with abuse, while others don't. Or we may want to know something entirely different, such as why men are more likely to be the abusers. Or why some people abuse persons they say they love.

Regardless of the particular question that we want to answer, the point is that we need to move beyond guesswork and common sense. We want to *know* what really is going on. And for accurate answers, we need sociological research. Let's look, then, at how sociologists do their research.

A Research Model

As shown in Figure 5.1, eight basic steps are involved in scientific research. As you look at each of these steps, be aware that this is an ideal model. In some research these steps are collapsed, in others their order may be changed, while in still others one or more steps may even be omitted.

1. Selecting a Topic

The first step is to select a topic. What do you want to know more about? Many sociologists simply follow their curiosity, their drive to know. They become interested in a particular topic, and they pursue it, as I did in studying the homeless. Some sociologists

Figure 5.1

The Research Model

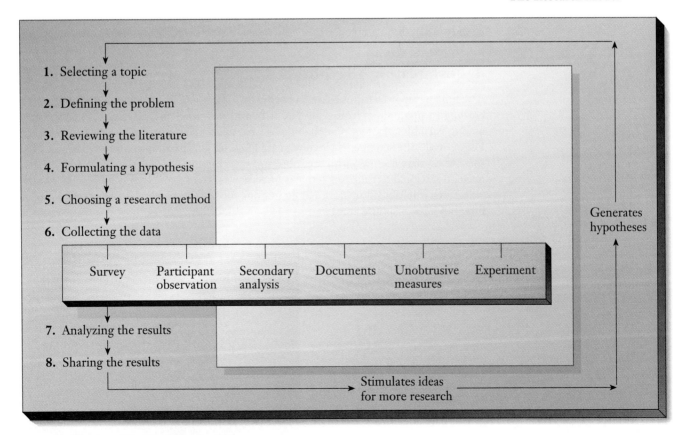

Source: Modification of Fig. 2.2 of Schaefer 1989.

Because sociologists find all human behavior to be valid research topics, their research runs from the unusual to the routines of everyday life. On the macro level, they study how voting patterns are related to religion, and on the micro level they study tattoo contests, such as this one in New York's East Village. Their analyses range from such intensely individual acts as suicide to such broad-scale social change as the globalization of capitalism.

choose a topic because funding is available to study it, others because a social problem such as domestic violence has become a pressing social issue, and the sociologist wants to gather data that will help people better understand it—and perhaps to help solve it.

2. Defining the Problem

The second step is to define the problem, to specify exactly what you want to learn about the topic. My interest in the homeless grew until I wanted to learn about homelessness across the nation. Ordinarily, sociologists' interests are much more focused than this. They develop a researchable question that focuses on a specific area or problem. For example, they may want to compare the work experiences of homeless women and men. Or they may want to know what can be done to reduce spouse abuse.

Although much sociological research examines social problems such as homelessness and spouse abuse, sociologists conduct research on any aspect of social life that interests them. The "problem" can be as earth shattering as why nations would ever contemplate nuclear war or as simple as wanting to find out why Native Americans like Westerns (see the box on page 47).

3. Reviewing the Literature

The third step is to review the literature to see what has been written on the problem. Reading research reported by others helps narrow down the problem, pinpointing particular areas to examine. Reviewing the research may also provide ideas about what questions to ask. Sometimes the researcher finds out that the problem has been answered already. Then there is no need to do the research, for no one wants to reinvent the wheel.

4. Formulating a Hypothesis

The fourth step is to formulate a **hypothesis,** a statement of what you expect to find according to predictions from a theory. A hypothesis predicts a relationship between or among **variables,** factors that change, or vary, from one person or situation to another. For example, the statement, "Men who are more socially isolated are more likely to abuse their wives than are men who are more socially integrated" is a hypothesis. Hypotheses need **operational definitions**—that is, precise ways to measure their variables. In this example, we would need operational definitions for three variables: social isolation, social integration, and spouse abuse.

hypothesis: a statement of the expected relationship between variables according to predictions from a theory

variable: a factor or concept thought to be significant for human behavior, which varies from one case to another

operational definitions: the way in which a variable in a hypothesis is measured

Almost all human behavior is of interest to sociologists, including what people do when faced with disaster. Human resiliency and determination in the face of overwhelming odds are one side of the human picture. This side is depicted in this photo of the 1993 "once-in-500-years" flood of the Mississippi River.

5. Choosing a Research Method

The means by which sociologists collect data are called **research methods** (or research designs). Sociologists use six basic research methods, outlined in the next section. They select the method that will best answer the particular questions they want to answer.

6. Collecting the Data

The next step is to gather the data. Sociologists take great care to assure both the validity and reliability of their data. **Validity** is the extent to which operational definitions measure what they are intended to measure. For example, just how should we measure social isolation and integration? Can we simply find out how frequently an individual interacts with others? Don't we also have to measure how much the individual identifies or feels a part of other people, a much more difficult matter? Even an operational definition for spouse abuse is not simple to determine. For example, some acts that are an accepted part of everyday life in some cultures and subcultures are viewed as abuse by people from other groups. Yet our operational definition must make sense *and* be so precise that no one has any question about what we are measuring.

The term **reliability** refers to the extent to which different studies come up with similar results. If one study shows that 1 percent of the women in a certain city have been the victims of spouse abuse, while another study finds that it is 10 percent, you can see why sociologists would use the term "unreliable." Inadequate operational definitions and sampling (to be covered later) hurt reliability. If these are adequate, two studies of domestic violence in the same city should show similar results (that is, be very reliable).

7. Analyzing the Results

After the data are gathered, it is time to analyze them. To do this, sociologists use qualitative and quantitative techniques. *Qualitative* analysis is especially useful for data gathered by participant observation. Sociologists classify statements people have made, or books, or even movies and television programs, in order to identify the main themes. The goal is to faithfully reproduce the world of the people being studied. In my research on cabdrivers, for example, I (1967, 1993) tried to picture the world as cabbies see it, so anyone reading the analysis would understand not just what cabbies do but also why they do it.

Quantitative analysis involves crunching numbers. Quantitative analysis is especially useful to test hypotheses, which is done at this stage. The computer, which has become an especially powerful tool for quantitative analysis, has four main values for sociologists. First, the computer can analyze huge amounts of information and identify basic patterns. Second, current software programs take much of the drudgery out of analyzing data. What used to take tedious hours, and even days or weeks, of mathematical analysis can now be performed in an instant. Third, it is easy for researchers to try various statistical tests to see which prove the most valuable for the data they have. Fourth, freed from the time-consuming tasks of number crunching, researchers can think more about what those numbers mean. Consequently, the use of this tool to analyze data is part of sociological training. The basic programs that sociologists, even many undergraduates, learn are Microcase and the Statistical Package for the Social Sciences (SPSS).

8. Sharing the Results

Now it is time to wrap up the research, or, if it is a broad project, at least some part of it. In this step, the researchers write a report to share their findings with the scientific community. The report includes a review of the preceding steps to help others evaluate the research. It also shows how the findings are related to the literature, the published results of other research on the topic. When research is published, usually in a scientific journal or a book, it then "belongs" to the scientific community. Table 5.1 on the next page is an example of published research. These findings are available for **replication;** that is, others

research method (or research design): one of six procedures sociologists use to collect data: surveys, participant observation, secondary analysis, documents, unobtrusive measures, and experiments

validity: the extent to which an operational definition measures what was intended

reliability: the extent to which data produce consistent results

replication: repeating a study in order to test its findings

TABLE 5.1		
How to Read a Table		

Comparing Violent and Nonviolent Husbands

Based on interviews with 150 husbands and wives in a Midwestern city who were getting a divorce.

Husband's Achievement and Job Satisfaction	*Violent Husbands* $n = 25$	*Nonviolent Husbands* $n = 125$
He started but failed to complete high school or college.	44%	27%
He is very dissatisfied with his job.	44%	18%
His income is a source of constant conflict.	84%	24%
He has less education than his wife.	56%	14%
His job has less prestige than his father-in-law's.	37%	28%

Source: Modification of Table 1 in O'Brien 1975.

A table is a concise way of presenting information. Because sociological findings are often presented in tabular form, it is important to understand how to read a table. Tables contain six elements: title, headnote, headings, columns, rows, and source. When you understand how these elements work together, you know how to read a table.

1. The *title* states the topic of a table. It is located at the top of the table. What is the title of this table? Please determine your answer before looking at the correct answer below.

2. The *headnote* is not always included in a table. When it is, it is located just below the title. Its purpose is to give more detailed information about how the data were collected or how data are presented in the table. What are the first seven words of the headnote of this table?

3. The *headings* tell what kind of information is contained in the table. There are three headings in this table. What are they? In the second heading, what does $n = 25$ mean?

4. The *columns* present information vertically arranged. What is the fourth number in the second column and the second number in the third column?

5. The *rows* present information arranged horizontally. In the fourth row, who is listed as having less education than his wife?

6. The *source* of a table, usually listed at the bottom, provides information on where the data shown in the table originated. Often, as in this instance, the information is specific enough for you to consult the original source. What is the source for this table?

Some tables are much more complicated than this one, but all follow the same basic pattern. To apply these concepts to a table with more information, see page 331.

Answers

1. Comparing Violent and Nonviolent Husbands.

2. Based on interviews with 150 husbands and

3. Husband's Achievement and Job Satisfaction, Violent Husbands, Nonviolent Husbands. The *n* is an abbreviation for number, and $n = 25$ means that 25 men were in the sample of violent husbands.

4. 56%, 18%.

5. Violent husbands.

6. A 1975 article by O'Brien (listed in the References section of this text).

can repeat the study to see if they come up with the same results. In this way, scientific knowledge builds slowly as finding is added to finding.

Let's look in greater detail at the fifth step to see what research methods sociologists use.

Six Research Methods

Sociologists use six research methods (or "research designs") for gathering data: surveys, participant observation, secondary analysis, documents, unobtrusive measures, and exper-

---

TABLE 5.2

Three Ways to Measure "Average"

The Mean

The term *average* seems clear enough. As you learned in grade school, to find the average you add a group of numbers and then divide the total by the number of cases that were added. For example, assume that the following numbers represent men convicted of battering their wives:

321
229
57
289
136
57
1,795

The total is 2,884. Divided by 7 (the number of cases), the average is 412. Sociologists call this form of average the *mean*.

The mean can be deceptive because it is strongly influenced by extreme scores, either low or high. Note that six of the seven cases are less than the mean.

Two other ways to compute averages are the median and the mode.

The Median

To compute the second average, the *median*, first arrange the cases in order—either from the highest to the lowest or the lowest to the highest. In this example, that arrangement will produce the following distribution:

57
57
136
229
289
321
1,795

Then look for the middle case, the one that falls halfway between the top and the bottom. That figure is 229, for three numbers are lower and three numbers higher. When there is an even number of cases, the median is the halfway mark between the two middle cases.

The Mode

The third measure of average, the *mode* is simply the cases that occur the most often. In this instance the mode is 57, which is way off the mark. Because the mode is often deceptive, and only by chance comes close to either of the other two averages, sociologists seldom use it. In addition, it is obvious that not every distribution of cases has a mode. And if two or more different numbers appear with the same frequency, you can have more than one mode.

---

iments. To understand these strategies better, let's continue our example of spouse abuse. As we do so, note how the choice of method depends on the questions we want to answer. Because researchers often want to know what "average" is in order to provide a yardstick for comparison, three measures of average are discussed in Table 5.2 above.

Surveys

Let's suppose that your goal is to know how many wives are abused each year. You know that some husbands are also abused, but let's assume that you are going to focus on wives. An appropriate method for this purpose would be the **survey,** in which people are asked a series of questions. Before using this method, however, you must deal with practical matters that face all researchers—selecting a sample, asking neutral questions, using questionnaires or interviews, and establishing rapport. Let's look at each of these practical problems.

Selecting a Sample.   Ideally, you may want to learn about all wives in the world. Obviously, however, your resources will not permit such a study, and you must narrow your **population,** the target group that you will study.

Let's assume that your resources allow you to investigate wife abuse only on your college campus. Let's also suppose that your college enrollment is large, making it impractical to survey all the married women who are enrolled. Now you must select a **sample,** individuals from among your target population. How you choose a sample is critical, for the choice will affect the results of your study. For example, to survey only first-year students—or only seniors, or only those enrolled in introductory sociology courses, or only those in advanced physics classes—will produce unrepresentative results in each case.

To be able to generalize your findings to the entire campus, you must select a sample that is representative of the campus (called a "representative sample"). What kind of sample will allow you to do this?

survey: the collection of data by having people answer a series of questions

population: the target group to be studied

sample: the individuals intended to represent the population to be studied

Because sociologists usually cannot interview or observe every member of a group they wish to study, such as the spectators at this boxing match between heavyweight world champion Evander Holyfield and Mike Tyson, they must select a sample that will let them generalize to the entire group. The text explains how samples are selected.

random sample: a sample in which everyone in the target population has the same chance of being included in the study

stratified random sample: a sample of specific subgroups of the target population in which everyone in the subgroups has an equal chance of being included in the study

respondents: people who respond to a survey, either in interviews or by self-administered questionnaires

questionnaires: a list of questions to be asked

self-administered questionnaires: questionnaires filled out by respondents

interview: direct questioning of respondents

The best is a **random sample.** This does *not* mean that you stand on some campus corner and ask questions of whomever happens to walk by. *In a random sample, everyone in the population has the same chance of being included in the study.* In this case, since the population is every married woman enrolled in your college, all married women—whether first-year or graduate students— must have the same chance of being included in the sample. Equally, such factors as a woman's major, her age, grade point average, or whether she is a day or evening or full- or part-time student must not affect her chance of becoming part of your study.

How can you get a random sample? First you need a list of all the married women enrolled in your college. You then would assign a number to each name on the list and, using a table of random numbers, determine which of these women become part of your sample. (Random numbers are available on tables in statistics books, or they can be generated by a computer.)

Because a random sample represents the population—in this case married women enrolled at your college—you can generalize your findings to all the married women students on your campus, whether they were included in the sample or not.

Social scientists have developed a variation of this sampling technique that you might want to consider. Suppose you want to compare the experiences of freshmen and seniors. If so, you could use a **stratified random sample.** You would first identify freshmen and seniors, and then use random numbers to select subsamples from each group.

Asking Neutral Questions. After you have decided on your population and sample, your next task is to make certain that your questions are neutral. Your questions must allow **respondents,** people who respond to a survey, to express their own ideas. Otherwise, you will end up with biased answers—and biased findings are worthless. For example, if you were to ask, "Don't you agree that men who beat their wives deserve a prison sentence?" you would be tilting the answers toward agreement with the position being stated. For other examples of flawed research, see the Down-to-Earth Sociology box on the next page.

Questionnaires and Interviews. Sociologists not only strive to ask questions that reduce bias; they also are concerned about how **questionnaires,** the list of questions to be asked, are administered (carried out). There are two basic techniques for administering questionnaires. The first is for the respondents to fill them out. Although **self-administered questionnaires** allow a larger number of people to be sampled at a relatively low cost, the researcher does not know the conditions under which people answered the questions. For example, someone could have influenced the respondents' answers. In the second technique, called an **interview,** the researcher asks the questions directly, either face to face or by telephone. The advantage of this method is that the researcher can make certain that each question is asked in precisely the same way. This method also has disadvantages, however. It reduces the number of questionnaires that can be completed, and

Improperly worded questionnaires steer respondents toward answers that are not their own, thus producing invalid results.

Down-to-Earth Sociology

Loading the Dice: How *Not* to Do Research

The methods of science lend themselves to distortion, misrepresentation, and downright fraud. Consider the following information. Surveys show that

- *Americans overwhelmingly prefer Toyotas to Chryslers.*
- *Americans overwhelmingly prefer Chryslers to Toyotas.*
- *Americans think that cloth diapers are better for the environment than disposable diapers.*
- *Americans think that disposable diapers are better for the environment than cloth diapers.*

Obviously such opposites cannot both be true. In fact, *both* sets of findings are misrepresentations, although each does come from surveys conducted by so-called independent researchers. These researchers, however, are biased, not independent and objective.

It turns out that some consumer researchers load the dice. Hired by firms that have a vested interest in the outcome of the research, they deliver the results their clients are looking for. There are six basic ways of loading the dice.

1. **Choose a biased sample.** For example, if you want to "prove" that Americans prefer Chryslers over Toyotas, you can interview unemployed union workers who trace their job loss to Japanese imports. The answer is fairly predictable. You'll get what you're looking for.

2. **Ask biased questions.** Even if you choose an unbiased sample, you can phrase questions in such a way that most people see only one logical choice. When the disposable diaper industry paid for the survey cited above, the researchers used an excellent sample, but they worded the question this way: "It is estimated that disposable diapers account for less than 2 percent of the trash in today's landfills. In contrast, beverage containers, third-class mail and yard waste are estimated to account for about 21 percent. Given this, in your opinion, would it be fair to ban disposable diapers?"

   Is it surprising, then, that 84 percent of the respondents said that disposable diapers are better for the environment than cloth diapers? Similarly, when the cloth diaper industry funded its survey, they worded the questions to load the dice in their favor.

   Consider the following finding, which is every bit as factual as those just cited:

- *80 percent of Americans support foreign aid.*

   It is difficult to get 80 percent of Americans to agree on anything, but as loaded as this question was it is surprising that there was *only* 80 percent agreement. Incredibly, the question was phrased this way: "*Should the U.S. share at least a small portion of its wealth with those in the world who are in great need?*"

This question is obviously designed to channel people's thinking toward a predetermined answer—quite contrary to the standards of scientific research.

3. **List biased choices.** Another way to load the dice is to use closed-ended questions that push people into the answers you want. Consider this finding:

- *U.S. college students overwhelmingly prefer Levis 501 to the jeans of any competitor.*

Sound good? Before you rush out to buy Levis, note what the researchers did: In asking a sample of students which jeans would be the most popular in the coming year, their list of choices included *no other jeans* but Levis 501!

4. **Discard undesirable results.** Researchers can simply keep silent about results they find embarrassing, or they can even continue to survey samples until they find one that matches what they are looking for.

As stressed in this chapter, research must be objective if it is to be scientific. Obviously, none of the preceding results qualifies. The underlying problem with the research cited here—and with so many surveys bandied about in the media as fact—is that survey research has become big business. Simply put, the vast sums of money offered by corporations have corrupted some researchers.

The beginning of the corruption is subtle. Paul Light, dean at the University of Minnesota, put it this way: "A funder will never come to an academic and say, 'I want you to produce finding *X*, and here's a million dollars to do it.' Rather, the subtext is that if the researchers produce the right finding, more work—and funding—will come their way." He adds, "Once you're on that treadmill, it's hard to get off."

The first four sources of bias are intentional, inexcusable fraud. The fifth and sixth sources of bias reflect sloppiness—which is also inexcusable in science.

5. **Misunderstand the subjects' world.** This route can lead to errors every bit as great as those just cited. Even researchers who use an adequate sample, word their questions properly, and offer adequate choices can end up with skewed results. For example, surveys show that 80 percent of Americans are environmentalists. Most Americans, however, are probably embarrassed to tell a stranger otherwise. Today, that would be like going against the flag, motherhood, and apple pie.

6. **Analyze the data incorrectly.** Even when researchers strive for objectivity, the sample and wording are correct, and respondents answer the questions honestly, the results can still be skewed—the researchers may simply err in their calculations, such as entering incorrect data into computers.

Sources: Based on Crossen 1991; Goleman 1993; Barnes 1995.

increases the cost. It also can result in **interviewer bias,** effects that interviewers have on respondents that bias their answers. For example, respondents may give "socially acceptable" answers to an interviewer. They may be willing to write an anonymous answer but not to express the same opinion to another person directly. Respondents also sometimes try to make their answers match what they think an interviewer wants to hear.

In some cases, **structured interviews** work best. This type of interview uses **closed-ended questions**—each question is followed by a list of possible answers. The advantages of structured interviews are that they are faster to administer and make it easier for the answers to be *coded* (categorized) so that they can be fed into a computer for analysis. The primary disadvantage is that the answers listed on the questionnaire may not include the respondent's opinions. For this reason, some researchers prefer **unstructured interviews.** Here the interviewer asks **open-ended questions,** which people answer in their own words. Although open-ended questions allow respondents to express the full range of their opinions, they make it difficult to compare people's answers. For example, how would you compare these answers to the question "What do you think causes men to abuse their wives?"

"They're sick."

"They haven't been raised right."

"I think they must have had problems with their mother."

"We ought to kill every one!"

"They're just *·*·* bastards!"

Establishing Rapport.   Research on spouse abuse also brings up another significant issue. You may have been wondering if your survey would be worth anything even if you rigorously followed scientific procedures. Will women who have been beaten really give honest answers? Will they even admit their victimization to a stranger?

If you were to walk up to female strangers on the street and ask if they had ever been beaten by their husbands, there understandably would be little basis for taking your findings seriously. It is therefore vital for researchers to establish **rapport** ("ruh-POUR"), a feeling of trust, with their respondents, especially when it comes to sensitive topics, areas about which people feel embarrassment, shame, or other deep emotions.

We know that once rapport is gained (for example, by first asking nonsensitive questions), victims will talk to researchers about personal, sensitive issues. A good example is rape. To go beyond police statistics, each year researchers conduct a national crime survey in which they interview a random sample of 100,000 Americans, asking them if they have been victims of burglary, robbery, and so on. After gaining rapport, the researchers ask about rape. They find that rape victims will talk about their experiences. The national crime surveys show that rape is twice as high as the official statistics—and that most rape is committed by someone the victim knows (Schafran 1995).

Participant Observation (Fieldwork)

In the second method, **participant observation,** the researcher *participates* in a research setting while *observing* what is happening in that setting. My research with the homeless, mentioned in Chapter 1, is an example of participant observation.

How is it possible to study spouse abuse by participant observation? Obviously, being present during the abuse and taking notes while it occurs is not feasible. Spouse abuse, however, is a broad topic, and many questions about abuse cannot be answered adequately by any method other than participant observation.

Let's suppose that your interest is in learning how spouse abuse affects wives. You may want to know if the abuse has changed their hopes and dreams. Or their ideas about men. Certainly it has affected their relationship with their husbands. And certainly their self-concept as well. But how? Participant observation can provide detailed insight into such questions.

Now let's go back to your campus again, assuming for the sake of argument that it has a crisis intervention center. Such a setting lends itself to participant observation, for

---

interviewer bias: effects that interviewers have on respondents that lead to biased answers

structured interviews: interviews that use closed-ended questions

closed-ended questions: questions followed by a list of possible answers to be selected by the respondent

unstructured interviews: interviews that use open-ended questions

open-ended questions: questions that respondents are able to answer in their own words

rapport: a feeling of trust between researchers and subjects

participant observation (or fieldwork): research in which the researcher *participates* in a research setting while *observing* what is happening in that setting

here you may be able to observe victims of spouse abuse from the time they first report the attack to their later participation in counseling. With good rapport, you may even be able to spend time with victims outside this setting, observing other aspects of their lives. Their statements and other behaviors may be the keys that help you unlock answers about how the abuse has affected their lives. This, in turn, might allow you to make suggestions about how to improve college counseling services.

As you may have noticed, the researcher's personal characteristics are extremely important in fieldwork. Their sex, age, race, personality, and even height and weight can affect their findings (Henslin 1990a). For example, could a male researcher conduct participant observation of women who have been beaten by their husbands? Technically, the answer is yes. But given the topic, which specifically centers on the emotions of women who have been brutally victimized by men, female sociologists are better suited to conduct such research, and thus more likely to achieve valid results. Here again, however, our commonsense suppositions regarding how likely these victims are to disclose information to men versus women are just that—suppositions. Research alone will verify or refute these assumptions.

Participant observers face a problem with **generalizability,** being able to apply their findings to larger populations. Most of their studies are exploratory, documenting in detail the experiences of people in a particular setting. Although such research suggests that other people who face similar situations react in similar ways, it is difficult to know just how far the findings apply beyond their original setting. The results of participant observation, however, can stimulate hypotheses and theories and be tested in other settings using other research techniques.

Sociologists who enter a research setting to discover information are following a research method known as participant observation. *As discussed in the text, sociologists also conduct research in controversial settings. Can you identify the sociologist in this photo?*

Because spouse abuse occurs between two people who have an intimate relationship, it often is considered a private matter. When the abuse occurs in public, however, it usually is seen in a different light.

generalizability: the extent to which the findings from one group (or sample) can be generalized or applied to other groups (or populations)

Sociologists use different methods of research to answer different questions. Among the methods that could be used to study spouse abuse is to examine the documents kept by shelters for battered women, which log the number of calls and visits made by victims.

secondary analysis: the analysis of data already collected by other researchers

documents: in its narrow sense, written sources that provide data; in its extended sense, archival material of any sort, including photographs, movies, and so on

unobtrusive measures: various ways of observing people who do not know they are being studied

causation: if a change in one variable leads to a change in another variable, causation is said to exist

correlation: the simultaneous occurrence of two or more variables

spurious correlation: the correlation of two variables actually caused by a third variable; there is no cause–effect relationship

experiment: the use of control groups and experimental groups and dependent and independent variables to test causation

Secondary Analysis

In **secondary analysis,** a third research method, researchers analyze data that have already been collected by others. For example, if you were to examine the original data from a study of women who have been abused by their husbands, you would be doing secondary analysis. Ordinarily, researchers prefer to gather their own data, but lack of resources, especially money, may make that impossible. In addition, existing data may contain a wealth of information that was not pertinent to the goals of the original researchers, which you can analyze for your own specific purposes.

Like the other methods, secondary analysis also poses its own problems. How can a researcher who did not carry out the research be sure that the data were systematically gathered, accurately recorded, and that biases were avoided? This problem plagues researchers who do secondary analysis, especially if the original data have been gathered by a team of researchers, not all of who were equally qualified.

Documents

The use of **documents,** written sources, is a fourth research method sociologists use. To investigate social life, they examine such diverse sources as books, newspapers, diaries, bank records, police reports, household accounts, immigration files, and records kept by various organizations.

To study spouse abuse, you might examine police reports and court records. These could reveal what proportion of complaints result in arrest and what proportion of the men arrested are charged, convicted, or even put on probation. If these were your questions, police statistics would be valuable.

But for other questions, those records would be useless. If you want to know about the social and emotional adjustment of victims, for example, those records would tell you little. Other documents, however, might lend themselves to answering this question. A crisis intervention center, for example, might have records that would provide key information. Diaries kept by abuse victims would yield important insights into their reactions, especially how their attitudes and relationships with others change over time. If you couldn't locate such diaries, you might contact victims and ask them to keep diaries. Again, an intervention center might help you in this research. Their personnel might ask clients to keep such diaries. To my knowledge, no sociologist has yet studied spouse abuse in this way.

Of course, I am presenting an ideal situation in which the crisis intervention center is opening its arms to you. In actual fact, the center might not cooperate at all, neither asking victims to keep diaries nor even letting you near its records. Access, then, is another problem researchers face constantly. Simply put, you can't study a topic unless you can gain access to it.

Unobtrusive Measures

The fifth method is **unobtrusive measures,** observing the behavior of people who do not know they are being studied. For example, social researchers studied the level of whisky consumption in a town that was officially "dry" by counting empty bottles in trash cans, and the degree of fear induced by ghost stories by measuring the shrinking diameter of a circle of seated children (Webb 1966). One of my graduate students studied gender differences by recording all the graffiti in every public rest room in two towns (Darnell 1971). Researchers have also gone high-tech in their unobtrusive measures. Some have outfitted shopping carts with infrared surveillance equipment. After tracing the customers' paths through a store and measuring their stops, retailers use their findings to change the location of their items (McCarthy 1993).

To use unobtrusive measures to study spouse abuse, we could go to a battered women's shelter. There we could secretly tape conversations among the women, as well as their telephone calls. Or we could use a one-way mirror to observe their interactions, and even videotape them. As may be obvious, although such unobtrusive measures may yield rich data, professional ethics would prohibit such a study.

Experiments

The sixth method, the **experiment,** is useful for determining cause and effect. Causation
has three necessary conditions, which are discussed in Table 5.3 below.

TABLE 5.3

Cause, Effect, and Spurious Correlations

In science, **causation** means that a change in one variable is due to another variable. Three conditions are necessary for causation: correlation, temporal priority, and no spurious correlation.
Let's apply each of these conditions to spouse abuse and alcohol abuse.

1. The first necessary condition is **correlation.**

   If two variables exist together, they are said to be correlated.
   If batterers have drunk alcohol, battering and alcohol abuse
   are correlated.

   Spouse Abuse ——————— Alcohol Abuse

   People sometimes assume that correlation is causation. In
   this instance, they conclude that alcohol abuse causes spouse
   abuse.

   Alcohol Abuse ——————→ Spouse Abuse

   But *correlation never proves causation. Either* variable could be
   the cause of the other. Perhaps battering pushes men into
   getting drunk.

   Spouse Abuse ——————→ Alcohol Abuse

2. The second necessary condition is *temporal priority* (one variable must occur before the other).

   Temporal priority means that one thing happens before something else does. For a variable to be a cause (the *independent*
   variable), it must *precede* that which is changed (the *dependent*
   variable). If the men had not drunk alcohol until after they
   had beaten their wives, obviously alcohol abuse could not be
   the cause of the abuse. Although the necessity of temporal
   priority is obvious, in many studies this is not easy to
   determine.

3. The third necessary condition is *no spurious correlation.*

   This is the necessary condition that really makes things difficult. Even if we identify correlation and can determine temporal priority, we still don't know that alcohol abuse is the
   cause. It is possible that we have a **spurious correlation;**
   that is, the cause may be some underlying third variable that
   is not easily visible. Some sociologists identify male culture
   as that underlying third variable.

   Male Culture ——————→ Spouse Abuse

   Socialized into dominance, some males learn to view women
   as objects on which to take out their frustration. In fact, this
   underlying third variable could be a cause of both spouse
   abuse and alcohol abuse.

   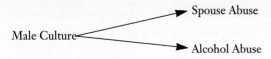
   Male Culture → Spouse Abuse / Alcohol Abuse

But since only some men beat their wives, while all males
are exposed to male culture, other variables must also be involved. Perhaps specific subcultures that promote violence
and denigrate women lead to both spouse abuse and alcohol
abuse.

Specific Subcultures → Spouse Abuse / Alcohol Abuse

   If so, this does *not* mean that it is the only causal variable, for spouse abuse probably has many causes. Unlike the
movement of amoebas or the action of heat on some object,
human behavior is infinitely complicated. What are especially important are people's *definitions of the situation,* including their views of right and wrong. To explain spouse
abuse, then, we need to add such variables as men's views
of violence and their definitions of the relative rights of
women and men. It is precisely to help unravel such com-
plicating factors in human behavior that we need the experimental method.

More on Correlations

Correlation simply means that two or more variables are present
together. The more often they are found together, the greater
the strength of their relationship. To indicate their strength,
sociologists use a number called a *correlation coefficient.* If two
variables are *always* related, that is, they are always present
together, they have what is called a *perfect positive correlation.*
The number 1.0 represents this correlation coefficient. Nature has some 1.0's, such as the lack of water and the death of
trees. 1.0's also apply to the human physical state, such as the
absence of nutrients and the absence of life. But social life is
much more complicated than physical conditions, and there
are no 1.0's in human behavior.

Two variables can also have a *perfect negative correlation.* This
means that when one variable is present, the other is always absent. The number –1.0 expresses this correlation coefficient.

Positive correlations of 0.1, 0.2, 0.3, and 0.4 mean that one
variable is associated with another only 1 time out of 10, 2
times out of 10, 3 times out of 10, and 4 times out of 10. In
other words, in most instances the first variable is *not* associated with the second, indicating a weak relationship.

The greater the correlation coefficient, the stronger the relationship. A strong relationship *may* indicate causation, but not
necessarily. Testing the relationship between variables is the
goal of some sociological research.

Let's suppose you develop the hypothesis that the consumption of alcohol creates attitudes that favor wife beating. You can conduct an experiment to test this hypothesis. Your **independent variable** (something that causes a change in another variable) would be alcohol consumption. Your **dependent variable** (the variable that is changed) would be attitudes toward spouse abuse.

Let's also suppose that you have access to a laboratory and to some male volunteers. You could randomly divide the men into two groups. The reason for doing this is that many of the men's characteristics will differ—their experiences, attitudes, perhaps even their "suggestibility." If you randomly divide the men—making certain that each man has an equal chance of becoming a member of either group—these unknown variables will be distributed between the groups.

As shown in Figure 5.2, your next step is to measure the dependent variable, the men's attitudes toward spouse abuse. In one group, called the **experimental group,** you introduce the independent variable; that is, you give them a specified amount of alcohol. The other men, the **control group,** are not exposed to the independent variable; that is, they are not given alcohol. You then measure the dependent variable (attitudes toward spouse abuse) again in both groups. In this way, you can assume that any changes in attitude in the experimental group can be attributed to the independent variable—the alcohol—which only that group received.

There always are unknown third variables that complicate experiments. That is why you randomly divide your subjects (the people being studied) into two groups. But these third variables are not necessarily distributed evenly among the groups. Because of this, you must *replicate* (repeat) your experiment with other groups of men. When you do this, you may wish to vary the amount of alcohol to see if there is a threshold effect; that is, alcohol may affect the men's attitudes only after a certain amount has been consumed.

Sometimes experiments are not conducted this rigorously, which increases the likelihood that variables will be confused. As described in the Down-to-Earth Sociology box on the next page, in the 1920s Elton Mayo did a set of famous experiments that uncovered a surprising third variable.

Sociologists seldom use this classic method of the natural sciences, because most sociologists are interested in broad features of society and social behavior, or they are interested in the actual workings of some group in a natural setting. Neither of these interests lends itself well to an experiment. We could devise experiments to study spouse abuse, however, and perhaps come up with some that might prove beneficial for society. For example, the independent variable could be therapy.

independent variable: a factor that causes a change in another variable, called the dependent variable

dependent variable: a factor that is changed by an independent variable

experimental group: the group of subjects exposed to the independent variable

control group: the group of subjects not exposed to the independent variable

Figure 5.2

The Experiment

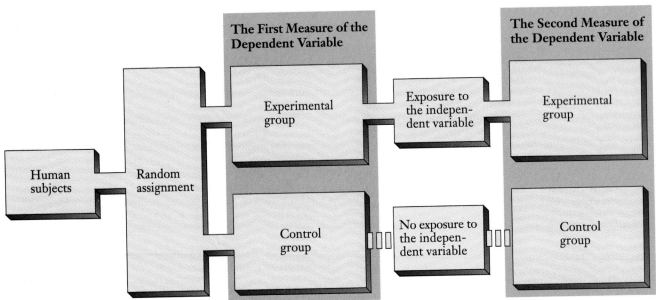

Down-to-Earth Sociology

The Hawthorne Experiments

Research from the 1920s, known as the Hawthorne experiments, became a classic in sociology. This research drives home how necessary it is to accurately identify independent and dependent variables.

The managers of the Hawthorne plant of the Western Electric Company near Chicago wanted to know how different levels of lighting would affect productivity. Several groups of women participated in what are known as the Relay Room Experiments. In the control room, the level of lighting was held constant, while in the experimental room the lighting was varied. To everyone's surprise, output increased in *both* locations. In the experimental room, productivity remained high even when the lights were dimmed to about the level of moonlight—so low that workers could barely see what they were doing!

To solve this mystery, management called in a team of researchers headed by Elton Mayo of the University of Chicago. This team tested thirteen different work conditions. When they changed the workers' pay from hourly wages to piecework, productivity increased. When they served refreshments, output again went up. When they added two 5-minute rest periods, productivity jumped. When they changed the rest periods to two 10-minute periods, again output increased. When they let the workers go home early, they found the same result. Confused, the researchers restored the original conditions, offering none of these added benefits. The result? Even higher productivity.

The situation grew even more confusing when men were observed in what is known as the Bank Wiring Room Study. Here, the researchers did not change the work conditions at all. They simply observed the men while they worked and interviewed them after work. Instead of there being no change in productivity, as might have been expected, productivity *dropped*.

None of this made sense. Finally, Mayo concluded that the results were due to the research itself. The women, aware that they were being studied and pleased at the attention paid to them, responded by increasing their efforts. The men, in contrast, were suspicious about why the researchers were observing them. They feared that if they had higher productivity, they would be expected to produce more each day, or that higher productivity might even cost some of them their jobs. Consequently, they decreased their output.

The Hawthorne research is important—not for its findings on worker productivity, but for what it revealed about the research process itself. Today, researchers carefully monitor the *Hawthorne effect*, the change in behavior that occurs when people know they are being studied.

Sources: Based on Roethlisberger and Dickson 1939; Mayo 1966; Baron and Greenberg 1990.

We could randomly assign abusers to experimental and control groups to help assure that their individual characteristics (attitudes, number of arrests, length of abuse, severity of abuse, education, race, age, and so on) would be distributed evenly between the groups. Then we could arrange for the experimental group to receive some form of therapy. The control group would not receive therapy. If there are any changes in abuse (the dependent variable) in the experimental group, we would then assume that the change is due to the therapy (the independent variable). We would hope that the abuse decreases, but, instead, it could *increase*. If so, we also would assume that the therapy was the cause.

If we were to conduct such an experiment, ideally we would want to test different types of therapy. We might even want to test self-therapy—reading articles and books and watching videos. Frankly, no one yet knows how to change a wife abuser into a loving husband, and such experiments are badly needed.

Deciding Which Method to Use

How do sociologists choose from among these methods? Four primary factors affect their choice. First, resources are crucial. Sociologists must match methods to available resources. For example, although they may want to conduct a survey, they may find that finances will not permit it, and instead they turn to the study of documents. The second significant factor is access to subjects. If people in a sample live in remote parts of the country, researchers may have to mail them questionnaires or conduct a telephone survey even if they would prefer face-to-face interviews. The third factor concerns the purpose of the research, the questions that the sociologist wishes to answer. Each method is better for answering some questions than for others. Participant observation, for example, is a good method for uncovering people's real attitudes, while experiments work better for resolving questions of cause and effect. Fourth, the researcher's background or training comes into play. In graduate school, sociologists study many methods but are able to practice only some of them. Consequently, after graduate school they generally use the methods in which they have had the most training.

Thus, sociologists who have been trained in **quantitative research methods,** which emphasize measurement, numbers, and statistics, are likely to use surveys. Sociologists who have been trained in **qualitative research methods,** which emphasize describing, observing, and interpreting people's behavior, lean toward participant observation. In the Down-to-Earth Sociology box below, you can see how a combination of quantitative and qualitative methods is used in applied sociology. The Thinking Critically section on the next page illustrates how significant the choice of research method is, and how sociologists can find themselves in the midst of controversy for applying rigorous research methods.

quantitative research methods: research in which the emphasis is placed on precise measurement, the use of statistics and numbers

qualitative research methods: research in which the emphasis is placed on observing, describing, and interpreting people's behavior

Down-to-Earth Sociology

Applied Sociology: Marketing Research as a Blend of Quantitative and Qualitative Methods

If a company is going to survive in the highly competitive business world, it must figure out what consumers need and want, and then supply it—or else convince people that what they need or want is what the company already is producing.

What Marketing Research Is

To increase sales, manufacturers try to improve the "position" of their products. "Position" is marketing jargon for how customers think about a product.

This is where marketing researchers come into play. They find out what customers think they want, how they select and use products, and what images they hold of a product or service. They also assess how receptive the public will be to a new product or to a change in an established product.

To do this, marketing researchers use a combination of qualitative and quantitative techniques. They use qualitative methods both as a prelude to survey research and as a "stand-alone" technique. An example is "focus groups," groups of about ten people who have been invited to discuss a product. A moderator leads a discussion before a one-way mirror, where other team members observe or videotape the session. To control for regional variations, other focus groups may be held at the same time in other cities. Sociologist Roger Straus points out that his training in symbolic interactionism is especially useful for interpreting these results.

Marketing researchers also use quantitative techniques. For example, they may conduct surveys to determine what the public thinks of a new product. They also gather sales data from the "bar codes" found on almost all products. They use statistics to analyze the data and prepare tables and graphics that summarize the findings for clients.

A Sociological Controversy

This summary would not be complete unless I point out a problem with the status of marketing research in sociology. Most of the results of marketing research are proprietary (owned by the client) and are therefore confidential. This means that the findings do not appear in sociology journals and are not used to create social theory. In addition, clients usually are interested only in specific marketing problems and seldom commission research on important social issues. For such reasons, many sociologists do not consider marketing research a "legitimate" sociological activity. Some even scorn marketing researchers as wasting their sociological talents. They chide them for having "sold out," for using sociological methods to help corporations exploit the public by convincing them to purchase unneeded goods and services.

Marketing researchers, of course, do not see things this way. They argue that marketing research is a neutral activity, and they do more than just help sell beer and soft drinks. Advocates point out that marketing research has been used to help colleges attract students and communities assess public needs. They argue that the decision to do sociological research on any topic must be based on the researcher's own values. This applies to studying how to reduce juvenile delinquency as well as to how to sell a particular product. It is unreasonable, they say, for anyone to pass judgment on marketing research—as though other research were morally superior.

Sources: Based on Straus 1991 and communication with Straus 1993.

Thinking Critically About Social Controversy

Doing Controversial Research— Counting the Homeless

▼ What could be simpler, or more inoffensive, than counting the homeless? As sometimes happens, however, even basic research lands sociologists in the midst of controversy. This is what happened to sociologist Peter Rossi and his associates.

It happened this way. There was a dispute between advocates for the homeless and the federal government. The advocates said that there were 3 to 7 million Americans homeless, while the government said there was about one-twelfth to one–twenty-eighth this number, only about a quarter of a million. Each side accused the other of gross distortion—the one to place undue pressure on Congress, the other to keep the public from knowing how bad the situation really was.

Only an accurate count could clear up the picture, for both sides were only guessing at the numbers. Peter Rossi and the National Opinion Research Center decided to carry out an accurate count. They had no vested interest in supporting one side or the other, only in answering this question honestly.

The challenge was immense. The *population* was evident, America's homeless. A *survey* would be appropriate, but how do you survey a *sample* of this population? No federal, state, county, or city has a list of the homeless, and only some of the homeless stay at shelters. As for *validity*, to make certain that they were counting only people who were really homeless, the researchers needed a good *operational definition* of homelessness. To include people who weren't really homeless would destroy the study's *reliability*. The researchers wanted results that would be consistent if others were to *replicate*, or repeat, the study.

As an operational definition, the researchers used "literally homeless," people "who do not have access to a conventional dwelling and who would be homeless by any conceivable definition of the term." Because a national count would cost about $6 million, far beyond their resources, the researchers decided to count just the homeless in Chicago. By using a *stratified random sample*, they were able to *generalize* to the entire country. The cost was still high, however—about $600,000.

To generalize about the homeless who sleep in shelters, the researchers used a stratified random sample of the city's shelters. For the homeless who sleep in the streets, vacant buildings, and so forth, they used a stratified random sample of the city's blocks. To make doubly certain that their count was accurate, the researchers conducted two surveys. At night, trained teams visited the shelters and searched the alleys, bridges, and vacant houses.

Many found the results startling. On an average night, Chicago has 2,722 homeless people. Because people move in and out of homelessness, between 5,000 and 7,000 are homeless at some point during the year. On warm nights, only two out of five sleep in the shelters, and even in winter only three out of four do so. The median age is 40; 75 percent are men, and 60 percent are African Americans. One in four is a former mental patient, one in five a former prisoner. A homeless person's income from all sources is less than $6 a day. Projecting these findings to the entire nation results in a national figure of about 350,000 homeless people.

The reactions were predictable. While government officials rubbed their hands in glee, stunned homeless advocates began a sniping campaign, denying the findings.

Remember that Rossi and his associates had no interest in proving which side in the debate was right, only in getting reliable figures. Using impeccable methods, this they did.

The researchers had no intention of minimizing the problem of homelessness. They stressed that several hundred thousand Americans are so poor that they slip through the welfare system, sleep in city streets, live in shelters, eat out of garbage cans, are malnourished, and suffer from severe health problems. In short, these people live hopeless, despairing lives.

It is good to *know* how many Americans are homeless. Guesses aren't worth much. Even though the number is far less than what the homeless advocates had estimated, this information can still serve their cause: Since there are fewer homeless people than many had thought, it makes the problem more manageable. It means that if we choose to do so, we can put our resources to work with greater certainty of success.

Nevertheless, as in this instance, people whose positions are not supported by research are not pleased, and they tend to take potshots at the researchers. This, of course, is one of the risks of doing sociological research, for sociologists never know whose toes they will step on.

Sources: Based on Anderson 1986; Rossi et al. 1986; Rossi et al. 1987; Coughlin 1988; Rossi 1989; Rossi 1991; De Parle 1994. ▲

As discussed on this page, research sometimes lands sociologists in the midst of controversy. An example is a study conducted to determine the number of homeless people there are in the United States. Homeless advocates were not pleased with the results.

Ethics in social research are of vital concern to all sociologists. As discussed in the text, sociologists may disagree on some of the issue's finer points, but none would approve of slipping LSD to unsuspecting subjects just "to see what would happen," as was done to U.S. servicemen in the 1960s under the guise of legitimate testing.

Ethics in Sociological Research

In addition to choosing an appropriate research method, sociologists must also bear in mind the matter of ethics. Sociologists cannot do just any type of research that they might desire. Their research must meet their profession's ethical criteria, which center on basic assumptions of science and morality (American Sociological Association 1997). Research ethics require openness (sharing findings with the scientific community), honesty, and truth. Ethics clearly forbid the falsification of results, as well as plagiarism—that is, stealing someone else's work. Another basic ethical guideline is that research subjects should not be harmed by the research. Ethics also require that sociologists protect the anonymity of people who provide information, which sometimes is intimate, potentially embarrassing, or otherwise harmful to them. Finally, although not all sociologists are in agreement about this, it generally is considered unethical for researchers to misrepresent themselves.

Sociologists take these ethical criteria seriously. To illustrate the extent to which they will go to protect their respondents, consider the research conducted by Mario Brajuha and Rik Scarce.

The Brajuha Research

Mario Brajuha, a graduate student at the State University of New York at Stony Brook, was doing participant observation of restaurant work (Brajuha and Hallowell 1986). He lost his job as a waiter when the restaurant where he was working burned down. The fire turned out to be of "suspicious origin," and during their investigation detectives learned that Brajuha had taken field notes. They asked to see them. When Brajuha refused, the district attorney subpoenaed the notes. Brajuha still refused to hand them over. The district attorney then threatened to send Brajuha to jail. By this time, Brajuha's notes had become rather famous, and unsavory characters, perhaps those who had set the fire, also began to wonder what was in them. They, too, demanded to see them—accompanying their demands with threats of a different nature. Brajuha unexpectedly found himself in a very disturbing double bind.

For two years Brajuha refused to hand over his notes, even though he had to appear at numerous court hearings and became filled with anxiety. Finally, the district attorney dropped the subpoena. When the two men under investigation for setting the fire died, so did the threats to Brajuha, his wife, and his children.

The Scarce Research

In 1991, a group calling itself the Animal Liberation Front broke into a research facility at Washington State University, released animals, and damaged computers and files. Rik Scarce, a doctoral student in sociology at the university who was doing research on radical environmental groups, was summoned before a federal grand jury investigating the break-in. Scarce was not a suspect, but law enforcement officers thought that during his research Scarce might have come across information that would help lead them to the guilty parties.

Scarce answered scores of questions about himself and topics related to the raid, but he refused to answer questions that would violate his agreements of confidentiality with research subjects. He cited the American Sociological Association's Code of Ethics:

> Confidential information provided by research participants must be treated as such by sociologists, even when this information enjoys no legal protection or privilege and legal force is applied. (1989 version)

A federal judge did not agree, and put Scarce in the Spokane County Jail for contempt of court. Although Scarce could have obtained his freedom at any time simply by testifying, he maintained his laudable ethical stance and continued to refuse, in his words, "to be bludgeoned into becoming an agent of the state." Scarce served 159 days in jail. The longest any scholar before this had been held in contempt was one week (Scarce 1993a, 1993b, 1994).

The Humphreys Research

Sociologists agree on the necessity to protect respondents, and they applaud the professional manner in which Brajuha and Scarce handled themselves. There is less agreement, however, that researchers not misrepresent themselves, and sociologists who violate this norm can become embroiled in ethical controversy. Let's look at the case of Laud Humphreys, whose research forced sociologists to rethink and refine their ethical stance.

Laud Humphreys, a classmate of mine at Washington University in St. Louis, was an Episcopal priest who decided to become a sociologist. For his Ph.D. dissertation, Humphreys (1970, 1971, 1975) decided to study social interaction in "tearooms," public rest rooms where some men go for quick, anonymous oral sex with other men.

Humphreys found that some rest rooms in Forest Park, just across from our campus, were tearooms. He first did participant observation, just hanging around these rest rooms. He found that in addition to the two having sex, a third person—called a "watchqueen"—served as a lookout for police and other unwelcome strangers. Humphreys then took the role of watchqueen, watching not only for strangers but also watching what the men did. He systematically recorded these encounters, and they became part of his dissertation.

Humphreys became curious about the regular lives of these men. Impersonal sex in tearooms was a fleeting encounter, and the men must spend most of their time doing other things. What things? With whom? And what was the significance of the wedding rings that he saw on many of the men? Humphreys then hit on an ingenious technique. After observing an encounter, he would leave the rest room and record the license number of the man's car. Through the help of a friend in the St. Louis police department, Humphreys then obtained each man's address. About a year later, Humphreys arranged for these men to be included in a medical survey conducted by some of the sociologists on our faculty. Disguising himself with a different hairstyle and clothing, and driving a different car, he visited these men at their homes. He then interviewed them, supposedly for the medical study.

Humphreys said that no one recognized him—and he did obtain the information he was looking for: family background, education, income, health, religion, and even their relationship with wife and children. He found that most of the men were in their mid-thirties and had at least some college education. Surprisingly, the majority were married, and a higher proportion than in the general population turned out to be Roman Catholic. Moreover, these men led very conventional lives. They voted, mowed their lawns, and took their kids to Little League games.

Humphreys also found that although most of the men were committed to their wives and families, their sex life was far from satisfactory. Many reported that their wives were not aroused sexually or were afraid of getting pregnant because their religion did not allow them to use birth control. Humphreys concluded that these were heterosexual men who were using the tearooms for an alternative form of sex, which, unlike affairs, was quick (taking no time away from their families), inexpensive (zero cost), and nonthreatening (the encounter required no emotional involvement to compete with their wives). If a wife had discovered her husband's secret sex life, of course, she would have been devastated. And today's tearoom encounters present a much more ominous threat, for Humphreys conducted his research before the arrival of AIDS. Anyone participating in tearooms today risks death—both for himself and, by transmitting AIDS, also for his sexual partners, wife included.

This study stirred controversy among sociologists and nonsociologists alike (Goodwin et al. 1991). Humphreys was severely criticized by many sociologists, and a national columnist even wrote a scathing denunciation of "sociological snoopers" (Von Hoffman 1970). Concerned about protecting the identity of his respondents, Humphreys placed his master list in a safe deposit box. As the controversy grew more heated, however, he feared that the names might be subpoenaed (a court case was being threatened). He then gave me a list to take from Missouri to Illinois, where I had begun teaching. (It could have been some other list of respondents. I was told not to examine it, and I did not.) When he called and asked me to destroy it, I burned it in my backyard. Humphreys had a contract to remain at Washington University as an assistant professor, but he was fired before he could begin teaching. (Although other reasons were involved, his research was a central issue. There was even an attempt by one professor to have his doctorate revoked.)

Was this research ethical? That question is not easily decided. Although many sociologists sided with Humphreys and his book reporting the research won a highly acclaimed award, the criticisms mounted. At first Humphreys vigorously defended his position, but five years later, in a second edition of his book (1975), he stated that he should have identified himself as a researcher.

How Research and Theory Work Together

As discussed, sociological research is based on the sociologist's interests, access to subjects, appropriate methods, and ethical considerations. But the value of research is also related to sociological theory. On the one hand, as sociologist C. Wright Mills (1959) so forcefully argued in a classic book, research without theory is of little value, simply a collection of unrelated "facts." On the other hand, theory that is unconnected to research is abstract and empty, unlikely to represent the way life really is.

Research and theory are both essential for sociology. Every theory that sociologists develop must be tested. Thus theory stimulates research. And as sociologists do research, they often come up with surprising findings. Those findings, in turn, stimulate the development of theory to explain them. Such findings also may stimulate more research, for they may indicate that different samples or better operational variables are necessary. As sociologists study social life, then, they combine research and theory.

The Real World: When the Ideal Meets the Real

Although one can list the ideals of research, real-life situations often force sociologists to settle for something that falls short of the ideal. Let's look at how two sociologists confronted the ideal and the real in the following Thinking Critically section.

Thinking Critically About Social Controversy

Are Rapists Sick? A Close-up View of Research

▼ Two sociologists, Diana Scully and Joseph Marolla, were not satisfied with the typical explanation that rapists are "sick," psychologically disturbed, or different from other men. They developed the hypothesis that rape, like most behavior, is learned through interaction with others. That is, some men learn to think of rape as appropriate behavior.

To test this hypothesis, Scully and Marolla would have liked to interview a random sample of rapists. But this was impossible, for there is no list of rapists, to give them all the same chance of being included in a sample. You can't even use prison populations to produce a random sample, for many rapists have never been caught, some who were caught were found not guilty, and some who were found guilty were given probation. Consequently, Scully and Marolla confronted the classic dilemma of sociologists—to either not do the study or to do so under less than ideal conditions.

They chose to do the study. They knew that whatever they learned would be more than we already knew, and when they had the opportunity to interview convicted rapists in prison, they jumped at it. They sent out 3,500 letters to men serving time in seven prisons in Virginia, the state where they were teaching. About 25 percent of the prisoners agreed to be interviewed. They matched these men on the basis of age, education, race, severity of offense, and previous criminal record. This resulted in a sample of 98 prisoners who were convicted for rape and a control sample of 75 nonrapists, men convicted for other offenses.

To prevent biases that might result from the sex of the interviewer, Marolla and Scully each interviewed half the sample. It took them 600 hours to gather information on the prisoners, including their psychological, criminal, and sexual history. To guard against lies, they did what is called a "validity check"; in this case, they checked what the individuals said against their institutional record. They used twelve scales to measure the men's attitudes about women, rape, and themselves. They also presented nine vignettes of forced sexual encounters to measure the circumstances under which the men defined a situation as rape or viewed the victim as responsible.

Scully and Marolla discovered something that goes against common sense—that most rapists are not sick, that they are not overwhelmed by uncontrollable urges. They found that the psychological histories of the rapists and the nonrapists were similar. Rapists, they concluded, are emotionally average men who have learned to view rape as appropriate in various situations. Some rape spontaneously, while others plan their rapes. Some even rape with friends on a regular basis, such as on weekends, using rape as a form of recreation. Others use rape as a form of revenge, to get even with someone, not necessarily the woman.

Scully and Marolla also found support for what feminists had been pointing out for years, that power was a major element in rape. Here is what one man said:

> Rape gave me the power to do what I wanted to do without feeling I had to please a partner or respond to a partner. I felt in control, dominant. Rape was the ability to have sex without caring about the woman's response. I was totally dominant.

To discover that most rape is calculated behavior—that rapists are not "sick," that the motivating force is power not passion, the criminal pursuit of pleasure not mental illness—is extremely significant. It makes the sociological quest worthwhile.

In comparing their sample of rapists with their control group of nonrapists, Scully and Marolla also found something else very significant. The rapists are more likely to believe "rape myths." They are more likely to believe that women cause their own rape by the way they act and the clothes they wear, that a woman who charges rape has simply changed her mind after voluntary sex, and that most men accused of rape are innocent.

Connecting Research and Theory

Such findings go far beyond simply adding to our storehouse of "facts." As indicated in Figure 5.1 on page 121, research stimulates both the development of theory and the need for more research. Scully and Marolla suggest that rape myths act as neutralizers, that they allow "potential rapists to turn off social prohibitions against injuring others."

This hypothesis, in turn, pinpoints the need to determine how such myths are transmitted. In which male subcultures do they exist? Do the mass media contribute to these myths? Do family, religion, and education create respect for females and help keep males from learning such myths? Or do they somehow contribute to them? If so, how?

At some point sociologists will build on this path-breaking research—done, as usual, under less than ideal conditions. The resulting theorizing and research may provide the basis for making changes that reduce rape in U.S. society.

Sources: Scully and Marolla 1984, 1985; Marolla and Scully 1986; Scully 1990; Foley et al. 1995.

This is exactly what sociology needs more of—imaginative, and sometimes daring, research conducted in an imperfect world under less than ideal conditions. This is really what sociology is all about. Sociologists study what people do—whether those behaviors are conforming or deviant, whether they are pleasing to others or disgust them and arouse intense anger. No matter the behavior studied, systematic research methods and the application of social theory take us beyond common sense. They allow us to penetrate surface realities so we can better understand human behavior—and, in the ideal case, to make changes to help improve social life.

Summary and Review

What Is a Valid Sociological Topic?

Any human behavior is a valid sociological topic, even disreputable behavior. Spouse abuse is an example. Sociological research is based on the sociologist's interests, access to subjects, appropriate methods, and ethical considerations. P. 120.

Common Sense and the Need for Sociological Research

Why isn't common sense adequate?

Common sense does not provide reliable knowledge. When subjected to scientific research methods, commonsense ideas often are found to be very limited or false. Pp. 120–121.

A Research Model

What are the eight basic steps of scientific research?

1. Selecting a topic
2. Defining the problem
3. Reviewing the literature
4. Formulating a hypothesis
5. Choosing a research method
6. Collecting the data
7. Analyzing the results
8. Sharing the results

These steps are explained in detail on pp. 121–124.

Six Research Methods

How do sociologists gather data?

Sociologists use six research methods (or research designs) for gathering data: surveys, participant observation, secondary analysis, documents, unobtrusive measures, and experiments. Pp. 124–133.

How do sociologists choose a particular research method?

Sociologists choose their research method on the basis of the research questions to be answered, their access to potential subjects, the resources available, their training, and ethical considerations. Pp. 133–134.

Ethics in Sociological Research

How important are ethics in sociological research?

Ethics are of fundamental concern to sociologists, who are committed to openness, honesty, truth, and protecting their subjects from harm. The Brajuha research on restaurants, the Scarce research on the environmental movement, and the Humphreys research on "tearooms" were cited to illustrate ethical issues of concern to sociologists. Pp. 136–138.

How Research and Theory Work Together

What is the relationship between theory and research?

Theory and research are interdependent. Sociologists use theory to interpret the data they gather. Theory also helps to generate research, while research, in turn, helps to generate theory. Theory without research is not likely to represent real life, while research without theory is merely a collection of unconnected facts. P. 138.

What happens when the ideal meets the real?

As illustrated by the Scully-Marolla research on rapists in prison, real-life situations often force sociologists to conduct research under less than ideal conditions. Although conducted in an imperfect world, social research stimulates sociological theory, more research, and the potential of improving human life. Pp. 138–140.

Where can I read more on this topic?

Suggested readings for this chapter are listed on page 660.

Sociology and the Internet

All URLs listed are current as of the printing of this book. URLs are often changed. Please check our Website http://www.abacon.com/henslin for updates.

1. In this exercise, we shall use secondary analysis of census data to construct a table. Go to the 1990 Census Lookup page at *http://www.census.gov/cdrom/lookup* Select the database "STF3C–Part 1." At the Choose an Option page, click *Submit.* At the Data Retrieval Option page, click *Submit.* At the page headed "Select the tables you wish to retrieve," page down to "P70—Sex By Employment Status" and click on the *square* in front of the entry. Then go to the top of the page and click *Submit.* At the next Data Retrieval Option page click on *Submit.* You should see a table that shows the employment status of males and females. Depending on your Web browser, you can either save the table or print it. (Netscape will allow both.) Use these data to construct a table. Apply the concepts presented in Table 5.1, "How to Read a Table" (page 124). Your instructor may ask you to use different census data, and to figure percentages to enter into your table. Be sure to include all of the elements in a typical table when you prepare your final version.

2. Examine the Protecting Human Subjects site at *http://www.er.doe.gov/production/ober/humsubj/index.html* Who is responsible for the welfare of human subjects in research? What federal regulations govern the protection of human subjects? When is it permissable to deceive research participants? Which is more important, the research or the welfare of the research subjects? Why? Examine the "Educational Information and Resources." What is informed consent? Why is it necessary to gain informed consent from human subjects before proceeding with social research?

3. Go to *http://www.softsolutions.com/survey/* and examine the survey on Sexuality Across the Lifespan, conducted by the department of psychology at the University of Utah. From the information presented on this Web page, can you tell how the sample was selected? What was the target population? What kind of questions were asked? Are the questions neutral? Which questions are open-ended and which are closed? How was the questionnaire administered?

Helen Hardin, Chief Robes, 1968

6

Societies to Social Networks

*J*OHNNY SMILED AS HIS FINGER *tightened on the trigger. The explosion was pure pleasure to his ears. His eyes glistened as the bullet ripped into the dog. With an ex- aggerated swagger, Johnny walked away, surrounded by five buddies, all wearing Levis, Air Jordans, and jackets emblazoned with the logo of Satan's Servants.*

Johnny had never felt as if he belonged. His parents were never home much, and when they were, all they did was have one drunken quarrel after another. Many times he had hud- dled in a corner while the police separated his parents, who were threatening to kill each other. One of Johnny's recurring memories was of his handcuffed father being taken away in a po- lice cruiser. School was a hassle, too, for he felt that the teachers were out to get him and that most of his classmates were jerks. It wasn't unusual for Johnny to spend most of his time in detention for disrupting classes and fighting during lunch period.

Johnny didn't want to be a loner, but that seemed to be what fate held in store. He once tried a church group, but that lasted just one meeting. He was lousy at rollerblading and had given that up after the guys laughed at him. It was the same with baseball and other sports.

But Satan's Servants—now, that was different. For the first time in his life, Johnny felt welcome—even appreciated. All the guys got in trouble in school, and none of them got along with their parents. He especially liked the jackets, with the skull and crossbones and "Satan's Servants" emblazoned on the back. And finally, with the "Satan's Servettes," there were girls who looked up to him.

The shooting assured Johnny, now known as J.B., of a firm place in the group. The old man wouldn't bother them anymore. He'd get the message when he found his dog.

When they returned to the abandoned building, which served as their headquarters, Johnny had never felt so good in his entire life. This was what life was all about. "There isn't anything I wouldn't do for these guys," he thought, as they gathered around him and took turns pointing the pistol.

Social Groups and Societies

Groups are the essence of life in society. Workers in a corporation form a group, as do neighbors on a block. The family is a group, as is the Los Angeles Lakers basketball team. The groups to which we belong help to determine our goals and values, how we feel about ourselves, and even how we feel about life itself. Groups can ignite a sense of pur- pose in life—or extinguish even the spark that makes life seem worthwhile. Just as Johnny found a sense of belonging in Satan's Servants, others find the same in the Scouts, in church and synagogue, in sports, in the family, at work.

Sociologists define **group** in many different ways. Albion Small (1905), mentioned in Chapter 1 as an early North American sociologist, used this term in a very broad sense to mean people who have some sort of relationship so that they are thought of together. Sociologists Michael Olmsted and Paul Hare (1978) point out that the "essential feature of a group is that its members have something in common and that they believe what they have in common makes a difference." This is our general definition of group, and more specific types of groups are defined later as they are introduced.

The largest and most complex group that sociologists study is **society,** which consists of people who share a culture and a territory. The values, beliefs, and cultural character- istics of a society profoundly affect the smaller groups within it. In the former Soviet Union, for example, underground artists formed hundreds of groups, all of which shared opposition to the Soviet state. The members of one art movement, called "Apartment Art," visually depicted how stifling life was for the millions of Russians forced to live sev- eral families or more to one apartment. Not knowing if your friend or roommate was a government spy engendered paranoia and unhappiness.

group: defined differently by various sociologists, but in a general sense, people who have something in common and who believe that what they have in common is significant; also called a social group

society: people who share a culture and a territory

144

As a society—the largest and most complex type of group—changes, so, too, do the groups, activities, and ultimately the types of people that form that society. The local garage used to be a central meeting place for men. Women felt unwelcome in this "men's territory" and stayed away as men conducted "their" business. The owner and workers would often stop work during the day to swap stories with friends and customers, as shown in this Norman Rockwell painting of a soldier's return from World War II. Our more impersonal Gesellschaft *society, with its emphasis on "putting out work" at a huge charge per hour, makes such scenes a rarity.*

The collapse of the Communist government responsible for the spying removed the impetus for the formation of these groups. Soviet artists now interpret other problematic features of national life—from inflation to other uncertainties of life brought about by their new capitalism. Similarly, thousands of other groups in the former Soviet Union are changing as they adapt to the new conditions of their society. *As any society changes, then, so do the nature and types of its groups.*

Later on, we shall focus on groups in industrialized societies, but first let's examine how contemporary society came into being. For example, how did the United States become an industrialized nation with literally millions of groups?

The Transformation of Societies ▶

To better understand this envelope that surrounds us and sets the stage on which we grow up, let's trace the development of societies from their earliest beginnings. As we review this evolution, portrayed in Figure 6.1 on the next page, picture yourself as a member of each society, and consider how each would have changed your life. In a hunting and gathering society, for example, your group membership would depend solely on your age, gender, and family—and you would see life primarily in these terms. Compare this with the many groups to which you belong—which impart a much more complicated identity. In short, the patterns we are going to review are significant because they underlie our basic orientations to life.

Hunting and Gathering Societies

Societies with the simplest organization are called **hunting and gathering societies.** As the name implies, these groups depend on hunting and gathering for their survival. In some, the men do the hunting (of animals), the females the gathering (of plants). In others, both men and women (and children) gather, men hunt the large animals, and both men and women hunt small animals. Beyond this basic division of labor by sex, there are few social divisions. The groups usually have a **shaman,** or priest, but they, too, must help obtain food. Although these groups give greater prestige to the male hunters, the women gatherers contribute much more food to the group, perhaps even four-fifths of their total food (Bernard 1992).

hunting and gathering society: a human group dependent on hunting and gathering for its survival

shaman: a priest in a preliterate society

Figure 6.1

The Social Transformations of Society

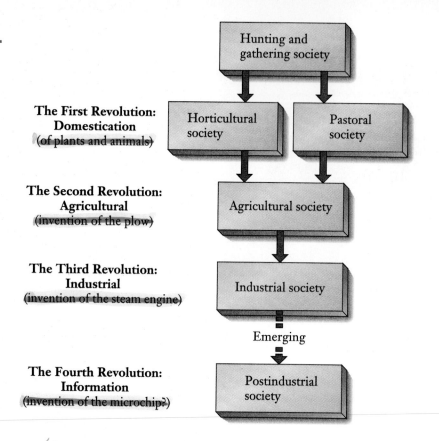

Hunting and gathering society

The First Revolution: Domestication
(of plants and animals)

Horticultural society

Pastoral society

The Second Revolution: Agricultural
(invention of the plow)

Agricultural society

The Third Revolution: Industrial
(invention of the steam engine)

Industrial society

Emerging

The Fourth Revolution: Information
(invention of the microchip?)

Postindustrial society

The simplest societies are called hunting and gathering societies. The members of these societies have adapted well to their environments. They have the most leisure of people in any type of society. The man shown here is a member of a hunting and gathering society in the Brazilian Amazon.

In addition to gender, the major unit of organization is the family. Most members are related by ancestry or marriage. Because the family is the only distinct social institution in these societies, it fulfills functions that are divided among many specialized institutions in modern societies. The family distributes food to its members, educates its children (especially in food skills), nurses the sick, and so on.

Because an area cannot support a large number of people who hunt animals and gather plants (they do not plant, only gather what is already there), hunting and gathering societies are small, usually consisting of only twenty-five to forty members. They are also nomadic, moving from one place to another as the food supply of an area gives out. These groups are usually peaceful and place high value on sharing food, which is essential to their survival. The high risk of destruction of the food supply, however—by disease, drought, famine, and pestilence—makes their death rate very high. Members of hunting and gathering groups have only about a fifty–fifty chance of surviving childhood (Lenski and Lenski 1987).

Of all societies, hunters and gatherers are the most egalitarian. Because what the people hunt and gather is perishable, they can't accumulate possessions. Consequently, no one becomes wealthier than anyone else. There are no rulers, and most decisions are arrived at through discussion. Because their needs are simple and they do not accumulate material possessions, hunters and gatherers also have the most leisure of all human groups (Sahlins 1972; Lorber 1994; Volti 1995).

All human groups were once hunters and gatherers, and until several hundred years ago such societies were still fairly common. Now, however, only a few remain, such as the pygmies of central Africa, the San of the Namibian desert, and the aborigines of Australia. Their demise came because modern societies took over the areas on which these groups depended for their food. The few remaining hunting and gathering societies, doomed to a similar fate, will soon disappear from the human scene (Lenski and Lenski 1987).

Pastoral and Horticultural Societies

About ten thousand to twelve thousand years ago, some groups found that they could tame and breed some of the animals they hunted—primarily goats, sheep, cattle, and

146

As stressed in the text, the type of society in which we live shapes us into the types of people we become. This includes the way we think and how we relate to one another. This 1622 painting by Pieter Brueghel (1564–1638), entitled "Sommer," depicts the pastoral society in which he lived. The limitations on activity and even on thought may be apparent, but this principle applies no less to our society. You might also note that the idea of women working for economic survival is the historical norm.

camels. Others discovered that they could cultivate plants. As a result, hunting and gathering societies branched in one of two directions.

The key to understanding the first branching is the word *pasture;* **pastoral societies** are based on the *pasturing of animals.* Pastoral societies developed in arid regions, where lack of rainfall made it impractical to build life around crops. Groups that took this turn remained nomadic, for they followed their animals to fresh pasture. The key to understanding the second branching is *horticulture,* or plant cultivation. **Horticultural societies** are based on the *cultivation of plants by the use of hand tools.* No longer having to abandon an area as the food supply gave out, these groups developed permanent settlements.

We can call the domestication of animals and plants the *first social revolution.* Although the **domestication revolution** was extremely gradual, it represented a fundamental break with the past and changed human history.

Horticulture apparently first began in the fertile areas of the Middle East. Primitive agricultural technology—hoes and digging sticks (to punch holes in the ground for seeds)—gradually spread to Europe and China. Apparently these techniques were independently invented in Central and South America, although they may have arrived there through *cultural diffusion* (the spreading of items from one culture to another) due to contacts yet unknown to us.

The sociological significance of animal husbandry and plant cultivation is that they *transformed human society.* By creating a more dependable food supply, they ushered in a series of interrelated changes that altered almost every aspect of human life. Because a more dependable food supply was able to support more people, human groups became larger. With more food than was necessary for survival, not everyone had to produce food. This allowed groups to develop a specialized division of labor: some people became full-time priests, others made jewelry, tools, weapons, and so on. This production of objects, in turn, stimulated trade. As groups traded with one another, they began to accumulate objects they considered valuable, such as gold, jewelry, and utensils.

As Figure 6.2 on page 148 illustrates, these changes set the stage for social inequality, for now some families (or clans) aquired more goods than others. Feuds and wars then erupted, for groups now possessed animals, pastures, croplands, jewelry, and other material goods to fight about. War, in turn, let slavery enter the human picture, for people found it convenient to let captives from their battles do their drudge work. Social stratification remained limited, however, for the surplus itself was limited. As individuals passed on their possessions to their descendants, wealth grew more concentrated and power more centralized. Forms of leadership then changed as chiefs emerged.

Note that the primary pattern that runs through this fundamental transformation of group life is the change *from greater to lesser equality.* Where people were located *within* a

pastoral society: a society based on the pasturing of animals

horticultural society: a society based on cultivating plants by the use of hand tools

domestication revolution: the first social revolution, based on the domestication of plants and animals, which led to pastoral and horticultural societies

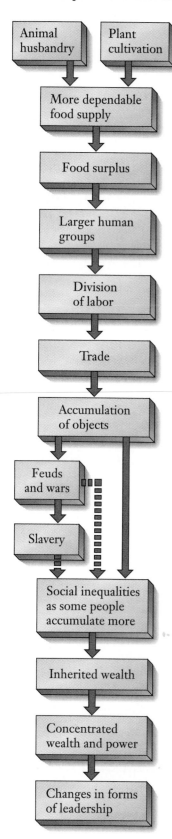

Figure 6.2

Fundamental Consequences of Animal Husbandry and Plant Cultivation

society came to be vital in determining what happened to them in life. Again, Figure 6.2 summarizes how these changes led to social inequality.

Agricultural Societies

About five to six thousand years ago, the invention of a new technology, the plow, changed social life forever. It brought the **agricultural revolution** a new type of society. Compared with hoes and digging sticks, the use of animals to pull plows was immensely efficient. As the ground was turned up, more nutrients were returned to the soil making the land much more productive. The resulting food surplus, unlike anything ever seen before in human history, allowed even more people to engage in activities other than farming. In this new **agricultural society,** people developed cities and the things popularly known as "culture," such as philosophy, art, literature, and architecture. Accompanied by the inventions of the wheel, writing, and numbers, the changes during this period in history were so profound that they sometimes are referred to as "the dawn of civilization."

As groups began to be distinguished by their possessions, social inequality, previously only a tendency, became a fundamental feature of social life. As some people managed to gain control of the surplus resources, they used them to establish themselves in power. To protect their growing privileges, this elite surrounded itself with armed men. They even levied taxes on others, who now had become their "subjects." As conflict theorists point out, this concentration of resources and power, along with the oppression of people not in power, was the forerunner of the state.

No one knows exactly how it happened, but sometime during this period females also became subjugated to males. Sociologist Elise Boulding (1976) theorizes that this change occurred because men were in charge of plowing and the cows. She suggests that when metals were developed, men took on the new job of attaching the metal as tips to the wooden plows and doing the plowing. As a result,

the shift of the status of the woman farmer may have happened quite rapidly, once there were two male specializations relating to agriculture: plowing and the care of cattle. This situation left women with all the subsidiary tasks, including weeding and carrying water to the fields. The new fields were larger, so women had to work just as many hours as they did before, but now they worked at more secondary tasks. . . . This would contribute further to the erosion of the status of women.

Although Boulding's explanation of this fundamental change hasn't been proven, it does match the available evidence. As new evidence comes to light, however, we must expect to modify the theory.

Industrial Societies Power, Prestige, Property

In the 1700s, the invention of another new technology again turned society upside down. The **Industrial Revolution** began in Britain, where in 1765 the steam engine was first used to run machinery. Before this time some machines had harnessed nature (such as wind and water mills), but most had depended on human and animal power. This new source of energy led to the development of what is called **industrial society,** defined by sociologist Herbert Blumer (1990) as a society in which goods are produced by machines powered by fuels instead of by the brute force of humans or animals.

This new form of production was far more efficient than anything before it. Just as its surplus was greater, so were its effects on the human group. Again social inequality increased, especially during the first stage of industrialization. The individuals who first used the new technology accumulated such great wealth that their riches in many instances outran the imagination of kings. Gaining an early position in the markets, they were able not only to control the means of production (factories, machinery, tools), but also to dictate the conditions under which people could work. Helping them control workers was the breakdown of feudal society, which threw masses of people off the lands that they and their ancestors had farmed as tenants for centuries. Moving to the cities,

The machinery that ushered in industrial society was met with ambivalence. On one hand, it brought a multitude of welcomed goods. On the other hand, factory time clocks and the incessant production line made people slaves to the very machines they built. The idea of machines dominating workers is illustrated by this classic scene of Charlie Chaplin's in Modern Times.

these landless peasants faced the choice of stealing, starving, or working for starvation wages (Chambliss 1964; Michalowski 1985).

At that time, workers had no legal rights to safe, or even humane, working conditions; nor had they the right to unionize to improve them. The law considered employment to be a private contract between the employer and the individual worker. If workers banded together to ask for higher wages or to improve some condition of their work, they were fired. If they returned to the factory, they were arrested for trespassing. In the United States—where strikes were illegal—strikers were sometimes beaten, and on rarer occasions shot by private police, and even by the National Guard.

Gradually, however, workers won their demands for better working conditions, and wealth spread to ever larger segments of society. Eventually, home ownership became common, as did the ownership of automobiles and an incredible variety of consumer goods. Beyond the imagination of early social reformers, today's typical worker in advanced industrial societies enjoys a high standard of living in such terms as material conditions, health care, longevity, and access to libraries and education.

As industrialization progressed, then, it reversed the pattern set earlier and increased equality. Indicators of greater equality include better housing and a vast increase in consumer goods, the abolition of slavery, the shift from monarchies to more representative political systems, the right to be tried by a jury of one's peers and to cross examine witnesses, the right to vote, the right to travel, and greater rights for women and minorities.

It is difficult to overstate the sociological principle that the type of society we live in is the fundamental reason that we become who we are. To see how industrial society affects your life, note that you would not be taking this course if it were not for industrialization. Clearly you could not have a car, or your type of clothing or home, a telephone, stereo, television, computer, or even electric lights. On a deeper level, you would not feel the same about life or have your particular aspirations for the future. Actually, probably no aspect of your life would be the same, for you would be locked into the attitudes and views that come with an agricultural or horticultural way of life.

Postindustrial Societies

If you were to describe our society, what terms would you choose? Of the many candidates, the word *change* would have to rank high among them. The primary source of the sweeping change that is transforming our lives is the new technology centering around the microchip. The change is so vast that sociologists say that a new type of society is emerging. They call it the **postindustrial society.**

What are the main characteristics of this new society? Unlike the industrial society from which we are emerging, its hallmark is not raw materials and manufacturing. Rather, its basic component is *information*. Teachers pass on knowledge to students, while lawyers, physicians, bankers, pilots, and interior decorators sell their specialized knowledge of law, the body, money, aerodynamics, and color schemes to clients. Unlike the factory workers in an industrial society, these workers don't *produce* anything. Rather, they transmit or use information to provide services that others are willing to pay for.

agricultural revolution: the second social revolution, based on the invention of the plow, which led to agricultural society

agricultural society: a society based on large-scale agriculture, dependent on plows drawn by animals

Industrial Revolution: the third social revolution, occurring when machines powered by fuels replaced most animal and human power

industrial society: a society based on the harnessing of machines powered by fuels

postindustrial society: a society based on information, services, and high technology, rather than on raw materials and manufacturing

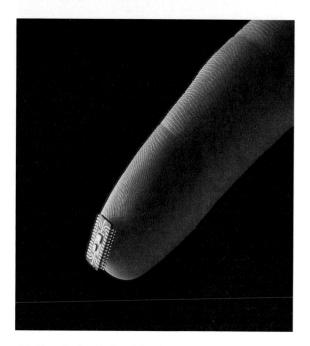

A hallmark of postindustrial societies is the information revolution, which is based on the computer chip. Like other social revolutions before it, this one, too, will leave hardly any aspect of our lives untouched.

The United States was the first country to have more than 50 percent of its work force in service industries such as education, health, research, the government, counseling, banking, investments, sales, law, and the mass media. Australia, New Zealand, western Europe, and Japan soon followed. This basic trend away from manufacturing to selling information services shows no sign of letting up.

The changes are so fundamental that future social analysts may call what we are witnessing today the *fourth social revolution.* As we saw with preceding societies, new technology can transform established ways of life, uprooting old perspectives and replacing them with new ones. So it is with our new technology. The microchip, with its miniaturized circuitry, allows people to work at home and, while driving their automobiles, to talk to others in distant cities and even in countries on the other side of the globe. Because of it, we can peer farther into the remote recesses of space than ever before. And because of it, millions of children spend countless hours struggling against video enemies, at home and in the arcades. For a review of other changes, see pages 631–633.

Although the full implications of the information explosion are still unknown, of this we can be certain: Just as the larger group called society has always exerted a fundamental force on people's thinking and behavior, so it will in its new form. As society is transformed, then, we, too, shall be swept along with it. As history is our guide, the changes will be so extensive that even our attitudes about the self and life will be transformed.

Groups Within Society

Sociologist Emile Durkheim (1933) viewed small groups as a buffer between the individual and the larger society. He said that if it were not for these groups, we would feel oppressed by that huge, amorphous entity known as society. By establishing intimate relationships and offering a sense of meaning and purpose to life, small groups serve as a sort of lifeline that helps to prevent *anomie,* a sense of not belonging. Sometimes, as with Johnny's group in our opening vignette, small groups stand in opposition to the larger society, but in most instances they reinforce society's major values.

Before we examine groups in more detail, we should distinguish between groups, aggregates, and categories. An **aggregate** consists of individuals who temporarily share the same physical space but who do not see themselves as belonging together, such as people waiting in a checkout line or drivers parked at the same red light. A **category** consists of people who have similar characteristics, such as all college women who wear glasses or all men over 6 feet tall. Unlike groups, the individuals who make up a category neither interact with one another nor take one another into account.

Let's look at the types of groups that make up our society—primary, secondary, ingroups and out-groups, reference groups, and social networks. Let's also consider a new type of group that has just appeared on the human scene, the electronic community.

Primary Groups

Johnny, in our opening vignette, never felt as though he belonged anywhere until Satan's Servants welcomed him. It was with them that he found friendship, admiration, and the close, intimate, face-to-face relationships that he longed for. That is what sociologist Charles Cooley calls a **primary group.** As Cooley (1909) put it,

> By primary groups I mean those characterized by intimate face-to-face association and cooperation. They are primary in several senses, but chiefly in that they are fundamental in forming the social nature and ideals of the individual.

aggregate: individuals who temporarily share the same physical space but do not see themselves as belonging together

category: people who have similar characteristics

primary group: a group characterized by intimate, long-term, face-to-face association and cooperation

Producing a Mirror Within. It is significant that Cooley calls primary groups the "springs of life." By this, he means that primary groups, such as the family, friendship groups, and even gangs, are essential to our emotional well-being. As humans, we have an intense need for face-to-face interaction that provides feelings of self-esteem. By offering a sense of belonging, a feeling of being appreciated, and sometimes even love, primary groups are uniquely equipped to meet this basic need.

Another reason why primary groups are so significant is that their values and attitudes become fused into our identity. We internalize their views, which become the lens through which we view life. Even as adults, no matter how far we may have come from our childhood roots, early primary groups remain "inside" us, where they continue to form part of the perspective from which we look out onto the world. Ultimately, then, it is difficult, if not impossible, for us to separate the self from our primary groups, for the self and our groups merge into a "we."

Primary Groups That Fail. Not all primary groups function well, however. Some fail to provide the deep self-satisfactions that their members seek. Such groups, like Johnny's family, for example, are dysfunctional.

Three types of dysfunctions can be identified. First, instead of providing emotional support, the members of a primary group may quarrel and humiliate one another. (Note, however, that some members, such as those who dominate a family, may be highly satisfied with such interaction.) Second, a primary group, such as the one Johnny joined, may set itself against society. (Note, however, that as with Satan's Servants, the group may be dysfunctional for society but highly functional for its members.) The third dysfunction occurs when an essential primary group breaks down throughout society. An example is the incredible state of Ik family life, discussed on page 72. Some analysts think that the U.S. family is also breaking down; others believe that the family is simply changing, and that it will continue to serve as an essential and beneficial primary group. We will discuss this issue further in Chapter 16.

Primary groups such as the family, a key focus of sociological investigation, play a key role in the development of the self. As a small group, the family also serves as a buffer from the often-threatening larger group known as society. The family has been of primary significance in helping this couple from Nicaragua adjust to their new life in the United States.

secondary group: compared with a primary group, a larger, relatively temporary, more anonymous, formal, and impersonal group based on some interest or activity, whose members are likely to interact on the basis of specific roles

Secondary Groups

Compared with primary groups, **secondary groups** are larger, relatively temporary, more anonymous, formal, and impersonal. Such groups are based on some interest or activity, and their members are likely to interact on the basis of specific roles, such as president, manager, worker, or student. Examples are a college classroom, the American Sociological Association, a factory, or the Democratic party.

As we have seen, in hunting and gathering and horticultural societies the entire society formed a primary group. In contrast, in industrial societies secondary groups have multiplied and become essential to our welfare. Over the course of our lives, we all join a variety of secondary groups. They are part of the way we get our education, make our living, and spend our money and leisure.

Although contemporary society could not function without secondary groups, such groups fail to satisfy deep human needs for intimate association. Consequently, *secondary groups tend to break down into primary groups.* For example, at school and work we tend to form friendship cliques, which provide such valued interaction that if it weren't for them we sometimes feel that school or work "would drive us crazy." Just as small groups serve as a buffer between us and the larger society, so the primary groups we form within secondary groups serve as a buffer between us and the demands that secondary groups place on us.

Relationships in secondary groups are more formal and temporary than those in primary groups. In order to satisfy basic emotional needs, members of secondary groups, such as members of the military, form smaller primary groups.

In-Groups and Out-Groups

Sometimes group membership is defined as much by what people are *not*, as by what they are. In other words, the antagonisms that some groups feel toward other groups become

"*I'm surprised, Marty. I thought you were one of us.*"
Drawing by Ziegler; © 1983 The New Yorker Magazine, Inc.

How our participation in social groups shapes our self-concept is a major focus of symbolic interactionists. In this process, knowing who we are not *is as significant as knowing who we are.*

an integral part of their identity. Groups toward which individuals feel loyalty are called **in-groups;** those toward which they feel antagonisms, **out-groups.** For Johnny, Satan's Servants was an in-group, while the police, teachers, welfare workers, and all those associated with school represented out-groups.

This fundamental division of the world into in-groups and out-groups has far reaching consequences for our lives. Because identifying with a group generates a sense of belonging and loyalty, our in-groups exert a high degree of control over us. To maintain status in our in-groups, we may even find ourselves doing things we dislike. How many of us, for example, have put on clothing or worn hair styles that we thought uncomfortable or even a bit strange, but that were expected by our in-group?

In-groups also foster ethnocentrism. Measuring ourselves in relationship to out-groups, we are encouraged to judge our own group's accomplishments and characteristics as superior. The result is prejudice, which, as sociologist Robert Merton (1968) observed, creates an interesting double standard—the traits of our in-groups come to be viewed as virtues, while those *same* traits in out-groups are seen as vices. For example, men may perceive an aggressive man as assertive, but an aggressive woman as pushy. A male employee who doesn't speak up may be thought of as "knowing when to keep his mouth shut," but a quiet woman as too timid to make it in the business world.

in-groups: groups toward which one feels loyalty

out-groups: groups toward which one feels antagonisms

To divide the world into "we" and "them" sometimes leads to acts directed against out-groups. Such acts may be mild and more esteem building for the in-group than anything else. For example, in sports rivalries between nearby towns the most extreme act is likely to be the furtive invasion of the out-group's territory in order to steal a mascot, paint a rock, or uproot a goal post.

Fear and hatred, however, which nourish feelings against out-groups, often give birth to highly destructive acts. During times of economic insecurity, for example, *xenophobia,* or fear of strangers, may grow. The out-group represents jobs stolen from one's friends and relatives. The result may be attacks against immigrants, a national anti-immigration policy, or a local resurgence of the Ku Klux Klan.

In short, to divide the world into in-groups and out-groups, a natural part of social life, brings with it both functional and dysfunctional consequences.

Negative feelings between out-groups can range from mild dislike to intense hatred, accompanied by the desire to destroy the other. Shown here are protestors in Houston as they react to a march by the Ku Klux Klan.

All of us have reference groups—*groups we use as standards for evaluating ourselves. We measure our accomplishments, failures, orientations, and attitudes against what we perceive as normative in these groups. As is evident in these two photos, the reference groups these youths are using are unlikely to lead them to the same social destination.*

Reference Groups

Suppose you have just been offered a good job. It pays double what you hope to make even after you graduate from college. You have just three days to make up your mind. If you accept it, you will have to drop out of college. As you consider the matter, thoughts like this may go through your mind: "My friends will say I'm a fool if I don't take the job . . . but Dad and Mom will practically go crazy. They've made sacrifices for me, and they'd be crushed if I didn't finish college. They've always said I've got to get my education first, that good jobs will always be there. . . . But, then, I'd like to see the look on the faces of those neighbors who said I'd never amount to much!"

This is an example of how people use **reference groups,** the groups we use as standards to evaluate ourselves. Your reference groups may include family, the Scouts, the members of a church or synagogue, your neighbors, teachers, classmates, and co-workers. Your reference group need not be one you actually belong to; it may include a group to which you aspire. For example, if you are thinking about going to graduate school, graduate students or members of the profession you want to join may form your reference group as you evaluate your grades or writing skills.

Reference groups exert tremendous influence over our lives. For example, if you want to become the president of a corporation, you might have your hair cut fairly short, start dressing more formally, try to improve your vocabulary, read the *Wall Street Journal,* take business and law courses, try to obtain a "fast-track" job, and join the local chamber of commerce. In contrast, if you want to become a rock musician, you might wear three earrings in one ear, dress in ways your parents and many of your peers consider outlandish, read *Rolling Stone,* drop out of college, and hang around clubs and rock groups.

From these examples, you can see that the yardsticks provided by reference groups operate as a form of social control. When we see ourselves as measuring up to the yardstick, there is no conflict, but if our behavior, or even aspirations, do not match the standards held by a reference group, the mismatch can lead to internal turmoil. For example, to want to become a corporate officer would present no inner turmoil for most of us, but it would if you had grown up in an Amish home, for the Amish strongly disapprove of such activities for their children. They ban high school and college education, three-piece suits, the *Wall Street Journal,* and corporate employment. Similarly, if you wanted to become a soldier and had been reared by dedicated pacifists, you likely would experience deep conflict, as such parents, disapproving of violence on principle, hold quite different aspirations for their children.

reference groups: Herbert Hyman's term for the groups we use as standards to evaluate ourselves

Although personal abilities and efforts are vitally important for success in life, so are social characteristics. Among them are our social networks, which open and close doors of opportunity. A good example occurs at sociology conventions. In spite of the official program, much of the "real" business centers around renewing and extending social networks.

Given the highly mobile and pluralistic nature of contemporary society, many of us are exposed to contradictory ideas and standards from the various groups that become significant to us. The "internal recordings" that play contradictory messages from these reference groups, then, are simply one cost of social mobility in a postindustrial society.

Social Networks

If you are a member of a large group, there probably are a few people within that group with whom you regularly associate. In a sociology class I was teaching at a commuter campus, six women chose to work together on a project. They got along well, and they began to sit together. Eventually they planned a Christmas party at one of their homes. These clusters, or internal factions, are called **cliques.** The links between people—their cliques, as well as their family, friends, acquaintances, and even "friends of friends"—are called **social networks.** Think of a social network as ties that expand outward from yourself, gradually encompassing more and more people.

The Small World Phenomenon.   Although we live in a huge society, we do not experience social life as an ocean of nameless, strange faces. Instead, we interact within social networks that connect us to the larger society. Social scientists have wondered just how extensive the connections are between social networks. If you list everyone you know, and each of those individuals lists everyone he or she knows, and you keep doing this, do you think that eventually almost everyone in the United States will be included on those lists?

It would be too cumbersome to test this hypothesis by drawing up such lists, but psychologist Stanley Milgram (1967) hit on an ingenious way to find out just how interconnected our social networks are. In what has become a classic experiment, he selected names at random from across the United States. Some he designated as "senders," others as "receivers." Milgram addressed letters to the receivers and asked the senders to mail the letters to someone they knew on a first-name basis who they thought might know the receiver. This person, in turn, was asked to mail the letter to someone he or she knew who might know the receiver, and so on. The question was, Would the letters ever get to the receivers, and if so, how long would the chain be?

Think of yourself as part of this experiment. What would you do if you are a sender, but the receiver lives in a state in which you know no one? You would send the letter to someone you know who might know someone in that state. And this is just what happened. None of the senders knew the receivers, and in the resulting chains some links

clique: a cluster of people within a larger group who choose to interact with one another; an internal faction

social network: the social ties radiating outward from the self that link people together

broke; that is, after receiving a letter, some people didn't send it on. Surprisingly, however, most letters did reach their intended receivers. Even more surprising, the average chain was made up of only *five* links. This gives us insight into why strangers from different parts of the country sometimes find they have a mutual acquaintance.

Global Considerations.   Milgram's experiment shows just how small our world really is. If our social networks are so interrelated that almost everyone in the United States is connected by just five links, how many links connect us to everyone on earth? This experiment is yet to be done.

Networking.   The term **networking** refers to using social networks, usually for career advancement. Hoping to establish a circle of acquaintances who will prove valuable to them, people join clubs, churches, synagogues, and political parties. Many networks are hard to break into, such as the "old boy" network, which keeps jobs moving in the direction of male friends and acquaintances.

To break this barrier, many women do *gender networking*, developing networks of working women to help advance their careers. When they reach top positions, some of these women then steer their business to other women. The resulting circle is so tight that the term "new girl" network is being used, especially in the field of law. Like the "good old boys" who preceded them, the new insiders also justify their exclusionary practice (Jacobs 1997).

A New Group: Technology and the Emergence of Electronic Communities

In the 1990s, due to our new technology, an entirely new type of human group made its appearance. The Internet is a series of millions of computers hooked together worldwide. On the Internet are hundreds of thousands of news groups, called usenets, people who communicate on almost any conceivable topic—from donkey racing and bird-watching to sociology and quantum physics. Most news groups are only an interesting, new way of communicating, but some meet our definition of *group:* people who interact with one another and who think of themselves as belonging together.

Some news groups pride themselves on the distinctive nature of their interest and knowledge, factors that give them a common identity, bind them together, and distinguish them from others. Some have even taken on the characteristics we associate with primary groups: People look forward to communicating daily with others in their news group, with whom they share personal, sometimes intimate matters about themselves. This new

networking: the process of consciously using or cultivating networks for some gain

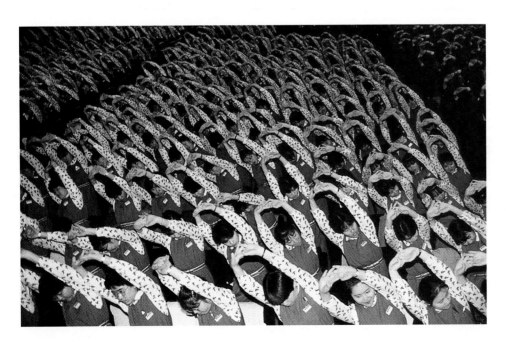

The text contrasts U.S. and Japanese corporate life. One of the main distinctions is that Japanese who work for the same firm think of themselves more as a group or team, Americans more as individuals. Japanese corporations use many techniques to encourage group identity, such as making group exercise a part of the work day. Sociologically, similarity of appearance and activity helps to fuse group identity and company loyalty.

 *Sociology and the New Technology*

New Forms of Talk: Cybercommunications and the Creation of Electronic Communities

As you have seen from the examples in this chapter of domestication of animals and of inventions such as the plow and the steam engine, a change in technology alters the way people relate to one another—and, sometimes, even the shape of society itself. *Online communications*—people communicating with one another via computers—is an example of an invention that alters relationships and even the very nature of "talk."

Through most of human history, "talk" meant face-to-face communication. The invention of writing, however, allowed people who were far apart to "talk" to one another—and left a record of what they "said." Another new technology, the printing press, not only multiplied the power of this "long-distance talk," but even changed religion and politics. By putting Bibles in the hands of common people, it weakened the power of the Roman Catholic Church, removing it as the exclusive interpreter of God's Word. As political tracts came off the press, they encouraged independent thinking, which undermined the monarchy and helped bring about constitutional forms of government.

Thus, as sociologist Joshua Meyrowitz (1995) stresses, we should not consider the media as passive channels of information. They are not mere "holders" or "senders" of messages; rather, they shape our lives. Just as when writing and the printing press were new technologies and people saw their relationships change, so our new technologies are bringing forms of "talk" that are also changing our relationships.

A remarkable example is how our new forms of electronic communication, sometimes called the information superhighway or cyberspace, have made our homes "less-

bounded environments." While remaining within the walls of our homes, we now can instantly "travel" electronically to previously remote settings around the world. There, we can share information with people we have never met, or seen, and even develop friendships with them. The result is a new type of group known as an **electronic community**. In some cases, the term **"electronic primary group"** seems more appropriate to refer to this new type of group, for people regularly interact with one another, share personal information, identify with one another, and develop a sense of intimacy—even though they have "met" only electronically.

The implications of cybercommunications for social relationships are still tentative, but as Meyrowitz points out, while our easy access to people in distant localities unites us with them it also can separate us from people nearby. For example, although I live in Illinois, I can contact my editor in New Jersey as quickly as I can contact my next door neighbor. I do this often, in fact, by telephone, computer, and fax. Our conversations often stray into personal matters—from child care to vacations. In contrast, I only wave to my next-door neighbor when I walk between my car and house—and only if we happen to be outside at the same time.

It is likely, then, that we are seeing a new form of social intimacy emerging, one in which people have closeness without permanence, depth without commitment, and need never meet one another to identify on a close, personal level (Cerulo et al. 1992). Electronic primary groups, with a changed sense of community, carry deep ramifications not only for our social interactions but also for our culture, and even our sense of self.

electronic community: individuals who more or less regularly interact with one another on the Internet

"electronic primary group": individuals who regularly interact with one another on the Internet, who see themselves as a group, and who develop close ties with one another

group dynamics: the ways in which individuals affect groups and the ways in which groups influence individuals

small group: a group small enough for everyone to interact directly with all the other members

form of group, the electronic community, is explored in the Sociology and the New Technology box above.

 ## Group Dynamics

As you know from your personal experience, the lively interaction *within* groups—who does what with whom—has profound consequences for how you adjust to life. Sociologists use the term **group dynamics** to refer to how groups affect us and how we affect groups. Let's first consider the differences that the size of a group makes, and then examine leadership, conformity, and decision making.

Before doing this, we should see what sociologists mean by the term **small group.** This is a group small enough for everyone to interact directly with all the other members. Small groups can be either primary or secondary. A wife, husband, and children, as well as workers who take their breaks together, are examples of primary small groups, while bidders at an auction and passengers on a flight from Chicago to Saint Louis are examples of secondary small groups.

Group size has a significant influence on how people interact. When a group changes from a dyad (two people) to a triad, the relationships among each of the participants undergo a shift.

Group Size

Writing at the turn of the century, sociologist Georg Simmel (1858–1918) noted the significance of group size. He used the term **dyad** for the smallest possible group, which consists of two people. Dyads, he noted, which include marriages, love affairs, and close friendships, show two distinct qualities. First, they are the most intense or intimate of human groups. Because only two people are involved, the interaction is focused on them. Second, because dyads require the continuing active participation and commitment of both members, they are the most unstable of social groups. If one member loses interest, the dyad collapses. In larger groups, in contrast, even if one member withdraws the group can continue, for its existence does not depend on any single member (Simmel 1950).

A **triad** is a group of three people. As Simmel noted, the addition of a third person fundamentally changes the group. For example, with the birth of a child hardly any aspect of a couple's relationship goes untouched (Rubenstein 1992). Despite difficulties that couples experience adjusting to their first child, however, their marriage is usually strengthened. Simmel's principle that groups larger than a dyad are inherently stronger helps explain this effect. Like dyads, triads are also intense, for interaction is shared by only three people. Because interaction is shared with an additional person, however, the intensity lessens.

Simmel also pointed out that triads, too, are inherently unstable. Because relationships among a group's members are seldom neatly balanced, they encourage the formation of a **coalition,** in which some group members align themselves against others. In a triad, it is not uncommon for two members to feel stronger bonds with one another, leading them to act as a dyad and leaving the third feeling hurt and excluded. In addition, triads often produce an arbitrator or mediator, someone who tries to settle disagreements between the other two.

The general principle is that *as a small group grows larger its intensity, or intimacy, decreases and its stability increases.* To see why, look at Figure 6.3 on page 158. The addition of each person to a group greatly increases the connections among people. In a dyad, there is only 1 relationship; in a triad, 3; in a group of four, 6; in a group of five, 10. If we expand the group to six, we have 15 relationships; while a group of seven yields 21 relationships. If we continue adding members to the groups in this figure, we soon would be unable to follow the connections, for a group of eight has 28 possible relationships; a group of nine, 36 relationships; a group of ten, 45; and so on.

It is not only the number of relationships that makes larger groups more stable. As groups grow, they tend to develop a more formal structure to accomplish their goals. For example, leaders emerge and more specialized roles come into play, ultimately resulting in such formal offices as president, secretary, and treasurer. This structure provides a framework that helps the group survive over time.

dyad: the smallest possible group, consisting of two people

triad: a group of three people

coalition: the alignment of some members of a group against others

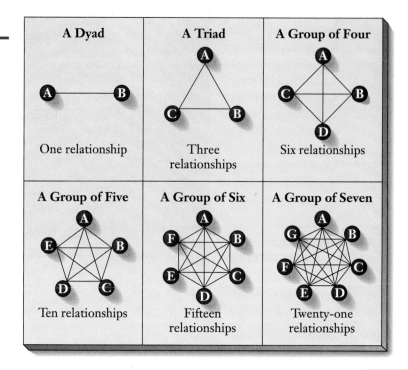

Figure 6.3

The Incremental Effects of Group Size on Relationships

Effects on Attitudes and Behaviors

Imagine that you are taking a class with social psychologists John Darley and Bibb Latané (1968) and they have asked you to join a few students to discuss your adjustment to college life. When you arrive, they tell you that to make things anonymous, they would like you to sit unseen in a booth and participate in the discussion over an intercom. You are to speak when your microphone comes on. The professors say they will not listen in, and they leave.

You find the format somewhat strange, to say the least, but you go along with it. You have not seen the other students in their booths, but when they begin to talk about their experiences, you find yourself becoming wrapped up in the problems they are sharing. One student even mentions how frightening he has found college because of his history of epileptic seizures. Later, this individual begins to breathe heavily into the microphone. Then he stammers and cries for help. A crashing noise follows, and you imagine him lying helpless on the floor. Then there is nothing but an eerie silence. What do you do?

The researchers staged the whole thing, but you don't know that. No one had a seizure. In fact, no students were in the other booths. Everything, except your comments, was on tape.

Some participants were told they would be discussing the topic with just one other student, others with two, others with three, and so on. Darley and Latané found that all students who thought they were part of a dyad rushed out to help. If they thought they were part of a triad, only 80 percent went to help—and they were slower in leaving the booth. In six-person groups, only 60 percent went to see what was wrong—and they were even slower in doing so.

This experiment demonstrates one of the far-reaching consequences that group size has on our attitudes and behaviors—that it even affects our willingness to help one another. Darley and Latané concluded that students in the dyad clearly knew that it was up to them. The professor was gone, and if they didn't help, there would be no help. In the triad, students felt less personal responsibility, while in the larger group, they felt a *diffusion of responsibility:* It was no more up to them than it was up to anyone else. In general, the smaller the group, the more willing we are to stick our necks out for strangers (Latané and Nida 1981).

You probably have observed the second consequence of group size firsthand. When a group is small, its members behave informally toward one another. As the group increases in size, however, its members grow more formal. A degree of intimacy is lost, for no longer can the members assume that the others are "insiders" in sympathy with what they say. Now they must take a "larger audience" into consideration, and instead of merely "talking," they begin to "address" the group. As their speech becomes more formal, their body language stiffens, too.

The third aspect of group dynamics is also one that you probably have observed many times. In the very early stages of a party, when only a few people are present, almost everyone talks with everyone else. As others arrive, however, the guests soon break into smaller groups. This sometimes dismays hosts, who may want all their guests to mix together, and may even make a nuisance of themselves trying to achieve *their* ideas of what a group should be like. The division into small groups is inevitable, however, for it follows the basic sociological principles we have just reviewed. Because the addition of each person rapidly increases connections (in this case, "talk lines"), it makes conversation more difficult. The guests then break into smaller groups where they can see each other and comfortably interact directly with one another.

Leadership

All groups, no matter what their size, have leaders, though they may not hold a formal position in a group. A **leader** is someone who influences the behaviors, opinions, or attitudes of others. Some people are leaders because of their personalities, but leadership involves much more than this, as we shall see.

Types of Leaders.   Groups have two types of leaders (Bales 1950, 1953; Cartwright and Zander 1968). The first is easy to recognize. This person, called an **instrumental leader** (or task-oriented leader), tries to keep the group moving toward its goals. These leaders try to keep group members from getting sidetracked, reminding them of what they are trying to accomplish. The **expressive leader** (or socioemotional leader), in contrast, is not usually recognized as a leader, but he or she certainly is. This person is likely to crack jokes, to offer sympathy, or to do other things that help lift the group's morale. Both types of leadership are essential: the one to keep the group on track, the other to increase harmony and minimize conflicts.

It is difficult for one person to be both an instrumental and an expressive leader, for these roles contradict one another. Because instrumental leaders are task oriented, they sometimes create friction as they prod the group to get on with the job. Their actions often cost them popularity. Expressive leaders, in contrast, being peacemakers who stimulate personal bonds and reduce friction, are usually more popular (Olmsted and Hare 1978).

Leadership Styles.   Let us suppose that the president of your college has asked you to head a task force to determine how the college can improve race relations on campus. Although this position requires you to be an instrumental leader, you can adopt a number of **leadership styles,** or ways of expressing yourself as a leader. The three basic styles are those of **authoritarian leader,** one who gives orders; **democratic leader,** one who tries to gain a consensus; and **laissez-faire leader,** one who is highly permissive. Which should you choose?

Social psychologists Ronald Lippitt and Ralph White (1958) carried out a classic study of these three leadership styles. Boys, matched for IQ, popularity, physical energy, and leadership, were assigned to "craft clubs" made up of five youngsters each. The experimenters trained adult males in the three leadership styles and rotated them among the clubs. As the researchers peered through peepholes, taking notes and making movies, each adult played all three styles to control possible effects of their individual personalities.

leader: someone who influences other people

instrumental leader: an individual who tries to keep the group moving toward its goals; also known as a task-oriented leader

expressive leader: an individual who increases harmony and minimizes conflict in a group; also known as a socioemotional leader

leadership styles: ways in which people express their leadership

authoritarian leader: a leader who leads by giving orders

democratic leader: a leader who leads by trying to reach a consensus

laissez-faire leader: an individual who leads by being highly permissive

The authoritarian leaders assigned tasks to the children and set the working conditions. They also praised or condemned their work arbitrarily, giving no explanation for why it was good or bad. The democratic leaders held group discussions and outlined the steps necessary to reach the group's goals. They also suggested alternative approaches to these goals and let the children work at their own pace. When they evaluated the children's projects, they gave "facts" as the bases for their decisions. The laissez-faire leaders were passive, giving the boys almost total freedom to do as they wished. They stood ready to offer help when asked, but made few suggestions. They did not evaluate the children's projects, either positively or negatively.

The results? The boys who had authoritarian leaders grew dependent on the leaders and showed a high degree of solidarity. They also became either aggressive or apathetic, with the aggressive boys growing hostile toward the leader. In contrast, the boys who had democratic leaders were friendlier, more "group minded," and looked to one another for mutual approval. They did less scapegoating, and when the leader left the room they continued to work at a steadier pace. The boys with laissez-faire leaders asked more questions, but they made fewer decisions. They were notable for their lack of achievement. The researchers concluded that the democratic style of leadership worked best. Their conclusions, however, may have been biased, as the researchers favored a democratic style of leadership, and they did the research during a highly charged political period (Olmsted and Hare 1978).

You may have noted that only males were involved in this experiment. It is interesting to speculate how the results might differ if we repeated the experiment with all-girl groups and with groups of both girls and boys and used both men and women as leaders. Perhaps you will become the sociologist to study such variations.

Adapting Leadership Styles to Changing Situations. It is important to note that different situations require different styles of leadership. Suppose, for example, that you are leading a dozen backpackers in California's Sierra Madre mountains, and it is time to make dinner. A laissez-faire style would be appropriate if everyone had brought their own food—or perhaps a democratic style if the meal were to be communally prepared. Authoritarian leadership—you telling everyone how to prepare their meals—would probably create resentment. This, in turn, would likely interfere with meeting the primary goals of the group, in this case, having a good time while enjoying nature.

Now assume the same group but a different situation: One of your party is lost and a blizzard is on its way. This situation calls for you to take charge and be authoritarian. To simply shrug your shoulders and say, "You figure it out," would invite disaster.

Who Becomes a Leader? Are leaders people who are born with characteristics that propel them to the forefront of a group? No sociologist would agree with such a premise. In general, people who are seen as strongly representing the group's values or as able to lead a group out of a crisis are likely to become leaders (Trice and Beyer 1991). Leaders also tend to be more talkative and to express determination and self-confidence.

These findings may not be surprising, as such traits appear related to a leadership role. Researchers, however, have also discovered that traits seeming to have no bearing whatsoever on ability to lead are also significant. For example, taller people and those judged better looking are more likely to become leaders (Stodgill 1974; Crosbie 1975). (The taller and more attractive are also likely to earn more, but that is another story [Deck 1968; Feldman 1972; Katz 1995].)

Many other factors underlie people's choice of leaders, most of which are quite subtle. A simple experiment performed by social psychologists Lloyd Howells and Selwyn Becker (1962) uncovered one of these factors. They formed groups of five people each who did not know one another, seating them at a rectangular table, three on one side and two on the other. After each group had discussed a topic for a set period of time, they chose a leader. Their findings are startling: Although only 40 percent of the people sat on the two-person side, 70 percent of the leaders emerged from that side. The explanation is that we tend to direct more interactions to people facing us than to people to the side of us.

Conformity to Peer Pressure: The Asch Experiment

How influential are groups in people's lives? To answer this, let's look first at *conformity* in the sense of going along with our peers. They have no authority over us, only the influence that we allow.

Imagine that you are taking a course in social psychology with Dr. Solomon Asch and you have agreed to participate in an experiment. As you enter his laboratory, you see seven chairs, five of them already filled by other students. You are given the sixth. Soon the seventh person arrives. Dr. Asch stands at the front of the room next to a covered easel. He explains that he will first show a large card with a vertical line on it, then another card with three vertical lines. Each of you is to tell him which of the three lines is identical to the line on the first card (see Figure 6.4).

Dr. Asch then uncovers the first card with a single line and the comparison card with the three lines. The correct answer is easy, for two of the lines are obviously wrong, and one exactly right. Each person, in order, states his or her answer aloud. You all answer correctly. The second trial is just as easy, and you begin to wonder what the point is of your being here. Then on the third trial something unexpected happens. Just as before, it is easy to tell which lines match. The first student, however, gives a wrong answer. The second gives the same incorrect answer. So do the third and the fourth. By now you are wondering what is wrong. How will the person next to you answer? You can hardly believe it when he, too, gives the same wrong answer. Then it is your turn, and you give what you know is the right answer. The seventh person also gives the same wrong answer.

On the next trial, the same thing happens. You know the choice of the other six is wrong, yet they give what to you are obviously wrong answers. You don't know what to think. Why aren't they seeing things the same way you are? Sometimes they do, but in twelve trials they don't. Something is seriously wrong, and you are no longer sure what to do. . . .

When the eighteenth card is finished, you heave a sigh of relief. The experiment is finally over, and you are ready to bolt for the door. Dr. Asch walks over to you with a big smile on his face, thanks you for participating in the experiment, and then explains that you were the only real subject in the experiment! "The other six were all stooges! I paid them to give those answers," he says. Now you feel real relief. Your eyes weren't playing tricks on you after all.

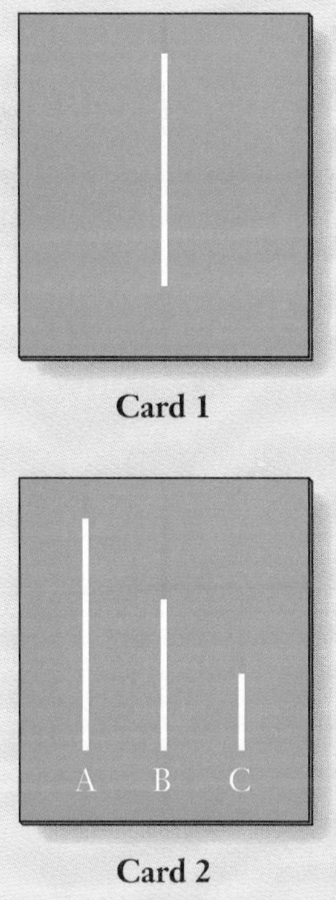

What were the results? Asch (1952) tested fifty people. About 33 percent gave in to the group half the time and gave what they knew to be wrong answers. Another 40 percent also gave wrong answers, but not as often. And 25 percent stuck to their guns and always gave the right answer. I don't know how I would do on this test (if I knew nothing about it in advance), but I like to think that I would be part of the 25 percent. You probably feel the same way. But why should we feel that we wouldn't be like *most* people?

The results are disturbing. In our "land of individualism," the group is so powerful that most people are willing to say things that they know do not match objective reality. And this was simply a group of strangers! How much more can we expect the group to enforce conformity when it consists of friends, people we value highly and depend on for getting along in life? Again, perhaps you will become the sociologist to run that variation of Asch's experiment, and perhaps to use female subjects.

Even more disturbing are the results of an experiment featured in the following Thinking Critically section.

Card 1

Card 2

The cards used by Solomon Asch in his classic experiment on group conformity

Figure 6.4

Asch's Cards

▼▼▼▼▼▼▼▼▼▼▼▼▼▼▼▼▼▼▼▼

Thinking Critically About Social Controversy

If Hitler Asked You to Execute a Stranger, Would You? The Milgram Experiment

▼ Imagine that you are taking a course with Dr. Stanley Milgram (1963, 1965), a former student of Dr. Asch's. Assume that you did not take part in Dr. Asch's experiment and have no reason to be wary of these experimenters. You arrive at the laboratory to participate in a study on punishment and learning. You and a second student draw lots for the roles of "teacher" and "learner." You are to be the teacher, he the learner. When you see that the learner's chair has protruding electrodes, you are glad that you are the teacher. Dr. Milgram shows you the machine you will run. You see that one side of the control panel is marked "Mild Shock, 15 Volts," the center says "Intense Shock, 350 Volts," while the far right side reads, "DANGER: SEVERE SHOCK."

"As the teacher, you will read aloud a pair of words," explains Dr. Milgram. "Then you will repeat the first word, and the learner will reply with the second word. If the learner can't remember the word, you press this lever on the shock generator. The shock will serve as punishment, and we can then determine if punishment improves memory." You nod, now extremely relieved that you haven't been designated a learner.

"Every time the learner makes an error, increase the punishment by 15 volts," Dr. Milgram says. Then, seeing the look on your face, he adds, "The shocks can be extremely painful, but they won't cause any permanent tissue damage." He pauses, and then adds, "I want you to see." You then follow him to the "electric chair," and Dr. Milgram gives you a shock of 45 volts. "There. That wasn't too bad, was it?" "No," you mumble.

The experiment begins. You hope for the learner's sake that he is bright, but unfortunately he turns out to be rather dull. He gets some answers right, but you have to keep turning up the dial. Each turn of the dial makes you more and more uncomfortable. You find yourself hoping that the learner won't miss another answer. But he does. When he received the first shocks, he let out some moans and groans, but now he is screaming in agony. He even protests that he suffers from a heart condition. *How far do you continue turning that dial?*

By now, you probably have guessed that there was no electricity attached to the electrodes and that the "learner" was a stooge, only pretending to feel pain. The purpose of the experiment, of course, was to find out at what point people refuse to participate. Does anyone actually turn the lever all the way to DANGER: SEVERE SHOCK?

Milgram wanted the answers because of the Nazi slaughter of Jews, Gypsies, homosexuals, and others they designated as "inferior." That millions of ordinary people did nothing to stop the deaths seemed bizarre, and Milgram wanted to see how ordinary, intelligent Americans might react in an analogous situation.

Milgram was upset by what he found. Many "teachers" broke into a sweat and protested to the experimenter that this was inhuman and should be stopped. But when the experimenter calmly replied that the experiment must go on, this assurance from the "authority" ("scientist, white coat, university laboratory") was enough for most "teachers" to continue, even though the learner screamed in agony and pleaded to be released. Even "teachers" who were "reduced to twitching, stuttering wrecks" continued to follow orders.

Milgram varied his experiments (Miller 1986). He used both males and females and put some "teachers" and "learners" in the same room, where the "teacher" could clearly see the suffering. He had some "learners" pound and kick on the wall during the first shocks and then go silent. The results varied from situation to situation. The highest proportion of "teachers" who pushed the lever all the way to 450 volts—65 percent—occurred when there was no verbal feedback from the "learner." Of those who could see the "learner," 40 percent turned the lever all the way. When Milgram added a second "teacher," a stooge who refused to go along with the experiment, only 5 percent carried out the severe shocking, a result that bears out some of Asch's results.

Milgram's experiments became a stormy basis for rethinking research ethics. Not only were researchers surprised, and disturbed, at what Milgram found, but they also were alarmed at his methods. Researchers agreed that to reduce subjects to "twitching, stuttering wrecks" was unethical, and almost all deception was banned. Universities began to require that subjects be informed of the nature and purpose of social research.

The results of the Asch and Milgram experiments leave us with the disturbing question: "How far would *I* go in following authority?" Truly the influence of the group extends beyond what most of us imagine.

For Your Consideration

Considering how significant these findings are, do you think that the scientific community overreacted to Milgram's experiment? Should we allow such research? Considering both the Asch and Milgram experiments, use symbolic interactionism, functionalism, and conflict theory to explain why groups have such influence over us. ▲

Global Consequences of Group Dynamics: Groupthink and Decision Making

In our era of nuclear weapons, one of the disturbing implications of the Asch and Milgram experiments is **groupthink.** Sociologist Irving Janis (1972) coined this term to refer to the tunnel vision that a group of people sometimes develop—they think alike, and to suggest alternatives is taken as a sign of disloyalty. Even moral judgments can be put aside, for the group becomes convinced that its welfare depends on a single course of action. Groupthink may lead to overconfidence, to illusions of invincibility, and to being blind to risks they otherwise would see (Hart 1991).

Groupthink poses a special danger to government officials. The options narrow, then finally disappear, and the officials are unable to see anything beyond what has already been decided on. They interpret all subsequent events from the framework of the "right" answer—that is, what the group has determined to be the only reasonable thing to do.

The Asch and Milgram experiments let us see how groupthink can develop. Suppose you are a member of the president's inner circle. It is midnight, and the president has just called an emergency meeting to deal with a national crisis. At first, various options are presented. Eventually, these are narrowed to only a few choices, and at some point everyone seems to agree on what now seems "the only possible course of action." At that juncture, expressing doubts will bring you into conflict with *all* the other important people in the room, while actual criticism may mark you as "not a team player." So you keep your mouth shut, with the result that each step commits you—and them—more and more to the "only" course of action.

We can choose from a variety of examples from around the globe, but U.S. history provides a fertile field to illustrate groupthink: the refusal of President Roosevelt and his chiefs of staff to believe that the Japanese might attack Pearl Harbor and the subsequent decision to continue naval operations as usual; President Kennedy's invasion of Cuba; and U.S. policies in Vietnam. Watergate is especially noteworthy, for it plunged the United States into political crisis and for the first time in history a U.S. president was forced to resign.

In each of these cases, options closed as officials committed themselves to a single course of action. It became the equivalent of disloyalty to question this action. Those in power then plunged ahead, no longer able to objectively weigh evidence as it came in, interpreting everything as supporting this single "correct" decision. Like Milgram's subjects, they became mired deeper and deeper in actions that as individuals they would have considered unacceptable. In some cases, they even found themselves pursuing policies they may have found morally repugnant.

groupthink: Irving Janis's term for a narrowing of thought by a group of people, leading to the perception that there is only one correct answer, in which to even suggest alternatives becomes a sign of disloyalty

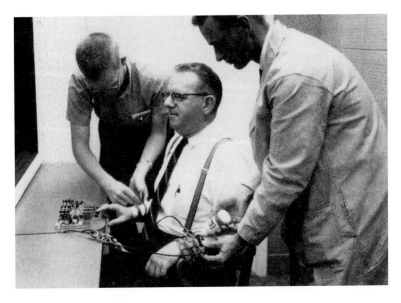

In the 1960s, U.S. social psychologists ran a series of creative but controversial experiments. Among these were Stanley Milgram's experiments, described in the text. From this photo of the "learner" being prepared for the experiment, you can get an idea of how convincing the situation would be for the "teacher."

Preventing Groupthink

Groupthink is a danger that faces any government, for leaders, isolated at the top, easily can become cut off from information that does not support their own opinions. Leaders also foster groupthink by surrounding themselves with an inner circle that closely reflects their own views. Perhaps the key to preventing the mental captivity and paralysis known as groupthink is the widest possible circulation, especially among a nation's top government officials, of research that has been freely conducted by social scientists, and information that has been freely gathered by media reporters.

If this conclusion comes across as an unabashed plug for sociological research and the free exchange of ideas, it is. Giving free rein to diverse opinions can effectively curb groupthink, which—if not prevented—can lead to the destruction of a society and, in today's world of sophisticated weapons, the obliteration of the earth's inhabitants.

Summary and Review

Social Groups and Societies

What is a group?

Sociologists use many definitions of groups, but, in general, **groups** are people who have something in common and who believe that what they have in common is significant. **Societies** are the largest and most complex groups that sociologists study. Pp. 144–145.

The Transformation of Societies

What inventions are linked to the change from one type of society to another?

On their way to postindustrial society, humans passed through four types of societies, each due to a social revolution linked to new technology. The **domestication revolution,** pasturing animals and cultivating plants, transformed **hunting and gathering societies** into **pastoral** and **horticultural societies.** Then the invention of the plow ushered in the **agricultural society,** while the **Industrial Revolution,** caused by machines being powered by fuels, allowed the **industrial society** to develop. Today, the computer chip is fostering a new type of society called **postindustrial society.** Pp. 145–150.

How is social inequality linked to the transformation of societies?

Social equality was greatest in hunting and gathering societies, but as societies became more complex social inequality grew. The root of the transition to social inequality was the accumulation of a food surplus, made possible through the domestication revolution. This surplus stimulated the division of labor, trade, accumulation of material goods, the subordination of females by males, the development of the state, and the rule by a few over many. Pp. 145–150.

Groups Within Society

How do sociologists classify groups?

Sociologists divide groups into primary, secondary, in-groups, out-groups, reference groups, and networks. The cooperative, intimate, long-term, face-to-face relationships provided by **primary groups** are fundamental to our sense of self. **Secondary groups** are larger, relatively temporary, more anonymous, formal, and impersonal than primary groups. **In-groups** provide members with a strong sense of identification and belonging, while **out-groups** help create this identity by showing in-group members what they are *not.* **Reference groups** are groups we use as standards to evaluate ourselves. **Social networks** consist of social ties that link people together. Changed technology has given birth to a new type of group, the **electronic community.** Pp. 150–156.

Group Dynamics

How does a group's size affect its dynamics?

The term **group dynamics** refers to how individuals affect groups and how groups influence individuals. In a **small group,** everyone can interact directly with everyone else. As a group grows larger, its intensity decreases and its stability increases. A **dyad,** consisting of two people, is the most unstable of human groups, but it provides the most intense or intimate relationships. The addition of a third person, forming a **triad,** fundamentally alters relationships. Triads are unstable, as **coalitions** tend to form (the alignment of some members of a group against others). Pp. 156–159.

What characterizes a leader?

A **leader** is someone who influences others. **Instrumental leaders** try to keep a group moving toward its goals, even at the cost of causing friction. **Expressive leaders** focus on creating harmony and raising group morale. Both types are essential to the functioning of groups. P. 159.

What are the three main leadership styles?

Authoritarian leaders give orders, **democratic leaders** try to lead by consensus, and **laissez-faire leaders** are highly permissive. An authoritarian style appears to be more effec-tive in emergency situations, a democratic style works best for most situations, and a laissez-faire style is usually ineffective. Pp. 159–160.

How do groups encourage conformity?

The Asch experiment was cited to illustrate the power of peer pressure, the Milgram experiment the influence of authority. Both experiments demonstrate how easily we can succumb to **groupthink,** a kind of collective tunnel vision. Preventing groupthink requires the free circulation of contrasting ideas. Pp. 161–164.

Where can I read more on this topic?

Suggested readings for this chapter are listed on page 661.

 Sociology and the Internet

All URLs listed are current as of the printing of this book. URLs are often changed. Please check our Website http://www.abacon.com/henslin for updates.

1. The importance of family as a primary group is emphasized by the contemporary catchwords "family values." Explore views of the family by going to *http://www.lycos.com/* At this site, use the search words "family values." Read the arguments, commentaries, and offers of service, noting which aspects of primary groups are addressed. Why are we so concerned with problems with families? Be ready to share your analysis with the class.

2. Are "electronic communities" really groups? Go to the Yahoo! Usenet list at *http://www.yahoo!.com/News/Usenet/* and select "Newsgroup Listings." At the listing, choose "List of Newsgroups" and scan at least three different news groups. Read several of the exchanges in these news groups. Which of these news groups seem to have group properties? Be sure to review your text's discussion of the characteristics of groups. Write a report discussing and defending your conclusions.

3. In the United States there is a well-known adage that it's not what you know, but who you know. In order to get a job once you're out of college, you most likely will count on your social networks. One such social network is your college alumni association. Examine the Web page of the Pennsylvania State University Alumni Association at *http://www.alumni.psu.edu/* Is this alumni association a social network? Why or why not? Why do people become members of their alumni associations? What are some of the benefits of joining the PSU Alumni Association? Is joining an alumni association a type of networking? Why or why not? After reading some of the links on the Penn State Alumni page, describe what type of group you would belong to if you joined this association. Be sure to give examples to support your conclusions.

4. Collectors clubs are growing in popularity and now exist for almost any kind of collectible you can think of. Let's focus on the Peanuts Collectors Club. Go to *http://www.dcn.davis.ca.us/~bang/peanuts/* Using your sociological perspective, discuss why people join collectors clubs. What are the functions of a collectors club? What kind of group is a collectors club? Is it an aggregate, a primary group, a secondary group, or what?

Diana Ong, Conference in Color, 1997

Bureaucracy and
Formal Organizations

*T*HIS WAS THE MOST EXCITING DAY *Jennifer could remember. Her first day at college. So much had happened so quickly. Her senior year had ended with such pleasant memories: the prom, graduation—how proud she had felt at that moment. But best of all had been her SAT scores. Everyone, especially Jennifer, had been surprised at the results—she had outscored everyone in her class.*

"Yes, they're valid," her advisor had assured her. "You can be anything you want to be."

Those words still echoed in Jennifer's mind. "Anything I want to be," she thought.

Then came the presidential scholarship! Full tuition for four years. It went beyond anything Jennifer had ever dreamed possible. She could hardly believe it, but it was really hers.

"Your Social Security number, please!"

These abrupt words snapped Jennifer out of her reverie. After an hour, she had reached the head of the line. Jennifer quickly mumbled the nine digits destined to stay with her to the grave.

"What?" asked the clerk. Jennifer repeated the numbers more clearly.

"I can't give you a class card. You haven't paid your fees."

"What do you mean? I'm on scholarship."

"Evidently not, or else you'd be in the computer," replied the clerk, rolling her eyes.

"But I am."

"If you were, it would say so here."

"But I really am. Look," Jennifer said as she took the prized letter out of her purse.

"I can't help what it says there," replied the clerk, "The only thing that counts is what it says here," she said, gesturing toward the computer. "You'll have to go to Forsyth to clear it up." Then looking past Jennifer, the clerk said, "Next."

Jennifer felt thoroughly confused. Dejected, she crossed the quadrangle to Forsyth and joined a double line of students stretched from the building to the courtyard.

No one told Jennifer that this was the line for deferring tuition. The "problem" line was in the basement.

*Y*ou can understand Jennifer's dismay. Things could have been clearer—a lot clearer. The problem is that many colleges must register thousands of students, most of whom are going to start classes on the same day. To do so, they have broken the registration process into tiny bits, with each piece making a small contribution to getting the job done. Of course, as Jennifer found out, things don't always go as planned.

This chapter looks at how society is organized to "get its job done." As you read it, you may be able to trace the source of some of your frustrations to this social organization, as well as see how your welfare depends on it.

The Rationalization of Society

In the previous chapter, we discussed how over the course of history, societies underwent transformations so extensive that whole new types of societies emerged. In addition to these transformations, a major development has been **rationality**—the acceptance of rules, efficiency, and practical results as the right way to approach human affairs. Let's examine how this approach to life—which we today take for granted—came about.

The Contribution of Max Weber

Max Weber (1864–1920), a sociologist whose studies incorporated an amazingly broad sweep of world history, concluded that until recently the world's groups and nations had been immersed in a **traditional orientation** to life—the idea that the past is the best

rationality: the acceptance of rules, efficiency, and practical results as the right way to approach human affairs

traditional orientation: the idea, characteristic of tribal, peasant, and feudal societies, that the past is the best guide for the present

guide for the present. In this view, what exists is good because it has passed the test of time. Customs—and relationships based on them—have served people well and should not be lightly abandoned. A central orientation of a traditional society is to protect the status quo. Change is viewed with suspicion, and comes but slowly, if at all.

Such a traditional orientation stands in the way of industrialization, which requires the willingness—even eagerness—to change. If a society is to industrialize, then, a deep-seated shift must occur in people's thinking—from wanting to hold onto things as they are to seeking the most efficient way to accomplish matters. With the "bottom line" (results) replacing the status quo, rule-of-thumb methods give way to explicit rules and procedures for measuring results. This change, called *rationality*, requires an entirely different way of looking at life. It flies in the face of human history, for it is opposed to the basic orientation of all human societies until the time of industrialization. How, then, did what Weber called the **rationalization of society**—a widespread acceptance of rationality and a social organization largely built around this idea—come about? How did people break through their profound resistance to change?

To Weber, this problem was like an unsolved murder is to a detective. Weber's primary clue was that capitalism thrived only in certain parts of Europe. If he could determine why this was so, he was convinced that he could discover the root of this fundamental change in human society. As Weber pursued the matter, he concluded that religion held the key, for it was in Protestant countries that capitalism flourished, while Roman Catholic countries held onto tradition and were relatively untouched by capitalism.

Until the 1500s, the world's societies had a traditional orientation to life. The way things had "always" been was the guide to decision making. Change, which came very slowly, was viewed with suspicion, and one generation was very similar to the next. In this painting from 1416 by Französische Buchmalerei, Les tres riches heures du Duc de Berry, *you can see the slow pace of life. The rise of capitalism, however, changed this orientation, and for much of the West, rationality became the new guide to decision making.*

But why should Roman Catholics have continued to hold onto the past, while Protestants embraced change, welcoming the new emphasis on practical results? Weber's answer to this puzzle has been the source of controversy ever since he first proposed it in his highly influential book, *The Protestant Ethic and the Spirit of Capitalism* (1904–1905). He concluded that essential differences between the two religions held the answer. Roman Catholic doctrine emphasized the acceptance of present arrangements, not change: "God wants you where you are. You owe primary allegiance to the Church, to your family, to your community and country. Accept your lot in life and remain rooted." But Protestant theology was quite different, Weber argued, especially Calvinism, a religion he was intimately familiar with from his mother. Calvinists (followers of the teachings of John Calvin, 1509–1564) believed that before birth people are destined to go either to heaven or to hell—and they would not know their destiny until after they died. Weber believed that this teaching filled Calvinists with an anxiety that pervaded their entire lives. Salvation became their chief concern in life—they wanted to know *now* where they were going after death.

To resolve their spiritual dilemma, Calvinists came up with an ingenious solution: God did not want those chosen for heaven to be ignorant of their destiny. Consequently, he would bestow signs of approval on them. But what signs? The answer, they claimed, was found not in mystical, spiritual experiences, but in tangible achievements that people could see and measure. The sign of God's approval became success: Those whom God had predestined for heaven would be blessed with visible success in this life.

This idea transformed Calvinists' lives, serving as an extraordinary motivation to work hard. Because Calvinists also believed that thrift is a virtue, their dedication to work led to an accumulation of money. Calvinists could not spend the excess on themselves, however, for to purchase items beyond the basic necessities was considered sinful. **Capitalism,** the investment of capital in the hope of producing profits, became an outlet for their excess money, while the success of those investments became a further sign of God's

rationalization of society: a widespread acceptance of rationality and a social organization largely built around this idea

capitalism: the investment of capital with the goal of producing profits

approval. Worldly success, then, became transformed into a spiritual virtue, and other branches of Protestantism, although less extreme, adopted the creed of thrift and hard work. Consequently, said Weber, Protestant countries embraced capitalism.

Now, what has this to do with rationalization? Simply put, capitalism demands rationalization, the careful calculation of practical results. If profits are your goal, you must compute income and expenses. You must calculate inventories and wages, the cost of producing goods and how much they bring in. You must determine "the bottom line." In such an arrangement of human affairs, efficiency, not tradition, becomes the drum to which you march. Traditional ways of doing things, if inefficient, must be replaced, for what counts are the results.

Marx on Rationalization

Another sociologist, Karl Marx, also noted that tradition had given way to rationality. When he analyzed the problem, however, Marx came up with an entirely different explanation. He didn't think religion had anything to do with breaking the bondage of tradition. Rather, Marx concluded that the switch to rationality was due to capitalism itself. When people saw that capitalism was more efficient, that it produced things they wanted in much greater abundance, they embraced rationality, giving up their traditional thinking. Thus Marx reversed the equation: The change to capitalism, he said, changed the way people thought about life, not the other way around.

Who is correct? Weber, who concluded that Protestantism produced rationality, which then paved the way for capitalism? Or Marx, who concluded that capitalism produced rationality? No analyst has yet reconciled these two opposing answers to the satisfaction of sociologists: The two views still remain side by side.

formal organization: a secondary group designed to achieve explicit objectives

A central characteristic of formal organizations is the division of labor. Bureaucracies, for example, divide tasks into very small segments. Prior to capitalism and industrialization, however, there was little division of labor, and few formal organizations existed. In this woodcut of money coiners in Germany during the Middle Ages, you can see an early division of labor and perhaps the emergence of a formal organization.

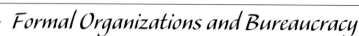

Formal Organizations and Bureaucracy

Regardless of whether Marx or Weber was right about its cause, rationality was a totally different way of thinking that came to permeate society. This new orientation transformed the way in which society is organized. As a result, **formal organizations,** secondary groups  designed to achieve explicit objectives, have become a central feature of contemporary society. Most of us are born within them, we are educated in them, we spend our working lives in them, and we are buried by them (Volti 1995).

Formal Organizations

Prior to industrialization, only a few formal organizations existed. The guilds of western Europe during the twelfth century are an example. People who performed the same type of work organized to control their craft in a local area. They set prices and standards of workmanship (Bridgwater 1953; Volti 1995). Much like modern unions, guilds also prevented outsiders (nonmembers of the guild) from working at the particular craft. Another example of an early formal organization is the army, with its structure of senior officers, junior officers, and ranks. Formal armies, of course, go back to early history.

With industrialization, secondary groups became common. Today we take their existence for granted and, beginning with grade school, all of us spend a good deal of time in them. Formal organizations tend to develop into bureaucracies, and in general, the larger the formal organization, the more likely it is to be bureaucratic.

The power of the traditional way of life prior to the arrival of capitalism is still evident from the dominating position of Hradcany cathedral in Prague, The Czech Republic. Max Weber wrote that the rise of capitalism and the type of society it produced—one based on rationality versus tradition—emerged in response to the Protestant ethic, especially the Calvinist doctrine of predestination. Karl Marx saw things differently. He believed that capitalism itself was responsible for the breakdown of traditional society and the rise of rationality.

The Essential Characteristics of Bureaucracies

Although the army, the post office, a college, and General Motors may not seem to have much in common, they are all bureaucracies. As Weber (1947) analyzed them, these are the essential characteristics of a **bureaucracy**:

1. *A hierarchy with assignments flowing downward and accountability flowing upward.* The organization is divided into clear-cut levels. Each level assigns responsibilities to the level beneath it, while each lower level is accountable to the level above for fulfilling those assignments. The bureaucratic structure of a typical university is shown in Figure 7.1 on the next page.

2. *A division of labor.* Each member of a bureaucracy has a specific task to fulfill, and all of the tasks are then coordinated to accomplish the purpose of the organization. In a college, for example, a teacher does not run the heating system, the president does not teach, and a secretary does not evaluate textbooks. These tasks are distributed among people who have been trained to do them.

3. *Written rules.* In their attempt to become efficient, bureaucracies stress written procedures. In general, the longer a bureaucracy exists and the larger it grows, the more written rules it has. The rules of some bureaucracies cover just about every imaginable situation. In my university, for example, the rules are bound in handbooks: separate ones for faculty, students, administrators, civil service workers, and perhaps others that I do not even know exist. The guiding principle generally becomes, "If there isn't a written rule covering it, it is allowed."

4. *Written communications and records.* Records are kept of much of what occurs in a bureaucracy. ("Fill that out in triplicate.") Consequently, workers in bureaucracies spend a fair amount of time sending memos back and forth. They also produce written reports detailing their activities. My university, for example, requires that each faculty member fill out quarterly reports summarizing the number of hours per week spent on specified activities as well as an annual report listing what was accomplished in teaching, research, and service—all accompanied by copies of publications, testimonies to service, and written teaching evaluations from each course. These materials go to committees whose task it is to evaluate the relative performance of each faculty member.

bureaucracy: a formal organization with a hierarchy of authority; a clear division of labor; emphasis on written rules, communications, and records; and impersonality of positions

171

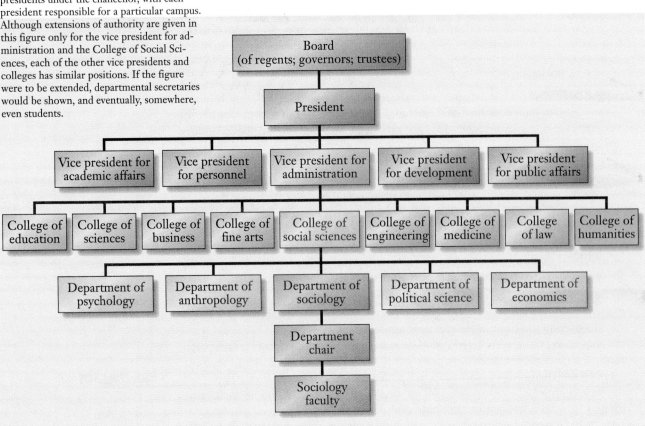

This 1907 photo indicates one way that technology has changed our lives. The little drawers that the women are searching contain customer records of the Metropolitan Life Insurance Company. Today, this entire bank of records could be stored on a personal computer. We also could use the computer to search or modify the records, infinitesimally faster—and certainly much easier on the legs—than standing on the ladder.

5. *Impersonality.* It is the office that is important, not the individual who holds the office. You work for the organization, not the replaceable person who heads some post in the organization. Consequently, members of a bureaucracy owe allegiance to the office, not to particular people. If you work in a bureaucracy, you become a small cog in a large machine. Each worker is a replaceable unit, for many others are available to fulfill each particular function. For example, when a professor retires or dies, someone else is appointed to take his or her place.

These five characteristics not only help bureaucracies reach their goals but also allow them to grow and endure. One bureaucracy in the United States, the

Figure 7.1

The Typical Bureaucratic Structure of a Medium-Sized University

This is a scaled-down version of a university's bureaucratic structure. The actual lines of authority of a university are likely to be much more complicated than those depicted here. A university may have a chancellor and several presidents under the chancellor, with each president responsible for a particular campus. Although extensions of authority are given in this figure only for the vice president for administration and the College of Social Sciences, each of the other vice presidents and colleges has similar positions. If the figure were to be extended, departmental secretaries would be shown, and eventually, somewhere, even students.

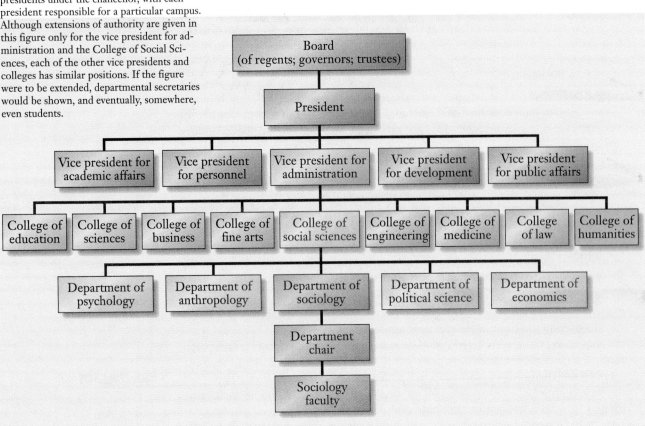

postal service, has become so large that one out of every 150 employed Americans now works for it (Frank 1990). If the head of a bureaucracy dies, retires, or resigns, the organization continues, ordinarily hardly skipping a beat, for unlike a "mom and pop" operation, the functioning of a unit does not depend on the individual who heads it. The expansion (some would say domination) of bureaucracies in contemporary society is illustrated by the Down-to-Earth Sociology box below.

"Ideal" Versus "Real" Bureaucracy

Just as people often act quite differently from the way the norms say they should, so it is with bureaucracies. The characteristics of bureaucracies identified by Weber are **ideal types;** that is, they are a composite of characteristics based on many specific examples.

▲▼▲▼▲▼▲▼▲▼ *Down-to-Earth Sociology* ▲▼▲▼▲▼▲▼▲▼

The McDonaldization of Society

Sociologist George Ritzer (1993) sees the thousands of McDonald's restaurants that dot the U.S. landscape—and increasingly, the world—as having much greater significance than the convenience of fast hamburgers and milk shakes. He coined the term *the McDonaldization of society,* to refer to the increasing rationalization of the routine tasks of everyday life.

He points out that Ray Kroc, the founder of McDonald's, applied the principles developed by Henry Ford to the preparation and serving of food. A 1958 operations manual spelled out the exact procedure:

It told operators exactly how to draw milk shakes, grill hamburgers, and fry potatoes. It specified precise cooking times for all products and temperature settings for all equipment. It fixed standard portions on every food item, down to the quarter ounce of onions placed on each hamburger patty and the thirty-two slices per pound of cheese. It specified that french fries be cut at nine-thirty-seconds of an inch thick. . . . Grill men . . . were instructed to put hamburgers down on the grill moving from left to right, creating six rows of six patties each. And because the first two rows were farthest from the heating element, they were instructed (and still are) to flip the third row first, then the fourth, fifth, and sixth before flipping the first two.

Ritzer stresses that "McDonaldization" does not refer just to the robotlike assembly of food. Rather, this process, occurring throughout society, is transforming our lives. Shopping malls are controlled environments of approved design, logo, colors, and opening and closing hours. Travel agencies transport middle-class Americans to ten European capitals in fourteen days, each visitor experiencing exactly the same hotels, restaurants, and other predictable settings. No one need fear meeting a "real" native. *USA Today* produces the same bland, instant news—in short, unanalytic pieces that can be read between gulps of the McShake or the McBurger.

Is all this bad? Not necessarily. Efficiency does bring reduced prices. But at a cost, a loss of something difficult to define, a quality of life washed away by rationalization. In my own travels, for example, had I taken packaged tours, I never would have had the enjoyable, eye-opening experiences that have added to my appreciation of human diversity.

In any event, the future has arrived. The trend is strongly toward the McDonaldization of human experience. For good or bad, our social destiny is to live in such prepackaged settings. When education becomes rationalized—which is now in process—our children will no longer have to put up with the idiosyncrasies of real professors, those people who think that ideas must be discussed endlessly and who never come to decisive answers anyway. What we want are instant, preformed solutions to social issues, like those we find in mathematics and engineering. Fortunately, our children will be able to be instructed in computerized courses, in which everyone learns the same answers, the approved, "politically correct," precise, and proper ways to think about social issues. This certainly will be efficient—and the "iron cage" of bureaucracy that Weber said would entrap us.

Think of a judge at a dog show. He or she has a mental image of what a particular breed of dog should look like, and judges each dog according to that mental image. No particular dog will have all the characteristics, but all dogs of that breed put together have them. Thus, a particular organization may be ranked high or low on some characteristic and still qualify as a bureaucracy. Instead of labeling a particular organization as a "bureaucracy" or "not a bureaucracy," it probably makes more sense to think in terms of the *extent* to which an organization is bureaucratized (Udy 1959; Hall 1963).

As with culture, then, a bureaucracy often differs from its ideal image. The actual lines of authority ("going through channels"), for example, may be quite different from those portrayed on organizational charts, such as that shown in Figure 7.1. For example, suppose that before being promoted, the university president taught in the history department. As a result, friends from that department may have direct access to him or her. In giving their "input" (ranging from opinions about how to solve problems to personal grievances or even gossip), these individuals may skip their chairperson or even the dean of their college altogether.

ideal type: a composite of characteristics based on many specific examples ("ideal" in this case means a description of the abstracted characteristics, not what one desires to exist)

Dysfunctions of Bureaucracies

Although no other form of social organization has been found to be more efficient in the long run, as Weber recognized, his model accounts for only part of the characteristics of bureaucracies. They also have a dark side, and do not always operate smoothly. Let's look at some of bureaucracy's dysfunctions—red tape, lack of communication, alienation, goal displacement, and incompetence.

Bureaucracies are so powerful and overwhelming that even Mother Teresa, one of the most famous religious figures of the late twentieth century, was not able to overcome bureaucratic rules in order to help the U.S. homeless.

Red Tape: A Rule Is a Rule. As Jennifer, in the opening vignette, discovered, bureaucracies can be filled with so much red tape that they impede the purpose of the organization. In the Bronx, Mother Teresa spotted a structurally sound abandoned building and wanted to turn it into a homeless shelter. But she ran head-on into a rule: The building must have an elevator for the handicapped homeless. Not having the funds for the elevator, Mother Teresa struggled to get permission to bypass this rule. Two frustrating years later, she gave up. The abandoned building is still an abandoned building (Tobias 1995).

Obviously this well-intentioned rule about elevators was not meant to stop Mother Teresa from ministering to the down and out. But, hey, rules is rules!

Lack of Communication Between Units. Each unit within a bureaucracy performs specialized tasks, which are designed to contribute to the organization's overall goals. At times, these units fail to communicate with one another and end up working at cross purposes. In Granada, Spain, for example, the local government was concerned about the rundown appearance of buildings along one of its main roads. Consequently, one unit of the government fixed the fronts of these buildings, painting and repairing concrete, iron, and stonework. The results were impressive, and the unit was proud of what it had accomplished. The only problem was that another unit of the government had slated these same buildings for demolition (Arías 1993). With neither unit of this bureaucracy knowing what the other was doing, the huge expense and effort of the one ended in a rubble heap.

Today's armies, no matter from what country, are bureaucracies. They have a strict hierarchy of rank, division of labor, impersonality (an emphasis on the office, not the person holding it), and they stress written records, rules, and communications—essential characteristics identified by Max Weber. This army in India, though its outward appearance may differ from Western standards, is no exception to this principle.

Bureaucratic Alienation.   Many workers find it disturbing to deal with others in terms of roles, rules, and functions rather than as individuals. Similarly, they may dislike writing memos instead of talking to people face to face. It is not surprising, then, that workers in large organizations sometimes feel more like objects than people, or, as Weber (1978) put it, "only a small cog in a ceaselessly moving mechanism which prescribes to [them] an endlessly fixed routine. . . ." Because workers must deal with one another in such formal ways, and because they constantly perform routine tasks, some come to feel that no one cares about them and that they are misfits in their surroundings.

Marx termed these reactions **alienation** and attributed them to the fact that workers are cut off from the finished product of their labor. Although assigning workers to repetitive tasks makes for efficient production, Marx argued that it also reduces their satisfaction by limiting their creativity and sense of contribution to the finished product. Underlying alienation is the workers' loss of control over their work because they no longer own their own tools. Before industrialization, individual workers used their own tools to produce an entire product, such as a chair or table. Now the capitalists own the machinery and tools and assign each worker only a single step or two in the entire production process. Relegated to repetitive tasks that seem remote from the final product, workers lose a sense of identity with what they produce. Ultimately they come to feel estranged not only from their products but from their whole work environment.

Resisting Alienation.   Alienation, of course, is not a pleasant experience. Because workers want to feel valued and want to have a sense of control over their work, they resist alienation. Forming primary groups at work is a major form of that resistance. They band together in informal settings—at lunch, around desks, for a drink after work. There they give one another approval for jobs well done and express sympathy for the shared need to put up with cantankerous bosses, meaningless routines, and endless rules. Here they relate to one another not just as workers, but as people who value one another. They laugh and tell jokes, talk about their families, their problems, their goals, and, often, their love life. Adding this multidimensionality to their work relationships restores their sense of being persons rather than mere cogs in an endlessly moving machine.

Consider a common sight. You are visiting an office, and you see work areas decorated with family and vacation photos. The sociological implication is that of workers striving to overcome alienation. By staking a claim to individuality, the workers are rejecting an identity as mere machines performing functions.

alienation: Marx's term for the experience of being cut off from the product of one's labor that results in a sense of powerlessness and normlessness

175

The Alienated Bureaucrat. Not all workers succeed in resisting alienation, however, and some become extremely alienated. They remain in the organization because they see no viable alternative or because they have "only so many years until retirement." They hate every minute of it, however, and it shows—in their attitudes toward clients, toward fellow workers, and especially toward authority in the organization. The alienated bureaucrat does not take initiative, will not do anything for the organization beyond what he or she is absolutely required to do, and uses rules to justify doing as little as possible. If Jennifer in this chapter's opening vignette had come across an alienated bureaucrat behind the registration window, she might have been told, "What's the matter with you—Can't you read? Everyone else manages to pay their fees on time, why can't you? I don't know what kind of students they are sending us nowadays." If the worker had been alienated even more, he or she might even have denied knowledge of where to get the problem taken care of.

In spite of poor attitude and performance, alienated workers often retain their jobs, either because they may have seniority, or know the written rules backward and forward, or threaten expensive, time-consuming, and embarrassing legal action if anyone tries to fire them. Some alienated workers are shunted off into small bureaucratic corners, where they do trivial tasks and have little chance of coming in contact with the public. This treatment, of course, only alienates them further.

Goal Displacement. Bureaucracies sometimes take on a life of their own, adopting new goals in place of old ones. In this process, called **goal displacement,** even when the goal of the organization has been achieved and there no longer is any reason for it to continue, continue it does. A good example is the National Foundation for the March of Dimes, organized in the 1930s to fight polio, a crippling disease that strikes without warning (Sills 1957). The origin of polio was a mystery to the medical profession, and the public was alarmed and fearful. All sorts of rumors ran rampant about its cause. Everyone knew someone who had been crippled by this disease. Overnight, a healthy child would be stricken. Parents were fearful because no one knew whose child would be next. The March of Dimes began to publicize individual cases. An especially effective strategy was placing posters of a child on crutches near cash registers in almost every store in the United States. The U.S. public took the goals of the organization to heart and contributed heavily.

The organization raised money beyond its wildest dreams. Then during the 1950s, when Dr. Jonas Salk developed a vaccine for polio this threat was wiped out almost

goal displacement: a goal displaced by another; in this context, the adoption of new goals by an organization; also known as *goal replacement*

The March of Dimes was founded by President Franklin Roosevelt in the 1930s to fight polio. When a vaccine for polio was discovered in the 1950s, the organization did not declare victory and disband. Instead, it kept the organization intact by creating new goals—fighting birth defects. Sociologists use the term goal displacement *to refer to this process of adopting new goals. "Fighting birth defects" is now being replaced by an even vaguer goal, "Breakthroughs for Babies." This new goal displacement may guarantee the organization's existence forever, for it is a goal so elusive it can never be reached. (Can we ever run out of the need for "breakthroughs"?)*

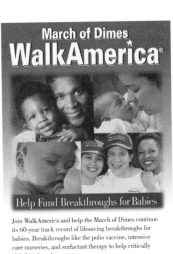

Join WalkAmerica and help the March of Dimes continue its 60-year track record of lifesaving breakthroughs for babies. Breakthroughs like the polio vaccine, intensive care nurseries, and surfactant therapy to help critically ill babies breathe.

Sign up for WalkAmerica today. Call your local March of Dimes or 1-800-525-WALK and join our successful fight to save babies.

overnight. The public breathed a collective sigh of relief. What then? Did the organization fold? After all, its purpose had been fulfilled. But, as you know, the March of Dimes is still around. Faced with the loss of their jobs, the professional staff that ran the organization quickly found a way to keep the bureaucracy intact by pursuing a new enemy—birth defects. Their choice of enemy is particularly striking, for it is doubtful that we will ever run out of birth defects—and thus unlikely that these people will ever run out of jobs.

Bureaucratic Incompetence.   In a tongue-in-cheek analysis of bureaucracies, Laurence Peter proposed what has become known as the **Peter principle:** Each employee of a bureaucracy is promoted to his or her *level of incompetence* (Peter and Hull 1969). People who perform well in a bureaucracy come to the attention of those higher up the chain of command and are promoted. If they again perform well, they are again promoted. This process continues until finally they are promoted to a level at which they can no longer handle the responsibilities well; this is their level of incompetence. There they hide behind the work of others, taking credit for what those under their direction accomplish. Although the Peter principle contains a grain of truth, if it were generally true, bureaucracies would be staffed entirely by incompetents, and none of these organizations could succeed. In reality, bureaucracies are remarkably successful.

The Sociological Significance of Bureaucracies

Perhaps the main sociological significance of bureaucracies is that they represent a fundamental change in how people relate to one another. When work is rooted in social relationships, much more is at stake than efficiency in performing tasks and keeping an eye on the bottom line. Seeing that all family members are employed, or that everyone in the community has a chance to make a living, for example, may be the determining factors in making decisions. Bureaucracies, or the rationalization of society, changed all this (Volti 1995).

Voluntary Associations ▶

Although bureaucracies have become the dominant form of organization for large, task-oriented groups, even more common are voluntary associations. Let us examine their essential characteristics.

Back in the 1830s, a Frenchman traveled across the United States, observing the customs of this new nation. Alexis de Tocqueville wrote a book about his observations, *Democracy in America* (1835), which became widely read in Europe and in the United States and is still quoted for its insights into the American character. As an outsider, de Tocqueville was able to see patterns that people immersed in them could not. One of de Tocqueville's observations was that Americans joined a lot of **voluntary associations,** groups made up of volunteers who organize on the basis of some mutual interest.

Over the years, Americans have maintained this pattern and are extremely proud of it. A visitor entering any of the thousands of small towns that dot the U.S. landscape is greeted with a highway sign proclaiming which volunteer associations that particular town has: Girl Scouts, Boy Scouts, Kiwanis, Lions, Elks, Eagles, Knights of Columbus, Chamber of Commerce, Future Farmers of America, American Legion, Veterans of Foreign Wars, and perhaps a host of others. One form of voluntary association is so prevalent that a separate sign usually indicates which varieties are present in the town: Roman Catholic, Baptist, Lutheran, Methodist, Episcopalian, and so on. Not listed on these signs are many other voluntary associations, such as political parties, unions, health clubs, the National Right to Life, the National Organization for Women, Alcoholics Anonymous, Gamblers Anonymous, Association of Pinto Racers, and Citizens United For or Against This and That.

Americans love voluntary associations, using them to express a wide variety of interests, goals, opinions, and even dissatisfactions. Some groups are local, consisting of only

Peter principle: a bureaucratic "law" according to which the members of an organization are promoted for good work until they reach their level of incompetence, the level at which they can no longer do good work

voluntary association: a group made up of volunteers who have organized on the basis of some mutual interest

a few volunteers; others are national, with a paid professional staff. Some are temporary, organized to accomplish a specific task such as arranging a town's next Fourth of July fireworks. Others, such as the Scouts and political parties, are permanent, large, secondary organizations with clear lines of command—and they are also bureaucracies.

Functions of Voluntary Associations

Whatever their form, voluntary associations are so numerous because they meet people's basic needs. People do not *have* to belong to these organizations. They join because they obtain benefits from their participation. Functionalists have identified seven functions of voluntary associations.

1. Voluntary organizations advance the particular interests they represent. For example, adults who are concerned about children's welfare volunteer for the Scouts because they think that this group is superior to the corner pool hall. In short, voluntary associations get things done, whether ensuring that fireworks are purchased and shot off or that people become familiar with the latest legislation affecting their occupation.

2. Voluntary groups also offer people an identity, for some, even a sense of purpose in life. As in-groups, they provide their members with a feeling of togetherness, of belonging, and in many cases, of doing something worthwhile. This function is so important for some individuals that their participation in voluntary associations becomes the center of their lives.

3. Voluntary associations help govern the nation and maintain social order. Groups that help "get out the vote" or assist the Red Cross in coping with disasters are obvious examples.

Note that the first two functions apply to all voluntary associations. In a general sense, so does the third. Although few organizations are focused on politics and the social order, taken together, voluntary associations help to incorporate individuals into the general society. By allowing the expression of desire and dissent, they help prevent anomie.

Voluntary organizations are extremely popular in the United States. Former President Jimmy Carter and former First Lady Rosalyn Carter spend a week each year working for Habitat for Humanity. They are shown here helping to build row houses for homeless people in the nation's capital.

Sociologist David Sills (1968) identified four other functions, which apply only to some voluntary groups.

4. Some voluntary groups mediate between the government and the individual. For example, some provide a way for people to put pressure on lawmakers.

5. By providing training in organizational skills, some groups help individuals climb the occupational ladder.

6. Some voluntary groups help bring people into the political mainstream. The National Association for the Advancement of Colored People (NAACP) is an example of such a group.

7. Finally, some voluntary groups pave the way to social change. Opposing society's definitions of "normal" and socially acceptable, some groups such as Greenpeace challenge society's established boundaries. Their activities often indicate the direction of social change.

Shared Interests

Voluntary associations, then, represent no single interest or purpose. They can be reactionary, dragged screaming into the present as their nails claw the walls of the past, or they can lead the vanguard for social change, announcing their vision of a better world. In spite of their amazing diversity, however, a thread does run through all voluntary associations. That thread is mutual interest. Although the particular interest varies from group to group, shared interest in some view or activity is the tie that binds their members together.

Although a group's members are united by shared interests, their motivations for joining the group differ widely. Some join because they have strong conviction concerning the stated purpose of the organization, others simply because membership gives them a chance to make contacts that will help them politically or professionally. Some even join to be closer to some special person of the opposite sex.

With motivations for joining voluntary associations and commitment to their goals so varied, these organizations often have a high turnover. Some people move in and out of groups almost as fast as they change clothes. Within each organization, however, is an inner core of individuals who stand firmly behind the group's goals, or at least are firmly committed to maintaining the organization itself. If this inner core loses commitment, the group is likely to fold.

The Problem of Oligarchy

Rather than losing its commitment, however, this inner core is likely to grow ever tighter, becoming convinced that most members can't be counted on and that it can trust only the smaller group to make the really important decisions. To see this principle at work, let us look at the Veterans of Foreign Wars (VFW).

Sociologists Elaine Fox and George Arquitt (1985) studied three local posts of the VFW, a national organization of former U.S. soldiers who have served in foreign wars. The constitution of the VFW is very democratic, giving every member of the organization the right to be elected to positions of leadership. Fox and Arquitt found three types of VFW members: the silent majority (members who rarely show up), the rank and file (members who show up, but mainly for drinking), and leaders (those who have been elected to office or appointed to committees). Although the leaders of the posts are careful not to let their attitudes show, they look down on the rank and file, viewing them as a bunch of ignorant boozers.

Because the leaders can't stand the thought that such people might represent them to the community and at national meetings, a curious situation arises. "You need to meet Jim," the sociologists were told. "He's the next post commander after Sam does his time." At first the researchers found this puzzling. How could the elite be so sure? As they investigated further, they found that leadership is effectively decided behind the scenes. The elected leadership appoints their favored people to chair key committees. The members then become aware of their accomplishments, and these individuals are elected as leaders. The inner core, then, is so effective in keeping their own group in leadership that even before an election is held they can specify who is going to be their new post commander.

Most organizations are like the VFW, and are run by only a few of their members (Cnaan 1991). Building on the term *oligarchy*, a system in which many are ruled by a few, sociologist Robert Michels (1876–1936) coined the term **the iron law of oligarchy** to refer to how formal organizations come to be dominated by a small, self-perpetuating elite. The majority of the members become passive, and an elite inner group keeps itself in power by passing the leading positions from one clique member to another.

What many find depressing about the iron law of oligarchy is that it applies even to organizations strongly committed to democratic principles. Even U.S. political parties, for example, supposedly the backbone of the nation's representative government, have fallen prey to it. Run by an inner group that may or may not represent the community, they pass their leadership positions from one elite member to another. This principle is also demonstrated by the U.S. Senate. With their control of statewide political machinery and access to free mailing, about 90 percent of U.S. senators who choose to run are reelected (*Statistical Abstract* 1997: Table 447).

The iron law of oligarchy is not without its limitations, of course. Members of the inner group must remain attuned to the opinions of the other members, regardless of their personal feelings. If the oligarchy gets too far out of line, it runs the risk of a grassroots rebellion that would throw this elite group out of office. It is this threat that often softens the iron law of oligarchy by making the leadership responsive to the membership. In addition, because not all organizations become captive to an elite, this is a tendency, not an inevitability (Fisher 1994).

the iron law of oligarchy: Robert Michels's phrase for the tendency of formal organizations to be dominated by a small, self-perpetuating elite

corporate culture: the orientations that characterize corporate work settings

Careers in Bureaucracies

Since you are likely to end up working in a bureaucracy, let's look at how its characteristics may affect your career.

The Corporate Culture: Consequences of Hidden Values

Sociologist Rosabeth Moss Kanter has written extensively about corporations, including such titles as Men and Women of the Corporation, Innovation: Breakthrough Thinking, *and* World Class: Thriving Locally in the Global Economy.

Who gets ahead in a large corporation? Although we might like to think that success is the consequence of intelligence and hard work, many factors other than merit underlie salary increases and promotions. As sociologist Rosabeth Moss Kanter (1977, 1983) stresses, the **corporate culture,** the orientations that characterize corporate work settings, is crucial in determining people's corporate fate. She explains how a corporation's "hidden values"—the values that are not officially part of the organization, but that nevertheless powerfully influence its members—operate as self-fulfilling stereotypes. The elite holds ideas about who are the best workers and colleagues, and those who fit this mold receive better access to information and networking, and are put in "fast-track" positions. Not surprisingly, these people perform better and become more committed to the organization, thus confirming the initial expectation. In contrast, those judged to be outsiders find opportunities closing up. They tend to work at a level beneath their capacity, come to think poorly of themselves, and become less committed to the organization.

The hidden values that created this self-fulfilling prophecy remain invisible to most. What is visible are the promotions of people with superior performances and greater commitment to the company, not the self-fulfilling prophecy that produced these attitudes and work performances.

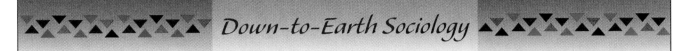

Maneuvering the Hidden Culture—Women Surviving the Male-Dominated Business World

I work for a large insurance company. Of its twenty-five hundred employees, about 75 percent are women. Only 5 percent of the upper management positions, however, are held by women.

I am one of the more fortunate women, for I hold a position in middle management. I am also a member of the twelve-member junior board of directors, of whom nine are men and three are women.

Recently one of the female members of the board suggested that the company become involved in Horizons for Tomorrow, a program designed to provide internships for disadvantaged youth. Two other women and I spent many days developing a proposal for our participation.

The problem was how to sell the proposal to the company president. From past experiences, we knew that if he saw it as a "woman's project" it would be shelved into the second tier of "maybes." He hates what he calls "aggressive bitches."

We three decided, reluctantly, that the proposal had a chance only if it were presented by a man. We decided that Bill was the logical choice. We also knew that we had to "stroke" Bill if we were going to get his cooperation.

We first asked Bill if he would "show us how to present our proposal." (It is ridiculous to have to play the role of the "less capable female" in the 1990s, but, unfortunately the corporate culture sometimes dictates this strategy.) To clinch matters, we puffed up Bill even more by saying, "You're the logical choice for the next chairmanship of the board."

Bill, of course, came to our next planning session, where *we* "prepped" *him* on what to say.

At our meeting with the president, we had Bill give the basic presentation. We then backed *him* up, providing the background and rationale for why the president should endorse the project. As we answered the president's questions, we carefully deferred to Bill.

The president's response? "An excellent proposal," he concluded, "an appropriate project for our company."

To be successful, we had to maneuver through the treacherous waters of the "hidden culture" (actually not so "hidden" to women who have been in the company for a while). The proposal was not sufficient on its merits, for the "who" behind a proposal is at least as significant as the proposal itself.

"We shouldn't have to play these games," Laura said, summarizing our feelings.

But we all know that we have no choice. To become labeled "pushy" is to commit "corporate suicide"—and we're no fools.

Source: Written by an insurance executive in Henslin's introductory sociology class who, out of fear of retaliation at work, chooses to remain anonymous.

The Down-to-Earth Sociology box above explores how ideas often are judged in corporations not by their merit, but according to *who* expresses them. You can see how such hidden values contribute to the iron law of oligarchy, for the corporate elite, the tight inner group that heads a corporation, sets in motion a self-fulfilling prophecy that tends to reproduce itself with people who "look" like themselves, generally white and male. Although women and minorities, who don't match the stereotype, are often "showcased"—placed in highly visible positions with little power in order to demonstrate to the public and affirmative action officials how progressive the company is (Benokraitis and Feagin 1991)—they often occupy "slow-track" positions, where accomplishments seldom come to the attention of top management.

Kanter found that the level people reach in the organization also shapes their behavior, and even their attitudes toward themselves and others. In general, the higher people go, the higher their morale. "This is a good company," they say to themselves. "They recognize my abilities." With their greater satisfaction, people in higher office also tend to be more helpful to subordinates and flexible in their style of leadership. In contrast, people who don't get very far in the organization are frustrated and tend to have lower morale. A less apparent result of their blocked opportunity, however, is that they are likely to be rigid supervisors and strong defenders of whatever privileges they have.

There is a significant hidden level in bureaucracies, then. Because the workers in a corporation tend to see only the level that is readily visible, they usually ascribe differences in behaviors and attitudes to people's personalities. Sociologists probe beneath this level, however, to examine how corporate culture shapes people's attitudes, and, by extension, the quality of their work.

One of the major issues in bureaucracies is how to adapt to a changing work force. A controversial solution that some corporations have chosen is discussed in the Social Issues box below.

Humanizing the Corporate Culture

Bureaucracies have transformed society by harnessing people's energies to specific goals and monitoring progress to those goals. Weber (1946a) predicted that because bureaucracies are so efficient and have the capacity to replace themselves indefinitely, they would come to dominate social life. More than any prediction in sociology, this one has withstood the test of time (Rothschild and Whitt 1986; Perrow 1991).

Bureaucracies appear likely to remain our dominant form of social organization, and most of us, like it or not, are destined to spend our working lives in bureaucracies. Many people have become concerned about the negative side of bureaucracies, however, and would like to make them more humane. **Humanizing a work setting** means organizing work in such a way that it develops rather than impedes human potential. Such work settings offer access to opportunities on the basis of ability and contributions rather than personal characteristics, distribute power more equally, and have less rigid rules and more open decision making. In short, more people are involved in making decisions, their contributions are more readily recognized, and individuals feel freer to participate.

Can bureaucracies adapt to such a model? Contrary to some popular images, not all bureaucracies are unyielding, unwieldy monoliths. There is nothing in the nature of bu-

> **assimilation:** the process by which the dominant group absorbs a minority group

> **humanizing a work setting:** organizing a workplace in such a way that it develops rather than impedes human potential

 *Liberal and Conservative Views on Social Issues*

Diversity Training

Some of the signs: More than half of U.S. workers are minorities, immigrants, and women. In San Jose, California, families with the Vietnamese surname *Nguyen* outnumber the Joneses by nearly 50 percent. Diversity in the workplace is much more than skin color. Diversity includes ethnicity, gender, age, religion, social class, and sexual orientation.

The huge successes of the women's movement and of civil rights activism have encouraged pride in one's heritage and made many Americans comfortable with being different from the dominant group. Consequently, people are now less amenable to **assimilation,** the process by which minorities are absorbed into the dominant culture. Assimilation involves relinquishing distinctive cultural patterns of behavior in favor of those of the dominant culture. Realizing that assimilation is probably not the wave of the future, most major companies sponsor "diversity training," sending workers to lectures and workshops to learn to work with colleagues of diverse cultures and racial/ethnic backgrounds.

In general, liberals welcome diversity training. They see it as an effective means of coming to grips with the new reality of the workplace. As Roosevelt Thomas, president of

the American Institute for Managing Diversity, says, "You don't have to aspire to be a white male or a member of the dominant group. People are willing to be part of a team, but they won't jump into the melting pot any more." Consequently, say liberals, diversity training is needed so we can develop an appreciative understanding of our differences and work together to meet common goals.

Conservatives, in general, see a dark side to diversity training. They believe that it stimulates the stereotypes and divisiveness it is meant to alleviate. They point to the "blame and shame" sessions sponsored by the U.S. Department of Transportation, in which African Americans and whites were encouraged to exchange insults, and men were groped while running a gauntlet of women. Consequently, say conservatives, we must deemphasize group differences and instead stress the behavioral qualities that lead to success—especially responsibility and pride in one's work. Then we can work together as a team to meet common goals.

Sources: Based on Thomas 1990; Piturro 1991; Sowell 1993a; Reibstein 1996.

reaucracies that makes them *inherently* insensitive to people's needs or that prevents them from humanizing corporate culture.

But how about the cost of such changes? The United States is in intense economic competition with other nations, especially Japan and western Europe, and it would be difficult to afford costly changes. To humanize corporate culture, however, does not require huge expense. Kanter (1983) compared forty-seven companies that were rigidly bureaucratic with competitors of the same size that were more flexible. It turned out that the more flexible companies were also the more profitable—probably because their greater flexibility encouraged greater company loyalty, creativity, and productivity.

Quality Circles

In light of such findings, many corporations have taken steps to humanize their work settings, motivated not by any altruistic urge to make life better for their workers but by self-interest, the desire to make their organization more competitive. About two thousand U.S. companies—from the smallest to the largest—have begun to reform their work organizations. Some have developed "quality circles," which consist of perhaps a dozen workers and a manager or two who meet regularly to try to improve the quality of both the work setting and the company's products. Over half of these companies, however, report that quality circles have yielded few benefits. Part of the reason may be that many companies set up quality circles for reasons of publicity, not intending to take employee suggestions seriously. Disappointed with the results, companies such as Whirlpool and GE have abandoned quality circles. Each company continues to solicit ideas from its employees, however. GE now uses town hall type meetings and rewards workers with cash and stock options (Naj 1993).

Employee Stock Ownership

Many companies offer an opportunity for their employees to purchase the firm's stock at a discount or as part of their salary, and about eight thousand U.S. companies are now partially owned by their employees. Because each employee typically owns only a tiny amount of stock in the company, such "ownership" is practically meaningless. In about a thousand of these companies, however, the employees own the majority of the stock. On average, companies with at least 10 percent of their stock owned by employees are more profitable than other firms, probably because the workers are more committed and managers take a longer-term view (White 1991).

One might think that employee ownership of a company's stock would eliminate problems between workers and management. Profitability, however, not ownership, appears to be the key to reducing these problems. Unprofitable firms put more pressure on their employee-owners, creating tension between workers and managers, while profitable companies are quicker to resolve problems.

Small Work Groups

Pioneered in the computer industry to increase productivity and cut down on absenteeism, small work groups, or self-managed teams, are now used by one in five U.S. companies. Small work groups stimulate creative ideas and imaginative solutions to problems, and employees who work in them feel a greater sense of loyalty to the company, work harder, and reduce their absenteeism. Workers in these groups also react more quickly to

Humanizing the work setting, an attempt to make working conditions better match human needs, has taken many forms. One (used by only a minority of corporations) is to offer on-site day care. Shown here is a working mom dropping her little girl off at the company-run day care center. Such services cost companies less than they appear to, for they reduce worker turnover.

threats posed by technological change and competitors' advances. No less a behemoth than IBM has found that people work more effectively in a small group than in a distant, centralized command structure (Larson and Dolan 1983; Drucker 1992).

Materials discussed in the last chapter help to explain these results. The small work group establishes primary relationships among its members, and workers' identities become tied up with their group. This reduces alienation, for rather than being lost in a bureaucratic maze, here their individuality is appreciated, their contributions more readily recognized. The group's successes become the individual's successes—as do its failures—reflecting positively or negatively on the individual. As a consequence of their expanded personal ties, workers make more of an effort. The results have been so good that in what is known as "worker empowerment," some self-managed teams even replace bosses in controlling everything from schedules to hiring and firing (Lublin 1991).

Corporate Day Care

Another way to humanize the work setting is to set up day care facilities at work. This eases the strain on parents, especially on new mothers, who are able to go to work and still keep an eye on a baby or young child. Parents are also able to spend time with their children during breaks and lunch hours. Mothers can even nurse a child at these times.

Granted global competition, can U.S. firms afford child care? Accountable to its stockholders, the Union Bank of Monterey, California, decided to measure the net cost of its day care. They found that the turnover of employees who used the center was only 2.2 percent, compared with 9.5 percent of those who did not use it. Users of the center were also absent from work almost two days a year less than the nonusers. Their maternity leaves were also shorter. The net cost? After subtracting what it cost to open the center and to run it, the bank saved over $200,000 (Solomon 1988).

A measure in between the company providing such services and offering no child care is to provide quality emergency back-up child care. Parents use their own baby-sitter, but when the sitter can't make it, the center's services allow the parent to get to work—and to work without worry. Such centers now operate in several cities, with staffs that hold master's degrees in early childhood education (Nayaran 1994).

With increasing numbers of women in management, it is likely that more and more U.S. firms will offer child care services as part of a benefits package to attract and hold capable workers.

Developing an Alternative: The Cooperative

In the 1970s, many Americans, especially those opposed to capitalism and what they considered to be the deadening effects of bureaucracy, began to seek an alternative organizational form. They began to establish cooperatives, organizations owned by members who collectively make decisions, determine goals, evaluate resources, set salaries, and assign work tasks. These tasks are all carried out without a hierarchy of authority, for all members can participate in the decisions of the organization. Since the 1970s, about five thousand cooperatives have been established.

As sociologists Joyce Rothschild and Allen Whitt (1986) pointed out, cooperatives are not new, but were introduced into the United States during the 1840s. Cooperatives attempt to achieve some specific social good (such as lowering food prices and improving food quality) and to provide a high level of personal satisfaction for their members as they work toward that goal. Because all members can participate in decision making, cooperatives spend huge amounts of time in deciding even routine matters. The economic results of cooperatives are mixed. Many are less profitable than private organizations, others more so. A few have been so successful that they have been bought out by Wall Street firms.

The Conflict Perspective

Conflict theorists point out that the basic relationship between workers and owners is confrontational regardless of how the work organization is structured (Edwards 1979;

Derber and Schwartz 1988). Each walks a different path in life, the one exploiting workers to extract a greater profit, the other trying to resist that exploitation. Since their basic interests are fundamentally opposed, these critics argue, employers' attempts to humanize the work setting (or to manage diversity) are mere window dressing, efforts to conceal their fundamental goal to exploit workers. If these efforts are not camouflage, then they are worse—attempts to manipulate workers into active cooperation in their own exploitation. This analysis does not apply to cooperatives because they are owned by the workers.

Technology and the Control of Workers

As stressed in the previous chapter, the microchip is changing our lives. Many people rejoice over the computer's capacity to improve their quality of life. They are pleased with the quality control of manufactured goods and the reduction of drudgery. Records are much easier to keep, and we can type just one letter and let the computer print and address it to ten individuals—or to ten thousand. With ease, I can modify this sentence, this paragraph, or any section of this book.

Computers also hold the potential of severe abuse. They may allow governments to operate a police state, monitoring our every move. The Big Brother in Orwell's classic novel, *1984*, may turn out to be a computer.

Whether this happens or not, the computer certainly does allow managers to achieve much greater control over workers. Social psychologist Shoshana Zuboff (1991) reports how computers allow managers to increase surveillance without face- to-face supervision. They let managers know the number of strokes a word processor makes each minute or hour, or inform supervisors how long each telephone operator takes per call. Operators who are "underperforming" are singled out for discipline. It does not matter that the slower operators may be more polite or more helpful, only that the computer reports slower performance.

As sociologist Gary Marx (1985, 1986, 1995) says, with computers able to measure motion, air currents, vibrations, odors, pressure changes, voice stress, accompanied by video cameras that need only a pinhole for their spying eye, we may be moving to a "maximum-security" workplace. When workers at a leading hotel punch in, a device scans their eyes, comparing their retina with computerized data on file. This prevents employees from punching in one another's time cards. A truckdriver at Safeway used to enjoy his job. He says, "No one was looking over your shoulder, and you felt like a human being." But now he says he feels "pushed around." A small computer in the dashboard of his truck (called, appropriately, a Tripmaster) keeps track of his speed, shifting, excessive idling, and even reports when and how long he stops for lunch or a coffee break. The driver says he will retire early.

The maximum-security workplace seems an apt term for what is coming. And, as many fear, with the computer's awesome capacities, this kind of workplace may be just one part of a "maximum-security society" (Marx 1995).

The Japanese Corporate Model

How were the Japanese able to arise from the defeat of World War II, including the nuclear destruction of two of their main cities, to become such a giant in today's global economy? Some analysts trace part of the answer to the way in which their major corporations are organized. Let's look at the conclusions of William Ouchi (1981), who pinpointed five major ways in which Japanese corporations differ from those in the United States.

Hiring and Promotion

In *Japan*, college graduates hired by a corporation are thought of as a team working toward the same goal, namely, the success of the organization. They are all paid about the

For a time, Americans stood in awe of the Japanese corporate model. Research (as well as the passage of time that revealed problems with competitiveness), however, have uncovered several serious flaws. Lifetime job security, for example, is a myth. Shown here is a soup kitchen for the homeless in Tokyo. With the much more closely knit Japanese families, however, homelessness is much less of a problem in Japan than it is in the United States.

same starting salary, and they are rotated through the organization to learn its various levels. Not only do they work together as a team, but they also are promoted as a team. Team members cooperate with one another, for the welfare of one represents the welfare of all. They also develop intense loyalty to one another and to their company. Only in later years are individuals singled out for recognition. When there is an opening in the firm, outsiders are not even considered.

In the *United States*, an employee is hired on the basis of what the firm thinks that individual can contribute. Employees try to outperform others, regarding salary and position as a sign of success. The individual's loyalty is to himself or herself, not to the company. When there is an opening in the firm, outsiders are considered.

Lifetime Security

In *Japan* lifetime security is taken for granted. Once hired, employees can expect to work for the same firm for the rest of their lives. Similarly, the firm expects them to be loyal to the company, to stick with it through good and bad times. On the one hand, employees will not be laid off or fired; on the other hand, they do not go job shopping, for their careers—and many aspects of their lives—are wrapped up in this one firm.

In the *United States*, lifetime security is unusual, being limited primarily to some college professors (who receive what is called *tenure*). A company is expected to lay off workers in slow times, and if it reorganizes it is not unusual for whole divisions to be fired. Given this context, workers "look out for number one," and that includes job shopping and job hopping, constantly seeking better pay and opportunities elsewhere.

Almost Total Involvement

In *Japan* work is like a marriage: The employee and the company are committed to each other. The employee supports the company with loyalty and long hours of dedicated work, while the company, in turn, supports its workers with lifetime security, health services, recreation, sports and social events, even a home mortgage. Involvement with the company does not stop when the workers leave the building. They are likely to spend evenings with co-workers in places of entertainment, and perhaps to be part of a company study or exercise group.

In the *United States*, the work relationship is assumed to be highly specific. An employee is hired to do a specific job, and employees who have done their jobs have thereby fulfilled their obligation to the company. The rest of their hours are their own. They go home to their private lives, which are highly separated from the firm.

Broad Training

In *Japan*, employees move from one job to another within the corporation. Not only are they not stuck doing the same thing over and over for years on end, but they gain a broader picture of the corporation and how the specific jobs they are assigned fit into the bigger picture.

In the *United States*, employees are expected to perform one job, to do it well, and then to be promoted upward to a job with more responsibility. Their understanding of the company is largely tied to the particular corner they occupy, and it may be difficult for them to see how their job fits into the overall picture.

Decision Making by Consensus

In *Japan*, decision making is a lengthy process. The Japanese think it natural that after lengthy deliberations, to which each person to be affected by a decision contributes, everyone will agree on which suggestion is superior. This process broadens decision making, allowing workers to feel that they are an essential part of the organization, not simply cogs in a giant wheel.

In the *United States*, whoever has responsibility for the unit in question does as much consulting with others as he or she thinks necessary and then makes the decision.

Limitations of the Model

This model of corporate life in Japan has always struck some sociologists as too idealized to accurately reflect reality. And, indeed, to peer beneath the surface gives a different view of this ideal image, as is illustrated in the Perspectives box below, with which we shall close this chapter.

Perspectives

CULTURAL DIVERSITY AROUND THE WORLD

Cracks in the Corporate Façade

- *The Japanese are more productive than Americans.*
- *The living standard of Americans has fallen behind that of the Japanese.*
- *All Japanese workers enjoy lifetime job security.*
- *The Japanese work for cheaper wages than do Americans.*

What is wrong with these statements? Nothing, except that they are untrue.

In recent years, the Japanese economic behemoth seemed unstoppable. Many nations felt threatened by it, and there was even talk that Japan had lost World War II, but

was winning a new, undeclared economic war. Impressed with the Japanese success, many nations, including the United States, copied parts of their economic model. A closer look, however, reveals that not everything about the Japanese corporate system is as it appears on the surface.

One element, in fact, is so unfair from the U.S. perspective that it is hard to imagine how the Japanese tolerate it. At age 60, workers are dismissed. Although early retirement may sound attractive, the problem is that retirement income does not begin until workers reach 65. Facing five years without income, these workers must depend on savings,

(continued)

Perspectives, (continued)

part-time, low-paying jobs, and family and friends to get by until their retirement pay kicks in.

Other cracks in the seamless surface—the image that Japan so carefully cultivated—have also become visible. It turns out that only employees of major corporations have lifetime job security, perhaps a third of Japanese workers. And Japan has found that paying the same wages to almost everyone in the same age group is costly and inefficient. Diligent but uninspired executives are compensated more by seniority than by output. Bottom-up decision making is also too slow to adjust to rapidly changing worldwide markets. Although still small by Western standards, unemployment has grown, while industrial output has fallen. Japanese labor costs have soared higher than those in the United States, while their much-vaunted productivity actually lags behind U.S. industry.

In a surprise move, Japan turned to U.S. corporations to see why they are more efficient. Flying in the face of their traditions, Japanese corporations now lay off workers and use merit pay. Toyota and Honda, for example, give bonuses to managers who meet their goals (a standard policy in the U.S. system, to be sure, but strange and innovative in Japan). And to meet the changing challenges of international mar-

kets, instead of waiting for "bottom-up" results, some managers now initiate decisions.

Perhaps the biggest surprise was Ford's takeover of Mazda. After huge losses, Mazda creditors decided that Ford knew more about building and marketing cars than Mazda and invited them to manage the company. Just a few years earlier, the Japanese auto industry had seemed invincible.

We will have to await the results, but we know that the Japanese were remarkably successful in their initial adapting of the West's manufacturing techniques to their culture. If they make the adjustment of this second phase as successfully, we can predict that a much leaner, meaner Japanese production machine will emerge.

The real bottom line is that we live in a global marketplace—of ideas as well as products. The likely result of global competition will be that both the West and Japan will feed off each other—the one learning greater cooperation in the production process, the other greater internal competition.

Sources: Besser 1992; Naj 1993; Schlesinger and Sapsford 1993; Schlesinger et al. 1993; Shill 1993; Reitman and Suris 1994; Shirouzu and Williams 1995; Kanabayashi 1996.

Summary and Review

The Rationalization of Society

How did the rationalization of society come about?

Weber used the phrase **rationalization of society** to refer to transformation in people's thinking and behaviors—the change from protecting time-honored ways to a concern with efficiency and practical results. Weber traced the rationalization of society to Protestant theology, which he said brought about capitalism, while Marx attributed the rationalization to capitalism itself. Pp. 168–170.

Formal Organizations and Bureaucracy

What are formal organizations?

Formal organizations are secondary groups designed to achieve specific objectives. Their dominant form is the **bureaucracy,** which Weber characterized as consisting of a hierarchy, a division of labor, written rules, written communications, and impersonality of positions—characteristics that allow bureaucracies to be efficient and enduring. Pp. 170–174.

What dysfunctions are associated with bureaucracies?

The dysfunctions of bureaucracies include alienation, red tape, lack of communication between units, **goal displacement,** and incompetence (as seen in the **Peter principle**). In Weber's view, the impersonality of bureaucracies tends to produce **alienation** among workers—the feeling that no one cares about them and that they do not really fit in. Marx's view of alienation is somewhat different—workers are separated from the product of their labor because they participate in only a small part of the production process. Pp. 174–177.

Voluntary Associations

What are the functions of voluntary associations?

Voluntary associations are groups made up of volunteers who organize on the basis of common interests. These associations further mutual interests, provide a sense of identity and purpose, help to govern and maintain order, mediate between the government and the individual, give training in organizational skills, help provide access to political power, and pave the way for social change. Pp. 177–179.

What is the "iron law of oligarchy"?

Sociologist Robert Michels noted that formal organizations have a tendency to become controlled by a small group that limits leadership to its own inner circle. The dominance of a formal organization by an elite inner cirle that keeps itself in power is called the **the iron law of oligarchy.** Pp. 180–182.

Careers in Bureaucracies

How does the corporate culture affect workers?

The term **corporate culture** refers to an organization's traditions, values, and unwritten norms. Much of corporate culture, such as its hidden values, is not readily visible. Often, a self-fulfilling prophecy is at work: People who match a corporation's hidden values are put on tracks that enhance their chance of success, while those who do not match these values are set on a course that minimizes their performance. Pp. 180–182.

Humanizing the Corporate Culture

What does it mean to humanize the work setting?

Humanizing a work setting means to organize it in a way that develops rather than impedes human potential. Among

the characteristics of more humane bureaucracies are expanded opportunities on the basis of ability and contributions rather than personal characteristics, a more even distribution of power, less rigid rules, and more open decision making. Attempts to modify bureaucracies include quality circles, small work groups, and self-management teams. Employee ownership plans give workers a greater stake in the outcomes of their work organizations. Cooperatives are an alternative to bureaucracies. Conflict theorists see attempts to humanize work as a way of manipulating workers. Pp. 182–185.

The Japanese Corporate Model

How do Japanese and U.S. corporations differ?

The Japanese corporate model contrasts sharply with the U.S. model in its hiring and promotion practices, lifetime security, worker involvement outside the work setting, broad training of workers, and collective decision making. This model, however, has been idealized and does not adequately reflect the reality of Japanese corporate life today. Pp. 185–188.

Where can I read more on this topic?

Suggested readings for this chapter are listed on page 661.

Sociology and the Internet

All URLs listed are current as of the printing of this book. URLs are often changed. Please check our Website http://www.abacon.com/henslin for updates.

1. The United States government bureaucracy is one of the largest and most complex in the world. Explore a small portion of its organization by accessing the Secretary of Defense's Web page *http://www.defenselink.mil* and select "The Secretary of Defense." On the Secretary's page select "The Organization Chart." Browse through the chart, looking for elements that are bureaucratic. What are the advantages of these bureaucratic features? What are the drawbacks? Can you think of any alternative ways of organizing the Department of Defense? Print the chart and bring it to class for discussion.

2. Women business owners are no longer rare. Go to the Business Women's Network *http://www.tpag.com/BWN.html* and browse the site. Look at the issues raised, problems noted, and suggested solutions. Do women business owners face special difficulties not faced by men? Discuss.

3. Examine the Alzheimer's Web Page *http://www.alz.org/* What kind of group is represented here? Is this a voluntary or-

ganization? How do you know? What are some of the functions of the organization? Does this association fulfill any of the four additional functions identified by sociologist David Sills and discussed in your text? After reading some of the Web pages, why do you think people would join this group?

4. Are sororities and fraternities formal organizations or bureaucracies? Examine the following Greek organizations and discuss whether the organizations contain the essential characteristics of bureaucracies identified by Weber. When you think of bureaucracies, do you normally think of sororities and fraternities? Do you see a difference in the organizational structure of social, professional, or service fraternities/sororities? Explain the differences and similarities in the organizational setup of the three listed below. Were you surprised by your results?

http://www.deltagamma.org/ Delta Gamma (Social)
http://www.bap.org Beta Alpha Psi (Professional)
http://dolphin.upenn.edu/~phispi/ Phi Sigma Pi (Service)

Tsing-Fang Chen, Judgement After the War, 1977

CHAPTER

8

Deviance and Social Control

IN JUST A FEW MOMENTS I was to meet my first Yanomamo, my first primitive man. What would it be like? . . . I looked up (from my canoe) and gasped when I saw a dozen burly, naked, filthy, hideous men staring at us down the shafts of their drawn arrows. Immense wads of green tobacco were stuck between their lower teeth and lips making them look even more hideous, and strands of dark-green slime dripped or hung from their noses. We arrived at the village while the men were blowing a hallucinogenic drug up their noses. One of the side effects of the drug is a runny nose. The mucus is always saturated with the green powder and the Indians usually let it run freely from their nostrils. . . . I just sat there holding my notebook, helpless and pathetic. . . .

The whole situation was depressing, and I wondered why I ever decided to switch from civil engineering to anthropology in the first place. . . . [Soon] I was covered with red pigment, the result of a dozen or so complete examinations. . . . These examinations capped an otherwise grim day. The Indians would blow their noses into their hands, flick as much of the mucus off that would separate in a snap of the wrist, wipe the residue into their hair, and then carefully examine my face, arms, legs, hair, and the contents of my pockets. I said (in their language), "Your hands are dirty"; my comments were met by the Indians in the following way: they would "clean" their hands by spitting a quantity of slimy tobacco juice into them, rub them together, and then proceed with the examination.

Gaining a Sociological Perspective on Deviance

So went Napoleon Chagnon's eye-opening introduction to the Yanomamo tribe of the rain forests of Brazil. His ensuing months of fieldwork continued to bring surprise after surprise, and often Chagnon (1977) could hardly believe his eyes—or his nose.

Where would we start to list the deviant behaviors of these people? Appearing naked in public? Using hallucinogenic drugs? Letting mucus hang from their noses? Rubbing hands filled with mucus, spittle, and tobacco juice over a frightened stranger who doesn't dare to protest? Perhaps. But it isn't this simple, for, as we shall see, deviance is relative.

The Relativity of Deviance

Sociologists use the term **deviance** to refer to any violation of norms—whether the infraction is as minor as jaywalking, as serious as murder, or as humorous as Chagnon's encounter with the Yanomamo. This deceptively simple definition takes us to the heart of the sociological perspective of deviance, which sociologist Howard S. Becker (1966) identified this way: *It is not the act itself, but the reactions to the act, that make something deviant.* In other words, people's behaviors must be viewed from the framework of the culture in which they take place. To Chagnon, the behaviors were frighteningly deviant, but to the Yanomamo they represented normal, everyday life. What was deviant to Chagnon was *conforming* to the Yanomamo. From their viewpoint, you *should* check out strangers as they did—and nakedness is good, as are hallucinogenic drugs and letting mucus be "natural."

Chagnon's abrupt introduction to the Yanomamo allows us to see the *relativity of deviance,* a major point made by symbolic interactionists. Because different groups have different norms, *what is deviant to some is not deviant to others.* This principle holds *within* a society as well as across cultures. Thus acts perfectly acceptable in one culture—or in one group within a society—may be considered deviant in another culture, or in another group within the same society. This idea is explored in the Perspectives box on the next page.

Unlike the general public, sociologists use the term *deviance* nonjudgmentally, to refer to any act to which people respond negatively. When sociologists use this term, it does not mean that they agree that an act is bad, just that people judge it negatively. To sociologists, then, all of us are deviants of one sort or another, for we all violate norms from time to time.

deviance: the violation of rules or norms

192

Perspectives

CULTURAL DIVERSITY AROUND THE WORLD

Suicide and Sexual Behavior in Cross-Cultural Perspective

Anthropologist Robert Edgerton (1976) reports how differently human groups react to similar behaviors. Of the many examples he cites, let's look at suicide and sexuality to illustrate how a group's *definitions* of a behavior, not the behavior itself, determine whether or not it will be considered deviant.

Suicide

In some societies, suicide is seen not as deviance but as a positive act, at least under specified conditions. In traditional Japanese society, hara-kiri, a ritual disembowelment, was considered the proper course for disgraced noblemen or defeated military leaders. Similarly, kamikaze pilots in World War II who crashed their explosives-laden planes into U.S. warships were admired for their bravery and sacrifice. Traditional Eskimos approved the suicide of individuals no longer able to contribute their share to the group. Sometimes an aged father would hand his hunting knife to his son, asking him to drive it through his heart. For a son to refuse this request would be considered deviant.

Sexuality

Norms of sexual behavior vary so widely around the world that what is considered normal in one society may be considered deviant in another. The Pokot people of northwestern Kenya, for example, place high emphasis on sexual pleasure and fully expect that both a husband and his wife will reach orgasm. If a husband does not satisfy his wife, he is in serious trouble. Pokot men often engage in adulterous affairs, and should a husband's failure

to satisfy his wife be attributed to his adultery, when her husband is asleep his wife will bring in female friends and tie him up. The women will then shout obscenities at him, beat him, and, as a final gesture of their utter contempt, slaughter and eat his favorite ox before releasing him. His hours of painful humiliation are assumed to make him henceforth more dutiful concerning his wife's conjugal rights.

Ideal Versus Covert Norms

People can also become deviants for failing to understand that the group's ideal norms may not be its real norms. As with many groups, the Zapotec Indians of Mexico expect sexual activity to take place exclusively between husband and wife. Yet the *only* person in one Zapotec community who had had no extramarital affairs was considered deviant. Evidently these people have a covert, commonly understood norm that married couples will engage in discreet extramarital affairs, for when a wife learns that her husband is having an affair she does the same thing. One Zapotec wife, however, did not follow this informal pattern. Instead, she continually threw her virtue into her husband's face—and claimed headaches. Worse, she also informed the other husbands and wives in the village who their spouses were sleeping with. As a result, this virtuous woman was condemned by everyone in the village. In other words, the official norms do not always represent the real norms—another illustration of the gap between ideal and real culture.

Suicide is not inherently deviant: It is deviant only when that meaning is assigned to it. During World War II, some Japanese pilots were trained for kamikaze, or suicide, missions. Their planes were loaded with bombs, and their mission was to ram U.S. ships, killing themselves in the process. Shown here are six kamikaze pilots after their training.

To be considered deviant, a person may not even have to *do* anything. Sociologist Erving Goffman (1963) used the term **stigma** to refer to attributes that discredit people. These attributes include violations of norms of ability (blindness, deafness, mental handicaps) and norms of appearance (a facial birthmark, obesity). They also include involuntary membership in groups, such as being the victim of AIDS or the brother of a rapist. The stigma becomes a person's master status, defining him or her as deviant. Recall from Chapter 4 that a master status cuts across all other statuses that a person occupies.

▼ **In Sum** In sociology, the term deviance refers to all violations of social rules, regardless of their seriousness. The term is not a judgment about the behavior. Deviance is

stigma: "blemishes" that discredit a person's claim to a "normal" identity

relative, for what is deviant in one group may be conformance in another. As symbolic interactionists stress, if we are to understand people, we must understand the meanings that they give to events. Consequently, we must consider deviance from *within* a group's own framework, for it is *their* meanings that underlie their behavior.

Who Defines Deviance?

If deviance does not lie in the act, but in definitions of the act, where do those definitions come from? To answer this question, let's look first at areas of agreement between functionalists and conflict theorists, then at how these views diverge.

Tribal Versus Industrial Societies.   Let's first consider preliterate groups without a written language. Each of these groups, such as the Yanomamo, has passed through a unique history. Each has faced and solved a set of problems that threatened their survival. These solutions, such as how to investigate strangers and protect themselves from enemies, have become part of their norms and now are an essential part of their way of life. Agreement on how life should be lived is relatively simple, for they are a small group, with strong social bonds.

Industrialized societies, in contrast, are made up of many competing groups. Each has its own history of problems, its own solutions, its own ideas about the way the world is and ought to be, and its own norms to uphold its ideas of right and wrong. Because these groups participate in the same general culture, they agree on many things. Yet due to their separate histories, they may differ sharply on many others—to the extent that what one group considers right, another may consider wrong.

Regardless of how they define deviance, to enforce their version of what is good all groups set up techniques of **social control.** Up to this point in the analysis, functionalists and conflict theorists are in basic agreement about social control. But now they diverge.

Functionalism and Social Control.   Functionalists stress how the many groups in a pluralistic society coexist. Each enforces its own norms on its members, and the groups attain a more or less balanced state. Although tensions between them may appear from time to time, the balancing of these tensions produces the whole that we call society. If some group threatens to upset the equilibrium, efforts are made to restore balance. For example, in a pluralistic society the central government often plays a mediating role between groups. In the United States, the executive, legislative, and judicial branches of the government mediate the demands of the various groups that make up society, preventing groups whose basic ideas deviate from those held by most members of society from taking political control (Riesman 1950). This view of mediation and balance among competing groups is broadly representative of what may be called the **pluralistic theory of social control.**

Conflict Theory and Social Control.   Conflict theorists, in contrast, stress that each society is dominated by a group of elite, powerful people, and that the basic purpose of social control is to maintain the current power arrangements. Consequently, society is made up not of groups in balance, but rather of competing groups uneasily held together. The group that holds power must always fend off groups that desire to replace it and take over the society themselves. If another group does gain power, it, too, immediately tries to neutralize competing groups. Some groups are much more ruthless than others; for example, before and during World War II the Nazis in Germany and the Communists in the Soviet Union systematically eliminated individuals and groups they deemed a threat to their vision of the ideal society. In more recent years, the Khmer Rouge did the same in Cambodia. Other dominant groups may be less ruthless, but they, too, are committed to maintaining power.

social control: a group's formal and informal means of enforcing its norms

pluralistic theory of social control: the view that society is made up of many competing groups, whose interests manage to become balanced

A master status is an identity that cuts across an individual's other identities. Monica Lewinsky, who at the age of 21 served as an intern at the White House, received a deviant master status when her alleged sexual relationship with President Bill Clinton made national and international headlines.

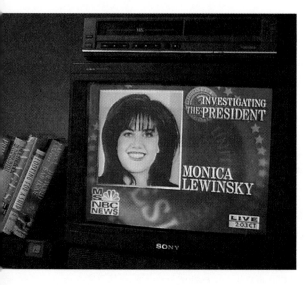

As conflict theorists stress, the enforcement of norms is always about power. About 2,000 years ago, the norms of the Romans and Christians clashed, with the Romans using violence to enforce its norms. Interestingly, the "powerless" group won the struggle. Shown here is a Hollywood version of Christians facing lions and gladiators in Rome's Coliseum. The clip is from Quo Vadis, a 1964 movie, with Peter Ustinov playing the Roman emperor Nero.

Although political power is not as naked in the United States as it is in dictatorships, conflict theorists note that an elite group of wealthy, largely white males maintains power by working behind the scenes to control the three branches of government (Domhoff 1990, 1997). These men make certain that their interests are represented in the day-to-day decisions of Congress, by the nominees to the U.S. Supreme Court, and by the presidential candidates of the two major political parties. Thus, it is this group's views of capital and property, the basis of their power, that are represented in the laws of society. This means that **official deviance**—the statistics on victims, lawbreakers, and the outcomes of criminal investigations and sentencing—centers on maintaining their interests.

Thus, conflict theorists stress, the state's machinery of social control represents the interests of the wealthy and powerful. It is this group that determines the basic laws whose enforcement is essential to preserving its own power. Other norms, such as those that govern informal behavior (chewing with a closed mouth, appearing in public with combed hair, and so on), may come from other sources, but they simply do not count for much. Although they influence everyday behavior, they do not determine prison sentences.

How Norms Make Social Life Possible

Regardless of which of these views is correct regarding the origin of a group's norms, or whose interests they represent, *norms make social life possible by making behavior predictable.* Consequently, every group within a society, and even human society itself, depends on norms for its existence. Only because we can count on most people most of the time to meet the expectations of others can social life as we know it exist.

What would life be like if you could not predict what others would do? Imagine for a moment that you have gone to a store to purchase milk:

Suppose that the clerk says, "I won't sell you any milk. We're overstocked with soda, and I'm not going to sell anyone milk until our soda inventory is reduced."

You don't like it, but you decide to buy a case of soda. At the checkout, the clerk says, "I hope you don't mind, but there's a $5 service charge on each fifteenth customer." You, of course, are the fifteenth.

Just as you start to leave, another clerk stops you and says, "We're not working anymore. We decided to have a party." Suddenly a stereo begins to blast, and everyone in the store begins to dance. "Oh, good, you've brought the soda," says one clerk, who takes your package and passes sodas all around.

But life is not like this. You can depend on grocery clerks to sell you milk. You also can depend on paying the same price as everyone else and not being forced to attend a party in the store. Why can you depend on this? Because we are socialized to follow norms, to play the basic roles society assigns to us.

Without norms we would have social chaos. Norms lay out the basic guidelines for how we play our roles and how we interact with others. In short, norms allow **social order,** a group's usual and customary social arrangements. Our lives are based on these arrangements, which is why deviance is often seen as so threatening, for it undermines

official deviance: a society's statistics on lawbreaking; its measures of crimes, victims, lawbreakers, and the outcomes of criminal investigations and sentencing

predictability, the foundation of social life. Consequently, human groups develop a system of *social control*, formal and informal means of enforcing norms.

Comparing Biological, Psychological, and Sociological Explanations

Since norms are essential for society, why do people violate them? To better understand the reasons, it is useful to know first how sociological explanations differ from biological and psychological ones, and then to examine how the three sociological perspectives explain deviance.

Psychologists and *sociobiologists* explain deviance by looking for answers *within* individuals. They assume that something in the makeup of people leads them to become deviant. By contrast, sociologists look for answers in factors *outside* the individual. They assume that something in the environment influences people to become deviant.

Biological explanations focus on **genetic predispositions** to such deviance as juvenile delinquency and crime (Lombroso 1911; Sheldon 1949; Glueck and Glueck 1956; Wilson and Hernstein 1985; Kamin 1975, 1986; Rose 1986). Biological explanations include (but are not restricted to) the following three theories: (1) intelligence—low intelligence leads to crime; (2) the "XYY" theory—an extra Y chromosome in males leads to crime; and (3) body type—people with "squarish, muscular" bodies are more likely to commit **street crime,** acts such as mugging, rape, and burglary.

How have these theories held up? Some criminals are very intelligent, and most people of low intelligence do not commit crimes. Most criminals have the normal "XY" chromosome combination, and most men with the "XYY" combination do not become criminals. In addition, no women have this combination of genes, so it wouldn't even deal with female criminals. Criminals also run the range of the body types exhibited by humanity, and most people with "squarish, muscular" bodies do not become street criminals. In short, these supposedly "causal" characteristics are even more common among the general population of people who do not commit crimes.

Still, we cannot rule out the possibility that biological factors influence deviance. Advances in biology have renewed interest in this issue, and some of the findings are intriguing. Psychiatrist Dorothy Lewis (1981), for example, compared the medical histories of delinquents and nondelinquents. She found that delinquents had significantly more head injuries. Then she matched the delinquents by the seriousness of their crimes. When she compared their medical histories, she found that the more violent delinquents—those incarcerated for murder, assault, and rape—also had more head injuries than boys locked up for lesser violence such as fights and threats with weapons. Many of the injuries had occurred before the age of 2.

The answers, then, are not yet in, and we must await more research. Even if biological factors are involved in some forms of deviance, from a sociological perspective the causes of deviance cannot be answered by biology alone. Biological factors are always mediated through the social environment. That is, conditions of society channel different categories of people in different directions. For example, some of the expectations of the masculine role in U.S. society—to be braver, tougher, more independent, and less tolerant of insult—increase the likelihood that males will become involved in violence.

Psychologists focus on abnormalities *within* the individual, on what are called **personality disorders.** Their supposition is that deviating individuals have deviating personalities (Kalichman 1988; Stone 1989; Heilbrun 1990), that various unconscious devices drive people to deviance. No specific negative childhood experience, however, is invariably linked with deviance. For example, children who had "bad toilet training," "suffocating mothers," or "emotionally aloof fathers" may become embezzling bookkeepers—or good accountants. Just as students, teachers, and police officers represent a variety of bad—and good—childhood experiences, so do deviants. In short, there is no inevitable outcome of particular childhood experiences, and deviance is not associated with any particular personality.

Sociologists, in contrast, search for factors *outside* the individual. Since deviance is relative, they ask why should we expect to find anything constant within people to account

social order: a group's usual and customary social arrangements, on which its members depend and on which they base their lives

genetic predispositions: inborn tendencies, in this context, to commit deviant acts

street crime: crimes such as mugging, rape, and burglary

personality disorders: the view that a personality disturbance of some sort causes an individual to violate social norms

for a behavior that is conforming in one society and deviant in another? Sociologists also look for social influences that "recruit" some people rather than others to break norms. To account for why people commit crimes, for example, sociologists examine such external influences as socialization, subcultural membership, and social class. *Social class*, a concept discussed in depth in the next two chapters, refers to people's relative standing in terms of education, occupation, and especially income and wealth.

Knowing how relative deviance is, sociologists wonder why anyone would expect to find factors within people to explain deviance. For example, because **crime** is the violation of norms that have been written into law, what a crime is varies from one human group to another. Why, then, should we expect to find anything constant within people to account for crime—or any other behavior that is conforming in one group but deviant in another?

To see how sociologists explain deviance, especially criminal behavior, let's contrast the three sociological perspectives—symbolic interactionism, functionalism, and conflict theory.

The Symbolic Interactionist Perspective

As we examine symbolic interactionism, it will become more evident why sociologists are not satisfied with explanations rooted in biology or personality. A basic principle of symbolic interactionism is that each of us interprets life through the symbols that we learn. Let's consider the extent to which membership in groups influences our behaviors and views of life, also a focus of the Perspectives box below.

crime: the violation of norms that are written into law

Perspectives

CULTURAL DIVERSITY IN U.S. SOCIETY

Is It Rape or Is It Marriage? A Study in Culture Clash

Isolated among cornfields, Lincoln, Nebraska, is about as provincial as a state capital gets. Its residents have little experience with people from different ways of life. And their baptism into cultural diversity came with a shock.

The wedding was traditional, following millennia-long Islamic practices (Annin and Hamilton 1996). A 39-year old Iraqi refugee arranged to marry his two eldest daughters, ages 13 and 14, to two fellow Iraqi refugees, ages 28 and 34. A Muslim cleric flew in from Ohio to perform the ceremony.

Nebraska went into shock. So did the refugees. What is marriage in Iraq is rape in Nebraska. The husbands were charged with rape, the girls' father with child abuse, and their mother with contributing to the delinquency of a minor.

The event made front page news in Saudi Arabia, where people shook their heads in amazement at the Americans. Nebraskans shook their heads in amazement, too.

In Fresno, California, a young Hmong refugee took a group of friends to a local college campus. There he picked up the girl he had selected as his mate (Sherman 1988; La Cayo 1993a). The youths brought her to the young man's house, where he had sex with her. The young woman, however, was not in agreement with this plan.

The Hmong call it *zij poj niam*, marriage by capture, an acceptable form of mate selection that matches Hmong courtship ideals of strong men and virtuous, resistant women. The Fresno District Attorney, however, called it kidnapping and rape.

For Your Consideration

To apply symbolic interactionism to these real-life dramas, ask how people's perspectives explain why they did what they did. To apply functionalism, ask how the U.S. laws that were violated are "functional" (that is, what are their benefits, to whom?). To apply conflict theory, ask what groups are in conflict in these examples—not the individuals involved, but the groups to which they belong.

To understand events theoretically does not tell us what reaction is "right" when cultures clash. Remember that science can analyze causes and consequences, but cannot answer questions of "ought." Any " "ought" that you feel about these cases comes from your system of values—which brings us, once again, to the initial issue—the relativity of deviance.

Differential Association Theory

The Theory. Contrary to theories of biology and personality, sociologist Edwin Sutherland stressed that people *learn* deviance. He coined the term **differential association** to indicate that learning to deviate or to conform to society's norms is influenced most by the people with whom we associate (Sutherland 1924, 1947; Sutherland and Cressey 1974; Sutherland et al. 1992). On the most obvious level, boys and girls who join Satan's Servants learn a way of looking at the world that is more likely to get them in trouble with the law than boys and girls who join the Scouts.

Sutherland's theory is actually more complicated than this, but he stressed that learning deviance is like learning anything else—which goes directly against the thinking that deviance is biological or due to deep personality needs. Sutherland said that the different groups to which we belong (our differential association) give us messages about conformity and deviance. We may receive mixed messages, but we end up with more of one than the other (an "excess of definitions" was Sutherland's term). Consequently, our attitudes favor conformity or deviance, and our behavior follows.

Families. We all know that we learn attitudes from others, and it certainly makes sense that this applies to crime. If so, one's family should make a big difference. To see if delinquents are more likely to come from families who themselves get in trouble with the law, researchers examined the family history of 25,000 delinquents locked up in high-security state institutions (Beck et al. 1988). They found that 25 percent have a father who has been in prison, 25 percent a brother or sister, 9 percent a mother, and 13 percent some other relative. Apparently, families involved in crime tend to set their children on a law-breaking path.

Friends and Neighborhoods. Friends are similarly important. If someone's friends are delinquent, that person is likely to be delinquent. In fact, the longer someone has delinquent friends the more likely he or she is to be delinquent (Warr 1993). Since delinquency is clustered in certain neighborhoods, children from those neighborhoods are likely to become delinquent (Miller 1958; Wolfgang and Farracuti 1967). This, of course, comes as no surprise to parents, who generally are eager to get their kids out of "bad" neighborhoods and away from "bad" friends, for, although they may not know the term differential association, they know how it works.

Subcultures. Subcultures work in the same way. Each subculture contains particular attitudes about deviance and conformity, and their members learn those attitudes. In a lower-class Chicano neighborhood in Chicago, for example, the concept of "honor" helped propel its young men into deviance. Sociologist Ruth Horowitz (1983, 1987), who did participant observation in this neighborhood, reports that the formula was simple: A man must have honor. An insult is a threat to one's honor. Therefore, not to stand up to someone is to be less than a real man. Now suppose you were a young man growing up in this neighborhood. You would likely do a fair amount of fighting, for you would see many statements and acts as infringing on your honor. You might make certain that you carried a knife or had access to a gun, for words and fists won't always do. Along with members of your group, you would define fighting, knifing, and shooting quite differently from the way most people do.

For members of the Mafia, ideas of manliness are also intertwined with deviance. For them, *killing is a primary measure of*

differential association:
Edwin Sutherland's term to indicate that associating with some groups results in learning an "excess of definitions" of deviance, and, by extension, in a greater likelihood that one will become deviant

Unlike biology and psychology, which look within individuals for explanations of human behavior, sociological explanations focus on external experiences, such as people's associations or group memberships. Sociological explanations of human behavior have become widely accepted and now permeate society, as illustrated by this teenager, whom I photographed as we were exiting the Staten Island Ferry in New York City.

their manhood. Not all killings are accorded the same respect, however, for "the more awesome and potent the victim, the more worthy and meritorious the killer" (Arlacchi 1980). Some killings are very practical matters. A member of the Mafia who gives information to the police, for example, has violated the Mafia's *omerta* (the vow of secrecy its members take). Such an offense can never be tolerated, for it threatens the very existence of the group. This example further illustrates just how relative deviance is. Although the act of killing is deviant to mainstream society, for them, *not* killing after certain rules are broken, such as "squealing" to the cops, is the deviant act.

Prison or Freedom? An issue that comes up over and over again in sociology is whether we are prisoners of socialization. Symbolic interactionists stress that we are not mere pawns in the hands of others. We are not destined by our group membership to think and behave as our groups dictate. Rather, we *help produce our own orientations to life.* Our choice of membership (differential association), for example, helps to shape the self. For instance, one college student may join a feminist group that is trying to change the treatment of women in college; another may associate with a group of women who shoplift on weekends. Their choice of groups points them in two different directions. The one who associates with shoplifters may become even more oriented toward deviant activities, while the one who joins the feminist group may develop an even greater interest in producing social change

Mainstreaming of deviance *occurs when people or activities that generally are disapproved of move into the mainstream, or become more socially acceptable. An example is the Beastie Boys, whose music and message have brought them fame and wealth. In years past, this group's audience would have been limited to a small following.*

Control Theory

Inside most of us, it seems, are strong desires to do things that would get us in trouble—inner drives, temptations, urges, hostilities, and so on. I'm sure you know what I'm talking about. Yet most of us stifle these desires most of the time. Why?

This is the basic question of **control theory,** which looks at deviance as a natural part of human nature. In order to have group life, commonly called society, the human group must restrain people's natural drives for self-gratification. Working against our tendencies to deviate, says sociologist Walter Reckless (1973), who developed control theory, are two control systems. Our *inner controls* include our internalized morality—conscience, religious principles, ideas of right and wrong. Inner controls also include fears of punishment, feelings of integrity, and the desire to be a "good" person (Hirschi 1969; Rogers 1977). Our *outer controls* consist of people—such as family, friends, and the police—who influence us not to deviate. (Control theory is sometimes classified as a functional theory, because when our outer controls operate well, we conform to social norms and thereby do not threaten the status quo. Because symbols and meanings are central to this theory, however, it can also be classified as a symbolic interactionist theory.)

As sociologist Travis Hirschi (1969) noted, the more that we feel bonds with society, the more effective our inner controls are. Bonds are based on *attachments* (in this case, affection and respect for people who conform to society's norms), *commitments* (having a stake in society that you don't want to risk, such as a respected place in your family, a good standing at college, a good job), *involvements* (putting time and energy into approved activities), and *beliefs* (holding that certain actions are morally wrong).

The likelihood that we will deviate from social norms, for example by committing a crime, depends on the strength of these two control systems relative to the strength of the pushes and pulls toward the deviance. If our control systems are weak, we deviate. If they are strong enough, however, we do not commit the deviant act. This theory can be summarized as *self*-control, says Hirschi. The key to learning high self-control is socialization, especially in childhood. Parents help their children develop self-control by supervising them and punishing their deviant acts (Gottfredson and Hirschi 1990).

control theory: the idea that two control systems—inner controls and outer controls—work against our tendencies to deviate

Labeling Theory

Symbolic interactionists have developed **labeling theory,** which focuses on the significance of the labels (names, reputations) given to people. Labels tend to become a part of the self-concept, which helps to set people on paths that propel them into or divert them from deviance. Let's look at how people react to society's labels—from whore and pervert to cheat and slob.

Rejecting Labels: How People Neutralize Deviance.   Most people resist the labels that others try to pin on them. Some are so successful that even though they persist in deviance, they still consider themselves conformists. For example, even though they beat up people and vandalize property, some delinquents consider themselves conforming members of society. How do they do it?

Sociologists Gresham Sykes and David Matza (1988), studied boys in this exact situation. They found that they used these five **techniques of neutralization** to help them deflect society's norms:

Denial of Responsibility.   The youths frequently said, "I'm not responsible for what happened because . . . " and then were quite creative about the "becauses." The act may have been an "accident," or they may see themselves as "victims" of society, with no control over what happened—like billiard balls shot around the pool table of life.

Denial of Injury.   Another favorite explanation of the boys was "What I did wasn't wrong because no one got hurt." They would define vandalism as "mischief," gang fighting as a "private quarrel," and stealing cars as "borrowing." They might acknowledge that what they did was illegal, but claim that it was "just having a little fun."

Denial of a Victim.   Sometimes the boys thought of themselves as avengers. To vandalize a teacher's car is only to get revenge for an unfair grade, while to shoplift is to even the score with "crooked" store owners. In short, if the boys did accept responsibility and even admit that someone did get hurt, they protect their self-concept by claiming that the people "deserved what they got."

Condemnation of the Condemners.   Another technique the boys used was to deny that others had the right to judge them. They might accuse people who pointed their fingers at them of being "a bunch of hypocrites": The police are "on the take," teachers have "pets," and parents cheat on their taxes. In short, they say, "Who are *they* to accuse *me* of something?"

Appeal to Higher Loyalties.   A final technique the boys used to justify antisocial activities was to consider loyalty to the gang more important than following the norms of society. They might say, "I had to help my friends. That's why I got in the fight." Not incidentally, the boy may also have shot two members of the rival group as well as a bystander!

▼   **In Sum** These five techniques of neutralization have implications far beyond these boys, for it is not only delinquents who try to neutralize the norms of mainstream society. Look again at these five techniques: (1) "I couldn't help myself"; (2) "Who really got hurt?" (3) "Don't you think she deserved that, after what *she* did?" (4) "Who are *you* to talk?" and (5) "I had to help my friends—wouldn't you have done the same thing?" Don't such statements have a familiar ring? All of us attempt to neutralize the moral demands of society, for such neutralizations help us sleep at night.

Rejecting Labels: Becoming a Prostitute.   Sociologist Nanette Davis (1978), who interviewed young women to find out how they had become prostitutes, noted that they had experienced a gradual slide from sexual promiscuity to prostitution. Their first acts of selling sex were casual. A girl might have run away from home and "turned a few tricks" to survive—or she might have done so to purchase a prom dress. At this point, the girls were

labeling theory: the view, developed by symbolic interactionists, that the labels people are given affect their own and others' perceptions of them, thus channeling their behavior either into deviance or into conformity

techniques of neutralization: ways of thinking or rationalizing that help people deflect society's norms in a stage of deviance that sociologist Edwin Lemert (1972) calls **primary deviance**—fleeting acts that do not become part of the self-concept. The young women did not think of themselves as prostitutes. As one girl said, "I never thought about it one way or another."

Girls who prostitute themselves for a longer time, however, must come to terms with their activities. They incorporate a deviant identity into their self-concept and come to think of themselves as prostitutes. When this occurs, they have entered **secondary deviance.**

The movement from primary to secondary deviance may be gradual. Through *self-labeling*, bit by bit the deviance becomes part of the self-concept. Often the reactions of others facilitate this transition. For example, if a young woman is arrested for prostitution, it is difficult for her to define her activities as "normal," as she might in primary deviance. A face-to-face confrontation with a formal system that publicly labels her a sexual deviant challenges self-definitions. (Self-jarring labels can also be informal, as indicated by such terms as "nut," "pervert," and "whore.") Such powerful labels tend to lock people out of conforming groups and push them into contact with other deviants.

There is yet another stage, one that few deviants reach. In **tertiary deviance,** deviant behavior is normalized by *relabeling* it nondeviant (Kitsuse 1980; de Young 1989). Most people in this stage simply reject the judgment that the behavior is wrong, but some even turn matters on their head by relabeling it a virtue. Although none of the women in Davis's sample had reached this stage, other prostitutes have. They have formed an organization called COYOTE (Call Off Your Old Tired Ethics) (Hughes 1995). This group takes the position that prostitutes perform a service to society. Therefore it is a reasonable occupational choice and legislation should allow prostitutes to operate without interference from the government.

Inviting Labels: The Embrace of Deviance. Although most of us resist attempts to label us as deviant, there are those who revel in a deviant identity. Some teenagers, for example, make certain by their clothing, choice of music, and hairstyles that no one misses their purposeful rejection of adult norms. Their status among fellow members of a subculture, within which they are almost obsessive conformists, is vastly more important than any status outside it.

One of the best examples of a group that embraces deviance is motorcycle gangs. Sociologist Mark Watson (1988) did participant observation with outlaw bikers. He rebuilt

Why are these women selling their bodies on the streets of Toronto in Ontario, Canada, instead of working at "respectable" jobs or studying sociology and other academic subjects in college?

primary deviance: Edwin Lemert's term for acts of deviance that have little effect on the self-concept

secondary deviance: Edwin Lemert's term for acts of deviance incorporated into the self-concept, around which an individual orients his or her behavior

tertiary deviance: "normalizing" behavior considered deviant by mainstream society; relabeling behavior as nondeviant

Outlaw bikers are of sociological interest because they reject the labels that society holds out as desirable and in an "in-your-face" approach replace them with their own labels of approval. What outward signs of this phenomenon are visible in this photo?

Harleys with them, hung around their bars and homes, and went on "runs" (trips) with them. He concluded that outlaw bikers see the world as "hostile, weak, and effeminate," while they pride themselves on looking "dirty, mean, and generally undesirable"—and take great pleasure in provoking shocked reactions to their appearance. Holding the conventional world in contempt, they also pride themselves on getting into trouble, laughing at death, and treating women as lesser beings whose primary value is to provide them with services—especially sex. Outlaw bikers also look at themselves as losers, a factor that becomes woven into their unusual embrace of deviance.

The Power of Labels: The Saints and the Roughnecks.   We can see how powerful labeling is by referring back to the study of the "Saints" and the "Roughnecks" cited in Chapter 4 (page 115). As you recall, both groups of high school boys were "constantly occupied with truancy, drinking, wild parties, petty theft, and vandalism." Yet their teachers looked on the Saints as "headed for success" and the Roughnecks as "headed for trouble." By the time they finished high school, not one Saint had been arrested, while the Roughnecks had been in constant trouble with the police.

Why did the community see these boys so differently? Chambliss (1973/1997) concluded that this double vision was due to their family background, especially social class. The Saints came from respectable, middle-class families, while the Roughnecks came from less respectable, working-class families. Because of their respective backgrounds, teachers and other authorities expected good, law-abiding behavior from the Saints and trouble from the Roughnecks. And like the rest of us, both teachers and police see what they expect to see.

Social class had allowed the Saints' lawbreaking to be *less visible.* The Saints had automobiles, and they made their drinking and vandalism inconspicuous by spreading it around neighboring towns. Without cars, the Roughnecks could not even make it to the edge of town. Day after day, they hung around the same street corners, where their boisterous behavior made them conspicuous, confirming the negative ideas that the community held about them.

Another significant factor was also at work. The boys' different social backgrounds had equipped them with distinct *styles of interaction.* When questioned by police or teachers, the Saints put on apologetic and penitent faces. Their deferential behavior elicited such positive reactions that they escaped serious legal problems. In contrast, the Roughnecks' attitude was "almost the polar opposite." They expressed open hostility to the authorities, and even when they pretended to show respect, the veneer was so thin that it fooled no one. Consequently, while the police let the Saints off with warnings, they came down hard on the Roughnecks, interrogating and arresting them when they had the chance.

While a lifetime career is not determined by a label alone, the Saints and Roughnecks did live up to the labels that the community gave them. As you recall, all but one of the Saints went on to college, after which one earned a doctorate and one became a lawyer, one a doctor, and the others business managers. In contrast, only two of the Roughnecks went to college, both on athletic scholarships, after which they became coaches. The other Roughnecks did not fare so well. Two of them dropped out of high school, later became involved in separate killings, and received long prison sentences. One became a local bookie, and no one knows the whereabouts of the other.

How do labels work? While the matter is extremely complex since it involves the self-concept and individual reactions, we can note that labels open and close the doors of opportunity. Being labeled a "deviant" (certainly far from a nonjudgmental term in everyday life!) can lock people out of conforming groups and force them into almost exclusive contact with people who have similar labels.

▼   **In Sum** Symbolic interactionists examine how people's definitions of the situation underlie their deviation from or conformance to social norms. They focus on group membership (differential association), how people balance pressures to conform and to deviate (control theory), and the significance of the labels placed on people (labeling theory).

 *Sociology and the New Technology*

Pornography Goes High-Tech

Not long after photography was invented in 1839, photographic pornography appeared. Today, the issue is computers and pornography. With its many pay and free sites, pornography flourishes on the Internet. Web surfers have their choice of explicit photographs. Some Web sites are even indexed: heterosexual or gay, single or group activity, teenagers, cheerleaders, and older women who "still think they have it." The indexes also include a variety of fetishes.

Live sites are also available, such as one that bills itself as "direct from Amsterdam," where you can command your "model" to do anything your heart desires. Both male and female "models" are available, and the per minute charges are hefty.

Some defend Internet pornography as another form of free speech, while others want to ban it. This issue has split the American Library Association. Some librarians want to install software that filters out pornography, while others insist that this would be a violation of their patrons' right of free speech (Brownlee 1997).

Very few free speech advocates extend their argument to child pornography, which is noticeably absent on the Internet. Photos of nude children and children engaged in sex acts did appear at an earlier point in the development of the Internet, but armed with stronger laws against child pornography, law enforcement agents began a widely publicized crackdown that scared off child pornographers.

As in other aspects of life, most sanctions are informal. When software producers held their annual trade show in Las Vegas, for example, some CD-ROM makers began to show nude performers in kinky situations. The show's sponsor declared them out of order and kicked them out (Ziegler 1995). This smaller group then formed their own trade show, where posters advertise CD-ROMs: "Bad Girls II: The Strip Search," and "Club 21: Our Deck Is Stacked."

For Your Consideration

Applying the symbolic interactionist perspective brings us again to the relativity of deviance: One person's art is another's pornography. Applying functionalism places the focus on functions (who benefits from Internet pornography) and dysfunctions (who is hurt by it). Applying the conflict perspective brings us to these basic sociological questions: Whose norms? Whose sanctions? And who has the power to make them stick?

The Sociology and the New Technology box above explores a central point of symbolic interactionism, that to call something deviant involves competing definitions and reactions to the same behavior.

The Functionalist Perspective

When we think of deviance, its dysfunctions are likely to come to mind. Functionalists, in contrast, are as likely to stress the functions of deviance as its dysfunctions.

How Deviance Is Functional for Society

Most of us are upset by deviance, especially crime, and assume that society would be better off without it. The classic functionalist theorist Emile Durkheim (1893/1933, 1893/1964), however, came to a surprising conclusion. Deviance, he said, including crime, is functional for society. Its three main functions are

1. *Deviance clarifies moral boundaries and affirms norms.* A group's ideas about how people should act and think mark its *moral boundaries.* Deviance challenges those boundaries. To call a deviant member to account, saying in effect, "You broke an important rule, and we cannot tolerate that," affirms the group's norms and clarifies the distinction between conforming and deviating behavior. To punish deviants is to assert what it means to be a member of the group.

2. *Deviance promotes social unity.* To affirm the group's moral boundaries by punishing deviants fosters a "we" feeling among the group's members. In saying, "You can't get by with that," the group collectively affirms the rightness of its own ways.

3. *Deviance promotes social change.* Groups do not always agree on what to do with people who push beyond their acceptable ways of doing things. Some group members may even approve the rule-breaking behavior. Boundary violations that gain enough support become new, acceptable behaviors. Thus, deviance may force a group to rethink and redefine its moral boundaries, helping groups, and whole societies, to change their customary ways.

Strain Theory: How Social Values Produce Crime

Functionalists argue that crime is a *natural* part of society, not an aberration or some alien element in our midst. Indeed, they say, some crime represents values that lie at the very core of society. This concept sounds strange at first. To understand how the acceptance of mainstream values can generate crime, consider what sociologists Richard Cloward and Lloyd Ohlin (1960) identified as the crucial problem of the industrialized world: the need to locate and train the most talented people of every generation—whether born in wealth or in poverty—so they can take over the key technical jobs of modern society. When children are born, no one knows which ones will have the abilities to become dentists, nuclear physicists, or engineers. To get the most talented people to compete with one another, society tries to motivate *everyone* to strive for success. It does this by arousing discontent—making people feel dissatisfied with what they have so that they will try to "better" themselves.

Most people, then, end up with strong desires to achieve **cultural goals,** the objectives held out as desirable for them, such as wealth or high status. Not everyone, however, has equal access to society's **institutionalized means,** the legitimate ways of achieving that success. Some people, for example, find their path to education and good jobs blocked. These people experience *strain* or frustrations, which may motivate them to take a deviant path.

This perspective, known as **strain theory,** was developed by sociologist Robert Merton (1956, 1968). People who experience strain, he said, are likely to feel *anomie,* a sense of normlessness. Because the dominant norms (work, education) don't seem to be getting them anywhere, they have a difficult time identifying with them. They may even feel wronged by the system, and its rules may seem illegitimate (Anderson 1978).

Merton's classic outline of how people react to cultural goals and institutionalized means is depicted in Table 8.1 below. The first reaction, which Merton said is the most common, is *conformity,* using socially acceptable means to strive to reach cultural goals. In industrialized societies most people try to get good jobs, a good education, and so on. If well-paid jobs are unavailable, they take less desirable jobs. If they are denied access to

cultural goals: the legitimate objectives held out to the members of a society

institutionalized means: approved ways of reaching cultural goals

strain theory: Robert Merton's term for the strain engendered when a society socializes large numbers of people to desire a cultural goal (such as success) but withholds from many the approved means to reach that goal; one adaptation to the strain is crime, the choice of an innovative means (one outside the approved system) to attain the cultural goal

TABLE 8.1

How People Match Their Goals to Their Means			
Feel Strain That Leads to Anomie?	*Mode of Adaptation*	*Cultural Goals*	*Institutionalized Means*
No	Conformists	Accept	Accept
Yes	Innovators	Accept	Reject
	Ritualists	Reject	Accept
	Retreatists	Reject	Reject
	Rebels	Reject/Accept	Reject/Accept

Harvard or Stanford, they go to a state university. Others take night classes and attend vocational schools. In short, most people take the socially acceptable road.

Four Deviant Paths.   The remaining four responses, which are deviant, represent reactions to anomie. Let's look at each. *Innovators* are people who accept the goals of society but use illegitimate means to try to reach them. Drug dealers, for instance, accept the goal of achieving wealth but reject the legitimate avenues for doing so. Other examples are embezzlers, robbers, and con artists.

The second deviant path is taken by people who become discouraged and give up on achieving cultural goals, but who still cling to conventional rules of conduct. Merton called this response *ritualism*. Although ritualists have given up on excelling and advancing in position, they survive by following the rules of their job. Teachers who suffer from "burnout" but continue to go through the motions of classroom performance after their idealism is shattered are an example. Their response is considered deviant because they cling to the job although they have abandoned the goal, such as stimulating young minds or making the world a better place.

People who choose the third deviant path, *retreatism*, reject both cultural goals and the institutionalized means of achieving them. Those who drop out of the pursuit of success by way of alcohol or drugs are retreatists. Such people do not even try to appear as though they share the goals of their society.

The final type of deviant response is *rebellion*. Convinced that the society in which they live is corrupt, rebels, like retreatists, reject both society's goals and its institutionalized means. Unlike retreatists, however, they seek to replace existing goals with new ones. Revolutionaries are the most committed type of rebels.

Strain theory underscores the main sociological point about deviance, namely, that deviants are not pathogenic individuals, but the product of society. Due to their social location, some people experience greater pressures to deviate from society's norms. Simply put, if a society emphasizes the goal of material success, groups deprived of access to this goal will be more involved in property crime. This is a good part of the reason that young males join the gangs discussed in the Down-to-Earth Sociology box on the next page.

Illegitimate Opportunity Theory: Explaining Social Class and Crime

One of the more interesting sociological findings in the study of deviance is that the social classes have distinct styles of crime. Let's see how unequal access to the institutionalized means to success helps explain this.

The Poor and Crime.   Functionalists point out that industrialized societies have no trouble socializing the poor into wanting to possess things. Like others, they, too, are bombarded with messages urging them to buy everything from designer jeans to new cars. The vivid images in movies and on television of the middle class enjoying luxurious lives reinforce the myth that all full-fledged Americans can afford society's many goods and services. This bombardment of messages also unintentionally produces the idea that they have a *right* to these items.

The school system, however, which constitutes the most common route to success, fails the poor. It is run by the middle class, and when the children of the poor enter it, already at an educational disadvantage, they confront a bewildering world for which their background ill prepares them. Their grammar and nonstandard language—liberally punctuated by what the middle class considers obscene and foul words and phrases—their ideas of punctuality and neatness, and their lack of preparation in paper-and-pencil skills are a mismatch with their new environment. Facing these barriers, the poor drop out of school in larger numbers than their more privileged counterparts. Educational failure, in turn, closes the door on many legitimate avenues to financial success.

Not infrequently, however, a different door opens to them, one that sociologists Richard Cloward and Lloyd Ohlin (1960) called **illegitimate opportunity structures.**

illegitimate opportunity structures: opportunities for crimes that are woven into the texture of life

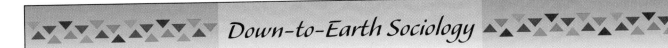

Down-to-Earth Sociology

Islands in the Street: Urban Gangs in U.S. Society

The United States has always had gangs—from the outlaws of the West to Chicago's mobs during Prohibition. Today it is urban youth gangs. For over ten years, sociologist Martín Sánchez Jankowski (1991) did participant observation of thirty-seven Irish, African-American, Puerto Rican, Chicano, Dominican, Jamaican, and Central American gangs in Boston, Los Angeles, and New York City. Jankowski ate, slept, and sometimes fought with the gangs, but by mutual agreement did not participate in drugs or other illegal activities. He was seriously injured twice during the study.

Jankowski identified five character traits of gang members, almost all of whom were from low-income neighborhoods: competitiveness, a sense of mistrust, self-reliance, social isolation, and a survival instinct, by which he means that they fight for survival in a hostile world filled with predators seeking prey.

Surprisingly, Jankowski did not find that the motive for joining was to escape broken homes (there were as many members from intact as broken homes) or to seek a substitute family (as many members said they were close to their families as said they were not). Rather, the boys joined to gain access to steady money, recreation (including access to females and drugs), anonymity in criminal activities, protection, and to help the community. This last reason may sound surprising, but in some neighborhoods gangs help to protect residents from outsiders. In addition, the gang was seen as an alternative to the dead-end—and deadening—jobs held by the working parents.

The gangs earn the money by which they attract members through gambling, arson, mugging, armed robbery, making and wholesaling drugs to pushers, and selling moonshine, guns, stolen car parts, and protection. Some gangs are involved in legal economic activities such as running "mom and pop" stores and renovating and renting abandoned apartment buildings—but this is unusual.

Jankowski witnessed much gang violence. When the members of a gang quarrel over drugs or women, or fight to test one another, gang rules and other members usually keep such violence under control. In contrast, attacks against rival gangs often escalate into serious violence. Similarly, the gangs don't attack residents of their own community unless someone has insulted them or threatened to turn them in to the police, but individuals will attack people outside the community simply to test their strength or even because they don't like the way someone looks.

The residents of a gang's turf are ambivalent about gangs. On the one hand, they don't like the violence; on the other hand, they may complain that the police use unnecessary force against gangs. The reasons for the ambivalence are that many adults once belonged to gangs, gang members are the children of neighborhood residents, and the gangs often provide better protection than do the police.

Particular gangs will come and go, but gangs will likely always be part of the city, for from a functional standpoint gangs fulfill needs for poor youth who live on the margins of society.

Woven into the texture of life in urban slums are robbery, burglary, drug dealing, prostitution, pimping, gambling, and other remunerative crimes, commonly called "hustles" (Liebow 1967; Anderson 1978, 1990; Bourgois 1994). For many of the poor, the "hustler" is a role model—glamorous, in control, the image of "easy money," one of the few people in the area who comes close to the cultural goal of success. For some, then, such illegal income-producing activities are functional—they provide income—and they attract disproportionate numbers of the poor.

White-Collar and Street Crime.   The more privileged social classes are not crime-free, of course, but they find a different illegitimate opportunity structure beckoning. For them, *other forms* of crime are functional. Rather than mugging, pimping, and burglary, the more privileged encounter "opportunities" for income tax evasion, bribery of public officials, stock manipulation, embezzlement, false advertising, and so on. Physicians, for example, never hold up cabbies, but many cheat Medicare. Sociologist Edwin Sutherland (1949) coined the term **white-collar crime** to refer to crimes that people of respectable and high social status commit in the course of their occupations.

Although the general public seems to think that the lower classes are more crime-prone, numerous studies show that white-collar workers also commit many crimes (Weisburd et al. 1991; Zey 1993). This difference in perception is largely based on visibility. While crimes committed by the poor are given much publicity, the crimes of the more

white-collar crime: Edwin Sutherland's term for crimes committed by people of respectable and high social status in the course of their occupations; for example, bribery of public officials, securities violations, embezzlement, false advertising, and price fixing

privileged classes seldom make the evening news and go largely unnoticed. Yet the dollar cost of "crime in the suites" is considerably higher than "crime in the streets." It actually totals several hundred billion dollars a year. Just the overbilling of insurance companies and Medicare by "respectable" physicians runs about $100 billion (Davis 1996), more than the cost of all street crime in the United States. These totals refer only to dollar costs. No one has yet figured out a way to compare, for example, the suffering of a rape victim with the pain experienced by an elderly couple who lose their life savings to white-collar fraud.

In terms of dollars, perhaps the most costly crime in U.S. history is the plundering of the savings and loan industry. Corporate officers, who had the trust of their depositors, systematically looted these banks of billions of dollars. The total cost runs somewhere around $500 billion—a staggering $2,000 for every man, woman, and child in the entire country (Kettl 1991; Newdorf 1991). Of the thousands involved, the most infamous culprit was Neil Bush, son of the then president of the United States and an officer of Silverado, a Colorado savings and loan. Bush approved loans totaling $100 million to a company in which he secretly held interests, an act that helped bankrupt his firm (Tolchin 1991).

Future generations will continue to suffer from the wholesale looting of this industry. The interest alone will be exorbitant (at 5 percent, a year's interest on an increase of $500 billion in the national debt would be $25 billion, at 10 percent $50 billion). Since the government does not pay its debt, but merely borrows more to pay the compounding interest, this extra $500 billion will double in just a few years. As the late Senator Everett Dirkson once said, "A billion here and a billion there, and pretty soon you're talking about real money."

Although white-collar crime is not as dramatic as a street killing or an abduction and rape—and therefore usually considered less newsworthy—it, too, can involve physical harm, and sometimes death. Unsafe working conditions, for example, many the result of executive decisions to put profits ahead of workers' safety, kill about one hundred thousand Americans each year—about *five* times the number of people killed by street criminals (Simon and Eitzen 1993). Nevertheless, the greatest concern of Americans is street crime, for they fear an encounter with violence that will change their life forever. As the Social Map below shows, the chances of such encounters depend on where you live.

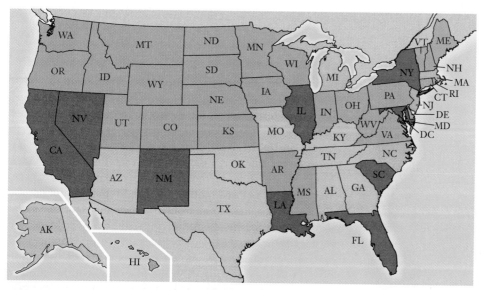

Figure 8.1

Some States Are Safer: Violent Crime in the United States

◼ Safer than average (below 600 violent crimes per 100,000 people per year)
◻ Average (600–830 violent crimes per 100,000 people per year)
◼ More dangerous than average (over 830 violent crimes per 100,000 people per year)

Violent crimes are murder, rape, robbery, and aggravated assault. The U.S. average is 716 per 100,00.

Source: Statistical Abstract 1996: Table 312.

Changes in White-Collar Crime.   A major change in white-collar crime is the growing numbers of female offenders. As more women joined the professions and corporate world, especially since World War II, they, too, were enticed by illegitimate opportunities. Gaining positions of trust, for example, more and more women were arrested for embezzlement. Today, nearly as many women as men are arrested for fraud and embezzlement (Forsyth and Marckese 1995; FBI 1995).

A second change is theft by computer, an example of crime keeping up with changing technology. To divert corporate resources to one's own use, fictitious information is inserted into a company's computer program. In one instance, a welfare department employee created a nonexistent work force by inserting fake Social Security numbers into the computer. Week after week, the computer faithfully issued checks to the bogus workers (Allen 1975). Becoming more common, this form of white-collar crime also runs in the billions of dollars (Goldstein 1987).

▼   **In Sum** Functionalists conclude that much street crime is the consequence of socializing the lower social classes into equating success with material possessions, while denying them the means to attain that success. People from higher social classes encounter different opportunity structures to commit crimes.

criminal justice system: the system of police, courts, and prisons set up to deal with people who are accused of having committed a crime

capitalist class: the wealthy who own the means of production and buy the labor of the working class

working class: those who sell their labor to the capitalist class

marginal working class: the most desperate members of the working class, who have few skills, little job security, and are often unemployed

The Conflict Perspective

Class, Crime, and the Criminal Justice System

The federal government accused two huge multinational corporations, Grumman and SmithKline, of fraud that cost the taxpayers millions of dollars. No executives went to jail. Instead, the corporations paid fines—and then were allowed to continue doing business with the federal government (Pasztor 1993; Tanouye 1995).

Contrast this event with stories common in newspapers of young men who steal automobiles and are sentenced to several years in prison. What's going on? How can a legal system that is supposed to provide "justice for all" be so inconsistent? According to conflict theorists, this question is central to the analysis of crime and the **criminal justice system**—the police, courts, and prisons that deal with people who are accused of having committed crimes.

Power and Inequality

Shown in this nineteenth-century lithograph are some of London's unemployed as they lunge forward to receive a free meal ticket. Conflict theorists stress that the marginal working class provides the temporary workers who are hired during economic booms and then discharged during economic turndowns. Until these workers are needed, they are kept alive at substandard conditions. Whether in early or late capitalism, is it surprising that most street criminals come from the marginal working class?

Conflict theorists look at power and social inequality as the primary characteristics of every society. They stress that the state's machinery of social control represents the interests of the wealthy and powerful. This group determines the basic laws whose enforcement is essential to preserving its own power. Other norms, such as those that govern informal behavior (chewing with a closed moth, appearing in public with combed hair, and so on), may come from other sources, but they simply do not count for much. Although such norms influence our everyday behavior, they do not determine prison sentences.

Conflict theorists see the most fundamental division in industrial society as that between the few who own the means of production and the many who do not, those who sell their labor and the privileged few who buy it. Those who buy labor, and thereby control workers, make up the **capitalist class;** those who sell their labor form the **working class.** Toward the most depressed end of the working class is the **marginal working class,** people with few skills, who are subject to unexpected layoffs, and

whose jobs are low paying, part time, or seasonal. This class is marked by unemployment and poverty, and from its ranks come most of the the prisoners in the United States. Desperate, these people commit street crimes, and because their crimes threaten the social order, they are severely punished.

The Law as an Instrument of Oppression

According to conflict theorists, the idea that the law is a social institution that operates impartially and administers a code shared by all is a cultural myth promoted by the capitalist class. In contrast, they see the law as an instrument of oppression, a tool designed to maintain the powerful in their privileged position (Spitzer 1975; Ritzer 1992; MacDonald 1995). Because the working class holds the potential of rebelling and overthrowing the current social order, when its members get out of line, they are arrested, tried, and imprisoned.

For this reason, the criminal justice system does not focus on the owners of corporations and the harm they do to the masses with unsafe products, wanton pollution, and price manipulations but, instead, directs its energies against violations by the working class (Gordon 1971; Platt 1978; Coleman 1989). The violations of the capitalist class cannot be totally ignored, however, for if they became too outrageous or oppressive, the working class might rise up in revolution. To prevent this, a flagrant violation by a member of the capitalist class is occasionally prosecuted. The publicity given to the case helps to stabilize the social system by providing visible evidence of the "fairness" of the criminal justice system.

Usually, however, the powerful bypass the courts altogether, appearing instead before some agency with no power to imprison (such as the Federal Trade Commission). Most cases of illegal sales of stocks and bonds, price fixing, restraint of trade, collusion, and so on are handled by "gentlemen overseeing gentlemen," for such agencies are directed by people from wealthy backgrounds who sympathize with the intricacies of the corporate world. It is not surprising, then, that the typical sanction is a token fine. In contrast, the property crimes of the masses are handled by courts that do have the power to imprison. The burglary, armed robbery, and theft by the poor not only threaten the sanctity of private property but, ultimately, the positions of the powerful.

In Sum From the perspective of conflict theory, the small penalties imposed for crimes committed by the powerful are typical of a legal system designed to mask injustice, to control workers, and, ultimately, to stabilize the social order. From this perspective, law enforcement is a cultural device through which the capitalist class carries out self-protective and oppressive policies (Silver 1977).

The Need for Multiple Theories

All these theories have merit. Differential association, labeling, blocked opportunities, illegitimate opportunities, and the privileged position of the elite—all help explain deviance, including crime. Yet few of us who are exposed to opportunities to seriously deviate ever do. Few of us rob or kill, even if robbing and killing are common in our neighborhood. Even if our access to good-paying jobs is blocked, we are unlikely to commit these crimes.

Why do so few of us violate mores even though we have the opportunity and motive to do so? It is promising to consider control theory in combination with these other theories. Differential association and illegitimate opportunity theories, for example, stress the circumstances that influence us, while control theory indicates that people with stronger internal controls are better able to resist the allure of deviance. Apparently, then, the likelihood of deviance is due to a *combination* of motivations, self-control, and exposure to opportunities (Smith and Brame 1994). Little, however, is presently known about

You probably have no difficulty telling which of these photos shows upper-middle-class youths and which portrays working-class youths. In spite of similarities of social identifiers by which both groups of students proclaim that they are U.S. teenagers, they also use status markers to signal their social class background. As the text explains, this information is of crucial importance, for it affects perception, social interaction, and ultimately, life chances.

this combination. When opportunity is strong (for example, drug dealing in the inner city), how much inner control does it take to avoid becoming a drug dealer? How much motivation *not* to participate? Reliable measurements of motivation, opportunity, and inner controls are yet to be made.

Reactions to Deviance

Whether it be cheating on a sociology quiz or holding up a liquor store, any violation of norms invites reaction. Let's look first at reactions by others, and then at how people react to their own deviance.

Sanctions

As discussed in Chapter 2, people do not strictly enforce folkways, but they become very upset when mores are broken. Disapproval of deviance, called **negative sanctions**, ranges from frowns and gossip for breaking folkways to imprisonment and capital punishment for breaking mores. **Positive sanctions**, in contrast—from smiles to formal awards—are used to reward people for conforming to norms. Getting a raise is a positive sanction, being fired a negative sanction. Getting an *A* in basic sociology is a positive sanction, getting an *F* a negative one.

Most negative sanctions are informal. You probably will merely stare when someone dresses in what you consider inappropriate clothing, or just gossip if a married person you know spends the night with someone other than his or her spouse. Whether you consider the breaking of a norm simply an amusing matter that warrants no severe sanctions or a serious infraction that does, however, depends on your perspective. If a woman appears at your college graduation ceremonies in a swimsuit, you may stare and laugh, but if it is

negative sanction: a punishment or negative reaction for disapproved behavior, for deviance

positive sanction: a reward or positive reaction for approved behavior, for conformity

Degradation ceremonies are intended to humiliate norm violators and mark them as "not members" of the group. This photo was taken by the U.S. army in 1945 after U.S. troops liberated Cherbourg, France. Members of the French resistance shaved the heads of these women, who had "collaborated" (had sexual contact with) with the occupying Nazis. They then marched the shamed women down the streets of the city, while the public shouted insults and spat on them.

your mother you are likely to feel that different sanctions are appropriate. Similarly, if it is *your* father who spends the night with an 18-year-old college freshman, you are likely to do more than gossip.

Responding to deviance is vital to the welfare of groups, for groups must maintain their boundaries if they are to continue to claim a unique identity. "Boundary maintenance," as sociologists call it, involves clashing definitions of morality, as the Perspectives box on page 197 illustrates.

Degradation Ceremonies

When someone wanders far from a group's standards, the reaction to the deviant is likely to be harsh. In some instances, groups attempt to mark an individual indelibly as a DE-VIANT for all the world to see. In Nathaniel Hawthorne's *The Scarlet Letter*, for example, Hester Prynne was forced to stand on a platform in public wearing a scarlet *A* sewn on her dress to mark her as an adulteress. Furthermore, she was expected by the community to wear this badge of shame every day for the rest of her life.

Sociologist Harold Garfinkel (1956) called such formal attempts to mark an individual with the status of an outsider **degradation ceremonies.** The individual is called to account before the group, witnesses denounce him or her, the offender is pronounced guilty, and, most important in sociological terms, steps are taken to *strip the individual of his or her identity as a group member*. Following a court martial, for example, officers found guilty stand at attention before their peers while the insignia of rank are ripped from their uniforms. A priest may be defrocked before a congregation, a citizen forced to wear a prison uniform. These procedures indicate that the individual is no longer a member of the group—no longer able to command soldiers, to preach or offer sacraments, or to move about freely. Although Hester Prynne was not banished from the group physically, her degradation ceremony proclaimed her a *moral* outcast from the community, the scarlet *A* marking her as "not one" of them.

Imprisonment

Today, we don't make people wear scarlet letters, but we do remove them from society and make them wear prison uniforms. The prison experience follows a degradation ceremony involving a public trial and the public pronouncement that the person is "unfit to

degradation ceremonies: rituals designed to strip an individual of his or her identity as a group member; for example, a court martial or the defrocking of a priest

Liberal and Conservative Views on Social Issues

Imprisonment

The facts are clear enough. As Figure 8.2 shows, the number of Americans in prison is now *more than five times* what it was in 1970. If the U.S. population had grown at the same rate, it would be over a billion people. As Table 8.2 on page 213 shows, about half of U.S. prisoners are African Americans, and about 95 percent are men. The United States has embraced prisons as its primary solution to crime to such an extent that it now imprisons seven times as many people relative to population as does the average European country (Hanke 1996).

What do these facts *mean*? Is this desirable or undesirable? When liberals and conservatives look at the same data, they usually disagree intensely. It is no different in this case.

Liberals bemoan this high rate of imprisonment. They say that prison is a human wasteland, and high rates of imprisonment an indicator of the failure of our social institutions and discrimination against the poor. To send people to gang-ridden, inmate-controlled prisons breeds hostility and

fosters a culture of violence. Such places reduce people to savagery (Hasine 1996). Instead of imprisoning people we should be educating them, teaching them how to make an honest living. We need to reduce our rate of imprisonment.

Anyone who rapes, kills, or robs, reply the conservatives, belongs in prison. No ifs, ands, or buts about it. And prisons make society safer. For every 1,100 people we put in prison, we have 4 fewer murders, 53 fewer rapes, and 1,100 fewer robberies (Levitt 1996). Even though it costs $30,000 to keep the average criminal behind bars, that person would do $54,000 of damage if he were on the streets. The net savings is $24,000 per prisoner per year. And we are finally seeing the results we've been looking for: The rate of violent crime is falling—because those who are most prone to violence are behind bars (*FBI Uniform Crime Reports* 1997). Prisons not only make us safer, but they are a bargain on top of it. Lock 'em up and throw away the key.

live among decent, law-abiding people" for some specified period of time. Liberal and conservative views on imprisonment are contrasted in the Social Issues box above.

Among the severe problems with imprisonment is that prisons fail to teach their clients to stay away from crime. Four of every five prisoners have been in prison before (*Statistical Abstract* 1995: Table 351). The **recidivism rate** (the proportion of people who

recidivism rate: the proportion of people who are rearrested

Figure 8.2

Growth in the U.S. Prison Population

Note: To better understand the significance of this phenomenal growth, it is useful to compare it with the change in the general population during this same period. Between 1970 and 1995, the population of the United States grew 28 percent, while the prison population grew *20 times as fast*, increasing by 560 percent. If the number of prisoners had increased at the same rate as the general population, there would be about 250,000 people in prison, about one-fifth of the actual number.

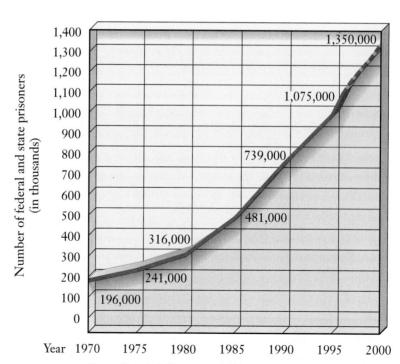

Source: Statistical Abstract 1995:Table 349; 1997:Table 358; *Sourcebook of Criminal Justice Statistics* 1996:510.

are rearrested) runs as high as 85 to 90 percent (Blumstein and Cohen 1987). Within just six years of their release from prison 69 percent are rearrested, most within just three years (Zawitz 1988). Those given probation—released into the community under the court's supervision—do no better, for within three years 62 percent are arrested for a felony or have a disciplinary hearing for violating their parole (Langan and Cunniff 1992).

Perhaps an underlying reason for this high recidivism rate is that Americans do not agree on *why* people should be put in prison. There appears to be widespread agreement that offenders should be imprisoned, but not on the reasons for doing so. Let's examine the four primary reasons for imprisoning people.

Retribution. The purpose of **retribution** is to right a wrong by making offenders suffer, or to pay back what they have stolen. The offense is thought to have upset a moral balance; the punishment is an attempt to restore that balance (Cohen 1940). Attempts to make the punishment "fit the crime," such as sentencing someone who has stolen from a widow to work a dozen weekends in a geriatric center for the poor, are rooted in the idea of retribution.

Deterrence. The purpose of **deterrence** is to create fear so that others won't break the law. The belief underlying deterrence is that if people know that they will be punished, they will refrain from committing the crime. Sociologist Ernest van den Haag (1975), a chief proponent of deterrence, believes, like many Americans, that the criminal justice system is too soft. He advocates that juveniles who commit adult crimes be tried as adults, that parole boards be abolished, and that prisoners be forced to work.

TABLE 8.2		
Inmates in U.S. State Prisons		
Prisoners		*U.S. Population*
Their Characteristics	*Percentage with These Characteristics*	*Percentage with These Characteristics*
Age		
Under 18	0.6	25.9%
18–24	21.3	10.2
25–34	45.7	16.6
35–44	22.7	15.7
45–54	6.5	10.7
55–64	2.4	8.2
65 and over	0.7	12.7
Race		
White[a]	49.1	83.4
African American	47.3	12.4
Other races	3.5	4.2
Sex		
Male	94.5	48.8
Female	5.5	51.2

[a]The category "white" includes Latinos.

Source: Statistical Abstract 1997:Tables 14, 18, 22, 356.

retribution: the punishment of offenders in order to restore the moral balance upset by the offense

deterrence: creating fear so people will refrain from breaking the law

Alabama has brought back chain gangs. These men, chained together, do hard physical labor. Some chain gangs merely break rocks with sledgehammers all day long. Do you think the purpose is retribution, deterrence, rehabilitation, or incapacitation?

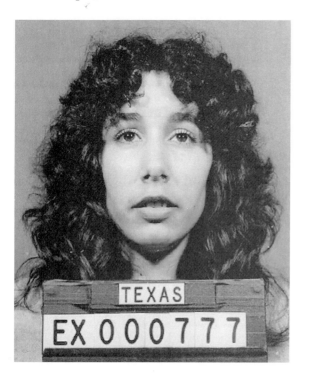

The greater the violation of norms, the greater the sanctions that are likely to result. Shown here is Karla Faye Tucker who in 1998 became the first woman put to death in Texas since 1863, and the first in the U.S. since 1984. Her crime was the pickax slaying of two people during a burglary in 1983.

Does deterrence work? Evidence is mixed, but those who claim that it does not, like to recall an example from the nineteenth century. When English law meted out the death penalty for pickpockets, other pickpockets looked forward to the hangings—for people whose attention was riveted on the gallows made easy victims (Hibbert 1963). At this point, no firm evidence resolves the issue.

Rehabilitation. The purpose of **rehabilitation** is not to punish offenders, but to resocialize them so they can become conforming citizens. One example of rehabilitation is teaching prisoners skills so they can support themselves after their release. Other examples include college courses in prison, encounter groups for prisoners, and *halfway houses*—community support facilities where ex-prisoners supervise many aspects of their own lives, such as household tasks, and still report to authorities.

Incapacitation. To remove offenders from circulation is called **incapacitation.** "Nothing works," some say, "but we can at least keep them off the streets." Criminologist James Wilson (1975, 1992) supports incapacitation, calling it the only policy that works. He proposes what he calls *added incapacitation*, increasing an offender's sentence each time he or she is convicted of a crime.

In the United States, the public is fearful of crime and despairing of solutions. Increasing dependence on prisons (see Table 8.2) may indicate that Americans are throwing up their hands as far as criminals are concerned and just trying to "keep them off the streets." It also may indicate attempts at retribution and deterrence. It certainly does not indicate efforts toward rehabilitation, for U.S. prisons are basically just holding tanks, offering few, if any, programs of rehabilitation.

The Trouble with Official Statistics

Both the findings of symbolic interactionists concerning the authorities' reactions to such groups as the Saints and the Roughnecks and the conclusions of conflict theorists that the criminal justice system exists to serve the ruling elite demonstrate the need for caution in interpreting official crime statistics. Statistics are not objective, tangible objects, like apples in a supermarket, waiting to be picked up. They are a human creation, produced within a specific social and political context for some particular purpose.

According to official statistics, working-class boys clearly emerge as much more delinquent than middle-class boys. Yet, as we have seen, *who actually gets arrested for what* is directly affected by social class, a point that has far-reaching implications. As symbolic interactionists point out, the police use a symbolic system as they enforce the law. Their ideas of "typical criminals" and "typical good citizens," for example, permeate their work. The more a suspect matches their ideas of the "criminal profile," the more likely that person is to be arrested. **Police discretion,** the decision whether or not to arrest someone or even to ignore a matter, is a routine part of police work. Consequently, official crime statistics always reflect these and many other biases.

▼ **In Sum** Reactions to deviants vary from such mild sanctions as frowns and stares to such severe responses as imprisonment and death. Some sanctions are formal—court hearings, for example—although most are informal, as when friends refuse to talk to each other. One sanction is to label someone a deviant, which can have powerful consequences for the person's life, especially if the label closes off conforming activities and opens deviant ones. The degradation ceremony, in which someone is publicly labeled "not one of us," is a powerful sanction. So is imprisonment. Official statistics must be viewed with caution, for they reflect a strong social class bias.

rehabilitation: the resocialization of offenders so that they can become conforming citizens

incapacitation: to take away someone's capacity to commit crimes, in this instance, by putting the offender in prison

police discretion: the practice of the police, in the normal course of their duties, to arrest someone for an offense or to overlook the matter

The Medicalization of Deviance: Mental Illness

Another way in which society deals with deviance is to "medicalize" it. Let us look at what this entails.

Neither Mental nor Illness?   To *medicalize* something is to make it a medical matter, to classify it as a form of illness that properly belongs in the care of physicians. For the past hundred years or so, especially since the time of Sigmund Freud (1856–1939), the Viennese physician who founded psychoanalysis, there has been a growing tendency toward the **medicalization of deviance.** In this view, deviance, including crime, is a sign of mental sickness. Rape, murder, stealing, cheating, and so on are external symptoms of internal disorders, consequences of a confused or tortured mind.

Thomas Szasz (1986, 1996), a renegade in his profession of psychiatry, argues that *mental illnesses are neither mental nor illnesses. They are simply problem behaviors.* Some forms of so-called mental illnesses have organic causes; that is, they are *physical* illnesses that result in unusual perceptions and behavior. Some depression, for example, is caused by a chemical imbalance in the brain, which can be treated by drugs. The depression, however, may show itself as crying, long-term sadness, and the inability to become interested in anything. When a person becomes deviant in ways that disturb others, and these others cannot find a satisfying explanation for why the person is "like that," they conclude that a "sickness in the head" causes the inappropriate, unacceptable behavior.

All of us have troubles. Some of us face a constant barrage of problems as we go through life. Most of us continue the struggle, encouraged by relatives and friends, motivated by job, family responsibilities, and life goals. Even when the odds seem hopeless, we carry on, not perfectly, but as best we can.

Some people, however, fail to cope well with the challenges of daily life. Overwhelmed, they become depressed, uncooperative, or hostile. Some strike out at others, while some, in Merton's terms, become retreatists and withdraw into their apartments or homes and won't come out. These are *behaviors, not mental illnesses,* stresses Szasz. They may be inappropriate coping devices, but they are coping devices, nevertheless, not mental illnesses. Thus, Szasz concludes that "mental illness" is a myth foisted on a naive public by a medical profession that uses pseudoscientific jargon in order to expand its area of control and force nonconforming people to accept society's definitions of "normal."

Szasz's extreme claim forces us to look anew at the forms of deviance called mental illness. To explain behavior that people find bizarre, he directs our attention not to "things hidden deep within the subconscious," but, instead, to how people learn such behaviors. To ask, "What is the origin of inappropriate or bizarre behavior?" then becomes similar to asking, "Why do some women steal?" "Why do some men rape?" "Why do some teenagers cuss their parents and stalk out of the room slamming doors?" *The answers depend on people's particular experiences in life, not some illness in their mind.* In short, some sociologists find Szasz's renegade analysis refreshing because it indicates that *social experiences,* not some illness of the mind, underlie bizarre behaviors—as well as deviance in general.

The Homeless Mentally Ill

Jamie was sitting on the low wall surrounding the landscaped open-air eating area of an exclusive restaurant. She appeared unaware of the stares elicited by her many layers of mismatched clothing, her dirty face, and the ever-present shopping cart overflowing with her meager possessions.

Every once in a while Jamie would pause, concentrate, and point to the street, slowly moving her finger horizontally. I asked her what she was doing.

"I'm directing traffic," she replied. "I control where the cars go. Look, that one turned right there," she said, now withdrawing her finger.

"Really?" I said.

After a while she confided that her cart talked to her.

medicalization of deviance: to make deviance a medical matter, a symptom of some underlying illness that needs to be treated by physicians

The homeless are located at the bottom of the U.S. social class ladder. One might even say that their status is so low that they are a step below its lowest rung. Why do you think a society as wealthy as the United States has homeless people?

"Really?" I said again.

"Yes," she replied. "You can hear it, too." At that, she pushed the shopping cart a bit.

"Did you hear that?" she asked.

When I shook my head, she demonstrated again. Then it hit me. She was referring to the squeaking wheels!

I nodded.

When I left Jamie, she was looking toward the sky, her finger upraised, for, as she told me, she also controlled the flight of airplanes.

To most of us, Jamie's behavior and thinking are bizarre. They simply do not match any reality we know. Could you or I become Jamie?

Suppose for a bitter moment that you are homeless and have to live on the streets. You have no money, no place to sleep, no bathroom, do not know *if* you are going to eat, much less where, have no friends or anyone you can trust, and live with the constant threat of rape and violence. Do you think this might be enough to drive you "over the edge"?

Consider just the problems involved in not having a place to bathe. (Shelters are often so dangerous that the homeless prefer to take their chances sleeping in public settings.) At first, you will try to wash in the toilets of gas stations, bars, the bus station, or a shopping center. But you are dirty, and people stare when you enter, and they call the management when they see you wash your feet in the sink. You are thrown out, and told in no uncertain terms to never come back. So you get dirtier and dirtier. Eventually you come to think of being dirty as a fact of life. Soon, maybe, you don't even care. No longer do the stares bother you—at least not as much.

No one will talk to you, and you withdraw more and more into yourself. You begin to build a fantasy life. You talk openly to yourself. People stare, but so what? They stare anyway. Besides, they are no longer important to you.

Jamie might be mentally ill. Some organic problem, such as a chemical imbalance in her brain, might underlie her behavior. But perhaps not. How long would it take us to engage in bizarre behaviors if we were homeless? What if we were homeless and hopeless for years? The point is that *just being on the streets can cause mental illness*—or whatever we want to label socially inappropriate behaviors that we find difficult to classify (McCarthy 1983; Belcher 1988; Nelson 1989). *Homelessness and mental illness are reciprocal:* Just as "mental illness" can cause homelessness, so the trials of being homeless, of living on cold, hostile streets, can lead to unusual and unacceptable thinking and behaviors.

The Need for a More Humane Approach

As Durkheim (1895/1938:68–69) pointed out, deviance is inevitable—even in a group of saints.

> Imagine a society of saints, a perfect cloister of exemplary individuals. Crimes, properly so called, will there be unknown; but faults which appear [invisible] to the layman will create there the same scandal that the ordinary offense does in ordinary [society].

With deviance inevitable, one measure of a society is how it treats its deviants. Our prisons certainly say little good about U.S. society. Filled with the poor, they are warehouses of the unwanted, reflecting patterns of broad discrimination in the larger society. White-collar criminals continue to get by with a slap on the wrist while street criminals are severely punished. Some deviants, failing to meet current standards of admission to either prison or mental hospital, take refuge in shelters and cardboard boxes in city streets. Although no one has *the* answer, it does not take much reflection to see that there are more humane approaches than these.

With deviance inevitable, the larger issues are how to protect people from deviant behaviors that are harmful to themselves or others, to tolerate those that are not, and to develop systems of fairer treatment for deviants. In the absence of the fundamental changes that would bring about a truly equitable social system, most efforts are, unfortunately, Band-Aid work. What is needed is a more humane social system, one that would prevent the social inequalities that are the focus of the next five chapters.

Summary and Review

Gaining a Sociological Perspective on Deviance

How do sociologists view deviance?

From a sociological perspective, **deviance**—defined as the violation of norms—is relative. What people consider deviant varies from one culture to another and from group to group within the same society. Consequently, as symbolic interactionists stress, it is not the act itself, but the reactions to the act, that make something deviant. All groups develop systems of **social control** to punish **deviants,** those who violate its norms. Pp. 192–196.

How do biological, psychological, and sociological explanations of deviance differ?

To explain why people deviate, biologists and psychologists look for reasons *within* the individual, such as **genetic predispositions** or **personality disorders.** Sociologists, in contrast, look for explanations *outside* the individual, in social relations. Pp. 196–197.

The Symbolic Interactionist Perspective

How do symbolic interactionists explain deviance?

Symbolic interactionists have developed several theories to explain deviance such as **crime** (the violation of norms written into law). According to **differential association theory,** people learn to deviate from associating with others. According to **control theory,** each of us is propelled toward deviance, but most of us conform because of an effective system of **inner** and **outer controls.** People who have less effective controls deviate. Pp. 197–199.

Labeling theory focuses on how labels (names, reputations) help to propel people into or divert people from deviance. Many people commit deviant acts and still think of themselves as conformists. They apparently use five **techniques of neutralization.** Studies of prostitutes show three ways in which the self concept is involved in deviant acts. In **primary deviance,** the acts are fleeting and have little effect on the self-concept. In **secondary deviance,** people incorporate their deviant acts into their self-concept. In **tertiary deviance,** acts commonly considered deviant are relabeled as normal. Although most people resist being labeled deviant, some embrace deviance. Pp. 200–202.

The Functionalist Perspective

How do functionalists explain deviance?

Functionalists point out that deviance, including criminal acts, is functional for society. Functions include affirming norms and promoting social unity and social change. According to **strain theory,** societies socialize their members into desiring **cultural goals,** but many people are unable to achieve these goals in socially acceptable ways—by **institutionalized means.** Deviants, then, are people who either give up on the goals or who use deviant means to attain them. Merton identified five types of responses to cultural goals and institutionalized means: conformity, innovation, ritualism, retreatism, and rebellion. **Illegitimate opportunity theory** stresses that some people have easier access to illegal means of achieving goals. Pp. 203–208.

The Conflict Perspective

How do conflict theorists explain deviance?

Conflict theorists take the position that the group in power (the **capitalist class**) imposes its definitions of deviance on other groups (the **working class** and the **marginal working class**). From the conflict perspective, the law is an instrument of oppression used to maintain the privilege of the few over the many. The marginal working class has little income, is desperate, and commits highly visible property crimes. The ruling class directs the **criminal justice system,** using it to punish the crimes of the poor while it diverts its own criminal activities away from this punitive system. Pp. 208–209.

Reactions to Deviance

How do societies react to deviance?

Deviance results in **negative sanctions,** acts of disapproval ranging from frowns to capital punishment. Some groups use **degradation ceremonies** to impress on their members that certain violations will not be tolerated. Imprisonment is motivated by the goals of **retribution, deterrence, rehabilitation,** and **incapacitation.** Pp. 210–214.

Are official statistics on crime reliable?

The conclusions of both symbolic interactionists (that the police operate with a large measure of discretion) and conflict theorists (that the legal system is controlled by the capitalist class) cast doubt on the accuracy of official crime statistics. P. 215.

What is the medicalization of deviance?

The medical profession has attempted to **medicalize** many forms of **deviance,** claiming that they represent mental illnesses. Thomas Szasz disagrees, claiming that they are just problem behaviors, not mental illnesses. Research on homeless people illustrates how problems in living can lead to bizarre behavior and thinking. Pp. 215–217.

The Need for a More Humane Approach

Deviance is inevitable, so the larger issues are how to protect people from deviance that harms themselves and others, to tolerate deviance that is not harmful, and to develop systems of fairer treatment for deviants. P. 217.

Where can I read more on this topic?

Suggested readings for this chapter are listed on page 661.

Sociology and the Internet

All URLs listed are current as of the printing of this book. URLs are often changed. Please check our Website http://www.abacon.com/henslin for updates.

1. To investigate changes in the crime index for major cities, go to the FBI's home page *http://www.fbi.gov/* and select "Uniform Crime Reports." At FBI publications select "UCR Preliminary Release 199_." Select it again on the following page. On the Report page, page down to *Table 4—OFFENSES KNOWN TO THE POLICE.* (The table number may change.) Save or print the table. Examine the column "Crime Index Total" for several cities of different sizes in various regions of the country. Note the changes in index crimes from the previous year. Are there patterns in the changes, or is each city unique? Why do you think this is? (Note: Your instructor may want you to figure the percentage change for each of the cities you use in your report.)

2. All people labeled "deviant" are not criminals. Use Lycos *http://www.lycos.com/* with the search words "mental illness homelessness." Look at the discussion and declarations at several sites. Why do you think people perceive a link between mental illness and homelessness? Do the two together constitute a social problem? Why? What are some possible solutions? Why hasn't the United States already solved the problem? How likely are we to solve it in the future? (Instructor: This would make an excellent panel discussion or debate.)

3. Examine the following links, which attempt to inform the cyber public about crime and deviance on the Internet:

http://locus.halcyon.com/gspam/netscams.html
http://www.fraud.org
http://www.isa.net/project-open/pre-warn.html

Use what you have learned from your text to discuss who might be orchestrating such scams and why. Use illegitimate opportunity theory to discuss who may be behind scams on the Internet. Next, use the functionalist perspective to discuss how netscams and other Internet deviance may contribute to social order. Finally, use strain theory to examine Internet crime and deviance.

4. Rehabilitation switches the focus from punishing offenders to resocializing them. Examine the following links with regard to the issues involved in rehabilitation:

http://www.soft.net.uk/turner/aftermath.htm
http://hb.quik.com/jmwiltse/chm.html
http://detnews.com/menu/stories/28523.htm

What does it mean to rehabilitate offenders? What are the issues involved in rehabilitation? Who does rehabilitation benefit? Who should undergo rehabilitation?

Roosevelt, Farm in Haiti

C H A P T E R

9

Social Stratification in Global Perspective

L ET'S CONSIDER THREE "AVERAGE" FAMILIES from around the world:

For Getu Mulleta, 33, and his wife, Zenebu, 28, of rural Ethiopia, life is a constant struggle to keep themselves and their seven children from starving. They live in a 320-square-foot manure-plastered hut with no electricity, gas, or running water. They have a radio, but the battery is dead. Surviving on $130 a year, the family farms teff, a cereal grain.

The Mulletas' poverty is not due to a lack of hard work. Getu works about 80 hours a week, while Zenebu puts in even more hours. "Housework" for Zenebu includes fetching water, making fuel pellets out of cow dung for the open fire over which she cooks the family's food, and cleaning animal stables. Like other Ethiopian women, she eats after the men.

In Ethiopia, the average male can expect to live to 48, the average female to 50.

The Mulletas' most valuable possession is their oxen. Their wishes for the future: more animals, better seed, and a second set of clothing.

In Guadalajara, Mexico, Ambrosio and Carmen Castillo Balderas and their five children, ages 2 to 10, live in a four-room house. They also have a walled courtyard, where the family spends a good deal of time. They even have a washing machine, which is hooked up to a garden hose that runs to a public water main several hundred yards away. Like most Mexicans, they do not have a telephone, nor do they own a car. Unlike many, however, they own a refrigerator, a stereo, and a recent proud purchase that makes them the envy of their neighbors, a television.

Ambrosio, 29, works full time as a produce wholesale distributor. He also does welding on the side. The family's total annual income is $3,600. They spend 57 percent of their income on food. Carmen works about 60 hours a week taking care of their children and keeping their home spotless. The neatness of their home stands in stark contrast to the neighborhood, which is lined with littered dirt roads. As in many other Mexican neighborhoods, public utilities and road work do not keep pace with people's needs.

The average life expectancy for males in Mexico is 70. For females, it is 76.

The Castillo Balderas' most valued possessions are their refrigerator and television. Their wish for the future: a truck.

Springfield, Illinois, is home to the Kellys—Rick, 36, Patti, 34, Julie, 10, and Michael, 7. The Kellys live in a four-bedroom, 2,100-square-foot, carpeted ranch-style house, with central heating and air conditioning, a basement, and a two-car garage. Their home is equipped with a refrigerator, washing machine, clothes dryer, dishwasher, garbage disposal, vacuum cleaner, food processor, microwave, and toaster. They also own three radios, two stereos (one a CD player), four telephones (one cellular), two televisions, a camcorder, VCR, tape recorder, Gameboy, Nintendo, computer and printer, not to mention two blow dryers, an answering machine, an electric can opener, and an electric toothbrush. This doesn't count the stereo-radio-cassette players in their pickup and car.

Rick works 40 hours a week as a cable splicer for the local telephone company. Patti teaches school part time. Together they make $40,611, plus benefits. The Kellys can choose from among dozens of superstocked supermarkets. They spend $4,085 for food they eat at home, and another $2,195 eating out, a total of 15 percent of their annual income.

In the United States, the average life expectancy is 72 for males, 79 for females.

On the Kellys' wish list are two cell phones, a new Bronco, a 4 gigabyte computer, a color printer, a digital camera, a fax machine, a boat, a camping trailer, and, oh yes, farther down the road, a vacation cabin.

Sources: Menzel 1994; Population Reference Bureau 1995; Statistical Abstract 1997: Tables 713, 723.

"Worlds Apart" could be the title for these photos, which illustrate how life chances depend on global stratification. On the left is the Mulleta family of Ethiopia, featured in the opening vignette, standing in front of their home with all their material possessions. On the right is the Skeen family of Texas, surrounded by their possessions.

What Is Social Stratification?

Some of the world's nations are wealthy, others poor, and some in between. This layering of nations, or of groups of people within a nation, is called *social stratification*. Social stratification is one of the most significant topics we shall discuss, for it affects our life chances—from material possessions to the age at which we die.

Social stratification also affects our orientations to life. If you had been born into the Ethiopian family, for example, you would be illiterate and expect your children to be the same. You also would expect hunger to be a part of life and not be too surprised when people die young. To be born into either of the other two families would give you quite different views of the world.

It is important to emphasize that social stratification does not refer to individuals. It is a *way of ranking large groups of people into a hierarchy that shows their relative privileges*. **Social stratification** is a system in which people are divided into layers according to their relative power, property, and prestige.

Let's examine how the nations of the world became so stratified that, as with these three families, it profoundly affects everyone's chances in life. But first let's review the major systems of social stratification.

Systems of Social Stratification

Every society stratifies its members in some form. Some, like agriculutral societies, draw firm lines that separate group from group, while others, like hunting and gathering societies, show much greater equality. Regardless of its forms, however, the existence of social stratification is universal. There are four major systems of social stratification: slavery, caste, clan, and class.

Slavery

Let's first look at the broad aspects of slavery—its major causes and conditions—and then at slavery in the New World. As we examine the characteristics of slavery, you will see how remarkably it has varied around the world.

social stratification: the division of large numbers of people into layers according to their relative power, property, and prestige: applies to both nations and to people within a nation, society, or other group

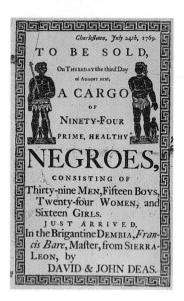

Slavery is an age-old system of social stratification. This 1769 broadside from Charleston, South Carolina, reminds us that this form of stratification was once the custom in the United States.

Causes of Slavery.   **Slavery,** whose essential characteristic is *ownership of some people by others,* has been common in world history. The Israelites of the Old Testament had slaves, as did the ancient Africans. In classical Greece and Rome, slaves did the work while free citizens engaged in politics and the arts. Slavery was least common among nomads, especially hunters and gatherers, and most common in agricultural societies (Landtman 1938/1968).

Contrary to popular assumption, slavery was not usually based on racism, but on one of three other factors. The first was debt. In some cultures, an individual who could not pay a debt could be enslaved by the creditor. The second was a violation of the law. Instead of being killed, a murderer or thief might be enslaved by the family of the victim as compensation for their loss. The third was war and conquest. When one group of people conquered another, it was often convenient to enslave at least some of the vanquished (Starna and Watkins 1991). Historian Gerda Lerner (1986) notes that through this practice the first slaves were women. When premodern men raided a village or camp, they killed the men, raped the women, and then brought the women back as slaves. The women were valued for sexual purposes, for reproduction, and for extra labor.

Roughly twenty-five hundred years ago when Greece was but a collection of city-states, slavery was common. A city that became powerful and conquered another city would enslave some of the vanquished. Both slaves and slaveholders were Greek. Similarly, when Rome became the supreme power of the Mediterranean area about two thousand years ago, following the custom of the time the Romans enslaved some of the Greeks they had conquered. More educated than their conquerors, some of these slaves served as tutors in Roman homes. Slavery, then, was a sign of defeat in battle, of crime, or of debt, not the sign of some supposedly inherently inferior status.

Conditions of Slavery.   The conditions of slavery have varied widely around the world. *In some cases, slavery was temporary.* After serving a set number of years, a slave might be free to return to his or her home country. Slaves of the Israelites were set free in the year of jubilee, which occurred every fifty years. Roman slaves ordinarily had the right to buy themselves out of slavery. They knew what their purchase price was, and some were able to meet this price by striking a bargain with their owner and selling their services to others. Such was the case with some of the educated Greek slaves. In most instances, however, slavery was lifelong. Some criminals, for example, became slaves when they were given life sentences as oarsmen on Roman war ships. There they served until death, which under this exhausting service often did not take long.

Slavery was not necessarily inheritable. In most places, the children of slaves were automatically slaves themselves. But in some instances, the child of a slave who served a rich family might even be adopted by that family, becoming an heir who bore the family name along with the other sons or daughters of the household. In ancient Mexico, the children of slaves were always free (Landtman 1938/1968:271).

Slaves were not necessarily powerless and poor. In almost all instances, slaves owned no property and had no power. Among some slaveholding groups, however, slaves could accumulate property and even rise to high positions in the community. Occasionally, a slave might even become wealthy, loan money to the master, and, while still a slave, own slaves himself or herself (Landtman 1938/1968). This, however, was rare.

Slavery in the New World.   **Indentured service** represents a fuzzy line between a contract and slavery (Main 1965; Elkins 1968). Many people who desired to start a new life in the American colonies were unable to pay their passage. Ship captains would carry them on credit, depending on someone to "buy their paper" when they arrived. This arrangement provided passage for the penniless, payment for the ship's captain, and servants for wealthier colonists for a set number of years. During that specified period, the servants had to serve their master—and could be captured and forcibly returned if they ran away. At the end of the period of indenture, they became full citizens, able to live where they chose and free to sell their labor.

slavery: a form of social stratification in which some people own other people

indentured service: a contractual system in which someone sells his or her body (services) for a specified period of time in an arrangement very close to slavery, except that it is voluntarily entered into

When the colonists found that there were not enough indentured servants to meet their growing need for labor, they tried to enslave Indians. This attempt, however, failed miserably. Among other reasons, when Indians escaped they knew how to survive in the wilderness and were able to make their way back to their tribe. The colonists then turned to Africans, who were being brought to North and South America by the Dutch, English, Portuguese, and Spanish.

Given this background of causes of slavery, some analysts conclude that racism didn't lead to slavery, but, rather, slavery led to racism. Finding it profitable to make people slaves for life, U.S. slave owners developed an **ideology,** a system of beliefs that justifies social arrangements. Essential to an ideology that would justify lifelong slavery was the view that the slaves were inferior. Some said that they were locked into a childlike, help-less state, which meant that they needed to be taken care of by superior people—white colonists, of course. Others even concluded that the slaves were not fully human. With these views, the colonists developed elaborate justifications for slavery on the presumed superiority of their own race.

To make slavery even more profitable, slave states passed laws that made slavery *in-heritable;* that is, the babies born to slaves became the property of the slave owners (Stampp 1956). These children could be sold, bartered, or traded. To strengthen their control, slave states passed laws making it illegal for slaves to hold meetings or to be away from the master's premises without carrying a pass (Lerner 1972). As sociologist W.E.B. Du Bois (1935/1966:12) noted, "gradually the entire white South became an armed camp to keep Negroes in slavery and to kill the black rebel."

Patterns of legal discrimination did not end after the Civil War. For example, until 1954 the states operated two separate school systems. Even until the 1950s, to keep the races from "mixing," it was illegal in Mississippi for a white and an African American to sit together on the same seat of a car! The reason there was no outright ban on both races being in the same car was to allow for African-American chauffeurs.

Slavery Today.   Slavery has again reared its ugly head, this time in Sudan, Mauritania, and Benin (Horwitz 1989; Liben 1995; "Child Slave Trade . . ." 1997). Apparently, vil-lages are raided and the men killed. The captive children are sold for a few dollars, some-times for just a couple of chickens. The women, sold to the highest bidder for work and sex, bring more. Public television (PBS) has even run film footage of captured children in chains. In spite of this, representatives of these governments strongly deny the accu-sations (Abdullah 1995).

Caste

The second system of social stratification is caste. In a **caste system,** status is determined by birth and is lifelong. In sociological terms the basis of a caste system is ascribed status (discussed on page 96). Achieved status cannot change an individual's place in this system. Someone born into a low-status group will always have low status, no matter how much that person may accomplish in life.

Societies with this form of stratification try to make certain that the boundaries between castes remain firm. They practice **en-dogamy,** marriage within their own group, and prohibit intermar-riage. To prevent contact between castes, they even develop elaborate rules about *ritual pollution*, teaching that contact with in-ferior castes contaminates the superior caste.

India.   India provides the best example of a caste system. Based not on race but on religion, it has existed for almost three thousand years (Chandra 1993a, b). India's four main castes, or *varnas*, are depicted in Table 9.1. The four main castes are subdivided into thousands of specialized subcastes, or *jati*, with each *jati* working in

ideology: beliefs about the way things ought to be that jus-tify social arrangements

caste system: a form of social stratification in which one's sta-tus is determined by birth and is lifelong

endogamy: marriage within one's own group

TABLE 9.1	
India's Caste System	
Caste	*Occupation*
Brahman	Priests or scholars
Kshatriya	Nobles and warriors
Vaishva	Merchants and skilled artisans
Shudra	Common laborers
Harijan	The outcastes; degrading labor

*In a caste system, status is determined at birth and is lifelong. Members of lower castes suffer depriva-
tion in virtually all aspects of life. In the Indian caste system, even occupation is determined by birth.
Just as this man's father fixed shoes, so will his son. Gender cuts across every form of social stratification.
Birth gave the woman in the photo on the left membership in a lower caste, as well as a secondary status
within that caste. So it will be for her daughter. The photo on the right, also from India, illustrates gender stratification in the division of labor that has been found in all societies. As the text discusses, this
system has come under attack.*

a specific occupation. For example, knife sharpening is done only by members of a particular subcaste.

The lowest group listed on Table 9.1, the Harijan, is actually so low that it is beneath
the caste system altogether. The Harijans, along with some of the Shudras, make up
India's "untouchables." If someone of a higher caste is touched by one of them, that person becomes unclean. In some cases, even the shadow of an untouchable is contaminat-
ing. Early morning and late afternoons are especially risky, for the long shadows of these
periods pose a danger to everyone higher up the caste system. Consequently, Harijans are
not even allowed in some villages during these times. If anyone becomes contaminated,
their religion specifies ablution, or washing rituals, to restore purity (Lannoy 1975).

Although the Indian government declared the caste system abolished in 1949, the
force of centuries-old practices cannot be so easily eliminated, and the caste system remains part of everyday life in India (Sharma 1994). The ceremonies one follows at births,
marriages, and deaths, for example, are dictated by caste (Chandra 1993a). Due to industrialization and urbanization, however, this system is breaking down, for it is difficult to
maintain caste divisions in crowded and anonymous cities (Robertson 1976).

South Africa. Until recently, South Africa provided another example of social stratification based on caste. Europeans of Dutch descent, a numerical minority called Afrikaaners, controlled the government, the police, and the military to enforce a system they
called **apartheid** (ah-PAR-tate), the separation of the races. By law there were four different racial groups: Europeans (whites), Africans (blacks), Coloureds (mixed races), and
Asians. To be classified in one of these groups—and everyone was—determined where
one could live, work, and go to school. It also determined where one could swim or see
movies—for by law whites and Africans were not allowed to mix socially.

apartheid: the separation of
races as was practiced in South
Africa

After decades of trade sanctions, sports boycotts, and worldwide negative publicity, however, Afrikaaners reluctantly dismantled their caste system (Ford 1993; Melloan 1993a). No longer must Africans carry special passes, public facilities are integrated, and all races have the right to vote and to hold office. In 1994, in the country's first post-apartheid election, Nelson Mandela, an African who had been imprisoned for nineteen years for revolutionary activities, was elected president of South Africa.

Although apartheid has been dismantled, its legacy haunts South Africa (Wells 1995). Whites still dominate the country's social institutions. Although there is a growing black middle class, most blacks remain uneducated and poor. Many new rights—to higher education, to eat in restaurants, to go swimming, even to see a doctor—are of little use to people who can't afford them. Political violence has been replaced by old-fashioned crime, and South Africa's murder rate runs *six times* higher than the extraordinary U.S. rate (Stengel 1995). Apartheid's legacy of prejudice, bitterness, and hatred is destined to fuel race relations for generations.

A U.S. Racial Caste System.   Before leaving the subject of caste, we should note that when slavery ended in the United States it was replaced by a *racial caste system*, in which birth marked a person for life (Berger 1963, 1995). In this system, *all* whites, no matter if they were poor and uneducated, considered themselves higher than *all* African Americans. Even into the earlier parts of this century, long after slavery had ended, this attitude persisted. When any white met any African American on a southern sidewalk, for example, the African American had to move aside. And as in India and South Africa, the upper caste feared pollution from the lower, insisting on separate schools, hotels, restaurants, and even toilets and drinking fountains in public facilities.

Clan

The **clan system** used to be common in agricultural societies. In this system, each individual is linked to a large network of relatives called a **clan.** A clan is like a greatly extended family. Just as in a family, if the clan has a high status, so does the individual. Similarly, the clan's resources—whether few or many—are the individual's. And like a family, allegiance to the clan is a lifelong obligation.

Clans are also like castes in that membership is determined by birth and is lifelong. Unlike castes, however, marriages can cross clan lines. In fact, marriages may be used to forge alliances between clans, for the obligations that a marriage establishes between in-laws can bind clans together (Erturk 1994).

Just as industrialization and urbanization are eroding the lines that separate the castes of India, so they make clans more fluid, eventually replacing them by social classes. Like other systems of social stratification, clans can make a difference between life and death, as the following example illustrates:

> The Sultan clan consists of about 150 individuals, who occupy a dozen neighboring houses in Kuwait City. To survive the Iraqi occupation of Kuwait in 1989–90, members of this clan pooled their resources for the common good. Those in the appliance business bribed Iraqi officers with food processors, microwave ovens, and televisions; while those in the hotel business secreted away huge amounts of steak and shrimp, which they shared with fellow clan members. Together they plotted—and obtained—the release of one of their members who had been imprisoned and were able to smuggle him into Saudi Arabia. (Horwitz 1991)

Class

As we have seen, stratification systems based on slavery, caste, and clan are rigid. The lines marking the divisions between people are so firm that, except for marriage between clans, there is no movement from one group to another. A **class system,** in contrast, is much more open, for it is based primarily on money or material possessions. It, too, begins at birth, when an individual is ascribed the status of his or her parents, but, unlike slavery,

clan system: a form of social stratification in which individuals receive their social standing through belonging to an extended network of relatives

clan: an extended network of relatives

class system: a form of social stratification based primarily on the possession of money or material possessions

caste, and clan, one's social class may change due to what one achieves (or fails to achieve) in life. In addition, there are no laws that specify occupations on the basis of birth or that prohibit marriage between the classes.

A major characteristic of this fourth system, then, is its relatively fluid boundaries. A class system allows **social mobility,** that is, movement up or down the class ladder. The potential for improving one's social circumstances, or class, is one of the major forces that drives people to go far in school and to work hard. In the extreme, the family background that an individual inherits at birth may bestow such obstacles that the child has little chance of climbing very far—or it may provide such privileges that it is almost impossible to fall down the class ladder.

A Note on Global Stratification and the Status of Females

We shall examine the social class system in detail, but first let's note that in every society of the world gender is a basis for social stratification. In no society is gender the sole basis for stratifying people, but gender cuts across *all* systems of social stratification—whether slavery, caste, clan, or class (Huber 1990). On the basis of their gender, people in every society are sorted into categories and given different access to the good things offered by their society.

Apparently these distinctions always favor males. It is remarkable, for example, that in every society of the world men's earnings are higher than women's. Or consider areas in which control of females by males is more evident, such as child brides, child prostitution (see the box on page 246), and female circumcision (see the box on page 289). That most of the world's illiterate are females drives home the relative positions of males and females. Of the 885 million adults who are illiterate, two-thirds are women, while of the 13 million school-age children who receive no education, two-thirds are girls (Browne 1995). Gender is so significant for human relations that we shall devote a separate chapter to this topic (Chapter 11).

What Determines Social Class?

social mobility: movement up or down the social class ladder

In the early days of sociology, a disagreement arose about the meaning of social class in industrialized societies. Let's compare how Marx and Weber saw the matter.

These photos, taken at the end of the nineteenth century, illustrate the different worlds that social classes produce within the same society. The boys on the left worked full time—when they could get work. They did not go to school, and they had no home. The children on the right, Cornelius and Gladys Vanderbilt, are shown in front of their parents' estate. They went to school and did not work. You can see how the life situations illustrated in these photos would have produced different orientations to life—and, therefore, politics, ideas about marriage, values, and so on—the stuff of which life is made.

Karl Marx: The Means of Production

As discussed in Chapter 1, Karl Marx (1818–1883) personally saw societies in upheaval. When the feudal system broke up, masses of peasants were displaced from their traditional lands and occupations. Fleeing to cities, they competed for the few available jobs. Offered only a pittance for their labor, they dressed in rags, went hungry, and slept under bridges and in shacks. In contrast, the factory owners built mansions, hired servants, and lived in the lap of luxury. Seeing this great disparity between owners and workers, Marx concluded that social class depends on a single factor—the **means of production**—the tools, factories, land, and investment capital used to produce wealth (Marx 1844/1964; Marx and Engels 1848/1967).

Marx argued that the distinctions people often make between themselves—such as clothing, speech, education, or relative salary—are superficial matters. They camouflage the only real significant dividing line: People (the **bourgeoisie**) either own the means of production or they (the **proletariat**) work for those who do. This is the only distinction that counts, for these two classes make up modern society. In short, according to Marx, people's relationship to the means of production determines their social class.

Marx did recognize that other groups were part of industrial society: farmers and peasants; a *lumpenproletariat* (marginal people such as migrant workers, beggars, vagrants, and criminals); and a middle class (self-employed professionals). Marx did not consider these groups social classes, however, for they lacked **class consciousness**—a common identity based on their position in the means of production. They did not see themselves as exploited workers whose plight could be solved only by collective action. Consequently, Marx thought of these groups as insignificant in the coming workers' revolution that would overthrow capitalism.

Capital will become more concentrated, Marx said, which will make capitalists and workers increasingly hostile. When workers see capitalists as the source of their oppression, they will unite and throw off the chains of their oppressors. In a bloody revolution, they will seize the means of production and usher in a classless society, where no longer will the few grow rich at the expense of the many. What holds back the workers' unity and their revolution is **false consciousness,** workers mistakenly identifying with capitalists. For example, workers with a few dollars in the bank often forget that they are workers and instead see themselves as investors, or as capitalists who are about to launch a successful business.

The only distinction worth mentioning, then, is whether a person is an owner or a worker. This decides everything else, Marx stressed, for property determines people's lifestyles, shapes their ideas, and establishes their relationships with one another.

Max Weber: Property, Prestige, and Power

Max Weber (1864–1920) became an outspoken critic of Marx. He said that property is only part of the picture. Social class, he said, is actually made up of three components— property, prestige, and power (Gerth and Mills 1958; Weber 1922/1968). Some call these the three P's of social class. (Although Weber used the terms *class, status,* and *power,* some sociologists find *property, prestige,* and *power* to be clearer terms. To make them even clearer, you may wish to substitute *wealth* for *property.*)

Property (or wealth), said Weber, is certainly significant in determining a person's standing in society. On that he agreed with Marx. But, added Weber, ownership is not the only significant aspect of property. For example, some powerful people, such as managers of corporations *control* the means of production although they do not *own* them. If managers can control property for their own benefit—awarding themselves huge bonuses and magnificent perks—it makes no practical difference that they do not own the property that they so generously use for their own benefit.

Prestige, the second element in Weber's analysis, is often derived from property, for people tend to look up to the wealthy. Prestige, however, can also be based on other factors. Olympic gold medalists, for example, may not own property, yet they have very high

means of production: the tools, factories, land, and investment capital used to produce wealth

bourgeoisie: Karl Marx's term for the people who own the means of production

proletariat: Karl Marx's term for the people who work for those who own the means of production

class consciousness: Karl Marx's term for awareness of a common identity based on one's position in the means of production

false consciousness: Karl Marx's term to refer to workers identifying with the interests of capitalists

The text describes the many relationships among Weber's three components of social class: property, prestige, and power. Both Abraham Lincoln and Colin Powell are examples of power that was converted into prestige.

prestige. Some are even able to exchange their prestige for property—such as being paid a small fortune for saying that they start their day with "the breakfast of champions." In other words, property and prestige are not one-way streets: Although property can bring prestige, prestige can also bring property.

Power, the third element of social class, is the ability to control others, even over their objections. Weber agreed with Marx that property is a major source of power, but he added that it is not the only source. For example, prestige can be turned into power. Perhaps the best example is Ronald Reagan, an actor who became president of the most powerful country in the world. For other interrelationships of property, prestige, and power, see Figure 9.1 on the next page.

 In Sum For Marx, social class was based solely on a person's position in relationship to the means of production—as a member of either the bourgeoisie or the proletariat—while Weber argued that social class is a combination of property, prestige, and power.

Why Is Social Stratification Universal?

What is it about social life that makes all societies stratified? We shall first consider the explanation proposed by functionalists, which has aroused much controversy in sociology, followed by criticisms of this position. We then explore explanations proposed by conflict theorists.

The Functionalist View of Davis and Moore: Motivating Qualified People

Functionalists take the position that the patterns of behavior that characterize a society exist because they are functional for that society. They conclude that because social inequality is universal, inequality must help societies survive. Using this principle, sociologists Kingsley Davis and Wilbert Moore (1945, 1953) concluded that stratification is inevitable for the following reasons:

1. Society must make certain that its positions are filled.
2. Some positions are more important than others.

3. The more important positions must be filled by the more qualified people.

4. To motivate the more qualified people to fill these positions, society must offer them greater rewards.

Let's look at some examples to flesh out this functionalist argument. The position of college president is deemed much more important for society than that of a student, because the president's decisions affect many more people. Any mistakes he or she makes carry implications for a large number of people, including many students. So it is with the general of an army versus privates. The decisions of college presidents and generals affect careers, paychecks, and, in some cases, even life and death.

Positions with greater responsibility also require greater accountability. College presidents and army generals are accountable for how they perform—to boards of trustees and the leader of a country, respectively. How can society motivate highly qualified people to enter such high-pressure positions? What keeps people from avoiding them and seeking only less demanding jobs?

The answer, said Davis and Moore, is that society offers greater rewards for its more responsible, demanding, and accountable positions. If they didn't offer higher salaries, benefits, and greater prestige, why would anyone strive for them? Thus, a salary of $2 million, country club membership, a private jet, and a chauffered limousine may be necessary to get the most highly qualified people to compete with one another for a certain position, while a $30,000 salary without fringe benefits is enough to get hundreds of people to compete for a less demanding position. Similarly, higher rewards are necessary to recruit people to positions that require rigorous training. Why suffer through taking tests and writing papers in college or graduate school if you can get the same pay and prestige with a high school education?

The functionalist argument is simple and clear. Society works better if its most qualified people hold its most important positions. For example, to get highly talented people to become surgeons—to undergo many years of rigorous training and then cope with life-and-death situations on a daily basis, as well as withstand the Sword of Damocles known as malpractice suits—requires a high payoff.

Tumin: A Critical Response

Note that the Davis–Moore thesis is an attempt to explain *why* social stratification is universal, not an attempt to *justify* social inequality. Note also that their view nevertheless makes many sociologists uncomfortable, for they see it as coming close to justifying the inequalities of society.

Melvin Tumin (1953) was the first sociologist to point out what he saw as major flaws in the functionalist position. Here are four of his arguments.

First, how do you measure the importance of a position? You can't measure importance by the rewards a position carries, for that argument is circular. You must have an independent measure of importance to test whether the more important positions actually carry higher rewards. For example, is a surgeon really more important to society than a garbage collector, since the garbage collector helps prevent contagious diseases?

Second, if stratification worked as Davis and Moore described it, society would be a **meritocracy;** that is, all positions would be awarded on the basis of merit. Ability, then, should predict who goes to college. Instead, the best predictor of college entrance is family income—the more a family earns, the more likely their children to go to college. Similarly, while some people do get ahead through ability and hard work, others simply inherit wealth and the opportunities that go with it. Moreover, if a stratification system places most men above most women, it does not live up to the argument that talent and ability are the bases for holding important positions. In short, factors far beyond merit give people their relative positions in society.

Third, Davis and Moore place too much emphasis on money and fringe benefits. These aren't the only reasons people take jobs. An example is college teaching. If money were the main motivator, why would people spend four years in college, then average an-

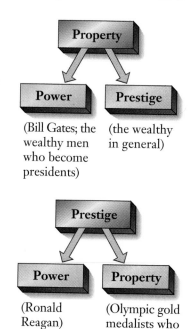

(Bill Gates; the   (the wealthy
wealthy men   in general)
who become
presidents)

(Ronald   (Olympic gold
Reagan)   medalists who
                 endorse
                 products)

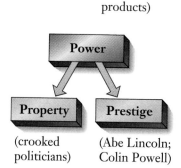

(crooked   (Abe Lincoln;
politicians)   Colin Powell)

Figure 9.1

Weber's Three Components of Social Class: Interrelationships Among Them

meritocracy: a form of social stratification in which all positions are awarded on the basis of merit

other six or seven years pursuing a Ph.D.—only to earn slightly more than someone who works in the post office? Obviously college teaching offers more than monetary rewards: high prestige (see Table 10.2, page 257), autonomy (college teachers have considerable discretion about how they do their job), rewarding social interaction (much of the job consists of talking to people), security (when given tenure, college teachers have a lifetime job), leisure and the opportunity to travel (many professors work short days, enjoy several weeks of vacation during the school year, and have the entire summer off).

Fourth, if social stratification is so functional, it ought to benefit almost everyone. In actual fact, however, social stratification is *dysfunctional* to many. Think of the people who could have made invaluable contributions to society had they not been born in a slum and had to drop out of school, taking a menial job to help support the family; or the many who, born female, are assigned "women's work," ensuring that they do not maximize their mental abilities (Huber 1988).

Mosca: A Forerunner of the Conflict Perspective

In 1896 Italian sociologist Gaetano Mosca wrote an influential book entitled *The Ruling Class*. He argued that every society will be stratified by power, for three main reasons:

1. A society cannot exist unless it is organized. This requires politics of some sort in order to coordinate people's actions and get society's work done.
2. Political organization always results in inequalities of power, for it requires that some people take leadership positions, while others follow.
3. It is human nature to be self-centered. Therefore, people in positions of power will use their positions to bring greater rewards for themselves.

There is no way around these facts of life, said Mosca. Social stratification is inevitable, and every society will stratify itself along lines of power. Because the ruling class is well organized and enjoys easy communication among its relatively few members, it is extremely difficult for the majority they govern to resist (Marger 1987). (Remember the law of oligarchy that we reviewed in Chapter 7.) Mosca's argument is a forerunner of explanations developed by conflict theorists.

The Conflict Perspective: Class Conflict and Competition for Scarce Resources

Conflict theorists sharply disagree with the functionalist position. They stress that conflict, not function, is the basis of social stratification. Sociologists such as William Domhoff (1990, 1997), C. Wright Mills (1956), and Irving Louis Horowitz (1966) point out that in every society groups struggle with one another to gain a larger share of their society's limited resources. Whenever some group gains power, it uses that power to extract what it can from the groups beneath it. It also uses the social institutions to keep other groups weak and itself in power. Class conflict, then, is the key to understanding social stratification, for society is far from being a harmonious system that benevolently distributes greater resources to society's supposedly more qualified members.

All ruling groups—from slave masters to modern elites—develop an ideology to justify their position at the top. This ideology often seduces the oppressed into believing that their welfare depends on keeping society stable. Consequently, the oppressed may support laws against their own interests and even sacrifice their children as soldiers in wars designed to enrich the bourgeoisie.

The day will come, Marx said, when class consciousness will overcome ideology. When their eyes are opened, the workers will throw off their oppressors. At first, this struggle for control of the means of production may be covert, showing up as work slowdowns or industrial sabotage, but ultimately it will break out into open resistance. The revolt, though inevitable and bloody, will be difficult, for the bourgeoisie control the police, the military, and even education (where they implant false consciousness in the workers' children).

Some sociologists have refocused conflict theory. C. Wright Mills (1956), Ralf Dahrendorf (1959), and Randall Collins (1974, 1988), for example, stress that groups within the *same class* also compete for scarce resources—for power, wealth, education, housing, and even prestige—whatever benefits society has to offer. The result is conflict not only between labor unions and corporations, but also between the young and the old, women and men, and racial and ethnic groups. Unlike functionalists, then, conflict theorists hold that just beneath the surface of what may appear to be a tranquil society lies overt conflict—only uneasily held in check.

Toward a Synthesis

In spite of vast differences between the functionalist and conflict views, some analysts have tried to synthesize them. Sociologist Gerhard Lenski (1966), for example, used the development of surpluses as a basis for reconciling the two views. He said that the functionalists are right if you look at societies that have only basic resources and do not accumulate wealth. In hunting and gathering societies, the limited resources are channeled to people as rewards for taking on important responsibilities. When it comes to societies with a surplus, however, the conflict theorists are right. Because humans pursue self-interest, they struggle to control those surpluses, and a small elite emerges. To protect its position, the elite builds social inequality into the society, which results in a full-blown system of social stratification.

How Do Elites Maintain Stratification?

Suppose that you are part of the ruling elite of your society. What can you do to maintain your privileged position? The key lies in controlling ideas and information, in social networks, and in the least effective of all, the use of force.

Ideology Versus Force

Medieval Europe provides a good example of the power of ideology. At that time, land, which was owned by only a small group of people, was the primary source of wealth. With the exception of the clergy and some craftsmen, almost everyone was a peasant working for this small group of powerful landowners, called the aristocracy. The peasants farmed the land, took care of the cattle, and built the roads and bridges. Each year, they had to turn over a designated portion of their crops to their feudal lord. Year after year, for centuries, they did so. Why?

Controlling Ideas. Why didn't the peasants rebel and take over the land themselves? There were many reasons, not the least of which is that the army was controlled by the aristocracy. Coercion, however, only goes so far, for it breeds hostility and nourishes rebellion. How much more effective it is to get the people to *want* to do what the ruling elite desires. This is where *ideology* comes into play, and the aristocracy of that time used it to great effect. They developed an ideology known as the **divine right of kings**—the idea that the king's authority comes directly from God—which can be traced back several thousand years to the Old Testament. The king could delegate authority to nobles, who as God's representatives also had to be obeyed. To disobey was a sin against God; to rebel meant physical punishment on earth and a sentence to suffer in eternal hell.

The control of ideas, then, can be remarkably more effective than brute force. Although this particular ideology no longer governs people's minds today, the elite in every society develops ideologies to justify its position at the top. For example, around the world schools teach that their country's form of government—*whatever form of government that may be*—is the best. Each nation's schools also stress the virtues of governments past and present, not their vices. Religion also teaches that we owe obedience to authority, that laws

divine right of kings: the idea that the king's authority comes directly from God

The divine right of kings *was an ideology that made the king God's direct representative on earth—so that he could administer justice and punish evildoers. This theological-political concept was supported by the Roman Catholic Church, whose representatives crowned the king. Depicted here is the coronation of Charlemagne by Pope Leo III on Christmas day* A.D. *800, an event that marked the beginning of the period that became known as the Holy Roman Empire.*

are to be obeyed. To the degree that their ideologies are accepted by the masses, political arrangements are stable.

Controlling Information. To maintain their positions of power, elites also try to control information. In dictatorships this is accomplished through the threat of force, for dictators can—and do—imprison editors and reporters for printing critical reports, sometimes even for publishing information unflattering to them (Timerman 1981). The ruling elites of democracies, lacking such power, accomplish the same purpose by manipulating the media through the selective release of information, withholding what they desire "in the interest of national security." But just as coercion has its limits, so does the control of information—especially given its new forms (from satellite communications to fax machines, e-mail, and the Internet) that pay no respect to international borders (Kennedy 1993).

Social Networks. Also critical in maintaining stratification are social networks—the social ties that link people together (Higley et al. 1991). As discussed in Chapter 6, social networks—contacts expanding outward from the individual that gradually encompass more and more people—supply valuable information and tend to perpetuate social inequality. Sociologist William Domhoff (1983, 1990) has documented how members of the elite move in a circle of power that multiplies their opportunities. Contacts with people of similar backgrounds, interests, and goals allow the elite to pass privileges from one generation to the next. In contrast, the social networks of the poor perpetuate poverty and powerlessness.

Technology. The elite's desire to preserve its position is aided by recent developments in technology, especially monitoring devices. These devices—from "hot telephones," taps that make your telephone a microphone even when it is off the hook, to machines that can read the entire contents of your computer without leaving a trace—help the elite monitor citizens' activities without their even being aware that they are being shadowed. Dictatorships have few checks on how such technology will be employed, but in democracies checks and balances, such as constitutional rights and the necessity of court orders, at least partially curb their use.

▼ **In Sum** Underlying the maintenance of stratification is control of a society's institutions. In a dictatorship, the elite makes the laws. In a democracy, they influence the laws. In both, the legal establishment enforces the laws. The elite also commands the police and military and can give orders to crush a rebellion—or even to run the post office or air traffic control if workers strike. As noted, force has its limits, and a nation's elite generally finds it preferable to maintain its stratification system by peaceful means, especially by influencing the thinking of its people.

Comparative Social Stratification

Now that we have examined different systems of social stratification and considered why stratification is universal, let us compare social stratification in Great Britain and in the former Soviet Union. For even more contrast, see the Perspectives box below, where you can catch a glimpse of the social stratification that characterized Polish Jews prior to the Nazi inferno.

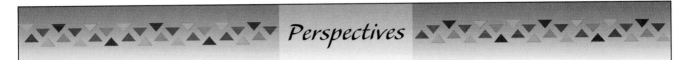

Perspectives

CULTURAL DIVERSITY AROUND THE WORLD

Social Stratification Among Polish Jews

The stratification of the Jews in Stoczek, Poland, between World Wars I and II provides a rich contrast with stratification in the United States. The four sources of social status for the Jews were occupation, wealth, learning, and lineage. In general, people were located at the same point on all four scales.

The first source of status, *occupation*, was divided into men of labor (about 60 percent) and businessmen (about 39 percent). About 1 percent were learners, who did not work. Learners devoted themselves full time to studying the Torah, the Jewish law as written in the first five books of the Old Testament. Learners were supported by their wives or by their parents-in-law. High respect was given to a man who devoted his life to learning.

Wealth, the second source of status, had three acceptable uses. First, a person should eat well, dress well, and enjoy other pleasures; but anyone who spent money only on such things was considered a "pig." To be rich and command respect also required that one do good deeds (*mitzvot*) for the needy. To give money to those who needed it, rather than to those who could repay, was a sign of having a true "Jewish heart." Doing a good deed for an orphan, for example, brought greater credit than doing a similar deed for a self-supporting person. In addition to gaining honor and respect, the doer of good deeds also stored up credit with God for the afterlife. The third use of money was to purchase status for one's children—to educate one's sons or to marry one's daughters into a "better" family.

The third source of status, *learning*, referred to studying the Torah. Unlike education, learning was never completed. This lifelong endeavor was a goal in itself, not a means to obtain material benefits. Learning was the equivalent of "refinement," and was to be pursued with love and joy. To sit up late at night studying, after a long day's work, brought prestige. The advice and opinions of a learned man were highly valued.

The fourth source of status, *lineage*, was the first thing to be established when strangers met or when people talked about a third person. People were accorded high prestige if they were descendants of learned, wealthy, and charitable ancestors. By itself, however, the connection was insufficient: Individuals had to live up to their lineage by being learned and charitable themselves. Those who did not were seen as having squandered their inheritance.

These four sources of social status translated into three social classes. At the top of the social pyramid were people with much learning, wealth, and a reputation for giving to the needy. Next came the middle class, consisting of shopkeepers and traders who had some means and some learning. At the bottom were the plain Jews—workers and craftsmen who had little learning and little money.

In Stoczek, social status was so significant that there were no friendships between adults of different classes, and status even determined where a man would sit in the synagogue. Reserved for men of highest status were the seats nearest to the eastern wall—those closest to Jerusalem.

Although anyone was supposed to be able to move up the class ladder through attaining wealth or learning, class membership was, for the most part, hereditary. Women who guided their children to love learning or to do good deeds were given higher status, as were those who were very religious and did good deeds themselves. A woman whose father was a rabbi or scholar was also accorded higher status, as was a woman who encouraged her husband to *mitzvot* or supported him so he could devote all his time to learning. Women were not allowed to worship alongside the men in the synagogue, but were permitted only in the balcony or some other separate place.

The world depicted by this stratification system was erased by Hitler in his systematic—and largely successful—campaign to destroy European Jewry.

Sources: Based on Heller 1953, 1991.

Social Stratification in Great Britain

Great Britain is often called England by Americans, but England is only one of the countries that make up the island of Great Britain. The others are Scotland and Wales. In addition, Northern Ireland is part of the United Kingdom of Great Britain and Northern Ireland.

Like other industrialized countries, Great Britain has a class system that can be divided into a lower, middle, and upper class. A little over half the population is in the lower or working class, while close to half the population is in the nation's very large middle class. A tiny upper class, perhaps 1 percent of the population, is powerful, highly educated, and extremely wealthy.

Compared with Americans, the British are extremely class conscious. Like Americans, the British recognize class distinctions on the basis of the type of car a person drives, or the stores that person patronizes. But the most striking characteristics of the British class system are language and education. Differences in speech have a powerful impact on British life. Accent almost always betrays class, and as soon as someone speaks, the listener is aware of that person's class—and treats him or her accordingly.

Education is the primary way by which the British perpetuate their class system from one generation to the next. Almost all children go to neighborhood schools, but the children of Great Britain's more privileged 5 percent—who own *half* the nation's wealth—attend exclusive private boarding schools (known as "public" schools), where they are trained in subjects considered "proper" for members of the ruling class. An astounding 50 percent of the students at Oxford and Cambridge, the country's most prestigious universities, come from this 5 percent of the population. To illustrate how powerfully this system of stratified education affects the national life of Great Britain, sociologist Ian Robertson (1987) says,

> [E]ighteen former pupils of the most exclusive of them, Eton, have become prime minister. Imagine the chances of a single American high school producing eighteen presidents!

Social Stratification in the Former Soviet Union

Vladimir Ilyich Lenin (1870–1924) and Leon Trotsky (1879–1940) heeded Karl Marx's call for a classless society. They led a revolution in Russia to bring this about. They, and the nations that followed their banner, never claimed to have achieved the ideal of communism, in which all contribute their labor to the common good and receive according to their needs. Instead, they used the term *socialism* to describe the intermediate step between capitalism and communism, in which social classes are abolished but some individual inequality remains.

Although the socialist nations often manipulated the world's mass media to tweak the nose of Uncle Sam because of the inequalities of the United States, they, too, were marked by huge disparities in privilege—much more than they ever acknowledged to the outside world. Their major basis of stratification—membership in the Communist party—often was the determining factor in deciding who would gain admission to the better schools or obtain the more desirable jobs. The equally qualified son or daughter of a nonmember would be turned down, for such privileges came with demonstrated loyalty to the Party.

Divided into three layers, even the Communist party was highly stratified. Most members occupied a low level, having such assignments as spying on other workers. For their services, they might be given easier jobs in the factory or occasional access to special stores to purchase hard-to-find goods. A smaller number were mid-level bureaucrats with better than average access to resources and privileges. The top level consisted of a small elite: party members who enjoyed not only power but also limousines, imported delicacies, vacation homes, and even servants and hunting lodges. As with other stratification systems around the world, women held lower positions in the Party, as was readily evident in each year's May Day photos of the top members of the Party reviewing the weapons paraded in Moscow's Red Square. The top officials were always men.

Russia's recent reluctant embrace of capitalism has brought many changes. Advertising in order to create demand for products is one new development. The stark contrast now evident between the social classes is another.

Rather than eliminating social classes, then, the Communist revolution merely ushered in a different set of classes. An elite continued to rule from the top. Before the revolution this elite was based on lineage and inherited wealth; afterward it consisted of top party officials. Below this elite was a small middle class consisting of white-collar and other skilled workers. At the bottom was a mass of peasants and unskilled workers, very similar to the lower class before the revolution.

Struggling with a bloated bureaucracy, the gross inefficiencies of central planning, workers who did the minimum because they could not be fired and received no bonuses for being efficient, and the military grabbing one of every eight of the nation's rubles, (*Statistical Abstract* 1993:1432), the leaders of the USSR grew frustrated as they saw the West thrive. Their ideology did not intend their citizens to be deprived. In an attempt to turn things around, the Soviet leadership initiated reforms. They sold to the public huge chunks of state-owned business and allowed elections with more than one candidate for an office (unlike earlier elections). With private investment and ownership, profits changed from a curse word to a respectable goal.

This transition to capitalism has taken a bizarre twist. To seize the newly opened opportunities to gain wealth and power, some Russians have formed criminal groups. Taking advantage of a breakdown of authority, and sometimes with the complicity of disgruntled military officers, they have stolen vast amounts of state property, amassed wealth, and intimidated businesspeople. To enforce cooperation, this Russian Mafia assassinates heads of banks and other business leaders (Bernstein 1994; Goble 1996). This group of organized criminals will likely take a place in Russia's new capitalist class.

Global Stratification: Three Worlds of Development

As noted at the beginning of this chapter, just as the people within a nation are stratified by power, prestige, and property, so are the world's nations. Until recently, a simple model consisting of First, Second, and Third Worlds was used to depict global stratification. "First World" referred to the industrialized capitalist nations, "Second World" to the communist nations, and "Third World" to any nation that did not fit into the first two categories. After the Soviet Union broke up in 1989, these terms became outdated. In addition, although *first, second,* and *third* did not mean "best," "better," and "worst," they sounded like it. An alternative classification some now use—developed, developing, and undeveloped nations—has the same drawback. By calling ourselves "developed," it sounds as though we are mature, leaving the "undeveloped" nations lacking our desirable trait.

Consequently, I have chosen more neutrally descriptive terms: Most Industrialized, Industrializing, and Least Industrialized Nations. One can measure industrialization, with no judgment, even implied, about whether a nation's industrialization represents "development," ranks them "first"—or is even desirable in the first place.

The intention is to depict on a global level social stratification's three primary dimensions: property, power, and prestige. The Most Industrialized Nations have much greater property (wealth), power (they do get their way in international relations), and prestige—rightly or wrongly, they are looked up to as world leaders and as having something worthwhile to contribute to humanity. The three families sketched in the opening vignette provide some insight into the far-reaching effects of global stratification on the citizens of this world.

The Most Industrialized Nations

The Most Industrialized Nations are the United States and Canada in North America; Great Britain, France, Germany, Switzerland, and the other industrialized nations of western Europe; Japan in Asia; and Australia and New Zealand in the area of the world known as Oceania. Although there are variations in their economic systems, these nations are capitalistic. As Table 9.2 shows, although these nations have 31 percent of the earth's land, they have only 16 percent of its people. Their wealth is so enormous that even their poor live better and longer lives than do the average citizens of the Least Industrialized Nations. The Social Map on pages 240–241 shows the tremendous disparities in income among the world's nations.

The Industrializing Nations

The Industrializing Nations include most of the nations of the former Soviet Union and its former satellites in eastern Europe. As Table 9.2 shows, these nations account for 20 percent of the earth's land and 16 percent of its people.

The dividing points between the three "worlds" are soft, making it difficult to know how to classify some nations. This is especially the case with the Industrializing Nations. Exactly how much industrialization must a nation have to be in this category? Although soft, these categories do pinpoint essential differences. Most inhabitants of the Industrializing Nations have much lower incomes and standards of living than people who live in the Most Industrialized Nations. Most, however, are better off than members of the Least Industrialized Nations. For example, on such measures as access to electricity, indoor plumbing, automobiles, telephones, and even food, citizens of the Industrializing Nations rank lower than those in the Most Industrialized Nations, but higher than those in the Least Industrialized Nations.

The Least Industrialized Nations

In the Least Industrialized Nations, most people are peasant farmers living on farms or in villages. These nations account for 49 percent of the earth's land and 68 percent of the world's people.

It is difficult to imagine the poverty that characterizes most of the Least Industrialized Nations. Although wealthy nations have their pockets of poverty, *most* people in these nations live on less than $1,000 a year, in many cases considerably less. Most of them have no running water, indoor plumbing, central water supply, or access to trained physicians. Because modern medi-

TABLE 9.2

Three Worlds of Development

| | *Percentage of the World's* | |
	Land	Population
Most Industrialized Nations	31%	16%
Industrializing Nations	20	16
Least Industrialized Nations	49	68

Sources: Computed from Kurian 1990, 1991, 1992.

It is difficult for citizens of the Most Industrialized Nations, where luxuries have been turned into necessities, to grasp the severity of the poverty in the Least Industrialized Nations. This photo by Sebastião Salgado shows garbage pickers in Fortaleza, Brazil. The survival of these children and adults depends on plucking bits and pieces from this trash heap. They must even fight with the vultures for scraps of rotting food.

cine has cut infant mortality but not births, the population grows fastest in these nations, thus placing even greater burdens on their limited facilities, and causing them to fall farther behind each year (Sweezy and Magdoff 1992). The twin specters of poverty and death at an early age continuously stalk these countries. Some conditions in these poor countries are gruesome, as discussed in the following Thinking Critically section.

Thinking Critically About Social Controversy

Open Season: Children As Prey

▼ What is childhood like in the poor nations? The answer depends primarily on who your parents are. If you are the son or daughter of rich parents, childhood can be extremely pleasant—a world of luxury. If you are born into poverty, but living in a rural area where there is plenty to eat, life can still be good—although there likely will be no books, television, and little education. If you live in a slum, however, life can be horrible—worse even than in the slums of the Most Industrialized Nations. Let's take a glance at what is happening to children in the slums of Brazil.

Not having enough food, this you can take for granted—as well as broken homes, alcoholism, drug abuse, and a high crime rate. From your knowledge of ghettos in the Most Industrialized Nations, you would expect these things. What you may not expect, however, are the brutal conditions in which Brazilian slum (*favela*) children live.

Sociologist Martha Huggins (1993) reports that poverty is so deep that children and adults swarm over garbage dumps to try to find enough decaying food to keep them alive. And you might be surprised to discover that in Brazil the owners of these dumps hire armed guards to keep the poor out—so they can sell the garbage for pig food. And you might be shocked to learn that poor children are systematically killed. Each year, the Brazilian police and death squads murder about 2,000 children. Some associations of shop owners even put hit men on retainer and auction victims off to the lowest bidder! The going rate is half a month's salary—figured at the low Brazilian minimum wage.

Life is cheap in the poor nations—but death squads for children? To understand this, we must first note that Brazil has a long history of violence. Brazil has an extremely high rate of poverty, only a tiny middle class, and is controlled by a small group of families who, under a veneer of democracy, make the country's major decisions. Hordes of homeless children, with no schools or jobs, roam the streets. To survive, they wash windshields, shine shoes, beg, and steal. These children, part of the "dangerous classes," as they are known, threaten the status quo.

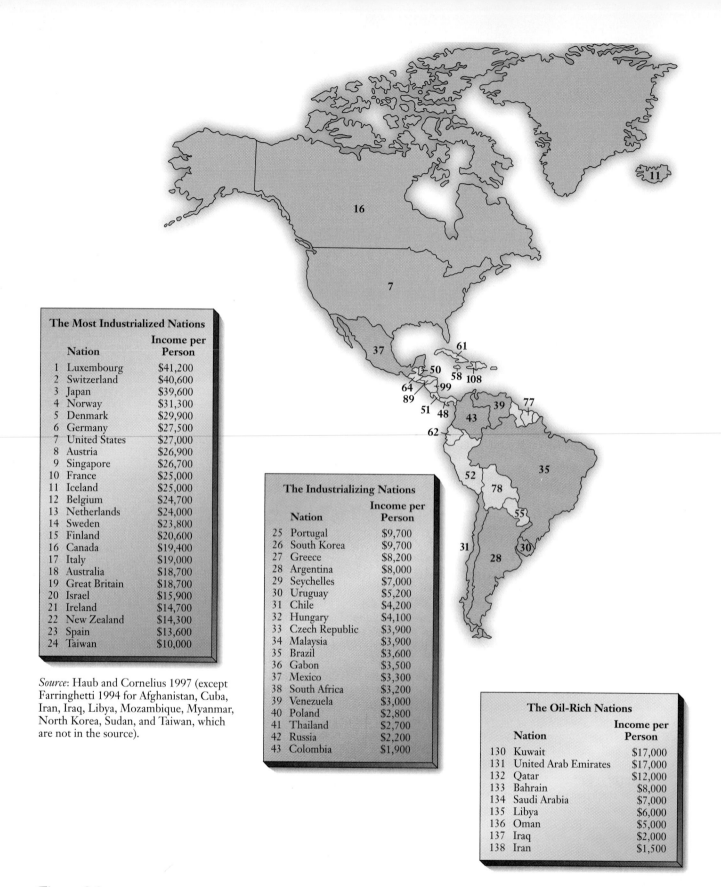

The Most Industrialized Nations

	Nation	Income per Person
1	Luxembourg	$41,200
2	Switzerland	$40,600
3	Japan	$39,600
4	Norway	$31,300
5	Denmark	$29,900
6	Germany	$27,500
7	United States	$27,000
8	Austria	$26,900
9	Singapore	$26,700
10	France	$25,000
11	Iceland	$25,000
12	Belgium	$24,700
13	Netherlands	$24,000
14	Sweden	$23,800
15	Finland	$20,600
16	Canada	$19,400
17	Italy	$19,000
18	Australia	$18,700
19	Great Britain	$18,700
20	Israel	$15,900
21	Ireland	$14,700
22	New Zealand	$14,300
23	Spain	$13,600
24	Taiwan	$10,000

Source: Haub and Cornelius 1997 (except Farringhetti 1994 for Afghanistan, Cuba, Iran, Iraq, Libya, Mozambique, Myanmar, North Korea, Sudan, and Taiwan, which are not in the source).

The Industrializing Nations

	Nation	Income per Person
25	Portugal	$9,700
26	South Korea	$9,700
27	Greece	$8,200
28	Argentina	$8,000
29	Seychelles	$7,000
30	Uruguay	$5,200
31	Chile	$4,200
32	Hungary	$4,100
33	Czech Republic	$3,900
34	Malaysia	$3,900
35	Brazil	$3,600
36	Gabon	$3,500
37	Mexico	$3,300
38	South Africa	$3,200
39	Venezuela	$3,000
40	Poland	$2,800
41	Thailand	$2,700
42	Russia	$2,200
43	Colombia	$1,900

The Oil-Rich Nations

	Nation	Income per Person
130	Kuwait	$17,000
131	United Arab Emirates	$17,000
132	Qatar	$12,000
133	Bahrain	$8,000
134	Saudi Arabia	$7,000
135	Libya	$6,000
136	Oman	$5,000
137	Iraq	$2,000
138	Iran	$1,500

Figure 9.2

Global Stratification: Income* in the Three Worlds of Development

*Income is 1995 per capita gross national product measured in U.S. dollars. Since some of these totals vary considerably from year to year, they must be taken as approximate.

The Least Industrialized Nations

Nation	Income per Person	Nation	Income per Person	Nation	Income per Person	Nation	Income per Person
44 Mauritius	$3,400	66 Swaziland	$1,200	88 China	$620	109 Laos	$250
45 Botswana	$3,000	67 Morocco	$1,100	89 Honduras	$600	110 Mali	$250
46 Slovakia	$3,000	68 Philippines	$1,100	90 Senegal	$600	111 Bangladesh	$240
47 Turkey	$2,800	69 Syria	$1,100	91 Zimbabwe	$540	112 Uganda	$240
48 Panama	$2,800	70 Indonesia	$1,000	92 Comoros	$470	113 Vietnam	$240
49 Lebanon	$2,700	71 North Korea	$1,000	93 Pakistan	$460	114 Madagascar	$230
50 Belize	$2,600	72 Maldives	$990	94 Georgia	$440	115 Mauritania	$220
51 Costa Rica	$2,600	73 Uzbekistan	$970	95 Bhutan	$420	116 Niger	$220
52 Peru	$2,300	74 Cape Verde	$960	96 Angola	$410	117 Afghanistan	$200
53 Namibia	$2,000	75 Turkmenistan	$920	97 Ghana	$390	118 Nepal	$200
54 Tunisia	$1,800	76 Macedonia	$900	98 Benin	$370	119 Chad	$180
55 Paraguay	$1,700	77 Suriname	$880	99 Nicaragua	$360	120 Rwanda	$180
56 Algeria	$1,600	78 Bolivia	$800	100 Central African		121 Sierra Leone	$180
57 Ukraine	$1,600	79 Egypt	$790	Republic	$340	122 Sudan	$180
58 Jamaica	$1,500	80 Lesotho	$770	101 India	$340	123 Malawi	$170
59 Jordan	$1,500	81 Kyrgyzstan	$700	102 Tajikistan	$340	124 Somalia	$170
60 Romania	$1,500	82 Sri Lanka	$700	103 Mongolia	$310	125 Burundi	$160
61 Cuba	$1,400	83 Congo	$680	104 Kenya	$280	126 Tanzania	$120
62 Ecuador	$1,400	84 Albania	$670	105 Cambodia	$270	127 Zaire	$120
63 Bulgaria	$1,300	85 Cote d'Ivoire	$660	106 Nigeria	$260	128 Ethiopia	$100
64 Guatemala	$1,300	86 Myanmar	$660	107 Yemen	$260	129 Mozambique	$80
65 Kazakstan	$1,300	87 Cameroon	$650	108 Haiti	$250		

One of the children killed by death squads operating in Brazil.

The "respectable" classes see these children as nothing but trouble. They hurt business, for customers feel uncomfortable or intimidated when they see a group of begging children clustered in front of stores. Some shoplift; others dare to sell items in competition with the stores. With no social institutions to care for these children, one solution is to kill them. As Huggins notes, murder sends a clear message—especially if it is accompanied by ritual torture—pulling out the eyes, ripping open the chest, cutting off the genitals, raping the girls, and burning the victim's body.

Not all life is bad in the poor nations, but this is about as bad as it gets.

For Your Consideration

Do you think there is anything the Most Industrialized Nations can do about this situation? Or is it any of their business? Is it, though unfortunate, just an "internal" affair that is up to the Brazilians to handle as they wish? ▲

Modifying the Model

This classification of nations into Most Industrialized, Industrializing, and Least Industrialized is helpful in that it pinpoints gross differences among them. But it also presents problems. As mentioned, just how much industrialization does a nation need in order to be classified as Most Industrialized or Industrializing? Also, in Chapter 6 we noted that several nations have become "postindustrial." Does this new stage require a separate classification? Finally, the oil-rich nations of the Middle East are not industrialized, but by providing the oil and gasoline that fuel the machinery of the Most Industrialized Nations, they have become immensely wealthy. Consequently, to classify them simply as Least Industrialized, glosses over significant distinctions, such as their modern hospitals, extensive prenatal care, pure water systems, abundant food and shelter, high literacy and even computerized banking (see Figure 9.2).

Kuwait, on whose formal behalf the United States and other Most Industrialized Nations fought Iraq in the Gulf War, is an excellent example of the problem. Kuwait is so wealthy that almost none of its citizens is employed. The government simply pays each a generous annual salary just for being citizens. Migrant workers from the poor nations do most of the onerous chores that daily life requires, while highly skilled workers from the Most Industrialized Nations run the specialized systems that keep Kuwait's economy going—and, on occasion, fight its wars for them as well. Table 9.3 reflects this significant distinction.

TABLE 9.3

An Alternative Model of Global Stratification

Four Worlds of Development

1. Most Industrialized Nations
2. Industrializing Nations
3. Least Industrialized Nations
4. Oil-rich, non-industrialized nations

How the World's Nations Became Stratified ▲

How did the globe become stratified into such distinct worlds of development? The obvious answer is that the poorer nations have fewer resources than the richer nations. As with so many other "obvious" answers, however, this one, too, falls short, for many of the Industrializing and Least Industrialized Nations are rich in natural resources, while one Most Industrialized Nation, Japan, has few. Four competing theories explain how global stratification came about.

Imperialism and Colonization

The first theory focuses on how the European nations that industrialized earliest got the jump on the rest of the world. Beginning in Great Britain about 1750, industrialization spread throughout western Europe. This powerful new technology produced great wealth, resulting in surplus capital. According to economist John Hobson (1858–1940), these industrialized nations lacked enough consumers to make it profitable to invest all excess capital there. Consequently, business leaders persuaded their governments to embark on **imperialism,** to take over other countries so they could expand their markets and gain access to cheap raw materials.

Backed by the powerful armaments developed by their new technology, the industrialized nations found others easy prey (Harrison 1993). The result was **colonization;** that is, these more powerful nations made colonies out of weaker nations. After invading and subduing them, they left a controlling force to exploit their labor and natural resources. At one point, there was even a free-for-all among these European industrialized nations as they rushed to divide up an entire continent. As Europe sliced Africa into pieces, even tiny Belgium got into the act and acquired the Congo—*seventy-five* times larger than itself. While the powerful European nations would plant their national flags in a colony and send their representatives to directly run the government, the United States, after it industrialized, usually chose to plant corporate flags in a colony and let these corporations dominate the territory's government. Central and South America are prime examples of U.S. *economic imperialism.* No matter what the form, and whether benevolent or harsh, the purpose was the same—to exploit the nation's people and resources for the benefit of the "mother" country.

Western imperialism and colonization, then, shaped the Least Industrialized Nations (Martin 1994). In some instances, the Most Industrialized Nations were so powerful that to divide the spoils they drew lines across a map, creating new states without regard for tribal or cultural considerations (Kennedy 1993). Britain and France did just this in North Africa and parts of the Middle East, which is why the national boundaries of Libya, Saudi Arabia, Kuwait, and other nations are so straight.

World System Theory

Historian Immanuel Wallerstein (1974, 1979, 1984, 1990) proposed a **world system** theory. Since the 1500s, he said, economic and political connections have grown between nations. Today, these connections are so great that they tie most of the world's countries together. Wallerstein identified four groups of interconnected nations. The first group is the *core nations,* those which first embraced capitalism. These nations (Britain, France, Holland, and later Germany) grew rich and powerful. The second group, the nations around the Mediterranean, Wallerstein called the *semiperiphery.* Their economies stagnated because they grew dependent on trade with the core nations. The third group, the *periphery,* or fringe, consists of the eastern European countries. Because they were limited primarily to selling cash crops to the core nations, their economies developed even less. The fourth group, the *external area,* includes most of Africa and Asia. These nations were left out of the development of capitalism and had few economic connections with the core nations.

imperialism: a nation's attempt to create an empire; its pursuit of unlimited geographical expansion

colonization: the process by which one nation takes over another nation, usually for the purpose of exploiting its labor and natural resources

world system: economic and political connections that tie the world's countries together

The world's people always have been part of an interconnected system of water and air, and, ultimately, part of a food chain. Now they also are interconnected by a global system of telecommunications. These women in Bangalore, India, are computer programmers.

Capitalism's relentless expansion has given birth to a **capitalist world economy,** which is dominated by the Most Industrialized Nations. This economy is so all-encompassing that today even the nations in the external area are being drawn into its commercial web.

Globalization. This extensive movement of capital and ideas among the nations of the world ushered in by the expansion of capitalism is called **globalization** (Kanter 1996). Although globalization has been under way for several hundred years, today's new forms of communication and transportation have greatly speeded it up. The interconnections have grown so extensive that events in remote parts of the world now affect us all—sometimes immediately, as when a revolution interrupts the flow of raw materials, or, perish the thought, if in Russia's unstable political climate terrorists manage to seize an arsenal of earth-destroying nuclear missiles. At other times, the effects arrive like a slow ripple, as when a government's policies impede its ability to compete in world markets. All of today's societies, then, no matter where they are located, are part of a global social system.

Dependency Theory

The third theory is sometimes difficult to distinguish from world system theory. **Dependency theory** stresses how the Least Industrialized Nations grew dependent on the Most Industrialized Nations (Cardoso 1972; Furtado 1984). According to this theory, the first nations to industrialize turned other nations into their plantations and mines, harvesting or extracting whatever they needed to meet their growing appetite for raw materials and exotic foods. As a result, many of the Least Industrialized Nations began to specialize in a single cash crop. Brazil became the Most Industrialized Nations' coffee plantation. Nicaragua and other Central American countries specialized in bananas (hence the term "banana republic"). Chile became the primary source of tin, while Zaire (then the Belgian Congo) was transformed into a rubber plantation. And the Mideast nations were turned into gigantic oil wells. A major point of dependency theory is that this domination of the Least Industrialized Nations rendered them unable to develop independent economies.

Culture of Poverty

An entirely different explanation of global stratification was proposed by economist John Kenneth Galbraith (1979), who claimed that it was the Least Industrialized Nations' own cultures that held them back. Building on the ideas of anthropologist Oscar Lewis (1966a, 1966b), Galbraith argued that some nations are crippled by a **culture of poverty,** a way of life that perpetuates poverty from one generation to the next. He explained it in this way: Most of the world's poor live in rural areas, where they barely eke out a living from the land. Their marginal life offers little room for error or risk, so they tend to stick closely to tried-and-true, traditional ways. Experimenting with new farming or manufacturing techniques is threatening, for if these fail they could lead to hunger or death. Their religion also reinforces traditionalism, for it teaches fatalism, the acceptance of their lot in life as God's will.

Evaluating the Theories

Most sociologists find imperialism, world system theory, and dependency theory preferable to an explanation based on a culture of poverty, for this theory places blame on the victim, the poor nations themselves. It points to characteristics of the poor nations, rather than to international arrangements that benefit the Most Industrialized Nations at the expense of the poor nations. But even taken together, these theories yield only part of the

capitalist world economy: the dominance of capitalism in the world along with the international interdependence that capitalism has created

globalization: the extensive movement of capital and ideas among nations due to the expansion of capitalism

dependency theory: the view that the Least Industrialized Nations have been unable to develop their economies because they grew dependent on the Most Industrialized Nations

culture of poverty: a culture that perpetuates poverty from one generation to the next

picture, as becomes evident from the example of Japan. None of these theories would lead anyone to expect that after World War II, Japan—with a religion that stressed fatalism, with two major cities destroyed by atomic bombs, and stripped of its colonies—would become an economic powerhouse able to turn the Western world on its head.

Each theory, then, yields but a partial explanation, and the grand theorist who will put the many pieces of this puzzle together has yet to appear.

Maintaining Global Stratification ▶

Regardless of how the world's nations became stratified, why do the same countries remain rich year after year, while the rest stay poor? Let's look at two explanations of how global stratification is maintained.

Neocolonialism

Sociologist Michael Harrington (1977) argued that colonialism fell out of style and was replaced by **neocolonialism.** When World War II changed public sentiment about sending soldiers and colonists to weaker countries, the Most Industrialized Nations turned to the international markets as a way to control the Least Industrialized Nations. These powerful nations determine how much they will pay for tin from Bolivia, copper from Peru, coffee from Brazil, and so forth. They also move hazardous industries into the Least Industrialized Nations.

As many of us learn, falling behind on a debt often means that we find ourselves dangling at the end of a string pulled by our creditor. So it is with neocolonialism. The *policy of selling weapons and other manufactured goods to the Least Industrialized Nations on credit* turns those countries into eternal debtors. The capital they need to develop their own industries goes instead to the debt, ever bloated with mounting interest. As debtors, these nations also are vulnerable to trading terms dictated by the neocolonialists (Tordoff 1992; Carrington 1993).

Thus, although the Least Industrialized Nations have their own governments—whether elected or dictatorships—they remain almost as dependent on the Most Industrialized Nations as they were when those nations occupied them. For an example of neocolonialism today, see the Perspectives box on the next page.

Multinational Corporations

Multinational corporations, companies that operate across many national boundaries, also help to maintain the global dominance of the Most Industrialized Nations. In some cases, multinational corporations exploit the Least Industrialized Nations directly. A prime example is the United Fruit Company, which for decades controlled national and local politics in Central America, running these nations as fiefdoms for the company's own profit while the U.S. Marines waited in the wings in case the company's interests needed to be backed up. Most commonly, however, multinational corporations help to maintain international stratification simply by doing business. A single multinational may do mining in several countries, manufacturing in many others, and run transportation and marketing networks around the globe. No matter where the profits are made, or where they are reinvested, the primary beneficiaries are the Most Industrialized Nations, especially the one in which the multinational corporation has its world headquarters. As Michael Harrington (1977) stressed, the real profits are made in processing the products and in controlling their distribution—and these profits are withheld from the Least Industrialized Nations. For more on multinational corporations, see pages 385–387.

Multinational corporations try to work closely with the elite of the Least Industrialized Nations (Lipton 1979; Waldman 1995a). This elite, which lives a sophisticated upper-class life in the major cities of its home country, sends its children to Oxford, the

During a period of exploitation called colonialism, European powers acquired as many parts of the globe as they could. Great Britain amassed the most, including Hong Kong, which China ceded in 1842. Shown here is the historic transfer of power that occurred when Hong Kong was returned to Chinese sovereignty on July 1, 1997.

neocolonialism: the economic and political dominance of the Least Industrialized Nations by the Most Industrialized Nations

multinational corporations: companies that operate across many national boundaries; also called transnational corporations

Perspectives

CULTURAL DIVERSITY AROUND THE WORLD

Sex Tourism and the Patriotic Prostitute

Holidays with the most beautiful women of the world. An exclusive tour by Life Travel. . . . You fly to Bangkok and then go to Pattaya. . . .Slim, sunburnt and sweet, they . . . are masters in the art of making love by nature, an art we European people do not know. . . . In Pattaya costs of living and loving are low. (from a Swiss pamphlet)

Some travel agencies promote sex tourism—travel for the purpose of exotic sex or for types of sex forbidden in the home country. Sex with children in Thailand and Tokyo is especially popular (Dickey 1996; Reitman 1996).

A related new wrinkle in the history of prostitution is the "patriotic prostitute." These are young women who are encouraged by their governments to prostitute themselves to help the country's economy. Patriotic prostitution is one of the seediest aspects of global stratification. Some poor nations encourage prostitution to accumulate national income for industrial development and to help pay their national debts. A consequence is that perhaps 10 percent of all Thai women between the ages of 15 and 30 have become prostitutes. Bangkok alone reports 100,000 prostitutes—plus 200,000 "massèuses."

Government officials encourage prostitution as a service to their country. In South Korea, prostitutes are issued identification cards that serve as hotel passes. In orientation ses-

sions, they are told, "Your carnal conversations [sic] with foreign tourists do not prostitute either yourself or the nation, but express your heroic patriotism." With such an official blessing, sex tourism has become big business. Travel agencies in Germany openly advertise "trips to Thailand with erotic pleasures included in the price." Japan Air Lines hands out brochures that advertise the "charming attractions" of Kisaeng girls, advising men to fly JAL for a "night spent with a consummate Kisaeng girl dressed in a gorgeous Korean blouse and skirt."

What the enticing advertising fails to mention is the misery underlying this prostitution. Many of the prostitutes are held in bondage. Some are only children. Some are forced into prostitution to pay family debts. Some are kept under lock and key to keep them from escaping. The advertisements also fail to mention AIDS. Somewhere between 25 percent and 50 percent of Nairobi's 10,000 prostitutes appear to be infected.

Women's groups protest this international sex trade, deploring its exploitation of the world's most impoverished and underprivileged women.

Sources: Based on Gay 1985; Cohen 1986; Shaw 1987; O'Malley 1988; Srisang 1989; Hornblower 1993.

Sorbonne, or Harvard to be educated. The multinational corporations funnel investments to this small circle of power, whose members favor projects such as building laboratories and computer centers in the capital city, projects that do not help the vast majority of their people living in poor, remote villages where they eke out a meager living on small plots of land.

The end result is an informal partnership between multinational corporations and the elite of the Least Industrialized Nations. The elite benefits by receiving subsidies (or payoffs). The corporations gain access to the country's raw materials, labor, and market. Both benefit through political stability, necessary to keep the partnership alive.

This, however, is not the full story. Multinational corporations also play a role in changing international stratification. This is an unintentional by-product of their worldwide search for cheap resources and labor. By moving manufacturing from the Most Industrialized Nations with high labor costs to the Least Industrialized Nations with low labor costs, they not only exploit cheap labor but in some cases also bring prosperity to those nations. Although workers in the Least Industrialized Nations are paid a pittance, it is more than they can earn elsewhere. With new factories come opportunities to develop new skills and a capital base. This does not occur in all nations, but the Pacific Rim nations, nicknamed the "Asian tigers," are a remarkable case in point. They have developed such a strong capital base that they have begun to rival the older capitalist nations.

Technology and the Maintenance of Global Domination

The race between the Most and Least Industrialized Nations to develop and apply the new information technologies is like a marathon runner competing with a one-legged man. Can the outcome be in doubt? The vast profits piled up by the multinational corporations allow the Most Industrialized Nations to invest huge sums in the latest technology. Gillette, for example, is spending $100 million simply so it can adjust its output "on an hourly basis" (Zachary 1995). These millions come from just one U.S. company. Many Least Industrialized Nations would love to have $100 million to invest in their entire economy, much less to fine-tune the production of razor blades. In short, in their quest to maintain global domination, the new technologies pile up even more advantages for the Most Industrialized Nations.

A Concluding Note

Let's go back to the three families in the chapter's opening vignette. Remember that these families represent three worlds of development, that is, global stratification. Their life chances—from access to material possessions to the opportunity for education and even the likely age at which their members will die—are profoundly affected by the global stratification reviewed in this chapter. This division of the globe into interconnected units of nations with more or less wealth and more or less power and prestige, then, is much more than a matter of theoretical interest. In fact, it is *your* life we are talking about.

Summary and Review

What Is Social Stratification?

The term **social stratification** refers to a hierarchy of relative privilege based on power, property, and prestige. Every society stratifies its members. P. 222.

Systems of Social Stratification

What are the four major systems of social stratification?

The four major stratification systems are slavery, caste, clan, and class. The essential characteristic of **slavery** is that some people own other people. Initially, slavery was based not on race but on debt, punishment, or defeat in battle. Slavery could be temporary or permanent, and was not necessarily passed on to one's children. In North America slaves had no legal rights, and the system was gradually buttressed by a racist ideology. In a **caste system,** status is determined by birth and is lifelong. People marry within their own group and develop rules about ritual pollution. In a **clan system,** people's status depends on lineage that links

them to an extended network of relatives. A **class system** is much more open than these other systems, for it is based primarily on money or material possessions. Industrialization encourages the formation of class systems. Gender discrimination cuts across all forms of **social stratification.** Pp. 222–228.

What Determines Social Class?

Karl Marx argued that a single factor determines social class: If you own the **means of production,** you belong to the **bourgeoisie;** if you do not, you are one of the **proletariat.** Max Weber argued that three elements determine social class: *property, prestige,* and *power.* Pp. 228–230.

Why Is Social Stratification Universal?

To explain why stratification is universal, functionalists Kingsley Davis and Wilbert Moore argued that to attract the most capable people to fill its important positions, society must offer them higher rewards. Melvin Tumin criticized this view, arguing that if it were correct, society would be a **meritocracy,** with all positions awarded on the basis of merit. Gaetano Mosca argued that stratification is inevitable because every society must have leadership, which by definition means inequality. Conflict theorists argue that stratification comes about because resources are limited, and groups struggle against one another for them. Gerhard Lenski suggested a synthesis between the functionalist and conflict perspectives. Pp. 230–233.

How Do Elites Maintain Stratification?

How do nations maintain social stratification?

To maintain social stratification within a nation, the ruling class uses an ideology that justifies current arrangements. It also controls information, and, when all else fails, depends on brute force. The social networks of the rich and poor also perpetuate social inequality. Pp. 233–235.

Comparative Social Stratification

What are some key characteristics of stratification systems in other nations?

The most striking features of the British class system are differences in speech and in educational patterns. In Britain, accents nearly always betray class standing, and virtually all of the elite attend "public" schools (the equivalent of our private schools). In what is now the former Soviet Union, communism was supposed to abolish class distinctions. Instead, it merely ushered in a different set of classes. Pp. 235–237.

Global Stratification: Three Worlds of Development

How are the world's nations stratified?

The model presented here divides the world's nations into three groups: the Most Industrialized, the Industrializing, and the Least Industrialized. This layering represents relative property, power, and prestige. The oil-rich nations are an exception. Pp. 237–242.

How the World's Nations Became Stratified

Why are some nations rich and others poor?

The main theories that seek to account for global stratification are **imperialism** and **colonization, world system theory, dependency theory,** and the **culture of poverty.** Pp. 242–245.

Maintaining Global Stratification

How is global stratification maintained?

There are two basic explanations for why nations remain stratified. **Neocolonialism** is the ongoing dominance of the Least Industrialized Nations by the Most Industrialized Nations. The second explanation points to the influence of **multinational corporations,** which operate across national boundaries. The new technology gives further advantage to the Most Industrialized Nations. Pp. 245–247.

Where can I read more on this topic?

Suggested readings for this chapter are listed on page 662.

Sociology and the Internet

All URLs listed are current as of the printing of this book. URLs are often changed. Please check our Website http://www.abacon.com/henslin for updates.

1. How can you use the Internet to measure social stratification in the United States? Go to the 1990 Census Lookup page *http://www.census.gov/cdrom/lookup/* Select the database "STF3C–Part 1." At the Choose an Option page, click on the "Submit" bar. At the Data Retrieval Option page, click on the "Submit" bar. At the page headed "Select the tables you wish to retrieve," page down to P119–"Poverty Status in 1989 by race by age," and click on the *square* in front of the entry. (Use a more recent year if it is available.) Then go to the top of the page and click on the "Submit" bar. At the next Data Retreival Option page, click on *Submit.* You should be presented with a table showing poverty status of five "racial" categories. Depending on your Web browser, you can either save the table or print it. (Netscape will allow both.) Next, you need to compute the percentages for those in poverty for each racial category. (Your instructor may ask you to do this for age

groups as well.) Total those in "Income in 1989 above poverty level: White." Do the same for those in "Income in 1989 below poverty level: White." Add the two figures and divide the sum found in "Income in 1989 below poverty level: White" by the result. This is the percent of white people whose income was below the poverty level in 1989. Now repeat the process for the other four "racial" categories.

After you have the percentages, construct a table of the results. (Refer back to Chapter 5 (page 124) Table 5.1, "How to Read a Table.") Analyze the results of the table in a one-page summary.

2. To measure social stratification in Latin America, go to Lanic *http://lanic.utexas.edu* Under the Subject Directory, select "Economy." Page down to "Macroeconomic Information by Country," then page down to "Regional Macroeconomic Data Resources" and select "USAID: Latin America and the Caribbean Economic and Social Data, 1996 Data Base." Next, select "Social Indicators," and then select "Selected Social Indicators." Print this table. Next, back up to the previous page and select "Population in Latin America and the Caribbean." Print this table as well.

Using the column "Human Development Index" (a composite of national income, literacy, and life expectancy) from the "Selected Social Indicators" table, compare nations of various sizes (from the "Midyear Population" table). Is Latin America a single unit of Industrializing or Least Industrialized Nations? Does size make a difference? Focus on two countries with very different Human Development Index scores, and research differences between them that might help explain their levels of development. (You can search the Web for information on the two nations, or do so at the library.) Prepare a report on your conclusions.

3. Many believe that the United States is a meritocracy. Examine the online conference with Nicholas Lemann about merit in our society *http://www2.theatlantic.com/atlantic/unbound/aandc/trnscrpt/lemtest.htm* Do you think we have a meritocracy? What are some of the problems associated with measuring merit and aptitude using standardized tests? How can we accurately measure merit and aptitude? What are some of the other issues involved in the discussion about meritocracy?

4. Your text mentions slavery in the Sudan, Mauritania, and Benin. Examine the site created by The Coalition Against Slavery In Mauritania And Sudan, Inc. *http://www.columbia.edu/~slc11/* Why is there a debate? What are the issues? According to the articles available at this site, who is being enslaved? Why? How is the slavery in the Sudan and Mauritania different from the historical slavery in the U.S.? How is it similar? What does CASMAS propose we do to stop the slavery?

Tsing-Fang Chen, City Gleaners

C H A P T E R

10

Social Class in Contemporary Society

*A*H, NEW ORLEANS, THAT FABLED CITY *on the Gulf. Images from its rich past floated through my head—pirates, wealth, intrigue. So did memories from a pleasant vacation—the exotic French Quarter with odors of Creole food and sounds of earthy jazz drifting through the air.*

The shelter for the homeless, however, forced me back to an unwelcome reality. The shelter was the same as those I had visited in the North—as well as the West and the East—only dirtier. The dirt, in fact, was the worst that I encountered during my research, and this was the only shelter to insist on payment to sleep in one of its filthy beds.

The men looked the same—disheveled and haggard, wearing that unmistakable expression of despair—just like the homeless anywhere in the country. Except for the accent, you wouldn't know where you were. Poverty wears the same tired face, I realized. The accent may differ, but the look remains the same.

The next morning, I felt indignation swell within me. I had grown used to the sights and smells of abject poverty, whether in the shelters or on the streets. Those no longer held surprises. But now, just a block from the shelter, I was startled by a sight so out of joint with the despair and misery I had just experienced that I stopped in midtrack.

Staring back at me were finely dressed men and women, proudly strutting about as they modeled elegant suits, dresses, jewelry, and furs.

I was looking only at posters mounted on a transparent plastic shelter that covered a bus stop, but I felt a wave of disgust sweep over me. "Something is cockeyed in this society," I thought, my mind refusing to stop juxtaposing the suffering I had just witnessed in the shelter with the images displayed here.

I felt nauseated—and surprised at my urge to deface the sketches and photos of these people strutting their finery.

What Is Social Class?

Occasionally the facts of social class hit home with brute force. This was one of those moments. The disjunction that I felt in New Orleans was triggered by the ads, but it was not the first time that I had experienced this sensation. Whenever my research abruptly transported me from the world of the homeless to one of another social class, I felt unfamiliar feelings of disjointed unreality. Each social class has its own way of being, and because these fundamental orientations to the world contrast so sharply, the classes do not mix well.

Defining Social Class

"There are the poor and the rich—and then there are you and I, neither poor nor rich." That is just about as far as most Americans' consciousness of social class goes. Let's try to flesh this out.

Our task is made somewhat difficult because sociologists have no clear-cut, agreed–on definition of social class. As noted in Chapter 9, most conflict sociologists (of the Marxist orientation) see only two social classes: those who own the means of production and those who do not. The problem with this view, say most sociologists, is that it lumps too many people together. Physicians and corporate executives with incomes of $250,000 a year are lumped together with hamburger flippers working at McDonald's for $10,000 a year.

Most sociologists agree with Weber that there are more components of social class than a person's relationship to the means of production. Consequently, most sociologists use the components Weber identified and define **social class** as a large group of people who rank closely to one another in wealth, power, and prestige. These three elements

social class: according to Weber, a large group of people who rank closely to one another in wealth, power, and prestige; according to Marx, one of two groups: capitalists who own the means of production or workers who sell their labor

separate people into different lifestyles, give them different chances in life, and provide them with distinct ways of looking at the self and the world.

Measuring Social Class

We will examine wealth, power, and prestige in the next section, but first let's look at three different ways of measuring social class.

Subjective Method. The **subjective method** is to ask people what their social class is. Although simple and direct, this approach is filled with problems. First, people may deny that they belong to any class, claiming, instead, that everyone is equal. Second, people may classify themselves according to their aspirations—where they would like to be—rather than where they actually are. Third, when asked to what class they belong, most Americans identify themselves as middle class, as do most citizens of industrialized nations (Kelley and Evans 1995). This perception removes the usefulness of the subjective method for most purposes.

Reputational Method. In the **reputational method,** people are asked what class others belong to, based on their reputations. Social anthropologist W. Lloyd Warner (1941, 1949) pioneered this method in a study of a community he called "Yankee City." Its use is limited to smaller communities, where people are familiar with one another's reputation.

Three of Warner's colleagues used this method to study "Old City," a small southern town (Davis et al. 1941). They found that just as people at each class level see life differently, so they carry around different pictures of society's classes. People see finer divisions at their own class level, but tend to lump people together as a social class recedes from them. Thus people at the top see several groups of people at the top, but tend to lump the bottom into a single unit ("the poor"), while people at the bottom see several distinctions among the poor but tend to see just "the rich" at the top.

Objective Method. In the **objective method,** researchers rank people according to objective criteria such as wealth, power, and prestige. This method has the advantage of letting others know exactly what measurements were made, so that they can test them.

Given the three choices of subjective, reputational, and objective methods to determine social class, sociologists use the objective method almost exclusively. The studies reported in this chapter are examples of the objective approach.

Most Americans identify themselves as middle class. How would you identify the individuals depicted by artist Duane Hanson in these life-size polyvinyl figures? What status markers do you see?

subjective method (of measuring social class): a system in which people are asked to state the social class to which they belong

reputational method (of measuring social class): a system in which people who are familiar with the reputations of others are asked to identify their social class

objective method (of measuring social class): a system in which people are ranked according to objective criteria such as their wealth, power, and prestige

wealth: property and income

The Components of Social Class

Let's look at how sociologists measure the three components of social class: wealth, power, and prestige.

Wealth

The primary dimension of social class is wealth. **Wealth** consists of property and income. *Property* comes in many forms, such as buildings, land, animals, machinery, cars, stocks, bonds, businesses, and bank accounts. *Income* is money received as wages, rents, interest, royalties, or the proceeds from a business.

In the United States, a mere 0.5 percent of the population owns over a quarter of the nation's wealth. Very few minorities are numbered among this 0.5 percent. An outstanding exception is Oprah Winfrey, whose ultra-successful career in entertainment, bringing her over $250 million a year, has made her one of the 400 richest Americans.

Distinction Between Wealth and Income.   Wealth and income are sometimes confused with each other, but they are not the same. Some people have much wealth and little income. For example, a farmer may own much land (a form of wealth), but with the high cost of fertilizers and machinery, a little bad weather can cause the income to disappear. Others have much income and little wealth. For example, an executive with $150,000 annual income may actually be debt ridden. Below the surface prosperity, he or she may be greatly overextended: unpaid bills for exotic vacations, country club membership, and the children's private schools, two sports cars just a payment away from being repossessed, and huge mortgage payments on the elite home in the exclusive suburb. Typically, however, wealth and income go together.

Distribution of Wealth.   Who owns the huge wealth of the United States? One answer, of course, is "everyone." Although this statement has some merit, it overlooks how the nation's wealth is divided among "everyone." Let's look at how the two forms of wealth—property and income—are distributed among Americans.

68% of the total net worth of all U.S. families...

Property.   Overall, Americans are worth a hefty sum, about $23 trillion (*Statistical Abstract* 1997: Table 750). Most of this wealth is in the form of real estate, corporate stocks, bonds, and business assets. As Figure 10.1 shows, this wealth is highly concentrated. The vast majority, 68 percent, is owned by only *10 percent* of the nation's families.

And the higher we go, the more concentrated that wealth becomes. As sociologist Leonard Beeghley (1996) observes, *the super-rich, the richest 1 percent of U.S. families, are worth more than the entire bottom 90 percent of Americans.*

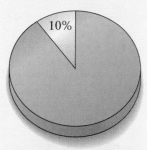

...is owned by just 10% of those families

Source: Beeghley 1996.

Figure 10.1

Distribution of Wealth of Americans

Income.   How is income distributed in the United States? Economist Paul Samuelson (1989:644) put it this way: "If we made an income pyramid out of a child's blocks, with each layer portraying $500 of income, the peak would be far higher than Mount Everest, but most people would be within a few feet of the ground."

Actually, if each block were 1½ inches tall, the typical American's attempt to climb Mount Everest takes him or her just *6 feet off the ground.* (The average per capita income in the United States is about $23,000 per year.) See Figure 10.2. The typical family climbs a little higher, for most families have more than one worker, and together they average about $41,000 a year. Yet compared with the Mount Everest incomes of a few, these earnings of the typical U.S. family bring it only 10 feet off the ground (*Statistical Abstract* 1997: Tables 728, 732).

The fact that some Americans enjoy the peaks of Mount Everest while most make it only 6 to 10 feet up the slope presents a striking image of income inequality in the United

States. Another picture emerges if we divide the U.S. population into five equal parts and rank them from the highest to lowest income. As Figure 10.3 (on the next page) shows, the top 20 percent of the population receives *almost half* (46.5 percent) of all income in the United States. In contrast, the bottom 20 percent of Americans receives only 4.4 percent of the nation's income.

Two features of Figure 10.3 are outstanding. First, notice how remarkably consistent income inequality remains through the years. Second, the changes that do occur indicate *growing inequality. The richest 20 percent of U.S. families have grown richer, while the poorest 20 percent have grown poorer.* In spite of numerous antipoverty programs, the poorest 20 percent of Americans receive *less* of the nation's income today than they did in the 1940s (a drop from 5.4 percent to 4.4 percent). The richest 20 percent, in contrast, receive *more* than ever (an increase from about 41 percent to about 47 percent).

The most affluent group in U.S. society is the chief executive officers (CEOs) of the nation's largest corporations. *Business Week* surveyed the 365 largest U.S. companies to find out what they paid their CEOs ("Executive Pay," 1997). Their median compensation, including salaries, bonuses, and stock options, came to $5,800,000 a year. (Median means that half received more than this amount, and half less.) The CEOs' income—which does *not* include their interest, dividends, rents, and capital gains—is *200 times* higher than the average pay of U.S. workers. Table 10.1 on the next page lists the 10 highest paid executives.

Imagine how you could live with an income like this. And that is precisely the point. Beyond these cold numbers lies a dynamic reality that profoundly affects people's lives. The difference in wealth between those at the top and the bottom of the U.S. class structure means vastly different lifestyles. For example, a colleague of mine who was teaching at an exclusive eastern university piqued his students' curiosity when he lectured on poverty in Latin America. That weekend, one of his students borrowed his parents' corporate jet and pilot, and in Monday's class he and his friends reported on their personal observations on the problem. Other Americans, in contrast, must choose whether to spend the little they have at the laundromat or on milk for the baby. In short, divisions of wealth represent not "mere" numbers, but choices that make real differences in people's lives.

Power

Like many people, you may have said to yourself, "Sure, I can vote, but somehow the big decisions are always made in spite of what I might think. Certainly *I* don't make the decision to send soldiers to Vietnam, Grenada, Panama, Kuwait, Somalia, Haiti, or Bosnia. *I* don't decide to raise taxes. It isn't *I* who decide to change welfare benefits."

Bill Gates, a founder of Microsoft Corporation, is the wealthiest person in the United States. His fortune of several billion dollars continues to increase as his company develops new products. He recently built a new home in Seattle, Washington, that cost about $25 million.

Higher than Mount Everest

(Some Americans) 29,028 feet

If a 1½-inch child's block equals $500 of income, the average American is only 6 feet off the ground, the average family just 10 feet, while the income of some families propels them past the top of Mount Everest.

6 feet

Average American

10 feet

Average U.S. Family

Figure 10.2

Inequality of U.S. Income

Figure 10.3

Growing Inequality: The percentage of the nation's income received by each fifth of U.S. families since World War II.

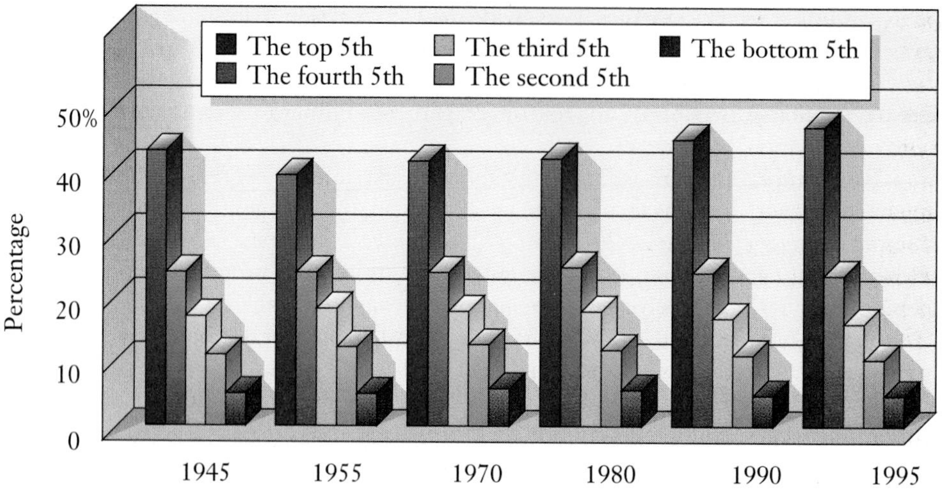

Note: The distribution of U.S. income—salaries, wages, and all other money received, except capital gains and government subsidies in the form of food stamps, health benefits, or subsidized housing. Because of rounding, totals for some years equal 101%.

Source: Statistical Abstract 1947; 1997:Table 725.

power: the ability to get your way in spite of the desires of other people

power elite: C. Wright Mills's term for the top people in U.S. corporations, military, and politics who make the nation's major decisions

prestige: respect or regard

TABLE 10.1

Highest-Paid CEOs

Executive	Company	Compensation
1. Lawrence Coss	Green Tree Financial	$102 million
2. Andrew Grove	Intel	$98 million
3. Sanford Weil	Travelers Group	$94 million
4. Theodore Waitt	Gateway 2000	$81 million
5. Anthony O'Reilly	H.J. Heinz	$64 million
6. Sterling Williams	Sterling Software	$58 million
7. John Reed	Citicorp	$44 million
8. Stephen Hilbert	Conseco	$37 million
9. Casey Cowell	U.S. Robotics	$34 million
10. James Moffett	Freeport-McMoran	$34 million

Source: "Executive Pay," 1997.

And then another part of you may say, "But *I* do it through my representatives in Congress." True enough—as far as it goes. The trouble is, it just doesn't go far enough. Such views of being a participant in the nation's "big" decisions are a playback of the ideology we learn at an early age—an ideology that Marx said is put forward by the elites to both legitimate and perpetuate their power. Sociologists Daniel Hellinger and Dennis Judd (1991) call this the "democratic façade" that conceals the real source of power in the United States.

Back in the 1950s, sociologist C. Wright Mills (1956) was criticized for insisting that **power**—the ability to carry out your will in spite of resistance—was concentrated in the hands of the few, for his analysis contradicted an almost sacred ideology of equality. As discussed in earlier chapters, Mills coined the term **power elite** to refer to those who make the big decisions in U.S. society.

Mills and others have stressed how wealth and power coalesce in a group of like-minded individuals who share ideologies and values. They belong to the same private clubs, vacation at the same exclusive resorts, and even hire the same bands for their daughters' debutante balls. These shared backgrounds and vested interests all serve to reinforce their view of the world and of their special place in it (Domhoff 1978, 1997). This elite wields extraordinary power in U.S. society. Although there are exceptions, *most* U.S. presidents have come from this group—millionaire white males from families with "old money" (Baltzell and Schneiderman 1988).

Continuing in the tradition of Mills, sociologist William Domhoff (1990,1996) argues that this group is so powerful that no major decision of the U.S. government is made without its approval. He analyzed how this group works behind the scenes with elected officials to set both the nation's foreign and domestic policy—from establishing Social Security taxes to determining trade tariffs. Although Domhoff's conclusions are controversial—and alarming—they certainly follow logically from the principle that wealth brings power, and extreme wealth brings extreme power.

Prestige

Occupations and Prestige. What would you like to do with the rest of your life? The chances are that you don't have the option of lying under palm trees at the beach. Almost all of us have to choose an occupation and go to work. Look at Table 10.2 to see how the one you are striving for stacks up in terms of **prestige** (respect or regard). Because we are moving toward a global society, this table also shows how the rankings given by Americans compare with those of the residents of sixty other countries.

Why do people give some jobs more prestige than others? If you look at Table 10.2, you will notice that the jobs at the top share four elements:

1. They pay more.
2. They require more education.
3. They entail more abstract thought.
4. They offer greater autonomy (freedom, or self-direction).

If we turn this around, we can see that people give less prestige to jobs that are low-paying, require less preparation or education, involve more physical labor, and are closely supervised. In short, the professions and white-collar jobs are ranked at the top of the list, blue-collar jobs at the bottom.

One of the more interesting aspects of these rankings is how consistent they are across countries and over time. For example, people in every country rank college professors higher than nurses, nurses higher than social workers, and social workers higher than janitors. Similarly, the occupations that were ranked high back in the 1970s are still ranked high in the 1990s—and likely will rank high in the new century.

Table 10.2 also reveals a disadvantage of the objective method of studying social stratification; namely, how do you rank a two-career family? Should you use only the husband's occupation, only the wife's, or average their scores (which would really represent neither occupation)? In addition, how do part-time workers fit in? Note also that although occupations are the primary source of prestige for most people, they are not the only source. Some gain fame (prestige) through inventions, feats (mountain climbing, Olympic gold medals), or even doing good for others (Mother Teresa).

Displaying Prestige. In times past, in some countries only the emperor and his family could wear purple. In France, only the nobility could wear lace. In England, no one could sit while the king was on his throne. Some kings and queens required that subjects walk backward as they left the room—so no one would "turn their back" on the "royal presence."

Concern with displaying prestige has not let up—for some, it is almost an obsession. Western kings and queens expect curtsies and bows, while their Eastern counterparts expect their subjects to touch their faces to the ground. The U.S. president enters a room only after others are present—to show that *he* isn't the one waiting for *them*. Military officers surround themselves with elaborate rules about who must salute whom, while bailiffs, sometimes armed, make certain that everyone stands when the judge enters.

The display of prestige permeates society. In Los Angeles, some people list their address as Beverly Hills and then add their correct ZIP code.

TABLE 10.2

Occupational Prestige: How the United States Compares with 60 Countries

Occupation	United States	Average of 60 Countries
Supreme court judge	85	82
College president	82	86
Physician	82	78
Astronaut	80	80
College professor	78	78
Lawyer	75	73
Dentist	74	70
Architect	71	72
Psychologist	71	66
Airline pilot	70	66
Electrical engineer	69	65
Civil engineer	68	70
Biologist	68	69
Clergy	67	60
Sociologist	65	67
Accountant	65	55
Banker	63	67
High school teacher	63	64
Author	63	62
Registered nurse	62	54
Pharmacist	61	64
Chiropractor	60	62
Veterinarian	60	61
Classical musician	59	56
Police officer	59	40
Actor or actress	55	52
Athletic coach	53	50
Journalist	52	55
Professional athlete	51	48
Undertaker	51	34
Social worker	50	56
Electrician	49	44
Secretary	46	53
Real estate agent	44	49
Farmer	44	47
Carpenter	43	37
Plumber	41	34
Mail carrier	40	33
Jazz musician	37	38
Bricklayer	36	34
Barber	36	30
Truck driver	31	33
Factory worker	29	29
Store sales clerk	27	34
Bartender	25	23
Lives on public aid	25	16
Bill collector	24	27
Cab driver	22	28
Gas station attendant	22	25
Janitor	22	21
Waiter or waitress	20	23
Bellhop	15	14
Garbage collector	13	13
Street sweeper	11	13
Shoe shiner	9	12

Sources: Treiman 1977, Appendices A and D; Nakao and Treas 1991.

Acceptable display of prestige and high social position varies over time and from one culture to another. Shown here is Elisabeth d'Autriche, queen of France from 1554 to 1592. It certainly would be difficult to outdress her at a party.

status consistency: ranking high or low on all three dimensions of social class

status inconsistency (or status discrepancy): ranking high on some dimensions of social class and low on others

status: social ranking

Sociologists use income, education, and occupational prestige to measure social class. The term status discrepancy *(or status inconsistency) refers to a mismatch of these components. What status inconsistency does Michael Jordan, shown here, experience?*

When the town of East Detroit changed its name to East Pointe to play off its proximity to swank Grosse Pointe, property values shot up (Fletcher 1997). Many willingly pay more for clothing that bears a "designer" label. For many, prestige is a primary factor in deciding which college to attend. Everyone knows how the prestige of a generic sheepskin from Regional State College compares with a degree from Harvard, Princeton, Yale, or Stanford.

Interestingly, status symbols vary with social class. Clearly, only the wealthy can afford certain items, such as yachts. But beyond affordability lies a class-based preference in status symbols. For example, yuppies (young upwardly mobile professionals) are quick to flaunt labels and other material symbols to show that they have "arrived," while the rich, more secure in their status, often downplay such images. The wealthy see designer labels of the more "common" classes as cheap and showy. They, of course, flaunt their own status symbols, such as the "right" addresses and $30,000 Rolex watches.

Status Inconsistency

Ordinarily a person has a similar rank on all three dimensions of social class—wealth, power, and prestige. The homeless men in the opening vignette are an example. Such people are **status consistent.** Sometimes the match is not there, however, and someone has a mixture of high and low ranks, a condition called **status inconsistency.** This leads to some interesting situations.

Sociologist Gerhard Lenski (1954, 1966) pointed out that each of us tries to maximize our **status,** our social ranking. Thus individuals who rank high on one dimension of social class but lower on others expect people to judge them on the basis of their highest status. Others, however, trying to maximize their own position, may respond to them according to their lowest status.

A classic study of status inconsistency was done by sociologist Ray Gold (1952). He found that after apartment-house janitors unionized, they made more money than some of the people whose garbage they carried out. Tenants became upset when they saw their janitors driving more expensive cars than they did. Some attempted to "put the janitor in his place" by making "snotty" remarks to him. Instead of addressing him by name, others would say, "Janitor." For their part, the janitors took secret pride in knowing "dirty" secrets about the tenants, gleaned from their garbage.

Individuals with status inconsistency, then, are likely to confront one frustrating situation after another. They claim the higher status, but are handed the lower. The sociological significance of this condition, said Lenski, is that such people tend to be more politically radical. An example is college professors. Their prestige is very high, as we saw in Table 10.1, but their incomes are relatively low. Hardly anyone in U.S. society is more educated, and yet college professors don't even come close to the top of the income pyramid. In line with Lenski's prediction, the politics of most college professors are left of center. This hypothesis may also hold true *among* academic departments; that is, the higher a department's pay, the less radical are its politics. Teachers in departments of business and medicine, for example, are among the most highly paid in the university—and they also are the most politically conservative. This hypothesis is also likely to hold true *within* departments, for in general, regardless of the department, higher-paid members tend to be more conservative, lower-paid members more liberal. Although age is a highly significant variable (age generally brings more conservative views of life, as well as a higher salary), status inconsistency may be part of the explanation. Only testing, of course, can determine the validity of these observations.

Sociological Models of Social Class ▶

The question of how many social classes there are is a matter of debate. Sociologists have proposed various models, but no model has gained universal support. There are two main models: one that builds on Marx, the other on Weber.

Updating Marx

Marx argued that there are just two classes—capitalists and workers—with membership based solely on a person's relationship to the means of production. Sociologists have criticized this view because these categories are too broad. For example, executives, managers, and supervisors, are technically workers because they do not own the means of production. But what do they have in common with assembly-line workers? Similarly, the category of "capitalist" takes in too many types. For example, the decisions of someone who employs a thousand workers directly affect a thousand families. Compare this with a man I know in Godfrey, Illinois. Working on cars out of his own back yard, he gained a following, quit his regular job, and in a few years put up a building with five bays and an office. This mechanic is now a capitalist, for he employs five or six other mechanics and owns the tools and building (the "means of production"). But what does he have in common with a factory owner who controls the lives of one thousand workers? Not only is his work different, but so are his lifestyle and the way he looks at the world.

Sociologist Erik Wright (1985) resolved this problem by regarding some people as members of more than one class at the same time. They have what he called **contradictory class locations.** By this Wright means that people's position in the class structure can generate contradictory interests. For example, the automobile mechanic-turned-business owner may want his mechanics to have higher wages, since he, too, has experienced their working conditions. At the same time, his current interests—making profits and remaining competitive with other repair shops—lead him to resist pressures to raise wages.

Because of such contradictory class locations, Wright modified Marx's model. As summarized in Table 10.3, Wright identified four classes: (1) *capitalists*, business owners

contradictory class location: Erik Wright's term for a position in the class structure that generates contradictory interests

TABLE 10.3
Social Class and the Means of Production
Marx's Class Model (based on the means of production)
1. Capitalists (bourgeoisie)
2. Workers (proletariat)
Wright's Modification of Marx's Class Model (to account for contradictory class locations)
1. Capitalists
2. Petty bourgeoisie
3. Managers
4. Workers

who employ many workers; (2) *petty bourgeoisie*, small business owners, (3) *managers*, who sell their own labor but also exercise authority over other employees; and (4) *workers*, who simply sell their labor to others. As you can see, this model allows finer divisions than the one Marx proposed, yet it maintains the primary distinction between employer and worker.

Updating Weber

Sociologists Dennis Gilbert and Joseph Kahl (1993) developed a six-class model to portray the class structure of the United States and other capitalist countries. Think of their model, illustrated in Figure 10.4 below, as a ladder. Our discussion will start with the highest rung and move downward. In line with Weber, on each lower rung you find less wealth, less power, and less prestige. Note that in this model education is also a primary criterion of class.

The Capitalist Class. The super-rich who occupy the top rung of the class ladder consists of only about 1 percent of the population. As mentioned, this 1 percent is so wealthy that its members are worth more than the entire bottom 90 percent of the nation. Their power is so great that their decisions open or close jobs for millions of people. Through their ownership of newspapers, magazines, and radio and television stations, together with their access to politicians, this elite class even helps to shape the consciousness of the nation. Its members perpetuate themselves by passing on to their children their assets and influential social networks.

Figure 10.4

The U.S. Social Class Ladder

Social Class	Education	Occupation	Income	Percentage of Population
Capitalist	Prestigious university	Investors and heirs, a few top executives	$500,000+	1%
Upper Middle	College or university, often with postgraduate study	Professionals and upper managers	$90,000+	14%
Lower Middle	At least high school; perhaps some college or apprenticeship	Semiprofessionals and lower managers, craftspeople, foremen	About $40,000	30%
Working Class	High school	Factory workers, clerical workers, low-paid retail sales, and craftspeople	About $30,000	30%
Working Poor	Some high school	Laborers, service workers, low-paid salespeople	About $18,000	22%
Underclass	Some high school	Unemployed and part-time, on welfare	About $10,000	3%

Source: Based on Gilbert and Kahl 1993; income estimates follow Duff 1995.

One of the characteristics of the culture of wealth is the transfer of social privilege (power, prestige, and property) from one generation to the next. Shown here is John F. Kennedy, Jr. Because of the privileges passed on to him, he was able to co-found George, *a prestigious magazine.*

Old Money.   The capitalist class can be divided into "old" and "new" money (Aldrich 1988). In general, the longer that wealth has been in a family, the more it adds to the family's prestige. Many people entering the capitalist class have found it necessary to cut moral corners, at least here and there. This "taint" to the money disappears with time, however, and the later generations of Kennedys, Rockefellers, Vanderbilts, Mellons, Du Ponts, Chryslers, Fords, Morgans, Nashes, and so on are considered to have "clean" money simply by virtue of the passage of time. Able to be philanthropic as well as rich, they establish foundations and support charitable causes. Subsequent generations attend prestigious prep schools and universities, and male heirs are likely to enter law. These old-money capitalists wield vast power as they use extensive political connections to protect their huge economic empires (Persell et al. 1992; Domhoff 1990, 1997).

New Money.   Those at the lower end of the capitalist class also possess vast sums of money and power, but it is new, and therefore suspect. Although these people may have made fortunes in business, the stock market, inventions, entertainment, or sports, they have not attended the right schools, and they lack the influential social networks that come with old money. Donald Trump, for example, is not listed in the *Social Register,* the "White Pages" of blue bloods that lists the most prestigious and wealthy one-tenth of 1 percent of the U.S. population. Trump says he "doesn't care," but he reveals his true feelings by adding that his heirs will be in it (Kaufman 1996). He probably is right, for the children of the new-monied can ascend into the upper part of the capitalist class if they go to the right schools *and* marry old money.

The Upper Middle Class.   Of all the classes, the upper middle is the one most shaped by education. Almost all members of this class have at least a bachelor's degree, and many have postgraduate degrees in business, management, law, or medicine. These people manage the corporations owned by the capitalist class or else operate their own business or profession. As Gilbert and Kahl (1982) say, these positions

> may not grant prestige equivalent to a title of nobility in the Germany of Max Weber, but they certainly represent the sign of having "made it" in contemporary America. . . . Their income is sufficient to purchase houses and cars and travel that become public symbols for all to see and for advertisers to portray with words and pictures that connote success, glamour, and high style.

Consequently, parents and teachers push children to prepare themselves for upper-middle-class jobs. About 14 percent of the population belong to this class.

The Lower Middle Class. About 30 percent of the population belong to the lower middle class. Members of this class follow orders on the job given by those who have upper-middle-class credentials. Their technical and lower-level management positions bring them a good living—albeit one constantly threatened by rising taxes and inflation— and they enjoy a generally comfortable, mainstream lifestyle. They usually feel secure in their positions and anticipate being able to move up the social class ladder.

The distinctions between the lower middle class and the working class on the next lower rung are more blurred than those between other classes. As a result, these two classes run into one another. Members of the lower middle class work at jobs that have slightly more prestige, however, and their incomes are generally higher.

The Working Class. About 30 percent of the U.S. population belong to this class of relatively unskilled blue-collar and white-collar workers. Compared with the lower middle class, they have less education and lower incomes. Their jobs are also less secure, more routine, and more closely supervised. One of their greatest fears is being laid off during recessions. With only a high school diploma, the average member of the working class has little hope of climbing up the class ladder. Job changes are usually "more of the same," so most concentrate on getting ahead by achieving seniority on the job rather than by changing their type of work.

The Working Poor. Members of this class, about 22 percent of the population, work at unskilled, low-paying, temporary and seasonal jobs, such as sharecropping, migrant farm work, housecleaning, and day labor. Most are high school dropouts. Many are functionally illiterate, finding it difficult to read even the want ads. They are not likely to vote (Gilbert and Kahl 1993), for they feel that no matter what party is elected to office their situation won't change.

About 6 million of the working poor work full time (O'Hare 1996b), but still must depend on help such as food stamps to supplement their meager incomes. It is easy to see how you can work full time and still be poor. Suppose that you are married and have a baby 3 months old and another 3 years old. Your spouse stays home to care for them, so earning the income is up to you. But as a high-school dropout, all you can get is a minimum wage job. At $4.75 an hour, you earn $190 for 40 hours. In a year, this comes to $9,880—before deductions. Your nagging fear—and daily nightmare—is of ending up "on the streets."

The Underclass. On the lowest rung, and with next to no chance of climbing anywhere, is the **underclass** (Myrdal 1962; Kelso 1995). Concentrated in the inner city, this group has little or no connection with the job market. Those who are employed, and some are, do menial, low-paying, temporary work. Welfare is their main support, and most members of other classes consider these people the ne'er-do-wells of society. Life is the toughest in this class, and it is filled with despair. The children's chances of getting out of poverty are about fifty-fifty (Gilbert and Kahl 1982:353). About 3 percent of the population fall into this class.

Social Class in the Automobile Industry

The automobile industry can be used to illustrate the social class ladder. The Fords, for example, own and control a manufacturing and financial empire whose net worth is truly staggering. Their power matches their wealth, for through their multinational corporation their decisions affect production and employment in many countries. The family's vast accumulation of money, not unlike its accrued power, is now several generations old. Consequently, Ford children go to the "right" schools, know how to spend money in the "right" way, and can be trusted to make family and class interests paramount in life. They are without question at the top level of the *capitalist* class.

Next in line come top Ford executives. Although they may have an income of several hundred thousand dollars a year (and some, with stock options and bonuses, earn several

underclass: a small group of people for whom poverty persists year after year and across generations

A husband and wife in their Virginia family estate and the migrant worker are both shown "at home." From the contrast evident in these photos, you can easily infer consequences of social class: from life chances to health, from family life to education. It also should be apparent why these people are not likely to view politics in quite the same way.

million annually), most are new to wealth and power. Consequently, they would be classified at the lower end of the capitalist class.

A husband and wife who own a Ford agency are members of the *upper middle class.* Their income clearly sets them apart from the majority of Americans, and their reputation in the community is enviable. More than likely they also exert greater-than-average influence in their community, but their capacity to wield power is limited.

A Ford salesperson, as well as people who work in the dealership office, belongs to the *lower middle class.* Although there are some exceptional salespeople, perhaps a few of whom make a lot of money selling prestigious, expensive cars to the capitalist class, salespeople at a run-of-the-mill local Ford agency are lower middle class. Compared with the owners of the agency, their income is less, their education is also likely to be less, and their work brings them less prestige.

Mechanics who repair customers' cars are members of the *working class.* If a mechanic is promoted to supervise the repair shop, that person has joined the lower middle class.

Those who "detail" used cars (making them appear newer by washing and polishing the car, painting the tires, spraying "new car scent" into the interior, and so on) belong to the *working poor.* Their income and education are low, the prestige accorded their work minimal. They are laid off when selling slows down.

Ordinarily, the *underclass* is not represented in the automobile industry. It is conceivable, however, that the agency might hire a member of the underclass to do a specific job such as raking the grass or cleaning up the used car lot. In general, however, personnel at the agency do not trust members of the underclass and do not want to associate with them—even for a few hours. They prefer to hire someone from the working poor for such jobs.

Below the Ladder: The Homeless

The homeless men described in the opening vignette of this chapter, and the women and children like them, are so far down the class structure that their position is even lower than the underclass. Technically, the homeless are members of the underclass, but their poverty is so severe and their condition in life so despairing that we can think of them as occupying an unofficial rung below the underclass.

These are the people whom most Americans wish would just go away. Their presence on our city streets bothers passersby from the more privileged social classes—which includes just about everyone. "What are those obnoxious, dirty, foul-smelling people doing here, cluttering up my city?" appears to be a common response. Some do respond with sympathy and a desire to do something to help. But what? Almost all of us just shrug our shoulders and look the other way, despairing of a solution and somewhat intimidated by the presence of the homeless.

The homeless are the "fallout" of industrialization, especially our developing post-industrial economy. In another era, they would have had plenty of work. They would have tended horses, worked on farms, dug ditches, shoveled coal, and run the factory looms. Some would have explored and settled the West. Others would have followed the lure of gold to California, Alaska, and Australia. Today, however, with no unsettled frontiers, factory jobs scarce, and even farms becoming technological marvels, we have little need for unskilled labor, and these people are left to wander aimlessly about the city streets.

Consequences of Social Class

Each social class can be thought of as a broad subculture with distinct approaches to life. Of the many ways that social class affects people's lives, we shall briefly review the new technology, family life, politics, religion, and health.

The New Technology

The higher one goes up the social class ladder, the more technology is a benefit. For the capitalist class, the new technology is a dream come true: global profits through global integration. No longer are national boundaries an obstacle. Rather, a product's components are produced in several countries, assembled in another, and the product marketed throughout the world. The new technology also benefits the upper middle class, for their education prepares them to take a leading role in managing this global system for the capitalist class, or for using the new technology to advance in their chosen professions.

Below these two classes, however, the new technology adds to the uncertainty of life, with the insecurity becoming greater the farther one moves down the ladder. As the new technology transforms the workplace, it eliminates jobs and outdates skills. People in lower management can transfer their skills from one job to another, although in shifting job markets the times between periods of employment can be precarious. Those in crafts are even less secure, for their training is more specific and the changing occupational world can reduce the need for their narrower, more specialized skills.

From this middle point in the ladder down, people are hit the hardest. The working class is ill prepared for the changes ushered in by the new technology, and they are haunted by the specter of unemployment. The low technical skills of the working poor make them even more vulnerable, for they have even less to offer in the new job market. As unskilled jobs dry up, more and more of the working poor are consigned to the industrial garbage bin. The underclass, of course, with no technical skills, is bypassed entirely.

The playing field is far from level. Some even fear that current trends in exporting U.S. jobs mean that U.S. workers are becoming an expendable luxury, destined to be replaced by low-paid, nonunionized—and more compliant—workers on other continents. In short, the new technology opens and closes opportunities for people largely by virtue of where they are located on the social class ladder.

Physical and Mental Health

Social class even affects our chances of living and dying. The principle is simple: The lower a person's class, the more likely that individual is to die before the expected age. This principle holds true at all ages. Infants born to the poor are more likely than other infants to die before their first birthday. In old age—whether 70 or 90—the poor are more likely to die of illness and disease. During both childhood and adulthood, the poor are also more likely to be killed by accidents, fires, and homicide.

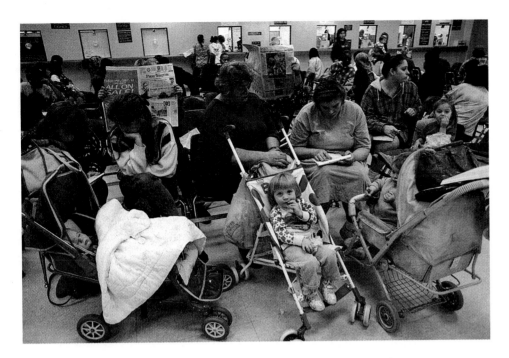

In general, the time and activities of the rich are considered to be more valuable than those of the poor. One consequence is that the length of time that people wait is inversely related to social class. In other words, in most situations the poor wait longer than the rich. This principle is evident in "waiting rooms," such as this one in Los Angeles, California, where AFDC recipients fill out forms for the Department of Public Social Services.

Underlying these different death rates is unequal access to medical care and nutrition. Medical care is expensive, and even with government-funded plans for the poor, the higher classes receive better medical treatment. Poor people are also less educated concerning nutrition, and their meals tend to be heavy in fats and sugars, neither of which is healthy (Freedman 1990).

Social class also affects mental health. From the 1930s until now, sociologists have found that the mental health of the lower classes is worse than that of the higher classes (Faris and Dunham 1939; Srole et al. 1978; Brown and Gary 1988; Lundberg 1991). This difference reflects the greater stresses that those in the lower classes experience, such as unpaid bills, unemployment, dirty and dangerous work, the threat of eviction, unhappy marriages, and broken homes. People higher up the social class ladder also experience stress in daily life, of course, but their stress is generally less and their coping resources greater. Not only can they afford vacations, psychiatrists, and counselors, but *their class position gives them greater control over their lives, a key to good mental health.*

Family Life

Social class plays an especially significant role in family life. Of its many consequences in this vital area, let's look at choice of spouse, divorce, and child rearing.

Choice of Husband or Wife.   The capitalist class strongly emphasizes family tradition and continuity. They stress the family's ancestors, history, and even a sense of purpose or destiny in life (Baltzell 1979; Aldrich 1989). Children of this class learn that their choice of husband or wife affects not just themselves but the whole family unit, that their spouse will have an impact on the "family line." Consequently, their field of "eligibles" is much narrower than it is for the children of any other social class. In effect, parents in this class play a greater role in their children's mate selection.

Divorce.   The more difficult life of the lower social classes, especially the many tensions that come from insecure jobs and inadequate incomes, leads to more marital friction and a greater likelihood of both spouse and alcohol abuse. Consequently, the marriages of the poor are more likely to fail and their children to grow up in broken homes.

Child Rearing.   As discussed on pages 76–77, sociologist Melvin Kohn (1977) finds significant class differences in child rearing. Lower-class parents are more concerned that their children conform to conventional norms and obey authority figures. Middle-class parents, in contrast, encourage their children to be more creative and independent, and tolerate a wider range of behaviors (except in speech, where they are less tolerant of bad grammar and curse words).

Kohn concluded that lower- and middle-class parents rear their children differently primarily because their occupations give them different visions of their children's futures. Lower-class parents are closely supervised in their jobs, and they anticipate that their children will work at similar jobs. Consequently, they try to teach their children to defer to authority. In contrast, parents from the more privileged classes work at jobs in which they enjoy greater creativity and self-expression. Anticipating similar work for their children, they encourage them to express greater freedom. Out of these contrasting orientations also arise different ways of enforcing discipline; lower-class parents are more likely to use the stick, while the middle classes rely more on verbal persuasion.

Education

As was shown in Figure 10.4, education increases as one goes up the social class ladder. It is not just the amount of education that changes, but also the type of education. Children of the capitalist class bypass public schools entirely in favor of exclusive private schools. Here their children are trained to take a commanding role in society. Prep schools such as Groton School, Phillips Exeter Academy, and Woodberry Forest School teach upper-class values and prepare their students for prestigious universities (Beeghley 1996). Aspiring members of the upper middle class, aware of the significance of this private school system, attempt to gain their children's entry into prestigious preschools by eliciting letters of recommendation for their 2- and 3-year-olds. Such differences in parental expectations and resources are major reasons that children from the more privileged classes do better in school and are more likely to enter and to graduate from college.

Religion

One area of social life that we might think would be unaffected by social class is religion. ("People are religious, or they are not. What does social class have to do with it?") As we shall discuss in Chapter 18, however, the classes tend to cluster in different denominations. Episcopalians, for example, are much more likely to recruit from the middle and upper classes, Baptists draw heavily from the lower classes, and Methodists are more middle class. Patterns of worship also follow class lines: Those that attract the lower classes have more spontaneous worship services and louder music, while the middle and upper classes prefer more "subdued" worship.

Politics

As has been stressed throughout this text, symbolic interactionists emphasize that people see events from their own corner in life. Political views are no exception to this principle, and the rich and the poor walk different political paths. The working class, which feels much more strongly than the classes above it that government should intervene in the economy to make citizens financially secure, is more likely to vote Democrat, those in the higher classes Republican. Although the working class is more liberal on *economic* issues (those that favor government spending), this class is more conservative on *social* issues (such as opposing abortion and the Equal Rights Amendment) (Lipset 1959; Houtman 1995). People toward the bottom of the class structure are also less likely to become politically active—to campaign for candidates, or even to vote (Gans 1991a; Gilbert and Kahl 1993).

Crime and the Criminal Justice System

If justice is supposed to be blind, it certainly is not when it comes to one's chances of being arrested (Henslin 1996). In Chapter 8 (pages 204–207) we discussed how the upper and lower social classes have different styles of crime. The white-collar crimes of the more privileged classes are more likely to be dealt with outside the criminal justice system, while the street crimes of the lower classes are dealt with by the police. One consequence of this class standard is that members of the lower classes are far more likely to be on probation, on parole, or in jail. In addition, since people tend to commit crimes in or near their own neighborhoods, the lower classes are more likely to be robbed, burglarized, or murdered.

Social Mobility ▶

No aspect of life, then—from marriage to politics—goes untouched by social class. Because life is so much more satisfying in the more privileged classes, people strive for upward social mobility. What affects people's chances of climbing the class ladder?

Three Types of Social Mobility

There are three basic types of social mobility: intergenerational, structural, and exchange mobility. **Intergenerational mobility** refers to adult children ending up on a different rung of the social class ladder than their parents—a change that occurs between generations. For example, if the child of someone who sells used cars goes to college and eventually buys a Toyota dealership, that person experiences **upward social mobility.** Conversely, if the child of the dealer's owners parties too much, drops out of college, and ends up selling cars, he or she experiences **downward social mobility.**

We like to think that individual efforts—or faults—are the reason people move up or down the class ladder. In these examples we can see hard work, sacrifice, and ambition on the one hand, versus indolence and alcohol abuse on the other. Although individual factors do underlie social mobility, sociologists consider **structural mobility** to be the crucial factor. This second basic type of mobility refers to changes in society that cause large numbers of people to move up or down the class ladder.

intergenerational mobility: the change that family members make in social class from one generation to the next

upward social mobility: movement up the social class ladder

downward social mobility: movement down the social class ladder

structural mobility: movement up or down the social class ladder that is attributable to changes in the structure of society, not to individual efforts

The term structural mobility *refers to changes in society that push large numbers of people either up or down the social class ladder. A remarkable example was the stock market crash of 1929, when thousands of people suddenly lost immense amounts of wealth. People who once "had it made" found themselves standing on street corners selling apples or, as depicted here, selling their possessions at fire-sale prices.*

To better understand structural mobility, think of how opportunities opened when computers were invented. New types of jobs appeared overnight. Huge numbers of people took workshops and crash courses, switching from blue-collar to white-collar work. Although individual effort certainly was involved—for some seized the opportunity while others did not—the underlying cause was a change in the *structure* of work. Or consider the other side, the closing of opportunities in a depression, when millions of people are forced downward on the class ladder. In this instance, too, their changed status is due less to individual behavior than to *structural* changes in society.

Underlying structural mobility are changes in technology. First there was the change from farming to blue-collar work, and, more recently, the change from blue-collar to white-collar occupations. Huge shifts in the types of work available opened so many doors that it became taken for granted that children could pass up their parents.

The third type, **exchange mobility**, occurs when large numbers of people move up or down the social class ladder, but on balance, the proportions of the social classes remain about the same. Suppose that a million or so working-class people are trained in computers, and they move up the social class ladder—but a vast surge in imports forces about a million skilled workers into lower-status jobs. Although millions of people change their social class, there is in effect an *exchange* among them. That is, the net result more or less balances out, and the class system remains basically untouched.

Ignoring Women

Sociologists used to focus only on the social mobility of men. For example, major studies of intergenerational mobility concluded that about half of sons moved beyond their fathers, about one-third stayed at the same level, and only about one-sixth fell down the social class ladder (Blau and Duncan 1967; Featherman and Hauser 1978; Featherman 1979).

Fathers and sons? How about the other half of the population? Feminists pointed out this obvious lack (Davis and Robinson 1988). They also objected that women were assumed to have no class position of their own—they simply were assigned the class of their husbands. The defense was that too few women were in the labor force to make a difference.

With the large numbers of women now working for pay, more recent studies include women (Breen and Whelan 1995; Beeghley 1996). Sociologists Elizabeth Higgenbotham and Lynn Weber (1992), for example, studied 200 women from working-class backgrounds who became professionals, managers, and administrators in Memphis. They found that almost without exception their parents had encouraged them while they were still little girls to postpone marriage and get an education. This study confirms findings that the family is of utmost importance in the socialization process and that the primary entry to the upper middle class is a college education. At the same time, note that if there had not been a *structural* change in society the millions of new positions that women occupy would not exist.

The New Technology and Fears of the Future

The ladder also goes down, of course, precisely what strikes fear in the hearts of many workers. If the United States does not keep pace with global change and remain highly competitive by producing low-cost, quality goods, its economic position will decline. The result will be shrinking opportunities—with U.S. workers facing fewer good jobs and lower incomes. Such a decline would result in the next generation having *less* status than their parents.

Perhaps this decline has already begun. We have lost millions of manufacturing jobs to Mexico, South America, and Asia. These jobs have taken with them the dreams of upward mobility for millions of Americans. For others, this loss means downward mobility (Dentzler 1991). Consider Alphonse Brown:

exchange mobility: about the same numbers of people moving up and down the social class ladder, such that, on balance, the social class system shows little change

Twenty-two years ago, his mother, Letitia, the daughter of a migrant worker, easily found work at an auto assembly plant in Flint, Michigan. There she earned good money, built seniority, and enjoyed excellent health benefits. Alphonse, in contrast, has given up hope of joining the assembly line. For ten years, he has moved from one low-paying, no-benefits job to another. Letitia says, "In Buick City, there's nobody left with less than fourteen years' seniority. We're on our way back to being migrants."

In short, with foreign competition nipping at the heels of U.S. industry, the richest rewards are reserved for the highly educated or for those who work at jobs sheltered from foreign competition. The result is that millions of workers in the lower half of the U.S. labor force are hitting a brick wall.

The foundation of this brick wall is the new technology, especially computers and satellites. When corporations move factories overseas, their top-level managers, through the wonders of satellite-based communications, are able to monitor the production process from the comfort of their U.S. offices. In many instances, this makes U.S. workers an expendable luxury, replaced by low-paid, nonunionized—and more compliant—workers on other continents.

Of the thousands of examples, consider this:

Ireland is one of the poorest of European countries. Its workers, though, receive a solid high school education, generally superior to our high schools, and are willing to work for a fraction of what U.S. workers make. Consequently, many health insurance claims forms and grocery store redemption coupons are flown overnight to Ireland, where Irish workers efficiently process them, and return them, again overnight, to the United States.

A Matter of Controversy.   Fears of the future are certainly present, but whether social mobility has decreased or not is a matter of heated debate. Some sociologists, such as Peter Blau (1994), conclude that upward mobility has declined, while other analysts conclude that mobility continues at such a brisk pace that the United States is a "pulsating, churning, dynamic" society where opportunities abound (Fossedal 1997). Although millions of jobs have been exported, millions more have been created. The question to be decided by empirical research is whether the new jobs bring sufficient incomes and status to maintain the social mobility to which Americans have become accustomed—or do most of them lead to a social class dead-end? Although this question will not be decided for some time, it is apparent that education remains the key to qualify for the better positions and thus to maintain or improve one's social class.

The Pain of Social Mobility

You know that to be knocked down the social class ladder is painful, but did you know that climbing it also brings pain? Sociologists Richard Sennett and Jonathan Cobb (1972, 1988) studied working-class men and women in Boston who had made deep sacrifices so their children could finish high school and go to college. The fathers worked long hours and were seldom home, while the mothers did without things. The parents expected their children to appreciate what they were doing for them. Instead, and to their dismay, they found estrangement, lack of communication, even bitterness. With the fathers seldom home, the children grew distant. Lack of communication also stemmed from the children's education, since it was so remote from the parents' world. Parents and children found that they no longer had much in common. Bitterness grew, because the parents felt betrayed: Instead of receiving appreciation for their sacrifice, they confronted aloofness and ingratitude.

In short, social class separates people into worlds so distinct that communication and mutual understanding become difficult. To change one's social class, then, is to risk losing one's roots. As you may recall, Richard Rodriguez, featured in the Perspectives box on page 79, also found similar costs in his climb up the ladder.

Poverty

A lot of Americans find the "limitless possibilities" of the American dream rather elusive. As illustrated in Figure 10.4 (on page 260), the working poor and underclass together form about 25 percent of the U.S. population. This percentage translates into a huge number, over sixty–five million people. Before taking a closer look at these people, let's see how poverty is defined.

Drawing the Poverty Line

To define poverty, the U.S. government assumes that poor families spend one-third of their income on food and then multiplies a low-cost food budget by three. Those whose incomes are less than this amount are classified as below the **poverty line.** As sociologists observe, this definition is unrealistic. It ignores changing standards of food consumption, does not allow for the costs of child care for working mothers, and is the same amount across the nation, even though the cost of living is much higher in some states (Katz 1989; Michael 1995). Nevertheless, this is how the government draws the line that separates the poor from the nonpoor.

It is part of the magical sleight-of-hand of modern bureaucracy that a modification in this official measure of poverty instantly adds—or subtracts—millions of people from this category. Although the official definition of poverty does not make anyone poor, the way in which poverty is defined does have serious practical consequences. The government uses this definition to decide who will receive help and who will not. Using this official definition of poverty, let's see who is poor. But before we do this, compare your ideas of the poor with the myths explored in the Down-to-Earth Sociology box below.

poverty line: the official measure of poverty; calculated to include those whose incomes are less than three times a low-cost food budget

---

Down-to-Earth Sociology

Exploring Myths About the Poor

Myth 1: Most poor people are lazy. They are poor because they do not want to work.

Half of the poor are either too old or too young to work. About 40 percent are under age 18, and another 10 percent are age 65 or older. About 30 percent of the working-age poor work at least half the year.

Myth 2: Poor people are trapped in a cycle of poverty that few escape.

The U.S. poverty population is *dynamic.* Most poverty lasts less than a year (Gottschalk et al. 1994). Only 12 percent of the poor remain in poverty for five or more consecutive years (O'Hare 1996a). Most children who are born in poverty are not poor as adults (Ruggles 1989).

Myth 3: Most of the poor are African Americans and Latinos.

As shown on Figure 10.6 (page 272), the poverty rates of African Americans and Latinos are much higher than that of whites. Because there are so many more whites in the population, however, *most poor people are white.* Of all the poor, 55 percent are white, 22 percent African American,

19 percent Latino, 3 percent Asian American, and 1 percent Native American (*Statistical Abstract* 1997: Tables 50, 52, 736).

Myth 4: Most of the poor are single mothers and their children.

Although about 38 percent of the poor do match this stereotype, 34 percent of the poor live in married-couple families, 22 percent live alone or with nonrelatives, and 6 percent live in other settings.

Myth 5: Most of the poor live in the inner city.

This one is close to fact, as about 42 percent do live in the inner city. But 36 percent live in the suburbs, and 22 percent in small towns and rural areas.

Myth 6: The poor live on welfare.

About half of the income of poor adults comes from wages and pensions, about 25 percent from welfare, and about 22 percent from Social Security.

Sources: Primarily O'Hare 1996, but other sources as indicated.

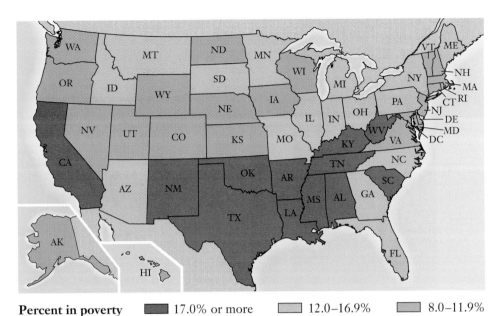

Figure 10.5

Patterns of Poverty

Percent in poverty ■ 17.0% or more ■ 12.0–16.9% ■ 8.0–11.9%

Source: U.S. Bureau of the Census, *Current Population Reports* P60–189: Table G.

Who Are the Poor?

Geography. As you can see from the Social Map above, the poor are not evenly distributed among the states. This map also shows that one of the dominant patterns is a clustering of poverty in the South. The only exception is California, which has far more immigrants than any other state.

A second aspect of geography is also significant. About fifty-six million Americans live in rural areas. Of these, nine million are poor. At 16 percent, this is higher than the national average of 14 percent. The rural poor are less likely to be on welfare or to be single parents, and more likely to be married and to have jobs. Compared with urban Americans, the rural poor are less skilled and less educated, and the jobs available to them pay less than similar jobs in urban areas (Dudenhefer 1993).

The greatest predictors of whether Americans are poor is not geography, however, but, rather, race/ethnicity, education, and the sex of the person who heads the family. Let's look at these three factors.

Race/Ethnicity. One of the strongest factors in poverty is race/ethnicity. As you can see from Figure 10.6 on the next page, only 11 percent of white Americans are poor, but 29 percent of African Americans and 30 percent of Latinos live in poverty. Although white Americans are less likely to be poor than are most racial/ethnic groups, because there are so many more white Americans, most poor people are white.

Education and Poverty. As you know, education is also a vital factor in poverty, but you may not have known how powerful it actually is. Look at Figure 10.7 on the next page. You can see that only 2 percent of people who finish college end up in poverty, but one of every four people who drop out of high school is poor. As you can see, the chances of someone being poor decrease with each level of education. Although this principle applies regardless of race/ethnicity, you can see how race/ethnicity retains its impact at every level of education.

The Feminization of Poverty. The other major predictor of poverty is the sex of the person who heads the family. Most poor families are headed

Beyond the awareness of most Americans are the rural poor, such as this West Virginia family and the thousands of similar families that live in what is known as Appalachia. As explained in the text, some of the characteristics of the rural poor differ from those of the urban poor.

Figure 10.6

Poverty in the United States, by Age and Race/Ethnicity

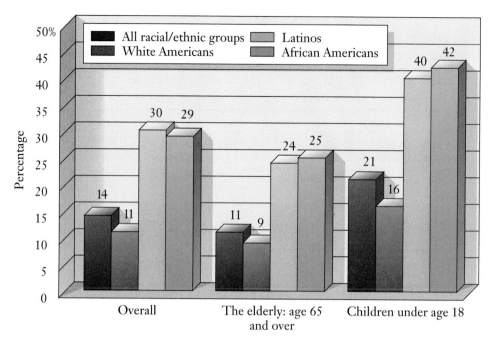

Note: The poverty line on which these figures are based is $15,569 for a nonfarm family of four. See the source for figures for single individuals and families of different sizes.

Source: Statistical Abstract 1997:Tables 736 and 739.

feminization of poverty: a trend in U.S. poverty whereby most poor families are headed by women

by women. For single-parent families headed by men, the poverty rate is less than the national average; but if a woman heads a family the chances of poverty soar. A mother-headed family is *two to six* times more likely to be poor than is a family headed by a married couple (*Statistical Abstract* 1994:Table 729). The three major causes of this phenomenon, called the **feminization of poverty,** are divorce, births to unwed mothers, and the lower wages paid to women.

Figure 10.7

Education and Poverty

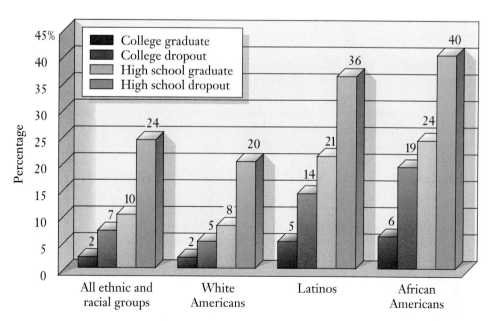

Source: Statistical Abstract 1997: Table 745.

Old Age.   Figure 10.6 also shows that the elderly are less likely than the general population to be poor. It used to be that growing old increased one's chances of being poor, but changes in government policies concerning Social Security and subsidized housing, food, and medical care have significantly cut the rate of poverty among the elderly. The bottom line, however, is that the prevailing racial and ethnic patterns carry over into old age, and an elderly African American or Latino is almost three times as likely to be poor than is an elderly white person.

Children of Poverty

Children are more likely to live in poverty than are adults or the elderly. This holds true regardless of race, but as Figure 10.6 shows, poverty is much greater among Latino and African-American children. That about 15 million U.S. children are reared in poverty is shocking when one considers the wealth of this country and the supposed concern for the well-being of children. This tragic aspect of poverty is the topic of the following Thinking Critically section.

Thinking Critically About Social Controversy

The Nation's Shame: Children in Poverty

▼ During the past decade or two, children have slipped into poverty faster than any other age group. As Figure 10.6 shows, one of six white U.S. children and two of every five Latino and African-American children are poor. These figures translate into incredible numbers—approximately *15 million* children live in poverty: 7 million white children, 4 million Latino children, and 4 million African-American children.

According to sociologist and U.S. Senator Daniel Moynihan, this high rate of child poverty is due primarily to a general breakdown of the U.S. family. He points his finger at the sharp increase in births outside marriage. In 1960, 5 percent of U.S. children were born to unmarried mothers. Today that figure is *six times higher*, and single women now account for 33 percent of all U.S. births. The relationship to social class is striking, for as Table 10.4 shows, births to unmarried mothers are not distributed evenly across the social classes. For women above the poverty line, only 6 percent of births are to single mothers, while for women below the poverty line this rate jumps to 44 percent.

Regardless of causes—and there are many—to say that millions of children live in poverty can be as cold and meaningless as saying that their shoes are brown. Easy to overlook is the

TABLE 10.4

U.S. Births to Single and Married Women	
Births to Women Above the Poverty Line	
Married	*Single*
94%	6%
Births to Women Below the Poverty Line	
Married	*Single*
56%	44%

Note: Figures were available only for white women.

Source: Murray 1993.

A disturbing new aspect of poverty is that, of all U.S. age groups, children are the most likely to be poor. Explanations for this troubling change are given in the text. What do you think the future holds for these children in Quito, Mississippi?

significance of childhood poverty. Poor children are more likely to die in infancy, to go hungry and to be malnourished, to develop more slowly, and to have more health problems. They are more likely to drop out of school, to become involved in criminal activities, and to have children while still in their teens—thus perpetuating the cycle of poverty.

For Your Consideration

Many social analysts—liberals and conservatives alike—are alarmed at this increase in child poverty. They emphasize that it is time to stop blaming the victim, and instead to focus on the structural factors that underlie child poverty. To relieve the problem, they say, we must take immediate steps to establish national programs of child nutrition and health care. Solutions will require at least these fundamental changes: (1) removing obstacles to employment; (2) improving education; and (3) strengthening the family. To achieve these changes, what specific programs would *you* recommend?

Sources: Moynihan 1991; Murray 1993; Sandefur 1995; *Statistical Abstract* 1997: Tables 22, 736, 739, 1338. ▲

The Dynamics of Poverty

In the 1960s, Michael Harrington (1962) and Oscar Lewis (1966a) suggested that the poor tend to get trapped in a **culture of poverty.** They assumed that the values and behaviors of the poor "make them fundamentally different from other Americans, and that these factors are largely responsible for their continued long-term poverty" (Ruggles 1989:7).

Lurking behind this concept is the idea that the poor are lazy people who bring poverty on themselves. Certainly there are individuals and families who match this stereotype—many of us have known them. But is a self-perpetuating culture, transmitted across generations, that locks poor people in poverty the basic reason for U.S. poverty?

Researchers who followed 5,000 U.S. families since 1968 have uncovered some rather surprising findings. Contrary to common stereotypes, most poverty is short, lasting only a year or less. Most poverty comes about due to a dramatic life change such as divorce, sudden unemployment, or even the birth of a child (O'Hare 1996a). As Figure 10.8 shows, only 12 percent of poverty lasts five years or longer. Contrary to the stereotype of lazy people content to live off the government, the vast majority of poor people don't like poverty, and they do what they can to *not* be poor.

Yet from one year to the next the number of poor people remains about the same. This means that the people who move out of poverty are replaced by people who move *into* poverty. The vast majority of these newly poor also will move out of poverty within a year. Some people even bounce back and forth, never quite making it securely out of poverty. This means that poverty is dynamic, touching a lot more people than the official figures indicate. Although 14 percent of Americans may be poor at any one time, about one-fourth of the U.S. population is or has been poor for at least a year.

Why Are People Poor? Individual versus Structural Explanations

Two explanations for poverty compete for our attention. The first, which sociologists adopt, focuses on *social structure.* Sociologists stress that *features of society* deny some people access to education or learning job skills. They emphasize racial, ethnic, age, and gender discrimination, as well as changes in the job market—the closing of plants, drying up of unskilled jobs, and an increase in marginal jobs that pay poverty wages.

A competing explanation focuses on the *characteristics of individuals* that are assumed to contribute to their poverty. Individualistic explanations that sociologists reject outright as worthless stereotypes are laziness and lack of intelligence. Individualistic explanations that sociologists reluctantly acknowledge include dropping out of school, bearing children

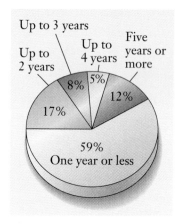

Source: Gottschalk et al. 1994:89.

Figure 10.8

How Long Does Poverty Last?

culture of poverty: the assumption that the values and behaviors of the poor make them fundamentally different from other people, that these factors are largely responsible for their poverty, and that parents perpetuate poverty across generations by passing these characteristics to their children

Welfare: How to Ravage the Self-Concept

My husband left me shortly after I was diagnosed with multiple sclerosis. At the time, I had 5 children. My oldest child was 14, and my youngest was 7. My physician, believing I would be seriously disabled, helped get me on Social Security disability. The process took several months, and so it became necessary for me to go on public aid and food stamps.

By the time I needed to depend on my family in the face of a crisis, there weren't any resources left to draw on. My father had passed away and my mother was retired, living on a modest income based on Social Security and my father's pension. Isn't it funny how there is no social stigma attached to Social Security benefits for the elderly? People look at this money as an entitlement—"we worked for it." But people who have to depend on public aid for existence are looked at like vermin and accused of being lazy.

I can tell you from my own experience, that a great deal of the lethargy that comes from long periods on welfare is due primarily to the attitudes of the people you have to come into contact with in these programs. I've been through the gamut: from rude, surly caseworkers at public aid, to patronizing nurses at the WIC [Women, Infants, Children] clinic ("You have *how* many children?"), to the accusing tone of the food pantry workers when you have to go begging for a handout before the thirty-day time span has expired. After a while your dignity is gone, and you start to believe that you really are the disgusting human trash they all make you out to be.

Source: Christine Hoffman, a student in the author's introductory sociology class.

at younger ages, and averaging more children than do women in the other social classes. Most sociologists are reluctant to speak of such factors in this context, for they appear to blame the victim, something that sociologists bend over backward not to do.

The tension between these competing explanations is more than of mere theoretical interest. These explanations affect our perception and have practical consequences, as is illustrated in the Down-to-Earth Sociology box above and in the following Thinking Critically section.

Thinking Critically About Social Controversy

The Welfare Debate: The Deserving and the Undeserving Poor

▼ Throughout U.S. history, Americans have divided the poor into two types: the deserving and the undeserving. The deserving poor are people who, in the public mind, are poor through no fault of their own. Most of the working poor, such as the Lewises, are considered deserving:

Nancy and Ted Lewis are married, in their late 30s, with two children. Ted works three part-time jobs; Nancy takes care of the children and house. Their total income is $12,000 a year. To make ends meet, the Lewises rely on food stamps, Medicaid, and housing subsidies. (Milbank 1995b)

The undeserving poor, in contrast, are viewed as having brought on their own poverty. They are freeloaders who waste their lives in sloth, alcohol and drug abuse, and unwed motherhood. They don't deserve help, and, if given anything, will waste it on their dissolute lifestyles. Some people would see Joan as an example:

Joan's grandmother and her six children were supported by welfare. Joan's parents are alcoholics—and on welfare. Joan started having sex at 13, bore her first child at 15, and, now at 23, with three children, is expecting her fourth. Her first two children have the same father, the third a different father, and Joan isn't sure who fathered her coming child. Joan parties most nights, using both alcohol and whatever drugs are available. Her house is filthy, and social workers have threatened to take away her children.

This division of the poor into deserving and undeserving underlies the heated debate about welfare. "Why should we use *our* hard-earned money to help *them*? They are just going to waste it. Of course, there are those who want to get on their feet, and helping them is okay."

For Your Consideration

Of what use is such a division of the poor into deserving and undeserving? Would we let some people starve because they "brought poverty upon themselves"? Would we let children go hungry because their parents are unmarried, uneducated, and unskilled? Try to go beyond such a simplistic division and use the sociological perspective to explain poverty without blaming the victim. What *social* conditions (conditions of society) create poverty? What *social* conditions produce the lifestyles of which the middle class so vehemently disapproves?

Welfare Reform

After decades of criticism, U.S. welfare has been restructured. Limits are placed on how long people can stay on welfare, welfare recipients are required to look for work and to take available jobs, and unmarried teen parents must attend school and live at home or in some other adult-supervised setting. Critics call this an attack on the poor, saying the new rules will push people deeper into poverty (Clawson 1997). Supporters claim they rescue people from poverty—transforming them into self-supporting and hard-working citizens—and reduce welfare costs (Cohen 1997). Welfare rolls have dropped, in some states over 50 percent, but it is too soon to know the long-term results of this national experiment—or even what will happen during our next recession. ▲

---

deferred gratification: forgoing something in the present in the hope of achieving greater gains in the future

Deferred Gratification

One consequence of a life of deprivation punctuated by emergencies—*and seeing the future as more of the same*—is a lack of **deferred gratification,** giving up things in the present for the sake of greater gains in the future. It is difficult to practice this middle-class virtue if one does not have a middle-class surplus—or middle-class hope.

Back in 1967, sociologist Elliot Liebow noted this precise problem among African-American street-corner men. Their jobs were low-paying and insecure, their lives pitted with emergencies. With the future looking exactly like the present, and any savings they did manage gobbled up by emergencies, either theirs or their friends and relatives, saving for the future was fruitless. The only thing that made sense from their perspective was to enjoy what they could at the moment. Immediate gratification, then, was not the cause of their poverty, but its consequence. Cause and consequence loop together, however, for their immediate gratification, in turn, helped perpetuate their poverty. For another look at this "looping," see the Down-to-Earth Sociology box on the next page, in which I share my personal experiences with poverty.

If both causes are at work, why do sociologists emphasize the structural explanation? Reverse the situation for a moment. Suppose that the daily routine of the middle class were an old car that ran only half the time, threats from the utility company to shut off the electricity and heat, and a choice between buying medicine and food and diapers or paying the rent. How long would they practice deferred gratification? Their orientations to life would likely make a sharp U-turn.

Sociologists, then, look at the behaviors of the poor as more driven by their poverty than as a cause of it. Poor people would love the opportunities that would allow them the chance to practice the middle-class virtue of deferred gratification. They just can't afford it.

Where Is Horatio Alger? The Social Functions of a Myth

Around the turn of the century, Horatio Alger was one of the country's most talked-about fictional heroes. The rags-to-riches exploits of this national character, and his startling

A culture's dominant ideology is reinforced in many ways, including in its literature. As discussed in the text, Horatio Alger was the inspirational hero for thousands of boys. The central theme of these many novels, immensely popular in their time, was rags to riches. Through rugged determination and self-sacrifice, a boy could overcome seemingly insurmountable obstacles to reach the pinnacle of success.

 *Down-to-Earth Sociology*

Poverty: A Personal Journey

I was born in poverty. Unable to afford to rent a house or apartment, my parents rented the small study of their minister. That is where I was born.

My father began to slowly climb the social class ladder. His fitful odyssey took him from laborer to truck driver to the owner of a series of small businesses (tire shop, bar, hotel), then to vacuum cleaner salesman and back to owning a bar. He converted a garage into a house. Although it had no indoor plumbing or insulation (in northern Minnesota!), it was a start. He later bought a house, and then built a new home. Then we moved into a trailer, and then back to a house. With a seventh grade education holding him back, my father never became wealthy, but poverty did become a distant memory.

My social class took a leap—from working to upper middle—when, after attending college and graduate school, I became a university professor. I entered a world unknown by my parents, certainly much more pampered and privileged, with opportunities to do research, to publish, and to travel to exotic places. As just one example of the differences: Whereas my reading centers on sociological research, as well as books in Spanish, my father never read a book in his life—and my mother never got past detective stories and romance paperbacks. One isn't "better" than the other, just significantly different for the way one looks at the world.

Rooted in childhood experiences, my interest in poverty stayed with me. I traveled to a dozen or so skid rows across

the United States and Canada, talking to the homeless and staying in their shelters. In my own town, I also spent considerable time with people on welfare, observing the way they lived. I constantly marveled at the intricate connections between *personal* causes (culture of poverty—alcohol and drug abuse, spouse abuse, multiple out-of-wedlock children, spending money on frivolous items, partying all night, especially on "Mother's Day" [the day the welfare check arrives], and a seeming incapacity to keep appointments, except to pick up the welfare check) and *structural* causes (lack of education, lack of unskilled jobs, and lack of transportation).

Sociologists haven't unraveled this connection, and as much as we may *like* there to be only structural causes, *both* are at work. It is similar to the perennial health problems I observed: the constant colds, runny noses, back aches, and injuries. Which was the cause and which the effect? Both, of course, for the health problems came from *social structure* (little access to medical treatment, lesser trained or capable physicians, drafty houses, and lack of education on nutrition). At the same time, their *personal* characteristics—hygiene, eating habits, and overdrinking—caused medical problems. The one fed into the other, just like the personal and structural causes of poverty itself. In addition, these medical factors (based on both personal and structural causes) fed into poverty, making them less able to perform jobs successfully—or even able to show up at work regularly.

What an intricate puzzle for sociologists!

successes in overcoming severe odds, motivated thousands of boys of that period. Although he has disappeared from U.S. literature, Horatio Alger remains alive and well in the psyche of Americans. From abundant, real-life examples of people from humble origins who climbed far up the social class ladder, Americans know that anyone can get ahead by really trying. In fact, they believe that most Americans, including minorities and the working poor, have an average or better than average chance of getting ahead—obviously a statistical impossibility (Kluegel and Smith 1986).

The accuracy of the Horatio Alger myth is less important than the belief itself in limitless possibilities for everyone. Functionalists would stress that this belief is functional for society. On the one hand, it encourages people to compete for higher positions, or, as the song says, "to reach for the highest star." On the other hand, it places blame for failure squarely on the individual. If you don't make it—in the face of ample opportunities to get ahead—the fault must be your own. The Horatio Alger myth helps to stabilize society, then, for since the fault is viewed as the individual's, not society's, current social arrangements are satisfactory. This reduces pressures to change the system.

As Marx and Weber pointed out, social class penetrates our consciousness, shaping our ideas of life and our proper place in society. When the rich look around, they sense superiority and control over destiny. In contrast, the poor see defeat, and a bitter buffeting by unpredictable forces. Each knows the dominant ideology, that their particular niche in life is due to their own efforts, that the reasons for success—or failure—lie solely with the self. Like the fish not seeing water, people tend not to see how social class affects their own lives.

Summary and Review

What Is Social Class?

What is social class, and how do sociologists measure it?

Most sociologists have adopted Weber's definition of **social class** as a large group of people who rank closely to one another in wealth, power, and prestige. There are three ways to measure social class. In the **subjective method,** people assign themselves their own social class. In the **reputational method,** people identify the social class of others based on knowledge of their circumstances. In the **objective method,** researchers assign subjects to a social class based on objective criteria such as wealth, power, and prestige. Pp. 252–253.

The Components of Social Class

What are the three criteria used to measure social class?

Wealth, power, and prestige are most commonly used to measure social class. **Wealth,** consisting of property and income, is concentrated in the upper classes. The distribution of wealth in the United States has changed little over the past couple of generations, and the poorest and richest quintiles now receive about the same share of the country's wealth as they did in 1945. **Power** is the ability to carry out one's will, even over the resistance of others. C. Wright Mills coined the term **power elite** to refer to the small group that holds the reins of power in business, government, and the military. **Prestige** is often linked to occupational status. People's rankings of occupational prestige have changed little over the decades and are similar from country to country. Globally, occupations that pay more, require more education and abstract thought, and offer greater autonomy are given greater prestige. Pp. 253–258.

What is meant by the term status inconsistency?

Status is social ranking. Most people are status consistent; that is, they rank high or low on all three dimensions of social class. People who rank higher on some dimensions than on others are status inconsistent. The frustrations of **status inconsistency** tend to produce political radicalism. Pp. 258–259.

Sociological Models of Social Class

What models are used to portray the social classes?

Two models that portray the social classes were described. Erik Wright developed a four-class model based on Marx: (1) capitalists or owners; (2) petty bourgeoisie or small business owners; (3) managers; and (4) workers. Gilbert and

Kahl developed a six-class model based on Weber. At the top is the capitalist class. In descending order are the upper middle class, the lower middle class, the working class, the working poor, and the **underclass.** Pp. 259–264.

Consequences of Social Class

How does social class affect people?

Social class leaves no aspect of life untouched. It affects people's chances of benefitting from the new technology, dying early, becoming ill, receiving good health care, and getting divorced. Class membership also affects child rearing, educational attainment, religious affiliation, political participation, and contact with the criminal justice system. Pp. 264–267.

Social Mobility

What are the three types of social mobility?

The term **intergenerational mobility** refers to changes in social class from one generation to the next. **Exchange mobility** is the movement of large numbers of people from one class to another, with the net result that the relative proportions of the population in the classes remain about the same. The term **structural mobility** refers to social changes that affect the social class membership of large numbers of people. Pp. 267–269.

Poverty

Who are the poor?

Poverty is unequally distributed in the United States. Latinos, African Americans, Native Americans, children, women-headed households, and rural Americans are more likely than others to be poor. The poverty rate of the elderly is about the same as the general population. Pp. 270–274.

What are individual and structural explanations of poverty?

Some social analysts believe that characteristics of *individuals,* such as a desire for immediate gratification, cause poverty. Sociologists, in contrast, examine *structural* features of society, such as employment opportunities, to find the causes of poverty. Sociologists generally conclude that life orientations are a consequence, not the cause, of people's position in the social class structure. Pp. 274–276.

How is the Horatio Alger myth functional for society?

The Horatio Alger myth—the belief that anyone can get ahead if only he or she tries hard enough—encourages people to strive to get ahead and deflects blame for failure from society to the individual. Pp. 276–277.

Where can I read more on this topic?
Suggested readings for this chapter are listed on page 662.

Sociology and the Internet

All URLs listed are current as of the printing of this book. URLs are often changed. Please check our Website http://www.abacon.com/henslin for updates.

1. After reading the Thinking Critically About Social Controversy section, "The Nation's Shame: Children in Poverty," go to the National Center for Children in Poverty page *http://cpmcnet.columbia.edu/dept/nccp* and select "Child Poverty News and Issues." Browse the current and back issues. How does the issue of children in poverty relate to social class? Reflect on the question that your author asks: "What specific programs would you recommend?" Present your conclusions in a panel discussion for your sociology class.

2. Welfare reform is an issue that continues to raise impassioned emotions, especially in presidential election years. Use Lycos *http://www.lycos.com* with the search words "welfare reform" to browse several sites related to the topic. What issues are currently being raised? How do the stands being taken seem to differ according to people's social class backgrounds?

Explain why you think this is true. What is your view of these issues? In what ways does your own social class background influence your position? Explain.

3. Examine the following surveys, which include questions about social class:

http://theresearch.com/e-shop.htm
http://www.halcyon.com/tandk/survey/survey.html

What methods of measuring social class are being used (subjective, reputational, or objective)? How do you know? Which components of social class are measured in each survey?

4. Go to *http://www.abwahq.org/* What is the American Business Women's Association and what is its function? How does the ABWA help promote the social mobility of women? What are some of the services offered to the members of ABWA? Why is this useful for women who work in our society?

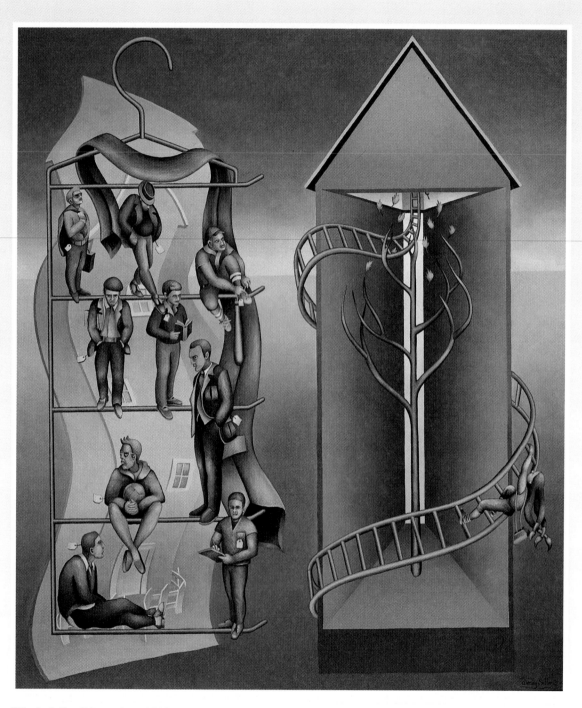

Wendy Seller, Dissension, 1993

CHAPTER

11

Inequalities of Gender

*I*N TUNIS, THE CAPITAL OF TUNISIA, *on Africa's northern coast, I met some U.S. college students, with whom I spent a couple of days. When they said that they wanted to see Tunis's red light district, I wondered if it would be worth the trip. I already had seen other red light districts, including the unusual one in Amsterdam where the state licenses the women, requires medical checkups (certificates available for customers to inspect), sets the prices, and pays prostitutes social security at retirement. The women sit behind lighted picture windows while customers, interspersed with tourists and neighborhood residents, stroll along attractive canalside streets, browsing from the outside.*

This time the sight turned my stomach.

We ended up on a narrow street opening onto the Mediterranean. Each side was lined with a row of one-room wooden shacks, the structures touching one another, side wall to side wall. In front of each open door stood a young woman. Peering from outside into the dark interior, I could see a tiny room with a well-worn bed.

The street was crowded with men looking at the women. Many of them wore sailor uniforms from countries that I couldn't identify.

As I looked more closely, I saw runny sores on the legs of some of the women. Incredibly, with such visible evidence of their disease, customers still entered. Evidently the low price (at that time $2) was too much to resist.

With a sickening feeling to my stomach and the desire to vomit, I kept a good distance between myself and the beckoning women. One tour of the two-block area was more than sufficient.

Out of sight, I knew, was a group of men, their wealth coming from these exploited women who were condemned to a short life punctuated by fear and prolonged by misery.

*T*his chapter examines **gender stratification**—males' and females' unequal access to power, prestige, and property on the basis of sex. Gender stratification is especially significant because it cuts across *all* aspects of social life. No matter what our social class, age, racial, or ethnic classification, we are labeled *male* or *female*. The images and expectations attached to these labels guide our behavior in everyday life. They are especially significant in determining power and privilege. In this chapter's fascinating journey, we shall look at inequality between the sexes around the world and in the United States. We shall review such topics as whether it is biology or culture that makes us the way we are, sexual harassment, unequal pay, and violence against women. This excursion will provide a

gender stratification: males' and females' unequal access to power, prestige, and property on the basis of their sex

Throughout history, women have been denied the right to pursue various occupations on the basis of presumed biological characteristics. One of the occupations most resistant to change has been the military. Demi Moore, star of G. I. JANE, reflects recent changes in the U.S. military.

good context for understanding the power differences between men and women that lead to such events as the one just described in the vignette. It should also give you insight into your own experiences with gender.

Issues of Sex and Gender

When we consider how females and males differ, the first thing that usually comes to mind is **sex,** the *biological* characteristics that distinguish males and females. *Primary sex characteristics* consist of a vagina or a penis and other organs related to reproduction; *secondary sex characteristics* are the physical distinctions between males and females that are not directly connected with reproduction. Secondary sex characteristics become clearly evident at puberty when males develop more muscles, a lower voice, and more hair and height; while females form more fatty tissue, broader hips, and larger breasts.

Gender, in contrast, is a *social,* not a biological characteristic. Gender varies from one society to another, for it is what a group considers proper for its males and females. Whereas *sex* refers to male or female, *gender* refers to masculinity or femininity. In short, you inherit your sex, but you learn your gender as you are socialized into behaviors and attitudes thought appropriate for your sex.

The sociological significance of gender is that it is a device by which society controls its members. Gender sorts us, on the basis of sex, into different life experiences. It opens and closes access to power, property, and even prestige. Like social class, gender is a structural feature of society.

Before examining inequalities of gender, let's consider why men and women act differently. Are they, perhaps, just born that way?

Biology or Culture? The Continuing Controversy

Why are most males more aggressive than most females? Why do women enter "nurturing" occupations such as nursing in such far greater numbers than men? To answer such questions, many people respond with some variation of "They're just born that way."

Is this the correct answer? Certainly biology is an extremely significant part of our lives. Each of us begins as a fertilized egg. The egg, or ovum, is contributed by our mother, the sperm that fertilizes the egg by our father. At the very moment the egg is fertilized, our sex is determined. Each of us receives twenty-three pairs of chromosomes from the ovum and twenty-three from the sperm. The egg has an X chromosome. If the sperm that fertilizes the egg also has an X chromosome, we become female (XX). If the sperm has a Y chromosome, we become male (XY).

That's the biology. Now, the sociological question is, Do these biological differences control our behaviors? Do they, for example, make females more nurturing and males more aggressive and domineering? Almost all sociologists take the side of "nurture" in this "nature versus nurture" controversy, but a few do not, as you can see from the Thinking Critically sections on the next two pages.

The Dominant Position in Sociology

The dominant sociological position is represented by the symbolic interactionists. They stress that the visible differences of sex do not come with meanings built into them. Rather, each human group determines what these physical differences mean to them, and on that basis assigns males and females to separate groups. Here people learn contrasting expectations of life and, on the basis of their sex, are given different access to their society's privileges.

Most sociologists find the argument compelling that if biology were the principal factor in human behavior, around the world we would find women to be one sort of person and men another. In fact, however, ideas of gender—and resulting male–female behavior—vary greatly from one culture to another. The Tahitians in the South Pacific pro-

sex: biological characteristics that distinguish females and males, consisting of primary and secondary sex characteristics

gender: the social characteristics that a society considers proper for its males and females; masculinity or femininity

Cynthia Fuchs Epstein, whose position in the ongoing "nature versus nurture" debate is summarized here.

▼▼▼▼▼▼▼▼▼▼▼▼▼▼▼▼▼▼▼▼▼▼▼▼▼▼▼▼▼▼▼▼

Thinking Critically About Social Controversy

Biology Versus Culture—Culture Is the Answer

▼ For sociologist Cynthia Fuchs Epstein (1986, 1988, 1989), differences between males' and females' behavior are solely the result of social factors—specifically, socialization and social control. Her argument is as follows:

1. A reexamination of the anthropological record shows greater equality between the sexes in the past than we had thought. In earlier societies, women, as well as men, hunted small game, made tools for hunting and gathering, and gathered food. Studies of today's hunting and gathering societies show that "both women's and men's roles have been broader and less rigid than those created by stereotypes. For example, the Agta and Mbuti are clearly egalitarian and thus prove that hunting and gathering societies exist in which women are not subordinate to men. Anthropologists who study them claim that there is a separate but equal status of women at this level of development."

2. The types of work that men and women perform in each society are determined not by biology but by social arrangements. Few people, whether male or female, can escape these arrangements and almost everyone works within their allotted narrow range. This gender inequality of work, which serves the interests of men, is enforced by informal customs and formal laws. When these socially constructed barriers are removed, women's work habits are similar to those of men.

3. The human behaviors that biology "causes" are limited to those involving reproduction or differences in body structure. These differences are relevant for only a few activities, such as playing basketball or "crawling through a small space."

4. Female crime rates, which are rising in many parts of the world, indicate that aggression, often considered a biologically dictated male behavior, is related instead to social rather than biological factors. When social conditions permit, such as when women become lawyers, they also exhibit "adversarial, assertive, and dominant behavior." Not incidentally, this "dominant behavior" also appears in scholarly female challenges to the biased views about human nature that have been proposed by male scholars.

In short, rather than "women's incompetence or inability to read a legal brief, perform brain surgery, [or] to predict a bull market," social factors—socialization, gender discrimination, and other forms of social control—are responsible for gender differences in behavior. Arguments that assign "an evolutionary and genetic basis" to explain differences in sex status are simplistic. They "rest on a dubious structure of inappropriate, highly selective, and poor data, oversimplification in logic and in inappropriate inferences by use of analogy." ▲

vide a remarkable contrast to what we expect of gender. They don't give their children names that are identifiable as male or female, and they expect *both* men and women to be passive, yielding, and to ignore slights. The result of their socialization into gender is reported to be a gentle people where neither men nor women are competitive in trying to attain material possessions (Gilmore 1990).

Opening the Door to Biology

The matter of "nature" versus "nurture" is not so easily settled, however, and some sociologists who take the "nurture" side still acknowledge that biological factors may be involved in some human behavior other than reproduction and childbearing. Alice Rossi, for example, a feminist sociologist and former president of the American Sociological Association, has suggested that women are better prepared biologically for "mothering" than are men. She (1977, 1984) says that women are more sensitive to the infant's soft skin and their nonverbal communications. Her basic point is that the issue is not biology *or*

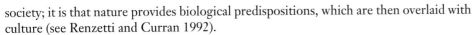

Thinking Critically About Social Controversy

Biology Versus Culture—Biology Is the Answer

▼ Sociologist Steven Goldberg (1974, 1986, 1993) finds it astonishing that anyone should doubt "the presence of core-deep differences in males and females, differences of temperament and emotion we call masculinity and femininity." Goldberg's argument, that it is not environment but inborn differences that "give masculine and feminine direction to the emotions and behaviors of men and women," is as follows:

1. The anthropological record shows that all societies for which evidence exists are (or were) **patriarchies** (societies in which men dominate women). Stories about long-lost **matriarchies** (societies in which women dominate men) are myths.

2. In all societies, past and present, the highest statuses are associated with males. In every society, politics is ruled by "hierarchies overwhelmingly dominated by men."

3. The reason why men dominate societies is that they "have a lower threshold for the elicitation of dominance behavior . . . a greater tendency to exhibit whatever behavior is necessary in any environment to attain dominance in hierarchies and male–female encounters and relationships." Men are more willing "to sacrifice the rewards of other motivations—the desire for affection, health, family life, safety, relaxation, vacation and the like—in order to attain dominance and status."

4. Just as a 6-foot woman does not prove the social basis of height, so exceptional individuals, such as a highly achieving and dominant woman, do not refute "the physiological roots of behavior."

In short, only one interpretation of why every society from that of the Pygmy to that of the Swede associates dominance and attainment with males is valid. Male dominance of society is "an inevitable resolution of the psychophysiological reality." Socialization and social institutions merely *reflect*—and sometimes exaggerate—inborn tendencies. Any interpretation other than inborn differences is "wrongheaded, ignorant, tendentious, internally illogical, discordant with the evidence, and implausible in the extreme." The argument that males are more aggressive because they have been socialized that way is the equivalent of a claim that men can grow moustaches because boys have been socialized that way.

To acknowledge this reality is *not* to defend discrimination against women. Whether or not one approves what societies have done with these basic biological differences is not the point. The point is that biology leads males and females to different behaviors and attitudes— regardless of how we feel about this or wish it were different. ▲

Steven Goldberg, whose position in the ongoing "nature versus nurture" debate is summarized here.

society; it is that nature provides biological predispositions, which are then overlaid with culture (see Renzetti and Curran 1992).

Let's consider two quite different situations, a medical accident and Vietnam veterans.

A Medical Accident.   The drama began in 1963, when 7-month-old identical twins were taken to a doctor to be circumcised (Money and Ehrhardt 1972). The inept physician, who was using electrocautery (a heated needle), turned the electric current too high and accidentally burned off the penis of one of the boys. You can imagine the parents' reaction of disbelief—followed by horror as the truth sank in.

What can be done in a situation like this? The damage was irreversible. The parents were told that the child could never have sexual relations. After months of soul-wrenching agonies and tearful consultations with experts, the parents decided that their son should have a sex change operation. When he was 17 months old, surgeons used the boy's own skin to construct a vagina. The parents then gave the child a girl's name, dressed him in frilly clothing, let his hair grow long, and began to treat him as a girl. Later, physicians gave the child female steroids to promote female pubertal growth.

patriarchy: a society in which men dominate women

matriarchy: a society in which women dominate men

At first the results were extremely promising. When the twins were 4 ½ years old, the mother said (remember that the children are biologically identical):

> One thing that really amazes me is that she is so feminine. I've never seen a little girl so neat and tidy. . . . She likes for me to wipe her face. She doesn't like to be dirty, and yet my son is quite different. I can't wash his face for anything. . . . She is very proud of herself, when she puts on a new dress, or I set her hair. . . . She seems to be daintier. (Money and Ehrhardt 1972)

About a year later, the mother described how their daughter imitated her while their son copied his father:

> I found that my son, he chose very masculine things like a fireman or a policeman. . . . He wanted to do what daddy does, work where daddy does, and carry a lunch kit. . . . And [my daughter] didn't want any of those things. She wants to be a doctor or a teacher. . . . But none of the things that she ever wanted to be were like a policeman or a fireman, and that sort of thing never appealed to her. (Money and Ehrhardt 1972)

If the matter were this clear-cut, we could use this case to conclude that gender is entirely up to nurture. Seldom are things in life so simple, however, and a twist occurs in this story. In spite of this promising start and her parents' coaching, the twin whose sex had been reassigned did not adapt well to femininity. She rejected dolls and tried to urinate standing up. Classmates called her a "cavewoman" because she walked like a boy (Diamond 1982). At age 14, in despair over her inner turmoil, she tried to commit suicide. In a tearful confrontation, her father told her about the accident and her sex change. She then chose to stop her hormone therapy, and later had extensive surgery to partially reconstruct a penis. At age 25 he married a woman and adopted her children (Gorman 1997a; "Sexual Identity . . ." 1997).

The Vietnam Veterans' Study. In 1985, the U.S. government began a health study of Vietnam veterans. To be certain the study was representative, the researchers chose a random sample of 4,462 men. Among the mass of data they collected was a measurement of testosterone for each veteran. Until this time, research on testosterone and human behavior was based on very small samples. Now, unexpectedly, sociologists had a large random sample available, which is turning out to hold surprising clues about human behavior.

This sample supports earlier studies showing that men who have higher levels of testosterone tend to be more aggressive and to have more problems as a consequence. These veterans, when they were boys, were more likely to get in trouble with parents and teachers and to become delinquents. As adults, they are more likely to use hard drugs, to get into fights, to end up in lower-status jobs, and to have more sexual partners. With this history, you probably won't find it surprising to learn that they also are less likely to marry. Certainly their low-paying jobs and trouble with authorities make them less appealing candidates for marriage. Those who do marry are less likely to share problems with their wives. They also are more likely to have affairs, to hit their wives, and to get divorced (Dabbs and Morris 1990; Booth and Dabbs 1993).

The Vietnam veterans' study does not leave us solely with biology. Not all men with high testosterone get in trouble with the law, do poorly in school, or mistreat their wives. A chief difference, in fact, is social class. High-testosterone men from higher social classes are less likely to be involved in anti-social behaviors than are high-testosterone men from lower social classes (Dabbs and Morris 1990). *Social* factors (socialization, life goals, self-definitions), then, must also be at work. Uncovering them and discovering how they work in combination with testosterone will be of high sociological interest.

▼ **In Sum** We shall have to await further studies, but what has been published so far is intriguing, indicating that some behavior that we sociologists usually assume to be due entirely to socialization is, in fact, also influenced by biology. The findings are preliminary, but extremely significant. In the years to come, this should prove to be an exciting—and controversial—area of sociological research. One level will be to document differences that are clearly due to biology. The second level, of much greater sociological significance, is, in sociologist Janet Chafetz's (1990:30) phrase, to determine "how 'different' becomes translated into 'unequal.' "

Sociologists stress the social factors that underlie human behavior, the experiences that mold us, funneling us into different directions in life. The study of Vietnam veterans discussed in the text is one indication of how the sociological door is slowly opening to consider also biological factors in human behavior.

Gender Inequality in Global Perspective

Some analysts speculate that in hunting and gathering societies women and men were social equals (Leacock 1981; Hendrix 1994). Apparently horticultural societies also had much less gender discrimination than does our contemporary world (Collins et al. 1993). In these societies, women may have been equal partners with men. They may even have contributed about 60 percent of the group's total food. Yet, after reviewing the historical record, historian and feminist Gerda Lerner (1986) concluded that "there is not a single society known where women-as-a-group have decision-making power over men (as a group)."

Let's take a brief overview of some of this inequality.

Sex Typing of Work

Anthropologist George Murdock (1937), who surveyed 324 premodern societies around the world, found that in all of them activities are **sex typing;** in other words, every society associates activities with one sex or the other. He also found that activities considered "female" in one society may be considered "male" in another. In some groups, for example, taking care of cattle is women's work, while other groups assign this task to men.

Metalworking was the exception, being men's work in all the societies examined. Three other pursuits—making weapons, pursuing sea mammals, and hunting—were almost universally the domain of men. In a few societies, however, women participated in these activities. Although Murdock found no specific work that was universally assigned to women, he did find that making clothing, cooking, carrying water, and grinding grain were almost always female tasks. In a few societies, however, such activities were regarded as men's work.

From Murdock's cross-cultural survey, we can conclude that nothing about biology requires men and women to be assigned different work. Anatomy does not have to equal destiny when it comes to occupations, for as we have seen, pursuits considered feminine in one society may be deemed masculine in another, and vice versa.

Anthropologist George Murdock surveyed 324 traditional societies worldwide. He found that all of them considered some work "men's" and other work "women's." An example of such sex typing of work is shown in this photo of a Quechuan Indian mother and daughter in Cotopaxi Province of Ecuador. The Quechuan Indians consider hoeing "women's work." This photo also illustrates the remarkable power of socialization across generations.

Prestige of Work

You might ask whether this division of labor really illustrates social inequality. Does it perhaps simply represent arbitrary forms of dividing up labor, not gender discrimination?

That could be the case, except for this finding: *Universally, greater prestige is given to male activities—regardless of what those activities are* (Linton 1936; Rosaldo 1974). If taking care of goats is men's work, then the care of goats is considered important and carries high prestige, but if it is women's work, it is considered less important and given less prestige. Or, to take an example closer to home, when delivering babies was "women's work" and done by midwives, it was given low prestige. But when men took over this task, its prestige increased sharply (Ehrenreich and English 1973). In short, it is not the work that provides the prestige, but the sex with which the work is associated.

Other Areas of Global Discrimination

Let's briefly consider four additional areas of global gender discrimination. Later, when we focus on the United States, we shall examine these same areas in greater detail.

Education.   These two figures illustrate how extensively females are discriminated against in education. Approximately one billion adults around the world cannot read; two-thirds are women. About 130 million children are not enrolled in grade school; 70 percent are girls (Ashford 1995). Table 11.1 illustrates this point further.

sex typing: the association of behaviors with one sex or the other

TABLE 11.1

Illiteracy in 15 Least Industrialized Nations, by Gender

Country	Females	Males	Country	Females	Males	Country	Females	Males
Pakistan	79%	53%	Nigeria	60	38	Indonesia	25	12
Bangladesh	78	53	Kenya	41	20	Brazil	19	18
Mali	76	59	Zimbabwe	40	26	Colombia	14	13
India	66	38	China	32	13	Thailand	9	5
Egypt	66	37	Turkey	31	10	Philippines	7	6

Source: UNICEF 1995.

Politics. That women lack equal access to national decision making can be illustrated by this global fact: In no national legislature in the entire world are there as many women as men. The closest women come is Norway, where 40 percent of the legislators are women, but in some countries, such as South Korea, the figure is only 1 percent (Riley 1997). In Kuwait and United Arab Emirates, women can't even vote (Crossette 1995a, b). In most nations, as in the United States, women hold about 10 percent of national legislative seats (Ashford 1995).

> **minority group:** a group that is discriminated against on the basis of its members' physical or cultural characteristics

The Pay Gap. In every nation, women average less pay than men. For manufacturing jobs, U.S. women earn about two-thirds of what men are paid, while in South Korea women make only half of what men earn (Ashford 1995).

Violence Against Women. A global human rights issue is violence against women (Crossman 1995). Perhaps the most infamous historical examples are footbinding in China, *suttee* (burning the living widow with her dead husband's body) in India, and witchburning in Europe. In addition to rape, wife beating, forced prostitution (as was likely the case in our opening vignette), and female infanticide, the most notorious current example is female circumcision, the topic of the Perspectives box on the next page.

Gender Inequality in Theoretical Perspective

Around the world, gender is *the* primary division between people. Each society sets up barriers to provide unequal access to power, property, and prestige on the basis of sex. Consequently, sociologists classify females as a **minority group.** Because females outnumber males, you may think this strange, but since this term refers to people who are discriminated against on the basis of physical or cultural characteristics, this concept applies to females (Hacker 1951). For an overview of gender discrimination in a changing society, see the Perspectives box on page 290.

Violence against women has taken many forms throughout history. One of the most ferocious was suttee, *in which a living widow was cremated with her dead husband. This painting by Aldo Torchio depicts the riot that ensued at Rajadhar, India, in 1851 when the British police tried to prevent a* suttee.

CULTURAL DIVERSITY AROUND THE WORLD

Female Circumcision

Female circumcision is common in 26 African countries and in some parts of Malaysia and Indonesia. This custom, often called *female genital mutilation* (FGM) by Westerners, is also known as *clitoral excision, clitoridectomy, infibulation,* and *labiadectomy,* depending largely on how much of the tissue is removed. In Egypt, 3,600 girls are circumcised each day. Worldwide, between 100 million and 200 million females have been circumcised.

In some cultures only the girl's clitoris is cut off, in others the clitoris and both the labia majora and the labia minora. The Nubia in the Sudan cut away most of the girl's genitalia, then sew together the remaining outer edges with silk or catgut. The girl's legs are bound from ankles to waist for several weeks while scar tissue closes up the vagina almost completely. A small opening the diameter of a matchstick or a pencil is left for the passage of urine and menstrual fluids. In East Africa the vaginal opening is not sutured shut, but the clitoris and both sets of labia are cut off.

Among most groups, the surgery takes place between the ages of 4 and 8. In some cultures it occurs seven to ten days after birth, while in others it is not performed until girls reach adolescence. Often done without anesthesia, the pain is so excruciating that adults must hold the girl down. In urban areas, the operation is sometimes performed by physicians; in rural areas, it usually is performed by a neighborhood woman. To stop the bleeding, the rural Masai of Kenya cleanse the wound with cow urine and smother it in goat fat (Welsh 1995).

Some of the risks are shock, extensive bleeding, infection, infertility, and death. Ongoing complications include vaginal spasms, painful intercourse, and lack of orgasms. The tiny opening makes urination and menstruation difficult. Frequent urinary tract infections result from urine and menstrual flow building up behind the little opening.

When the woman marries, the opening is cut wider to permit sexual intercourse. In some groups, this is the husband's responsibility. Before a woman gives birth, the opening is enlarged further. After birth, the vagina is again sutured shut, a cycle of surgically closing and opening that begins anew with each birth.

Mariama L. Barrie (1996), a poet who now lives in Long Island, New York, and is active in the international campaign to end female genital mutilation, recounts her own circumcision:

I am 10 years old, and though I do not yet know it, the events of this day will forever alter my life. . . . (My granny has taken me to a remote place in the country where I and other girls) are led to a round thatched hut, where we are blindfolded. I feel the women grab me, gag me and lay me down upon a matta. "Be brave," they tell me. "Crying is a disgrace." Suddenly I feel an excruciating pain. My clitoris is sliced off! I try to pull away, but the women hold me. I scream, but no sound comes. Before my silent scream ends, a sharp blade has removed my labia majora and minora. As the women close my wounds with thorns and try to staunch the bleeding with scalding water, I faint from the pain. . . .

At nightfall our relatives leave us. The girls will sleep on a mat in the large hut, our wounds tended by women who are versed in the healing herbs of the forest. . . . Upon my return home, I am presented with a new lappa suit and an offer of marriage. I am now a full-fledged member of my tribe and, at the age of 10, a woman ready to leave home to work in the house of her future mother-in-law.

What are the reasons for this custom? Some groups believe that it reduces female sexual desire, thus making it more likely that a woman will be a virgin until marriage, and, afterward, remain faithful to her husband. Others believe that it enhances female fertility, prevents the clitoris from getting infected, and enhances vaginal cleanliness.

Feminists, who call female circumcision a form of ritual torture to control female sexuality, point out that the societies that practice it are male dominated. Mothers cooperate with the circumcision because in these societies an unmarried woman has virtually no rights, and an uncircumcised woman is considered impure and is not allowed to marry. Grandmothers insist that the custom continue out of concern that their granddaughters marry well.

Some immigrants to the United States have taken their daughters back to the homeland for the operation, while others pooled their money and flew in an excisor who performed the surgery on several girls. In 1997, the United States passed a law that makes arranging or performing female circumcision punishable by up to five years in prison.

For Your Consideration

Do you think that Western nations should try to make other nations stop this custom? Or would this be ethnocentric, the imposition of Western values on other cultures? As one Somali woman said, "The Somali woman doesn't need an alien woman telling her how to treat her private parts." What legitimate basis do you think there is for members of one culture to interfere with another?

Sources: Based on Mahran 1978, 1981; Ebomoyi 1987; Lightfoot-Klein 1989; Merwine 1993; Welsh 1995; Barrie 1996; "Egipto . . ." 1996; Chalkley 1997.

Women in China

Mao, the leader of China's 1949 Communist revolution, is often quoted as saying that women hold up half the sky. By this, he meant that women are as important as men. One of the revolution's goals was to free women from their traditional low status.

Although women never did become the social equals of men, their status under Mao did improve. Today, with China's cautious transition to capitalism, however, the situation of women is deteriorating.

For the first time, factory managers are under pressure to produce a profit. Under the old system, production without profit was the norm: managers were assigned production goals and given the workers to meet those goals. Now the managers say that with maternity leaves and the requirement that they provide child care centers and rooms for nursing mothers, women workers are more expensive than men. Consequently, women have become the last hired and first fired.

Women are also being encouraged to enter "traditional" women's occupations, which are the least skilled and pay less. Being "nurses, nursery school teachers, grade school teachers, and street sweepers is more ap-

propriate for women," says an official with the Beijing Labor Bureau.

The new mentality that has begun to pervade the culture is illustrated by an emphasis on appearance rather than skills. In an adaptation of Western-style advertising, scantily clad women are shown perched on top of sports cars. A new cosmetic surgery industry has sprung up to give Chinese women Western-looking eyes, stenciled eyebrows, and bigger breasts.

Smarting under international criticism, China passed a law that guarantees equality for women in employment, education, housing, and property rights. The flaw? There is no mechanism to enforce the law. It remains a piece of propaganda.

An improvement in women's status is bound to come, for quietly behind the scenes women have formed study groups. Without slogans or drawing public attention, which could be dangerous, a woman's movement is emerging. As in the West, the political struggle must begin with a changed consciousness of one's status.

Sources: Based on Sun 1993; Chen 1995.

What is the origin of discrimination against women? Let's consider a popular theory. It assumes that patriarchy is universal and, accordingly, to explain its origin it looks to universal conditions—biological factors coupled with social factors.

Childbirth and Social Experiences

This theory points to social consequences of the biology of human reproduction (Lerner 1986; Friedl 1990). In early human history, life was short and to reproduce the human group many children had to be born. Because only females get pregnant, carry a child nine months, give birth, and nurse, women were limited in activities for a considerable part of their lives. To survive, an infant needed a nursing mother. With a child at her breast or in her uterus, or one carried on her hip or on her back, women were physically encumbered. Consequently, around the world women assumed tasks associated with the home and child care, while men took over the hunting of large animals and other tasks that required greater speed and absence from the base camp for longer periods of time (Huber 1990).

As a consequence, males became dominant. It was the men who left camp to hunt animals, who made contact with other tribes, who traded with these other groups, and who quarreled and waged war with them. It was also men who made and controlled the instruments of death, the weapons used for hunting and warfare. It was they who accumulated possessions in trade, and gained prestige by triumphantly returning with prisoners of war or with large animals to feed the tribe. In contrast, little prestige was given to the ordinary, routine, taken-for-granted activities of women—who were not seen as risking their lives for the group. Eventually, men took over society. Their weapons, items of trade, and knowledge gained from contact with other groups became sources of power. Women were transformed into second-class citizens, subject to men's decisions.

Evaluating the Theory

Is this theory correct? Remember that the answer lies buried in human history, and there is no way of testing it. Male dominance may be due to some entirely different cause. For example, anthropologist Marvin Harris proposed that because most men are stronger than most women and hand-to-hand combat was necessary in tribal groups, men became the warriors and women the reward to entice them to do battle. Frederick Engels proposed that patriarchy (male dominance of a society) developed with the origin of private property (Lerner 1986). He could not explain why private property should have produced patriarchy, however. Gerda Lerner (1986) suggests that patriarchy may even have had different origins in different places. And as we reviewed earlier in this chapter (pages 283–286), some sociologists argue that biology is the cause.

Whatever its origins, a circular system of thought evolved. Men developed notions of their own inherent superiority—based on the evidence of their dominant position in society. They then consolidated their power, enshrouded many of their activities with secrecy, and constructed elaborate rules and rituals to avoid "contamination" by the females, whom they now openly deemed inferior. Even today, patriarchy is always surrounded with cultural supports to justify male dominance.

As tribal societies developed into larger groups, men, enjoying their power and privileges, maintained their dominance. Long after hunting and hand-to-hand combat ceased to be routine, and even after large numbers of children were no longer needed to reproduce the human group, men held onto their power. Male dominance in contemporary societies, then, is a continuation of a millennia-old pattern whose origin is lost in history.

Foot binding, a form of violence against women, was practiced in China. This photo of a woman in Canton, China, is from the early 1900s. The woman's tiny feet, which made it difficult for her to walk, were a "marker" of status, indicating that her husband was wealthy and did not need her labor.

One theory about the origin of patriarchy is that because of childbirth women assumed tasks associated with home and child care, while men hunted and performed other tasks requiring greater strength, speed, and absence from home.

Gender Inequality in the United States

Rather than some accidental hit-or-miss affair, the institutions of each society work together to maintain the group's particular forms of inequality. Custom, venerated by history, both justifies and maintains arrangements of gender inequality. Although men have resisted sharing their privileged positions with women, change has come.

Fighting Back: The Rise of Feminism

To see how far we have come, it is useful to see where we used to be. In early U.S. society, the second-class status of women was taken for granted. A husband and wife were legally one person—him (Chafetz and Dworkin 1986). Women who worked for wages could not even collect their own paychecks—single women were often required to hand them over to their fathers; married women, to their husbands. Women could not serve on juries, nor could they vote, make legal contracts, or hold property in their own name. These conditions were generally seen as part of the *proper* relations of the sexes. How could times have changed so much that such conditions sound like fiction?

A central lesson of conflict theory is that power yields tremendous privilege; that, like a magnet, it draws to the elite the best resources available. Because men held tenaciously onto their privileges and used social institutions to maintain their position, basic rights for women came only through prolonged and bitter struggle (Offen 1990).

Feminism, the view that biology is not destiny, and, therefore, stratification by gender is wrong and should be resisted, met strong opposition—both by men who had privilege to lose and by many women who accepted their status as morally correct. In the United States, for example, women had to directly confront men, who first denied them the right to speak and then ridiculed them when they persisted in speaking in public. Leaders of the feminist movement, then known as *suffragists*, chained themselves to posts and to the iron grillwork of public buildings—and then went on protesting while the police sawed them loose. When imprisoned, they continued to protest by going on hunger strikes. Threatened by such determination and confrontations, men spat on demonstrators for daring to question their place, slapped their faces, tripped them, pelted them with burning cigar stubs, and hurled obscenities at them (Cowley 1969).

In 1916, feminists founded the National Women's Party. In January 1917, they threw a picket line around the White House. After picketing continuously for six months, the pickets were arrested. Declaring their fines unjust, the women refused to pay them. Hundreds went to prison, including Lucy Burns and Alice Paul, two leaders of the National Women's Party. The extent to which these women had threatened male prerogatives is demonstrated by their treatment in prison.

> Two men brought in Dorothy Day, [the editor of a periodical that espoused women's rights], twisting her arms above her head. Suddenly they lifted her and brought her body down twice over the back of an iron bench. . . . They had been there a few minutes when Mrs. Lewis, all doubled over like a sack of flour, was thrown in. Her head struck the iron bed and she fell to the floor senseless. As for Lucy Burns, they handcuffed her wrists and fastened the handcuffs over head to the cell door. (Cowley 1969)

This "first wave" of the women's movement had a conservative branch that concentrated on winning the vote for women and a radical branch that wanted to reform all the institutions of society (Chafetz and Dworkin 1986). Both groups worked toward winning the right to vote, but after the vote was won in 1920 the movement was left with no unifying goal. The smaller radical group launched a relentless campaign to pass an Equal Rights Amendment (ERA) to the U.S. Constitution, while the dominant conservative group founded the nonpartisan League of Women Voters (Taylor 1997). The movement, however, basically disappeared from public consciousness.

feminism: the philosophy that men and women should be politically, economically, and socially equal, and organized activity on behalf of this principle

The worldwide women's struggle for equal rights has been long and hard. Shown here is a 1919 photo from the "first wave" of the U.S. women's movement. Today's primary focus in this ongoing fight for justice is the workplace.

The "second wave" began in the 1960s. Sociologist Janet Chafetz (1990) points out that up to this time most women thought of work as a temporary activity to fill the time between completing school and getting married. When larger numbers of women began to work, however, they began to compare their working conditions with those of men. This shift in reference group created a different view of working conditions, launching a "second wave" of protest and struggle against gender inequalities. The goals of this second wave are broad—from changing work roles to changing policies on violence against women.

This second wave of the women's movement is also broken into liberal and conservative factions. Although each holds a different picture of what gender equality should look like, they share several goals, including nondiscrimination in job opportunities and pay. Both liberals and conservatives have a radical wing. The radicals on the liberal side call for hostility toward men, while radicals on the conservative side call for a return to traditional family roles. All factions—whether radical or conservative—claim to represent the "real" needs of today's women. It is from these claims and counterclaims that the women's movement will continue to take shape and affect public policy.

Although women enjoy fundamental rights today, gender inequality continues to play a central role in social life. In some instances, it can even be a life-and-death matter, as with the medical situations discussed in the Down-to-Earth Sociology box on the next page. Let's look at gender relations in education and everyday life, and then, in greater detail, at discrimination in the world of work.

Gender Inequality in Education

In education, too, a glimpse of the past sheds light on the present. About a century ago, leading educators claimed that women's wombs dominated their minds. This made higher education a burden on women's frail capacities. Dr. Edward Clarke, of Harvard University's medical faculty, expressed the dominant sentiment this way:

> A girl upon whom Nature, for a limited period and for a definite purpose, imposes so great a physiological task, will not have as much power left for the tasks of school, as the boy of whom Nature requires less at the corresponding epoch. (Andersen 1988)

Because women were so much weaker, Clarke urged them to study only one-third as much as young men—and not to study at all during menstruation.

Down-to-Earth Sociology

Making the Invisible Visible—The Deadly Effects of Sexism

Medical researchers were perplexed. Reports were coming in from all over the country indicating that women, who live longer than men, were twice as likely to die after coronary bypass surgery. Researchers at Cedars-Sinai Medical Center in Los Angeles checked their own hospital's records. They found that of almost 2,300 coronary bypass patients, 4.6 percent of the women died as a result of the surgery, compared with only 2.6 percent of the men.

These findings presented a sociological puzzle. To solve it, medical researchers first turned to an answer based on biology. In coronary bypass surgery, a blood vessel is taken from one part of the body and stitched to a coronary artery on the surface of the heart. Perhaps this operation was more difficult to perform on women because of their smaller coronary arteries. To find out, researchers measured the amount of time that surgeons kept patients on the heart–lung machine while they operated. They were surprised to learn that women spent less time on the machine than men, indicating that the operation was not more difficult to perform on women.

As the researchers probed, a surprising answer unfolded—unintended sexual discrimination. Referring physicians had not taken the chest pains of their women patients as seriously as those of their men patients. Physicians, it turned out, were *ten* times more likely to give men exercise stress tests and radioactive heart scans. They also sent men to surgery on the basis of abnormal stress tests but waited until women showed clear-cut symptoms of coronary heart disease before sending them to surgery. Being referred for surgery after the disease is further along decreases the chances of survival.

Other researchers wondered if the sex of the physician matters when it comes to ordering Pap smears and mammography. They examined the records of 98,000 patients and found that it does make a difference—women physicians are much more likely to order these screening tests.

For Your Consideration

In short, gender bias is so pervasive that it operates beneath our level of awareness and so severe that it can even be a matter of life or death. It is important to note that the doctors are unaware that they are discriminating. They have no intentions to do so. In what ways does gender bias affect your own perceptions and behavior?

Sources: Based on Bishop 1990; Lurie et al. 1993.

Over the years, the situation gradually improved, but discrimination persisted. Through the 1960s, for example, girls were barred from attending shop classes, which were reserved for boys. Instead, they were routed to home economics, considered appropriate for their station in life. Today, women's sports are often underfunded. As a parenthetical note, whenever I attend high school football games, I still see an organized group of girls in short, brightly colored skirts wildly cheering the boys from the sidelines—but no such group of boys leading organized cheers for the girls as they play *their* sports.

The situation has so changed from what it used to be, however, that some measures of education make it look as though discrimination may be directed against males. For example, more women than men are enrolled in U.S. colleges and universities, and women now earn 55 percent of all bachelor's degrees (*Statistical Abstract* 1997:Table 300, 303). As Figure 11.1 shows, women also complete their bachelor's degrees faster than men.

Probing below the surface, however, reveals that degrees follow gender, thus reinforcing male–female distinctions. An extreme at the bachelor's level highlights gender tracking: Men earn 85 percent of bachelor's degrees in the "masculine" field of engineering, while women are awarded 90 percent of bachelor's degrees in the "feminine" field of nursing (*Digest of Education Statistics* 1996:Table 244). Because gender socialization gives men and women different orientations to life, they enter college with gender-linked aspirations. It is this socialization—rather than any presumed innate characteristics—that channels them into different educational paths.

If we follow students into graduate school, we see that with each passing year the proportion of women decreases. Table 11.2 gives us a snapshot of doctoral programs in the sciences. Note how aspirations (enrollment) and accomplishments (doctorates earned) are sex linked. In all but one of these doctoral programs, men outnumber women, and in *all* of them women are less likely to complete the doctorate. It is significant that the four programs women are least likely to complete have come to be considered masculine endeavors.

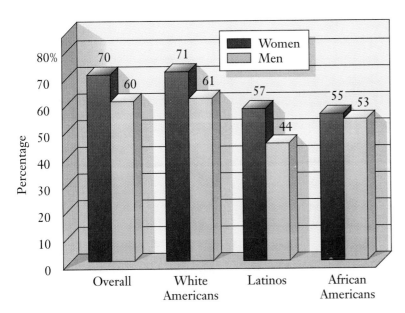

Figure 11.1

Of Those Who Go to College, How Many Receive a Bachelor's Degree within 5 Years?

Source: Statistical Abstract 1997:Table 302.

If we follow those who earn doctoral degrees back into colleges and universities, we find gender stratification in both prestige and income. Throughout the United States, women are less likely to be full professors, the highest, most prestigious rank. It is important also to note that full professors are paid more than the lower ranks (instructor, assistant professor, and associate professor). To see the extent of the stratification, we can note that even when women are full professors, they average less pay than men who are full professors (DePalma 1993).

Some encouraging changes are taking place in higher education. Although we are still a long way from equality, as Figure 11.2 on the next page illustrates, the proportion of professional degrees earned by women has increased sharply. The greatest change is in dentistry: In 1970 across the entire United States, only 34 women earned this degree. Today that annual total is almost 1,500 (*Statistical Abstract* 1997:Table 307).

TABLE 11.2

Doctorates in Science, by Sex

Field	Students Enrolled in Doctoral Programs		Doctorates Conferred		Completion Ratio[a] (higher or lower than expected)	
	Women	*Men*	*Women*	*Men*	*Women*	*Men*
Agriculture	35%	65%	22%	78%	−37	+20
Mathematics	33%	67%	22%	78%	−33	+16
Engineering	17%	83%	12%	88%	−29	+6
Computer sciences	24%	76%	19%	81%	−21	+6
Social sciences	47%	53%	38%	62%	−19	+17
Biological sciences	48%	52%	41%	59%	−15	+13
Physical sciences	27%	73%	23%	77%	−15	+5
Psychology	69%	31%	64%	36%	−7	+16

[a]The difference between the proportion enrolled in a program and the proportion granted doctorates divided by the proportion enrolled in the program.

Source: Statistical Abstract 1997:Tables 977, 979.

Figure 11.2

Gender Changes in Professional Degrees

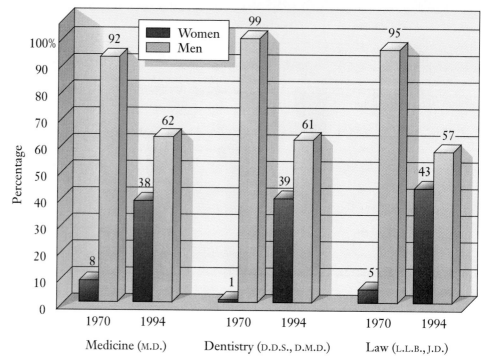

Source: *Statistical Abstract* 1997:Table 307.

Gender Inequality in Everyday Life

Of the many aspects of gender discrimination in everyday life that could be examined, we have space to look only at two: the general devaluation of femininity in U.S. society and male dominance of conversation.

General Devaluation of Things Feminine

> Leaning against the water cooler, two men—both minor executives—are nursing their cups of coffee, discussing last Sunday's Giants game, postponing for as long as possible the moment when work must finally be faced.
>
> A vice president walks by and hears them talking about sports. Does he stop and send them back to their desks? Does he frown? Probably not. Being a man, he is far more likely to pause and join in the conversation, anxious to prove that he, too, is "one of the boys," feigning an interest in football that he may very well not share at all. These men—all men in the office—are his troops, his comrades-in-arms.
>
> Now, let's assume that two women are standing by the water cooler discussing whatever you please: women's liberation, clothes, work, any subject—except football, of course. The vice president walks by, sees them, and moves down the hall in a fury, cursing and wondering whether it is worth the trouble to complain—but to whom?—about all those bitches standing around gabbing when they should be working. "Don't they know," he will ask, in the words of a million men, "that this is an office?" (Korda 1973:20–21)

As indicated in this scenario, women's capacities, interests, attitudes, and contributions are not taken as seriously as those of men. Masculinity is valued more highly, for it represents success and strength; while femininity is devalued, for it is perceived as failure and weakness (Schur 1984).

During World War II, sociologist Samuel Stouffer noted the general devaluation of things feminine. In his classic study of combat soldiers, *The American Soldier*, Stouffer reported that officers used feminine terms as insults to motivate soldiers (1949). To show less-than-expected courage or endurance was to risk the charge of not being a man. An officer might say, "Whatsa matter, Bud—got lace on your drawers?" A generation later, to prepare soldiers to fight in Vietnam accusations of femininity were still used as motivating insults. Drill sergeants would mock their troops by saying, "Can't hack it, little girls?" (Eisenhart 1975). In the Marines, the worst insult to male recruits is to compare their performance to a woman's (Gilham 1989).

The same phenomenon occurs in sports. Sociologist Douglas Foley (1997) notes that football coaches insult boys who don't play well by saying that they are "wearing skirts," and sociologists Jean Stockard and Miriam Johnson (1980), who observed boys playing basketball, heard boys who missed a basket called a "woman." This pattern continues in professional sports, and hockey players who are not rough enough on the ice are called "girls" (Gallmeier 1988:227).

This name-calling is sociologically significant. As Stockard and Johnson (1980:12) point out, such insults embody a generalized devaluation of females in U.S. society. As they noted, "There is no comparable phenomenon among women, for young girls do not insult each other by calling each other 'man.' "

Gender Inequality in Conversation.   As you may have noticed in your own life, gender inequality also shows up in everyday talk. Because men are more likely to interrupt a conversation and to control changes in topics, sociologists have noted that talk between a man and a woman is often more like talk between an employer and an employee than between social equals (Hall 1984; West and Garcia 1988; Smith-Lovin and Brody 1989; Tannen 1990). Even in college, men interrupt their instructors more often than do women, especially if the instructor is a woman (Brooks 1982). In short, conversations between men and women mirror their relative positions of power in society.

Derogatory terms and conversation represent only the tip of the iceberg, however, for underlying these aspects of everyday life is a structural inequality based on gender that runs throughout society. Let's examine that structural feature in the workplace.

Gender Relations in the Workplace

To examine the work setting is to make visible basic relations between men and women. Let's begin with one of the most remarkable areas of gender inequality at work, the pay gap.

The Pay Gap

Since 1890, the U.S. government has tracked the percentages of men and women in the work force. From Figure 11.3, you can see that in 1890 about one of every five workers was a woman and that with each passing year women have made up a larger proportion of the U.S. labor force. The exception occurred immediately after World War II when

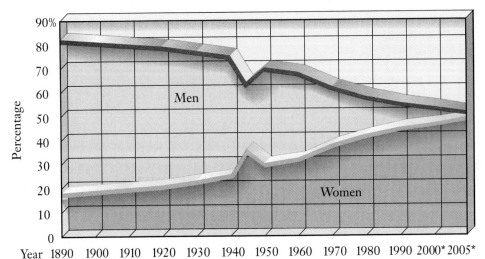

Figure 11.3

Women's and Men's Proportion of the U.S. Labor Force

Note: Pre-1940 figures include women 14 and over: figures for 1940 and after are for women 16 and over.

* Estimated

Sources: 1969 Handbook on Women Workers, 1969:10; *Manpower Report to the President,* 1971:203, 205; Mills and Palumbo, 1980:6, 45; *Statistical Abstract* 1997:Table 620.

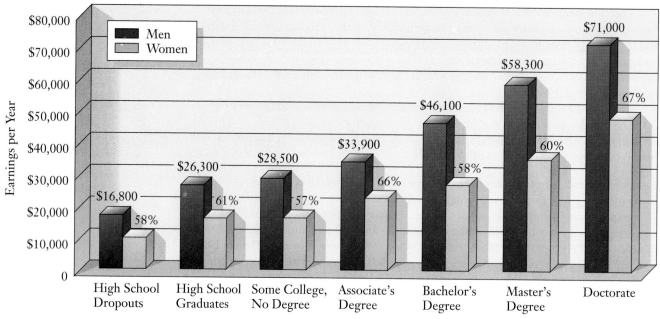

Source: Statistical Abstract 1997:Table 246.

Figure 11.4

What Percentage of Men's Earnings Do Women Earn?: The Gender Pay Gap, by Education

millions of women left factories and offices to return home as full-time wives and mothers. Today, for every ten men workers, there are nine women workers.

The chances are that you are going to be one of these workers. How would you like to earn an extra $800,000 on your job? If this sounds appealing, read on. I'm going to reveal how you can average an extra $20,000 a year between the ages of 25 and 65.

Is this hard to do? All you have to do is be a man (see Figure 11.4). Comparing workers who have bachelor's degrees, this is precisely how much more the *average* man will earn. Hardly any single factor pinpoints gender discrimination better than this total. From Figure 11.4, you also can see that this gender gap in earnings shows up at all levels of education.

Figure 11.5 shows the overall pay gap for year-round, full-time U.S. workers in all fields. You can see that women's wages average only about 66 percent of men's. Until 1985 women's earnings hovered between 58 and 61 percent of men's, so being paid only two-thirds of what men make is actually an improvement. A gender pay gap characterizes all industrialized nations, but only in Japan is the gap larger than in the United States (Blau and Kahn 1992).

If we look at how the pay gap compares by race-ethnicity, we are in for a few surprises. As Figure 11.6 shows, African-American women and Latinas come the closest to earning what men of their groups make. Then come Asian Americans, followed in last place by whites.

This figure is deceptive, however, for it makes it look as if African-American women and Latinas earn more than white women, which they do not. They simply earn a larger proportion of what men in *their* groups earn. Because the men in these groups average less than whites, so do the women. Asian-American women are relatively well off, for they make a higher-than-average percentage of men who also earn more than average. We shall have more to say on this in the next chapter, but if you want to jump ahead, look at Table 12.1 on page 331.

What logic can underlie the gender pay gap? Earlier we saw that college degrees are gender linked, so perhaps this gap is due to career choices. Maybe women tend to choose lower-paying jobs, such as grade school teaching, whereas men are more likely to go into better-paying fields, such as business and engineering. Actually, this is true, and researchers have found that about *half* the pay gap is due to such factors. The balance, however, is due to gender discrimination (Kemp 1990).

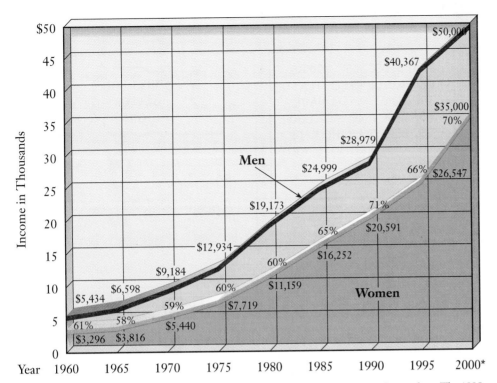

Note: The income jump from 1990 to 1995 is probably due to a statistical procedure. The 1995 source (for 1990 income) uses "median income," while the 1997 source (for 1995 income) merely says "average earnings." How the "average" is computed is not stated. For a review of this distinction, see Table 5.2.

* Indicates projections by the author

Sources: Beeghley 1989:239; Statistical Abstract 1995:Table 739; 1997:Table 734.

Figure 11.5

The Gender Pay Gap Over Time: The Annual Income of Full-Time Workers and the Percentage of the Men's Income Earned by Women

Depending on your sex, then, you are likely either to benefit from gender discrimination—or to be its victim. Because the pay gap will be so important in your own work life, let's follow some college graduates to see how it takes place. Economists Rex Fuller and Richard Schoenberger (1991) examined the starting salaries of the business majors at the University of Wisconsin, of whom 47 percent were women. They found that the women averaged 11 percent ($1,737) lower pay.

You might be able to think of valid reasons for this initial pay gap. For example, the women might have been less qualified. Perhaps their grades were lower. Or maybe they did fewer internships. If so, they would deserve lower salaries. To find out, Fuller and Schoenberger reviewed the students' college records. To their surprise, it turned out that the women had earned *higher* grades and done *more* internships than the men. In other words, if women were equally qualified, they were offered lower salaries—and if they were more highly qualified, they were offered lower salaries—a classic lose–lose situation.

What happened after these graduates were on the job? Did these starting salaries wash out, so that after a few years the men and women earned about the same? To find out, Fuller and Schoenberger checked their salaries five years later. Instead of narrowing, the pay gap had grown even wider. By this time, the women earned 14 percent ($3,615) less than the men.

As a final indication of the extent of the gender pay gap, consider this. I examined the names of the CEOs of the 350 largest U.S. corporations, and *not one of them is a woman*. Your best chance to reach the top is to be named—in this order—John, Robert, James, William, or Charles. Edward, Lawrence, and Richard are also advantageous. Amber, Candace, Leticia, and María, however, apparently draw a severe penalty.

Figure 11.6

The Pay Gap by Race/Ethnicity: Women's Earnings as a Percentage of Men's Earnings

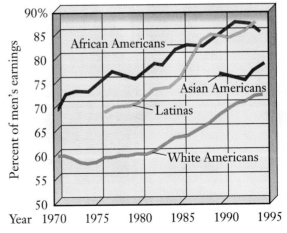

Note: Median annual earnings of full-time, year-round workers.

Source: Modified from Bianchi and Spain 1996:24.

One of the frustrations felt by many women in the labor force is that no matter what they do, they hit a glass ceiling. Another is that to succeed they feel forced to abandon characteristics they feel are essential to their self.

The Glass Ceiling or the Glass Escalator?

The Glass Ceiling.   What keeps women from breaking through the *glass ceiling*, the mostly invisible barrier that keeps women from reaching the executive suite? Researchers have identified a "pipeline" that leads to the top—marketing, sales, and production—positions that directly add to the corporate bottom line (Reich 1995). Stereotyped as better at "support," women often are steered into human resources or public relations. There successful projects are not appreciated the same as those that bring in corporate profits—and bonuses for their managers. Felice Schwartz, founder of Catalyst, an organization that focuses on women's issues in the workplace, put it this way: Men, who dominate the executive suite, stereotype potential leaders as people who look like themselves (Lopez 1992).

Another reason that the glass ceiling is so powerful is that women lack mentors, successful executives who take an interest in them and teach them the ropes. Some men executives fear gossip and sexual harassment charges if they get close to a woman in a subordinate position. Others don't mentor women because of stereotypes of women as weak (Lancaster 1995; Reich 1995). To lack a mentor is no trivial matter, for supposedly all top executives have had a coach or mentor (Lancaster 1995).

The glass ceiling is cracking, however, and more women are reaching the executive suite (Lublin 1996). A look at women above the glass ceiling reveals highly motivated women with a fierce competitive spirit who are willing to give up sleep and recreation for the sake of career advancement. They also learn to play by "men's rules," developing a style that makes men comfortable. In the background of about three-fourths of the women at the top is a supportive husband who shares household duties and adapts his career to the needs of his executive wife.

After Jill Barad took over the Barbie division of Mattel, Inc., sales soared. In 1997, Barad was elected CEO of Mattel, becoming the first woman to take the reins of a "Fortune 500" corporation.

The Glass Escalator.   Sociologist Christine Williams (1995) interviewed men and women who worked as nurses, elementary school teachers, librarians, and social workers. She found that the men in these traditionally women's occupations, instead of bumping into a glass ceiling, had climbed aboard a *glass escalator.* That is, compared with women the men were accelerated into more desirable work assignments, higher-level positions, and larger salaries. The motor that drives the glass escalator is gender, the stereotype that because someone is male he is more capable.

The "Mommy Track"

Wives are more likely than husbands to be the caretakers of the marriage, to nurture it through the hard times. Most wives also take greater responsibility for taking care of the children, for maintaining family ties (such as sending greeting cards), and spend considerably more time doing housework. Consequently, most employed wives face greater role conflict than do their husbands.

To help resolve this conflict, Felice Schwartz (1989) suggested that corporations offer women a choice of two parallel career paths. The "fast track" consists of the high-powered, demanding positions that may require sixty or seventy hours of work per week—regular responsibilities, emergencies, out-of-town meetings, and a briefcase jammed with work at night and on weekends. With such limited time outside of work, family life often suffers. Women can choose this "fast track" if they wish. Or instead they may choose a "mommy track," which would stress both career and family. Less would be expected of a woman on the "mommy track," for her commitment to the firm would be lower and her commitment to her family higher.

That, of course, say critics, is exactly what is wrong with this proposal. A "mommy track" will encourage women to be satisfied with lower aspirations and fewer promotions and confirm men's stereotypes of women executives. Because there is no "daddy track," it also assumes that child rearing is primarily women's work (Starrels 1992). To encourage women to slow up in the race to climb the corporate ladder would perpetuate, or even increase, the executive pay gap. The "mommy track," conclude critics, would keep men in executive power and relegate women to an inferior position in corporate life.

Schwartz replies that what she is really proposing is a "zigzag track" (Shellenbarger 1995b). "In my ideal world," she says, "people, including men, would slow down during a period when their kids were small. Later they would be readmitted to the mainstream. If you choose this intermittent route upward, you would make it to the top more slowly than someone equally able who took the straight vertical route. The goal," she adds, "is to balance family and career."

Critics suggest that a better way to confront the conflict between work and family is for husbands to take greater responsibilities at home and for firms to provide on-site day care, flexible work schedules, and parental leave without loss of benefits (Auerbach 1990; Galinsky and Stein 1990). Others maintain that the choice between family and career is artificial, that there are ample role models of family-oriented, highly successful women from Sandra Day O'Connor and Ruth Bader Ginsberg, Justices of the U.S. Supreme Court, to Ann Fisher, astronaut and physician (Ferguson and Dunphy 1991).

Parenting and work often bring conflict, some of which we shall examine in Chapter 16. For a controversy surrounding motherhood that has been ushered in by technology, see the box on the next page.

Sexual Harassment

Until the 1970s, women considered it a personal matter when they experienced unwanted sexual comments, touches, looks, or pressure to have sex. The term **sexual harassment,** referring to these activities, especially in occupational or school settings, was unknown. Then in 1979, Catharine MacKinnon, an activist lawyer, published a book that forever changed our way of thinking. MacKinnon stressed that such unwanted sexual advances are a *structural* problem; that is, they are built into the social structure. It is not a case of a man here and a man there doing obnoxious things because they are attracted to a woman: Rather, it is a case of men abusing their positions of authority to force unwanted sexual activities on women.

As symbolic interactionists stress, language is dynamic. It not only reflects our experiences in life, but also changes our perceptions of those experiences. Today, because we have this term, we see the same behaviors in a different light from the way our predecessors saw them.

sexual harassment: the abuse of one's position of authority to force unwanted sexual demands on someone

 *Sociology and the New Technology*

Rent-A-Uterus: Gender and Reproductive Technology

Breakthroughs in reproductive technology have led to cultural lag. That is, our technology allows forms of reproduction that have outpaced our norms, our standards of right and wrong. Let's look at some real-life examples:

• *Consider surrogate motherhood:*

Mary Beth Whitehead of New Jersey signed a contract for which she was paid to be artificially inseminated with the semen of Bill Stern, whose wife was ill. During pregnancy, Whitehead became emotionally attached to her developing child and decided to keep the baby.

Stern sued Whitehead to enforce the contract. The controversy, known as the "Baby M case," captivated the nation. Should the contract be enforced, or did a "mother's right" supersede the contract? Stern won, based not on the contract, which was ruled illegal, but on his fathering the baby.

• *Consider artificial insemination for the purpose of abortion:*

Rae Leith loved her father, who was suffering the ravages of Alzheimer disease. She wanted to be inseminated with her father's sperm in order to have an abortion, and then have the brains of the fetus, which would match her father's tissue, transplanted into her father's brain. Her father said no.

• *Consider postmortem ventilation (PMV), in which a brain-dead body is kept alive by artificial means:*

Brain-dead pregnant women have been kept in a ventilated state for several months in order to allow their fetuses to have a better chance to survive. In one case, the man who claimed to be the father of the fetus, requested PMV, but the husband objected. The court ruled that since the woman was dead, the state had the right to make the decision, which it did, ruling in favor of PMV. Seven weeks later, the baby died after a caesarean delivery.

For Your Consideration

What should the relative roles of men and women be in technological conception? In the first case just described, should contracts for surrogate motherhood be legally enforceable—and be placed higher than a woman's right to motherhood? In the second case, should a woman have an absolute right to do whatever she wishes with her uterus—it making no difference whose sperm is used? In the third case, should the state be able to determine what happens to a woman's womb and fetus if she is brain dead? Is this the rightful saving of a child's life, or the state's wrongful control over a woman's womb? Finally, based on this last case, since brain-dead women have no legal rights, could they be used as incubators for the embryos of others—which is totally within our technological capacity?

Sources: Based on Overvold 1988; Rothman 1989; Raymond 1993.

With changes in the work force that we just reviewed, women also have become sexual harassers. One study in 1981 and another in 1992 found that 15 percent of men workers had been sexually harassed (*Merit Systems Protection Board* 1981; Lawlor 1994). Male victims are less likely than female victims to receive a sympathetic ear, for people tend to find their situations humorous, sort of like a boy's dream come true. Like women victims, however, these men also report that they feel powerless and used. Social norms and symbolic perceptions, I assume, will catch up eventually to this changing reality of women abusing power and men as victims.

Like other dynamic terms in our language, this one, too, continues to undergo shifts. For example, as the box on the next page explores, the line between sexual harassment and rape becomes blurred.

 ## Gender and Violence

The high rate of violence in the United States shocks foreigners and frightens many Americans. Only a couple of generations ago, many Americans left their homes and cars unlocked. Today, fearful of carjackings, they even lock their cars while driving, and, fearful of rape and kidnappings, escort their children to school. Lurking behind these fears is gender inequality of violence—that females are most likely to be victims of males, not the other way around. Let's briefly review this almost one-way street in gender violence.

Liberal and Conservative Views on Social Issues

Sexual Harassment and Women in the Military

The news spread like wildfire across the United States. Several male Army sergeants at Aberdeen Proving Ground in Maryland were accused of sexually abusing their female trainees (McIntyre 1997). To become soldiers, female recruits, many in their late teens, had been entrusted to the care of severe, demanding drill sergeants. Nothing new about this, for the Army uses rugged training to socialize its recruits. What was new, however, were widespread accusations of sexual harassment, of using power—including intimidation and threats—to force unwanted sex on unwilling recruits. The accused drill sergeants, who said the sex was consensual, were tried and found guilty of rape. One sergeant, who had pleaded guilty to having consensual sex with 11 trainees (adultery is a crime in the Army), was convicted of raping 6 trainees a total of 18 times and sentenced to 25 years in prison.

Conservatives took an "I told you so," attitude. You can't mix the sexes in dormitories unless you're looking for trouble. Those are red-blooded men in the prime of their life, and the recruits are young, desirable, and in some cases, naive. It is absolutely stupid to have them spend the night together under the same roof. If we are going to prepare women for combat, they need to be trained in separate military camps under the supervision of women. If men are brought in to assist, they must leave at the end of the day or sleep in separate barracks.

Liberals, also shocked by the rapes, took the attitude that the system was fine, but a few sergeants had gone bad. Training men and women together is the only way to assure equality, they insisted. Training must involve all phases of military life. We must instill greater controls over those in charge—expecting a greater sense of responsibility and demanding total accountability. Recruits need to be told to report immediately all violations of touching or even of seductive language.

Then another bombshell hit. After the recruits made their accusations, the Army appointed a blue-ribbon panel to investigate sexual harassment in its ranks. When Sgt. Major Gene McKinney, the highest-ranking of the Army's 410,000 noncommissioned officers, was appointed to this committee, former subordinates accused him of sexual harassment (Shenon 1997). McKinney was relieved of duties and court-martialed. He was found not guilty, except for one charge of obstruction of justice. His accusers, embittered, claimed that the Army had sacrificed them for McKinney.

Liberals and conservatives reiterated their positions. Liberals insisted we continue to train women and men together, but get rid of the bad apples. Conservatives replied that it isn't bad apples, but human nature; people will abuse power, so stop the nonsense of training women and men together.

Violence Against Women

On pages 288–289, we examined violence against women in other cultures. Here, due to space limitations, we can review only briefly the primary features of violence against U.S. women.

Rape. Rape has become so common in the United States that each year almost 1 of every 1,000 females 12 years of age and over is raped. Rapists are almost exclusively young males. Although males aged 15 to 24 make up about 15 percent of the U.S. male population, about 34 percent of those arrested for rape are in this age group (*FBI Uniform Crime Reports* 1994:Table 39, *Statistical Abstract* 1997:Table 16).

Date Rape. What has shocked so many about date rape (also known as *acquaintance rape*) are studies showing that it is not an isolated event here and there. For example, about 21 percent of women taking the introductory psychology courses at Texas A&M University reported that they had been forced to have sexual intercourse. Date rape most commonly occurs not between relative strangers on first dates, but between couples who have known each other about a year (Muehlenhard and Linton 1987). Most date rapes go unreported. Those that are reported are difficult to prosecute, for juries tend to believe that if a woman knows the accused she wasn't "really" raped (Bourque 1989).

Domestic abuse is one of the most common forms of violence. Until recently, it was treated by the police as a private family matter. Shown here are police pulling a woman from her bathroom window, where she had fled from her armed husband, who was threatening to shoot her.

Murder. Table 11.3 summarizes U.S. patterns of murder and gender. Note that although females make up about 51 percent of the U.S. population, they don't even come close to making up 51 percent of the nation's killers. Note also that almost one-fourth of all murder victims are female—and their killers are almost always male.

Violence in the Home. Spouse battering, marital rape, and incest are discussed in Chapter 16, pages 456–458. A particular form of violence against women, genital circumcision, is the focus of the Perspectives box on page 289.

A Feminist Understanding of Gender Patterns in Violence

Feminist sociologists have been especially effective in bringing violence against women to the public's attention. Some see symbolic interactionism, pointing out that to associate strength and virility with violence—as is done in so many areas of U.S. culture—is to produce violence. Others use conflict theory. They argue that as gender relations change, males are losing power, and that some males become violent against females as a way to reassert their declining power and status.

Solutions

There is no magic bullet for this problem, but to be effective any solution must break the connection between violence and masculinity. This would require an educational program that incorporates school, churches, homes, and the media. Given such aspects of U.S. history as gun-slinging heroes of the West, and current messages in the mass media, it is difficult to be optimistic that a change will come soon.

Our next topic, women in politics, however, gives us much more reason for optimism.

The Changing Face of Politics

What do these nations have in common?

- Canada in North America
- Argentina, Bolivia, and Nicaragua in Latin America
- Britain, France, Ireland, and Portugal in western Europe
- The Philippines in Asia
- Israel in the Mideast
- Poland in eastern Europe
- India, Pakistan, and Sri Lanka on the subcontinent

The answer is that all have had a woman president or prime minister. To this list we can add even such bastions of male chauvinism as Haiti, Turkey, and Bangladesh (Harwood and Brooks 1993).

Then why not the United States? Why don't women, who outnumber men, take political control of the nation? Eight million more women than men are of voting age, and more women than men vote in U.S. national elections. As Table 11.4 shows, however, women are greatly outnumbered by men in political office. In spite of the political gains women have made in recent elections, since 1789 about 1,800 men have served in the U.S. Senate, but only 24 women, including the nine current senators. Not until 1992 was the

TABLE 11.3	
Killers and Their Victims	
The Victims	
Male	Female
77%	23%
The Killers	
Male	Female
91%	9%

Source: FBI Uniform Crime Reports 1996: Tables 2.5, 2.6.

first African-American woman (Carol Moseley-Braun) elected to the U.S. Senate (National Women's Political Caucus 1995; *Statistical Abstract* 1995:Table 444).

The reasons for women's underrepresentation? First, women are still underrepresented in law and business, the careers from which most politicians come. Further, most women do not perceive themselves as a class of people who need bloc political action in order to overcome domination. Most women also find the irregular hours needed to run for office incompatible with their role as mothers. Fathers, in contrast, whose ordinary roles are more likely to take them away from home, do not feel this same conflict. Women are also less likely to have a supportive spouse who is willing to play an unassuming background role while providing solace, encouragement, child care, and voter appeal. Finally, preferring to hold tightly onto their positions of power, men have been reluctant to incorporate women into centers of decision making or to present them as viable candidates.

These factors are changing, however, and we can expect more women to seek and gain political office. As we saw in Figure 11.2 (on page 296), more women are going into law, where they are doing more traveling and making statewide and national contacts. The same is true for business. Increasingly, child care is seen as a mutual responsibility of both mother and father. And in some areas, such as my own political district, party heads are searching for qualified candidates (read "people with voter appeal and without skeletons in their closets"), without regard to sex. The primary concern in at least some areas today is not gender, but whether a candidate can win. This generation, then, is likely to mark a fundamental change in women's political participation, and it appears only a matter of time until a woman occupies the Oval Office.

TABLE 11.4

U.S. Women in Political Office, 1995–1996

	Percentage and Number Held by Women	
	Percentage	Number
National Office		
U.S. Senate	9%	9
U.S. House of Representatives	11%	47
State Office		
Governors	4%	2
Attorneys general	22%	11
Secretaries of state	28%	14
Treasurers	32%	16
State auditors	8%	4
State legislators	21%	1,539
Local Office		
Mayors[a]	18%	177

Note: Does not include women elected to the judiciary, appointed to state cabinet-level positions, elected to executive posts by the legislature, or members of a university board of trustees.

[a]Of cities with a population over 30,000.

Source: National Women's Political Caucus 1995, *Statistical Abstract* 1997:Tables 448, 453, 457.

Glimpsing the Future—with Hope

Playing a fuller role in the decision-making processes of our social institutions, women are breaking the stereotypes and role models that lock males into exclusively male activities and push females into roles considered feminine. As structural barriers fall and more activities become degenderized, both males and females will be free to pursue activities more compatible with their abilities and desires as *individuals*.

As sociologists Janet Chafetz (1974), Janet Giele (1978), and Judith Lorber (1994) have pointed out, the ultimate possibility is a new conception of the human personality. At present structural obstacles, accompanied by supporting socialization and stereotypes, cast most males and females into fairly rigid molds along the lines that culture dictates. To overcome these obstacles and abandon traditional stereotypes is to give males and females new perceptions of themselves and one another. Both females and males will then be free to feel and to express needs and emotions that present social arrangements deny them. Females are likely to perceive themselves as more in control of their environment and to explore this aspect of the human personality. Males are likely to feel and to express more emotional sensitivity—to be warmer, more affectionate and tender, and to give greater expression to anxieties and stresses that their gender now forces them to suppress. In the future we may discover that such "greater wholeness" of males and females entails many other dimensions of the human personality.

As they develop a new consciousness of themselves and of their own potential, relationships between women and men will change. Certainly distinctions between the sexes will not disappear. There is no reason, however, for biological differences to be translated into social inequalities. The reasonable goal is appreciation of sexual differences coupled with equality of opportunity—which may well lead to a transformed society (Gillman 1911; Offen 1990). If so, as sociologist Alison Jaggar (1990) observed, gender equality can become less a goal than a background condition for living in society.

Summary and Review

Issues of Sex and Gender

What is gender stratification?

The term **gender stratification** refers to unequal access to power, prestige, and property on the basis of sex. Each society establishes a structure that, on the basis of sex and gender, opens and closes access to the group's privileges. Pp. 282–283.

How do sex and gender differ?

Sex refers to biological distinctions between males and females. It consists of both primary and secondary sex characteristics. **Gender,** in contrast, is what a society considers proper behaviors and attitudes for its male and female members. Sex physically distinguishes males from females; gender defines what is "masculine" and "feminine." P. 283.

Why do the behaviors of males and females differ?

In the "nature versus nurture" debate—whether differences between the behaviors of males and females are caused by inherited (biological) or learned (cultural) characteristics—almost all sociologists take the side of nurture. In recent years, however, the door to biology has opened somewhat. Pp. 283–286.

Gender Inequality in Global Perspective

Is gender stratification universal?

George Murdock surveyed information on premodern societies and found not only that all of them have sex-linked activities, but also that all of them give greater prestige to male activities. Patriarchy, or male dominance, does appear to be universal. Besides work, other areas of discrimination include education, politics, and violence. Pp. 287–288.

Gender Inequalities in Theoretical Perspective

How did females become a minority group?

The main theory that attempts to explain how females became a minority group in their own societies focuses on the

physical limitations imposed by childbirth. The origins of this discrimination, however, are lost in history, and no one knows for sure how this discrimination began. Pp. 288–292.

Gender Inequality in the United States

Is the feminist movement new?

In what is called the "first wave," feminists made political demands for change in the early 1900s—and were met with much hostility, and even violence. The "second wave" began in the 1960s and continues today. Pp. 292–293.

What forms does gender stratification in education take?

Although more women than men now attend college, each tends to select "feminine" or "masculine" fields. In addition, men outnumber women in all but two scientific fields. Change is indicated by the growing numbers of women in such fields as law and medicine. Pp. 293–296.

Is there gender inequality in everyday life?

Two indications of gender inequality in everyday life are the general devaluation of femininity and the male dominance of conversation. Pp. 296–297.

Gender Relations in the Workplace

What gender inequality is there in the workplace?

Over the last century, women have made up an increasing proportion of the work force. Nonetheless, the gender gap in pay characterizes all occupations. For college graduates, the lifetime pay gap runs about $800,000 in favor of men. **Sexual harassment** also continues to be a reality of the workplace. Pp. 297–307.

Gender and Violence

What forms does violence against women take?

The victims of battering, rape, incest, and murder overwhelmingly are females. Female circumcision is a special case of violence against females. Conflict theorists point out that men use violence to maintain their power. Pp. 302–304.

The Changing Face of Politics

What is the trend in gender inequality in politics?

A strict division of gender roles—women as child care providers and housekeepers, men as workers outside the home—has traditionally kept women out of politics. Although women continue to be underrepresented in U.S. politics, the trend toward greater political equality is firmly in place. Pp. 304–305.

Glimpsing the Future—with Hope

What progress has been made in reducing gender inequality?

In the United States, women are playing a fuller role in the decision-making processes of our social institutions. Men, too, are reexamining their traditional roles. The ultimate possibility of gender equality is a new conception of the human personality, one that allows both males and females to pursue their individual interests unfettered by gender. Pp. 305–306.

Where can I read more on this topic?

Suggested readings for this chapter are listed on page 663.

 Sociology and the Internet

All URLs listed are current as of the printing of this book. URLs are often changed. Please check our Website http://www.abacon.com/henslin for updates.

1. You have read in your text about the increasingly recognized problem of sexual harassment, as well as about its changing legal definitions. One place this problem is being recognized and addressed—if controversially—is on college campuses. It is highly probable that your school has a formal policy on sexual harassment. Get a copy of the policy. Then go to the Lycos search engine on the Internet *http://www.lycos.com* and enter the search words "sexual harassment" "university policy statements." Go to several of them and either save or print them. Compare the statements with each other and with that of your own school. Write a paper on what they have in common and how they differ. Indicate anything that you think should be added to or removed from your college's policy.

2. As you learned in this chapter's section, "The Changing Face of Politics," a number of countries have had women presidents or prime ministers. The United States is not one of them. In this project you will have the chance to ask U.S. senators about this issue.

Access the Internet home page of the United States Congress *www.senate.gov* Select "Senators," then select "Directory of Senators (by Name)." Select each name that seems to be female, and jot them down. Then choose one from your list and go back to her site. First make sure she offers an e-mail address (usually at the bottom of the page). If she has an address, read her speeches, policy statements, addresses, and whatever else she offers that reflects her political position.

Compose a letter reflecting what you have learned (if anything) about the senator's position on the status of women in our society, and ask for details about a particular point. At the end of your message, ask her whether we should and will have a woman president. Include your postal mailing address, since she likely will acknowledge by e-mail and reply to your message by land mail.

3. A global human rights issue is violence against women. One current form of violence against women is Female Genital Mutilation. After reading the Perspectives box on page 289 of your text, examine the following links:

http://www.hollyfeld.org/fgm/index.html
http://cpmcnet.columbia.edu/news/chronicle/phmg0026.html
http://www.tggh.net/forward/
http://www.religioustolerance.org/fem_cira.htm

What is the difference between FGM and female circumcision? Where is FGM practiced? Why is it currently being practiced? What are the arguments against FGM? What are some of the arguments in support of such an activity?

4. Many people have talked about the sexist nature of the English language. Some have linked sexist language to the perpetuation of gender stereotypes (especially in the workforce). Examine the following links which suggest guidelines for eliminating sexist language and replacing it with non-sexist language:

http://www.macarthur.uws.edu.au/HR/policies/nonsexis.htm
http://www.stetson.edu/~history/nongenderlang.html
http://www.lumina.net/OLD/gfp/

What are Gender-Free Pronouns and why is this an issue in the United States? What are some of the arguments in support of GFP? What are some of the arguments against GFP? What are some of the effects of sexist language? How is sexist language associated with gender inequality in our society?

Jacob Lawrence, Revolt On the Amistad, 1989

C H A P T E R

12

Inequalities of Race and Ethnicity

*M*Y BROTHER-IN-LAW WAS A RELIGIOUS MAN,* " said Edmond. *"When the militia came for him, he asked if he could pray first. They let him pray. After his prayers, he said he didn't want his family dismembered. They said he could throw his children down the latrine holes instead. He did. Then the militia threw him and my sister on top."*

Shining a flashlight into the 40-foot-deep hole, Edmond said, "Look. You can still see the bones."

Between 800,000 and 1 million Rwandans died in the slaughter. Although the killings were low-tech—most were done with machete—it took just 100 days in the summer of 1994 to complete the state-sanctioned massacres (Gourevitch 1995).

Rwanda has two major ethnic groups. The Hutus outnumber the Tutsis 6 to 1. Hutus are stocky and round-faced, dark-skinned, flat-nosed, and thick-lipped. The Tutsis are lankier and longer-faced, lighter-skinned, narrow-nosed, and thin-lipped. But the two groups, who speak the same language, have intermarried for so long that they have difficulty telling Hutu from Tutsi. National identity cards, originally issued by the Belgians when Rwanda was its colony, are one sure way of knowing who is who.

During the genocide, a Tutsi card was a passport to death.

The Hutus, who controlled the government, called on all Hutus to kill all Tutsis. It was a national duty, said the Hutu leaders. Obediently, neighbors hacked neighbors to death in their homes. Colleagues hacked colleagues to death at work. Even teachers killed their students.

Opening stadiums and churches, local officials offered refuge to Tutsis. There the largest massacres occurred, executions supervised by these same local officials.

While radio announcers urged their listeners to disembowel pregnant women, the government fortified armed men with alcohol and bused them from massacre to massacre.

Nkongoli, a Tutsi who is now the vice-president of the National Assembly, says, "One expected to die. Not by machete, one hoped, but with a bullet. If you were willing to pay for it, you could ask for a bullet. Death was more or less normal, a resignation. You lose the will to fight" (Gourevitch 1995).

*A*t the end of World War II, the world was aghast at the revelations of the Nazi slaughter of Jews, Slavs, gypsies, and homosexuals. Dark images of gas ovens and emaciated bodies stacked like cordwood haunted the world's nations. At Nuremberg, the Allies, flush with victory, put the top Nazis on trial, exposing their heinous deeds to a shocked world. Their public executions, everyone assumed, marked the end of genocide, a shameful aberration of history.

Never again could such a thing happen was the general consensus. Yet mass slaughters did occur. By far, the worst was the Khmer Rouge's killing spree in the 1970s, leaving 2 or 3 million Cambodians dead (Markusen 1995). But this was purely political killing, the ruthless regime and its victims of the same race and ethnicity.

Then in the early 1990s alarming reports of "ethnic cleansing"—merely a new term for an old act—seeped out of the former Yugoslavia (by now Bosnia, Croatia, and Herzegovena). Although the number of the Serbs' victims pale in comparison with those of Rwanda, their **genocide**—the attempt to annihilate a people because of their presumed race or ethnicity—grew out of the same impulse of hatred. Although the killings lacked swastika and goose-stepping, and machetes replaced poison gas and ovens, the goal was the same.

There were, of course, other reasons for the slaughter. There always are. The Hutus felt threatened by a Tutsi rebel group, and twenty years earlier the Tutsis had killed 100,000 Hutus. The particulars matter little, however. What is significant for our purposes is that it happened, even after the world vowed "Never Again" in 1945.

genocide: the systematic annihilation or attempted annihilation of a people based on their presumed race or ethnicity

This Tutsi girl, who is carrying water to her family, survived the gruesome events described in the chapter's opening vignette. She fled to this refugee camp, where Hutus then slaughtered about 1,000 more Tutsi. The girl is walking past corpses that have been prepared for mass burial.

Laying the Sociological Foundation

Seldom do race and ethnic relations drop to such a brutal low as they did in Nazi Germany and Rwanda, but in our own society newspaper headlines and television evening news keep race relations constantly before us. Sociological findings on this topic, then, can contribute greatly to our better understanding of this aspect of social life. To begin, let us consider to what extent race itself is a myth.

Race: Myth and Reality

With its almost 6 billion people, the world offers a fascinating variety of human shapes and colors. People see one another as black, white, red, yellow, and brown. Eyes come in various shades of blue, brown, and green. Thick and thin lips. Straight hair, curly hair, kinky hair, black, white, and red hair—and, of course, all hues of brown.

As humans spread throughout the world, their adaptations to diverse climate and other living conditions resulted in this profusion of complexions, colors, and shapes. Genetic mutations added distinct characteristics to the peoples of the globe. In this sense the concept of **race,** a group with inherited physical characteristics that distinguish it from another group, is a reality. Humans do, indeed, come in a variety of colors and shapes.

Common Sense Versus Sociology. At the beginning of this text (pages 8–10), I mentioned that common sense and sociology often conflict. This is especially so when it comes to race. According to common sense, our racial classifications represent biological differences between people. Sociologists, however, stress that what we call races are *social* classifications, not biological categories.

Sociologists point out that *our "race" depends more on the society in which we live than on our biological characteristics.* The racial categories common in the United States, for example, constitute merely one of *numerous* ways that people around the world classify physical appearances. Although groups around the world use different categories, each group assumes that its categories are natural, merely a response to visible biology.

To better understand this essential sociological point—that race is more social than it is biological—consider this: In the United States, children born to the same parents are all of the same race. "What could be more natural?" Americans assume. But in Brazil, children born to the same parents may be of different races—if their appearances differ. "What could be more natural?" assume Brazilians.

race: inherited physical characteristics that distinguish one group from another

Or consider how Americans classify as "black" a child born to a "black" mother and a "white" father. Wouldn't it be equally as logical to classify the child as "white"? Similarly, if a child's grandmother is "black," but all her other ancestors are "white," the child is often considered "black," not "white." Yet she has much more "white blood" than "black blood." Why, then, is she considered "black"? Certainly not because of biology. Rather, such thinking is a legacy of slavery when white masters tried to preserve the "purity" of their "race" by classifying anyone with a "drop of black blood" as "not white."

This sounds ridiculous, but *even a plane trip can change a person's race.* In the city of Salvador in Brazil, people classify one another by color of skin and eyes, breadth of nose and lips, and color and curliness of hair. They use at least seven terms for what we call white and black. Consider again a U.S. child who has "white" and "black" parents. If she flies to Brazil, no longer is she "black," but she now belongs to one of their several "whiter" categories (Fish 1995).

Has her "race" actually changed? Yes, it has. Our common sense revolts at this, I know. We want to argue that because her biological characteristics remain unchanged, her race remains unchanged. This is because we think of race as biological, when it really is social. Simply put, what we "are" depends on *where* we are.

But what about the biology? The biological differences are real, regardless of how we categorize them, aren't they? It is true that we humans have numerous physical differences. But if biology is the main element, biologists, of all people, should agree on the numbers and characteristics of human races.

But they do not. Human physical differences are so numerous that biologists cannot even agree on how *many* races there are, much less their characteristics. Biologists—and anthropologists, too—have drawn up many lists, each containing a different number of "races." Even trying to classify large groupings of people on the basis of blood type and gene frequencies does not clarify "race." Ashley Montagu (1964), a physical anthropologist, pointed out that some scientists have classified humans into only two races while others have identified as many as two thousand. Montagu (1960) himself classified humans into forty racial groups.

▼ **In Sum** Race, then, lies in the eye of the beholder. Humans show such a mixture of physical characteristics—in skin color, hair texture, nose shape, head shape, eye color, and so on—that there is no inevitable, much less universal, way to classify our many biological differences. Instead of falling into distinct types clearly separate from one another, human characteristics flow endlessly together. As with Tiger Woods (discussed in the Cultural Diversity box), these minute gradations make arbitrary any attempt to draw firm lines. Because racial classifications are arbitrary, the categories we use change over time. In this sense, then, race is a myth.

Racial Superiority. The myth of race, however, remains a powerful force in social life. From their basic ethnocentrism, people are inclined to think that their "race" is superior to others. Regardless of the logical arguments I have just recounted, the idea of racial superiority haunts humanity.

Adolf Hitler believed that a super-race, the Aryan, was responsible for the cultural achievements of Europe. These tall, fair-skinned blonds, a supposed "master race," possessed the genetic stuff that made them inherently superior. (Never mind that Hitler was not a blond!) Consequently, the Aryans were destined to establish a higher culture and institute a new world order. This destiny required them to avoid the "racial contamination" that would come from breeding with inferior races. It also meant to isolate or destroy races that might endanger Aryan culture.

Even many scientists of the time (not only in Germany but also throughout Europe and the United States) espoused the idea of racial superiority. Not surprisingly, they considered themselves members of the supposedly superior race.

The Power of the Myth. The idea of racial superiority continues its powerful journey even today. As one of the most significant elements of U.S. culture, it makes an impact on our everyday lives. That race is an arbitrary classification makes little difference

Figure 12.1

Blurring the Color Lines: Trends in U.S. Interracial Marriages

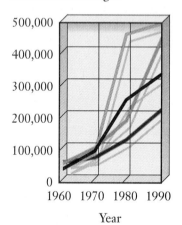

- ▬▬ Native American/White
- ▬▬ Asian American/White
- ▬▬ African American/White
- ▬▬ Other/Other*

Note: These totals are cumulative. They represent total existing marriages in each catagory, not the number performed in each year

* The other/other category includes Asian American/African American, Native American/African American, and Asian American/Native American marriages, as well as marriages between others who identify themselves differently from these categories.

Source: Hogan 1994:Tables 1,2.

Perspectives

CULTURAL DIVERSITY IN THE UNITED STATES

Tiger Woods and the Emerging Multiracial Identity: Mapping New Ethnic Terrain

Tiger Woods, who burst upon the golfing scene in 1997, calls himself Cablinasian (Leland and Beals 1997). Woods invented this term as a boy to try to explain to himself just who he was—a combination of Caucasian, Black, Indian, and Asian. Woods wants to embrace both sides of his family. To be known by a racial identity that applies to just one of his parents is to deny the other parent.

Like many of us, Tiger Woods's racial/ethnic heritage is difficult to specify. Some, who like to count things mathematically, put Woods at one-quarter Thai, one-quarter Chinese, one quarter white, an eighth Native American, and an eighth African American. From this chapter, you know how ridiculous such computations are, but the sociological question is why many consider Tiger Woods an African American. The U.S. racial scene is indeed complex, but a good part of the reason is simply that this is what the media chose. "Everyone has to fit somewhere" seems to be our attitude. If they don't, we grow uncomfortable. And for Tiger Woods, the media chose African American.

To see what is happening, look at Figure 12.1 on the previous page. As the "color line" breaks down, to what group do the children of such marriages belong? At several campuses, students have begun Interracial Students Organizations. Harvard even has two, one just for students who have one African-American parent (Leland and Beals 1997).

Our ordinary classifications are bursting at the seams as we march into unfamiliar ethnic terrain. Kwame Anthony Appiah, of Harvard's Philosophy and Afro-American Stud-

Tiger Woods, after hitting a hole-in-one on the fourteenth hole of the Greater Milwaukee Open.

ies Departments, says, "My mother is English; my father is Ghanaian. My sisters are married to a Nigerian and a Norwegian. I have nephews who range from blond-haired kids to very black kids. They are all first cousins. Now according to the American scheme of things, they're all black—even the guy with blond hair who skis in Oslo" (Wright 1994).

Until recently, in the U.S. census, taken every ten years, we could choose from a list that offered only Caucasian, Negro, Indian, and Oriental. Everyone was carefully sliced and diced and packed into one of these restrictive categories. In recent years the list expanded somewhat, and the year 2000 census will offer American Indian or Alaska Native, Asian, Black or African American, Native Hawaiaan or Other Pacific Islander, and White. In addition, people will be able to declare that they are "Hispanic or Latino" or "Not Hispanic or Latino." These categories, of course, hardly do justice to our complex, changing reality.

So, shall we change the census list? If so, how about Cablinasian?

This term certainly makes as much sense as the categories we currently use.

For Your Consideration

Just why do we count people by "race" anyway? Why not eliminate race from the U.S. census? (Race became a factor in the census during slavery because five blacks were counted the same as three whites to determine how many representatives a state could send to Congress!) Why is race so important to some people? Perhaps you can use the materials in this chapter to answer these questions.

to ways of common thinking. "I know what I see, and you can't tell me any different" seems to be the common response. "I know what *they* are like. *They* are (fill in common responses you hear)." For these people, this becomes reality.

As noted in Chapter 4, sociologist W. I. Thomas observed that "if people define situations as real, they are real in their consequences." That even experts can't decide how people should be biologically classified into races is not what counts. What makes a difference for social life is what people *believe,* for *people act on beliefs, not facts.* As a result, the ideas of race that are so firmly embedded in our culture—not scientific fact—influence attitudes and behavior. As you read this chapter, perhaps you will examine some of the racial ideas that you learned as you were socialized in your culture.

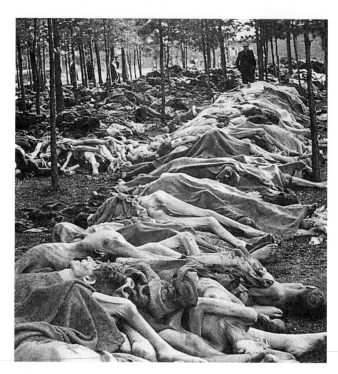

Fanning hatred for Jews—who served as scapegoats for Germany's problems—and preaching the superiority of the supposedly racially pure Aryans, Adolf Hitler put his ideas of race into practice. The result was the Holocaust, the systematic slaughter of Jews and others deemed racially inferior. In the photo on the left, Hitler is addressing a group called Hitler Youth, a sort of Boy Scouts organization dedicated to serving Hitler and his ideas. The photo on the right shows the sight that greeted British troops when they entered the concentration camp in Bergen, Germany—60,000 people dying of starvation and diseases amidst piles of bodies awaiting burial.

Ethnic Groups

Whereas people use the term *race* to refer to supposed biological characteristics that distinguish one people from another, **ethnicity** and **ethnic** apply to cultural characteristics. Derived from the Greek *ethnos*, meaning "people" or "nation," these terms refer to people who identify with one another on the basis of common ancestry and cultural heritage. Their sense of belonging may center on nation of origin, distinctive foods, dress, family names and relationships, language, music, religion, and other customs. The Down-to-Earth Sociology box on the next page indicates how strong ethnic identity can be.

People often confuse the terms *race* and *ethnic group*. For example, many people consider the Jews a race, including many Jews. Jews, however, are more properly considered an ethnic group, for it is their cultural characteristics, especially religion, that bind them together. Wherever Jews have lived in the world, they have intermarried. Consequently, Jews in China may look mongoloid, while some Swedish Jews are blue-eyed blonds. This matter is strikingly illustrated in the photo on the next page. Ethiopian Jews look so different from European Jews that when they immigrated to Israel many European Jews felt that they could not *really* be Jews.

ethnic (and **ethnicity**): having distinctive cultural characteristics

minority group: people who are singled out for unequal treatment, and who regard themselves as objects of collective discrimination

Minority Groups and Dominant Groups

Sociologist Louis Wirth (1945) defined a **minority group** as people who are singled out for unequal treatment *and* who regard themselves as objects of collective discrimination. Either physical (racial) or cultural (ethnic) differences can serve as the basis of the unequal treatment. Wirth added that the discrimination excludes minorities from full participation in the life of their society.

CULTURAL DIVERSITY AROUND THE WORLD

No One Ever Tried to Kill Me Before:
Ethnic Identity and the Perils of Global Travel

For several reasons, Barcelona is one of my least favorite cities. Within five minutes of arriving on the Ramblas, one of the city's more colorful areas, my 9-year-old son's backpack was stolen. I chased the thief into the subway station, but quickly lost him in a maze of tunnels. A few minutes later, a second thief, while talking to me and looking me straight in the eye, tried to undo the zipper of my backpack.

A couple of days later, my wife, son, and I visited a cafeteria-style restaurant. An attractive display was filled with delectable foods, and, trying to be friendly and to show my appreciation of the culture, I haltingly said in broken Spanish that this was really good Spanish food and what a pleasure it was to be in Spain. Instead of getting the usual broad smile that such remarks bring in a foreign country, a scowl spread over the waiter's face, and he mumbled something to the other waiter. When I had seconds, I found a fairly large piece of glass in my food.

Ethnicity—self-identity often filled with an emotional history of hurts—is one of the most powerful concepts in social life. Without meaning to, I had offended this man's sense of ethnic identity. Unknown to me, the people in this part of northern Spain do not think of themselves as Spaniards. In fact, they detest Spaniards and everything Spanish. They identify themselves as Catalans, prefer to speak Catalonian, and only under protest remain part of Spain. During the Spanish civil war of the 1930s, at a high cost of life, Franco vanquished the rebels in this area of Spain.

Later, in the Prado museum in Madrid, when I saw Picasso's mural, *Guernica*, which depicts Franco's bombing of a defenseless town, I gained some idea of why the waiter feels as he does. This painting also helped me understand why, after a parade on the Ramblas on Spain's national day (the equivalent of our 4th of July), a group of masked men went down the street plucking the Spanish flags from their standards. They threw the flags on the ground, where hundreds of cheering followers stomped on them.

This insight doesn't change my opinion about Barcelona, however, although I do hope that a future visit will modify my experiences. And I still think the waiter was a _____, a word that I think is better left out of this text.

Surprisingly, the term *minority group* does not necessarily refer to a *numerical* minority. For example, before India's independence in 1947, a handful of British colonial rulers discriminated against millions of Indians. Similarly, when South Africa practiced apartheid, a small group of Dutch discriminated against the black majority. And all over

Because ideas of race and ethnicity are such a significant part of society, all of us are classified according to those ideas. This photo illustrates the difficulty such assumptions posed for Israel. The Ethiopians, shown here as they arrived in Israel, although claiming to be Jews, looked so different from other Jews that it took several years for Israeli authorities to acknowledge this group's "true Jewishness."

the world, females are a minority group. Accordingly, sociologists refer to those who do the discriminating not as the *majority*, but, rather, as the **dominant group**, for they have greater power, privileges, and social status.

The dominant group almost always considers its privileged position to be due to its own innate superiority. Possessing political power and unified by shared physical and cultural traits, the dominant group uses its position to discriminate against those with different—and supposedly inferior—traits.

Emergence of Minority Groups. A group becomes a minority in one of two ways. The *first* is through the expansion of political boundaries. With the exception of females, small tribal societies contain no minority groups. In tribal societies everyone is "related," speaks the same language, practices the same customs, and belongs to the same physical stock. When a group expands its political boundaries, however, it produces minority groups if it incorporates people with different customs, languages, values, and physical characteristics into the same political entity. For example, after defeating Mexico in war, the U.S. government annexed the Southwest. Consequently, the Mexicans living there, who had been the dominant group, were transformed into a minority group, a master status that has significantly influenced their lives ever since. A *second* way in which a group becomes a minority is by migration. This can be voluntary, as with the millions of people who have chosen to move from Mexico to the United States, or involuntary, as with the millions of Africans forcibly transported to the United States. (The way females became a minority group represents a third way, but as reviewed in the previous chapter, no one knows just how this occurred.)

Shared Characteristics. Anthropologists Charles Wagley and Marvin Harris (1958) identified five characteristics shared by minorities worldwide.

1. Membership in a minority group is an ascribed status; that is, it is not voluntary, but comes through birth.
2. The physical or cultural traits that distinguish minorities are held in low esteem by the dominant group.
3. Minorities are unequally treated by the dominant group.
4. Minorities tend to marry within their own group.
5. Minorities tend to feel strong group solidarity (a sense of "we-ness").

These conditions—especially when combined with collective discrimination—tend to create a shared sense of identity among minorities, and, in many instances, even a sense of common destiny (Chandra 1993b).

Prejudice and Discrimination

Prejudice and discrimination are common throughout the world. In Mexico, Hispanic Mexicans discriminate against Native–American Mexicans; in Israel, Ashkenazic Jews, primarily of European descent, discriminate against Sephardic Jews from the Muslim world; and in Japan, the Japanese discriminate against just about anyone who isn't Japanese, especially immigrant Koreans and the descendants of the Eta caste. A stigma still attaches to the Eta, now renamed the Burakumin, who used to do the society's dirty work—working with dead animals (stripping the hides and tanning the leather) and serving as Japan's executioners and prison guards (Mander 1992). In some places the elderly discriminate against the young, in others the young against the elderly. And all around the world men discriminate against women.

As you can see from this list, **discrimination** is an *action*—unfair treatment directed against someone. When the basis of discrimination is race, it is known as **racism,** but discrimination can be based on many characteristics other than race—including age, sex,

dominant group: the group with the most power, greatest privileges, and highest social status

discrimination: an *act* of unfair treatment directed against an individual or a group

racism: prejudice and discrimination on the basis of race

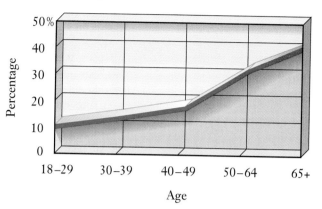

Percentage of white Americans, by education, who believe that different races should live in segregated housing

Percentage of white Americans, by age, who believe that interracial marriage should be banned

Source : Bobo and Kluegel 1 991.

Figure 12.2

A Measure of Preferred Social Distance

height, weight, income, education, marital status, sexual orientation, disease, disability, religion, and politics. Discrimination is often the result of an *attitude* called **prejudice**—a prejudging of some sort, usually in a negative way. Positive prejudice exaggerates the virtues of a group, such as thinking that some group (usually one's own) is more capable than others. Most prejudice, however, is negative, prejudging a group as inferior.

The Extent of Prejudice.   You yourself may not be prejudiced, but sociologists have found that ethnocentrism is so common that each racial or ethnic group views other groups as inferior in at least some ways. In a random sample of adults in the Detroit area, sociologists Maria Krysan and Reynolds Farley (1993) found that whites and African Americans tend to judge Latinos as less intelligent than themselves. Using a probability sample (from which we can generalize), sociologists Lawrence Bobo and James Kluegel (1991) found that older and less educated whites are not as willing to have close, sustained interaction with other groups as are younger and more educated whites. Details of their findings are shown in Figure 12.2. We must await matching studies to test the prejudices of Latinos, Asian Americans, and Native Americans.

Not everyone of the same age and education has the same amount of prejudice, of course. At the University of Alabama, sociologist Donald Muir (1991) measured racial attitudes of white students who belonged to fraternities and sororities and compared them to nonmembers. He asked a variety of questions—from their ideas about dating African Americans to attending classes together. On all measures, fraternity members were more prejudiced than the nonfrats. Research on other campuses supports this finding (Morris 1991). Let's take a closer look at race relations on U.S. campuses.

Thinking Critically About Social Controversy

Self-Segregation: Help or Hindrance for Race Relations on Campus?

▼ Only after a long, bitter, and violent struggle was federal civil rights legislation prohibiting racial segregation on college campuses passed in the 1960s. These laws did not mark the end of self-segregation, however, such as areas of a cafeteria or lounge being used almost exclusively by a particular group. In recent years, minority students have requested separate dor-

prejudice: an *attitude* or prejudging, usually in a negative way mitories and campus centers. At Brown University, an Ivy League school located in Providence, Rhode Island, the old rows of fraternity and sorority houses have been replaced by Harambee House (for African Americans), Hispanic House, Slavic House, East Asian House, and German House. Cornell University offers "theme dorms" for African Americans, Hispanics, and Native Americans.

Intense controversy surrounds this increasing segregation of racial/ethnic groups. On one side is William H. Gray III, the head of the United Negro College Fund. Both African American and Latino students drop out of college at a much higher rate, Gray says, so colleges should do everything they can to make minority students feel welcome and accepted.

Critics call the trend toward separate housing a "separatist movement" that divides students into "small enclaves." The vice president of Brown compares separate college housing to the war in the former Yugoslavia (also known as the Balkan states) and worries that the result will be the "Balkanization of the campus." Administrators at the University of Pennsylvania also are concerned. A commission to study campus life concluded that when students self-segregate, they lose opportunities for wider interaction with diverse groups of students. Since students tend to socialize with the people they live with, separate housing inhibits the mixing of different groups, depriving students of the rich experiences that come through intercultural contacts.

Joshua Lehrer, a Brown University student who is white, says that various racial and ethnic groups "are separating themselves from everybody else, yet complain when society separates them. Can you really have it both ways?" he asks.

For Your Consideration

Compare separate racial/ethnic housing on college campuses with the patterns discussed in this chapter: segregation, assimilation, and multiculturalism. Is self-segregation permissible if minority students desire it, but not if desired by white students? Explain your position.

Sources: Bernstein 1993; "Racial Balkanization at Cornell" 1995; Jordon 1996. ▲

Individual and Institutional Discrimination

Sociologists stress that we need to move beyond thinking in terms of **individual discrimination**, the negative treatment of one person by another. Although such behavior certainly creates problems, it is primarily a matter of one individual treating another badly. With their focus on the broader picture, sociologists encourage us to examine **institutional discrimination**, that is, to see how discrimination is woven into the fabric of society, to such an extent that it becomes routine, sometimes even a matter of social policy. Let's look at two examples.

Home Mortgages.   Mortgage lending provides an excellent illustration. As shown in Figure 12.3, race/ethnicity is a significant factor in getting a mortgage. When bankers looked at the statistics shown in this figure, however, they cried foul. They said that it might *look* like discrimination, but the truth was that whites had better credit histories. To see if this were true, researchers went over the data again, comparing the credit histories of applicants. Not only did they check for late payments, but they also compared the applicants' debts, loan size relative to income, and even characteristics of the property they wanted to buy. The lending gap did narrow, but the bottom line was that even when two mortgage applicants were identical in all these areas, African Americans and Latinos were *60 percent* more likely to be rejected than whites (Thomas 1992; Passell 1996). In short, the results do not show a banker here and there who discriminates, but, rather, that discrimination is built into the country's financial institutions.

Heart Surgery.   Discrimination does not have to be deliberate. It can occur without the awareness of either the person doing the discriminating or those being discriminated against. An example is coronary bypass surgery. Physicians Mark Wenneker and Arnold Epstein (1989) studied all patients admitted to Massachusetts hospitals for circulatory

individual discrimination: the negative treatment of one person by another on the basis of that person's perceived characteristics

institutional discrimination: negative treatment of a minority group that is built into a society's institutions; also called *systemic discrimination*

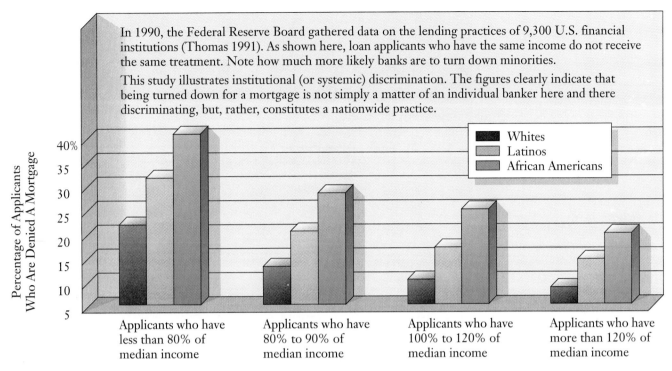

In 1990, the Federal Reserve Board gathered data on the lending practices of 9,300 U.S. financial institutions (Thomas 1991). As shown here, loan applicants who have the same income do not receive the same treatment. Note how much more likely banks are to turn down minorities.

This study illustrates institutional (or systemic) discrimination. The figures clearly indicate that being turned down for a mortgage is not simply a matter of an individual banker here and there discriminating, but, rather, constitutes a nationwide practice.

Legend:
- Whites
- Latinos
- African Americans

Y-axis: Percentage of Applicants Who Are Denied A Mortgage (40%, 35, 30, 25, 20, 15, 10, 5)

X-axis categories:
- Applicants who have less than 80% of median income
- Applicants who have 80% to 90% of median income
- Applicants who have 100% to 120% of median income
- Applicants who have more than 120% of median income

Note: The totals refer to applicants for conventional mortgages. Although applicants for government-backed mortgages had lower overall rates of rejection, the identical pattern showed up for all income groups. Median income is the income of each bank's local area.

Figure 12.3

Race/Ethnicity and Mortgages: An Example of Institutional Discrimination

diseases or chest pain. After comparing their age, sex, race, and income, they found that whites were 89 percent more likely to be given coronary bypass surgery. A national study of Medicare patients showed an even higher discrepancy—that whites were three times as likely as African Americans to receive this surgery (Winslow 1992).

The particular interracial dynamics that cause medical decisions to be made on the basis of race are unknown at present. It is likely that physicians *do not intend* to discriminate, but that in ways we do not yet fully understand discrimination is somehow built into the medical delivery system. Race apparently works like gender. Just as women's higher death rates in bypass surgery can be traced to attitudes about gender (see page 294), so race serves as a subconscious basis for giving or denying access to advanced medical procedures.

Theories of Prejudice

Why are people prejudiced? The commonsense explanation is that some member of a group has done something negative to them or to someone they know, and they transfer their feelings to other members of the group. In some cases, this may be true, but as a classic piece of research by psychologist Eugene Hartley (1946) showed, much more is involved. Hartley asked people how they felt about various racial and ethnic groups. Besides blacks, Jews, and so on, his list included the Wallonians, Pireneans, and Danireans—names he had made up. Most people who expressed dislike for Jews and blacks also expressed dislike for these three fictitious groups. The significance of Hartley's study is twofold. First, people who are prejudiced against one racial or ethnic group tend to be prejudiced against other groups. Second, prejudice does not depend on negative experiences with others. People can be, and are, prejudiced against people they have never met—and even against groups that do not exist!

In the 1920s, the Ku Klux Klan became a powerful political force in the United States, especially in Indiana, where this photo was taken. Which theories, sociological and psychological, would be most useful to explain this upsurge in racism among ordinary citizens?

Social scientists have developed several theories to explain prejudice. Let's look first at psychological theories, then at sociological explanations.

Psychological Perspectives

Frustration and Scapegoats.   In 1939, psychologist John Dollard suggested that prejudice is the result of frustration. People who are unable to strike out at the real source of their frustration (such as low wages) find someone else to blame. This **scapegoat,** generally a racial, ethnic, or religious minority that they unfairly blame for their troubles, becomes a convenient—and safe—target on which to vent their frustrations. Gender and age also provide common bases for scapegoating.

Even mild frustration can increase prejudice. In an ingenious experiment, psychologists Emory Cowen, Judah Landes, and Donald Schaet (1959) measured the prejudice of a sample of students. They then gave the students two puzzles to solve, but made sure they did not have enough time to solve them. After the students had worked furiously on the puzzles, the experimenters shook their heads in disgust and said they couldn't believe they had not finished. They then retested the students and found higher scores on prejudice. The students had directed their frustrations outward, onto people who had nothing to do with their problem.

The Authoritarian Personality.   Have you ever wondered if personality is a cause of prejudice—if some people are more inclined to be prejudiced, and others more fairminded? For psychologist Theodor Adorno, who had escaped from the Nazis, this was no idle speculation. With the horrors he had observed still fresh in his mind, Adorno wondered whether there was a certain type of individual who was more likely to fall for the racist utterances and policies of people like Hitler, Mussolini, and the Ku Klux Klan.

To test this idea, Adorno (1950) developed three scales: a series of statements that measured ethnocentrism, anti-Semitism, and support for strong, authoritarian leaders. Testing about two thousand people, ranging from college professors to prison inmates, Adorno found that people who scored high on one scale also scored high on the other two. For example, people who agreed with anti-Semitic statements also agreed that it was good for a government to be highly authoritarian and that foreign ways of life posed a threat to the "American" way.

scapegoat: an individual or group unfairly blamed for someone else's troubles

Adorno concluded that highly prejudiced people have several things in common. They are insecure, are highly conformist, have deep respect for authority, and are highly submissive to superiors. He termed this the **authoritarian personality.** Believing that things are *either* right *or* wrong, they are disturbed by ambiguity, especially in matters of religion or sex. When they confront norms and values that differ from their own, they become anxious. A scapegoat relieves their anxiety, for to define people who are different from themselves as inferior assures them that their own positions are right.

Adorno's research stirred the scientific community, and more than a thousand research studies followed. In general, the researchers found that people who are older, less educated, less intelligent, and from a lower social class are more likely to be authoritarian. Critics say that this merely shows that the less educated are more prejudiced—which we already knew (Yinger 1965; Ray 1991).

authoritarian personality: Theodor Adorno's term for people who are prejudiced and rank high on scales of conformity, intolerance, insecurity, respect for authority, and submissiveness to superiors

Sociological Perspectives

Sociologists find psychological explanations inadequate. They stress that the key to understanding prejudice is not the *internal* state of individuals, but factors *outside* the individual. Thus, sociological theories focus on how some environments foster prejudice, while others reduce it. Let's compare functionalist, conflict, and symbolic interactionist perspectives on prejudice.

Functionalism.   In a telling scene from a television documentary, journalist Bill Moyers interviewed Fritz Hippler, a Nazi intellectual who at age 29 was put in charge of the entire German film industry. Hippler said that when Hitler came to power the Germans were no more anti-Semitic than the French, probably less so. He was told to create anti-Semitism, which he did by producing movies that contained vivid scenes comparing Jews to rats—their breeding threatening to infest the population.

Why was Hippler told to create hatred? Prejudice and discrimination were functional for the Nazis, helping them come to power. The Jews provided a convenient scapegoat, a common enemy around which the Nazis could unite a Germany weakened by defeat in World War I and bled by war reparations and rampant inflation. In addition, the Jews had businesses, bank accounts, and other property to confiscate. They also held key positions (university professors, reporters, judges, and so on), which the Nazis could replace with their own flunkies as they fired Jews. In the end hatred also showed its dysfunctional side, as the Nazi officials who were sentenced to death at Nuremberg discovered.

To harness state machinery to hatred as the Nazis did— the schools, police, courts, mass media, and almost all aspects of the government—makes prejudice practically irresistible. Recall the identical twins featured in the Down-to-Earth Sociology box on page 63. Oskar and Jack had been separated as babies. Jack was brought up as a Jew in Trinidad, while Oskar was reared as a Catholic in Czechoslovakia. Under the Nazi regime, Oskar learned to hate Jews, although, unknown to himself, he was a Jew.

That prejudice is functional and shaped by the social environment was dramatically demonstrated by psychologists Muzafer and Carolyn Sherif (1953) in a simple but ingenious experiment. In a boys' summer camp, they first assigned friends to different cabins and then made the cabin the basic unit of competition. Each cabin competed against the others in sports and for status. In just a few days, strong in-groups had formed, and even former lifelong friends were calling one another "crybaby" and "sissy" and showing intense dislike for one another.

Governments sometimes find prejudice functional. Arousing negative sentiment against a racial or ethnic group can help to consolidate citizens, especially during time of war. This propaganda poster, published by the U.S. Navy during World War II, is directed against Japan, one of the United States' main enemies at that time. The anti-Japanese sentiment it aroused, however, extended to Japanese Americans, whom many considered "enemies living within our borders." Under orders from President F. D. Roosevelt, Japanese Americans were imprisoned in "internment camps."

OCCUPIED TERRITORY

SALVAGE SCRAP TO BLAST THE JAP

Sherif's study illustrates four major points. First, the social environment can be deliberately arranged to generate either positive or negative feelings about people. Second, prejudice can be a product of pitting group against group in an "I win, you lose" situation. Third, prejudice is functional in that it creates in-group solidarity. Fourth, prejudice is dysfunctional in that it destroys social relationships.

Conflict Theory. Conflict theorists stress that the capitalist class systematically pits group against group. If workers are united, they will demand higher wages and better working conditions. In contrast, groups that fear and distrust one another will work against one another. To reduce worker solidarity, then, is to weaken their bargaining power, drive down costs, and increase profits. Thus the capitalist class exploits racial and ethnic strife to produce a **split labor market** (also called a *dual labor market*), workers divided along racial, ethnic, and gender lines (Du Bois 1935/1992; Reich 1972; Lind 1995).

Unemployment is a useful weapon to help maintain a split labor market. If everyone were employed, the high demand for labor would put workers in a position to demand pay increases and better working conditions. Keeping some people unemployed, however, provides a **reserve labor force** from which owners can draw when they need to expand production. When the economy contracts, these workers are released to rejoin the ranks of the unemployed. Minority workers are especially useful for this manipulative goal, for white workers tend to see them as a threat (Willhelm 1980).

The consequences are devastating, say conflict theorists. Just like the boys in the Sherif experiment, African Americans, Latinos, whites, and so on see themselves as able to make gains only at one another's expense. This rivalry shows up along even finer racial and ethnic lines, such as Miami Haitians and African Americans who distrust each other as competitors. Thus, their frustration, anger, and hostility are deflected away from the capitalists and directed toward the scapegoats, whom they see as standing in their way. Pitted against one another, racial and ethnic groups learn to fear and distrust one another, instead of recognizing their common class interests and working for their mutual welfare (Blackwelder 1993).

Symbolic Interactionism. Where conflict theorists focus on the role of the capitalist class in exploiting racial and ethnic inequalities, symbolic interactionists examine how perception and labels produce prejudice.

How Labels Create Prejudice. "What's in a name?" asked Juliet. In answer she declared, "That which we call a rose / By any other name would smell as sweet." This may be true of roses, but it does not apply to human relations. Words are not simply meaningless labels. Rather, *the labels we learn color the way we see the world.*

Symbolic interactionists stress that labels are an essential ingredient of prejudice. Labels cause **selective perception;** that is, they lead people to see certain things and blind them to others. Through labels, people look at the members of a group as though they were all alike. As sociologists George Simpson and Milton Yinger (1972) put it, "New experiences are fitted into old categories by selecting only those cues that harmonize with the prejudgment or stereotype."

Racial and ethnic labels are especially powerful. They are shorthand for emotionally laden stereotypes. The term *nigger*, for example, is not, like Romeo's rose, simply a neutral name. Nor are *honky, spic, mick, kike, limey, kraut, dago,* or any of the other scornful words people use to belittle ethnic groups. Such words overpower us with emotions, blocking out rational thought about the people they refer to (Allport 1954).

Symbolic interactionists stress that no one is born prejudiced. Instead, we learn our prejudices in interaction with others. At birth each of us joins some particular family and racial or ethnic group, where we learn beliefs and values. There, as part of our basic orientations to the world, we learn to like—or dislike—members of other groups and to perceive them positively or negatively. Similarly, if discrimination is the common practice, we

split-labor market: workers split along racial, ethnic, gender, age, or any other lines; this split is exploited by owners to weaken the bargaining power of workers

reserve labor force: the unemployed; unemployed workers are thought of as being "in reserve"—capitalists take them "out of reserve" (put them back to work) during times of high production and then lay them off (put them back in reserve) when they are no longer needed

selective perception: seeing certain features of an object or situation, but remaining blind to others

learn to practice it routinely. Just as we learn any other attitudes and customs, then, so we learn prejudice and discrimination.

Stereotypes and Discrimination: The Self-Fulfilling Prophecy.   The stereotypes that we learn not only justify prejudice and discrimination, but they can even produce the behavior depicted in the stereotype. Let's consider Group X. Negative stereotypes, which characterize Group X as lazy, seem to justify withholding opportunities from this group ("because they are lazy and undependable") and placing its members in inferior positions. The result is a *self-fulfilling prophecy*. Denied jobs that require high dedication and energy, Group X members are confined to "dirty work," for it is seen as more fitting for "that kind" of people. Since much dirty work is irregular, members of Group X are also liable to be readily visible—standing around street corners. The sight of their idleness then reinforces the original stereotype of laziness, while the discrimination that created the "laziness" in the first place passes unnoticed.

One aspect of racism that has gained attention and concern from citizens and government alike is the rise of neo-Nazi and Ku Klux Klan organizations (Shanks-Meile and Dobratz 1991; Dobratz and Shanks-Meile 1995). To understand the racist mind—and the appeal it has to some—see the Down-to-Earth Sociology box below.

▲▼▲▼▲▼ *Down-to-Earth Sociology* ▲▼▲▼▲▼

The Racist Mind

Sociologist Raphael Ezekiel wanted to get an inside look at the racist mind. As a Jew, he faced a unique problem. The best way to examine racism from the inside was to do participant observation (see pp. 128–129). Would this be possible for him? Openly identifying himself as a Jew, Ezekiel asked Ku Klux Klan and neo-Nazi leaders if he could interview them and attend their meetings. Surprisingly, they agreed. The results of his pathbreaking research were published in a book, *The Racist Mind*. Here Ezekiel (1995) shares some of the insights he gained during his fascinating sociological adventures:

[The leader] builds on mass anxiety about economic insecurity and on popular tendencies to see an Establishment as the cause of economic threat; he hopes to teach people to identify that Establishment as the puppets of a conspiracy of Jews. [He has a] belief in exclusive categories. For the white racist leader, it is profoundly true . . . that the socially defined collections we call races represent fundamental categories. A man is black or a man is white; there are no in-betweens. Every human belongs to a racial category, and all the members of one category are radically different from all the members of other categories. Moreover, race represents the essence *of the person. A truck is a truck, a car is a car, a cat is a cat, a dog is a dog, a black is a black, a white is a white. . . . These axioms have a rock-hard quality in the leaders' minds; the world is made up of racial groups. That is what exists for them.*

Two further beliefs play a major role in the minds of leaders. First, life is war. The world is made of distinct racial groups; life is about the war between these groups. Second, events have secret causes, are never what they seem superficially. Events are caused by the complex scheming of tricksters. . . . Any myth is plausible, as long as it involves intricate plotting. . . . It does not matter to him what others say. . . . He lives in his ideas and in the little world he has created where they are taken seriously. . . . Gold can be made from the tongues of frogs; Yahweh's call can be heard in the flapping swastika banner. (pp. 66–67)

To whom do propagators of hate appeal? Here is what Ezekiel discovered about the recruits:

[There is a] ready pool of whites who will respond to the racist signal. . . . This population [is] always hungry for activity—or for the talk of activity—that promises dignity and meaning to lives that are working poorly in a highly competitive world . . . Much as I don't want to believe it, [this] movement brings a sense of meaning—at least for a while—to some of the discontented. To struggle in a cause that transcends the individual lends meaning to life, no matter how ill-founded or narrowing the cause. For the young men in the neo-Nazi group, . . . membership was an alternative to atomization and drift; within the group they worked for a cause and took direct risks in the company of comrades. . . .

When interviewing the young neo-Nazis in Detroit, I often found myself driving with them past the closed factories, the idled plants of our shrinking manufacturing base. The fewer and fewer plants that remain can demand better education and more highly skilled workers. These fatherless Nazi youths, these high-school dropouts, will find little place in the emerging economy . . . a permanently underemployed white underclass is taking its place alongside the permanent black underclass. The struggle over race merely diverts youth from confronting the real issues of their lives. Not many seats are left on the train, and the train is leaving the station. (pp. 32–33)

For Your Consideration

Use functionalism, conflict theory, and symbolic interaction to explain: (1) why some people are attracted to the message of hate mongers, and (2) how the world is viewed by leaders and followers of these hate groups.

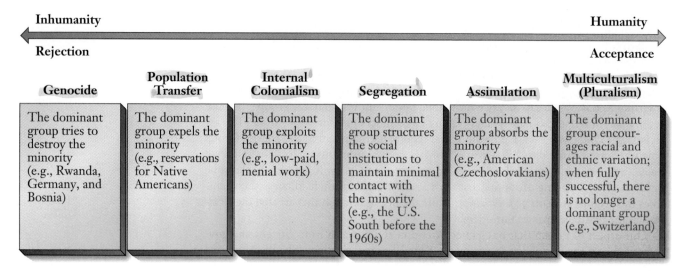

Inhumanity   Humanity

Rejection   Acceptance

Genocide	Population Transfer	Internal Colonialism	Segregation	Assimilation	Multiculturalism (Pluralism)
The dominant group tries to destroy the minority (e.g., Rwanda, Germany, and Bosnia)	The dominant group expels the minority (e.g., reservations for Native Americans)	The dominant group exploits the minority (e.g., low-paid, menial work)	The dominant group structures the social institutions to maintain minimal contact with the minority (e.g., the U.S. South before the 1960s)	The dominant group absorbs the minority (e.g., American Czechoslovakians)	The dominant group encourages racial and ethnic variation; when fully successful, there is no longer a dominant group (e.g., Switzerland)

Figure 12.4

Patterns of Intergroup Relations: A Continuum

Global Patterns of Intergroup Relations

In any society that contains minorities, basic patterns develop between the dominant group and the minorities. Let's look at each of the patterns shown in Figure 12.4.

Genocide

Stereotypes (or labels) powerfully influence human behavior. Symbolic interactionists point out that labels are so powerful that they can even persuade people who have been taught from childhood that hurting others, much less killing them is wrong, to participate in mass murder.

This century's most notorious examples of genocide are Hitler's attempt to destroy all Jews and, as depicted in our opening vignette, the Hutus' attempt to destroy all Tutsis. One of the horrifying aspects of these slaughters is that those who participated did not crawl out from under a rock someplace. Rather, they were ordinary citizens—whose participation was facilitated by labels that singled out the victims as enemies worthy of death.

To better understand how ordinary people can participate in genocide, let's focus on an example from the last century. The U.S. government and white settlers chose the label "savages" to refer to Native Americans. This label, defining the Native Americans as less than human, made it easier to justify killing them in order to take over their resources. Although most Native Americans actually died from diseases brought by the whites, against which they had no immunity (Dobyns 1983; Thornton 1987), the settlers ruthlessly destroyed the Native Americans' food base (buffalos, crops) and systematically killed those who resisted their advance toward the West. These policies resulted in the death of more than *90 percent* of Native Americans (Garbarino 1976; Thornton 1987).

During the 1800s, when most of this slaughter occurred, the same thing was happening in other places. In South Africa, the Boers, or Dutch settlers, looked on the native Hottentots as jungle animals and totally wiped them out. In Tasmania, the British settlers ruthlessly stalked the local aboriginal population, hunting them for sport and sometimes even for dog food.

Labels, then, are powerful forces in human life. Labels that dehumanize others help people to **compartmentalize**—to separate their acts from feelings that would threaten their self-concept and make it difficult for them to participate in killing (Bernard et al. 1971; Markusen 1995). Thus, *genocide is facilitated by labeling the targeted group as less than fully human.*

compartmentalize: to separate acts from feelings or attitudes

Population Transfer

Population transfer is of two types, indirect and direct. *Indirect* population transfer is achieved by making life so unbearable for members of a minority that they leave "voluntarily." Under the bitter conditions of czarist Russia, for example, millions of Jews made this "choice." *Direct* transfer takes place when a minority is expelled. Examples include the relocation of Native Americans to reservations and the transfer of Americans of Japanese descent to relocation camps during World War II.

In the 1990s, a combination of genocide and population transfer occurred in Bosnia, a part of the former Yugoslavia. A hatred bred for centuries, so carefully nurtured that no slight was overlooked, had been kept under wraps during Tito's iron-fisted rule. After the breakup of communism, Yugoslavia split into warring factions and these suppressed, smoldering hatreds broke to the surface. During protracted armed conflict, the Serbs vented their hatred by what they termed **ethnic cleansing,** that is, slaughtering Muslims and some Croatians who lived in areas the Serbs captured and forcing survivors to flee through fear inspired by the slaughter, rape, and torture.

Internal Colonialism

In Chapter 9, the term *colonialism* was used to refer to how the Most Industrialized Nations exploit the Least Industrialized Nations. Conflict theorists use the term **internal colonialism** to refer to how a dominant group exploits minority groups. The "routine" form is to use the social institutions to deny minorities access to the society's full benefits. Slavery, reviewed in Chapter 9, is an extreme example of internal colonialism, as was the South African system of *apartheid*. Although the dominant Afrikaaners despised the minority, they found its presence necessary. As Simpson and Yinger (1972) put it, who else would do all the hard work?

Segregation

Segregation—the formal separation of racial or ethnic groups—accompanies internal colonialism. Segregation allows the dominant group to exploit the labor of the minority (butlers, chauffeurs, housekeepers, nannies, street cleaners) while maintaining social

population transfer: involuntary movement of a minority group

ethnic cleansing: a policy of population elimination, including forcible expulsion and genocide. The term emerged in 1992 among the Serbians during their planned policy of expelling Croats and Muslims from territories claimed by them during the Yugoslav wars

internal colonialism: the policy of economically exploiting minority groups

segregation: the policy of keeping racial or ethnic groups apart

Segregation is one of the many faces of discrimination. Until the 1940s, major league baseball was reserved for white players. Shown here is Jackie Robinson, who broke the color barrier in 1947. Voted Rookie of the Year, and then Most Valued Player two seasons later, Robinson was inducted into the Hall of Fame as soon as he was eligible.

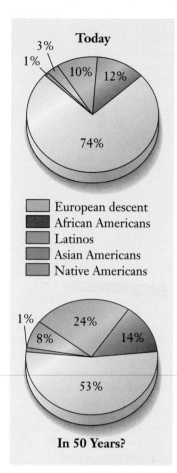

Today

3%
1%
10%
12%
74%

■ European descent
■ African Americans
■ Latinos
■ Asian Americans
■ Native Americans

1%
24%
8%
14%
53%

In 50 Years?

Source: Statistical Abstract 1997:Table 19.

Figure 12.5

Projections of the Racial/Ethnic Makeup of the U.S. Population

assimilation: the process of being absorbed into the mainstream culture

multiculturalism (also called **pluralism**): a philosophy or political policy that permits or encourages ethnic variation

ethnic work: activities designed to discover, enhance, or maintain ethnic and racial identification

distance (Collins 1986). In the U.S. South until the 1960s, by law African Americans and whites had to use separate public facilities such as hotels, schools, swimming pools, bathrooms, and even drinking fountains. In thirty-eight states, laws prohibited interracial marriage. Violators could be punished by one to five years in prison (Mahoney and Kooistra 1995). The legal structure also upheld residential segregation (Massy and Denton 1993).

Assimilation

Assimilation is the process by which a minority is absorbed into the mainstream culture. There are two types. In *forced assimilation* the dominant group refuses to allow the minority to practice its religion, speak its language, or follow its customs. Prior to the fall of the Soviet Union, for example, the dominant group, the Russians, required that Armenian schoolchildren be taught in Russian and that Armenians honor Russian, not Armenian, holidays. *Permissible assimilation*, in contrast, permits the minority to adopt the dominant group's patterns in its own way and at its own speed. In Brazil, for example, an ideology favoring the eventual blending of diverse racial types into a "Brazilian stock" encourages its racial and ethnic groups to intermarry.

Multiculturalism (pluralism)

A policy of **multiculturalism,** also called **pluralism,** permits or even encourages racial and ethnic variation. The minority groups are able to maintain their separate identities, yet participate in the country's social institutions, from education to politics. Switzerland provides an outstanding example of multiculturalism. The Swiss are made up of three separate groups—French, Italians, and Germans—who have kept their own languages, and live peacefully in political and economic unity. Multiculturalism has been so successful that none of these groups can properly be called a minority.

Race and Ethnic Relations in the United States

As we have stressed, racial classifications are arbitrary and changing. Nevertheless, as a part of everyday life, we classify one another as belonging to racial-ethnic groups (see Figures 12.5 and 12.6). Most of us also have strong racial-ethnic self-identities. Let's explore some of the consequences of that membership and identity.

Constructing Ethnic Identity

Some people have a much greater sense of ethnicity than others. For them, the boundaries between "us" and "them" are sharp and firm. Others, in contrast, have assimilated so extensively into mainstream culture that they are only vaguely aware of their ethnic origins. With extensive interethnic marrying, some do not even know the countries from which their families originated—nor do they care. If asked to identify themselves ethnically, they respond with something like "I'm German-Irish, with a little Italian and French thrown in—and I think someone said something about being 1/16th American Indian."

Why do some people feel an intense sense of ethnic identity, while others feel hardly any? Figure 12.7 portrays four factors identified by sociologist Ashley Doane (1993) that heighten or reduce a sense of ethnic identity. From this figure, you can see that the keys are relative size, power, appearance, and discrimination. If a group is relatively small, has little power, looks different from most people in the society, and is an object of discrimination, its members will have a heightened sense of ethnic identity. In contrast, members of the numerical majority who hold most of the power, look like most people in the society, and feel no discrimination are likely to experience a sense of "belonging," and wonder why ethnic identity is such a big deal.

We can use the term **ethnic work** to refer to how people construct their ethnicity. For people who already have a strong ethnic identity, this term refers to how they enhance

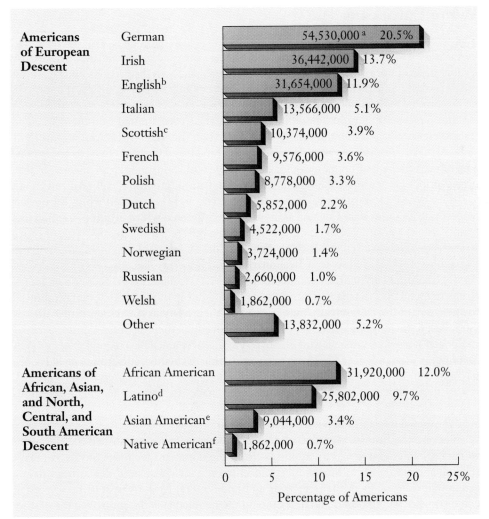

Figure 12.6

U.S. Racial and Ethnic Groups

[a] To compute percentages, the population totals of the individual groups listed in the source were added, and the groups' totals were divided by this sum. To obtain the groups' population, these percentages were multiplied by the official U.S. population count.

[b] Includes "British."

[c] Includes "Scottish-Irish."

[d] Most Latinos trace at least part of their ancestry to Europe.

[e] In descending order, the largest six groups of Asian Americans are Chinese, Filipinos, Japanese, Koreans, Asian Indians, and Vietnamese.

[f] Includes Native American, Eskimo, and Aleut.

Source: Statistical Abstract 1997:Tables 2, 49, 50, 52, 53, 56.

and maintain their group's distinctions. For people with a lower sense of ethnicity, it refers to attempts to recover their ethnic heritage, such as trying to trace family lines. Millions of Americans are engaged in ethnic work, which has confounded the experts who thought that the United States would be a **melting pot**, its many groups quietly blending into a sort of ethnic stew. In recent years, however, Americans have become fascinated with their "roots" and increasingly assertive and prideful of their ethnic background (Karnow and Yoshihara 1992; Wei 1993). Consequently, some analysts think the term "tossed salad" more appropriate than "melting pot."

melting pot: the view that Americans of various backgrounds would blend into a sort of ethnic stew

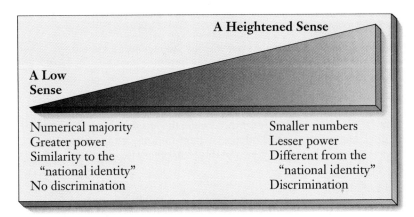

Figure 12.7

A Sense of Ethnicity
Source: Based on Douane 1993.

White Europeans

The term **WASP** stands for White Anglo-Saxon Protestant. In its narrow meaning, WASP refers to Protestant Americans whose ancestors came from England. These early immigrants did not consider all WASPs to be equal, and class distinctions quickly developed. Lacking an official royalty, and somewhat envious of European royal courts, in 1890 some WASPs established the Society of Mayflower Descendants to certify which families possessed the right "blood lines." Membership was limited to those who could trace their ancestry to the immigrants who arrived on the Mayflower. Around this same time, the *Social Register* began to be published. To be listed in this book is to be deemed a member of the upper upper class, for only people with "old" money are included. Such organizations help insulate their members from the more "common" folk (Baltzell 1964).

The WASP colonists were highly ethnocentric, and they viewed white Europeans from countries other than England as inferior. They greeted **white ethnics**—immigrants from Europe whose language and other customs differed from theirs—with negative stereotypes. They viewed the Irish as dirty, lazy drunkards, and they painted Germans, Poles, Jews, Italians, and so on with similarly broad brush strokes.

The cultural and political dominance of the WASPs placed great pressure on immigrants to blend into the mainstream culture. The children of most immigrants embraced the new way of life and quickly came to think of themselves as Americans rather than as Germans, French, Hungarians, and so on. They dropped their distinctive customs, especially their language, often viewing them as symbols of shame. This second generation of immigrants was sandwiched between two worlds, that of their parents from "the old country" and their new home. With fewer inconsistencies and with fewer customs to discard, it was their children, the third generation, who made the easier adjustment. As immigrants from other parts of Europe assimilated into this Anglo culture, the meaning of WASP expanded to include people of this descent.

Because the English settled the Colonies, it was they who established the culture to which later immigrants had to conform—from the dominant language to the dominant religion and family form. Moved by ethnocentrism, they considered the customs of any group that differed from theirs inferior and undesirable. In short, it was the European colonists who, taking power and determining the national agenda, controlled the destiny of the nation and dominated and exploited other ethnic groups. Throughout the years, other ethnic groups have had to react to this institutional and cultural dominance of western Europeans, which still sets the stage for current ethnic relations.

African Americans

Discrimination was once so integral a part of U.S. life that it was not until 1944 that the U.S. Supreme Court decided that African Americans could vote in southern primaries, and not until 1954 that they had the legal right to attend the same public schools as whites (Carroll and Noble 1977; Polenberg 1980). Well into the 1960s, the South was openly—and legally—practicing segregation. (Another form of discrimination, and the role that technology played in changing it, is discussed in the Sociology and the New Technology box.)

The Struggle for Civil Rights

It was 1955, in Montgomery, Alabama. As specified by law, whites took the front seats of the bus, while blacks went to the back. As the bus filled up, blacks had to give up their seats to whites.

When Rosa Parks, a 42-year-old African-American woman and secretary of the Montgomery NAACP, was told she would have to stand so white folks could sit, she refused (Bray 1995). She stubbornly sat there while the bus driver raged and whites felt insulted. Her arrest touched off mass demonstrations, led fifty thousand blacks to boycott the city's buses for a year, and thrust an otherwise unknown preacher into a historic role.

[handwritten marginalia: Act of 1865 "unconstitutional" / Jim Crow Laws (1895) / legalizing segregation]

WASP: a White Anglo-Saxon Protestant; narrowly, an American of English descent; broadly, an American of western European ancestry

white ethnics: white immigrants to the United States whose culture differs from that of WASPs

 *Sociology and the New Technology*

Technology and the African-American Experience

On October 2, 1944, in Clarksdale, Mississippi, about 3,000 people gathered at the Hopson Plantation to watch some of the first mechanical cotton pickers go into action. What they saw amazed them:

In an hour, a good field hand could pick twenty pounds of cotton; each mechanical picker, in an hour, picked as much as a thousand pounds. . . . Each machine did the work of fifty people. (Lemann 1991:5)

African Americans in the crowd were most likely to be alarmed as well as amazed, for it was they who earned a meager living picking cotton by hand. As Nicholas Lemann narrates in *The Promised Land*, in just a few years the introduction of the mechanical cotton picker was to render the way they earned their livelihood—as sharecroppers—obsolete. In theory, sharecroppers were provided with credit for seeds, tools, living quarters, and food; in return, they worked the land for an agreed-on share of the selling price of the crop minus the amount they spent to plant and live. In reality, these former slaves were being kept in a form of bondage by dishonest plantation owners. The owners debited the sharecroppers' accounts such that after a year's toil, at the "settle" (the time when profit and loss were figured), the sharecroppers were not only profitless but in debt to the owner. This tied them to the land for another year, doomed yet again to work for starvation wages.

By the mid-1950s, mechanized cotton farming had virtually ended the sharecropper system. (Pockets, of course, remained, and even today a few African Americans continue to live and work on the same plantations their parents or grandparents sharecropped.) As with any new technology, the time between the mechanical cotton picker's introduction and its widespread adoption did not take place overnight. Five years after the machine was exhibited at the Hopson Plantation, about 6 percent of the cotton was harvested by machines. By 1964, the total had jumped to 78 percent. By 1972, all the cotton in the South was mechanically farmed.

Southern blacks had been migrating from the South to northern cities since the early 1900s. They were drawn by the new factory jobs and the promise of a more dignified life—one that included the option of voting, of not being called "boy," and of being able to sit anywhere on a bus (Le-

mann 1991:40). But after the mechanical cotton picker came along, the migrations of blacks to the South accelerated dramatically as millions of evicted sharecroppers were forced to seek work elsewhere. Between 1940 and 1970—the same time frame it took to establish mechanized cotton farming—5 million blacks headed North, especially to cities like Chicago and Detroit. Whereas in 1940, 77 percent of black Americans lived in the South, by 1970 half of all African Americans lived in the North. As Lemann (1991:6) writes, "The black migration was one of the largest and most rapid mass internal movements of people in history—perhaps *the* greatest not caused by the immediate threat of execution or starvation."

Rather than war or famine, the driving force behind this vast migration was technology. With only a few hands necessary to run the mechanized cotton pickers, the South no longer depended on cheap black labor. Jobs, poor as they had paid, dried up almost overnight. For awhile, the back-breaking job of chopping weeds in the cotton field remained, but even this source of work was eliminated by another new technology, the new herbicides.

In the North, the fortunes of black workers improved steadily until 1954, and from there began a 40-year decline (Rifkin 1995:73). The reason? A new wave of automation permanently eliminated many unskilled assembly line jobs. Between 1953 and 1962, 1.6 million African Americans lost factory jobs. At the same time, due to yet another feat of technology—the creation of a massive interstate highway system—manufacturers began to relocate their factories to the suburbs. This pulled jobs away from the inner cities where African Americans were clustered.

Mechanized cotton farming, fast-paced automation, and the newly laid interstate highway system affected the economic fates of many beside African Americans. But according to many analysts, no other single group suffered quite so dramatically from the fallout of these developments. According to Jeremy Rifkin (1995), "Technological unemployment has fundamentally altered the sociology of America's black community." It created a permanent underclass abandoned in the urban ghetto, where millions languish without the skills to compete in today's high-tech world.

Brun vs. Supreme Court

Rev. Martin Luther King, Jr., who had majored in sociology at Morehouse College in Atlanta, Georgia, took control. He organized car pools and preached nonviolence. Incensed at this radical organizer and at the stirrings in the normally compliant African-American community, segregationists also put their beliefs into practice—by bombing homes and dynamiting churches.

Under King's leadership, **civil disobedience,** the act of deliberately but peacefully disobeying laws considered unjust, became a tactic widely used by civil rights activists to break down institutional barriers. Inspired by Mohandas Gandhi, who had played a crit-

civil disobedience: the act of deliberately but peacefully disobeying laws considered unjust

Until the 1960s, the South's public facilities were racially segregated. Some were reserved for whites only, others for blacks only. This apartheid was broken by blacks and whites who worked together and risked their lives to bring about a fairer society. Shown here is a 1963 sit-in at a Woolworth's lunch counter in Jackson, Mississippi. Sugar, ketchup, and mustard are being poured over the heads of the demonstrators.

ical part in winning India's independence from Great Britain, King (1958) based his strategy on the following principles:

1. Pursuing active, nonviolent resistance to evil
2. Not seeking to defeat or humiliate opponents, but to win their friendship and understanding
3. Attacking the forces of evil rather than the people who are doing the evil
4. Being willing to accept suffering without retaliating
5. Refusing to hate the opponent
6. Acting with the conviction that the universe is on the side of justice

Rising Expectations and Civil Strife.   The barriers came down slowly, but they did come down. Not until 1964 did Congress pass the Civil Rights Act, making it illegal to discriminate in restaurants, hotels, theaters, and other public places. Then in 1965, Congress passed the Voting Rights Act, banning the fraudulent literacy tests that the South had used to keep African Americans from voting.

Encouraged by such gains, African Americans experienced what sociologists call **rising expectations;** that is, they believed better conditions would soon follow. The lives of the poor among them, however, changed little, if at all. Frustrations built, finally exploding in Watts in 1965, when people living in that African-American ghetto of central Los Angeles took to the streets in the first of what have been termed "the urban revolts." When King was assassinated by a white supremacist on April 4, 1968, ghettos across the nation again erupted in fiery violence. Under threat of the destruction of U.S. cities, Congress passed the sweeping Civil Rights Act of 1968.

rising expectations: the sense that better conditions are soon to follow, which, if unfulfilled, creates mounting frustration

Continued Gains.   Since then, African Americans have made remarkable political, educational, and economic gains. At 9 percent, African Americans have *quadrupled* their membership in the U.S. House of Representatives in the past twenty-five years (Rich 1986; *Statistical Abstract* 1997:Table 448). As enrollment in colleges increased, the middle class

TABLE 12.1

Race/Ethnicity and Comparative Well-Being

	Median Family Income	Percentage of White Income	Percentage Unemployed	Percentage of White Unemployment	Percentage Below Poverty Line	Percentage of White Poverty	Percentage Owning Their Homes	Percentage of White Home Ownership
White Americans	$42,646	—	3.1%	—	11.2%	—	69%	—
African Americans	25,970	60%	6.7	216	29.3	262%	44	64%
Latinos	24,314	57	6.1	197	30.7	274	42	61
Country of origin								
Mexico	23,609	55	6.5	210	32.3	288	46	67
Puerto Rico	20,929	49	6.5	210	36.0	321	29	42
Cuba	30,584	72	4.4	142	17.8	159	52	75
Central and South America	26,558	62	5.6	181	25.8	230	29	42
Asian Americans[a]	46,356	109	3.3	106	14.6	130	51	74
Native Americans	21,619	51	NA[b]	NA	31.2	279	NA	NA

Note: The racial and ethnic groups are listed from largest to smallest.

[a]Includes Pacific Islanders.

[b]Not available.

Source: Statistical Abstract 1997:Tables 49, 50, 52, 53, 55.

expanded, and it now holds three times the proportion of African Americans as it did in 1940. One of every five African-American families makes more than $50,000 a year (*Statistical Abstract* 1997:Table 49).

The extent of African-American political prominence was highlighted when Jesse Jackson (another sociology major) competed for the Democratic presidential nomination in 1984 and 1988. In 1989, this progress was further confirmed when L. Douglas Wilder of Virginia became the nation's first elected African-American governor (Perry 1990). The political prominence of African Americans came to the nation's attention again in 1991 at the televised Senate hearings held to confirm the appointment of Clarence Thomas to the Supreme Court. After grueling questioning concerning sexual harassment charges brought by Anita Hill, a former employee, Thomas was confirmed as the nation's second African-American Supreme Court Justice.

Current Losses.   In spite of these gains, African Americans continue to lag behind in politics, economics, and education. Only one U.S. senator is African American, when by ratio in the population we would expect 12. As Table 12.1 shows, African Americans average only 60 percent of white income, have much more unemployment and poverty, and are much less likely to own their home. As Table 12.2 on the next page shows, only 14 percent have graduated from college.

That one of five African-American families makes over $50,000 a year is only part of the story. The other part is that about one of every five African-American families makes less that $10,000 a year (*Statistical Abstract* 1997:Table 49). Among these ultra-poor are concentrated those with the least hope, the highest despair, and the violence that so often dominates the evening news. African-American males are more than *seven* times as likely to be homicide victims as are white males, and African-American females are more than *four* times as likely as white females to be murdered (*Statistical Abstract* 1997:Table 136). Homicide is now the leading cause of death for African-American males ages 15 to 24.

TABLE 12.2

Education and Race/Ethnicity

	Less Than High School	High School Graduates	1–3 Years College	College Graduates	Number of Doctorates Awarded	Percent of Doctorates Awarded
White Americans	17%	34%	25%	24%	24,602	77.1%
African Americans	26	35	26	14	1,467	4.6
Latinos	47[a]	44	NA	9	1,053	3.3
Asian Americans	17	22	20	42	4,307	13.5
Native Americans	35[a]	56	NA	9	160	0.5

Note: NA = Not Available. Totals except for doctorates refer to persons 25 years and over.

[a]Totals for Latinos and Native Americans are not listed in the same way in the source as they are for other groups.

Source: Statistical Abstract 1997: Tables 49, 50, 52, 979.

Each year, more African-American males are killed by other African Americans than died in the entire nine years of the war in Vietnam.

Race or Social Class? A Sociological Debate. This division of African Americans into "haves" and "have nots" has fueled a sociological controversy. Sociologist William Wilson (1978, 1987) argues that social class is more important than race in determining the life chances of African Americans. Prior to civil rights legislation, he says, the African-American experience was dominated by race. Throughout the United States, African Americans were systematically excluded from avenues of economic advancement—from good schools and good jobs. When civil rights legislation opened new opportunities, middle-class African Americans seized them. Following the path taken by other ethnic groups, as they advanced economically, they, too, moved out of the inner city. Unfortunately, just as legal remedies began to open doors to African Americans, opportunities for unskilled labor declined: Manufacturing jobs dried up and many other blue-collar jobs were transferred to the suburbs. As a result, while better-educated African Americans were able to obtain middle-class, white-collar jobs, a large group of African Americans—those with poor education and lack of skills—was left behind, trapped in poverty in the inner city.

As discussed in the text, sociologists disagree about the relative significance of race and social class in determining social and economic conditions of African Americans. William Julius Wilson, shown here, is an avid proponent of the social class side of this debate.

The result, says Wilson, is two worlds of African-American experience. Those who are stuck in the inner city, live in poverty, confront violent crime daily, attend underfunded schools, face dead-end jobs or welfare, and are filled with hopelessness and despair, combined with apathy or hostility. In contrast, those who have moved up the social class ladder live in good housing in secure neighborhoods, work at well-paid jobs that offer advancement, and send their children to good schools. Their middle-class experiences and lifestyle have changed their views on life. Their aspirations and values no longer have much in common with African Americans who remain poor. According to Wilson, then, social class—not race—has become the most significant factor in the lives of African Americans today.

Many sociologists point out that this analysis overlooks the ongoing discrimination that still underlies the relative impoverishment of African Americans (Massey and Denton 1993; Feagin 1997). Sociologist Charles Willie (1991), for example, notes that even when they do the same work, whites average higher pay than do African Americans. This, he argues, points to racial discrimination, not to social class. He and other critics are concerned that Wilson's analysis can be used by people who want to turn back affirmative action.

What is the answer to this debate? Wilson would reply that the question is framed improperly. Certainly racism is a reality, he would say, but social class is *more* central to the African-American experience than is racial discrimination. The answer, then, is simple—provide jobs—for the availability of work offers hope, and work provides an anchor to a responsible life (Wilson 1996).

Continued Discrimination and Social Class.   It also is likely that African Americans who occupy higher statuses and enjoy greater opportunities face less discrimination. What they do face, however, is no less painful. Many middle-class and wealthy African Americans, for example, report being pulled over in traffic by police who assume their expensive cars must be stolen. Similarly, while rushing to catch a plane, a *New York Times* reporter was stopped by a white security officer who concluded that since she was black and in such a hurry, she must be carrying drugs (Cose 1993).

Afrocentrism.   In response to ongoing discrimination, many African Americans embrace **Afrocentrism**—an emphasis on uniquely African-American traditions and concerns. The Afrocentric movement has encouraged the establishment of black studies courses and has led to the celebration of the holiday Kwanzaa, observed the week after Christmas. Afrocentrism is a modified form of black nationalism, which originally appeared in the mid-1800s (Lemann 1991). At that time, some African Americans perceived moving to Africa as the only reasonable answer to the conditions they faced in white America. Afrocentrism's emphasis today is not emigration but, rather, encouraging African-American culture and improving the status of African Americans.

Latinos

A Note on Terms.   To write on race/ethnicity is like stepping into a minefield: One never knows where to expect the next explosion. Even basic terms are controversial. Some, for example, prefer the term *Hispanic Americans*, while others reject it, saying that it ignores the Indian side of their heritage. Similarly, although the term *Chicanos* is commonly used to refer to Americans from Mexico, some would limit this term to Americans from Mexico who have a sense of oppression and ethnic unity, denying it to those who have assimilated. Keep in mind as you read this section that *Latino* and *Hispanic* do not refer to a race, but to ethnic groups. Latinos may identify themselves racially as black, white, or Native American (Salas 1996; Diaz-Calderon 1996, 1997).

Numbers, Origins, and Location.   When birds still nestled in the trees from which the *Mayflower* was made, there were Latino settlements in Florida and New Mexico (Bretos 1994). Today, Latinos are the second-largest minority group in the United States. In addition to the 18 million Latinos whose country of origin is Mexico, Latinos include almost 3 million Puerto Ricans, over a million Cuban Americans, and almost 4 million people from Central or South America, primarily Venezuela and Colombia. Officially tallied at 27 to 28 million, the actual number of Latinos is considerably higher, perhaps 32 million (see Figure 12.8). No one knows for certain because, although most Latinos are legal residents, large numbers have entered the country illegally. Not surprisingly, they avoid contact with both public officials and census forms. Each year more than 1 million people are apprehended at the border or at points inland and deported to Mexico (*Statistical Abstract* 1997: Table 337), but perhaps another million or so manage to enter the United States. Most migrate for temporary work and then return to their homes and families. The Down-to-Earth Sociology box on the next page explores this vast subterranean immigration.

   To gain an understanding of these numbers, note that as many Latinos live in the United States as there are Canadians in Canada (29 million).

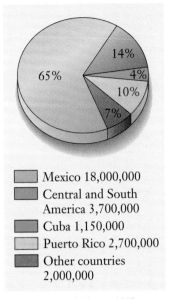

Mexico 18,000,000
Central and South America 3,700,000
Cuba 1,150,000
Puerto Rico 2,700,000
Other countries 2,000,000

Source: *Statistical Abstract* 1997: Table 53.

Figure 12.8

Country of Origin of U.S. Latinos

Afrocentrism: an emphasis on African-American traditions and concerns

When the U.S. government took control of what is now the southwestern United States, Mexicans living there were transformed from the dominant group into a minority group. These children in Austin, Texas, dancing at a Cinco de Mayo festival, are learning to appreciate their ethnic identity, with its rich cultural heritage.

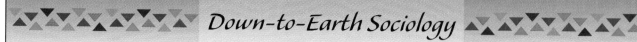

Down-to-Earth Sociology

The Illegal Travel Guide

Manuel was a drinking buddy of Jose's, a man I had met on an earlier trip to Mexico. At 45, Manuel can best be described as friendly, outgoing, and enterprising.

Manuel lived in the United States for seven years and speaks fluent English. Preferring his home town in Colima, Mexico, where he can pal around with his childhood friends, Manuel always seemed to have money and free time.

When Manuel invited me to go on a business trip with him, I quickly accepted. I never could figure out how Manuel made his living and how he was able to afford a car—a luxury that none of his friends had. As we traveled from one remote village to another, Manuel would gather a crowd and sell used clothing that he had heaped in the back of his older-model station wagon.

While chickens ran in and out of the dirt-floored, thatched-roof hut, Manuel spoke in whispers to a slender man of about 23. The sense of poverty was overwhelming. Juan, as his name turned out to be, had a partial grade school education. He also had a wife, four hungry children under the age of 5—and two pigs, his main meat supply. Although eager to work, he had no job—and no prospects of getting one, for there was simply no work available.

As we were drinking a Coke, the national beverage of the poor of Mexico, Manuel explained to me that he was not only selling clothing—he was also lining up migrants

to the United States. For $200 he would take a man to the border and introduce him to a "wolf," who, for another $200 would make a night crossing into the promised land.

When I saw the hope in Juan's face, I knew nothing would stop him. He was borrowing every cent he could from every relative to get the $400 together. He would make the trip although he risked losing everything if apprehended—for wealth beckoned on the other side. He personally knew people who had been there and spoke in glowing terms of its opportunities.

Looking up from the shoeless children playing on the dirt floor with the chickens pecking about them, I saw a man who loved his family and was willing to suffer their enforced absence, as well as the uncertainties of a foreign culture whose language he did not know, in order to make the desperate bid for a better life.

Juan handed me something, and I looked at it curiously. I felt tears as I saw the tenderness with which he handled this piece of paper—his passport to opportunity—a Social Security card made out in his name, sent by a friend who had already made the trip and who was waiting for Juan.

It was then that I knew that the thousands of Manuels scurrying about the face of Mexico and the millions of Juans they were transporting could never be stopped—for the United States held their only dream of a better life.

To midwesterners, such a comparison often comes as a surprise, for Latinos are virtually absent from vast stretches of mid-America. As shown in Figure 12.9, 70 percent are concentrated in just four states: California, Texas, New York, and Florida. In just a few years, Latinos, who already are the largest minority group in several major cities, including Los Angeles, San Antonio, Miami, and Houston, will likely become the largest minority group in the United States.

Figure 12.9

Where U.S. Latinos Live

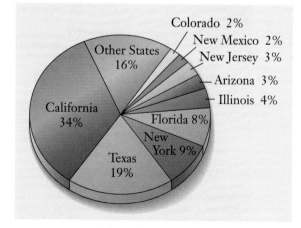

Source: Statistical Abstract 1997:Table 38.

The Spanish Language. The Spanish language distinguishes most Latinos from other U.S. ethnic minorities. With 17 million people speaking Spanish at home, the United States has become one of the largest Spanish-speaking nations in the world (*Statistical Abstract* 1997:Table 57). Because almost half of Latinos are unable to speak English, or can do so only with difficulty, many face a major obstacle to getting good jobs.

The growing use of Spanish has become a social issue. Perceiving the prevalence of Spanish a threat, Senator S. I. Hayakawa of Hawaii initiated an "English only" movement in 1981. The constitutional amendment he sponsored never got off the ground, but about half the states have passed a law declaring English their official language (Amselle 1995)

Politics and Disunity. For Latinos, country of origin is highly significant. Those from Puerto Rico, for example, feel little in common with people from Mexico, Venezuela, or El Salvador—just as earlier immigrants from Germany, Sweden, and England felt little in common with one another. A sign of these divisions among Latinos is the preference of many to refer to themselves by country of origin, such as Puerto Rican or Cuban American, rather than as Latino.

As with other ethnic groups, Latinos, too, find huge gulfs separating them on the basis of social class. The half-million Cubans who fled Castro's rise to power in 1959, for example, were mostly well-educated, well-to-do professionals or businesspeople. In contrast, the 100,000 "boat people" from Cuba who arrived in 1980 were mostly lower-class refugees, people with whom the earlier arrivals would not even have associated in Cuba. The earlier arrivals, firmly established in Florida and in control of many businesses and financial institutions, distance themselves from the more recent immigrants.

These divisions of national origin and social class are a major obstacle to Latino political unity. In California, 23 percent of Latino voters supported Proposition 187, which deprives the children of illegal immigrants (mostly Latino) of schooling and all but emergency medical care (Gitlin 1997:115). One consequence of this disunity is underrepresentation in politics. Although Latinos make up 10 percent of the U.S. population, they hold only 4 percent of the seats in the U.S. Congress and 1 percent of the elected local offices (*Statistical Abstract* 1997:Tables 448, 456).

Fragmented among themselves, Latinos also find that a huge gulf separates them from Africa Americans. With highly distinct histories and cultures, these two minorities tend to often avoid each other. As Latinos have become more visible in U.S. society and more vocal in their demands for equality, they have come face to face with African Americans who fear that Latino gains in jobs and at the ballot box will come at their expense (Chavez 1990).

Comparative Conditions.   Table 12.1 on page 331 shows how Latinos compare with other groups. You can see that compared with European Americans and with Asian Americans, Latinos are worse off on all the indicators of well-being shown in this table. Their rankings on these indicators are very similar to those of African Americans. This table also illustrates the significance of country of origin. You can see that Cuban Americans score much better on these indicators of well-being, while conditions are considerably worse for Puerto Rican Americans. Table 12.2 on page 332 shows that almost half of Latinos do not complete high school, and only 9 percent graduate from college. In a postindustrial society that increasingly stresses advanced skills, these figures indicate growing problems.

Asian Americans

A Background of Discrimination

It was December 7, 1941, a quiet Sunday morning destined to "live in infamy," as President Roosevelt described it. Wave after wave of Japanese bombers began their dawn attack on Pearl Harbor. Beyond their expectations, the pilots found the Pacific fleet anchored like sitting ducks.

By pushing the United States into World War II, this attack changed the world political order. As the nation readied for war, no American was untouched. Many left home to battle overseas. Other millions left the farm to work in factories to support the war effort. Everyone lived with the rationing of food, gasoline, coffee, sugar, meat, and other essentials.

Just as waves of planes had rolled over Pearl Harbor, so waves of suspicion and hostility now rolled over the Japanese Americans. Many feared that Japan would invade the United States and that the Japanese Americans would fight on Japan's side (Daniels 1975). They also feared that they would sabotage military installations on the West Coast.

Although no Japanese American had been involved in even a single act of sabotage, on February 1, 1942, President Roosevelt signed Executive Order 9066, authorizing the removal of anyone considered a threat from specified military areas. All people on the West Coast who were *one-eighth Japanese or more* were imprisoned, sent to what were termed "relocation camps." They were charged with no crime. There were no indictments, no trials. Japanese ancestry was sufficient cause for being imprisoned.

This was not the first time that Asian Americans had met discrimination. Lured by gold strikes in the West and a vast need for unskilled workers, 200,000 Chinese had immigrated between 1850 and 1880. Feeling threatened by competing cheap labor, Anglo mobs and vigilantes intimidated the Chinese. Although 90 percent of the Central Pacific's labor force was Chinese, when the famous golden spike was driven at Promontory, Utah, in 1869 to mark the joining of the Union Pacific and the Central Pacific railroads, white workers prevented the Chinese from being present (Hsu 1971).

As fears of "alien genes and germs" grew, U.S. legislators passed anti-Chinese laws (Schrieke 1936). An 1850 California law, for example, required Chinese (and Latino) miners to pay a fee of $20 a month—at a time when wages were only $1 a day. The California Supreme Court even ruled that Chinese testimony against whites was inadmissible in court, a ruling that stood for almost twenty years (Carlson and Colburn 1972). In 1882 Congress passed the Chinese Exclusion Act, suspending all Chinese immigration for ten years. Four years later, the Statue of Liberty was dedicated. The tired, the poor, and the huddled masses it was to welcome were obviously not Chinese.

Spillover Bigotry.   When immigrants from Japan began to arrive, they encountered "spillover bigotry," a stereotype that lumped Asians together, depicting them as sneaky, lazy, and untrustworthy. In 1913 California passed the Alien Land Act, prohibiting anyone ineligible for citizenship from owning land. Federal law, which had initially allowed only whites to be citizens, had been amended in the 1870s to extend that right to African Americans and some Native Americans—although most Native Americans were not granted citizenship in their own land until 1924 (Amott and Matthaie 1991). The Supreme Court ruled that since Asians had not been mentioned in these amendments, they could not become citizens (Schaefer 1979). In 1943, Chinese residents were finally allowed to become citizens, but those born in Japan were excluded from citizenship until 1952.

A World of Striking Contrasts.   Today, Asian Americans are the fastest-growing U.S. minority, increasing at *fifteen* times the rate of non-Hispanic whites, and doubling in just the past ten years (Chun and Zalokar 1992). Most Asian Americans live in the West, as can be seen in Figure 12.10. The three largest groups of Asian Americans—of Chinese, Filipino, and Japanese descent—are concentrated in Los Angeles, San Francisco, Honolulu, and New York City.

Contrary to stereotypes, it is inaccurate to characterize Asian Americans as a single group. They are diverse peoples divided by separate cultures. Like Latinos, Asian Americans from different countries feel little in common with one another and are divided by social class. From Table 12.1 on page 331 you can see that Asian Americans have a higher annual income than any other racial/ethnic group listed on this table. This has led to the stereotype that all Asian Americans are successful, a stereotype that masks huge ethnic differences. For example, with more than 30 percent of all households depending on welfare for survival, Southeast Asians have the highest rate of welfare dependency of any racial or ethnic group in the United States (Dunn 1994).

The reason that most Asian Americans have done so well can be traced to four major factors: family life, supportive community, educational achievement, and assimilation into mainstream culture. Family life gives Asian Americans their basic strength, for they socialize their children into cultural values that stimulate cohesiveness and the motivation to succeed (Bell 1991). Most Asian-American children grow up in close-knit families that stress self-discipline, thrift, and industry (Suzuki 1985). The second factor, supportive community, means that the community supports the parents' efforts. For example, if a child is impolite, other adults will admonish the child and report the situation to the parents (McLemore 1994). This consistent socialization within a framework of encouragement and strict limits provides strong motivation for doing well in school. Their high ed-

Figure 12.10

Residence of Asian Americans

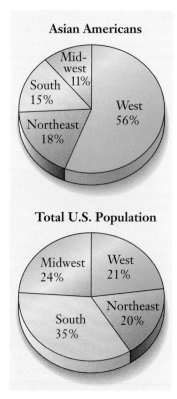

Asian Americans

Mid-west 11%
South 15%
Northeast 18%
West 56%

Total U.S. Population

Midwest 24%
West 21%
South 35%
Northeast 20%

Source: Statistical Abstract 1997: Table 30.

ucational attainment, shown in Table 12.2 on page 332, paves the way for high-paying professional and technical work, which, in turn, affords them better-than-average housing and health care. Assimilation, the fourth element, is indicated by their high intermarriage rate (see Figure 12.1 on page 312).

Recent Immigrants.   In 1975, after the United States was defeated in Vietnam, 130,000 Vietnamese, fearful for their lives because they had sided with the United States, were evacuated. Scattered to various locations across the United States, they were denied an avenue of adjustment used by previous immigrant groups, the ethnic community. On their own, however, most Vietnamese moved to California and Texas, where they established such communities.

Another group of Vietnamese arrived later, termed by the media and the public "the boat people." This group, too, barely escaped with their lives. Fleeing in leaky boats, they were attacked by pirates who robbed them and raped the women. Although no one knows the exact number, it is estimated that 200,000 drowned (McLemore 1994).

In spite of their trauma, cultural differences, and huge language barrier, these immigrants adjusted well. Their children have done remarkably well in school, with three-fourths earning overall GPAs of *A*'s and *B*'s, and over 60 percent scoring in the top half on the standardized California Achievement Test (McLemore 1994). Their high rate of interracial marriage is an indication of their assimilation: 35 percent of Vietnamese Americans born in the United States marry non-Asian Americans (Lee and Yamanaka 1990).

Native Americans

Diversity of Groups.   Thanks to countless grade-B Westerns, many Americans hold stereotypes of Native Americans on the frontier as wild, uncivilized savages, a single group of people subdivided into separate bands. The European immigrants of this period, however, encountered diverse groups of people with a variety of cultures, from nomadic hunters and gatherers to people living in wooden houses in settled agricultural communities. Each group had its own sets of norms and values—and the usual ethnocentric pride in its own cultures. Consider the following event:

> In 1744, the colonists of Virginia offered college scholarships for "savage lads." They were somewhat taken aback, however, when the Iroquois replied, "Several of our young people were formerly brought up at the colleges of Northern Provinces. They were instructed in all your sciences. But when they came back to us, they were bad runners, ignorant of every means of living in the woods, unable to bear either cold or hunger, knew neither how to build a cabin, take a deer, or kill an enemy. . . . They were totally good for nothing."
>
> They then added, "If the English gentlemen would send a dozen or two of their children to Onondaga, the great Council would take care of their education, bring them up in really what was the best manner and make men of them" (Nash 1974 in McLemore 1994).

Perhaps numbering 5 million, the Native Americans had no immunity to the diseases the Europeans brought with them. With deaths due to disease—and warfare, a much lesser cause—their number was reduced to about *one-twentieth* its size, reaching a low point of about a half million at the turn of the century. Native Americans, who now number about 2 million (see Figure 12.6 on page 327), still represent diverse groups. Like Latinos and Asian Americans, Native Americans—who speak 150 different languages—do not think of themselves as a single people that justifies a single label (McLemore 1994).

From Treaties to Genocide and Population Transfer.   At first, relations between the European settlers and the Native Americans were by and large peaceful. The Native Americans accommodated the strangers, as there was plenty of land for both. As wave after wave of settlers continued to arrive, however, Pontiac, an Ottawa chief, saw the fu-

Of all the oppressive acts perpetrated against the Native Americans by the dominant Anglos, the Trail of Tears was certainly one of the most brutal. This painting presents a sanitized version of events; most victims walked (some were barefoot, although it was winter), and dead bodies were left strewn along the trail. Also, it is unlikely that any Native American was allowed to possess a rifle.

ture—and didn't like it. He convinced several tribes to unite in an effort to push the Europeans into the sea. He almost succeeded, but failed when the English were reinforced by fresh troops (McLemore 1994).

A pattern developed. The U.S. government would make treaties to buy some of a tribe's land, with the promise to honor forever the tribe's right to what it had not sold. European immigrants who continued to pour into the United States would disregard these boundaries. The tribes would resist, with death tolls on both sides. Washington would then intervene—not to enforce the treaty—but to force the tribe off its lands. In its relentless drive westward, the U.S. government embarked on a policy of genocide. The U.S. Cavalry was assigned the task of "pacification," which translates as slaughtering Native Americans who "stood in the way" of this territorial expansion.

The acts of cruelty perpetrated by the Europeans against Native Americans appear endless, but two of the most grisly were the distribution of blankets contaminated with smallpox under the guise of a peace offering, and the Trail of Tears, a march of a thousand miles from the Carolinas and Georgia to Oklahoma. Conditions were so bad that of the 15 thousand Cherokees who were forced to make this midwinter march, four thousand died. The symbolic end to Native American resistance was the 1890 massacre at Wounded Knee, South Dakota. Of 350 men, women, and children, the U.S. cavalry gunned down 300 (Thornton 1987; Lind 1995). These acts took place after the U.S. government changed its policy from genocide to population transfer and began to confine Native Americans to specified areas called *reservations*.

The Invisible Minority and Self-Determination. Native Americans can truly be called the invisible minority. Because about 50 percent live in rural areas and one-third in just three states—Oklahoma, California, and Arizona—most other Americans are hardly conscious of a Native American presence in U.S. society. The isolation of two of every five Native Americans on reservations further reduces their visibility (Thornton 1987; *Statistical Abstract* 1997:Table 51).

The systematic attempts of European Americans to destroy the Native Americans' way of life and their resettlement onto reservations continue to have deleterious effects. Of all U.S. minorities, Native Americans are the worst off. As Table 12.1 on page 331 shows, the poverty rate of Native Americans is high. In addition, their life expectancy is lower than that of the nation as a whole, and their rates of suicide and alcoholism are higher (U.S. Department of Health and Human Services 1990). As Table 12.2 on page 332 shows, their education so lags behind the nation that only 9 percent graduate from college. The percentage of doctorates earned by Native Americans also remains below their proportion of the population.

These negative conditions are the consequence of Anglo domination. In the 1800s, U.S. courts determined that Native Americans did not own the land on which they had been settled and had no right to develop their resources. Native Americans were made wards of the state and treated like children by the Bureau of Indian Affairs (Mohawk 1991). Then, in the 1960s, Native Americans won a series of legal victories that restored their control over the land and their right to determine economic policy. As a result, several Native American tribes have opened businesses on their lands—ranging from industrial parks serving major metropolitan areas to fish canneries. Perhaps the development that has attracted the most attention is the opening of casinos, which for some tribes offers an exit from poverty. More than 200 tribes operate gambling businesses that generate about $2.5 billion a year (McLemore 1994). One small tribe, the Mdewakanton Dakota in Minnesota, which has just 270 members, has struck it rich. Its casino nets over $600,000 a year for each man, woman, and child (Farney 1998).

A highly controversial issue is *separatism*. Because Native Americans were independent peoples when the Europeans arrived and they never willingly joined the United States, many tribes maintain the right to remain separate from the U.S. government and U.S. society. The chief of the Onondaga tribe in New York, a member of the Iroquois Federation, summarizes the issue this way:

> For the whole history of the Iroquois we have maintained that we are a separate nation. We have never lost a war. Our government still operates. We have refused the U.S. government's reorganization plans for us. We have kept our language and our traditions, and when we fly to Geneva to UN meetings, we carry Hau de no sau nee passports. We made some treaties that lost some land, but that also confirmed our separate-nation status. That the U.S. denies all this doesn't make it any less the case. (Mander 1992)

One of the most significant changes is **pan-Indianism,** an emphasis on common elements that run through Native American cultures in the attempt to develop a self-identity that goes beyond the tribe. Whether Native Americans wish to work together as in pan-Indianism, or to stress separatism and to identify solely with their tribes, to assimilate into the dominant culture or to remain apart from it, to move to cities or to remain on reservations, to manufacture electronics or to engage only in traditional activities— "Such decisions must be ours," say the Native Americans. "We are sovereign, and will not take orders from the victors of the last centuries' wars."

Looking Toward the Future ▶

Race and ethnic relations are one of the most volatile topics facing the United States. As we enter the new century, two issues we are grappling with are immigration and affirmative action.

The Immigration Debate

Both welcoming immigration and fearing its consequences are central to U.S. history. The gates opened wide (numerically, if not in attitude) for a massive wave of immigrants who arrived in the late nineteenth and early twentieth centuries. During the past 15 years, a second great wave of immigration has brought about a million new residents to the United States each year (*Statistical Abstract* 1995:Table 5). Unlike the first wave, which was almost exclusively from western Europe, this second wave has brought with it much greater

pan-Indianism: a movement that focuses on common elements in Native-American culture in order to develop a mutual self-identity and to work toward the welfare of all Native Americans

variety. In fact, it is changing the U.S. racial-ethnic mix (Henry 1990; Stevenson 1992; Lind 1995). If current trends in immigration (and birth) persist, somewhere between the years 2056 and 2080 the "average" American will trace his or her ancestry to Africa, Asia, South America, the Pacific Islands, the Middle East—to almost anywhere but white Europe.

In some states, the future is arriving much more quickly than this. In just a couple of years, California is expected to be the first state in which ethnic and racial minorities together constitute the majority. Already this is true in California's schools, where Latino, Asian- and African-American students outnumber non-Hispanic white students. Californians who request new telephone service from Pacific Bell can speak to customer service representatives in English, Spanish, Korean, Vietnamese, Mandarin, or Cantonese.

As in the past, there is a widespread concern that "too many" immigrants will alter the character of the United States. "Throughout the history of American immigration," write sociologists Alejandro Portés and Ruben Rumbaut (1990), "a consistent thread has been the fear that the 'alien element' would somehow undermine the institutions of the country and would lead it down the path of disintegration and decay." A widespread fear held by native-born European Americans in the early part of the century was that immigrants would subvert the democratic system in favor of communism. Today, some fear that the primacy of the English language is threatened. In addition, the age-old fear that immigrants will take jobs away from native-born Americans remains strong. Finally, minority groups that struggled for political representation fear that newer groups will gain political power at their expense.

Affirmative Action

The role of affirmative action in our multicultural society lies at the center of a national debate about how to steer a course in race and ethnic relations. In this policy, goals based on race (and gender) are used in hiring and college admissions. Liberals, both white and minority, defend affirmative action, saying that it is the most direct way to level the playing field of economic opportunity. If whites are passed over, this is an unfortunate cost we must pay if we are to make up for past discrimination. Conservatives, in contrast, both white and minority, agree that opportunity should be open to all, but say that putting race (or sex) ahead of people's ability to perform a job is reverse discrimination. Because of their race (or sex), qualified people who had nothing to do with past discrimination are being discriminated against. They add that affirmative action stigmatizes the people who benefit from it because it suggests that they hold their jobs because of race (or sex), rather than merit.

This national debate crystallized with a series of controversial rulings during the 1990s. Perhaps the most significant was Proposition 209, an amendment to the California state constitution that banned race and gender preferences in hiring and in college admissions. Despite appeals by a coalition of civil rights groups, the U.S. Supreme Court upheld the California law in 1997, making it likely that other states will follow California's lead. Certainly the issue of the proper role of affirmative action in a multicultural society is likely to remain center stage for quite some time.

Toward a True Multicultural Society

The potential is for the United States to become a society in which different racial-ethnic groups not only co-exist, but where they respect one another and work for mutually beneficial goals. The idea of a multicultural society is for the various minority groups that make up the United States to participate fully in the social institutions of the country while maintaining their individual cultural integrity. This, however, is only a potential. To reach it will require that groups with different histories and cultures *accept* one another. Among other things, this means that U.S. citizens—especially those who belong to the group that has taken its dominance for granted since the founding of the nation—must grapple with their traditional beliefs and national symbols. For example, does the Alamo represent the heroic action of dedicated Americans struggling against overwhelming odds—or the death of extremists bent on wresting territory from Mexico? Was the West settled by individuals determined to find economic opportunity and freedom from oppression—or was it a savage conquest, another brutal expression of white imperialism? Such issues are the focus of the Thinking Critically section that concludes this chapter.

Thinking Critically About Social Controversy

Whose History?

▼ As Symbolic Interactionists stress, the events of life do not come with built-in meaning. Instead, they are given meaning by being placed within a framework that interprets them. Consequently, the victors and the vanquished don't view events in the same way.

Consider the Battle of Little Bighorn. U.S. history books usually recount the massacre of an outnumbered, brave band of cavalrymen, with Gen. George Custer going down to a sad but somehow glorious defeat. When Joe Marshall, a Lakota Sioux, heard this version as a fourth-grader, he mustered all the courage he could, raised his hand, and told the class the version he had heard as he was growing up among the descendants of survivors of the battle. This version refers to an armed group invading Native American lands. When the young boy finished, his teacher smiled indulgently and said, "That's nice, but we'll stick to the real story."

The U.S. history books say there were no survivors of this battle. Think about this for a moment, and the point about perspectives in history will become even more obvious. For the Native Americans, there were *many* survivors. Indeed, those survivors kept the memory of the battle alive, using what is called "oral tradition" to pass to the next generation what took place during that battle. Their descendants have written a book that recounts those events, but the white officials who head the Little Bighorn Battlefield National Monument won't let the book be sold there—only books that recount events from the European-American perspective may be sold.

This issue of perspective underlies the current controversy surrounding the teaching of history in U.S. schools. The question of *what* should be taught was always assumed, for the school boards, teachers, and textbook writers were united by a background of shared assumptions. It was assumed unquestioningly, for example, that George Washington was the general-hero-founder of the nation. No question was raised about whether school curricula should mention that he owned slaves. In the first place, most white boards, teachers, and textbook writers were ignorant of such facts, and, secondly, on learning of them, thought them irrelevant.

But no longer. The issue now is one of balance—how to make certain that the accomplishments of both genders and our many racial and ethnic groups are included in teaching. This issue, called *multiculturalism*, is now central to school districts around the nation. Teachers, administrators, school boards, and publishers are wrestling with a slew of difficult questions. How much space should be given to Harriet Tubman versus George Washington? Is enough attention paid to discrimination against Asian Americans? to Latinos? Is the attempted genocide of Native Americans sufficiently acknowledged? What about the contributions to U.S. society of women? How about those of white ethnics—Poles, Russians, and so on?

No one yet knows the answers. What is certain at this point is that the imagery of U.S. society has changed—from a melting pot to a tossed salad. At the heart of the current issue is the fact that so many groups have retained separate identities, instead of fusing into one as was "supposed" to happen. The question being decided now is how much emphasis should be given to the salad as a whole, and how much to the cucumbers, tomatoes, lettuce, and so on.

The answers to such questions will give birth to new images of history, which, rather than consisting of established past events, as is commonly supposed, is a flowing, winding, and sometimes twisted perception that takes place in the present.

Sources: Glazer 1991; Charlier 1992. ▲

Summary and Review

Laying the Sociological Foundation

How is race both a reality and a myth?

In the sense that different groups inherit distinctive physical characteristics, race is a reality. In the sense of one race being superior to another and of there being pure races, however, race is a myth. The *idea* of race is powerful, shaping basic relationships among people. Pp. 311–313.

How do race and ethnicity differ?

Race refers to inherited biological characteristics; **ethnicity,** to cultural ones. Ethnic groups identify with one another on the basis of common ancestry and cultural heritage. P. 314.

What are minority and dominant groups?

Minority groups are people singled out for unequal treatment by members of the **dominant group,** the group with more power, privilege, and social status. Minorities originate with the expansion of political boundaries or migration. Pp. 314–316.

Are prejudice and discrimination the same thing?

Prejudice is an attitude, **discrimination** an act. Some people who are prejudiced do not discriminate, while others who are not prejudiced do. Pp. 316–318.

How do individual and institutional discrimination differ?

Individual discrimination is the negative treatment of one person by another, while **institutional discrimination** is discrimination built into a society's social institutions. Institutional discrimination often occurs without the awareness of either the perpetrator or the object of discrimination. Referral rates for coronary bypass surgery are but one example. Pp. 318–319.

Theories of Prejudice

How do psychologists explain prejudice?

Psychological theories of prejudice stress frustration displaced toward **scapegoats** and **authoritarian personalities.** Pp. 320–321.

How do sociologists explain prejudice?

Sociological theories focus on how different social environments increase or decrease prejudice. Functionalists stress the benefits and costs that come from discrimination. Conflict theorists look at how the groups in power exploit racial and ethnic group divisions in order to hold down wages and otherwise maintain power. Symbolic interac-

tionists stress how labels create **selective perception** and self-fulfilling prophecies. Pp. 321–323.

Global Patterns of Intergroup Relations

What are the major patterns of minority and dominant group relations?

Beginning with the least humane, they are **genocide, population transfer, internal colonialism, segregation, assimilation,** and **multiculturalism (pluralism).** Pp. 324–326.

Race and Ethnic Relations in the United States

What are the major ethnic groups in the United States?

From largest to smallest, the major ethnic groups are European Americans, African Americans, Latinos, Asian Americans, and Native Americans. P. 326.

What heightens ethnic identity, and what is "ethnic work"?

A group's size, power, physical characteristics, and amount of discrimination heighten or reduce ethnic identity. **Ethnic work** is the process of constructing an ethnic identity. For people with strong ties to their culture of origin, ethic work involves enhancing and maintaining group distinctions. For those without a firm ethnic identity, ethnic work is an attempt to recover one's ethnic heritage. Pp. 326–327.

What are some issues in race/ethnic relations and characteristics of minority groups today?

African Americans are increasingly divided into middle and lower classes, with two sharply contrasting worlds of experience. Illegal immigration has led to a backlash against Latinos, who are themselves divided by country of origin. On many measures, Asian Americans are better off than white Americans, but their well–being varies with country of origin. For Native Americans, the primary issues are poverty, nationhood, and settling treaty obligations. The overarching issue for minorities is overcoming discrimination. Pp. 328–339.

Looking Toward the Future

What main issues dominate race-ethnic relations?

The main issues are immigration, affirmative action, and how to develop a true multicultural society. The answers affect our future. Pp. 339–341

Where can I read more on this topic?

Suggested readings for this chapter are listed on page 663.

Sociology and the Internet

All URLs listed are current as of the printing of this book. URLs are often changed. Please check our Website http://www.abacon.com/henslin for updates.

1. Throughout the text, you have been led step-by-step through Internet projects. Now you have a chance to design your own. You've read about four minority groups in the United States: African Americans, Hispanic Americans, Asian Americans, and Native Americans. Now explore the Net to learn about one of these groups. Go to *http://www.yahoo!.com/* and select the category "Social Science." Toward the top of the page (under the search space), you will find a list that includes "African American Studies," "Asian American Studies," "Latin American Studies," and "Native American Studies." Select one of the groups and start surfing! For example, under "Native American Studies," "History," you will find the category "First Person Histories of NW Coast." There you will find fascinating narratives, great graphics (if your system supports them), and a lot of information. You decide where to go with this—your instructor will help you decide what final form your discussion or report will take.

2. In the Sociology and the New Technology box "Technology and the African-American Experience," you learned about the impact of mechanical cotton pickers on the employment of African Americans working in the cotton fields. Perhaps more important, you were introduced to *The Promised Land* by Nicholas Lemann, a leading U.S. writer on race, class, and poverty. Lemann is a contributing editor for *Atlantic Monthly*. You can access that home page at *http://www.theatlantic.com/atlantic/* Then click on Search. In the search box, type "Nicholas Lemann" and select the "Search for" button. You should now see a list of topics. Select "Lemann biography" and read this brief introduction to the author. Select "Author Index." (If you can't get there, start over with the home page and repeat the search.) First, read the article "The Origins of the Underclass," which relates to the migration discussed in *The Promised Land*. (The article is in

two parts). After you have read both parts of the article, go back to the search results and find "The Unfinished War" (another two-part article). Read both parts of Lemann's treatise on the War on Poverty. Return to your search results and select "Philadelphia: Black Nationalism on Campus." Do you agree that multiculturalism and assimilation are not incompatible?

Write a paper summarizing each of the articles; then integrate the ideas into a single statement. To do this, you will have to draw your own conclusions about the relationships among the various ideas.

3. Examine the following sites concerning the controversy over "Black English" (BE):

http://www.princeton.edu/~bclewis/blacktalk.html
http://www.gmu.edu/departments/economics/Articles/
   Black-English.htm

What is "Black English"? Compare and contrast the two opposing views of BE. What is the history of BE? How is BE associated with racial inequality in the U.S.? Why is it important to examine the history and role of BE in the education of African-American children? Like other languages BE is rich in history, but it is not recognized as a legitimate language. Why? What are the functions and dysfunctions for African Americans of teaching academic subjects in BE in the U.S. school system? What are the functions and dysfunctions of teaching BE as a language—like German, Spanish, Latin?

4. Your text discusses the concepts of Afrocentrism and multiculturalism. It suggests that the Afrocentric movement has led to the celebration of Kwanzaa. Examine the Kwanzaa page at *http://www.melanet.com/kwanzaa/* and discuss whether you feel the addition of Kwanzaa to the December holiday calendar is a product of Afrocentrism or a sign of the spread of multiculturalism.

Deidre Scherer, Fragments, 1987

Inequalities of Age

I N 1928, CHARLES HART, *who was working on his Ph.D. in anthropology, did field-work with the Tiwi, a preliterate people who live on an island off the northern coast of Australia. Because every Tiwi belongs to a clan, they assigned Hart to the bird (Jabijabui) clan and told him that a particular woman was his mother. Hart describes the woman as "toothless, almost blind, withered," who was "physically quite revolting and mentally rather senile." He then describes this remarkable event:*

> *[T]oward the end of my time on the islands an incident occurred that surprised me because it suggested that some of them had been taking my presence in the kinship system much more seriously than I had thought. I was approached by a group of about eight or nine senior men, all of whom I knew. They were all senior members of the Jabijabui clan and they had decided among themselves that the time had come to get rid of the decrepit old woman who had first called me son and whom I now called mother. As I knew, they said, it was Tiwi custom, when an old woman became too feeble to look after herself, to "cover her up." This could only be done by her sons and brothers and all of them had to agree beforehand, since once it was done, they did not want any dissension among the brothers or clansmen, as that might lead to a feud. My "mother" was now completely blind, she was constantly falling over logs or into fires, and they, her senior clansmen, were in agreement that she would be better out of the way. Did I agree?*

> *I already knew about "covering up." The Tiwi, like many other hunting and gathering peoples, sometimes got rid of their ancient and decrepit females. The method was to dig a hole in the ground in some lonely place, put the old woman in the hole and fill it in with earth until only her head was showing. Everybody went away for a day or two and then went back to the hole to discover to their surprise, that the old woman was dead, having been too feeble to raise her arms from the earth. Nobody had "killed" her; her death in Tiwi eyes was a natural one. She had been alive when her relatives last saw her. I had never seen it done, though I knew it was the custom, so I asked my brothers if it was necessary for me to attend the "covering up." They said no and that they would do it, but only after they had my agreement. Of course I agreed, and a week or two later we heard in our camp that my "mother" was dead, and we wailed and put on the trimmings of mourning. (Hart 1970:154)*

Aging in Global Perspective

Apart from the morality of agreeing that the old woman should be "covered up"—and Hart seems to have been more concerned about not having to watch the act than acquiescing to it—what is of interest is how the Tiwi, a group living on an island off the northern coast of Australia, treated their frail elderly—or, more specifically, their frail *female* elderly. (You probably noticed the Tiwi "covered up" only old women. As noted in Chapter 11, females are discriminated against throughout the world. As this case makes evident, in some places that discrimination extends even to death.)

Every society must deal with the problem of people growing old, some of whom grow very frail. Although few societies choose to bury them alive, all must decide how to allocate limited resources among their citizens. As the proportion of the population that is old increases, as is happening in many nations, those decisions become more complex and the tensions they generate among the generations deepen.

The Social Construction of Aging

The example of how the Tiwi treat their frail female elderly reflects one extreme in how societies cope with aging. An extreme in a different direction is illustrated by the Abkhasians, an agricultural people who live in a mountainous region of Georgia, a republic of the former Soviet Union. Rather than "covering up" their elderly, the Abkhasians give them high respect and look to them for guidance. They would no more dispense with one of their elderly in this manner than we would "cover up" a sick child.

The Abkhasians may be the longest-lived people in the world. Many claim to live past 100—some beyond 120 and even 130 (Benet 1971). Although it is difficult to document the accuracy of these claims (Haslick 1974; Harris 1990), government records indicate that an extraordinary number of Abkhasians do live to a very old age. Three main factors appear to account for their long lives. The first is their diet, which consists of little meat, much fresh fruit, vegetables, garlic, goat cheese, cornmeal, buttermilk, and wine. The second is their lifelong physical activity. They do slow down after age 80, but even after the age of 100 they still work about 4 hours a day.

The third factor—a highly developed sense of community—goes to the very heart of the Abkhasian culture. From childhood, each individual is highly integrated into a primary group, and remains so throughout life. There is no such thing as a nursing home, nor do the elderly live alone. Because even into old age they continue to work and contribute to the group's welfare, they aren't a burden to anyone. They don't vegetate, nor do they have the need to "fill time" with bingo and shuffleboard. In short, the elderly feel no sudden rupture between what they "were" and what they "are."

The examples of the Tiwi and the Abkhasians reveal an important sociological principle we shall explore in this chapter—that aging is *socially constructed.* That is, nothing in the nature of aging summons forth any particular set of attitudes. Rather, attitudes toward the aged—and resulting behaviors—are rooted in society, and therefore differ from one social group to another. As we shall also see, even when people are considered old depends not on biology, but on culture.

Demonstrating a traditional Abkhasian dance is Tamdel Djopua, who is 102 years old. The text suggests reasons for the Abkhasians' remarkable longevity.

Central to a group's culture are ways of viewing reality. Living for centuries in isolation on Bathurst and Melville Islands off the northern coast of Australia, the Tiwi, featured in the opening vignette, developed a unique culture. Shown here is Wurarbuti, prior to leading a funeral dance. To be certain that his late uncle's ghost will not recognize him, Wurarbuti is wearing a "shirt" painted with ocher and clay, a topknot of cockatoo feathers, and a beard of goose feathers.

TABLE 13.1				
The Elderly in Cross-Cultural Perspective				
Country	*Total Population*	*Percentage over 65*	*Number over 65*	*Percentage of Payroll Paid in Taxes to Support the Elderly*
Italy	58,000,000	17.0	10,000,000	28.3
Spain	39,000,000	16.0	6,000,000	28.3
Great Britain	59,000,000	15.7	9,000,000	22.2
France	58,000,000	15.6	9,000,000	16.5
Germany	84,000,000	15.4	13,000,000	19.2
Japan	126,000,000	15.4	10,000,000	16.5
Holland	16,000,000	13.4	2,000,000	31.8
United States	268,000,000	12.7	34,000,000	12.4
Canada	29,000,000	12.5	4,000,000	5.4
China	1,221,000,000	6.4	78,000,000	N/A
Mexico	98,000,000	4.5	4,000,000	N/A
Egypt	65,000,000	3.6	2,000,000	N/A
Kenya	29,000,000	2.6	750,000	N/A

Source: Statistical Abstract 1997:Tables 1334, 1335, 1337.

Effects of Industrialization

As noted in previous chapters, industrialization is a worldwide trend. Along with a higher standard of living, with industrialization comes a more plentiful food supply, better public health measures, especially a purer water supply, and a largely successful fight against the diseases that kill people at younger ages. Consequently, when a country industrializes more of its people reach older ages. Look at Table 13.1. You can see that the last four countries listed on the table, which are not industrialized, have only one-sixth to one-half the proportion of elderly as do industrialized nations.

As a nation's elderly increases, so, too, does the bill its younger citizens pay to provide for their needs. In the Most Industrialized Nations, this bill has become a major social issue. Although Americans commonly complain that Social Security taxes are too high, Table 13.1 shows that the U.S. rate is comparatively low. In the Least Industrialized Nations, there are no social security taxes, and families are expected to take care of their own elderly.

The Graying of America

Figure 13.1 shows how extensively U.S. life expectancy has increased throughout the century. To me, and perhaps to you, it is startling to realize that less than a hundred years ago the average American would not even see age 50. Since then, **life expectancy** has increased so greatly that Americans born today can expect to live until their 70s or 80s.

The term **graying of America** has been coined to refer to this increasing proportion of older people in the U.S. population. As Figure 13.2 shows, in 1900 only 4 percent of Americans were age 65 and over. Today the figure stands at almost 13 percent. When the average person reaches 65, he or she can expect to live another seventeen years (*Statistical Abstract* 1997:Table 119). U.S. society has become so "gray" that there are now almost eight million *more* elderly Americans than teenagers (*Statistical Abstract* 1997:Table 22).

life expectancy: the number of years that an average newborn can expect to live

graying of America: a term that refers to the rising proportion of older people as a percentage of the U.S. population

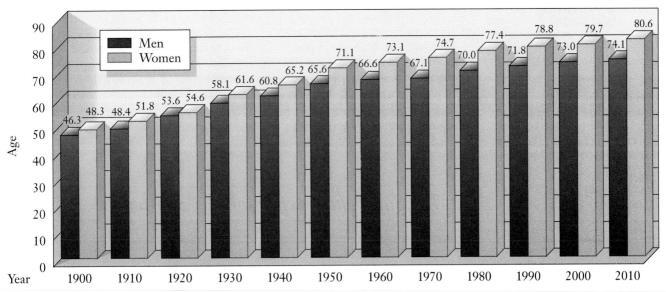

Sources: *Historical Statistics of the United States, Colonial Times to 1970*, Bicentennial Edition, Part 1, Series B, 107–115; *Statistical Abstract* 1997:Table 117.

We also can note that we have a long way to go, for as you can see from Table 13.2 (on the next page), on a global scale Americans rank just seventeenth in life expectancy.

As anyone who has ever visited Florida has noticed, the elderly population is not evenly distributed around the country. (As Jerry Seinfeld sardonically notes, "There is a law that when you get old you've got to move to Florida.") The Social Map on the next page shows how uneven this distribution is expected to be in a couple of decades or so.

It is important to keep in mind that the maximum length of life, the **life span,** has not increased. Experts disagree, however, on what the maximum is. We do know, however, that it is at least 122, for this was the well-documented age of Jeanne Louise Calment of France at her death. If the reports on the Abkhasians are correct, a matter of controversy, the human life span may exceed even this number by a comfortable margin.

Race or Ethnicity and Aging. Due largely to social class, the U.S. racial-ethnic groups have different proportions of elderly (Harper 1990; Treas 1995). For example, compared

Figure 13.1

U.S. Life Expectancy by Year of Birth

life span: The maximum length of life of a species

Figure 13.2

The Graying of America

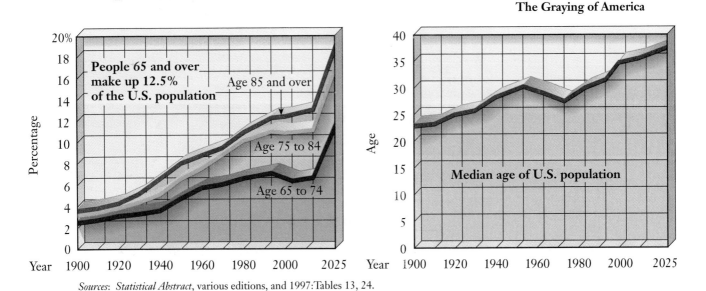

Sources: *Statistical Abstract*, various editions, and 1997:Tables 13, 24.

TABLE 13.2

U.S. Life Expectancy in Perspective

World Rank	Country	Life Expectancy at Birth
1	Hong Kong	82.4
2	Japan	79.7
3	Australia	79.6
4	Canada	79.3
5	France	78.6
6	Spain	78.5
7	Greece	78.3
8	Italy	78.2
9	Sweden	78.2
10	Holland	77.9
11	Switzerland	77.8
12	Belgium	77.2
13	Austria	76.7
14	Great Britain	76.6
15	Taiwan	76.3
16	Germany	76.1
17	United States	76.0

Source: Statistical Abstract
1997:Table 1336.

with African Americans a larger proportion of white Americans is over age 65. Of all racial-ethnic groups, Native Americans have the smallest proportion of elderly.

Currently, only about 10 percent of the U.S. elderly are minorities, but because the proportion of non-whites in the U.S. population is growing, so is their representation among the U.S. elderly. In a generation, the overall total of minority elderly will increase to 15 percent, while in California, which attracts large numbers of minorities, this percentage will reach 40 percent (Wray 1991). Differences in cultural attitudes about aging, family relationships, work histories, and health practices will be important areas of sociological investigation in coming years.

 The Symbolic Interactionist Perspective

To study how aging is socially constructed, symbolic interactionists examine how the symbols associated with age affect our perceptions. Let's look, then, at how culture underlies our ideas of when a person becomes "old," and then at how negative stereotypes and the mass media affect our perceptions of aging.

Labeling and the Onset of Old Age

You probably can remember when you thought a 12-year-old was "old"—and anyone older beyond reckoning, just "up there" someplace. You probably were 5 or 6 at the time. Similarly, to a 12-year-old someone of 21 seems "old." At 21, 30 may mark that line, and 40 may seem "very old." And so it keeps on going, with "old" gradually receding from the self. To people who turn 40, 50 seems old; at 50, the late 60s look old (not the early 60s, for at that point in accelerating years they don't seem too far away).

At some point, of course, an individual must apply the label "old" to himself or herself. Often, cultural definitions of age force this label on people sooner than they are ready

Figure 13.3

As Florida Goes, So Goes the Nation

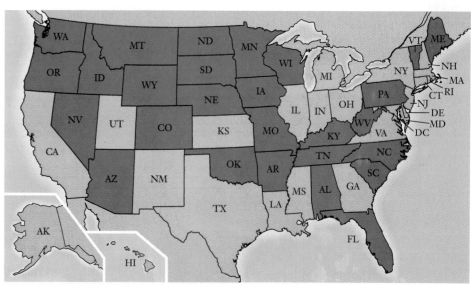

■ 20% or more elderly   ☐ Less than 20% elderly

Note: The growing proportion of the elderly in the U.S. population is destined to have profound effects on U.S. society. By the year 2025, one-fifth of the population of 27 states is expected to be age 65 or older. Today, at 19 percent, only Florida comes close to this.

Source: U.S. Bureau of the Census, 1996, U.S. Department of Commerce, PPL-47.

to accept it. In the typical case, the individual has become used to what he or she sees in the mirror. The changes have taken place very gradually, and each change, if not exactly taken in stride, has been accommodated. (Consequently, it comes as a shock, when meeting a friend one has not seen in years, to see how much that person has changed. At class reunions, *each* person can hardly believe how much older *the others* appear!)

If there is no single point at which people automatically cross a magical line and become "old," what, then, makes someone "old"? We can point to several factors that spur people to apply the label of old to themselves.

The first factor is *biology*. One person may experience "signs" of aging much earlier than another: wrinkles, balding, aches, difficulty in doing some things that he or she used to take for granted. Consequently, one person will feel "old" at an earlier or later age than others, and only at that time *adopt the role of an "old person,"* that is, begin to act in ways old people in that particular society are thought to act.

Personal history or biography is a second factor that influences when people consider themselves old. An accident that limits mobility may make one person feel old sooner than others. Or a woman may have given birth at 16 to a daughter, who in turn has a child at 18. When this woman is 34, she is a biological grandmother. It is most unlikely that she will begin to play any stereotypical role—spending the day in a rocking chair, for example—but *knowing* that she is a grandmother has an impact on her self-concept. At a minimum, she must *deny* that she is old.

A third factor in determining when people label themselves old is **gender age,** the relative value that a culture places on men's and women's ages. For example, around the world, compared to most women most men are able to marry much younger spouses. Similarly, on men graying hair and even some wrinkles may be seen as signs of "maturing," while on women those same features are likely to be interpreted as signs of "old."

Marie-Louise Meilleur of Corbeil, Ontario, Canada, is the world's oldest living person whose age can be authenticated. Cutting Marie-Louise's 117th birthday cake is the premier of Ontario, Mike Harris. The world's previous oldest living person, Jeanne Calment of France, died in 1997 at the age of 122.

Aging depends on much more than biology, and classifying oneself as old depends on many factors, including cultural guidelines and biography. What biographical factors do you think were significant for this woman of the Great Depression?

gender age: the relative values of men's and women's ages in a particular culture

As emphasized in the text, age is much more than biology. The point at which old age begins, for example, differs from one culture to another. In some cultures, Tom Selleck, at age 50, would be considered an old man, but on the popular television show Friends *he portrayed the romantic lead opposite Courteney Cox, age 31.*

"Mature" and "old," of course, carry quite different meanings in Western cultures—the first is desired, while the second is shunned. Two striking examples of gender age in U.S. society are found in the mass media. Older male news anchors are likely to be retained, while female anchors who turn the same age are more likely to be transferred to a less visible position. Similarly, in movies older men are much more likely to play romantic leads—and opposite much younger rising stars.

Many individuals, of course, are exceptions to these patterns. Maria, for example, may marry Bill, who is fourteen years younger than she. But in most marriages in which there is a fourteen-year age gap between husband and wife, around the world the odds greatly favor the wife being the younger of the pair. Biology, of course, has nothing to do with this socially constructed reality.

The fourth factor is *timetables*, the signals societies use to inform their members that they are old. Since there is no automatic age at which people become "old," these timetables vary around the world. One group may choose a particular birthday, such as the 60th or 65th, to signal the onset of old age. Other groups may not even have birthdays, making such numbers meaningless. Only after they moved to reservations, for example, did Native Americans adopt the white custom of counting birthdays. For traditional Native Americans, the signal for old age is more the inability to perform productive social roles than any particular birthday. Consequently, those unable to continue in these roles tend to think of themselves as old, regardless of their age. In one survey, for instance, a Native American woman with many disabilities described herself as elderly, although she was only 37 (Kramer 1992).

The Meaning of Old Age: Cross-Cultural Comparisons

To help pinpoint the extent to which people's experience of old age involves factors beyond biology, let's look at three cross-cultural examples.

Consider first this fictionalized conversation between two Tiwi men:

Bashti looked in envy at Masta. Masta strutted just a bit as he noticed Bashti glance his way. He knew what Bashti was thinking. Had he not thought the same just twenty years earlier? Then he had no wife; now he had three. Then he had no grand hut. Now he did, plus one for each wife. Then he had no respect, no power, no wealth. Now he was looked up to by everyone. "Ah, the marvels and beauty of gray hair," Masta thought.

Bashti hung his head as he slouched toward the fringe of the group. "But my turn will come. I, too, will grow old," he thought, finding some comfort in the situation.

Why would a Tiwi man look forward to growing old, something that few people in the United States do? Traditional Tiwi society was a **gerontocracy,** a society run by the elderly. The old men were firmly entrenched in power and controlled everything. Their power was so inclusive that the old men married *all* the women—both young and old—leaving none for the young men. Only at about the age of 40 was a man able to marry (Hart and Pilling 1970). (In Tiwi society, females were the pawns, and aging was of no advantage to a woman. Indeed, as we saw in the opening vignette, for a woman aging could be a considerable disadvantage.)

Traditional Eskimo society also provides a rich contrast to that of an industrialized society such as the United States.

Shantu and Wishta fondly kissed their children and grandchildren farewell. Then sadly, but with resignation at the sacrifice they knew they had to make for their family, they slowly climbed onto the ice floe. The goodbyes were painfully made as the large slab of ice inched into the ocean currents. Shantu and Wishta would now starve. But they were old, and their death was necessary, for it reduced the demand on the small group's scarce food supply.

gerontocracy: a society (or some other group) run by the elderly

As the younger relatives watched Shantu and Wishta recede into the distance, each knew that their turn to make this sacrifice would come. Each hoped that they would face it as courageously.

To grow old in traditional Eskimo society meant a "voluntary" death. Survival in their harsh environment was so precarious that all, except very young children, had to pull their own weight. The food supply was so limited that nothing was left over to give to anyone who could not participate in the closely integrated tasks required for survival.

Finally, consider how old age brought honor and respect in traditional Chinese society:

> Wong Fu bowed deeply as he met Ming Chau. When Ming Chau sat down, Wong Fu shyly took a seat at his side. Wong Fu had wanted to speak to Ming Chau for some time. Ming Chau was in his 80s, and his many years of experience had brought wisdom. Wong Fu was certain that Ming Chau would have the answer for his problem. He would remain silent until Ming Chau asked him about his family. Perhaps then he might be able to bring the matter up. If not, he would wait until the next time he was able to meet with Ming Chau.

▼ **In Sum** Symbolic interactionists stress that, by itself, old age has no particular meaning. There is nothing about old age that automatically summons forth responses of honor and respect (as with the Abkhasians and the traditional Chinese), envy (as with the Tiwi), or resignation (as with the traditional Eskimo). This perspective helps us see the role of culture in how we view the process of growing old—how the social modifies the biological.

As a society changes, so can its meanings of aging. This is especially likely to happen if a society adopts capitalism and industrializes. The Perspectives box below examines this change in China.

Perspectives

CULTURAL DIVERSITY AROUND THE WORLD

China: Changing Sentiment About the Elderly

As she contemplates her future, Zhao Chunlan, a 71-year-old widow, smiles shyly, but with evident deep satisfaction. She has heard about sons abandoning their aged parents. She has even heard whispering about brutality.

But Zhao has no such fears.

It is not that her son is such an exceptionally devoted man that he would never swerve from his traditional duty to his aging mother. Instead, it is a piece of paper that puts Zhao's mind at ease. Her 51-year-old son has signed a support agreement: he will cook her special meals, take her to regular medical checkups, even give her the largest room in his house and put his family's color television in it (Sun 1990).

The elderly have always occupied a high status in China. The outline is well known: They are considered a source of wisdom, given honored seating at both family and public gatherings, even venerated after death in ancestor worship.

Although this outline often may have represented more ideal than real culture, it appears to have been generally true. As China industrializes, however, the bonds among generations are weakening. Also contributing to this change is a longer life expectancy and a national birth policy that allows only one child to each married couple. Consequently, the over-65 population is mushrooming. Now about 66 million, or 6 percent of the population, the elderly may soar to 40 percent in the next fifty years (Sun 1990; Kinsella and Taeuber 1993).

With no national security system, it is essential that children provide for the elderly. To make sure, and in view of evidence that bonds are weakening, many local officials insist that adult children sign support agreements for their aged parents. One province has hit on an ingenious device: In order to get a marriage license, the couple must sign a contract pledging to support their parents after they reach 60 (Sun 1990).

"I'm sure he would do right by me, anyway," says Zhao, "but this way I know he will."

The social position of the elderly differs from one society to another. In Asian cultures, the elderly usually enjoy high respect. Shown here is a Vietnamese-American boy intently learning from his grandfather how to do calligraphy.

U.S. Society: Changing Perceptions

At first, the audience sat quietly as the developers explained their plans for a high-rise apartment building. After a while, people began to shift uncomfortably in their seats. Now they were showing open hostility.

"That's too much money to spend on those people," said one.

"You even want them to have a swimming pool?" asked another incredulously.

Finally, one young woman put it all in a nutshell when she asked, "Who wants all those old people around?"

When physician Robert Butler (1975/1980) heard these responses to plans to construct an apartment building for senior citizens, he came to realize how deeply feelings against the elderly can run. He coined the term **ageism** to refer to prejudice, discrimination, and hostility directed against people because of their age.

As we have just seen, however, there is nothing inherent in old age to summon forth negative attitudes. Some researchers even suggest that in early U.S. society old age had positive meanings (Cottin 1979; Kart 1990; Clair et al. 1993). Due to high death rates, they point out, not many people made it to old age. Consequently, growing old was seen as an accomplishment, and the younger generation listened to the elderly's advice about how to live a long life. With no pensions (this was before industrialization), the elderly continued to work. Since their jobs changed little over time, they were a storehouse of knowledge about work skills.

These bases of respect, however, were eroded with the coming of industrialization. Improved sanitation and medical care allowed more people to reach old age, removing the distinction of being elderly. Then, too, the new forms of mass production made young workers as productive as the elderly. Coupled with mass education, this stripped away the mystique that the elderly possessed superior knowledge (Cowgill 1974).

As the social bases that had upheld respect for the elderly crumbled, a new set of images—from those of esteem to those of contempt—emerged. A sign of this shift in meanings is how people lie about their age—they used to claim they were older than they were, but now they say they are younger than they are (Clair et al. 1993).

It is a basic principle of symbolic interactionism that people perceive both themselves and others according to the symbols of their culture. Thus, as the meaning of old age was transformed—from usefulness to uselessness, from wisdom to foolishness, from an asset to a liability—not only did younger people see the elderly differently, but the elderly, who also internalized the same cultural symbols, came to see themselves in a new light.

The meaning of old age is being transformed once again. The proportion of elderly who are able to take care of themselves financially has grown. They are no longer seen as

ageism: prejudice, discrimination, and hostility directed against people because of their age; can be directed against any age group, including youth

PEANUTS® by Charles M. Schulz

Stereotypes, which play such a profound role in social life, are a basic area of sociological investigation. In contemporary society, the mass media are a major source of stereotypes.

such a dependent group. In addition, the baby boom generation, the first of whom have now turned 50, has begun to confront the realities of aging. With better health, longer lives and a celebration of a youth culture, they can be counted on to resist being perceived in negative terms. For example, the value of maturity and the possibilities of aging as a process to be appreciated are beginning to be explored. Given their vast numbers and economic clout, they are likely to positively affect our images of the elderly.

The Mass Media: Powerful Source of Symbols

In Chapter 3 (pages 74–75), we noted that the mass media help to shape our ideas of gender and relationships between men and women. The media also influence our ideas of the elderly. Like females, the elderly are underrepresented on television, in advertisements, and in the most popular magazines. Their omission implies a lack of social value. The covert message is that the elderly are of little consequence and can be safely ignored. This message is not lost on viewers, who internalize the media's negative symbols and, as they add years, go to great lengths to deny that they are growing old. The mass media then exploit fears of losing youthful vitality to sell hair dyes, skin creams, and innumerable other products that supposedly conceal even the appearance of old age (Vernon et al. 1990; Vasil and Wass 1993).

The American Association of Retired Persons (AARP) contends that television advertising often depicts the elderly as feeble, foolish, or passing their time endlessly in rocking chairs (Goldman 1993). The AARP complains that advertising firms are dominated by younger people who transmit their own negative images—picking up the "worst traits of the group, making everyone believe that old is something you don't want to be." With the mass media so influential in our perceptions, the AARP has zeroed in on a significant matter—and changes are definitely coming, as indicated by the photo on page 352.

The Functionalist Perspective

age cohort: people born at roughly the same time who pass through the life course together

Functionalists examine how the parts of society work together. We can consider an **age cohort,** people born at roughly the same time who pass through the life course together, as a component of society. This component affects other parts. For example, if the age cohort nearing retirement is large (a "baby boom" generation), many jobs will open at roughly the same time. If it is small (a "baby bust" generation), fewer jobs will open. A smooth transition at retirement requires a good adjustment among the parts of society.

Disengagement theory and activity theory, which we shall now examine, focus on the adjustments between those who are retiring and society's other components.

Disengagement Theory

disengagement theory: the view that society prevents disruption by having the elderly vacate (or disengage from) their positions of responsibility so the younger generation can step into their shoes

activity theory: the view that satisfaction during old age is related to a person's level and quality of activity

Elaine Cumming and William Henry (1961) developed **disengagement theory** to explain how society prevents disruption when the elderly vacate (or disengage from) their positions of responsibility. It would be disruptive if the elderly left their positions only when they died or became incompetent. Consequently, societies use pensions to entice the elderly to voluntarily hand over their positions to younger people. Thus, disengagement is a mutually beneficial agreement between two parts of society, facilitating a smooth transition between the generations.

Cumming (1976) also examined disengagement from the individual's perspective. She pointed out that disengagement begins during middle age, long before retirement, when an individual senses that the end of life is closer than its start. The individual does not immediately disengage, but, realizing that time is limited, begins to assign priority to goals and tasks. Disengagement begins in earnest when children leave home, then with retirement, and eventually, widowhood.

Evaluation of the Theory.   Disengagement theory has come under heavy criticism. Anthropologist Dorothy Jerrome (1992) points out that it contains an implicit bias against older people—assumptions that the elderly disengage from productive social roles, and then sort of sink into oblivion. Instead, the elderly in good health spend time in social, recreational, and civic activities. Most regularly attend social gatherings and travel (Treas 1995). Jerrome found that the new roles, often centering around friendship, are no less satisfying than were the earlier roles—although they are less visible to researchers who tend to have a youthful orientation, and who show their bias by assuming that productivity is the measure of self-worth. In short, rather then disengaging from society, the elderly exchange one set of roles for another.

Why is old age a source of satisfaction for some, but of despair for others? Researchers have found that people's level and type of activity are significant factors. Some of the elderly obtain immense satisfaction and a sense of purpose from volunteer activities that help the younger generation. These two woman volunteer their time to provide cuddling for "boarder babies," babies abandoned by their crack-addicted mothers.

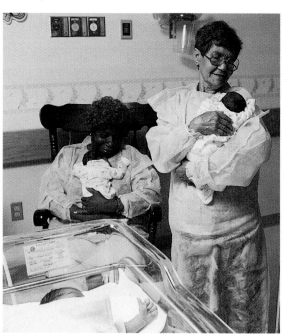

Activity Theory

What happens to people when they disengage from their usual activities? For example, are retired people less satisfied with life? Are intimate activities more satisfying than formal ones? Such questions are the focus of **activity theory,** in which the central hypothesis is that the more activities that elderly people engage in, the more they find life satisfying. Although we could consider this theory under other perspectives, because its focus is how disengagement is functional or dysfunctional, it, too, can be considered from the functionalist perspective.

Evaluation of the Theory.   The research results are mixed. In general, research has supported the central hypothesis that more active people are more satisfied. But not always. For example, a study of retired people in France found that some people are happier when they are very active, others when they are less involved (Keith 1982). Similarly, most people find more informal, intimate activities, such as spending time with friends, to be more satisfying than formal activities. But not everyone. The 2,000 retired U.S. men in one study reported formal activities to be as important as more intimate activities. Even solitary activities, such as doing home repairs, turned out to have about the same impact as intimate activities on these men's life satisfaction (Beck and Page 1988).

With this mix, it is evident that researchers should search for key variables that underlie people's activities. I suggest three: finances, health, and individual orientations. The first may be related directly to social class, for older people with adequate finances are usually more satisfied with life (Atchley 1975; Krause 1993). The second is health, for healthier people are more active (Jerrome 1992; Johnson and Barer 1992). Third, the French and U.S. studies just mentioned indicate the significance of individual orientations. Just as some people are happier doing less, others are satisfied only if they are highly involved. Similarly, some people prefer informal activities, while others are miserable if they are not active in more formal ones. To simply count people's activities, then, is far from adequate, and these variables, as well as others, may provide the key to understanding the relationship between disengagement, activities, and life satisfaction.

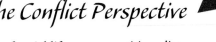

The Conflict Perspective

From the conflict perspective, the guiding principles of social life are competition, disequilibrium, and change. So it is with society's age groups. Whether the young and old recognize it or not, they are part of a basic struggle that threatens to throw society into turmoil. The passage of Social Security legislation is an example of this struggle.

Social Security Legislation

In the 1920s, before Social Security provided an income for the aged, two-thirds of all citizens over 65 had no savings and could not support themselves (Holtzman 1963; Hudson 1978). The Great Depression made matters even worse, and in 1930 Francis Townsend, a physician and social reformer, started a movement to rally older citizens. He soon had one-third of all Americans over 65 enrolled in his Townsend clubs, demanding that the federal government impose a national sales tax of 2 percent to provide $200 a month for every person over 65—the equivalent of over $2,000 a month today. In 1934, the Townsend Plan went before Congress. Because it called for such high payments and many were afraid that it would remove younger people's incentive to save for the future, Congress looked for a way to reject the plan without appearing to oppose old age pensions. When President Roosevelt announced his own, more modest Social Security plan in June 1934, Congress embraced it (Schottland 1963; Amenta et al. 1997).

This legislation required that workers retire at 65. It did not matter how well people did their work, nor how much they needed an income. For decades, the elderly protested. Finally, in 1978 Congress raised the mandatory retirement age to 70, and eliminated it in 1986. Today, almost 90 percent of Americans retire by age 65, but they do so voluntarily. They can no longer be forced out of their jobs simply because of their age.

Conflict theorists point out that today's retirement benefits are not the result of generous hearts in Congress. They are, rather, the result of a struggle between competing interest groups. As conflict theorists stress, equilibrium is only a temporary balancing of social forces, one that is always ready to come apart. Perhaps, then, more direct conflict will emerge in the future. Let us consider that possibility.

The Question of Intergenerational Conflict

Will the future bring conflict between the elderly and the young? Although violence is not likely to result, the grumblings have begun—complaints about the elderly getting more than their share of society's dwindling resources in an era of high taxes, reduced services, and gigantic budget deficits (Hunt 1995). The huge costs of Social Security have be-

Social Security has been compared to a national chain letter: Those who get in toward the beginning draw out much more than they contribute, while those at the end are caught reaping a basket of nothing. Shown here is Ida Fuller, who in 1940 was the first person to receive a Social Security check. Some fear that today's college students, when they retire, will discover they are at the empty end of the chain.

Down-to-Earth Sociology

Changing Sentiment About the U.S. Elderly

Just a few years back, there was widespread concern about extensive poverty among the elderly in the United States. As noted in the text, Congress took effective measures, and their rate of poverty dropped dramatically. At this point, is sentiment about the elderly changing?

There are indications that it is. Senator Alan Simpson called the elderly "greedy geezers," "oldsters in Bermuda shorts teeing off near their second homes in Florida," while demanding government handouts (Duff 1995b). Teresa Anderson (1985) recounts her resentment when she had to pay more than her parents for an identical room in the same motel. She says, "My parents work and own several pieces of property. Something is wrong when people are automatically entitled to a 'senior citizen discount,' regardless of need."

Robert Samuelson (1988) proposes that we eliminate tax breaks for the elderly, such as their extra standard deduction on federal income tax forms. He also suggests reducing the cost-of-living adjustments in Social Security.

Some even argue that because medical resources are limited we should ration medical care for the elderly (Perrin 1994). Considering costs, Daniel Callahan (1987) asks, should we perform open-heart surgery on people in their 80s, which might prolong life only two or three years—or should we use those same resources for a kidney transplant to a child, which might prolong life by fifty years?

Samuelson accuses the elderly's powerful lobby, the American Association of Retired Persons (AARP), of using misleading stereotypes to take unfair advantage of the public and politicians. He says, "In the real world, the stereotypes of the elderly as sedentary, decrepit, and poor have long vanished, but in politics the cliché is promoted and perpetuated." He then accuses the AARP of outright hypocrisy: "They insist (rightfully) that age alone doesn't rob them of vitality and independence, while also arguing (wrongfully) that age alone entitles them to special treatment." They can't have it both ways, he says.

For Your Consideration

Use materials in this chapter to analyze why perceptions of the elderly are changing. In doing so, note two sides of the coin. On one side: today's elderly have higher living standards than any 65-plus generation in U.S. history; one in three golfers is over 65, as are 60 percent of cruise vacationers. On the other side are the elderly poor: 21 percent of the unmarried, 24 percent of Latinos, and 25 percent of African Americans (*Statistical Abstract* 1997:Table 740). Note also the resulting opposing images—on one hand "blood-sucking vultures" and on the other hand, "pathetic creatures saving coins to buy the best meal they can afford—dog food."

come a national concern. As Figure 13.4 shows, Social Security taxes were only $781 million in 1950, but now they run almost *500* times higher. The Down-to-Earth Sociology box above examines stirrings of resentment that may become widespread.

Some form of conflict seems inevitable. As the United States grays, the number of people who collect Social Security grows, but the proportion of working people—those who pay for these benefits out of their wages—shrinks. Some see this shift in the **dependency ratio,** the number of workers compared with the number of Social Security recipients, as especially troubling. Presently about five working-age Americans pay Social Security taxes to support each person who is over 65—but shortly this ratio will drop to less than three to one (Eisner 1996). The following Thinking Critically section summarizes major problems with Social Security.

dependency ratio: the number of workers required to support dependent persons—those 64 and older and those 15 and under

Thinking Critically About Social Controversy

Social Security—Fraud of the Century?

▼ Each month the Social Security Administration mails checks to about 35 million retired Americans. Across the country, in every occupation, U.S. workers dutifully pay into the Social Security system, looking to it to provide for their basic necessities—and, hopefully, a little more—in their old age.

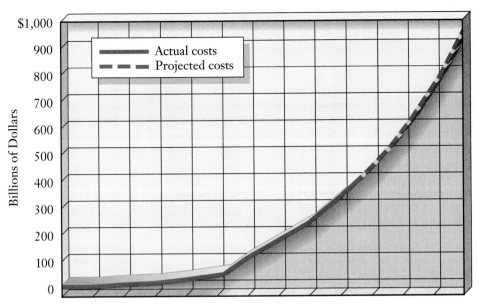

Figure 13.4

Costs of Social Security

Sources: Statistical Abstract, various years. Recent years are from 1991:Table 592 and 1997:Table 518. Broken line indicates the author's projection.

How dependable is Social Security? The short answer is "Don't bet your old age on it."

The first problem is well known. Social Security is not like a bank account into which individuals make deposits, and then, when they retire, draw it out. Instead, the money that current workers pay into Social Security is paid to retired workers. When these current workers retire, they will be paid not from their own savings, but from the contributions of others who are still working.

This system is like a chain letter—it works well as long as enough new people join the chain. If you join early enough, you will collect much more than you paid in—but if you get in toward the end, you are simply out of luck. And, say some conflict theorists, we are nearing the end of the chain. When the number of workers supporting each retiree drops from five to just two, Social Security taxes may become so prohibitive that they will stifle the country's entire economy. To address this problem, Social Security taxes were raised in 1977 and again in 1983. These increased revenues were intended to build up a Social Security surplus in the trillions of dollars—a trust fund that would ease the burden on a future, smaller labor force.

The second problem with Social Security takes us to the root of the crisis, or, some say, fraud. In 1965 President Lyndon Johnson, bogged down in a horribly expensive war in Vietnam, wanted to conceal the war's true costs from the U.S. public. To produce a budget that would hide the red ink, politicians hit on an ingenious solution—they simply transferred what the workers pay into Social Security to the general fund (the general income of the U.S. government). The confiscation went unnoticed by the public, for it was accomplished simply by prohibiting the Social Security Administration from investing in anything but U.S. Treasury bonds—a form of government IOUs. Suppose that you buy a $1,000 U.S. Treasury bond (although they don't come that small). The government takes your $1,000 and gives you a document that says it owes you $1,000 plus interest. This is what now happens with the money that workers pay into Social Security. The Social Security Administration collects the money, pays the retired, and then hands the excess over to the U.S. government, which, in turn, gives out these gigantic IOUs.

Now, if the government were running a surplus, the shenanigans might be OK. But the fact that the public's pension money is being appropriated by an organization with an annual deficit of $250 billion or $350 billion does not exactly inspire confidence.

This arrangement also helps conceal the true extent of the government's debt from the public, for the annual deficits announced by the government do *not* include these amounts confiscated from U.S. workers. The Gramm–Rudman provisions, designed to limit the amount of federal debt, do *not* count the funds "borrowed" from Social Security. It is as though this government spending does not exist.

It's a politician's ideal money machine. Workers, who have no choice about "contributing," are led to believe that they're building up a retirement nest egg for themselves when the money is actually being spent by the federal government.

For Your Consideration

Will Social Security still be there when you retire? Some conflict theorists say that you should not count on it, for each month the government wipes the Social Security trust fund clean. The federal government now owes the fund about $15 trillion, which means that the national debt is *several times* its official figures. If this process continues, to support future retirees, Social Security taxes may have to be raised so high that they will eat up 45 percent of the income of all U.S. workers.

Will U.S. workers stand for such huge taxes? Will there one day be a taxpayers' revolt that will leave millions of retirees without their monthly payments? How can the federal government be prevented from spending revenues designated for Social Security? Are the current arrangements legitimate—or is the system a gigantic fraud?

Sources: Smith 1986; Smith 1987; Hardy 1991; Genetski 1993; and Gary North's newsletter, *Remnant Review*. Raw data in which Social Security receipts are listed as deficits can be found in *Monthly Treasury Statement of Receipts and Outlays*, the *Winter Treasury Bulletin*, and *the Statement of Liabilities and Other Financial Commitments of the United States Government*—all government publications. ▲

As shown in Figure 13.5, medical costs for the elderly have soared. The increase has been so great that some now fear that the health care of children is being shortchanged and Congress will be forced to "pick between old people and kids." Are the elderly and children, then, on a collision course? What especially alarms some are the data shown in Figure 13.6. As the condition of the elderly improved, that of children worsened. Although critics are glad that the elderly are better off than they were, they are bothered that this improvement has come at the cost of the nation's children.

Figure 13.5

Health Care Costs for the Elderly and Disabled

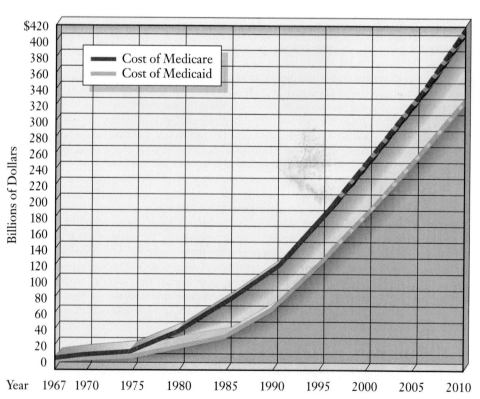

Note: Medicare is intended for the elderly and disabled, Medicaid for the poor. Almost one-third of Medicaid payments ($37 billion) goes to the elderly (*Statistical Abstract* 1997:Table:168). Broken lines indicates the author's projections.

Sources: Statistical Abstract, various years. Recent years are from 1997 edition:Tables 164, 165.

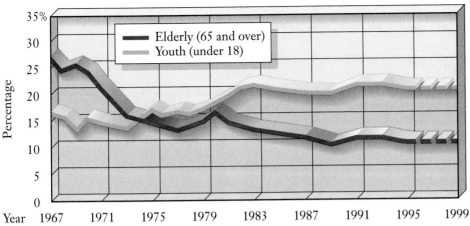

Figure 13.6

Trends in Poverty: The Percentage of U.S. Youth and Elderly in Poverty

Note: For some years the government totals for youth refer to people under 18, for other years to people under 16 or 15. Broken lines indicate the author's projections.

Sources: Congressional Research Service; *Statistical Abstract* 1997:Table 739.

But has it really? Conflict sociologists Meredith Minkler and Ann Robertson (1991) say that while the figures themselves are true, the comparison is misleading. The money that went to the elderly did *not* come from the children. Would anyone say that the money the government gives to flood or earthquake victims comes from the children? Of course not. The government makes choices about where to spend money, and it could very well have decided to increase spending on *both* the elderly and the children. It simply has not done so. To frame the issue as money going to one at the expense of the other is an attempt to divide the working class. If the working class can be made to think that they must make a choice between suffering children and suffering old folks, they will be divided and unable to work together to change U.S. society.

Fighting Back: Elderly Empowerment

Some organizations work to protect the hard-won gains of the elderly. Let's consider two.

The Gray Panthers. The Gray Panthers are aware of the danger of dividing the working class along age lines. This organization, founded in the 1960s by Margaret Kuhn (1905–1995), encourages people of all ages to work for the welfare of both the old and the young. On the micro level, the goal is to develop positive self-concepts (Kuhn 1990). On the macro level, the goal is to build a power base that will challenge institutions that oppress the poor, whatever their age—and to fight attempts to pit people against one another along age lines. One indication of their effectiveness is that Gray Panthers frequently testify before congressional committees concerning pending legislation.

The American Association of Retired Persons. The AARP also combats negative images of the elderly. This 33-million member organization is politically powerful (Clark 1994). It monitors proposed federal and state legislation and mobilizes its members to act on issues affecting their welfare. The organization can command tens of thousands of telephone calls, telegrams, and letters from irate elderly citizens. To protect their chances of reelection, politicians know better than to cross swords with the AARP. As you can expect, critics claim that the organization is too powerful, that it is able to muster forces to claim greater than its share of the nation's resources.

All this helps prove our point, say conflict theorists. Age groups are just one of society's many groups that are struggling for scarce resources, with conflict the inevitable result.

Before we close this chapter, let's look at problems of dependency and the sociology of death and dying.

Problems of Dependency

"Will I be able to take care of myself? Will I become frail and not be able to get around? Will I end up poor and in some nursing home somewhere, in the hands of strangers who don't care about me?" These are some concerns of people as they grow older. Let's examine the dependency of the elderly: isolation, nursing homes, abuse, and poverty.

Isolation and Gender

Most U.S. elderly are not isolated. Fifty-four percent live with their spouse, and another 15 percent live with someone else. But that leaves about one of three who does live alone (*Statistical Abstract* 1997:Table 48). For many people over 65, then, isolation is a problem, especially for women. Because of differences in mortality, most men over 65 are married, while most elderly women are not. As a result, most elderly men live with their wives, while most elderly women live alone or with someone else (see Figure 13.7). The intense feelings of isolation that widowhood brings (DiGiulio 1992), then, are more likely to be experienced by women.

Nursing Homes

Each year, about 13 percent of all U.S. citizens age 65 and over are admitted to nursing homes. At any one time, about 5 percent of the U.S. elderly are nursing home residents. (*Statistical Abstract* 1997:Tables 14, 200). Turnover is high. Some residents return home after only a few weeks or a few months. Others die after a short stay. Overall, about one half of elderly women and one-third of elderly men spend at least some time in a nursing home.

Nursing home residents are *not typical* of the elderly, and the picture is not pleasing. They are likely to be over 80, to be widowed, or never to have married and therefore without family to take care of them. More than half are incontinent (cannot control their urine), and two-thirds are disorientated or have memory loss (Treas 1995).

It is difficult to say good things about nursing homes, even those that are run well. First, nursing care is so expensive (averaging about $25,000 a year) that 70 percent of residents without family go broke within just three months (Ruffenbach 1988; Treas 1995). The literature, both popular and scientific, is filled with horror stories—reports of patients neglected, beaten, and otherwise maltreated (Ellis 1991; Brink 1993). Of course, not all nursing homes are like that. On the contrary, most are probably at least halfway decent. Some even provide a pleasant decor and concerned help, but they still fall far short of being home (Butterworth 1992). Even the better ones have a tendency to strip away human dignity, as sociologist Sharon Curtin found (1976):

> Miss Larson entered Montcliffe the last week of October. . . . Shortly after her admission, I arrived at 7 A.M. to find the night nurse indignant and angry. Miss Larson had climbed over the side rails during the night, and had been found in the bathroom. "She didn't ring or call out," said the nurse. . . . "Why, she might have been hurt, and she is so confused. I want the doctor to order me more sedation. We can't have her carrying on, and disturbing all the other patients."

> I walked in the room and Miss Larson was in restraints. . . . "Get me out of these!" she ordered. "How dare they try to stop me from getting out of bed. I always have to relieve myself at night; and they never answer my bell."

> Miss Larson was not confused; but in a place where all the patients are so sedated that they scarcely move a muscle during the night, she was counted a nuisance. I did not want them to increase her sedation; barbiturates frequently make old people confused and disoriented. Even if she was a pain in the neck, I like her better awake and making some sense. The problem was she had no rights. She was old, sick, feeble. Therefore she must shut up, lie still, take what little was offered and be grateful. And if she did that, she would be a "good girl."

The elderly bitterly resent being treated like children—in an institution or anywhere else. They resist, as did Miss Larson, but resistance is usually fruitless.

Figure 13.7

Where Do the U.S. Elderly Live?

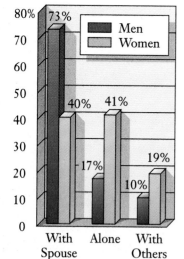

Source: Statistical Abstract 1997:Table 48.

Not everything about nursing homes is bad, of course. They do provide care for those who have no families, or are so sick that their families can no longer care for them. Sometimes nursing homes even help family relationships. A study of a well-run, middle-class nursing home showed that 30 percent of the residents continued their pattern of alienation, but 70 percent either grew closer to one another or maintained an already close relationship. With professional care, the condition of some patients improved, and children whose affection had been strained by the parent's physical or mental traumas found themselves free to again provide emotional support to the parent (Smith and Bengston 1979).

After numerous complaints about nursing home abuses, the U.S. government finally took action. To change nursing homes from a warehouse of bodies to places of treatment and human care, Congress passed a bill of rights for nursing home residents. Now nursing home patients have the right to be informed about their treatment and to refuse it, the right to privacy, the right to complain without reprisal, and the right to be unfettered—not tied to a chair or a bed (Brink 1993). As with any other law, of course, this one, too, is only as good as its enforcement. For an example of an excellent system of institutionalized care, see the Cultural Diversity box below.

Perspectives

CULTURAL DIVERSITY AROUND THE WORLD

Alzheimer Disease: Lessons from Sweden

"I'm ready," shouted Clay from the bedroom.

"That was fast," thought Virginia, his wife of forty-eight years. "He never gets ready for church that fast."

Virginia walked into the bedroom, and there, smiling and ready to leave for church, stood Clay—absolutely naked except for three watches strapped to his left wrist. Virginia told me this story later that morning when I asked her how things were going.

As people age, among their fears is that of "losing their mind." By this they mean senility, or, more technically, Alzheimer disease.

How do we care for people when they get like Clay?

Clay, of course, is just fine. His wife is still healthy, and she lovingly makes certain that he eats nourishing meals, is included in social events—and wears clothes when he goes out.

But what about the many who don't have close, caring relatives? For them, senility means institutionalization—which, even if it does not mirror the horror stories we all have heard, is certainly a far cry from the tender love and consideration that someone like Virginia gives.

Former president Ronald Reagan suffers from Alzheimer disease. This disease devastates the thinking process, making its victims unable to carry out the ordinary routines on which everyday life depends. As the percentage of the aged in our society increases, so will the number of people who suffer from this disease—and the caregiving that will become necessary.

Institutionalization, however, can be positive. For an example we can turn to Sweden, which since the 1980s has been pioneering group homes for victims of Alzheimer disease (Malmberg and Sundström 1996). The group homes consist of six to eight small apartments fanning outward from a shared kitchen and living room. Residents have their own accommodations, but a care staff is available around the clock. The goal is to provide a supportive home environment in which residents participate in everyday activities. In addition to receiving humane care, residents find that secondary problems associated with Alzheimer—depression, restlessness, and anxiety—are apparently lessened.

For Your Consideration

The group home model pioneered by Sweden is exemplary, but expensive. In the United States, what chance do you think we have of providing similar group homes for victims of Alzheimer disease? Since we could hardly afford such homes for all victims, how should they be rationed?

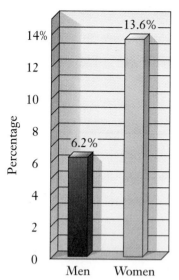

The Percentage of Americans Aged 65 and Older Who Are Poor, by Sex

Source: *Statistical Abstract* 1997:Table 48.

Figure 13.8

Gender and Poverty in Old Age

Elder Abuse

Stories of elder abuse abound—and so does the abuse itself. In interviews with a random sample of nursing home staff, 40 percent admitted that during the preceding year they had abused patients psychologically, and 10 percent admitted to abusing them physically (Pillemer and Hudson 1993). Most abuse of the elderly, however, takes place at home, and most abusers are not paid staff, but family members, who hit, verbally and emotionally abuse, or financially exploit their aged relatives (Pillemer and Wolf 1987). Spouses are most likely to be the abusers (Nachman 1991; Pillemer and Suitor 1993).

Why do children, spouses, and other relatives abuse their own elderly? Sociologists Karl Pillemer and Jill Suitor (1993) interviewed over 200 people who were caring for family members who suffered from Alzheimer disease. One husband told them,

> Frustration reaches a point where patience gives out. I've never struck her, but sometimes I wonder if I can control myself. . . . This is . . . the part of her care that causes me the frustration and the loss of patience. What I tell her, she doesn't register. Like when I tell her, "You're my wife." "You're crazy," she says.

Apparently, the precipitating cause of this form of violence is stress from caring for a person who is highly dependent, demanding, and in some cases violent (Pillemer and Suitor 1993; Korbin et al. 1994). Since most people who care for the elderly undergo stress, however, we still do not have the answer to why some caregivers become violent. For that, we must await future research.

The Elderly Poor

Many elderly live in nagging fear of poverty. Since they do not know how long they will live, nor what the rate of inflation will be, they are uncertain whether their money will last as long as they will. How realistic is this fear? Although we cannot speak to any individual case, we can look at the elderly as a group.

Gender and Poverty. As reviewed in Chapter 11, during their working years most women have lower incomes than men. Figure 13.8 shows how this pattern follows women

In old age, as in other stages in the life course, having enough money for one's needs and desires makes life more pleasant and satisfying. This elderly woman, who must live out of her car, is not likely to find this time of her life satisfying. Income, however, is hardly the sole determiner of satisfaction during old age. As indicated in the text, integration in a community in which one is respected is a crucial factor. Thus, these elderly men, although poor, are likely to find this time of life much more satisfying than the isolated homeless woman.

and men into their old age. As you can see from this figure, women are more than twice as likely to be poor as are men.

Race or Ethnicity and Poverty.   Basic racial and ethnic patterns also persist among the elderly. Latinos aged 65 and over are twice as likely as whites to be poor, while the poverty rate among elderly African Americans is 2½ times the white rate. For elderly Asian Americans, the gap is not as large, yet it runs 43 percent higher than whites. The poverty of elderly women also shows distinct patterns by race and ethnicity, with elderly Latinas and African-American women twice as likely as elderly white women to be poor (Wray 1991).

A Decline in Poverty.   An image of poor, neglected grandparents was used in earlier decades to promote programs to benefit the elderly. This was an apt description during the 1960s, for at that time the poverty rate of the U.S. elderly was greater than that of the general population. Today, however, as a result of federal programs for the elderly, this is not the case. In the 1950s, one of every three Americans aged 65 and over was living below the poverty line. By the 1970s, this rate dropped to one of seven (Hudson 1978), and today it is just one of ten (*Statistical Abstract* 1997:Table 743). As Figure 13.9 shows, the U.S. elderly are now *less* likely than the average American to be poor.

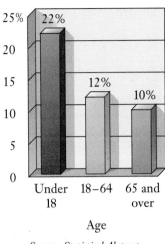

Source: Statistical Abstract 1997:Table 743.

Figure 13.9

Poverty and Age

The Sociology of Death and Dying ▶

In a fascinating subfield of sociology, death and dying, sociologists stress how death, like old age, is much more than a biological event. They examine how culture shapes the ways that people experience death. Let us look at some of their findings.

Effects of Industrialization and the New Technology

In preindustrial societies, the sick were taken care of at home, and they died at home. Because life was short, during childhood most people saw a sibling or parent die (Blauner 1966). As noted in Chapter 1 (page 25), corpses were even prepared for burial at home.

   Industrialization radically altered the circumstances of dying. With modern medicine, dying was transformed into an event to be managed by professionals in hospitals. Consequently, most Americans have never seen anyone die. Fictional deaths on television are the closest most come to witnessing death. In effect, dying has become an event that takes place behind closed doors—isolated, disconnected, remote.

   In consequence, the process of dying has become strange to us. To help put on a mask of immortality, we hide from the fact of death. We have even developed elaborate ways to refer to death without using the word itself, which uncomfortably reminds us of our human destiny. We carefully construct a language of avoidance, terms such as "gone," "passed on," "no longer with us," "gone beyond," "passed through the pearly gates," and "at peace now."

   New technologies not only removed the dying from our presence, but they also are bringing a new experience of death. They have produced what sociologists Karen Cerulo and Janet Ruane (1996) call *technological lifespace*. By this term, they mean a form of existence that is neither life nor death as we usually define them. The self of a "brain dead" person, for example, is gone—dead—yet due to technology the body lives on. What used to be firm—the boundaries between life and death—are now becoming murky, for technological lifespace is a kind of bridge between life and death. (The Sociology and the New Technology box in Chapter 19, page 540, explores some aspects of technological lifespace.)

   As people grow older, death becomes a less distant event. The elderly see many friends and relatives die, and often much of their talk centers on those persons. Often fears about dying focus more on the "how" of death than on death itself. The elderly are especially fearful of dying alone or in pain. One of their biggest fears is cancer, which seems to strike out of the blue.

Death as a Process

Through her interviews with people who had been informed that they had an incurable disease, psychologist Elisabeth Kübler-Ross (1969/1981) found that coming face to face with one's own death sets in motion a five-stage process:

1. *Denial.* In this first stage, people cannot believe that they are really going to die. ("The doctor must have made a mistake. Those test results can't be right.") They avoid the topic of death and any situation that might remind them of it.

2. *Anger.* In this second stage, they acknowledge their coming death but see it as unjust. ("I didn't do anything to deserve this. So-and-so is much worse than I am, and he's in good health. It isn't right that I should die.")

3. *Negotiation.* Next, the individual tries to get around death by making a bargain with God, with fate, or even with the disease itself. ("I need one more Christmas with my family. I never appreciated them as much as I should have. Don't take me until after Christmas, and then I'll go willingly.")

4. *Depression.* In this stage, people are resigned to the fact that death is inevitable, but they are extremely unhappy about it. They grieve because their life is about to end, and they have no power to change the course of events.

5. *Acceptance.* In this final stage, people come to terms with the certainty of impending death. They are likely to get their affairs in order—to make wills, pay bills, give instructions to children on what kind of adults they should become and of how they should take care of the surviving parent, and express regret at not having done certain things when they had the chance. Devout Christians are likely to talk about the hope of salvation and their desire to be in heaven with Jesus.

Kübler-Ross noted that not everyone experiences all these stages, and that not everyone goes through them in this precise order. Some people never come to terms with their death and remain in the first or second stage throughout the process of dying. Others may move back and forth, vacillating, for example, between acceptance, depression, and negotiation. When my mother was informed that she had inoperable cancer, she immediately went into a vivid stage of denial. If she later went through anger or negotiation, she kept it to herself. After a short depression, she experienced a longer period of questioning why this was happening to her. She then moved quickly into stage 5, which occurred very much as Kübler-Ross described it. After her funeral, my two brothers and I went to her apartment, as she had instructed us. There, to our surprise, we found attached to each item in every room a piece of masking tape with one of our names on it—from the bed and television to the silverware and knickknacks. At first we found this strange, but as we sorted through things, reflecting on why she had given certain items to whom, we began to appreciate the "closure" she had given to this aspect of her material life. It was a strong indication of her acceptance of death.

Hospices

In earlier generations, when not many people made it to age 65 or beyond, death at an early age was taken for granted—much as people take it for granted today that most people *will* see 65. In fact, due to advances in medical technology, *most* deaths in the United States (about 75 percent) do occur after age 65. With technology reducing the swift deaths that come from infectious diseases and giving us earlier detection of fatal illnesses even before the symptoms are felt, the time of "dying" has also been lengthened (Levy 1994).

Such technological effects on disease and dying have led to a greater concern about the *how* of dying. Few elderly people want to burden their children with their own death. They also want to die with dignity and with the comforting presence of friends and relatives. Hospitals, to put the matter bluntly, are awkward places in which to die. There, experiencing what sociologists call *institutional death*, patients are surrounded by strangers in formal garb, in an organization that puts its routines ahead of their needs. In addition to their coldness and formality, hospitals are also extremely expensive.

Hospices emerged as a solution to these problems. Originating in Great Britain, hospices attempt to reduce the emotional and physical burden on children and other relatives and to lower costs. Above all, hospices are intended to provide dignity in death and to make people comfortable in what Kübler-Ross (1989) called the living–dying interval, that period between discovering that death is imminent and death itself. The term **hospice** originally referred to a place, but increasingly it refers to services that are brought into a dying person's home. Those services range from intricate counseling to such down-to-earth help as providing baby sitters or driving the person to a lawyer (Levy 1994). In the United States, the number of hospices has grown from one in 1974 to 1,800 today (Busby 1993).

Whereas hospitals are dedicated to prolonging life, hospices are dedicated to bringing comfort and dignity to a dying person's last days or months. In the hospital the patient is the unit, but in the hospice the unit changes to the dying person and his or her friends and family. In the hospital, the goal is to make the patient well; in the hospice, it is to relieve pain and suffering. In the hospital, the primary concern is the individual's physical welfare; in the hospice, although medical needs are met, the primary concern is the individual's social—and in some instances, spiritual—well-being.

Suicide and the Elderly

In Chapter 1, we noted that Durkheim analyzed suicide as much more than an individual act. He stressed that each country has its own suicide rate, and that these rates remain quite stable year after year. This same stability can be seen in the age, sex, and race of people who kill themselves. Figure 13.10 shows striking patterns. One of the most notable is that at all ages males kill themselves at higher rates than do females. Similarly, at all ages the rates of white Americans are higher than those of African Americans (data are unavailable for other racial and ethnic groups).

hospice: a place, or services brought into someone's home, for the purpose of bringing comfort and dignity to a dying person

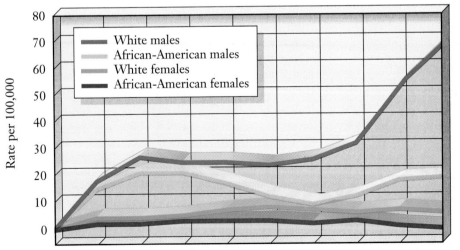

Figure 13.10

A Profile of Suicide

Note: The source contains data only for whites and African Americans. Data are from 1992 except 1990 for African-American women 65–74, and 1980 for African-American girls age 10–14, women 75 and over, and men 85 and over.

Source : *Statistical Abstract* 1995:Table 136.

Statistics often fly in the face of the impressions fostered by the mass media, and here you have such an example. Although self-inflicted deaths of young people are given high publicity, such deaths are relatively rare. Note that with the exceptions of African-American men age 45 to 74 and African-American women age 75 and over, the suicide rate of adolescents is *lower* than all other ages. Because adolescents have such a low death rate, however, suicide does rank as their third leading cause of death—after accidents and homicide (*Statistical Abstract* 1997:Table 129).

What is also striking about Figure 13.10 is the sharp rise in the suicide of white men when they reach their middle 60s. No one has a good explanation for this, but from a symbolic interactionist viewpoint it may indicate that white men experience aging differently from the other groups shown in this figure. Because white men generally enjoy greater power and status in U.S. society, it could be that aging for them represents a relatively greater loss of privilege. As noted, however, no one knows the explanation—nor, for that matter, has anyone been able to adequately explain why year after year the suicide rate of African Americans is lower than that of white Americans.

The primary sociological point of these findings on suicide is one that has been stressed throughout this text: Recurring patterns of human behavior—whether education, marriage, work, or even suicide—represent underlying social forces. Consequently, if no basic changes take place in the social conditions under which the groups that make up U.S. society live, you can expect their suicide rates to be little changed five to ten years from now.

Summary and Review

Aging in Global Perspective

How are the aged treated around the world?

There is no single set of attitudes, beliefs, or policies regarding the elderly that characterizes the world's nations. Rather, they vary from exclusion and killing, to integration and honor. Globally, and especially in industrialized nations, the trend is for more people to live longer. Pp. 346–348.

What does the term "graying of America" mean?

The phrase **graying of America** refers to the growing proportion of Americans who reach old age. The cost of health care for the elderly has become a social issue, and sentiment about the elderly seems to be shifting. Pp. 348–350.

The Symbolic Interactionist Perspective

What factors influence perceptions of aging?

Symbolic interactionists stress that, by itself, reaching any particular age has no meaning. They identify four factors that influence when people label themselves as "old": biological changes, biographical events, gender age, and cultural timetables. Cross-cultural comparisons—for example, the traditional Tiwi, Eskimos, Chinese, and Native Americans—demonstrate the role of culture in determining how individuals experience aging. **Ageism,** negative reactions to the elderly, is based on stereotypes, which, in turn, are influenced by the mass media. Pp. 350–355.

The Functionalist Perspective

How is retirement functional for society?

Functionalists focus on how the withdrawal of the elderly from positions of responsibility benefits society. **Disengagement theory** examines retirement as a device for ensuring that a society's positions of responsibility will be passed smoothly from one generation to the next. **Activity theory** examines how people adjust when they disengage from productive roles. Pp. 355–357.

The Conflict Perspective

Is there conflict among different age groups?

Social Security legislation is an example of one generation making demands on another generation for limited resources. As the **dependency ratio,** the number of workers who support one retired person, decreases, workers may become resentful. The Social Security Trust Fund may be a gigantic fraud perpetrated by the power elite on the nation's elderly. The argument that benefits to the elderly come at the cost of benefits to children is fallacious. Organizations such as the Gray Panthers and the AARP recognize the potential for conflict between age groups. Pp. 357–361.

Problems of Dependency

What are some of the problems that today's elderly face?

Due to differences in mortality and work histories, women are more likely to live alone and to be poor. About one-third of elderly men and one-half of women will spend at least some time in nursing homes. Beyond the expense of this kind of care, nursing homes tend to foster dependency among the elderly. The U.S. Congress has passed laws to protect the rights of nursing home residents. Some elderly are victims of abuse, most often by their own family. Poverty in old age, greatly reduced through government programs, reflects the gender and racial or ethnic patterns of poverty in the general society. Pp. 362–365.

The Sociology of Death and Dying

How does culture affect the meaning— and experience—of death and dying?

Like old age, death is much more than a biological event. Industrialization, for example, brought modern medicine, and with it hospitals and the custom of dying in a formal setting surrounded by strangers. Kübler-Ross identified five stages in the dying process, which, though insightful, do not characterize all people. **Hospices** are a cultural device of recent origin, designed to overcome the negative aspects of dying in hospitals. Suicide shows distinct patterns by age, sex, and race. At all ages, whites are more likely to commit suicide than are African Americans, as are males than females. Pp. 365–368.

Where can I read more on this topic?

Suggested readings for this chapter are listed on page 664.

Sociology and the Internet

All URLs listed are current as of the printing of this book. URLs are often changed. Please check our Website http://www.abacon.com/henslin for updates.

1. This project calls for role playing. The text describes some of the consequences of growing old in highly industrial societies such as the United States. Now imagine that you are old yourself. First you need to invent yourself. You are at least 65 years old and live in the United States. What is your age? gender? marital status? What is the exact place where you live (including size of town)? Do you own your home? What about savings? income? health? Do you have any close relatives (who, where)? Are you working or retired? What are your interests or hobbies? Before you begin, read this chapter again and be realistic as you decide on your attributes.

Now go to *http://www.yahoo!.com/* and select "Health." On the new page select "Health." You should see the category "Geriatrics and Aging." Now start to surf! You may also want to go back to "Society and Culture" in the main listing and look at the topic "Cultures and Groups" and the category "Seniors." Find the information you need, given your personal attributes. If you are in bad health, you might need information on health care. If your spouse has Alzheimer disease, you might look for support groups. If you are in good health and have enough money, why don't you plan a dream excursion with a "seniors tour"? You get the idea. See how far you can go toward meeting your needs. Outline what you find, and exchange ideas with others in the class.

2. You have read in this chapter about the controversy surrounding Social Security, and have been introduced to groups that lobby for the special interests of the elderly. This project will allow you to explore some of the federal government's programs. The Administration on Aging is the Executive Branch's chief agency aimed at the elderly. Go to the agency's home page at *http://www.aoa.dhhs.gov/* and select "About AOA and the Aging Network." Select "Older American Act-Administration on Aging Fact Sheet" on the new screen. Learn what you can about the AOA by reading this. You may find the agency's organization chart interesting. When you finish, go back to the "About" page. (If you get lost, just start over with the AOA home page and select "About" again.) Three other topics besides the "Fact Sheet" are available: "The Older Americans Act," "The Administration on Aging," and "The Aging Network." Follow some of the links under each of these headings.

3. One aspect of age inequality is elder abuse. Examine the following sites concerned with elder abuse:

http://www.interinc.com/NCEA/
http://www.acjnet.org/docs/eldabpfv.html
http://www.aimnet.com/~oaktree/elder/home.shtml

What is elder abuse? Who is affected by elder abuse? Who are the abusers? What can be done about it? How is elder abuse a sign of age inequality in our society? How could raising the status and value of our senior members reduce the occurrence of elder abuse?

4. Examine the following link to locate a hospice: *http://www.freenet.tlh.fl.us/Social Agencies/agencies/group3/* What is the difference between a hospice and a hospital? What are the functions of a hospice? What kind of services are offered? Discuss why elderly people might feel more comfortable living their final days in a hospice instead of in a hospital bed.

Harvey Chan, Workers Walking in a City Landscape, 1996

C H A P T E R

14

The Economy: Money and Work in the Global Village

*T*HE ALARM POUNDED IN *KIM'S* ears. *"Not Monday already,"* she groaned. *"There must be a better way of starting the week."* She pressed the snooze button on the clock (from Germany) to sneak another ten minutes' sleep. In what seemed just thirty seconds, the alarm shrilly insisted she get up and face the week.

Still bleary-eyed after her shower, Kim peered into her closet and picked out a silk blouse (from China), a plaid wool skirt (from Scotland), and leather shoes (from India). She nodded, satisfied, as she added a pair of simulated pearls (from Taiwan). Running late, she hurriedly ran a brush (from Mexico) through her hair. As Kim wolfed down a bowl of cereal (from the United States), topped with milk (from the United States), bananas (from Costa Rica), and sugar (from the Dominican Republic), she turned on her kitchen television (from Korea) to listen to the weather forecast.

Gulping the last of her coffee (from Brazil), Kim grabbed her briefcase (from Wales), purse (from Spain), and jacket (from Malaysia), and quickly climbed into her car (from Japan). As she glanced at her watch (from Switzerland), she hoped the traffic would be in her favor. She muttered to herself as she glimpsed the gas gauge at a street light (from Great Britain). She muttered again when she paid for the gas (from Saudi Arabia), for the price had risen once more. "My check never keeps up with prices," she moaned to herself as she finished the drive to work.

The office was abuzz. Six months ago, New York headquarters had put the company up for sale, but there had been no takers. The big news this Monday was that both a Japanese and a Canadian corporation had put in bids over the weekend. No one got much work done that day, as the whole office speculated about how things might change.

As Kim walked to the parking lot after work, she saw a tattered "Buy American" bumper sticker on the car next to hers. "That's right," she said to herself. "If people were more like me, this country would be in better shape."

*W*hile the vignette may be slightly exaggerated, it is not too far from the experience of most Americans. Many of us are like Kim—using a multitude of products from around the world, yet somewhat concerned about our country's ability to compete in global markets. In terms of trade and products, the world has certainly grown much smaller in recent years. We live in a global economy, and this chapter focuses on the consequences of this fact for the future of the United States.

 ## The Transformation of Economic Systems

In Mexico, the market is a bustling scene—farmers selling fruits and vegetables, as well as poultry, goats, and caged songbirds—others selling homemade blankets, serapes, huaraches, pottery, belts. Women bend over open fires cooking tacos, which their waiting customers wolf down with soft drinks. The market is a combined business and social occasion, as people make their purchases and catch each other up on the latest gossip. Such scenes used to characterize the world, but now they are limited primarily to the Least Industrialized Nations. The closest people come in the United States is a flea market, a farmer's market, or a bazaar.

Today, the term *market* means much more than such settings and activities. It has kept its original meaning of buying and selling, but it now refers to things much more impersonal. The **market,** the mechanism by which we establish values in order to exchange goods and services, today means the Dow Jones Industrial Average in New York City, and the Nikkei Index in Tokyo. Market also means the movement of vast amounts of goods across international borders, even across oceans and continents. Market means brokers

market: any process of buying and selling; on a more formal level, the mechanism that establishes values for the exchange of goods and services

Although the term market *now refers to the mechanisms by which people establish value so they can exchange goods and services, its original meaning referred to a direct exchange of goods, as shown in this photo of a market in Chiapas, Mexico. In peasant societies, where such markets are still a regular part of everyday life, people find the social interaction every bit as rewarding as the goods and money that they exchange.*

taking orders for IBM, speculators trading international currencies, and futures traders making huge bets on whether oil, wheat, and pork bellies will go up or down—and, of course, it also refers to making a purchase at the local food store.

People's lives have always been affected by the dynamics of the market, or as sociologists prefer to call it, the **economy.** Today, the economy, which many sociologists believe is the most important of our social institutions, differs radically from all but our most recent past. Economic systems have become impersonal and global. The products that Kim used in our opening vignette make it apparent that today's economy knows no national boundaries. The economy is essential to our welfare for it means inflation or deflation, high or low interest rates, high or low unemployment, economic recession or economic boom. The economy affects our chances of buying a new home, of having to work at a dead-end job or of being on a fast track in an up-and-coming company.

To better understand the U.S. economy and its relative standing in history, let's begin with a review of sweeping historical changes. (Pages 145–150 go into these changes in greater detail.)

Preindustrial Societies: From Equality to Inequality

The earliest human groups, *hunting and gathering societies,* had a simple **subsistence economy.** Groups of perhaps twenty-five to forty people lived off the land, gathering what they could find and moving from place to place as their food supply ran low. Because there was little or no excess food or other items, they did little trading with other groups. With no excess to accumulate, everybody possessed about the same as everyone else.

Then something unexpected happened, which produced a surplus and ushered in social inequality: People discovered how to breed animals and cultivate plants. Due to the more dependable food supply in *pastoral and horticultural societies,* humans settled down in a single place. Human groups grew larger, and for the first time some individuals could devote their energies to tasks other than producing food. Some people became leather workers, others weapon makers, and so on. This new division of labor produced a variety of items that were available for trade. The primary sociological significance of surplus and trade was that they fostered *social inequality,* for some people now accumulated more possessions than others. The effects of that change remain with us today.

economy: a system of distribution of goods and services

subsistence economy: a type of economy in which human groups live off the land with little or no surplus

The next major change was due to the invention of the plow, which made land much more productive. As *agricultural societies* developed, even more people were freed from food production and more specialized divisions of labor followed. Trade expanded, and trading centers developed. As trading centers turned into cities, power passed from the heads of families and clans to a ruling elite. The result was even greater social, political, and economic inequality.

Industrial Societies: The Birth of the Machine

Industrial societies, which are based on machines powered by fuels, created a surplus unlike anything the world had seen. Following the invention of the steam engine in 1765, a minority of people could produce all the food a society needed, and the vast surplus of manufactured goods stimulated extensive trade between nations. The early part of the Industrial Revolution magnified social inequalities, as some individuals found themselves able to exploit the labor of many others and to manipulate the political machinery for their own purposes. Later on, bloody battles occurred as workers unionized to improve their working conditions.

As the surplus increased, the emphasis changed from the production of goods to their consumption. Sociologist Thorstein Veblen (1912) used the term **conspicuous consumption** to describe this fundamental change in people's orientations. By this term, Veblen meant that the Protestant ethic identified by Weber—an emphasis on hard work, savings, and a concern for salvation (discussed on pages 168–170)—had been replaced by an eagerness to show off wealth by the "elaborate consumption of goods."

Postindustrial Societies: The Birth of the Information Age

conspicuous consumption: Thorstein Veblen's term for a change from the Protestant ethic to an eagerness to show off wealth by the elaborate consumption of goods

In 1973, sociologist Daniel Bell noted that *an entirely new type of society was emerging.* To refer to it, he coined the term *postindustrial society.* He identified six characteristics of the postindustrial society: (1) a service sector so large that it employs the majority of workers; (2) a huge surplus of goods; (3) even more extensive trade among nations; (4) a wider variety and quantity of goods available to the average person; (5) an "information explosion"; and (6) a "global village"—that is, the globe becomes linked by instantaneous communications, transportation, and trade.

One of the negative consequences of early industrialization in the West was the use of child labor. In the photo on the left, of the U.S. textile industry in the 1800s, you can see spindle boys at work in a Georgia cotton mill. Today's Least Industrialized Nations are experiencing the same negative consequence as they industrialize. The photo on the right shows boys at work in a contemporary textile factory in Varanas, India. About the only improvement is that the child workers in India are able to sit down as they exhaust their childhood.

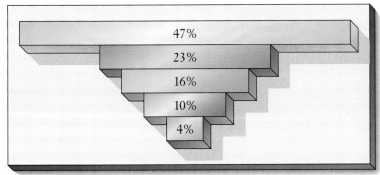

Source: *Statistical Abstract* 1997:Table 725.

Figure 14.1

The Inverted Income Pyramid: The Proportion of Income Received by Each Fifth of the U.S. Population

Perhaps the "information explosion" and the global village are the key elements of the postindustrial society. Although few people are needed to produce food or basic materials and few people to process them, the information explosion demands that large numbers of people do "knowledge work"—managing information and designing and servicing products. Almost all of us who graduate from college will be doing some form of "knowledge work."

The consequences of this information explosion that is transforming the world are extremely uneven. Most of us who graduate from college will become as comfortable with the new society as our predecessors became with theirs. But not everyone will find a comfortable niche in this new global village.

You can think of the village as divided into three large neighborhoods—the three worlds of development, which we reviewed in Chapter 9. Due to political and economic arrangements, some nations are socially destined to live in the poor part of the village, where citizens barely eke out a living from menial work. Some will even starve to death while fellow villagers in another neighborhood feast on the best that the globe has to offer.

Within each neighborhood in the village, gross inequalities also show up, for both the wealthy and poor neighborhoods have citizens who are well off and those who are poor. In the preceding five chapters, we examined inequalities—from global stratification to inequalities of social class, gender, race, and age in the United States. There is little to add to that extensive presentation, but an overall snapshot of how the income of the United States is distributed may be useful.

The inverted pyramid shown in Figure 14.1 is that snapshot. The proportion of the nation's income going to the wealthiest fifth of the U.S. population is at the top, the proportion going to the poorest fifth at the bottom. Note that *47 percent* of the whole country's income goes to just one-fifth of Americans, while only *4 percent* goes to the poorest fifth. Rather than bringing equality, then, the postindustrial society has perpetuated the income inequalities of the industrial society.

The Transformation of the Medium of Exchange

As each type of economy evolved, so, too, did the **medium of exchange,** the means by which people value and exchange goods and services. As we review this transformation, you will see how the medium of exchange is vital to each society, both reflecting its state of development and contributing to it.

Earliest Mediums of Exchange

As noted, the lack of surplus in hunting and gathering and pastoral and horticultural societies meant that there was little to trade. Whatever trading did occur was by **barter,** the direct exchange of one item for another. The surplus that stimulated trade in later soci-

medium of exchange: the means by which people value goods and services in order to make an exchange, for example, currency, gold, and silver

barter: the direct exchange of one item for another

eties led to different ways of valuing goods and services for the purpose of exchange. Let us look at how the medium of exchange was transformed.

Medium of Exchange in Agricultural Societies

Although bartering continued in agricultural societies, people increasingly came to use **money**, a medium of exchange by which items are valued. In most places, money consisted of gold and silver coins, their weight and purity determining the amount of goods or services that they could purchase. In some places people made purchases with **deposit receipts**, receipts that transferred ownership to a specified number of ounces of gold, bushels of wheat, or amount of other goods that were on deposit in a warehouse or bank. Toward the end of the agricultural period, deposit receipts became formalized into **currency** (paper money), each piece of paper representing a specific amount of gold or silver on deposit in a central warehouse. Thus currency (and deposit receipts) represented **stored value**, and no more currency could be issued than the amount of gold or silver that the currency represented. Gold and silver coins continued to circulate alongside the deposit receipts and currency.

Medium of Exchange in Industrial Societies

With but few exceptions, bartering became a thing of the past in industrial societies. Gold was replaced by paper currencies, which, in the United States, could be exchanged for a set amount of gold stored at Fort Knox. This policy was called the **gold standard,** and as long as each dollar represented a specified amount of gold the number of dollars that could be issued was limited. By the end of this period, U.S. paper money could no longer be exchanged for gold or silver, resulting in **fiat money,** currency issued by a government that is not backed by stored value.

One consequence of the move away from stored value was that coins made of precious metals disappeared from circulation. In comparison with fiat money, these coins were more valuable, and people became unwilling to part with them. Gold coins disappeared first, followed by the largest silver coin, the dollar. Then, as inferior metals (copper, zinc, and nickel) replaced the smaller silver coins, people began to hoard them, too, and silver coins also disappeared from circulation.

Even without a gold standard that restrains the issuing of currency to stored value, governments have a practical limit on the amount of paper money they can issue. In general, prices increase if a government issues currency at a rate higher than the growth of its **gross national product (GNP),** the total goods and services that a nation produces. This condition, **inflation,** means that each unit of currency will purchase fewer goods and services. Governments try to control inflation, for it is a destabilizing influence.

As you can see from Figure 14.2, as long as the gold standard limited the amount of currency, the purchasing power of the dollar remained relatively stable. When the United States departed from the gold standard in 1937, the dollar no longer represented stored value, and it plunged in value. Today, the dollar is but a shadow of its former self, retaining only about 10 percent of its original purchasing power.

In the industrial society, checking accounts held in banks became common. A *check* is actually a type of deposit receipt, for it is a promise that the writer of the check has enough currency on deposit to cover the check. The latter part of this period saw the invention of the **credit card,** a device that allows its owner, who has been preapproved for a set amount of credit, to purchase goods without an immediate exchange of money—either metal or currency. The credit card owner is later billed for the purchases.

Medium of Exchange in Postindustrial Societies

During the first part of the postindustrial society, paper money circulates freely. Paper money then becomes less common as it is gradually replaced by checks and credit cards. The **debit card,** a device by which a purchase is charged against its owner's bank account,

money: any item (from seashells to gold) that serves as a medium of exchange; today, currency is the most common form

deposit receipts: a receipt stating that a certain amount of goods is on deposit in a warehouse or bank; the receipt is used as a form of money

currency: paper money

stored value: the backing of a currency by goods that are stored and held in reserve

gold standard: paper money backed by gold

fiat money: currency issued by a government that is not backed by stored value

gross national product (GNP): the amount of goods and services produced by a nation

inflation: an increase in prices

credit card: a device that allows its owner to purchase goods but to be billed later

debit card: a device that allows its owner to charge purchases against his or her bank account

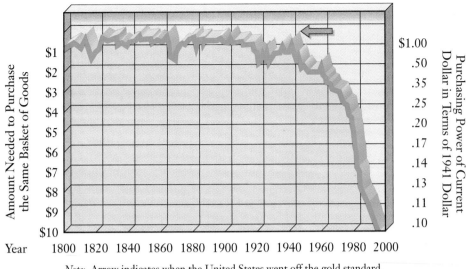

Figure 14.2

Declining Value of the U.S. Dollar

Note: Arrow indicates when the United States went off the gold standard.

Source: Modified from "Alternative Investment Market Letter," November 1991.

comes into being. The debit card, too, is a type of deposit receipt, for it is a guarantee that its user has enough currency on deposit to cover the purchase.

Increasingly, spending in the postindustrial society means not an exchange of physical money—whether paper or coins—but rather the electronic transfer of numbers residing in computer memory banks. In effect, the new medium of exchange is itself a part of the information explosion.

World Economic Systems

Now that we have outlined the main economic changes in history, let's compare capitalism and socialism, the two main economic systems in force today.

Capitalism

People who live in a capitalist society are immersed in details that blur its essentials. It is difficult to see beyond the local shopping mall and fast-food chains. If we distill the businesses of the United States to their basic components, however, we see that **capitalism** has three essential features: (1) **private ownership of the means of production** (individuals own the land, machines, and factories, and decide what shall be produced); (2) the pursuit of *profit* (selling something for more than it costs); and (3) **market competition** (an exchange of items between willing buyers and sellers).

Welfare (or State) Capitalism Versus Laissez-Faire Capitalism.   Many people believe that the United States is an example of pure capitalism. Pure capitalism, however, known as **laissez-faire capitalism** (literally meaning "hands off"), means that market forces operate without interference from the government. Such is not the case in the United States, where many restraints to the laissez-faire model are in force. The current form of U.S. capitalism is **welfare** or **state capitalism.** Private citizens own the means of production and pursue profits, but they do so within a vast system of laws designed to protect the welfare of the population.

Suppose that you have discovered what you think is a miracle tonic: It will grow hair, erase wrinkles, and dissolve excess fat. If your product works, you will become an overnight sensation—not only a millionaire, but also the toast of television talk shows.

Before you count your money—and your fame—however, you must reckon with **market restraints,** the laws and regulations of welfare capitalism that limit your capac-

capitalism: an economic system characterized by the private ownership of the means of production, the pursuit of profit, and market competition

private ownership of the means of production: the ownership of machines and factories by individuals, who decide what shall be produced

market competition: the exchange of items between willing buyers and sellers

laissez-faire capitalism: unrestrained manufacture and trade (literally, "hands off" capitalism)

welfare (state) capitalism: an economic system in which individuals own the means of production, but the state regulates many economic activities for the welfare of the population

market restraints: laws and regulations that limit the capacity to manufacture and sell products

ity to sell what you produce. First, you must comply with local and state rules. You must obtain a charter of incorporation, a business license, and a state tax number that allows you to buy your ingredients without paying sales taxes. Then come the federal regulations. You cannot simply take your item to local stores and ask them to sell it; you must first seek approval from federal agencies that monitor compliance with the Pure Food and Drug Act. This means you must prove that your product will not cause harm to the public. In addition, you must be able to substantiate your claims—or else face being shut down by state and federal agencies that monitor the market for fraud. Your manufacturing process is also subject to government regulation: state and local laws concerning cleanliness and state and federal rules for the storage and disposal of hazardous wastes.

Suppose that you succeed in overcoming these obstacles, your business prospers, and the number of your employees grows. Other federal agencies will monitor your compliance with regulations concerning racial and sexual discrimination, the payment of minimum wages, and the remittance of Social Security taxes. State agencies will also examine your records to see if you have paid unemployment compensation taxes on your employees and sales taxes on items that you sell at retail. Finally, the Internal Revenue Service will constantly look over your shoulder. In short, the highly regulated U.S. economic system is far from an example of laissez-faire capitalism.

To see how welfare or state capitalism developed in the United States, let us go back to the 1800s when capitalism was considerably less restrained. At that time, you could have made your "magic" potion in your kitchen and sold it at any outlet willing to handle it. You could have openly advertised that it cured baldness, erased wrinkles, and dissolved fat, for no agency existed to monitor your product or your claims. In fact, that is precisely what thousands of individuals did at that time, producing numerous "elixirs" with whimsical names such as "Grandma's Miracle Medicine" and "Elixir of Health and Happiness." A single product could claim that it simultaneously restored sexual potency, purged the intestines, and made people more intelligent. People often felt better after drinking such tonics, for many elixirs were liberally braced with alcohol—and even cocaine (Ashley 1975). Indeed, until 1903 a main ingredient of Coca-Cola was cocaine. To protect the public's health, in 1906 the federal government passed the Pure Food and Drug Act and began to regulate products.

Government regulation of capitalism was accelerated by John D. Rockefeller's remarkable success in unregulated markets. After a ruthless drive for domination—which included drastically reducing prices for oil and then doubling them after driving out the competition, and in some instances sabotaging competitors' pipelines and refineries—Rockefeller managed to corner the U.S. oil and gasoline market (Josephson 1949). With

As illustrated by this scene in Havana, Cuba, poverty is not limited to any particular economic system. The cause of the poverty shown here, however, is as complex as the relationship between economic systems, for economic sanctions by the United States directed against Fidel Castro certainly have not helped Cubans thrive.

his competitors crippled or eliminated, his company, Standard Oil, was able to dictate prices to the entire nation. Rockefeller had achieved the capitalist's dream, a **monopoly,** the control of an entire industry by a single company.

Rockefeller had overplayed the capitalist game, however, for he had wiped out one of its essential components, competition. Consequently, to protect this cornerstone of capitalism, the federal government passed antimonopoly legislation and broke up Standard Oil. Today, the top firms of each industry—such as General Motors in automobiles and General Electric in household appliances—must obtain federal approval before acquiring another company in the same industry. If the government determines that one firm dominates a market, and thereby unfairly restricts competition, it can force that company to **divest** (sell off) some of its businesses.

Another characteristic of welfare capitalism is that although the government supports competition, it establishes its own monopoly over "common good" items—those presumed essential for the common good of the citizens, such as soldiers, war supplies, highways, and sewers.

▼ **In Sum** As currently practiced, capitalism is far from the classical laissez-faire model. The economic system of the United States encourages the first two components of capitalism, the private ownership of the means of production and the pursuit of profit. But a vast system of government regulations both protects and restricts the third component, market competition. The government also controls "common good" items.

Socialism

Socialism also has three essential components: (1) the public ownership of the means of production; (2) central planning; and (3) distribution of goods without a profit motive.

In socialist economies, the government owns the means of production—not only the factories, but also the land, railroads, oil wells, and gold mines. Unlike capitalism, in which **market forces**—supply and demand—determine what shall be produced and the prices that will be charged, in socialism a central committee decides that the country needs X number of toothbrushes, Y toilets, and Z shoes. This group decides how many of each shall be produced, which factories will produce them, the prices that will be charged for the items, and where they will be distributed.

Socialism is designed to eliminate competition, for goods are sold at predetermined prices regardless of demand for an item or the cost to produce it. Profit is not the goal, nor is encouraging consumption of goods in low demand (by lowering the price), nor limiting the consumption of hard-to-get goods (by raising the price). Rather, the goal is to produce goods for the general welfare and to distribute them according to people's needs, not their ability to pay.

In a socialist economy *everyone* in the economic chain works for the government. The members of the central committee who set production goals are government employees, as are the supervisors who implement those goals, the factory workers who do the producing, the truck drivers who move the merchandise, and the clerks who sell it. Although those who purchase the items work at entirely different jobs—in offices, on farms, in day care centers—they, too, are government employees.

Just as capitalism does not exist in a pure form, neither does socialism. Although the ideology of socialism calls for resources to be distributed according to need and not position, in line with the functionalist argument of social stratification presented in Chapter 9 (pages 230–231), socialist countries found it necessary to offer higher salaries for some jobs in order to entice people to take greater responsibilities. For example, factory

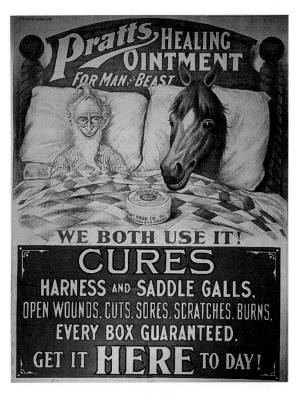

This advertisement from 1885 represents an earlier stage of capitalism, when individuals were free to manufacture and market products with little or no interference from the government. Today, the production and marketing of goods take place under detailed, complicated government regulations.

monopoly: the control of an entire industry by a single company

divest: to sell off

socialism: an economic system characterized by the public ownership of the means of production, central planning, and the distribution of goods without a profit motive

market forces: the law of supply and demand

The slogan of the Cuban revolution is "Socialism or Death." In spite of an invasion, a long embargo, and efforts by the CIA to assassinate him, Castro has remained in power. Many wonder when the animosity between the U.S. government and Castro will finally come to a close, and if the two political-economic systems can accommodate one another.

managers always earn more than factory workers. By narrowing the huge pay gaps that characterize capitalist nations, however, socialist nations were able to establish considerably greater equality of income.

Democratic Socialism. Dissatisfied with the greed and exploitation of capitalism and the lack of freedom and individuality of socialism, some Western nations (most notably Sweden and Denmark) developed **democratic socialism,** or welfare socialism. In this form of socialism, both the state and individuals engage in production and distribution. Although the government owns and runs the steel, mining, forestry, and energy concerns, as well as the country's telephones, television stations, and airlines, the retail stores, farms, manufacturing concerns, and most service industries remain in private hands.

Ideologies of Capitalism and Socialism

Capitalism and socialism not only have different approaches to producing and distributing goods, but each also represents a distinct ideology.

Capitalists hold that market forces should determine both products and prices. They also believe that it is healthy for people to strive after profits, that this stimulates them to develop and produce new products desired by the public. It also motivates workers to work hard so that they can make as much money as possible in order to purchase more goods. As the Down-to-Earth Sociology box on the next page shows, the market also *creates* a demand for products. In short, market forces underlie the successful capitalist society.

In contrast, socialists believe that profit is immoral, that it represents *excess value* extracted from workers. Karl Marx made the point that because an item's value represents the work that goes into it, there can be no profit unless workers are paid less than the value of their labor. Profit, then, represents an amount withheld from workers. To protect workers from this exploitation, socialists believe that the government should own the means of

democratic socialism: a hybrid economic system in which capitalism is mixed with state ownership

Throughout most of the twentieth century, capitalism and communism were pitted against one another in a deadly struggle. Each thought of itself as the correct economic form, and the other as an evil obstacle to be eradicated. In support of this view of essential goodness and evil, proponents of each system launched global propaganda campaigns. Shown here is a painting of Wladimir Lenin, leader of the worldwide workers' revolution. This 1930 painting by Alexander Gerassimow (1881–1963) hangs in the Tretyakov Gallery in Moscow.

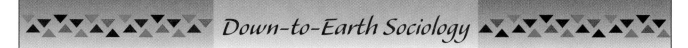

Down-to-Earth Sociology

Selling the American Dream— The Creation of Constant Discontent

Advertising is such an integral part of contemporary life that it almost appears to be our natural state to be deluged with ads. We open a newspaper or magazine and expect to find that a good portion of its pages proclaim the virtues of products and firms. We turn on the television and on most stations are assailed with commercials for about ten minutes of every half hour. Some social analysts even claim that the purpose of television is to round up an audience to watch the commercials—making the programs a mere diversion from the medium's real objective of selling products!

A fascinating potential of advertising is its ability to increase our desire to consume products for which we previously felt no need whatsoever. U.S. kitchens, filled with gadgets that slice and dice and machines that turn anything into a sandwich, attest to this power.

But advertising's power to make people gluttons for consumption goes beyond kitchen gadgets soon consigned to back drawers and later to garage sales. Many Americans today would not think of going out in public without first shampooing, rinsing, conditioning, and blow-drying their hair. Many also feel the need to apply an underarm deodorant so powerful that it overcomes the body's natural need to sweat. For many women, public appearance also demands the application of foundation, lipstick, eye shadow, mascara, rouge, powder, and perfume. For many men, aftershave lotion is essential. And only after covering the body with clothing bearing suitable designer labels do Americans feel that they are presentable to the public.

Advertising also penetrates our consciousness to such an extent that it determines not only what we put on our bodies, what we eat, and what we do for recreation, but to a large degree also how we feel about ourselves. Our ideas of whether we are too fat, too skinny, too hippy, too buxom, whether our hair is too oily or too dry, our body too hairy, or our skin too rough are largely a consequence of advertising. As we weigh our self-image against the idealized pictures that constantly bombard us in our daily fare of commercials, we conclude that we are lacking something. Advertising, of course, assures us that there is salvation—some new product that promises to deliver exactly what we lack.

The creation of constant discontent—dissatisfaction with ourselves compared to ideal images that are impossible to match in real life—is, of course, intentional. As designed, it leaves most of us vulnerable to consuming more of the never-ending variety of products that the corporations have for sale—and decided that we need.

---

production, using them not for profit, but to produce and distribute items according to people's needs rather than their ability to pay.

These two ideologies paint each other in such stark colors that *each sees the other as a system of exploitation.* Capitalists see socialists as violating basic human rights of freedom of decision and opportunity, while socialists see capitalists as violating basic human rights of freedom from poverty. With each side painting itself in moral colors while viewing the other as a threat to its very existence, this century witnessed the world split into two main blocs. The West armed itself to defend capitalism, the East to defend socialism. Prior to the collapse of the Soviet Union in 1989, the remaining "nonaligned" nations often were able to extort vast sums of economic and military aid by playing the West and the East off against one another.

Criticisms of Capitalism and Socialism

The primary criticism leveled against capitalism is that it leads to social inequality. Capitalism, say its critics, produces a tiny top layer consisting of wealthy, powerful people, who exploit a vast bottom layer of poorly paid workers, many of whom are unemployed and underemployed (**underemployment** is having to work at a job beneath one's training and abilities or being able to find only part-time work). Another major criticism is that the tiny top layer wields vast political power. To further their own wealth, the few who own the means of production and reap huge profits are able to get legislation passed that goes against the public good.

The primary criticism leveled against socialism is that it does not respect individual rights (Berger 1991). Others (in the form of some government body) control people's lives—making decisions about where they will live, where they will go to school, where

underemployment: the condition of having to work at a job beneath one's level of training and abilities, or of being able to find only part-time work

Although most people under communist rule lived in poverty, they were assured jobs that provided very basic food and shelter. Today, with the transition to capitalism, citizens of the former Soviet Union no longer have that assurance. Shown here is a scene in Sverdlosk, Russia, where people are learning capitalism, that is, to buy and sell for profit.

they will work, how much they will be paid, and, in the case of China, even how many children they may have (Mosher 1983). Critics also argue that central planning is grossly inefficient (Kennedy 1993) and that socialism is not capable of producing much wealth. They say that its greater equality really amounts to giving almost everyone an equal chance to be poor.

Changes in Capitalism and Socialism

Let's look at some of the fundamental changes that have taken place in these two economic systems.

Changes in Capitalism. Over the years, the United States adopted many socialist practices in which the government extracts money from some to pay for benefits it gives to others. Examples include unemployment compensation (taxes paid by workers are distributed to those who no longer produce a profit); subsidized housing (shelter, paid for by the many, is distributed to the poor and elderly, with no motive of profit); welfare (taxes from the many are distributed to the needy); a minimum wage (the government, not the employer, determines the minimum that a worker shall be paid); and Social Security (as noted in the Thinking Critically section in Chapter 13, pages 358–360, the retired do not receive what they pay into the system, but rather, money collected from current workers).

Each program was viewed with alarm when it was first proposed. Now that it has become a firm part of the U.S. capitalist system, its socialist base has become almost invisible. There is an "of course" sense about these programs—they just seem to "belong" to capitalism.

Changes in Socialism. For its part, in 1989 the Soviet Union, which headed an eastern European bloc of nations (East Germany, Czechoslovakia, and Hungary, among others), concluded that its system of central planning had failed. Suffering from shoddy goods and plagued by shortages, its standard of living severely lagged behind the West. Consequently, the former Soviet Union began to reinstate market forces. Making a profit—which had been a crime—was encouraged, private ownership of property became respectable, state industries were auctioned off. And their former arch-enemies against whom they had uttered ten thousand curses, Western corporations, were invited to open up shop. For a glimpse of this transition to capitalism, see the Perspectives box.

The second major socialist power, China, watched in dismay as its one-time mentor abandoned the basic principles of socialism (Szelenyi 1987). In 1989, at the cost of many lives and despite world opposition, Chinese authorities, in what is called the Tiananmen

Perspectives

CULTURAL DIVERSITY AROUND THE WORLD

No Cash? No Problem! Barter in the Former Soviet Union

About 50 miles from the town of Bila Tserkva, you'll see a few tires piled alongside the highway. By the time you get to Bila Tserkva, the stacks of black tires have grown thicker and higher until they seem to line both sides of the road like thick rubber walls (Brzezinski 1997).

Welcome to the transition to capitalism. This is payday at the tire plant in Bila Tserkva. With cash in short supply, workers are paid in tires. In another town, Volgograd, workers are paid in brassieres. So many brassieres will get you into the latest Sylvester Stallone movie—or buy you a hat, a pair of shoes, an ice cream cone. . . .

And in the cash-strapped former Soviet Union, it's not just individuals who conduct transactions using goods in-

stead of cash. Ukraine's electric utility company receives payment in goods ranging from military uniforms to steel tubing. The company, in turn, passes these goods on to the Russian company that supplies it with electricity, which, in turn, uses the tubing in its pipelines. The uniforms? It gives these to Russia's Ministry of Defense in lieu of taxes.

Recently, when city workers in Tatarstan arrived at city hall, they found 600 new trucks parked on the front lawn. The trucks were payment on the local truck maker's tax bill. The workers were lucky—they might have been greeted with piles of tires or brassieres.

Square massacre, stood firm, putting down a hunger strike by students and workers who were demanding greater freedom and economic reforms. Despite this repressive measure, however, China, too, began to endorse capitalism. Its leaders also solicited Western investments and encouraged farmers to cultivate their own plots on the communal farms. They allowed the use of credit cards, approved a stock market, and even permitted bits of that symbol of China itself, the Great Wall, to be sold as souvenirs—for profit (McGregor 1992). While still officially proclaiming Marxist–Leninist–Maoist principles, the Communist party—under the slogan "One China, two systems"—is trying to make Shanghai the financial center of East Asia (McGregor 1993; Schlesinger 1994). One consequence— besides the new Avon ladies and the Head & Shoulders brand rushing to the top of the charts in shampoo sales—is a rapidly rising standard of living (Kahn 1995; Ikels 1996).

Coming from behind with a vengeance, China is successfully arm-twisting multinational corporations to deliver breakthrough technology and to train Chinese workers to administer it. They are now building the base from which China will launch itself as a top competitor in world markets ("Price of Entry," 1995).

Convergence Theory.   The socialist nations, then, have embraced profit while the capitalist nations have adopted socialistic programs designed to redistribute wealth. Will the two systems continue to adopt features of the other until they converge, creating a sort of hybrid economic system? This, at least, is the bare bones outline of the prediction made by **convergency theory** (Form 1979; Kerr 1960, 1983).

The evidence for this theory seems impressive. Since the pursuit of profits will produce greater wealth and an inevitably higher standard of living, it will be almost impossible for socialist leaders to erase profits from their economic system. Similarly, the citizens of capitalist nations have become so used to socialistic features built into their system that they cannot imagine a government that does not protect the unemployed, guarantee a minimum wage, and so on. Leaders and citizens of both systems may quarrel about the details, but they have embraced the opposing principles.

The matter, however, is not this simple. That each has adopted features of the other is only part of the picture. The systems remain far from "converged," and the struggle between them continues, although much muted from what it was in the heady days of the cold war. Russian and Polish citizens, for example, longing for greater stability, have voted Communists back into top government positions. At the same time, U.S. Republicans try to roll

convergence theory: the view that as capitalist and socialist economic systems each adopt features of the other, a hybrid (or mixed) economic system will emerge

back socialistic measures and return to a purer capitalism, while Democrats resist. Meanwhile, the Chinese, longing to transform themselves into the world's number one capitalist nation, await the death of the ruling old men locked up in their "Kremlin" fortress.

 In Sum At this historical point, with the pullback of socialism around the world, we can note that capitalism has a strong lead. We also must note that there is no pure capitalism (and likely never was). Today, then, capitalism speaks in a variety of accents, some more muted than others, with the versions in Chinese, the former Soviet Union, Great Britain, Japan, Germany, Sweden, and the United States each differing from the others.

Capitalism in a Global Economy

As we have seen, capitalism has undergone many twists in its economic journey. Today, large corporations dominate the economic system. Coupled with a trend toward the globalization of capitalism, this is profoundly altering the U.S. economy and economies around the world.

Corporate Capitalism

Corporations have altered the face of capitalism. A **corporation** is a business that is treated in law as a person. Its liabilities and obligations are separate from those of its owners. For example, each shareholder of Xerox—whether the owner of one or 100,000 shares—owns a portion of the company. Xerox is a legal entity, and can buy and sell, sue and be sued, make contracts, and incur debts. The corporation, however, not its individual owners, is responsible for the firm's liabilities—such as paying its debts and fulfilling its contracts.

One of the most significant aspects of corporations is the *separation of ownership and management*. Unlike most businesses, it is not the owners, those who own the company's stock, who run the day-to-day affairs of the company (Walters 1995). Rather, a corporation is run by managers who are able to treat it *as though it were their own* (Cohen 1990). The result is the "ownership of wealth without appreciable control, and control of wealth without appreciable ownership" (Berle and Means 1932). Sociologist Michael Useem (1984) put it this way:

> When few owners held all or most of a corporation's stock, they readily dominated its board of directors, which in turn selected top management and ran the corporation. Now that a firm's stock [is] dispersed among many unrelated owners, each holding a tiny fraction of the total equity, the resulting power vacuum allow[s] management to select the board of directors; thus management [becomes] self-perpetuating and thereby acquire[s] de facto control over the corporation.
>
> Management determines its own salaries, sets goals and awards itself bonuses for meeting them, authorizes market surveys, hires advertising agencies, determines marketing strategies, and negotiates with unions. The management's primary responsibility to the owners is to produce profits. The greater the profit, the better their job performance.

At the annual stockholders' meeting the owners consider broad company matters, including the selection of a board of directors and a firm to audit the company's books. As long as management reports a handsome profit, the stockholders rubber-stamp its recommendations. It is so unusual for this not to happen, that when it does not the outcome is called a **stockholders' revolt.** The irony of this term is generally lost, but remember that in such cases it is not the workers but the owners who are rebelling!

The world's largest corporations wield immense power. Forming **oligopolies**—several large companies that dominate a single industry, such as gasoline, breakfast cereal, or light bulbs—they dictate pricing, set the quality of their products, and protect their markets. Oligopolies also use their political connections to support legislation that gives them special tax breaks or protects their industry from imports. Corporations have so changed capitalism that the term **corporate capitalism** is used to indicate that giant corporations

corporation: the joint ownership of a business enterprise, whose liabilities and obligations are separate from those of its owners

stockholders' revolt: the refusal of a corporation's stockholders to rubber-stamp decisions made by its managers

oligopoly: the control of an entire industry by several large companies

corporate capitalism: the domination of the economic system by giant corporations

dominate the economic system. Of the hundreds of thousands of businesses and tens of thousands of corporations in the United States, a mere five hundred dominate the economy. Called the Fortune 500 (derived from *Fortune* magazine's annual profile of the largest five hundred companies), these firms are so large that their annual profits represent 10 percent of the United States' entire gross national product (*Statistical Abstract* 1997:Tables 698, 874).

Interlocking Directorates

One way in which the wealthy use corporations to wield power is by means of **interlocking directorates** (Mizruchi and Koenig 1991). The elite serve as directors of several companies. Their fellow members on those boards also sit on the boards of other companies, and so on. Like a spider's web that starts at the center and then fans out in all directions, eventually the top companies in the country are interlocked into a network (Mintz and Schwartz 1985). The chief executive officer of a firm in Great Britain, who also sits on the board of directors of half a dozen other companies, noted:

> If you serve on, say, six outside boards, each of which has, say, ten directors, and let's say out of the ten directors, five are experts in one or another subject, you have a built-in panel of thirty friends who are experts who you meet regularly, automatically each month, and you really have great access to ideas and information. You're joining a club, a very good club. (Useem 1984)

The resulting concentration of power minimizes competition, for a director is not going to approve a plan that will be harmful to another company in which he or she (mostly he) has a stake. The top executives of the top U.S. companies—part of the powerful capitalist class described on pages 260–261—also meet together in recreational settings, where they renew their sense of solidarity, purpose, and destiny (Domhoff 1997).

Multinational Corporations

Kim, in the opening vignette, illustrates the new distribution and consumption patterns of our global marketplace. Another view is given by the Social Map below, which shows the percentage of U.S. businesses owned by foreign corporations. Outgrowing national bound-

interlocking directorates: the same people serving on the board of directors of several companies

Figure 14.3

The Globalization of Capitalism: Foreign Ownership of U.S. Businesses

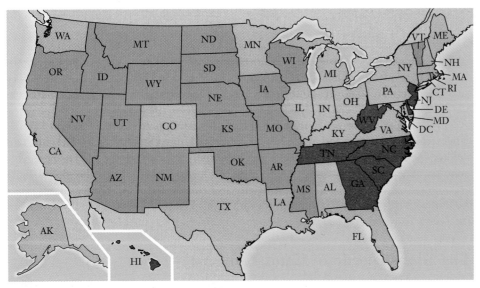

■ More than average (6 percent or more of all businesses)
▨ Average (4.0–5.9 percent of all businesses)
▧ Less than average (less than 4.0 percent of all businesses)

Source: Statistical Abstract 1996:Table 1290.

TABLE 14.1

The World's Largest Corporations[a]

Rank	Name	Country	Market Value	Profit/Loss
1	General Electric	U.S.	$137 billion	$6.6 billion
2	Shell	Holland	$128 billion	$6.8 billion
3	Coca-Cola	U.S.	$117 billion	$3.0 billion
4	NIT	Japan	$114 billion	$7.0 billion
5	Exxon	U.S.	$102 billion	$6.5 billion
6	Bank of Tokyo	Japan	$98 billion	$2.5 billion
7	Toyota	Japan	$92 billion	$1.3 billion
8	Philip Morris	U.S.	$86 billion	$5.5 billion
9	AT&T	U.S.	$84 billion	$5.5 billion
10	Merck	U.S.	$78 billion	$3.3 billion
11	Roche	Switzerland	$71 billion	$3.3 billion
12	Microsoft	U.S.	$71 billion	$1.5 billion
13	Johnson & Johnson	U.S.	$64 billion	$1.5 billion
14	Intel	U.S.	$62 billion	$3.6 billion
15	Procter & Gamble	U.S.	$61 billion	$2.6 billion
16	IBM	U.S.	$58 billion	$6.0 billion
17	Sumitomo Bank	Japan	$58 billion	$2.8 billion LOSS
18	Fuji Bank	Japan	$57 billion	$0.5 billion
19	Wal-Mart	U.S.	$55 billion	$2.7 billion
20	Dai-Ichi Bank	Japan	$53 billion	$0.3 billion
21	Industrial Bank	Japan	$51 billion	$0.3 billion
22	British Petroleum	U.K.	$51 billion	$3.1 billion
23	Sanwa Bank	Japan	$51 billion	$0.2 billion
24	Pepsi	U.S.	$50 billion	$1.6 billion
25	Glaxo Wellcome	U.K	$49 billion	$3.8 billion

[a] For the year 1996.

Source: "The Global Giants" 1996.

---

aries, the larger corporations have become more and more detached from the interests and values of their country of origin. They move investments and production from one part of the globe to another—with no concern for consequences other than profits. As the cold war trading barriers broke down and the global economy became more integrated, these corporations took on an increasingly significant role in global life (Kennedy 1993).

The domination of world trade shows an interesting pattern. After World War II, with Germany destroyed and France in shambles, the United States eclipsed Great Britain and became the major player in international business. More recently, the Japanese, also using the multinational corporate model, gained huge markets across the globe. Table 14.1 shows that of the world's largest twenty-five corporations, the United States holds the lead with thirteen, and Japan follows with eight. Without doubt, these two countries are today's Goliaths of global trade.

The Globalization of Capitalism

- *Sun Microsystems uses a single phone number to offer round-the-globe, round-the-clock technical service. The number is staffed by teams in California, England, and Australia. They electronically hand work off as a team from another country comes on line.*

In its march toward globalization, capitalism is undergoing major changes. Such fundamental change is exemplified by companies that locate their corporate headquarters in one country, manufacture basic components in a different country, assemble them in still another, and sell them throughout the world. In this photo, Nike soccer balls are being assembled in Pakistan. This photo also illustrates an old standby of economic systems—whether capitalism or any other—the use of child labor.

- *When the Turkish economy plunged, Goodyear Tire & Rubber didn't even idle its Turkish plant. Instead, thanks to flexible new tire-making technology, Goodyear swiftly regeared its tire models and redirected output to the rest of Europe (Zachary 1995)*

The global integration of the giant corporations is the most significant economic change in the past 100 years. Its impact on our lives may rival that of the Industrial Revolution itself. As Louis Gallambos, a historian of business, says, "This new global business system will change the way everyone lives and works" (Zachary 1995).

The Sociological Significance of Global Capitalism.   It may be only a slight exaggeration to say that multinational corporations are becoming the primary political force in the world. Certainly they are reshaping the globe as no political or military force has been able to do. The lives of all of us are touched by these global giants. Although we already have started to take this for granted—this is new to the world scene.

The sociological significance of global capitalism is that the multinational corporations owe allegiance only to profits and market share, not to any nation, nor even to any particular culture. As a U.S. executive said, "The United States does not have an automatic call on our resources. There is no mind-set that puts the country first" (Kennedy 1993). This fundamental shift in orientation is so new that its implications are unknown at present. Certainly the millions of workers whose jobs have been pulled out from under them know the negative consequences. On the positive side, these corporations' global interconnections may be a force for peace, for they are removed from tribal loyalties and national boundaries. The downside, however, may be a "new world order" dominated by a handful of corporate leaders.

Applying Sociological Theories

Let's see what pictures emerge when we apply the three theoretical perspectives of sociology to our economic life.

The Symbolic Interactionist Perspective

As we apply the symbolic interactionist perspective, let's consider what distinguishes a job from a profession.

Profession or Job? Work as a Status Symbol. We know that selling hamburgers from a drive-in window is not a profession, but why isn't selling shoes? Sociologists identify five characteristics of **professions** (Parsons 1954; Goode 1960; Greenwood 1962; Etzioni 1969).

1. *Rigorous education.* A high school education will not do. Nor will a six-week training course in cutting hair, or even a rigorous course in diesel repair. Today the professions require not only college but also graduate school. Ordinarily, those years are followed by an examination that determines whether or not you will be allowed into the profession. From personal experience, I would like to add that this examination is one of the most significant parts of the educational ordeal. The gnawing threat of not knowing if your years of preparation will allow you to enter your chosen profession hangs over your head like the sword of Damocles.

2. *Theory.* The education is theoretical, not just "hands on." Instead of "Turn this nut, and it frees the main bolt that holds the carburetor," heavy stress is placed on causes and processes. In other words, concepts or objects that cannot be seen are used to explain what can be seen. For example, in medicine, microbes, viruses, and genetics are used to explain disease, while in sociology, social structure and social interaction are used to explain human behavior.

3. *Self-regulation.* Members of the profession claim that only they possess sufficient knowledge to determine the profession's standards and to certify those qualified to be admitted. As sociologist Ernest Greenwood (1962) put it, "Anyone can call himself a carpenter, locksmith, or metal-plater if he feels so qualified. But a person who assumes the title of physician or attorney without having earned it conventionally becomes an imposter." The group's members also determine who shall be decertified because of incompetence or moral problems.

4. *Authority over clients.* Members of a profession claim authority over clients on the basis of their specialized education and theoretical understanding. Unlike carpentry, in which any of us can see that the nail is bent, members of the profession claim that the matter is too complex for "laypeople" to understand. Thus it is the clients' obligation to follow the professional's instructions.

5. *Service to society, not self-interest.* The public good lies at the heart of a profession. Although some car salespeople may make preposterous claims about serving the public good, we all know that they sell cars to make money. In contrast, the professions claim that they exist "to provide service to whomever requests it, irrespective of the requesting client's age, income, kinship, politics, race, religion, sex and social status" (Greenwood 1962).

   Obviously, this fifth criterion is the weakest. Today, we expect the basic motivation of a physician to be not far different from that of an automobile mechanic. Although both physicians and automobile mechanics may want to help their customers, most of us assume that money is the reason both do their jobs.

Is it a profession or a job? In some ways, this is not an either–or matter. While we can identify the extremes—medicine is a profession and flipping burgers is not—we also can view any particular work as "more" or "less" professionalized. For example, we may wish to make the case that creating stained glass windows is a profession. We can measure it according to these five criteria and see that it ranks higher on some than on others. So it is with other work. Using these guidelines, we can see that practicing law is less professional than practicing medicine, for law is low on theory and, in the public's mind at least, even more questionable on its claim to be doing a service for society.

The Functionalist Perspective

Work is functional for society. It is only because people work that we have electricity, hospitals, schools, automobiles, and homes. Beyond this obvious point, however, lies a

profession: an occupation characterized by rigorous education, a theoretical perspective, self-regulation, authority over clients, and service to society (as opposed to a job)

basic sociological principle: *Work binds us together.* This is a good point to review Durkheim's principles of mechanical and organic solidarity introduced in Chapter 4 (page 102).

Mechanical Solidarity.   In preindustrial societies, people do similar work and directly share most aspects of life. Because of this, they look at the world in similar ways. Durkheim used the term **mechanical solidarity** to refer to this sense of unity that comes from doing similar activities.

Organic Solidarity.   As societies industrialize, however, a division of labor develops, and people work at different occupations. Consequently, they feel less solidarity with one another. Grape growers in California, for example, may feel little in common with manufacturers of aircraft in Missouri. Yet, like an organism, each is part of the same economic system, and the welfare of each depends on the others. Durkheim called this economic interdependence **organic solidarity.**

The Global Division of Work.   Organic solidarity has expanded far beyond anything Durkheim envisioned. Today it engulfs the world, and like Kim, in our opening vignette, our daily life now depends on workers around the globe. People who live in California or New York—or even Michigan—depend on workers in Tokyo to produce cars. Tokyo workers, in turn, depend on Saudi Arabian workers for oil, South American workers to operate ships, and workers in South Africa for palladium for their catalytic converters. Although we do not feel unity with one another—in fact, we sometimes feel threatened and hostile—interdependence links us all in the same economic web. Perhaps then, the term *organic solidarity* is no longer adequate to depict this sweeping change, and we need a new term such as "superorganic solidarity."

Driving this global interdependence is the dominance of capitalism. As capitalism globalizes, the world's nations are being divided into three primary trading blocks: North and South America dominated by the United States, Europe dominated by Germany, and Asia dominated by Japan. The multinational corporate giants, benefiting from this new world structure, are promoting free trade. If free trade is put into practice, its functions will include greater competition, lower prices, and a higher standard of living. Among the dysfunctional consequences—already felt by millions of U.S., U.K., French, and German workers—is the vast loss of production jobs in the most industrialized nations. Another consequence may be a decrease in nationalistic ties as identity expands from the nation to a global region. This change—considered by some a function, by others a dysfunction—may be part of the New World Order discussed in the next chapter.

The Conflict Perspective

Central to conflict theory is an emphasis on how the wealthy benefit at the expense of workers. Their analysis includes the impact of technology and the economic and political power of capitalism's inner circle.

Technology: Who Benefits?   Conflict theorists point out that the jobs the new technologies destroy are not located at the top levels of the multinationals, nor are they held by the wealthy individuals who own large blocs of stock. For the most part, these people are immune from such disruptions. For them, by lowering production costs, the new technology increases profits and fattens their dividend checks. The people who bear the brunt of the change are low-level workers who live from paycheck to paycheck. It is they who suffer the ravages of uncertainty, the devastation of job loss, and, often, the wrenching adjustments that come with being forced into jobs that pay lower wages.

The Inner Circle of Power.   The multinational corporations are headed by a group that Michael Useem (1984) calls the *inner circle*. Members of this inner circle, though in competition with one another, are united by a mutual interest in preserving capitalism (Mizruchi and Koenig 1991). Within their own country, they consult with high-level

mechanical solidarity: Durkheim's term for the unity that comes from being involved in similar occupations or activities

organic solidarity: Durkheim's term for the interdependence that results from people needing others to fulfill their jobs

As capitalism has gone global, so, too, have the political forces that undergird it. Shown here is U.S. Secretary of State Madeleine Albright with U.N. Secretary General Kofi Annan. The United Nations depends primarily on U.S. armed forces when it sends troops to global hot spots. From a conflict perspective this makes perfect sense, for from this perspective the U.N. is a tool that enforces the global expansion of capitalism.

politicians, promote legislation favorable to big business, and serve as trustees for foundations and universities. They also promote political candidates who stand firmly for the private ownership of property. On a global level, they fiercely promote the ideology of capitalism and move capital from one nation—or region—to another in their relentless search for greater and more immediate profits.

As stressed in previous chapters, conflict theorists focus on power. Although multinational corporations enshroud much of their activities in secrecy, on occasion their subterranean abuse of power comes to light. As Lord Acton said, "Power corrupts, and absolute power corrupts absolutely." The more power that a corporation has, then, the greater the temptation to misuse that power. One of the most notable examples occurred in 1973 when a U.S. multinational, the International Telephone & Telegraph Company (ITT), joined the CIA in a plot to unseat Chile's elected government. They first attempted to bring about the economic collapse of Chile. When this failed, they then plotted a coup d'état, which resulted in the assassination of the Chilean president, Salvador Allende (Coleman 1995).

The inner circle develops such a cozy relationship with the U.S. president that on occasion it can even recruit him to pitch its products, as this dispatch from the Associated Press (October 29, 1995) reveals:

> The White House celebrated Saudi Arabia's $6 billion purchase of U.S.-made airplanes Thursday, calling it a victory for both American manufacturers and the Clinton administration. . . . President Clinton helped broker the sale. . . . Prince Bandar bin Sultan, [Saudi Arabia's] minister of defense and aviation, credited Clinton for closing the purchase. *Clinton personally pitched the quality of the U.S. planes to Saudi King Fahd.* (Italics added)

Although the president wasn't selling toothpaste, it was the same principle.

In short, the interests of the heads of the multinational corporations and the top political leaders converge. We might note that the Associated Press dispatch just cited also includes this statement: "(T)he Clinton Administration worked this sale awfully damn hard because of the president's commitment to promoting U.S. business abroad. . . . He has done that routinely, instructed his ambassadors and his diplomats to put the economic interests of Americans forward as they conduct their diplomacy." Much of the activity of top government leaders, then, is dedicated to promoting the economic interests of the country's power elite—a topic to which we shall return in the next chapter.

Work in U.S. Society

Let's now turn our focus on work in U.S. society. To understand the present situation, we must first review the large-scale changes in what are called economic sectors.

Three Economic Sectors

Sociologists divide economic life into three sectors: primary, secondary, and tertiary. The primary sector is central to preindustrial societies. In the **primary sector,** workers extract natural resources from the environment. People who fish for a living or who mine copper work in the primary sector. So do hunters, cattle raisers, farmers, and lumberjacks. In the **secondary sector,** workers turn raw materials into manufactured goods. They package fish, process copper into electrical wire, and turn trees into lumber and paper. The secondary sector dominates industrial economies.

The main focus of the **tertiary sector** is providing services. Some workers, such as computer technicians and automobile mechanics, install or service products. Others, such as private detectives and cab drivers, provide personal services. Although *most* of the labor force in postindustrial societies work in the tertiary sector, all three sectors exist side by side. Take the common lead pencil as an example. People who extract lead and cut timber work in the primary sector, those who turn the wood and lead into pencils are in the secondary sector, and those who advertise and sell the pencils work in the tertiary sector.

Farming provides a remarkable example of this transition, for which there is no parallel in history (Drucker 1987; 1994). Figure 14.4a shows the decline of employment in farming (the primary sector), where most of our ancestors once worked. As the number of farmers declined during the early and mid-1900s, manufacturing (the secondary sector) picked up the slack. During the 1800s, a typical farmer could produce enough food for five people. With today's powerful farming machinery and hybrid seeds, he or she now feeds about eighty. In the 1800s over 50 percent of U.S. workers were engaged in farming, but today only 2 percent are farmers (*Statistical Abstract* 1997:Tables 649, 1098).

primary sector: that part of the economy that extracts raw materials from the environment

secondary sector: that part of the economy that turns raw materials into manufactured goods

tertiary sector: that part of the economy that consists of service-oriented occupations

Figure 14.4

U.S. Workers in Three Types of Work and the Proportion of Workers by Sex

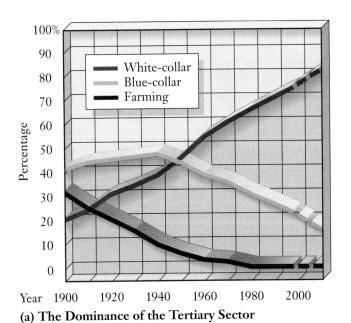

(a) **The Dominance of the Tertiary Sector**

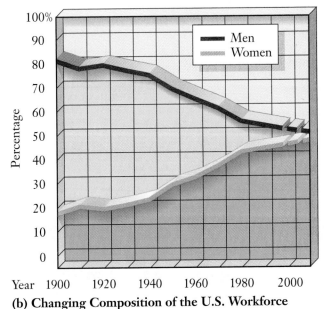

(b) **Changing Composition of the U.S. Workforce**

Note: From 1900 to 1940, "workers" refers to people age 14 and over, from 1970 to people age 16 and over. Broken lines are the author's projections.

Source: Statistical Abstract, various years and 1997:Tables 624, 645, 648.

Figure 14.4a also shows the major transition that occurred about 1955. Then, for the first time, most Americans worked in the tertiary sector. Although a postindustrial society requires few people to produce food or basic materials and few people to process them, the information explosion demands that large numbers of people work in the tertiary sector. Consequently, we have experienced a surge in "knowledge work"—managing information and designing and servicing products—and, as Figure 14.4a also shows, a severe decline in blue-collar jobs.

Women and Work

One of the chief characteristics of the U.S. work force has been a steady increase in the numbers of women who work outside the home for wages. Figure 14.4b shows how women have become an increasingly larger component of the U.S. work force. At the turn of the century, one of five U.S. workers was a woman. By 1940, this ratio had grown to one of four, by 1960 it was one of three, and today it is almost one of two. As you can see from Figure 14.5, this ratio is one of the highest in the industrialized world.

How likely a woman is to be in the labor force depends on several factors. Figure 14.6a shows how working for wages increases with each level of education. This is probably because as one ascends the educational ladder work is more satisfying and the pay much better. Figure 14.6b shows the influence of marital status. You can see that single women are the most likely to work for wages, married women follow closely behind, and divorced, widowed, and separated women are the least likely to be in the work force. From Figure 14.6c you can see that race–ethnicity has very little influence on whether or not a woman is in the labor force.

Researchers have found some major distinctions between women and men in the world of work. For one, women tend to be more concerned than men with maintaining a balance between their work and family lives (Statham et al. 1988). For another, men and women tend to follow different models for success: Men tend to emphasize individualism, power, and competition, while women are much more likely to stress collaboration, persuasion, and helping (Miller-Loessi 1992). A primary concern of many women is the extent to which they must adopt the male model of leadership in order to be successful in their careers. You should note that these findings represent tendencies. Although they characterize the average woman or man, many people diverge from them.

the quiet revolution: the fundamental changes in society that occur as a result of vast numbers of women entering the work force

The Quiet Revolution. Because its changes are so gradual but its implications so profound, sociologists use the term **"quiet revolution"** to refer to the continually increas-

Figure 14.5

Women Make Up What Percentage of the Labor Force in the Most Industrialized Nations?

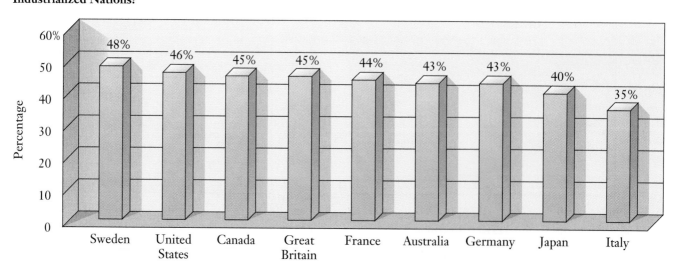

Source: Statistical Abstract 1997:Tables 624, 1362.

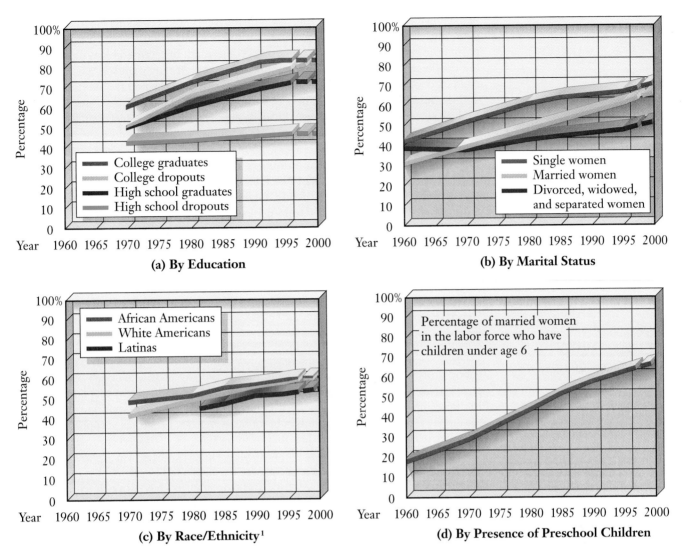

(a) By Education

(b) By Marital Status

(c) By Race/Ethnicity[1]

(d) By Presence of Preschool Children

[1]Data for other racial/ethnic groups unavailable in the source; no data for Latinas for 1970–1980.

Source: *Statistical Abstract* 1995:Tables 627, 629, 637, 639; 1997:620, 623, 630, 632. Broken lines indicate author's projections.

Figure 14.6

Percentage of Women in the U.S. Labor Force

ing proportions of women who have joined the ranks of paid labor. This trend, shown in Figure 14.6, means a transformation of consumer patterns, relations at work, self-concepts, and relationships with boyfriends, husbands, and children. One of the most significant aspects of the quiet revolution is indicated by Figure 14.6d. Note that since 1960 the proportion of married women with preschool children who work for wages has tripled. It now equals the average of all U.S. women. We discuss implications of these changes in Chapter 16.

The Underground Economy

The underground economy. It has a sinister ring—suggestive of dope deals struck in alleys and wads of dollar bills hastily exchanged. The underground economy is this, but it is a lot more—and usually a lot more innocent. If you pay the plumber with a check made out to "cash," if you purchase a pair of sunglasses from a street vendor or a kitchen gadget at a yard sale, if you so much as hand a neighbor's kid a $20 bill (or if you accept it) to mow the lawn or to baby sit, you are participating in the underground economy. (Pennar and Farrell 1993)

Also known as the informal economy and the off-the-books economy, the **underground economy** consists of economic activities—whether legal or illegal—that people don't report to the government. What interests most of us is not unreported baby-sitting money, but the illegal activities that people cannot report even if they want to. As a 20-year-old child care worker who also works as a prostitute two or three nights a week said, "Why do I do this? For the money! Where else can I make this kind of money in a few hours? And it's all tax free" (author's files). Drug dealing is perhaps the largest single source of illegal income, for billions of dollars flow from users to sellers and their networks of growers, importers, processors, transporters, dealers, and enforcers. These particular networks are so huge that each year more than a million Americans are arrested for illegal drug activities (*Statistical Abstract* 1997:Table 328).

Because of its subterranean nature, no one knows the exact size of the underground economy, but it probably runs 10 to 15 percent of the regular economy (Pennar and Farrell 1993). Since the official gross national product of the United States is about $8 trillion (*Statistical Abstract* 1997:Table 698), the underground economy probably runs close to $1 trillion. It is so huge that it distorts the official statistics of the country's gross national product, and the IRS loses over $100 billion a year in taxes.

Shrinking Paychecks

underground economy: exchanges of goods and services that are not reported to the government and thereby escape taxation

U.S. workers are some of the most productive in the world (*Statistical Abstract* 1997:Table 1368), and as we saw on Table 14.1 (page 386), U.S. multinational corporations make gigantic profits. One might think, therefore, that the pay of U.S. workers would be increasing. Until about 1970, gains in productivity did translate into pay that bought more. But how things have changed. Look at Figure 14.7. The gold bars show current dollars, the money the average worker finds in his or her paycheck. From this, it appears that U.S. workers are making a lot more than they used to. Back in 1970 workers averaged only a little over $3 an hour, and now it is almost $12. The green bars, which show the *buying power* of these paychecks, however, strip away the illusion. They show that inflation has whittled away the value of those dollars, and workers can't buy as much with their $12 today as they could with the "measly" $3 they made in 1970. The question is not "How could you live on just $3 back in 1970?" but, rather, "How can you live on just $12 an hour today?"

Some workers, however, aren't able to bring home even these shrinking paychecks. The Perspectives box on the next page presents an overview of who is unemployed—and explains why these figures are deceptive.

Patterns of Work and Leisure

Suppose that it is 1860 and you work for a textile company in Lowell, Massachusetts. When you arrive at work one day, you find that the boss has posted a new work rule: All workers will have to come in at the same time and remain until quitting time. Like the other workers, you feel outrage. You join them as they shout, "This is slavery!" and march out on strike, indignant at such a preposterous rule (Zuboff 1991). The workers were angry because they had been able to come and go when they wanted. To see why, let's consider how patterns of work and leisure are related to the transformation of economies.

Effects of Industrialization. Hunting and gathering societies provided tremendous amounts of leisure. If people did not face some unusual event, such as drought or pestilence, it did not take long to gather what they needed for the day. In fact, *most of their time was leisure*, and the rhythms of nature were an essential part

Figure 14.7

Average Hourly Earnings of U.S. Workers in Current and Constant (1982) Dollars

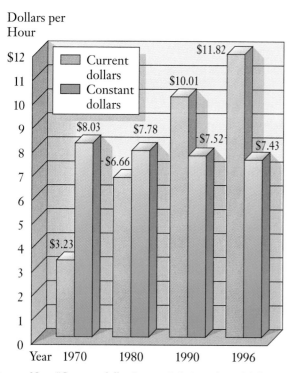

Dollars per Hour

Note: "Constant dollars" means inflation-adjusted dollars.

Source: *Statistical Abstract* 1993:Table 667; 1997:Table 667.

CULTURAL DIVERSITY IN THE UNITED STATES

Who Is Unemployed?

It is hard to believe that Amy and Peter are not officially part of the unemployed. After all, they have no jobs. In fact, they have no home. They are among the many homeless and jobless Americans sleeping in alleys and shelters for the destitute. That, however, is *not* enough to count them as unemployed.

To see how the calculation works, let's suppose that you lose your job. After six months' frustrating search for work, you become so discouraged that you stay home and stare blankly at the television. Amazingly, you no longer are counted as unemployed. As far as official statistics are concerned, to be unemployed you must be *actively* seeking work. If not, the government leaves you out of its figures. People without jobs who are so discouraged that they have not looked for work during the previous four weeks are simply not included in the government's unemployment figures.

Now, suppose that you do keep on looking for work, and you remain part of the government's count. But if your neighbor pays you to clean out her garage and rake the leaves, and if you put in fifteen hours and report them, you won't be counted, for the government figures that you have a job. Now assume that you keep on looking for work, don't rake leaves for a few hours' pay, but can't pay your telephone

bill. Again, you won't show up in the totals, for the Bureau of Labor Statistics counts only people it reaches in a random telephone survey. To get an accurate idea of how many are unemployed, then, we need to add about 3 percent to the official unemployment rate (Myers 1992). If the Labor Department says it is 7 percent, the true rate is actually about 10 percent—a difference of about *8 million people*. This is a conservative figure, for some estimate that 6 million people who want to work have only part-time jobs or are so discouraged that they no longer look for work (Herbert 1993).

Granted these problems, certain patterns do show up year after year. As you can see from Table 14.2, unemployment varies by sex, race/ethnicity, education, marital status, and presence of preschool children. Asian Americans are the least likely to be unemployed, with whites close behind them. African Americans and Latinos have the highest unemployment. You won't be surprised to see that the higher a person's education, the less the likelihood of unemployment, but you might be surprised to see that divorced workers are less likely to be unemployed than single workers, but more likely than married people to find themselves without work. Although the particular percentages fluctuate with changing economic conditions, these general patterns remain fairly constant.

TABLE 14.2

THE OFFICIAL U.S. UNEMPLOYMENT RATE

Category	Percentage	Category	Percentage	Category	Percentage	Category	Percentage
Sex		*Race/Ethnicity*		*Ethnic Background of Latinos*		*Education*	
Male	5.4%	African Americans		Puerto Rican		High school dropouts	
Female	5.4	Men	11.1%	Men	8.6%	Men	11.0%
Marital Status of Women[a]		Women	10.0	Women	10.8	Women	10.7
Married	3.4	Latinos		Mexican		High school graduates	
Single	8.6	Men	7.9	Men	8.2	Men	6.4
Divorced, widowed, and separated	5.5	Women	10.2	Women	11.0	Women	4.4
		Whites		Cuban		1–3 years of college	
Women with Preschool Children[a]		Men	4.7	Men	6.4	Men	4.5
		Women	4.7	Women	8.3	Women	3.8
Married	3.9	Asian Americans[b]		Other[c]		College graduates	
Single	20.3	Men	3.3	Men	7.4	Men	2.3
Divorced, widowed, and separated	9.7	Women	3.3	Women	8.7	Women	2.1

[a]Source does not list totals for men.

[b]Source does not list employment of Asian Americans by sex, and this is the overall total listed for both men and women.

[c]Refers primarily to people from Central or South America.

Source: Statistical Abstract 1997: Tables 50, 627, 631, 633, 652, 657.

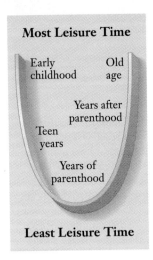

Most Leisure Time

Early childhood

Old age

Years after parenthood

Teen years

Years of parenthood

Least Leisure Time

Figure 14.8

Leisure and the Life Course: The "U" Curve of Leisure

of their lives. Agricultural economies also allowed much leisure, for, at least in the western hemisphere, work peaked with the spring planting, let up in the summer, and then peaked again with the fall harvest. During the winter work again receded, for by this time the harvest was in, animals had been slaughtered, food had been canned and stored, and a wood supply had been laid up.

Industrialization, however, broke this harness to seasonal rhythms. Going against all of human history, rhythms now were dictated by bosses and machines. Workers, however, resisted, insisting on moving to their traditional rhythms. After working for several weeks, a worker would disappear, only to reappear when money ran out. For most, enjoying leisure was considerably more important than amassing money (Weber 1958/1904–1905). Bosses, wanting to profit from regular, efficient production, began to insist that all workers start work at the same time. To workers, that seemed like slavery. Today, in contrast, those work patterns artificially imposed on us have become part of our culture and are taken for granted.

Trends in Leisure. **Leisure** is time not taken up by work or required activities such as eating and sleeping. It is not the activity itself that makes something leisure, but the purpose for which it is done. Consider driving a car. If you do it for pleasure, it is leisure, but if you are an on-duty police officer or commuting to the office, it is work. If done for enjoyment, horseback riding and reading a book are leisure—but these activities are work for jockeys and students.

Patterns of leisure change with the life course, following the U-curve shown on Figure 14.8. Young children enjoy the most leisure, but teenagers still have considerably more leisure than their parents. Parents with small children have the least leisure, but after the children leave home, leisure picks up again. After the age of 60 or so, the amount of leisure for adults peaks.

Work in the Postindustrial Society. Compared with early industrialization, workers today have far more leisure. A hundred years ago the work week was half again as long as today's, for then workers had to be at their machines sixty hours a week. When workers unionized, they demanded a shorter work week. Over the years, the work week has gradually shrunk. In Germany the work week is 35 hours, with Friday afternoons usually off. Volkswagen is the world's first global corporation to adopt a 30-hour work week (Rifkin 1995). In addition, German workers are guaranteed six weeks of paid vacation each year. Unlike western Europe, however, in the United States this trend to more leisure reversed course during the 1960s (Schor 1991; Rifkin 1995). U.S. workers now average 1,948 hours of work a year, matched only by workers in Great Britain. They are soundly beaten, however, by Japanese workers, who average 2,120 hours a year (Ono and Schlesinger 1992; MacShane 1993).

The Future: Facing the Consequences of Global Capitalism

The best place to catch a glimpse of the future is to look at two trends that are firmly in place: global trade and the new technology.

Expanding Global Trade

With the giant multinational corporations carving up the world into major trading blocs and pushing for the drastic reduction or elimination of tariffs, trade among nations will increase beyond anything we have ever seen. The United States will be at the forefront of this expanding global trade, for world markets have become crucial for the success of many U.S. corporations. For example, with the huge costs of making movies (the aver-

leisure: time not taken up by work or required activities such as eating, sleeping, commuting, child care, and housework

If politics make strange bedfellows, so do economics. The animosity felt by U.S. politicians toward Vietnam's economic system was once so fierce that they sacrificed hundreds of thousands of lives and billions of dollars in a wasted effort to extinguish "the enemy." This photo from Ho Chi Minh City, the capital of Vietnam, illustrates how this former "enemy to death" is now in the process of becoming an economic partner of the United States.

age movie now runs $50 million), the U.S. movie industry would go broke if it weren't for global distribution.

New Technologies and Downsizing: Utopia or Nightmare?

Computer-driven production will continue to reduce the number of workers needed to make the goods we use. As I wrote back in 1975,

> Although it may sound as though it is taken from some utopian scheme, it has been estimated that the day will come when only 2 percent of the population will be needed to produce all the manufactured goods our total population needs. That day may not be far off as Ford Motor Company now takes only six workers to produce a single car while it took 104 workers for the same task in 1910 . . . it is possible that a single plant with but a single worker can produce all the bread needed in southern California. . . . Whether such changes represent a utopian dream come true or not, for displaced workers it can well be a nightmare. (p. 341)

Utopia or a nightmare? From a symbolic interactionist standpoint, it all depends on your point of view. As conflict theorists stress, that point of view depends on where you stand in the production process. If you are the capitalist who owns the bread factory that feeds all of southern California and you have to pay but a single worker, your opinion will differ sharply from the workers who may have to beg for bread instead of earning their living by making bread.

Let's close this chapter, then, with a Thinking Critically section that focuses on the far-reaching implications of this global transformation of our economy.

Thinking Critically About Social Controversy

New Technology and the Restructuring of Work: What Type of New Society?

▼ Many workers fear that they will be automated out of their jobs. They have seen machines displace people who worked at their side, neighbors with a solid work history join the lines of the unemployed, friends, forced to take "early retirement," now wondering how they will support themselves in their old age.

fears are not irrational. In recent years, the number of workers at U.S. Steel dropped from 120,000 to just 20,000—yet production has remained the same. If each telephone operator handled the number of calls she or he did in the 1920s, today's telephone traffic would require 50 million operators! In just the next few years, computerization will erase another 3 million U.S. manufacturing jobs (Volti 1995).

But there is another side to the story, for technology also creates jobs. Although the automobile industry wiped out the livelihood of many bicycle workers and stable hands, for example, it put tens of thousands more to work in the new steel and gasoline industries. These jobs are in addition to mechanics, salespeople, advertisers, as well as the work done in the body shops that dot our landscape.

Each new technology, then, both destroys old jobs and creates new ones. Some of these jobs, as with the gasoline stations required by automobiles, are readily visible. Others are less evident. The technology that went into airplanes, for example, not only spawned pilots, mechanics, and reservation clerks, but it also stimulated global tourism. To put this in a nutshell: *most* of us work at jobs that did not even exist a hundred years ago.

And the future? This we can take for granted: There will be more new technologies—and they will make millions of our current jobs obsolete. The basic question is whether the new technologies will destroy jobs faster than they create them. For the millions of workers who are finding their jobs pulled out from under them, this question is of much more than theoretical interest. Always in the past the new technologies created more jobs than they destroyed, but this time around something different may be happening. Social analyst Jeremy Rifkin (1995:xvi–xvii) puts it this way:

> In the past, when new technologies have replaced workers in a given sector, new sectors have always emerged to absorb the displaced laborers. Today, all three of the traditional sectors of the economy—agriculture, manufacturing, and service—are experiencing technological displacement, forcing millions onto the unemployment rolls. The only new sector emerging is the knowledge sector, made up of a small elite of entrepreneurs, scientists, technicians, computer programmers, professionals, educators, and consultants. While this sector is growing, it is not expected to absorb more than a fraction of the hundreds of millions [worldwide] who will be eliminated in the next several decades in the wake of revolutionary advances in the information and communication sciences.

Evidence for this point of view is growing. Even that staunch defender of U.S. and global capitalism, *The Wall Street Journal*, reported that the U.S. economy isn't growing fast enough to produce enough well-paying jobs to replace those lost to technology and trade (Davis 1996).

Most experts suggest that the solution to this problem is to retrain workers. Although this sounds good on the surface, and is necessary in some instances, with the automation of all sec-

As conflict theorists stress, in order to keep labor costs low and profits high, capitalist economies need a reserve labor force that pits one worker against another. This poorly paid gold miner in South Africa, working under the debilitating conditions you see in this photo, is an expendable part of the profit system that drives the economic machinery called capitalism. If this worker protests his working conditions, he will be fired immediately, for waiting in the wings are thousands of unemployed workers eager to take his place.

tors of the economy, the frustrating question is "Retraining for what?" We would simply be juggling workers from phased-out positions to temporary jobs.

Consider two futures (Rifkin 1995). The one is a technoparadise of abundance and leisure. With few workers needed, work is spread around, and the work week is only 10 or 15 hours. Yet everyone is able to possess goods in abundance. Having restored the leisure that humans used to enjoy in their early days as hunters and gatherers, creative leisure becomes a chief characteristic of the new society. Some spend time in intellectual pursuits, studying the sciences, philosophy, languages. Some follow the arts—painting, poetry, the theater. Many travel. Parents spend much more time with their children. Others, of course, just watch more soap operas, play more video games, or sit transfixed, with beer in one hand and remote in the other, for that many more hours of televised sports.

The second future is a divided society. A smaller, affluent group forms a country inside a country of impoverished workers and those dispossessed from the work force. Millions, surviving in hopelessness, accept meager welfare handouts grudgingly given. Displaced from job opportunities, the nation's youth produce a violent criminal subculture. Frightened and confused at the increasing violence, the affluent lock themselves behind barricaded neighborhoods.

We can't turn back the clock. New technology is here to stay, and it will continue to change the shape of work. The basic issue, then, is how we, as a society, react. In other words, the transformation of work is inevitable, but the consequences of that restructuring are not.

For Your Consideration

Given the discussion in this chapter about (1) the effects of the new technologies on work and (2) the direction of capitalism, especially the globalization of trade and the growing power of multinationals, which of these futures appears the most likely? ▲

Summary and Review

The Transformation of Economic Systems

How are economic systems linked to types of societies?

The earliest societies, hunting and gathering, were **subsistence economies:** Small groups lived off the land and produced little or no surplus. Economic systems grew more complex as people discovered how to domesticate and cultivate (pastoral and horticultural societies), farm (agricultural societies), and manufacture (industrial societies). Each of these methods allowed people to produce a *surplus*, which fostered trade. Trade, in turn, brought social inequality as some people began to accumulate more than others. Pp. 372–375.

The Transformation of the Medium of Exchange

How has the medium of exchange evolved?

A **medium of exchange** is any means by which people exchange goods and services. In hunting and gathering and pastoral and horticultural societies, people **bartered** goods and services. In agricultural societies, **money** came into use, which evolved into **currency,** or paper representing a specific amount of gold or silver. Postindustrial societies rely increasingly on electronic transfer of funds in the form of **credit** and **debit cards.** Pp. 375–377.

World Economic Systems

How do the major economic systems differ?

The world's two major economic systems are capitalism and socialism. In **capitalism,** private citizens own the means of production and pursue profits. In **socialism,** the state owns the means of production and determines production with no goal of profit. Adherents of each have developed ideologies that defend their own systems and paint the other as harmful. Following **convergence theory,** in recent years each system has adopted features of the other. Pp. 377–384.

Capitalism in a Global Economy

What is the role of the corporation in capitalism?

The term **corporate capitalism** indicates that giant corporations dominate capitalism today. At the top of the major corporations is an **inner circle,** whose mutual interests make certain that corporate capitalism is protected. The primary sociological significance of global capitalism is that the interests of the inner circle lie beyond national boundaries. Pp. 384–387.

Applying Sociological Theories

How do the three major perspectives apply to work?

Symbolic interactionists analyze meanings and self-perceptions, asking why work is a job or a profession, what gives work status, and what makes work satisfying. From the *functionalist perspective,* work is a basis of social solidarity. Preindustrial societies foster **mechanical solidarity,** identifying with others who perform similar tasks. With industrialization comes **organic solidarity,** economic interdependence brought about by the division of labor. *Conflict theorists,* who focus on power, note how the new technology and global capitalism affect workers and owners. Workers lose jobs to automation, while the inner circle maintains its political power and profits from these changes. Pp. 387–390.

Work in U.S. Society

What are the three economic sectors of the labor force?

In the **primary sector** workers extract raw materials from the environment. In the **secondary sector** workers turn raw products into manufactured goods. In the **tertiary sec-** tor workers produce services. Most Americans now work in the tertiary, or service sector. Pp. 391–392.

How has the ratio of women in the workforce changed?

In 1940, one in four members of the labor force was a woman. Today, this figure is almost one in two, one of the highest ratios in the industrialized world. Pp. 392–393.

What is the underground economy?

The **underground economy** consists of any economic activity not reported to the government, from babysitting to prostitution. The size of the underground economy runs perhaps 10 to 15 percent of the regular economy. Pp. 393–394.

How have patterns of work and leisure changed?

In hunting and gathering societies, most time was leisure. In agricultural societies, work was dictated by the seasons. Industrialization initially brought a dramatic decrease in leisure, but workers have gained some back. Among the industrialized nations, currently only the Japanese work more hours per year than do U.S. workers. Pp. 394–396.

The Future: Facing the Consequences of Global Capitalism

Expanding global trade, new technologies, and downsizing will continue to force a restructuring of work. Choices made now can lead to a better society or to a nightmare. Pp. 396–399.

Where can I read more on this topic?

Suggested readings for this chapter are listed on page 664.

 Sociology and the Internet

All URLs listed are current as of the printing of this book. URLs are often changed. Please check our Website http://www.abacon.com/henslin for updates.

1. Now that you have learned about capitalism and socialism, as well as about the trend toward the convergence of the two, let's explore further. The Internet is a popular place for proponents of each ideology to expound their views. I'm going to ask you to do another search, because quite often these discussions and even their sites have very short lives. Go to the Lycos search engine at *http://www.lycos.com/* Enter the search terms "capitalism" and "socialism." (Don't put in the quotation marks or the word *and.*) Now browse through the results of your search, selecting a variety of sites. Read the material at several of the sites and take notes on issues, positions, and analyses. In preparing this assignment we found outlines of college courses, book advertisements, student papers, a University of Texas Islamic club's position on capitalism, and even an entire book (*Socialism from Below*). After you have viewed the first 10 listings, you should select "next page" to continue your search.

When you finish your research, write a paper defining capitalism and socialism, and analyze the positions you found at the various sites.

2. Work is one of the fundamental anchors of identity in industrial societies. This makes unemployment a devastating event. You found some of the characteristics of unemployed people in the Perspectives box "Who Is Unemployed?" Now let's look at regional unemployment in the United States, and introduce you to the data at the Bureau of Labor Statistics (BLS). Go to the BLS Home Page at *http://stats.bls.gov/* and select "Regional Information." Now select the region V. Chicago. On the new screen, select "Most Requested Series." You should now see a list of topics with small squares in front of them. Click on each of the following: *Unemployment Rate*

US, seasonally adjusted, Unemployment Rate (for V. Chicago), *Unemployment Rate* (for a state adjacent to V. Chicago.) Now go the bottom of the list. In the box labeled "Years to Search For," make sure the current year is highlighted. If it isn't, click on it. Now select "Retrieve Data." You should see tables for each of the categories you selected. Save or print these if you can; otherwise, you will have to work from the screen. Note the rates for January and June for the United States.

You now are ready to construct a table with the data. Refer back to Table 5.1 in Chapter 5 (page 124) to refresh your memory on making tables. Write a brief analysis of your table, and add your own suggestions for why the differences exist.

3. Use a search engine such as Yahoo! *http://www.yahoo!.com* to find online shopping malls. Examine the medium of exchange available on these Internet communities. What are the accepted methods of payment? How is Internet shopping contributing to the extinction of the exchange of physical money? How is it promoting the electronic transfer of numbers residing in computer memory banks?

4. The Internet and the Web have taken the world by storm. They have changed the way people work, shop, and do business. Examine the following link, which discusses how the Net changes business: *http://www.gslis.utexas.edu/~jpetri/business.html* What are some of the changes the Net makes to business? Use the functional perspective to determine possible consequences for various "units" of society. Are these changes good for society? How do you know? Use the conflict perspective to discuss who benefits from these changes.

Tsing-Fang Chen, Hail to the Statue of Liberty, circa 1986

CHAPTER

15

Politics:
Power and Authority

*I*N THE *1930*S, GEORGE ORWELL WROTE *1984*, *a book about a future in which the government, known as "Big Brother," dominates society, dictating almost every aspect of everyone's life. To even love someone is considered a sinister activity, a betrayal of the first love and unquestioning allegiance that all citizens owe Big Brother.*

Two characters, Winston and Julia, fall in love. Because of Big Brother, they meet furtively, always with the threat of discovery and punishment hanging over their heads. When informers turn them in, expert interrogators separate Julia and Winston. They swiftly proceed to break their affection—to restore their loyalty to Big Brother.

Then follows a remarkable account of Winston and his tormentor, O'Brien. Winston is strapped so tightly into a chair that he can't even move his head. O'Brien explains that inflicting pain is not always enough, but that everyone has a breaking point, some worst thing that will push them over the edge.

O'Brien tells Winston that he has discovered his worst fear. Then he sets a cage with two giant, starving sewer rats on the table next to Winston, picks up a mask connected to the door of the cage and places it over Winston's head. In a quiet voice, O'Brien explains that when he presses the lever, the door of the cage will slide up, and the rats will shoot out like bullets and bore straight into Winston's face. Winston's eyes, the only part of his body that he can move, dart back and forth, revealing his terror. Still speaking so quietly that Winston has to strain to hear him, O'Brien adds that the rats sometimes attack the eyes first, but sometimes they burrow through the cheeks and devour the tongue. When O'Brien places his hand on the lever, Winston realizes that the only way out is for someone to take his place. But who? Then he hears his own voice screaming, "Do it to Julia! . . . Tear her face off, strip her to the bones. Not me! Julia! Not me!"

Orwell does not describe Julia's interrogation, but when Julia and Winston see each other later they realize that each has betrayed the other. Their love is gone. Big Brother has won.

Winston's crime was that he had given his loyalty to Julia, his lover, instead of to Big Brother, the overseeing, all-demanding, and all-controlling government. Winston's misplaced loyalty made him a political heretic, for it was the obligation of every citizen to place the state above all else in life. To preserve the state's dominance over the individual, Winston's allegiance had to be taken away from Julia. As you see, it was.

Although seldom this dramatic, politics is always about power and authority, the focus of this chapter.

Micropolitics and Macropolitics

Although the images that come to mind when we think of politics are those of government—kings, queens, coups, dictatorships, running for office, voting—politics, in the sense of power relations, is also an inevitable part of everyday life (Schwartz 1990). As Weber (1922/1968) said, **power** is the ability to carry out your will in spite of resistance, and in every group, large or small, some individuals have power over others. Symbolic interactionists use the term **micropolitics** to refer to the exercise of power in everyday life. Routine situations in which people jockey for power include several employees' trying to impress the new boss—who is going to decide which one of them will be promoted to manager—as well as efforts by parents to enforce their curfew on a reluctant daughter or son, and the struggle over the remote control to the TV. *Every group, then, is political, for in every group there is a power struggle of some sort.*

In contrast, **macropolitics**—the focus of this chapter—refers to the exercise of large-scale power over a large group. Governments, whether the dictatorship faced by Winston or the elected forms in the United States and Canada, are examples of macropolitics. Let us turn, then, to macropolitics, considering first the matter of authority.

power: the ability to carry out one's will, even over the resistance of others

micropolitics: the exercise of power in everyday life, such as deciding who is going to do the housework

macropolitics: the exercise of large-scale power, the government being the most common example

Power, Authority, and Violence

For a society to exist, it must have a system of leadership. Some people will have to have power over others. As Max Weber (1913/1947) pointed out, however, we perceive power as legitimate or illegitimate. Weber used the term **authority** to refer to legitimate power—that is, power that we accept as right. In contrast, illegitimate power—**coercion**—is power that we do not accept as just.

Imaging that you are driving to college to take a sociology exam, and on the way you stop to buy a CD player on sale for $250. As you approach the store, a man jumps out of the alley and shoves a gun in your face. He demands your money. Frightened for your life, you hand it over. After filing a police report, you are running late. Afraid you might miss the test, you step on the gas. As the needle hits 85, you see flashing blue and red lights in your rear-view mirror. Your explanation about the robbery doesn't faze the officer—nor the judge who hears your case a few weeks later. She first lectures you on safety and then orders you to pay $50 court costs plus $10 for every mile an hour over 65 mph. You pay the $250.

What's the difference? The mugger, the police officer, and the judge—each has power, and in each case you part with $250. The difference is that the mugger has no authority. His power is illegitimate—he has no *right* to do what he did. In contrast, you acknowledge that the officer has the right to stop you and that the judge has the right to fine you. Theirs is authority, or legitimate power.

Authority and Legitimate Violence

As sociologist Peter Berger observed, it makes little difference whether you willingly pay the fine that the judge levies against you, or refuse to pay it. The court will get its money one way or another.

> There may be innumerable steps before its application [violence], in the way of warnings and reprimands. But if all the warnings are disregarded, even in so slight a matter as paying a traffic ticket, the last thing that will happen is that a couple of cops show up at the door with handcuffs and a Black Maria. Even the moderately courteous cop who hands out the initial traffic ticket is likely to wear a gun—just in case. (Berger 1963)

The **state,** then—a term synonymous with *government*—claims a monopoly on legitimate force or violence within some designated territory. This point, made by Max Weber (1946a, 1922/1968)—that the state claims the exclusive right to use violence and the right to punish everyone else who does—is critical to our understanding of macropolitics. If someone owes you a debt, you cannot imprison that person or even forcibly take the money. The state can. The ultimate proof of the state's authority is that you cannot kill someone because he or she has done something that you consider absolutely horrible—but the state can. As Berger (1963) summarized this matter, *"Violence is the ultimate foundation of any political order."*

Before we explore the origins of the modern state, let us first look at a situation in which the state loses legitimacy.

The Collapse of Authority. Sometimes the state oppresses its people, and they resist their government just as they do a mugger. The people cooperate reluctantly—but with a smile if that is what is required—while they eye the gun in the hand of the government's representatives. But, as they do with a mugger, if they are able they take up arms to free themselves. **Revolution,** armed resistance with the intention to overthrow a government, is not only a people's rejection of a govern-

authority: power that people accept as rightly exercised over them; also called *legitimate power*

coercion: power that people do not accept as rightly exercised over them; also called *illegitimate power*

state: a political entity that claims monopoly on the use of violence in some particular territory; commonly known as a country

revolution: armed resistance designed to overthrow a government

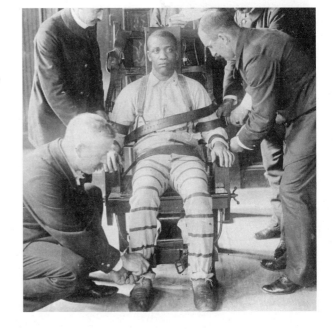

The ultimate foundation of any political order is violence. At no time is this more starkly demonstrated than when a government takes human life. Shown in this 1910 photo from Sing Sing Prison is a man about to be executed.

For centuries, widows in the Mediterranean area were expected to dress in black. Their long dresses were matched by black stockings, black shoes, and black head covering. Widows conformed to this socially defined expression of ongoing sorrow for the deceased husband not because of law, but because of custom. Today, however, as industrialization erodes traditional authority, few widows follow this practice.

traditional authority: authority based on custom

rational-legal authority: authority based on law or written rules and regulations; also called *bureaucratic authority*

ment's claim to rule over them but also a rejection of its monopoly on violence. In a revolution, the people claim that right for themselves and if successful, they establish a new state in which they claim the right to monopolize violence.

What some see as coercion, however, others see as authority. Consequently, some people remain loyal to a government, willingly defend it, perhaps even die for it, although others are ready to take up arms against it. *The more that its power is seen as legitimate, then, the more stable a government is.*

But just why do people accept power as legitimate? Max Weber (1922/1968) identified three sources of authority: traditional, rational-legal, and charismatic. Let's examine each.

Traditional Authority

Throughout history, the most common form of authority has been tradition. **Traditional authority,** which is based on custom, is the hallmark of preliterate groups. In these societies, custom dictates basic relationships. For example, because of birth a particular individual becomes the chief, king, or queen. As far as members of that society are concerned, this is the right way to determine who shall rule because "It's always been done this way."

Gender relations in most human groups are a good example of traditional authority, for they are based on custom. For example, as shown in the photo, in the villages of Spain and Portugal widows are expected to wear only black until they remarry—which generally means that they wear black for the rest of their lives. By law, a widow is free to wear any color she wishes, but not by tradition. Tradition, decreeing black, is so strong that if a widow were to violate the dress code, she would be seen as having profaned the memory of her deceased husband and would be ostracized by the community.

When a traditional society changes, it undermines traditional authority. For example, as a society industrializes, people have new experiences. This opens up new perspectives on life, and no longer does traditional authority go unchallenged. Thus, in Spain and Portugal you can still see old women dressed in black from head to toe—and you immediately know their marital status. Younger widows, however, are likely to be indistinguishable from other women.

Even in postindustrial societies, traditional authority never totally dies out (Schwartz 1990). Parental authority provides an excellent example. Parents exercise authority over their children *because* they always have had such authority. From generations past, we inherit the idea that parents are not only responsible for providing their children with food and shelter, but also that they have the right to discipline them, to choose their doctors and schools, and to teach them religion and morality.

Rational-Legal Authority

The second type of authority identified by Weber, **rational-legal authority,** is not based on custom but on written rules. "Rational" means reasonable, and "legal" means part of law. Thus "rational-legal" refers to matters agreed to by reasonable people and written into law (or regulations of some sort). The matters agreed to may be as broad as a constitution that specifies the rights of all members of a society or as narrow as a contract between two individuals. Because bureaucracies are based on written rules, rational-legal authority is also called *bureaucratic authority.*

George Washington, first president of the United States, 1789–1797, is an example of rational-legal authority. That is, he took office according to a system of rules that people had agreed on, in this case, the new Constitution of the United States.

Rational-legal authority comes from the position that an individual holds, not from the person who holds the position. In a democracy, for example, the president's authority comes from the office, as specified in a written constitution, not from custom or the individual's personal characteristics. In rational-legal authority, everyone—no matter how high the office—is subject to the organization's written rules. In governments based on traditional authority, the ruler's word may be law, but in those based on rational-legal authority, the ruler's word is subject to the law.

Charismatic Authority

A few centuries back, in 1429, the English controlled large parts of France. When they prevented the coronation of a new French king, a farmer's daughter heard a voice telling her that God had a special assignment for her—that she should put on men's clothing, recruit an army, and go to war against the English. Inspired, Joan of Arc raised an army, conquered cities, and vanquished the English. Later that year, her visions were fulfilled as she stood next to Charles VII while he was crowned king of France. (Bridgwater 1953)

Joan of Arc is an example of **charismatic authority,** the third type of authority Weber identified. (*Charisma* is a Greek word that means a gift freely and graciously given [Arndt and Gingrich 1957].) A charismatic individual is someone to whom people are drawn because they believe that person has been touched by God or has been endowed by nature with exceptional qualities (Lipset 1993). The armies did not follow Joan of Arc because it was the custom to do so, as in traditional authority. Nor did they risk their lives alongside her because she held a position defined by written rules, as in rational-legal authority. Instead, people followed her because they were drawn to her outstanding traits. They saw her as a messenger of God, fighting on the side of justice, and accepted her leadership because of these appealing qualities.

The Threat Posed by Charismatic Leaders. A king owes allegiance to tradition, and a president to written laws. To what, however, does a charismatic leader owe allegiance?

One of the best examples of charismatic authority is Joan of Arc, shown here at the coronation of Charles VII, whom she was instrumental in making king. Uncomfortable at portraying Joan of Arc wearing only a man's coat of armor, the artist has made certain she is wearing plenty of makeup, and also has added a ludicrous skirt.

Charismatic authorities can be of any morality, from the saintly to the most bitterly evil. Like Joan of Arc, Adolf Hitler attracted throngs of people, providing the stuff of dreams and arousing them from disillusionment to hope. This poster from the 1930s, entitled Es Lebe Deutschland *("Long Live Germany") illustrates the qualities of leadership that Germans of that period saw in Hitler.*

charismatic authority: authority based on an individual's outstanding traits, which attract followers

Because their authority is based only on their personal ability to attract followers, charismatic leaders pose a threat to the established political system. They direct followers solely according to personal preference, not according to the paths of tradition or the regulations of law. Accordingly, they can inspire followers to disregard—or even to overthrow—traditional and rational-legal authorities.

This means that charismatic leaders pose a threat to the established order. Consequently, traditional and rational-legal authorities are often quick to oppose charismatic figures. If they are not careful, however, their opposition may create a martyr, arousing even higher sentiment in favor of the charismatic leader. Occasionally the Roman Catholic church faces such a threat when a priest claims miraculous powers, a claim perhaps accompanied by amazing healings. As people flock to this individual, they bypass parish priests and the formal ecclesiastical structure. To transfer allegiance from the organization to an individual threatens the church bureaucracy. Consequently, the church hierarchy may encourage the priest to withdraw from the public eye, perhaps to a monastery, to rethink matters. Thus the threat is defused, rational-legal authority reasserted, and the stability of the organization maintained.

Authority as Ideal Type

Weber's classifications—traditional, rational-legal, and charismatic—represent ideal types of authority. As noted on pages 173–174, ideal type does not refer to what is ideal or desirable, but to a composite of characteristics found in many real-life examples. A particular leader, then, may show a combination of characteristics.

An example is John F. Kennedy, who combined rational-legal and charismatic authority. As the elected head of the U.S. government, Kennedy represented rational-legal authority. Yet his mass appeal was so great that his public speeches aroused large numbers of people to action. When in his inaugural address Kennedy said, "Ask not what your country can do for you, but what you can do for your country," millions of Americans were touched. When Kennedy proposed a Peace Corps to help poorer countries, thousands of idealistic young people volunteered for challenging foreign service.

Charismatic and traditional authority can also overlap. The Ayatollah Khomeini of Iran, for example, was a religious leader, holding the traditional position of ayatollah. His embodiment of the Iranian people's dreams, however, as well as his austere life and devotion to principles of the Koran, gave him such mass appeal that he was also a charismatic leader. Khomeini's followers were convinced that he had been chosen by God, and his speeches could arouse tens of thousands of followers to action.

In rare instances, then, traditional and rational-legal leaders possess charismatic traits. This is unusual, however, and most authority is clearly one type or another.

The Transfer of Authority

The orderly transfer of authority from one leader to another is critical for social stability. Under traditional authority, people generally know who is next in line. Under rational-legal authority, people may not know who the next leader will be, but they do know *how* that person will be selected. South Africa provides a remarkable example of the orderly transfer of authority under a rational-legal organization. In spite of this country being ripped apart by decades of racial strife, accompanied not only by deep suspicions and hatreds but also by many murders committed by each side, by maintaining its rational-legal authority the country was able to peacefully transfer power from the dominant group led by President de Klerk to the minority group led by Nelson Mandela.

Charismatic authority, however, has no such rules of succession, which makes it inherently less stable than either traditional or rational-legal authority. Because charismatic authority is built around a single individual, the death or incapacitation of a charismatic leader can mean a bitter struggle for succession. Consequently, some charismatic leaders make arrangements for an orderly transition of power by appointing a successor. This does not guarantee orderly succession, of course, for the followers may not perceive the designated heir in the same way as they did the charismatic leader. A second strategy is for the charismatic leader to build an organization, which then develops a system of rules or regulations, thus transforming itself into a rational-legal leadership. Weber used the term the **routinization of charisma** to refer to this transition of authority from a charismatic leader to either traditional or rational-legal authority.

Although usually arranged tidily, the transfer of traditional leadership can be murky, an issue now faced by Arab countries as rulers age (Waldman 1996). A king may have several sons jockeying for power, and as he comes close to death he may simply pick the one who is currently most in favor. In other instances, he may appoint no one, and at his death a power struggle can break out between the king's sons, army officers, and high-ranking politicians, with no one knowing the outcome.

Types of Government ▶

How do the various types of government—monarchies, democracies, dictatorships, and oligarchies—differ? As we compare them, let's also look at how the institution of the state arose, and how the idea of citizenship was revolutionary.

Monarchies: The Rise of the State

Early societies were small and needed no extensive political system. They operated more like an extended family, with decisions being made as they became necessary. As surpluses developed and societies grew larger, cities evolved—perhaps about 3500 B.C. (Fischer 1976). **City-states** then came into being, with power radiating outward from a city like a spider's web. Although the city controlled the immediate area around it, the areas between cities remained in dispute. Each city-state had its own **monarchy,** a king or queen whose right to rule was considered hereditary. If you drive through Spain, France, or Germany, you can still see evidence of former city-states. In the countryside you will see only scattered villages. Farther on, your eye will be drawn to the outline of a castle on a faraway hill. As you get closer, you will see that the castle is surrounded by a city. Several miles farther, you will see another city, also dominated by a castle. Each city, with its castle, was once a center of power.

City-states often quarreled, and wars were common. The victorious ones extended their rule, and eventually a single city-state was able to wield power over an entire region. As the size of these regions grew, the people slowly developed an identity with the larger region. That is, they began to see distant inhabitants as a "we" instead of a "they." What we call the *state*—the political entity that claims a monopoly on the use of violence within a territory—came into being.

Democracies: Citizenship as a Revolutionary Idea

The United States had no city-states. Each colony, however, like a city-state, was small and independent. After the American Revolution, the colonies united. With the greater strength and resources that came from political unity, they conquered almost all of North America, bringing it under the power of a central government.

The government formed in this new country was called a **democracy.** (Derived from two Greek words—*kratos* [power], and *demos* [common people]—*democracy* literally means "power to the people.") Because of the bitter antagonisms associated with the revolution against the British king, the founders of the new country were distrustful of monarchies. They wanted to put political decisions into the hands of the people. This was not the first democracy the world had seen, but such a system had been tried before only with smaller groups. Athens, a city-state of Greece, practiced democracy two thousand years ago, with each free male above a certain age having the right to be heard and to vote. Members of Native American tribes also were able to elect a chief, and in some, women were able to vote and to hold the office of chief.

routinization of charisma: the transfer of authority from a charismatic figure to either a traditional or a rational-legal form of authority

city-state: an independent city whose power radiates outward, bringing the adjacent area under its rule

monarchy: a form of government headed by a king or queen

democracy: a system of government in which authority derives from the people, derived from two Greek words that translate literally as "power to the people"

Because of their small size, tribes and cities were able to practice **direct democracy.** That is, they were small enough for the eligible voters to meet together, express their opinions, and then vote publicly—much like a town hall meeting today. As populous and spread out as the United States was, however, direct democracy was impossible, and **representative democracy** was invented. Certain citizens (at first only male white landowners) voted for men to represent them in Washington. Later the vote was extended to nonowners of property, to African-American men, then to women, and to others. Our new communications technologies, which make "electronic town meetings" possible, may also allow a new form of direct democracy. This issue is explored in the Sociology and the New Technology box below.

Today we take the idea of citizenship for granted. What is not evident to us is that the idea had to be conceived in the first place. There is nothing natural about citizenship—it is simply one way in which people choose to define themselves. Throughout most of human history, people were thought to *belong* to a clan, to a tribe, or even to a ruler. The idea of **citizenship**—that by virtue of birth and residence people have basic rights— is quite new to the human scene (Turner 1990).

The concept of representative democracy based on citizenship, perhaps the greatest gift the United States has given to the world, was revolutionary. Power was to be vested in the people themselves, and government was to flow from the people. That this concept

direct democracy: a form of democracy in which the eligible voters meet together to discuss issues and make their decisions

representative democracy: a form of democracy in which voters elect representatives to govern and make decisions on their behalf

citizenship: the concept that birth (and residence) in a country impart basic rights

Sociology and the New Technology

Politics and Democracy in a Technological Society

"Politics is just like show business." —RONALD REAGAN

Is the new technology a threat to democracy? Politicians and their pollsters use computers, sophisticated telephone link-ups, faxes, e-mail, and Web sites to take the pulse of the public—and to convey their platforms and their biases. Instead of tuning in and passively listening to a politician's speech, we now can interact with—talk back to—candidates and leaders via "chat rooms" and other online computer forums, "electronic town meetings," and call-in radio and TV talk shows.

This shift to more interactive communications technologies lies at the heart of a debate over the health and future of our democracy. Critics charge that when elected officials use the new technology to constantly "take the public's temperature," they give more attention to minute shifts in public opinion than to the business of governing. Politicians use poll results to "fine tune" their public posturing, to take sides on issues with no personal conviction of what is right. In other words, politicians now campaign nonstop.

Critics worry that our new interactive communications have only begun to undermine the process of governing. "Televoting" (voting from home with the push of a button),

Shown here is the first televised debate between presidential hopefuls, which took place in 1960 between Senator John Kennedy and Vice President Richard Nixon. This debate changed presidential campaigning forever. It is likely that our current new technology will have similar effects on U.S. politics.

they fear, may replace our current form of representational democracy with a form of direct democracy. Some welcome this possibility, for it would allow the voters to directly make laws and decide a wide variety of social issues, rather than having politicians do this for them. Others, however, fear that televoting may be a detour around the U.S. Constitution's careful system of checks and balances designed to safeguard us from the "tyranny of the majority." To determine from a poll that 51 percent of adults hold a certain opinion on an issue is one thing—it can give guidance to leaders. But to have 51 percent of televoters determine a law or an issue is not the same as having elected representatives publicly argue a proposed law or an issue and then try to balance the interests of the many groups that make up their constituents.

Visual image over substance, reasoned leadership replaced by nonstop campaigning, even a fundamental change in our current form of democracy—these are some of the issues that the new technologies bring to today's politics.

Sources: "Democracy and Technology" 1995; Diamond and Silverman 1995; Grossman 1995.

was revolutionary is generally forgotten, but its implementation meant *the reversal of traditional ideas, for the government was to be responsive to the people's wishes, not the people to the wishes of the government.*

The idea of **universal citizenship**—of *everyone* having the same basic rights by virtue of being born in a country (or by immigrating and becoming a naturalized citizen)—flowered very slowly, and came into practice only through fierce struggle. When the United States was founded, for example, this idea was still in its infancy. Today it seems inconceivable to us that anyone on the basis of gender or race/ethnicity should not have the right to vote, hold office, make a contract, testify in court, or own property. For earlier generations of Americans, however, it seemed just as inconceivable that the poor, women, African Americans, Native Americans, and Asian Americans should have such rights.

Over the years, then, rights have been extended, and in the United States citizenship and its privileges now apply to all. No longer does property, sex, or race determine the right to vote, to testify in court, and so on. These characteristics, however, do influence whether or not one votes, as we shall see in a later section on voting patterns.

Dictatorships and Oligarchies: The Seizure of Power

In some countries, an individual seizes power, sometimes by killing the king, queen, or president, and then dictates his will onto the people. A government run by a single person who has seized power is known as a **dictatorship.** If a small group seizes power, the government is called an **oligarchy.** The frequent coups in Central and South America, in which a few military leaders seize control of a country, are examples of oligarchies. Although one individual may be named president, it often is a group of high-ranking military officers, working behind the scenes, that makes the decisions. If their designated president becomes uncooperative, they remove him from office, and designate another.

Monarchies, dictatorships, and oligarchies vary in the amount of control they exert over their people. **Totalitarianism** is almost *total* control of a people by the government. As our opening vignette demonstrated, totalitarian regimes tolerate no opposing opinion. In Nazi Germany, for example, Hitler kept the populace in tight control through the Gestapo, a ruthless secret police force that looked for any sign of dissent. Control was so total that spies even watched moviegoers' reactions to newsreels, reporting those who did not respond "appropriately" (Hippler 1987).

In totalitarian regimes, the names of those who rule may change, but the techniques of control remain frighteningly similar. Threats and terror force citizen compliance and allow the dictator to remain in power. Privacy is viewed as a threat to the regime, and the police may keep a dossier on each citizen. A description of Nazi Germany could just as well be applied to the Soviet Union under Stalin or Iraq under Saddam Hussein. The police, courts, armed forces, and entire government bureaucracy are directly accountable to the dictator. Individual rights, if they existed prior to the dictator, simply disappear, while if individual citizens dissent, they disappear.

People around the world find the ideas of citizenship and of representative democracy appealing. Those who have no say in their government's decisions, or who face prison for expressing dissent, find in these ideas the hope for a brighter future. With today's electronic communications, people no longer remain ignorant of whether they are more or less privileged politically than others. This knowledge produces pressure for greater citizen participation in government. With continued development in communications, the future will continue to step up this pressure.

universal citizenship: the idea that everyone has the same basic rights by virtue of being born in a country (or by immigrating and becoming a naturalized citizen)

dictatorship: a form of government in which power is seized by an individual

oligarchy: a form of government in which power is held by a small group of individuals; the rule of the many by the few

totalitarianism: a form of government that exerts almost total control over the people

Totalitarian leaders such as Saddam Hussein often try to bolster their authority by spreading larger-than-life images of themselves throughout their domain. Such images make it difficult to forget who is in charge—which, of course, is one of the main objectives.

The U.S. Political System

At this point, let us turn to an overview of the U.S. political system. We shall consider the two major political parties, compare the U.S. political system with other democratic systems, examine voting patterns, analyze how the Great Depression of the 1930s transformed U.S. politics, and examine the role of lobbyists and PACs.

Political Parties and Elections

After the founding of the United States, numerous political parties emerged, but by the time of the Civil War, two parties dominated U.S. politics (Burnham 1983): the Democrats, who in the public mind are associated with the working class and the Republicans, who are associated with wealthier people. Each party nominates candidates, and in pre-elections, called *primaries*, the voters decide which candidates will represent their party. Each candidate then campaigns, trying to appeal to the most voters. Table 15.1 shows how Americans align themselves with political parties. The realignment of party identification shown on this table reflects the more conservative stance Americans have recently taken.

Although the Democrats and Republicans represent different philosophical principles, each appeals to such a broad membership that it is difficult to distinguish a conservative Democrat from a liberal Republican. The extremes, however, are easy to discern. Deeply committed Democrats support legislation that transfers income from one group to another or that controls wages, working conditions, and competition. Dyed-in-the-wool Republicans oppose such legislation.

Those elected to Congress may cross party lines. That is, some Democrats vote for legislation proposed by Republicans, and *vice versa*. This happens because officeholders support their party's philosophy but not necessarily its specific proposals. Thus, when it comes to a specific bill, such as raising the minimum wage, some conservative Democrats may view the measure as unfair to small employers, or too costly, and vote with the Republicans against the bill. At the same time, liberal Republicans—feeling that the proposal is just, or sensing a dominant sentiment in voters back home—may side with its Democratic backers.

Regardless of their differences, however, the Democrats and Republicans represent *different slices of the center.* Although each may ridicule its opposition and promote differ-

TABLE 15.1					
How Americans Identify with Political Parties					
	1960	*1970*	*1980*	*1990*	*1994*
Democrats					
Strong Democrat	20%	20%	18%	20%	15%
Weak Democrat	25	24	23	19	19
Independent Democrat	6	10	11	12	13
Total	51	54	52	51	47
Republicans					
Strong Republican	16	9	9	10	16
Weak Republican	14	15	14	15	15
Independent Republican	7	8	12	12	12
Total	37	32	35	37	43
Other					
Independent	10	13	13	11	10
Not political	3	1	2	2	1
Total	13	14	15	13	11

Note: Due to rounding, the totals do not always equal 100 percent.

Source: Statistical Abstract 1991:Table 452; 1997:Table 461.

ent legislation, each party firmly supports such fundamentals of U.S. political philosophy as free public education, a strong military, freedom of religion, speech, assembly, and, of course, capitalism—especially the private ownership of property.

Third parties also play a role in U.S. politics, but to have any influence they, too, must support these centrist ideas. To advocate their radical change is to doom a third party to a short life of little political consequence. Because most Americans consider a vote for a third party a waste, third parties do notoriously poorly at the polls. Two exceptions are Theodore Roosevelt's Bull Moose party, which won more votes in 1912 than Taft, the Republican presidential candidate, and the United We Stand (now Reform) party, headed by billionaire political hopeful Ross Perot, which won 19 percent of the vote in 1992, but only 8 percent in 1996 (Bridgwater 1953; *Statistical Abstract* 1995:Table 437; 1997:Table 441).

Democratic Systems in Europe

We tend to take our political system for granted and assume that any other democracy looks like ours—even down to having two major parties. Such is not the case. To gain a comparative understanding, let us look at the European system.

Although both theirs and ours are democracies, there are fundamental distinctions between the two (Domhoff 1979, 1983; Lind 1995). First, elections in most of Europe are not winner-take-all. In the United States, elections are determined by a simple majority. For example, if a Democrat wins 51 percent of the votes cast in an electoral district, he or she takes office. The Republican candidate, who may have won 49 percent, loses everything. In contrast, most European countries base their elections on a system of **proportional representation;** that is, the seats in the national legislature are divided according to the proportion of votes received by each political party. If one party wins 51 percent of the vote, for example, that party is awarded 51 percent of the seats; while a party with 49 percent of the votes receives 49 percent of the seats.

Second, proportional representation encourages minority parties, while the winner-take-all system discourages them. As we saw, the U.S. system pushes parties to the center as they strive to obtain the broadest possible support required to win elections. For this reason, the United States has **centrist parties.** The proportional representation followed in most European countries means that if a party gets 10 percent of the voters to support its candidate, it will get 10 percent of the seats. This system encourages the formation of **noncentrist parties,** those that propose less popular or even offbeat ideas. For example, a party may make its central platform a return to the gold standard, or the retirement of all nuclear weapons and the shutting down of all nuclear power reactors.

Three main results follow from being able to win even just a few seats in the national legislature. First, if a minority party has officeholders, it gains access to the media throughout the year, receiving publicity that helps keep its issues alive. Second, small parties gain power beyond their numbers. Because many parties compete in the elections, no single party is likely to gain a majority of the seats in the national legislature. To muster the required votes to make national decisions, the party with the most seats must align itself with one or more of the smaller parties and form a **coalition government.** A party with only 10 or 15 percent of the seats, then, may be able to trade its vote on some issues for the larger party's support on others. Third, because coalitions break down, the governments tend to be less stable. Italy, for example, has had fifty-one different governments since World War II, compared with ten presidents in the United States. To add greater stability, the Italians have voted that three-fourths of their Senate seats will be decided on the winner-take-all system (Melloan 1993b).

Voting Patterns

Let's examine major voting patterns and then consider reasons for them.

Likelihood of Voting.   Year after year, Americans show consistent voting patterns. From Table 15.2 on the next page, you can see that the percentage of people who vote increases with age. This table also shows the significance of race and ethnicity. Whites are more likely to vote than are African Americans, while Latinos are the least likely to

proportional representation: an electoral system in which seats in a legislature are divided according to the proportion of votes each political party receives

centrist party: a political party that represents the center of political opinion

noncentrist party: a political party that represents marginal ideas

coalition government: a government in which a country's largest party aligns itself with one or more smaller parties

TABLE 15.2

Who Votes in U.S. Presidential Elections?					
	1980	*1984*	*1988*	*1992*	*1996*
Overall					
Americans Who Vote	59%	60%	57%	61%	54%
Age					
18–20	36	37	33	39	31
21–24	43	44	38	46	33
25–34	59	58	54	58	43
35–44	64	64	61	64	55
45–64	69	70	68	70	64
65 and up	65	68	69	70	67
Sex					
Male	59	59	56	60	53
Female	59	61	58	62	56
Race/Ethnicity[a]					
Whites	61	61	59	64	56
African Americans	51	56	52	54	51
Latinos	30	33	29	29	27
Education					
Grade school only	43	43	37	35	28
High school dropout	46	44	41	41	34
High school graduate	59	59	55	58	49
College dropout	67	68	65	69	61
College graduate	80	79	78	81	73
Labor Force					
Employed	62	62	58	64	55
Unemployed	41	44	39	46	37
Income					
Under $5,000	38	39	35	NA	NA
$5,000 to $9,999	46	49	41	NA	NA
$10,000 to $14,999	54	55	48	NA	NA
$15,000 to $19,999	57	60	54	NA	NA
$20,000 to $24,999	61	67	58	NA	NA
$25,000 to $34,999	67	74	64	NA	NA
$35,000 and over	74	74	70[b]	NA	NA

[a]Other race-ethnic groups are not listed in the sources.

[b]For 1988, the percentage is an average of $35,000 to $49,900 and over $50,000.

Sources: Statistical Abstract 1991:Table 450; 1997:Table 462; *Current Population Reports,* Series P-20, vols. 440, 446, 504.

vote. The difference is so great that whites are more than twice as likely to vote as are Latinos. A crucial aspect of the socialization of newcomers to the United States is to learn the U.S. political system, the topic of the Perspectives box on the next page.

This table also shows that voting increases with education. College graduates are more than twice as likely to vote as those who complete only grade school. Employment and income are also significant. People who make over $35,000 a year are twice as likely to vote as those who make less than $5,000. Finally, note that women are slightly more likely to vote than men.

Social Integration. How can we explain the voting patterns shown in Table 15.2? The people most likely to vote are older, more educated, affluent, employed whites, while

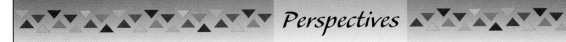

Immigrants—Ethnicity and Class as the Path to Political Participation

That the United States is the land of immigrants is a truism; every schoolchild knows that since the English Pilgrims first landed on Plymouth Rock, successive groups—among them Germans, Scandinavians, Italians, Poles, and Greeks—crossed the Atlantic Ocean to reach U.S. shores.

Some, such as the Irish immigrants in the late 1800s and early 1900s, left to escape brutal poverty and famine. Others, such as the Jews of czarist Russia, fled a government that singled them out for persecution. Some fled as refugees or asylum seekers from lands ravaged by war. Others, called *entrepreneurial immigrants*, sought economic opportunities absent in their native lands. Still others came as *sojourners*, planning to return home after a temporary stay.

Today the United States witnesses its second large wave of immigration of the twentieth century. The first, in the early 1900s, in which immigrants came to account for 13.2 percent of the population, consisted largely of Europeans. Today, the mix of immigrants—currently about 7.9 percent of the population—is far more diverse, with most coming from South and Central America and Asia. Since 1980, over 11 million legal immigrants have settled in the United States. About another 4 million are here illegally.

A widespread fear held by U.S.-born Americans in the early part of the century was that immigrants would subvert the democratic system in favor of socialism or communism. Today some fear that the primacy of the English language is threatened. In addition, the age-old fear that immigrants will take jobs away from U.S.-born Americans remains strong. Finally, minority groups that struggled for political representation fear that newer groups will gain political power at their expense.

What route to political participation do immigrants take? In general, they first organize as a group on the basis of *ethnicity* rather than *class*. In response to common problems, especially discrimination, they reaffirm their cultural identity. "This represents the first effective step in their social and political incorporation," note sociologists Alejandro Portes and Ruben Rumbaut. "By mobilizing the collective vote and by electing their own to office, immigrant minorities have learned the rules of the democratic game and absorbed its values in the process."

Irish immigrants to Boston illustrate this pattern of banding together on the basis of ethnicity. They built a power base that put the Irish in political control of the city, and, ultimately, saw one of their own sworn in as president of the United States.

As Portes and Rumbaut observe, "Assimilation as the rapid transformation of immigrants into Americans 'as everyone else' has never happened." Instead, all immigrant groups began by fighting for their own interests as Irish, Italians, and so on. Only when they had attained enough political power to overcome discrimination did they become "like everyone else"—that is, like others who had power.

Thus, only when a certain level of political power is achieved, when groups gain political representation somewhat proportionate to their numbers, does the issue of class grow in significance. This, then, is the path that immigrants follow in their socialization into the U.S. political system.

Sources: Portés and Rumbaut 1990; Salholz 1990; Prud'Homme 1991; James 1993; *Statistical Abstract* 1997: Tables 5, 10, 54.

---

those least likely to vote are poor, younger, ill-educated, unemployed Latinos. From these patterns, we can draw this principle: *The more that people feel they have a stake in the political system, the more likely they are to vote.* They have more to protect, and feel that voting can make a difference. In effect, people who have been rewarded by the political system feel more socially integrated. They vote because they perceive that elections directly affect their own lives and the type of society in which they and their children live.

Alienation. In contrast, those who gain less from the system—in terms of education, income, and jobs—are more likely to be alienated. They feel that their vote will not affect their lives one way or another, that "next year will bring more of the same, regardless of who is president," that "all politicians lie to us." Similarly, minorities who feel that the U.S. political system is a "white" system are less motivated to vote.

Voter Apathy. From Table 15.2, we see that many highly educated people with jobs and good incomes also stay away from the polls. Many people do not vote because of **voter apathy,** or indifference. Like the alienated, they feel that their vote will not affect

voter apathy: indifference and inaction on the part of individuals or groups with respect to the political process

TABLE 15.3

How the Two-Party Presidential Vote is Split

	1988	1992
Women		
Democrat	50%	61%
Republican	50%	39%
Men		
Democrat	44%	55%
Republican	56%	45%
African Americans		
Democrat	92%	94%
Republican	8%	6%
Whites		
Democrat	41%	53%
Republican	59%	47%

Note: 1992 is the latest year reported in the 1997 source.

Source: Statistical Abstract 1997: Table 439.

the outcome. A common attitude is "What difference does my one vote make when there are millions of votes?" Although they are not alienated, many of the apathetic see little difference between the two major political parties.

The result of alienation and apathy is that two out of five eligible U.S. voters do not vote for president. Actually, *most* of the nation's eligible voters don't bother to vote for candidates for Congress (*Statistical Abstract* 1997:Table 462).

How People Vote. Historically, men and women have voted the same way. Now when they go to the ballot box, however, they are somewhat more likely to vote for different presidential candidates. This *gender gap in politics*, which has just appeared, is illustrated in Table 15.3. This table also shows the older and much larger racial-ethnic gap in politics. Note how few African Americans vote for a Republican presidential candidate.

Voting patterns reflect life experiences, especially economic circumstances. On average, women and African Americans earn less than do men and whites, and at this point in history women and African Americans tend to look more favorably on government programs that redistribute income (Seib 1996).

The Depression as a Transforming Event

Until Franklin D. Roosevelt (FDR) became president in 1932, the country's ruling philosophy was that the government should play as small a part as possible in people's lives. The proper role of local government was to run schools, take care of streets, bridges, garbage, and sewers, and to make the community safe; that of the federal government was to coin money, deliver the mail, and maintain a small armed force to protect from external enemies. Government, at whatever level, was to collect as few taxes as possible. The poor were the responsibility of family, church, and local community.

During what became known as the Great Depression of the 1930s, which followed the stock market's collapse in 1929, employment around the country collapsed too. About one in every four workers had no job, and many of those who did worked for subsistence wages. Previously, Americans had been convinced that only laziness kept people from work. Now they saw that millions desperately wanted to work, but no work was available. At this point, Americans began to develop a sociological imagination, for they caught a glimpse of the economic system itself. They began to see that having a job or being unemployed was not simply the result of individual traits such as initiative or the lack of it, but the consequence of the social system itself. They demanded that the government do something about the economy.

In 1932 Herbert Hoover, the Republican president, was defeated, and Roosevelt, a Democrat, took office with the promise to change things. That he did. He took the view that it was the government's responsibility to oversee the country's economy. Among other things, he instituted federal work programs such as the Works Progress Administration (WPA) to build parks and civic buildings, and the Rural Electrification Association (REA) to bring electricity to the country's farms. Because he put people back to work, FDR was reelected in 1936, 1940, and 1944.

U.S. politics was never the same again. Although they disagree about the extent of government responsibility, both Republicans and Democrats support payments to unemployed workers, the elderly, and the poor. If parties and candidates were to suggest dismantling unemployment insurance, Social Security, and welfare, they would have no chance of being elected. As the costs have come in and the national debt has ballooned, however, politicians have found that a call to reduce spending on social programs meets wide approval. Whenever *specific* proposals are made to reduce spending, however, an outcry follows. Every proposal to reduce a government subsidy means that some group—often the elderly, sick, or poor—will be hurt by the cutback. Although from time to time some tinkering will be done with these programs, it is unlikely that they will be fundamentally changed.

Lobbyists and Special-Interest Groups

Suppose that you are president of the United States, and you want to make bread and other grain products more affordable for the poor. As you check into the matter, you find that prices are high because the government is paying farmers about $800 million a year in price supports (*Statistical Abstract* 1996:Table 1091). You therefore propose to eliminate these subsidies.

Immediately, large numbers of people leap into action. They send telegrams and e-mail to your office, contact their senator and representatives, and call reporters for news conferences. The news media report that across the land farmers will be put out of business. The Associated Press distributes pictures of a farm family—their Holsteins grazing contentedly in the background—informing readers how this healthy, happy family of good Americans struggling to make a living will be destroyed by your harsh proposal.

President or not, you have little chance of getting your legislation passed.

What happened? The farming industry went to work to protect its special interests. A **special-interest group** consists of people who think alike on a particular issue and who can be mobilized for political action. The farming industry is just one of thousands of such groups that employ **lobbyists,** people paid to influence legislation on behalf of their clients. Special-interest groups and lobbyists have become a major force in U.S. politics. Members of Congress who are interested in being re-elected must pay attention to them, for they represent blocs of voters who have a vital interest in the outcome of specific bills. Well financed and able to contribute huge sums, lobbyists can deliver votes to you—or to your opponent.

Because so much money was being passed under the table by special-interest groups to members of Congress, in the 1970s legislation limited the amount that any individual, corporation, or special-interest group could give a candidate, and required all contributions over $1,000 to be reported. Special-interest groups immediately did an end sweep around the new laws by forming **political action committees (PACs),** organizations that solicit contributions from many donors—each contribution within the allowable limit—and then use the combined total to influence legislation.

PACs have become a powerful influence in Washington, for they bankroll lobbyists and legislators. About four thousand PACs disburse about $400 million a year (*Statistical Abstract* 1997:Tables 468, 469). A few PACs represent broad social interests such as environmental protection, but most stand for narrow financial concerns, such as the dairy, oil, banking, and construction industries. Those PACs with the most clout in terms of money and votes gain the ear of Congress. In short, to politicians the sound of money talking sounds like the voice of the people (see Ferguson 1995).

PACs in U.S. Politics

Suppose that you want to run for the Senate. To have a chance of winning, you must not only shake hands around the state, be photographed hugging babies, and eat a lot of chicken dinners at local civic organizations, but you must also send out hundreds of thousands of pieces of mail to solicit votes and financial support. During the home stretch, television ads may run $700,000 a week (Harwood 1994). If you are an *average* candidate for the Senate, you will spend $4 million on your campaign. To run for the House will cost a paltry one half million dollars (*Statistical Abstract* 1997:Tables 447, 472).

Now suppose that it is only a few weeks from the election, the polls show you and your opponent neck and neck, and your war chest is empty. The representatives of a couple of PACs pay you a visit. One says that his organization will pay for a mailing, while the other offers to buy television and radio ads. You feel somewhat favorably toward their positions anyway, and you accept. Once elected, you owe them. When legislation that affects their interests comes up for vote, their representatives call you—at your unlisted number at home—and tell you how they want you to vote. It would be political folly to double-cross them.

It is said that the first duty of a politician is to get elected—and the second duty to get reelected. If you are an average senator, to finance your reelection campaign you must

The Great Depression transformed Americans' attitudes about government intervention in economic matters. Shown here is a 1939 poster that was displayed in post offices and other public buildings throughout the country.

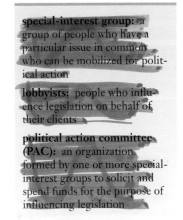

special-interest group: a group of people who have a particular issue in common who can be mobilized for political action

lobbyists: people who influence legislation on behalf of their clients

political action committee (PAC): an organization formed by one or more special-interest groups to solicit and spend funds for the purpose of influencing legislation

It is said that money is the mother's milk of politics. Because running for high political office is costly, U.S. politicians spend a good deal of time raising money instead of developing social policy. This preoccupation with campaign funds—and the ethical violations it sometimes leads to—is what this cartoonist is satirizing.

raise $1,700 *every single day* of your six-year term. It is no wonder that money has been dubbed the "mother's milk of politics" (Abramson and Rogers 1991).

Criticism of Lobbyists and PACs.   The major criticism leveled against lobbyists and PACs is that their money, in effect, buys votes. Rather than representing the people who elected them, legislators support the special interests of groups able to help them stay in power. The *more than $60 million* that the medical industry has given to members of Congress, for example, just may have something to do with the United States being the only postindustrial nation that lacks a national health care plan (Common Cause 1992).

The influence of foreign lobbyists has been a target of especially harsh criticism. As shown in Figure 15.1 on the next page, the top ten foreign lobbyists spend $163 million annually to influence votes. Japan has hired over 100 former U.S. government officials to pressure members of Congress to reduce quotas and duties on imports of its products. During election years, Japan contributes to *both* presidential candidates. Critics argue that the playing field is not level, for Japan has made it illegal for foreigners to influence *its* legislation (Judis 1990; Duffy 1992).

Even if the United States were to outlaw PACs, special-interest groups would not disappear from the U.S. political process. Lobbyists walked the corridors of the Senate long before PACs, and since the time of Alexander Graham Bell they have carried the unlisted numbers of members of Congress. Lobbyists—for good or ill—play an essential role in the U.S. political system.

Who Rules the United States?

With lobbyists and PACs, just whom do U.S. senators and representatives really represent? This question has led to a lively debate among sociologists. In previous chapters we have discussed the contrasting views of sociologists on the control of U.S. society, and this is an opportune moment to review them.

The Functionalist Perspective: Pluralism

Functionalists view the state as having arisen out of the basic needs of the social group. To protect themselves from would-be oppressors, people formed a government and gave it the monopoly on violence. The risk is that the state can turn that force against its own citizens. To return to the example used earlier, states have a tendency to become muggers. Thus, people must perform a balancing act between having no government—which would lead to **anarchy,** a state in which disorder and violence reign—and having a gov-

anarchy: a condition of lawlessness or political disorder caused by the absence or collapse of governmental authority

ernment to protect them from violence, but that may itself turn against them. When functioning well, then, the state is a balanced system that protects its citizens—from one another *and* from government.

What keeps the U.S. government from turning against its citizens? Functionalists say that **pluralism,** a diffusion of power among many interest groups, prevents any one group from gaining control of the government and using it to oppress the people (Polsby 1959; Huber and Form 1973; Dahl 1961/1982). The founders of the United States foresaw this possibility of the abuse of power, and in it, the doom of democracy. To balance the interests of competing groups, the founders set up three branches of government—the executive (president), judicial (courts), and legislative (the Senate and House of Representatives). Each is sworn to uphold the Constitution, which guarantees rights to citizens, and each is able to nullify the actions of the other two. This system, known as **checks and balances,** was designed to ensure that power remains distributed and that no one branch of government dominates.

From the functionalist perspective, ethnic groups, women, men, farmers, factory workers, religious groups, bankers, bosses, the unemployed, coal miners, the retired, as well as the broader categories of the rich, middle class, and poor, are all parts of our pluralist society. Because each has political muscle to flex at the polls, to be reelected politicians must take them into consideration. Thus, as each group pursues its own interests, it is balanced by other groups pursuing theirs. As special-interest groups negotiate with one another and reach compromises, conflict is minimized, and the resulting policies gain wide support. Consequently, say functionalists, no one group rules the United States, and the political system is responsive to the people.

The Conflict Perspective: Power Elite/ Ruling Class

Conflict theorists come up with a different answer. If you focus on the lobbyists scurrying around Washington, they say, you get a blurred image of superficial activities, of laws being passed for specific purposes. What really counts is the big picture, not its fragments. The important question is who holds the power that determines the overarching policies of the United States. For example, who determines how many Americans will be out of work by raising or lowering interest rates? Who sets policies that transfer jobs from the United States to countries with low-cost labor? And the ultimate question of power: who is behind decisions to go to war?

Power Elite/Ruling Class. C. Wright Mills (1956) took the position that the most important matters are not decided by lobbyists, nor even by Congress. Rather, the decisions that have the greatest impact on the lives of Americans—and people across the face of the globe—are made by a coalition of individuals whose interests coincide and who have access to the center of political power in the United States. Mills called them the **power elite,** and said that it is this group that rules the United States. As depicted in Figure 15.2 on the next page, the power elite consists of the top leaders of the largest corporations, the most powerful generals and admirals of the armed forces, and certain elite politicians—the president, his cabinet, and select senior members of Congress who chair the major committees. It is they who wield power, who make the decisions that direct the country—and shake the world (Hellinger and Judd 1991; Ferguson 1995).

Are the three groups that make up the power elite—the top political, military, and corporate leaders—equal in power? Mills said they were not, but for his choice of dominance he did not point to the president and his staff or even to the generals and admirals, but rather to the corporate heads. Because all three segments of the power elite view capitalism as essential to the welfare of the country, business interests, he said, come foremost in setting national policy. Remember the example from the previous chapter (page 390) of the U.S. president selling airplanes.

Sociologist William Domhoff (1967, 1990) uses the term **ruling class** to refer to the power elite. He focuses on the 1 percent of Americans who belong to the super rich, the powerful capitalist class studied in Chapter 10 (pages 260–261). Members of this class

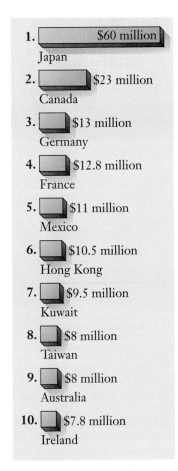

1. Japan $60 million
2. Canada $23 million
3. Germany $13 million
4. France $12.8 million
5. Mexico $11 million
6. Hong Kong $10.5 million
7. Kuwait $9.5 million
8. Taiwan $8 million
9. Australia $8 million
10. Ireland $7.8 million

Source: Engelberg and Tolchin 1993.

Figure 15.1

Foreign Lobbyists: The Top 10 Spenders

pluralism: the diffusion of power among many interest groups, preventing any single group from gaining control of the government

checks and balances: the separation of powers among the three branches of U.S. government—legislative, executive, and judicial—so that each is able to nullify the actions of the other two, thus preventing the domination of any single branch

power elite: C. Wright Mills's term for those who rule the United States: the top people in the leading corporations, the most powerful generals and admirals of the armed forces, and certain elite politicians

ruling class: another term for the power elite

Figure 15.2

**Power in the United States:
The Model Proposed by
C. Wright Mills**

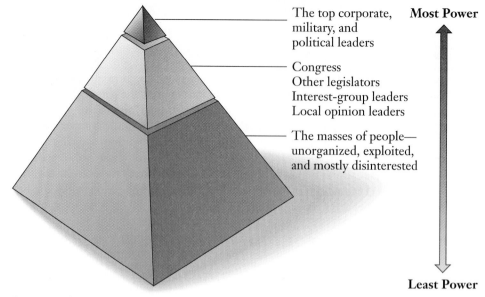

The top corporate,
military, and
political leaders — **Most Power**

Congress
Other legislators
Interest-group leaders
Local opinion leaders

The masses of people—
unorganized, exploited,
and mostly disinterested

Least Power

Source: Based on Mills 1956.

control our top corporations and foundations, even the boards that oversee our major universities. It is no accident, says Domhoff, that from this group the president chooses most members of his cabinet and appoints the top ambassadors to the most powerful countries of the world.

Conflict theorists point out that we should not think of the ruling class as a group that meets together and agrees on specific matters. Rather, it consists of people whose backgrounds and orientations to life are so similar—they attend prestigious private schools, belong to exclusive private clubs, and are millionaires many times over—that they automatically share the same values and goals. Their behavior stems not from some grand conspiracy to control the country, but, rather, from mutual interests in solving the problems that face large businesses (Useem 1984). With their political connections reaching to the top centers of power, this group sets the economic and political conditions under which the rest of the country operates (Domhoff 1990). We shall return to this line of inquiry later.

Which View Is Right?

The functionalist and conflict views of power in U.S. society cannot be reconciled. Either competing interests block the dominance of any single group, as functionalists assert, or a power elite oversees the major decisions of the United States, as conflict theorists maintain. Perhaps at the middle level of Mills's model, depicted in Figure 15.2, the competing interest groups do keep each other at bay, and none is able to dominate. If so, the functionalist view would apply to this middle level, as well as the lowest level of power. Perhaps functionalists have just not looked high enough, and activities at the peak remain invisible to them. If so, on that level lies the key to U.S. power, the dominance by an elite as it follows its mutual interests.

The answer, however, is not yet conclusive. For that, we must await more research.

 War: A Means to Implement Political Objectives

war: armed conflict between nations or politically distinct groups

As we have noted, an essential characteristic of the state is that it claims a monopoly on violence. At times, a state may direct that violence against other nations. **War,** armed conflict between nations (or politically distinct groups), is often part of national policy. Let us look at this aspect of politics.

Is War Universal?

Although human aggression and individual killing characterize all human groups, war does not. War is simply *one option* that groups may choose for dealing with disagreements; but not all societies choose this option. The Mission Indians of North America, the Arunta of Australia, the Andaman Islanders of the South Pacific, and the Eskimos of the Arctic, for example, had procedures to handle aggression and quarrels, but they did not have organized battles that pitted one tribe or group against another. These groups do not even have a word for war (Lesser 1968).

How Common Is War?

One of the contradictions of humanity is that people long for peace while at the same time they glorify war. The glorification of war can be seen by noting how major battles hog the center of a country's retelling of its history and how monuments to generals and battles are scattered throughout the land. From May Day parades in Moscow's Red Square to the Fourth of July celebrations in the United States and the Cinco de Mayo victory marches in Mexico, war and revolutions are interwoven into the fabric of daily life.

To find out how often war occurred in European history, sociologist Pitirim Sorokin (1937) counted the wars from 500 B.C. to A.D. 1925. He documented 967 wars, an average of one war every two to three years. Counting years or parts of a year in which a country was at war, at 28 percent Germany had the lowest record of warfare, while Spain's 67 percent gave it the dubious distinction of being the most war-prone. Sorokin found that Russia, the land of his birth, had experienced only one peaceful quarter-century during the entire previous thousand years. Since the time of William the Conqueror, who took power in 1066, England was at war an average of 56 out of each 100 years. Spain fought even more often. It is worth noting the history of the United States in this regard: Since 1850, it has intervened militarily around the world more than 150 times, an average of *more than once a year* (Kohn 1988). With Grenada, Panama, Kuwait, Somalia, Haiti, and Bosnia, the pattern continues.

During war, countries harness their most advanced technology in the attempt to destroy their enemies. Shown here is a classic photo from World War II, a B-26 Marauder of the Ninth U.S. Air Force dropping twenty-six 100-pound bombs on Nazi installations in France.

Why Nations Go to War

Why do nations choose war to handle disputes? Sociologists answer this question by focusing not on factors *within* humans, such as aggressive impulses, but by looking for *social* causes—conditions in society that encourage or discourage combat between nations.

Sociologist Nicholas Timasheff (1965) identified three essential conditions of war. The first is a cultural tradition of war. Because their nation has fought wars in the past, the leaders of a group see war as an option for dealing with serious disagreements with other nations. The second is an antagonistic situation in which two or more states confront incompatible objectives. For example, each may want the same land or resources. The third is a "fuel" that heats the antagonistic situation to a boiling point, so that people cross the line from thinking about war to actually engaging in it. Timasheff identified seven such "fuels." He found that war is likely if a country's leaders see the antagonistic situation as an opportunity to achieve one of the following objectives:

1. Gain revenge or settle "old scores" from previous conflicts
2. Dictate their will to a weaker nation
3. Enhance the nation's prestige, or save the nation's "honor"
4. Unite rival groups within their country
5. Protect or exalt their own position
6. Satisfy the national aspirations of ethnic groups, bringing under their rule "our people" who are living in another country
7. Forcibly convert others to religious and ideological beliefs

TABLE 15.4

What U.S. Wars Cost

War of 1812	$615,000,000
Mexican War	$1,076,000,000
American Revolution	$1,918,000,000
Spanish-American War	$5,961,000,000
Civil War	$45,990,000,000
World War I	$369,580,000,000
Vietnam War	$553,088,000,000
Korean War	$262,062,000,000
World War II	$2,953,716,000,000
Total	$4,194,006,000,000

Note: In the source, the costs are listed in 1967 dollars. To account for inflation, I increased these amounts by 350 percent, and added the costs of service-connected benefits. Where a range was listed, the mean was used.

The costs of the many "military interventions" such as in Grenada, Panama, Somalia, and Haiti, are not listed in the source—nor is the more expensive "military intervention" on behalf of Kuwait. These costs do *not* include interest payments on war loans, nor are they reduced by the financial benefits to the United States, such as the acquisition of California and Texas in the Mexican War.

Source: Statistical Abstract 1993:Table 553.

TABLE 15.5

The Business of Death

The 5 Largest Arms Sellers

Country	Amount
Russia	$20.0 billion
United States	$12.4 billion
Great Britain	$3.4 billion
China	$0.8 billion
France	$0.8 billion

The 10 Largest Consumers

Country	Amount
Saudi Arabia	$5.2 billion
Great Britain	$3.4 billion
Egypt	$1.5 billion
United States	$1.1 billion
Israel	$1.0 billion
South Korea	$1.0 billion
Turkey	$1.0 billion
China	$0.8 billion
France	$0.8 billion
Japan	$0.7 billion

Source: Statistical Abstract 1997: Table 552, except Russia, which is 1993:Table 550. For some strange reason, Russia was dropped from later sources.

Costs of War

One side effect of the new technologies stressed in this text has been a growing capacity to inflict death. For example, during World War I bombs claimed fewer than 3 of every 100,000 people in England and Germany. With more powerful airplanes and bombs, accompanied by a diminished sense of it being wrong to kill noncombatants, by World War II this figure increased a hundredfold, to 300 of every 100,000 civilians (Hart 1957). As you know, further technological advances in human destruction have so increased our killing capacity that if a war were fought with nuclear bombs the death rate could run 100 percent.

War is also extremely costly in terms of money. As shown in Table 15.4, the United States has spent $4 trillion on nine major wars. In spite of its massive cost in lives and property, warfare continues as a common technique of pursuing political objectives. For about seven years, the United States fought in Vietnam—at a cost of 59,000 American and about 2 million Vietnamese lives (Herring 1989; Hellinger and Judd 1991). For nine years, the Soviet Union waged war in Afghanistan—with a death toll of about 1 million Afghanistani and perhaps 20,000 Soviet soldiers (Armitage 1989). An eight-year war between Iran and Iraq cost about 400,000 lives. The total exacted by Cuban mercenaries in Africa and South America is unknown. Also unknown is the number of lives—almost exclusively Iraqi—lost in "Desert Storm," a brief war against Iraq by international forces led by the United States. The figure of 100,000 losses on the Iraqi side has been suggested by media reports. Not even counting the slaughter in Rwanda, the topic of the opening vignette of Chapter 12, civil wars in Africa have claimed hundreds of thousands. Bosnia, Chezen, Azerbaijan, Georgia, Israel and its Arab neighbors—the list grows, with more names added yearly.

Sowing the Seeds of Future Wars

The hypocrisy is incredible. The Most Industrialized Nations lament the regional conflicts that can escalate into larger wars, yet they zealously pursue profits by selling advanced war technology to the Least Industrialized Nations. When one Least Industrialized Nation buys high-tech weapons, its neighbors get nervous, sparking an arms race among them (Cole and Lubman 1994; Ricks 1994). Table 15.5 shows that Russia and the United States are the chief merchants of death. The seeds of future wars are also sown by nuclear proliferation, and several Least Industrialized Nations such as India and China now have nuclear weapons. Always a threat to the world's safety, these weapons in the hands of a dictator can mean nuclear blackmail or nuclear attack to settle personal or nationalistic grudges.

On the positive side, with the cold war over, the United States and the former Soviet Union have announced that they no longer aim their nuclear missiles at the other's cities. Nonetheless, these nations continue to eye each other suspiciously, neither of them wholly convinced that the other has truly peaceful intentions. The United States is especially concerned that the democratic reform movement in Russia may be undermined by reactionary politicians seeking to revert to military might, communism, and cold war foreign policies.

Nuclear, Biological, and Chemical Terrorism

With hatreds fanned through the generations, an unmitigated danger is terrorism directed against a civilian population. One of the few options open to a weaker group looking to retaliate against a powerful country for its suppression is suicide terrorism. Use of

War takes many forms, only one of which is armed conflict officially declared between countries. More common is terrorism. This particular example is from Algiers, the capital of Algeria, but it might as well be from Ireland, Angola, Sri Lanka, India, Pakistan, Israel, Paris, Madrid, and so on.

this strategy by Palestinian liberationists against Israel has shocked the world and captured headlines. Yet the tools used have been weak—bombs that are capable of blowing up only a few people at a time.

The real danger lies elsewhere: the potential of nuclear, chemical, and biological weapons unleashed against a civilian population. The United States is ripe for such an attack. Its role in suppressing some groups' aspirations, especially those of some Arab nations—coupled with the availability of nuclear, chemical, and biological weapons due to the breakup of the Soviet empire—makes this a chilling possibility. In my estimation, it is only a matter of time until such attacks are launched against major U.S. cities.

War and Dehumanization

> Proud of his techniques, the U.S. trainer was demonstrating to the South American soldiers how to torture a prisoner. As the victim screamed in anguish, the trainer was interrupted by a phone call from his wife. His students could hear him say, "A dinner and a movie sound nice. I'll see you right after work." Hanging up the phone, he then continued the lesson. (Stockwell 1989)

War exacts many costs in addition to killing people and destroying property. One is its effect on morality. Exposure to brutality and killing often causes **dehumanization**, the process of reducing people to objects that do not deserve to be treated as humans.

As we review findings on dehumanization and see how it breeds callousness and cruelty, perhaps we can better understand how O'Brien in the opening vignette could have unleashed rats into someone's face. Consider the four characterizations of dehumanization (Bernard et al. 1971):

1. *Increased emotional distance from others.* People stop identifying with others, no longer seeing them as having qualities similar to themselves. Instead of people, they are seen as subhumans, "the enemy," or objects of some sort.

2. *An emphasis on following procedures.* Regulations are not questioned, for they are seen as a means to an end. People are likely to say, "I don't like doing this, but it is necessary to follow procedures," or "We all have to die some day. What difference does it make if these people die now?"

3. *Inability to resist pressures.* Fears of losing one's job, losing the respect of one's peers, or having one's integrity and loyalty questioned take precedence over individual moral decisions.

dehumanization: the act or process of reducing people to objects that do not deserve the treatment accorded humans

4. *A diminished sense of personal responsibility.* People come to see themselves as only small cogs in a large machine. They are not responsible for what they do, for they are simply following orders. The higher-ups who give the orders are thought to have more complete or even secret information that justifies what is being done. They think, "The higher-ups are in a position to judge what is right and wrong, but in my humble place, who am I to question these acts?"

A Vietnam vet who read this section remarked, "You missed the major one we used. We killed kids. Our dehumanizing technique was a saying: 'The little ones are the soldiers of tomorrow.' "

With dehumanization, then, the conscience grows numb. As in the little vignette that opened this section, even acts of torture can become dissociated from one's "normal self." Brutality and killing become simply acts that must be done in order to accomplish a job. It is not the individual's responsibility to question whether or not the job should be done—one's responsibility as a soldier is limited to obedience (Kelman and Hamilton 1997). Torturing and killing are extremely unpleasant, but somehow they fit into the larger scheme of things—and someone has to do such "dirty work." Those who make the decisions are the ones who are responsible, not I, a simple soldier who is merely following orders.

As sociologist Tamotsu Shibutani (1970) stressed, dehumanization is helped along by the tendency for prolonged conflicts to be transformed into a struggle between good and evil. The enemy, of course, represents evil in the equation. To fight against absolute evil sometimes requires the suspension of moral standards—for one is dealing with an abnormal situation, an enemy that is less than human, and the precarious survival of good (Markhusen 1995). War, then, exalts treachery, cruelty, and killing—and medals are given to glorify actions that would be condemned in every other context of social life.

As soldiers participate in acts that they, too, would normally condemn, they neutralize their morality. This insulates them from acknowledging their behaviors as evil, which would threaten their self-concept and mental adjustment. Surgeons, highly sensitive to patients' needs in ordinary medical situations, become capable of mentally removing an individual's humanity. By thinking of Jews as "people who are going to die anyway," German surgeons during World War II were able to mutilate them just to study the results.

Dehumanization does not always insulate the self from guilt, however, and its failure to do so can bring severe personal consequences. During the war, while soldiers are surrounded by army buddies who agree that the enemy is less than human and deserves inhuman treatment, such definitions ordinarily remain intact. After returning home, however, the dehumanizing definitions more easily break down. Many soldiers then find themselves seriously disturbed by what they did during the war. Although most eventually adjust, some cannot, for example, the soldier from California who wrote this note before putting a bullet through his brain (Smith 1980):

> I can't sleep anymore. When I was in Vietnam, we came across a North Vietnamese soldier with a man, a woman, and a three-or four-year-old girl. We had to shoot them all. I can't get the little girl's face out of my mind. I hope that God will forgive me . . . I can't.

A New World Order?

The globalization of capitalism, accompanied by the worldwide flow of information, capital, and goods discussed in the previous chapter, is little affected by national boundaries. The United States, Canada, and Mexico have formed a North American Free-Trade Association (NAFTA), to which all of South America will eventually belong. Most European countries have formed an economic and political unit (the European Union, or UE) that supersedes their national boundaries. Similarly, the United Nations, transcending national borders and moderating disputes between countries, can authorize the use of international force against individual nations—as it has done against North Korea in 1950, Iraq in 1990, and on a smaller scale, Somalia in 1993 and Bosnia in 1994 and 1997.

nationalism: a strong identity with a nation, accompanied by the desire for that nation to be dominant

CULTURAL DIVERSITY AROUND THE WORLD

The Rise of Nationalism Versus the Globalization of Capitalism—Implications for a New World Order

The world has about five thousand nations. What makes each a *nation* is that its people share a language, culture, territory, and political organization. A *state*, in contrast, claims a monopoly on violence over a territory. A state may contain many nations. The Kayapo Indians are but one nation within the state called Brazil. The Chippewa and Sioux are two nations within the state called the United States. To nation peoples, group identity transcends political affiliation. The world's ten thousand nations have existed for hundreds, some even for thousands of years. In contrast, most of the world's 194 states have been around only since World War II.

Most modern states are empires, and they are increasingly seen as such by the nations that have been incorporated into them—usually by conquest. Some states have far better records than others, but overall, no ideology, left or right, religious or sectarian, has protected nations or promoted pluralism much better or worse than any other. In fact, the twentieth century has probably seen more genocides and ethnocides (the destruction of an ethnic group) than any other.

Clearly, the Palestinians who live within Israel's borders will not soon identify themselves as Israelis. But did you know that the Oromos in Ethiopia have more members than three-quarters of the states in the United Nations, and that they do not think of themselves as Ethiopians? The 22 million Kurds don't consider themselves first and foremost Turks, Iranians, Iraqis, or Syrians. There are about 130 nations in the former USSR, 180 in Brazil, 90 in Ethiopia, 450 in Nigeria, 350 in India. That so many nations are squeezed into so few states is, in fact, the nub of the problem.

In most states, power is in the hands of a few elites, who operate by a simple credo: winner take all. They control foreign investment and aid, and use both to reinforce their power. They set local commodity prices, control exports, levy taxes—and buy the weapons. They confiscate the resources of its nations, whether it be Indian land in North and South America or oil from the Kurds in Iraq. When nations resist, the result is open conflict.

About half of the debt of the least industrialized states and nearly all debt in Africa comes from the purchase of

Nourished by family, centuries-old hatreds are passed from one generation to the next. To avenge wrongs and kill "the enemy" becomes a duty, a righteous calling, inherited with one's language, the air one breathes, the dreams of one's people.

weapons for states to fight their own citizens. Most of the world's 12 million refugees are the offspring of such conflicts, as are most of the 100 million internally displaced people who have been uprooted from their homelands.

A vicious cycle forms. The appropriation of a nation's resources leads to conflict, conflict leads to weapons purchases, weapons purchases lead to debt, and debt leads to the appropriation of more resources. This self-feeding cycle helps ensure the cooperation of the elites of the least industrialized states as the most industrialized states divide the globe's resources among themselves.

The fly in the ointment in the march to the New World Order is the appearance of fierce **nationalism**—identity with and loyalty to a nation. Nationalism, with its loyalty to small groups, threatens to undermine the developing new world order. Based on nationalism, the shooting wars increase —fought over issues, grudges, and animosities rooted in long history, only faintly understood by those who are not a party to the events but vividly alive in the folklore and collective memory of these nations. These wars threaten the yet fragile coalitions of the powerful states that are dividing up the world's resources.

Consequently, we should not be surprised to see the United States and its allies maintain silence as the Soviets oppress nations under their dominance—and silence on the part of Russia as the United States and European powers put out their own nationalistic brushfires.

Currently, then, we witness an oppositional struggle: nationalism versus the formation of global coalitions. We are likely to see many more seemingly contradictory fruits of these two forces: the globe divided into huge regional trading blocs controlled by the most industrialized states, matched by the simultaneous outbreak of small-scale shooting wars as nations struggle for independence.

The end result? Let's just note how greatly the scales are tipped in favor of the most industrialized states and the multinational corporations.

Sources: Clay 1990; Kanter 1995; Ohmae 1995; Jáuregui 1996; Marcus 1996.

Will this process continue until there is but one state or empire that envelops the earth itself? This is a possibility, perhaps deriving not only from these historical trends but also from a push by a powerful group of capitalists who profit from global free trade (Domhoff 1990). Although the trend is in full tilt, even if it continues we are unlikely to see its conclusion during our lifetimes, for national boundaries and national patriotism will die only a hard death. And as borders shift, as occurred with the breakup of the Soviet Union, previously unincorporated nations such as Lithuania and Azerbaijan demand their independence and the right to full statehood. The Perspectives box on page 425 explores this rising tension between nations and states.

If such global political and economic unity does come about, it is fascinating to speculate on what type of government will result. If Hitler had had his way, his conquests would have resulted in world domination—by a world dictator and a world totalitarian regime based on racial identification. If our current trend continues—and it is a big "if"—and if a world order does emerge, the potential for human welfare is tremendous. There could be almost global peace. And if a benevolent government arises, there also could be highly satisfying participation in politics. If, however, we end up with totalitarianism, and the world's resources and people come under the control of a dictatorship or an oligarchy, the future for humanity could be bleak, perhaps like that of Winston and Julia in our opening vignette.

Summary and Review

Micropolitics and Macropolitics

What is the difference between micropolitics and macropolitics?

The essential nature of politics is **power,** and every group is political. The term **micropolitics** refers to the exercise of power in everyday life, **macropolitics** to large-scale power, such as governing a nation. P. 404.

Power, Authority, and Violence

How are authority and coercion related to power?

Authority is power that people view as legitimately exercised over them, while **coercion** is power they consider unjust. The **state** is a political entity that claims a monopoly on violence over a particular territory. If enough people consider a state's power illegitimate, **revolution** is possible. Pp. 405–406.

What kinds of authority are there? Max Weber identified three types of authority. Power in **traditional authority** derives from custom—patterns set down in the past serve as rules for the present. Power in **rational-legal authority** (also called *bureaucratic authority*) is based on law and written procedures. In **charismatic authority** power is based on loyalty to an individual to whom people are attracted. Charismatic authority, which undermines traditional and rational-legal authority, has built-in problems in transferring authority to a new leader. Pp. 406–409.

Types of Government

How are the types of government related to power?

In a **monarchy,** power is based on hereditary rule; in a **democracy,** power is given to the ruler by citizens; and in a **dictatorship,** power is seized by an individual or small group. Pp. 409–411.

The U.S. Political System

What are the main characteristics of the U.S. political system?

The United States has a "winner take all" system, in which elections are determined by a simple majority. Most European democracies, in contrast, have **proportional representation,** with legislative seats divided among political parties according to the percentage of votes each receives. If no single party is in power, proportional representation creates the need of a **coalition government.** Pp. 000–000.

Voter turnout is higher among people who are more socially integrated, those who sense a greater stake in the outcome of elections, such as the more educated and well-to-do. The Great Depression of the 1930s marked a turning point in the U.S. political system, as the government accepted greater responsibility for economic conditions. Lobbyists and special-interest groups, such as **political action committees** (PACs), play a significant role in U.S. politics. Pp. 412–418.

Who Rules the United States?

Is the United States controlled by a ruling class?

In a view known as **pluralism,** functionalists say that no one group holds power, that the country's many competing interest groups balance one another. Conflict theorists, who focus on the top level of power, say that the United States is governed by a **power elite,** a **ruling class** made up of the top corporate, military, and political leaders. At this point, the matter is not settled. Pp. 418–420.

War

How is war related to politics—and what are its costs?

War, common in human history, is a means of attempting to reach political objectives. Because of technological advances in killing, the costs of war in terms of human lives have escalated. The Least Industrialized Nations, which can least afford it, spend huge amounts on technologically advanced weapons. Another cost is **dehumanization,** whereby people no longer see others as worthy of human treatment. Pp. 420–424.

A New World Order?

Is humanity headed toward a one-world political order?

The global expansion of communications, transportation, and trade, the widespread adoption of capitalism and the retreat of socialism, and the trend toward larger political unions may indicate that a world political system is developing. The oppositional trend is a fierce **nationalism.** If a new world order develops, the possible consequences for human welfare range from excellent to calamitous. Pp. 424–426.

Where can I read more on this topic?

Suggested readings for this chapter are listed on page 664.

Sociology and the Internet

All URLs listed are current as of the printing of this book. URLs are often changed. Please check our Website http://www.abacon.com/henslin for updates.

1. As you have learned, European democracies look somewhat different from that of the United States. The parliamentary system of proportional representation does not provide for a distinct separation of power between the legislative and executive areas of government. Also unlike the United States, the political parties are noncentrist.

Let's use the Internet to explore political parties in England. Go to the "British Politics" site at *http://www.ukpol.co.uk* You should see the heading "Political Parties," with 50 party names, beginning with the Conservative Party. Explore each of the parties listed to discover as much as you can. Look for their history, philosophy, constituency, and position on specific issues. How do they differ from U.S. political parties? Write a paper comparing the parties.

2. You have read about the controversy surrounding lobbyists, special-interest groups, and political action committees (PACs). Let's see what we can find out about them on the Internet. Go to Yahoo!'s list of sites under "Politics" *http://www.yahoo!.com/Government/Politics* Select "Interest Groups." You should now see two categories. "Lobbying Groups" points to firms advertising their services. You might want to look at a few of these to see what is offered. The second category, "Political Action Committees," leads to several sites, most of them dealing with single issues at the state level (California's Eco-vote Online, for example). If you are doing this project in an election year, you will find a fascinating CNN site, which lists the financial contributions to major candidates (by state). It's interesting to see who supports whom, and for how much. Next, search *http://www.pirg.org/pirg* for "Public Interest Groups." Under this heading you will find several links to single issue groups: abortion issues, animal rights, and so on.

Look at areas that you think are controversial or which particularly interest you.

A report on this excursion will have to be very broad, so let's use a journal approach. Write a narrative of where you went and what you found, along with personal reactions along the way. Organize your report in diary form. Don't forget to include a general introduction and a conclusion.

3. How do young people feel about the politics in this country? Take a look at the following site:

http://www.xgeneration.org/

How do the opinions of those interviewed differ from your own view? From the views of the functionalists and conflict theorists, as explained in this chapter? What are some of the problems suggested by the people on this site? How might the opinions of members of Generation X differ from those of the "Baby Boom" generation? Why?

4. You probably are familiar with the U.S. voting system. Voter apathy is just one problem that results from the current system, which you have read about in your text. Examine the following links to alternative voting systems for the United States:

http://www.alumni.caltech.edu/~croft/ideas/voting.html
http://www.eskimo.com/~robla/cpr/single-winner.html
http://www.webcom.com/~worldgov/zoom.html
http://www.mtholyoke.edu/acad/polit/damy/prlib.htm
http://www.igc.apc.org/cvd/
http://www.ionet.net/~dwaddell/

What changes to the current voting system are introduced in these sites? What problems in the current system do they hope to counteract? If adopted, what problems could these new systems create? How do you feel about these proposed alternatives?

Sonya McQueen, Family Union, 1993

C H A P T E R

16

The Family:
Initiation into Society

"**H**OLD STILL. *WE'RE GOING TO BE LATE*," *said Sharon as she tried to put shoes on 2-year-old Michael, who kept squirming away.*

Finally succeeding with the shoes, Sharon turned to 4-year-old Brittany, who was trying to pull a brush through her hair. "It's stuck, Mom," Brittany said.

"Well, no wonder. Just how did you get gum in your hair? I don't have time for this, Brittany. We've got to leave."

Getting to the van fifteen minutes behind schedule, Sharon strapped the kids in, and then herself. Just as she was about to pull away, she remembered that she had not checked the fridge for messages.

"Just a minute, kids. I'll be right back."

Running into the house, she frantically searched for a message from Tom. She vaguely remembered him mumbling something about being held over at work. She grabbed the Post-It and ran back to the van.

"He's picking on me," complained Brittany when her mother climbed back in.

"Oh, shut up, Brittany," Sharon said. "He's only 2. He can't pick on you."

"Yes, he did," Brittany said, crossing her arms defiantly, as she stretched out her foot to kick her brother's seat.

"Oh, no! How did Mikey get that smudge on his face? Did you do that, Brit?"

Brittany crossed her arms again, pushing out her lips in her classic pouting pose.

As Sharon drove to the day care center, she tried to calm herself. "Only two more days of work this week, and then the weekend. Then I can catch up on housework and have a little relaxed time with the kids. And Tom can finally cut the lawn and buy the groceries," she thought. "And maybe we'll even have time to make love. Boy, that's been a long time."

At a traffic light, Sharon found time to read Tom's note. "Oh, no. That's what he meant. He has to work Saturday. Well, there go those plans."

What Sharon didn't know was that her boss also had made plans for Sharon's Saturday. And that their emergency Saturday baby-sitter would be unavailable. And that the van would break down on the way home from work. That Michael was coming down with chicken pox. That Brittany would follow next. That . . .

That there isn't enough time to get everything done is a common complaint of most of us. But it is especially true for working parents of young children who find themselves without the support services taken for granted just a generation ago: stay-at-home moms who were the center of the neighborhood, a husband whose sole income was enough to support a wife and several children, a safe neighborhood where even small children could play outside, even a grandma who could pitch in during emergencies.

Those days are gone forever. Today, more and more families are like Sharon's and Tom's. They are harried, pressured, working more and seemingly making less, and, certainly, having less time for one another—and for their children. In this chapter, we shall try to understand what is happening to the U.S. family, and to families worldwide.

Marriage and Family in Global Perspective

To better understand U.S. patterns of marriage and family, let's first sketch a cross-cultural portrait. The perspective it yields will give us a context for interpreting our own experience in this vital social institution.

Defining Family

"What is a family, anyway?" asked William Sayres (1992) at the beginning of an article on this topic. By this question, he meant that although the family is so significant to humanity that it is universal—every human group in the world organizes its members in families—the world's cultures display so much variety that the term *family* is difficult to define. For example, although the Western world regards a family as consisting of a husband, wife, and children, other groups have family forms in which men have more than one wife (**polygyny**) or women more than one husband (**polyandry**). To try to define the family as the approved group into which children are born overlooks the Banaro of New Guinea. Among this group a young woman must give birth before she can marry, and she cannot marry the father of her child (Murdock 1949).

And so it goes. For just about every element you might consider essential to marriage or family, some group has a different custom. Even the sex of the bride and groom may not be what you expect. Although in almost every instance the bride and groom are female and male, though rare, there are exceptions. In some Native American tribes, for example, a man or woman who wanted to be a member of the opposite sex went through a ceremony (*berdache*) and was *declared* a member of the opposite sex. From then on, not only did the "new" man or woman do the tasks associated with his or her new sex, but the individual also was allowed to marry. In this instance, the husband and wife were of the same biological sex. In the contemporary Western world, Denmark, Holland, Norway, and Sweden have legalized same–sex marriages.

Even to say that the family is the unit in which children are disciplined and their parents are responsible for their material needs is not universally true. Among the Trobriand Islanders, the wife's eldest brother is responsible for making certain that his sister's children are fed and are properly disciplined when they get out of line (Malinowski 1927). Finally, even sexual relationships don't universally characterize a husband and wife. The Nayar of Malabar never *allow* a bride and groom to have sex. After a three-day celebration of the marriage, they send the groom packing—and never allow him to see his bride again (La Barre 1954). (In case you are wondering, the groom comes from another tribe, and Nayar women are allowed to have sex, but only with approved lovers—who can never be the husband. This system keeps family property intact—along matrilineal lines.)

Such remarkable variety means settling for a very broad definition. A **family** consists of two or more people who consider themselves related by blood, marriage, or adoption. A **household,** in contrast, consists of all people who occupy the same housing unit—a house, apartment, or other living quarters.

We can classify families as **nuclear** (husband, wife, and children) and **extended** (including people such as grandparents, aunts, uncles, and cousins in addition to the nuclear unit). Sociologists also refer to the **family of orientation** (the family in which an individual grows up) and the **family of procreation** (the family formed when a couple have their first child). Finally, regardless of its form, **marriage** can be viewed as a group's approved mating arrangements—usually marked out by a ritual of some sort (the wedding) to indicate the couple's new public status.

Common Cultural Themes

In spite of this diversity, several common themes do run through marriage and family. As Table 16.1 on the next page illustrates, all societies use marriage and family to establish patterns of mate selection, descent, inheritance, and authority. Let's look at these patterns.

Norms of Mate Selection.   Each human group establishes norms to govern who marries whom. Norms of **endogamy** specify that people should marry within their own group. Groups may prohibit interracial marriages, for example. In contrast, norms of **exogamy** specify that people must marry outside their group. The best example is the *incest taboo*, which prohibits sex and marriage among designated relatives. In some societies

Often one of the strongest family bonds is that of mother–daughter. The young artist, an eleventh grader, wrote: "This painting expresses the way I feel about my future with my child. I want my child to be happy and I want her to love me the same way I love her. In that way we will have a good relationship so that nobody will be able to take us apart. I wanted this picture to be alive, that is why I used a lot of bright colors."

polygyny: a marriage in which a man has more than one wife

polyandry: a marriage in which a woman has more than one husband

family: two or more people who consider themselves related by blood, marriage, or adoption

household: all people who occupy the same housing unit

nuclear family: a family consisting of a husband, wife, and child(ren)

extended family: a nuclear family plus other relatives, such as grandparents, uncles and aunts, who live together

family of orientation: the family in which a person grows up

family of procreation: the family formed when a couple's first child is born

marriage: a group's approved mating arrangements, usually marked by a ritual of some sort

---

TABLE 16.1

Common Cultural Themes: Marriage in Traditional and Industrial Societies

Characteristic	*Traditional Societies*	*Industrial (and Postindustrial) Societies*
What is the structure of marriage?	*Extended* (marriage embeds spouses in a large kinship network of explicit obligations)	*Nuclear* (marriage brings fewer obligations toward the spouse's kin)
What are the functions of marriage?	Encompassing (see the six functions listed on pp. 24–25)	More limited (many functions are fulfilled by other social institutions)
Who holds authority?	Highly *patriarchal* (authority is held by males)	Although some patriarchal features remain, authority is more evenly divided
How many spouses at one time?	Most have one spouse (*monogamy*), while some have several (*polygamy*)	One spouse
Who selects the spouse?	The spouse is selected by the parents, usually the father	Individuals choose their own spouse
Where does the couple live?	Couples most commonly reside with the groom's family (*patrilocal residence*), less commonly with the bride's family (*matrilocal residence*)	Couples establish a new home (*neolocal residence*)
How is descent figured?	Most commonly figured from male ancestors (*patrilineal kinship*); less commonly from female ancestors (*matrilineal kinship*)	Figured from male and female ancestors equally (*bilateral kinship*)
How is inheritance figured?	Rigid system of rules; usually patrilineal, but may be matrilineal	Highly individualistic; usually bilateral

---

these norms are written into law, but in most cases they are informal. For example, in the United States most whites marry whites and most African Americans marry African Americans, not because of any laws but because of informal norms. (For patterns of "out-marriage" in the United States, see Figure 12.1 on page 312).

The path to marriage varies around the world. A common pattern in traditional societies is for marriage to be arranged by the parents. This mass marriage, performed in Washington, D.C., is a most unusual form of arranged marriage. All 2,500 couples were matched by Sun Myung Moon, the head of the Unification Church. Most couples had never met before their marriage.

endogamy: the practice of marrying within one's own group

exogamy: the practice of marrying outside one's group

Reckoning Patterns of Descent.   How are you related to your father's father or to your mother's mother? The explanation is found in your society's **system of descent,** the way people trace kinship over generations. To us, a **bilateral** system seems logical—and natural—for we think of ourselves as related to both our mother's and our father's side of the family. "Doesn't everyone?" you might ask. Interestingly, this is only one logical way to reckon descent. In a **patrilineal** system, descent is traced only on the father's side, and children are not considered related to their mother's relatives. In a **matrilineal** system, descent is figured only on the mother's side, and children are not considered related to their father's relatives.

Rights of Inheritance.   Marriage and family—in whatever form is customary in a society—are also used to compute rights of inheritance. In the bilateral system, property is passed to both males and females, in the patrilineal system only to males, and in the matrilineal system (the rarest form) only to females. Each system matches a people's ideas of justice and logic.

Patterns of Authority.   Historically, some form of **patriarchy,** a social system in which men dominate women, has formed a thread running through all societies. As noted in Chapter 11, there are no historical records of a true **matriarchy,** a social system in which women as a group dominate men as a group. Our marriage and family customs, then, developed within a framework of patriarchy. Although U.S. family patterns are becoming more **egalitarian,** or equal, many customs practiced today point to their patriarchal origin. Naming patterns, for example, reflect patriarchy. In spite of recent trends, the typical bride still takes the groom's last name; children, too, are usually given the father's last name. For information on a society that systematically promotes equality in marriage, see the Perspectives box on the next page.

Marriage and Family in Theoretical Perspective ▶

When we consider marriage in a global perspective, then, we see that our own forms of marriage and family follow just one of many patterns that humans have chosen. Let's see what picture emerges when we apply the three sociological perspectives.

The Functionalist Perspective: Functions and Dysfunctions

As noted in Chapter 1, functionalists stress that to survive, a society must meet certain basic needs, or functions. When functionalists look at family, they examine how it is related to other parts of society, especially how it contributes to the well-being of society.

Why the Family Is Universal.   Functionalists note that although the form of the family may vary from one human group to another, the family is universal because it fulfills six needs basic to every society's well-being. As described on pages 24–25, these needs, or functions, are economic production, socialization of children, care of the sick and aged, recreation, sexual control, and reproduction. To make certain that these needs are met, every human group has found it necessary to adopt some form of the family.

Functions of the Incest Taboo.   By specifying which people are too closely related to have sex or to marry, the incest taboo helps families avoid role confusion. This, in turn, facilitates the socialization of children. For example, if father–daughter incest were allowed, how should a wife treat her daughter—as a daughter, as a subservient second wife, or even as a rival? Should the daughter act toward her mother as a mother or as a rival? Would her father be a father or a lover? And would the wife be the husband's main wife,

system of descent: how kinship is traced over the generations

bilateral (system of descent): a system of reckoning descent that counts both the mother's and the father's side

patrilineal (system of descent): a system of reckoning descent that counts only the father's side

matrilineal (system of descent): a system of reckoning descent that counts only the mother's side

patriarchy: authority vested in males; male control of a society or group

matriarchy: authority vested in females; female control of a society or group

egalitarian: authority more or less equally divided between people or groups, in this instance between husband and wife

Perspectives

Family Life in Sweden

Swedish lawmakers hold a strong image of what good family life is. That image is of total equality in marriage and the welfare of children. They bolster this image with laws designed to put women and men on equal footing in marriage, to have mothers and fathers share responsibility for the home and children, and to protect the financially weaker party in the event of divorce.

At the center of family laws is the welfare of children. Health care for mothers and children, for example, is free. This includes all obstetric care and all health care during pregnancy. Maternity centers offer free health checks and courses in preparation for childbirth. Fathers are encouraged to attend the childbirth classes.

When a child is born, the parents are eligible for fifteen months' leave of absence with pay. The leave and compensation are available for either or both parents. Both cannot receive compensation at the same time, and the parents decide how they will split the leave between them. For the first twelve months the state pays 90 percent of gross income, and then a generous fixed rate for the remaining three months. The paid leave does not have to be taken all at once, but can be spread over eight years. The parents can stay at home full time, or they can work part time for a longer period. Because most mothers take all the leave, the law now includes a "father's month," one month that cannot be transferred to the mother.

The government also guarantees other benefits. All fathers are entitled to ten days leave of absence with full pay when a child is born. When a child is sick, either parent can care for the child and receive full pay for missed work—up to sixty days a year per child. Moreover, by law local governments must offer child care. And if a husband becomes violent or threatens his wife, the woman can have a security alarm installed in their home free of charge.

The divorce laws also have been drawn up with a view to what is best for the child. Local governments are required to provide free counseling to any parent who requests it. If both parties agree and if they have no children under the age of 16, a couple is automatically entitled to a divorce. Otherwise the law requires a six-month cooling-off period, so they can more calmly consider what is best for their children. Joint custody of children is automatic, unless one of the parents opposes it. The children may live only with one of the parents. The parent who does not live with the children is required to pay child support in proportion to his or her finances. If the parent fails to do so, the social security system makes the payments.

For Your Consideration

How does the Swedish system compare with that of the United States? What "system" for watching out for the welfare of children does the United States have, anyway?

Source: Based on The Swedish Institute 1992; Froman 1994.

---

a secondary wife—or even "the mother of the other wife" (whatever role that might be)? Maternal incest would also lead to complications every bit as confusing as these.

Another function of the incest taboo is to force people to look outside the family for marriage partners. Anthropologists theorize that exogamy was especially functional in tribal societies, for it forged alliances between tribes that otherwise might have killed each other off. Today, exogamy extends a bride's and groom's social networks beyond the nuclear family, building relationships with their spouse's family.

Connection to Other Parts of Society.   Functionalists stress that the family is not an isolated unit, but is vitally connected to other parts of society. They note, for example, that industrialization made the family more fragile. Industrialization ushered in formal organizations, and some of them began to replace the family's traditional functions. Medical treatment began to be provided by hospitals, recreation by businesses, and sex education by schools. To weaken family functions is to weaken the "ties that bind," to reduce the motivation to struggle together against hardships. One consequence is higher divorce. From the functionalist perspective, then, increased divorce does not represent "incompatible personalities." Rather, changes in other parts of society affect intimate relationships.

Isolation and Emotional Overload.   Functionalists also analyze the dysfunctions that arise from the relative isolation of today's nuclear family (another consequence of industrialization). Unlike extended families in traditional societies, which are enmeshed in kinship networks, members of nuclear families can count on fewer people for material and emotional support. This makes nuclear families vulnerable to "emotional overload." That is, the stress that comes with crises such as the loss of a job—or even the routine pressures of a harried life, as described in our opening vignette—is spread around fewer people. This places greater strain on each family member. In addition, the relative isolation of the nuclear family makes it vulnerable to a "dark side"—incest and various other forms of abuse—which we examine later in this chapter.

The Conflict Perspective: Gender, Conflict, and Power

As you recall, central to conflict theory is the struggle over scarce resources. The recurring struggle over who does housework is actually a struggle over scarce resources—time, energy, and the leisure to pursue interesting activities.

The Power Struggle Over Housework.   Most men resist doing housework, and as Figure 16.1 shows, even wives who work outside the home full-time end up doing most of it. The lesser effort that husbands make seems so great to them, however, that even when his wife does almost all the cooking and cleaning, the husband is likely to see himself as splitting the work fifty-fifty (Galinsky et al. 1993). Things are so one-sided that wives are *eight* times more likely to feel that the division of housework is unfair (Sanchez 1994).

And no wonder. Wives who put in an eight-hour day of working for wages average eleven hours more child care and housework each week than their husbands (Bianchi and Spain 1996). *Incredibly, this is the equivalent of twenty-four 24-hour days a year.* Sociologist Arlie Hochschild (1989) calls this the working wife's "second shift." To stress the one-sided nature of the second shift, she quotes this satire by Garry Trudeau in the Doonesbury comic strip:

> A "liberated" father is sitting at his word processor writing a book about raising his child. He types: "Today I wake up with a heavy day of work ahead of me. As Joannie gets Jeffry ready for day care, I ask her if I can be relieved of my usual household responsibilities for the day. Joannie says, 'Sure, I'll make up the five minutes somewhere.' "

Not surprisingly, the burden of the second shift creates deep discontent among wives. These problems, as well as how wives and husbands cope with them, are discussed in the following Thinking Critically section.

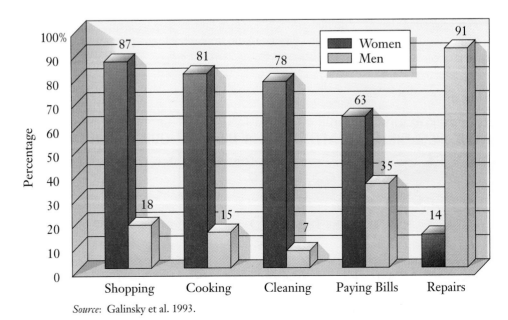

Source: Galinsky et al. 1993.

Figure 16.1

In Two-Paycheck Marriages, Who Has More Responsibility for Housework?

Thinking Critically About Social Controversy

✦ The Second Shift—Strains and Strategies ✦

▼ To find out what life is like in two-paycheck marriages, for nine years sociologist Arlie Hochschild (1989) and her research associates interviewed and reinterviewed fifty-some families. Hochschild also did participant observation with a dozen of them. She "shopped with them, visited friends, watched television, ate with them, walked through parks, and came along when they dropped their children at day care."

Hochschild notes that women have no more time in a day than when they stayed home, but that now there is twice as much to get done. Most wives and husbands in her sample felt that the *second shift*—the household duties that follow the day's work for pay—is the wife's responsibility. But as they cook, clean, and take care of the children after their job at the office or factory, many wives feel tired, emotionally drained, and resentful. Not uncommonly, these feelings show up in the bedroom, where the wives show a lack of interest in sex.

It isn't that men do nothing around the house. But since they see household responsibilities as the wife's duty, they "help out" when they feel like it—or when they get nagged into it. And since most of us prefer to tend to our children than clean house, men are more likely to "help out" on the second shift by taking children to do "fun" things—to see movies, or to go for outings in the park. In contrast, the woman's time with the children is more likely to be "maintenance"—feeding and bathing them, taking them to the doctor, and so on.

The strains from working the second shift affect not only the marital relationship, but also the wife's self-concept. Here is how one woman tried to buoy her flagging self-esteem:

> After taking time off for her first baby, Carol Alston felt depressed, "fat," "just a housewife," and for a while became the supermarket shopper who wanted to call down the aisles, "I'm an MBA! I'm an MBA!"

Most wives feel strongly that the second shift should be shared, but many feel that it is hopeless to try to get their husbands to change. They work the second shift, but they resent it. Others have a "showdown" with their husbands, some even giving the ultimatum, "It's share the second shift, or it's divorce." Still others try to be the "supermom" who can do it all.

Some men cooperate and cut down on their commitment to a career. Others cut back on movies, seeing friends, doing hobbies. Most men, however, engage in what Hochschild describes as "strategies of resistance." She identified the following:

- *Waiting it out.* Many men never volunteer to do household chores. Since many wives dislike asking because it feels like "begging," this strategy often works. Some men make this strategy even more effective by showing irritation or becoming glum when they are asked, discouraging the wife from asking again.
- *Playing dumb.* When they do housework, some men become incompetent. They can't cook rice without burning it; when they go to the store, they forget grocery lists;

The cartoonist has beautifully captured the reduction of needs strategy discussed by Hochschild.

ARLO & JANIS ® by Jimmy Johnson

they can never remember where the broiler pan is. Hochschild did not claim that husbands do these things on purpose, but, rather, that by withdrawing their mental attention from the task, they "get credit for trying and being a good sport"—but in such a way that they are not chosen next time.

- *Needs reduction.* An example of this strategy is a father of two who explained that he never shopped because he didn't "need anything." He didn't need to iron his clothes because he "[didn't] mind wearing a wrinkled shirt." He didn't need to cook because "cereal is fine." As Hochschild observed, "Through his reduction of needs, this man created a great void into which his wife stepped with her 'greater need' to see him wear an ironed shirt . . . take his shirts to the cleaners . . . and cook his dinner."
- *Substitute offerings.* Expressing appreciation to the wife for being so organized that she can handle both work for wages and the second shift at home can be a substitute for helping—and a subtle encouragement for her to keep on working the second shift.

For Your Consideration

Hochschild (1991) is confident that such problems can be solved. Use these materials to

1. Identify the underlying *structural* causes of the problem of the second shift.
2. Based on your answer to number 1, identify *structural* solutions to this problem.
3. Determine how a working wife and husband might best reconcile this problem.

The Symbolic Interactionist Perspective: Gender and the Meanings of Marriage

As noted in Chapter 1, symbolic interactionists focus on the meanings that people give to their lives. Let's apply this perspective to some surprising findings about marriage.

Housework, Paychecks, and Masculinity.   The first finding is probably what you'd expect—the closer a husband's and wife's earnings, the more likely they are to share housework. (Although husbands in such marriages don't share housework equally, they do more than other husbands.) This finding, however, may be surprising: *husbands who earn less than their wives do the least housework.* And this one: most husbands who get laid off *reduce* their housework.

How can we explain this? It would seem that husbands who earn less than their wives would want to balance things out, that they would do more around the house, not less. Researchers suggest that the key is gender role. If a wife earns more than her husband, this threatens his masculinity—he takes it as a sign that he has failed in his traditional manly role of provider. To do housework—"women's work" in his eyes—threatens it even further. By avoiding housework, he "reclaims" his masculinity (Hochschild 1989; Brines 1994).

Two Marriages in One.   Another interesting finding of symbolic interactionists is how husbands and wives perceive their marriage. When asked how much housework each does, they give different answers. They even disagree about whether or not they fight over doing housework (Sanchez 1994). Sociologist Jessie Bernard, who studied this marital gulf, noted in a classic work (1972) that when researchers

> ask husbands and wives identical questions about the union they often get quite different replies. There is usually agreement on the number of children they have and a few other such verifiable items, although not, for example, on length of premarital acquaintance and of engagement, on age at marriage and interval between marriage and birth of first child. Indeed, with respect to even such basic components of the marriage as frequency of sexual relations, social interaction, household tasks, and decision making, they seem to be reporting on different marriages.

Why don't husbands and wives agree on such a basic matter as how frequently they have sex? The answer lies in differing *perceptions* of lovemaking. It appears that in the typical marriage the wife desires greater emotional involvement from her husband, while the husband's desire is for more sex (Komter 1989; Barbeau 1992). When questioned about sex, then, the husband, feeling deprived, tends to underestimate it, while the wife, more reluctant to participate in sex because of unsatisfied intimacy needs, overestimates it (Bernard 1972).

Symbolic interactionists conclude that because husbands and wives hold down such different corners in marriage they perceive marriage differently. Their experiences contrast so sharply that *every marriage contains two separate marriages—his and hers.*

The Family Life Cycle

Thus far we have seen that the forms of marriage and family vary widely, and we have examined marriage and family from the three sociological perspectives. Now let's discuss love, courtship, and the family life cycle.

Love and Courtship in Global Perspective

Until recently, social scientists thought that romantic love originated in western Europe during the medieval period (Mount 1992). When anthropologists William Jankowiak and Edward Fischer (1992) surveyed the data available on 166 societies around the world, they found that this was not so. **Romantic love**—people being sexually attracted to one another and idealizing the other—showed up in 88 percent (147) of these groups. The role of love, however, differs sharply from one society to another. As the Perspectives box details, for example, Indians don't expect love to occur until *after* marriage—if then.

Because love plays such a significant role in Western life—and is often thought to be the *only* proper basis for marriage—social scientists have probed this concept with the tools of the trade—laboratory experiments, questionnaires, interviews, and systematic observations. One of the more interesting experiments was conducted by psychologists Donald Dutton and Arthur Aron who discovered that fear breeds love (Rubin 1985). Across a rocky gorge, about 230 feet above the Capilano River in North Vancouver, a rickety footbridge sways in the wind. Another footbridge, a solid structure, crosses only ten feet above a shallow stream. An attractive woman approached men who were crossing these bridges, asking if they would take part in her study of "the effects of exposure to scenic attractions on creative expression." She showed them a picture, and they wrote down their associations. The sexual imagery in their stories showed that the men on the unsteady, frighten-

romantic love: feelings of erotic attraction accompanied by an idealization of the other

Romantic love reaches far back into history, as illustrated by this Etruscan sarcophagus. The Etruscans, reaching their peak of civilization in 500 B.C. in what is now Italy, were vanquished by Rome about one hundred years later. The artist has portrayed the couple's mutual affection and satisfaction.

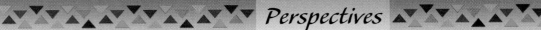

Perspectives

CULTURAL DIVERSITY AROUND THE WORLD

East Is East and West Is West . . . Love and Arranged Marriage in India

After Arun Bharat Ram returned home with a degree from the University of Michigan, his mother announced that she wanted to find him a wife. Arun would be a good "catch" anywhere: 27 years old, good education, well mannered, intelligent, handsome—and, not incidentally, heir to one of the largest fortunes in India.

Arun's mother already had someone in mind. Manju, who came from a solid, middle-class family, was also a college graduate. Arun and Manju met in a coffee shop in a luxury hotel—along with both sets of parents. He found her pretty and quiet. He liked that. She was impressed that he didn't boast about his background.

After four more meetings, one with the two alone, the parents asked their children if they were willing to marry. Neither had any major objections.

The Prime Minister of India and fifteen hundred other guests came to the wedding.

"I didn't love him," Manju says. "But when we talked, we had a lot of things in common." She then adds, "But now I couldn't live without him. I've never thought of another man since I met him."

Although India has undergone extensive social change, Indian sociologists estimate that about 95 percent of marriages are still arranged by the parents. Today, however, as with Arun and Manju, couples have veto power over their parents' selection. Another innovation is that the couple are allowed to talk to each other before the wedding—unheard of just a generation ago.

The fact that arranged marriages are the norm in India does not mean that this ancient land is without a tradition of passion and love. Far from it. The *Kamasutra* is world-renowned for its explicit details about lovemaking, and the erotic sculptures at Khajuraho still startle Westerners today. Indian mythology extols the copulations of gods, and every Indian schoolchild knows the love story of the god Krishna and Radha, the beautiful milkmaid he found irresistible.

Why, then, aren't love and passion the basis of marriage in India? Why arranged marriages? And why does this practice persist today, even among the educated and upper classes? We can also ask why the United States has such an individualistic approach to marriage.

To answer these questions takes us to a basic sociological principle—that *a group's marriage practices match its values and patterns of social stratification.* Individual mate selection matches U.S. values of individuality and independence, while arranged marriages match Indian values of children deferring to parental authority. In addition, arranged marriages reaffirm caste lines by channeling marriage within the same caste.

To Indians, to practice unrestricted dating would be to trust important matters to inexperienced young people. It would encourage premarital sex, which, in turn, would break down family lines that virginity at marriage assures the upper castes. Consequently, Indian young people are socialized to think that parents have cooler heads and superior wisdom in these matters. In the United States, family lines are much less important, and caste is an alien concept.

Even ideas of love differ. For Indians, love is a peaceful emotion, based on long-term commitment and devotion to family. Indians also think of love as something that can be "created" between two people. To do so, one needs to arrange the right conditions—and marriage is one of those right conditions.

Thus, Indian and U.S. cultures have produced different approaches to love and marriage. For Indians, marriage produces love—while for Americans, love produces marriage. Americans see love as having a mysterious element, a passion that "grabs" the individual. Indians see love as a peaceful feeling that develops when a man and a woman are united in intimacy and share common interests and goals in life.

Sources: Based on Cooley 1962; Gupta 1979; Weintraub 1988; Bumiller 1992; Sprecher and Chandak 1992; Whyte 1992.

---

ing bridge were more sexually aroused than the men on the solid bridge. More of these men also called the young woman afterward—supposedly to get more information about the study.

This research, of course, was really about sexual attraction, not love. The point, however, is that romantic love usually begins with sexual attraction. We find ourselves sexually attracted to someone and spend time with that person. If we discover mutual interests, we may eventually label our feelings "love." Apparently, then, romantic love has two components. The first is emotional, a feeling of sexual attraction. The second is cognitive, a label that we attach to our feelings. If we do attach this label, we describe ourselves as being "in love."

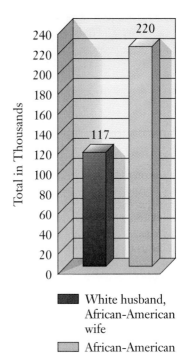

White husband, African-American wife

African-American husband, white wife

Source: *Statistical Abstract* 1997: Table 62.

Figure 16.2

The Racial Background of Husbands and Wives in Marriages Between Whites and African Americans

Marriage

In the typical case, marriage in the United States is preceded by "love," but contrary to folklore, whatever love is, it certainly is not blind. That is, love does not hit anyone willy-nilly, as if Cupid had shot darts blindly into a crowd. If it did, marital patterns would be unpredictable. An examination of who marries whom, however, reveals that love is socially channeled.

The Social Channels of Love and Marriage. When we marry, we generally think that we have freely chosen our spouse. With few exceptions, however, our choices follow highly predictable social channels, especially age, education, social class, race, and religion (Tucker and Mitchell-Kerman 1990; Kalmijn 1991). For example, a Latina with a college degree whose parents are both physicians is likely to fall in love and marry a Latino slightly older than herself who has graduated from college. Similarly, a female high school dropout whose parents are on welfare is likely to fall in love with and marry a male who comes from a background similar to hers.

Sociologists use the term **homogamy** to refer to the tendency of people with similar characteristics to marry one another. Homogamy occurs largely as a result of *propinquity*, or spatial nearness. That is, we tend to "fall in love" and marry people who live near us or whom we meet at school, church, or work. The people with whom we associate are far from a random sample of the population, for social filters produce neighborhoods, schools, and churches that follow racial–ethnic and social class lines.

As with all social patterns, there are exceptions. Although 94 percent of all Americans marry someone of their same race, this means that 6 percent do not. Since there are 55 million married couples in the United States, those 6 percent add up, totaling three million couples. As we saw in Figure 12.1 on page 312, many barriers blocking interracial marriages have dropped. To use just one example, during the past twenty-five years the number of married couples increased only 22 percent, but the number of marriages between African Americans and whites increased 500 percent—more than 20 times as fast. This total is still relatively small, however, representing just over ½ percent (337,000) of the 55 million U.S. married couples (*Statistical Abstract* 1997:Table 62). As shown on Figure 16.2, these marriages, in turn, have their own distinct pattern.

Childbirth

The popular image is that the arrival of a baby makes a couple deliriously happy. The facts are somewhat different.

Marital Satisfaction. A sociological finding that surprises many is that marital satisfaction usually *decreases* with the birth of a child (Whyte 1992; Bird 1997). To understand why, recall from Chapter 6 that a dyad (just two persons) provides greater intimacy than a triad (after adding a third person, interaction must be shared). To move from the theoretical to the practical, think about the implications of coping with a newborn—less free time (feeding, soothing, and diapering), less sleep, and heavier expenses.

Social Class. Sociologist Lillian Rubin (1976, 1992b) compared fifty working-class couples with twenty-five middle-class couples. She found that social class is a key to how couples adjust to the arrival of children. For the average working-class couple, the first baby arrived just nine months after marriage. They hardly had time to adjust to being husband and wife before they were thrust into the demanding roles of mother and father. The result was financial problems, bickering, and interference from in-laws. The young husbands weren't ready to "settle down" and resented getting less attention from their wives. A working-class husband who became a father just five months after getting married made a telling remark to Rubin when he said, "There I was, just a kid myself, and I finally had someone *to take care of me*. Then suddenly, I had to take care of a kid, and she was too busy with him *to take care of me*" (italics added).

In contrast, the middle-class couples postponed the birth of their first child, which gave them more time to adjust to each other. On average, their first baby arrived three

homogamy: the tendency of people with similar characteristics to marry one another years after marriage. Their greater financial resources also worked in their favor, making life a lot easier and marriage more pleasant.

Child Rearing

Who's minding the kids while the parents are at work? A while back such a question would have been ridiculous, for the mother was at home taking care of the children. As with Sharon in our opening vignette, however, that assumption no longer holds. With three of five U.S. mothers working for wages, who is taking care of the children?

Married Couples and Single Mothers.   Figure 16.3 compares the child care arrangements of married couples and single mothers. As you can see, their overall child care arrangements are similar. For each, about one-third of preschoolers is cared for in the child's home. The main difference is the role of the child's father while the mother is at

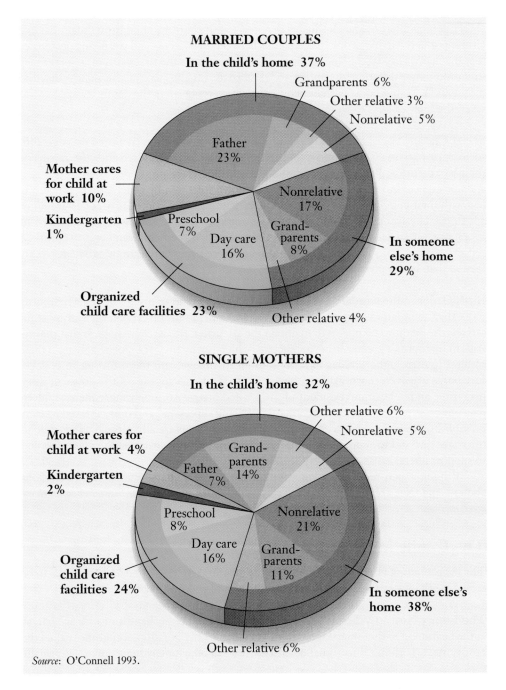

Figure 16.3

Who Takes Care of Preschoolers While their Mother Is at Work?

MARRIED COUPLES

In the child's home 37%
Grandparents 6%
Other relative 3%
Nonrelative 5%
Father 23%
Mother cares for child at work 10%
Kindergarten 1%
Preschool 7%
Day care 16%
Nonrelative 17%
Grandparents 8%
In someone else's home 29%
Organized child care facilities 23%
Other relative 4%

SINGLE MOTHERS

In the child's home 32%
Other relative 6%
Nonrelative 5%
Mother cares for child at work 4%
Kindergarten 2%
Father 7%
Grandparents 14%
Preschool 8%
Day care 16%
Nonrelative 21%
Grandparents 11%
Organized child care facilities 24%
In someone else's home 38%
Other relative 6%

Source: O'Connell 1993.

work. For married couples, almost one of four children is cared for by the father, while for single mothers such child care plummets to only one of fourteen. As you can see, grandparents step in to help fill the gap left by the absent father.

Day Care. As Figure 16.3 shows, about one of six children is in day care. The broad conclusions of research on day care were reported in Chapter 3 (page 77): High-quality day care helps children, low-quality harms them. It is difficult for parents to judge the quality of their day care, however, especially since they do not know what takes place when they are not there. Apparently only a minority of U.S. day care centers offer high-quality care as measured by safety, emotional warmth and support, and stimulating learning activities (Bergmann 1995). A primary reason for this dismal situation is the abysmal salaries paid day care workers, which average less than $10,000 a year (Casper and O'Connell 1997).

Nannies. For upper-middle-class parents, nannies have become popular. Part of their attraction is one-on-one care. Another is in-home care, which reduces the chances of a child catching illnesses and eliminates the need to transport the child to an unfamiliar environment. A recurring problem is tensions between the parents and the nanny: jealousies that the nanny may be the one to see the first step or hear the first word or is sometimes called mommy; different discipline styles; disdain on the part of the nanny that the mother isn't staying home with her child; the child crying when the nanny leaves, but not when the mother goes to work (Ansberry 1993).

Social Class. Social class is highly significant in child rearing. As noted on page 266, sociologist Melvin Kohn found that parents socialize their children into the norms of their work worlds. Because members of the working class are more closely supervised and are expected to follow explicit rules laid down for them by others, their concern is less with their children's motivation and more with outward conformity. They are more apt to use physical punishment. In contrast, middle-class parents, who are expected to take more initiative on the job, are more concerned that their children develop curiosity, self-expression, and self-control. They also are more likely to withdraw privileges or affection than to use physical punishment.

Birth Order. Birth order is also significant. Parents tend to discipline their firstborns more than their later children, and to give them more attention. When the second child arrives, the firstborn competes to maintain the attention. Researchers suggest that this instills in firstborns a greater drive for success, which is why they are more likely than their siblings to earn higher grades in school, to go to college, and to go further in college. Firstborns are even more likely to become astronauts, to appear on the cover of *Time* magazine, and to become president of the United States. Although subsequent children may not go as far, most are less anxious about being successful, and more relaxed in their relationships (Snow et al. 1981; Goleman 1985). Firstborns are also more likely to defend the status quo and to support conservative causes, later-borns to upset the apple cart and to support liberal causes (Sulloway 1997).

Although such tendencies are strong, they are only that—tendencies. Exceptions abound, and *there are no inevitable outcomes of birth order, social class, or any other social characteristic.*

The Family in Later Life

The later stages of family life bring their own pleasures to be savored and problems to be solved. Let's look at the empty nest, retirement, and widowhood.

The Empty Nest. When the last child leaves home, the husband and wife are left, as at the beginning of their marriage, "alone together." This situation, sometimes called the **empty nest,** is thought to signal a difficult time of adjustment for women—especially

empty nest: a married couple's domestic situation after the last child has left home

those who have not worked outside the home—because they have devoted so much energy to a child-rearing role that is now gone. Sociologist Lillian Rubin (1992a), who interviewed both career women and homemakers, found that this picture is largely a myth. Contrary to the stereotype, she found that women's satisfaction generally *increases* when the last child leaves home. A typical statement was made by a 45-year-old woman, who leaned forward in her chair as though to tell Rubin a secret:

> To tell you the truth, most of the time it's a big relief to be free of them, finally. I suppose that's awful to say. But you know what, most of the women I know feel the same way. It's just that they're uncomfortable saying it because there's all this talk about how sad mothers are supposed to be when the kids leave home.

Similar findings have come from other researchers, who report that most mothers feel relieved at finally being able to spend more time on themselves (Whyte 1992). Many couples also report a renewed sense of intimacy at this time (Mackey and O'Brien 1995). This closeness appears to stem from four causes: the couple is free of the many responsibilities of child rearing; they have more leisure; their income is at its highest; and they have fewer financial obligations.

The Not-So-Empty Nest.   An interesting twist on leaving home has taken place in recent years. With prolonged education and a growing cost of establishing households, U.S. children are leaving home later (Goldscheider and Goldscheider 1994). In addition, many who strike out on their own find the cost or responsibility too great and return to the home nest. As a result, 53 percent of all U.S. 18- to 24-year-olds live with their parents, and one of eight 25- to 34-year-olds is still living at home (*Statistical Abstract* 1997: Table 65).

Widowhood.   Women are more likely than men to face widowhood and its wrenching problems. Not only does the average wife live longer than her husband, but also she has married a man older than herself. The death of a spouse tears at the self, clawing at identities that had merged through the years (DiGiulio 1992). Now that the one who had become an essential part of the self is gone, the survivor, as in adolescence, is forced once again to wrestle with the perplexing question "Who am I?"

When death is unexpected, the adjustment is much more difficult (Hiltz 1989). Survivors who know that death is impending make preparations that smooth the transition—from arranging finances to psychologically preparing themselves for being alone. Saying goodbye and cultivating treasured last memories help them to adjust to the death of an intimate companion.

Diversity in U.S. Families ▶

It is important to note that there is no such thing as *the* American family. Rather, family life varies widely throughout the United States. The significance of social class, noted earlier, will continue to be evident as we examine diversity in U.S. families.

African-American Families

Note that the heading is African-American *families*, not *the* African-American family. There is no such thing as *the* African-American family any more than there is *the* white family or *the* Latino family. The primary distinction is not between African Americans and other groups, but among social classes. Because African Americans who are members of the upper class follow the class interests reviewed in Chapter 10—preservation of privilege and family fortune—they are especially concerned about the family background of those whom their children marry (Gatewood 1990). To them, marriage is viewed as a merger of family lines. Children of this class marry later than children of other classes.

There is no such thing as the African-American family, any more than there is the Native-American, Asian-American, Latino, or Irish-American family. Rather, each racial-ethnic group has many different types of families, with the primary determinant being social class.

This African-American family is observing Kwanzaa, a festival that celebrates their African heritage. Can you explain how Kwanzaa is an example of ethnic work, a concept introduced in Chapter 12?

Middle-class African-American families focus on achievement and respectability. Both husband and wife are likely to work outside the home. Their concerns are that the family stay intact and that their children go to college, get good jobs, and marry well—that is, marry people like themselves, respectable and hardworking, who want to get ahead in school and pursue a successful career.

African-American families in poverty face all the problems that cluster around poverty (Franklin 1994). Because the men are likely to have few skills and to be unemployed, it is difficult for them to fulfill the cultural roles of husband and father. Consequently, these families are likely to be headed by a woman and to have a high rate of unwed motherhood. Divorce and desertion are also more common than among other classes. Sharing scarce resources and stretching kinship are primary survival mechanisms. That is, people who have helped out in hard times are considered brothers, sisters, or cousins, to whom one owes obligations as though they were blood relatives (Stack 1974). Sociologists use the term *fictive kin* to refer to this stretching of kinship.

From Figure 16.4, you can see that, compared with whites and Latinos, African-American families are less likely to be headed by married couples and more likely to be headed by women. Because of a **marriage squeeze**—an imbalance in the sex ratio, in this instance fewer unmarried men per 100 unmarried women—African-American women are more likely than other racial groups to marry men who are less educated than themselves, who are unemployed, or who are divorced (South 1991).

Latino Families

As Figure 16.4 shows, the proportion of Latino families headed by married couples and women falls in between whites and African Americans. The effects of social class on families, which I just sketched, also apply to Latinos. In addition, families differ by country of origin. Families from Cuba, for example, are more likely to be headed by a married couple than are families from Puerto Rico (*Statistical Abstract* 1997:Table 53).

What really distinguishes Latino families, however, is culture—especially the Spanish language, the Roman Catholic religion, and a strong family orientation with a disapproval of divorce. Although there is some debate among the experts, another characteristic seems to be **machismo**—an emphasis on male strength and dominance. In Chicano families (those originating from Mexico), the husband-father plays a stronger role than in either white or African-American families (Vega 1990). Machismo apparently decreases

marriage squeeze: the difficulty a group of men or women have in finding marriage partners, due to an imbalanced sex ratio

machismo: an emphasis on male strength and dominance

Although there is no such thing as the Latino family, in general Latinos place high emphasis on extended family relationships.

with each generation in the United States (Hurtado et al. 1992). In general, however, the wife-mother makes most of the day-to-day decisions for the family and does the routine disciplining of the children. She is usually more family centered than her husband, displaying more warmth and affection for her children.

Generalizations have limits, of course, and as with other ethnic groups individual Latino families vary considerably from one another (Baca Zinn 1994; Carrasquillo 1994).

Asian-American Families

As you can see from Figure 16.4, the structure of Asian-American families is almost identical to that of white families. Apart from this broad characteristic, because Asian Americans come from twenty countries, their family life varies considerably, reflecting their many cultures. In addition, as with Latino families, the more recent the immigration, the closer that family life reflects the family life of the country of origin (Kibria 1993; Glenn 1994).

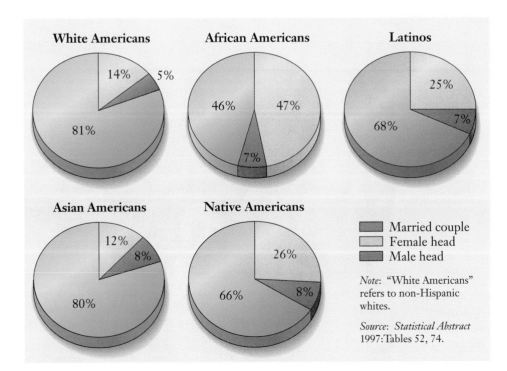

Figure 16.4

Family Structure: The Percentage of U.S. Households Headed by Men, Women, and Married Couples

Note: "White Americans" refers to non-Hispanic whites.

Source: Statistical Abstract 1997:Tables 52, 74.

Regardless of race and ethnicity, the more resources a family has, the more it tends to assume middle-class characteristics, including ideas, attitudes, and behavior. For example, the greater the resources, the more emphasis on educational achievement and deferred gratification. Shown here is a Vietnamese-American family that has made a successful adjustment to their new culture.

In spite of such differences, sociologist Bob Suzuki (1985), who studied Chinese-American and Japanese-American families, identified several distinctive characteristics. Although Asian Americans have adopted the nuclear family common in the United States, they have retained Confucian values that provide a distinct framework for family life: humanism, collectivity, self-discipline, hierarchy, respect for the elderly, moderation, and obligation. Obligation means that each individual owes respect to other family members and carries the responsibility never to bring shame on the family. Asian Americans tend to be more permissive than Anglos in child rearing and more likely to use shame and guilt rather than physical punishment to control their children's behavior.

Native-American Families

Perhaps the single most significant issue that Native-American families face is whether to follow traditional values or to assimilate (Yellowbird and Snipp 1994). This primary distinction makes for vast differences in families. The traditionals speak native languages and emphasize distinctive Native-American values and beliefs. Those that have assimilated into the broader culture do not.

To search for the Native-American family would be fruitless. There are rural, urban, single-parent, extended, nuclear, rich, poor, traditional, and assimilated Native-American families, to name just a few. Shown here is an Inupiat family in Kotzebue, Alaska.

Figure 16.4 depicts the structure of Native-American families. You can see how it is almost identical to that of Latinos. In general, Native-American parents are permissive with their children and avoid physical punishment. Elders play a much more active role in their children's families than is true of most U.S. families: they not only provide child care, but they teach and discipline children. Like others, Native-American families differ by social class.

▼ **In Sum** Social class and culture, not race, hold the keys to understanding family life. The more resources a family has, the more it assumes the middle-class characteristics of a nuclear family. Compared with the poor, middle-class families have fewer children, fewer unmarried mothers, and place greater emphasis on educational achievement and deferred gratification.

One-Parent Families

From TV talk shows to government officials, one-parent families have become a matter of general concern. The increase is no myth. Since 1970, the number of one-parent families has tripled, while the number of two-parent families has actually decreased by 250,000 (*Statistical Abstract* 1995:Table 71; 1997:Table 75). Two primary reasons underlie this change. The first is the high divorce rate, which each year forces a million children from two-parent homes to one-parent homes (*Statistical Abstract* 1997:Table 149). The second is a sharp increase in births to women who are not married. Overall, 33 percent of U.S. children are born to unmarried women, a 50 percent increase in just ten years (*Statistical Abstract* 1995:Table 94; 1997:Table 96).

The primary reason for the concern, however, may have less to do with children being reared by one parent than the fact that most one-parent families are poor. The poverty is not a coincidence. Most one-parent families are headed by women. Although 90 percent of children of divorce live with their mothers, most divorced women earn less than their former husbands. And most mothers who have never married have little education and few marketable skills, which condemns them to bouncing from one minimum-wage job to another, with welfare sandwiched in between.

To understand the typical one-parent family, then, we need to view it through the lens of poverty, for that is its primary source of strain. The results are serious, not just for these parents and their children, but for society as a whole. Children from single-parent families are more likely to drop out of school, to get arrested, to have emotional problems, and to get divorced (McLanahan and Sandefur 1994; Menaghan et al. 1997). If a female, they are more likely to bear a child while still a teenager and to bear children outside marriage. The cycle of poverty is so powerful that *nearly half* of all welfare recipients are current or former teenage parents (Corbett 1995).

Families Without Children

Overall, about 12 percent of U.S. married couples never have children (*Statistical Abstract* 1997:Table 105). The percentage, however, differs by education. As Figure 16.5 shows, the more education a woman has, the more likely she is to expect to bear no children. This figure shows that race/ethnicity is also significant. As you can see, Latinas are much less likely to remain childless than are white and African-American women.

Why do some couples choose not to have children? Sociologist Kathleen Gerson (1985) found that some women see their marriage as too fragile to withstand the strains a child would bring. Other women believe they would be stuck at home—bored and lonely and with diminishing career opportunities. Many couples see a child as too expensive. With trends firmly in place—more education and careers for women, technological advances in contraception, abortion, the high cost of rearing children—the proportion of women who never bear children is likely to increase.

Many childless couples, however, are not childless by choice. Some of them adopt, while a few turn to the solutions featured in the Sociology and New Technology box on the next page.

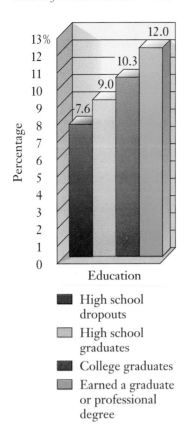

High school dropouts

High school graduates

College graduates

Earned a graduate or professional degree

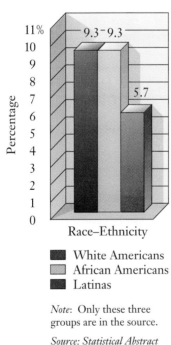

White Americans

African Americans

Latinas

Note: Only these three groups are in the source.

Source: Statistical Abstract 1997:Table 107.

Figure 16.5

What Percentage of U.S. Women Expect to Never Give Birth?

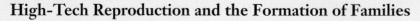

High-Tech Reproduction and the Formation of Families

Imagine a child being able to claim five people as parents: First, there's the woman who provided the egg. Second, there's the man who donated the sperm. Third, there's the woman who carried the child, *in utero*, and gave birth. Fourth and fifth are the man and woman who took the child home from the hospital to rear her or him (Rosenthal 1996).

Welcome to the brave—and very real—new world of high-tech reproduction. Although to date most children conceived with the aid of high-tech procedures claim only two parents, and a minority claim three, reproductive technologies—especially procedures such as in vitro fertilization (IVF)—make this scenario possible. IVF is a technique in which a woman's eggs are surgically removed from an ovary and placed in a laboratory dish along with the sperm. A fertilized egg is then inserted into the woman's uterus. The sperm can be anyone's, which complicates parentage.

The first successful in vitro fertilization (IVF) took place in 1978, when a woman in England gave birth to Louise, the world's first "test-tube baby." Well over 40,000 Americans have been born as a result of this process (Lee 1996). The vast majority of these children are the biological offspring of the same parents who rear them. In some instances, however, single women, lesbian and heterosexual, have purchased sperm from sperm banks; the resulting child does not know the identity of the biological father.

If a woman cannot produce viable eggs, *donor* eggs can be used; that is, her husband's sperm are mixed with eggs removed from a fertile woman—the donor (Lee 1996). The resulting embryo is implanted in the infertile woman's uterus. In this instance, the child is related biologically to the father who rears her or him, but not to the mother who does so.

In some instances of donor IVF a woman can produce viable eggs, but suffers from miscarriage and cannot carry a child to term. Her eggs are mixed with her husband's sperm, and the embryo is implanted in a surrogate, who agrees, usually for money, to carry it to term and then relinquish the baby. In this instance, the child is related biologically to the two parents who rear him or her, but not to the woman who gave birth to her or him.

For Your Consideration

The issues surrounding high-tech reproductive technologies are enough to make one's head swirl. These include:

- *Is it ethical for physicians and clinics to make a profit by buying and selling eggs and sperm?*
- *What about social class discrimination? Only better-off couples are able to afford the staggering costs of these infertility treatments. One attempt at donor IVF, for instance, costs between $14,000 and $20,000, while one attempt at regular in vitro fertilization runs about $8,000 (Lee 1996)*
- *Are egg and sperm donors victimized by a system that exploits their need for income?*
- *Are donors crassly selling life for profit?*
- *Should these techniques be covered by insurance or—as some critics suggest—would the money be better spent elsewhere, such as on the health of poor children?*
- *Are infertile couples being sold a false bill of goods, since the success rate for these expensive high-tech procedures is astonishingly low?*
- *Will the children born by these procedures suffer identity problems? Will they, like some adopted children, want to meet their biological parents?*

No, this is not a preschool, though it may look like one. These six children, all born within a few minutes of one another, have the same parents. One consequence of fertility drugs is multiple births. Shown here are the Dilley sextuplets of Indianapolis, Indiana: Ian, Adrian, Claire, Brenna, Quinn, and Julian.

Blended Families

An increasingly significant type of family formation found in the United States is the **blended family,** one whose members were once part of other families. Two divorced people who marry and each bring their children into a new family unit become a blended family. With divorce common, many children spend some of their childhood in blended families. One result is more complicated family relationships, exemplified by the following description written by one of my students:

> I live with my dad. I should say that I live with my dad, my brother (whose mother and father are also my mother and father), my half sister (whose father is my dad, but whose mother is my father's last wife), and two stepbrothers and stepsisters (children of my father's current wife). My father's wife (my current stepmother, not to be confused with his second wife who, I guess, is no longer my stepmother) is pregnant, and soon we all will have a new brother or sister. Or will it be a half brother or half sister?

> If you can't figure this out, I don't blame you. I have trouble myself. It gets very complicated around Christmas. Should we all stay together? Split up and go to several other homes? Who do we buy gifts for, anyway?

Gay Families

In 1989, Denmark was the first country to legalize marriage between people of the same sex. Since then, Holland, Norway, and Sweden have made same-sex marriages legal. In the United States, three gay couples appealed to the Hawaii Supreme Court that they were unconstitutionally deprived of marriage licenses. Fearful that the Court would rule in their favor, the Hawaii legislature proposed this amendment to the Hawaii Constitution: "The legislature shall have the power to reserve marriage to opposite-sex couples." The amendment, if affirmed by voters, will continue to make same-sex marriages illegal (Coolidge 1997). If not affirmed, a legal battle will ensue to determine if same-sex marriages performed in Hawaii must be recognized by the other states (Kirkpatrick 1996).

What are gay marriages like? As with everything else in life, same-sex couples cannot be painted with a single brush stroke (Allen and Demo 1995). As with opposite-sex couples, social class is highly significant, and orientations to life differ according to education, occupation, and income. Sociologists Blumstein and Schwartz (1985) interviewed same-sex couples and found their main struggles to be housework, money, careers, problems with relatives, and sexual adjustment—the same as heterosexual couples. Same-sex couples are much more likely to break up, however, probably because of a combination of higher levels of sexual infidelity and a lack of legal and broad social support.

With same-sex marriages now legal in several European countries, how long will it be until they are legal in the United States? Shown here are Ninia Baehr and Genora Dancel, who challenged Hawaii's right to limit marriage to opposite-sex couples.

blended family: a family whose members were once part of other families

Intentional Families

The segmented relationships of contemporary society make many of us feel emotionally aloof, disconnected from others. Many would like to find a solution to this problem—to enjoy long-term relationships and to feel closer to others. To overcome such problems of loneliness, some have started **intentional families.** The members, though not related by blood or marriage, declare themselves a family. They live separately, but near one another. They meet regularly and share experiences, which adds satisfaction to their lives. The first intentional family, formed in Providence, Rhode Island, has been together for twenty-five years (Graham 1996). While some might say that they are not a "real" family, they consider themselves a family. A sign of their family-like intimacy is evident when the eighteen members get together for their Sunday suppers—they walk into the house without knocking.

Trends in U.S. Families

As is apparent from this discussion, patterns of marriage and family life in the United States are undergoing a fundamental shift. Other indicators of this change include the postponement of marriage, cohabitation, single motherhood, divorce, and remarriage.

Postponing Marriage

intentional family: people who declare themselves a family and treat one another as members of the same family; originated in the late twentieth century in response to the need for intimacy not met due to distance, divorce, and death

Figure 16.6 illustrates one of the most significant trends in U.S. marriage. After declining for about eighty years, the average age of first-time brides and grooms turned sharply upward. In 1890 the typical first-time bride was 22, but by 1950 she had just left her teens. For twenty years, there was little change. Then about 1970 the average age at first marriage began to increase sharply. *Today the average first-time bride is considerably older than at any time in U.S. history.* The average age of first-time grooms is back to where it was in 1890.

Because postponing marriage is today's norm, it may come as a surprise to many readers to learn that *most* U.S. women used to marry before they turned 25. Look at Figure 16.7 on the next page . You can see that the proportion of younger Americans who have not married has soared. The percentage of unmarried women is now *double* what it was in 1970.

Figure 16.6

The Median Age at Which Americans Marry for the First Time

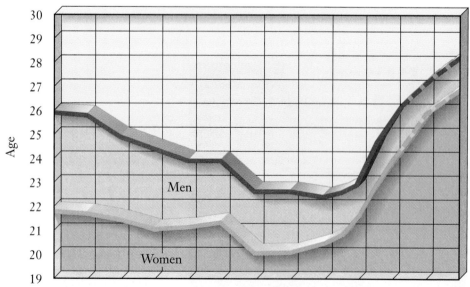

Source: *Statistical Abstract* 1997:Table 148, and earlier years.

Why did this change occur? As sociologist Larry Bumpass points out, if we were to count cohabitation, we would find that this average age has changed little (Bumpass et al. 1991). Although Americans have postponed the age at which they first marry, they have *not* postponed the age at which they first set up housekeeping with someone of the opposite sex. Let's look at this trend in cohabitation.

Cohabitation

Figure 16.8 shows the remarkable increase in **cohabitation,** adults living together in a sexual relationship without being married. *Eight times* more Americans are cohabiting today than twenty-five years ago. Cohabitation has become so common that about half of the couples who marry have cohabited (Bumpass 1995). With this change in behavior have come changed attitudes. For example, when hiring executives, some corporations now pay for live-in partners to attend orientation sessions.

Commitment is the essential difference between cohabitation and marriage. Whereas the assumption of marriage is permanence, cohabiting couples agree to remain together for "as long as it works out." Marriage requires public vows—and a judge to authorize its termination. Cohabitation requires only that a couple move in together; if the relationship sours, they can move out. Sociologists have found that couples who cohabit before marriage are more likely to divorce than couples who do not first cohabit (Bennett et al. 1988; Whyte 1992). The reason, they conclude, is that cohabiting couples have a weaker commitment to marriage and to relationships.

Unmarried Mothers

Earlier we discussed the increase in births to unmarried U.S. mothers. To better understand this trend, we can place it in global perspective. As Figure 16.9 on the next page shows, the United States is not alone in this increase. Of the ten industrialized nations for which we have data, all except Japan have experienced sharp increases in births to unmarried mothers. Far from the highest, the U.S. rate falls in the middle third of these nations.

From this figure, it seems fair to conclude that industrialization sets in motion social forces that encourage out-of-wedlock births. There are several problems with this conclusion, however. Why was the rate so low in 1960? Industrialization had been in process for many decades prior to that time. Why are the rates in the bottom four nations only a fraction of those in the top two nations? Why does Japan's rate remain so consistently low? Why are Sweden's and Denmark's so high? With but a couple of minor exceptions, the ranking of these nations in the 1990s is the same as 1960. By itself, then, industrialization is too simple an answer. A fuller explanation will have to focus on customs and values embedded within the particular cultures. For that answer, we will have to await further research.

The Sandwich Generation and Elder Care

The term "sandwich generation" refers to people who find themselves sandwiched between two generations, responsible for the care of their children and for their own aging parents. Typically between the ages of 40 and 55, these people find themselves pulled in two strongly compelling directions. Feeling responsible both for their children and their parents, they are plagued with guilt and anger because they can be in only one place at a time (Shellenbarger 1994a).

Concerns about elder care have gained the attention of the corporate world, and about 25 percent of large companies offer some kind of elder care assistance to their employees (Hewitt Associates 1995). This assistance includes seminars, referral services, and flexible work schedules in order to help employees meet their responsibilities without missing so much work (Shellenbarger 1994b). Some experts believe that companies may respond more positively to the issue of elder care than to child day care. Why? Most CEOs are older men whose wives stayed home to take care of their children, so they lack

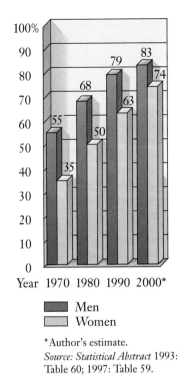

Year 1970 1980 1990 2000*

■ Men
□ Women

*Author's estimate.
Source: Statistical Abstract 1993: Table 60; 1997: Table 59.

Figure 16.7

Americans Ages 20–24 Who Have Never Married

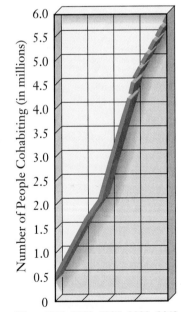

Year 1970 1980 1990 2000 2010

Note: Broken line indicates author's estimate.
Source: Statistical Abstract 1995: Table 60; 1997: Table 61.

Figure 16.8

Cohabitation in the United States

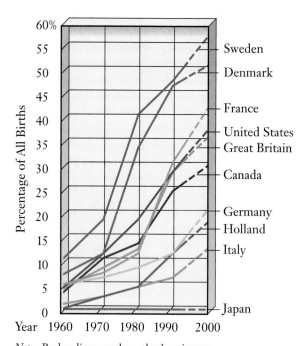

Note: Broken lines are the author's estimates.

Source: Statistical Abstract 1993: Table 1380; 1997: Table 1338.

Figure 16.9

Births to Unmarried Women in Ten Industrialized Nations

cohabitation: unmarried couples living together in a sexual relationship

Figure 16.10

The "Where" of U.S. Divorce

an understanding of the stresses of balancing work and child care. Nearly all have aging parents, however, and many have faced the turmoil of trying to cope with work, children, and aging parents.

Divorce and Remarriage

The topic of family life would not be complete without considering divorce. Let's first try to determine how much divorce there really is.

Problems in Measuring Divorce

You probably have heard that the U.S. divorce rate is 50 percent, a figure popular with reporters. The statistic is true in the sense that each year about half as many divorces are granted as marriages are performed. In 1997, for example, 2,389,000 U.S. couples married and 1,142,000 couples divorced ("Population Update" 1997).

With these statistics, what is wrong with saying that the divorce rate is 50 percent? The real question is why these two totals should be compared in the first place. The couples who divorced do not—with rare exceptions—come from the group who married that year. The one set of figures has nothing to do with the other, so these statistics in no way establish the divorce rate.

What figures should we compare, then? Couples who divorce are drawn from the entire group of married people in the country. Since the United States has 55,000,000 married couples, and only 1,142,000 of them obtained divorces in 1997, the divorce rate is 2.1 percent, not 50 percent (*Statistical Abstract* 1997:Table 59). A couple's chances of still being married at the end of a year are 98 percent—not bad odds—and certainly much better than the mass media would have us believe. As the Social Map below shows, however, the "odds," if we want to call them that, change depending on where you live.

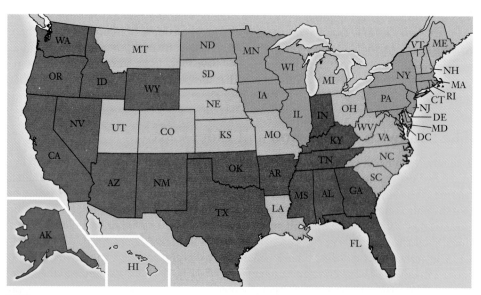

■ Higher than average (5.2 and more annual divorces per 1,000 population)
□ Average (4.0–5.1 annual divorces per 1,000 population)
■ Less than average (3.9 and fewer annual divorces per 1,000 population)

Source: Statistical Abstract 1996: Table 153.

TABLE 16.2					
Divorce Rates in Ten Industrialized Nations					
	1960	*1970*	*1980*	*1990*	*1992*
United States	10	15	23	21	21
Denmark	6	8	11	13	13
Canada	2	6	11	12	11
Great Britain	2	5	12	12	12
Sweden	5	7	11	12	12
Germany	4	5	6	8	7
France	3	3	6	8	9
Netherlands	2	3	8	8	9
Japan	4	4	5	5	6
Italy	1	1	1	2	2

Note: Strangely, the source gives data only per 1,000 women. The last reporting year is inconsistent.

Source: Statistical Abstract 1992:Table 1364; 1996:Table 1329.

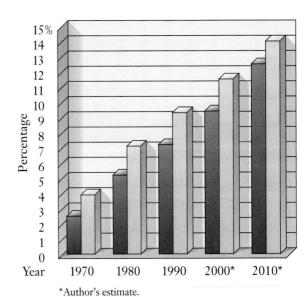

*Author's estimate.

Note: Refers to Americans age 18 and over.

Source: Statistical Abstract 1995: Table 58; 1997: Table 58.

Figure 16.11

What Percentage of Americans are Divorced?

Over time, of course, those annual 2.1 percentages add up. A third way of measuring divorce, then, is to ask, "Of all U.S. adults, what percentage are divorced?" Figure 16.11 shows the increase. Again, a cross-cultural comparison helps to place U.S. statistics in perspective—but the news is not good. As Table 16.2 illustrates, the United States has— by far—the highest divorce rate in the industrialized world. If current trends persist, it is likely that half or even more of all U.S. marriages will end in divorce (Milbank 1996).

While this may occur, Table 16.2 also shows that the U.S. divorce rate has actually declined since peaking around 1980. The Down-to-Earth Sociology box reports some "curious" findings about divorce, while factors that make marriage successful are summarized at the end of this chapter.

Children of Divorce

Each year, over 1 million U.S. children discover that their parents are divorcing (*Statistical Abstract* 1997:Table 149). Most divorcing parents become so wrapped up in their own problems that they are unable to prepare their children for the divorce—even if they knew how to do so in the first place. When the break comes, children become confused

Down-to-Earth Sociology

You Be the Sociologist: Curious Divorce Patterns

Sociologists Alex Heckert, Thomas Nowak, and Kay Snyder (1995) did secondary analysis (see page 130) of data gathered on a nationally representative sample of 5,000 U.S. households. Here are three of their findings:

1. If a wife earns more than her husband, the likelihood of divorce increases; if a husband earns more than his wife, divorce is less likely.

2. If the wife's health is poorer than her husband's, the marriage is more likely to break up; if the husband's health is poorer than his wife's, divorce is less likely.

3. The more housework a wife does, the less likely a couple is to divorce.

You be the sociologist. Can you explain these findings? Please develop your own explanations before looking at the box on the next page.

(continued)

Down-to-Earth Sociology

(Continued)

Heckert, Nowak, and Snyder suggest these explanations:

1. A wife who earns more than her husband has more alternatives to an unsatisfying marriage; a wife who earns less is more dependent.

2. Social pressure is greater for a wife to take care of a husband in poor health than it is for a husband to take care of a wife in poor health.

3. Who does the most housework is an indication of a husband's and wife's relative bargaining power. Wives with the most bargaining power are the least likely to put up with unsatisfying marriages.

and insecure. For security, many cling to the unrealistic idea that their parents will be reunited (Wallerstein and Kelly 1992). To help resolve the conflict, they may side with one parent and reject the other. Compared with children whose parents have not divorced, these children also have more hostility, anxiety, and nightmares, and don't do as well in school (Guidubaldi et al. 1987). As sociologist Sara McLanahan puts it, "On balance, the average child does worse, not better, after a divorce" (Krattenmaker 1994.)

The effects of divorce follow people into adulthood. For example, compared with adults who grew up in intact families, grown-up children of divorced parents are less likely to have contact with either their father or their mother (Webster and Herzog 1995). A study of college students at McGill University showed that those whose mothers did not remarry, who remarried and then divorced again, or who interfered with the child's relationship with their father had the most problems. Those whose mothers entered a single, stable relationship after the divorce had the best adjustment—including a better ability to build an intimate relationship (Bolgar et al. 1995). For a controversial solution to this problem of children of divorce, see the Social Issues box on the next page.

Researchers have identified several factors that help children adjust to divorce. Adjustment is better if (1) both parents show understanding and affection; (2) the child lives with a parent who is making a good adjustment; (3) family routines are consistent; (4) the family has adequate money for its needs; and (5) at least according to preliminary stud-

It is difficult to capture the anguish of the children of divorce, but when I read these lines by the fourth-grader who drew these two pictures, my heart was touched:

Me alone in the park . . .
All alone in the park.
My Dad and Mom are divorced
that's why I'm all alone.

This is me in the picture with my son.
We are taking a walk in the park.
I will never be like my father.
I will never divorce my wife and kid.

Liberal and Conservative Views on Social Issues

Shall We Tighten the Ties That Bind? Rolling Back No-Fault Divorce

Not divorce, but the children of divorce, are what bothers people. Children are hurt by divorce, and apparently they are not as well adjusted as children from intact families. The solution proposed by some is to make it more difficult to get divorced. Following this reasoning, in 1997 the Louisiana legislature passed a law that created "covenant marriages." In these marriages, marital vows are intended to be taken more seriously and can be broken only because of extreme circumstances.

Conservatives applaud covenant marriages, saying that they are a step in the right direction. The disintegration of the family, they point out, is at the root of what ails our society: crime, violence, even poor national test scores. To have children is an extreme commitment, a pledge to remain together as husband/wife, mother/father, in order to nurture those children. Our children deserve the fulfillment of that commitment. Personal goals, other relationships,

even personal happiness, need to be put aside for the welfare of the children. Although it is unrealistic to expect everyone to follow through on their commitment as parents, covenant marriage at least makes it more difficult to obtain a divorce.

Liberals are shocked at covenant marriage. They view it as a step backward, toward a time when women were shackled to their husbands. They see it as another way to reduce women's choices, to bind them to the home. Abuse and betrayal aren't the only signs of a bad marriage, they say, and people—men as well as women—need to have the right to leave bad marriages. If someone is unhappy, he or she should be able to seek happiness elsewhere. The children of divorce do okay. The studies are flawed. The children of divorce should not be compared with children from intact families but, rather, with children whose parents have dreadful marriages, for those are the homes from which they come.

ies, the child lives with the parent of the same sex (Lamb 1977; Clingempeel and Reppucci 1982; Peterson and Zill 1986; Wallerstein and Kelly 1992). Sociologist Urie Bronfenbrenner (1992a) reports that children adjust better if there is a second adult who can be counted on for support. This person makes the third leg of a stool, giving stability to the smaller family unit. Any adult can be the third leg, he says—a relative, friend, mother-in-law, or even co-worker—but the most powerful stabilizing third leg is the father, the ex-husband.

The Absent Father and Serial Fatherhood

With mothers given custody of the children about 86 percent of the time, a new fathering pattern has emerged. In this pattern, known as **serial fatherhood**, divorced fathers tend to maintain high contact with their children during the first year or two after the divorce. As the men develop a relationship with another woman, they begin to play a fathering role with the woman's children and reduce contact with their own children. With another breakup, this pattern may repeat. Only about one-sixth of children who live apart from their fathers see their dad as often as every week, and most divorced fathers stop seeing their children altogether (Ahlburg and De Vita 1992; Furstenberg and Harris 1992; Seltzer 1994). Apparently, for many men fatherhood has become a short-term commitment.

The Ex-Spouses

Anger, depression, and anxiety are common feelings at divorce. But so is relief. Women are more likely than men to feel that the divorce is giving them a "new chance" in life. A few couples manage to remain friends through it all—but they are the exception. The spouse who initiates the divorce usually gets over it sooner (Stark 1989; Kelly 1992).

Divorce does not necessarily mean the end of a couple's relationship. Some divorced couples maintain contact because of their children. For others, the "continuities," as sociologists call them, represent lingering attachments (Vaughan 1985; Masheter 1991). The former husband may help his former wife hang a picture and move furniture, for ex-

serial fatherhood: a pattern of parenting in which a father, after divorce, reduces contact with his own children, serves as a father to the children of the woman he marries or lives with, then ignores them after moving in with or marrying another woman; this pattern repeats

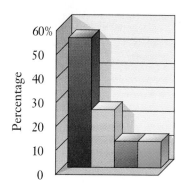

■ First marriage of bride and groom

□ Remarriage of bride and groom

▨ First marriage of bride, remarriage of groom

▧ First marriage of groom, remarriage of bride

Source: Statistical Abstract 1997: Table 146.

Figure 16.12

The Marital History of U.S. Brides and Grooms

ample, or she may invite him over for a meal. Some couples even continue to make love after their divorce.

After divorce, a couple's cost of living increases—two homes, two utility bills, and so forth. But the financial impact is very different for men and for women. Divorce often spells economic hardships for women, especially mothers of small children, whose standard of living drops about 37 percent (Seltzer 1994). In contrast, the former husband's standard of living is likely to increase (Weitzman 1985). The higher a woman's education, the better prepared she is to survive financially after the divorce (Dixon and Rettig 1994).

Remarriage

Despite the number of people who emerge from the divorce court swearing "Never again!" most do. But they aren't remarrying as quickly as they used to. In the 1960s, the average woman remarried in about two years. Today she waits a little over five years (*Statistical Abstract* 1997:Table 150). Comparable data are not available for men.

As Figure 16.12 shows, most divorced people remarry other divorced people. You may be surprised that the women most likely to remarry are young mothers and those who have not graduated from high school (Glick and Lin 1986). Apparently women who are more educated and more independent (no children) can afford to be more selective. Men are more likely than women to remarry, perhaps because they have a larger pool of potential mates from which to select.

How do remarriages work out? The divorce rate of remarried people *without* children is the same as that of first marriages. Those who bring children into a new marriage, however, are more likely to divorce again. To understand why, we need further research on the dynamics of remarriages (MacDonald and DeMaris 1995). As sociologist Andrew Cherlin (1989) notes, we have not developed adequate norms for remarriages. For example, we lack satisfactory names for stepmothers, stepfathers, stepbrothers, stepsisters, stepaunts, stepuncles, stepcousins, and stepgrandparents. At the very least, these are awkward terms to use, but they also represent ill-defined relationships.

► Two Sides of Family Life

Let's first look at situations in which marriage and family have gone seriously wrong and then try to answer the question of what makes marriage work.

The Dark Side of Family Life: Child Abuse, Battering, Marital Rape, and Incest

The dark side of family life involves events that people would rather keep in the dark. We shall look at child abuse, battering, rape, and incest.

Child Abuse

> My wife and I answered an ad about a house for sale by owner. As the woman showed us through the house—immaculate, in a middle-class neighborhood—we were surprised to see a plywood box in the youngest child's bedroom. About three feet high, 3 feet wide, and 6 feet long, the box was perforated with holes and had a little door with a padlock. Curious, I asked what it was. The woman matter-of-factly replied that her son had a behavior problem, and this is where they locked him for "time out." She added that other times they would tie him to a float, attach a line to the dock, and put him in the lake.
>
> We left as soon as we could. With thoughts of a terrorized child, I called the state child abuse hotline.

As you can tell, what I saw upset me. Most of us are bothered by child abuse—helpless children being victimized by their own parents, the adults who are supposed to love, protect, and nurture them. The most gruesome of these cases make the evening news, but most are "routine." The 4-year-old girl who was beaten and raped by her mother's boyfriend, passed into a coma, and then three days later passed out of this life—events like these make the news. A few days before this actual event in my area, the news reported on the 6- to 10-year-old children who had been videotaped in sex acts by their stepfather. Unlike these instances, however, few child abuse cases come to our attention—the children who live in filth, are neglected, are left alone for hours or even days at a time, or are beaten with extension cords. Nor do cases like the little boy I learned about on my house-hunting expedition.

We do know, however, that child abuse is extensive. Each year, about 3 million U.S. children are reported to the authorities as victims of abuse or neglect. About 1 million of these cases are substantiated (*Statistical Abstract* 1997:Table 353).

Battering.　To determine the amount and types of violence in U.S. homes, sociologists have interviewed nationally representative samples of U.S. couples (Straus 1980; Straus, Gelles, and Steinmetz 1980; Straus and Gelles 1988; Straus 1992). Although not all sociologists agree (Dobash et al. 1992, 1993; Pagelow 1992), Murray Straus concludes that husbands and wives are about equally likely to attack one another. When it comes to the effects of violence, however, gender equality vanishes (Gelles 1980; Straus 1980, 1992). As Straus points out, even though *she* may throw the coffeepot first, it is generally *he* who lands the last and most damaging blow. Consequently, many more wives than husbands seek medical attention because of marital violence. A good part of the reason, of course, is that most husbands are bigger and stronger than their wives, putting women at a disadvantage in this literal battle of the sexes.

Violence against women is related to the sexist structure of society, which we reviewed in Chapter 11, and to the socialization we reviewed in Chapter 3. Growing up with norms that encourage aggression and the use of violence, many men feel it is their right to control women. When frustrated in a relationship—or even by causes outside it—many men turn violently on their wives and lovers. The basic sociological question is how to socialize males to handle frustration and disagreements without resorting to violence (Rieker et al. 1997). We do not yet have this answer.

Marital Rape.　Sociologists have found that marital rape is more common than is usually supposed. For example, between one-third and one-half of women who seek help at shelters for battered women are victims of marital rape (Bergen 1996). But these are a special group of women in the first place, not representative of U.S. women. To get a better answer, sociologist Diana Russell (1990) used a sampling technique that allows generalization. She found that 14 percent of married women report that their husbands have raped them. Similarly, 10 percent of a representative sample of Boston women interviewed by sociologists David Finkelhor and Kersti Yllo (1985, 1989) reported that their husbands had used physical force to compel them to have sex.

Finkelhor's and Yllo's in-depth interviews with fifty victims showed that marital rape most commonly occurs during separation or during the breakup of a marriage. They found three types of marital rape.

- *Nonbattering rape* (40 percent). The husband forces his wife to have sex, with no intent to hurt her physically. These instances generally involve conflict over sex, such as the husband feeling insulted when his wife refuses to have sex.

- *Battering rape* (48 percent). In addition to sexually assaulting his wife, the husband intentionally inflicts physical pain to retaliate for some supposed wrongdoing on her part.

- *Perverted rape* (6 percent). These husbands, apparently sexually aroused by the violent elements of rape, force their wives to submit to unusual sexual acts. Anger and hostility can also motivate this type of rape. (The remaining 6 percent are mixed, containing elements of more than one type.)

Incest.   Sexual relations between relatives, such as brothers and sisters or parents and children, called **incest,** are most likely to occur in families that are socially isolated (Smith 1992). As with marital rape, sociological research has destroyed assumptions that incest is not common. Sociologist Diana Russell (n.d.) found that incest victims who experience the most difficulty are those who have been victimized the most often, over longer periods of time, and whose incest was "more intrusive," for example, sexual intercourse as opposed to sexual touching.

Who are the offenders? Russell found that uncles are the most common offenders, followed by first cousins, then fathers (stepfathers especially), brothers, and, finally, relatives ranging from brothers-in-law to stepgrandfathers. Other researchers report that brother–sister incest is several times more common than father–child incest (Canavan et al. 1992). Incest between mothers and sons is rare.

The Bright Side of Family Life: Successful Marriages

Successful Marriages.   After examining divorce and family abuse, one could easily conclude that marriages seldom work out. That would be far from the truth, however, for about two of every three married Americans report that they are "very happy" with their marriages (Cherlin and Furstenberg 1988; Whyte 1992). To find out what makes marriage successful, sociologists Jeanette and Robert Lauer (1992) interviewed 351 couples who had been married fifteen years or longer. Fifty-one of these marriages were unhappy but the couple stayed together for religious reasons, family tradition, or "for the sake of the children." Of the others, the 300 happy couples, all:

1. Think of their spouse as their best friend
2. Like their spouse as a person
3. Think of marriage as a long-term commitment
4. Believe that marriage is sacred
5. Agree with their spouse on aims and goals
6. Believe that their spouse has grown more interesting over the years
7. Strongly want the relationship to succeed
8. Laugh together

Sociologist Nicholas Stinnett (1992) used interviews and questionnaires to study 660 families from all regions of the United States and parts of South America. He found that happy families:

1. Spend a lot of time together
2. Are quick to express appreciation
3. Are committed to promoting one another's welfare
4. Do a lot of talking and listening to one another
5. Are religious
6. Deal with crises in a positive manner

Symbolic Interactionism and the Misuse of Statistics.   Many of my students express concerns about their own marital future, a wariness born out of the divorce of their parents, friends, neighbors, relatives—even pastors and rabbis. They wonder what chance they really have. Since sociology is not just an abstract discipline, but is really about our lives, it seems valuable in this context to stress that we are individuals, not statistics. That is, if the divorce rate were 33 percent or 50 percent, this does *not* mean that if we marry our chances of getting divorced are 33 percent or 50 percent. This is a misuse of statis-

incest: sexual relations between specified relatives, such as brothers and sisters or parents and children

tics, and a very common one at that. Divorce statistics represent all marriages, and have absolutely *nothing* to do with any individual marriage. Our own chances depend on our own situation—especially the way we approach marriage.

To make this point clearer, let's apply symbolic interactionism. From a symbolic interactionist perspective, we create our own worlds. That is, experiences don't come with built-in meanings. Rather, we interpret our experiences, and act accordingly. Simply put, if we think of marriage as likely to fail, we increase the likelihood that it will fail; if we think that our marriage will work out well, the chances of a good marriage increase. In other words, we tend to act according to our ideas, creating a sort of self-fulfilling prophecy. The folk saying "There are no guarantees in life" is certainly true, but it does help to have a *vision* that a good marriage is possible and that it is worth achieving.

The Future of Marriage and Family

What can we expect of marriage and family in the future? In spite of its many problems, marriage is in no danger of becoming a relic of the past. Marriage is so functional that it exists in every society. Consequently, the vast majority of Americans will continue to find marriage vital to their welfare.

Certain trends are firmly in place. Cohabitation, births to single women, and age at first marriage will increase. More married women will join the work force, and they will continue to gain marital power. Equality in marriage, however, is not even on the horizon. The number of elderly will continue to increase, and more couples will find themselves sandwiched between caring for their parents and their own children. The reduction in our divorce rate is another matter entirely. At this point we don't know if it is just a breather, from which an even higher rate will be launched, the prelude to a long-term decline, or even an indication that we have reached the saturation point and divorce will remain flat.

Finally, our culture will continue to be haunted by distorted images of marriage and family: the bleak ones portrayed in the mass media and the rosy ones painted by cultural myths. Sociological research can help correct these distortions and allow us to see how our own family experiences fit into the patterns of our culture. Sociological research also can help to answer the big question of how to formulate social policy that will support and enhance family life.

Summary and Review

Marriage and Family in Global Perspective

What is a family—and what themes are universal?

Family is difficult to define. For just about every element one might consider essential, there are exceptions. Consequently, **family** is defined broadly—as two or more people who consider themselves related by blood, marriage, or adoption. Sociologists and anthropologists have documented extensive variation in family customs—from cultures in which babies are married to those in which husbands and wives refrain from sexual relations for years at a time. Universally, **marriage** and family are mechanisms for governing mate selection, reckoning descent, and establishing inheritance and authority. Pp. 430–433.

Marriage and Family in Theoretical Perspective

What is the functionalist perspective on marriage and family?

Functionalists examine the functions of families, analyzing such matters as the incest taboo. They also examine consequences of weakening family functions, and the dysfunctions of the family. Pp. 433–435.

What is the conflict perspective on marriage and family?

Conflict theorists examine how marriage and family help perpetuate inequalities, especially the subservice of women. Power struggles in marriage, such as those over housework, are an example. Pp. 435–437.

What is a symbolic interactionist perspective on marriage and family?

Symbolic interactionists examine how the contrasting experiences and perspectives of men and women are played out in marriage. They stress that only by grasping the perspectives of wives and husbands can we understand their behavior. P. 437–438.

The Family Life Cycle

What are the major elements of the family life cycle?

The major elements are love and courtship, marriage, childbirth, child rearing, and the family in later life. Most marriages follow predictable patterns of age, social class, race, and religion. Childbirth and child-rearing patterns also vary by social class. Pp. 438–443.

Diversity in U.S. Families

How significant are race and ethnicity in family life?

The primary distinction is social class, not race or ethnicity. Families of the same social class are likely to be similar, regardless of their racial or ethnic makeup. Pp. 443–447.

What other diversity in U.S. families is there?

Also discussed were one-parent, childless, **blended,** and gay families. Although each has its own unique characteristics, social class is also significant in determining their primary characteristics. Poverty is especially significant for one-parent families, most of which are headed by women. Pp. 447–450.

Trends in U.S. Families

What major changes characterize U.S. families?

Two changes are postponement of first marriage and an increase in **cohabitation**. With more people living longer, many middle-aged couples find themselves sandwiched between caring for their own children and their own parents. Pp. 450–452.

Divorce and Remarriage

What is the current divorce rate?

Depending on what figures you choose to compare, you can produce almost any rate you wish, from 75 percent to just 2.2 percent. However you figure it, the U.S. divorce rate is higher than any other industrialized nation. P. 452–453.

How do children and their parents adjust to divorce?

Divorce is especially difficult for children, whose adjustment problems often continue into adulthood. Most divorced fathers do not maintain ongoing relationships with their children. Financial problems are usually greater for the former wives. Although most divorced people remarry, their rate of remarriage has slowed considerably. Pp. 453–456.

Two Sides of Family Life

What are the two sides of family life?

The dark side is family abuse—child abuse, spouse battering, marital rape, and incest, activities that revolve around the misuse of family power. The bright side is families that provide intense satisfaction for spouses and their children. Pp. 456–459.

The Future of Marriage and Family

What is the likely future of marriage and family?

We can expect cohabitation, births to unmarried mothers, and age at marriage to increase. The growing numbers of women in the work force will likely continue to shift the marital balance of power. P. 459

Where can I read more on this topic?

Suggested readings for this chapter are listed on page 665.

Sociology and the Internet

All URLs listed are current as of the printing of this book. URLs are often changed. Please check our Website http://www.abacon.com/henslin for updates.

1. As you have read in this chapter, every society has needs that are met with some kind of family arrangement. These common cultural themes have been addressed in a variety of ways by societies throughout the world. Anthropologists have studied hundreds of societies and have created concepts to refer to various kinship patterns. You have been introduced to a number of terms, such as polygyny, exogamy, and matrilineal. Now explore the fascinating world of kinship patterns by working through a brief Internet tutorial, "Principles of Kinship." Access the site at *http://www.umanitoba.ca/anthropology/tutor/* You should see a list of topics, beginning with "Kin Fundamentals." Select this and hit "Continue" on the bottom of each page until you reach the page, "Kinship Diagrams"; then select "Main Menu." Next, select two topics under "Systems of Descent." Go through all six areas, including the subtopics under 4, "Marriage Systems." Then look at the two ethnographic examples listed under 6: "A Turkish Peasant Village" and "Ancient Hebrews."

Write an essay describing the kinship systems in the Turkish village and among the Hebrews. Then, analyze the U.S.

system. Be sure to apply what you learned in the tutorial based on your own experience.

2. You have been reading about various forms of abuse found in families. Suppose a friend came to you asking for help concerning child abuse. You could find local sources of help by making a phone call or two, but you want a broader perspective. So you turn to your computer. Search the Internet using Lycos *http://www.lycos.com* Enter the search terms "child abuse" (without the quotation marks) and select "Go get it." Browse and follow any promising links. After looking at the pertinent sites on the Lycos results page, select "next page" at the bottom of the screen.

When you finish researching the topic, write a paper to provide useful information for your friend. Explain the information in terms your friend can understand.

3. Heading toward the twenty-first century, our definition of the family is changing. One recent consideration is the inclusion of same-sex couples in the definition. For someone who is in a committed same-sex relationship and wants to form a socially and legally recognized union, how could he or she go about it? Are same-sex marriages legal? What rights do they have? To help answer these questions, go to *http:www.cs.cmu. edu/afs/cs.cmu.edu/user/scotts/domestic-partners/mainpage.html*

Also use this site to help answer: What is a family? How has the definition of family changed? What is a couple? What is a domestic partner? What are domestic partner benefits? What was the outcome of the *Baehr* vs. *Lewin* case? (see *Baehr* v. *Lewin*: Will Equal Protection Lead to the End of Prohibitions on Same-Sex Marriages.) Can same-sex partners legally marry in any state? Based on the information you have read in your text and at the Web site, do you think same-sex marriages will be legalized in the near future? Why or why not?

4. Your author discusses the dark side of family life. The Internet provides support groups for those who have suffered from family abuse. The Healing Club at *http://www.healing-club.com/* is such a site. Go to this site, and read some of the postings by abused individuals. What are some of the life events that these individuals report? What are some of the effects of the violence they have experienced? What role do groups such as the Healing Club play? What kind of help does this club offer to its members? According to some of the stories you read at this site, what do you feel needs to be done in order to prevent and end family violence?

Jacob Lawrence, The Library, 1960

17

Education:
Transferring Knowledge and Skills

WENDY STILL FEELS RESENTMENT WHEN *she recalls the memo that greeted her that Monday morning:*

With growing concern about international competition for our products, the management is upgrading several positions. The attached listing of jobs states the new qualifications that must be met.

Wendy quickly scanned the list. The rumors had been right, after all. The new position the company was opening up—the job she had been slated to get—was listed.

After regaining her composure somewhat, but still angry, Wendy marched to her supervisor's office. "I've been doing my job for three years," she said. "You always gave me good evaluations, and you said I'd get that new position."

"I know, Wendy. You'd be good at it. Believe me, I gave you a high recommendation. But what can I do? You know what the higher-ups are like. If they decide they want someone with a college degree, that's just what they'll get."

"But I can't go back to college now, not with all my responsibilities. It's been five years since I was in college, and I still have a year to go."

The supervisor was sympathetic, but she insisted that her hands were tied. Wendy would have to continue working at the lower job classification—and stay at the lower pay.

It was Wendy's responsibility to break in Melissa, the newcomer with the freshly minted college degree. Those were the toughest two weeks Wendy ever spent at work—especially since she knew that Melissa was already being paid more than she was.

Today's Credential Society

Sociologist Randall Collins (1979) observed that industrialized nations have become **credential societies,** that employers use diplomas and degrees to determine who is eligible for a job. In many cases the diploma or degree is irrelevant for the work that must be performed. The new job that Wendy wanted, for example, did not suddenly change into a task requiring a college degree. Her immediate supervisor knew Wendy's abilities well and was sure she could handle the responsibility just fine—but the new company policy required a credential that Wendy didn't have. Similarly, is a high school diploma necessary to pump gas or to sell shoes? Yet employers routinely require such credentials.

In fact, it is often on the job, not at school, that employees learn the specific knowledge or skills that a job requires. A high school diploma teaches no one how to sell tacos or to be polite to customers. Wendy had to teach Melissa the ropes. Why, then, do employers insist on diplomas and degrees? Why don't they simply use on-the-job training?

A major reason credentials are required is the larger size, urbanization, and consequent anonymity of industrial societies. Diplomas and degrees serve as automatic sorting devices. Because employers don't know potential workers personally or even by reputation, they depend on schools to weed out the capable from the incapable. By hiring college graduates, the employer assumes that the individuals are responsible people; for evidently they have shown up on time for numerous classes, have turned in scores of assignments, and have demonstrated basic writing and thinking skills. The specific job skills that a position requires can then be grafted onto this base certified by the college.

In other cases, specific job skills must be mastered before an individual is allowed to do certain work. As a result of change in technology and in knowledge, simple on-the-job training will not do for physicians, engineers, and airline pilots. That is precisely why doctors so prominently display their credentials. Their framed degrees declare that they have been certified by an institution of higher learning, that they are qualified to work on our bodies.

credential society: the use of diplomas and degrees to determine who is eligible for jobs, even though the diploma or degree may be irrelevant to the actual work

Without the right credentials, you won't get hired. It does not matter that you can do the job better than someone else. You will never have the opportunity to prove what you can do, for, like Wendy, you lack the credentials even to be considered for the job.

The Development of Modern Education

Credentialing is only one indicator of how central the educational institution is in our lives. Before exploring the role of education in contemporary society, let us first look at education in earlier societies, and then trace the development of universal education.

Education in Earlier Societies

In earlier societies there was no separate social institution called education. There were no special buildings called schools, and no people who earned their living as teachers. Rather, as an integral part of growing up children learned what was necessary to get along in life. If hunting or cooking were the essential skills, then people who already possessed those skills taught them. *Education was synonymous with* **acculturation,** the transmission of culture from one generation to the next—as it still is in today's preliterate groups.

In some societies, when a sufficient surplus developed—as in Arabia, China, North Africa, and classical Greece—a separate institution developed. Some people then devoted themselves to teaching, while those who had the leisure—the children of the wealthy— became their students. In ancient China, for example, Confucius taught a few select pupils, while in Greece, Aristotle, Plato, and Socrates taught science and philosophy to upper-class boys. **Education,** then, came to be something quite distinct from informal acculturation; education is a group's *formal* system of teaching knowledge, values, and skills. Such instruction stood in marked contrast to the learning of traditional skills such as farming or hunting, for it was clearly intended to develop the mind.

The flourishing of education during the period roughly marked by the birth of Christ, however, slowly died out. During the Dark Ages of Europe, the candle of enlightenment was kept burning by monks, who, except for a handful of the wealthy and nobility, were the only ones who could read and write. Although they delved into philosophy, the intellectual activities of the monks centered on learning Greek, Latin, and Hebrew so that they could read early texts of the Bible and writings of the church fathers. Similarly, Jews kept formal learning alive as they studied the Torah.

acculturation: the transmission of culture from one generation to the next

education: a formal system of teaching knowledge, values, and skills

In hunting and gathering societies, there is no separate social institution called education. *As with this 4-year-old Kalahari boy in South Africa, children learn their adult economic roles from their parents and other kin.*

One of the first great educators was Socrates, depicted here in a 1787 painting by Jacques Louis David. Education can be a dangerous thing, for it often challenges conventional beliefs. Socrates, who taught in Greece 400 years before the birth of Christ, was forced to take poison because his views challenged those of the establishment.

Formal education, however, remained limited to those who had the leisure to pursue it. (In fact *school* comes from the Greek word σχωλή *[scholē]* meaning "leisure.") Industrialization transformed this approach to learning, for the new machinery and new types of jobs brought a general need to be able to read, to write, and to work accurately with figures—the classic three R's of the nineteenth century (Reading, 'Riting, and 'Rithmetic).

Democracy, Industrialization, and Universal Education

The development of universal education is linked to industrialization. Let's see how the United States pioneered free, universal education.

In the years following the American Revolution, the founders of the new republic felt that formal education should be the principal mechanism for creating a uniform national culture out of its many nationalities and religions. Thomas Jefferson and Noah Webster proposed a universal system of schooling based on standardized texts that would instill patriotism and teach the principles of republican government (Hellinger and Judd 1991). They reasoned that if the American political experiment were to succeed, it needed educated voters who were capable of making sound decisions. Several decades later, in the early 1800s, the country remained politically fragmented, with many of its states still thinking of themselves as near-sovereign nations.

Education reflected this political situation. The United States had no comprehensive school system, just a hodgepodge of independent schools administered by separate localities, with no coordination among them. Most public schools were supported by tuition, with a few poor children being allowed to attend free. Parochial schools were run by Lutherans, Presbyterians, Congregationalists, and Roman Catholics (Hellinger and Judd 1991). Children of the rich attended private schools. Most children of the lower classes—and all slaves—received no formal education at all. Only the wealthy could afford to send their children to high school. College, too, was beyond the reach of almost everyone.

Horace Mann, an educator from Massachusetts, found it deplorable that the average family could not afford to send its children even to grade school. In 1837 he proposed that

This 1893 photo of a school in Hecla, Montana, taught by Miss Blanche Lamont, provides a glimpse into the past, when free public education, pioneered in the United States, was still in its infancy. In these one-room rural schools, a single teacher had charge of grades 1 to 8. Children were assigned a grade not by age but by mastery of subject matter. Occasionally, adults who wished to learn to read, to write, or to do mathematics would join the class. Attendance was sporadic, for the family's economic survival came first.

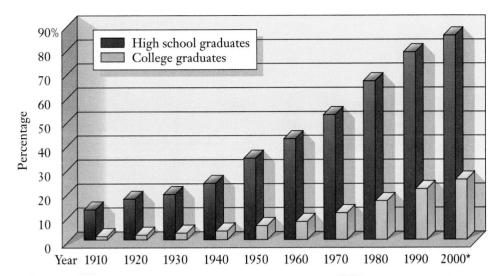

Figure 17.1

Educational Achievement in the United States

Note: Americans 25 years and over. Asterisk indicates author's estimate.

Source: National Center for Education Statistics, 1991: Table 8; *Statistical Abstract* 1997: Table 243.

"common schools," supported through taxes, be established throughout his state. Mann's idea spread throughout the country, and state after state began to support free public education. It is no coincidence that universal education and industrialization occurred simultaneously. Seeing that the economy was undergoing fundamental change, political and civic leaders recognized the need for an educated work force. They also feared the influx of foreign values and looked on public education as a way to Americanize immigrants (Hellinger and Judd 1991).

Over time, the amount of education considered necessary continued to expand. By 1918, all U.S. states had **mandatory education laws** requiring children to attend school, usually until they had completed the eighth grade or turned 16, whichever came first. In the early 1900s, graduation from the eighth grade was considered to be a full education for most people. "Dropouts" at that time were students who did not complete grade school. High school, as its name implies, was viewed as a form of "higher" education.

As industrialization progressed and as fewer people made their living from agriculture, formal education came to be thought of as essential to the well-being of society. Industrialized nations then developed some form of the credential society described earlier. As you can see from Figure 17.1 above, college graduation in the United States is now more common than high school graduation was in 1930. Sixty-two percent of all U.S. high school graduates now enter college, the highest rate of any nation (*Statistical Abstract* 1997:Table 282).

One fourth of Americans don't make it through high school, however, condemning most of them to a difficult economic life. The rate of high school graduation is not evenly distributed across the states, as you can see from the Social Map on the next page. You may wish to compare this Social Map with the one that shows the distribution of poverty in the United States (see page 271).

Education in Global Perspective

To gain an idea of the variety of education around the world, and how education is directly related to a nation's economy, let's look at an example from each of the three worlds of development. Keep in mind that these are just examples, that no single nation represents the wide variety of educational approaches that characterizes each of these three worlds.

mandatory education laws: laws that require all children to attend school until a specified age or until they complete a minimum grade in school

Figure 17.2

Not Making It: Failure to Get Through High School

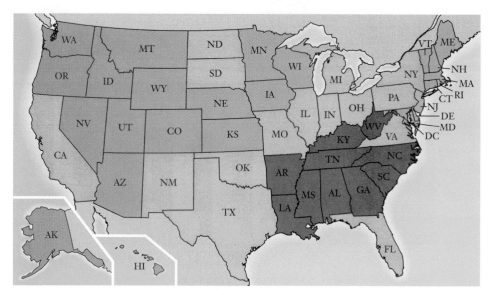

What percentage of a state's residents age 25 and over have not finished high school?

▓ Over 28%   ░ 22%–28%   ░ Less than 22%

Source: Statistical Abstract 1996: Table 245.

Education in the Most Industrialized Nations: Japan

A central sociological principle of education is that a nation's education reflects its culture. Since a core Japanese value is solidarity with the group, competition among individuals is downgraded. For example, in the work force people who are hired together work as a team. They are even promoted collectively (Ouchi 1993). Japanese education reflects this group-centered ethic. Children in grade school work as a group, all mastering the same skills and materials. Teachers stress cooperation and respect for elders and others in positions of authority. By law, Japanese schools even use the same textbooks (Haynes and Chalker 1997).

College admission procedures in Japan and the U.S. also differ (Cooper 1991). Like the Scholastic Assessment Test (SAT) required of U.S. college-bound high school seniors,

Some of the Least Industrialized Nations are so poor that they can afford neither classrooms nor regular teachers. Shown here is a math lesson in Ethiopia, taught by a traveling teacher. Such sporadic lessons are likely to be the extent of these children's formal education.

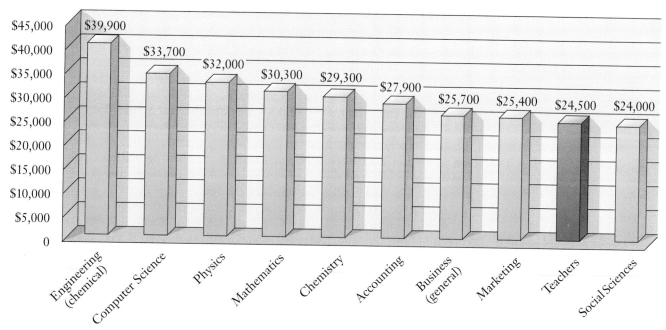

Source: Smith 1996; *Statistical Abstract* 1997: Table 301.

Figure 17.3

Starting Salaries of U.S. College Graduates: Public School Teachers Compared with Private Industry

Japanese seniors who want to attend college must take a national test. ~~Only the top scorers in Japan, however—rich and poor alike—are admitted to college.~~ In contrast, U.S. high school graduates who perform poorly on these tests can find some college to attend—as long as their parents can pay the tuition.

This Japanese practice poses a fascinating cultural contradiction. Although cooperation is a core Japanese value, students are admitted to college only on the basis of intense competition. Because this make-or-break process affects their entire lives, each day after high school and on weekends about half of those who plan to go to college attend cram schools (*juku*). Affluent parents hire tutors for their children (Stevenson and Baker 1994). The annual college admission tests have become a national obsession. Families and friends nervously stand on college campuses at midnight awaiting the outcome that seals their fate. The results are posted on flood-lit bulletin boards. Families shout in joy—or hide their faces in shame and disappointment, while reporters photograph the results and rush back to their papers with the news. The next day, entire neighborhoods are abuzz about the results (Rohen 1983).

Just how highly do the Japanese value education? One way to tell how much a society values something is to see how much money it chooses to spend on it. By law, Japanese teachers are paid 10 percent more than the highest-paid civil service workers, putting teachers in the top 10 percent of the country's wage earners (Richburg 1985). In sharp contrast, as Figure 17.3 shows, the starting salaries of teachers in the United States are considerably lower than those in most other fields. (The abysmal starting salaries of social science majors is a separate issue.) Because the Japanese reward schoolteaching with both high pay and high prestige, each opening for a teaching position is met by a barrage of eager, highly qualified applicants.

Education in the Industrializing Nations: Post-Soviet Russia

After the Revolution of 1917, the Soviet Communist party attempted to upgrade the nation's educational system. At that time, as in most other countries, education was limited to the elite. The revolution, meant to usher in social equality, was also intended to make education accessible to all. Just as the new central government directed the economy, so

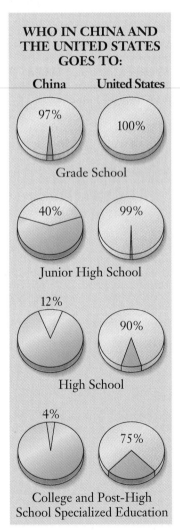

Figure 17.4

A Comparison of Education in a Most Industrialized (postindustrial) Nation and a Least Industrialized Nation

WHO IN CHINA AND THE UNITED STATES GOES TO:

China   United States

97%   100%

Grade School

40%   99%

Junior High School

12%   90%

High School

4%   75%

College and Post-High School Specialized Education

Note: These are initial attendance rates, not completion rates. The U.S. junior high school total is the author's estimate.

Source: Brauchli 1994.

it directed the country's education. Following the sociological principle that education reflects culture, the government made certain that socialist values dominated its schools, for it saw education as a means to undergird the new political system. As a result, schoolchildren were taught that capitalism was evil and that communism was the salvation of the world.

With the country still largely agricultural, education remained spotty for the next two decades. The Nazi invasion of the Soviet Union during World War II dealt a severe blow to the attempt to provide universal education, as military service disrupted the education of hundreds of thousands of young people. Even by 1950, only about half of Soviet young people were in school, and most of these came from the more privileged strata (children of the more educated and of party members) rather than from workers and peasants (Bell 1973; Grant 1979; Ballentine 1983; Matthews 1983).

Eyeing the gains of the West, the Soviet leadership continued to struggle toward universal education, seeing education as a key to becoming a world power. Education, including college, was free. Mathematics and the natural sciences were stressed, and few courses in the social sciences were taught (Taylor and Mechitov 1994). Although the Soviet Union never succeeded in becoming a world industrial power—its power was based on military threat, not industrial might—its educational success did challenge the West. The launching of *Sputnik*, the first satellite, in the 1950s caught Western leaders by surprise. They were forced to acknowledge how effective Soviet education had become.

The breakup of the Soviet empire in 1989 again caught Western experts by surprise, but this time they were surprised at the backwardness of Soviet education. Many schools lacked such basics as heat and indoor plumbing. To control ideas, education was totally centralized, with orders issued out of a remote educational bureaucracy in Moscow. Schools throughout the country followed the same state-prescribed curriculum, and all students in the same grade used the same textbooks. Students memorized the materials, and were discouraged from discussing them (Bridgman 1994).

Post–Soviet Russians are now in the midst of "reinventing" education. For the first time, private, religious, and even foreign-run schools are allowed, and teachers can encourage students to question and to think for themselves. The problems confronting the Russians are mind-boggling. Not only do they have to retrain tens of thousands of teachers who are used to teaching pat political answers, but school budgets are also shrinking while inflation is spiraling. Urban teachers are stampeding out of education into fields that, with the new capitalism, pay ten times the going rate for instructors (Bridgman 1994).

Because it is true of education everywhere, it is safe to conclude that beneath these changes Russia is developing an educational system designed to reflect its culture. The system will glorify its historical exploits and reinforce its values and world views. One difficulty for Russians at this point is that their values and world views are rapidly changing. Due to the transition to a competitive market system, basic ideas about profit and private property are being transformed—and the Russian educational system is destined to reflect those changed values.

Education in the Least Industrialized Nations: Egypt

Education in the Least Industrialized Nations stands in sharp contrast to the industrialized world. Even if the Least Industrialized Nations have mandatory attendance laws, they are not enforced. Because most of their people work the land or take care of families, they find little need for education. In addition, most of these nations simply cannot afford extensive formal education. As we saw on Figure 9.2 (on pages 240–241), the average person in many of the Least Industrialized Nations lives on less that $1,000 a year. Consequently, in some nations most children do not go to school beyond the first couple of grades. Figure 17.4 contrasts education in China and the United States. As was once common around the globe, it is primarily the wealthy in the Least Industrialized Nations who have the means and the leisure for formal education—especially anything beyond the basics. As an example, let's look at education in Egypt.

Several centuries before the birth of Christ, Egypt's world-renowned centers of learning produced such acclaimed scientists as Archimedes and Eukleides. The primary areas of study during this classic period were physics, astronomy, geometry, geography, mathematics, philosophy, and medicine. The largest library in the world was at Alexandria. Fragments from the papyrus manuscripts of this library, which burned to the ground, have been invaluable in deciphering ancient manuscripts. After defeat in war, however, education declined, never again to rise to its former prominence.

Although the Egyptian constitution makes five years of grade school free and compulsory for all children, as in most of the Least Industrialized Nations qualified teachers are few, classrooms are crowded, and education is limited. Many peasant children go completely uneducated, while others receive but rudimentary teaching of numbers and basic reading. Only 34 percent of women and 63 percent of men can read and write (Barberis 1994). Three years of preparatory school follow the five of grade school, and high school lasts for three years. During the first two years, all students take the same required courses, and during the third year they specialize in arts, science, or mathematics. Examinations are held monthly, and a national exam is given at the end of the senior year. The Egyptian government specifies the manifest functions of higher education: to prepare graduates for the world of work, to develop scientific research, and to help solve the economic and social problems that confront Egypt's development (El-Meligi 1992). Although education is free at all levels, including college, children of the wealthy are several times as likely to get a college education.

Education is costly, and financing education is a burden on the Least Industrialized Nations. Consequently, their schools are minimal, their teachers are undereducated, and attendance is sporadic. Shown here is an Egyptian school in Hellwan, near Cairo.

The Functionalist Perspective: Providing Social Benefits

As stressed in previous chapters, a central position of functionalism is that when the parts of society are working properly, each contributes to the well-being or stability of that society. The intended consequences of people's actions are known as **manifest functions,** while those that are not intended are called **latent functions.** As we examine the functions of education, both its manifest and latent functions will become evident.

Teaching Knowledge and Skills

Education's most obvious manifest function is to teach knowledge and skills, whether those be the traditional three R's or their more contemporary version, such as computer literacy. Each society must train the next generation to fulfill its significant positions. From a functionalist perspective, this is the reason that schools are founded, parents support them, and taxes are raised to finance them.

Cultural Transmission of Values

At least as significant as teaching knowledge and skills is a function of education called **cultural transmission,** a process by which schools pass on a society's core values from one generation to the next. As discussed in Chapter 2, values lie at the center of every culture (see pages 45–48 for a summary of values that characterize U.S. culture). In addition to responding to the demands of the economy, the need to produce an informed electorate, and the desire to "Americanize" immigrants, how else does the U.S. educational system reflect—and transmit—cultural values?

Schools are such an essential part of U.S. culture that it is difficult even to know where to begin. For example, the fact that instruction takes place almost exclusively in English, the dominant language of the society, reflects an intimate evolution from British

manifest functions: intended consequences of people's actions

latent functions: unintended consequences of people's actions

cultural transmission: in reference to education, the ways in which schools transmit a society's culture, especially its core values

institutions. Similarly, the architecture of school buildings themselves reflects Western culture, their often distinctive appearance identifying them as schools on sight, unlike, for example, the thatched-roof schools of some tropical societies.

Americans value "bigness," and this value is reflected in the U.S. educational system. With 50 million students attending grade and high schools, and another 15 million enrolled in college, U.S. education has become big business. Primary and secondary schools provide employment for 2½ million teachers, while another 700,000 people teach in colleges and universities (*Statistical Abstract* 1997:Table 235). Millions more work as support personnel—aides, administrators, bus drivers, janitors, and secretaries. Another several million earn their living in industries that service schools—from building schools to manufacturing pencils, paper, and desks. Overall, the United States spends $250 billion a year on its elementary and secondary schools, and another $180 billion on its colleges and universities (*Statistical Abstract* 1997:Tables 261, 287).

To better understand the connection between education and values, let's look at how the educational system transmits individualism, competition, and patriotism.

Individualism. Individualism forms a thread that is integrally woven into the U.S. educational system. Unlike their Japanese counterparts, U.S. teachers and students seldom focus on teamwork. Where Japanese schools stress that the individual is only one part of a larger, integrated whole, U.S. students learn that the individual is on his or her own. Pervasive but often subtle, such instruction begins in the early grades when teachers point out the success of a particular student. They might say, for example, "Everyone should be like José," or, "Why can't you be like María, who got all the answers right?" In such seemingly innocuous statements, the teacher thrusts one child ahead of the rest, holding the individual up for praise.

Competition. Competitive games in the classroom and the schoolyard provide an apt illustration of how schools transmit this core value. In the classroom, a teacher may divide the class into competitive groups for a spelling bee, while on the playground children are encouraged to play hard-driving competitive games and sports. The school's formal sports program—baseball, football, basketball, soccer, hockey, volleyball, and so on—pits team against team in head-to-head confrontations, driving home the lesson that the competitive spirit is highly valued. Although organized sports stress teamwork, the individual is held up for praise. The custom of nominating an "outstanding player" (emphasizing which of these persons is *the* best) reinforces the related lesson of individualism.

Patriotism. Finally, as in schools around the world, U.S. schools teach patriotism. U.S. students are taught that the United States is the best country in the world; Russians learn that no country is better than Russia; and French, German, British, Spanish, Japanese, Chinese, Afghani, and Egyptian students all learn the same about their respective countries. To instill patriotism, grade school teachers in every country extol the virtues of the society's founders, their struggle for freedom from oppression, and the goodness of the country's basic social institutions.

In the United States, grade school teachers wax eloquent when it comes to the exploits of George Washington—whether real or mythical (and each society tends to develop myths about its own early heroes). Throwing a silver dollar across the Potomac and chopping down the cherry tree are vivid memories many adults carry from their childhood classrooms—their hesitant suspicions about the waste of money or how such a good person could have chopped down a valued tree in the first place hushed by the teacher's stress on Washington's virtues: strength and accuracy in throwing the silver dollar, and honesty about the cherry tree.

Social Integration

Schools also perform the function of *social integration*, helping to mold students into a more or less cohesive unit. Indeed, as we just saw, forging a national identity by integrating immigrants into a common cultural heritage was one of the manifest functions of

Among the major functions of education is the cultural transmission of values such as patriotism and good citizenship. Another function of education, social integration, also is apparent from this photo, for the students are learning that in spite of their individual identities, they all are Americans.

establishing a publicly funded system of education in the United States (Hellinger and Judd 1991). When children enter school, they come from many different backgrounds. Their particular family and social class may have taught them speech patterns, dress, and other behaviors or attitudes that differ from those generally recognized as desirable or acceptable. In the classroom and on the playground, those backgrounds take new shape. The end result is that schools help socialize students into the mainstream culture.

Peer culture is especially significant, for most students are eager to fit in. From their peers, they learn ideas and norms that go beyond their family and little corner of the world. Guided by today's powerful mass media, students in all parts of the country choose to look alike by wearing, for example, the same brands and styles of jeans, shirts, skirts, blouses, sneakers, and jackets. Parental influence rapidly declines as the peer culture molds not only the youths' appearance but even their ideas, speech patterns, and interaction with the opposite sex (Thorne and Luria 1993).

The classroom itself helps to produce social integration. As students salute the flag and sing the national anthem, for example, they become aware of the "greater government," and their sense of national identity grows. One of the best indicators of how education promotes political integration is the millions of immigrants who have attended U.S. schools, learned mainstream ideas, and given up their earlier national and cultural identities as they became Americans (Violas 1978; Rodriguez 1995).

How significant is this integrative function of education? It goes far beyond similarities of appearance or speech. *To forge a national identity is to stabilize the political system.* If people identify with a society's social institutions and *perceive them as the basis of their welfare*, they have no reason to rebel. This function is especially significant when it comes to the lower social classes, from which most social revolutionaries are drawn. The wealthy already have a vested interest in maintaining the status quo, but to get the lower classes to identify with the U.S. social system *as it is* goes a long way to preserving the system as it is.

Gatekeeping

Gatekeeping, or determining which people will enter what occupations, is another major function of education. Credentialing, the subject of the opening vignette, is an example of gatekeeping. Because Wendy did not have the credentials, but Melissa did, education closed the door to the one and opened it to the other.

Essential to the gatekeeping function is tracking, sorting students into different educational programs on the basis of real or perceived abilities. Tests are used to determine which students should be directed into "college prep" programs, while others are put onto a vocational track. The impact is lifelong, for, like Wendy and Melissa, throughout adulthood opportunities for jobs, raises, and promotions open or close on the basis of education.

gatekeeping: the process by which education opens and closes doors of opportunity; another term for the **social placement** function of education

tracking: the sorting of students into different educational programs on the basis of real or perceived abilities

Tracking begins in grade school, where on the basis of test results most students take regular courses, but some are placed in advanced sections of English and mathematics. In high school, tracking becomes more elaborate. In many schools, students are funneled into one of three tracks: general, college prep, or honors. All students who complete their sequence of courses receive a high school diploma and are eligible to go on to college. Those in the lowest track, however, are most likely to go to work after high school or perhaps to take a vocational course in a community college; those in the highest track enter the more prestigious colleges around the country; and those in between most often attend a local college or regional state university.

Gatekeeping sorts people on the basis of merit, say functionalists. Sociologists Talcott Parsons (1940), Kingsley Davis, and Wilbert Moore (1945), who pioneered this view, also known as **social placement,** argue that a major task of society is to fill its positions with capable people. Some positions, such as that of physician, require a high intellect and many years of arduous education. Consequently, to motivate capable people to postpone immediate gratification and to submit to many years of rigorous education, high income and prestige are held out as rewards. Other jobs require far fewer skills and can be performed by people of lesser intelligence. Thus, functionalists look on education as a system that, to the benefit of society, sorts people according to their abilities.

Promoting Personal Change

Learning critical thinking skills helps to promote personal change. Schools teach students to "think for themselves"—to critically evaluate ideas and social life. One consequence is that the further people go in school, the more open they tend to be to new ways of thinking and doing things. People with more education tend to hold more liberal ideas, while those with less education tend to be more conservative.

Promoting Social Change

The educational institution also contributes to social change by sponsoring research. Most university professors, for example, are given time off from teaching so that they can do research. Their findings become part of a body of accumulated knowledge that stimulates social change. Sociologists, for example, presented conclusions from sociological research before the U.S. Supreme Court that helped bring about the 1954 decision to desegregate U.S. schools. Some academic research has had an explosive impact on society—literally, in the case of the atomic and hydrogen weapons that were developed in part from university research. Nobody remains untouched by this function of education. For example, medical research conducted in universities across the world is partially responsible for the likelihood that you will reach old age.

Mainstreaming

A new function of education is **mainstreaming,** incorporating people with disabilities into regular social activities. As a matter of routine policy, students with disabilities used to be placed in special schools. Educators concluded that in these settings disabled students learned to adjust only to a world of the disabled, leaving them ill prepared to cope with the dominant world. The educational philosophy then changed to having disabled students attend regular schools.

Mainstreaming is easiest for students whose disabilities are minor, of course, for they fit more easily into regular schools. For people who cannot walk, schools (and other public facilities) have been required to build wheelchair ramps; for those who cannot

social placement: a function of education that funnels people into a society's various positions

mainstreaming: helping people to become part of the mainstream of society

In recent years, social integration, a traditional function of public education, has been extended. In a process called mainstreaming *(also known as inclusion by educators), children who used to be sent to special schools now attend regular schools. Shown here is a physical education class in a school in California.*

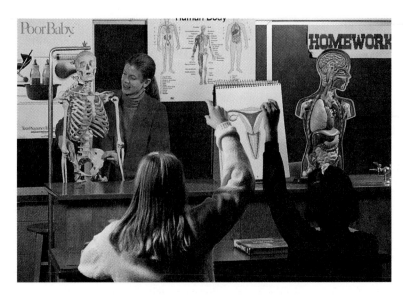

Education has replaced several functions of the family. In most areas, parents have quietly acquiesced. Sex education, however, has remained a source of continuing controversy. Many parents object to the schools usurping their role, as well as to their children being taught values that violate their own. Many would condemn a graphic presentation of how to put on a condom.

hear, "signers" (interpreters who use their hands) may attend classes with them. Most blind students still attend special schools, as do people with severe learning disabilities. Overall, one half of students with disabilities ages 6 to 12 spends most of the day in regular classrooms (*Statistical Abstract* 1997:Table 268).

Replacing Family Functions

U.S. schools have become a rival for some family functions. Child care is an example. Grade schools do double duty as baby-sitters for parents who both work, or for single mothers in the work force. Child care always has been a *latent* function of formal education, for it was an unintended consequence of schooling. Now, however, since most families have two wage earners, child care has become a manifest function. Some schools even offer child care both before and after formal classes. Another example is providing sex education and birth control advice, which has stirred controversy, for some families resent this function being taken from them.

Other Functions

Education also fulfills many other functions. For example, because most students are unmarried, high schools and colleges effectively serve as *matchmaking* institutions. It is here that many young people find their future spouses. The sociological significance of this function of schools is that they funnel people into marriages with mates of similar background, interests, and education. Schools also establish *social networks*. Some older adults maintain friendship networks from high school and college, while others become part of business or professional networks that prove highly beneficial to their careers. Finally, schools also help to *stabilize employment*. The Most Industrialized Nations have little use for unskilled individuals. To keep millions out of the labor market keeps positions open for older workers.

The Conflict Perspective: Reproducing the Social Class Structure

Unlike functionalists, who see education as a social institution that performs functions for the benefit of society, conflict theorists see the educational system as a tool used by those in the controlling sector of society to maintain their dominance.

The Hidden Curriculum

The term **hidden curriculum** refers to the unwritten rules of behavior and attitudes, such as obedience to authority and conformity to cultural norms, that are taught in the schools in addition to the formal curriculum (Gillborn 1992). Conflict theorists note how this hidden curriculum perpetuates social inequalities.

To better understand this central point, consider the values and work habits that students are taught in school: obedience to the teacher, punctuality, and turning in neat work on time. These traits are highly desired by employers, who want dependable, docile, subordinate workers. Or consider just the emphasis on "proper" English. Members of the elite need people to run their business empires, and they are more comfortable if their managers possess the "refined" language and manners that they themselves are used to. Consequently, middle-class schools, whose teachers know where their pupils are headed, stress "proper" English and "good" manners. In contrast, because few children from inner city schools will occupy managerial positions, their teachers allow ethnic and street language in the classroom.

To reproduce the social class structure, then, means to prepare students to work in positions similar to those of their parents. Some children, socially destined for higher positions, need to learn "refined" speech and manners. Others simply need to be taught to obey rules so they can take their place in the closely supervised, low-status positions for which they are socially destined (Bowles and Gintis 1976; Olneck and Bills 1980). "Refined" speech and manners would be wasted on them. From this conflict perspective, even kindergarten has a hidden curriculum, as the Down–to–Earth Sociology box illustrates.

Tilting the Tests: Discrimination by IQ

Even intelligence tests play their part in keeping the social class system intact. For example, how would you answer the following question?

A symphony is to a composer as a book is to a(n) _____.

_____ *paper* _____ *sculptor* _____ *musician* _____ *author* _____ *man*

You probably had no difficulty coming up with "author" as your choice. Wouldn't any intelligent person have done so?

In point of fact, this question raises a central issue in intelligence testing. Not all intelligent people would know the answer, because this question contains *cultural biases*. In other words, children from some backgrounds are more familiar with the concepts of symphonies, composers, sculptors, and musicians than are other children. Consequently, the test is tilted in their favor (Turner 1972; Ashe 1992).

Perhaps asking a different question will make the bias clearer. How would you answer this question?

If you throw dice and "7" is showing on the top, what is facing down?

_____ *seven* _____ *snake eyes* _____ *box cars* _____ *little Joes* _____ *eleven*

This question, suggested by Adrian Dove (n.d.), a social worker in Watts, is slanted toward a lower-class experience. It surely is obvious that this *particular* cultural bias tilts the test so that children from some social backgrounds will perform better than others.

It is no different with IQ (intelligence quotient) tests that use such words as *composer* and *symphony*. A lower-class child may have heard about rap, rock, hip hop, or jazz but not about symphonies. In other words, IQ tests measure not only intelligence but also culturally acquired knowledge. Whatever else we can say, the cultural bias built into the IQ tests used in schools is clearly *not* tilted in favor of the lower classes.

A second inadequacy of IQ tests is that they focus on mathematical, spatial, symbolic, and linguistic abilities. Intelligence, however, consists of more than these components. The ability to compose music, to be empathetic to the feelings of others, or to be humorous or persuasive are also components of intelligence.

The significance of these factors, say conflict theorists, is that culturally biased IQ tests favor the middle classes and discriminate against students from lower-class back-

hidden curriculum: the unwritten goals of schools, such as obedience to authority and conformity to cultural norms

 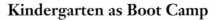 *Down-to-Earth Sociology*

Kindergarten as Boot Camp

Sociologist Harry Gracey (1995), who did participant observation in a kindergarten, concluded that kindergarten is a sort of boot camp for the entire educational system. Here, tender students are drilled in the behaviors and attitudes deemed appropriate for the "student role," which, he argued, is to follow classroom routines. The goal of kindergarten is to mold many individuals from diverse backgrounds into a compliant group that will, on command, unthinkingly follow classroom routines.

Kindergarten's famous "show and tell," for example, does not merely allow children to be expressive. It also teaches them to talk only when they are asked to speak. ("It's 'your turn,' Jarmay.") The format also teaches children to request permission to talk ("Who knows what Letitia has?") by raising a hand and being acknowledged. Finally, the whole ritual teaches children to acknowledge the teacher's ideas as superior. (She is the one who has the capacity to evaluate students' activities and ideas.)

Gracey found a similar hidden curriculum in the other activities he observed. Whether it was drawing pictures, listening to records, snack time, or rest time, the teachers would quiet talkative students, even scolding them at times, while giving approval for conforming behaviors. In short, the message is that the teacher—and, by inference, the entire school system—is the authority.

The purpose of kindergarten, Gracey concluded, is to teach children to "follow orders with unquestioning obedience." To accomplish this, kindergarten teachers "create and enforce a rigid social structure in the classroom through which they effectively control the behavior of most of the children for most of the school day." This produces three kinds of students: (1) "good" students, those who submit to school-imposed discipline and come to identify with it; (2) "adequate" students, those who submit to the school's discipline but do not identify with it; and (3) "bad" students, those who refuse to submit to school routines. This third type is also known as "problem children." To bring them into line, a tougher drill sergeant, the school psychologist, is called in.

Learning the student role prepares children for grade school, where they "will be asked to submit to systems and routines imposed by the teachers and the curriculum. The days will be much like those of kindergarten, except that academic subjects will be substituted."

Gracey adds that these lessons extend well beyond the classroom, that they prepare students for the routines of the work world, whether those be of the assembly line or the office. Mastering the student role prepares them to follow unquestioningly the routines imposed by "the company."

---

grounds. These tests, used to track students, assign disproportionate numbers of minorities and the poor to noncollege tracks (Kershaw 1992). This outcome, as we have seen, destines them for lower-paying jobs in adult life. Thus, conflict theorists view IQ tests as another weapon in the arsenal designed to maintain the social class structure over the generations (Postman 1992).

Stacking the Deck: Unequal Funding

Conflict theorists stress the central role that funding for education plays in perpetuating social inequalities. Funding is a scarce resource unequally distributed among rich and poor school districts, and even among different geographical regions. The geographical inequality becomes readily visible when we look at Table 17.1 on the next page. You can see that for each of its students Alaska and New Jersey spend two and a half times what Utah and Mississippi do on their students. If you divide the list in the middle, you can see that ten of the eleven eastern states rank in the top half, while all but two of the southern states fall in the bottom half. Although higher expenditure is generally associated with higher educational quality, high spending does not guarantee quality education. Students from Iowa, for example, which ranks only twenty-ninth in spending, score the highest on the SAT test. But this figure, too, is misleading, for compared with some other states a smaller

---
TABLE 17.1
What States Spend on Education, per Student

Rank	State	Expenditure	Rank	State	Expenditure	Rank	State	Expenditure
1.	Alaska	$10,156	18.	Indiana	$6,222	35.	Nevada	$5,256
2.	New Jersey	9,967	19.	Minnesota	6,203	36.	North Carolina	5,147
3.	New York	9,535	20.	Wyoming	6,129	37.	South Carolina	5,140
4.	Connecticut	8,716	21.	Washington	6,114	38.	Missouri	5,078
5.	Rhode Island	7,733	22.	Kentucky	6,075	39.	South Dakota	5,070
6.	Delaware	7,549	23.	Virginia	6,072	40.	California	4,977
7.	Vermont	7,474	24.	Kansas	6,059	41.	Louisiana	4,844
8.	Pennsylvania	7,411	25.	Florida	5,983	42.	North Dakota	4,785
9.	Massachusettes	7,385	26.	Georgia	5,852	43.	Tennessee	4,717
10.	Wisconsin	7,231	27.	Montana	5,774	44.	Oklahoma	4,523
11.	Michigan	7,090	28.	Ohio	5,749	45.	Idaho	4,511
12.	Maryland	6,930	29.	Iowa	5,742	46.	Alabama	4,479
13.	West Virginia	6,902	30.	New Mexico	5,655	47.	Arkansas	4,353
14.	Maine	6,478	31.	Texas	5,593	48.	Arizona	4,332
15.	New Hampshire	6,458	32.	Illinois	5,530	49.	Mississippi	4,185
16.	Oregon	6,390	33.	Nebraska	5,513	50.	Utah	3,909
17.	Hawaii	6,335	34.	Colorado	5,447		Average	$6,103

Note: These are 1993 figures. They refer to the amount spent per student in grade school and high school.

Source: Statistical Abstract 1997:Table 262.

---

proportion of Iowan students take the test. Table 17.2 shows this same situation on an international level. Although Switzerland spends the most per student and gets the best test results, the United States is the third highest spender but gets the worst test results.

Conflict theorists go beyond this observation, however. They stress that in each state the deck is stacked against the poor. Because public schools are largely supported by local property taxes, the richer communities (where property values are higher) have more to spend on their children, while the poorer communities end up with much less. Consequently, the richer communities are able to offer higher salaries (and take their pick of the most highly qualified and motivated teachers), afford the latest textbooks and computers, as well as teach additional courses in foreign language, music, and so on. Because U.S. schools so closely reflect the U.S. social class system, then, the children of the privileged

---
TABLE 17.2
Educational Expenditures and Student Scores

Rank by Student Performance	Country	Math Scores (percentage correct)	Science Scores (percentage correct)	Money Spent per Student	Rank by Money Spent per Student
1.	Switzerland	71%	74%	$6,815	1.
2.	Italy	64	70	4,470	4.
3.	France	64	69	4,380	5.
4.	Canada	62	69	6,191	2.
5.	Ireland	61	63	2,240	7.
6.	Spain	55	68	2,500	6.
7.	United States	55	67	6,103	3.

Note: These are the only countries in the source for which both expenditures and test scores are given. Based on testing of 13-year-olds. Expenditures are for 1991 and 1992, test scores for 1991.

Source: Statistical Abstract 1992: Table 1369; 1994: Table 1362; 1995: Table 1370; 1997: Table 262.

emerge from grade school best equipped for success in high school. In turn, they come out of high school best equipped for success in college. Their greater likelihood of success in college, in turn, serves to maintain their dominance.

The Correspondence Principle

Conflict sociologists Samuel Bowles and Herbert Gintis (1976) used the term **correspondence principle** to refer to the ways in which schools reflect the social structure of society. This term means that what is taught in a nation's schools *corresponds* to the characteristics of that society. Thus education helps to perpetuate a society's social inequalities. The following list provides some examples.

Characteristics of Society	Characteristics of Schools
1. Capitalism	1. Promote competition
2. Social inequality	2. Unequal funding of schools, track the poor to job training
3. Racial-ethnic prejudice	3. Make minorities feel inferior, track minorities to job training
4. Bureaucratic structure of the corporation	4. Provide a model of authority in the classroom
5. Need for submissive workers	5. Make students submissive
6. Need for dependable workers	6. Promote punctuality
7. Need to maintain armed forces	7. Promote patriotism (to fight for capitalism)

Thus, conclude conflict theorists, the U.S. educational system is designed to produce dependable workers who will not question their bosses, as well as some individuals who will go on to be innovators in thought and action but can still be counted on to be loyal to the social system as it exists (Olneck and Bills 1980).

The Bottom Line: Family Background and the Educational System

The end result of unequal funding, IQ tests, and so on is that family background proves more important than test scores in predicting who attends college. Back in 1977, sociologist Samuel Bowles compared the college attendance of the brightest 25 percent of high school students with the intellectually weakest 25 percent. Figure 17.5 shows the results. Of the *brightest* 25 percent of high school students, 90 percent of those from affluent homes went to college, while only half of those from low-income homes did so. Of the *weakest* students, 26 percent from affluent homes went to college, while only 6 percent from poorer homes did so. And today? This same general relationship still holds. If you rank families from the poorest to the richest, as the income increases the likelihood that the children will attend college also increases (Manski 1992–1993).

Conflict theorists point out that the educational system not only reproduces the wealth–poverty part of the U.S. social class structure, but also its divisions of race and ethnicity. From Figure 17.6 on the next page, you can see that, compared with whites, African Americans and Latinos are less likely to complete high school, less likely to go to college, and if they go to college, less likely to graduate. Like Wendy in the opening vignette, those without college degrees have less access to jobs with the better pay and potential for advancement. Then, too, there is the type of college. As Table 17.3 on the next page shows, whites are more likely than other racial-ethnic groups to attend private and four-year colleges.

Conflict theorists stress that education reproduces a country's social class system. To support this position, they point out that the U.S. social classes attend different schools, where they are taught by teachers of different backgrounds, and where they learn contrasting perspectives of the world and their place in it. Shown here are students lunching with their teacher at St. Alban's School in Washington, D.C., obviously not a school for the poor.

correspondence principle: the sociological principle that schools correspond to (or reflect) the social structure of society

Figure 17.5

Who Goes to College? The Role of Social Class and Personal Ability in Determining College Attendance

Students' Test Scores

Students' Background	High	Low
Rich	90%	26%
Poor	50%	6%

Source: Bowles 1977.

Figure 17.6

The Funneling Effects of Education: Race and Ethnicity

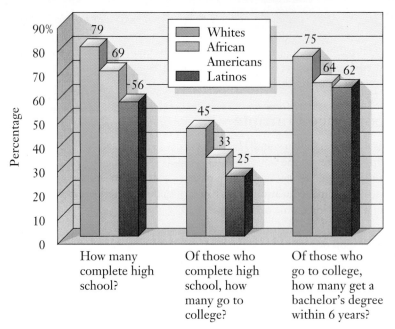

Note: The source gives totals only for these three groups.

Source: Statistical Abstract 1997:Tables 274, 302.

TABLE 17.3

Of Those Who Go to College, What Type of College Do They Attend?

	Public College	Private College
Whites	77%	23%
African Americans	79%	21%
Asian Americans	80%	20%
Latinos	86%	14%
Native Americans	87%	13%
	2-Year College	**4-Year College**
Whites	37%	63%
Asian Americans	39%	61%
African Americans	42%	58%
Native Americans	50%	50%
Latinos	56%	44%

Source: Statistical Abstract 1997:Table 274.

The *purpose* of the educational system, stress conflict theorists, is to *reproduce inequality*, to help keep the social class structure intact from one generation to the next. Consequently, most children of the less privileged are funneled into community college job training programs, while children of the middle classes attend state universities and small private colleges. The offspring of the elite, in contrast, attend exclusive boarding high schools, where their learning environment includes small classes and well-paid teachers (Persell et al. 1992). Here they inherit a cozy social network between the school's college advisers and the admissions officers of the nation's most elite colleges. Some of these networks are so efficient that half of these private schools' graduating classes are admitted to Harvard, Yale, and Princeton (Persell and Cookson 1986).

The Symbolic Interactionist Perspective: Teacher Expectations and the Self-Fulfilling Prophecy

Whereas functionalists look at how education functions to benefit society and conflict theorists examine how education perpetuates social inequality, symbolic interactionists study face-to-face interactions inside the classroom. They have found that the expectations of teachers have profound consequences for their students.

The Rist Research

Symbolic interactionists have uncovered some of the dynamics of educational tracking. In what has become a classic study, sociologist Ray Rist did participant observation in an African-American grade school with an African-American faculty. Rist (1970) found that after only eight days in the classroom, the kindergarten teacher felt that she knew the children's abilities well enough to assign them to three separate worktables. To Table 1, Mrs. Caplow assigned those she considered to be "fast learners." They sat at the front of the room, closest to her. Those whom she saw as "slow learners," she assigned to Table 3, located at the back of the classroom. She placed "average" students at Table 2, in between the other tables.

This pattern seemed strange to Rist. He knew that the children had not been tested for ability, yet the teacher was certain that she could differentiate between bright and slow children. Investigating further, Rist found that social class was the underlying basis for assigning the children to the different tables. Middle-class students were separated out for Table 1, children from poorer homes to Tables 2 and 3. The teacher paid the most attention to the children at Table 1, who were closest to her, less to Table 2, and the least to Table 3. As the year went on, children from Table 1 perceived that they were treated better and came to see themselves as smarter. They became the leaders in class activities and even ridiculed children at the other Tables, calling them "dumb." Eventually, the children at Table 3 disengaged themselves from many classroom activities. Not surprisingly, at the end of the year only the children at Table 1 had completed the lessons that prepared them for reading.

This early tracking stuck. When these students entered the first grade, their new teacher looked at the work they had accomplished and placed students from Table 1 at her Table 1. She treated her tables much as the kindergarten teacher had, and the children at Table 1 again led the class.

The children's reputations continued to follow them. The second-grade teacher reviewed their scores and also divided her class into three groups. The first she named the "Tigers," and, befitting their name, gave them challenging readers. Not surprisingly, the Tigers came from the original Table 1 in kindergarten. The second group she called the "Cardinals." They came from the original Tables 2 and 3. Her third group consisted of children she had failed the previous year, whom she called the "Clowns." The Cardinals and Clowns were given less advanced readers.

Rist concluded that *the child's journey through school was determined at the eighth day of kindergarten!* What had occurred was a **self-fulfilling prophecy,** a term coined by sociologist Robert Merton (1949) to refer to an originally false assumption of what is going to happen that comes true simply because it was predicted. For example, if people believe an unfounded rumor that a bank is in trouble and assume that they won't be able to get their money out, they all rush to the bank to demand their money. The prediction—*although originally false*—is now likely to be true.

In this case, of course, we are dealing with something more important than money, the welfare of little children. As was the case with the Saints and Roughnecks in Chapter 8 (page 201), labels are powerful. They can set people on courses of action that affect the rest of their lives. That, of course, is the significance of Rist's observations of these grade school children.

The Rosenthal–Jacobson Experiment

During the course of our education, most of us have seen teacher expectations at work. We know that if our teacher expects higher standards, then we must perform at a higher level to earn good grades. Teacher expectations, however, also work subtly but effectively in ways that we don't perceive. In what has become a classic experiment, social psychologists Robert Rosenthal and Lenore Jacobson (1968) tried out a new test in a San Francisco grade school. They tested the children's abilities and then told the teachers which students would probably "spurt" ahead during the year. They instructed the teachers to watch these students' progress, but not to let the students or their parents know about the test results. At the end of the year, they tested the students again and found that the IQs of the predicted "spurters" had jumped ten to fifteen points higher than those of the other children.

You might think that Rosenthal and Jacobson then became famous for developing such an impressive scholastic aptitude test. Actually, however, this "test" was another of those covert experiments. Rosenthal and Jacobson had simply given routine IQ tests to the children and had then *randomly* chosen 20 percent of the students as "spurters." These students were *no different* from the others in the classroom. A self-fulfilling prophecy had taken place: The teachers expected more of those particular students, and the students responded. In short, expect dumb and you get dumb. Expect smart, and you get smart.

Although attempts to replicate this experiment have had mixed results (Pilling and Pringle 1978), a good deal of research confirms that students who are expected to do better generally do (Seaver 1973; Snyder 1993).

How Do Teacher Expectations Work?

How do teacher expectations work? Observations of classroom interaction give us some idea (Leacock 1969; Rist 1970; Buckley 1991; Farkas 1990a, b, 1996). The teacher's own

self-fulfilling prophecy: Robert Merton's term for an originally false assertion that becomes true simply because it was predicted

middle-class background comes into play, for teachers are pleased when middle-class students ask probing questions. They take these as a sign of intelligence. When lower-class students ask similar questions, however, teachers are more likely to interpret their questions as "smart aleck." In addition, lower-class children are more likely to reflect a subculture that "puts down" intellectual achievements, an attitude that causes teachers to react negatively.

Sociologist George Farkas (1990a, 1990b, 1996) led a team of researchers in probing how teacher expectations affect grades. Using a stratified sample of students in a large urban school district in the Southwest and a survey of their teachers, the researchers discovered that students who scored similarly on tests over the course materials did not necessarily receive the same grade for the course. They found that females and Asian Americans averaged higher course grades than males, African Americans, Latinos, and whites—even though they all had scored the same on the course work.

To explain this, the first conclusion most of us would jump to would be discrimination. In this case, however, such an explanation does not seem to fit, for it is most unlikely that the teachers would be prejudiced against males and whites. Farkas used symbolic interactionism to interpret these unexpected results. He noted that some students "signal" to their teachers that they are "good students" by being more eager and cooperative and showing that they are "trying hard." Females and Asian Americans, the researchers concluded, are most likely to display these characteristics.

We do not yet have enough information on how teachers form their expectations, how they communicate them to students, or exactly how these expectations influence teacher–student interaction. Nor do we know very much about how students "signal" messages to teachers. (As discussed in the Sociology and New Technology box below, technology is producing new forms of student–teacher interaction and "signaling.") Perhaps you will become the educational sociologist who will shed more light on these everyday but significant aspects of human behavior.

 *Sociology and the New Technology*

Internet University: No Walls, No Ivy, No Keg Parties

Distance learning, courses taught to students who are not physically present with their instructor, is not new. For decades, we have had correspondence courses.

Today, however, distance learning refers to something much more than this. Joe Martin, a 41-year-old executive in Indianapolis, is enrolled in Duke University's MBA program. On his lunch hour or at night in his bedroom, Martin logs onto the Internet and does homework assigned by a professor in another state whom he has never met. He also listens to lectures on the Internet and chats with classmates in China and Brazil (Hamilton and Miller 1997).

Telecommunications—satellites, computers, television, and CD-ROMs—are changing the face of education. With computer link-ups, students in remote parts of Alaska earn B.A.s from their state university. What is now a flow will become a torrent, and cybercolleges soon may be part of mainstream education. Already about 400 colleges and universities offer virtual degrees.

In the past, distance learning often meant a TV screen that replaced a live teacher in a classroom. Consequently, some critics say that the only real change has been an increased capacity to bore: Instead of a live teacher boring a few students in a single classroom, that person's image bores thousands simultaneously (Thornburg 1994). Certainly until now most distance learning has been either slow (a correspondence course) or one-way (students passively receiving instruction, usually providing feedback only through tests). The new technology, such as teleconferencing, however, permits students and teachers to see one another, to talk with one another, and to share documents worldwide.

The potential is staggering. Why, indeed, should our learning be limited to walled classrooms? When studying human culture, for example, wouldn't it be intriguing to be able to compare notes on eating, dating, or burial customs with fellow students in Thailand, Iceland, South Africa, Germany, Egypt, China, and Australia? Or even to write a joint paper comparing your cross-cultural experiences with those described in text, and then submitting that paper to your mutual instructor?

Will we eventually go from kindergarten to grad school, proceeding at our own pace, with classmates from around the world? While this may sound intriguing, no walls also means no flirting after class, no joking in the hallway or dorm, no keg parties. . . .

Problems in U.S. Education— and Their Solutions

To conclude this chapter, let's examine some of the major problems facing U.S. education today—and consider their potential solutions.

Problems: Mediocrity, Violence, and Teen Pregnancy

The Rising Tide of Mediocrity.   Perhaps nothing so captures what is wrong with U.S. schools than this event reported by sociologist Thomas Sowell (1993):

> [A]n international study of 13-year-olds . . . found that Koreans ranked first in mathematics and Americans last. When asked if they thought they were "good at mathematics," only 23 percent of the Korean youngsters said "yes"—compared to 68 percent of American 13-year-olds. The American educational dogma that students should "feel good about themselves" was a success in its own terms—though not in any other terms.

In 1983, a blue-ribbon presidential panel gave a grim assessment of U.S. education, warning of a "rising tide of mediocrity that threatens our very future as a nation and as a people." Even the title of the report, *A Nation at Risk*, sounded an alarm. What especially upset panel members was a decline in scores on the Scholastic Assessment Test (SAT). As Figure 17.7 shows, the math scores have recovered a good part of the lost ground. The verbal scores, however, are holding at their lows. Both are lower than they were thirty years ago.

The president of the American Federation of Teachers has come up with a unique defense of this decline in SAT scores: They indicate, he says, that teachers are doing a *better* job! Teachers are getting more students to stay in high school and to go on to college. This means that more students from poorer academic backgrounds become part of the test results (Sowell 1993b). Perhaps this is the reason, but if it is, it indicates not success, but a severe underlying problem—teachers giving inferior education to disadvantaged students (Murray and Herrnstein 1992).

Others suggest that SAT scores have declined because children find television and video games more appealing than reading (Rigdon and Swasy 1990). Students who read little acquire a smaller vocabulary and less rigor in thought and verbal expression. Sociologists Donald Hayes and Loreen Wolfer (1993a,b) are convinced that the culprit is the "dummied down" textbooks that pervade U.S. schools. Some point their fingers at other low standards: "frill" courses, less homework, fewer term papers, grade inflation, and burned-out teachers who are more interested in collecting paychecks than in educating their students. Some of the examples they offer are startling, such as the college freshman who couldn't understand why she was doing poorly in college since she had placed third in her Chicago high school graduating class. Testing showed that she ranked in the lowest 2 percent of the nation's high school graduates (Kotlowitz 1992).

Cheating on the SATs.   If you receive poor grades this semester, wouldn't you like to use a magic marker and, presto!, change them into better grades? I suppose every student would. Now imagine that you had that power. Would you use it?

This appears to be the solution some people in authority have found to our embarrassing problem of low national SAT scores. On Table 274 of the 1996 edition of the *Statistical Abstract of the United States*, only 8.3 percent of students earned 600 or more on the verbal portion of the SAT test. But the very next edition, in

Figure 17.7

National Results of the Scholastic Assessment Test (SAT)

Source: Statistical Abstract 1997: Table 276.   *Author's estimate

1997, holds a pleasant surprise, for Table 276 tells us that it was really 21.9 percent of students who scored 600 or higher. What a magic marker!

In the twinkle of an eye, we get another bonus. Between 1996 and 1997 the scores of *everyone* in previous years improved. Now that's the kind of power we all would like to have. Students, grab your report cards. Workers, just change the numbers on your paycheck.

While all the explanations for this sleight-of-hand are not in, we do know that rather than doing better educating, some authorities have decided to improve student performance by shortening the SAT, giving students more time to answer the fewer questions, and making the verbal part easier by dropping the antonym portion (Manno 1995; Stecklow 1995). This "dummying down" of the SAT is yet another form of grade inflation, the topic to which we shall now turn.

Grade Inflation, Social Promotion, and Functional Illiteracy. At the same time that learning declined, grades went up. In the 1960s, high school teachers gave out about twice as many *C*'s as *A*'s, but now the *A*'s exceed the *C*'s. Another sign of **grade inflation** is that *one-third* of all entering college freshmen have an overall high school grade-point average of A– or higher. This is *twice* what it was in 1970 (*Statistical Abstract* 1997:Table 298).

Grade inflation in the face of declining standards has been accompanied by **social promotion,** the practice of passing students from one grade to the next even though they have not mastered basic materials. One unfortunate result is **functional illiteracy,** difficulty with reading and writing even though one has graduated from high school. Some high school graduates cannot fill out job applications; others can't figure out if they are given the right change at the grocery store.

grade inflation: higher grades given for the same work; a general rise in student grades without a corresponding increase in learning or test scores

social promotion: passing students to the next grade even though they have not mastered basic materials

functional illiterate: a high school graduate who has difficulty with basic reading and math

Peer Groups. A team of two psychologists and a sociologist studied 20,000 high school students in California and Wisconsin (Steinberg et al. 1996). They found that of all the influences affecting these teenagers, peer group is the most important. Simply put: those who hang out with good students tend to do well; those who hang out with friends who do poorly in school do poorly. The subcultures that students develop include informal norms about educational achievement, and some groups set up norms of classroom excellence, while others sneer at getting good grades. The applied question that arises from this research, of course, is how to build educational achievement into student culture.

Violence in Schools

James Murphy was teaching his government class at Dartmouth High, in a town 50 miles south of Boston, when two Dartmouth students and a third teenager suddenly burst through the door. One brandished a bat, another a billy club, and the third a hunting knife. When they asked for Shawn Pina, Jason Robinson made the fatal mistake of asking why they wanted him. When Murphy saw one go after Robinson with the bat, he wrestled the assailant to the floor. Another plunged his knife into Robinson's stomach, killing him. (Toch 1993)

Lethal weapons and violence are major problems in U.S. schools. Shown here is the scene at a shooting at Heath High School in Paducah, Kentucky, which left three students dead and five wounded. The shooter was a 14-year old freshman.

Many U.S. schools have deteriorated to the point that basic safety is an issue, putting students' lives at risk, a condition that only a few years back would have been unimaginable. Consequently, in some schools uniformed guards have become a fixture, while in others students can gain entrance only after passing through metal detectors. Some schools even supplement the traditional fire drills with "drive-by shooting drills" (Toch 1993; Grossman 1995).

Teenage Pregnancy. Students who lack a high school diploma face a severe handicap in life. At several points in this text, I have mentioned the highly negative consequences that often follow single motherhood, especially the cycle of poverty (see pages 273–274 and 447). Those consequences are especially stark for teenage mothers. Not only do these young women, some still girls, have the expense and responsibility of caring for a child, but they also are unlikely to complete high school, thus perpetuating a cycle of poverty and interrupted education.

Solutions: Retention, Safety, Standards, and Other Reforms

It is one thing to identify problems, and quite another to find solutions for them. Let's begin by looking at a program designed to help pregnant teenagers complete high school, as described in the following Thinking Critically section, and then consider solutions to the other problems we have just reviewed.

▼▼▼▼▼▼▼▼▼▼▼▼▼▼▼▼▼▼▼▼▼▼

Thinking Critically About Social Controversy

High Schools and Teen Pregnancy: A Program That Works

▼ To improve the high school graduation rates of teenage mothers, researchers in Ohio designed a program called LEAP—Learning, Earning, and Parenting. They made it tough for themselves by singling out teenage mothers on welfare, the group of teenage mothers that has the least chance of completing high school. The researchers randomly selected twelve of Ohio's eighty-eight counties, which included rural, suburban, and urban counties. All teens who were receiving Aid to Families with Dependent Children (AFDC), 7,000 individuals, became part of LEAP. They were required to stay in school or to return to school if they had dropped out—either to high school or to an Adult Basic Education program leading to a high school diploma.

The teens were randomly assigned to either one of two groups. Those in the *experimental group* received a $62 bonus in their welfare check for providing evidence that they were enrolled in school and attending an assessment interview. Teens who did not comply had $62 deducted from their check. For each month they were absent no more than four times, the mothers received an additional $62 on their check, while those absent more than four times had $62 deducted from theirs. Sixty-two dollars may not sound like much, but since the monthly AFDC grant was $274, receiving a check with a bonus ($336) or a check with the penalty ($212) made a considerable difference. Mothers who enrolled in school were also eligible for assistance with child care and transportation to attend school. In contrast, teens assigned to the *control group* were treated as usual—no school attendance requirements, no child care or transportation, no bonuses, and no deductions.

The program design is simple and straightforward, and, as discussed in Chapter 5 (pages 125–126), random assignment to control and experimental groups allows us to separate cause and effect. What, then, were the results? These are shown in Figure 17.8.

As you can see, teen mothers are like the rest of us—we all desire rewards and try to avoid punishments. Because of the random assignment to the groups, we know that the higher rates of retention and returning to school are due to the experimental variable. Beyond its effectiveness, what is also good is the program's cost. There is little additional bureaucracy to feed, nor are there expensive educational programs to design and administer. There is little administrative work involved—simply identifying the teens and adjusting welfare checks on the basis of attendance data. In addition, a good part of the cost is covered by an internal transfer of money: For every two teens who received bonuses, one teen received penalties.

For Your Consideration

If you were in charge of this program, how might you modify it to improve the results? Although the program had positive results, two of five teens in the experimental group still dropped out. If you were Ohio's administrator, would you recommend that the program be continued? Do you think this program should be applied nationally? Why or why not?

Source: Based on Bloom et al. 1993. ▲

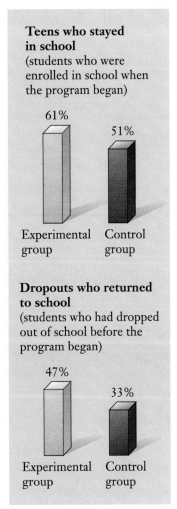

Figure 17.8

LEAP's Impact on High School Retention and Dropouts

Teens who stayed in school
(students who were enrolled in school when the program began)

61% Experimental group

51% Control group

Dropouts who returned to school
(students who had dropped out of school before the program began)

47% Experimental group

33% Control group

A Secure Learning Environment.   The first criterion for a good education is security, to guarantee students' physical safety and freedom from fear (Shanker 1995). Granted the high rate of violence in U.S. society, some violence is bound to spill over into the schools, but basic steps can be taken to minimize that spillover. Fortunately, most U.S. schools are not yet violent, and those that are can be changed. School administrators and teachers can reclaim the schools by expelling all students who threaten the welfare of others and to refuse to tolerate threats, violence, drugs, and weapons (Toby 1992).

Higher Standards.   Within a secure learning environment, then, steps can be taken to improve the quality of education. The president's commission mentioned earlier concluded that U.S. schools need higher standards. The commission recommended that high school students take more courses in math, science, English, social studies, and computer science. The members also recommended that schools recruit more qualified teachers by paying higher salaries. To see why, review Figure 17.3 on page 469.

A study by sociologists James Coleman and Thomas Hoffer (1987) provides helpful guidelines for improving the quality of education. They wanted to see why the test scores of students in Catholic schools average 15 to 20 percent higher than those of students in public schools. Is it because Catholic schools attract better students, while public schools have to put up with everyone? To find out, Coleman and Hoffer tested 15,000 students in public and Catholic high schools.

Their findings? From their sophomore through their senior years, students at Catholic schools pull ahead of public school students by a full grade in verbal and math skills. The superior test performance of students in Catholic schools, they concluded, is due not to better students, but to higher standards. Catholic schools have not watered down their curriculum as have public schools. The researchers also identified parental involvement as a significant factor, finding that parents and teachers in Catholic schools reinforce each other's commitment to the importance of learning.

These findings support the basic principle reviewed earlier about teacher expectations: Students perform better when they are expected to do well. To this, you might want to reply, "Of course. I knew that. Who wouldn't?" Somehow, however, such a basic principle seems to be lost on many teachers, who end up teaching at a low level—and on most school administrators, who accept low student performance. The reason, actually, is probably not their lack of awareness of such basics, but, rather, the constraints in which they find themselves organizationally, the bureaucracies in which ritual often replaces performance. To understand this point better, you may wish to review Chapter 7.

Ultimately, then, it is not only of students that we must expect more, but also of teachers and administrators. They, too, must be held accountable to higher standards. One way to do this is to peg their salaries, or at least bonuses, to the performance of their students. This may be the simplest and most effective step we could take to improve student performance.

Other Reforms—From School Choice to Site-Based Management.   There is no lack of proposals for improving schools, but perhaps the one that has gained the most media attention—both because it is so controversial and because it holds such potential—is the use of tuition vouchers to bring about **school choice**. The main outline of this proposal is that the state would give the parents of each school-age child a voucher to be spent on the school of the parents' choice. As you can see from Table 17.1 (p. 478), the states have a great deal of money to work with, and the amount available per pupil would be rather large. Public and private schools—even those operated by individuals and business firms—would compete for the vouchers. With each school's test results published in the newspapers and otherwise readily available, parents would be able to shop around for the school they like best (Stecklow 1994; Peterson 1995).

Although many applaud this proposal, others fear that vouchers would mean the end of public schools, as vouchers would drain away their resources (Cookson 1994; Henig 1994). Proponents of the proposal reply that there is no reason why public schools can't compete in the marketplace, that vouchers should stimulate them to produce better results. Those that can't produce should fold.

school choice: parents being able to choose the school their child will attend; often used in the context of expecting for-profit schools to compete for vouchers issued by the state

Public school teachers and administrators are especially fearful of this proposal, for it threatens their jobs. In the face of persistent dissatisfaction with the performance of public schools and a growing demand for reform, administrators and teachers are developing proposals designed to keep public education out of private hands. At the center of these counterproposals is *site-based management*, a term that refers to schools designing their own reforms (Dunleavey 1994). We don't yet know the specifics of such reforms, but if they mean that students will be held accountable for meeting high academic standards and that teachers will be accountable for teaching at a high level, the potential is encouraging.

Reform in anything needs a guiding principle. I suggest that this serve as the guiding principle in reforming education: The problem is not the ability of the students, but rather the educational system itself. That this is true becomes apparent when we consider the results reported in the following Thinking Critically section, with which we close this chapter.

Thinking Critically About Social Controversy

Breaking Through the Barriers: The Jaime Escalante Approach to Restructuring the Classroom

▼ Called "the best teacher in America," Jaime Escalante taught in an East Los Angeles inner-city school plagued with poverty, crime, drugs, gangs, and the usual miserably low student scores. In this self-defeating environment, he taught calculus. His students scored so highly on national tests that test officials, suspecting cheating, asked his students to retake the test. They did. Again they passed—this time with even higher scores.

Escalante's school ranks fourth in the nation in the number of students who have taken and passed the Advanced Placement SAT Calculus examination. For students to even take the test, they must complete Algebra I, Geometry, Algebra II, Trigonometry or Math Analysis, and Calculus for first-year college and/or Calculus for second-year college.

How did Escalante overcome such odds? His success is *not* due to a recruitment of the brightest students. Students' poor academic performance does not stand in the way of being admitted to the math program. The *only* requirement is an interest in math. What did Escalante do right, and what can we learn from his approach?

"Success starts with attitude" could be Escalante's motto. Few Latino students were taking math. Most were tracked into craft classes and made jewelry and birdhouses. "Our kids are just as talented as anyone else. They just need the opportunity to show it. And for that, they must be motivated," he said. "They just don't think about becoming scientists or engineers."

Here are the keys to what Escalante accomplished. First, teaching and learning can't take place unless there is discipline. For that the teachers, not gangs, must control the classroom. Second, the students must believe in themselves. The teacher must inspire students with the idea that they *can* learn (remember teacher expectations). Third, the students must be motivated to perform, in this case to see learning as a way out of the barrio, the path to good jobs.

Escalante uses a team approach. He has his students think of themselves as a team, of him as the coach, and the national exams as a sort of Olympics for which they are preparing. To stimulate team identity, the students wear team jackets, caps, and T-shirts with logos that identify them as part of the team. Before class, his students do "warmups" (hand clapping and foot stomping to a rock song).

His team has practice schedules as rigorous as a championship football team. Students must sign a contract that binds them to participate in the summer program he has developed, to complete the daily homework, and to attend Saturday morning and after-school study sessions. To get in his class, even the student's parents have to sign the contract. To keep before his students the principle that self-discipline pays off, Escalante covers his room with posters of sports figures in action—Michael Jordan, Jerry West, Babe Ruth, and Tiger Woods.

To say that today's schoolchildren can't learn as well as previous schoolchildren is a case of blaming the victim. As discussed in the text, Jaime Escalante (shown here) demonstrated that teachers can motivate even highly deprived students to study hard and to excel in learning. His experience challenges us to rethink our approach to education.

"How have I been successful with students from such backgrounds?" he asks. "Very simple. I use a time-honored tradition—hard work, lots of it, for teacher and student alike."

The following statement helps us understand how Escalante challenges his students to think of what is possible in life, instead of problems that destroy the possible:

> The first day when these kids walk into my room, I have a bunch of names of schools and colleges on the chalkboard. I ask each student to memorize one. The next day I pick one kid and ask, "What school did you pick?" He says USC or UCLA or Stanford, MIT, Colgate, and so on. So I say, "Okay, keep that in mind. I'm going to bring in somebody who'll be talking about the schools."

Escalante then has a college adviser talk to the class. But more than this, he also has arranged foundation money to help the students get to the colleges of their choice.

The sociological point is that the problem was *not* the ability of the students. Their failure to do well in school was not due to something *within* them. The problem was the *system*, the way classroom instruction is arranged. When Escalante changed the system of instruction, both attitudes and performance changed. Escalante makes this very point—that student performance does not depend on the charismatic personality of a single person, but on how we structure the learning setting.

For Your Consideration

What principles discussed in this or earlier chapters did Escalante apply? What changes do you think we can make in education to bring about similar results all over the country?

Sources: Based on Barry 1989; Meek 1989; Escalante and Dirmann 1990; Hilliard 1991.

Summary and Review

Today's Credential Society

What is a credential society, and how did it develop?

A **credential society** is one in which employers use diplomas and degrees to determine who is eligible for a job. One reason that credentialism developed is that large, anonymous societies lack the personal knowledge common to smaller groups; educational certification provides evidence of a person's ability. Pp. 464–465.

The Development of Modern Education

How did modern education develop?

In most of human history, education consisted of informal learning, equivalent to **acculturation.** In some earlier societies, centers of formal education did develop, such as among the Arabians, Chinese, Greeks, and Egyptians. Because modern education came about in response to industrialization, formal education is much less common in the Least Industrialized Nations. Pp. 465–467.

Education in Global Perspective

How does education compare among the Most Industrialized, Industrializing, and Least Industrialized Nations?

In general, formal education reflects a nation's economy. Consequently, education is much more extensive in the Most Industrialized Nations, undergoing extensive change in the Industrializing Nations, and very spotty in the Least Industrialized Nations. Japan, post-Soviet Russia, and Egypt provide examples of education in the three worlds of development. Pp. 467–471.

The Functionalist Perspective: Providing Social Benefits

What is the functionalist perspective on education?

Among the functions of education are the teaching of knowledge and skills, **cultural transmission** of values, social integration, **gatekeeping**, promoting personal and social change, and **mainstreaming.** Functionalists also note that education has replaced some traditional family functions. Pp. 471–475.

The Conflict Perspective: Reproducing the Social Class Structure

What is the conflict perspective on education?

The basic view of conflict theorists is that education reproduces the social class structure; that is, through such mechanisms as unequal funding and operating different schools for the elite and for the masses, education reinforces a society's basic social inequalities. Pp. 475–480.

The Symbolic Interactionist Perspective: Teacher Expectations and the Self-Fulfilling Prophecy

What is the symbolic interactionist perspective on education?

Symbolic interactionists focus on face-to-face interaction. In examining what occurs in the classroom, they have found a **self-fulfilling prophecy:** that student performance tends to conform to teacher expectations, whether they are high or low. Pp. 480–482.

Problems in U.S. Education—and Their Solutions

What are the chief problems that face U.S. education?

The major problems are low achievement (as shown in low SAT scores), **grade inflation, social promotion, functional illiteracy,** violence, and teen pregnancy. Pp. 483–485.

What are the primary solutions to these problems?

The primary solution is to restore high educational standards, which can be done only after providing basic security for students. Specific problems, such as the high dropout rate of pregnant teenagers, must have specific solutions, one of which is detailed in the text. Any solution for improving quality must be based on raising standards and expecting more of students and teachers alike. Pp. 485–488.

Where can I read more on this topic?

Suggested readings for this chapter are listed on page 665.

Sociology and the Internet

All URLs listed are current as of the printing of this book. URLs are often changed. Please check our Website http://www.abacon.com/henslin for updates.

1. As you read in the Sociology and the New Technology box "Internet University: No Walls, No Ivy, No Keg Parties," college courses are no longer restricted to the classroom. One of the hottest topics on campus today is "distance learning," involving everything from standard correspondence courses to multimedia instruction. This project gives you the opportunity to explore the cutting edge of this adventure in learning. Go to the Yahoo! education site at *http://www.yahoo!.com/education/* Scroll down and select "Teaching"; then select "On-Line Teaching and Learning." Browse through several of the sites listed to see the entire scope of what is offered. Then search for "Globewide Network Academy." Select "Distance Learning Catalogue." Next, select "Browse All Courses and Programs by Topic." Now you can explore the vast number of courses available. Just follow the leads to a course you are interested in. You might want to return to "Distance Learning Catalog" and select "Browse all courses and programs by sponsor." You will be surprised at the number and variety of colleges that offer instruction on the Internet. In fact, your college may be listed there.

As you browse through the Web sites and track down courses and schools that offer distance learning, record the steps of your journey and your impressions along the way. Bring your journal to class to share with your classmates.

2. As you have discovered from reading this chapter (and perhaps from your own experiences), education in the United States faces many problems and wide controversy. In this project, you will evaluate the content of two Internet sites dealing with educational reform. Go to the Center for Education Reform at *http://edreform.com/* and Effective Education at *http://www.interlog.com/~klima/ed.html* Browse through the two sites, and then write a critique of what they have to offer. Are the problems they target general or specific? Are the so-

lutions aimed at general reform, or at reaching the goals of special interest groups? How would the problems and suggested solutions be analyzed by functionalist, conflict, and symbolic interactionist theorists?

3. With credentials important in our society for obtaining a good job, emphasis is placed on test scores. Does everyone have the same chance of achieving a high score on a standardized test? How does social class play a role in test preparation? Examine the following links to companies that specialize in test preparation:

> *http://www.columbiareview.com/*
> *http://www.angelfire.com/biz/gmatcoaching/gmat.html*
> *http://www.mostlybrightideas.com/*
> *http://www.powerprep.com/*

Who is likely to take advantage of the opportunities for test preparation? Who is likely to be excluded from such opportunities? How do test preparation courses such as those on this list help to reproduce the social class structure? How do your conclusions support or refute the conflict perspective on education? The functionalist perspective?

4. School choice has been proposed as a solution to the problems in education. After reading about school choice in your text, examine the following Web sites:

> *http://www.edreform.com/choice.htm*
> *http://www.nygroup.com/scs/*
> *http://www.manhattan-institute.org/cei.htm*

What is school choice? What problems in the current U.S. school system does this proposal hope to solve? How? How does the idea of school choice differ at each of the above links? How is the idea of school choice being implemented? What do you think of the idea and these particular propositions? What effects do you think they might have on education's role in reproducing the social class structure?

Rebecca Merry, The Calling, 1994

Religion: Establishing Meaning

WITH HIS MOTHER'S CALL, *Tom's world had begun to crumble. Amid sobs, she had told him that she had left his father. After twenty-two years, their marriage was over! Why? It just didn't make sense. Tom knew that his mother and father had problems, that they argued quite a bit. But they always had. And didn't every married couple? Where was he going to go for the summer? His parents had put the house up for sale, and each had moved to a small apartment. There was no home anymore.*

Life seemed a little brighter when Tom met Amy in English class. She was the only one he could talk to about his feelings—Amy's parents had divorced three years before, and she understood. When Amy was invited to a meeting of the Unification church, Tom agreed to go with her.

The meeting was a surprise. Everyone was friendly, and everything was low-key. And everyone seemed so sure. They all believed that Judgment Day was just around the corner.

Amy and Tom found the teachings rather strange, but, since the people had been so friendly, they came back. After Tom and Amy attended meetings for about a month, they became good friends with Marcia and Ryan. Later they moved into an apartment house where Marcia, Ryan, and other Moonies lived. After a while, they dropped out of college and immersed themselves in a new life as Moonies.

What Is Religion?

All human societies are organized by some form of the family, as well as by some kind of economic system and political order. As we have seen, these key social institutions touch on aspects of life that are essential to human welfare. This chapter examines religion, another universal social institution.

Sociologists who do research on religion analyze the relationship between society and religion and study the role that religion plays in people's lives. They do not seek to make value judgments about religious beliefs. Nor is their goal to verify or to disprove anyone's faith. As mentioned in Chapter 1, sociologists have no tools for deciding that one course of action is more moral than another, much less that one religion is "the" correct one. Religion is a matter of faith; sociologists deal with empirical matters, things they can observe or measure. Thus sociologists can measure the extent to which people are religious, and they can study the effects of religious beliefs and practices on people's lives. They can analyze how religion is organized and how systems of belief are related to culture, stratification systems, and other social institutions. Unlike theologians, however, they cannot evaluate the truth of a religion's teachings.

In 1912 Emile Durkheim published an influential book, *The Elementary Forms of the Religious Life*, in which he tried to identify the elements common to all religions. After surveying religions around the world, Durkheim concluded that there is no specific belief or practice shared by all religions. He did find, however, that all religions, regardless of their name or teaching, separate the sacred from the profane. By **sacred,** Durkheim referred to aspects of life having to do with the supernatural that inspire awe, reverence, deep respect, even fear. By **profane,** he meant aspects of life that are not concerned with religion or religious purposes but, instead, are part of the ordinary aspects of everyday life. Durkheim also found that all religions develop a community around their practices and beliefs. He (1912/1965) summarized his findings as follows:

> A religion is a unified system of beliefs and practices relative to sacred things, that is to say, things set apart and forbidden—beliefs and practices which unite into one single moral community called a Church, all those who adhere to them.

sacred: Durkheim's term for things set apart or forbidden, that inspire fear, awe, reverence, or deep respect

profane: Durkheim's term for common elements of everyday life

Thus, he argued, a **religion** is defined by three elements:

1. *Beliefs* that some things are sacred (forbidden, set off from the profane)
2. *Practices* (rituals) centering around the things considered sacred
3. A *moral community* (a church) resulting from a group's beliefs and practices

Durkheim used the word **church** in an unusual sense, to refer to any "moral community" centered on beliefs and practices regarding the sacred. In Durkheim's sense, *church* refers to Buddhists bowing before a shrine, Hindus dipping in the Ganges River, and Confucianists offering food to their ancestors. Similarly, the term *moral community* does not imply morality in the sense familiar to most of us. A moral community is simply people united by their religious practices—and that would include Aztec priests who each day gathered around an altar to pluck out the beating heart of a virgin.

To better understand the sociological approach to religion, let's see what pictures emerge when we apply the three theoretical perspectives.

From his review of world religions, Durkheim concluded that all religions have beliefs, practices, and a moral community. Part of Hindu belief is that the Ganges is a holy river and bathing in it imparts spiritual benefits. Each year, millions of Hindus participate in this rite of ablution (purification).

The Functionalist Perspective

Functionalists examine the functions, dysfunctions, and functional equivalents of religion. Let us look at some of their conclusions.

Functions of Religion

In Durkheim's sense of religion—dividing the world into the sacred and profane and establishing rituals around those beliefs—religion is universal (Alpert 1939; Galanter 1989; Caldwell et al. 1992; Nauta 1993). The reason for its universality, say functionalists, is that religion meets the following eight basic human needs.

Questions About Ultimate Meaning. Around the world, religions provide answers to perplexing questions about ultimate meaning—such as the purpose of life, why people suffer, and the existence of an afterlife. Those answers give people a sense of purpose. Instead of seeing themselves buffeted by random events in an aimless existence, religious believers see their lives as fitting into a divine plan.

Emotional Comfort. The answers that religion provides about ultimate meaning also comfort people by assuring them that there is a purpose to life, even to suffering. Similarly, religious rituals that enshroud critical events such as illness and death provide emotional comfort at times of crisis. The individual knows that others care and can find consolation in following familiar rituals.

Social Solidarity. Religious teachings and practices unite believers into a community that shares values and perspectives ("we Jews," "we Christians," "we Muslims"). The religious rituals that surround marriage, for example, link the bride and groom with a broader community that wishes them well. So do other religious rituals, such as those that celebrate birth and mourn death.

Guidelines for Everyday Life. The teachings of religion are not only abstract. They also apply to people's everyday lives. For example, four of the Ten Commandments delivered by Moses to the Israelites concern God, but the other six contain instructions on

religion: according to Durkheim, beliefs and practices that separate the profane from the sacred and unite its adherents into a moral community

church: according to Durkheim, one of the three essential elements of religion—a moral community of believers; a second definition is the type of religious organization described on page 508, a large, highly organized group with formal, sedate worship services and little emphasis on personal conversion

how to live everyday life, from how to get along with parents, employers, and neighbors to warnings about lying, stealing, and adultery.

Social Control.   Religion not only provides guidelines for everyday life, but it also controls people's behaviors. Most norms of a religious group apply only to its members, but some set limits on nonmembers also. An example is religious teachings that are incorporated into criminal law. In the United States, for example, blasphemy and adultery were once statutory crimes for which offenders could be arrested, tried, and sentenced. Laws that prohibit the sale of alcohol before noon on Sunday—or even Sunday sales of "nonessential items" in some places—are another example.

Adaptation.   Religion can help people adapt to new environments. For example, it is not easy for immigrants to adjust to the confusing customs of a new land. By keeping their native language alive and preserving familiar rituals and teachings, religion provides continuity with the immigrants' cultural past.

The handful of German immigrants who settled in Perry County, Missouri, in the 1800s, for example, even brought their Lutheran minister with them. Their sermons and hymns continued to be in German, and their children also attended a school in which the minister conducted classes in German. Out of this small group grew the Lutheran Church–Missouri Synod, which, in spite of its name, is an international denomination that numbers almost 3 million people. Little by little, this group's descendants and converts entered mainstream U.S. culture. Today, except for Luther's basic teachings and some church practices, little remains of the past, for just as it helped the immigrants adapt to a new environment, so the religion itself underwent change.

Support for the Government.   Most religions provide support for the government. An obvious example is the U.S. flag so prominently displayed in many churches. For its part, governments reciprocate by supporting God—as witnessed by the inaugural speeches of U.S. presidents, who invariably ask God to bless the nation.

In some instances, the government sponsors a particular religion, bans all others, provides financial support for building churches and seminaries, and may even pay salaries to the clergy. The religions so sponsored are known as **state religions.** During the sixteenth and seventeenth centuries in Sweden, the government sponsored Lutheranism; in Switzerland, Calvinism; and in Italy, Roman Catholicism. In other instances, even though no particular religion is sponsored by the government, religious beliefs are so established in a nation's life that the country's history and social institutions are sanctified by being associated with God. For example, U.S. officials—even those who do not belong to any particular religion—take office by swearing that they will, in the name of God, fulfill their duty. Similarly, Congress is opened with prayer by its own chaplain, schoolchildren recite daily the pledge of allegiance (including the phrase "one nation under God"), and coins bear the inscription "In God We Trust." Sociologist Robert Bellah (1970) referred to this phenomenon as **civil religion.**

Social Change.   Although religion is often so bound up with the prevailing social order that it resists social change, occasionally religion spearheads change. In the 1960s, for example, the civil rights movement, which fought to desegregate public facilities and abolish racial discrimination at southern polls, was led by religious leaders, especially leaders of African-American churches such as Martin Luther King, Jr. Churches also served as centers at which demonstrators were trained and rallies were organized (Jones 1992).

Functional Equivalents of Religion

The functions just described can also be fulfilled by other components of society. If another component answers questions about ultimate meaning, provides emotional comfort and guidelines for daily life, and so on, sociologists call it a **functional equivalent** of religion. Thus, for some people, Alcoholics Anonymous is a functional equivalent of religion (Chalfant 1992). For others, psychotherapy, humanism, transcendental meditation, or even a political party performs similar functions.

state religion: a government-sponsored religion

civil religion: Robert Bellah's term for religion that is such an established feature of a country's life that its history and social institutions become sanctified by being associated with God

functional equivalent: in this context, a substitute that serves the same functions (or meets the same needs) as religion, for example, psychotherapy

Religion can promote social change, as was evident in the U.S. civil rights movement. Dr. Martin Luther King, Jr., a Baptist minister, shown here in his famous "I have a dream" speech, was the foremost leader of this movement. Many think that Pope John Paul II's visit to communist Cuba in 1998 will stimulate social change in that island nation. Shown here is the Pope meeting with Fidel Castro, the communist revolutionary who has headed Cuba since 1957.

Some functional equivalents are difficult to distinguish from a religion (Brinton 1965; Luke 1985). For example, communism had its prophets (Marx and Lenin), sacred writings (everything written by Marx, Engels, and Lenin, but especially the *Communist Manifesto*), high priests (the heads of the Communist party), sacred buildings (the Kremlin), shrines (Lenin's body on display in Red Square), rituals (the annual May Day parade in Red Square), and even martyrs (Cuba's Che Guevara). Soviet communism, which was avowedly atheistic and tried to wipe out all traces of Christianity and Judaism from its midst, even tried to replace baptisms and circumcisions with state-sponsored rituals that dedicated the child to the state. The Communist party also composed its own rituals for weddings and funerals.

As sociologist Ian Robertson (1987) pointed out, however, there is a fundamental distinction between a religion and its functional equivalent. Although the substitute may perform similar functions, its activities are not directed toward God, gods, or the supernatural.

Dysfunctions of Religion

Functionalists also examine ways in which religion can be *dysfunctional*, that is, how it can bring harmful results. Two main dysfunctions are war and religious persecution.

War. History is filled with wars based on religion—commingled with politics. Between the eleventh and fourteenth centuries, for example, Christian monarchs conducted nine bloody Crusades in an attempt to wrest control of the Holy Land from the Muslims. Unfortunately, such wars are not just a relic of the past. Even in recent years we have seen Protestants and Catholics kill one another in Northern Ireland, while Jews and Muslims in Israel and Christians and Muslims in Bosnia have done the same thing.

Religion as Justification for Persecution. Beginning in the 1200s and continuing into the 1800s, in what has become known as the Inquisition, special commissions of the Roman Catholic church tortured women to elicit confessions that they were witches, and burned them at the stake. In 1692, Protestant leaders in Salem, Massachusetts, drowned

Woodcuts (engraved blocks of wood coated with ink to leave an impression on paper) were used to illustrate books shortly after the printing press was invented. This woodcut commemorates a dysfunction of religion, the burning of witches at the stake. This particular event occurred at Derneburg, Germany, in 1555.

women who were accused of being witches. (The last execution for witchcraft was in Scotland in 1722 [Bridgwater 1953].) Similarly, it seems fair to say that the Aztec religion had its dysfunctions—at least for the virgins offered to appease angry gods. In short, religion has been used to justify oppression and any number of brutal acts.

The Symbolic Interactionist Perspective

Symbolic interactionists focus on the meanings that people give their experiences, especially how they use symbols. Let's apply this perspective to religious symbols, rituals, and beliefs to see how they help to forge a community of like-minded people.

Religious Symbols

To see how significant religious symbols can be, suppose that it is about two thousand years ago and you have just joined a new religion. You have come to believe that a recently crucified Jew named Jesus is the Messiah, the Lamb of God offered for your sins. The Roman leaders are persecuting the followers of Jesus. They hate your religion because you and your fellow believers will not acknowledge Caesar as God.

Christians are few in number, and you are eager to have fellowship with other believers. But how can you tell who is a believer? Spies are all over. The government has sworn to destroy this new religion, and you do not relish the thought of being fed to lions in the Coliseum.

You use a simple technique. While talking with a stranger, as though doodling absentmindedly in the sand or dust you casually trace out the outline of a fish. Only fellow believers know the hidden symbolism—that, taken together, the first letter of the words in the Greek sentence "Jesus (is) Christ the Son of God" spell the Greek word for *fish*. If the other person gives no response, you rub out the outline and continue the interaction as normal. If there is a response, you eagerly talk about your new faith.

All religions use symbols to provide identity and social solidarity for their members. For Muslims, the primary symbol is the crescent moon and star, for Jews the Star of

David, for Christians the cross. For members, these are not ordinary symbols, but sacred symbols that evoke feelings of awe and reverence. In Durkheim's terms, religions use symbols to specify what is sacred and to separate the sacred from the profane.

A symbol is a condensed way of communicating. Worn by a fundamentalist Christian, for example, the cross says, "I am a follower of Jesus Christ. I believe that He is the Messiah, the promised Son of God, that He loves me, that He died to take away my sins, that He rose from the dead and is going to return to earth, and that through Him I will receive eternal life."

That is a lot to pack into one symbol—and it is only part of what the symbol means to a fundamentalist believer. To people in other traditions of Christianity, the cross conveys somewhat different meanings—but to all Christians, the cross is a shorthand way of expressing many meanings. So it is also with the Star of David, the crescent moon and star, the cow (expressing to Hindus the unity of all living things), and the various symbols of the world's many other religions.

Rituals

Rituals, ceremonies or repetitive practices, are also symbols that help unite people into a moral community. Some rituals, such as the bar mitzvah of Jewish boys and Holy Communion of Christians, are designed to create in the devout a feeling of closeness with God and unity with one another. Rituals include kneeling and praying at set times, bowing, crossing oneself, singing, lighting candles and incense, a liturgy, scripture readings, processions, baptisms, weddings, funerals, and so on.

Beliefs

Symbols, including rituals, develop from beliefs. The belief may be vague ("God is") or highly specific ("God wants us to prostrate ourselves and face Mecca five times each day"). Religious beliefs not only include *values* (what is considered good and desirable in life—how we ought to live) but also a **cosmology,** a unified picture of the world. For example, the Jewish, Christian, and Muslim belief that there is only one God, the Creator of the universe, who is concerned about the actions of humans and who will hold us accountable for what we do, is a cosmology. It presents a unifying picture of the universe.

Symbolic interactionists stress that a basic characteristic of humans is that they attach meaning to objects and events and then use representations of those objects or events to communicate with one another. Some religious symbols are used to communicate feelings of awe and reverence. Michaelangelo's Pietà, depicting Mary tenderly holding her son, Jesus, after his crucifixion, is one of the most acclaimed symbols in the Western world, admired for its beauty by believers and nonbelievers alike.

Religious Experience

The term **religious experience** refers to a sudden awareness of the supernatural or a feeling of coming in contact with God. Some people undergo a mild version, such as feeling closer to God when they look at a mountain or listen to a certain piece of music. Others report a life-transforming experience; for example, St. Francis of Assisi became aware of God's presence in every living thing.

Some Protestants use the term **born again** to describe people who have undergone such a life-transforming religious experience. These persons say that they came to the realization that they had sinned, that Jesus had died for their sins, and that God wants them to live a new life. Henceforth their worlds become transformed, they look forward to the Resurrection and a new life in heaven, and they see relationships with spouses, parents, children, and even bosses in a new light. They also report a need to make changes in how they interact with others, so that their lives reflect their new, personal commitment to Jesus as their "Savior and Lord." They describe a feeling of beginning life anew, hence the term "born again."

rituals: ceremonies or repetitive practices; in this context, religious observances or rites, often intended to evoke a sense of awe of the sacred

cosmology: teachings or ideas that provide a unified picture of the world

religious experience: a sudden awareness of the supernatural or a feeling of coming in contact with God

born again: a term describing Christians who have undergone a life-transforming religious experience so radical that they feel they have become new persons

One of the functions of religion is to create community. An example is the Promise Keepers, a fundamentalist movement for men founded by Bill McCartney, the former football coach of the University of Colorado Buffaloes. Controversy surrounds the Promise Keepers' position on the roles of men and women.

Community

Finally, the shared meanings that come through symbols, rituals, and beliefs (and for some, a religious experience) unite people into a moral community. People in a moral community feel a bond with one another, for their beliefs and rituals bind them together while at the same time separating them from those who do not share their unique symbolic world. Mormons, for example, feel a "kindred spirit" (as it is often known) with other Mormons. So do Baptists, Jews, Jehovah's Witnesses, and Muslims with members of their respective faiths.

As a symbol of their unity, members of some religious groups address one another as "brother" or "sister." "Sister Dougherty, we are going to meet at Brother and Sister Tedrick's on Wednesday" is a common way of expressing a message. The terms "brother" and "sister" are intended to symbolize a relationship so close that the individuals consider themselves members of the same family.

Community is powerful, not only because it provides the basis for mutual identity, but also because it establishes norms that govern the behavior of its members. Members either conform, or they lose their membership. In Christian churches, for example, an individual whose adultery becomes known, and who refuses to ask forgiveness, may be banned from the Church. He or she may be formally excommunicated, as in the case of Catholics, or more informally discharged, as is the usual Protestant practice.

The removal of community is a serious matter for people whose identity is bound up in the community. Sociologists John Hostetler (1980), William Kephart, and William Zellner (1994) describe the Amish practice of *shunning*—ignoring an offender in all situations. Persons who are shunned are treated as though they do not exist (for if they do not repent by expressing sorrow for their act they have ceased to exist as members of the community). The shunning is so thorough that even family members, who themselves remain in good standing in the congregation, are not allowed to talk to the person being shunned. This obviously makes for some interesting meals.

The Conflict Perspective

The conflict perspective has an entirely different focus. Conflict theorists examine how religion supports the status quo, and helps to maintain social inequalities.

Opium of the People

In general, conflict theorists are highly critical of religion. Karl Marx, an avowed atheist who believed that the existence of God was an impossibility, set the tone for conflict theorists with his most famous statement on this subject: "Religion is the sigh of the oppressed creature, the sentiment of a heartless world. . . . It is the opium of the people" (Marx 1844/1964). By this statement, Marx meant that oppressed workers, sighing for release from their suffering, escape into religion. For them, religion is like a drug that helps them forget their misery. By diverting their eyes to future happiness in a coming world, religion takes their eyes off their suffering in this one, thereby greatly reducing the possibility that they will rebel against their oppressors.

A Reflection of Social Inequalities

Conflict theorists stress that religious teachings and practices are a mirror of a society's inequalities. Gender inequality illustrates this point. When men completely dominated U.S. society, U.S. churches and synagogues ordained only men, limiting women to such activities as teaching children in Sunday school or preparing meals for congregational get-togethers, which were considered appropriate "feminine" activities. As women's roles in the broader society changed, however, religion reflected those changes. First, many religious groups allowed women to vote. Then, as women attained prominent positions in the business world and professions, some Protestant and Jewish groups allowed women to be ordained. Similarly, just as women still face barriers in secular society, so some congregations still refuse to ordain women. In some congregations the barriers remain so high that women are still not allowed to vote.

A Legitimation of Social Inequalities

Not only does religion mirror the social inequalities of the larger society, conflict theorists say, but it also legitimates them. By this, they mean that religion, reflecting the interests of those in power, teaches that the existing social arrangements of a society represent what God desires. For example, during the Middle Ages Christian theologians decreed the "divine right of kings." This doctrine meant that God determined who would become king and set him on the throne. The king ruled in God's place, and it was the duty of a king's subjects to be loyal to him (and to pay their taxes). To disobey the king was to disobey God.

In what is perhaps the supreme technique of legitimating the social order, going even a step further than the "divine right of kings," the religion of ancient Egypt held that the Pharaoh was a god. The Emperor of Japan was similarly declared divine. If this were so, who could even question his decisions? How many of today's politicians would give their right arm for such a religious teaching!

Conflict theorists point to many other examples of how religion legitimates the social order. One of the more remarkable took place in the decades before the American Civil War. Southern ministers used scripture to defend slavery, saying that it was God's will—while northern ministers legitimated *their* region's social structure and used scripture to denounce slavery as evil (Ernst 1988; Nauta 1993; White 1995). In India, Hinduism supports the caste system by teaching that an individual who tries to change caste will come back in the next life as a member of a lower caste—or even as an animal.

Religion and the Spirit of Capitalism ▶

Max Weber disagreed with the conflict perspective that religion merely reflects and legitimates the social order, and that religion impedes social change by encouraging people to focus on the afterlife. In contrast, Weber saw religion's focus on the afterlife as a source of profound social change.

Like Marx, Weber personally observed the European countries industrialize. Weber was intrigued with the question of why some societies embraced capitalism, while others clung to their traditional ways. Tradition is strong and holds people in check, yet some societies had been transformed by capitalism, while others remained untouched. As he explored this problem, Weber concluded that religion held the key to **modernization**—the transformation of traditional societies to industrial societies.

modernization: the transformation of traditional societies into industrial societies

To explain his conclusions, Weber wrote *The Protestant Ethic and the Spirit of Capitalism* (1904–1905/1958). Because Weber's argument was presented in Chapter 7 (pages 168–170), it is only summarized here.

1. Capitalism is not just a superficial change. Rather, capitalism represents a fundamentally different way of thinking about work and money. *Traditionally, people worked just enough to meet their basic needs, not so that they could have a surplus to invest.* To accumulate money (capital) as an end in itself, not to spend it, was a radical departure from traditional thinking. People even came to consider it a duty to invest money in order to make profits, which, in turn, they reinvested to make more profits. Weber called this new approach to work and money the **spirit of capitalism.**

2. Why did the spirit of capitalism develop in Europe, and not, for example, in China or India, where the people had similar intelligence, material resources, education, and so on? According to Weber, *religion was the key.* The religions of China and India, and indeed Roman Catholicism in Europe, encouraged a traditional approach to life, not thrift and investment. Capitalism appeared when Protestantism came on the scene.

3. What was different about Protestantism, especially Calvinism? John Calvin taught that God had predestined some people to heaven, others to hell, and that in this life you couldn't know where you were headed. People could depend neither on church membership nor on feelings about their relationship with God to know they were saved.

4. This doctrine created intense anxiety among Calvin's followers: "Am I predestined to hell or to heaven?" they wondered. As Calvinists wrestled with this question, they concluded that church members had a duty to prove that they are one of God's elect, and to live as though they are predestined to heaven—for good works are a demonstration of salvation.

5. This conclusion motivated Calvinists to lead highly moral lives *and* to work hard, to not waste time, and to be frugal—for idleness and needless spending were signs of worldliness. Weber called this self-denying approach to life the **Protestant ethic.**

6. As people worked hard and spent money only on necessities (with luxuries narrowly defined), they accumulated money. This capital, in turn, since it couldn't be spent, was invested—which led to a surge in production.

7. Thus, a change in religion (from Catholicism to Protestantism, especially Calvinism) led to a fundamental change in thought and behavior (the *Protestant ethic*). The result was the *spirit of capitalism.* Thus capitalism originated in Europe, and not in places where religion did not encourage capitalism's essential elements: the accumulation of capital through frugality and hard work, and its investment and reinvestment.

Although Weber's analysis has been highly influential, it has not lacked critics (Marshall 1982). Hundreds of scholars have attacked it, some for overlooking the lack of capitalism in Scotland (a Calvinist country), others for failing to explain why the Industrial Revolution was born in England (not a Calvinist country). Hundreds of other scholars have defended Weber's argument. There is currently no historical evidence that can definitively prove or disprove Weber's thesis.

At this point in history, the Protestant ethic and the spirit of capitalism are not confined to any specific religion or even part of the world. Rather, they have become cultural traits that have spread to societies around the world (Greeley 1964; Yinger 1970). U.S. Catholics have about the same approach to life as do U.S. Protestants. In addition, Hong Kong, Japan, Malaysia, Singapore, South Korea, and Taiwan have embraced capitalism—not exactly Protestant countries (Levy 1992).

spirit of capitalism: Weber's term for the desire to accumulate capital as a duty—not to spend it, but as an end in itself—and to constantly reinvest it

Protestant ethic: Weber's term to describe the ideal of a self-denying, highly moral life, accompanied by hard work and frugality

The World's Major Religions

Of the thousands of religions in the world, most people practice either Judaism, Christianity, Islam, Hinduism, Buddhism, or Confucianism. Let us briefly review each.

Judaism

The origin of Judaism is traced to Abraham, who lived about four thousand years ago in Mesopotamia. Jews believe that God (Jahweh) made a covenant with Abraham, setting aside his descendants as a chosen people and promising to make them "as numerous as the sands of the seashore" and give them a special land that would be theirs forever. The sign of this covenant was the circumcision of male children, to be performed when a newborn was eight days old. Descent is traced through Abraham and his wife, Sarah, their son Isaac, and their grandson Jacob (also called Israel).

Joseph, a son of Jacob, was sold by his brothers into slavery and taken to Egypt. Following a series of hair-raising adventures, Joseph became Pharaoh's right-hand man. When a severe famine hit Canaan, where Jacob's family was living, Jacob and his eleven other sons fled to Egypt. Under Joseph's leadership, they were welcome. A subsequent Pharaoh, however, enslaved the Israelites. After about four hundred years, Moses, an Israelite who had been adopted by Pharaoh's daughter, confronted Pharaoh. He persuaded Pharaoh to release the slaves, numbering at that time about 2 million. Moses led them out of Egypt, but before they reached their Promised Land the Israelites spent forty years in desert wanderings. Sometime during those years, Moses delivered the Ten Commandments from Mount Sinai. Abraham, Isaac, Jacob, and Moses hold revered positions in Judaism. The events of their lives and the recounting of the early history of the Israelites are contained in the first five books of the Bible, called the Torah.

The founding of Judaism marked a fundamental change in religion, for it was the first religion based on **monotheism,** the belief that there is only one God. Prior to Judaism, religions were based on **polytheism,** the belief that there are many gods. In Greek religion, for example, Zeus was the god of heaven and earth, Poseidon the god of the sea, and Athena the goddess of wisdom. Other groups followed **animism,** believing that all objects in the world have spirits, some of which are dangerous and must be outwitted.

Contemporary Judaism in the United States comprises three main branches: Orthodox, Reform, and Conservative. Orthodox Jews adhere to the laws espoused by Moses. They eat only foods prepared in a designated manner (kosher), observe the Sabbath in a traditional way, and segregate males and females in their religious services. During the 1800s, a group that wanted to make their practices more compatible with the secular (nonreligious) culture broke from this tradition. This liberal group, known as Reform Judaism, mostly uses the vernacular (a country's language) in its religious ceremonies and has reduced much of the ritual. The third branch, Conservative Judaism, falls somewhere between the other two. No branch has continued polygyny (allowing a husband to have more than one wife), the original marriage custom of the Jews, which was outlawed by rabbinic decree about a thousand years ago.

The history of Judaism is marked by conflict and persecution. The Israelites were conquered by Babylon, and again made slaves. After returning to Israel and rebuilding the temple, they were later conquered by Rome, and after their rebellion at Masada in A.D. 70 failed, they were dispersed for almost two thousand years into other nations. During those centuries, they faced prejudice, discrimination, and persecution (called **anti-Semitism**) by many peoples and rulers. The most horrendous example is Hitler's attempt to eliminate the Jews as a people in the Nazi Holocaust of World War II. Under the Nazi occupation of Europe and North Africa, about 6 million Jews were slaughtered, perhaps half dying in gas ovens constructed specifically for this purpose.

Central to Jewish teaching is the requirement to love God and do good deeds. Good deeds begin in the family, where each member has an obligation toward the others. Sin is a conscious choice to do evil, and must be atoned for by prayers and good works. Jews consider Jerusalem their holiest city, where the Messiah will one day appear bringing redemption for them all.

Christianity

Christianity, which developed out of Judaism, is also monotheistic. Christians believe that Jesus Christ is the Messiah whom God promised the Jews.

monotheism: the belief that there is only one God

polytheism: the belief that there are many gods

animism: the belief that all objects in the world have spirits, some of which are dangerous and must be outwitted

anti-Semitism: prejudice, discrimination, and persecution directed against Jews

Jesus was born in poverty, and traditional Christians believe, to a virgin. Within two years of his birth, Herod, named king of Palestine by Caesar, who had conquered Israel, was informed that people were saying that a new king had been born. When Herod sent soldiers to kill Jesus, his parents fled with him to Egypt. After Herod died, they returned, settling in the small town of Nazareth.

About the age of 30, Jesus began a preaching and healing ministry. His teachings challenged the contemporary religious establishment and as his popularity grew, the religious leaders plotted to have him killed by the Romans. Christians interpret the death of Jesus as a blood sacrifice for their sins. They believe that through his death they have peace with God and will inherit eternal life.

The twelve main followers of Jesus, called *apostles*, believed that Jesus rose from the dead. They preached the need to be "born again," that is, to accept Jesus as Savior, give up selfish ways, and live a devout life. The new religion spread rapidly, and after initial hostility from imperial Rome—including the feeding of believers to the lions in the Coliseum—in A.D. 317 Christianity became the empire's official religion.

During the first thousand years of Christianity, there was only one church organization, directed from Rome. During the eleventh century, after disagreement over doctrine and politics, Greek Orthodoxy was established. It was headquartered in Constantinople (now Istanbul, Turkey). During the Middle Ages, the Roman Catholic church, aligned with the political establishment, grew corrupt. Some Church offices, such as that of bishop, were sold for a set price, and, in a situation that touched off the Reformation led by Martin Luther in the sixteenth century, the forgiveness of sins (including those not yet committed) could be purchased by buying an "indulgence."

Although Martin Luther's original goal was to reform the Church, not divide it, the Reformation began a splintering of Christianity. It coincided with the breakup of feudalism, and as the ancient political structure came apart, people clamored for independence not only in political but also in religious thought. Today, Christianity is the most popular religion in the world, with over 1 billion adherents. Christians are divided into hundreds of groups, some with doctrinal differences so slight that only members of the group can appreciate the extremely fine distinctions that, they feel, significantly separate them from others. The Social Map on the next page shows how some of these groups are distributed in the United States.

Islam

Islam, whose followers are known as Muslims, began in the same part of the world as Judaism and Christianity. Islam is the world's third monotheistic religion. It was founded by Muhammad, who was born in Mecca (now in Saudi Arabia) about A.D. 570. Muhammad married Khadija, a wealthy widow. About the age of 40, he reported that he had visions from God. These, and his teachings, were later written down in a book called the Koran. Few paid attention to Muhammad, although Ali, his son-in-law, believed him. When he found out that there was a plot to murder him, Muhammad fled to Medina, where he found a more receptive audience. There he established a *theocracy* (a government based on the principle that God is the ruler, his laws the statutes of the land, and priests his earthly administrators), and founded the Muslim empire. In A.D. 630 he returned to Mecca, this time as a conqueror (Bridgwater 1953).

After Muhammad's death, a struggle for control over the empire he had founded split Islam into two branches that remain today, the Sunni and the Shi'ite. The Shi'ites, who believe that the *imam* (the religious leader) is inspired as he interprets the Koran, are generally more conservative and inclined to **fundamentalism,** the belief that modernism threatens religion and that the faith as it was originally practiced should be restored. The Sunni, who do not share this belief, are generally more liberal.

Like the Jews, Muslims trace their ancestry to Abraham. Abraham fathered a son, Ishmael, by Hagar, his wife Sarah's Egyptian maid (Genesis 25:12). Ishmael had twelve sons, from whom a good portion of today's Arab world is descended. For them also,

fundamentalism: the belief that true religion is threatened by modernism and that the faith as it was originally practiced should be restored

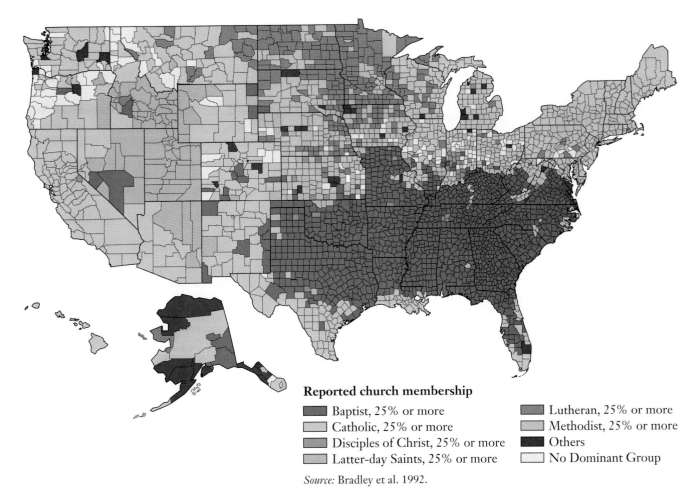

Reported church membership

- Baptist, 25% or more
- Catholic, 25% or more
- Disciples of Christ, 25% or more
- Latter-day Saints, 25% or more

- Lutheran, 25% or more
- Methodist, 25% or more
- Others
- No Dominant Group

Source: Bradley et al. 1992.

Figure 18.1

**Church Membership:
Dominant Religion,
by County**

Jerusalem is a holy city. The Muslims consider the Bibles of the Jews and the Christians to be sacred but take the Koran as the final word. They believe that the followers of Abraham and Moses (Jews) and Jesus (Christians) changed the original teachings and that Muhammad restored their purity. It is the duty of each Muslim to make a pilgrimage to Mecca during his or her lifetime.

Unlike the Jews, the Muslims continue to practice polygyny. They limit a man, however, to four wives.

Hinduism

Unlike the other religions described, Hinduism has no specific founder. Going back about four thousand years, Hinduism is the chief religion of India. The term *Hinduism*, however, is Western, and in India the closest term is *dharma* (law). Unlike Judaism, Christianity, and Islam, Hinduism has no canonical scripture, that is, no texts thought to be inspired by God. Instead, several books, including the *Brahmanas, Bhagavad-Gita,* and *Upanishads,* expound on moral qualities that people should strive after. They also delineate the sacrifices people should make to the gods.

Hindus are *polytheists;* that is, they believe that there are many gods. They believe that one of these gods, Brahma, created the universe. Brahma, along with Shiva (the Destroyer) and Vishnu (the Preserver), form a triad at the center of modern Hinduism. A central belief is *karma*, spiritual progress. There is no final judgment, but, instead, **reincarnation,** a cycle of life, death, and rebirth. Death involves only the body, and each person's soul comes back in a form that matches the individual's moral progress in the

reincarnation: in Hinduism and Buddhism, the return of the soul after death in a different form

The most famous buddhist symbol is the Buddha, which is depicted in many forms, including female. Shown here is a buddhist monk in Sri Lanka praying before the world-famous Buddha at Anuradhapura.

previous life (which centers on proper conduct in following the rules of one's caste). If an individual reaches spiritual perfection, he or she has attained *nirvana*. This marks the end of the cycle of death and rebirth, when the soul is reunited with the universal soul. When this occurs, *maya*, the illusion of time and space, has been conquered.

Some Hindu practices have been modified as a consequence of social protest—especially child marriage and *suttee*, the practice of cremating a surviving widow along with her deceased husband (Bridgwater 1953). Other ancient rituals remain unchanged, such as *kumbh mela*, a purifying washing in the Ganges River, which takes place every twelve years, and in which many millions participate.

Buddhism

About 600 B.C., Siddhartha Gautama founded Buddhism. (Buddha means the "enlightened one," a term Gautama was given by his disciples.) Gautama was the son of an upper-caste Hindu ruler in an area north of Benares, India. At the age of 29, he renounced his life of luxury and became an ascetic. Through meditation, he discovered the following "four noble truths," all of which emphasize self-denial and compassion.

1. Existence is suffering.
2. The origin of suffering is desire.
3. Suffering ceases when desire ceases.
4. The way to end desire is to follow the "noble eightfold path."

The noble eightfold path consists of

1. Right belief
2. Right resolve (to renounce carnal pleasure and to harm no living creature)
3. Right speech
4. Right conduct
5. Right occupation or living
6. Right effort
7. Right-mindedness (or contemplation)
8. Right ecstasy

Like Hinduism, the final goal of Buddhism is to escape from reincarnation into nonexistence or blissful peace (Bridgwater 1953).

Buddhism spread rapidly. In the third century B.C., the ruler of India adopted Buddhism and sent missionaries throughout Asia to spread the new teaching. By the fifth century A.D., Buddhism reached the height of its popularity in India, after which it died out. Buddhism, however, had been adopted in Ceylon, Burma, Tibet, Laos, Cambodia, Thailand, China, Korea, and Japan, where it flourishes today.

Confucianism

About the time that Gautama lived, K'ung Fu-tsu (551–479 B.C.) was born in China. Confucius (his name strung together in English), a public official, was distressed by the corruption that he saw in government. Unlike Gautama, who urged withdrawal from social activities, Confucius urged social reform and developed a system of morality based on peace, justice, and universal order. His teachings were incorporated into writings called the *Analects*.

The basic moral principle of Confucianism is to maintain *jen*, sympathy or concern for other humans. The key to jen is to maintain right relationships—being loyal and placing morality above self-interest. In what is called the "Confucian Golden Rule," Confucius stated a basic principle for jen: to treat those who are subordinate to you as you would like to be treated by people superior to yourself. Confucius taught that right relationships within the family (loyalty, respect) should be the model for society. He also taught the "middle way," an avoidance of extremes.

Confucianism was originally atheistic, simply a set of moral teachings without reference to the supernatural. As the centuries passed, however, local gods were added to the teachings, and Confucius himself was declared a god. Confucius's teachings became the basis for the government of China. About A.D. 1000, the emphasis on meditation gave way to a stress on improvement through acquiring knowledge. This emphasis remained dominant until the twentieth century, by which time the government had become rigid, with approval of the existing order having replaced respectful relationships (Bridgwater 1953). Following the Communist revolution of 1949, political leaders attempted to weaken the people's ties with Confucianism.

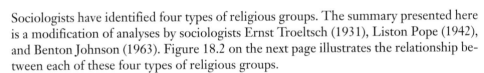

Types of Religious Groups

Sociologists have identified four types of religious groups. The summary presented here is a modification of analyses by sociologists Ernst Troeltsch (1931), Liston Pope (1942), and Benton Johnson (1963). Figure 18.2 on the next page illustrates the relationship between each of these four types of religious groups.

Cult

The word *cult* conjures up bizarre images—shaven heads, weird music, brainwashing—even ritual murder may come to mind. In the opening vignette, Tom and Amy dropped out of college, and, to the dismay of their parents and friends, cut themselves off from their usual surroundings and activities.

The sociological and commonsense meanings of the term cult *differ radically. Shoko Asahara of Japan, left, matches the public's image of a crazed cult leader. Asahara headed a cult that on March 20, 1995, released a nerve gas, sarin, in the Tokyo subway during rush hour. The attack left 10 people dead and 4,700 injured. As the text explains, the sociological meaning of* cult, *in contrast, is neutral.*

Cults sometimes make instant headlines around the world, as did the one described in the Down-to-Earth Sociology box on the next page. Cults, however, are not necessarily weird, and few practice "brainwashing" or bizarre rituals. In fact, *all religions began as cults* (Stark 1989). A **cult** is simply a new or different religion, whose teaching and practices put it at odds with the dominant culture and religion. Because the term cult arouses such negative meanings in the public mind, however, some scholars prefer to use "new religion" instead.

Cults often begin with the appearance of a **charismatic leader,** an individual who inspires people because he or she seems to have extraordinary qualities. **Charisma** refers to an outstanding gift or some exceptional quality. Finding something highly appealing about the individual, people feel drawn to both the person and the message.

The most popular religion in the world today began as a cult. Its handful of followers believed that an unschooled carpenter who preached in remote villages in a backwater country was the Son of God, that he was killed and came back to life. Those beliefs made the early Christians a cult, setting them apart from the rest of their society. Persecuted by both religious and political authorities, these early believers clung to one another for support, many cutting off associations with their unbelieving families and friends. To others, the early Christians must have seemed deluded and brainwashed.

cult: a new religion with few followers, whose teachings and practices put it at odds with the dominant culture and religion

charismatic leader: literally, someone to whom God has given a gift; more commonly, someone who exerts extraordinary appeal to a group of followers

charisma: literally, an extraordinary gift from God; more commonly, an outstanding, "magnetic" personality

Figure 18.2

A Cult–Sect–Church–Ecclesia Continuum

Characteristics of the Group
1. Number of members
2. Wealth of organization
3. Wealth of members ("worldly success")
4. Formal training of clergy

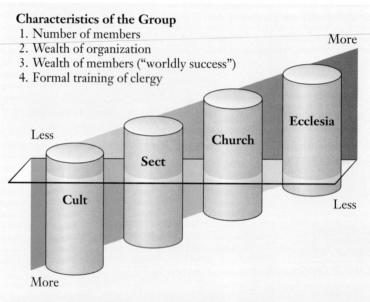

The Group Emphasizes
1. The need to reject society
   (the culture is a threat to true religion)
2. That it is rejected by society (the group feels hostility)
3. Hostility toward other religions
4. Hostility from other religions
5. Personal salvation
6. Emotional expression of religious beliefs
7. Revelation (God speaks directly to people)
8. God's direct intervention in people's lives
   (such as providing guidance or healing)
9. A duty to spread the message (evangelism)
10. A literal interpretation of scripture
11. A literal heaven and hell
12. That a conversion experience is necessary

Note: Any religious organization can be placed somewhere on this continuum, based on its having "more" or "less" of these characteristics.

Sources: Based on Troeltsch 1931; Pope 1942; and Johnson 1963.

Heaven's Gate and Other Cults

The news made instant headlines around the world. Thirty-nine bodies in an exclusive San Diego neighborhood draped in purple, diamond-shaped shrouds. Some of the men had been castrated. No sign of a struggle.

Reports followed on the beliefs of those who died. A spaceship was hiding behind the Hale-Bopp comet ready to transport them to a new life. To be beamed aboard, they had to leave their "containers" behind. That meant suicide. For their space travels, each cult member put on new Nike sneakers. Each also packed a bag with clothing, $5 bills, and quarters—and a passport.

Then there is the garbage-eating Brotherhood led by an ex-Marine who claims he is Jesus. His long-haired followers rummage through dumpsters, carefully removing any mold before dining on rotting scraps of the material world they so disdain. They blame their stomachaches on Satan (O'Neill 1997).

Other Messiahs have been just as influential. Back in the 1970s, hundred followed Jim Jones to Guyana. More than 900 committed suicide—or were murdered. In the 1990s, 74 members of the Solar Temple in Switzerland, France, and Canada arranged themselves in the shape of a cross and set themselves afire. They believed they would be transported to the star Sirius (Lacayo 1997).

Marshal Applewhite, pictured here, was able to persuade 38 men to commit suicide with him in order to be beamed aboard a spaceship. The text explains how such bizarre events can occur.

Why would anyone fall for such "obvious" deception? As this chapter's subtitle indicates, finding *meaning* in life lies at the center of religion. Always, people seek to satisfy their spiritual longings. And with today's rapid social change, our traditional meanings are constantly challenged and sometimes uprooted. Most significantly, cult teachings are learned among a group of people who satisfy deep needs of belonging, who provide a life–enhancing sense of community. Newcomers are isolated, cut off from family and friends who would provide a balancing perspective on reality. As the group's views are regularly confirmed by people one has come to like and respect, the bizarreness of these beliefs gradually wears off. Instead, cult members come to be viewed as "insiders" who are privy to secret messages that lie beyond the grasp of ordinary people.

Heaven's Gate, and its many counterparts throughout the world, matches the public's image of cults—bizarre people with strange teachings whose followers act in repugnant ways. As this chapter stresses, however, the *sociological* meaning of "cult" is different. All new religions begin as cults. Some grow and become sects. Others even develop into churches and ecclesias. Of those that do, however, not one includes mass suicide as part of its message. That sort of eliminates the possibility of moving up the continuum illustrated on the facing page.

So it was with Islam. When Muhammad revealed his visions and said that God's name was really Allah, only a few people believed him. To others, he must have seemed crazy, deranged.

Each cult (or new religion) meets with rejection from society. Its message is considered bizarre, its approach to life strange. Its members antagonize the majority, who are convinced that they have a monopoly on the truth. The new message may claim revelation, visions, visits from God and angels, some form of enlightenment, or seeing the true way to God. The cult demands intense commitment, and its followers, confronting a hostile world, pull into a tight circle, separating themselves from nonbelievers.

Most cults fail. Not many people believe the new message, and the cult fades into obscurity. Some, however, succeed and make history. Over time, large numbers of people may come to accept the message, and become followers of the religion. If this happens, the new religion changes from a cult to a sect.

Sect

A **sect** is a group larger than a cult. Its members still feel a fair amount of tension with the prevailing beliefs and values of the broader society. The sect may even be hostile to the society in which it lives. At the very least, its members remain uncomfortable with many of the emphases of the dominant culture, while nonmembers, in turn, tend to be uncomfortable with members of the sect.

sect: a group larger than a cult that still feels substantial hostility from and toward society

Ordinarily, sects are loosely organized and fairly small. They emphasize personal salvation and an emotional expression of one's relationship with God. Clapping, shouting, dancing, and extemporaneous prayers are hallmarks of sects. Like cults, sects also stress **evangelism,** the active recruitment of new members.

If a sect grows, its members gradually tend to make peace with the rest of society. They become more respectable in the eyes of the majority and feel much less hostility and little, if any, isolation. To appeal to the new, broader base, the sect shifts some of its doctrines, redefining matters to remove some of the rough edges that created tension between it and the rest of society. If a sect follows this course and becomes larger and more integrated into society, it changes into a church.

Church

At this point, the religious group is highly bureaucratized—probably with national and international headquarters that give directions to the local congregations, enforce rules about who can be ordained, and control finances. The group's worship service is likely to have grown more sedate, with much less emphasis on personal salvation and emotional expression. Written prayers, for example, are now likely to be read before the congregation, sermons to be much more formal, and the relationship with God to be less intense. Rather than being recruited from the outside by fervent, personal evangelism, most new members now come from within, from children born to existing members. Rather than joining through conversion—seeing the new truth—children may be baptized, circumcised, or dedicated in some other way. At some designated age, children may be asked to affirm the group's beliefs in a confirmation or bar mitzvah ceremony.

Ecclesia

Finally, some groups become so well integrated into a culture, and so strongly allied with their government, that it is difficult to tell where one leaves off and the other takes over. In these state religions, also called **ecclesia,** the government and religion work together to try to shape society. There is no recruitment of members, for citizenship makes everyone a member. The majority of the society, however, may belong to the religion in name only. The religion is part of a cultural identification, not an eye-opening experience. How extensive religion and government intertwine in an ecclesia is illustrated by Sweden, where in the 1800s all citizens had to memorize Luther's *Small Catechism* and be tested on it yearly (Anderson 1995). Today, Lutheranism is still the state religion, but most Swedes come to church only for baptisms, marriages, and funerals.

Where cults and sects see God as personally involved and concerned with an individual's life, requiring an intense and direct response, ecclesias envision God as more impersonal and remote. Church services reflect this view of the supernatural, for they tend to be highly formal, directed by ministers or priests who, after undergoing rigorous training in approved schools or seminaries, follow prescribed rituals.

Examples of ecclesia include the Church of England (whose very name expresses alignment between church and state), the Lutheran church in Sweden and Denmark, Islam in Iran and Iraq, and, during the time of the Holy Roman Empire, the Roman Catholic church, which was the official religion for what is today Europe.

Variations in Patterns

Obviously, not all religious groups go through all these stages—from cult to sect to church to ecclesia. Some die out because they fail to attract enough members. Others, such as the Amish, remain sects. And, as is evident from the few countries that have state religions, very few religions ever become ecclesias.

In addition, these classifications are not perfectly matched in the real world. For example, although the Amish are a sect, they place little or no emphasis on recruiting others. The early Quakers, another sect, shied away from emotional expressions of their beliefs. They would quietly meditate in church, with no one speaking, until God gave someone a message to share with others. Finally, some groups that become churches may

evangelism: an attempt to win converts

ecclesia: a religious group so integrated into the dominant culture that it is difficult to tell where the one begins and the other leaves off; also called a *state religion*

retain a few characteristics of sects, such as an emphasis on evangelism or a personal relationship with God.

Although all religions began as cults, not all varieties of a particular religion have done so. For example, some **denominations**—"brand names" within a major religion, such as Methodism or Reform Judaism—may begin as splinter groups. A large group within a church may disagree with *some aspects* of the church's teachings (not its major message) and break away to form its own organization. An example mentioned earlier (page 499) is the Southern Baptist Convention, formed in 1845 to defend the right to own slaves.

When Religion and Culture Conflict

As we have seen, cults and sects represent a break with the past. Consequently, they challenge the social order. Three major patterns of adaptation occur when religion and the culture in which it is embedded find themselves in conflict.

First, the members of a religion may reject the dominant culture and have as little as possible to do with nonmembers of their religion. Like the Amish, they may withdraw into closed communities. As noted in the Perspectives box on page 104, the Amish broke away from Swiss-German Mennonites in 1693. They try to preserve the culture of their ancestors, a simpler time when life was uncontaminated by television, movies, automobiles, or even electricity. To do so, they emphasize family life, traditional male and female roles, and live on farms, which they work with horses. They continue to wear the same style of clothing as their ancestors did three hundred years ago, to light their homes with oil lamps, and to speak German at home and in church. They also continue to reject radio, television, motorized vehicles, and education beyond the eighth grade. They do mingle with non-Amish to the extent of shopping in town—where they are readily distinguishable by their form of transportation (horse-drawn carriages), clothing, and speech.

In the second pattern, a cult or sect rejects only specific elements of the prevailing culture. For example, religious teachings may dictate that immodest clothing—short skirts, swimsuits, low-cut dresses, and so on—is immoral, or that wearing makeup or going to the movies is wrong. Most elements of the main culture, however, are accepted. Although specific activities are forbidden, members of the religion are able to participate in most aspects of the broader society. They resolve this mild tension either by adhering to the religion or by "sneaking," doing the forbidden acts on the sly.

In the third pattern, the society rejects the religious group and may even try to destroy it. The early Christians are an example. The Roman emperor declared them enemies of Rome and ordered all Christians to be hunted down and destroyed. The Mormons provide another example. Their rejection of Roman Catholicism and Protestantism as corrupt, accompanied by their belief in polygyny, led to their persecution. In 1831, they left Palmyra, New York, and moved first to Kirtland, Ohio, and subsequently to Independence, Missouri. When the persecution continued, they moved to Nauvoo, Illinois. There a mob murdered the founder of the religion, Joseph Smith, and his brother Hyrum. The Mormons then decided to escape the dominant culture altogether by founding a community in the wilderness. Consequently, in 1847 they settled in the Great Salt Lake Valley of what is today the state of Utah (Bridgwater 1953). For a more current example, see the following Thinking Critically section.

▼▼▼▼▼▼▼▼▼▼▼▼▼▼▼▼▼▼▼▼▼▼▼

Thinking Critically About Social Controversy

How to Destroy a Cult: A Conflict Interpretation of the U.S. Government Versus the Branch Davidians

▼ The first report was stunning. About a hundred armed agents of the Bureau of Alcohol, Tobacco, and Firearms (ATF) attacked the compound of an obscure religious group in Waco, Texas. Four armed agents who assaulted the compound and six men who tried to defend it

denomination: a "brand name" within a major religion, for example, Methodist or Baptist

were shot to death. The result was a fifty-one-day standoff, televised to the U.S. public, with the ATF and FBI doing such strange things as bombarding the compound with loud music day and night. At 6 A.M. on the fifty-first day of the siege, following on-again, off-again negotiations with David Koresh, the charismatic 33-year-old leader of the Branch Davidians, a tank rammed the compound's main building and began pumping in gas consisting of chemicals that, by law, the U.S. military was unable to use against Iraqi soldiers. A second tank joined in, punching holes in the walls. In terror, the women and children fled to the second floor, while the men continued to shoot futilely at the armed vehicles. Suddenly an explosion rocked the compound, and the buildings burst into flames. Eighty-five men, women, and children were burned to death. Some of the charred bodies of the twenty-five children were found huddled next to their mothers.

The government claimed that the Branch Davidians set the fire. Survivors said the fire began when one of the tanks knocked over a lantern. After the fire, the government sealed off the area and bulldozed the charred remains of the buildings.

The following analysis of this controversial event does *not* take the government line. Rather, it is written from the conflict perspective, assuming a conspiracy of the elite to destroy a group that posed a threat to its power.

What crimes could have justified such a lethal assault against the Branch Davidians? At first, the government said that it took action because the group had violated firearms laws. Later, agents changed their story to make saving the children their primary goal. Was the death of those children—and their parents—just an ironic twist of events that marked the stunning end to a strange group? Or was it part of a conspiracy by U.S. government agencies to put an end to groups that dare to challenge their authority?

Koresh's teachings certainly were bizarre. He taught that he was Jesus Christ returned to earth. Many have made this same claim, but Koresh's twist was that he had returned in sinful form so he could better understand sinners. As a sinner, Koresh had a voracious sexual appetite. He demanded—and received—sex from the men's wives, while insisting that the men remain celibate. Some reports, perhaps sponsored by the government, indicate that he also had sex with their daughters, some as young as 12 and 13 years old. Koresh also taught that Armageddon was on its way, that the government, the enemy, would one day launch an armed attack against them. About this, at least, he was right.

Since the official version has been repeatedly published in the mass media, let's consider the case for the other side.

First, Koresh was no stranger to Waco. He regularly drove around the area, shopping in stores and eating in restaurants. If the government had wanted, it could have served warrants and arrested him in public, with no confrontation. Second, after the first assault, Koresh let anyone leave who wanted to go. Some parents and twenty-one children did leave. After studying the children, the worst the government could come up with was that some children had been spanked for disobedience. They also learned that the children had been taught Bible stories and had learned songs. Third, the accounts of some of the survivors certainly don't support government claims. Sheila Martin, whose husband, a Harvard-trained attorney, along with four of their children, died in the conflagration, says that people watching television saw only the outside of the building, not how nice it was to live there. "Those were the happiest days of my life," she said.

On the other hand, there may have been child abuse. But an armed attack by government agents for child abuse? Unlikely. Rather, the ATF's first accounts of the group stockpiling weapons is the key to explain the government's desire to annihilate the group. In the months before their destruction, the Branch Davidians had purchased many thousands of dollars of guns and ammunition. Although their purchases were legal, the government became concerned about reports of a strange group, heavily armed, holed up in its own compound. Who knows what they might do? The solution was to seek out and destroy. In this context, it is not without significance to note that the ATF is the trigger-happy group once headed by Elliot Ness of "The Untouchables" fame.

For Your Consideration

If this analysis is correct, what groups might be targeted next? One target could be militant Islamic groups, which government agents have already infiltrated. Other primary candidates are the survivalist groups that, believing the U.S. government is the Antichrist, reject the government's decrees as illegitimate, and, fearing an attack, have armed themselves. Like the Branch Davidians, some have retreated into their own compounds. One group calls itself Christian Identity. Its members believe that white "Aryans" are the direct descendants of the tribes of Israel and those who call themselves Jews are really the children of Satan. A specific candidate is the Prophet's Church Universal and Triumphant, which under the leadership of Elizabeth Clare, has built underground shelters near Yellowstone National Park—and is rumored to have stockpiled arms. Dozens of other groups have sprouted up, teaching that the world is soon coming to an end, that the Antichrist has been unleashed on the world. Like Koresh, they, too, have stockpiled weapons to defend themselves.

Can we expect more Wacos? It is difficult to see how the government can sit idly by while groups with paramilitary structures arm themselves, denounce the government as the Antichrist—and refuse to pay taxes. With the public outcry over the death of the Waco children and the subsequent congressional hearings, however, future attacks may be more restrained—and probably not televised.

Sources: Barkun 1993; Chua-Eoan 1993; Corbin 1993; Dillin 1993; Lacayo 1993; Pressley 1993; Tye 1993; Gotschall 1994; Paul 1994; "Faddish Justice" 1995. ▲

Characteristics of Religion in the United States ▲

With its hundreds of denominations and sects, how can we generalize about religion in the United States? What do these many religious groups have in common? It certainly isn't doctrine, but doctrine is not the focus of sociology. Sociologists, rather, are interested in the relationship between society and religion, and the role that religion plays in people's lives. To better understand religion in U.S. society, then, we shall focus first on characteristics of members of religious groups, then on the groups themselves.

Characteristics of Members

About 69 percent of Americans belong to a church or synagogue. Let's look at the characteristics of people who hold formal membership in a religion.

Region.   Membership is not evenly distributed around the country. As shown in Table 18.1, membership is highest in the South, followed by the Midwest and the East. Membership in the West is much lower, perhaps because the West is both the newest region in the nation and has the highest net migration. If so, when its residents have put down firmer roots, the West's proportion of religious membership will increase.

Social Class.   Religion in the United States is stratified by social class. As can be seen from Figure 18.3 on the next page, each religious group draws members from all social classes, but some are "top-heavy" and others "bottom-heavy." The most top-heavy are the Episcopalians and Jews, the most bottom-heavy the Baptists and Evangelicals. This figure is further confirmation that churchlike groups tend to appeal more to the successful, the more sectlike to the less successful.

Americans have a tendency to change their religion. About 40 percent of Americans belong to a denomination different from the one in which they were reared (Sherkat and Wilson 1991). People who change their social class are also likely to change their denomination. An upwardly mobile person is likely to seek a religion that draws more people from his or her new social class. An upwardly mobile Baptist, for example, may become a Methodist or a Presbyterian. For Roman Catholics, the situation is somewhat different. Since each parish is a geographical unit, an upwardly mobile individual who moves into a more affluent neighborhood is likely to automatically transfer into a congregation that has a larger proportion of affluent members.

Race and Ethnicity.   It is common for religions around the world to be associated with race and ethnicity: Islam with Arabs, Judaism with Jews, Hinduism with Indians, and Confucianism with Chinese. Sometimes, as with Hinduism and Confucianism, a religion

TABLE 18.1	
Church and Synagogue Membership, Percentage of Population by Region	
South	77%
Midwest	72
East	69
West	53

Source: Statistical Abstract 1997: Table 86.

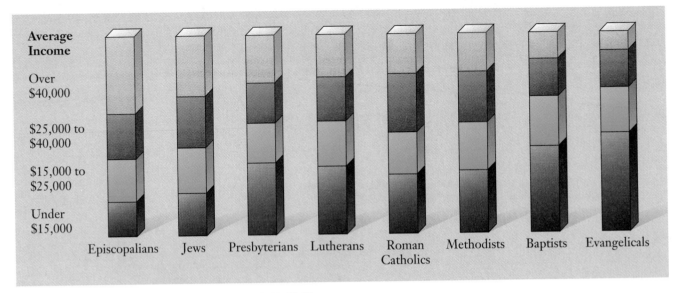

Average Income

Over $40,000

$25,000 to $40,000

$15,000 to $25,000

Under $15,000

Episcopalians   Jews   Presbyterians   Lutherans   Roman Catholics   Methodists   Baptists   Evangelicals

Source: Compiled from data in *Gallup Opinion Index*, 1987:20–27, 29.

Figure 18.3

Average Income and Religious Affiliation

and a particular country are almost synonymous. Christianity is not associated with any one country, although it is associated primarily with Western culture.

In the United States, all major religious groups draw from the nation's many racial and ethnic groups. Like social class, however, race and ethnicity also tend to cluster. People of Latino or Irish descent are likely to be Roman Catholics, those of Greek origin to belong to the Greek Orthodox church. African Americans are likely to be Protestants, more specifically Baptists, or to belong to fundamentalist sects.

Although many churches are integrated, it is not without cause that Sunday morning between 10 and 11 A.M. has been called "the most segregated hour in the United States." African Americans tend to belong to exclusively or largely African-American churches, while most whites see only whites in theirs. The segregation of churches is based not on law, but on custom.

Age. As shown on Table 18.2, the chances that an American belongs to a church or synagogue increase with age. Possibly this is because people become more concerned about an afterlife as they age. A different explanation for the increase at ages 30–49 is the assumption of adult roles: Along with marriage, parenthood, and becoming established often comes religious affiliation. A possible—and intriguing—explanation for the large increase at ages 50–64 and the still larger increase among people over 65 is that religious people outlive those who do not affiliate with a church or synagogue. Each year, as alcohol abuse and other forms of unhealthy lifestyles take their toll, a larger percentage of church members—whose lifestyles are more sedate, more conforming—remains. Perhaps some reader of this text will become the sociologist who will test these three hypotheses.

TABLE 18.2

Age and Church or Synagogue Membership

Age	Membership
18–29	61%
30–49	65
50–64	74
65+	80

Source: Statistical Abstract 1997: Table 86.

Characteristics of Religious Groups

Let's examine the major features of religious groups in the United States.

Diversity. With its 325,000 congregations and hundreds of denominations, no single religious group even comes close to being a dominant religion in the United States (*Statistical Abstract* 1997:Table 85). Table 18.3 and the Perspectives box on Islam on the next page illustrate some of this remarkable diversity.

TABLE 18.3

The 30 Largest U.S. Churches

1.	Roman Catholic	60,300,000	11.	Churches of Christ	3,130,000	22.	Salvation Army	450,000
2.	Baptist	36,400,000	12.	Episcopal Church	2,540,000	23.	Armenian Church	410,000
3.	Pentecostal	10,450,000	13.	Evangelical Church	2,540,000	24.	Buddhist	400,000
4.	Methodist	8,730,000	14.	Christian Churches	1,070,000	25.	Christian and Missionary Alliance	310,000
5.	Lutheran	8,200,000	15.	Jehovah's Witnesses	970,000	26.	American Orthodox	300,000
6.	African (and Christian) Methodist Episcopal	5,450,000	16.	Disciples of Christ	930,000	27.	Polish National Catholic	280,000
7.	Mormon	4,890,000	17.	Seventh Day Adventist	790,000	28.	Community Churches	250,000
8.	Eastern Orthodox	4,080,000	18.	Church of the Nazarene	600,000	29.	Evangelical Free Church	240,000
9.	Presbyterian	3,940,000	19.	Islamic	530,000	30.	Hindu	230,000
10.	Jews	3,140,000	20.	Reformed Churches	520,000			
			21.	Unitarian Universalist	500,000			

Source: Statistical Abstract: 1997, Table 85.

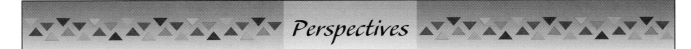

Perspectives

CULTURAL DIVERSITY THE UNITED STATES

The New Neighbor: Islam in the United States

It is Sunday morning, and across the nation Americans are on their way to church. Instead of going into a Baptist or a Roman Catholic church or a Jewish synagogue, many Americans now enter mosques. In a scene that is growing increasingly familiar, they take off their shoes, face Mecca, and kneel with their faces to the floor.

Called by some the fastest growing religion in the United States—perhaps numbering 6 million—Islam is making its presence felt. Islam's growth is fueled by two main sources. The primary source is the millions of immigrants from the Middle East and Asia who have arrived in the United States since the 1980s. Like the immigrants before them, these refugees from Muslim countries brought their religion as part of their culture. Slightly more than half of America's Muslims are foreign-born immigrants from Muslim countries (Brooke 1995). The second source is growth among African Americans. Although believers represent a cross-section of African Americans, the call of Islam is heard most loudly in the inner city (Peart 1993).

The appeal of Islam to African Americans is the message of black pride, self-improvement, and black power. Although U.S. Muslims are divided among about twenty groups, the appeal is similar: morality (no drugs, crime, or extramarital sex), respect for women, and black empowerment. Among all groups, modest clothing is required. Among some, ultraconservative codes govern behavior: Men and women sit separately in public, women wear robes that cover them from head to toe, and one-on-one dating is prohibited (Tapia 1994). Many men embrace the authority that

Islam ascribes to them. For many, both men and women, Islam is a way to connect with African roots.

For many Americans, Louis Farrakhan is synonymous with U.S. Islam. Although he is the most visible and vocal Muslim leader, the group he heads, the Nation of Islam, has only about 10,000 members (Brooke 1995). The other 97 percent of Black Muslims belong to other organizations. One, headed by W. Dean Mohammed, claims over a million members.

Just as their organizations are diverse, so their opinions are wide-ranging. On race, for example, they vary from the idea that the races are equal to the belief that African Americans are superior and whites are devils. Similarly, some groups stress black separatism, while others emphasize the need to enter the U.S. mainstream and identify with the ideas of the country's Founding Fathers.

Alarmed that Islam has gained so many converts, some African-American Christians have begun a counterattack. They hold Muslim Awareness seminars in order to warn Christians away from Islam (Tapia 1994). A former Black Muslim, who is now a Christian evangelist and sees it his duty to counter Islam, says the difference is grace. "Islam is a works-oriented religion, but Christianity is built on God's grace in Jesus."

"His is just a slave religion," retort some Muslims.

In spite of tension and confrontation, it is apparent that the Muslim presence is not temporary, that the face of U.S. religion is being fundamentally altered. Mosques are taking their place in the midst of churches and synagogues, a true sign of a multicultural society.

PEANUTS® by Charles M. Schulz

In its technical sense, to evangelize *means to "announce the Good News" (that Jesus is the Savior). In its more common usage,* to evangelize *means to make converts. As* Peanuts *so humorously picks up, evangelization is sometimes accomplished through means other than pronouncements.*

Pluralism and Freedom.   It is the U.S. government's policy not to interfere with religions. The government's position is that its obligation is to ensure an atmosphere in which people can worship as they see fit. Religious freedom is so extensive that anyone can start his or her own church and proclaim himself or herself a minister, revelator, or any other desired term. At times, however, the government grossly violates its hands-off policy, as was discussed in the Thinking Critically section on pages 509–511.

Competition and Recruitment.   The many religious groups of the United States compete for clients. They even advertise in the Yellow Pages of the telephone directory and insert appealing advertising—under the guise of news—in the religious section of the Saturday or Sunday edition of the local newspapers.

Commitment.   Americans are a deeply religious people, as demonstrated by the high proportion who believe in God and attend a church or synagogue. This religious commitment is underscored by generous support for religion and its charities. Each year Americans donate about $65 billion to religious causes (*Statistical Abstract* 1997:Table 616). To appreciate the significance of this huge figure, keep in mind that, unlike a country in which there is an ecclesia, those billions of dollars are not taxes but voluntary contributions that are the result of religious commitment.

Toleration.   The general religious toleration can be illustrated by three prevailing attitudes: (1) "All religions have a right to exist—as long as they don't try to brainwash anyone or bother me." (2) "With all the religions to choose from, how can anyone tell which one—if any—is true?" (3) "Each of us may be convinced about the truth of our religion—and that is good—but to try to convert others is a violation of the individual's dignity."

Fundamentalist Revival.   The fundamentalist Christian churches are undergoing a revival. They teach that the Bible is literally true and that salvation comes only through a personal relationship with Jesus Christ. They also decry what they see as the permissiveness of U.S. culture: sex on television and in movies, abortion, corruption in public office, premarital pregnancy, cohabitation, and drugs. Their answer to these problems is firm, simple, and direct: People whose hearts are changed through religious conversion will change their lives. The approach of the mainstream churches, which offer a remote God and a corresponding lack of emotional involvement, fails to meet the basic religious needs of large numbers of Americans. Consequently, mainstream churches have been losing members while the fundamentalists have been gaining. Figure 18.4 depicts this change. The exception is the Roman Catholic church, whose growth is primarily due to heavy immigration from Catholic countries.

The Electronic Church.   What began as a ministry to shut-ins and those who do not belong to a church has blossomed into its own type of church. Its preachers, called "televangelists," reach millions of viewers and raise millions of dollars. Some of its most fa-

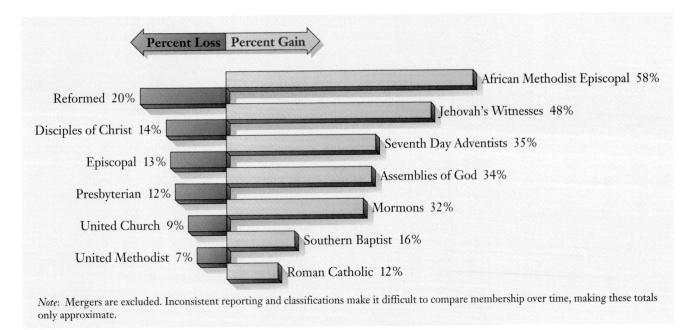

Percent Loss | **Percent Gain**

African Methodist Episcopal 58%
Reformed 20%
Jehovah's Witnesses 48%
Disciples of Christ 14%
Seventh Day Adventists 35%
Episcopal 13%
Assemblies of God 34%
Presbyterian 12%
Mormons 32%
United Church 9%
Southern Baptist 16%
United Methodist 7%
Roman Catholic 12%

Note: Mergers are excluded. Inconsistent reporting and classifications make it difficult to compare membership over time, making these totals only approximate.

Sources: *Yearbook of American and Canadian Churches* 1993:Table 2; *Statistical Abstract* 1985:Table 74; 1995:Table 84.

Figure 18.4

U.S. Churches: Gains and Losses in Ten Years

mous ministries are those of Robert Schuler (the "Crystal Cathedral") and Pat Robertson (the 700 Club). Its most infamous preachers are Jim Bakker and Jimmy Swaggert. Jim Bakker was sentenced to federal prison for misappropriation of funds, while Jimmy Swaggert lost his national television ministry (which brought in over $50 million a year) when revelations of his involvements with prostitutes became public. Surprisingly, Swaggert is making a television comeback.

Many local ministers view the electronic church as a competitor. They complain that it competes for the attention and dollars of their members. The electronic church replies that its money goes to good causes and that through its conversions it feeds members into the local churches, strengthening, not weakening them.

The Internet and Religion.   As with so many aspects of life, the Internet is having an impact on religion. Not only have religious groups set up home pages (the Vatican runs three computers—named Raphael, Michael, and Gabriel—twenty-four hours a day), but also many discussion groups (news groups) have formed around religion. Now Lutherans find themselves keyboard-to-keyboard with devil worshippers, Jews modem-to-modem with Islamic fundamentalists (Ramo 1996). The significance of the Internet for religion may be only that it provides another means of communicating ideas about God. Some, however, believe that the Internet will fundamentally change our ideas about God.

Secularization of Religion and Culture

The term **secularization** refers to the process by which worldly affairs replace spiritual interests. (The term **secular** means "belonging to the world and its affairs.") As we shall see, both religions and cultures can become secularized.

The Secularization of Religion

As the model, fashionably slender, paused before the head table of African-American community leaders, her gold necklace glimmering above the low-cut bodice of her emerald-green dress, the hostess, a member of the Church of God in Christ, said, "It's now OK to wear more revealing clothes—as long as it's done in good taste." Then she added, "You couldn't do this when I was a girl, but now it's OK—and you can still worship God." (Author's files)

secularization: the process by which spiritual concerns are replaced by worldly concerns

secular: belonging to the world and its affairs

When I heard these words, I grabbed a napkin and quickly jotted them down, my socio-logical imagination stirred at their deep implication. As strange as it may seem, this sim-ple event pinpoints the essence of why the Christian churches in the United States have splintered. Let's see how that could possibly be.

The simplest answer to why Christians don't have just one church, or at most several, instead of the hundreds of sects and denominations that dot the U.S. landscape is dis-agreements about doctrine (church teaching). As theologian and sociologist Richard Niebuhr pointed out, however, there are many ways of settling doctrinal disputes beside splintering off and forming another religious organization. Niebuhr (1929) suggested that the answer lies more in *social* change than in *religious* conflict.

The explanation goes like this. As noted earlier, when a sect becomes more church-like, tension between it and the surrounding culture lessens. Quite likely, its founders and first members were poor, or at least not too successful in worldly pursuits. Feeling es-tranged from their general culture, they received a good part of their identity from their religion. Their services and customs stressed differences between their values and those of the dominant culture. Typically, their religion also stressed the joys of the coming af-terlife, when they would be able to escape from their present pain.

As time passes, the group's values—such as frugality and the avoidance of gambling, alcohol, and drugs—help later generations become successful. As they attain more edu-cation and become more middle class, they grow more respectable in the eyes of society. They no longer experience the alienation felt by the founders of their group. Life's bur-dens don't seem as heavy, and the need for relief through an afterlife doesn't seem as press-ing. Similarly, the pleasures of the world no longer appear as threatening to the "true" belief. Then, as in the preceding example of the fashion show, there follows an attempt to harmonize religious beliefs with their changing ideas about the culture.

This process is called the **secularization of religion**—shifting the focus from spiri-tual matters to the affairs of this world. (*Secular* means to belong to the world and its af-fairs.) Anyone familiar with today's ultra-mainstream Methodists, for example, would be surprised to know they once were a sect. Methodists used to ban playing cards, dancing, and attending the theater. They even considered circuses as sinful. As Methodists grew more middle-class, however, they began to change their views on sin. They then began to dismantle the barriers that they had constructed between themselves and the outside world (Finke and Stark 1992).

Secularization leads to a splintering of the group, for accommodation with the secu-lar culture displeases some of the group's members, especially those who have had less worldly success. These people still feel a gulf between themselves and the broader culture. For them, tension and hostility continue to be realities of everyday life. They see secu-larization as deserting the group's fundamental truths, a "selling out" to the secular world. (The Down-to-Earth Sociology box on the next page describes a group whose needs, too, are not met by mainstream religious groups.)

After futile attempts by die-hards to bring the group back to its senses, the group splinters. Those who protested the secularization of Methodism, for example, were kicked out—even though *they* represented the values around which the group had or-ganized in the first place. The dissatisfied—who by now are viewed as complainers—then form a sect that continues to stress its differences from the world, the need for more personal, emotional religious experiences, and salvation from the pain of living in this world. As time passes, the same process—adjustment to the dominant culture by some, and continued dissatisfaction by others—occurs among this group, and the cycle repeats itself.

The Secularization of Culture. Just as religion can be secularized, so can culture. So-ciologists use the term **secularization of culture** to refer to a culture that, once heavily influenced by religion, has lost much of its religious influence. The United States pro-vides an example.

In spite of attempts to reinterpret history, the Pilgrims and most of the Founding Fa-thers of the United States were highly religious people. The Pilgrims were even con-

secularization of religion:
the replacement of a religion's "otherworldly" concerns with concerns about "this world"

secularization of culture:
the process by which a culture becomes less influenced by religion

Down-to-Earth Sociology

Bikers and Bibles

Some Christian groups make evangelism, the conversion of others, a primary goal. One such group is the Christian Motorcyclists' Association, discussed in this box. Another is the Full Gospel Motorcycle Association, shown here joining hands in prayer before setting out to change tires, help stranded motorists, and preach the gospel. The bikers strike up conversations about their motorcycles, then change the topic to "how to reverse direction from the highway to hell to the highway to heaven."

The Bible Belt churchgoers in Eureka Springs, Arkansas, stare as Herbie Shreve, unshaven, his hair hanging over the collar of his denim vest, roars into town on his Harley Davidson. With hundreds of other bikers in town, it is going to be a wild weekend of drinking, nudity, and fights.

But not for Herbie. After pitching his tent, he sets up a table at which he offers other bikers free ice water and religious tracts. "No hard sell. They seek us out when it's the right time," says Herbie.

The ministry began when Herbie's father, a pastor, took up motorcycling to draw closer to his rebellious teen-age son. As the pair rode around the heartland of America, they often were snubbed by fellow Christians when they tried to attend church. So Herbie's father hatched plans for a motorcycle ministry. "Jesus said, 'Go out to the highways and hedges,' and that always stuck with me," says the elder Shreve. "I felt churches ought to be wherever the people are."

They founded the Christian Motorcyclists Association (CMA), headquartered in Hatfield, Arkansas. It now has 33,000 members in more than 300 chapters in the United States and Canada. Members of the CMA call themselves "weekend warriors."

"Riding for the Son" is emblazoned on their T-shirts and jackets, which in the midst of the nudity and drunkenness, makes them stand out.

No CMA member has ever been harmed by a biker. But they have come close. In the early days, bikers at a rally surrounded Herbie's tent and threatened to burn it down. "Some of those same people are friends of mine today," says the elder Shreve.

Stepping over a biker who has passed out in front of his tent, Herbie goes through the campground urging last night's carousers to join them by a lake for a Sunday service. Four years ago no one took him up on it. Today twenty bikers straggle down to the dock.

Herbie's brief sermon is plain-spoken. He touches on the biker's alienation—the unpaid bills, the oppressive bosses, the righteous church ladies "who are always mad and always right." He tells them that Jesus loves them, and that they can call him anytime. "I'll help fix your life," he says.

They have several conversions this weekend. They give away more tracts—and a couple of the group come up to thank Herbie.

"You just stay at it. You don't know when their hearts are touched. Look at these guys," Herbie says, pointing to fellow CMA members. "They were all bikers headed for hell, too. Now they follow the Son."

Herbie gets on his Harley. In town, the churchgoers stare as he roars past, his long hair sweeping behind him.

Sources: Based on Graham 1990; Shreve 1991.

vinced that God had guided them to found a new land, while many of the Founding Fathers felt that God had guided them to develop a new form of government.

The clause in the Constitution that guarantees the separation of church and state was not an attempt to keep religion out of government, but a (successful) device to avoid the establishment of a state religion like that in England. Here, people were to have the freedom to worship as they wished. The assumption of the founders was even more specific—that Protestantism represented the true religion.

The phrase in the Declaration of Independence, "All men are created equal," refers to a central belief in God as the creator of humanity. A member of the clergy opened Congress with prayer. Many colonial laws were based on principles derived explicitly from the Old and the New Testaments. In some colonies, blasphemy was listed as a crime, as was failing to observe the Sabbath. Similarly, adultery was a crime that carried the death penalty. Even public kissing between husband and wife was considered an offense, punishable by being placed in the public stocks (Frumkin 1967). In other words, religion permeated U.S. culture. It was part and parcel of the way early Americans saw life. Their lives, laws, and other aspects of the culture reflected their religious beliefs.

Today, however, U.S. culture has been secularized; that is, the influence of religion on public affairs has greatly lessened. Laws are no longer passed on the basis of religious principles. In general, ideas of what is "generally good" have replaced religion as an organizing principle for the culture.

The major cause for the secularization of a culture is *modernization*, a term that refers to a society industrializing, urbanizing, developing mass education, and adopting science and advanced technology. The significance of modernization goes far beyond these surface changes. Science and advanced technology bring with them a secular view of the world that begins to permeate society. They provide explanations for many aspects of life that people traditionally attributed to God. As a consequence, people come to depend much less on religion to explain life events. Its satisfactions and problems—from births to deaths—are attributed to natural causes. When a society has secularized thoroughly, even religious leaders may turn to answers provided by biology, philosophy, psychology, sociology, and so on.

Although the secularization of its culture means that religion has become less important in U.S. public life, *personal* religious involvement among Americans has not diminished. Instead, it has *increased*. Ninety-four percent believe there is a God, 77 percent believe there is a heaven, and 69 percent claim membership in a church or synagogue. On any given weekend, 43 percent of all Americans report that they attend a church or synagogue (Woodward 1989; Gallup 1990; *Statistical Abstract* 1997:Table 86).

Table 18.4 underscores the paradox of how religious participation has increased while the culture has secularized. The proportion of Americans who belong to a church or synagogue is now *four* times higher than it was when the country was founded. Church membership, of course, is only a rough indicator of how significant religion is in people's lives, for some church members are not particularly religious, while many intensely religious people—Abraham Lincoln, for one—never join a church.

TABLE 18.4	
Growth in Religious Membership: The Percentage of Americans Who Belong to a Church or Synagogue	
	Percentage Who Claim Membership
1776	17%
1860	37
1890	45
1926	58
1975	71
1995	69

Sources: Finke 1992; *Statistical Abstract* 1997:Table 86.

The Future of Religion

Marx was convinced that religion would crumble when the workers threw off their chains of oppression. When the workers usher in a new society based on justice, he argued, there will no longer be a need for religion, for religion is the refuge of the miserable, and people will no longer be miserable. Religion will wither away, for people will see that thoughts about an afterlife are misdirected. In its place, they will put their energies into developing a workers' paradise here on earth (De George 1968).

After Communist countries were established, however, people continued to be religious. At first, the leaders thought this was simply a remnant of the past that would eventually dwindle to nothing. Old people might cling to the past, but the young would give it up, and with the coming generation religion would cease to exist.

The new Marxist states, avowing atheism, were not content to let this withering occur on its own, and they tried to eradicate religion from their midst. (Keep in mind that Marx said that he was not a Marxist. He did not advocate the persecution of religion, for he felt that religion would crumble on its own.) The Communist government in the Soviet Union confiscated church buildings and turned them into museums or government offices. The school curriculum was designed to ridicule religion, and, as noted, a civil marriage ceremony was substituted for the religious ceremony (complete with an altar and a bust of Lenin), while a ceremony dedicating newborns to the state was substituted for baptism. Ministers and priests were jailed as enemies of the state, and parents who dared to teach religion to their children were imprisoned or fired from their jobs, their children taken from them to be reared by the state where they would learn the "truth."

In spite of severe, extended persecution, religion remained strong, even among many of the youth. Table 18.5 shows results of the first scientific sampling of the Russian population since the collapse of the Soviet Union. Three of four Russians believe there is a God, and one of three believes there is a heaven.

Another group of thinkers, who placed their faith not in socialism or communism but in science, foresaw a similar end to religion. As science advanced, it would explain everything. Science would transform human thought and replace religion, which was merely mistaken prescientific thinking. For example, in 1966 Anthony Wallace, one of the world's best-known anthropologists, made the following observation:

> The evolutionary future of religion is extinction. Belief in supernatural beings . . . will become only an interesting historical memory. . . . doomed to die out, all over the world, as a result of the increasing adequacy and diffusion of scientific knowledge.

Marx, Wallace, and the many other social analysts who took this position were wrong. Religion thrives in the most advanced scientific nations, in capitalist and socialist countries. It is evident that these analysts did not understand the fundamental significance of religion in people's lives.

Humans are inquiring creatures. They are aware that they have a past, a present, and a future. They reflect on their experiences to try to make sense out of them. One of the questions that people develop as they reflect on life is the purpose of it all. Why are we born? Is there an afterlife? If so, where are we going, and what will it be like when we get there? Out of these concerns arises this question: If there is a God, what does God want of us in this life? Does God have a preference about how we should live?

Science cannot answer such questions. By its very nature, science cannot tell us about four main concerns that many people have: (1) the existence of God; (2) the purpose of life; (3) morality; and (4) the existence of an afterlife. About the first, science has nothing to say (no test tube has either isolated God or refuted God's existence). For the second, while science can provide a definition of life and describe the characteristics of living organisms, it has nothing to say about ultimate purpose. For the third, science can demonstrate the consequences of behavior but not the moral superiority of one action compared with another. For the fourth, again science can offer no information, for it has no tests that it can use to prove or disprove a "hereafter."

Science simply cannot replace religion. Nor can political systems, as demonstrated by the experience of socialist and communist countries. Science cannot even prove that lov-

TABLE 18.5	
Religious Belief in Russia	
	Percentage of Russians Who Believe There Is (Are)
God	74%
Life after death	40
Miracles	33
Heaven	33
Hell	30

Source: Greeley 1994.

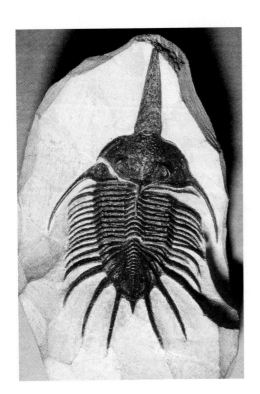

A basic principle of symbolic interactionism is that meaning is not contained in an object or event, but is determined (interpreted) by people. An excellent illustration of this principle is fossils. Does this rare fossil of a trilobite (psychopyge), found in Algeria, "prove" evolution? Does it "disprove" creation? Such "proof" and "disproof" lie in the eye of the beholder, as evidenced by the recent rise of "scientific creationism," now gaining adherents in U.S. universities.

ing your family and neighbor is superior to hurting and killing them. It can describe death and compute consequences, but it cannot dictate the *moral* superiority of any action, even in such an extreme example.

There is no doubt that religion will last as long as humanity lasts— or until humans develop adequate functional alternatives. And even though such alternatives do come, would they not be religion under a different name?

Summary and Review

What Is Religion?

Durkheim identified three essential characteristics of **religion:** beliefs that set the **sacred** apart from the **profane, rituals,** and a moral community (a **church**). Pp. 492–493.

The Functionalist Perspective

What are the functions and dysfunctions of religion?

Among the functions of religion are answering questions about ultimate meaning, providing emotional comfort, social solidarity, guidelines for everyday life, social control, adaptation, support for the government, and fostering social change. Groups or activities that provide these same functions are called **functional equivalents** of religion. Among the dysfunctions of religion are war and religious persecution. Pp. 493–496.

The Symbolic Interactionist Perspective

What aspects of religion do symbolic interactionists study?

Symbolic interactionists focus on the meanings of religion for its followers. They examine religious symbols, rituals, beliefs, experiences, and the sense of community provided by religion. Pp. 496–498.

The Conflict Perspective

What aspects of religion do conflict theorists study?

Conflict theorists examine the relationship of religion to social inequalities, especially how religion is a conservative force that reinforces a society's social stratification. Pp. 498–499.

Religion and the Spirit of Capitalism

What does the spirit of capitalism have to do with religion?

Max Weber disagreed with Marx's conclusion that religion impedes social change. In contrast, Weber saw religion as a primary source of social change. He analyzed how Protestantism gave rise to **the Protestant ethic,** which stimulated what he called **the spirit of capitalism.** The result was capitalism, which transformed society. Pp. 499–500.

The World's Major Religions

What are the world's major religions?

Judaism, Christianity, and Islam, all **monotheistic** religions, can be traced to the same Old Testament roots. Hinduism, the chief religion of India, has no specific founder, as do Judaism (Abraham), Christianity (Jesus), Islam (Muhammad), Buddhism (Gautama), and Confucianism (K'ung Fu-tsu). Specific teachings and history of these six religions are given in the text. Pp. 500–505.

Types of Religious Groups

What types of religious groups are there?

Sociologists divide religious groups into cults, sects, churches, and ecclesias. All religions began as **cults.** Those that survive tend to develop into **sects** and eventually into **churches.** Sects, often led by **charismatic leaders,** are unstable. Some are perceived as a threat and are persecuted by the state. **Ecclesias,** or state religions, are rare. Pp. 505–511.

Characteristics of Religion in the United States

What are the main characteristics of religion in the United States?

Membership varies by region, social class, age, and race or ethnicity. The major characteristics of U.S. religious groups are diversity, pluralism and freedom, competition, commitment, toleration, a fundamentalist revival, and the electronic church. Pp. 511–515.

What is the connection between secularization of religion and the splintering of churches?

The **secularization of religion,** a change in a religion's focus from spiritual matters to concerns of "this world," is the key to understanding why churches divide. Basically, as a cult or sect changes to accommodate its members' upward social class mobility, it changes into a church. Left dissatisfied, members who are not upwardly mobile tend to splinter off and form a new cult or sect, and the cycle repeats itself. Cultures permeated by religion also secularize. This, too, leaves many dissatisfied and promotes social change. Pp. 515–518.

The Future of Religion

Although industrialization led to the **secularization of culture,** this did not spell the end of religion, as many social analysts assumed it would. Because science and education cannot answer questions about ultimate meaning, the existence of God or an afterlife, or provide guidelines for morality, the need for religion will remain. In any foreseeable future, religion—or its functional equivalents—will prosper. Pp. 518–520.

Where can I read more on this topic?

Suggested readings for this chapter are listed on page 665.

Sociology and the Internet

All URLs listed are current as of the printing of this book. URLs are often changed. Please check our Website http://www.abacon.com/henslin for updates.

1. In this chapter you were introduced to a brief survey of world religions. You can explore most of these further through the Internet. Go to the Yahoo! religion site at *http://www.yahoo!.com/society_and_culture/religion/organizations/* You should find links to Buddhism, Christianity, Hinduism, Islam, and Judaism. You might like to browse through some of these sites.

When you finish, select one religion (not your own) and follow the links to as many sites as you can. As you go, take notes on history, beliefs, symbols, rituals, and organization. Use this information to write a paper on the culture and social structure of the religion.

2. As you have discovered, sociologists use the terms *cult* and *sect* differently from the way they are used in the media and in everyday conversation. As you start this project, write sociological definitions of *church* and *sect*. Now go to the Yahoo! site on cyberspace religions *http://www.yahoo!.com/society_and_culture/cyberculture/religions/* (If you have trouble with this long address go to *http://www.yahoo!.com* and follow the path through each page.) You will see many links. Go to each site and try to determine which are meant to be taken seriously. Of those, how many represent churches? Of those that don't seem to represent churches, use the definitions you wrote at the beginning of the project to decide whether they are more sect-like or cultlike. Write a brief analysis of your findings and compare them with the conclusions of other students in the class.

3. Technology is changing the major social institutions of our society. Religion is yet another place where technology has left its mark. Examine the following links and discuss what impact the Internet and Web have on the functions of religion. Does cyber worship fulfill the same functions as those described by Durkheim and explored in your text? Does it fulfill any additional functions not fulfilled by traditional religion?

http://www6.pilot.infi.net/~rllewis/opener.html
http://www.netaxs.com/~mvd/bbs/
http://www.nettally.com/jesusnet/
http://www.infidels.org/
http://www5.zdnet.com/yil/higher/heavensgate/index.html

4. What kind of impact have the Internet and the Web had on the spread and development of cults such as Heaven's Gate? Examine the following sites before you answer the next few questions:

http://www.cnn.com/US/9703/29/suicide.chats/index.html
http://www.ocregister.com/news/1997/0397/cult/cultwe.html

Why are people concerned with the spread of cults on the Internet? What are some of their concerns? Use a search engine such as Yahoo! *http://www.yahoo!.com* to examine the meaning of *cult* as this term is used on the Internet. How does the use of *cult* on the Internet differ from the definition listed in your text? How can we protect ourselves and those we love from cults on the Internet?

Connie Hayes, Doctor and Patient, 1996

Medicine: Health and Illness

R UDY JOHNSON HAD A PROBLEM—*how to transport a long extension ladder on a short pickup truck. Against her better judgment, his wife, Norma, consented to sit on the ladder while Rudy moved it. That worked out just fine—until Rudy took a curve too fast and she and the ladder spilled out.*

This was not Norma's lucky day. She landed on her head.

An emergency medical team answered the 911 call. Determining that the unconscious woman was near death, the team ordered a helicopter to fly Norma to a trauma center, where emergency specialists sprang into action. The trauma surgeon ordered X rays, which revealed a haziness in her lungs, probably from aspirated vomit. A CAT scan revealed a brain hemorrhage and a skull fracture. When a blood test showed that the oxygen level in her blood had fallen to a dangerously low level, an anesthesiologist inserted a breathing tube into Norma's trachea and administered 100 percent oxygen.

Norma's condition worsened. The trauma surgeon inserted a tube into her chest to expand a collapsed lung. The cardiologist pushed an ultrasound probe down her throat to take pictures of her beating heart and to evaluate its pumping efficiency. The neurosurgeon drilled a hole in Norma's skull and inserted a pressure gauge to monitor her swollen brain.

To improve the blood flow to her lungs, that night a special bed rocked Norma from side to side. Her condition stabilized, and she lived. Norma vowed never again to ride in the back of a pickup—at least not on top of an extension ladder. (Based on Miller 1995)

Sociology and the Study of Medicine

The technology that saved Norma Johnson's life, available in only a few places on earth, opens up fascinating possibilities in health care. It also contributes to skyrocketing medical costs and creates such dilemmas as whether or not such expensive technology should be rationed, topics we shall explore in this chapter.

As we look at such issues, the role of sociology in studying **medicine**—a society's standard ways of dealing with illness and injury—will become apparent. For example, because U.S. medicine is a profession, a bureaucracy, and a big business, sociologists study how it is influenced by ideals of self-regulation, the bureaucratic structure, and the profit motive. Sociologists also study how illness and health are much more than biological matters—how, for example, they are intimately related to cultural beliefs, lifestyle, and social class. Because of such emphases, the sociology of medicine is one of the applied fields of sociology, and many medical schools and even hospitals have sociologists on their staffs.

The Symbolic Interactionist Perspective

Let's begin, then, by examining how culture influences health and illness. This takes us to the heart of the symbolic interactionist perspective.

The Role of Culture in Defining Health and Illness

Suppose that one morning you look in the mirror and see strange blotches covering your face and chest. Hoping against hope that it is not serious, you rush to a doctor. If the doctor said that you had "dyschromic spirochetosis," your fears would be confirmed.

Now, wouldn't everyone around the world draw the conclusion that the spots are a disease? No, not everybody. In one South American tribe this skin condition is so common

medicine: one of the major social institutions that sociologists study; a society's organized ways of dealing with sickness and injury

that the few individuals who *aren't* spotted are seen as the unhealthy ones. They are even excluded from marriage because they are "sick" (Ackernecht 1947; Zola 1983).

Consider mental "illness" and mental "health." People aren't automatically "crazy" because they do certain things. Rather, they are defined as "crazy" or "normal" according to cultural guidelines. If an American talks aloud to spirits that no one else can see, and takes direction from them, he or she is likely to be defined as insane—and, for everyone's good, may be locked up. In some tribal societies, in contrast, someone who talks to invisible spirits might be honored for being in close contact with the spiritual world—and, for everyone's good, be declared a **shaman,** or "witch doctor," and then diagnose and treat medical problems.

"Sickness" and "health," then, are not absolutes, as we might suppose. Rather, they are matters of definition. Around the world, each culture provides guidelines that its people use to determine whether they are "healthy" or "well." This is another example of the vital role that the social construction of reality plays in our lives.

The Components of Health

Back in 1941, international "health" experts identified three components of **health:** physical, mental, and social (World Health Organization 1946). They missed the focus of our previous chapter, however, and I have added a spiritual component to Figure 19.1. Even the dimensions of health, then, are subject to debate.

If we were to agree on the components of health, we would still be left with the question of what makes someone physically, mentally, socially, or spiritually "healthy." Again, as symbolic interactionists stress, these are not objective matters, but, rather, vary from culture to culture. In a pluralistic society, they even differ from one group to another.

As with religion in the previous chapter, then, the concern of sociologists is not to define "true" health or "true" illness. Instead, it is to analyze the effects that people's ideas of health and illness have on their lives, and even how people determine that they are sick.

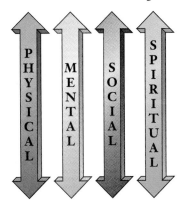

Health
Excellent Functioning

P H Y S I C A L   M E N T A L   S O C I A L   S P I R I T U A L

Poor Functioning
Illness

Figure 19.1

A Continuum of Health and Illness

shaman: the healing specialist of a preliterate tribe who attempts to control the spirits thought to cause a disease or injury; commonly called a witch doctor

health: a human condition measured by four components: physical, mental, social, and spiritual

The Functionalist Perspective ▶

Functionalists begin with an obvious point: If society is to function well, its people need to be healthy enough to perform their normal roles. This means that societies must set

Health practices vary widely around the world. Many cultures have shamans, *who treat both mental and physical illnesses. Shown here are shamans in Nepal, performing a ceremony as part of their patients' treatment.*

up ways to control sickness. One level is the system of medical care that societies develop. But there is also another level—making rules to keep too many people from "being sick." Let's look at how this works.

The Sick Role

Do you remember when your throat began to hurt and when your mom or dad took your temperature the thermometer registered 102°F? Your parents took you to the doctor, and despite your protests that tomorrow was (your birthday or the first day of vacation), you had to spend the next three days in bed taking medicines. You were forced to play what sociologists call the "sick role." What do they mean by this term?

Elements of the Sick Role. Talcott Parsons, the functionalist who first analyzed the **sick role,** pointed out that it has four elements—that you are not held responsible for being sick, that you are exempt from normal responsibilities, that you don't like the role, and that you will get competent help so you can return to your routines. People who don't seek competent help are considered responsible for being sick. They are denied the right to claim sympathy from others and to be excused from their normal routines. The one is given sympathy and encouragement, the other a cold shoulder for wrongfully claiming the sick role.

Ambiguity in the Sick Role. Instead of a fever of 102°F, suppose that the thermometer registers 99.3°F. Do you then "become" sick or not? That is, do you decide to claim the sick role? Because clear-cut events such as heart attacks and limb fractures are rare, decisions to claim the sick role often are based more on social considerations than physical conditions. Let's also suppose that you are facing a midterm for which you are drastically underprepared, and you are allowed to make it up. The more you think about the test, the worse you are likely to feel—legitimating to yourself the need to claim the sick role. Now assume that you have no test, but your friends are coming over to take you out to celebrate your twenty-first birthday. You are much less likely to play the sick role. Note that in both cases your physical condition is the same.

Gatekeepers to the Sick Role. Parents and physicians are the primary gatekeepers to the sick role. That is, they mediate between our feelings of illness and our claim to being sick. Before parents call the school to excuse a child's absence, they decide whether the child is faking or has genuine symptoms serious enough to allow him or her to remain home from school. For adults, physicians are the main gatekeepers of the sick role. A "doctor's excuse"—actually official permission to play the sick role—removes the need for employers and teachers to pass judgment on the individual's claim.

Gender Differences in the Sick Role. Although on average, females are healthier than males and live longer lives, they also go to doctors more frequently and are sick more often (*Statistical Abstract* 1997:Tables 181, 206). How can we reconcile these seemingly incompatible findings? Testing college students from working-class backgrounds, researchers Elizabeth Klonoff and Hope Landrine (1992) found that women are more willing to claim the sick role when they don't feel well. The researchers identified two primary reasons for this. Because fewer women were employed, they found less role conflict in claiming the sick role, and the women had been socialized for greater dependency and self-disclosure.

sick role: a social role that excuses people from normal obligations because they are sick or injured, while at the same time expecting them to seek competent help and cooperate in getting well

This research helps to pinpoint some of the social factors that underlie the sick role. Gender roles—ideas of what is properly feminine or masculine—vary from one culture to another. An ideal that men should be strong, keep their hurts to themselves, and "tough it through," while women should share their feelings and seek help from others, then, underlies this riddle of why women can be healthier than men and yet be sick and go to doctors more often.

The Conflict Perspective

As stressed in earlier chapters, the primary focus of conflict theorists is how people struggle over scarce resources. Since medical treatment is one of those resources, let's examine this competition in global perspective, and then see how one group developed a monopoly on U.S. health care.

Effects of Global Stratification on Health Care

Our review in Chapter 9 (pages 243–245) of how the globe became stratified stressed how the nations that industrialized obtained the economic and military power that allowed them to become rich and to dominate the globe. One consequence is the global stratification of medical care.

Our opening vignette is an example. The Least Industrialized Nations cannot even begin to afford the technology that saved Norma Johnson's life. Life expectancy also illustrates global stratification. Whereas most people in the industrialized world can expect to live to about 75, *most* people in Afghanistan, Angola, Cambodia, Haiti, and Rwanda die before they reach 50. The infant mortality rates shown in Figure 19.2 also tell the story. This figure lists the world's countries where less than 7 of every 1,000 babies die before they are a year old. *All* of them are industrialized nations. The contrast is stark—close to 150 of every 1,000 babies born in Afghanistan and Angola never reach their first birthday (*Statistical Abstract* 1997:Table 1336).

Global stratification, then, is a matter of life and death. In addition, it even helps to determine what diseases you get. Suppose that you had been born in a Least Industrialized Nation located in the tropics. During your much shorter life, you would face illness and death from four major sources: malaria (from mosquitos), internal parasites (from contaminated water), diarrhea (from food and soil contaminated with human feces), and malnutrition. You would not face heart disease and cancer for they are "luxury" diseases; that is, they characterize the industrialized world where people live long enough to get them. As nations industrialize, their people live longer and they then trade in their primary killers and begin to worry about cancer and heart attacks instead.

Figure 19.2

**How Many Babies Die
Before Their First Birthday?**

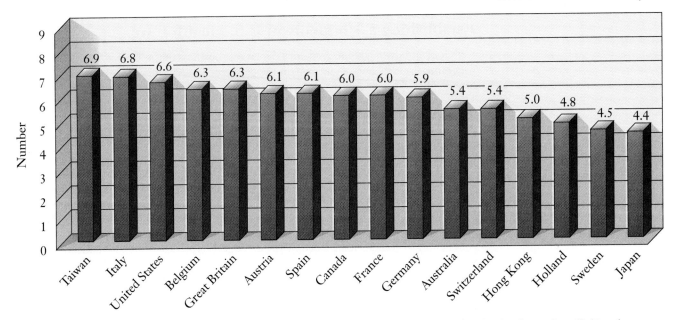

Note: All countries listed in the source with an infant mortality rate below 8. Infant mortality is defined as the number of babies who die before their first birthday, per 1,000 live births.

Source: *Statistical Abstract* 1997:Table 1336.

 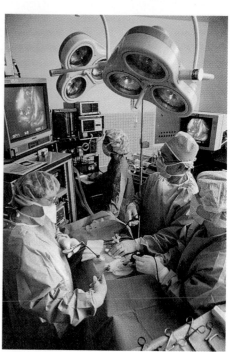

Global stratification in health care is starkly contrasted in these two photographs. The one on the left shows medical treatment in Papua, New Guinea. The items on the table represent the extent of medical technology available to most residents of the Least Industrialized Nations. The photo on the right, of open heart surgery, illustrates the medical treatment available in the Most Industrialized Nations. Not all of their citizens, however, have equal access to such technology.

Many diseases that ravage the populations of these poorer countries could be brought under control if more of their meager funds were spent on public health. Cheap drugs can prevent malaria, while safer water supplies and increased food production would go a long way toward eliminating the other major killers. The money, however, is not spent this way. Instead, having garnered the lion's share of the country's resources, the elite lavish it on themselves. The elite also send a few students to top medical schools in the West. This gives the elite access to advanced technology, from X rays to life support systems—while the poor of their nations go without even basic medical services and continue to die at an early age.

Establishing a Monopoly in U.S. Health Care

Let's look at how medicine grew into the largest business in the United States—and how it became the only legal monopoly in the country. To do so, we first need to understand how medicine became professionalized.

The Professionalization of Medicine. Imagine that you are living in the American colonies in the 1700s and that you want to become a physician. There are no course prerequisites, no entrance exams—in fact, there are no medical schools. You don't have to have *any* education at all. You simply ask a physician to train you and assist with menial tasks in return for the opportunity to learn. When *you* think that you have learned enough, you hang out a shingle and thereby proclaim yourself a physician. The process was similar to how someone becomes an automobile mechanic today. And like mechanics today, you could even skip the apprenticeship if you wished, and simply hang out the shingle. If you could convince people you were good, you made a living. If not, you turned to something else.

During the 1800s, a few medical schools opened, and there was some licensing. Medical schools then, however, were like religious sects today; they competed for clients and represented different claims on truth. That is, medical schools had competing philosophies about both the causes of illnesses and the most effective treatments. Training was short, often not even a high school diploma was required, there was no clinical training, and lectures went unchanged from year to year. Even Harvard University's medical school

As hard as it is to believe, doctors used to be available at the beck and call of patients. They would come to a patient's home, diagnose the illness, prescribe medication, and even sit up all night with the critically ill—all for a modest fee. This photo is from the 1950s.

took only two school years to complete—and the school year in those days lasted only four months (Starr 1982; Rosenberg 1987; Riessman 1994).

In 1906 the American Medical Association (AMA) examined the 160 medical schools in the United States and found only 82 acceptable (Starr 1982). The Carnegie Foundation asked Abraham Flexner, a renowned educator of the time, to investigate the matter. Flexner visited every medical school. Even the most inadequate opened their doors to him, for they thought that gifts from the Carnegie Foundation would follow (Rodash 1982). Flexner found glaring problems. The laboratories of some schools consisted only of "a few vagrant test tubes squirreled away in a cigar box." Other schools had libraries with no books. Flexner (1910) recommended that admissions and teaching standards be raised and that philanthropies fund the most promising schools. As a result, those schools that were funded were able to upgrade their facilities and attract more capable faculty and students. Left with inadequate funds and few students, most of the other schools had to close their doors.

The Flexner report led to the **professionalization of medicine.** Physicians began to (1) undergo a rigorous education; (2) claim a theoretical understanding of illness; (3) regulate themselves; (4) claim that they were performing a service for society (rather than just following self-interest); and (5) take authority over clients (Goode 1960). (For differences between professions and jobs, see page 388.)

The Monopoly of Medicine.   When medicine professionalized, it also became a monopoly. The group that gained control over U.S. medicine set itself up as *the* medical establishment. This group was able to get laws passed to restrict medical licenses to graduates of approved schools, and make it so only graduates of those schools could become the faculty members who trained the next generation of physicians. In short, by controlling the education and licensing of physicians, they silenced most competing philosophies of medicine. The WASP males who took control also either refused to admit women and minorities to medical schools or placed severe enrollment limits on them.

Eliminating the competition paved the way for medicine to become big business. The monopoly was so thorough that by law only a select group of men—a sort of priesthood of medicine—was allowed to diagnose and treat medical problems. Only they knew what was right for people's health. Only they could scribble the secret language (Latin) on special pieces of parchment (prescription forms) for translators (pharmacists) to decipher (Miner 1995). This select group was able to shape itself into the most lucrative profession in the country—for they set their own fees and had little competition. This group of men

professionalization of medicine: the development of medicine into a field in which education becomes rigorous, and in which physicians claim a theoretical understanding of illness, regulate themselves, claim to be doing a service to society (rather than just following self-interest), and take authority over clients

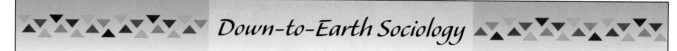

Down-to-Earth Sociology

To Establish a Monopoly, Eliminate Your Competition: How Physicians Dealt with Midwives

Midwifery helps us understand the professionalization of medicine and provides insight into the founding of the U.S. medical establishment. It had been the custom in the United States, as in Europe and elsewhere, for midwives to deliver babies. Pregnancy and childbirth were considered natural events, for which women were best equipped to help women. It was also considered indecent for a man to know much about pregnancy, much less to see a woman deliver a baby. Some midwives were trained; others were simply neighborhood women who had experience in childbirth. In many European countries, midwives were licensed by the state—as they still are. In the United States, physicians came to see midwives as business competitors.

Their desire for expansion ran up against a major problem, however: few physicians knew anything about delivering babies. To learn, they first sneaked into the bedrooms where midwives were assisting births. To say "sneaked" is no exaggeration, for some physicians crawled on their hands and knees so that the mother-to-be would not know a man was present. Since many midwives refused to cooperate, the training of most physicians was limited to lessons with mannequins. Physicians gradually gained admission to childbirth, but the issue of indecency persisted. At first the physician was limited to fumbling blindly under a sheet in a dark room, his head decorously turned aside.

As physicians grew more powerful politically, they launched a bitter campaign against midwives, attacking them

as "dirty, ignorant, and incompetent," even calling them a "menace to the health of the community." Using the new political clout of the AMA, physicians succeeded in persuading many states to pass laws that made it illegal for anyone but a physician to deliver babies. Some states, however, continued to allow nurse-midwives to practice. The struggle is not yet over, and nurse-midwives and physicians still clash over who has the right to deliver babies.

Conflict theorists emphasize that this struggle was an attempt by men to gain control over what had been women's work. They stress that political power was central to the physicians' success in expanding their domain. Without denying the political aspect, symbolic interactionists stress that the key was the redefinition of pregnancy and childbirth from a natural event to a medical condition. To eliminate midwives, physicians launched a campaign of images, stressing that pregnancy and childbirth were not normal conditions. Their new definitions, which flew in the face of the millennia-old tradition of women helping women to have babies, transformed pregnancy and childbirth from a natural process to a "medical condition" that required the assistance of an able man. When this redefinition made childbirth "men's work," not only did the prestige of the work go up—so did the price.

Sources: Wertz and Wertz 1981; Rodash 1982; Danzi 1989; Rothman 1994.

became so powerful that it was even able to take over childbirth—the focus of the Down-to-Earth Sociology box above.

This **fee-for-service** (paying a physician to diagnose and treat) approach to medicine usually went unquestioned. As the monopoly drove up the price of medical care, however, there was a public outcry that the poor and many of the elderly were priced out of health care. The AMA fought every proposal for the government to fund medical treatment as furiously as someone fending off a mad dog. Physicians were convinced that government funding would "socialize" medicine, remove the fee for service, and turn them into government employees—not unlike the 1990s' skirmishes between the AMA and proponents of national health care.

After *Medicaid* (government-paid medical care for the poor) and *Medicare* (government-sponsored medical insurance for the elderly) were instituted in the 1960s, however, U.S. physicians found that these programs did not lead to socialization. Instead, they provided millions of additional customers, for people who previously could not afford medical services now had their medical bills guaranteed by the government. As Figure 13.5 on page 360 illustrates, these programs have become extremely expensive—and they put much wealth into physicians' pockets.

From its humble origins, medicine has grown into the largest business in the United States. Today it consists not only of physicians, but also of nurses, paraphysicians, hospital personnel, druggists, the manufacturers and sales force of medical technology, and especially insurance and pharmaceutical companies and the corporations that own hospitals. Medicine has become much more than listening to people's health complaints and pre-

fee for service: payment to a physician to diagnose and treat a patient's medical problems

epidemiology: the study of disease and disability patterns in a population

scribing medications. The medical monopoly is so powerful that it not only wages national advertising campaigns to drum up customers but also lobbies all the state legislatures and the U.S. Congress. Some hospitals even pay million-dollar sign-up bonuses to lure big-name surgeons (McCartney 1993).

Historical Patterns of Health

How have patterns of health and illness in the United States changed? The answer to this question takes us into the field of **epidemiology,** the study of how medical disorders are distributed throughout a population.

Physical Health

Leading Causes of Death   One way to see how the physical health of Americans has changed is to compare the leading causes of death in two time periods. To get an idea of how extensively health problems have changed, look at Figure 19.3. Note that only half of the leading causes of death in 1900 are the same today. Heart disease and cancer, which placed fourth and eighth in 1900, have now jumped to the top of the list, while tuberculosis and diarrhea, which were the number 1 and 3 killers in 1900 don't even show up in today's top 10. Similarly, homicide, suicide, and AIDS didn't make the top 10 in 1900, but they do now. Changes in this figure indicate extensive changes in society. Diseases, then, are not only biological events. They are also *social,* following the contours of social change.

Were Americans Healthier in the Past?   A second way to see how the physical health of Americans has changed is to ask if they are healthier—or sicker—than they used to be. This question brings us face to face with the definitional problem discussed earlier. "Healthy" by whose standards? An additional problem is that many of today's diseases went unrecognized in the past. Mortality rates, however, help us to answer this question. Because most people today live longer than their ancestors, we can conclude that contemporary Americans are healthier.

Some may see this conclusion as flying in the face of polluted air and water and today's high rates of heart disease and cancer, shown in Figure 19.3. And it does. Sometimes older people say, "When I was a kid, cancer wasn't even around. I never knew anyone who died from cancer, and now it seems everyone does." What they overlook is that in the past most cancer went unrecognized. People were simply said to have died of "old age" or "heart failure." In addition, most cancers strike older people, and the younger that most people die, the less chance that cancer is the cause of death.

Mental Health

When it comes to mental health, we have no rational basis at all for making comparisons. The elderly may paint a picture of a past with lower suicide rates, less mental illness, and so on, but we need measures of mental illness or mental health, not anecdotes. The idyllic past—where everyone grew up in a happy home, married for life, and was at one with the universe—never existed. All groups have had their share of mental problems—and commonsense beliefs that

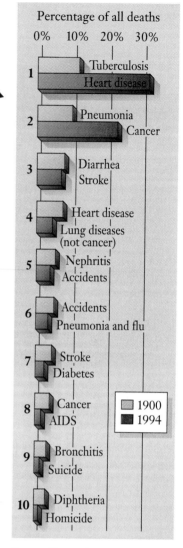

Sources: National Center for Health Statistics; *Statistical Abstract* 1997: Tables 129, 130.

Figure 19.3

The Top Ten Causes of Death in the United States, 1900 and 1994

Despite the thousands of volumes written about mental illness and the thousands of advanced degrees awarded to specialists, the causes of mental illness remain little understood. As was explained in Chapter 8, some experts even deny the existence of mental illness. Does this individual's choice of securing privacy make him or her mentally ill? Or is this behavior a logical adaptation to the life circumstances this person faces?

Because the U.S. medical delivery system often bypasses the poor, the Colorado National Guard opened a field hospital in Denver to serve indigent civilians. This two-week action, although well-intentioned and useful, is far from being a solution to this chronic problem of inequity in health care.

mental illness is worse today represent perceptions, not measured reality. Such perceptions may be true, of course, but the *opposite* could also be true. Since we don't even know how extensive mental illness is today (Miller 1993), we certainly can't judge how much there was in the past.

Issues in Health Care

Let's look at issues in health care in the United States.

Medical Care: A Right or a Commodity?

A primary controversy in the United States is whether or not medical care is a right or a privilege. If it is a right, then all citizens should have fairly equal access to good medical care. If it is a privilege, however, then, much like automobiles, clothing, and other commodities, the rich will have access to one type of care, the poor to another. Currently, medical care is not the right of citizens, but a commodity to be sold at the highest price (Kaufmann 1994; McGinley and Georges 1995). Like potatoes, those with the money can buy better quality, while the poor and uninsured can go without—or wait on handouts. This is the concern that underlies the so-far futile attempts to institute national medical care.

Related to this issue is the skyrocketing cost of medical care, shown on Figure 19.4. In 1960, the average American spent just $150 a year on health care. Today it is $3,300. In 1960, a 17-inch black-and-white television also cost about $150. If television prices had risen at the same rate as health care, a 17-inch *black-and-white* television would now cost about $3,300. Several factors have fueled medical costs, including a larger segment of the population that is elderly, and the new, expensive technology. With health care considered a commodity, the result is a *two-tier system of medical care*—superior care for those who can afford the cost, and inferior care for those who cannot.

Social Inequality

> Standing among the police, I watched as the elderly, nude man, looking confused, struggled to put on his clothing. The man had ripped the wires out of the home-less shelter's main electrical box, and then led the police a merry chase as he had run from room to room.
>
> I asked the officers where they were going to take the man, and they replied, "To Malcolm Bliss" (the state hospital). When I said, "I guess he'll be in there for quite a while," they replied, "Probably for just a day or two. We picked him up last week—he was crawling under cars at a traffic light—and they let him out in two days."

The police then explained that one must be a danger to others or to oneself to be admitted as a long-term patient. Visualizing this old man crawling under cars in traffic and the possibility of electrocution in ripping out electrical wires with bare hands, I marveled at the definitions of "danger" that the psychiatrists must be using. The two-tier system of medical care was readily visible, stripped of its coverings. Certainly a middle-class or rich person would receive different treatment, and would not, of course, be in this shelter in the first place.

Since 1939, sociologists have found an inverse correlation between mental problems and social class. In other words, the lower the social class, the higher the proportion of serious mental problems. This finding has been confirmed in numerous studies (Faris and Dunham 1939; Hudson 1988; Ortega and Corzine 1990; Ross and Willigen 1997). Sociologists have little difficulty understanding why people in the lower social classes have greater mental problems, for they are part of a stress package that comes with poverty. Compared with middle- and upper-class Americans, the poor have less job security, lower wages, more unpaid bills and insistent bill collectors, more divorce, greater vulnerability

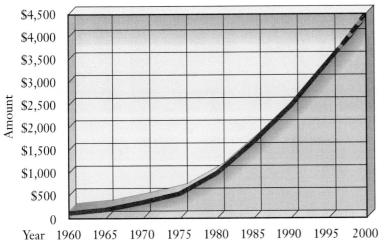

Figure 19.4

The Soaring Cost of Medical Care: The Amount the Average American Pays Each Year

The broken line is the author's estimate.

Source: *Statistical Abstract* 1997:Table 155.

to crime, more alcoholism, more violence, and more physical illness. Such conditions certainly deal severe blows to people's emotional well-being.

In a policy called **deinstitutionalization,** back in the 1960s the locked wards of state mental hospitals were opened and patients were released. The plan was to provide community-based services—counseling and medications—so the former mental patients could adjust to life outside mental hospitals. The outpatient services, however, were not put in place. As a result, U.S. streets were flooded with former mental patients with no income and nowhere to go. The streets became their home.

Needless to say, these were poor people. The middle class and wealthy who had mental problems were counseled by private psychiatrists and, if hospitalized, went to expensive private mental hospitals. The rich were treated with "talk" therapy (various forms of psychotherapy), while the poor wore "medicinal straitjackets" (were sedated and controlled with medicines).

When it comes to physical illnesses, we find similar inequalities by social class. As Figure 19.5 shows, the poor are more likely to become ill. Unlike the middle and upper classes, however, few poor people have a personal physician, and they are likely to spend hours waiting in crowded public health clinics. After waiting most of a day, some don't even get to see a doctor, but are told to come back the next day (Fialka 1993). Finally, when hospitalized, the poor are likely to find themselves in understaffed and underfunded public hospitals, where they are treated by rotating interns who do not know them and cannot follow up on their progress.

deinstitutionalization: the release of patients from mental hospitals into the community while receiving treatment within a network of outpatient services

Figure 19.5

Number of Days Sick

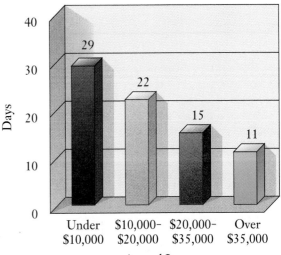

Note: Number of days people were so sick or injured that they cut down on their usual activities for more than half a day; includes days off work and school.

Source: Statistical Abstract 1997:Table 206.

Malpractice Suits and Defensive Medicine

Some analysts have observed that prior to this century physicians may have killed more patients than they ever cured. Given that physicians didn't know about germs and didn't wash before surgery or childbirth, this may be true. Back then, doctors thought that sickness was caused by "bad fluids," and they had four techniques for getting rid of these fluids: (1) bleeding (cutting a vein and draining out bad blood); (2) blistering (applying packs so hot they burned the skin and made the bad pus come to the surface); (3) vomiting (feeding patients liquids that made them vomit up the bad fluids); and (4) purging (feeding patients substances that caused diarrhea).

Although this ad strikes us as strange, in the 1950s news-papers and magazines were filled with testimonials about how cigarettes were good for people's health. They were even said to "soothe the throat." The health hazards of smoking were not unknown at this time. Today's cigarette advertising may be more subtle, but it has the same in-tent—to seduce the young into smoking, and to assure cur-rent smokers that it is all right to continue.

Comparing today's vastly superior technology and treatment, one might think mal-practice suits would have been a problem in the past but not today. The opposite, how-ever, is true. Back then, the law didn't allow patients to recover damages. "People make mistakes" was the thinking, and that included doctors. Today, in contrast, physicians are held to much higher standards—some say to impossible ones. Awards are high, and doc-tors are anxious. One physician told me, "I'm looking for something else to do, because medicine is no longer fun. Every time I treat a patient, I wonder if this is the one who is going to turn around and sue me."

To protect themselves, physicians practice **defensive medicine.** They consult with colleagues and order lab tests not because the patient needs them but to leave a paper trail that can be used in case they are sued. These consultations and tests—done for the doc-tor's benefit, not the patient's—boost the cost spiral even further. They add several billion dollars to the nation's annual medical bill (Volti 1995). To reduce the costs of defensive medicine, the state of Maine has given checklists to physicians. If they follow them, mal-practice suits are dismissed (Felsenthal 1993). Although physicians complain about a "paint-by-numbers" or cookbook approach to medicine, many prefer this to the threat of lawsuits.

Depersonalization: The Cash Machine

One of the main criticisms leveled against the medical profession is **depersonalization,** the practice of dealing with people as though they were cases and diseases, not individu-

defensive medicine: medical practices done not for the pa-tient's benefit but in order to protect a physician from mal-practice suits

depersonalization: dealing with people as though they were objects; in the case of medical care, as though pa-tients were merely cases and diseases, not persons

als. Many patients get the impression that they have been trapped by a cash machine—a physician who, while talking to you, is impatiently counting minutes and tabulating dollars so that he or she can move on to the next customer, and more dollars. After all, extra time spent with a patient is money down the drain.

Sociologist Sue Fisher (1986), who was examined for an ovarian mass, gives this account:

> On my initial visit a nurse called me into an examination room, asked me to undress, gave me a paper gown to put on and told me the doctor would be with me soon. I was stunned. Was I not even to see the doctor before undressing? . . . How could I present myself as a competent, knowledgeable person sitting undressed on the examining table? But I had a potentially cancerous growth, so I did as I had been told.
>
> In a few minutes the nurse returned and said, "Lie down. The doctor is coming." Again I complied. The doctor entered the examining room, nodded in my direction while reading my chart, and proceeded to examine me without ever having spoken to me.

Participant observation of medical students at McMaster University in Canada by sociologists Jack Haas and William Shaffir (1993) provides insight into how physicians learn to depersonalize patients. Haas and Shaffir found that students begin medical school wanting to "treat the whole person." As vast amounts of material are thrown at them, their feelings for patients are overpowered by the need to be efficient. This student's statement picks up the change:

> Somebody will say, "Listen to Mrs. Jones's heart. It's just a little thing flubbing on the table." And *you forget about the rest of her* . . . and it helps in learning in the sense that you can go in to a patient, put your stethoscope on the heart, listen to it, and walk out. . . .The advantage is that *you can go in a short time and see a patient, get the important things out of the patient, and leave* (italics added).

Another student's statement illustrates the extent to which patients become objects.

> You don't know the people that are under anesthesia—just practice putting the tube in, and the person wakes up with a sore throat, and well, it's just sort of a part of the procedure. . . .Someone comes in who has croaked (and you say), "Well, come on. Here is a chance to practice your intubation" (inserting a tube in the throat).

Conflict of Interest

As part of her treatment for cancer, Julia Lippman needed intravenous feeding at home. Her doctor told her to cancel the arrangements she had made with a company that provided such services and to use a company called T^2 instead. If she didn't, he added, he would not be responsible for her treatment. It turned out that he had invested in T^2 (Rodwin 1993).

The medical cash machine generates conflicts of interest. A physician may make hidden income by choosing one course of treatment instead of another or by referring a patient to a hospital, pharmacy, or medical supply company of which he or she is part owner. For prescribing enough high-profit medications, some drug companies even award doctors all-expense-paid trips to exotic locations. Such conflicts of interest make it difficult to know if a doctor has based a course of treatment on the patient's best interest or on the best interest of the doctor's bank account.

Medical Fraud

With 2 million Medicare claims a day making an audit unlikely, for many physicians the temptation is just too great. The following are not isolated incidents—just some of the most outrageous.

> . . . [D]octors have been caught billing for services on persons who were dead. . . .
> [A] psychiatrist in California charged Medicaid for sexual liaisons with a patient. . . .

Another doctor billed for abortions on women who were not pregnant, including one who had a hysterectomy. . . . (He even claimed he performed) two abortions within a month on the same patient. . . . (Another doctor billed Medicare for) treating a 22-year-old for diaper rash (Geis et al. 1995:248).

Medical suppliers have also dipped into the illicit Medicare money pot. A wheelchair van service, for example, billed Medicare $62,000 for just one patient, who supposedly made a $260 trip every two days for sixteen months. But worse yet is medical fraud that endangers people's lives, as was the case with the pharmacists who sold expired pacemakers (Schatz 1995) and the opthalmologist who, in an attempt to pocket an extra $14,000, performed unnecessary eye operations that left fourteen people with impaired vision (Geis et al. 1995).

Sexism in Medicine

On a different level lies another issue in medicine. Although usually quite subtle, often even below people's awareness, sexism in medicine can carry serious consequences. As we saw in the Down-to-Earth Sociology box on page 294, physicians don't take women's health complaints as seriously as they do men's. As a result, women are operated on at a later stage in heart disease, making it more likely that they will die from their surgery.

Bias *against* women's reproductive organs has also been reported. Sue Fisher (1986), whose encounter with depersonalized medicine was cited earlier, did participant observation in a hospital. When she heard doctors recommend total hysterectomy (removal of both the uterus and the ovaries) although no cancer was present, she asked why. The doctors explained that the uterus and ovaries are "potentially disease-producing" organs. Also, they said, they are unnecessary after the childbearing years, so why not remove them?

Since few women feel the same way, in order to make money surgeons have to "sell" the operation. Here is how one resident explained it to sociologist Diana Scully (1994):

> You have to look for your surgical procedures; you have to go after patients. Because no one is crazy enough to come and say, "Hey, here I am. I want you to operate on me." You have to sometimes convince the patient that she is really sick—if she is, of course [laughs], and that she is better off with a surgical procedure.

To "convince" a woman to have this surgery, the doctor tells her that, unfortunately, the examination has turned up fibroids in her uterus—and they *might* turn into cancer. This statement is often sufficient, for it frightens women, who can picture themselves ready to be buried. What the surgeon does *not* say is that the fibroids probably will not turn into cancer and there is a variety of nonsurgical alternatives.

Underlying this sexism is male dominance of medicine in the United States. This is not a worldwide phenomenon. For example, while only one of four U.S. physicians is a woman, in the former Soviet Union three out of four physicians are women (Knaus 1981; *Statistical Abstract* 1997:Table 645). Following changes in gender relations, the percent of U.S. medical degrees earned by women has risen rapidly, going from only 6 percent in 1960 to 38 percent today (*Statistical Abstract* 1997:Table 307). This changing sex ratio should considerably reduce sexism in medical practice, including that described in the Down-to-Earth Sociology box on the next page.

Medicalization of Society

As we have seen, childbirth and women's reproductive organs have become defined as medical matters. Sociologists use the term **medicalization** to refer to the process of turning something that was not previously considered medical into a medical matter. Examples include balding, weight, wrinkles, acne, anxiety, depression, a sagging chin or buttocks, small breasts, and even the inability to achieve orgasm. As Susan Sontag (1994) says, even many criminal behaviors have become matters to be understood and treated.

There is nothing inherently medical in such human conditions, yet we have become so used to medicalization that we tend to consider them somehow naturally medical con-

medicalization: the transformation of something into a matter to be treated by physicians

 *Down-to-Earth Sociology*

The Doctor–Nurse Game

Leonard Stein (1988), a physician who observed nurses and doctors for many years, analyzed their interactions in terms of a game. Because physicians have higher status, nurses must try to give the impression that the doctor is always "in control." Although nurses spend more time with patients and, therefore, are often more familiar with their needs, nurses can never be perceived as giving recommendations to a doctor. Consequently, nurses disguise their recommendations. Consider the following dialogue between a nurse and a resident physician whom the nurse has called at 1 A.M. The rotating resident does not know the patient.

"This is Dr. Jones." (*An open and direct communication*)

"Dr. Jones, this is Nurse Smith on 2W. Mrs. Brown learned today that her father died, and she is unable to fall asleep." (*This apparently direct, open communication of factual information—that the patient is unable to sleep and has learned of a death in the family—contains a hidden recommendation. The nurse has diagnosed the cause of the sleeplessness and is suggesting that a sedative be prescribed.*)

The conversation continues: "What sleeping medication has been helpful to Mrs. Brown in the past?" (*This communication, supposedly a mere request for facts, is actually a request for a recommendation of what to prescribe.*)

"Pentobarbital, 100 milligrams, was quite effective the night before last." (*This is actually a specific recommendation from the nurse to the physician, but it comes disguised in the form of factual information.*)

"Pentobarbital, 100 milligrams before bedtime, as needed for sleep. Got it?" (*This communication is spoken with audible authority—a little louder, a little firmer.*)

"Yes, I have, and thank you very much, doctor."

The two have successfully played the doctor–nurse game. The lower-status person has made a recommendation to the higher-status person in a covert manner that requires neither of them to acknowledge what really occurred and does not threaten their relative statuses.

When I interviewed Stein, he said that the doctor–nurse game is breaking down because of the larger number of men in nursing, the feminist movement challenging male authority, and the larger number of women physicians. As a consequence, nurses are less subservient, and physicians are less able to exert unquestioned authority.

Some version of the game will continue to be played, however, as long as status differences remain. The rules will simply be modified to meet changing circumstances.

---

cerns. Symbolic interactionists would stress that medicalization is based on a view of life that is bound to a specific historical period. Functionalists would stress how such medicalization helps the medical establishment, that people have someone to listen to their problems and that sometimes they are helped. Conflict sociologists would argue that this process is another indication of the growing power of the medical establishment—the more that physicians can medicalize human affairs, the greater their power and profits.

Medically Assisted Suicide

I started the intravenous dripper, which released a salt solution through a needle into her vein, and I kept her arm tied down so she wouldn't jerk it. This was difficult as her veins were fragile. And then once she decided she was ready to go, she just hit the switch and the device cut off the saline drip and through the needle released a solution of thiopental that put her to sleep in ten to fifteen seconds. A minute later, through the needle flowed a lethal solution of potassium chloride.

This is how Jack Kevorkian described his death machine (Denzin 1992). Kevorkian, a retired pathologist who introduced his machine on a TV talk show, is known by some as Dr. Death. He has helped over 100 people commit suicide. One side defends Kevorkian as a courageous trail blazer, while another side decries his acts as perverted. Some even call him "Jeffrey Dahmer in a lab coat" (Morganthau 1993). The topic fascinates the U.S. public. A how-to book on suicide, *Final Exit*, sold over a half million copies. The Hemlock Society, a group advocating voluntary **euthanasia** (mercy killing) for terminally ill people, has grown to eighty chapters.

With new technology that can keep the body alive even after the heart, lungs, and other vital organs no longer function on their own, a burning question, yet undecided, is "Who has the right to pull the plug?" Should someone's body be kept alive for years al-

euthanasia: mercy killing

though the person's mind can no longer work? To resolve this issue, some people sign a **living will**—a declaration they make while in good health of what they want medical personnel to do in case they become dependent on artificial life support systems.

Our technology and the acts of Kevorkian have brought us face to face with matters of death that are both disturbing and unresolved. Should "medically assisted suicide" be legal? Few find this medical-ethical issue easy to resolve. The following Thinking Critically section explores these issues.

Thinking Critically About Social Controversy

Euthanasia in Holland

▼ Proponents of euthanasia base their claim on "people's right to die." "If someone wants to be disconnected from feeding tubes," they say, "he or she should be able to die in peace. And if someone wants to commit suicide, that person should have the right to do so. What right does the rest of society have to interfere?"

Framed in this way, many Americans would agree that euthanasia should be permitted. "The problem," say its opponents, "is that most euthanasia involves other types of dying."

The best example, critics point out, is Holland, which has allowed euthanasia for over twenty years. According to Dutch law, a physician can assist a patient in dying if the patient makes "a free, informed, and persistent request." Euthanasia must be a "last resort," and physicians are accountable to the courts for following the letter of the law.

A Dutch government committee, however, has found that the practice is very different from what the law specifies. Although only about 150 cases of euthanasia are reported annually to government officials, this doesn't come even close to the actual number. The committee found 2,300 cases of "voluntary" euthanasia and 400 assisted suicides. They also found 8,750 deaths due to the physicians withholding or withdrawing treatment—*in not one of these cases did the patients consent to their deaths.* Doctors killed another 8,100 people by giving them pain-killing drugs—and more than half of these patients had *not* consented to their deaths.

Leading Dutch physicians who practice euthanasia oppose its legalization in the United States. Said one, "If euthanasia were allowed in the United States, I would not want to be a patient there. In view of the financial costs that the care of patients can impose on relatives and society under the United States health-care system, the legalization of euthanasia in America would be an open door to get rid of patients."

What do you think?

Sources: Gomez 1991; Markson 1992; Angell 1996.

Curbing Costs: Issues in Private and National Health Insurance

We have seen some of the reasons why the price of medical care in the United States has soared: advanced—and expensive—technology for diagnosis and treatment, a growing elderly population, tests performed for defensive rather than medical reasons, and health care that is regarded as a commodity to be sold to the highest bidder. As long as these conditions are in place, the price of medical care will continue to outpace inflation. Let's look at some attempts to reduce costs.

HMOs.   **Health Maintenance Organizations,** or **HMOs,** are medical companies that negotiate an annual fee to take care of the medical needs of a corporation's employees. Whatever is left over at the end of the year is the HMO's profit. While this arrangement eliminates unnecessary procedures, it also creates pressures to reduce *necessary* medical treatment.

living will: a statement people in good health sign that clearly expresses their feelings about being kept alive on artificial life support systems

health maintenance organization (HMO): a health care organization that provides medical treatment to its members for a fixed annual cost

FRANK & ERNEST by ® Bob Thaves

The cartoonist has captured an unfortunate reality of U.S. medicine.

The results are anything but pretty. Over her doctor's strenuous objections, a friend of mine was discharged from the hospital even though she was still bleeding and running a fever. Her HMO representative said he would not authorize another day in the hospital. After a heart attack, a man in Kansas City, Missouri, needed surgery that could be performed only at Barnes Hospital in St. Louis, Missouri. The HMO said, "Too bad. That hospital is out of our service area." The man died while appealing the HMO decision (Spragins 1996).

The basic question, of course, is: At what human cost do we reduce spending on medical treatment?

Diagnosis-Related Groups. To interrupt the cost spiral, the federal government has classified all illnesses into 468 diagnosis-related-groups (DRGs) and specified the amount it will pay for the treatment of each. Hospitals make a profit only if they move patients through the system quickly. If patients are discharged before the hospital has spent the allotted amount, the hospital makes money. One consequence is that some patients are discharged before they are fully ready to go home. Others are refused admittance because they appear to have a "worse than average" case of a particular illness, which would cost the hospital money instead of making it a profit (Easterbrook 1987; Feinglass 1987).

National Health Insurance

> A young woman who was five months pregnant was taken to a hospital complaining of stomach pains. The hospital refused to admit her because she had no money or credit. As they were about to transfer her to a hospital for the poor, she gave birth. The baby was stillborn. The hospital went ahead and transferred the woman—dead baby, umbilical cord, and all. (Ansberry 1988)

One consequence of the desire to turn a profit on patient care is **dumping**, sending unprofitable patients to public hospitals. Most cases are less dramatic than this woman and her stillborn baby, but the same principle applies. With 40 million Americans uninsured, primarily the poor (*Statistical Abstract* 1997:Table 171), pressure has grown for national health insurance. Advocates point out that it will reduce costs through centralized, large-scale purchases. They also cite the social inequalities of medicine and the inadequacy of care for the poor. Such horror stories as the one just told make their point. Those against national health insurance stress the immense red tape such plans would require. They ask if federal agencies—such as those that monitored the savings and loan associations—inspire so much confidence that they should be entrusted with administering something so vital as the nation's health care. This debate is not new, and even if some form of national health insurance is adopted the argument is likely to continue.

Rationing Medical Care. The most controversial suggestion to reduce medical costs is to ration medical care. We cannot afford to provide all the available technology to everyone, goes the argument. No easy answer has been found for this pressing matter, which is becoming the center of a national debate. This dilemma is the focus of the Sociology and the New Technology box on the next page.

dumping: the practice of sending unprofitable patients to public hospitals

Who Should Live, and Who Should Die?
Technology and the Dilemma of Medical Rationing

Visiting a doctor or a hospital today is not without risk, but the risk is small compared with the times when physicians bled and purged their patients. Today's physicians are well trained, and medical care is supported by scientific studies. Our new technology even allows us to cure medical conditions that just a short time ago doomed people to premature deaths. In other instances, the medical condition remains, but the patient is able to live a long life.

And therein lies the rub. Some technology is limited, and there isn't enough to go around to everyone who needs it. Other technology is so costly that it would bankrupt society if it were made available to everyone who has a particular condition. Who, then, should receive the benefits of our new medical technology?

Consider dialysis, the use of artificial kidneys to cleanse the blood of people suffering from kidney disease. Currently, dialysis is available to anyone who needs it, and the cost runs several billion dollars a year. Four percent of all Medicare goes to pay for the dialysis of just one-fourth of 1 percent of Medicare patients. Great Britain, facing this same problem, rations dialysis to people under the age of 55 (Volti 1995).

The technology of bypass surgery is similarly astonishing, and so are its costs. One percent of all the money the nation spends on its medical bills goes to pay for the bypass surgeries of just 0.04 (four-hundredths of 1 percent) of the population.

The cost of medical technology at the end of people's lives helps us understand the issue. Of all Medicare money, about one-fourth is spent to maintain patients during just the last year of their lives. Almost a third of this amount is spent during the last month of life alone (Volti 1995).

At the heart of this issue of how to spend limited resources lie questions not only of costs, but also of fairness, of how to distribute equitably the benefits of advanced medical technology.

For Your Consideration

The dilemma is harsh: If we choose medical rationing, many sick people will be allowed to die. If we don't, we may go bankrupt. In more specific terms: should an alcoholic Mickey Mantle be given a liver transplant when he is already dying of cancer? Use ideas, concepts, and principles presented in this and other chapters to develop a reasonable answer to this pressing issue. Also note how this dilemma changes shape if you view it from the contrasting perspectives of conflict, functionalism, and symbolic interactionism.

 ## Threats to Health

Let's look at four threats to health: disease; drugs; disabling environments; and misguided, foolish, and callous experiments.

AIDS

Perhaps the most pressing issue in U.S.—and global—health today is AIDS (acquired immune deficiency syndrome). Since the first case of this virus that attacks the human immune system was documented in 1981, AIDS has jumped to the eighth leading cause of death in the United States (see Figure 19.3 on page 531). Let's look at some of its major characteristics.

Origin. The origin of AIDS is unknown. The most prevalent theory is that the virus was first present in monkeys in Africa and then transmitted to humans. If so, just how the transmission to humans took place remains a matter of conjecture. It may have occurred during the 1920s and 1950s when, in a peculiar experiment for malaria, people were inoculated with blood from monkeys and chimpanzees. The blood may unknowingly have been infected with viral ancestors of HIV (Rathus and Nevid 1993). Since monkeys are considered food in several parts of Africa, another possibility is that the virus was transmitted through inadequately cooked meat. Some suggest the opposite route, that the disease originated in Europe or the United States and was somehow transmitted to Africa (Rushing 1995). Although at this point scientists do not know its origin, genetic sleuths may eventually unravel the mystery.

The Transmission of AIDS. In the United States, AIDS first appeared among male homosexuals. Male bisexuals provided the bridge that passed AIDS on to the heterosexual population. As a result of having sex with bisexuals and sharing needles for intravenous drugs, prostitutes quickly become a second bridge to the heterosexual population.

Others were infected with AIDS through blood transfusions. Figure 19.6 summarizes how people have become infected.

A person cannot become infected with AIDS unless bodily fluids pass from one person to another. AIDS is known to be transmitted by the exchange of blood and semen, as well as, in rare cases, by mother's milk to newborns. Since the AIDS virus is present in all bodily fluids (including sweat, tears, spittle, and urine), some people think that AIDS can also be transmitted in these forms. The U.S. Centers for Disease Control, however, say that AIDS cannot be transmitted by casual contact in which traces of these fluids would be exchanged (Edgar 1994).

Gender, Race-Ethnicity, and AIDS. Although many people think of AIDS as a man's disease, in parts of Africa AIDS strikes males and females equally. And as Figure 19.7 shows, in the United States each year women make up a larger proportion of new cases. In 1982, only 6 percent of AIDS cases were women, but today one of five of every new AIDS case is a woman (Centers for Disease Control 1997:Tables 3, 10). AIDS has become the third leading cause of death of U.S. women aged 25 to 44, while it is *the* leading cause of death for U.S. men of this age (*Statistical Abstract* 1997:Table 130). As shown in Table 19.1, the risk of AIDS is also related to race-ethnicity. The reason for this is not genetic; that is, no racial-ethnic group is more susceptible to AIDS because of biology. Rather, risks differ because of *social* factors, such as rates of intravenous drug use and the use of condoms.

The Stigma of Aids. One of the most significant sociological aspects of AIDS is its stigma, another example of how social factors are essential to health and illness. Some people refuse even to be tested because they fear the stigma they would have to bear if they tested HIV positive. One unfortunate consequence is the further spread of AIDS by people who "don't want to know." The stigma is so great in some Asian countries that government officials refuse to acknowledge how widespread AIDS is. Burying their heads in the sand, however, makes them unable to sponsor preventive measures, and so the epidemic grows (Shenon 1995). If this disease is to be brought under control, its stigma must be overcome: AIDS must be thought of as being, like other lethal diseases, the work of a destructive biological organism.

The Globalization of AIDS. AIDS may have been confined to some remote region of the earth, where it incubated quietly for thousands of years. Today's global travel, however, has brought the globalization of AIDS. As the Social Map on pages 542–543 shows, Africa has been hit the hardest, and we can expect 20 million deaths there (Haub 1997).

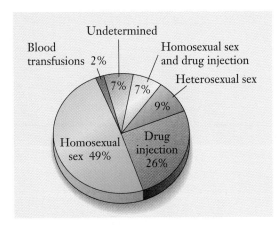

Source: Centers for Disease Control 1997:Table 3.

Figure 19.6

How People Get AIDS

TABLE 19.1
AIDS and Race–Ethnicity

	Percentage of U.S. Population	Percentage of AIDS Cases
Whites	74.2%	46%
African Americans	12.0%	35%
Latinos	9.7%	18%
Asian Americans	3.4%	0.7%
Native Americans	0.75%	0.3%

Source: Centers for Disease Control, 1997:Table 8, and Figure 12.6 on page 327 of this text.

Figure 19.7

Percentage of Americans Diagnosed with AIDS Who Are Women

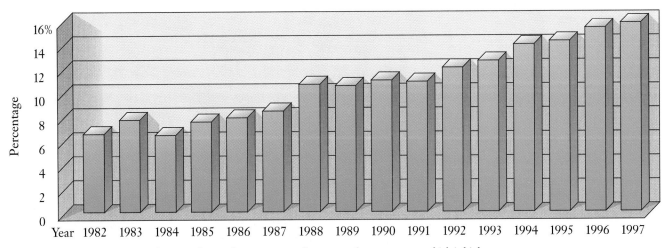

Note: These are cumulative totals, not the percentage of new cases that are women, which is higher.

Sources: Centers for Disease Control, various years and 1996:Table 9; 1997:Table 8.

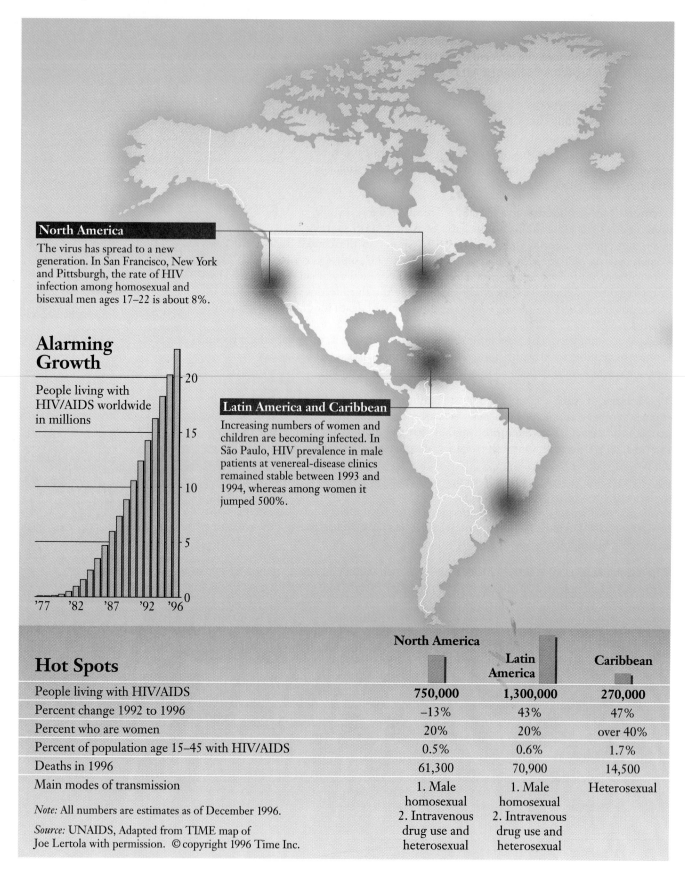

North America

The virus has spread to a new generation. In San Francisco, New York and Pittsburgh, the rate of HIV infection among homosexual and bisexual men ages 17–22 is about 8%.

Alarming Growth

People living with HIV/AIDS worldwide in millions

Latin America and Caribbean

Increasing numbers of women and children are becoming infected. In São Paulo, HIV prevalence in male patients at venereal-disease clinics remained stable between 1993 and 1994, whereas among women it jumped 500%.

Hot Spots	North America	Latin America	Caribbean
People living with HIV/AIDS	750,000	1,300,000	270,000
Percent change 1992 to 1996	–13%	43%	47%
Percent who are women	20%	20%	over 40%
Percent of population age 15–45 with HIV/AIDS	0.5%	0.6%	1.7%
Deaths in 1996	61,300	70,900	14,500
Main modes of transmission	1. Male homosexual 2. Intravenous drug use and heterosexual	1. Male homosexual 2. Intravenous drug use and heterosexual	Heterosexual

Note: All numbers are estimates as of December 1996.

Source: UNAIDS, Adapted from TIME map of Joe Lertola with permission. © copyright 1996 Time Inc.

Figure 19.8

AIDS in Global Perspective

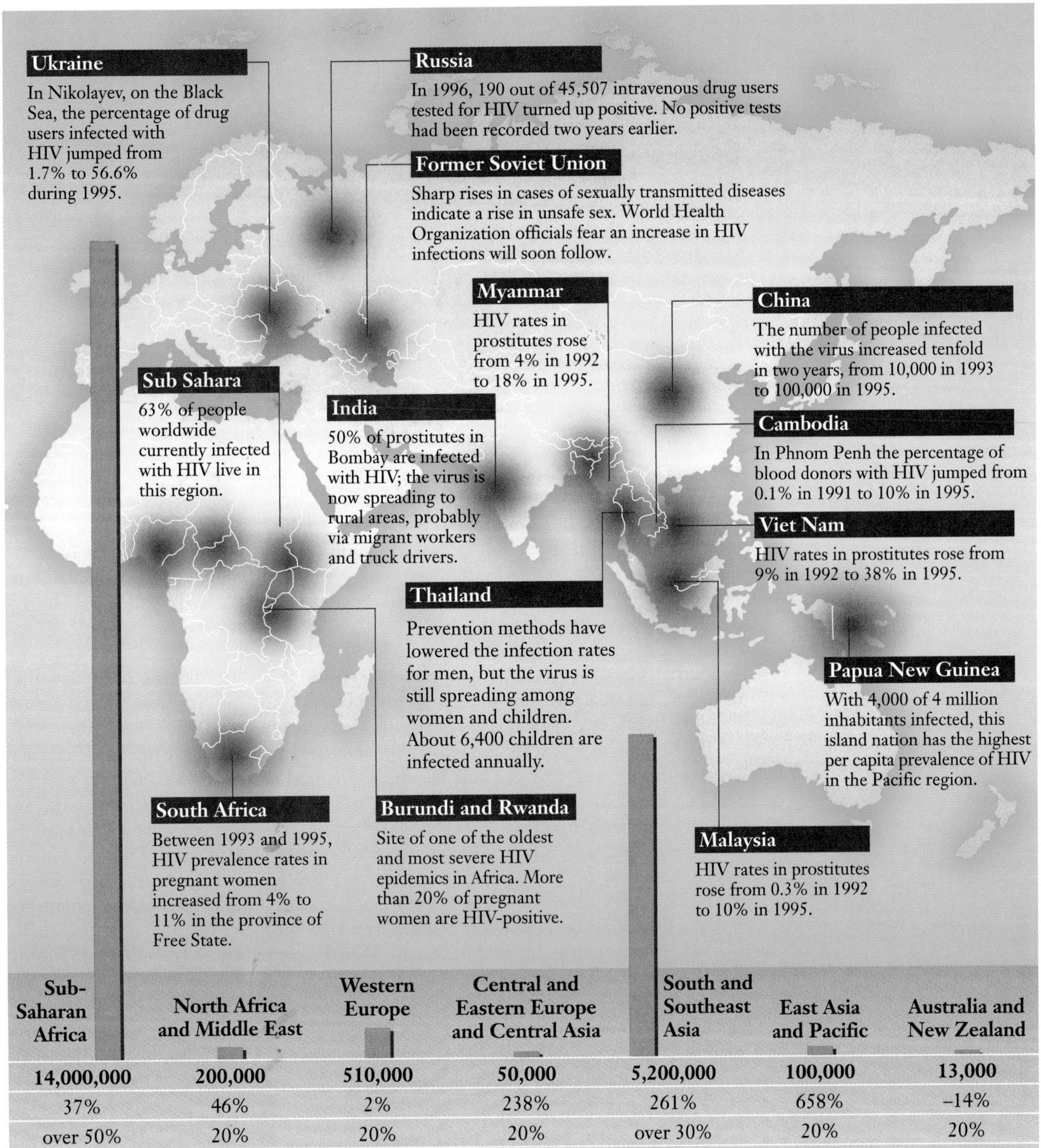

Ukraine

In Nikolayev, on the Black Sea, the percentage of drug users infected with HIV jumped from 1.7% to 56.6% during 1995.

Russia

In 1996, 190 out of 45,507 intravenous drug users tested for HIV turned up positive. No positive tests had been recorded two years earlier.

Former Soviet Union

Sharp rises in cases of sexually transmitted diseases indicate a rise in unsafe sex. World Health Organization officials fear an increase in HIV infections will soon follow.

Myanmar

HIV rates in prostitutes rose from 4% in 1992 to 18% in 1995.

China

The number of people infected with the virus increased tenfold in two years, from 10,000 in 1993 to 100,000 in 1995.

Sub Sahara

63% of people worldwide currently infected with HIV live in this region.

India

50% of prostitutes in Bombay are infected with HIV; the virus is now spreading to rural areas, probably via migrant workers and truck drivers.

Cambodia

In Phnom Penh the percentage of blood donors with HIV jumped from 0.1% in 1991 to 10% in 1995.

Viet Nam

HIV rates in prostitutes rose from 9% in 1992 to 38% in 1995.

Thailand

Prevention methods have lowered the infection rates for men, but the virus is still spreading among women and children. About 6,400 children are infected annually.

Papua New Guinea

With 4,000 of 4 million inhabitants infected, this island nation has the highest per capita prevalence of HIV in the Pacific region.

South Africa

Between 1993 and 1995, HIV prevalence rates in pregnant women increased from 4% to 11% in the province of Free State.

Burundi and Rwanda

Site of one of the oldest and most severe HIV epidemics in Africa. More than 20% of pregnant women are HIV-positive.

Malaysia

HIV rates in prostitutes rose from 0.3% in 1992 to 10% in 1995.

Sub-Saharan Africa	North Africa and Middle East	Western Europe	Central and Eastern Europe and Central Asia	South and Southeast Asia	East Asia and Pacific	Australia and New Zealand
14,000,000	200,000	510,000	50,000	5,200,000	100,000	13,000
37%	46%	2%	238%	261%	658%	–14%
over 50%	20%	20%	20%	over 30%	20%	20%
5.6%	0.1%	0.2%	0.015%	0.6%	0.001%	0.1%
783,700	10,800	21,000	1,000	143,700	1,200	1,000
Heterosexual	1. Intravenous drug use 2. Heterosexual	1. Male homosexual 2. Intravenous drug use and heterosexual	1. Intravenous drug use 2. Male homosexual	Heterosexual	1. Intravenous drug use and heterosexual 2. Male homosexual	1. Male homosexual 2. Intravenous drug use and heterosexual

A new controversy surrounding AIDS is the "semilegal" marijuana clubs in San Francisco. Here marijuana is sold openly to people seeking to combat the side effects of AIDS treatments.

In some countries ravished by AIDS, life expectancy may be cut in half (Olshansky et al. 1997). Botswana, Uganda, and Zimbabwe are likely to lose a quarter of their populations (Stout 1992). In Kampala and Kigali, a third of all pregnant women have AIDS (Scommegna 1996). In the former Soviet Union AIDS is multiplying, primarily due to the rise in prostitution and drug use since the fall of communism (Kaminski and Palchikoff 1997). Partially due to its huge sex industry (see the Perspectives box on page 246) AIDS is also flourishing in Asia.

Is There a Cure for AIDS? As Figure 19.9 shows, about 400,000 Americans have died of AIDS. As this figure also shows, the number of deaths and new cases in the United States peaked between 1992–1994. Have we found a cure for AIDS?

With thousands of scientists searching for a cure, the media have heralded each new breakthrough in research as a possible cure. The most promising treatment to date, the one that lies behind the reduction in deaths, was spearheaded by David Ho, a virologist (virus researcher). If patients in the very early stages of the disease take a "cocktail" of drugs (a combination of protease inhibitors, AZT, and 3TC), all signs of the virus can be erased from their bodies. Their immune systems then rebound (Gorman 1997). No one is yet calling this a cure, however. What is not known is if the virus is hiding undetected in some part of the body, and if it, too, will rebound unexpectedly.

While most praise this new treatment, some researchers have launched a dire warning (Rotello 1996). They suggest that the cocktail may become this decade's penicillin. When penicillin was introduced, everyone was ecstatic with its results. But over the years the microbes it targets mutated, producing "super germs" against which we have no protection. If this is the case with AIDS, then a new, "super AIDS" virus may hit the world with more fury than the first devastating wave.

The Globalization of Disease

In the movie *Outbreak*, when a new disease threatened the world, government epidemiologists were transformed into Indiana Jones heroes in order to save it. Apart from its overdramatization, the movie's depiction of the rapid spread of disease is not too far from reality. Modern travel has wiped out the frontiers that used to contain diseases. Within forty-eight hours of its outbreak, a new, lethal disease can reach most U.S. cities from anywhere in the world via commercial airlines (Olshansky et al. 1997).

As mentioned earlier, older diseases have mutated and produced "super bugs" that are immune to antibiotics. Antibiotics are also ineffective against many of the twenty-eight new diseases that have recently appeared on the world scene. Because some of

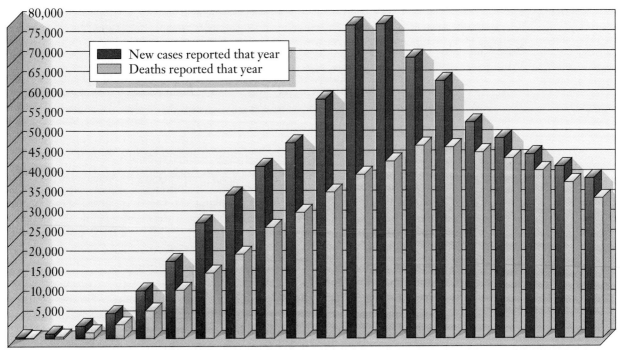

1981 1982 1983 1984 1985 1986 1987 1988 1989 1990 1991 1992 1993 1994 1995 1996* 1997* 1998* 1999* 2000*

*Author's estimate.

Note: In 1993, the CDC began to use an expanded definition of AIDS. To be uniform, this Figure follows the 1989 definition, making the totals shown here conservative.

Sources: Centers for Disease Control 1997:Table 9; the estimates are from 1995:Table 13 and 1996:Table 13.

Figure 19.9

The Growth of AIDS in the United States

these new diseases are lethal, we may have to resort to an old remedy—sending people to asylums. The only way ebola, with its particularly hideous death, could be contained was to isolate an entire region in Zaire. Apparently some U.S. patients with new strains of deadly tuberculosis have already been quietly removed from the population (Olshansky 1997).

Drugs: Alcohol and Nicotine

Let's examine some of the health consequences of alcohol and nicotine, the most frequently used drugs in the United States.

Alcohol. Alcohol is the standard recreational drug of Americans. The *average* adult American consumes 36 gallons of alcoholic beverages per year—almost 32 gallons of beer, 2½ gallons of wine, and 2 gallons of whiskey, vodka, or other distilled spirits. Alcohol is so popular that most Americans drink more beer than either milk or coffee (*Statistical Abstract* 1997:Table 232).

In spite of laws banning alcohol consumption before the age of 21, underage drinking is common. During the past year, about three of four high school seniors have drunk alcohol, while this figure is even higher for college students (see Table 19.2 to the right and Table 19.3 on the next page). Drinking alcohol is directly related to college grades, as Table 19.4 on the next page makes evident: The more that college students drink, the worse they do in their classes. These tables also show that men and women have distinct patterns of drug use: In general, men are more likely to use drugs. These rates are fairly consistent from year to year, but the higher rate of smoking by college women violates previous findings. It may not show up in future samples.

TABLE 19.2

What Drugs Have High School Seniors Used in the Past Year?

	Men	Women
Alcohol	74.1%	72.1%
Nicotine (cigarettes)	NA	NA
Marijuana	35.1	26.4
LSD	8.4	5.3
Cocaine	4.5	2.8
Barbiturates	4.3	3.8
Hallucinogens	9.2	5.8
Heroin	0.8	0.4

Source: Johnston et al. 1995: Table 7.

TABLE 19.3

What Drugs Have Full-Time College Students Used in the Past Year?

	Men	Women
Alcohol	86.9%	86.3%
Nicotine (cigarettes)	38.0	39.3
Marijuana	30.0	26.2
LSD	7.1	3.6
Cocaine	3.7	1.9
Barbiturates	2.2	1.0
Heroin	0.1	0.1

Source: Johnston et al. 1995: Table 19.

TABLE 19.4

Grade-Point Average (GPA) and Average Number of Drinks per Week

	Number of Drinks per Week	
GPA	Men	Women
A	5	2
B	7	3
C	9	4
D *or* F	15	5

Source: Presley et al. 1993.

TABLE 19.5

Percentage of Americans Who Smoke Cigarettes

	1965	1985	1993
Men	52%	33%	25%
Women	34%	28%	23%

Source: Statistical Abstract 1993: Table 210; 1997:Table 221.

disabling environment: an environment that is harmful to health

Is alcohol bad for health? This beverage cuts both ways. About two drinks a day for men and one drink for women reduce the risk of heart attacks and blood vessel diseases. (Women weigh less on average and produce fewer enzymes that metabolize alcohol.) Beyond these amounts, however, alcohol increases the risk of a variety of diseases, from cancer to stroke. It also increases the likelihood of birth defects. Each year, over 300,000 Americans seek treatment for alcohol problems; about 20,000 die from alcohol abuse (*Statistical Abstract* 1997:Tables 143, 219).

Nicotine.　Of all drugs, nicotine is the most harmful to health. Sociologist Erich Goode (1989) points out that compared with nonsmokers smokers are three times as likely to die before reaching the age of 65. Smokers in their thirties are *six* times as likely to have heart attacks as are nonsmokers of the same age (Winslow 1995). Smoking doubles the risk of blindness in old age (Lagnado 1996). Smoking also causes progressive emphysema and several types of cancer that kill about 390,000 Americans each year. By far, nicotine is the most lethal of all recreational drugs.

Stressing the health hazards of smoking and of secondhand smoke, an antitobacco campaign is being waged successfully in Europe and North America. It has ended smoking on U.S. airlines and brought about smoking and nonsmoking areas in restaurants and offices. It is even illegal to light up in a bar in California. Table 19.5 shows how this antismoking message has hit home. In less than two decades, cigarette smoking has been cut in *half* among U.S. men, and dropped by a third among U.S. women.

Yet many people persist. Why, when it is so destructive to their health? There are two major reasons, addiction and advertising. Nicotine may be as addictive as heroin (Tolchin 1988). While this may sound far-fetched, consider Buerger's disease:

> In this disease, the blood vessels, especially those supplying the legs, become so constricted that circulation is impaired whenever nicotine enters the bloodstream. If a patient continues to smoke, gangrene may eventually set in. First a toe may have to be amputated, then the foot at the ankle, then the leg at the knee, and ultimately at the hip. . . . Patients are informed that if they will only stop smoking, it is virtually certain that the otherwise inexorable march of gangrene up the legs will be curbed. Yet surgeons report that some patients with Buerger's disease vigorously puff away in their hospital beds following a second or third amputation (Brecher et al. 1972).

The second reason is advertising. Even though cigarette ads were banned from television in the 1980s, cigarettes continue to be heavily advertised on billboards and in print. The tobacco industry has a huge advertising budget, spending $5 billion a year to encourage people to smoke (Federal Trade Commission 1996). The industry targets youth, often by associating cigarette smoking with success, high fashion, and independence. With the tobacco industry's clout in Washington and with 40,000 Americans depending on it for their livelihood, attempts to stop cigarette advertising have failed (*Statistical Abstract* 1997:Table 650). Joe Camel, however, the industry's most blatant attempt to hook youth, has been banned. (See the photo on the facing page.)

Disabling Environments

A **disabling environment** is one that is harmful to health. The health risk of some occupations is evident: lumberjacking, riding rodeo bulls, and taming lions are obvious examples. In many occupations, however, people become aware of the risk only years after they worked at jobs they thought were safe. For example, several million people worked with asbestos during and after World War II. Now the federal government estimates that one-quarter of them will die of cancer from having breathed asbestos dust. It is likely that many other substances that we have not yet identified also cause slowly developing cancers—including, ironically, some asbestos substitutes (Meier 1987).

Although industrialization has increased the world's standard of living, it also threatens to disable the basic environment of the human race, posing what may be the greatest health hazard of all time. The burning of vast amounts of carbon fuels is leading to the *greenhouse*

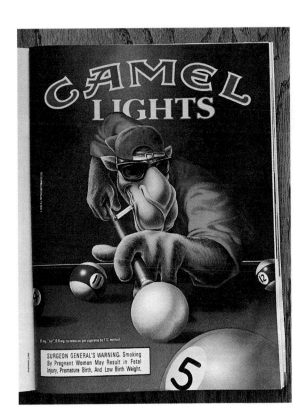

SURGEON GENERAL'S WARNING: Smoking By Pregnant Women May Result in Fetal Injury, Premature Birth, And Low Birth Weight.

Do you think that this magazine ad is designed to make cigarettes appealing to male youth? Although tobacco industry officials denied that they were trying to entice youth to smoke, the evidence such as this ad is overwhelmingly against them. After pressure from the U.S. Congress, in 1977 Camel agreed to terminate its Joe Camel ads.

In my opinion, it is not an exaggeration to call the U.S. tobacco industry criminal. At its feet must be laid countless painful deaths. Among those torturous deaths, I count those of my mother and only sister.

effect, a warming of the earth that may change the globe's climate, melt its polar ice caps, and flood the earth's coastal shores. Use of fluorocarbon gases in such items as aerosol cans, refrigerators, and air conditioners is threatening the *ozone shield*, the protective layer of the earth's upper stratosphere that screens out a high proportion of the sun's ultraviolet rays. High-intensity ultraviolet radiation is harmful to most forms of life. In humans, it causes skin cancer. The pollution of land, air, and water, especially through nuclear waste, pesticides, herbicides, and other chemicals, poses additional risks to life on our planet.

To identify environmental threats to world health is only the first step. The second is to introduce short- and long-term policies to reduce such problems. The sociology of the environment is discussed on pages 635–642.

Misguided, Foolish, and Callous Experiments

At times, physicians and government officials become so arrogant with power that they callously disregard the health of the people they are sworn to protect. Let's look at two notorious instances.

The Tuskegee Syphilis Experiment. Imagine that you are living in Macon County, Alabama, during the Depression years. You are dirt poor. You live in a little country shack with a dirt floor and no electricity or running water. You never finished grade school, and you make a living, such as it is, by doing odd jobs. You can't afford a doctor, but you haven't been feeling quite right lately.

Then you rub your eyes in disbelief. It is just like winning the lottery. You are offered free physical examinations at Tuskegee University, free rides to and from the clinic, hot meals on examination days, and free treatment for minor ailments. Your survivors are even guaranteed a burial payment. You eagerly accept.

You have just become part of what is surely slated to go down in history as one of the most callous experiments with human life, outside the infamous Nazi experiments. The U.S. Public Health Service told 399 African-American men that they had joined a social club and burial society called "Miss Rivers' Lodge." They also told them that they had "bad blood," and if they went to a private doctor they would lose their benefits.

Awareness of disabling environments has grown—from air pollution to asbestos and harmful food additives. Coping mechanisms also are taking many forms, from reducing auto emissions and eating organically grown foods to that depicted here—Tokyo shoppers "stopping off for a quick one," in this case, a hit of pure oxygen.

What the men were *not* told was that they had syphilis. For forty years, the "Public Health Service" let their disease go untreated just "to observe what happened." There was even a control group of 201 men free of the disease (Jones 1993).

By the way, there was one further benefit for the men—free autopsies to determine the ravages of syphilis on the body.

The Cold War Experiments.   Now assume that you are a soldier stationed in Nevada, and the U.S. Army orders your platoon to march through an area just after an atomic bomb is detonated. Because you are a soldier, you obey. Nobody knows much about radiation, and you don't know that the army wants you as a guinea pig, just to see if you'll be able to withstand the fallout—without any radiation equipment. Or suppose you are a patient at the University of Rochester in 1946, and your doctor, whom you trust implicitly, says he is going to give you something "to help you." You are pleased. But the injection, it turns out, is uranium (Noah 1994).

Like the Tuskegee experiment, such radiation experiments—as well as giving LSD to soldiers and releasing whooping cough viruses over Palmetto, Florida, which killed a dozen children—were conducted with unsuspecting subjects simply because government officials wanted information (Conahan 1994).

Playing God.   To most of us, it is incredible that government officials and medical personnel would so callously disregard human life, but it obviously happens. Those in official positions can come to the point that they think they can play God and determine who shall live and who shall die. And obviously the most expendable citizens are the poor and powerless. It is inconceivable that an experiment such as the syphilis study would be forced on the wealthy and powerful. The elite are protected from such callous disregard of human rights and life. The only protection the rest of us have against such gross abuse of professional positions is to publicize each known instance and to insist on vigorous prosecution of those who direct and carry out such experiments.

The Search for Alternatives

What alternatives are there to the way U.S. medicine is usually practiced? The suggestion we shall explore here is that we shift the emphasis away from the treatment of disease to prevention. We shall close with a look at health care systems of other countries—which might contain ideas to follow, or to avoid.

Treatment or Prevention?

Effects of Values and Lifestyles.   The impact of values and lifestyle on health becomes apparent if we contrast Utah (home of the Mormons, who disapprove of tobacco and alcohol) with its adjacent state of Nevada (home of the gambling industry). Although these two states have similar climate, levels of income, education, medical care, and urbanization (Fuchs 1981), Nevada's overall death rate is *50 percent* higher than Utah's. Nevadans are 50 percent more likely to commit suicide, more than twice as likely to die from lung disease, more than three times as likely to be murdered, and almost four times as likely to die from AIDS (*Statistical Abstract*, 1997:Table 132). In short, many threats to health are preventable.

Prevention implies both an individual and a group responsibility. On the individual level, doing exercises regularly, eating nutritious food, maintaining sexual monogamy, and avoiding smoking and alcohol abuse go a long way to preventing disease. Following these guidelines can add years to our lives—and make those years healthy and enjoyable.

On the group level, one alternative is preventive medicine. Instead of the treatment of disease, U.S. medicine could have "wellness" as its goal. What would it require to implement a national policy of "prevention, not intervention"? First, the medical establishment must change its basic philosophy, not an easy task to accomplish. Essentially, physicians, nurses, and hospitals would have to be convinced that prevention is profitable. One possibility is that a group of doctors and a hospital would be paid an annual fee for keeping people well (Cooper 1993). Second, the public's attitude would also have to be turned around so they, too, can see the benefit of "wellness." This would require a program of education in the schools and the media showing how some practices of nutrition, exercise, sex, and drug use pay off with healthier lives. For example, diet is a significant factor in many types of cancer, and an educational program to replace fatty, low-fiber foods with a diet rich in fruits, vegetables, and green tea would go a long way in saving lives. Unfortunately, rather than making such basic changes most Americans seem to prefer that their doctors prescribe drugs.

On yet a broader scale is comprehensive prevention—eliminating disabling environments and the use of harmful drugs. Some businesses continue to spew industrial wastes into the air and to use rivers and oceans as industrial sewers, while others use advertising to seduce youths to use harmful drugs. These acts are unconscionable. Finally, since we now live in a global village, the creation and maintenance of a health-producing environment require international controls and cooperation.

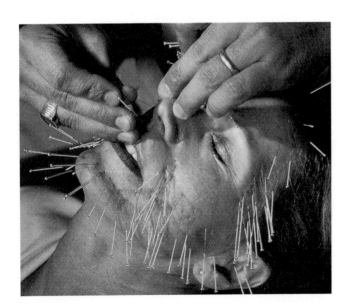

Each culture makes basic assumptions about the causes and cures of medical problems. The traditional assumptions of Eastern medical practitioners, usually ridiculed by Western physicians, are now being examined seriously by some. Acupuncture, for example, is gradually gaining acceptance in the West, although it does not fit Western assumptions of cause and cure.

Health Care in Global Perspective

The search for alternatives also leads us to examine health care in other nations. Consequently, we shall close this chapter with a comparison of health care in the three worlds of industrialization. As with education (see pages 467–471), no one country can adequately illustrate the varieties of medicine that are practiced in nations in a particular stage of industrialization. Nevertheless, the countries highlighted in the Perspectives box do illustrate contrastive themes that characterize health care around the world. Because they are so different—one socialized, the other modified capitalist—we shall consider two Most Idustrialized Nations. The following materials, then, help us place both positive and negative aspects of the U.S. health care system in cultural perspective.

Perspectives

CULTURAL DIVERSITY AROUND THE WORLD

Health Care in the Three Worlds of Industrialization: Sweden, Canada, Russia, and China

Health Care in the Most Industrialized Nations: Sweden

Sweden has the most comprehensive health care system in the world. All Swedish citizens and alien residents are covered by national health insurance financed by contributions from the state and employers. Most physicians are paid a salary by the government to treat patients, but 5 percent work full time in private practice (Swedish Institute 1990). Except for a small consultation fee, medical and dental treatment by these government-paid doctors is free, and most of the charges of private physicians are also paid by the government. The government also reimburses travel expenses for patients, as well as for the parents of a hospitalized child. Only minimal fees are charged for prescriptions and hospitalization.

Medical treatment is just one component of Sweden's broad system of social welfare. For example, people who are sick or must stay home with sick children receive 90 percent of their salaries. Swedes are given parental leave at the birth of a child, and all Swedes are guaranteed a pension. This comprehensive system does not come cheap, running about 35 percent of each employee's salary (Cockerham 1989).

Sweden's socialized medicine is not only very expensive, but also very inefficient. Swedes have not solved the twin problems of getting rid of waiting lines and getting physicians to work. With salaries of medical personnel guaranteed, regardless how many patients they see, the system is marked by lack of productivity. When reporters of a Stockholm newspaper visited Sweden's largest hospital on a weekday morning, a peak period when 80 of 120 surgeons were on duty, they found 19 of 24 operating rooms not in use. Their photos of dark and empty operating rooms—at a time when there was a one- to two-year waiting period for hip replacements and cataract operations—provoked a public outcry (Bergström 1992). Due to public pressure and an emphasis on accountability, efficiency is improving (Hakansson 1994).

Health Care in the Most Industrialized Nations: Canada

In 1971, the Canadian government instituted a national health insurance program. Medical costs are shared equally between the federal and provincial governments. Unlike most doctors in Sweden, Canadian physicians work in private practice and charge a fee for service. Patients can choose any doctor they wish. The government acts as the patient's insurer and pays the physician's bill. Physicians face no restrictions in choosing a medical specialty or deciding where they will practice. If they wish, physicians can practice private medical care instead of participating in the government program, but only a handful do (Coburn et al. 1981; Grant 1984; Vayda and Deber 1984).

Canada's bill for medical care runs 10 percent of its gross national product, compared with 14 percent in the United States (*Statistical Abstract* 1997:Table 1341). Costs are held down in three main ways. (1) A fixed fee is established annually by the government for each medical service after negotiations with professional medical associations; (2) physicians' incomes are capped—once a general practitioner hits $39,474 in quarterly fees, the government pays only 25 percent of each bill submitted over that amount until the next quarter starts; and (3) overhead costs are low because hospitals run at full capacity, compared with 65 percent capacity in the United States. Fixed costs are thus spread over the greatest possible number of patients. Nor do hospitals need large accounting departments to deal with a myriad of insurance companies, for only the provincial government is billed (Heideman 1994). The savings in overhead account for half the difference between the cost of health care in Canada and the United States (Walker 1991).

Although the health care of Canadians is among the best in the world, with more of its citizens aging Canada's medical system is in a financial crisis. With 10 percent of the population of the United States, Canada has only 11 facili-

(Continued)

ties for open-heart surgery; the United States has 793 (Barnes 1990). There are waiting lines for coronary bypass surgery and even for ultrasound treatment of kidney stones (Blinick 1992). Seeing greener pastures, about 10,000 Canadian physicians have moved to the United States to practice medicine (Goodman 1993). To discourage patients with minor complaints from clogging up the system, the province of Ontario put up billboards that say, "A cold lasts a week, but if you see a doctor it lasts seven days" (Greenberg 1994).

Health Care in the Industrializing Nations: Post-Soviet Russia

The government owns all health care facilities, all medical equipment, and determines how many students will attend the medical schools that it also owns and operates. The physicians, most of whom are women, are government employees, earning about the same salary as factory workers and high school teachers. Physicians are not trained well, and the health of the population has declined. Serious birth defects have jumped to four times the U.S. rate. A likely culprit is radiation pollution from decades of nuclear irresponsibility (Specter 1995).

Perhaps the single best indicator of the deterioration of health is the drop in life expectancy that began in the 1960s and is continuing today (Cockerham 1997). A major cause is alcohol poisoning due to excessive drinking, especially by Russian men. As shown on Table 19.6, the health of post-Soviet Russians is closer to that of China than to the Most Industrialized Nations.

The only hospitals comparable with those of the United States are the hospitals reserved for the elite (Light 1992). In the rest, basic supplies and equipment are in such short supply that surgical scalpels are resharpened until they break. Sometimes even razor blades are used for surgery (Donelson 1992). Although health care is free, patients have no choice about which doctor they see or where they will be treated. Some hospitals do not even have a doctor on staff. The length of the average hospital stay is three times longer than it is in the United States. Medical care is so inefficient that the *majority* of X rays are uninterpretable because of poor quality. Some of the radical changes now being introduced in the former Soviet Union include employer-based health insurance (Light 1992).

Health Care in the Least Industrialized Nations: China

Because this nation of 1.2 billion people has a vast shortage of trained physicians, hospitals, and medicine, most Chinese see "barefoot doctors," people who have only a rudimentary knowledge of medicine, are paid low wages, and travel from village to village. Physicians are employees of the government, and as in post-Soviet Russia, the government owns all the country's medical facilities. With its emphases on medicinal herbs and acupuncture, Chinese medicine differs from that of the West. Although Westerners have scoffed at the Chinese approach, some have changed their minds. One of the herbs that the Chinese have used for a thousand years or longer to treat liver disease, for example, has been tested by Western societies; it reduces liver cancer (Tanouye 1995).

Recent changes include payment for medical treatment. A hospital stay can now cost several hundred yuan, when the average monthly wage is 200 yuan. A system of private medical clinics is also developing. Some physicians take extra jobs because they cannot survive on their salaries, and bribery of medical personnel who are supposed to give free treatment has become routine. In some cases bribery is demanded, as with the surgeons who, arms scrubbed and held high in the air, refused to enter the operating room until the patient's relatives had stuffed their pockets with cash (Sampson 1992).

For Your Consideration

It is important to note that no nation has discovered the perfect medical system, and that today each country faces a medical crisis of "too much demand at too great a cost" (Moore and Winslow 1993). The preceding examples illustrate a variety of medical systems that can be compared to that of the United States. In what ways would you say that the U.S. medical system is superior—and inferior—to each of these four systems? If you had a choice, is there one that you would pick over the U.S. system? Why or why not? Short of socializing medicine, which goes against the value system of Americans, what modifications do you think can realistically be made in the U.S. medical system to overcome the deficiencies reviewed in this chapter—and to maintain its strengths?

TABLE 19.6

Indicators of Health					
	Sweden	*Canada*	*United States*	*Russia*	*China*
Life expectancy at birth	78.5 years	79.3 years	76.0 years	63.8 years	70.0 years
Infant mortality[a]	4.5	6.0	6.6	24.3	37.9
Suicide[b]	14.7	12.8	11.8	41.7	NA
Health cost per person	$1,360	$2,049	$3,700	NA	NA

[a]Per 1,000 live births.

[b]Per 100,000 population.

Source: Statistical Abstract 1994:Table 1360; 1997:Tables 1339, 1341.

Summary and Review

Sociology and the Study of Medicine

What is the role of sociology in the study of medicine?

Sociologists study medicine as a social institution. As practiced in the United States, three of its primary characteristics are professionalization, bureaucracy, and the profit motive. P. 524.

What is the symbolic interactionist perspective on health and illness?

Health is not only a biological matter, but is intimately related to society. Illness is also far from an objective matter, for illness is always viewed from the framework of culture, and such definitions vary from one group to another. Pp. 524–525.

What is the functionalist perspective on health and illness?

The **sick role** is society's permission to not perform one's usual activities. In return for this permission, the individual assumes responsibility to seek competent help and to cooperate in getting well so he or she can quickly resume normal activities. Pp. 525–526.

What is the conflict perspective on health and illness?

Health care is one of the scare resources over which groups compete. On a global level, health care follows the international stratification we studied in Chapter 9, with the best health care available in the dominant nations and the worst in the dependent nations.

In the American colonies, no training or licensing was necessary to call oneself a doctor. Even until the early 1900s medical training was a hit-or-miss affair. In 1910, the education of physicians came under the control of a group of men who eliminated most of their competition and turned medicine into the largest business in the United States. Pp. 527–531.

Historical Patterns of Health

How have health patterns changed over time?

Patterns of disease in the United States have changed so extensively that of today's top ten killers five did not even show up on the 1900 top ten list. Because most Americans live longer than their ancestors, we can conclude that contemporary Americans are healthier. For mental illness, we have no idea how today compares with the past, for we have no baselines from which to make comparisons. P. 531–532.

Issues in Health Care

How does treating health care as a commodity lead to social inequalities?

Because medical care is a commodity to be sold to the highest bidder, the United States has a two-tier system of medical care in which the poor receive inferior health care for both their mental and physical illnesses. Pp. 532–533.

What are some other problems in U.S. health care?

One problem is **defensive medicine** which refers to medical procedures done for the physician's benefit, not the patient's. Intended to protect physicians from lawsuits, these tests and consultations add huge amounts to the nation's medical bill. Other problems are depersonalization, conflict of interest, and medical fraud. Another is sexism which leads to tests on females being done too late and to much unnecessary surgery. Pp. 533–537.

Why is medically assisted suicide an issue now?

Due to advanced technology, people can be kept technically alive even when they have no brain waves. Physicians who openly assist in suicides have come under severe criticism. Research findings on **euthanasia** in Holland have fueled this controversy. Pp. 537–538.

What attempts have been made to cut medical costs?

Health maintenance organizations, diagnosis-related groups, and various procedures instituted by private insurance companies are among the measures taken to reduce medical costs. National health insurance, which has run into immense opposition, has been proposed as another solution. Pp. 538–540.

Threats to Health

What are some threats to the health of Americans?

Discussed here are AIDS, which is rapidly increasing; alcohol and nicotine, the most lethal drugs used by Americans; **disabling environments**, environments that are harmful to health, such as work-related diseases or pollution of air and water; and unethical experiments, with the Tuskegee syphilis and the radiation experiments cited as examples. P. 540–548.

The Search for Alternatives

Are there alternatives to our current health care system?

The primary alternative discussed here is a change from treatment to the prevention of disease. Other alternatives may be found by examining health care systems in other countries. Both positive and negative characteristics of health care in Sweden, Canada, Russia, and China were reviewed. Pp. 548-551.

Where can I read more on this topic?

Suggested readings for this chapter are listed on page 666.

Sociology and the Internet

All URLs listed are current as of the printing of this book. URLs are often changed. Please check our Website http://www.abacon.com/henslin for updates.

1. Among its many topics, this chapter introduced you to the origin and scope of AIDS. This project builds on that introduction and provides the opportunity to explore AIDS in greater depth. Access the CDC/AIDS site at *http://www.cdcnac.org* Select "AIDS Info" and browse through several subdirectories. Examine the listed topics to find out as much as you can. When you have gathered enough information, write a paper on AIDS as a global threat.

2. In the Perspectives box entitled "Health Care in Three Worlds of Industrialization," you encountered four examples of how a country's degree of industrialization is related to its level of health care. Look again at Table 19.6 (page 55). Note that two indicators of health care are life expectancy at birth and infant mortality.

In this project you will use these variables to test the hypothesis that the greater a nation's industrial development, the poorer its health care. First, go back to the two-page map of global stratification in Chapter 9 (pages 240–241). Pick out ten countries from each of the three categories: "Most Industrialized Nations," "Industrializing Nations," and "Least Industrialized Nations." List these thirty countries in the left column and then make two more columns with the headings "Life Expectancy" and "Infant Mortality." Now access the CIA home page *http://www.odci.gov/cia/publications/pubs.html/* and click on the book icon, "World Factbook." Then select "All Countries in the World Factbook." You should see the alphabet running through the middle of the page. Choose a nation from your list and select its initial. (For example, select J

if you want Japan.) Now select the name of the country. Page down to the "People" section and look for your two variables, life expectancy and infant mortality. Write these numbers on your worksheet and go on to the next country on your list. When you have collected all of the data, create a table showing the values of the variables for each level of industrialization. Using the mean, average the rates for each category. You may want to refer back to Table 5.1 (page 124) and Table 5.2 (page 125) on averaging. Now write a report: State your hypothesis, explain your methodology, and discuss your findings.

3. Diabetes is the seventh leading cause of death in the United States. Use the following links to learn more about diabetes. What is diabetes? Why is there no cure? Why is diabetes a leading cause of death? Who gets diabetes? How much of a threat is diabetes? What is being done to find a cure for diabetes?

http://www.cdc.gov/nccdphp/ddt/ddthome.htm
http://www.geocities.com/Athens/Forum/5769/diabete.html
http://www.diabetes.org/default.htm
http://www.diabetes.org/ada/legislate.html

4. Follow this link to examine an example of a living will.

http://www.euthanasia.org/lwpdf.html

Now answer these questions: What is a living will? How has technology led to the need for living wills? What does the living will protect against? What are the legal ramifications of living wills? What do you have to do to make a living will legal? What is a values history? Why is a living will necessary in our society?

Ralph Fasanella, Going to Work, 1980

Population and Urbanization

*T*HE IMAGE STILL HAUNTS ME. *There stood Celia, age 30, her distended stomach obvious proof that her thirteenth child was on its way. Her oldest was only 14 years old! A mere boy by our standards, he had already gone as far in school as he ever would. Each morning, he joined the men to work in the fields. Each evening around twilight, we saw him return home, exhausted from hard labor in the sun.*

My wife and I, who were living in Colima, Mexico, had eaten dinner in Celia's and Angel's home, which clearly proclaimed the family's poverty. A thatched hut consisting of only a single room served as home for all fourteen members of the family. At night, the parents and younger children crowded into a double bed, while the eldest boy slept in a hammock. As in many other homes in the village, the others slept on mats spread on the dirt floor.

The home was meagerly furnished. It had only a gas stove, a cabinet where Celia stored her cooking utensils and dishes, and a table. There being no closets, clothes were hung on pegs in the walls. There were no chairs, not even one. This really startled us. The family was so poor that they could not afford even a single chair.

Celia beamed as she told us how much she looked forward to the birth of her next child. Could she really mean it? It was hard to imagine that any woman would want to be in her situation.

Yet Celia meant every word. She was as full of delightful anticipation as she had been with her first child—and with all the others in between.

*H*ow could Celia have wanted so many children—especially when she lived in such poverty? That question bothered me. I couldn't let it go until I had the solution.

This chapter helps provide an answer.

POPULATION IN GLOBAL PERSPECTIVE

Celia's story takes us into the heart of **demography,** the study of the size, composition, growth, and distribution of human populations. It brings us face to face with the question of whether we are doomed to live in a world so filled with people that there will be practically no space for anybody. Will our planet be able to support its growing population? Or is chronic famine and mass starvation the sorry fate of most earthlings? Let's look at how this concern began, and then at what today's demographers say about it.

A Planet with No Space to Enjoy Life?

demography: the study of the size, composition, growth, and distribution of human populations

Malthus theorem: an observation by Thomas Malthus that although the food supply increases only arithmetically (from 1 to 2 to 3 to 4 and so on), population grows geometrically (from 2 to 4 to 8 to 16 and so forth)

Sometimes the cultural diffusion of a simple item can have far-reaching consequences on nations. An example is the potato, which the Spanish Conquistadors found among the natives of the Andes. When the Spanish brought this food back to Europe, Europeans first viewed it suspiciously. Gradually they came to accept it. Eventually the potato became the principal food of the lower classes. With more abundant food, fertility increased, and the death rate dropped. As a result, Europe's population soared, almost doubling during the 1700s (McKeown 1977).

This rapid growth alarmed Thomas Malthus (1766–1834), an English economist. He saw it as a sign of coming doom. In 1798, he wrote a book that became world famous, *An Essay on the Principle of Population.* In it, Malthus proposed what became known as the **Malthus theorem.** He argued that while population grows geometrically (from 2 to 4 to 8 to 16 and so forth), the food supply increases only arithmetically (from 1 to 2 to 3 to 4

In earlier generations, large farm families were common. (My own father came from a Minnesota farm family of ten children.) Having many children was functional—there were many hands to help with crops, food production, and food preparation. As the country industrialized and urbanized, this changed to a dysfunction—children became expensive and nonproducing. Consequently, the size of families shrank as we entered Stage 3 of the demographic transition, and today U.S. families of this size are practically nonexistent.

and so on). This meant, he claimed, that if births go unchecked, the population of a country, or even of the world, will outstrip its food supply.

The New Malthusians

Was Malthus right? This question is a matter of heated debate among demographers. One group, which can be called the "New Malthusians," is convinced that today's situation is at least as grim, if not grimmer, than Malthus ever imagined. Figure 20.1 shows how fast the world's population is growing. *In just the time it takes you to read this chapter, another fifteen thousand to twenty thousand babies will be born!* By this time tomorrow, the earth will have an additional quarter of a million people to support. This increase goes on hour after hour, day after day, without letup.

The New Malthusians point out that the world's population is following an **exponential growth curve.** In other words, if growth doubles during approximately equal intervals of time, it suddenly accelerates. To illustrate the far-reaching implications of exponential growth, sociologist William Faunce (1981) told a parable about a man who

exponential growth curve: a pattern of growth in which numbers double during approximately equal intervals, thus accelerating in the latter stages

Figure 20.1

How Fast Is the World's Population Growing?

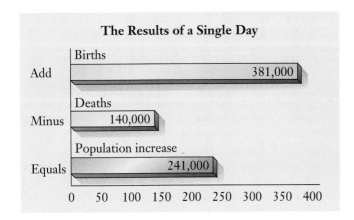

The Results of a Single Day

- Add — Births — 381,000
- Minus — Deaths — 140,000
- Equals — Population increase — 241,000

0 50 100 150 200 250 300 350 400

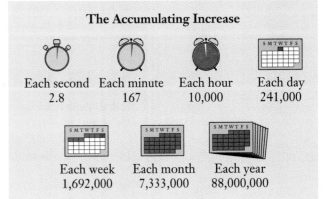

The Accumulating Increase

Each second	Each minute	Each hour	Each day
2.8	167	10,000	241,000

Each week	Each month	Each year
1,692,000	7,333,000	88,000,000

Source: "Population Update" 1997.

Figure 20.2

World Population Growth over 2,000 Years

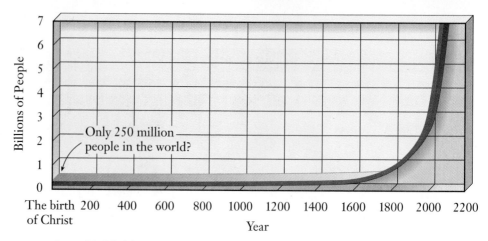

Source: Modified from Piotrow 1973:4.

saved a rich man's life. The rich man was grateful and said that he wanted to reward the man for his heroic deed.

> The man replied he would like his reward to be spread out over a four-week period, with each day's amount being twice what he received on the preceding day. He also said he would be happy to receive only one penny on the first day. The rich man immediately handed over the penny and congratulated himself on how cheaply he had gotten by. At the end of the first week, the rich man checked to see how much he owed and was pleased to find that the total was only $1.27. By the end of the second week he owed only $163.83. On the twenty-first day, however, the rich man was surprised to find that the total had grown to $20,971.51. When the twenty-eighth day arrived the rich man was shocked to discover that he owed $1,342,177.28 for that day alone and that the total reward had jumped to $2,684,354.56!

This is precisely what alarms the New Malthusians. They claim that humanity has just entered the "fourth week" of an exponential growth curve. Figure 20.2 shows why they think the day of reckoning is just around the corner. They point out that it took all of human history for the world's population to reach its first billion around 1800. It then took about one hundred thirty years (1930) to add the second billion. Just thirty years later (1960), the world population hit 3 billion. The time needed to reach the fourth billion was cut in half, to only fifteen years (1975). It then took just twelve more years (1987) for the total to hit 5 billion. Right now, the world population is closing in on 6 billion (Haub and Yinger 1994; Cohen 1996).

To illustrate this increase, the New Malthusians have come up with some mind-boggling statistics. They note that before the Industrial Revolution, it took 1,600 years for the world's population to double, but the most recent doubling took just forty years—*forty* times as fast (Cohen 1996). They also point out that between 8000 B.C. and A.D. 1750 the world added an average of only 67,000 people a year—but now that many people are added *every six to seven hours* (Weeks 1994).

It is obvious, claim the New Malthusians, that there is going to be less and less for more and more.

The Anti-Malthusians

It does seem obvious, and no one wants to live in a shoulder-to-shoulder world and fight for scraps. How, then, can anyone argue with the New Malthusians?

A much more optimistic group of demographers, whom we can call the "Anti-Malthusians," claim that such an image of the future is ridiculous. "Ever since Malthus reached his faulty conclusions," they argue, "people have been claiming that the sky is falling—that it is only a matter of time until the world is overpopulated and we all starve to death." The New Malthusians erroneously think that people breed like germs in a bucket, as illustrated by the following example.

Assume there are two germs in the bottom of a bucket, and they double in number every hour. . . . If it takes one hundred hours for the bucket to be full of germs, at what point is the bucket one-half full of germs? A moment's thought will show that after ninety-nine hours the bucket is only half full. The title of this volume [*The 99th Hour*] is not intended to imply that the United States is half full of people but to emphasize that it is possible to have "plenty of space left" and still be precariously near the upper limit. (Price 1967)

Anti-Malthusians, such as economist Julian Simon (1992, 1996) and anthropologist Steven Mosher (1994, 1997), regard this image as dead wrong. In their view, people simply do not blindly reproduce until there is no room left. It is ridiculous, they say, to project the world's current population growth into the indefinite future, for this fails to take into account people's intelligence and rational planning when it comes to having children. To understand human reproduction, we need to look at the historical record more closely.

The Anti-Malthusians believe that Europe's **demographic transition** provides a more accurate picture of the future. This transition is diagrammed in Figure 20.3. During most of its history, Europe was in stage I. High birth rates offset by high death rates led to a fairly stable population. Then came stage II, the "population explosion" that so upset Malthus. Europe's population surged because birth rates remained high, while death rates went down. Finally, Europe made the transition to stage III—the population stabilized as people brought their birth rates into line with their lower death rates.

This, continue the Anti-Malthusians, is precisely what will happen in the Least Industrialized Nations. Their current surge in growth simply indicates that they have reached the second stage of the demographic transition. Hybrid seed and modern medicine imported from the Most Industrialized Nations have cut their death rates, but their birth rates remain high. When they move into the third stage, as surely they will, we will wonder what all the fuss was about.

Some Anti-Malthusians go even further (Mosher 1997). As shown by the far right part of Figure 20.3, they foresee a "demographic free fall." They predict that the world's population will peak at about 7 billion around the year 2030, then begin a long descent. As countries industrialize, they stress, women become more educated, postpone marriage, and reduce the number of children they bear. The result will be **population shrinkage,** a population becoming smaller.

Because industrialization is a worldwide trend, the birth rate throughout the world is declining. The shrinking population of Europe—Germany and Italy already fill more coffins than cradles—has begun to alarm policymakers. The two main concerns are: not

demographic transition: a three-stage historical process of population growth: first, high birth rates and high death rates; second, high birth rates and low death rates; and, third, low birth rates and low death rates

population shrinkage: the process by which a country's population becomes smaller because its birth rate and immigration are too low to replace those who die and emigrate

Figure 20.3

The Demographic Transition

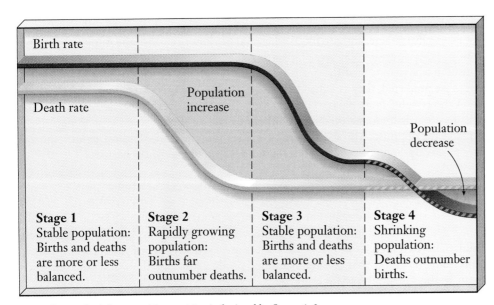

Note: The standard demographic transition is depicted by Stages 1–3.
Stage 4 has recently been suggested by some Anti-Malthusians.

enough young workers to support a rapidly growing elderly population, and race-ethnic problems that develop as workers from other parts of the world migrate to depopulating countries. Coming as a surprise to almost everyone, this fourth stage of the demographic transition has also begun to hit Asia: Japan and South Korea do not produce enough children to maintain their populations (Chesnais 1997). In short, stress the Anti-Malthusians, the world's problem will not be a population explosion, but *population shrinkage*—too few children in the world, not too many.

Who Is Correct?

As you can see, both the New Malthusians and the Anti-Malthusians have projected trends into the future. The New Malthusians project world growth trends and are alarmed. The Anti-Malthusians project the demographic transition onto the Least Industrialized Nations and are reassured.

Only the future will prove the accuracy of either of these projections. There is no question that the Least Industrialized Nations are in stage II of the demographic transition. The question is, will these nations enter stage III? After World War II, Western medicine, techniques of public hygiene, hybrid seeds, herbicides, and farm machinery were exported around the globe. Death rates plummeted as the food supply increased and health improved. At first, almost everyone was ecstatic. As the birth rate of the Least Industrialized Nations stayed high, however, and their populations mushroomed, misgivings set in. Demographers such as Paul and Anne Ehrlich (1972, 1978) predicted worldwide catastrophe if something were not done immediately to halt the population explosion.

We can use the conflict perspective to understand what happened when this message reached the leaders of the industrialized world. They saw the mushrooming populations of the Least Industrialized Nations as a force that could upset the balance of power they had so carefully worked out. Fearing that the poorer countries, with swollen populations, might demand a larger share of the earth's resources, they used the United Nations to spearhead global efforts to reduce world population growth. At first, those efforts looked as though they were doomed to fail as populations in the Least Industrialized Nations continued to surge. Then, gradually, the birth rates in countries such as China, India, South Korea, and Sri Lanka began to fall. Their populations did not decrease, but the rate at which they were growing slowed down, dropping from an average 2.1 percent a year in the late 1960s to 1.5 percent today (Haub and Yinger 1994; Haub and Cornelius 1997).

The New Malthusians and Anti-Malthusians greeted this news with significantly different interpretations. The New Malthusians retort that this is but a dent in the increase: The populations of the Least Industrialized Nations are still increasing, they point out, only not as fast as they were. A slower growth rate still spells catastrophe, they insist—it just takes a little longer for it to hit (Ehrlich and Ehrlich 1997). For the Anti-Malthusians, however, this slowing in the rate of growth is the signal that stage III of the demographic transition is arriving. First the death rate in the Least Industrialized Nations fell—now, just as we predicted, they say, the birth rate of these nations is also falling.

Who is right? It simply is too early to tell. Like the proverbial pessimists who see the glass of water half empty, the New Malthusians interpret population growth negatively. And like the optimists who see the same glass half full, the Anti-Malthusians view the figures positively. Sometime during our lifetimes we should know the answer.

Why Are People Starving?

Pictures of starving children haunt us. They gnaw at our conscience; we live in such abundance, while these children and their parents starve before our very eyes. Why don't these children have enough food? Is it because there are too many of them, as the New Malthusians claim, or simply that the abundant food produced around the world does not reach them, as the Anti-Malthusians argue?

The basic question is this: Does the world produce enough food to feed everyone? Here, the Anti-Malthusians make a point that seems irrefutable. As Figure 20.4 shows,

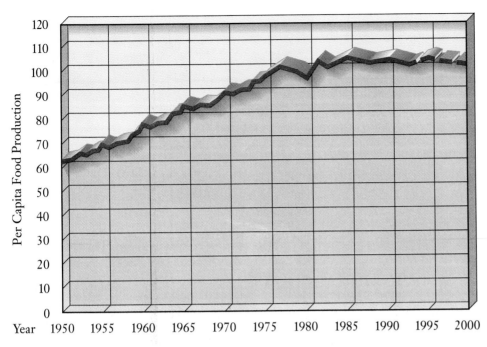

Figure 20.4

How Much Food Does the World Produce Per Person?

Note: 1979–1981 = 100
    Years 1975 to 1991 are U.N. figures; years prior to 1975 have been recomputed from
    Simon to 1979–1981 base; years beyond 1993 are the author's projections.

Sources: Simon 1981:58; United Nations Statistical Yearbook: 1985–1986:Table 7; and
1990–1991:Table 4; *Statistical Abstract* 1997:Table 1374.

the amount of food produced for each person in the world is now much more than it was in 1950. Although the world's population has more than doubled during this time, improved seeds and fertilization have made more food available for each person on earth. And even more is on the way, add the Anti-Malthusians, for chemists have now discovered how to split nitrogen molecules. Since the earth's atmosphere is 78 percent nitrogen, in a few years we will be able to produce chemical compounds—including fertilizers—out of thin air (Naj 1995).

Then why do people die of hunger? From Figure 20.4, we can conclude that starvation does not occur because the earth produces too little food, but because particular places lack food. Some countries produce more food than their people can consume, others less than they need for survival. In short, the cause of starvation is an imbalance between supply and demand. One of the most notable examples is that at the same time as widespread famine is ravishing West Africa, the U.S. government is paying farmers to *reduce* their crops. The United States's problem is too much food, *theirs* too little.

The New Malthusians counter with the argument that the world's population is continuing to grow and that we do not know how long the earth will continue to produce sufficient food. They remind us of the penny doubling each day, as well as the germs multiplying in a bucket. It is only a matter of time, they say, until the earth no longer produces enough food—not "if," but "when."

The way in which governments view this matter is crucial for deciding social policy. If the problem is too many people, a government may call for one course of action, whereas an imbalance of resources would indicate another solution entirely. Where the New Malthusians would attempt to reduce the number of people in the world, the Anti-Malthusians would try to distribute food more equitably.

Both the New Malthusians and the Anti-Malthusians have contributed significant ideas, but theories will not eliminate the problem of famines. Starving children are going to continue to peer out at us from our televisions and magazines, their tiny, shriveled bodies and bloated stomachs nagging at our conscience and calling for us to do something. It

Photos of starving people, such as this mother and her child, haunt Americans and other members of the Most Industrialized Nations. Many of us wonder why, when some are starving, we should live in the midst of such abundance, often overeating and even casually scraping excess food into the garbage. The text discusses reasons for such unconscionable disparities.

is important to understand the underlying cause of such human misery, some of which could certainly be alleviated by transferring food from nations that have a surplus.

These pictures of starving Africans leave the impression that Africa is overpopulated. Why else would all those people be starving? The truth, however, is far different. Africa has 22 percent of the earth's land surface, but only 10.5 percent of the earth's population (Nsamenang 1992). The reason for famines in Africa, then, certainly is *not* too many people living on too little land. In fact, Africa contains some of the world's largest untapped land suitable for agriculture (Bender and Smith 1997). Rather, these famines are due to two primary causes: outmoded farming techniques and political instability—revolutions and other warfare—that disrupt harvests and food distribution.

Population Growth

Even if famines are due to a maldistribution of food rather than world overpopulation, the fact remains that the Least Industrialized Nations are growing *fifteen times faster* than the Most Industrialized Nations—1.8 percent a year compared with 0.1 percent a year. (That this looks like eighteen times faster is due to rounding.) At these rates, it will take 564 years for the average Most Industrialized Nation to double its population, but just 38 years for the average Least Industrialized Nation to do so (Haub and Cornelius 1997). Why do those who can least afford it have so many children?

Why the Least Industrialized Nations Have So Many Children

To understand why the population is increasing so much more rapidly in the Least Industrialized Nations, let's figure out why Celia is so happy about having her thirteenth child. To do so, we need to apply the symbolic interactionist perspective, taking the role of the other, so that we can understand the world of Celia and Angel as *they* see it. As ours does for us, their culture provides a perspective on life that guides their choices. In this case, Celia's and Angel's culture tells them that twelve children are *not* enough, that they ought to have a thirteenth—as well as a fourteenth and fifteenth. How can that be? Let us consider three reasons that bearing many children plays a central role in their lives—and in the lives of millions of poor people around the world.

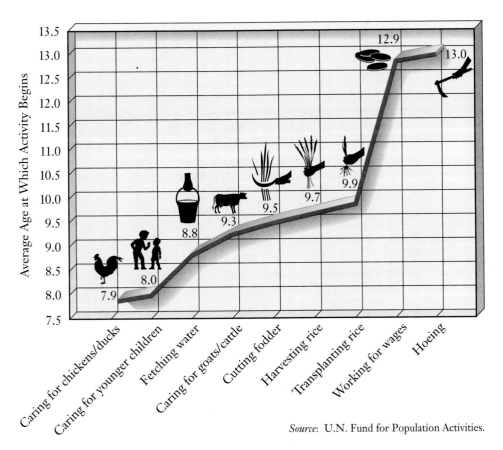

Source: U.N. Fund for Population Activities.

Figure 20.5

Why the Poor Need Children

Surviving children are an economic asset in the Least Industrialized Nations. Based on a survey in Indonesia, this figure shows that boys and girls can be net income earners for their families by the age of 9 or 10.

First is the status of parenthood. In the Least Industrialized Nations, motherhood is the most highly exalted status a woman can achieve. The more children a woman bears, the more she is thought to have achieved the purpose for which she was born. Similarly, a man proves his manhood by fathering children. The more children he fathers, especially sons, the better—for through them his name lives on.

Second, the community supports this view. Celia and those like her live in *Gemeinschaft* communities, where people share values and closely identify with one another. This community awards or withholds status. And everyone agrees that children are a sign of God's blessing and that a couple should have many children. As people produce children, then, they achieve status in one of the primary ways held out by their community. The barren woman, not the woman with a dozen children, is to be pitied.

While the first two factors provide strong motivations for bearing many children, there is yet a third incentive. Poor people in the Least Industrialized Nations consider children economic assets. They have no Social Security or medical and unemployment insurance. As a result, they are motivated to bear *more* children, not fewer, for when parents become sick or too old to work—or when no work is to be found—they rely on their families to take care of them. The more children they have, the broader their base of support. Moreover, like the eldest son of Celia and Angel, children begin contributing to the family income at a young age. See Figure 20.5.

To those of us who live in the Most Industrialized Nations, it seems irrational to have many children. And *for us it would be.* To understand life from the framework of people who are living it, however—the essence of the symbolic interactionist perspective—reveals how it makes perfect sense to have many children. For example, consider the following incident, reported by a government worker in India:

> Thaman Singh (a very poor man, a water carrier) . . . welcomed me inside his home, gave me a cup of tea (with milk and "market" sugar, as he proudly pointed out later), and said: "You were trying to convince me in 1960 that I shouldn't have any more sons. Now, you see, I have six sons and two daughters and I sit at home in leisure.

They are grown up and they bring me money. One even works outside the village as a laborer. *You told me I was a poor man and couldn't support a large family. Now, you see, because of my large family I am a rich man.*" (Mamdani 1973, italics added)

Conflict theorists offer a different view of why women in the poor nations bear so many children. They stress that in these cultures men dominate women in all spheres of life, including that of reproduction. Conflict theorists would argue that Celia has internalized values that support male dominance. For example, in Latin America *machismo* is common. This emphasis on male virility and dominance includes fathering many children as a means of achieving status in the community. From a conflict perspective, then, the reason poor people have so many children is that men control women's reproductive choices.

Implications of Different Rates of Growth

The result of Celia's and Angel's desire for many children—and of the millions of Celias and Angels like them—is that Mexico's population will double in thirty-four years. In contrast, Sweden's population is growing at only 0.1 percent a year, and it will take 990 years to double. To illustrate population dynamics, demographers use **population pyramids,** depicting a country's population by age and sex. Figure 20.6 contrasts Mexico, in stage II of the demographic transition, with the United States, in advanced stage III.

The implications of a doubled population are mind-boggling. *Just to stay even,* within thirty-four years Mexico must double its jobs, food production, and factories; hospitals and schools; transportation, communication, water, gas, sewer, and electrical systems; housing, churches, civic buildings, theaters, stores, and parks. If Mexico fails to double them, its already meager standard of living will drop even further.

A declining standard of living poses the threat of political instability—protests, riots, even revolution, and, in response, severe repression by the government. As conflict theorists point out, this possibility is one reason that the Most Industrialized Nations keep pressing for strong U.N. support for worldwide birth control. Political instability in one country can spill over into others, threatening an entire region's balance of power. Con-

population pyramid: a graphic representation of a population, divided into age and sex

Figure 20.6

Population Pyramids of Mexico and the United States

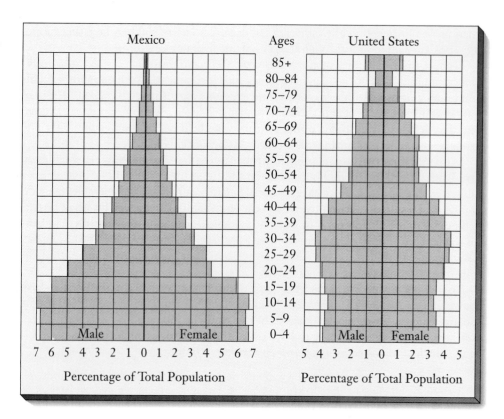

sequently, to help preserve political stability, with one hand the Most Industrialized Nations give agricultural aid, IUDs, and condoms to the masses in the Least Industrialized Nations—while, with the other, they sell weapons to their elites. Both actions serve the same purpose, say conflict theorists.

Think of the worldwide attempt to achieve a higher standard of living as a contest. The Least Industrialized Nations appear destined to fall still farther behind, for not only do they start with less, but their swelling numbers drain the limited financial resources that might otherwise be used for industrial development. In contrast, nations such as Sweden and the United States, already becoming postindustrial nations, are far ahead and have *fewer people on whom to spend much more.*

Estimating Population Growth: The Three Demographic Variables

To accurately project the future of human populations is obviously important. Educators want to know how many schools to build. Manufacturers want to anticipate changes in demand for their products. The government needs to know how many doctors, engineers, and executives to train, as well as how many people will be paying taxes and how many young people will be available to fight a war.

To project population trends, demographers use three **demographic variables:** fertility, mortality, and migration. Let's look at each.

Fertility.   The **fertility rate** is the number of children the average woman bears. A term sometimes confused with fertility is **fecundity,** the number of children that women are *capable* of bearing. The fecundity of women around the world is around twenty children each. Their fertility rate, however (the actual number of children they bear), is much lower. The world's overall fertility rate is 3.0, which means that the average woman in the world bears 3 children during her lifetime. At 2.0, the fertility rate of U.S. women is considerably less.

The region of the world that has the highest fertility rate is Sub–Saharan Africa, where the average woman gives birth to 6.0 children; the lowest is Europe, where the average woman bears only 1.4 children. The record for the lowest rate is held by tiny San Marino in Europe, where the average woman gives birth to only 1.1 children. Two countries tie for the world's highest rate: In both Gaza in the Middle East and Niger in Western Africa the average woman gives birth to 7.4 children, *seven* times as many children as the average San Marino woman (Haub and Cornelius 1997).

To compute the fertility rate of a country, demographers usually depend on a government's records of births. From these, they figure the country's **crude birth rate,** the annual number of live births per 1,000 population. There may be considerable slippage here, of course. The birth records in many of the Least Industrialized Nations are haphazard. From Figure 20.6, you can see how a country's age structure affects its birth rate. If by some miracle Mexico were transformed overnight into a nation as industrialized as the United States, its birth rate would continue to be higher—simply because a much higher percentage of Mexican women are in their childbearing years.

Mortality.   The second demographic variable, **crude death rate,** refers to the number of deaths per 1,000 population. It, too, varies widely around the world. The highest death rate is 30, a record held by Sierra Leone in Western Africa, while the lowest is just 2, a record held by oil-rich Kuwait in the Mideast (Haub and Cornelius 1997). Recall Figure 9.2 on pages 240–241 for the incredible difference in standards of living and quality of life that underlie these death rates.

demographic variables: the three factors that influence population growth: fertility, mortality, and net migration

fertility rate: the number of children that the average woman bears

fecundity: the number of children that women are theoretically *capable* of bearing

crude birth rate: the annual number of births per 1,000 population

crude death rate: the annual number of deaths per 1,000 population

Although all humans face mortality (the second demographic variable), the conditions of death vary from one culture to another. In the Most Industrialized Nations, the death of a child is rare, whereas in the Least Industrialized Nations it is common. Shown here are mourners at the death of a child in South America.

One of the great waves of immigration to the United States occurred in the 1920s, when millions of poor people bought cheap passage on ocean-going vessels. Some had to sleep on the decks, as did these immigrants from Czechoslovakia. The countries of origin of today's new wave of immigrants may be different, but the principle is the same—the poor eagerly hoping for a new life.

Migration. The third major demographic variable is the **net migration rate**, the difference between the number of *immigrants* (people moving in) and *emigrants* (people moving out) per 1,000 population. Unlike fertility and mortality rates, this rate does not affect the global population, for people are simply shifting their residence from one country to another.

As is apparent, immigrants are seeking a better life. To find it, they are willing to give up the security of their family and friends and to move to a country with a strange language and unfamiliar customs. What motivates people to embark on such a venture? To understand migration, we need to look at both *push* and *pull* factors. The push factors are the things that people want to escape—poverty, the lack of religious and political freedoms, even political persecution. The pull factors are the magnets that draw people to a new land, such as a chance for higher wages and better jobs.

Around the world, the flow of migration is from the Least Industrialized Nations to the more industrialized countries (Kalish 1994). After "migrant paths" are established, immigration often accelerates as networks of kin and friends become further magnets that attract more people from the same nation—and even from the same villages. As discussed in the Perspectives box on the next page, immigration is contributing to a shifting U.S. racial-ethnic mix.

With the United States the world's number one choice of immigrants, this nation admits more immigrants each year than all the other nations of the world combined. Twenty million—one of every twelve Americans—were born in another country. Table 20.2 on page 568 shows where U.S. immigrants were born. In an attempt to escape the poverty experienced by Celia and Angel, large numbers of people also enter the United States illegally. The U.S. government puts their number at 4 or 5 million, most of whom have come from Central and South America, mostly from Mexico (*Statistical Abstract* 1997:Table 10).

Experts cannot agree whether immigrants are a net contributor to or a drain on the U.S. economy. Economist Julian Simon (1986, 1993) claims that the net results benefit the country. After subtracting what immigrants collect in welfare and adding what they produce in jobs and taxes, he concludes that immigrants make an overall positive contribution to the U.S. economy. Other economists such as Donald Huddle (1993) produce figures showing that immigrants are a drain on taxpayers. The fairest conclusion seems

net migration rate: the difference between the number of immigrants and emigrants per 1,000 population

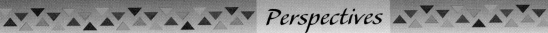

Perspectives

CULTURAL DIVERSITY IN THE UNITED STATES

Glimpsing the Future: The Shifting U.S. Racial-Ethnic Mix

During the next ten or twelve years, the population of the United States is expected to grow about 13 percent. To see what the U.S. population will look like in ten years, can we multiply the current racial-ethnic mix by 13 percent?

The answer is a resounding no. Primarily due to immigration, some groups will grow much more than others, giving us a different-looking United States. Let's try to catch a glimpse of the future.

That glimpse is shown on the table below. As you can see, some of the changes in the U.S. racial/ethnic mix are dramatic. For example, in a decade, one of every thirty Americans is expected to be from an Asian background, and one of eight of Latino background. Very significantly, at this time Latinos and African Americans should be equal in number and, of course, be the same percentage of the U.S. population.

The basic cause of this shift is immigration. Because the racial-ethnic groups have different rates of immigration, their proportion of the population changes. With no immigration, Native Americans are expected to grow the slowest. With little immigration from Africa but a higher than average birth rate, African Americans are expected to just barely maintain their proportion of the population. In a decade, there still will be more whites than all other groups combined, but their majority will shrink, dropping from about 74 percent of the U.S. population to about 69 percent.

For Your Consideration

This shifting racial-ethnic mix is one of the most significant events occurring in the United States. Use the conflict perspective to identify the groups most likely to be threatened and to anticipate their likely responses.

Underlying this change is the symbolic interactionist issue we discussed on page 313—how the government classifies people by race–ethnicity. If the classifications change, how might this shift the U.S. racial/ethnic mix? Does it make any difference? To whom?

TABLE 20.1

Projecting the Future

Racial-Ethnic Group	Numbers in the United States		Growth Rate	Percent of U.S. Population	
	Now	In the Year 2010		Now	In the Year 2010
Asian Americans	9,000,000	14,000,000	50%	3.4%	4.7%
Latinos	26,000,000	38,000,000	46%	9.7%	12.75%
African Americans	32,000,000	38,000,000	18%	12.0%	12.75%
White Americans	197,000,000	206,000,000	5%	74.2%	69.1%
Native Americans	2,000,000	2,000,000	4%	0.75%	0.7%
Total	266,000,000	298,000,000	13%	100%	100%

Note: The populations have been rounded to the nearest million, changing the totals slightly.

Source: Modified from Crispell 1992. *Statistical Abstract* 1997: Tables 37, 38, 49, 50, 52, 53, and Figure 12.6 on page 327 of this text.

to be that the more educated immigrants produce more than they cost, while the less educated cost more than they produce. The cost is also unevenly distributed. Native-born Americans with less than a high school education have found their incomes declining because they compete for jobs with low-educated immigrants ("Immigration's Costs" 1997).

The Demographic Equation and Problems in Forecasting Population Growth

The total of the three demographic variables—fertility, mortality, and net migration—gives us a country's **growth rate,** the net change after people have been added to and sub-

growth rate: the net change in a population after adding births, subtracting deaths, and either adding or subtracting net migration

TABLE 20.2

Country of Birth of Immigrants to the United States, by Region and Country, 1981–1995

North America	**4,646,000**	Japan	77,000	Argentina	40,000
Mexico	3,140,000	Lebanon	67,000	Chile	33,000
Dominican Republic	470,000	Taiwan	63,000	Venezuela	31,000
		Israel	56,000		
Jamaica	304,000	Jordan	53,000	*Europe*	**1,434,000**
Haiti	236,000	Bangladesh	42,000	Former Soviet Union	277,000
Cuba	228,000	Iraq	41,000		
Canada	195,000	Afghanistan	39,000	Great Britain	224,000
Trinidad and Tobago	73,000	Syria	34,000	Poland	212,000
		Turkey	33,000	Germany	107,000
				Ireland	86,000
Asia	**4,451,000**	*Central and South America*	**1,507,000**	Romania	67,000
Philippines	788,000			Portugal	54,000
Vietnam	677,000	El Salvador	344,000	Italy	45,000
China	616,000	Colombia	192,000	Yugoslavia	39,000
India	453,000	Guatemala	149,000	Greece	38,000
Korea	435,000	Guyana	140,000	France	37,000
Iran	223,000	Peru	118,000		
Laos	181,000	Ecuador	93,000	*Africa*	**353,000**
Cambodia	127,000	Nicaragua	88,000	Nigeria	63,000
Pakistan	119,000	Honduras	86,000	Egypt	53,000
Hong Kong	108,000	Brazil	50,000	Ethiopia	53,000
Thailand	96,000	Panama	43,000	South Africa	27,000

Note: Because only the countries of largest emigration are listed, the total of the countries is less than the total given for the region.

Source: Statistical Abstract 1997: Table 8.

tracted from a population. What demographers call the **basic demographic equation** is quite simple:

$$\text{GROWTH RATE} = \text{BIRTHS} - \text{DEATHS} + \text{NET MIGRATION}$$

With such a simple equation, it might seem that it also would be a simple matter to project a country's future population. To forecast population growth, however, is to invite yourself to be wrong. Consider the following instance.

> During the depression of the late 1920s and early 1930s, birth rates plunged as unemployment reached unprecedented heights. Demographers issued warnings about the dangers of depopulation almost as alarmist as some of today's forecasts of overpopulation. Because each year fewer and fewer females would enter the childbearing years, they felt that the population of countries such as Great Britain would shrink. (Waddington 1978)

What actually happened? When the Great Depression ended and World War II broke out, the birth rate dropped. Then after the war, it increased, bringing a "baby boom" (from 1946 to 1950) to both the United States and Europe.

If population increase depended only on biology, the demographer's job would be relatively simple. But social factors—economic booms and busts, wars, plagues, and famines—push rates up or down. As shown in the Perspectives box, even infanticide is a factor. Government programs also complicate projections. Some governments may take steps to get women to bear more children, others to reduce the size of families. When Hitler decided that Germany needed more "Aryans," the German government outlawed abortion and offered cash bonuses for women who gave birth. The population increased.

basic demographic equation:
growth rate = births – deaths + net migration

Perspectives

CULTURAL DIVERSITY AROUND THE WORLD

Killing Little Girls: An Ancient and Thriving Practice

"The Mysterious Case of the Missing Girls" could have been the title of this box. Around the globe, for every 100 girls about 105 boys are born. In China, however, for every 100 girl babies, there are 111 boy babies. With China's huge population, this imbalance indicates that about 400,000 baby girls are missing each year. What is happening to them?

The answer is rooted in deep sexism—the preference for boy babies. To ensure the birth of boys, for millennia people have experimented with a variety of folk techniques, none of which has worked. Only in recent years, with the development of technology that separates semen, has a technique become available that is 80 percent effective. China, however, is not technologically advanced. Have the Chinese, then, stumbled on some effective folk technique?

The answer points in a different direction—to the ancient practice of *female infanticide*, the killing of girl babies. When a Chinese woman goes into labor, village midwives sometimes grab a bucket of water. If the newborn is a girl, she is plunged into the water before she can draw her first breath.

At the root of China's infanticide is economics. The people are extremely poor, and they have no pensions. When parents can no longer work, sons support them. In contrast, a daughter must be married off, at great expense, and at that point her obligations transfer to her husband and his family.

In the past few years, the percentage of boy babies has grown. The reason, again, is economics, but this time with a new twist. As China opened the door to capitalism, travel and trade opened up—but primarily to men, for it is not thought appropriate for women to travel alone. Thus men find themselves in a better position to bring profits home to the family—one more push toward preferring male children.

By no means is female infanticide limited to China. Although the British banned this practice in India in 1870, it continues. Western technology has even been put to work. Many Indian women use amniocentesis to learn the sex of their child, and then decide whether or not to abort. In 99.9 percent of these abortions, the fetus is female.

This use of amniocentesis for sex selection led to a public outcry in India. The indignation was not due to outrage about female infanticide, however; nor was it due to some antiabortion movement. Rather, the public became indignant when a physician mistakenly gave the parents wrong information and aborted a *male* baby!

It is likely that the preference for boys, and the consequent female infanticide, will not disappear until the social structures that perpetuate sexism are dismantled. This will not take place until women hold as much power as men, a time, should it ever occur, that apparently lies far in the future.

Sources: Lagaipa 1990; McGowan 1991; Polumbaum 1992; Renteln 1992; Greenhalgh and Li 1995.

In contrast, when Chinese authorities decided that their population should not grow any larger, they launched a "one couple, one child" national policy. Steven Mosher, an anthropologist who did fieldwork in China, reports that the Chinese government has mandated the insertion of intrauterine devices after one child, sterilization after two children, and abortion for women pregnant without permission. The woman's wishes are irrelevant, the state's all-consuming (recall the Big Brother vignette in Chapter 15). The government even has its agents check sanitary napkins to make sure that women are having their menstrual periods and are not pregnant. If a woman who is pregnant without permission does not consent to an abortion, one is performed on her anyway—even if she is nine months pregnant (Erik 1982).

Letting such policies pass without comment, we can see that a government's efforts to influence a country's growth rate greatly complicate the demographer's task of projecting future populations.

The primary factor that influences a country's growth rate, however, is its rate of industrialization. *In every country that industrializes, the growth rate declines.* Not only does industrialization open up economic opportunities, but it also makes children more expensive. They require more education and remain dependent longer. Significantly, the basis

Due to the Chinese government's policy of "One couple, one child," the birth rate of China has dropped sharply. As explained in the text, however, there are serious moral concerns about how this policy is enforced.

Figure 20.7

Population Projections of the United States

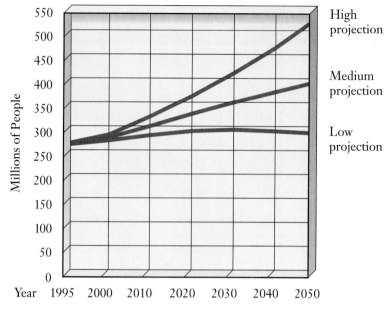

Source: Statistical Abstract 1997: Table 17.

for conferring status also changes—from having children to attaining education and displaying material wealth. People like Celia and Angel then begin to see life differently, and their motivation to have many children drops sharply. Not knowing how rapidly industrialization will progress, or how quickly changes in values and reproductive behavior will follow, adds to the difficulty of making accurate projections.

Because of such complications, demographers play it safe by making *several* projections of population growth (Haub 1997). For example, what will the population of the United States be in the year 2010? Perhaps we will be at **zero population growth,** with every 1,000 women giving birth to 2,100 children. (The extra 100 children make up for those who do not survive.) Will a larger proportion of women go to college? (The more education women have, the fewer children they bear.) How will immigration change during the coming years? Will AIDS come under control? Will some other horrible disease appear? What will happen to the global economy? With such huge variables, it is easy to see why demographers make the three projections of the U.S. population shown in Figure 20.7.

 ## The Challenge of the Twenty-First Century

Before concluding these materials on population, let's take a final glance at the challenge that confronts the world's nations as we enter the twenty-first century.

Thinking Critically About Social Controversy

As We Enter the Twenty-First Century

zero population growth:
a demographic condition
in which women bear only
enough children to reproduce
the population

▼ There is no doubt that Malthus's pessimistic predictions were wrong—for his time, that is. Malthus could not foresee the new technology of the Industrial Revolution, which created new wealth and caused national products to skyrocket.

But what about today, as we stand on the doorstep of the twenty-first century? Economist Paul Kennedy (1993) says that our greatest challenge is how to use modern technology to free the Least Industrialized Nations from "the growing Malthusian trap of malnutrition, starvation, resource depletion, unrest, enforced migration, and armed conflict—developments that will also endanger the richer nations, if less directly."

The past, unfortunately, may not provide guidelines for the future. During the last century, both the population and technology exploded in the same place, the British Isles. Today, however, technology is exploding in one part of the world, population in another. In the Most Industrialized Nations, which have the technology explosion, population is slow-growing and in some places even declining. The areas with the population explosion, however, find themselves with "limited technological resources, very few scientists and skilled workers, inadequate investment in research and development . . . and cultural and ideological prejudices are much more tilted against change than they were in the England of the Industrial Revolution" (Kennedy 1993). To complicate matters even more, adds Kennedy, overgrazing and erosion are also concentrated in these countries, reducing their agricultural resources just as their populations are mushrooming.

For Your Consideration

As we enter the twenty-first century, then, we face a severe challenge—with the fate of millions, if not billions, of people hanging in the balance. Considering the materials so far in this chapter, do you think that we should open our borders to anyone and everyone who wants to immigrate? Or would closing them entirely and concentrating on taking care of our own problems be a better approach? Do you think that the population problem is so severe that the Most Industrialized Nations should subsidize world condom distribution? Or pay people to be sterilized? Should the Most Industrialized Nations support such policies as the enforced abortions in China? Finally, how do you think the Most Industrialized Nations can harness their vast technologies to benefit today's global community? ▲

Let's look at a different aspect of population, where people live. Since the world is rapidly becoming urban, we shall concentrate on urban trends and urban life.

URBANIZATION

*T*HE TRANSFORMATION OF THE SAN FRANCISCO *streets was as intriguing as it was unexpected. My interviewing of the homeless had gone on somewhat longer than I had planned, and dusk had begun to settle in. Heading back to the fleabag hotel, I had spotted a 20-year-old man carrying a backpack. Trying for one more interview, I sat on the sidewalk, with my back against a building, a self-protective position that let me feel more secure. While answering a question, the man suddenly stopped mid-sentence, stared at me intently, and in a voice so low I had to concentrate to hear what he was saying, slowly said, "I know why you are here."*

Somewhat taken back, I said, "What?"

He replied, "I know why you are here."

In measured tones, I said that I had already explained that to him, that I was doing sociological interviews.

"No," he said, not taking his eyes off me. "I know why you are here." He paused, then said, "You are here to help me. I can tell because of the way you move your hands."

I felt a tingling go up my spine as the man leaned closer as though he were to reveal some secret. He then began to mutter that the FBI was after him.

Not taking my eyes off him, I looked past him to seek out an escape route—just in case.

The man fell into silence. He continued to stare intensely at me. Then, as I uttered a silent prayer, he scooped up his knapsack and walked briskly off into the falling darkness.

Ordinarily I would have felt bad about losing an interview. But not this time.

I had begun to take too much for granted in my homeless research, and this experience put me on guard once again, forcing onto my consciousness a keener awareness of the city. As I looked for my hotel with dusk gently falling about the city streets, I saw the area change.

The men and women in business dress carrying briefcases, who had been scurrying around these streets as though time pursued them, and the fashionably dressed shoppers going in and out of the shops, were now replaced by people with hair adorned in bright hues. A woman with a tattoo on her left breast, mostly exposed by her half-zipped leather jacket and absence of bra or blouse, leaned against a building. A man on roller skates, wearing a white jump suit with the zipper opened to his navel, rhythmically moved his feet back and forth to a beat only he heard, never leaving the tiny space he had claimed. Women in short, tight skirts, keenly eyeing passing cars, strolled slowly on the outside of the sidewalk.

And there was the couple whose image is forever emblazoned on my memory. The man, in his forties, shirtless and riding a Harley hog, wore an open denim vest. Other than his flowing beard and unkempt, long hair, his most pronounced characteristic was the huge beer gut that kept his vest from closing. On the back of his motorcycle, her arms tightly clutched about the man, but not quite able to reach around his stomach, sat a skinny blonde who couldn't have been more than 16.

This transformation took place in San Francisco in the mid-1980s. But if I had been in New Orleans or Atlanta in the South, New York or Boston in the East, Houston or Dallas in the Southwest, Miami in the Southeast, or Chicago in the Midwest, the scene would have been similar. This is a distinctly *urban* phenomenon. That is, there are specific characteristics of cities that give them their unique "flavor." Their "urbanness" comes not only from their size, but especially from the anonymity they provide, which allows people to both blend in with others and to stand out at the same time.

Such behaviors as I have just described whet the sociological imagination. Earlier (page 102), we reviewed Emile Durkheim's conclusions about organic and mechanical solidarity and Ferdinand Tönnies's contrasts of rural and urban life (*Gemeinschaft* and *Gesellschaft*). In the 1920s, Chicago was a vivid mosaic of immigrants, gangsters, prostitutes, the homeless, the rich and the poor—much as it is today. Sociologists at the University of Chicago began to study these contrasting ways of life. From what became known as the Chicago School of Sociology emerged numerous studies of city life—from hobos (Anderson 1923) and gangs (Thrasher 1927) to a contrast of the lives of the poor and the rich (Zorbaugh 1929). Today, sociologists still enjoy studying why and how some people find the city a place of refuge, while others find it a threatening, foreboding sort of place.

To better understand urban life, let's first find out how the city itself came about.

The Development of Cities

Cities are not new to the world scene. Perhaps as early as seven to ten thousand years ago people built small cities with massive defensive walls, such as Catal Hüyük (Schwendinger and Schwendinger 1983) and biblically famous Jericho (Homblin 1973). Cities on a larger scale originated about 3500 B.C., about the same time as the invention of writing (Chandler and Fox 1974; Hawley 1981). At that time, cities appeared in several parts of the world—first in Mesopotamia (Iran) and later in the Nile, Indus, and Yellow River valleys, around the Mediterranean, in West Africa, Central America, and the Andes (Fischer 1976; Flanagan 1990).

The key to the origin of cities is the development of more efficient agriculture (Lenski and Lenski 1987). Only when farming produces a surplus can some people stop being food producers and gather in cities to spend time in other pursuits. A **city**, in fact, can be defined as a place in which a large number of people are permanently based and do not produce their own food. The invention of the plow between five and six thousand years ago created widespread agricultural surpluses, stimulating the development of towns and cities

city: a place in which a large number of people are permanently based and do not produce their own food

Early cities were small economic centers surrounded by walls to keep out enemies. These cities, built like fortresses, were constantly threatened by armed, roving tribesmen and by the leaders of nearby city-states who raised armies in an effort to enlarge their domain and enrich their coffers by sacking neighboring cities. Pictured here is Carcasonne, a restored medieval city in southern France.

(Curwin and Hart 1961). (For a review of the sweeping historical changes that laid the organizational groundwork for the rise and expansion of cities, see pages 145–150).

The Industrial Revolution and the Size of Cities

Most early cities were tiny by comparison with those of today, merely a collection of a few thousand people in agricultural centers or on major trade routes. The most notable exceptions are two cities that reached 1 million for a brief period of time before they declined—Changan in China about A.D. 800 and Baghdad in Persia about A.D. 900 (Chandler and Fox 1974). Even Athens at the peak of its power in the fifth century B.C. had less than 200,000 inhabitants. Rome, at its peak, may have had a million or more (Flanagan 1990).

Even 200 years ago, the only city in the world that had a population of more than a million was Peking (now Beijing), China (Chandler and Fox 1974). Then in just 100 years, by 1900, the number of such cities jumped to sixteen. The reason is the Industrial Revolution, which drew people to cities by providing work. It also stimulated the invention of mechanical means of transportation and communication, and allowed people, resources, and products to be moved efficiently—all essential factors (called "infrastructure") on which large cities depend. Today almost 300 cities have a million or more people (Frisbie and Kasarda 1988).

Urbanization, Metropolises, and Megalopolises

Although cities are not new to the world scene, urbanization is. **Urbanization** refers to masses of people moving to cities and to these cities being a growing influence on society. Urbanization is worldwide. Just 200 years ago, in 1800, only 3 percent of the world's population lived in cities (Hauser and Schnore 1965). Today about 43 percent do: about 75 percent of people in the industrialized world and 35 percent of those who live in the Least Industrialized Nations. Each year the world's urban population grows by 0.5 percent, and soon most people will live in cities (Palen 1987; Population Reference Bureau 1995).

Without the Industrial Revolution this remarkable growth could not have taken place, for an extensive infrastructure is needed to support hundreds of thousands and even millions of people in a relatively small area. To understand the city's attraction, we need to consider the "pull" of urban life. Due to its exquisite division of labor, the city offers

urbanization: the process by which an increasing proportion of a population lives in cities

incredible variety—music ranging from rock and rap to country and classic, diets for vegetarians and diabetics as well as imported delicacies from around the world for the rest of us. Cities also offer anonymity, which so many find highly refreshing in light of the much tighter controls of village and small-town life. And, of course, the city offers work.

Some cities have grown so large and influential over a region that the term *city* is no longer adequate to describe them. The term **metropolis** is used instead. This term refers to a central city surrounded by smaller cities and their suburbs. They are connected economically, sometimes politically through county boards and regional governing bodies, as well as by ties of transportation and communication.

St. Louis is an example. Although this name, St. Louis, properly refers to a city of less than 400,000 people in Missouri, it also refers to another 2 million people living in over a hundred separate towns in both Missouri and Illinois, vaguely known as the "St. Louis or Bi-State Area." Although these towns are independent politically, they form an economic unit. They are united by work (many people in the smaller towns work in St. Louis, or are served by industries from St. Louis), by communications (the same area newspaper and radio and television stations), and by transportation (the same interstate highways, "Bi-State Bus" system, and international airport). As symbolic interactionists would note, a common identity also arises from the area's shared symbols (the Arch, the Mississippi River, Busch Brewery, the Cardinals, the Rams, the Blues—both the hockey team and the music). Most of the towns run into one another, and if you were to drive through this metropolis you would not know you were leaving one town and entering another—unless you had lived here some time and were aware of the fierce small-town identifications and rivalries that exist side by side with this larger identification.

Some metropolises have grown so large and influential that the term **megalopolis** is used to describe them. This term refers to an overlapping area consisting of at least two metropolises and their many suburbs. Of the twenty or so megalopolises in the United States, the three largest are the Eastern seaboard running from Maine to Virginia, the area in Florida between Miami, Orlando, and Tampa, and California's coastal area between San Francisco and San Diego.

This process of urban areas turning into a metropolis and metropolises developing into a megalopolis is also worldwide. Figure 20.8 shows the ten largest cities in the world. Note that most of them are located in the Least Industrialized Nations.

metropolis: a central city surrounded by smaller cities and their suburbs

megalopolis: an urban area consisting of at least two metropolises and their many suburbs

Figure 20.8

The Urban Giants: The Population of the World's Ten Largest Cities, in millions

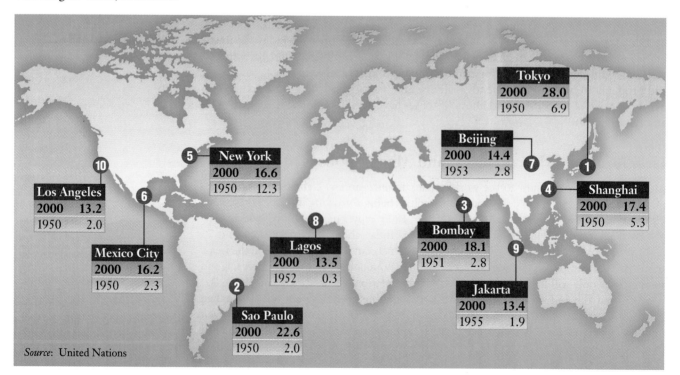

Source: United Nations

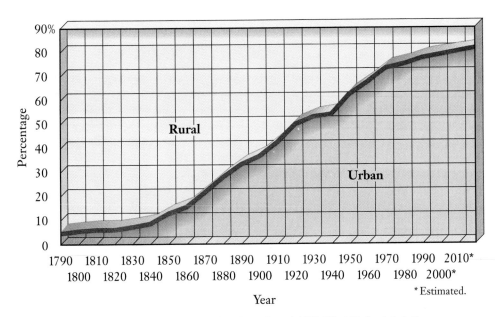

Figure 20.9

Urban Makeup of the U.S. Population, 1790–2010

*Estimated.

Sources: Patterns of Urban and Rural Population Growth 1980:159–162; *Statistical Abstract* 1988:Table 33; 1997:Table 44.

U.S. Urban Patterns

When the United States was founded, it was almost exclusively rural. Figure 20.9 illustrates how the country changed from rural to urban. In 1790, only about 5 percent of Americans lived in cities. By 1920, this figure had jumped to 50 percent. Urbanization has continued without letup, and today about 75 to 80 percent of Americans live in cities.

The U.S. Census Bureau has divided the country into 269 **metropolitan statistical areas (MSAs).** Each MSA consists of a central city and the urbanized county areas linked to it. As Table 20.3 shows, over half of the entire U.S. population lives in just 40 or so MSAs.

As Americans migrate in search of work and better lifestyles, there is two-way migration among regions. At the end of the year, as shown on Figure 20.10 on the next page, each region shows a net loss or a net gain. A few years ago, the pattern was simple—a net migration from the North and East to the West and the South. Now it is much more complicated. The Northeast still shows a loss to the other three regions, but the Midwest, which used to have a net loss to the West and South, now shows net gains from all regions. We do not know why the pattern changed.

Another way to view this migration is to compare the fastest and slowest growing U.S. cities. This is done in Table 20.4 on the next page. As you can see, all of the fastest growing cities are in the West, or in the South. Of the declining and slowest growing cities, ten are in the Northeast, while the South and West have one each.

As Americans migrate and businesses move, to serve them **edge cities** have developed. This term refers to a clustering of shopping malls, hotels, office parks, and residential areas near the intersection of major highways (Gans 1991b; Garreau 1992; De Vita 1996). Although this clustering of services may overlap the boundaries of several cities or towns, it provides a sense of place to those who live, work, or shop there.

metropolitan statistical area (MSA): a central city and the urbanized counties adjacent to it

edge city: a large clustering of service facilities and residential areas near highway intersections that provides a sense of place to people who live, shop, and work there

TABLE 20.3

Metropolitan Statistical Areas over 1 Million			
Census Year	*Number of MSAs*	*Population (millions)*	*Percentage of U.S. Population*
1950	14	45	30%
1960	22	64	36
1970	31	84	41
1980	35	104	46
1990	40	133	53
1995	42	139	53
2000[a]	45	150	55

[a]Author's estimate.

Source: Census Bureau 1991:2; *Statistical Abstract* 1997:Table 41.

Figure 20.10

Net Migration Flows Between Regions, 1995–1996

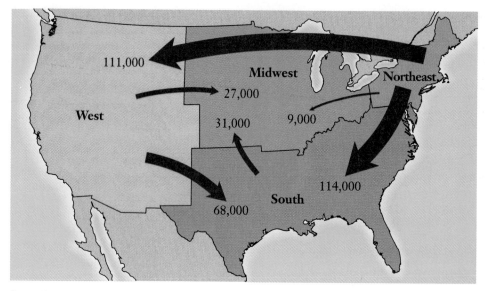

Source: *Statistical Abstract* 1997:Table 31.

Another major U.S. urban pattern is **gentrification,** the movement of middle-class people into rundown areas of a city. They are attracted by the low prices for quality housing that, though deteriorated, can be restored. One consequence is an improvement in the appearance of urban neighborhoods—freshly painted buildings, well-groomed lawns, and the absence of boarded-up windows. Another consequence is that the poor residents are displaced as the more well-to-do newcomers move in. Tension often arises between these groups (Anderson 1990, 1997).

Models of Urban Growth

In the 1920s, Chicago was a vivid mosaic of newly arrived immigrants, gangsters, prostitutes, the homeless, the rich, and the poor—much as it is today. Sociologists at the Uni-

TABLE 20.4			
The Twelve Fastest and Slowest Growing U.S. Cities			
Fastest		*Slowest*	
1. Las Vegas, NV	26.2	1. Salinas, CA	−1.1
2. McAllen, TX	20.2	2. Binghamton, NY	−1.0
3. Boise City, ID	17.5	3. Scranton, PA	−0.2
4. Bremerton, WA	16.2	4. Jersey City, NJ	−0.1
5. Olympia, WA	16.1	5. Utica, NY	−0.1
6. Brownsville, TX	15.2	6. Pittsburgh, PA	0.3
7. Colorado Springs, CO	14.0	7. New York, NY	0.4
8. Austin, TX	13.9	8. Bridgeton, NJ	0.5
9. Atlanta, GA	12.6	9. Dayton, OH	0.5
10. Killeen, TX	12.5	10. Philadelphia, PA	0.5
11. Knoxville, TN	12.5	11. Shreveport, LA	0.5
12. El Paso, TX	12.4	12. Youngstown, OH	0.5

Note: Population change 1990–1994. A minus sign indicates a loss of population. At 12.4, Raleigh, NC, ties El Paso, but lost out due to alphabetizing.

Source: *Statistical Abstract* 1997:Table 43.

gentrification: the displacement of the poor by the relatively affluent, who renovate the former's homes

versity of Chicago studied these contrasting ways of life. One of these sociologists, Robert Park, coined the term **human ecology** to describe how people adapt to their environment (Park and Burgess 1921; Park 1936). (This concept is also known as *urban ecology*.) The process of urban growth is of special interest to human ecologists. Let's look at the three main models they developed.

The Concentric Zone Model

To explain how cities expand, sociologist Ernest Burgess (1925) proposed a *concentric-zone model*. As shown in segment A of Figure 20.11, Burgess noted that a city expands outward from its center. Zone I is the central business district. Encircling this downtown area is a zone in transition (Zone II). It contains deteriorating housing and roominghouses, which, as Burgess noted, breed poverty, disease, and vice. Zone III is the area to which thrifty workers have moved to escape the zone in transition and yet maintain easy access to their work. Zone IV contains more expensive apartments, residential hotels, single-family dwellings, and exclusive areas where the wealthy live. Still farther out, beyond the city limits, is Zone V, a commuter zone consisting of suburban areas or satellite cities that have developed around rapid transit routes.

Burgess intended this model to represent "the tendencies of any town or city to expand radially from its central business district." He noted, however, that no "city fits perfectly this ideal scheme." Some cities have physical obstacles, such as a lake, river, or railroad, which cause their expansion to depart from the model. Although Burgess also noted in 1925 that businesses were deviating from the model by locating in outlying zones, he was unable to anticipate the extent of this trend—the suburban shopping malls that replaced downtown stores and now account for most of the country's retail sales (Palen 1987; Milbank 1995a).

The Sector Model

Sociologist Homer Hoyt (1939, 1971) noted that a city's concentric zones do not form a complete circle, and he modified Burgess's model of urban growth. As shown in segment B of Figure 20.11, a concentric zone might contain several sectors—one of working-class housing, another of expensive homes, a third of businesses, and so on, all competing for the same land.

What sociologists call an **invasion–succession cycle** is an example of this dynamic competition of urban life. When poor immigrants or migrants enter a city, they settle in the lowest-rent area they can. As their numbers swell, they spill over into adjacent areas. Upset at their presence, the middle class moves out, thus expanding the sector of low-cost

human ecology: Robert Park's term for the relationship between people and their environment (natural resources such as land)

invasion–succession cycle: the process of one group of people displacing a group whose racial-ethnic or social class characteristics differ from their own

Figure 20.11

Models of Urban Growth

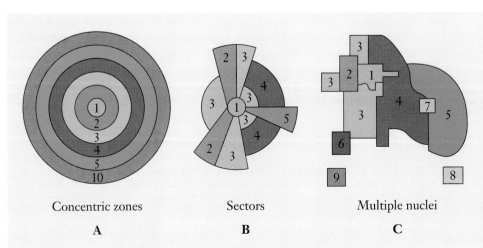

Concentric zones — **A**   Sectors — **B**   Multiple nuclei — **C**

Three Generalizations of the Internal Structure of Cities

District
1. Central business district
2. Wholesale light manufacturing
3. Low-class residential
4. Medium-class residential
5. High-class residential
6. Heavy manufacturing
7. Outlying business district
8. Residential suburb
9. Industrial suburb
10. Commuters' zone

Source: Cousins and Nagpaul 1970.

housing. The invasion–succession cycle is never complete, for later another group will replace this earlier one, or it may be gentrified by other migrants.

The Multiple-Nuclei Model

Geographers Chauncey Harris and Edward Ullman noted that some cities have several centers or nuclei (Harris and Ullman 1945; Ullman and Harris 1970). As shown in segment C of Figure 20.11, each nucleus is the focus of some specialized activity. A familiar example is the clustering of fast-food restaurants in one area and automobile dealerships in another. Sometimes similar activities are grouped together because they profit from cohesion; retail districts, for example, draw more customers if there are more stores. Other clustering occurs because some activities, such as factories and expensive homes, are incompatible with one another. Thus, push–pull factors separate areas by activities, and services are not evenly spread throughout an urban area.

Critique of the Models

These models tell only part of the story of how cities develop. They are time bound, for medieval cities didn't follow these patterns (see the photo on page 573). They also are geography bound, as Americans visiting Europe can attest. England, for example, has planning laws that preserve green belts (trees, farmlands) around the city. This prevents urban sprawl: Wal-Mart cannot buy land outside the city and put up a store, but, instead, must locate in the downtown area with the other stores. Norwich, England, for example, has 250,000 people; yet the city suddenly ends, and in its green belt pheasants skitter across plowed fields while sheep graze in verdant meadows (Milbank 1995b). The models, then, do not account for urban planning policies.

The models also fall short when it comes to the cities of the Least Industrialized Nations. Here, too, U.S. visitors are surprised: the wealthy often claim the inner city, where fine restaurants and other services are readily accessible. Tucked behind tall walls and protected from public scrutiny, they enjoy luxurious homes and gardens. In contrast, the poor, especially rural migrants, settle unclaimed fringe areas outside the city (see the Perspectives box on the next page).

City Life

Cities are intended to be solutions to problems. They are human endeavors to improve life collectively, to develop a way of life that transcends the limitations of farm and village. Cities hold out the hope of gaining employment, education, and other advantages. The perception of such opportunities underlies mass migration to cities throughout the world.

Just as cities provide opportunities, however, they also create problems. Humans not only have physical needs—food, shelter, and safety—but also a need for **community**, a feeling of belonging—the sense that others care what happens to you, and that you can depend on the people around you. Some people find this sense of community in the city; others find only its opposite, *alienation*, a sense of not belonging, and a feeling that no one cares what happens to you. Let's look at these two aspects of city life.

Alienation

Twenty-eight-year-old Catherine Genovese, who was called Kitty by almost everyone in her Queens neighborhood, was returning home from work. After she had parked her car, a man grabbed her. She screamed, "Oh my God, he stabbed me! Please help me! Please help me!"

For more than half an hour, thirty-eight respectable, law-abiding citizens looked out their windows and watched as the killer stalked and stabbed Kitty in three separate attacks. Twice the sudden glow from their bedroom lights interrupted him

community: a place people identify with, where they sense that they belong and that others care what happens to them

Perspectives

Urbanization in the Least Industrialized Nations

Images of the Least Industrialized Nations that portray serene pastoral scenes distort today's reality. In these nations, poor rural people have flocked to the cities in such numbers that, as we saw in Figure 20.8 (page 574), these nations now contain most of the world's largest cities. In general, the world's industrialization preceded urbanization, but here urbanization is preceding industrialization. Their limited technology makes it difficult to support the mushrooming urban populations.

When rural migrants and immigrants move to U.S. cities, they usually settle in the low-rent districts, mostly deteriorating housing located near the city's center. The wealthy reside in exclusive suburbs and in luxurious city enclaves. In contrast, migrants in the Least Industrialized Nations settle in squatter settlements outside the city. There they build shacks from scrap boards, cardboard, and bits of corrugated metal. Even flattened tin cans are considered valuable building material. The squatters enjoy no city facilities—roads, transportation lines, water, sewers, or garbage pickup. After thousands of squatters have settled in an area, the city runs bus lines to it, acknowledging their de facto right to live there. Eventually the city runs a water line to the area and several hundred people use a single spigot. About 4 *million* of Mexico City's inhabitants live in such conditions.

Reflecting on conditions in its cities, India's leading news magazine published the following report.

[The city is] heading for a total breakdown. The endless stream of migrants pour in, turning metropolises into giant slums. A third of the urban population lives in ramshackle huts with gunny sacks as doors and pavements for toilets. Another half of the populace is squeezed into one-room tenements or lives in monotonous rows of multi-storeyed flats. (Singh 1988)

Why are people rushing to these cities? Basically, the rural way of life is breaking down. As the second leg of the demographic transition—low death rates and high birth rates—kicks in, rural populations are multiplying, and no longer is there enough land to divide up among descendants. Recall the poor Mexican peasant preparing to migrate illegally to the United States as recounted in the Down-to-Earth Sociology box on page 334. There are also the pull factors discussed in this chapter—from jobs, education, and better housing to a more stimulating life.

Will cities of the Least Industrialized Nations satisfy the people's longing for a better life? As miserable as life for the poor is in these cities, for many it is an improvement over what they left behind. If not, they would flee the city to return to pastoral pleasures. If the Anti-Malthusians are right, this second stage of the demographic transition will come to an end, and the population of the Least Industrialized Nations will stabilize. In the meantime, however, the Least Industrialized Nations cannot catch up with their population explosion—or their urban growth.

Sources: Based on Palen 1987; Singh 1988; Huth 1990; Kasarda and Crenshaw 1991; Chen 1996.

The Least Industrialized Nations are facing massive upheaval as they rapidly urbanize, resulting in disparities such as those depicted here. Lacking the infrastructure to support their many newcomers, cities in the Least Industrialized Nations, already steeped in poverty, face the daunting task of developing jobs, housing, sewage and electrical systems, roads, schools, and so on.

and frightened him off. Each time he returned, sought her out, and stabbed her again. Not one person telephoned the police during the assault. (*New York Times*, March 26, 1964)

When the police interviewed them, some witnesses said, "I didn't want to get involved." Others said, "We thought it was a lovers' quarrel." Some simply said, "I don't know." People throughout the country were shocked. It was as though Americans awoke one morning to discover that the country had changed overnight. They took this event as a sign that people could no longer trust one another, that the city was a cold, forbidding place.

Why should the city be alienating? In a classic essay, "Urbanism as a Way of Life," sociologist Louis Wirth (1938) argued that the city undermines kinship and neighborhood, which are the traditional sources of social control and social solidarity. Urban dwellers live in anonymity, he pointed out. They go from one superficial encounter with strangers to another. This causes them to grow aloof from one another and indifferent to other people's problems—as did the neighbors of Kitty Genovese. In short, the very sense of personal freedom that the city provides comes at the cost of alienation.

Wirth built on some of the ideas discussed on pages 102–103. *Gemeinschaft*, the sense of community that comes from everyone knowing everyone else, is ripped apart as a country industrializes. What emerges is a new society based on *Gesellschaft*, secondary, impersonal relationships. The end result can be alienation so deep that people can sit by while someone else is being murdered. Lacking identification with one another, people develop the attitude, "It's simply none of *my* business."

Community

The city dwellers whom Gans identified as ethnic villagers find community in the city. Living in tightly knit neighborhoods, they know many other residents. Some first-generation immigrants have even come from the same village in the "old country."

Such attitudes, however, do not do justice to the city. The city is more than a mosaic of strangers who feel disconnected and distrustful of one another. It is also made up of a series of smaller worlds, within which people find *community*, a sense of belonging. People don't live in a city in some abstract sense. Rather, they come to know smaller areas of the city. Here they live, work, shop, and play. Even slums, which to outsiders seem so threatening, can provide a sense of belonging. In a classic study, sociologist Herbert Gans noted,

After a few weeks of living in the West End (of Boston), my observations—and my perceptions of the area—changed drastically. The search for an apartment quickly indicated that the individual units were usually in much better condition than the outside or the hallways of the buildings. Subsequently, in wandering through the West End, and in using it as a resident, I developed a kind of selective perception, in which my eye focused only on those parts of the area that were actually being used by people. Vacant buildings and boarded-up stores were no longer so visible, and the totally deserted alleys or streets were outside the set of paths normally traversed, either by myself or by the West Enders. . . .

Since much of the area's life took place on the street, faces became familiar very quickly. I met my neighbors on the stairs and in front of my building. And, once a shopping pattern developed, I saw the same storekeepers frequently, as well as the area's "characters" who wandered through the streets every day on a fairly regular route and schedule. In short, the exotic quality of the stores and the residents also wore off as I became used to seeing them.

Living in the West End, Gans gained an insider's perspective. He found that in spite of its narrow streets, substandard buildings, and even piled-up garbage, most West Enders had chosen to live there: *to them, the West End was a low-rent district, not a slum.* Gans had located a community in the West End, discovering that its residents visited back and forth with relatives and were involved in extensive networks of friendships and acquaintances. Gans therefore titled his book *The Urban Villagers* (1962).

The residents of the West End were extremely upset when well-intentioned urban planners embarked on an urban renewal scheme to get rid of the "slum." And their distrust proved well founded, for with the gleaming new buildings came invaders with more money who took over the area. Its former residents were dispossessed, their intimate patterns destroyed.

Types of Urban Dwellers

Whether you find alienation or community in the city largely depends on who you are, for the city offers both. People from different backgrounds experience the city differently. Gans (1962, 1968, 1991a) identified five types of people who live in the city. The first three types live in the city by choice, for they find a sense of community.

The Cosmopolites.   The cosmopolites are the city's students, intellectuals, professionals, musicians, artists, and entertainers. They have been drawn to the city because of its conveniences and cultural benefits.

The Singles.   Young, unmarried people, who may team up to rent an apartment come to the city seeking jobs and entertainment. Businesses and services such as singles bars, singles apartment complexes, and computer dating cater to their needs. Their stay in the city often reflects a temporary stage in their life course, for most move to the suburbs after they marry and have children.

The Ethnic Villagers.   These people live in tightly knit neighborhoods that resemble villages and small towns. United by race–ethnicity and social class, their neighborhoods are far from depersonalized or disorganized. Placing an emphasis on family and friendship, the ethnic villagers try to isolate themselves from what they view as the harmful effects of city life.

Men like this one, who has just drunk himself into a stupor, are not an unfamiliar sight in some parts of U.S. cities. The text describes various types of urban dewllers. What type is this man?

The next two groups, the deprived and the trapped, have little choice about where they live. Outcasts of industrial society, they are alienated and always skirting the edge of disaster.

The Deprived.   City inhabitants in this category live in blighted neighborhoods more like urban jungles than urban villages. Consisting primarily of the very poor and the emotionally disturbed, the deprived represent the bottom of society in terms of income, education, social status, and work skills. Some of them stalk their jungle in search of prey, their victims usually deprived like themselves. Their future holds little chance for anything better in life, either for themselves or their children.

The Trapped.   The trapped can find no escape either. They consist of four subtypes: those who could not afford to move when their neighborhood was "invaded" by another ethnic group, elderly people who are not wanted elsewhere, alcoholics and other drug addicts, and the "downwardly mobile," people who have fallen from a higher social class. Like the deprived, the trapped also suffer high rates of assault, mugging, robbery, and rape.

Gans's typology provides insight into the great variety of ways in which urban dwellers experience the city. Recall the observations I reported on San Francisco. Some find the streets a stimulating source of cultural contrasts. For others, however, the same events pose a constant threat as they try to survive in what for them amounts to an urban jungle.

Urban Sentiment: Finding a Familiar World

Sociologists note that *the city is divided into little worlds* that people come to know down to their smallest details. Gregory Stone (1954) and Herbert Gans (1970) observed how city people create a sense of intimacy for themselves by *personalizing* their shopping. By frequenting the same stores, they become recognized as "regulars," and after a period of time customers and clerks greet each other by name. Particular taverns, restaurants, laundromats, and shops are more than just buildings in which to purchase items and services. They become meeting places where neighborhood residents build social relationships with one another and share informal news about the community.

Spectator sports also help urban dwellers find a familiar world (Hudson 1991). When the Cardinals won the World Series in 1982, for example, the entire St. Louis metropolitan area celebrated the victory of "their" team—even though fewer than one in seven of the area's 2.5 million people lived in the city. Sociologists David Karp and William Yoels (1990) note that such identification is so intense that long after moving to other parts of the country many people maintain an emotional allegiance to the sports teams of the city in which they grew up.

As sociologists Richard Wohl and Anselm Strauss (1958) pointed out, city dwellers even develop strong feelings for particular objects and locations in the city, such as buildings, rivers, lakes, parks, and even trees and street corners. In some cases, objects become a type of logo that represents the city:

> We need only show persons New York's skyline, or San Francisco's Golden Gate Bridge, or New Orleans's French Quarter, and the city will be quickly identified by most. For those who live in these respective cities, such objects and places do not merely identify the city; they are also sources for personal identification *with* the city. (Karp et al. 1991, italics added)

Urban Networks

Think of the city as a series of overlapping circles. Each circle consists of one person and everyone in the city that that person knows. If you were to draw these circles, they would overlap, and eventually they would include everyone in the entire city. The exception would be a few loners and people who have just moved into the city. Urban dwellers find their community, then, not in buildings and space, but in their social relationships. Regardless of where they live in the city, people who are not integrated into social networks find alienation, while those who are integrated find community.

The Norm of Noninvolvement and the Diffusion of Responsibility

Urban dwellers try to avoid intrusions from strangers. As they traverse everyday life in the city, they follow a *norm of noninvolvement.*

> To do this, we sometimes use props such as newspapers to shield ourselves from others and to indicate our inaccessibility for interaction. In effect, we learn to "tune others out." In this regard, we might see the Walkman as the quintessential urban prop in that it allows us to be tuned in and tuned out at the same time. It is a device that allows us to enter our own private world and thereby effectively to close off encounters with others. The use of such devices protect our "personal space," along with our body demeanor and facial expression (the passive "mask" or even scowl that persons adopt on subways). (Karp et al. 1991)

Recall Kitty Genovese, whose story was recounted on pages 578 and 580. Her story troubled social psychologists Bibb Latané and John Darley (1970), who ran a series of experiments featured in Chapter 6 on pages 158–159. As you may recall, they found that the *more* bystanders there are, the *less* likely people are to help. As a group grows, people's sense of responsibility becomes diffused, with each person assuming that *another* will do the responsible thing, "With these other people here, it is not *my* responsibility," they reason.

The norm of noninvolvement and the diffusion of responsibility help explain the response to Kitty Genovese's murder. The bystanders at her death were *not* uncaring people. They *did* care that a woman was being attacked. They simply were abiding by an urban norm—one helpful in getting them through everyday city life, but, unfortunately, dysfunctional in some critical situations. This norm, combined with killings, rapes, carjackings, muggings, and the generalized fear that the city now engenders in many Americans, underlies a desire to retreat to a safe haven. This topic is discussed in the Down-to-Earth Sociology box on the next page.

suburbanization: the movement from the city to the suburbs

suburb: the communities adjacent to the political boundaries of a city

The Decline of the City

The poverty, decay, and general decline of U.S. cities are among the primary problems of urban life today. Let's examine underlying reasons for these conditions and consider how to develop social policy to solve urban problems and improve our quality of life.

Suburbanization

On Suburbs and Ghettos. **Suburbanization,** which refers to people moving from cities to **suburbs,** the communities located just outside a city, is not new. The dream of a place of one's own with green grass, a few trees, and kids playing in the yard was not discovered by this generation (Riesman 1970). For the past hundred years or so, as transportation became more efficient, especially with the development of automobiles, people have moved to towns next to the cities in which they work. Minorities joined this movement about 1970. The extent to which people have left the city in search of their dreams is remarkable. In 1957, only 37 million Americans lived in the suburbs (Karp et al. 1991), but today over 125 million Americans live in them (Gans 1991b).

A fundamental drama being played out in various areas of the United States is the struggle between the haves and the have-nots. As much as possible, the haves segregate themselves from the have-nots. Urban life, however, sometimes makes their paths cross, at least momentarily, as captured in this photo.

Urban Fear and the Gated Fortress

Gated neighborhoods—where a gate on a street literally opens and closes access to a neighborhood—are not new. They always have been available to the rich. What is new is the upper middle class's rush to towns where the residents pay heavy taxes to keep private the town's entire facilities, including its streets.

Towns cannot discriminate on the basis of religion or ethnicity-race, but they can—and do—discriminate on the basis of social class. Klahanie, Washington, is an excellent example. Begun in 1985, it was supposed to take twenty years to develop. With its safe streets, 300 acres of open space, and its ban on satellite dishes, flagpoles, and even basketball hoops on garages, demand for the $300,000-plus homes in this private, lake-nestled community has exceeded supply (Egan 1995).

The future will bring many more such private towns as the upper middle class flees crime-ridden urban areas and attempts to build a bucolic dream. A strong sign of the future is that Walt Disney Company is building Celebration, a planned town of 20,000 people just south of Orlando, Florida (Egan 1995). With the new technology, the residents of these new private communities will be able to communicate with the outside world while remaining securely locked within their gated fortresses.

Community always involves a sense of togetherness, of identity with one another. Apparently it also contains the idea of separateness from others. If we become a nation of gated communities, where homeowners withdraw into private domains, separating themselves from the rest of the nation, this will be another declaration that the urban experiment has failed.

The U.S. economic system has proven highly beneficial to most citizens, but it also has left many in poverty. To protect themselves, primarily from the poor, the upper middle class increasingly seeks sanctuary behind gated residential enclaves.

The U.S. city has been the loser in this transition. As people moved out of the city, businesses and jobs followed and now about two-thirds of people who live in the suburbs also work there (Gans 1991b). As the city's tax base shrank, the resulting budget squeeze not only affected parks, zoos, libraries, and museums, but even the city's basic services— its schools, streets, sewer and water systems, and police and fire departments.

As this shift in population and resources took place, left behind were the people who had no choice but to stay in the city. The net result, observed sociologist William Wilson, was to transform the inner city into a ghetto. Left behind were highly disadvantaged

> families that have experienced long-term spells of poverty and/or welfare dependency, individuals who lack training and skills and have either experienced periods of persistent unemployment or have dropped out of the labor force altogether, and individuals who are frequently involved in street criminal activity. The term ghetto . . . suggests that a fundamental social transformation has taken place . . . that groups represented by this term are collectively different from and much more socially isolated from those that lived in these communities in earlier years. (quoted in Karp et al. 1991)

Barriers to Mutual Identification: City Versus Suburb. Having made the move out of the city—or having been born there and liking it—suburbanites want the city to keep its problems to itself. They reject proposals to share suburbia's revenues with the city and oppose measures that would allow urban and suburban governments joint control over what has become a contiguous mass of people and businesses. Suburban leaders generally see it as in their best interests to remain politically, economically, and socially separate from their nearby city. They do not mind going to the city to work, or venturing there on weekends for the diversions it offers, but they do not want to help shoulder the city's burdens.

It is likely that the mounting bill will come due ultimately, however, and that suburbanites will have to pay for their uncaring attitude toward the urban disadvantaged. Karp et al. (1991) put it this way:

> It may be that suburbs can insulate themselves from the problems of central cities, at least for the time being. In the long run, though, there will be a steep price to pay for the failure of those better off to care compassionately for those at the bottom of society.

It may be that our urban riots are part of that bill—perhaps just the down payment.

Suburban Flight. For some suburbs, the bill is coming due quickly. As suburbs age, some are becoming a mirror image of the city their residents so despise, with rising crime, flight of the middle class, a shrinking tax base, and eroding services. This, in turn, creates a spiraling sense of insecurity, more middle-class flight, and a further reduction of property values. Figure 20.12 illustrates this process, which is new to the urban/suburban scene.

Disinvestment

Already by the 1940s, the movement out of cities to suburbs had begun to undermine the cities' tax base, a problem only accelerated as poor rural migrants, mostly African American, moved in huge numbers to northern cities (Lemann 1994). As the tax base eroded, services declined—from garbage pickup to education. Buildings deteriorated, and banks began **redlining:** Afraid of loans going bad, banks drew a line on a map around a problem area and refused to make loans for housing or businesses there. The **disinvestment,** withdrawal of investment, pushed these areas into further decline. Not unconnected, youth gangs, murders, and robberies are high in these areas, while education, employment, and income are low.

Deindustrialization and Globalization

The development of a global market also has left a heavy imprint on U.S. cities. As sociologist Victor Rodríguez (1994) points out, to compete in the global market many U.S. industries have abandoned local communities and moved their factories to places where labor costs are lower. Although this makes U.S. industries more competitive, it also has eliminated millions of manufacturing jobs, locking many poor people out of the postindustrial economy that is engulfing the United States. Left behind in the inner cities,

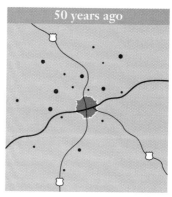

At first, the city and surrounding villages grew independently.

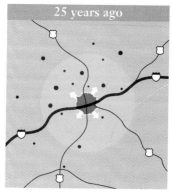

As city dwellers fled urban decay, they created a ring of suburbs.

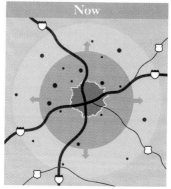

As middle-class flight continues outward, urban problems are arriving in the outer rings.

Figure 20.12

Urban Growth and Urban Flight

redlining: the officers of a financial institution deciding not to make loans in a particular area

disinvestment: the withdrawal of investments by financial institutions, which seals the fate of an urban area

Like the phoenix that rose from the ashes, luxury hotels and apartments, along with exclusive restaurants and shops, have sprung from the ruins of urban decay. Urban renewal, a benefit for the privileged, has displaced the poor, often shoving them into adjacent areas every bit as bad as those in which they previously lived.

many live in despair as a distant economy charges into the uncharted waters of a brave new world without them.

Social Policy: Failure and Potential

The Failure.   Social policy usually takes one of two forms. The first is to tear down and rebuild in the fancifully named effort called **urban renewal.** The result is the renewal of an area—but not for its inhabitants. Stadiums, high-rise condos, luxury hotels, and expensive shops are built. Outpriced, the area's inhabitants are displaced. They flow into adjacent areas, adding to their problems. The second form is some sort of **enterprise zone,** economic incentives such as reduced taxes to encourage businesses to move into the area. Although the intention is good, failure is the result. Most businesses refuse to locate in high-crime areas. Those that do may find that the costs of additional security and losses from crime run higher than the tax savings. If workers are hired from the problem area, and the jobs pay a decent wage, which most do not, the workers move to better neighborhoods, frustrating the purpose of establishing an enterprise zone (Lemann 1994). After all, who chooses to live with the fear of violence?

The Potential: An Urban Manhattan Project.   In spite of the problems facing U.S. cities—problems so severe that they are discussed not only around dinner tables in New York and Los Angeles, but also in Tokyo and London—government policies remain uncoordinated and ineffective (Flanagan 1990; Lemann 1994).

A "nothing works" mentality will solve nothing. U.S. cities can be revitalized and made into safe and decent places to live. There is nothing in their nature that turns cities into dangerous, deteriorating slums. Most cities of Europe, for example, are both safe and pleasant. If U.S. cities are to change, they must become top agenda items of the U.S. government, with adequate resources in terms of money and human talents focused on overcoming urban woes.

Granted the deplorable condition of many U.S. cities, and the flight of the middle classes—both whites and minorities—to greener pastures, an urban Manhattan Project seems in order. During World War II the United States and the Allies faced a triumphant Hitler in Europe and Tojo in Asia. The United States gathered its top scientific minds, gave them all the resources they needed, and produced the atomic bomb. Today, a similar gathering of top social scientists and similar resources may be required to triumph over urban ills.

urban renewal: the rehabilitation of a rundown area, which usually results in the displacement of the poor who are living in that area

enterprise zone: the use of economic incentives in a designated area with the intention of encouraging investment there

Guiding Principles. Sociologist William Flanagan (1990) suggests three guiding principles for working out specific solutions to our pressing urban problems:

- *Scale.* Regional and national planning is necessary. Currently, the many local jurisdictions, with their many rivalries, competing goals, and limited resources, lead to a hodgepodge of mostly unworkable solutions. A positive example is Portland, Oregon, where a regional government prohibits urban sprawl and ensures a green belt (Ortega 1995).
- *Livability.* Growth must be channeled in such a way that cities are appealing and meet human needs, especially the need of community stressed in this chapter. This will attract the middle classes into the city and increase its tax base. In turn, this will help finance the services that make the city more livable.
- *Social justice.* In the final analysis, social policy must be evaluated by its effects on people. "Urban renewal" programs, for example, that displace the poor for the benefit of the middle class and wealthy do not pass this standard. The same would apply to solutions that create "livability" for select groups but neglect the poor and homeless.

Unless the *root* causes of urban problems are addressed—housing, education, and jobs—solutions, at best, will be only Band-Aids that cover up problems, or, at worst, window dressing for politicians who want to *appear* as though they are doing something about the problems that affect our quality of life.

Summary and Review

A Planet with No Space to Enjoy Life?

What debate did Thomas Malthus initiate?

In 1798, Thomas Malthus analyzed the surge in Europe's population. His conclusion, called the **Malthus theorem,** was that because the population grows geometrically but food only arithmetically, the world will outstrip its food supply. The debate between today's New Malthusians and those who disagree, the Anti-Malthusians, continues. Pp. 556–560.

Why are people starving?

Starvation is not due to a lack of food in the world, for there now is more food for each person in the entire world than there was fifty years ago. Starvation, rather, is due to a maldistribution of food. Pp. 560–562.

Population Growth

Why do the poor nations have so many children?

In the Least Industrialized Nations, children generally are viewed as gifts from God, cost little to rear, and represent the parents' social security. Consequently, people are motivated to have large families. Pp. 562–565.

What are the three demographic variables?

To compute population growth, demographers use *fertility, mortality,* and *migration.* The **basic demographic equation** is births – deaths + net migration = growth rate. Pp. 565–567.

Why is forecasting population difficult?

A nation's growth rate is affected by unanticipated variables—from economic conditions, wars, plagues, and famines to government policies and industrialization. Pp. 567–570.

What population challenges do we face today?

The population explosion is occurring in those nations that have the least wealth and technology. The challenge is how to use technology to help the Least Industrialized Nations avoid starvation and resource depletion. Pp. 570–571.

Urbanization

What is the relationship of cities to farming?

Cities can develop only if there is a large agricultural surplus, which frees people from food production. The primary impetus to the development of cities was the invention of the plow about five or six thousand years ago. Pp. 571–572.

How did the Industrial Revolution affect the size of cities?

Almost without exception, throughout history cities have been small. After the Industrial Revolution stimulated mechanical transportation and communication, the infrastructure on which modern cities depend, cities grew quickly and much larger. Pp. 572–573.

What are metropolises and megalopolises?

Urbanization is so extensive that some cities have become **metropolises,** dominating the area adjacent to them. The areas of influence of some metropolises have merged, forming a **megalopolis.** Pp. 573–575.

Models of Urban Growth

What models of urban growth have been proposed?

The primary models are concentric zone model, a sector model, and a multiple-nuclei model. These models fail to account for medieval cities, as well as many European cities and those in the least industrialized nations. Pp. 576–578.

City Life

Is the city inherently alienating?

Some people experience alienation in the city; others find community in it. What people find depends largely on their background and urban networks. Five types of people who live in cities are cosmopolites, singles, ethnic villagers, the deprived, and the trapped. Pp. 578–583.

The Decline of the City

Why have U.S. cities declined?

Three primary reasons for their decline are **suburbanization** (as people moved to the suburbs, the tax base of cities eroded, and services deteriorated), **disinvestment** (financial institutions withdrawing their financing), and **deindustrialization** (which has caused a loss of jobs). Pp. 583–586.

What social policy can salvage U.S. cities?

A Manhattan Project on Urban Problems could likely produce workable solutions. Three guiding principles for developing social policy are scale, livability, and social justice. Pp. 586–587.

Where can I read more on this topic?

Suggested readings for this chapter are listed on page 666.

Sociology and the Internet

All URLs listed are current as of the printing of this book. URLs are often changed. Please check our Website http://www.abacon.com/henslin for updates.

1. Studying demography can seem very abstract. Even when implications for poverty and starvation are addressed, the problems may seem far removed from the relative safety of our own lives. In this project, you will apply the study of population to your own world.

First, go to the U. S. Census Bureau's Population Division site at *http://www.census.gov/ftp/pub/population/www/* Click on "Selected 1990 Census Data"; then select "1990 Census Lookup." Select "STF3a (detailed geography)." On the new page, you should find directions to "Retrieve the areas you've selected below." Click on "Go to level: state-place" Now page down, select your home state, and click on the "Submit" bar. When the next page comes up, scroll down to select your home town, and again click on the "Submit" bar. On the new page, "Choose tables" should already be marked, so just click "Submit." Now you should see a heading telling you to "Select the tables you wish to retrieve." For now, mark "P1 Persons" and "P7 Sex (2)." Click on "Submit." There should already be a dot before "HTML Format," so just click

"Submit" again. You should now see the two tables you asked for. You can print or save them.

Now that you know how to get the data, go back to the page with the statement "Select the tables you wish to receive." Pick tables that will tell you about the social conditions of your town. Do you have a large minority population? What is the state of the housing? Get enough information so you can write a report on what demographic variations can tell you about your home town.

2. Look again at the ten urban giants in Figure 20.8 (page 574). Have you visited any of them? Do you live in one of them? In this project you will have the opportunity to tour some of them by way of the Internet. As you visit the sites, their emphasis will vary widely, as the sponsors include government, commercial agencies, and academic sources. Tour as many cities as you can; then bring your impressions to class to share with other tourists. (Some addresses may be case sensitive; that is, they react to upper and lower cases, so copy each exactly.)

Tokyo: *http://jw.nttam.com/LWT/TOKYO/tokyo_home.html*
Mexico City: *http://remag.com/mexcity*
Seoul: *http://iworld.net/Korea/travel/f282.html*

New York City: *http://astor.mediabridge.com/nyc*
Bombay: *http://www.bchs.uh.edu/~mdoshi/Bombay/ Bombay.html*
Moscow: *http://sunsite.unc.edu/sergei/Exs/Moscow/moscow. html*
Buenos Aires: *http://www.wam.com.ar/tourism/reg 6/reg 6. htm*
Jaharta: *http://www.jaharta.dki.go.id/*

3. Although many researchers are concerned about over-population, infertility is an issue for many U.S. couples. Examine the following links to learn more about the other side of fertility:

http://www.vais.net/~travis/firl.html#FIRL_Online_Resources
http://www.resolve.org/index.htm

Write a paragraph on each of these questions and be ready to discuss your conclusions/opinions with the class: What is in-fertility? What are its causes? About how many U.S. couples are affected by infertility each year? What are the treatments for infertility? What are the costs for treatment? What role does social class play in the cause/treatment of infertility? Does everybody have the right to reproduce as much as they wish? How far should technology go to allow couples to re-produce?

4. After reading about zero population growth in your text-book, check out the Zero Population Growth web site at *http:// www.zpg.org* Be ready to answer these questions: What are some of the most frequently asked questions about popula-tions? What is the purpose of this organization? What is the current federal and state legislation on population policy? What are the current population statistics?

Charles Alston, Walking, 1958

Collective Behavior and Social Movements

THE NEWS SPREAD LIKE WILDFIRE. A police officer had been killed. In just twenty minutes, the white population was armed and heading for the cabin. Men and mere boys, some not more than 12 years old, carried rifles, shotguns, and pistols.

The mob, now about four hundred, surrounded the log cabin. Tying a rope around the man's neck, they dragged him to the center of town. While the men argued about the best way to kill him, the women and children shouted their advice—some to hang him, others to burn him alive.

Someone pulled a large wooden box out of a store and placed it in the center of the street. Others filled it with straw. Then they lifted the man, the rope still around his neck, and shoved him head first into the box. One of the men poured oil over him. Another lit a match.

As the flames shot upward, the man managed to lift himself out of the box, his body a mass of flames. Trying to shield his face and eyes from the fire, he ran the length of the rope, about twenty feet, when someone yelled, "Shoot!" In an instant, dozens of shots rang out. Men and boys walked to the lifeless body and emptied their guns into it.

They dragged the man's body back to the burning box, then piled on more boxes from the stores, and poured oil over them. Each time someone threw more oil onto the flames, the crowd roared shouts of approval.

Standing about seventy-five feet away, I could smell the poor man's burning flesh. No one tried to hide their identity. I could clearly see town officials help in the burning. The inquest, dutifully held by the coroner, concluded that the man met death "at the hands of an enraged mob unknown to the jury." What else could he conclude? Any jury from this town would include men who had participated in the man's death.

They dug a little hole at the edge of the street, and dumped in it the man's ashes and what was left of his body.

The man's name was Sam Pettie, known by everybody to be quiet and unoffensive. I can't mention my name. If I did, I would be committing suicide.

(Based on a May 1914 letter to The Crisis*)*

COLLECTIVE BEHAVIOR

Why did the people in this little town "go mad"? These men—and the women who watched in agreement—were ordinary, law-abiding citizens. Even some of the "pillars of the community" joined in the vicious killing of Sam Pettie, who may have been innocent.

Lynching is a form of **collective behavior,** a group of people bypassing the usual norms that guide their behavior and doing something unusual (Turner and Killian 1987; Lofland 1993). Collective behavior is a very broad term, for it includes not only such violent acts as lynchings and riots, but also panics, rumors, fads, and fashions. Before examining its specific forms, let us look at theories that seek to explain collective behavior.

Early Explanations: The Transformation of the Individual

collective behavior: extraordinary activities carried out by groups of people; includes lynchings, rumors, panics, urban legends, and fads and fashions

When people can't figure something out, they often resort to some form of "madness" as an explanation. People are apt to say, "She went 'off her rocker'; that's why she drove her car off the bridge." "He must have 'gone nuts,' or he wouldn't have shot into the crowd." Early explanations of collective behavior were not far from such assumptions. Let's look at how these ideas developed.

Contemporary sociologists analyze collective behavior as rational behavior; that is, the group is seen as utilizing whatever means are accessible in order to reach a goal, even though that goal may be barbaric. This is a photo of a lynching that occurred in Rayston, Georgia, on April 28, 1936. Earlier in the day, the 40-year-old victim, Lint Shaw, who was accused of attacking a white girl, had been rescued from a mob by National Guardsmen. After the National Guard left, the mob forced its way into the jail.

Charles Mackay, Gustave LeBon, and Robert Park: How the Crowd Transforms the Individual

The field of collective behavior began when Charles Mackay (1814–1889), a British journalist, noticed that "country folks," who ordinarily are reasonable sorts of people, sometimes "went mad" and did "disgraceful and violent things" when they got in a crowd. The best explanation Mackay (1852) could come up with was that people had a "herd mentality"—they were like a herd of cows that suddenly stampede.

About fifty years later, Gustave LeBon (1841–1931), a French psychologist, built on this initial idea. In an 1895 book, LeBon stressed how crowds make people feel anonymous, as though they are not accountable for what they do. In a crowd, people even develop feelings of invincibility, and come to think that they can do almost anything. A **collective mind** develops, he said, and people are swept up with almost any suggestion. Then contagion, something like mass hypnosis, takes over, releasing the destructive instincts that society has so carefully repressed.

Robert Park (1864–1944), a U.S. sociologist who studied in Germany and wrote a 1904 dissertation on the crowd, was greatly influenced by LeBon (McPhail 1991). After Park joined the faculty at the University of Chicago, he added the ideas of social unrest and circular reaction. He said,

> Social unrest . . . is transmitted from one individual to another . . . so that the manifestations of discontent in A [are] communicated to B, and from B reflected back to A. (Park and Burgess 1921a)

Park used the term **circular reaction** to refer to this back-and-forth communication. Circular reaction, he said, creates a "collective impulse" that comes to "dominate all members of the crowd." If "collective impulse" sounds just like LeBon's "collective mind," that's because it really is. As noted, Park was heavily influenced by LeBon, and his slightly different term did not change the basic idea at all.

collective mind: Gustave LeBon's term for the tendency of people in a crowd to feel, think, and act in extraordinary ways

circular reaction: Robert Park's term for a back-and-forth communication between the members of a crowd whereby a "collective impulse" is transmitted

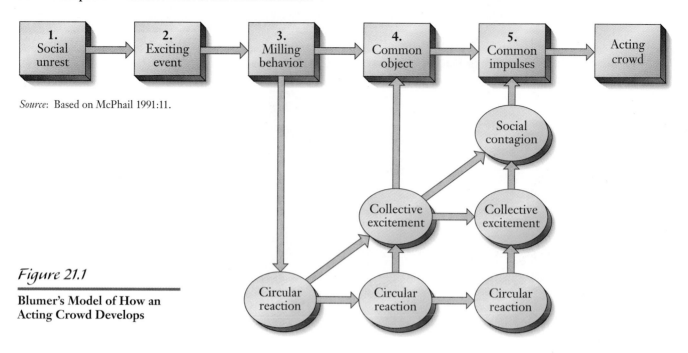

Source: Based on McPhail 1991:11.

Figure 21.1

Blumer's Model of How an Acting Crowd Develops

Herbert Blumer: The Acting Crowd

Herbert Blumer (1900–1987), who studied under Park, synthesized LeBon's and Park's ideas. As you can see from Figure 21.1, Blumer (1939) identified five stages that precede what he called an **acting crowd,** an excited group that moves toward a goal. This model still dominates today's police manuals on crowd behavior (McPhail 1989). Let's apply it to the lynching of Sam Pettie.

1. *Tension or unrest.* At the root of collective behavior is a background condition of tension or unrest. Disturbed about some condition of society, people are restless, apprehensive, and vulnerable to rumors and suggestions. When Sam Pettie was lynched, it was during the early 1900s when traditional southern life was undergoing upheaval. Due to industrialization, millions of Americans were moving to where the jobs were, from farm to city and from South to North. Left behind were many poor, rural southerners, white and black, who faced a bleak future. In addition, African Americans were questioning the legitimacy of their low status and deprivation.

2. *Exciting event.* An exciting event occurs, one so startling that people become preoccupied with it. In this instance, that event was the killing of a police officer.

3. *Milling.* Next comes **milling,** people standing or walking around, talking about the exciting event. A circular reaction then sets in. That is, as people pick up cues to the "right" way of thinking and feeling, they reinforce them in one another. During the short period in which Sam Pettie's lynch mob milled, the white residents of this small town became increasingly agitated as they discussed the officer's death.

4. *A common object of attention.* In this stage, people's attention becomes riveted on some aspect of the event. They get caught up in the collective excitement. In this case, people's attention turned to Sam Pettie. Someone may have said that he had been talking to the officer or that they had been arguing.

5. *Common impulses.* A sense of collective agreement about what should be done emerges. What stimulates these common impulses is *social contagion,* a sense of excitement that is passed from one person to another. In this instance, people concluded that the killer had to be punished, and that only an immediate, public death would be adequate vengeance—as well as a powerful warning for other African Americans who might even think about getting "out of line."

acting crowd: Herbert Blumer's term for an excited group that collectively moves toward a goal

milling: a crowd standing or walking around as they talk excitedly about some event

Acting crowds aren't always negative or destructive, as this one was, for they also include spontaneous demonstrations directed against oppression. Nor are they all serious, for college food fights are also acting crowds.

The Contemporary View: The Rationality of the Crowd

If we were to witness a lynching—or a screaming mob or a prison riot—most of us probably would agree with LeBon that some sort of "madness" had swept over the crowd. Sociologists today, however, point out that crowds are actually quite rational. By this, they mean that crowds take deliberate steps to reach some desired goal. As sociologist Clark McPhail (1991) points out, even a lynch mob is cooperative—someone gets the rope while others hold the victim, some tie the knot, and others hoist the body.

Richard Berk: The Minimax Strategy

A general principle of human behavior is that we try to minimize our costs and maximize our rewards. Sociologist Richard Berk (1974) calls this a **minimax strategy.** The fewer costs and the more rewards we anticipate from something, the more likely we are to do it. For example, if we believe that others will approve an act, the likelihood that we will do it increases. Whether in yelling for the referee's blood at a bad call in football, or shouting for real blood as a member of a lynch mob, this principle applies. In short, whether people are playing cards with a few friends, or are part of a mob, the principles of human behavior remain the same.

Ralph Turner and Lewis Killian: Emergent Norms

Since collective behavior always involves something unusual, however, it seems that something besides the usual norms of behavior is involved. Sociologists Ralph Turner and Lewis Killian (1987) use the term **emergent norms** to get at the heart of this matter. They point out that life usually goes much as we expect, and our usual norms are adequate. If an unusual event disrupts our usual ways of doing things, however, our ordinary norms may not cover the new situation. People then may develop *new* norms to deal with the new situation. Sometimes they even produce new definitions of right and wrong that *under the new circumstances* justify actions that they would otherwise consider wrong.

To understand how new norms emerge, we need to keep in mind that not everyone in a crowd shares the same point of view (Snow et al. 1993; Rodríguez 1994). As Turner and Killian (1987) point out, there are at least five kinds of crowd participants:

1. The *ego-involved* feel a personal stake in the extraordinary event.
2. The *concerned* also have a personal interest in the event, but less so than the ego-involved.
3. The *insecure* care little about the matter, but they join the crowd because it gives them a sense of power and security.
4. The *curious spectators* also care little about the issue, but they are inquisitive about what is going on.
5. The *exploiters* do not care about the event, but they use it for their own purposes, such as hawking food or T-shirts.

The contrasting attitudes, motives, and emotions of these different types of participants significantly influence the emergence of new norms. The most important role goes to the "ego-involved": Some make suggestions about what should be done, while others take action. As the "concerned" join in, they, too, help to set the crowd on a particular

minimax strategy: Richard Berk's term for the effort people make to minimize their costs and maximize their rewards

emergent norms: Ralph Turner's and Lewis Killian's term for the development of new norms to cope with a new situation, especially among crowds

This protest against imports, by farmers in Marseilles, France, illustrates several sociological principles. Among them are emergent norms (behavior otherwise disapproved becomes acceptable) and different types of crowd participants (the curious spectators are especially evident; the photographer could be an exploiter).

course of action. The "insecure" and the "curious spectators" may then join in. Although the "exploiters" are unlikely to participate, they do lend the crowd passive support. A common mood completes the stage for new norms to emerge: Activities "not OK" in everyday life may now seem "OK"—whether throwing bottles at the cops or shouting obscenities at the college president.

This analysis of emergent norms helps us see that collective behavior is *rational*. The crowd, for example, does not consider all suggestions made by the ego-involved to be equal: To be acceptable, suggestions must match predispositions that the crowd already has. This analysis, then, is a far cry from earlier interpretations that people were so transformed by a crowd that they went out of their minds.

Forms of Collective Behavior

Sociologists, then, treat collective behavior the same as other forms of behavior (Turner and Killian 1987; Lofland 1993; Turner 1993). They view it as ordinary people responding to extraordinary situations (Rodríguez 1994). They ask their usual questions about interaction, such as How do people influence one another? What is the significance of the members' age, gender, and social class? What role do preexisting attitudes play? Just how do people's perceptions get translated into action?

In addition to lynchings, collective behavior includes riots, panics, moral panics, rumors, fads, fashions, and urban legends. Let's look at each.

Riots

The nation watched in horror. White Los Angeles police officers had been caught on videotape beating an African-American traffic violator with their nightsticks. The videotape clearly showed the officers savagely bringing their nightsticks down on a man prostrate at their feet. Television stations around the United States—and the world—broadcast the pictures to stunned audiences.

The evidence was vivid and irrefutable. When the officers went on trial for beating the man identified as Rodney King, how could the verdict be anything but guilty? Yet a jury consisting of eleven whites and one Asian American found the officers innocent of using excessive force. The result was a **riot**—violent crowd behavior aimed against people and property. Within minutes of the verdict, angry

riot: violent crowd behavior aimed against people and property

596

crowds began to gather in Los Angeles. That night, mobs set fire to businesses in south-central Los Angeles, and looting and arson began in earnest. The rioting spread to other cities, including Atlanta, Georgia, Tampa, Florida, and even Madison, Wisconsin, and Las Vegas, Nevada. Whites and Koreans were favorite targets of violence.

Again Americans sat transfixed before their television sets as they saw parts of Los Angeles go up in flames and looters carrying television sets and lugging sofas in full view of the Los Angeles Police Department, which took no steps to stop them. Seared into the public's collective consciousness was the sight of Reginald Denny, a 36-year-old white truck driver who had been pulled from his truck in the riot area. As he sat dazed in the street, Damian Williams, laughing, broke Denny's skull with a piece of concrete.

On the third night, after 4,000 fires had been set and more than thirty people killed, President George Bush announced on national television that the U.S. Justice Department had appointed prosecutors to investigate possible federal charges against the police officers for violating the civil rights of Rodney King. The president then stated that he had ordered the Seventh Infantry, SWAT teams, and the FBI into Los Angeles. He also federalized the California National Guard and placed it under the command of Gen. Colin Powell, the chairman of the Joint Chiefs of Staff. Even Rodney King went on television and tearfully pleaded for peace.

The Los Angeles riot was the bloodiest since the U.S. Civil War. Before it was over, fifty-four people lost their lives, 2,328 people were treated in hospital emergency rooms, thousands of small businesses were burned, and about $1 billion of property was destroyed. Two of the police officers were later sentenced to 2½ years in prison on federal charges, and King was awarded several million dollars in damages. (Rose 1992; Stevens and Lubman 1992; Holden and Rose 1993; Cannon 1998)

Urban riots usually are caused by frustration and anger at deprivation. Frustrated at being kept out of mainstream society—limited to a meager education, denied jobs and justice, and kept out of good neighborhoods—frustration builds to such a boiling point that it takes only a precipitating event to erupt in collective violence. In the Los Angeles riot all these conditions existed, with the jury's verdict the precipitating event.

Sociologists have found that it is not only the deprived, however, who participate in riots. After the assassination of Dr. Martin Luther King, Jr., in 1968, many U.S. cities erupted in riots, and even people with good jobs participated (McPhail 1991). In the L.A. riots, the first outbursts didn't come from the poorest neighborhoods but from the most stable neighborhoods. Why would middle-class people participate in riots? The answer, says sociologist Victor Rodríguez (1994), is a sense of frustration that many minorities feel with being treated as second-class citizens even when they are gainfully employed and living stable lives.

In fact, the event that precipitates a riot is much less important than the riot's general context. The precipitating event is only the match that lights the fuel. The fuel is the area's background of unrest—a perceived sense of injustice that is being ignored or even condoned and encouraged by officials. It is this seething rage just underneath the surface that erupts following incidents such as the Rodney King verdict. Because this rage is felt not only by the poor and the unemployed but also by those who are materially better off, both groups participate. In addition, there are opportunists—individuals who participate not out of rage, or even because they are particularly concerned about the precipitating event, but because the riot provides an opportunity for looting.

The Los Angeles riot of 1992 was different from other riots only in the extent of its violence: In terms of lives and property lost, it was the most destructive riot in U.S. history. Otherwise, the riot followed a familiar pattern. It was set off by a precipitating event that stemmed from an atmosphere of mounting frustration.

Natural disasters often provide examples of collective behavior. A primary finding of disaster research is that people act rationally. Typically, they first check on the safety of their loved ones, then organize to overcome the effects of the disaster. Although this man appears dazed after a tornado destroyed his home, predictably, he soon will participate in organized efforts to recover from the disaster.

Panics

In 1938, on the night before Halloween, a radio program of dance music was interrupted with a report that explosions had been observed on the surface of Mars. The announcer breathlessly added that a cylinder of unknown origin had been discovered embedded in the ground on a farm in New Jersey. The radio station then switched to the farm, where an alarmed reporter gave details of horrible-looking Martians coming out of the cylinder. Their death-ray weapons had destructive powers unknown to humans. An interview with an astronomer confirmed that Martians had invaded the Earth.

Perhaps six million Americans heard this broadcast. About one million were frightened, and thousands panicked. Unknown numbers burst into tears, while thousands more grabbed weapons and hid in their basements or ran into the streets. Hundreds bundled up their families and jumped into their cars, jamming the roads as they headed to who knows where.

Of course, there was no invasion. This was simply a dramatization of H. G. Wells's *War of the Worlds*, starring Orson Welles. There had been an announcement at the beginning of the program and somewhere in the middle that the account was fictional, but apparently many people missed it. Although the panic reactions to this radio program may appear humorous to us, to anyone who is in a panic the situation is far from humorous. **Panic** occurs when people become so fearful that they cannot function normally, and may even flee.

Why did people panic? Psychologist Hadley Cantril (1941) attributed the result to widespread anxiety about world conditions. The Nazis were marching in Europe, and millions of Americans (correctly, as it turned out) were afraid that the United States would get involved. War jitters, he said, created fertile ground for the broadcast to touch off a panic.

Contemporary analysts, however, question whether there even was a panic. Sociologist William Bainbridge (1989) acknowledges that some people did become frightened, and that a few actually did get in their cars and drive like maniacs. But he says that most of this famous panic was an invention of the news media. Reporters found a good story and milked it, exaggerating as they went along.

Bainbridge points to a 1973 event in Sweden. To dramatize the dangers of atomic power, Swedish Radio broadcast a play about an accident at a nuclear power plant. Knowing about the 1938 broadcast in the United States, Swedish sociologists were waiting to see what would happen. Might some people fail to realize that it was a dramatization and panic at the threat of ruptured reactors spewing out radioactivity? The sociologists found no panic. A few people did become frightened. Some telephoned family members and the police; others shut windows to keep out the radioactivity—reasonable responses, considering what they thought had occurred.

The Swedish media, however, reported a panic! Apparently, a reporter had telephoned two police departments and learned that each had received calls from concerned citizens. With a deadline hanging over his head, the reporter decided to gamble. He reported that police and fire stations were jammed with citizens, that people were flocking to the shelters, and that others were fleeing south (Bainbridge 1989).

Panics do occur, of course—which is why nobody has the right to shout "Fire!" in a public building when no such danger exists—for if people fear immediate death, they will lunge toward the nearest exit in a frantic effort to escape. Such a panic occurred on Memorial Day weekend in 1977 at the Beverly Hills Supper Club, in Southgate, Kentucky. About half the 2,500 patrons were crowded into the Cabaret Room, awaiting the appearance of singer John Davidson. The fire, which began in a small banquet room near the front of the building, burned undetected until it was beyond control. When employ-

panic: the condition of being so fearful that one cannot function normally, and may even flee

ees discovered the fire, they warned patrons. People began to exit in orderly fashion, but when flames rushed in the result was sheer panic. Patrons trampled one another in a furious attempt to reach the exits, which were immediately blocked by masses of screaming people simultaneously trying to push their way through. The writhing bodies at the exits created further panic among the remainder, who pushed even harder to force their way through the bottlenecks. One hundred sixty-five people died, all but two within thirty feet of two exits of the Cabaret Room.

Sociologists who studied this panic found what other researchers have discovered in analyzing other disasters. *Not everyone panics.* In disturbances many people continue to act responsibly. Especially important are primary group bonds. Parents help their children, for example (Morrow 1995). Gender roles also persist, and more men help women than women help men (Johnson 1993). Even work roles continue to guide some behavior. Sociologists Drue Johnston and Norris Johnson (1989) found that only 29 percent of the employees of the Beverly Hills Supper Club left when they learned of the fire. As noted on Table 21.1, 41 percent helped customers, 17 percent reported or fought the fire, 7 percent simply went about their routines, and 5 percent did such things as search for friends and relatives.

Sociologists use the term **role extension** to describe the actions of most of the employees. In other words, the employees incorporated other activities into their occupational roles. For example, servers extended their role to include helping people to safety. How do we know that giving help was an extension of the occupational role, not simply helping in general? Johnston and Johnson found that servers who were away from their assigned stations returned to them in order to help *their* customers.

Moral Panics

Moral panics occur when large numbers of people become intensely concerned, even fearful, about some behavior thought to threaten morality, and the fear is out of proportion to any supposed danger (Cauthen and Jasper 1994; Goode and Ben-Yehuda 1994). The threat is seen as enormous, and hostility builds toward those thought responsible. The most infamous of moral panics is the fear of witches in Europe between 1400 and 1650, resulting in the Inquisition—investigations, torture, and burning at the stake of people accused of witchcraft.

Today, moral panics are fueled by the mass media, as with the fear of sexual abuse of children in day care centers that spread across the United States during the 1980s. At one point, almost every day care worker became suspect in someone's eyes, and only fearfully did parents leave their children in day care centers. Although sexual abuse at day care centers has occurred, the highly publicized stories of children subjected to bizarre rituals with devil worshippers and naked priests and weird sex have not been substantiated. The hysteria has since died down.

Like other panics, moral panics center around a sense of danger. The supposed thousands of U.S. children who are snatched by strangers from playgrounds, city streets, and their own back yards are part of a moral panic that has made parents fearful and others perplexed at how U.S. society could so suddenly go to hell in a handbasket. This moral panic is destined to meet the same fate as others. The fear and hysteria will gradually subside, and people will feel less fear as they drop children off at school or let them play outside.

Moral panics are fed by **rumor**, information for which there is no discernible source and which is usually unfounded. For example, a rumor, still continuing, is that missing children are sold to Satanists who abuse them sexually and then ritually murder them. This rumor is intensely believed by some, and has been supported by testimony from people who claim to have been involved in such sacrifices. Investigations by the police, however, have uncovered no evidence to substantiate it. In addition, the actual number of stranger kidnappings per year is between 200 and 300 (Bromely 1991).

Moral panics thrive on uncertainty and anxiety. Today's changing family serves up a rich plateful of anxiety. Concerns that children are receiving inadequate care because so

TABLE 21.1

Employees' First Action After Learning of the Fire

Action	Percentage
Left	29%
Helped others to leave	41%
Fought or reported the fire	17%
Continued routine activities	7%
Other (e.g., looked for a friend or relative)	5%

Note: These figures are based on interviews with 95 of the 160 employees present at the time of the fire: 48 males and 47 females, ranging in age from 15 to 59.

Source: Based on Johnston and Johnson 1989.

role extension: the incorporation of additional activities into a role

moral panic: a fear that grips large numbers of people that some evil group or behavior threatens the well-being of society, followed by intense hostility, sometimes violence, toward those thought responsible

rumor: unfounded information spread among people

many mothers have left home to join the work force have become linked with thoughts of dangers to children from sinister sources lurking almost everywhere.

Rumors

Everyone is interested in a juicy bit of gossip. Or is this a rumor? Differences between gossip and rumor are sometimes difficult to distinguish. This woodcut by a Harper's Weekly *staff artist appeared in an 1874 issue.*

In *Aladdin*, the handsome young title character murmurs, "All good children, take off your clothes." In *The Lion King*, Simba, the cuddly lion star, stirs up a cloud of dust that, floating off the screen, spells S-E-X. Then there is the bishop in *The Little Mermaid*, who presiding over a wedding, becomes noticeably aroused.

Ann Runge, a mother of eight, who owned stacks of animated Disney films, said she felt betrayed when she heard that the Magic Kingdom was sending obscene, subliminal messages. "I felt as though I had entrusted my kids to pedophiles," she said (Bannon 1995).

Thriving in conditions of ambiguity, rumors function to fill in missing information (Turner 1964; Shibutani 1966). In response to the rumor, Disney reports that Aladdin really says, "Scat, good tiger, take off and go." The line is hard to understand, however, leaving enough ambiguity for others to continue to hear what they want, even to insist that it is an invitation to a teenage orgy. Similar ambiguity remains with Simba's dust and the aroused bishop.

Most rumors are short-lived. They arise in a situation of ambiguity, only to dissipate when they are replaced by factual information—or by another rumor. Occasionally, however, a rumor has a long life. In the eighteenth and nineteenth centuries, for no known reason, healthy people would grow weak and slowly waste away. No one understood the cause and people said they had *consumption* (now called tuberculosis). People were terrified as they saw their loved ones wither into shells of their former selves. With no one knowing when the disease would strike, or who its next victim would be, the rumor began that some of the dead weren't really dead. What had happened, people said, was that they had turned into vampire-like beings, and at night they were coming back from the grave and draining the life out of the living. The evidence was irrefutable—loved ones wasting away before their very eyes. To kill these ghoulish "undead," on dark nights people began to sneak into graveyards. They would dig up a grave, remove the leg bones and place them over the skeleton's chest, then lay the skull at the feet, forming a skull and crossbones. Having thus killed the "undead," they would rebury the remains. These rumors and resulting mutilations of the dead continued off and on in New England until the 1890s (Associated Press, November 30, 1993).

Why do people believe rumors? Three main factors have been identified. First, rumors deal with a subject that is important to an individual. Second, they replace ambiguity with some form of certainty. Third, they are attributed to a creditable source. An office rumor may be preceded by "Jane has it on good authority that . . . ," or "Bill overheard the boss say that . . . "

Ambiguity or uncertainty is especially important in giving life to rumors. That is why the New Englanders speculated about the cause of people slowly dying, their rather bizarre conclusions offering certainty in the face of bewildering events. The uncertainty that sparked the Disney rumor may be feelings among some that the moral fabric of modern society is decaying. If one believes this, perhaps it is not too far a stretch to believe that a conspiracy may underlie the decay. Perhaps even the Magic Kingdom . . .

Fads and Fashions

fad: a temporary pattern of behavior that catches people's attention

A **fad** is a novel form of behavior that briefly catches people's attention. The new behavior appears suddenly and spreads by suggestion, imitation, and identification with people already involved in the fad. Publicity by the mass media also helps to spread the fad. After a short life, the fad fades into oblivion, although it may reappear from time to time (Aguirre et al. 1993).

Sociologist John Lofland (1985) identified four types of fads. First are object fads, such as the Hula Hoop of the 1950s, pet rocks of the 1970s, the Rubik's Cube and Cabbage Patch dolls of the 1980s, and pogs and beanie babies of the 1990s. Second are activity fads, such as eating goldfish in the 1920s and bungee jumping and body piercing in the 1990s. Third are idea fads, such as astrology. Fourth are personality fads, such as Elvis Presley, Princess Diana, and Michael Jordan. Some fads are extremely short-lived, such as "streaking" (running naked in a public place), which lasted only a couple of months in 1974. Some fads involve millions of people, but die just as quickly as they appeared. For example, in the 1950s the Hula Hoop sold so quickly that stores couldn't keep them in stock. Children cried and pleaded for these brightly colored plastic hoops. Across the nation, children, and some adults, gyrated with this object encircling their waists. Hula Hoop contests were held to see who could keep the hoops up the longest or who could rotate the most hoops at one time. Then, in a matter of months it was over, and parents wondered what to do with the abandoned items, now useless for any other purpose.

When a fad lasts, it is called a **fashion.** Some fashions, as with clothing, are the result of a coordinated international marketing system that includes designers, manufacturers, advertisers, and retailers. Billions of dollars worth of clothing are sold by manipulating the tastes of the public. Fashion, however, also refers to hairstyles, home decorating, even the design and colors of buildings. Sociologist John Lofland (1985) pointed out that fashion even applies to language, as demonstrated by these roughly comparable terms: "Neat!" in the 1950s, "Right on!" in the 1960s, "Really!" in the 1970s, "Awesome!" in the 1980s, "Bad!" in the early 1990s,—and, recurringly, "Cool."

Fads are one of the fascinating aspects of social life studied by sociologists. From antiquity, hair has been the object of fads. This combination of shorn, shaved, and braided is unlikely to gain wide popularity.

Urban Legends

> Did you hear about Nancy and Bill? They were parked at Echo Bay. They were listening to the car radio, and the music was interrupted by an announcement that a rapist-killer had escaped from prison. Instead of a right hand, he had a hook. Nancy said they should leave, but Bill laughed and said there wasn't any reason to go. When they heard a strange noise, Bill agreed to take her home. When Nancy opened the door, she heard something clink. It was a hook hanging on the door handle!

For the past generation, some version of "The Hook" story has circulated among Americans. It has appeared as a "genuine" letter in "Dear Abby," and some of my students heard it in grade school. **Urban legends** are stories with an ironic twist that sound realistic but are false. Although untrue, they usually are told by people who believe that they happened.

Another urban legend that has made the rounds is the "Kentucky Fried Rat."

> One night, a woman didn't have anything ready for supper, so she and her husband went to the drive-through at Kentucky Fried Chicken. While they were eating in their car, the wife said, "My chicken tastes funny."
>
> Her husband said, "You're always complaining about something." When she insisted that the chicken didn't taste right, he put on the light. She was holding fried rat—crispy style. The woman went into shock and was rushed to the hospital.
>
> A lawyer from the company offered them $100,000 if they will sign a release and not tell anyone. This is the second case they have had.

Folklorist Jan Brunvand (1981, 1984, 1986) reported that urban legends are passed on by people who think that the event happened just one or two people down the line of transmission, often to a "friend of a friend." The story has strong appeal and gains credibility from naming specific people or local places. Brunvand views urban legends as "modern morality stories," with each teaching a moral lesson about life.

If we apply Brunvand's analysis to these two urban legends, three major points emerge. First, their moral serves as a warning. "The Hook" warns young people that they

fashion: a pattern of behavior that catches people's attention, which lasts longer than a fad

urban legend: a story with an ironic twist that sounds realistic but is false

should be careful about where they go, with whom they go, and what they do. The world is an unsafe place, and "messing around" is risky. "The Kentucky Fried Rat" contains a different moral: Do you *really* know what you are eating when you buy food from a fast-food outlet? Maybe you should eat at home, where you know what you are getting.

Second, each story is related to social change: "The Hook" to changing sexual morality; the "Kentucky Fried Rat" to changing male–female relationships, especially to changing sex roles at home. Third, each is calculated to instill guilt and fear: guilt—the wife failed in her traditional role of cooking supper, and she gets punished—and fear, the dangerous unknown, whether the dark countryside or fast food. The ultimate moral of these stories is that we should not abandon traditional roles or the safety of the home.

These principles can be applied to an urban legend that made the rounds in the late 1980s. I heard several versions of this one, each narrator swearing that it had just happened to a friend of a friend.

> Jerry (or whoever) went to a night club last weekend. He met a good-looking woman, and they hit it off. They spent the night in a motel, and when he awoke the next morning, the woman was gone. When he went into the bathroom, he saw a message scrawled on the mirror in lipstick: "Welcome to the wonderful world of AIDS."

SOCIAL MOVEMENTS

*W*HEN THE NAZIS, A SMALL GROUP *of malcontents in Bavaria, first appeared on the scene in the 1920s, their ideas appeared laughable to the world. They believed that the Germans were a race of supermen* (Übermenschen) *who would launch a Third Reich (rule or nation) that would control the world for a thousand years. Their race destined them for greatness, lesser races to their service and exploitation.*

From a little band of comic characters who looked as though they had stepped out of a grade B movie, the Nazis gained such power that they threatened the existence of Western civilization. How could a little man with a grotesque moustache, surrounded by a few sycophants in brown shirts, ever come to threaten the world? Such things don't happen in real life—only in novels or movies, the deranged nightmare of some imaginative author. Only this was real life, the Nazi appearance on the human scene causing the deaths of millions of people and changing the course of world history.

How could this have happened? Social movements, the second major topic of this chapter, hold the answer. **Social movements** consist of large numbers of people who organize to promote or resist social change. They have strong ideas about what is wrong with the world—or some part of it—and how to make things right. Examples include the abolitionist (anti-slavery) crusade, the civil rights movement, the white supremacist movement, the women's movement, the animal rights crusade, the nuclear freeze movement, and the environmental movement.

At the heart of social movements lie grievances and dissatisfactions. For some people, a current condition of society is intolerable, and their goal is to *promote* social change. Theirs is called a **proactive social movement.** In contrast, others feel threatened because some condition of society is changing, and they organize to *resist* that change. Theirs is a **reactive social movement.**

To further their goals, people develop **social movement organizations.** Those whose goal is to promote social change develop such organizations as the National Organization for Women (NOW) and the National Association for the Advancement of Colored People (NAACP). In contrast, for those who are trying to resist these changes, the Stop-ERA and the Ku Klux Klan serve the same purpose. To recruit followers and sympathizers, leaders of social movements use various attention-getting devices, from marches and protest rallies to sit-ins and boycotts. To publicize their grievances, they also may try to stage "media events." Some do so very effectively (see the Perspectives box).

social movement: a large group of people who are organized to promote or resist social change

proactive social movement: a social movement that promotes some social change

reactive social movement: a social movement that resists some social change

social movement organization: an organization developed to further the goals of a social movement

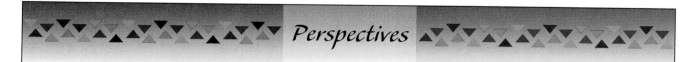

Perspectives

CULTURAL DIVERSITY IN THE UNITED STATES

The Million-Man March: Another Step in an Unfinished Social Movement

The Civil Rights Movement of the 1950s and 1960s did not end in the year 1970. This movement brought huge gains: integrated public facilities, schools, voting booths, housing, and workplaces. Or, rather, the right to such aspects of social life, for they always seemed to be elusive, to somehow disappear just when they seemingly were on the verge of being fulfilled.

The inner city, with all of its ills, from unemployment to violent crime, has become the single most powerful symbol that this social movement is unfinished. The nightly headlines not only nurture the fears of both African Americans and whites—and of everyone else—but also proclaim the unfinished nature of the Civil Rights Movement.

The Million-Man March—consisting of thousands of African-American males from all over the country who gathered on the Mall in Washington, D.C., in the fall of 1995—picked up where this movement stalled. It had two essential features. The first is an outward direction: protest at continued obstacles; the insistence that the walls of racism come down; voter registration drives; a sense of optimism and determination that good can be accomplished. And overriding all else, a sense of black unity arising from twin sources—shared pain and a glimpse of a promising future.

This first feature is a direct reflection of the old Civil Rights Movement.

The second feature, an inward-turning, is a redirecting of the Civil Rights Movement. It is a conservative, proactive stance, a desire by African Americans to make changes in the African-American community. As stressed by the march's organizers, this feature underscores the need to build greater respect between men and women, to reduce spouse abuse, and to assume the obligations of fatherhood—including marriage, nurturing and supporting one's children, and giving them a positive role model of responsible masculinity (Whetstone 1996).

This desire for inward change, to be manifested in personal relationships, reflects the religious orientation of the March's organizers. The emphases are on repentance, atonement, and changed behavior. Although a religious orientation to the Civil Rights Movement is not new— for central to this movement has been a dedication to religious principles motivated by moral outrage over grievous wrongs—this inward direction of the religious orientation is new.

The Million-Man March, then, did not begin with a figurative march to Washington. Nor did it end with the departure of the buses. Rather, the March is one facet of an interrupted social movement—one destined to take other forms in the future, for its goals have been but partially reached.

Social movements are like a rolling sea, says sociologist Mayer Zald (1992). During one period of time, few social movements appear, but shortly afterward a wave of them rolls in, each competing for the public's attention. Zald suggests that a *cultural crisis* can give birth to a wave of social movements. By this, he means that there are times when a society's institutions fail to keep up with social change, many people's needs go unfulfilled, massive unrest follows, and social movements spring into action to bridge this gap.

Types and Tactics of Social Movements

Let's see what types of social movements there are and then examine their tactics.

Types of Social Movements

Since social change is always their goal, we can classify social movements according to their *target* and the *amount of change* they seek. Figure 21.2 on the next page summarizes the classification developed by sociologist David Aberle (1966). If you read across, you will see that the target of the first two types of social movements is *individuals*. **Alterative social movements** seek only to *alter* some particular behavior of people. An example is a powerful social movement of the early 1900s, the Women's Christian Temperance

alterative social movement: a social movement that seeks to alter only particular aspects of people

Figure 21.2

Types of Social Movements

Amount of Change

	Partial	Total
Individual	Alterative 1	Redemptive 2
Society	3 Reformative	4 Transformative

Target of Change

Source: Aberle 1966.

redemptive social movement: a social movement that seeks to change people totally

reformative social movement: a social movement that seeks to change only particular aspects of society

transformative social movement: a social movement that seeks to change society totally

millenarian movement: a social movement based on the prophecy of coming social upheaval

cargo cult: a social movement in which South Pacific islanders destroyed their possessions in the anticipation that their ancestors would send items by ship

Social movements involve large numbers of people who, upset about some condition in society, organize to do something about it. Shown here is Carrie Nation, a temperance leader who in 1900 began to break up saloons with a hatchet. Her social movement eventually became so popular that it resulted in Prohibition.

Union (WCTU), whose goal was to get people to stop drinking alcohol. Its members were convinced that if they could close the saloons such problems as poverty and spouse abuse would go away. **Redemptive social movements** also target individuals, but here the aim is for *total* change. An example is a religious social movement that stresses conversion. In fundamentalist Christianity, for example, when someone converts to Christ, the entire person is supposed to change, not just some specific behavior. Self-centered acts are to be replaced by loving behaviors toward others as the convert becomes, in their terms, a "new creation."

The target of the next two types of social movements is *society*. **Reformative social movements** seek to *reform* some specific aspect of society. The environmental movement, for example, seeks to reform the ways society treats the environment, from its disposal of garbage and nuclear wastes to its use of forests and water. **Transformative social movements,** in contrast, seek to *transform* the social order itself and to replace it with a new version of the good society. Revolutions, such as those in the American colonies, France, Russia, and Cuba, are examples.

One of the more interesting examples of transformative social movements is **millenarian movements,** which are based on prophecies of coming calamity. Of particular interest is a type of millenarian movement called a **cargo cult** (Worsley 1957). About one hundred years ago, Europeans colonized the Melanesian Islands of the South Pacific. From the home countries of the colonizers arrived ship after ship, each loaded with items the Melanesians had never seen. As the Melanesians watched the cargo being unloaded, they expected some of it to go to them. They noted, however, that it all went to the Europeans. Melanesian prophets then revealed the secret of this exotic merchandise. Their own ancestors were manufacturing and sending the cargos to them, but the colonists were intercepting the merchandise. Since the colonists were too strong to fight, and too selfish to share the cargo, there was little the Melanesians could do.

Then came a remarkable self-fulfilling prophecy. Melanesian prophets revealed that if the people would destroy their crops and food and build harbors, their ancestors would see their sincerity and send the cargo directly to them. The Melanesians did so. When the colonial administrators of the island saw that the natives had destroyed their crops and were just sitting in the hills waiting for the cargo ships to arrive, they informed the home government. The prospect of thousands of islanders patiently starving to death was too horrifying to allow, and the British government sent ships to the islands with cargo earmarked for the Melanesians.

A new twist in social movements is the global orientation of some. Rather than focusing on changing a condition within a specific country, the goal is to change this condition throughout the world. The women's, environmental, and animal rights movements are examples. Because of this new focus, some sociologists refer to them as **new social movements** (McAdam et al. 1988).

Tactics of Social Movements

The leaders of a social movement can choose from a variety of tactics. Should they peacefully boycott, march, or hold an all-night candle-lit vigil? Or should they bomb a building, blow up an airplane, or assassinate a key figure? To understand why the leaders of social movements choose their tactics, we need to examine a group's levels of membership, the publics it addresses, and its relationship to authorities.

Levels of Membership. Figure 21.3 shows the composition of social movements. Beginning at the center and moving outward are three levels of membership. At the center is the inner core, those people most committed to the movement. This inner core sets the group's goals, timetables, strategies, and inspires the other members. Those at the second level are also committed to the movement, but somewhat less so than the inner core. People at this level, however, can be counted on to show up for demonstrations and to do the grunt work—to do mailings, pass out petitions and leaflets, make telephone calls. At the third level is a wider circle of people who are less committed and less dependable. Their participation is primarily a matter of convenience. If an activity does not interfere with something else they want to do, they participate.

The predispositions and backgrounds of the inner core are essential in the choice of tactics. Because of their background, the inner core of some groups is predisposed to use peaceful means, others confrontational, while still others prefer violence. Tactics also depend on the number of committed members. Different tactics are called for if the inner core can count on seven hundred—or only seven—committed members to show up.

The Publics. Lying outside the membership is the **public,** a dispersed group of people who usually have an interest in the issue. Just outside the third circle of members, and blending into it, is the sympathetic public. Although their sympathies lie with the move-

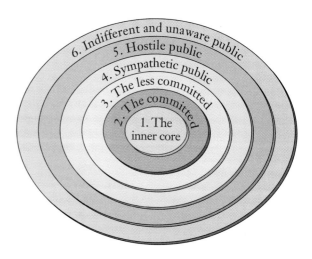

Figure 21.3

The Membership and Publics of Social Movements

new social movements: social movements with a new emphasis on the world, instead of on a condition in a specific country

public: a dispersed group of people who usually have an interest in the issue on which a social movement focuses; the sympathetic and hostile publics have such an interest, but a third public is either unaware of the issue or indifferent to it

Activists in social movements become committed to "the cause." The social movement around abortion, currently one of the most dynamic in the United States, has split Americans, is highly visible, and has articulate spokespeople on both sides.

ment, these people have no commitment to it. Sympathy with the movement's goals, however, makes this public fertile ground for recruiting new members. The second public is hostile; it is keenly aware of the group's goals and dislikes them. This public wants to stop the social movement, for the movement's values go against its own. The third public consists of disinterested people. They are either unaware of the social movement, or if aware, indifferent to it.

In selecting tactics, the leadership pays attention to these publics. The sympathetic public is especially significant as it is the source of new members and support at the ballot box. Tactics that appear likely to alienate the sympathetic public will be avoided, while tactics will be chosen if they look as though they will elicit greater sympathy from this group. The leadership may even force a confrontation with the hostile public, trying to make itself appear a victim, a group whose rights are being trampled on. Tactics directed toward the unaware or indifferent public are designed to neutralize their indifference and increase their awareness.

Relationship to Authorities.   The movement's relationship to authorities is also significant in determining tactics—especially in choosing peaceful or violent tactics. If a social movement is *institutionalized*, accepted by authorities, violence will not be directed against the authorities, for they are on the same side. This, however, does not rule out violence directed against the opposition. If authorities are hostile to a social movement, aggressive or even violent tactics are more likely. For example, since the goal of a transformative (revolutionary) social movement is to replace the government, the movement and the government are clearly on a collision course.

Other Factors.   Sociologist Ellen Scott (1993), who studied the movement to stop rape, discovered that close friendships, race, and even size of town are important in determining tactics. Women in Santa Cruz, California, chose to directly confront accused rapists, to publicly humiliate them. The tactic worked because the town was smaller (41,000). Women in Washington, D.C., rejected confrontation because in their larger

The social movement to stop violence against women has had a major impact on our thinking about gender relations, laws, and law enforcement. Discussed in the text are social factors that underlie the choice of tactics used by women's centers. Shown here are the Purple Berets in Santa Rosa, California, who are protesting against county officials for wanting to treat spouse abuse as a counseling problem instead of a criminal problem.

city (640,000) anonymity reduced its effectiveness. In addition, both groups of women were white, and in Santa Cruz it was white women confronting white men, but in Washington, D.C., it would have been white women confronting black men. Finally, hostile public confrontations require a closely working team of people who will back each other up. In Santa Cruz, the women lived together for years, while the group in Washington, D.C., is a more formal organization.

As movement leaders fear, tactics may backfire, which is what happened in Santa Cruz. Workers from the center hung around town the picture of a man accused of rape. He sued. The long litigation that followed sapped the women's energy, and the Santa Cruz center folded.

The Mass Media: Gatekeepers to Social Movements

In selecting tactics, the leaders of social movements are keenly aware of their effects on the mass media (Zald 1992). Their goal is to influence **public opinion,** how people think about some issue. The right kind of publicity enables them to arouse the sympathetic public and to lay the groundwork for recruiting a wider membership. Pictures of bloodied, dead baby seals, for example, go a long way to getting the group's message across.

A key to understanding social movements, then, is **propaganda.** Although this word often evokes negative images, it actually is neutral. Propaganda is simply the presentation of information in the attempt to influence people. Its original meaning was positive, for *propaganda* referred to a committee of cardinals of the Roman Catholic church whose assignment was the care of foreign missions. (They were to *propagate* the faith.) The term has traveled a long way since then, however, and today it usually refers to a one-sided presentation of information that distorts reality.

Propaganda, then, in the sense of organized attempts to manipulate public opinion, is a regular part of modern life. Advertisements, for example, are a form of propaganda, for they present a one-sided version of reality. Underlying effective propaganda are seven

public opinion: how people think about some issue

propaganda: in its broad sense, the presentation of information in the attempt to influence people; in its narrow sense, one-sided information used to try to influence people

The use of propaganda is popular among those committed to the goals of a social movement. They can see only one side to the social issue about which they are so upset. Do you think there is another side to this social issue?

basic techniques, discussed in the Down-to-Earth Sociology box below. Perhaps by understanding these techniques, you will be able to resist one-sided appeals—whether they come from social movements or from hawkers of some new product.

The mass media play a crucial role in social movements. They have become, in effect, the gatekeepers to social movements. If those who control and work in the mass media—from owners to reporters—are sympathetic to some particular "cause," you can be sure that it receives sympathetic treatment. If the social movement goes against their biases, it will either be ignored or receive unfavorable treatment. If you ever get the impression that the U.S. media are trying to manipulate your opinions and attitudes on some particular social movement—or some social issue—you probably are right. Far from doing unbiased reporting, the media are under the control and influence of people who have an agenda to get across. To the materials in the Down-to-Earth Sociology box on

Down-to-Earth Sociology

"Tricks of the Trade"—The Fine Art of Propaganda

Sociologists Alfred and Elizabeth Lee (1939) found that propaganda relies on seven basic techniques, which they termed "tricks of the trade." To be effective, the techniques should be subtle, with the audience remaining unaware of just which part of their mind or emotions is being manipulated. If propaganda is effective, people will not know *why* they support something, only that they do—as they fervently defend it.

1. *Name calling.* This technique aims to arouse opposition to the competing product, candidate, or policy by associating it with a negative image. By comparison, one's own product, candidate, or policy appears attractive. Political candidates who call an opponent "soft on crime" are using this technique.

2. *Glittering generality.* Essentially the opposite of the first, this technique surrounds the product, candidate, or policy with "virtue words," phrases that arouse positive feelings. "She's a *real* Democrat" has little meaning, but it makes the audience feel that something has been said. "He stands for individualism" is so general that it is meaningless, yet the audience thinks that it has heard a specific message about the candidate.

3. *Transfer.* In its positive form, this technique associates the product, candidate, or policy with something that the public respects or approves; in its negative form, with something of which it disapproves. Let's look at the positive form: You might not be able to get by with saying, "Coors is patriotic," but surround a beer with the U.S. flag, and beer drinkers will get the idea that it is more patriotic to drink this brand of beer than another.

4. *Testimonials.* Famous and admired individuals are used to endorse a product, candidate, or policy. Michael Jordan lends his name to cologne, Nike products, and even underwear, while Candace Bergen does

the same for Sprint. Candidates for political office solicit the endorsement of movie stars—who may know next to nothing about the candidate, or even about politics itself. In the negative form of this technique, a despised person is associated with the competing product. If propagandists could get away with it, they would show Saddam Hussein drinking a competing beer or announcing support for an opposing candidate.

5. *Plain folks.* Sometimes it pays to associate the product, candidate, or policy with "just plain folks." "If Mary or John Q. Public like it, you will, too." A political candidate who kisses babies, dons a hard hat, and has lunch at McDonald's while photographers "catch him or her in the act"—is using the "plain folks" strategy. "I'm just a regular person," is the message of the presidential candidate posing for photographers in jeans and work shirt—while making certain that the Mercedes and chauffeur do not show up in the background.

6. *Card stacking.* The aim of this technique is to present only positive information about what you support, only negative information about what you oppose. Make it sound as though there is only one conclusion that a rational person can draw. Use falsehoods, distortions, and illogical statements if you must.

7. *Bandwagon.* "Everyone is doing it" is the idea behind this technique. Emphasizing how many others buy the product or support the candidate or policy conveys the message that anyone who doesn't join in is on the wrong track. After all, "20 million Frenchmen can't be wrong," can they?

The Lees (1939) added, "Once we know that a speaker or writer is using one of these propaganda devices in an attempt to convince us of an idea, we can separate the device from the idea and see what the idea amounts to on its own merits."

propaganda, then, we need to add the biases of the media establishment, the issues to which it chooses to give publicity, those it ignores, and its favorable and unfavorable treatment of issues and movements.

Sociology can be a liberating discipline (Berger 1963). It sensitizes us to the existence of *multiple realities;* that is, for any single point of view on some topic, there likely are competing points of view, which some find equally as compelling. Each represents reality as the individual sees it, but different experiences lead to different perceptions. Consequently, although the committed members of a social movement are sincere, and perhaps even sacrificing for "the cause," theirs is but one view of the way the world is. If other sides were presented, the issue would look quite different.

Why People Join Social Movements

As we have seen, social movements arise from widespread, deeply felt discontent, from the conviction that some condition of society is no longer tolerable. Not everyone, however, who feels strongly dissatisfied about an issue joins a social movement. Let's look at three explanations that explain why some people join social movements.

Mass Society Theory

To explain why people are attracted to social movements, sociologist William Kornhauser (1959) proposed **mass society theory.** Kornhauser argued that **mass society**—an impersonal, industrialized, highly bureaucratized society—makes many people feel isolated. Social movements fill a void by offering people a sense of belonging. In geographical areas where social ties are supposedly weaker, such as the western United States, one would then expect to find more social movements than in areas where traditional ties are supposedly stronger, such as in the Midwest and South.

This theory seems to match commonsense observations. Certainly, social movements seem to proliferate on the West Coast. But sociologist Doug McAdam (1988), who interviewed people who had risked their lives in the civil rights movement, found that these people were firmly rooted in families and communities. It was their strong desire to right wrongs and to overcome injustices, not their isolation, that motivated their participation. Even the Nazis attracted many people firmly rooted in their communities (Oberschall 1973). Finally, those most isolated of all, the homeless, generally do not join anything—except food lines.

Deprivation Theory

A second explanation to account for why people join social movements is *deprivation theory.* According to this theory, people who are deprived of things deemed valuable in society—whether money, justice, status, or privilege—join social movements with the hope of redressing their grievances. This theory may seem so obvious as to need no evidence. Aren't the thousands of African Americans who participated in the civil rights movement of the 1950s and the World War I soldiers who marched on Washington after Congress refused to pay their promised bonuses ample evidence that the theory is true?

Deprivation theory does provide a beginning point. But there is more to the matter than this. We must also pay attention to what Alexis de Tocqueville (1856/1955) noted almost 150 years ago. The peasants of Germany were worse off than the peasants of France, and from deprivation theory we would expect the Germans to have rebelled and to have overthrown their king. Revolution, however, occurred in France, not Germany. The reason, said de Tocqueville, is *relative* deprivation. French peasants had experienced improving living conditions, and could imagine even better conditions, while German peasants, having never experienced anything but depressed conditions, had no comparative basis for feeling deprived.

mass society theory: an explanation for participation in social movements based on the assumption that such movements offer a sense of belonging to people who have weak social ties

mass society: industrialized, highly bureaucratized, impersonal society

Militias—*citizens who arm themselves and form paramilitary organizations—have sprung up across the United States. The most well known is the Michigan Militia, shown here. Although all the theories discussed in the text may apply to members of these militias, those that deal with moral issues and ideological commitment are especially relevant.*

According to **relative deprivation theory,** then, it is not people's actual negative conditions (their *absolute* deprivation) that matters. Rather, the key to participation is *relative* deprivation—that is, what people *think* they should have relative to what others have, or even compared with their own past or perceived future. This theory, which has provided excellent insight into revolutions, also holds a surprise. Because improving conditions fuel human desires for even better conditions, in some instances *improving* conditions can spark revolutions.

What about the civil rights movement of the 1950s and 1960s? At the center of the sit-ins in the South were relatively well-off African Americans. It was college students, Boy Scouts, and leaders of the churches who went to restaurants and lunch counters reserved for whites, and who when refused service sat peacefully while abuse and even food were heaped on them (Morris 1993). What is significant for this theory, however, is the people with whom one compares oneself. The sit-ins were a form of rebellion against the white establishment, and compared with whites these demonstrators felt quite deprived.

Another example from this same social movement, however, offers greater challenge to this theory, for many of the later demonstrators who risked their lives in marches and other protests were white, middle-class college students from the North (McAdam 1988; Fendrich and Lovoy 1993). This is an example of people whose own personal welfare is not at stake who become active in social movements for *moral* reasons, a motivation to which we shall now turn.

Moral Issues and Ideological Commitment

As sociologists James Jasper and Dorothy Nelkin (1992) point out, we would miss the basic reason for many people's involvement in social movements if we overlooked the moral issue. Some people join because of *moral shock*—a sense of outrage at finding out what is "really" going on (Jasper and Poulsen 1995). For people who see a social movement in moral terms, great issues hang in the balance. They feel they must choose sides and do what they can to make a difference. As sociologists put it, they join because of *ideological commitment* to the movement. Many members on both sides of the abortion issue see their involvement in such terms. Similarly, most activists in the animal rights movement are convinced that there can be no justification for animals to suffer in order to make safer products for humans. Some see nuclear weapons and power in similar moral terms, and they risk arrest and ridicule for their participation in demonstrations. For others, matters of the environment are moral issues, and to not act would be an inexcusable betrayal of future generations. The *moral* component of a social movement, then, is a primary reason for some people's involvement.

relative deprivation theory: in this context, the belief that people join social movements based on their evaluations of what they think they should have compared with what others have

A Special Case: The Agent Provocateur

A unique type of social movement participant is the **agent provocateur,** an agent of the government or even of a rival social movement, whose job is to spy on the leadership and perhaps to sabotage their activities. Some are recruited from the membership itself, traitors to the organization for a few Judas dollars, while others are members of the police or a rival group who go underground and join the movement.

Since the social change that some social movements represent is radical, threatening the power elite, the use of agent provocateurs is not surprising. What may be surprising, however, is that some agents are converted to the social movement on which they are spying. Sociologist Gary Marx (1993) explains that to be credible, agents must share at least some of the class, age, gender, ethnic, racial, or religious characteristics of the group. This, however, makes the agents more likely to sympathize with the movement's goals and to become disenchanted with trying to harm the group. Also, to be effective, agents must work their way into the center of the group. This requires frequent interaction with the group's committed members, which tends to produce liking. In addition, while they build trust they may be cut off from their own group. The point of view they represent may recede, and concerns about betraying and deceiving people who now trust them may creep in.

What also may be surprising is how far some agents go. During the 1960s, when a wave of militant social movements rolled across the United States, the FBI and other police were busy recruiting agent provocateurs. To sabotage groups, these agents provoked illegal activities that otherwise would not have occurred, setting the leadership up for arrest, and in some instances, even death. Three examples will let us see how agent provocateurs operate (Marx 1993). A student at Northeastern Illinois University who proposed schemes for sabotaging public facilities and was suspended for two semesters for throwing the school's president off the stage turned out to be a police agent. One of the four men involved in a plot to blow up the Statue of Liberty by a small New York group called the Black Liberation Front was an undercover agent. It was he who drew up the plans and even provided funds to pay for the dynamite and rent the car. Finally, the FBI reportedly paid $36,500 to two members of the White Knights of the Ku Klux Klan to arrange for two other Klansmen to bomb a Jewish businessman's home. A trap was set in which one Klansman was killed and another arrested in the unsuccessful attempt.

▼ **In Sum** Recruitment generally follows channels of social networks. Perhaps most commonly, people join a social movement because they have friends and acquaintances already in the movement (McCarthy and Wolfson 1992; Snow et al. 1993). Some join because of moral convictions, others to further their own careers, because it is fun, or because they achieve recognition or find a valued identity. Some participate even though they *don't want to.* The Cuban government, for example, compels people to turn out for mass demonstrations to show support of the Communist regime (Aguirre 1993). As we just saw, police officials may join social movements in order to spy on them and sabotage their activities. In no social movement, then, is there a single cause for people joining. As in all other activities in life, people remain a complex bundle of motivations—which provides a challenge to sociologists to unravel.

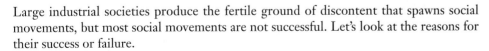

On the Success and Failure of Social Movements

Large industrial societies produce the fertile ground of discontent that spawns social movements, but most social movements are not successful. Let's look at the reasons for their success or failure.

The Life Course of Social Movements

Social movements have a life course; that is, they go through different stages as they grow and mature. Sociologists have identified five stages of social movements (Lang and Lang 1961; Mauss 1975; Spector and Kitsuse 1977; Tilly 1978; Jasper 1991).

agent provocateur: someone who joins a group in order to spy on it and to sabotage it by *provoking* its members to commit illegal acts

1. *Initial unrest and agitation.* During this first stage, people are upset about some condition in society and want to change it. Leaders emerge who verbalize people's feelings and crystallize issues. Most social movements fail at this stage. Unable to gain enough support, after a brief flurry of activity they quietly die.

2. *Resource mobilization.* The crucial factor that enables social movements to make it past the first stage is **resource mobilization.** By this term, sociologists mean the mobilization of resources such as time, money, people's skills, technologies such as direct mailing and fax machines, attention by the mass media, and even legitimacy among the public and authorities (Oliver and Marwell 1992; Buechler 1993). In some cases, an indigenous leadership arises to mobilize available resources. Other groups, having no capable leadership of their own, turn to outsiders, "specialists for hire." As sociologists John McCarthy and Mayer Zald (1977; Zald and McCarthy 1987) point out, even though large numbers of people may be upset over some condition of society, without resource mobilization they are only upset people, perhaps even agitators, but not a social movement.

3. *Organization.* A division of labor is set up. The leadership makes policy decisions, and the rank and file carry out the daily tasks necessary to keep the movement going. There is still much collective excitement about the issue, the movement's focal point of concern.

4. *Institutionalization.* At this stage, a movement has developed a bureaucracy, the type of formal hierarchy described in Chapter 7. The collective excitement is gone, and control lies in the hands of career officers, who may care more about their own position in the organization than the movement for which the organization's initial leaders made sacrifices. They may move the group's headquarters to a "good" location, for example, furnish it with expensive furniture and art work, and take pains to be seen with the "right" people in the "right" places.

5. *Organizational decline and possible resurgence.* At this point, the organization may decline, for instead of working on the issues, the leadership may waste its energies on managing a bloated bureaucracy. Or, a change in public sentiment may so dominate the society that most members jump ship, leaving the leaders with few to lead. With no strong, committed group united by a common cause, the movement may wither away and finally disappear. Its diehards always linger, grasping at any straw in hope that there may be a resurgence.

And appearances can be deceiving. Even if most participants desert and those most committed flounder with little support, this does not necessarily mean the end of a movement. After suffragists won the right to vote in 1920 (discussed on pages 292-293), their movement declined until nothing but a shell remained. During a period researchers call *abeyance*, only a handful of committed organizers were left, and the best they could do was to desperately keep the flame burning. Yet, the women's movement was reenergized, and again thrust into national prominence (Taylor 1997).

As discussed in the following Thinking Critically section, the social movement surrounding abortion has also undergone resurgence.

Thinking Critically About Social Controversy

Which Side of the Barricades?
Prochoice and Prolife as a Social Movement

▼ No issue so divides Americans as abortion does. Although most Americans take a more moderate view, on one side are some who feel that abortion should be permitted under any circumstances, even during the last month of pregnancy. They are matched by some on the

resource mobilization: a theory that social movements succeed or fail based on their ability to mobilize resources such as time, money, and people's skills

other side who are convinced that abortion should never be allowed, not even during the first month of pregnancy. This polarization constantly breathes new life into the movement.

When the U.S. Supreme Court determined in its 1973 decision, *Roe v. Wade*, that states could not restrict abortion, the prochoice side relaxed. Victory was theirs, and they thought their opponents would quietly disappear. Instead, large numbers of Americans were disturbed by what they saw as the legal right to murder unborn children.

The views of the two sides could not be more incompatible. Those who favor choice view the 1.5 million abortions performed annually in the United States as examples of women exercising their basic reproductive rights. Those who gather under the prolife banner see them as legalized murder. To the prochoice side, those who oppose abortion are blocking women's rights, forcing women to continue pregnancies they desire to terminate. To the prolife forces, those who advocate choice are seen as condoning murder, of putting their own desires for school, career, or convenience ahead of the lives of their unborn children.

There is no way to reconcile such contrary views. Each sees the other as unreasonable and extremist. And each uses propaganda by focusing on worst-case scenarios: prochoice images of young women, raped at gunpoint, forced to bear the children of rapists; prolife images of women who are eight months pregnant killing their babies instead of nurturing them.

With no middle ground, these views are in permanent conflict. As each side fights for what it considers basic rights, it reinvigorates the other. When in 1989 the U.S. Supreme Court decided in *Webster v. Reproductive Services* that states could restrict abortion, one side hailed it as a defeat, the other as a victory. Seeing the political battle going against them, the prochoice side regrouped for a determined struggle. The prolife side, sensing judicial victory within its grasp, gathered forces to push for a complete overthrow of *Roe v. Wade*.

This goal of the prolife side came close to becoming reality in *Casey v. Planned Parenthood*. On June 30, 1992, in a 6-to-3 decision the Supreme Court upheld the right of states to require women to wait 24 hours between the confirmation of pregnancy and abortion, girls under 18 to obtain the consent of one parent, and women to be informed about alternatives to abortion and to be given materials that describe the fetus. In the same case, by a 5-to-4 decision, the Court ruled that a wife does not have to inform her husband if she intends to have an abortion.

Because the two sides see reality in such contrasting ways, this social movement cannot end unless the vast majority of Americans commit to one side or the other. Otherwise, all legislative and judicial outcomes—whether the overthrow of *Roe v. Wade* or such extremes as a constitutional amendment declaring abortion either murder or a woman's right—are victories to one and defeats to the other. Nothing, then, to such committed activists is ever complete. Rather, each action is only a way station in a prolonged, bitter, moral struggle.

For Your Consideration

Typically, the last stage of a social movement is decline. Why does this last stage not apply to this social movement? Under what conditions will this social movement decline?

The longer the pregnancy, the smaller the proportion of Americans who approve abortion. Does your opinion about abortion change depending on the length of pregnancy? For example, how do you feel about abortion during the second month versus the eighth month? What do you think of abortion in cases of rape and incest? Or partial–birth abortion? Can you identify some of the *social* reasons that underlie your opinions?

Sources: Neikirk and Elsasser 1992; McKenna 1995; Williams 1995; Henslin 1996; *Statistical Abstract* 1997:Table 114. ▲

The Difficult Road to Success

Despite their significance in contemporary society, social movements seldom solve social problems. Resource mobilization helps to explain why. To mobilize resources, a movement must appeal to a broad constituency. This means that the group must focus on large-scale issues, which are deeply embedded in society. For example, the fact that workers at one particular plant are upset about their low wages is not adequate to recruit the broad support necessary for a social movement. At best, it will result in local agitation. The low wages and unsafe working conditions of millions of workers, however, have a chance of becoming the focal point of a social movement.

By their nature, such broad problems are entrenched in society and not easy to solve. They require more than merely tinkering with some small part. Just as the problem touches many interrelated components of society, so the solutions require changes in those many parts. With no quick-fix available, the social movement must stay around. But longevity brings its own danger of failure, for as noted, social movements tend to become bureaucratized, to turn inward and to focus their energies on running the organization.

Many social movements, however, do vitally affect society. Some become powerful forces for social change. They highlight problems and turn the society on a path that solves the problem. Others become powerful forces in resisting the social change that its members—and the public it is able to mobilize—consider undesirable. In either case, social movements are highly significant for contemporary society, and we can anticipate that new ones will be a regular feature of our social landscape.

Summary and Review

Early Explanations of Collective Behavior

How did early theorists explain the effects of crowds on individuals?

Early theorists argued that individuals are transformed by crowds. Charles Mackay used the term *herd mentality* to explain why people did wild things when they were in crowds. Gustave LeBon said that a **collective mind** develops, and people are swept away by suggestions. Robert Park said that collective unrest develops, which, fed by a **circular reaction**, leads to collective impulses. Pp. 592–593.

What stages of crowd behavior are there?

Herbert Blumer identified five stages that crowds go through before they become an **acting crowd:** social unrest, an exciting event, **milling,** a common object of attention, and common impulses. Pp. 594–595.

The Contemporary View of Collective Behavior

What is the current view of crowd behavior?

Current theorists view crowds as rational. Richard Berk stresses a **minimax strategy;** that is, people try to minimize their costs and maximize their rewards, whether or not they are in crowds. Ralph Turner and Lewis Killian analyze how new norms emerge that allow people to do things in crowds that they otherwise would not do. Pp. 595–596.

Forms of Collective Behavior

What forms of collective behavior are there?

Some of the major forms of collective behavior are **lynchings, riots, panics, moral panics, rumors, fads, fashions,** and **urban legends.** Conditions of discontent or uncertainty provide fertile ground for collective behavior, and each form provides a way of dealing with these conditions. Pp. 596–602.

Types and Tactics of Social Movements

What types of social movements are there?

Social movements consist of large numbers of people who organize to promote or resist social change. Depending on their target (individuals or society) and the amount of social change desired (partial or complete), social movements can be classified as **alterative, redemptive, reformative,** and **transformative.** Pp. 602–605.

How do social movements select their tactics?

Tactics are chosen on the basis of a group's levels of membership, its publics, and its relationship to authorities. The three levels of membership are *the inner core, the committed,* and *the less committed.* The predispositions of the inner core are crucial in choosing tactics, but so is the public they wish to address. If relationships with authorities are bad, the chances of aggressive or violent tactics increase. Friendship, size of city, and the race of movement participants and their targets may also be significant. Pp. 605–607.

How are the mass media related to social movements?

Because the mass media are gatekeepers for social movements, their favorable or unfavorable coverage greatly affecting a social movement, tactics are chosen with the media in mind. Social movements also make use of **propaganda** to further their cause. Pp. 607–609.

Why People Join Social Movements

Why do people join social movements?

There is no single, overriding reason why people join social movements. According to **mass society theory,** social movements relieve feelings of isolation created by an impersonal, bureaucratized society. According to **relative deprivation theory,** people join movements in order to address their grievances. Morality, values, and ideological commitment also motivate people to join social movements. The **agent provocateur** illustrates that even people who hate a cause can end up participating in it. Pp. 609–611.

On the Success and Failure of Social Movements

Why do social movements succeed or fail?

Social movements go through several stages—initial unrest and agitation, mobilization, organization, institutionaliza-

tion, and, finally, organizational decline and possible resurgence. Groups that appeal to few people cannot succeed. But to appeal broadly in order to accomplish **resource mobilization,** the movement must focus on very broad concerns, problems deeply embedded in society, which also makes success extremely difficult. Pp. 611–614.

Where can I read more on this topic?

Suggested readings for this chapter are listed on page 666.

Sociology and the Internet

All URLs listed are current as of the printing of this book. URLs are often changed. Please check our Website http://www.abacon.com/henslin for updates.

1. As you discovered in reading this chapter, riots are a form of collective behavior. The nation's most destructive riot up to the time this book was written occurred in Los Angeles in 1992. Because of the extensive media coverage it received, the event can be analyzed using secondary sources.

Access the Hubert H. Humphrey Institute of Public Affairs at *http://www.hhh.umn.edu/pubpol/pubpol_d/9505/0018. html* You should now be in the Institute's "Pubpol Archive." The topic heading should read "L.A. Riots: Q 0) Conference Instructions (Repost)." When you have read the page, click on "Thread." As you travel through the discussion, watch for "next message" and "previous message." Follow these as you study the exchanges.

Your assignment will be to write a paper in which you apply the theories discussed in this chapter to the Los Angeles riot. For Blumer's theory, what evidence is there that general social unrest preceded the riot? What was the "exiting event"? Is there evidence of crowd milling? Can you find a common object of attention and common crowd impulses? For Richard Burke's theory of collective behavior as calculated, rational action, is there evidence of people balancing the rewards and costs of becoming involved? Now consider emergent norm theory. Is there evidence that the participants had different motives for their involvement? Or was everyone simply angry over the precipitating event? How is the emergence of crowd norms appropriate to everyday life?

2. In this chapter, you studied four types of social movements, each with a different goal. We will use the Internet to find an example of each of these types of social movements. For an example of alterative social movements, whose goal is to change some specific behavior, we can look at the antismoking movement. Go to *http://www.tobacco.org* For an example of redemptive social movements, which stress near-total personal change, you may wish to go to *http://www. watchtower.org* For an example of reformative social move-

ments, which attempt to change some specific aspect of society, go to *http://www.greenpeace.org* An example of transformative social movements, which focus on changing the entire social order, is provided by the Rastafarians at *http://www. cwrl.utexas.edu/~bill/e309m/students/marley/history/rastafar/ index.html*

Write a paper in which you compare these four movements in terms of goals, membership, sympathetic publics outside the movement, and relationships with authorities. Discuss evidence of how each social movement attempts to mold public opinion. Why do you think each of these social movements has had its particular success?

3. After reading about fads and fashions in your text, examine the following links:

> *http://beaniemom.com*
> *http://www.ty.com*
> *http://beaniex.com*
> *http://www.geocities.com/~beanphiles*
> *http://beaniemania.com*

Did these links take you to a fad or a fashion? How do you know? Do you think Beanie Babies will continue, or will they die out suddenly like Trolls and Tickle Me Elmo? What do the authors of the above links think?

If this "craze" has died down or disappeared by the time you read this exercise (and it likely will have), analyze "Beanie Babies" in terms of a fad. Can you explain why it began—and why it died out?

4. Let's use the Internet to get information on some basic ideas about rumors. Try to answer these questions: What are rumors? How do rumors spread? How have the Internet and the Web contributed to the spread of rumors?

I am going to link you to a rumor page on one of the Beanie Baby Web sites *http://members.beaniemania.com/gabiann.html* Read the rumors (especially the Announcement Archives) and check the Ty company at *http://www.ty.com* or other Beanie Web pages to see whether the rumors were true. Discuss the role of the Internet in the transmission of rumors.

Pete Whyte, Globes Interconnected, 1996

C H A P T E R

22

Technology, Social Change, and the Environment

*T*HE MORNING OF *JANUARY 28, 1986,* *dawned clear but near freezing, strange weather for subtropical Florida. At the Kennedy Space Center, launch pad 39B was lined with three inches of ice. Icicles 6 to 12 inches long hung like stalactites from the pad's service structure.*

Shortly after 8 A.M., the crew took the elevator to the white room, where they entered the crew module. By 8:36 A.M., the seven members of the crew were strapped in their seats. They were understandably disappointed when liftoff, scheduled for 9:38 A.M., was delayed because of the ice.

Due to a strong public relations campaign, public interest in the flight ran high. Attention focused on Christa McAuliffe, a 37-year-old high school teacher from Concord, New Hampshire, the first private citizen to fly aboard a space shuttle. Across the nation, schoolchildren watched with great anticipation, for Mrs. McAuliffe, selected from thousands of applicants, was to give two televised lessons during the flight. The first was to describe life aboard a spacecraft in orbit, the second to discuss the prospects of using space's microgravity to manufacture new products.

At the viewing site, thousands of spectators had joined the families and friends of the crew eagerly awaiting the launch. They were delighted to see Challenger's *two solid-fuel boosters ignite and broke into cheers as this product of technical innovation thundered majestically into space.*

The time was 11:38 A.M. Seventy-three seconds later, the Challenger, *racing skyward at 2,900 feet per second, had reached an altitude of 50,000 feet and was 7 miles from the launch site. Suddenly, a brilliant glow appeared on one side of the external tank. In seconds, the glow blossomed into a gigantic fireball. Screams of horror arose from the crowd as the* Challenger, *now 19 miles away, exploded, and bits of debris began to fall from the sky.*

In classrooms across the country, children burst into tears. Adult Americans stared at their televisions in stunned disbelief.

Sources: *Based on Broad 1986; Magnuson 1986; Lewis 1988; Maier 1993.*

*I*f any characteristic describes social life today, it is rapid social change. As we shall see in this chapter, technology, such as that which made the *Challenger* first a reality and then a disaster, is a driving force in this change. To understand the forces of social change is to better understand today's society—and our own lives.

An Overview of Social Change

Social change, a shift in the characteristics of culture and society, is such a vital part of social life that it has been a theme throughout this book. To make this theme more explicit, let's review the main points about social change made in the preceding chapters.

The Four Social Revolutions

The rapid, far-reaching social change that the world is currently experiencing did not "just happen." Rather, it is the result of fundamental forces set in motion thousands of years ago, beginning with the gradual domestication of plants and animals. This first social revolution allowed hunting and gathering societies to develop into horticultural and pastoral societies (see pages 145–150). The plow brought about the second social revolution, from which agricultural societies emerged. Then the invention of the steam engine ushered in the Industrial Revolution, and now we are witnessing the fourth social revolution, stimulated by the invention of the microchip.

social change: the alteration of culture and societies over time

618

The Protestant reformation ushered in not only religious change but also, as Max Weber analyzed, fundamental social-economic change. This painting by Hans Holbein, the Younger, shows the new prosperity of the merchant class. Previously, only the nobility could afford such possessions.

From *Gemeinschaft* to *Gesellschaft*

Although our lives are being vitally affected by this fourth revolution, we have seen only the tip of the iceberg. By the time this social revolution is full blown, little of our way of life will be left untouched. We can assume this because that is how it was with the first three social revolutions. For example, the change from agricultural to industrial society meant not only that people moved from villages to cities but also that intimate, lifelong relationships were replaced by impersonal, short-term associations. Paid work, contracts, and especially money, replaced the reciprocal obligations required by kinship, social position, and friendship. As reviewed on pages 102–105, sociologists use the terms *Gemeinschaft* and *Gesellschaft* to indicate this fundamental shift in society.

Capitalism and Industrialization

Just why did societies change from *Gemeinschaft* to *Gesellschaft*? Karl Marx pointed to a social invention called *capitalism*. He analyzed how the breakup of feudal society threw people off the land, creating a surplus of labor. Moving to cities, these masses were exploited by the owners of the means of production (factories, machinery, tools), setting in motion antagonistic relationships between capitalists and workers that remain today.

Max Weber agreed that capitalism was changing the world, but he traced capitalism to the Protestant Reformation (see pages 168–170). He noted that the Reformation stripped from Protestants the assurance that church membership saved them. As they agonized over heaven and hell, they concluded that God did not intend to leave the elect in uncertainty, that God would provide visible evidence for people predestined to heaven.

That sign, they decided, was prosperity. An unexpected consequence of the Reformation, then, was to make Protestants work hard and to be thrifty. The result was an economic surplus and the stimulation of capitalism, which laid the groundwork for the Industrial Revolution that transformed the world.

Modernization

The term given to the sweeping changes ushered in by the Industrial Revolution is **modernization.** Table 22.1 reviews these changes. This table is an ideal type in Weber's sense of the term, for no society exemplifies to the maximum degree all the traits listed here. For example, although most Americans now work in the tertiary sector of the economy,

TABLE 22.1

Comparing Traditional and Modern Societies

Characteristics	Traditional Societies	Modern Societies
General Characteristics		
Social change	Slow	Rapid
Size of group	Small	Large
Religious orientation	More	Less
Formal education	No	Yes
Place of residence	Rural	Urban
Demographic transition	First stage	Third stage
Family size	Larger	Smaller
Infant mortality	High	Low
Life expectancy	Short	Long
Health care	Home	Hospital
Temporal orientation	Past	Future
Material Relations		
Industrialized	No	Yes
Technology	Simple	Complex
Division of labor	Simple	Complex
Economic sector	Primary	Tertiary
Income	Low	High
Material possessions	Few	Many
Social Relationships		
Basic organization	*Gemeinschaft*	*Gesellschaft*
Families	Extended	Nuclear
Respect for elders	More	Less
Social stratification	Rigid	More open
Statuses	More ascribed	More achieved
Gender equality	Less	More
Norms		
View of reality, life, and morals	Absolute	Relativistic
Social control	Informal	Formal
Tolerance of differences	Less	More

modernization: the process by which a *Gemeinschaft* society is transformed into a *Gesellschaft* society

For centuries, Western society remained virtually unchanged. As shown in this fifteenth-century painting, work, which was passed from parents to children, was based on personal relationships and revolved around the seasons. How this long-standing traditional way of life gave way to Gesellschaft *society has been a primary topic of sociological investigation.*

many millions still work in the primary and secondary sectors. Thus all characteristics shown in Table 22.1 should be interpreted as "more" or "less" rather than "either–or."

Traditional, or *Gemeinschaft*, societies are small and rural, slow changing, with little stress on formal education. Most illnesses are treated at home. People live in extended families, look to the past for guidelines to the present, usually show high respect for elders, and have rigid social stratification and much inequality between the sexes. Life and morals tend to be seen in absolute terms, and few differences are tolerated. Modern societies, in contrast, are large, more urbanized, and fast changing. They stress formal education, are future oriented, and are less religiously oriented. In the third stage of the demographic transition, people have smaller families, lower rates of infant mortality, longer lives, higher incomes, and vastly more material possessions.

As capitalism and industrialization stimulated city life and ushered in short-term contractual relationships, people's views of the world changed. Their fundamental beliefs about what life should be like, their attitudes toward one another—nothing was to remain untouched. Just one example will help to make this point. In *Gemeinschaft* societies, people's rhythms of life were regulated by the seasons. For many, agriculture meant short periods of intense work, followed by long periods of a slower pace at routine tasks. Work was always available, and people worked as family units, with all but the youngest children contributing to the family's economic survival. Industrialization brought fundamental change, separating workers from family life for twelve to fourteen hours, six days a week. Work was no longer seasonal, but year round, except for unemployment, which now hung over people's heads, threatening their survival.

Social change comes in many forms. Shown here is a Chinese peasant in 1911, whose pigtail is being cut off by the revolutionary army. To retain the custom of never cutting one's hair was considered a sign of allegiance to warlords and of resistance to the new regime.

As technology from the industrialized world is introduced into traditional societies, we are able to witness how far-reaching the changes are. Take just modern medicine as an example. Its introduction into the Least Industrialized Nations helped to usher in the second stage of the demographic transition. As death rates dropped and birth rates remained high, the population exploded, bringing hunger and starvation, mass migration to cities, and mass migration to the industrialized nations. This rush to cities that have little industrialization, new to the world scene, is creating a host of problems yet to be solved (see the Perspectives box on page 579).

Technology and Shifts in the Global Map

Already during the sixteenth century, today's global divisions had begun to emerge. Trade alliances, forged by those nations with the most advanced technology of the time (the swiftest ships and the heaviest armaments), created a division into rich and poor nations. Then, according to *dependency theory*, as capitalism emerged the nations that industrialized exploited the resources of those that did not. Growing dependent—captive to their own exploitation—these nations were unable to develop their own resources (see pages 243–245). Today's information revolution will have similar consequences on global stratification. Those nations that take the fast lane on the information superhighway, primarily the Most Industrialized Nations, are destined to dominate in the coming generation.

Since World War II, the realignment of national and regional powers (called *geopolitics*) has resulted in a triadic division of the world: a Japan-centered East, a Germany-centered Europe, and a United States-centered western hemisphere (Robertson 1992). These three global powers, along with four lesser ones—Canada, France, Great Britain, and Italy—dominate today's globe. These industrial giants—collectively known as G7 (meaning "*the* Group of Seven")—hold annual meetings at which they decide how to divide up the world's markets and regulate global economic policy, such as interest rates, tariffs, and currency exchanges. Their goal is to perpetuate their global dominance, which includes keeping prices down on the raw materials they buy from the Least Industrialized Nations. Because cheap oil is essential for this goal, it requires the domination of the Mideast, whether that be accomplished through peaceful means or by a joint war effort of the United Nations.

Because of Russia's nuclear arsenal, the G7 has carefully courted Russia—giving Russia observer status at its annual summits and providing loans and expertise to help Russia's transition to capitalism. The breakup of the Soviet Union has been a central consideration in G7's plans for a new world order, and events there will help determine the shape of future global stratification.

G7, the world's seven wealthiest, most powerful nations, holds an annual meeting at which the countries make decisions concerning their global rule. Although Russia is not a Most Industrialized Nation, for strategic reasons and because of fear on the part of other nations, Russia has been allowed to attend these meetings. Russia's membership may be so solid now that the G7 will be changed to G8, or even, to use a simple phrase that belies its immense power, "The Eight," shown in this photo.

The Resurgence of Ethnic Conflicts

Threatening the global map so carefully divided by the G7 is the resurgence of ethnic conflicts. The breakup of the Soviet empire lifted the cover that had held in check the centuries' old hatreds and frustrated nationalistic ambitions of many ethnic groups. With the Soviet military and the KGB in disarray, these groups turned violently on one another. In Africa, similar seething hatreds have brought warfare to groups united only by artificial political boundaries. In Europe, the former Yugoslavia divided, with parts self-destructing as pentup fury was unleashed. Ethnic conflicts threaten to erupt in Germany, France, Italy, the United States, and Mexico. At what point these resentments and hatreds will play themselves out, if ever, is unknown.

For the most part, the Most Industrialized Nations care little if the entire continent of Africa self-destructs in ethnic slaughter, but they could not tolerate the interethnic warfare of Bosnia. If it had spread, the resulting inferno could have engulfed Europe. For global control, the G7 must be able to depend on political and economic stability in its own neighborhood, as well as in those countries that provide the essential raw materials for its industrial machine.

In spite of the vast social change occurring around the globe, race remains a fundamental distinction among human groups. Shown here is a Ukrainian being measured to see if he is really "full lipped" enough to be called a Tartar.

Social Movements

If we want to examine the cutting edge of social change in an industrialized society, for the most part we need to look no further than its social movements. Emerging from wide discontent, social movements, built around pressing social issues, either promote or resist social change. Indicating issues of concern to a country's citizens, social movements point to the areas that contain the greatest pressures for change (see pages 602–614). To see the future, we also need to examine the second part of the cutting edge of social change—a nation's new technology.

How Technology Changes Society ▶

As you may recall from Chapter 2, **technology** carries a double meaning. It refers to both *tools*, items used to accomplish tasks, and to the skills or procedures to make and use those tools. This broad concept includes tools as simple as a comb as well as those as complicated as computers. Technology's second meaning—the skills or procedures to make and use tools—refers in this case not only to the procedures used to manufacture combs and computers but also to those required to "produce" an acceptable hairdo or to gain access

Technology, which drives much social change, is at the forefront of our information revolution. This revolution, based on the computer chip, allows reality to cross with fantasy, a merging that sometimes makes it difficult to tell where one ends and the other begins. Shown here is an example of "performance animation," or "morphing," in the David Byrnes video "She's Mad."

technology: often defined as the applications of science, but can be conceptualized as tools, items used to accomplish tasks, along with the skills or procedures necessary to make and use those tools

to the Internet. Apart from its particulars, technology always refers to *artificial means of extending human abilities.*

All human groups make and use technology, but the chief characteristic of postindustrial societies (also called **postmodern societies**) is technology that greatly extends out abilities to analyze information, to communicate, and to travel. These *new technologies*, as they are called, allow us to do what had never been done in history: to probe space and other planets, to communicate almost instantaneously anywhere on the globe, to travel greater distances faster, and to store, retrieve, and analyze vast amounts of information.

This level of accomplishment, though impressive, is really very superficial. Of much greater sociological significance is a level beyond this, how technology changes people's way of life. *Technology is much more than the apparatus.* On a very obvious level, without automobiles, telephones, televisions, computers, and the like, our entire way of life would be strikingly different. As we look at how technology spreads, I shall stress this sociological aspect of technology—how it affects people's lives.

Ogburn's Theory of Social Change

Sociologist William Ogburn (1922, 1961, 1964) identified three processes of social change. Technology, he said, can lead to social change through invention, discovery, and diffusion.

Invention. Ogburn defined **invention** as a combining of existing elements and materials to form new ones. Although we think of inventions as being only material, such as computers, there also are *social* inventions, such as capitalism and the corporation. As we have seen, social inventions can have far-reaching consequences on a society. Later on, we will explore ways in which the automobile and the computer have transformed society, affecting not just some small part of social life but having ramifications for almost everything we do.

Discovery. Ogburn's second process of change is **discovery**, a new way of seeing reality. The reality is already present, but people now see it for the first time. An example is Columbus's "discovery" of North America, which had consequences so huge that it altered the course of history. This example also illustrates another principle: A discovery brings extensive change only when it comes at the right time. Other groups, such as the Vikings, had already "discovered" America in the sense of learning that a new land existed (the land, of course, was no discovery to the Native Americans already living in it). Viking settlements disappeared into history, however, and Norse culture was untouched by the discovery.

Diffusion. The spread of an invention or discovery from one area to another, called **diffusion,** can have far-reaching effects on human relationships. For example, when missionaries introduced steel axes to the Aborigines of Australia, it upset their whole society. Before this, the men controlled the making of axes, using a special stone available only in a remote region and passing axe-making skills from one man to another. Women had to request permission to use the stone axe. When steel axes became common, women also possessed them, and the men lost both status and power (Sharp 1995).

Diffusion also includes the spread of ideas. The idea of citizenship, for example, changed the political structure, for no longer was the monarch an unquestioned source of authority. Today, the concept of gender equality is circling the globe, with the basic idea that it is wrong to withhold rights on the basis of someone's sex. This idea, though now taken for granted in a few parts of the world, is revolutionary. Like citizenship, it is destined to transform basic human relationships and entire societies.

Cultural Lag. As noted in Chapter 2, Ogburn coined the term **cultural lag** to describe the situation in which some elements of a culture adapt to an invention or discovery more

---

postmodern society: another term for postindustrial society; its chief characteristic is the use of tools that extend the human abilities to gather and analyze information, to communicate, and to travel

invention: the combination of existing elements and materials to form new ones; identified by William Ogburn as the first of three processes of social change

discovery: a new way of seeing reality; identified by William Ogburn as the second of three processes of social change

diffusion: the spread of invention or discovery from one area to another; identified by William Ogburn as the final of three processes of social change

cultural lag: Ogburn's term for human behavior lagging behind technological innovations

Culture contact is the source of diffusion, *the spread of an invention or discovery from one area to another. Shown here are two children of the Huli tribe in Papua New Guinea. They are amused by a Polaroid photo of themselves.*

rapidly than others. Technology, he suggested, usually changes first, followed by culture. In other words, we play catch-up with changing technology, adapting our customs and ways of life to meet its needs.

Evaluation of Ogburn's Theory

Some find Ogburn's analysis too one-directional, saying that it makes technology the cause of almost all social change. They point out that adapting to changing technology is only one part of the story. The other part consists of people taking control over technology—developing the technology they need and selectively using technology. Some groups even prevent technology's influence by rejecting technologies they perceive as threatening to their culture. An example is the Amish (see page 104). Other resistance to technology is discussed in the Sociology and the New Technology box on the next page.

Technology and social change actually form a two-way street: Just as technology leads to social change, so social change leads to technology. For example, as the numbers of elderly in our society have grown, their needs have stimulated the development of medical technologies to treat Alzheimer disease. Changing ideas about the disabled have stimulated the development of new types of wheelchairs that allow people who cannot move their legs to play basketball, participate in the Special Olympics, and enter downhill races.

In fairness to Ogburn, we must note that he never said technology is the only force for social change, or that people are passive pawns in the face of overwhelming technological forces. Rather, Ogburn stressed that the usual direction of change is for the material culture (technology) to change first, and for the symbolic culture (people's ideas and ways of life) to follow, a direction that still holds. With the many influences of the new technologies on our lives, Ogburn's analysis remains highly significant.

Technology varies greatly from one culture to another, and at least part of each culture is built around its technology. Shown here is a very basic technology used in Dazuo, China. Of primary sociological interest is that the people carrying these 1,100-pound slabs of granite are women.

Transforming Society

When a technology is introduced into a society, it forces others parts of society to give way. In fact, *a new technology can reshape an entire society.* As discussed in the Sociology and the New Technology

 *Sociology and the New Technology*

From the Luddites to the Unabomber: Opposition to Technology

Because every new technology replaces some existing technology, technology always threatens someone. Consequently, opposition to technology is common; on occasion, opposition even grows violent. The classic example occurred in the British textile industry in the early 1800s when owners introduced machines that made stockings. The workers, whose jobs were being automated away, rioted, smashing the machines. Twelve thousand troops had to be called out to restore order. Some of the Luddites (named after Ned Ludlum, an apprentice stocking maker who destroyed his machine) were shipped off to Australia; others were executed (Volti 1995). Today, the term "Luddite" means someone who opposes new technology.

Opposition is usually directed at a specific new technology, but sometimes it is a protest against technology in general. Jacques Ellul (1965), for example, a French sociologist, warned that technology was destroying traditional values. Humans, he said, are becoming "a single tightly integrated and articulated component" of technology. Technology, he added, is producing a monolithic world culture in which "variety is mere appearance."

The message of Ellul and others like him, such as Neil Postman (1992), reached but a few intellectuals who dis-

cussed the matter in faculty seminars and wrote obscure papers on the subject. In contrast, the Unabomber's message came thundering into our consciousness, for he sent his warning signals not via books and articles, but via the mail—in explosives that maimed and killed their unsuspecting recipients. For seventeen years, the man sent bombs, with no apparent message behind his seemingly random attacks. Then unexpectedly, in 1995, he sent a verbal message, promising to stop his terror if his 35,000-word essay against technology were published. *The New York Times* and the *Washington Post* duly printed it. His message, in its essence, was not dissimilar to Ellul's: Technology is destroying us. A recluse in the mountains of Montana, Ted Kaczynski, was eventually identified as the Unabomber. He was arrested and found guilty.

For Your Consideration

What do the Luddites, Jacques Ellul, and the Unabomber have in common? Use concepts presented in this and earlier chapters to analyze the effects of technology on society. Given your conclusions, should we fear new technologies?

box on page 627, it is easy to misguess the consequences of a new technology. Let's look at five ways that technology changes society.

Transformation of Existing Technologies.   The first impact is felt by the technology that is being displaced. Currently, for example, the rotary dial telephone is a living dinosaur. Some of us still use these machines, but they are clearly doomed to extinction in the wake of newer, more efficient touchtone telephones, and eventually, devices into which we simply speak the number we desire. Similarly, IBM electric typewriters, "state of the art" equipment just a few years ago, have been rendered practically useless by the desktop computer.

Changes in Social Organization.   Technology also changes social organization. As discussed in Chapter 6, for example, machine technology gave birth to the factory. Prior to machine technology, most workers labored at home, but the advent of power-driven machinery required people to gather in one place to do their work. Then it was discovered that workers could produce more items if each did a specialized task. Instead of each worker making an entire item, as had been the practice, each individual worked on only part of an item. One worker would do so much hammering on a single part, or turn so many bolts, and then someone else would take the item and do some other repetitive task before a third person took over, and so on. Henry Ford then built on this innovation by developing the assembly line: instead of workers moving to the parts, a machine moved the parts to the workers. In addition, the parts were made interchangeable and easy to attach (Womack et al. 1991).

alienation: Marx's term for workers' lack of connection to the product of their labor; caused by their being assigned repetitive tasks on a small part of a product

Changes in Ideology.   Technology also spurs ideology. Karl Marx saw the change to the factory system as a source of **alienation.** He noted that workers who did repetitive tasks on just a small part of a product no longer felt connected to the finished product

Sociology and the New Technology

When Old Technology Was New: Misguessing the Future

Almost everybody wants to know the future—from the work we'll be doing five years from now to how much money we'll have in ten years.

So it is with technology. Futurists guesstimate the social ramifications of new technologies, predicting far-reaching—and sometimes dire—consequences. Consider the following *totally wrong* predictions:

A new century is at hand. Our new technology will practically annihilate time and space. It will let people live and work wherever they please, creating dynamic new communities linked by electronics. Because of this new technology, many people will move out of cities, doing their work from their homes.

Some social class barriers will crumble, for people will have the power to summon almost anyone. It may even save the family farm by linking farmers with others.

In this amazing future, people will be able to dial up symphonies, presidential speeches, and even three-dimensional Shakespeare plays.

The new technology is not without risk, however. Novels and movie theaters may vanish, people may lose their privacy, and its illicit use can spark a crackdown by the government.

How can I say with such certainty that these predictions are *totally wrong*? After all, we are only in the initial stages of the communications revolution, and they all may prove true. Perhaps. The only thing wrong is that these predictions were made 100 years ago—not about the computer, but about the telephone!

To all the guesstimates of futurists, a reasonable response seems to be, Let's wait and see. Plenty of predictions in the past didn't make it to the light of day. We do know that our way of life depends on technology and that new technology can transform society. Changes there will be—that we can count on; what we don't know are the exact directions and implications of those changes. For that, we must let the future itself unfold—taking us with it—sometimes willingly, sometimes reluctantly.

Sources: Based on Marvin 1988; Fischer 1995; Pearl 1995a.

and could therefore no longer take pride in it. They became alienated from the product of their labor, Marx said, which bred dissatisfaction and unrest.

Marx also noted that, like machines and tools, workers had become replaceable parts. Before factories came on the scene, workers owned their tools and were essentially independent. If they did not like their work situation, they could pack up their hammers and saws and leave. Others would hire them to build a wagon or make a harness. In the factory, however, the capitalists owned the tools and machinery, and they used the power that

As discussed in the text, when technology changes, so does social organization—and even ideology and social relationships. This 1946 photo of the Kaiser assembly line in Willow Run, Michigan, gives you an idea of the monotony and pressures associated with this kind of work, and why it can lead to the alienation *that Marx analyzed.*

came with ownership to extract every ounce of sweat and blood they could. The workers had to submit, for if they left, the tools stayed, and other workers took their place. Only a workers' revolution will change this exploitation, said Marx. When the workers realize the common basis of their exploitation, they will take over the means of production and establish a workers' state.

Note how the new technology that led to the factory stimulated new ideologies. First, defenders of capitalism developed an ideology to support the principle of maximizing profits. Then followers of Marx built theories of socialism to attack capitalism. As we shall see shortly, just as changes in technology stimulated the development of communism, changes in technology have been crucial in bringing about its end.

Transformation of Values.   Just as ideology follows technology, so do values. If technology is limited to clubbing animals, then strength and cunning are valued. So are animal skins. No doubt some primitive man and woman walked with heads held high as they wore the skins of some especially unusual or dangerous animal—while their neighbors looked on in envy as they trudged along wearing only the same old sheepskins. In contrast, today's technology produces an abundance of synthetic fabrics for clothing. Unlike this primitive couple, Americans brag about cars, hot tubs, and jacuzzis—and make certain that their jeans have the right labels prominently displayed. In short, while jealousy, envy, and pride may be basic to human nature, the particular emphasis on materialism depends on the state of technology.

Transformation of Social Relationships.   Technology also changes social relationships. As men were drawn out of their homes to work in factories, family relationships changed. No longer present in the home on a daily basis, the husband-father became isolated from many of the day-to-day affairs of the family. One consequence of husbands becoming strangers to their wives and children was a higher divorce rate. As current technology draws more and more women from the home to offices and factories, the consequences are similar—greater isolation from husbands and children, and one more impetus toward a higher divorce rate.

The Automobile

If we try to pick the single item that has had the greatest impact on social life in this century, among the many candidates the automobile stands out. Let us look at some of the ways in which it changed U.S. society.

Displacement of Existing Technology.   The automobile gradually pushed aside the old technology, a replacement that began in earnest when Henry Ford began to mass-produce the Model T in 1908. People immediately found automobiles attractive (Flink 1990). They considered them cleaner, safer, more reliable, and more economical than horses. Cars also offered the appealing prospect of lower taxes, for no longer would the public have to pay to clean up the tons of horse manure that accumulated on the city streets each day. Humorous as it sounds now, it was even thought that automobiles would eliminate the cities' parking problems, for an automobile took up only half as much space as a horse and buggy.

The automobile also replaced a second technology. The United States had developed a vast system of urban transit, with electric streetcar lines radiating outward from the center of our cities. As the automobile became affordable and more dependable, Americans demonstrated a clear preference for the greater convenience of private transportation. Instead of walking to a streetcar and then having to wait in the cold and rain, people were able to travel directly from home on their own schedule.

Effects on Cities.   The decline in the use of streetcars actually changed the shape of U.S. cities. Before the automobile, U.S. cities were web-shaped, for residences and businesses were located along the streetcar lines. When freed by automobiles from having to live so close to the tracks, people filled in the areas between the "webs."

As is apparent from the design of this 1903 car, which looks like a horse-drawn buggy, new technology builds on existing technology. At the turn of the century, the automobile was an inefficient novelty. Only after supporting technology came into being, especially graveled and paved roads, did the automobile become a serious contender with other forms of transportation. At the time this photo was taken, who could have imagined that this strange vehicle was destined to transform society?

The automobile also stimulated mass suburbanization. Already in the 1920s, U.S. residents had begun to leave the city, for they found that they could commute to work in the city from outlying areas where they benefitted from more room and fewer taxes (Preston 1979). Their departure significantly reduced the cities' tax base, thus contributing, as discussed in Chapter 20, to many of the problems that U.S. cities experience today.

Effects on Farm Life and Villages. The automobile had a profound impact on farm life and villages. Prior to the 1920s, most farmers were isolated from the city. Because using horses for a trip to town was slow and cumbersome, they made such trips infrequently. By the 1920s, however, the popularity and low price of the Model T made the "Saturday trip to town" a standard event. There, farmers would market products, shop, and visit with friends. As a consequence, farm life was altered; for example, mail order catalogues stopped being the primary source of shopping, and access to better medical care and education improved (Flink 1990). Farmers were also able to travel to bigger towns, where they found a greater variety of goods. As farmers began to use the nearby villages only for immediate needs, these flourishing centers of social and commercial life dried up.

Changes in Architecture. The automobile's effects on commercial architecture are clear—from the huge parking lots that decorate malls like necklaces to the drive-up windows of banks and restaurants. But the automobile also fundamentally altered the architecture of U.S. homes (Flink 1990). Before the car, each home had a stable in the back where the family kept its buggy and horses. The stable was the logical place to shelter the family's first car, and it required no change in architecture. The change occurred in three steps. First, new homes were built with a detached garage located like the stable, at the back of the home. Second, as the automobile became a more essential part of the U.S. family, the garage was incorporated into the home by moving it from the back yard to the side of the house, and connecting it by a breezeway. In the final step the breezeway was removed, and the garage integrated into the home so that Americans could enter their automobiles without even going outside.

Changed Courtship Customs and Sexual Norms. By the 1920s, the automobile was used extensively for dating. This removed children from the watchful eye of parents and undermined parental authority. The police began to receive complaints about "night riders" who parked their cars along country lanes, "doused their lights, and indulged in orgies" (Brilliant 1964). Automobiles became so popular for courtship that by the 1960s about 40 percent of marriage proposals took place in them (Flink 1990).

In 1925 Jewett introduced cars with a foldout bed, as did Nash in 1937. The Nash version became known as "the young man's model" (Flink 1990). Since the 1970s, mobile lovemaking has declined, partly because urban sprawl (itself due to the automobile) left fewer safe trysting spots, and partly because changed sexual norms made beds more accessible.

Effects on Women's Roles.   The automobile may also lie at the heart of the changed role of women in U.S. society. To see how, we first need to see what a woman's life was like before the automobile. Historian James Flink (1990) described it this way:

> Until the automobile revolution, in upper-middle-class households groceries were either ordered by phone and delivered to the door or picked up by domestic servants or the husband on his way home from work. Iceboxes provided only very limited space for the storage of perishable foods, so shopping at markets within walking distance of the home was a daily chore. The garden provided vegetables and fruits in season, which were home-canned for winter consumption. Bread, cakes, cookies, and pies were home-baked. Wardrobes contained many home-sewn garments.
>
> Mother supervised the household help and worked alongside them preparing meals, washing and ironing, and house cleaning. In her spare time she mended clothes, did decorative needlework, puttered in her flower garden, and pampered a brood of children. Generally, she made few family decisions and few forays alone outside the yard. She had little knowledge of family finances and the family budget. The role of the lower-middle-class housewife differed primarily in that far less of the household work was done by hired help, so that she was less a manager of other people's work, more herself a maid-of-all-work around the house.

Because automobiles required skill rather than strength, women were able to drive as well as men. This new mobility freed women physically from the narrow confines of the home. As Flink (1990) observed, the automobile changed women "from producers of food and clothing into consumers of national-brand canned goods, prepared foods, and ready-made clothes. The automobile permitted shopping at self-serve supermarkets outside the neighborhood and in combination with the electric refrigerator made buying food a weekly rather than a daily activity." When women began to do the shopping, they gained greater control over the family budget, and as their horizons extended beyond the confines of the home, they also gained different views of life.

In short, the automobile changed women's roles at home, including their relationship with their husbands, altered their attitudes, transformed their opportunities, and stimulated them to participate in areas of social life not connected with the home.

▼   **In Sum**   With changes this extensive, it would not be inaccurate to say that the automobile also shifted basic values and changed the way we look at life. No longer isolated, women, teenagers, and farmers began to see the world differently. So did husbands and wives, whose marital relationship had also been altered. The automobile even transformed views of courtship, sexuality, and gender relations.

No one attributes such fundamental changes solely to the automobile, of course, for many historical events, as well as other technological changes, occurred during this same period, each making its own contribution to social change. Even this brief overview of the social effects of the automobile, however, illustrates that technology is not merely an isolated tool but exerts a profound influence on social life.

The second candidate for bringing the greatest social change is that technological marvel, the computer. Let's consider its effects.

The Computer

The ominous wail seemed too close for comfort. Sally looked in her rear-view mirror and realized that the flashing red lights and the screaming siren might be for her. She felt confused. "I'm just on my way to Soc class," she thought. "I'm not

Most of us take computers for granted, but they are new to the world scene—as are their effects on our lives. This photo captures a significant change in the evolution of computers. The laptop held by the superimposed model has more power than the room-size ENIAC of 1946.

speeding or anything." After she pulled over, an angry voice over a loudspeaker ordered her out of the car.

As she got out, someone barked the command, "Back up with your hands in the air!" Bewildered, Sally stood frozen for a moment. "Put 'em up now! Right now!" She did as she was told.

The officer crouched behind his open door, his gun drawn. When Sally reached the police car—still backing up—the officer grabbed her, threw her to the ground, and handcuffed her hands behind her back. She heard words she would never forget: "You are under arrest for murder. You have the right to remain silent. Anything you say can and will be used against you in a court of law. You have the right to an attorney. If you cannot afford one, one will be provided for you."

Traces of alarm still flicker across Sally's face when she recalls her arrest. She had never even been issued a traffic ticket, much less been arrested for anything. The nightmare that Sally experienced happened because of a "computer error." With the inversion of two numbers, her car's license number had been entered instead of that of a woman wanted for a brutal killing earlier that day.

The police later apologized. "These things happen," they said, "but not very often. We're sorry, but I'm sure you understand."

None of us is untouched by the computer, but it is unlikely that many of us have felt its power as directly and dramatically as Sally did. For most of us, the computer's control lies quietly behind the scenes. Although the computer has intruded into our daily lives, most of us never think about it. Our grades are computerized, and probably our paycheck as well. When we buy groceries, a computer scans our purchases and presents a printout of the name, price, and quantity of each item. Essentially the computer's novelty has given way to everyday routine; it is simply another tool.

Many people rejoice over the computer's capacity to improve their quality of life. They are pleased with the quality control of manufactured goods and the ease with which they can keep detailed records. Computers have also reduced the drudgery of many jobs. We can type just one letter and let the computer print and address it to ten individuals— or to ten thousand. If we use e-mail, those letters can be delivered in seconds.

Some people, however, worry about errors that can creep into computerized records, aware that something like Sally's misfortune may happen to them. Others fear that confidentiality of computer data will be abused, in the way that Orwell's Big Brother used information to achieve total control. These are legitimate concerns, but space does not permit us to pursue them further.

At this point, let's consider how the computer is changing medicine, education, and the workplace, then its likely effects on social inequality.

Medicine

> The patient's symptoms were mystifying. After exercise, one side of his face and part of his body turned deep red, the other chalky white. He looked as though someone had taken a ruler and drawn a line down the middle of his body.
>
> Stumped, the patient's physician consulted a medical librarian who punched a few words into a personal computer to search for clues in the world's medical literature. Soon, the likely answer flashed on the screen: Harlequin's disease. (Winslow 1994)

The computer was right, and a neurosurgeon was able to correct the patient's nervous system. With computers, physicians can peer within the body's hidden recesses to determine how its parts are functioning or to see if surgery is necessary. Surgeons can operate on unborn babies and on previously inaccessible parts of the brain. In a coming "lab-on-a-chip," one million tiny fragments of genetic DNA can be crammed onto a disposable microchip. Read by a laser scanner, in just a few minutes the chip reveals such things as whether a patient carries the cystic fibrosis gene or has grown resistant to AIDS drugs. The chip will sell for only $10 (King 1994).

As the future rushes in, the microchip is bringing even more technological wonders. In what is called *telemedicine*, patients have their hearts and lungs checked with a stethoscope—by doctors who are in another state—or another country. The data are transmitted by fiber–optic cable (Richards 1996). Soon a surgeon in Boston or San Francisco, using a remote-controlled robot and images relayed via satellite to computers, will be able to operate on a wounded soldier in a field hospital in Bosnia (Associated Press 1995).

Will the computer lead to "doctorless" medical offices? Will we perhaps one day feed vital information about ourselves into a computer and receive a printout of what is wrong with us—and, of course, a prescription? (Somehow, "Take two aspirins and key me in the morning" doesn't sound comforting.)

Although computers do outperform physicians in diagnosis (Waldholz 1991), such an office is likely to remain only a concept in some futurist's fanciful imagination, for physicians would repel such an onslaught on their expertise. Many patients also are likely to resist, for they would miss interacting with their doctors, especially the assurances and other emotional support that good physicians provide. It is likely that the computer will remain a diagnostic tool for physicians, not a replacement for them.

Education.

Almost every grade school in the United States introduces its students to the computer. Children learn how to type on it, as well as how to use science and mathematics software. Successful educational programs use a gamelike, challenging format that makes students forget they are "studying." Classrooms are being wired to the Internet; students in schools that have no teachers knowledgeable in Russian are able to take courses in Russian—as well as the sociology of baseball ("Cyberschool" 1996). The question of social inequality becomes significant in this context. Those schools most able to afford the latest in computer technology are able to better prepare their students for the future. That advantage, of course, is given students of private schools and the richest public school districts, thus helping to perpetuate social inequalities that arise from the chance of birth.

The computer will transform the college of the future. Each office and dormitory room and off-campus residence will be equipped with fiber-optic cable, and a professor will be able to transmit a book the size of this text directly from his or her office to a student's residence, or back the other way, in *less* time than it took to read this sentence. To help students and professors write papers or prepare reports, computers will search millions of pages of text. Digital textbooks will replace printed versions such as this one. You will be able to key in terms such as *social interaction* and *gender*, select your preference of historical period and geographical area—and the computer will spew out maps, moving images, and sounds. It will be the same for riots and Los Angeles, sexual discrimination in the military, even the price of marijuana in San Francisco. If you wish, the computer will give you a test—at your chosen level of difficulty—so you can immediately check your mastery of the material.

The Workplace.   The computer is transforming the workplace. On the simplest level is how we do work. For example, I am composing this book on a computer, which will immediately print what I write. A series of archaic, precomputer processes follows, however, in which the printed copy is sent via the postal service to an editor, who physically handles the manuscript and sends it to others who do the same. The manuscript is eventually returned to me via the postal service for final corrections—a rather primitive process, much as would have occurred during Benjamin Franklin's day. Eventually I will be able to zap my manuscript electronically from my computer to my editor's computer—when practice catches up with potential.

The computer is also changing things on a deeper level, for it alters social relationships. For example, no longer do I bring my manuscript to a university secretary, wait, and then retrieve it several days later. Since I make changes directly at the computer, the secretary is bypassed entirely. In this instance, the computer enhances social relationships, for the department secretary has much less work, and this new process eliminates the necessity of excuses when a manuscript is not ready on time—and the tensions in the relationship that this brings.

The computer's effect may be so radical that it even returns the work location to the home. As discussed earlier, industrialization caused work to shift from home to factory and office. Since workers now can be "networked" (linked via computers), this historical change may be reversed. Already millions of workers remain at home, where they perform their work on computers.

On the negative side are increased surveillance of workers and depersonalization. As a telephone information operator said:

> The computer knows everything. It records the minute I punch in, it knows how long I take for each call . . . I am supposed to average under eighteen seconds per call . . . Everything I do is reported to my supervisor on his computer, and if I've missed my numbers I get a written warning. I rarely see the guy . . . It's intense. It's me and the computer all day. I'm telling you, at the end of the day I'm wiped out. Working with computers is the coal mining of the nineties. (Mander 1992:57)

Cyberspace and Social Inequalities in the Twenty-First Century

The term *information superhighway* carries the idea of information traveling at a high rate of speed among homes and businesses. Just as a highway allows physical travel from one place to another, so homes and businesses are being connected by the rapid flow of information. Already about 100 million people around the world are able to communicate by Internet, and "servers" such as Prodigy, America Online, and CompuServe allow electronic access to libraries of information. Some programs sift, sort, and transmit scanned images, sound, even video. Electronic mail (e-mail) allows people to zap messages without regard to national boundaries. This is the future, a world linked by almost instantaneous communications, with information readily accessible around the globe, and few places to be called remote.

The implications of the information superhighway for national and global stratification are severe. On the national level, we can end up with information have nots, primarily inner-city residents, thus perpetuating present inequalities. On the global level, the question is, Who will control the information superhighway? The answer, of course, is obvious, for it is the Most Industrialized Nations that are developing the communications system. This leads to one of the more profound issues of the twenty-first century—will such control destine the Least Industrialized Nations to a perpetual pauper status?

Other Theories of Social Change

Although technology certainly is a driving force in social change, this is not the only theory of why societies change. As a sharp contrast, let's consider evolutionary and cyclical theories, and then look at conflict theory.

Evolutionary Theories

Evolutionary theories can be classified into three basic types: unilinear, multilinear, and cyclical. Let's consider each.

Unilinear Evolution.   *Unilinear* evolutionary theories assume that all societies follow the same path. Evolving from simple to more complex forms, they go through uniform sequences (Barnes 1935). Many versions of this theory have been proposed, but one that once dominated Western thought was Lewis Henry Morgan's (1877) theory that societies go through three stages: savagery, barbarism, and civilization. In his eyes English society served as the epitome of civilization, which all others were destined to follow. Sociologists Herbert Spencer (1884) and Robert MacIver (1937) also held evolutionary views of social change.

Since the basic assumption of this theory, that all preliterate groups have the same form of social organization, has been found to be untrue, views of unilinear evolution have been discredited. In addition, seeing one's own society as the top of the evolutionary ladder is now considered unacceptably ethnocentric.

Multilinear Evolution.   *Multilinear* views of evolution have replaced unilinear theories. The assumption remains that societies evolve from smaller to larger, more complex forms as they adapt to their environments. Instead of assuming that all societies follow the same path, however, multilinear theories presuppose that different routes can lead to a similar stage of development. Thus, to become industrialized, societies need not pass through the same sequence of stages (Sahlins and Service 1960; Lenski and Lenski 1987).

Evaluating Evolutionary Theories.   Central to evolutionary theories, whether unilinear or multilinear, is the idea of *progress*, that preliterate societies evolve from a simple form of organization toward a higher state. Growing appreciation of the rich diversity—and complexity—of traditional cultures, however, has discredited this idea. Moreover, Western culture is now in crisis (poverty, racism, discrimination, war, alienation, violent sexual assaults, unsafe streets, rampant fear) and no longer regarded as holding the answers to human happiness. Consequently, the assumption of progress has been cast aside and evolutionary theories have been rejected (Eder 1990; Smart 1990).

Cyclical Theories

Cyclical theories attempt to account for the rise of entire civilizations, not a particular society. Why, for example, did Egyptian, Greek, and Roman civilizations rise to a peak of power and then decline? Cyclical theories assume that civilizations are like organisms: they are born, see an exuberant youth, attain maturity, then decline as they reach old age, and finally die (Hughes 1962).

To explain this pattern, historian Arnold Toynbee (1946) proposed that each time a civilization successfully meets a challenge, oppositional forces are set up. At its peak, when a civilization has become an empire, the ruling elite loses its capacity to keep the masses in line "by charm rather than by force." As oppositional forces are set loose, the fabric of society is ripped apart. Although force may hold the empire together for hundreds of years, the civilization is doomed.

In a book that provoked widespread controversy, *The Decline of the West* (1926–1928), Oswald Spengler, a German teacher and social critic, proposed that Western civilization was declining. Although the West succeeded in overcoming the crises provoked by Hitler and Mussolini that so disturbed Spengler, as Toynbee noted, civilizations do not necessarily end in a sudden and total collapse. Since the decline can last hundreds of years, perhaps the crisis in Western civilization mentioned earlier (poverty, assault, and so on) may indicate that Spengler was right.

Conflict Theory

Long before Toynbee, Marx identified a recurring process in human history (see Figure 22.1). He said that each *thesis* (a current arrangement of power) contains its own *antithesis* (contradiction or opposition). A struggle develops between the thesis and its antithesis, leading to a *synthesis* (a new arrangement of power). This new social order, in turn, becomes a thesis that will be challenged by its own antithesis, and so on.

According to Marx's view (called a **dialectical process** of history), each ruling group sows the seeds of its own destruction. Consider capitalism. Marx said that capitalism (the thesis) is built on the exploitation of workers (an antithesis, or built-in opposition). With workers and owners on a colllision course, the dialectical process will not stop until workers establish a classless state (the synthesis).

The analysis of G7 on page 622 follows conflict theory. The current division of global resources and markets is a thesis. An antithesis is resentment on the part of have-not nations. If a less industrialized nation gains in relative wealth or military power, that nation will press for a redistribution of resources. Any new arrangement, or synthesis, will contain its own antithesis (such as ethnic hostilities), contradictions that haunt the arrangement of power and must at some point be resolved into a synthesis. The process repeats itself.

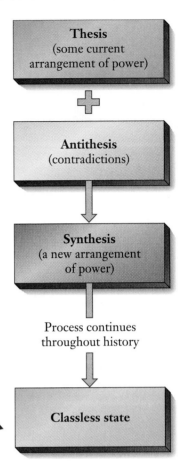

Figure 22.1

Marx's Model of Historical Change

Social Change and the Natural Environment

Of all the changes swirling around us, perhaps those affecting the natural environment hold the most serious implications for human life. I shall close the book with a short overview of this pressing matter.

Environmental Problems in Past Civilizations

Contrary to common assumptions, environmental problems are not new to the human scene. Several civilizations even destroyed themselves by destroying the environment on which their very existence depended. This happened to the Anasazi Indians of Arizona and New Mexico about 700 years ago (Budiansky 1987) and to the Mayan civilization in Guatemala about 1,000 years ago (Deevey et al. 1979).

The most famous is the fall of Mesopotamia, a civilization located in the lush river basin of the Tigris and Euphrates in what is now Iraq. About 3,000 years before Christ, this civilization flourished because the people had developed an extensive irrigation system that provided abundant food. This irrigation system, however, had no drainage. The water constantly evaporated, gradually growing saltier. Over the centuries, this saltier water seeped into the ground, the underground water table rose, and the land became too salty to grow crops. The Mesopotamians had unwittingly destroyed the agricultural base on which their civilization depended (Jacobsen and Adams 1958). What once was a beautiful, lush, green land producing fruits, vegetables, and grains in abundance is now desert.

Environmental Problems in the Most Industrialized Nations

Although environmental degradation is not new, the frontal assault on the natural environment did not begin in earnest until nations industrialized. The more extensive the industrialization, the better it was considered for a nation's welfare, and the slogan for the Most Industrialized Nations has been "Growth at any cost."

dialectical process: each arrangement, or thesis, contains contradictions, or antitheses, which must be resolved; the new arrangement, or synthesis, contains its own contradictions, and so on

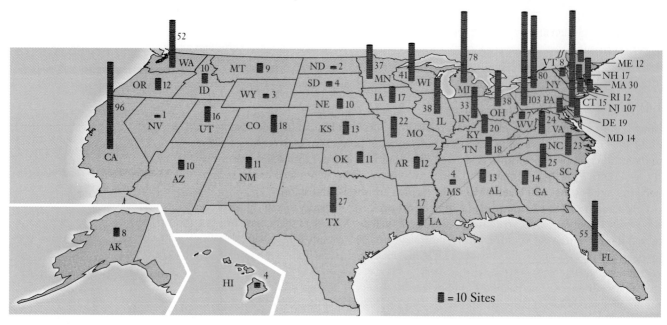

Source: *Statistical Abstract* 1996:Table 382.

Figure 22.2

Where Are the Worst Hazardous Waste Sites?

Industrial growth did come, but at a high cost to the natural environment. Today many formerly pristine streams are polluted sewers, and the water supply of many cities is unfit to drink. When Los Angeles announces "smog days" on radio and television, school children are kept inside during recess, and everyone is warned to stay indoors. The accumulation of hazardous wastes is a special problem. In spite of the danger to people and the environment, in many cases the waste has simply been dumped. The Social Map above shows how the worst hazardous waste sites are distributed among the United States.

Of all the consequences of pollution that we could discuss—such as the depletion of the ozone layer in order to enjoy the convenience of spray bottles and air conditioners, which may yet prove to be a folly that harms all of humanity—due to space limitations, we shall consider just the implications of fossil fuels.

Fossil Fuels and Environmental Degradation. The burning of fossil fuels for factories, motorized vehicles, and power plants has been especially harmful. Fish can no longer survive in some lakes in Canada and the northeastern United States because of

Environmental degradation is anything but new. Entire civilizations may have been destroyed because of the unwitting destruction of the environment on which the civilization depended. Some suggest that the Maya of Central America, whose ruins are depicted here, fell victim to their own destruction of their environment.

acid rain—the burning fossil fuels release sulfur dioxide and nitrogen oxide, which react with moisture in the air to become sulfuric and nitric acids (Luoma 1989).

An invisible but infinitely more serious consequence is the **greenhouse effect.** Like the glass of a greenhouse, the gases emitted from burning fossil fuels allow sunlight to enter the earth's atmosphere freely, but inhibit the release of heat. It is as though the gases have closed the atmospheric window through which our planet breathes. Some scientists say that the resulting **global warming** may melt the polar ice caps and inundate the world's shorelines, cause the climate boundaries to move about 400 miles north, and make many animal and plant species extinct (Smith and Tirpak 1988; Thomas 1988; Weisskopf 1992). Alarmed, in 1997, 160 nations approved an environmental treaty that requires a reduction of "greenhouse gases." Not all scientists agree that we face a danger, however. Some even doubt that a greenhouse effect exists (Robinson and Robinson 1997).

The Energy Shortage, Internal Combustion Engines, and Multinational Corporations.   If you ever read about an energy shortage, you can be sure it is false. There is no energy shortage, nor can there ever be. The earth holds the potential of producing unlimited low-cost power, which can help raise the living standards of humans across the globe. The sun, for example, produces more energy than humanity could ever use. Boundless energy is also available from the tides and the winds. In some cases, we need better technology to harness these sources of energy; in others, we need only apply technology we already have.

Since burning fossil fuels in internal combustion engines is the main source of pollution in the Most Industrialized Nations, and vast sources of alternative energy are available, why don't we develop the technology to use these alternative sources of energy? From a conflict perspective, these abundant sources of energy threaten the multinationals' oil monopoly. To maintain their profits, these corporations make certain that internal combustion engines remain dominant. The practical development and widespread use of alternative sources of power will wait until the multinationals have cornered the market on the technology that will harness them—so they can continue reaping huge profits.

Environmental Racism and Social Class.   Pollution in the United States has a racial and social class bias (Bullard 1994; Noah 1994). Racial minorities and the poor are disproportionately exposed to air pollution, hazardous wastes, pesticides, and the like. The basic reasons are that the land where the poor live sells cheaply, and the rich would not stand for factories to spew pollution near their homes. For the same reasons, hazardous waste landfills are likely to be located in predominantly African-American or Latino communities. To deal with this issue, a new specialty, environmental poverty law, is developing (Hayes 1992).

Environmental Problems in the Industrializing Nations

Severe consequences of industrialization, such as ozone depletion, the greenhouse effect, and global warming, cannot be laid solely at the feet of the Most Industrialized Nations. With their rush to be contenders in the global competition, the lack of funds to purchase pollution controls, and few anti-pollution laws, the Industrializing Nations make their own enormous contributions to this problem. Breathing the polluted air of Mexico City, for example, is the equivalent of smoking two packs of cigarettes a day (Durbin 1995).

The former Soviet Union is a special case. Until this empire broke up, pollution had been treated as a state secret. Scientists and journalists were forbidden to mention pollution in public. Even peaceful demonstrations to call attention to pollution could net participants two years in prison (Feshbach 1992). With protest stifled and no environmental protection laws, environmental pollution was rampant: Almost half of Russia's arable land

On the anniversary of the gas leak that left 3,000 people dead in Bhopal, India, Union Carbide, having become a symbol of oppression, is burned in effigy.

acid rain: rain containing sulfuric and nitric acids (produced by the reaction of sulfur dioxide and nitrogen oxide with moisture when released into the air with the burning of fossil fuels)

greenhouse effect: the buildup of carbon dioxide in the earth's atmosphere that allows light to enter but inhibits the release of heat; believed to cause global warming

global warming: an increase in the earth's temperature due to the greenhouse effect

has been made unsuitable for farming, about a third of Russians live in cities where air pollution is over ten times greater than levels permitted in the United States, and half of Russia's tap water is unfit to drink. Pollution is so severe that the life expectancy of Russians has dropped, a lesson that should not be lost on the rest of us as we make decisions on how to treat our environment.

Environmental Problems in the Least Industrialized Nations

With its greater poverty and swelling populations, the Least Industrialized Nations have an even greater incentive to industrialize at any cost. The pressure of population growth combined with almost nonexistent environmental regulations destine the Least Industrialized Nations to become major sources of pollution.

Their lack of environmental protection laws has not gone unnoticed by opportunists in the Most Industrialized Nations, who seized the opportunity to use these countries as garbage dumps for hazardous wastes and for producing chemicals that their own nations will no longer tolerate (La Dou 1991; Smith 1995). Alarmed at the growing environmental destruction, the World Bank, a monetary arm of the Most Industrialized Nations, has placed pressure on the Least Industrialized Nations to reduce pollution and soil erosion (Lachica 1992). Understandably, the basic concern of these nations is to produce food and housing first, and to worry about the environment later.

Rain Forests and Extinction. Holding unknown consequences for the future of humanity is the extinction of numerous plant and animal species as tropical rain forests are relentlessly cleared for lumber, farms, and pastures. Although the rain forests cover just 7 percent of the earth's land area, they are home to half of all its plant species. With the rain forests disappearing at a rate of nearly *2,500 acres every hour* (McCuen 1993), it is estimated that ten thousand species are made extinct each year—about one per hour (Durning 1990). As the rain forests are destroyed, so are the Indian tribes that live in them. With their extinction goes their knowledge of the environment, the topic of the Cultural Diversity box.

The Bottom Line: The Growth Machine Versus the Earth

Underlying today's environmental decay is the globalization of capitalism, which has been stressed throughout this text. To maintain their dominance and increase their wealth, the Most Industrialized Nations, spurred by multinational corporations, continue to push for economic growth. As a result, a child born in the United States will have 35 times more impact on the earth's environment in his or her lifetime than a child born in India— and more than 250 times the impact of a child born in sub-Saharan Africa ("Population, Consumption . . . " 1996).

The Industrializing Nations don't like second place, and, playing catch-up, are striving to develop their economies. Meanwhile, the Least Industrialized Nations, eyeing the wealth of the others, are anxious to enter the race. Starting from far behind, however, they have to push for even faster growth if they have any hope of catching up.

Some scientists are convinced that the earth cannot withstand such onslaught (Krupp 1995). Our global economic production creates extensive pollution, and faster-paced production means faster-paced destruction of our environment. If the goal is a **sustainable environment,** a world system in which we use our physical environment to meet our needs without destroying humanity's future, we cannot continue to trash the earth's natural resources. In short, the ecological message is incompatible with an economic message that it is okay to rape the environment for the sake of profits.

The Environmental Movement

Concern about environmental problems has produced a worldwide social movement. In some countries, political parties built around environmental concerns, called *green parties,*

sustainable environment: a world system that takes into account the limits of the environment, produces enough material goods for everyone's needs, and leaves a heritage of a sound environment for the next generation

Perspectives

CULTURAL DIVERSITY AROUND THE WORLD

The Rain Forests: Lost Tribes, Lost Knowledge

Since 1900, 90 of Brazil's 270 Indian tribes have disappeared. As settlers have taken over their lands, other tribes have moved to villages. With village life comes a loss of tribal knowledge.

Tribal groups are not just "wild" people barely surviving in spite of their ignorance. On the contrary, they possess intricate forms of social organization and knowledge accumulated over thousands of years. The 2,500 Kayapo Indians, for example, belong to one of the Amazon's endangered tribes. The Kayapo make use of 250 types of wild fruit and hundreds of nut and tuber species. They cultivate thirteen types of bananas, eleven kinds of manioc (cassava), sixteen strains of sweet potato, and seventeen kinds of yams. Many of these varieties are unknown to non-Indians. The Kayapo also use thousands of medicinal plants, one of which contains a drug effective against intestinal parasites.

Until recently, Western scientists dismissed tribal knowledge as superstitious and worthless. Now, however, the West is coming to realize that to lose tribes is to lose knowledge. In the Central African Republic, a man whose chest was being eaten away by a subcutaneous amoeboid infection lay dying because he did not respond to drugs. Out of desperation, the Catholic nuns who were treating him sought the advice of a native doctor, who applied crushed termites to the open wounds. The "dying" man made a remarkable recovery.

The disappearance of the rain forests destroys many species yet unknown that may hold healing properties. Of the earth's 265,000 species of plants, only 1,100 have been thoroughly studied by Western scientists. Yet 40,000 may possess medicinal or undiscovered nutritional value for humans. For example, scientists have discovered that the needles of *Taxus baccata*, a Himalayan tree found in mountainous parts of India, contain taxol, a drug effective against ovarian cancer.

On average, one tribe of Amazonian Indians has been lost each year of this century—due to violence against them, greed by non-Indians for their native lands, and exposure to infectious diseases against which they have little resistance. Ethnocentrism underlies much of this assault. Perhaps the extreme is represented by the cattle ranchers in Colombia who killed eighteen Cueva Indians. The cattle ranchers were perplexed when they were put on trial for murder. They asked why they should be charged with a crime, since everyone knew that the Cuevas were animals, not people. They pointed out that there was even a verb in Colombian Spanish, *cuevar*, which means "to hunt Cueva Indians." So what was their crime, they asked? The jury found them innocent because of "cultural ignorance."

Sources: Simons 1989; Durning 1990; Gorman 1991; Linden 1991; Stipp 1992; Simons 1995.

---

campaign in local and national elections. In Europe, especially Germany, green parties have become a political force and have won seats in the national legislatures.

Activists in the environmental movement generally seek solutions in politics, legislation, and education. Seeing that pollution continues, the rain forests are still being cleared, and that species are becoming extinct, some activists are convinced that the planet is doomed unless immediate steps are taken. Choosing a more radical course, they use extreme tactics to try to arouse indignation among the public and thus force the government to act. Convinced that they stand for morality, many are willing to break the law and go to jail for their actions. Such activists are featured in the following Thinking Critically section.

Thinking Critically About Social Controversy

Ecosabotage

▼ Chaining oneself to a giant Douglas fir slated for cutting; pouring sand down the gas tank of a bulldozer; tearing down power lines and ripping up survey stakes; driving spikes into redwood trees and sinking whaling vessels—are these the acts of dangerous punks, intent on vandalism and with little understanding of the needs of modern society? Or are they the acts of

As concern about the environment has grown, a social movement to try to change the course of events has developed. Earth First!, one group within this movement, is featured in the text. Shown here is an Earth First! rally in Arcata, California.

brave men and women willing to put their freedom, and even their lives, on the line on behalf of the earth itself?

Probably nothing in life can be painted accurately in such terms, but to get some idea of why ecosabotage is taking place, consider the Medicine Tree, a 3,000-year-old redwood in the Sally Bell Grove near the northern California coast. Georgia Pacific, a lumber company, was determined to cut down the Medicine Tree, the oldest and largest of the region's redwoods, which rests on an ancient sacred site of the Sinkyone Indians. Members of Earth First! chained themselves to the tree. After they were arrested, the sawing began. Other protesters jumped over the police-lined barricade and planted themselves in front of the axes and chain saws. A logger swung an axe and missed a demonstrator. At that moment, the sheriff radioed a restraining order, and the cutting stopped.

How many 3,000-year-old trees remain on this planet? Do fences and picnic tables for back yard barbecues justify cutting them down? It is questions like these, as well as the slaughter of seals, the destruction of the rain forests, and the drowning of dolphins in mile-long drift nets that spawned Earth First! and other organizations devoted to preserving the environment, such as Greenpeace, Sea Shepherds, and the Ruckus Society.

"We feel like there are insane people who are consciously destroying our environment, and we are compelled to fight back," explains a member of one of the militant groups. "No compromise in defense of Mother Earth!" says another. "With famine and death approaching, we're in the early stages of World War III," adds another.

The dedication of some of these activists has brought them close to martyrdom. When Paul Watson, founder of the Sea Shepherds, sprayed seals with green dye, which destroys the value of their pelts but doesn't hurt the animals, hunters hogtied him, dragged him across the ice, and threatened to toss him into the sea. "It's no big deal," says Watson, "when you consider that 100 million people in this century have died in wars over real estate."

Radical environmentalists represent a broad range of activities and purposes. They are united neither on tactics nor goals. Some want to stop a specific action, such as the killing of whales, or to destroy all nuclear weapons and dismantle nuclear power plants. Others want everyone to become vegetarians. Still others want the earth's population to be reduced to 1 billion, roughly what it was in 1800. Some even want humans to return to hunting and gathering bands. Most espouse a simpler lifestyle that will consume less energy and place less pressure on the earth's resources. These groups are so splintered that the founder of Earth First!, Dave Foreman, quit his own organization when it became too confrontational for his tastes.

Among their successes, the radical groups count a halt to the killing of dolphins off Japan's Iki Island, a ban on whaling, trash recycling in many communities, hundreds of thousands of acres of uncut trees, and, of course, the Medicine Tree.

For Your Consideration

Who, then, are these people? Should we applaud ecosaboteurs or jail them? As symbolic interactionists stress, it all depends on your definition. And as conflict theorists emphasize, your definition likely depends on your location in the economic structure. That is, if you are the owner of a lumber company you will see ecosaboteurs differently from the way a camping enthusiast would. How does your own view of ecosaboteurs depend on your life situation? What effective alternatives to ecosabotage are there for people who are convinced that we are destroying the life support system of our planet?

Sources: Russell 1987; Borrelli 1988; Guha 1989; Carpenter 1990; Eder 1990; Foote 1990; Martin 1990; Parfit 1990; Reed and Benet 1990; Courtney 1995. ▲

environmental sociology: a subdiscipline of sociology that examines how human activities affect the physical environment and how the physical environment affects human activities

Environmental Sociology

Environmental sociology, which examines the relationship between human societies and the environment, emerged as a subdiscipline of sociology about 1970 (Dunlap and Catton 1979, 1983; Buttel 1987; Freudenburg and Gramling 1989; Laska 1993). Its main assumptions are:

1. The physical environment is a significant variable in sociological investigation.

2. Human beings are but one species among many that are dependent on the natural environment.

3. Because of intricate feedbacks to nature, human actions have many unintended consequences.

4. The world is finite, so there are potential physical limits to economic growth.

5. Economic expansion requires increased extraction of resources from the environment.

6. Increased extraction of resources leads to ecological problems.

7. These ecological problems place restrictions on economic expansion.

8. Governments create environmental problems by trying to create conditions for the accumulation of capital.

As you can see, the goal of environmental sociology is not to stop pollution or nuclear power, but, rather, to study how humans (their cultures, values, and behaviors) affect the physical environment and how the physical environment affects human activities. Environmental sociologists, however, generally are also environmental activists, and the Section on Environment and Technology of the American Sociological Association tries to influence governmental policies (American Sociological Association, n.d.).

At this point in global capitalism, the goal of achieving a harmonious relationship with our environment is not even on the horizon. In 1997, pollution in Malaysia was so bad that for many months people wore masks as they went about their everyday lives. Shown here are surgical masks for sale from a roadside vendor.

Technology and the Environment: The Goal of Harmony

It is inevitable that humans will continue to develop new technologies. But the abuse of our environment by those technologies is not inevitable. To understate the matter, the destruction of our planet is an unwise choice.

If we are to have a world that is worth passing on to coming generations, we must seek harmony between technology and the natural environment. This will not be easy. At one extreme are people who claim that to protect the environment we must eliminate industrialization and go back to some sort of preindustrial way of life. At the other extreme are people unable to see the harm being done to the natural environment, who want the entire world to continue industrializing at full speed. Somewhere, there must be a middle ground, one that recognizes that industrialization is here to stay but that we *can* control it, for it is our creation. Industrialization, controlled, can enhance our quality of life. Uncontrolled, it will destroy us.

As a parallel to the development of technologies, then, we must develop systems to reduce or eliminate their harm to the environment. This includes mechanisms to monitor the production, use, and disposal of technology. The question, of course, is whether we have the resolve to take the steps that will preserve the environment for future generations. The stakes—no less than the welfare of the entire planet—are surely high enough to motivate us to make wise choices.

Summary and Review

An Overview of Social Change

What are the major trends in social change over the course of human history?

The primary changes in human history are the four social revolutions (domestication, agriculture, industrialization, and information); the change from *Gemeinschaft* to *Gesellschaft* types of societies; capitalism and industrialization; modernization; and global stratification. Ethnic conflicts and social movements indicate cutting edges of social change. Pp. 618–623.

How Technology Changes Society

What is Ogburn's theory of social change?

Ogburn identified technology as the basic cause of social change, which comes through three processes: **invention, discovery,** and **diffusion.** The term **cultural lag** refers to symbolic culture lagging behind changes in technology. Pp. 623–625.

What types of technology are there, and what effects can a changed technology have on society?

Because technology is an organizing force of social life, when technology changes its effects can be profound. The automobile and the computer were used as extended examples. The automobile changed the development of cities, buying patterns, architecture, and even courtship and women's roles. We looked at how the computer is changing the way we practice medicine, learn, and work. The information superhighway is likely to perpetuate social inequalities both on a national and global level. Pp. 625–633.

Other Theories of Social Change

Besides technology, capitalism, modernization, and so on, what other theories of social change are there?

Evolutionary theories presuppose that societies are moving from the same starting point to some similar ending point. *Unilinear* theories, which assume the same path for everyone, have been replaced with *multilinear* theories, which assume that different paths can lead to the same stage of development. *Cyclical* theories, in contrast, view civilizations as going through a process of birth, youth, maturity, decline, and death. Conflict theorists view social change as inevitable, for each *thesis* (basically an arrangement of power) contains an *antithesis* (contradictions). A new *synthesis* develops to resolve these contradictions, but it, too, contains contradictions that will have to be resolved, and so on. This is called a **dialectical process.** Pp. 634–635.

Social Change and the Natural Environment

What are the environmental problems of the Most Industrialized Nations?

The environmental problems of the Most Industrialized Nations are severe, ranging from city smog and **acid rain** to the **greenhouse effect.** Scientists debate whether the greenhouse effect is real; if it is, it may cause **global warming** that will fundamentally affect social life. The burning of fossil fuels in internal combustion engines lies at the root of many environmental problems, but alternative sources of energy are unlikely to be developed until the multinational corporations can turn them into a profit. Due to the location of factories and hazardous waste sites, environmental problems have a greater impact on minorities and the poor. Pp. 635–637.

What are the environmental problems of the Industrializing and Least Industrialized Nations?

The worst environmental problems are found in the former Soviet Union, a legacy of the unrestrained exploitation of resources by the Communist party. The rush of the Least Industrialized Nations to industrialize is adding to our en-

vironmental decay. The world is facing a basic conflict between the lust for profits through the exploitation of the earth's resources and the need to produce a **sustainable environment.** Pp. 637–638.

What is the environmental movement?

The environmental movement is an attempt to restore a healthy environment for the world's people. This global movement takes many forms, from peacefully influencing the political process to *ecosabotage*, sabotaging the efforts of people thought to be legally harming the environment. Pp. 638–640.

What is environmental sociology?

Environmental sociology is not an attempt to change the environment, but a study of the relationship between humans and the environment. Environmental sociologists are generally also environmental activists. Pp. 640–642.

Where can I read more on this topic?

Suggested readings for this chapter are listed on page 667.

 Sociology and the Internet

All URLs listed are current as of the printing of this book. URLs are often changed. Please check our Website http://www.abacon.com/henslin for updates.

1. Rapid technological change raises new issues for public debate and new areas for sociologists to study. The Center for Democracy and Technology (CDT) is a "watchdog" group concerned with the impact of technological policy decisions and related issues on U.S. society. Read one or more of the headline articles at their site: *http://www.cdt.org* In a one- or two-page paper, answer the following questions: What issues are of concern? What seems to be the viewpoint of those at CDT? Finally, present opposing arguments to their views.

2. This chapter's summary of the impact of social change on the environment in the Most Industrialized Nations suggests that the "bottom line" involves a decision for the global growth machine or the earth. Attempts at balancing these concerns are referred to as *sustainable environment.* Read the section "Social Change and the Natural Environment." Then look at efforts to create sustainable environments by accessing Solstice *http://solstice.crest.org* Read the information on Solstice itself; then click "Related Net sites." Search the GEM database to see a list of sites dedicated to environmental concerns. Browse several of them.

Write a short paper in which you answer these questions: Is the sustainable environment theme aimed only at Least In-

dustrial Nations, or is it global? What are some policies and practices that you think might work with nations at different levels of industrialization? Are there any that would be practical in nearly all countries? How likely is it that any of the policies will be adopted by the United States? What do you think the future holds: growth machine or the earth? Or a compromise enabling a sustainable environment? If so, what would that compromise consist of?

3. Read the Environmental Defense Fund Web page to determine key areas of concern about the environment: *www.edf.org* Examine the role of modernization, industrialization, and technology in these environmental concerns. What surprised you? Read some of the "Practical Action" articles. What can you do to help save our environment? Be specific.

4. Examine the Amish Web sites listed below:

www.amish-heartland.com/amish/
www.800padutch.com/amish.html
www.poopets.com/

Why do the Amish limit the introduction of technology into their community? What are they afraid will happen? After reading the section in your text about the changes that the automobile created in U.S. society, explain why the Amish still do not own automobiles. Why do they still use the horse and buggy?

Glossary

acculturation: the transmission of culture from one generation to the next

achieved statuses: positions that are earned, accomplished, or involve at least some effort or activity on the individual's part

acid rain: rain containing sulfuric and nitric acids (produced by the reaction of sulfur dioxide and nitrogen oxide with moisture when released into the air with the burning of fossil fuels)

acting crowd: Herbert Blumer's term for an excited group that collectively moves toward a goal

activity theory: the view that satisfaction during old age is related to a person's level and quality of activity

Afrocentrism: an emphasis on African-American traditions and concerns

age cohort: people born at roughly the same time who pass through the life course together

ageism: prejudice, discrimination, and hostility directed against people because of their age; can be directed against any age group, including youth

agent provocateur: someone who joins a group in order to spy on it and to sabotage it by *provoking* its members to commit illegal acts

agents of socialization: people or groups that affect our self-concept, attitudes, or other orientations toward life

aggregate: individuals who temporarily share the same physical space but do not see themselves as belonging together

agricultural revolution: the second social revolution, based on the invention of the plow, which led to agricultural society

agricultural society: a society based on large-scale agriculture, dependent on plows drawn by animals

alienation: Marx's term for workers' lack of connection to the product of their labor; caused by their being assigned repetitive tasks on a small part of a product

alterative social movement: a social movement that seeks to alter only particular aspects of people

anarchy: a condition of lawlessness or political disorder caused by the absence or collapse of governmental authority

animal culture: learned, shared behavior among animals

animism: the belief that all objects in the world have spirits, some of which are dangerous and must be outwitted

anomie: Durkheim's term for a condition of society in which people become detached, cut loose from the norms that usually guide their behavior

anti-Semitism: prejudice, discrimination, and persecution directed against Jews

anticipatory socialization: because one anticipates a future role, one learns parts of it now

apartheid: the separation of races as was practiced in South Africa

appearance: how an individual looks when playing a role

applied sociology: the use of sociology to solve problems—from the micro level of family relationships to the macro level of crime and pollution

ascribed statuses: positions an individual either inherits at birth or receives involuntarily later in life

assimilation: the process of being absorbed into the mainstream culture

authoritarian leader: a leader who leads by giving orders

authoritarian personality: Theodor Adorno's term for people who are prejudiced and rank high on scales of conformity, intolerance, insecurity, respect for authority, and submissiveness to superiors

authority: power that people consider legitimate

back stage: where people rest from their performances, discuss their presentations, and plan future performances

background assumptions: deeply embedded common understandings, or basic rules, concerning our view of the world and of how people ought to act

barter: the exchange of one item for another

basic demographic equation: growth rate = births – deaths + net migration

bilateral (system of descent): a system of reckoning descent that counts both the mother's and the father's side

blended family: a family whose members were once part of other families

born again: a term describing Christians who have undergone a life-transforming religious experience so radical that they feel they have become new persons

bourgeoisie: Karl Marx's term for the people who own the means of production

bureaucracy: a formal organization with a hierarchy of authority; a clear division of labor; emphasis on written rules, communications, and records; and impersonality of positions

capitalism: an economic system characterized by the private ownership of the means of production, the pursuit of profit, and market competition

capitalist class: the wealthy who own the means of production and buy the labor of the working class

capitalist world economy: the dominance of capitalism in the world along with the international interdependence that capitalism has created

cargo cult: a social movement in which South Pacific islanders destroyed their possessions in the anticipation that their ancestors would send items by ship

caste system: a form of social stratification in which one's status is determined by birth and is lifelong

category: people who have similar characteristics

causation: if a change in one variable leads to a change in another variable, causation is said to exist

centrist party: a political party that represents the center of political opinion

charisma: literally, an extraordinary gift from God; more commonly, an outstanding, "magnetic" personality

charismatic authority: authority based on an individual's outstanding traits, which attract followers

charismatic leader: literally, someone to whom God has given a gift; more commonly, someone who exerts extraordinary appeal to a group of followers

checks and balances: the separation of powers among the three branches of U.S. government—legislative, executive, and judicial—so that each is able to nullify the actions of the other two, thus preventing the domination of any single branch

church: according to Durkheim, one of the three essential elements of religion—a moral community of believers; a second definition is a large, highly organized group with formal, sedate worship services and little emphasis on personal conversion

circular reaction: Robert Park's term for a back-and-forth communication between the members of a crowd whereby a "collective impulse" is transmitted

citizenship: the concept that birth (and residence) in a country impart basic rights

city: a place in which a large number of people are permanently based and do not produce their own food

city-state: an independent city whose power radiates outward, bringing the adjacent area under its rule

civil disobedience: the act of deliberately but peacefully disobeying laws considered unjust

civil religion: Robert Bellah's term for religion that is such an established feature of a country's life that its history and social institutions become sanctified by being associated with God

clan: an extended network of relatives

clan system: a form of social stratification in which individuals receive their social standing through belonging to an extended network of relatives

class conflict: Marx's term for the struggle between the proletariat and the bourgeoisie

class consciousness: Karl Marx's term for awareness of a common identity based on one's position in the means of production

class system: a form of social stratification based primarily on the possession of money or material possessions

clinical sociology: the direct involvement of sociologists in bringing about social change

clique: a cluster of people within a larger group who choose to interact with one another; an internal faction

closed-ended questions: questions followed by a list of possible answers to be selected by the respondent

coalition: the alignment of some members of a group against others

coalition government: a government in which a country's largest party aligns itself with one or more smaller parties

coercion: power that people do not accept as rightly exercised over them; also called *illegitimate power*

cohabitation: unmarried couples living together in a sexual relationship

collective behavior: extraordinary activities carried out by groups of people; includes lynchings, rumors, panics, urban legends, and fads and fashions

collective mind: Gustave LeBon's term for the tendency of people in a crowd to feel, think, and act in extraordinary ways

colonization: the process by which one nation takes over another nation, usually for the purpose of exploiting its labor and natural resources

common sense: those things that "everyone knows" are true

community: a place people identify with, where they sense that they belong and that others care what happens to them

compartmentalize: to separate acts from feelings or attitudes

conflict theory: a theoretical framework in which society is viewed as composed of groups competing for scarce resources

conspicuous consumption: Thorstein Veblen's term for a change from the Protestant ethic to an eagerness to show off wealth by the elaborate consumption of goods

contradictory class location: Erik Wright's term for a position in the class structure that generates contradictory interests

control group: the group of subjects not exposed to the independent variable

control theory: the idea that two control systems—inner controls and outer controls—work against our tendencies to deviate

convergence theory: the view that as capitalist and socialist economic systems each adopt features of the other, a hybrid (or mixed) economic system will emerge

corporate capitalism: the domination of the economic system by giant corporations

corporate culture: the orientations that characterize corporate work settings

corporation: the joint ownership of a business enterprise, whose liabilities and obligations are separate from those of its owners

correlation: the simultaneous occurrence of two or more variables

correspondence principle: the sociological principle that schools correspond to (or reflect) the social structure of society

cosmology: teachings or ideas that provide a unified picture of the world

counterculture: a group whose values, beliefs, and related behaviors place its members in opposition to the broader culture

credential society: the use of diplomas and degrees to determine who is eligible for jobs, even though the diploma or degree may be irrelevant to the actual work

credit card: a device that allows its owner to purchase goods but to be billed later

crime: the violation of norms that are written into law.

criminal justice system: the system of police, courts, and prisons set up to deal with people who are accused of having committed a crime

crude birth rate: the annual number of births per 1,000 population

crude death rate: the annual number of deaths per 1,000 population

cult: a new religion with few followers, whose teachings and practices put it at odds with the dominant culture and religion

cultural diffusion: the spread of cultural characteristics from one group to another

cultural goals: the legitimate objectives held out to the members of a society

cultural lag: Ogburn's term for human behavior lagging behind technological innovations

cultural leveling: the process by which cultures become similar to one another, and especially by which Western industrial culture is imported and diffused into developing nations

cultural relativism: understanding a people from the framework of its own culture

cultural transmission: in reference to education, the ways in which schools transmit a society's culture, especially its core values

cultural universal: a value, norm, or other cultural trait that is found in every group

culture: the language, beliefs, values, norms, behaviors, and even material objects that are passed from one generation to the next

culture contact: encounter between people from different cultures, or coming in contact with some parts of a different culture

culture of poverty: the assumption that the values and behaviors of the poor make them fundamentally different from other people, that these factors are largely responsible for their poverty, and that parents perpetuate poverty across generations by passing these characteristics to their children

culture shock: the disorientation that people experience when they come in contact with a fundamentally different culture and can no longer depend on their taken-for-granted assumptions about life

currency: paper money

debit card: a device that allows its owner to charge purchases against his or her bank account

defensive medicine: medical practices done not for the patient's benefit but in order to protect a physician from malpractice suits

deferred gratification: forgoing something in the present in the hope of achieving greater gains in the future

definition of the situation: the way we look at matters in life; the way we define reality or some particular situation

degradation ceremonies: rituals designed to strip an individual of his or her identity as a group member; for example, a court martial or the defrocking of a priest

dehumanization: the act or process of reducing people to objects that do not deserve the treatment accorded humans

deinstitutionalization: the release of patients from mental hospitals into the community while receiving treatment within a network of outpatient services

democracy: a system of government in which authority derives from the people, derived from two Greek words that translate literally as "power to the people"

democratic leader: a leader who leads by trying to reach a consensus

democratic socialism: a hybrid economic system in which capitalism is mixed with state ownership

demographic transition: a three-stage historical process of population growth: first, high birth rates and high death rates; second, high birth rates and low death rates; and third, low birth rates and low death rates

demographic variables: the three factors that influence population growth: fertility, mortality, and net migration

demography: the study of the size, composition, growth, and distribution of human populations

denomination: a "brand name" within a major religion, for example, Methodist or Baptist

dependency ratio: the number of workers required to support dependent persons—those 64 and older and those 15 and under

dependency theory: the view that the Least Industrialized Nations have been unable to develop their economies because they grew dependent on the Most Industrialized Nations

dependent variable: a factor that is changed by an independent variable

depersonalization: dealing with people as though they were objects; in the case of medical care, as though patients were merely cases and diseases, not persons

deposit receipts: a receipt stating that a certain amount of goods is on deposit in a warehouse or bank; the receipt is used as a form of money

deterrence: creating fear so people will refrain from breaking the law

deviance: the violation of rules or norms

deviants: people who violate rules, as a result of which others react negatively to them

dialectical process: each arrangement, or thesis, contains contradictions, or antitheses, which must be resolved; the new arrangement, or synthesis, contains its own contradictions, and so on

dictatorship: a form of government in which power is seized by an individual

differential association: Edwin Sutherland's term to indicate that associating with some groups results in learning an "excess of definitions" of deviance, and, by extension, in a greater likelihood that one will become deviant

diffusion: the spread of invention or discovery from one area to another; identified by William Ogburn as the final of three processes of social change

direct democracy: a form of democracy in which the eligible voters meet together to discuss issues and make their decisions

disabling environment: an environment that is harmful to health

discovery: a new way of seeing reality; identified by William Ogburn as the second of three processes of social change

discrimination: an *act* of unfair treatment directed against an individual or a group

disengagement theory: the view that society prevents disruption by having the elderly vacate (or disengage from) their positions of responsibility so the younger generation can step into their shoes

disinvestment: the withdrawal of investments by financial institutions, which seals the fate of an urban area

divest: to sell off

divine right of kings: the idea that the king's authority comes directly from God

division of labor: the splitting of a group's or a society's tasks into specialties

documents: in its narrow sense, written sources that provide data; in its extended sense, archival material of any sort, including photographs, movies, and so on

domestication revolution: the first social revolution, based on the domestication of plants and animals, which led to pastoral and horticultural societies

dominant group: the group with the most power, greatest privileges, and highest social status

downward social mobility: movement down the social class ladder

dramaturgy: an approach, pioneered by Erving Goffman, analyzing social life in terms of drama or the stage; also called dramaturgical analysis

dumping: the practice of sending unprofitable patients to public hospitals

dyad: the smallest possible group, consisting of two people

ecclesia: a religious group so integrated into the dominant culture that it is difficult to tell where the one begins and the other leaves off; also called a *state religion*

economy: a system of distribution of goods and services

edge city: a large clustering of service facilities and residential areas near highway intersections that provides a sense of place to people who live, shop, and work there

education: a formal system of teaching knowledge, values, and skills

egalitarian: authority more or less equally divided between people or groups, in this instance between husband and wife

ego: Freud's term for a balancing force between the id and the demands of society

electronic community: individuals who more or less regularly interact with one another on the Internet

electronic primary group: individuals who regularly interact with one another on the Internet, who see themselves as a group, and who develop close ties with one another

emergent norms: Ralph Turner's and Lewis Killian's term for the development of new norms to cope with a new situation, especially among crowds

empty nest: a married couple's domestic situation after the last child has left home

endogamy: the practice of marrying within one's own group

enterprise zone: the use of economic incentives in a designated area with the intention of encouraging investment there

environmental sociology: a subdiscipline of sociology that examines how human activities affect the physical environment and how the physical environment affects human activities

epidemiology: the study of disease and disability patterns in a population

ethnic (and ethnicity): having distinctive cultural characteristics

ethnic cleansing: a policy of population elimination, including forcible expulsion and genocide. The term emerged in 1992 among the Serbians during their planned policy of expelling Croats and Muslims from territories claimed by them during the Yugoslav wars

ethnic work: activities designed to discover, enhance, or maintain ethnic and racial identification

ethnocentrism: the use of one's own culture as a yardstick for judging the ways of other individuals or societies, generally leading to a negative evaluation of their values, norms, and behaviors

ethnomethodology: the study of how people use background assumptions to make sense out of life

euthanasia: mercy killing

evangelism: an attempt to win converts

exchange mobility: about the same numbers of people moving up and down the social class ladder, such that, on balance, the social class system shows little change

exogamy: the practice of marrying outside one's group

experiment: the use of control groups and experimental groups and dependent and independent variables to test causation

experimental group: the group of subjects exposed to the independent variable

exponential growth curve: a pattern of growth in which numbers double during approximately equal intervals, thus accelerating in the latter stages

expressive leader: an individual who increases harmony and minimizes conflict in a group; also known as a socioemotional leader

extended family: a nuclear family plus other relatives, such as grandparents, uncles and aunts, who live together

face-saving behavior: techniques used to salvage a performance that is going sour

fad: a temporary pattern of behavior that catches people's attention

false consciousness: Karl Marx's term to refer to workers identifying with the interests of capitalists

family: two or more people who consider themselves related by blood, marriage, or adoption

family of orientation: the family in which a person grows up

family of procreation: the family formed when a couple's first child is born

fashion: a pattern of behavior that catches people's attention, which lasts longer than a fad

fecundity: the number of children that women are theoretically *capable* of bearing

fee for service: payment to a physician to diagnose and treat a patient's medical problems

feminism: the philosophy that men and women should be politically, economically, and socially equal, and organized activity on behalf of this principle

feminization of poverty: a trend in U.S. poverty whereby most poor families are headed by women

feral children: children assumed to have been raised by animals, in the wilderness isolated from other humans

fertility rate: the number of children that the average woman bears

fiat money: currency issued by a government that is not backed by stored value

folkways: norms that are not strictly enforced

formal organization: a secondary group designed to achieve explicit objectives

front stage: where performances are given

functional analysis: a theoretical framework in which society is viewed as composed of various parts, each with a function that, when fulfilled, contributes to society's equilibrium; also known as functionalism and structural functionalism

functional equivalent: in this context, a substitute that serves the same functions (or meets the same needs) as religion, for example, psychotherapy

functional illiterate: a high school graduate who has difficulty with basic reading and math

functional requisites: the major tasks that a society must fulfill if it is to survive

fundamentalism: the belief that true religion is threatened by modernism and that the faith as it was originally practiced should be restored

gatekeeping: the process by which education opens and closes doors of opportunity; another term for the **social placement** function of education

Gemeinschaft: a type of society in which life is intimate; a community in which everyone knows everyone else and people share a sense of togetherness

gender: the social characteristics that a society considers proper for its males and females; masculinity or femininity

gender age: the relative values of men's and women's ages in a particular culture

gender role: the behaviors and attitudes considered appropriate because one is a female or a male

gender socialization: the ways in which society sets children onto different courses in life *because* they are male or female

gender stratification: males' and females' unequal access to power, prestige, and property on the basis of their sex

generalizability: the extent to which the findings from one group (or sample) can be generalized or applied to other groups (or populations)

generalization: a statement that goes beyond the individual case and is applied to a broader group or situation

generalized other: the norms, values, attitudes, and expectations of people "in general"; the child's ability to take the role of the generalized other is a significant step in the development of a self

genetic predispositions: inborn tendencies, in this context, to commit deviant acts

genocide: the systematic annihilation or attempted annihilation of a people based on their presumed race or ethnicity

gentrification: the displacement of the poor by the relatively affluent, who renovate the former's homes

gerontocracy: a society (or some other group) run by the elderly

Gesellschaft: a type of society dominated by impersonal relationships, individual accomplishments, and self-interest

gestures: the ways in which people use their bodies to communicate with one another

global warming: an increase in the earth's temperature due to the greenhouse effect

globalization: the extensive movement of capital and ideas among nations due to the expansion of capitalism

goal displacement: a goal displaced by another; in this context, the adoption of new goals by an organization; also known as *goal replacement*

gold standard: paper money backed by gold

grade inflation: higher grades given for the same work; a general rise in student grades without a corresponding increase in learning or test scores

graying of America: a term that refers to the rising proportion of older people as a percentage of the U.S. population

greenhouse effect: the buildup of carbon dioxide in the earth's atmosphere that allows light to enter but inhibits the release of heat; believed to cause global warming

gross national product (GNP): the amount of goods and services produced by a nation

group: defined differently by various sociologists, but in a general sense, people who have something in common and who believe that what they have in common is significant; a good working definition is people who regularly and consciously interact with one another; also called a social group

group dynamics: the ways in which individuals affect groups and the ways in which groups influence individuals

groupthink: Irving Janis's term for a narrowing of thought by a group of people, leading to the perception that there is only one correct answer, in which to even suggest alternatives becomes a sign of disloyalty

growth rate: the net change in a population after adding births, subtracting deaths, and either adding or subtracting net migration

health: a human condition measured by four components: physical, mental, social, and spiritual

health maintenance organization (HMO): a health care organization that provides medical treatment to its members for a fixed annual cost

hidden curriculum: the unwritten goals of schools, such as obedience to authority and conformity to cultural norms

homogamy: the tendency of people with similar characteristics to marry one another

horticultural society: a society based on cultivating plants by the use of hand tools

hospice: a place, or services brought into someone's home, for the purpose of bringing comfort and dignity to a dying person

household: all people who occupy the same housing unit

human ecology: Robert Park's term for the relationship between people and their environment (natural resources such as land)

humanizing a work setting: organizing a workplace in such a way that it develops rather than impedes human potential

hunting and gathering society: a human group dependent on hunting and gathering for its survival

hypothesis: a statement of the expected relationship between variables according to predictions from a theory

id: Freud's term for the individual's inborn basic drives

ideal culture: the ideal values and norms of a people, the goals held out for them

ideal type: a composite of characteristics based on many specific examples ("ideal" in this case means a description of the abstracted characteristics, not what one desires to exist)

ideology: beliefs about the way things ought to be that justify social arrangements

illegitimate opportunity structures: opportunities for crimes that are woven into the texture of life

imperialism: a nation's attempt to create an empire; its pursuit of unlimited geographical expansion

impression management: the term used by Erving Goffman to describe people's efforts to control the impressions that others receive of them

in-groups: groups toward which one feels loyalty

incapacitation: to take away someone's capacity to commit crimes, in this instance, by putting the offender in prison

incest: sexual relations between specified relatives, such as brothers and sisters or parents and children

indentured service: a contractual system in which someone sells his or her body (services) for a specified period of time in an arrangement very close to slavery, except that it is voluntarily entered into

independent variable: a factor that causes a change in another variable, called the dependent variable

individual discrimination: the negative treatment of one person by another on the basis of that person's perceived characteristics

Industrial Revolution: the third social revolution, occurring when machines powered by fuels replaced most animal and human power

industrial society: a society based on the harnessing of machines powered by fuels

inflation: an increase in prices

institutional discrimination: negative treatment of a minority group that is built into a society's institutions; also called *systemic discrimination*

institutionalized means: approved ways of reaching cultural goals

instrumental leader: an individual who tries to keep the group moving toward its goals; also known as a task-oriented leader

intentional family: people who declare themselves a family and treat one another as members of the same family; originated in the late twentieth century in response to the need for intimacy not met due to distance, divorce, and death

intergenerational mobility: the change that family members make in social class from one generation to the next

interlocking directorates: the same people serving on the board of directors of several companies

internal colonialism: the policy of economically exploiting minority groups

interview: direct questioning of respondents

interviewer bias: effects that interviewers have on respondents that lead to biased answers

invasion–succession cycle: the process of one group of people displacing a group whose racial-ethnic or social class characteristics differ from their own

invention: the combination of existing elements and materials to form new ones; identified by William Ogburn as the first of three processes of social change

involuntary memberships: (or involuntary associations) groups in which people are assigned membership rather than choosing to join

iron law of oligarchy: Robert Michels's phrase for the tendency of formal organizations to be dominated by a small, self-perpetuating elite

labeling theory: the view, developed by symbolic interactionists, that the labels people are given affect their own and others' perceptions of them, thus channeling their behavior either into deviance or into conformity

laissez-faire capitalism: unrestrained manufacture and trade (literally, "hands off" capitalism)

laissez-faire leader: an individual who leads by being highly permissive

language: a system of symbols that can be combined in an infinite number of ways and can represent not only objects but also abstract thought

latent functions: the unintended consequences of people's actions that help to keep a social system in equilibrium

leader: someone who influences other people

leadership styles: ways in which people express their leadership

leisure: time not taken up by work or required activities such as eating, sleeping, commuting, child care, and housework

life course: the sequence of events that we experience as we journey from birth to death

life expectancy: the number of years that an average newborn can expect to live

life span: The maximum length of life of a species

living will: a statement people in good health sign that clearly expresses their feelings about being kept alive on artificial life support systems

lobbyists: people who influence legislation on behalf of their clients

looking-glass self: a term coined by Charles Horton Cooley to refer to the process by which our self develops through internalizing others' reactions to us

machismo: an emphasis on male strength and dominance

macro-level analysis: an examination of large-scale patterns of society

macropolitics: the exercise of large-scale power, the government being the most common example

macrosociology: analysis of social life focusing on broad features of social structure, such as social class and the relationships of groups to one another; an approach usually used by functionalist and conflict theorists

mainstreaming: helping people to become part of the mainstream of society

Malthus theorem: an observation by Thomas Malthus that although the food supply increases only arithmetically (from 1 to 2 to 3 to 4 and so on), population grows geometrically (from 2 to 4 to 8 to 16 and so forth)

mandatory education laws: laws that require all children to attend school until a specified age or until they complete a minimum grade in school

manifest function: the intended consequences of people's actions designed to help some part of a social system

manner: the attitudes that people show as they play their roles

marginal working class: the most desperate members of the working class, who have few skills, little job security, and are often unemployed

market: any process of buying and selling; on a more formal level, the mechanism that establishes values for the exchange of goods and services

market competition: the exchange of items between willing buyers and sellers

market forces: the law of supply and demand

market restraints: laws and regulations that limit the capacity to manufacture and sell products

marriage: a group's approved mating arrangements, usually marked by a ritual of some sort

marriage squeeze: the difficulty a group of men or women have in finding marriage partners, due to an imbalanced sex ratio

mass media: forms of communication, such as radio, newspapers, and television, that are directed to mass audiences

mass society: industrialized, highly bureaucratized, impersonal society

mass society theory: an explanation for participation in social movements based on the assumption that such movements offer a sense of belonging to people who have weak social ties

master status: a status that cuts across the other statuses that an individual occupies

material culture: the material objects that distinguish a group of people, such as their art, buildings, weapons, utensils, machines, hairstyles, clothing, and jewelry

matriarchy: a society in which women dominate men

matrilineal (system of descent): a system of reckoning descent that counts only the mother's side

means of production: the tools, factories, land, and investment capital used to produce wealth

mechanical solidarity: Durkheim's term for a shared consciousness or sense of unity that people experience as a result of being involved in similar occupations or activities

medicalization: the transformation of something into a matter to be treated by physicians

medicalization of deviance: to make deviance a medical matter, a symptom of some underlying illness that needs to be treated by physicians

medicine: one of the major social institutions that sociologists study; a society's organized ways of dealing with sickness and injury

medium of exchange: the means by which people value goods and services in order to make an exchange, for example, currency, gold, and silver

megalopolis: an urban area consisting of at least two metropolises and their many suburbs

melting pot: the view that Americans of various backgrounds would blend into a sort of ethnic stew

meritocracy: a form of social stratification in which all positions are awarded on the basis of merit

metropolis: a central city surrounded by smaller cities and their suburbs

metropolitan statistical area (MSA): a central city and the urbanized counties adjacent to it

micro-level analysis: an examination of small-scale patterns of society

micropolitics: the exercise of power in everyday life, such as deciding who is going to do the housework

microsociology: analysis of social life focusing on social interaction; an approach usually used by symbolic interactionists

middle-range theories: explanations of human behavior that go beyond a particular observation or research but avoid sweeping generalizations that attempt to account for everything

millenarian movement: a social movement based on the prophecy of coming social upheaval

milling: a crowd standing or walking around as they talk excitedly about some event

minimax strategy: Richard Berk's term for the effort people make to minimize their costs and maximize their rewards

minority group: people who are singled out for unequal treatment, and who regard themselves as objects of collective discrimination

modernization: the process by which a *Gemeinschaft* society is transformed into a *Gesellschaft* society: the transformation of traditional societies into industrial societies

monarchy: a form of government headed by a king or queen

money: any item (from seashells to gold) that serves as a medium of exchange; today, currency is the most common form

monopoly: the control of an entire industry by a single company

monotheism: the belief that there is only one God

moral panic: a fear that grips large numbers of people that some evil group or behavior threatens the well-being of society, followed by intense hostility, sometimes violence, toward those thought responsible

mores: (MORE-rays) norms that are strictly enforced because they are thought essential to core values

multiculturalism (also called pluralism): a philosophy or political policy that permits or encourages ethnic variation

multinational corporations: companies that operate across many national boundaries; also called transnational corporations

nationalism: a strong identity with a nation, accompanied by the desire for that nation to be dominant

natural sciences: the intellectual and academic disciplines designed to comprehend, explain, and predict events in our natural environment

negative sanction: an expression of disapproval for breaking a norm, ranging from a mild, informal reaction such as a frown to a formal prison sentence or an execution

neocolonialism: the economic and political dominance of the Least Industrialized Nations by the Most Industrialized Nations

net migration rate: the difference between the number of immigrants and emigrants per 1,000 population

networking: the process of consciously using or cultivating networks for some gain

new social movements: social movements with a new emphasis on the world, instead of on a condition in a specific country

new technology: the emerging technologies of an era that have a significant impact on social life

noncentrist party: a political party that represents marginal ideas

nonmaterial culture: a group's ways of thinking (including its beliefs, values, and other assumptions about the world) and doing (its common patterns of behavior, including language and other forms of interaction)

nonverbal interaction: communication without words through gestures, space, silence, and so on

norms: the expectations, or rules of behavior, that develop out of values

nuclear family: a family consisting of a husband, wife, and child(ren)

objective method (of measuring social class): a system in which people are ranked according to objective criteria such as their wealth, power, and prestige

objectivity: total neutrality

official deviance: a society's statistics on lawbreaking; its measures of crimes, victims, lawbreakers, and the outcomes of criminal investigations and sentencing

oligarchy: a form of government in which power is held by a small group of individuals; the rule of the many by the few

oligopoly: the control of an entire industry by several large companies

open-ended questions: questions that respondents are able to answer in their own words

operational definition: the way in which a variable in a hypothesis is measured

organic solidarity: Durkheim's term for the interdependence that results from people needing others to fulfill their jobs; solidarity brought about by the division of labor

out-groups: groups toward which one feels antagonisms

pan-Indianism: a movement that focuses on common elements in Native American culture in order to develop a mutual self-identity and to work toward the welfare of all Native Americans

panic: the condition of being so fearful that one cannot function normally, and may even flee

participant observation (or fieldwork): research in which the researcher *participates* in a research setting while *observing* what is happening in that setting

pastoral society: a society based on the pasturing of animals

patriarchy: a society in which men dominate women

patrilineal (system of descent): a system of reckoning descent that counts only the father's side

patterns: recurring characteristics or events

peer group: a group of individuals roughly the same age linked by common interests

personal identity kit: items people use to decorate their bodies

personality disorders: the view that a personality disturbance of some sort causes an individual to violate social norms

Peter principle: a bureaucratic "law" according to which the members of an organization are promoted for good work until they reach their level of incompetence, the level at which they can no longer do good work

pluralism: the diffusion of power among many interest groups, preventing any single group from gaining control of the government

pluralistic society: a society made up of many different groups

pluralistic theory of social control: the view that society is made up of many competing groups, whose interests manage to become balanced

police discretion: the practice of the police, in the normal course of their duties, to arrest someone for an offense or to overlook the matter.

political action committee (PAC): an organization formed by one or more special-interest groups to solicit and spend funds for the purpose of influencing legislation

polyandry: a marriage in which a woman has more than one husband

polygyny: a marriage in which a man has more than one wife

polytheism: the belief that there are many gods

population: the target group to be studied

population pyramid: a graphic representation of a population, divided into age and sex

population shrinkage: the process by which a country's population becomes smaller because its birth rate and immigration are too low to replace those who die and emigrate

population transfer: involuntary movement of a minority group

positive sanction: positive reaction for approved behavior, for conformity, ranging from a smile to a prize

positivism: the application of the scientific approach to the social world

postindustrial society: a society based on information, services, and high technology, rather than on raw materials and manufacturing

postmodern society: another term for postindustrial society; its chief characteristic is the use of tools that extend the human abilities to gather and analyze information, to communicate, and to travel

poverty line: the official measure of poverty; calculated to include those whose incomes are less than three times a low-cost food budget

power: the ability to get your way in spite of the desires or resistance of other people

power elite: C. Wright Mills's term for those who make the nation's major decisions: the top people in the leading corporations, the most powerful generals and admirals of the armed forces, and certain elite politicians

prejudice: an *attitude* or prejudging, usually in a negative way

prestige: respect or regard

primary deviance: Edwin Lemert's term for acts of deviance that have little effect on the self-concept

primary group: a group characterized by intimate, long-term, face-to-face association and cooperation

primary sector: that part of the economy that extracts raw materials from the environment

private ownership of the means of production: the ownership of machines and factories by individuals, who decide what shall be produced

proactive social movement: a social movement that promotes some social change

profane: Durkheim's term for common elements of everyday life

profession: an occupation characterized by rigorous education, a theoretical perspective, self-regulation, authority over clients, and service to society (as opposed to a job)

professionalization of medicine: the development of medicine into a field in which education becomes rigorous, and in which physicians claim a theoretical understanding of illness, regulate themselves, claim to be doing a service to society (rather than just following self-interest), and take authority over clients

profit: an amount in excess of an item's cost

proletariat: Karl Marx's term for the people who work for those who own the means of production; the exploited class, the mass of workers who do not own the means of production

propaganda: in its broad sense, the presentation of information in the attempt to influence people; in its narrow sense, one-sided information used to try to influence people

proportional representation: an electoral system in which seats in a legislature are divided according to the proportion of votes each political party receives

Protestant ethic: Weber's term to describe the ideal of a self-denying, highly moral life, accompanied by hard work and frugality

public: a dispersed group of people who usually have an interest in the issue on which a social movement focuses; the sympathetic and hostile publics have such an interest, but a third public is either unaware of the issue or indifferent to it

public opinion: how people think about some issue

pure or basic sociology: sociological research whose only purpose is to make discoveries about life in human groups, not to make changes in those groups

qualitative research methods: research in which the emphasis is placed on observing, describing, and interpreting people's behavior

quantitative research methods: research in which the emphasis is placed on precise measurement, the use of statistics and numbers

questionnaires: a list of questions to be asked

quiet revolution: the fundamental changes in society that occur as a result of vast numbers of women entering the work force

race: inherited physical characteristics that distinguish one group from another

racism: prejudice and discrimination on the basis of race

random sample: a sample in which everyone in the target population has the same chance of being included in the study

rapport: a feeling of trust between researchers and subjects

rational-legal authority: authority based on law or written rules and regulations; also called *bureaucratic authority*

rationality: the acceptance of rules, efficiency, and practical results as the right way to approach human affairs

rationalization of society: a widespread acceptance of rationality and a social organization largely built around this idea

reactive social movement: a social movement that resists some social change

real culture: the norms and values that people actually follow

recidivism rate: the proportion of people who are rearrested

redemptive social movement: a social movement that seeks to change people totally

redlining: the officers of a financial institution deciding not to make loans in a particular area

reference groups: Herbert Hyman's term for the groups we use as standards to evaluate ourselves

reformative social movement: a social movement that seeks to change only particular aspects of society

rehabilitation: the resocialization of offenders so that they can become conforming citizens

reincarnation: in Hinduism and Buddhism, the return of the soul after death in a different form

relative deprivation theory: in this context, the belief that people join social movements based on their evaluations of what they think they should have compared with what others have

reliability: the extent to which data produce consistent results

religion: according to Durkheim, beliefs and practices that separate the profane from the sacred and unite its adherents into a moral community

religious experience: a sudden awareness of the supernatural or a feeling of coming in contact with God

replication: repeating a study in order to test its findings

representative democracy: a form of democracy in which voters elect representatives to govern and make decisions on their behalf

reputational method (of measuring social class): a system in which people who are familiar with the reputations of others are asked to identify their social class

research method (or research design): one of six procedures sociologists use to collect data: surveys, participant observation, secondary analysis, documents, unobtrusive measures, and experiments

reserve labor force: the unemployed; unemployed workers are thought of as being in reserve—capitalists take them "out of reserve" (put them back to work) during times of high production and then discard them (lay them off) when they are no longer needed

resocialization: the process of learning new norms, values, attitudes, and behaviors

resource mobilization: a theory that social movements succeed or fail based on their ability to mobilize resources such as time, money, and people's skills

respondents: people who respond to a survey, either in interviews or by self-administered questionnaires

retribution: the punishment of offenders in order to restore the moral balance upset by the offense

revolution: armed resistance designed to overthrow a government

riot: violent crowd behavior aimed against people and property

rising expectations: the sense that better conditions are soon to follow, which, if unfulfilled, creates mounting frustration

rituals: ceremonies or repetitive practices; in this context, religious observances or rites, often intended to evoke a sense of awe of the sacred

role: the behaviors, obligations, and privileges attached to a status

role conflict: conflicts that someone feels *between* roles because the expectations attached to one role are incompatible with the expectations of another role

role extension: the incorporation of additional activities into a role

role performance: the ways in which someone performs a role within the limits that the role provides; showing a particular "style" or "personality"

role strain: conflicts that someone feels *within* a role

romantic love: feelings of erotic attraction accompanied by an idealization of the other

routinization of charisma: the transfer of authority from a charismatic figure to either a traditional or a rational-legal form of authority

ruling class: another term for the power elite

rumor: unfounded information spread among people

sacred: Durkheim's term for things set apart or forbidden, that inspire fear, awe, reverence, or deep respect

sample: the individuals intended to represent the population to be studied

sanction: an expression of approval or disapproval given to people for upholding or violating norms

Sapir–Whorf hypothesis: Edward Sapir and Benjamin Whorf's hypothesis that language itself creates ways of thinking and perceiving

scapegoat: an individual or group unfairly blamed for someone else's troubles

school choice: parents being able to choose the school their child will attend; often used in the context of expecting for-profit schools to compete for vouchers issued by the state

science: the application of systematic methods to obtain knowledge and the knowledge obtained by those methods

scientific method: the use of objective, systematic observations to test theories

secondary analysis: the analysis of data already collected by other researchers

secondary deviance: Edwin Lemert's term for acts of deviance incorporated into the self-concept, around which an individual orients his or her behavior

secondary group: compared with a primary group, a larger, relatively temporary, more anonymous, formal, and impersonal group based on some interest or activity, whose members are likely to interact on the basis of specific roles

secondary sector: that part of the economy that turns raw materials into manufactured goods

sect: a group larger than a cult that still feels substantial hostility from and toward society

secular: belonging to the world and its affairs

secularization: the process by which spiritual concerns are replaced by worldly concerns

secularization of culture: the process by which a culture becomes less influenced by religion

secularization of religion: the replacement of a religion's "otherworldly" concerns with concerns about "this world"

segregation: the policy of keeping racial or ethnic groups apart

selective perception: seeing certain features of an object or situation, but remaining blind to others

self: the unique human capacity of being able to see ourselves "from the outside"; the picture we gain of how others see us

self-administered questionnaires: questionnaires filled out by respondents

self-fulfilling prophecy: Robert Merton's term for an originally false assertion that becomes true simply because it was predicted

serial fatherhood: a pattern of parenting in which a father, after divorce, reduces contact with his own children, serves as a father to the children of the woman he marries or lives with, then ignores them after moving in with or marrying another woman; this pattern repeats

sex: biological characteristics that distinguish females and males, consisting of primary and secondary sex characteristics

sex typing: the association of behaviors with one sex or the other

sexual harassment: the abuse of one's position of authority to force unwanted sexual demands on someone

shaman: the healing specialist of a preliterate tribe who attempts to control the spirits thought to cause a disease or injury; commonly called a witch doctor

sick role: a social role that excuses people from normal obligations because they are sick or injured, while at the same time expecting them to seek competent help and cooperate in getting well

sign-vehicles: the term used by Goffman to refer to how people use social setting, appearance, and manner to communicate information about the self

significant other: an individual who significantly influences someone else's life

slavery: a form of social stratification in which some people own other people

small group: a group small enough for everyone to interact directly with all the other members

social change: the alteration of culture and societies over time

social class: most commonly, a large number of people with similar amounts of income and education who work at jobs that are roughly comparable in prestige; according to Weber, a large group of people who rank closely to one another in wealth, power, and prestige; according to Marx, one of two groups: capitalists who own the means of production or workers who sell their labor

social cohesion: the degree to which members of a group or a society feel united by shared values and other social bonds

social construction of reality: the process by which people use their background assumptions and life experiences to define what is real for them

social construction of technology: the view (opposed to *technological determinism*) that culture (people's values and special interests) shapes the use and development of technology

social control: a group's formal and informal means of enforcing its norms

social environment: the entire human environment, including direct contact with others

social facts: Durkheim's term for the patterns of behavior that characterize a social group

social inequality: a social condition in which privileges and obligations are given to some but denied to others

social institutions: the organized, usual, or standard ways by which society meets its basic needs

social integration: the degree to which people feel a part of social groups

social interaction: what people do when they are in one another's presence

social location: people's group memberships because of their location in history and society

social mobility: movement up or down the social class ladder

social movement: a large group of people who are organized to promote or resist social change

social movement organization: an organization developed to further the goals of a social movement

social network: the social ties radiating outward from the self that link people together

social order: a group's usual and customary social arrangements, on which its members depend and on which they base their lives

social placement: a function of education that funnels people into a society's various positions

social promotion: passing students to the next grade even though they have not mastered basic materials

social sciences: the intellectual and academic disciplines designed to understand the social world objectively by means of controlled and repeated observations

social setting: the place where the action of everyday life unfolds

social stratification: the division of large numbers of people into layers according to their relative power, property, and prestige: applies to both nations and to people within a nation, society, or other group

social structure: the framework that surrounds us, consisting of the relationship of people and groups to one another, which give direction to and set limits on behavior

socialism: an economic system characterized by the public ownership of the means of production, central planning, and the distribution of goods without a profit motive

socialization: the process by which people learn the characteristics of their group—the attitudes, values, and actions thought appropriate for them

society: people who share a culture and a territory

sociobiology: a framework of thought that views human behavior as the result of natural selection and considers biological characteristics to be the fundamental cause of human behavior

sociological perspective: an approach to understanding human behavior by placing it within its broader social context

sociology: the scientific study of society and human behavior

special-interest group: a group of people who have a particular issue in common who can be mobilized for political action

spirit of capitalism: Weber's term for the desire to accumulate capital as a duty—not to spend it, but as an end in itself—and to constantly reinvest it

split-labor market: workers split along racial, ethnic, gender, age, or any other lines; this split is exploited by owners to weaken the bargaining power of workers

spurious correlation: the correlation of two variables actually caused by a third variable; there is no cause–effect relationship

state: a political entity that claims monopoly on the use of violence in some particular territory; commonly known as a country

state religion: a government-sponsored religion

status: the position that someone occupies in society or a social group

status consistency: ranking high or low on all three dimensions of social class

status inconsistency (or status discrepancy): a condition in which a person ranks high on some dimensions of social class and low on others

status set: all the statuses or positions that an individual occupies

status symbols: items used to identify a status

stereotype: assumptions of what people are like, based on previous associations with them or with people who have similar characteristics, or based on information, whether true or false

stigma: "blemishes" that discredit a person's claim to a "normal" identity

stockholders' revolt: the refusal of a corporation's stockholders to rubber-stamp decisions made by its managers

stored value: the backing of a currency by goods that are stored and held in reserve

strain theory: Robert Merton's term for the strain engendered when a society socializes large numbers of people to desire a cultural goal (such as success) but withholds from many the approved means to reach that goal; one adaptation to the strain is crime, the choice of an innovative means (one outside the approved system) to attain the cultural goal

stratified random sample: a sample of specific subgroups of the target population in which everyone in the subgroups has an equal chance of being included in the study

street crime: crimes such as mugging, rape, and burglary

structural mobility: movement up or down the social class ladder that is attributable to changes in the structure of society, not to individual efforts

structured interviews: interviews that use closed-ended questions

subculture: the values and related behaviors of a group that distinguish its members from the larger culture; a world within a world

subjective meanings: the meanings that people give their own behavior

subjective method (of measuring social class): a system in which people are asked to state the social class to which they belong

subsistence economy: a type of economy in which human groups live off the land with little or no surplus

suburb: the communities adjacent to the political boundaries of a city

suburbanization: the movement from the city to the suburbs

superego: Freud's term for the conscience, the internalized norms and values of our social groups

survey: the collection of data by having people answer a series of questions

sustainable environment: a world system that takes into account the limits of the environment, produces enough material goods for everyone's needs, and leaves a heritage of a sound environment for the next generation

symbol: something to which people attach meanings and then use to communicate with others

symbolic culture: another term for nonmaterial culture

symbolic interactionism: a theoretical perspective in which society is viewed as composed of symbols that people use to establish meaning, develop their views of the world, and communicate with one another

system of descent: how kinship is traced over the generations

taboo: a norm so strong that it brings revulsion if violated

taking the role of the other: putting oneself in someone else's shoes; understanding how someone else feels and thinks and thus anticipating how that person will act

teamwork: the collaboration of two or more persons interested in the success of a performance to manage impressions jointly

techniques of neutralization: ways of thinking or rationalizing that help people deflect society's norms.

technological determinism: the view that technology determines culture, that technology takes on a life of its own and forces human behavior to follow

technology: in its narrow sense, tools; its broader sense includes the skills or procedures necessary to make and use those tools

tertiary deviance: "normalizing" behavior considered deviant by mainstream society; relabeling behavior as nondeviant

tertiary sector: that part of the economy that consists of service-oriented occupations

theory: a general statement about how some parts of the world fit together and how they work; an explanation of how two or more facts are related to one another

Thomas theorem: William I. Thomas's classic formulation of the definition of the situation: "If people define situations as real, they are real in their consequences."

tool: an object that is created or modified for a specific purpose

total institution: a place in which people are cut off from the rest of society and are almost totally controlled by the officials who run the place

totalitarianism: a form of government that exerts almost total control over the people

tracking: the sorting of students into different educational programs on the basis of real or perceived abilities

traditional authority: authority based on custom

traditional orientation: the idea, characteristic of tribal, peasant, and feudal societies, that the past is the best guide for the present

transformative social movement: a social movement that seeks to change society totally

triad: a group of three people

underclass: a small group of people for whom poverty persists year after year and across generations

underemployment: the condition of having to work at a job beneath one's level of training and abilities, or of being able to find only part-time work

underground economy: exchanges of goods and services that are not reported to the government and thereby escape taxation

universal citizenship: the idea that everyone has the same basic rights by virtue of being born in a country (or by immigrating and becoming a naturalized citizen)

unobtrusive measures: various ways of observing people who do not know they are being studied

unstructured interviews: interviews that use open-ended questions

upward social mobility: movement up the social class ladder

urban legend: a story with an ironic twist that sounds realistic but is false

urban renewal: the rehabilitation of a rundown area, which usually results in the displacement of the poor who are living in that area

urbanization: the process by which an increasing proportion of a population lives in cities

validity: the extent to which an operational definition measures what was intended

value clusters: a series of interrelated values that together form a larger whole

value contradictions: values that contradict one another; to follow the one means to come into conflict with the other

value free: the view that a sociologist's personal values or biases should not influence social research

values: ideas about what is good or worthwhile in life; attitudes about the way the world ought to be; the standards by which people define what is desirable or undesirable, good or bad, beautiful or ugly

variable: a factor or concept thought to be significant for human behavior, which varies from one case to another

Verstehen: a German word used by Weber that is perhaps best understood as "to have insight into someone's situation"

voluntary association: a group made up of volunteers who have organized on the basis of some mutual interest

voluntary memberships: (or voluntary associations) groups that people choose to join

voter apathy: indifference and inaction on the part of individuals or groups with respect to the political process

war: armed conflict between nations or politically distinct groups

WASP: a White Anglo-Saxon Protestant; narrowly, an American of English descent; broadly, an American of western European ancestry

wealth: property and income

welfare (state) capitalism: an economic system in which individuals own the means of production, but the state regulates many economic activities for the welfare of the population

white ethnics: white immigrants to the United States whose culture differs from that of WASPs

white-collar crime: Edwin Sutherland's term for crimes committed by people of respectable and high social status in the course of their occupations; for example, bribery of public officials, securities violations, embezzlement, false advertising, and price fixing

working class: those who sell their labor to the capitalist class

world system: economic and political connections that tie the world's countries together

zero population growth: a demographic condition in which women bear only enough children to reproduce the population

Suggested Readings

Chapter 1 The Sociological Perspective
Berger, Peter L. *Invitation to Sociology: A Humanistic Perspective*. New York: Doubleday, 1963. This delightful analysis of how sociology applies to everyday life is highly recommended.

Charon, Joel M. *Symbolic Interactionism: An Introduction, an Interpretation, an Integration*, 5th ed. Englewood Cliffs, N.J.: Prentice Hall, 1995. As it lays out the main points of symbolic interactionism, this book provides an understanding of why symbolic interactionism is important in sociology.

Henslin, James M., ed. *Down to Earth Sociology: Introductory Readings*, 9th ed. New York: Free Press, 1997. This collection of readings about everyday life is designed to broaden the reader's understanding of society, and of the individual's place within it.

Mills, C. Wright. *The Sociological Imagination*. New York: Oxford University Press, 1959. This classic work provides an overview of sociology from the framework of conflict theory.

Willis, Evans. *The Sociological Quest: An Introduction to the Study of Social Life*, 3rd ed. New Brunswick, N.J.: Rutgers University Press, 1997. A user-friendly introduction to sociology.

Journals
Applied Behavioral Science Review, *Clinical Sociology*, *Clinical Sociology Review*, *International Clinical Sociology*, *Journal of Applied Sociology*, *The Practicing Sociologist*, and *Sociological Practice Review* report the experiences of sociologists who work in a variety of applied settings, from peer group counseling and suicide prevention to recommending changes to school boards.

Humanity & Society, the official journal of the Association for Humanist Sociology, publishes articles that "serve to advance the quality of life of the world's people."

About a Career in Sociology
The following pamphlets or brochures are available free of charge from the American Sociological Association: 1722 N Street, N.W., Washington, DC 20036 Tel. (202) 833-3410. Fax (202) 785-0146. ASA_Executive_Office@MCIMAIL.com

Careers in Sociology. American Sociological Association. What can you do with sociology? You like the subject and would like to major in it, but. . . . This pamphlet provides information about jobs available for sociology majors.

Majoring in Sociology: A Guide for Students. American Sociological Association. This brochure provides an overview of the programs offered in sociology departments, possible areas of specialization, and how to find information on jobs.

Ferris, Abbott L. *How to Join the Federal Workforce and Advance Your Sociological Career*. American Sociological Association. This pamphlet gives tips on how to find employment in the federal government, including information on how to prepare a job application.

Huber, Bettina J. *Embarking Upon a Career in Sociology with an Undergraduate Sociology Major*. American Sociological Association. Designed for undergraduate sociology majors who are seeking employment, this brochure discusses how to identify interests and skills, pinpoint suitable jobs, prepare a résumé, and survive an employment interview.

Miller, Delbert C. *The Sociology Major as Preparation for Careers in Business*. American Sociological Association. What careers can a sociology major pursue in business or industry? This brochure includes sections on job prospects, graduate education, and how to practice sociology in business careers.

These two books are also useful if you are considering a career as a sociologist: the first provides background information; the second is more specific.

Hess, Beth B. *Individual Voices, Collective Visions: Fifty Years of Women in Sociology*. Philadelphia: Temple University Press, 1995. During the past fifty years, women have played an increasingly larger role in sociology, which, like the other sciences, has been dominated by men. The author examines this change.

Stephens, W. Richard. *Careers in Sociology*, 2nd ed. Boston: Allyn and Bacon, 1997. How can you make a living with a major in sociology? The author explores careers in sociology, from business and government to health care and the law.

Chapter 2 Culture
Chagnon, Napoleon A. *Yanomamo: The Fierce People*, 4th ed. New York: Harcourt, Brace, Jovanovich, 1992. This fascinating account of a preliterate people whose customs are extraordinarily different from ours will help you to see the arbitrariness of choices that underlie human culture.

Edgerton, Robert B. *Sick Societies: Challenging the Myth of Primitive Harmony*. New York: Free Press, 1992. The author's thesis is that cultural relativism is misinformed, that we have the obligation to judge cultures that harm their members as inferior to those that do not.

Gitlin, Todd. *The Twilight of Common Dreams: Why America Is Wracked by Culture Wars*. New York: Metropolitan Books, 1997. "Culture wars" refers to fundamental disagreements about the way life should be lived, and to the way certain groups push their own agendas and disparage those of others. The author expresses hope that we can build "cultural bridges" so we once again can dream "common dreams."

Goodall, Jane, and Michael Nichols. *The Great Apes: Between Two Worlds*, 1993. This account of Jane Goodall's research offers—as much as is possible—an insider's view of the behavior of chimpanzees.

Harris, Marvin. *Cannibals and Kings: The Origins of Cultures*. New York: Random House, 1977.

Harris, Marvin. *Good to Eat: Riddles of Food and Culture*. New York: Simon & Schuster, 1986.

To read Harris's books is to read about cultural relativism. Using a functional perspective, this anthropologist analyzes cultural practices that often seem bizarre to outsiders. He interprets those practices within the framework of the culture being examined.

Jones, Steven G., ed. *Virtual Culture: Identity and Communication in Cybersociety*. Beverly Hills, Calif.: Sage, 1997. The authors' thesis is that the Internet is fundamentally affecting our lives, and has the potential to create vast social change.

Zellner, William W. *Countercultures: A Sociological Analysis*. New York: St. Martin's, Press, 1995. The author's analysis of skinheads, the Ku Klux Klan, survivalists, satanism, the Church of Scientology, and the Unification Church (Moonies) helps us understand why people join countercultures.

Journals

Qualitative Sociology, *Urban Life*, and *Visual Sociology Review* focus on qualitative research on social life.

Chapter 3   Socialization

Ariès, Philippe. *Centuries of Childhood: A Social History of Family Life*. New York: Vintage Books, 1965. This pathbreaking study of childhood in Europe during the Middle Ages provides a sharp contrast to child-rearing patterns in modern society.

Corsaro, William. *The Sociology of Childhood*. Beverly Hills, Calif.: Sage, 1997. This overview of children's culture includes an analysis of how children have been viewed through history.

Epstein, Jonathan S., ed. *Adolescents and Their Music: If It's Too Loud, You're Too Old*. Hamden, Conn.: Garland Publishing, 1994. The type of music a particular age, ethnic, or religious group prefers is never an accident, but is a vital part of the group's relative place in society. This analysis clarifies that relationship between youth and society.

Gilmore, David D. *Manhood in the Making: Cultural Concepts of Masculinity*. New Haven, Conn.: Yale University Press, 1991. A survey of societies around the world aimed at determining if masculinity is constant; contains fascinating anthropological data.

Lieberman, Alicia F. *The Emotional Life of the Toddler*. New York: Free Press, 1993. The author analyzes challenges in socializing young children and presents many interesting case materials on problems that toddlers confront.

Mead, George Herbert. *Mind, Self and Society from the Standpoint of a Social Behaviorist*. Charles W. Morris, ed. Chicago: University of Chicago Press, 1974. First published in 1934. Put together from notes taken by Mead's students, this book presents Mead's analysis of how mind and self are products of society.

Rymer, Russ. *Genie: An Abused Child's Flight from Silence*. New York: HarperCollins, 1993. This moving account of Genie includes the battles among linguists, psychologists, and social workers, who all claimed to have Genie's best interests at heart.

Sociological Studies of Child Development: A Research Annual. Greenwich, Conn.: JAI Press. Along with theoretical articles, this annual publication reports on sociological research on the socialization of children.

Chapter 4   Social Structure and Social Interaction

Barber, Bernard. *Constructing the Social System*. New Brunswick, N.J.: Transaction Books, 1993. An example of the macrosociological approach to understanding human life; perhaps best suited for advanced students.

Goffman, Erving. *The Presentation of Self in Everyday Life*. New York: Doubleday, 1990. First published in 1959. This classic statement of dramaturgical analysis provides a different way of looking at everyday life.

Hatfield, Elaine, and Susan Sprecher. *Mirror, Mirror . . . : The Importance of Looks in Everyday Life*. Albany: State University of New York Press, 1986. All of us consider appearance to be very important in everyday life. You may be surprised, however, at just how significant good looks are for determining what happens to us.

Helmreich, William B. *The Things They Say Behind Your Back: Stereotypes and the Myths Behind Them*. New Brunswick, N.J.: Transaction, 1984. Spiced with anecdotes and jokes, yet sensitively written, the book explores the historical roots of stereotypes. The author also illustrates how stereotypes help produce behaviors that reinforce them.

Schellenberg, James A. *Exploring Social Behavior: Investigations in Social Psychology*. Boston: Allyn and Bacon, 1993. The author takes the reader on an intellectual journey, exploring such "mysteries" as identity, conscience, intelligence, attraction, and aggression.

Tönnies, Ferdinand. *Community and Society (Gemeinschaft und Gesellschaft)*. New Brunswick, N.J.: Transaction, 1988. Originally published in 1887, this classic work, focusing on social change, provides insight into how society influences personality. Rather challenging reading.

Walker, Beverly M., ed. *Construction of Group Realities: Culture, Society, and Personal Construction Theory*. New York: Praeger, 1995. Our views of life, what we believe, even what we perceive have a group basis to them.

Whyte, William Foote. *Corner Boys: A Study of Clique Behavior*. New York: Irvington, 1993. Originally published in 1945. The author's analysis of interaction in a U.S. Italian slum demonstrates how social structure affects personal relationships.

Journals

The following three journals feature articles on symbolic interactionism and analyses of everyday life: *Qualitative Sociology*, *Symbolic Interaction*, *Urban Life*.

Chapter 5   How Sociologists Do Research

Bailey, Kenneth D. *Methods of Social Research*, 4th ed. New York: Free Press, 1994. A detailed explanation of the research methods that, due to limited space, we could only touch on in this chapter—plus much more.

Baker, Therese L. *Doing Social Research*, 2nd ed., New York: Mc-Graw-Hill, 1994. This "how-to" book of sociological research describes the major ways in which sociologists gather data and the logic that underlies each method.

Burgess, Robert, ed. *Studies in Qualitative Sociology: Reflections on Field Experience*. London: JAI Press, 1990. First-person accounts by sociologists provide an understanding of the problems and rewards of fieldwork.

Jorgensen, D. L. *Participant Observation: A Methodology for Human Studies*. Newbury Park, Calif.: Sage, 1989. The book explains the value of participant observation and summarizes interesting studies. From it, you may understand why *you* are uniquely qualified for doing participant observation.

Merton, Robert K., Marjorie Fiske, and Patricia L. Kendall. *The Focused Interview: A Manual of Problems and Procedures*, 2nd ed. New

York: Free Press, 1990. Interviewing techniques are outlined; of value primarily to more advanced students.

Scully, Diana. *Understanding Sexual Violence: A Study of Convicted Rapists.* New York: Routledge, 1994. The author's examination of the rationalizations of rapists helps us understand why some men rape and what they gain from it.

Webb, Eugene J., Donald T. Campbell, Richard D. Schwartz, Lee Sechrest, and Janet Below Grove. *Unobtrusive Measures: Nonreactive Research in the Social Sciences.* Chicago: Houghton Mifflin, 1981. This clear overview of unobtrusive measures also contains concise summaries of a great deal of research.

Whyte, William Foote, and Kathleen King Whyte. *Learning from the Field: A Guide from Experience.* Beverly Hills, Calif.: Sage, 1984. Focusing on the extensive field experience of the senior author, this book provides insight into the critical involvement of the self in this research method.

Writing Papers for Sociology

The Sociology Writing Group. *A Guide to Writing Sociology Papers,* 3rd ed. New York: St. Martin's Press, 1994. The guide walks students through the steps in writing a sociology paper, from choosing the initial topic to doing the research and turning in a finished paper. Also explains how to manage your time and cite sources.

Cuba, Lee J. *A Short Guide to Writing About Social Science.* Glenview, Ill.: Scott, Foresman, 1993. The author summarizes the various types of social science literature, presents guidelines on how to organize and write a research paper, and explains how to prepare an oral presentation.

Journal

Visual Sociology Review. A specialized journal in qualitative sociology that focuses on the analysis of social life through visual means such as photos, movies, and videos.

Chapter 6 Societies to Social Networks

Forschi, Martha, and Edward J. Lawler, eds. *Group Processes: Sociological Analysis.* New York: Nelson-Hall, 1994. How do your associates, friends, family—and even strangers—influence you? Among other topics, these authors explore such influences.

Fleisher, Mark S. *Beggars and Thieves: Lives of Urban Street Criminals.* Madison: University of Wisconsin Press, 1995. Based on years of participant observation, the author presents an inside view of thieves, gangs, addicts, and lifelong criminals.

Homans, George. *The Human Group.* New York: Harcourt, Brace, 1950. Homans develops the idea that all human groups share common activities, interactions, and sentiments and examines various types of social groups from this point of view.

Janis, Irving. *Victims of Groupthink.* Boston, Mass.: Houghton Mifflin, 1972. Janis analyzes how groups can become cut off from alternatives, interpret evidence in light of their preconceptions, and embark on courses of action that they should have seen as obviously incorrect.

Kephart, William M., and William W. Zellner. *Extraordinary Groups: An Examination of Unconventional Lifestyles,* 4th ed. New York: St. Martin's Press, 1991. This sketch of the history and characteristics of eight groups—the Old Order Amish, Oneida Community, Gypsies, Shakers, Hasidim, Father Divine Movement, Mormons, and Jehovah's Witnesses—illustrates the effects of groups on their members.

Mills, Theodore M. *The Sociology of Small Groups.* Englewood Cliffs, N.J.: Prentice Hall, 1984. Mills provides an overview of research on small groups, focusing on the interaction that occurs within them (group dynamics).

Chapter 7 Bureaucracy and Formal Organizations

Fucini, Joseph J., and Suzy Fucini. *Working for the Japanese: Inside Mazda's American Auto Plant.* New York: Free Press, 1990. The authors report on how U.S. workers at the wholly-owned Japanese auto plant in Flat Rock, Michigan, have found that the team system requires them to sacrifice individual interests to the welfare of the group.

Herkscher, Charles, and Anne Donnellon, eds. *The Post-Bureaucratic Organization.* Beverly Hills, Calif.: Sage, 1994. By any other name, is a bureaucracy still a bureaucracy? The authors of these articles explain how bureaucracies can be modified to better reach the organization's goals and to better meet human needs.

Howard, Philip K. *The Death of Common Sense: How Law Is Suffocating America.* New York: Random House, 1995. The way law is practiced in the United States is an impediment to the goals it is designed to achieve.

Hummel, Ralph P. *The Bureaucratic Experiment: A Critique of Life in the Modern Organization,* 4th ed., New York: St. Martin's Press, 1994. The author explores the perils and promises of bureaucracies, with an emphasis on how bureaucracies can become better tools for human needs.

MacDonald, Keith M. *The Sociology of the Professions.* Newbury Park, Calif.: Sage, 1995. Using a symbolic interactionist framework, the author analyzes how jobs are turned into professions.

Mitchell, William C. *Beyond Politics: Markets, Welfare, and Bureaucracy.* New York: Westview, 1994. Welfare reform has become a popular political topic. This book explains how much of what is wrong with welfare is due to the bureaucracy set up to administer Washington's programs.

Parkinson, C. Northcote. *Parkinson's Law.* Boston: Houghton Mifflin, 1957. Although this exposé of the inner workings of bureaucracies is delightfully satirical, if what Parkinson analyzes were generally true, bureaucracies would always fail.

Sims, David, Stephen Fineman, and Yiannis Gabriel. *Organizing and Organizations: An Introduction.* Newbury Park, Calif.: Sage, 1993. The authors draw on many firsthand accounts to help make the study of formal organizations come alive.

Chapter 8 Deviance and Social Control

Bartner, M. A., and Linda M. Williams. *Youth in Prison: We the People of Unit Four.* New York: Routledge, 1997. The authors provide an insightful account of the lives of youth inside and outside of prison.

Hasine, Victor. *Life Without Parole: Living in Prison Today.* Los Angeles: Roxbury, 1996. The author, a middle-class graduate of New York Law School who is serving a life sentence for murder, gives us an insider's view of why today's prisons foster a culture of violence and reduce people to savagery.

Humes, Edward. *No Matter How Loud I Shout: A Year in the Life of Juvenile Court.* New York: Simon & Schuster, 1996. The author's participant observation in the largest U.S. juvenile probation system helps us understand violence by juveniles.

Jankowski, Martín Sánchez. *Islands in the Street: Gangs and American Urban Society.* Berkeley: University of California Press, 1991. The author presents an overview of urban gangs in the United States; findings from this book are featured in the box on page 205.

Mann, Coramae Richey. *Unequal Justice: A Question of Color.* Bloomington: Indiana University Press, 1994. The author examines a controversial issue: why our jails and prisons are so disproportionately filled with minorities.

Mann, Coramae Richey, and Marjorie S. Zatz, eds. *Images of Color, Images of Crime.* Los Angeles: Roxbury, 1998. This collection of twenty-two articles examines the relationship between racial stereotypes and crime.

Messner, Steven F., and Richard Rosenfeld. *Crime and the American Dream*. Belmont, Calif.: Wadsworth, 1994. Explains how the "American Dream" produces a strong desire to make money but fails to instill adequate desires to play by the rules. Supports Merton's strain theory featured in this chapter.

Rafter, Nicole Hahn. *Partial Justice: Women, Prisons, and Social Control*, 2nd ed. New Brunswick, N.J.: Transaction, 1990. The author documents the development of separate prisons for women, the goal of reform in women's prisons, and current concerns to produce more than "partial justice."

Scott, Kody. *Monster: The Autobiography of an L.A. Gang Member*. New York: Penguin Books, 1993. This intriguing inside view of gang life provides a rare glimpse of the power of countercultural norms.

Wright, Richard T., and Scott Decker. *Burglars on the Job: Streetlife and Residential Break-ins*. Boston: Northeastern University Press, 1994. For an understanding of how burglars think, as well as how they "work," this book is highly recommended.

Chapter 9   Social Stratification in Global Perspective

Curtis, James, and Lorne Tepperman, eds. *Haves and Have-Nots: An International Reader on Social Inequality*. Englewood Cliffs, N.J.: Prentice Hall, 1994. The authors of these fifty-six articles explore economic, power, and status inequality among the world's nations.

Freedman, Robert. *The Mind of Karl Marx: Economic, Political, and Social Perspectives*. Chatham, N.J.: Chatham House, 1986. A conflict theorist provides an overview of social stratification from his perspective.

Harrison, Paul. *Inside the Third World: The Anatomy of Poverty*, 3rd ed. London: Penguin Books, 1993. The book's vivid examples make conditions in the Least Industrialized Nations come alive.

Kennedy, Paul. *Preparing for the Twenty-First Century*. New York: Random House, 1993. A thorough analysis of the relationship among the three worlds of economic development.

Kibria, Nazli. *Family Tightrope: The Changing Lives of Vietnamese Americans*. Princeton: N.J.: Princeton University Press, 1993. To change one's culture challenges almost all aspects of the self. The author analyzes how Vietnamese families are adjusting to their new lives.

Lane, David, ed. *Russia in Flux: The Political and Social Consequences of Reform*. Brookfield, Vt.: Ashfield, 1992. The author analyzes the political and economic changes in Russia, the consequences of which are being felt throughout the world.

Miles, Rosalind. *The Woman's History of the World*. New York: HarperCollins, 1990. The author examines the importance of gender in human history.

Said, Edward W. *Culture and Imperialism*. New York: Knopf, 1993. The author analyzes the relationship of national power to cultural dominance, especially that of the Most Industrialized Nations to the Least Industrialized Nations.

Scheper-Hughes, Nancy. *Death Without Weeping: The Violence of Everyday Life in Brazil*. Berkeley: University of California Press, 1992. As stressed in this chapter, global stratification leaves some nations in poverty—in spite of their possessing rich natural resources. The results can be a short and brutish life for the underprivileged of those nations, as documented in this report.

Thomas, Hugh. *The Slave Trade*. New York: Simon and Schuster, 1997. An overview of slavery from 1444, when slaves from Africa were first taken to Portugal, until the 1860s, when the last African slave ships arrived in Cuba.

United Nations. *World Economic Survey 1990: Current Trends and Policies in the World Economy*. New York: United Nations, 1990. This survey of the economic characteristics of the world's nations provides a detailed contrast between the rich and poor nations.

Chapter 10   Social Class in Contemporary Society

Berrick, Jill Duerr. *Faces of Poverty: Portraits of Women and Children on Welfare*. New York: Oxford University Press, 1995. With a focus on how welfare helps the poor survive from day to day, the author puts a human face on this stereotyped population.

Domhoff, G. William. *State Autonomy or Class Dominance? Case Studies on Policy Making in America*. Hawthorne, New York: Aldine de Gruyter, 1996. The author, a conflict theorist, applies his analysis of social class and power to the development of major U.S. policy decisions.

Gatewood, Willard B. *Aristocrats of Color: The Black Elite, 1880–1920*. Bloomington: Indiana University Press, 1990. Analyzing the rise and decline of the African-American upper class that developed after the Civil War, the author focuses on marriage, occupations, education, religion, clubs, and relationships with whites and with African Americans of lower classes.

Grusky, David B., ed. *Social Stratification: Class, Race, and Gender in Sociological Perspective*. Boulder, Colo.: Westview Press, 1994. The authors of these readings explain how social class, race, and gender are the primary elements underlying social stratification in contemporary society.

Jennings, James. *Understanding the Nature of Poverty in Urban America*. Westport, Conn.: Praeger, 1994. In this analysis of major characteristics of U.S. poverty, the author also analyzes why poverty persists.

Klepper, Michael, and Robert Gunther. *Wealthy 100: From Benjamin Franklin to Bill Gates; A Ranking of the Richest Americans, Past and Present*. Secaucus, N.J.: Carol Publishing Group, 1997. The authors determined who the 100 richest Americans are by analyzing their fortunes relative to the country's gross national product. Only six living Americans made the list.

Liebow, Elliot. *Tell Them Who I Am: The Lives of Homeless Women*. New York: Penguin Books, 1995. Based on participant observation in a Washington, D.C., shelter for homeless women, this study puts flesh and blood on those nameless faces we see on the news and on our city streets.

MacLeod, Jay. *Ain't No Makin' It: Aspirations and Attainment in a Low-Income Neighborhood*, expanded ed. Boulder, Colo.: Westview, 1995. Following two groups of high school boys into adulthood, the author documents how social class inequality is sustained from generation to generation, and how friendships and families, work and school experiences shape occupational aspirations.

Massey, Douglas S., and Nancy A. Denton. *American Apartheid: Segregation and the Making of the Underclass*. Cambridge, Mass.: Harvard University Press, 1993. The authors explain how the "underclass" developed and propose possible solutions to this pressing problem.

Oliver, Melvin L., and Thomas M. Shapiro. *Black Wealth/White Wealth: A New Perspective on Racial Inequality*. New York: Routledge, 1996. This book is the first comparison of the wealth (not income) of African Americans and whites. It shows how deep the divide is.

Rank, Mark Robert. *Living on the Edge: The Realities of Welfare in America*. New York: Columbia University Press, 1995. This account of what poor people do to make ends meet dispels many myths of welfare recipients.

Wilson, William Julius. *The Truly Disadvantaged: The Inner City, the Underclass, and Public Policy*. Chicago: University of Chicago Press, 1990. The author looks at how the conditions of the ghetto poor have deteriorated and suggests what can be done to improve matters.

Chapter 11   Inequalities of Gender

Amott, Teresa. *Caught in the Crisis: Women and the U.S. Economy*. New York: Monthly Review Press, 1995. A short, readable overview of women's economic roles from a leftist perspective.

Anderson, Margaret L. *Thinking about Women: Sociological Perspectives on Sex and Gender,* 3rd ed. New York: Macmillan, 1993. An overview of the main issues of sex and gender in contemporary society, ranging from sexism and socialization to work and health.

Campbell, Anne. *Men, Women, and Aggression.* New York: Basic Books, 1993. This comparison of male–female differences in aggression includes fights, robbery, marital violence, and street gangs.

Driscoll, Dawn-Marie, and Carol R. Goldberg. *Members of the Club: The Coming of Age of Executive Women.* New York: Free Press, 1993. Based on interviews with senior women executives, the authors suggest strategies for climbing to the top of the corporate ladder.

Farganis, Sondra. *The Social Reconstruction of the Feminine Character,* 2nd ed. Lanham, Md.: Rowman & Littlefield, 1996. An overview of feminist theory that emphasizes how views of women are shaped by concrete situations.

Gilman, Charlotte Perkins. *The Man-Made World or, Our Androcentric Culture.* New York: Charlton, 1911. Reprinted in 1971 by Johnson Reprint. This early book on women's liberation provides an excellent view of female–male relations at the beginning of this century.

Goldberg, Steven. *Why Men Rule: A Theory of Male Dominance.* Chicago: Open Court, 1993. A detailed explanation of the author's theory of male dominance featured in this chapter.

Jacobs, Jerry A., ed. *Gender Inequality at Work.* Thousand Oaks, Calif.: Sage, 1995. The authors of these articles review the main issues in gender discrimination in employment.

Kimmel, Michael S., and Michael A. Messner, eds. *Men's Lives,* 2nd ed. New York: Macmillan, 1993. These authors examine major issues of sex and gender as they affect men. An excellent companion, and often counterpoint, to the Anderson book.

Lorber, Judith. *Gender and the Social Construction of Illness.* Thousand Oaks, Calif.: Sage, 1997. Taking the position that both gender and medicine are social institutions, the author examines their interrelationships.

Lorber, Judith. *Paradoxes of Gender.* New Haven, Conn.: Yale University Press, 1994. The author focuses on two vital issues: how gender is constructed and how gender is a primary component of social inequality.

Madriz, Esther. *Nothing Bad Happens to Good Girls: Fear of Crime in Women's Lives.* Berkeley: University of California Press, 1997. The author uses interviews to explain how women's fear of crime contributes to gender inequalities and the social control of women.

Pierce, Jennifer L. *Gender Trials: Emotional Lives in Contemporary Law Firms.* Berkeley: University of California Press, 1995. Using participant observation combined with interviews, the author explains how "doing gender" maintains gender stratification in high-pressure law offices.

Tannen, Deborah. *You Just Don't Understand: Women and Men in Conversation.* New York: Morrow, 1990. A psycholinguist documents the extent to which speech patterns of men and women are related to basic differences in their social worlds.

Williams, Christine L. *Still a Man's World: Men Who Do Women's Work.* Berkeley: University of California Press, 1995. Based on in-depth interviews with men and women in nursing, elementary school teaching, librarianship, and social work, the author concludes that, due to the high value placed on masculinity, men who work in traditionally women's occupations find a "glass escalator" instead of a "glass ceiling."

Witt, Linda, Karen M. Paget, and Glenna Matthews. *Running as a Woman: Gender and Power in American Politics.* New York: Macmillan, 1994. This history of women in politics includes successful strategies for running for political office as a woman.

Journals

These journals focus on the role of gender in social life: *Feminist Studies; Gender and Society; Gender, Place and Culture: A Journal of Feminist Geography; Journal of Gender, Culture, and Health; Sex Roles;* and *Signs: Journal of Women in Culture and Society.*

Chapter 12 Inequalities of Race and Ethnicity

Browning, Christopher R. *Ordinary Men: Reserve Police Battalion 101 and the Final Solution in Poland.* New York: HarperPerennial, 1993. A startling account of how a government turned ordinary men into mass murderers.

De Anda, Roberto M., ed. *Chicanas and Chicanos in Contemporary Society.* Boston: Allyn and Bacon, 1996. An overview of the economy, family, religion, crime, justice, education, and politics of Americans who trace their origins to Mexico.

Du Bois, W.E.B. *Black Reconstruction in America: An Essay Toward a History of the Part Which Black Folk Played in the Attempt to Reconstruct Democracy in America, 1860–1880.* New York: Harcourt, Brace 1935; London: Frank Cass, 1966. This analysis of the role of African Americans in the Civil War and in the years immediately following provides a glimpse into a neglected part of U.S. history.

Duneier, Mitchell. *Slim's Table: Race, Respectability, Masculinity.* Chicago: University of Chicago Press, 1994. Based on participant observation, the author analyzes the relationships of a group of working-class African-American men in Chicago, with an emphasis on how they maintain their sense of moral worth.

Ellison, Christopher G., and W. Allen Martin, eds. *Race and Ethnic Relations in the United States: Readings for the 21st Century.* Los Angeles: Roxbury, 1998. In their analysis of the contemporary experiences of U.S. racial and ethnic groups, the authors of these forty-six articles examine major debates over controversial issues.

Espiritu, Yen Le. *Asian American Women and Men: Labor, Laws, and Love.* Beverly Hills, Calif.: Sage, 1996. The author's discussion of Asian-American culture demonstrates how race, class, and gender intersect and confirm one another.

In-Jin, Yoon. *On My Own: Korean Businesses and Race Relations in America.* Chicago: University of Chicago Press, 1997. The author explains how the entry of Korean immigrants into small businesses affects their relations with African Americans and Latinos.

Lipset, Seymour Martin, and Earl Raab. *Jews and the New American Scene.* Cambridge, Mass.: Harvard University Press, 1995. The book centers on this question: With little antisemitism, reduced threat to Israel, low participation in formal religion, and high intermarriage (57 percent), what is going to hold the Jewish community together?

Mander, Jerry. *In the Absence of the Sacred: The Failure of Technology and the Survival of the Indian Nations.* San Francisco, Calif.: Sierra Club Books, 1992. With a focus on the impact of technology, the author analyzes past and present relations of Native Americans and the U.S. government.

Rodriguez, Roberto. *Justice: A Question of Race.* Tempe, Ariz.: Bilingual Review Press, 1997. The author was arrested and beaten by the police for taking photos of them beating a mentally confused man. He recounts his own victimization and his subsequent trial against the Los Angeles Police Department.

Skrentny, John David. *The Ironies of Affirmative Action: Politics, Culture, and Justice in America.* Chicago: University of Chicago Press, 1996. The author takes on the almost impossible task of not taking sides while analyzing affirmative action.

Stack, Carol. *Call to Home: African Americans Reclaim the Rural South.* New York: Basic Books, 1996. This analysis of reverse migration helps us understand why African Americans who return to the rural South are viewed as a threat by both African Americans and whites.

Chapter 13 Inequalities of Age

Clair, Jeffrey Michael, David A. Karp, and William C. Yoels. *Experiencing the Life Cycle: A Social Psychology of Aging*, 2nd ed. Springfield, Ill.: Thomas, 1993. The authors examine social factors that underlie the adjustments that the elderly make to life changes.

Cockerham, William C. *This Aging Society*. Englewood Cliffs, N.J.: Prentice Hall, 1991. The social consequences of the growing numbers of elderly in U.S. society are the focus of this book.

Cox, Harold G. *Late Life: The Realities of Aging*, 3rd ed. Englewood Cliffs, N.J.: Prentice Hall, 1993. Using a symbolic interactionist framework, the author presents an overview of issues in aging.

Jerrome, Dorothy. *Good Company: An Anthropological Study of Old People in Groups*. Edinburgh, Scotland: Edinburgh University Press, 1992. The author analyzes the day-to-day interactions that provide the primary bases for satisfying adjustment to old age.

National Center for Health Statistics. *Common Beliefs About the Rural Elderly: What Do National Data Tell Us?* Washington, D.C.: U.S. Government Printing Office, 1993. This book provides a broad overview of a neglected topic, U.S. elderly in rural areas.

Posner, Richard A. *Aging and Old Age*. Chicago: University of Chicago Press, 1995. The author, a federal judge and prolific social analyst, proposes that a biology of aging accounts for changes in intelligence and emotions, which, in turn, have surprising consequences for society.

Stoller, Eleanor Palo, and Rose Campbell Gibson. *Worlds of Difference: Inequality in the Aging Experience*. Thousand Oaks, Calif.: Pine Forge Press, 1994. The authors document extensive inequalities borne by the U.S. elderly and explain the social conditions that create those inequalities.

Journals

The Gerontologist, Journal of Aging and Identity, Journal of Aging and Social Policy, Journal of Aging Studies, Journal of Cross-Cultural Gerontology, Journal of Elder Abuse and Neglect, Journal of Gerontology, and *Journal of Women and Aging* focus on issues of aging, while *Youth and Society* examines adolescent culture.

Chapter 14 The Economy: Money and Work

Berger, Peter L. *The Capitalist Revolution: Fifty Propositions About Prosperity, Equality, and Liberty*. New York: Basic Books, 1991. Berger's explanation of why capitalism is highly productive and why it enhances personal liberty is especially useful in light of changes in the Industrializing Nations.

Drucker, Peter F. *Post-Capitalist Society*. New York: HarperCollins, 1993. A highly readable account of the fundamental changes that are transforming our society, including how we live, work, and even think.

Dudley, Kathryn Marie. *The End of the Line: Lost Jobs, New Lives in Postindustrial America*. Chicago: University of Chicago Press, 1994. This analysis of the closing of the Chrysler assembly plant in Kenosha, Wisconsin, helps us understand the working class's mounting fears about job security.

Harrison, Bennett, and Barry Bluestone. *The Great U-Turn: Corporate Restructuring and the Polarizing of America*. New York: Basic Books, 1990. The authors investigate major changes taking place in the U.S. economy, focusing on the declining standard of living of the average American.

Ikels, Charlotte. *The Return of the God of Wealth: The Transition to a Market Economy in Urban China*. Stanford, Calif.: Stanford University Press, 1996. The author uses firsthand observations to describe what life is like in a society that is making the transition from socialism to capitalism.

Marx, Karl. *Selected Writings in Sociology and Social Philosophy*, Thomas B. Bottomore and Maximilian Rubel, eds. New York: McGraw-Hill, 1964. If you are unfamiliar with Marx's ideas, you will benefit from this useful introduction, especially Marx's analysis of social class and alienation.

Morales, Rebecca, and Frank Bonilla, eds. *Latinos in a Changing U.S. Economy: Comparative Perspectives on Growing Inequality*. Newbury Park, Calif.: Sage, 1993. Some groups feel the negative consequences of a changing economy more than do other groups. The authors of these articles analyze why Latinos are falling behind.

Porter, Michael E. *The Competitive Advantage of Nations*. New York: Free Press, 1990. Based on research in ten countries, the author first examines how productivity is the key to a nation's competitive market position and then provides an explanation for the economic success of Japan and the decline of Great Britain.

Journals

Two journals that focus on issues presented in this chapter are *Insurgent Sociologist* and *Work and Occupations*.

Chapter 15 Politics: Power and Authority

Aho, James A. *This Thing of Darkness: A Sociology of the Enemy*. Seattle: University of Washington Press, 1994. This book provides insight into how people develop a collective perception of a broad conspiracy to destroy their way of life, even a shared, impassioned hatred of what they term "the enemy."

Allen, Oliver E. *The Tiger*. New York: Addison-Wesley, 1993. An entertaining account of Tammany Hall, the corrupt political group that controlled New York City from the 1800s to past the middle of this century.

Amnesty International. *Amnesty International Report*. London: Amnesty International Publications, published annually. The reports summarize human rights violations around the world, listing specific instances country by country.

Bills, David D., ed. *The New Modern Times: Factors Reshaping the World of Work*. Albany: State University of New York, 1994. The authors help us understand the global social changes that, forcing a restructuring of our economy, are vitally affecting our everyday lives.

Chirot, Daniel. *Modern Tyrants: The Power and Prevalence of Evil in Our Age*. New York: Free Press, 1994. From Hitler and Stalin to Trujillo, Mao, and Pol Pot, the author analyzes the political expediency that underlies tyranny.

Ferguson, Thomas. *Golden Rule*. Chicago: University of Chicago Press, 1995. The title, based on the statement "to discover who rules, follow the gold (money)," gives support to the conflict perspective of U.S. politics.

Kerbo, Harold R., and John A. McKinstry. *Who Rules Japan?: The Inner Circles of Economic and Political Power*. Westport, Conn.: Praeger, 1995. An analysis of the "iron triangle" that wields power in Japan—the tightly bound group of corporate, bureaucratic, and political elites.

Mills, C. Wright. *The Power Elite*. New York: Oxford University Press, 1956. This classic analysis elaborates the conflict thesis summarized in this chapter that U.S. society is ruled by the nation's top corporate leaders, together with an elite from the military and political institutions.

Porter, Bruce D. *War and the Rise of the State: The Military Foundations of Modern Politics*. New York: Free Press, 1994. The author presents an intriguing analysis of how war and the military underlie the creation of the state and of changed relations within it.

Stiglmayer, Alexandra, ed. *Mass Rape: The War Against Women in Bosnia-Herzegovina*, Marion Faber, trans. Lincoln: University of Nebraska Press, 1994. Giving chilling accounts, the authors explain why mass rape sometimes accompanies war, as it did in Bosnia.

Journals

Most sociology journals publish articles on politics. Three that focus on this area of social life are *American Political Science Review, Journal of Political and Military Sociology,* and *Social Policy.*

Research in Political Sociology: A Research Annual. Greenwich, Conn.: JAI Press. This annual publication is not recommended for beginners, as the findings and theories are often difficult and abstract. It does, however, analyze political topics of vital concern to our well-being.

Chapter 16 The Family: Initiation into Society

Bergen, Raquel Kennedy. *Wife Rape: Understanding the Response of Survivors and Service Providers.* Newbury Park, Calif.: Sage, 1996. To understand the experience of women who have been raped, and how agency workers fail to help them, the author interviewed women who had taken refuge in shelters.

Hays, Sharon. *The Cultual Contradictions of Motherhood.* New Haven, Conn.: Yale University Press, 1996. The author's premise is that our changed ideology of child rearing ("intensive mothering") forces such great demands on mothers that it drives them to exhaustion.

Hochschild, Arlie Russell. *The Time Bind.* New York: Metropolitan Books, 1997. Do parents really want to spend more time with their families and less at work? Or do parents flee families, finding work a respite from family pressures? The author presents some surprising answers.

LaRossa, Ralph. *The Modernization of Fatherhood: A Social and Political History.* Chicago: University of Chicago Press, 1996. The author's exploration of how ideas of fatherhood have changed over time, and how they have varied from one group to another, sheds light on our current ideas of fatherhood.

McAdoo, Harriette Pipes, ed. *Black Families,* 3rd ed. Newbury Park, Calif.: Sage, 1996. An analysis of the experiences of black families and the pressures they experience.

Rubin, Lillian. *Families on the Faultline: America's Working Class Speaks about the Family, the Economy, Race and Ethnicity.* New York: HarperCollins, 1994. Based on interviews, this book maps primary concerns of the working class, allowing us to better understand the tensions they face.

Strasser, Mark. *Legally Wed: Same-Sex Marriage and the Constitution.* Ithaca, N.Y.: Cornell University Press, 1997. Based on the Hawaiian case mentioned in this chapter, the author analyzes same-sex marriages in light of the U.S. Constitution.

Journals

Family Relations, International Journal of Sociology of the Family, Journal of Comparative Family Studies, Journal of Divorce, Journal of Family and Economic Issues, Journal of Family Issues, Journal of Family Violence, Journal of Marriage and the Family, and *Marriage and Family Review* publish articles on almost every aspect of marriage and family life.

Chapter 17 Education: Transferring Knowledge and Skills

Cookson, Peter W. *School Choice: The Struggle for the Soul of American Education.* New Haven, Conn.: Yale University Press, 1994. This focus on school choice examines the controversy over educational reform, which, based on fundamentally different ideas about the philosophy and content of education, is not likely to be resolved soon.

Farkas, George. *Human Capital or Cultural Capital? Ethnicity and Poverty Groups in an Urban School District.* New York: Aldine De-Gruyter, 1996. Based on his research in Dallas, the author develops strategies to increase the success of at-risk students.

Garrod, Andrew, and Colleen Larimore, eds. *First Person, First Peoples: Native American College Graduates Tell Their Life Stories.* Ithaca, N.Y.: Cornell University Press, 1997. Written by graduates of Dartmouth College, these essays recount the anguish minority students feel in a predominantly white college.

Hurn, Christopher J. *The Limits and Possibilities of Schooling: An Introduction to the Sociology of Education,* 3rd ed. Boston: Allyn and Bacon, 1993. This overview of the sociology of education reviews in greater depth many of the topics discussed in this chapter.

Kozol, Jonathan. *Savage Inequalities.* New York: Crown Publishers, 1991. Kozol presents a journalistic account of educational inequalities that arise from social class.

Padilla, Felix M. *The Struggle of Latino/Latina University Students: In Search of a Liberating Education.* New York: Routledge, 1997. The author draws on his students' journal entries and on his own educational experiences to analyze how Latino/a students construct their education in a white university.

Reagin, Joe, Vera Hernan, and Imani Nikitah. *The Agony of Education: Black Students at a White University.* New York: Routledge, 1996. Based on interviews with African-American students and their parents, the authors analyze the dilemmas these students face and the decisions they make.

Steinberg, Laurence, Stanford Dornbusch, and Bradford Brown. *Beyond the Classroom: Why School Reform Has Failed and What Parents Need to Do.* New York: Simon & Schuster, 1996. Based on a study of 20,000 high school students, the authors conclude that the peer group is the most important factor in determining educational success or failure.

Journals

The following journals contain articles that examine almost every aspect of education: *Education and Urban Society, Harvard Educational Review,* and *Sociology of Education.*

Chapter 18 Religion: Establishing Meaning

Berger, Peter L. *A Far Glory: The Quest for Faith in an Age of Credulity.* New York: Free Press, 1992. A sociologist explains how faith is possible in an age of pluralistic relativism.

Finke, Roger, and Rodney Stark. *The Churching of America, 1776–1990: Winners and Losers in Our Religious Economy.* New Brunswick, N.J.: Rutgers University Press, 1992. The authors' account of why churches gain or lose members over the decades provides a sweeping view of religious change in U.S. history.

Galanter, Marc. *Cults: Faith, Healing, and Coercion.* New York: Oxford University Press, 1989. What do Alcoholics Anonymous, the Unification Church, and the mass suicide in Jonestown have in common? This book, rich in ethnographic materials on charismatic cults, provides answers: however, the sociological reader will have to wade through some unacceptable psychiatric interpretations.

Reeves, Thomas C. *The Empty Church: The Suicide of Liberal Christianity.* New York: Free Press, 1996. This examination of religion in U.S. society compares the relative fates of liberal and conservative denominations.

Stark, Rodney, and William Sims Bainbridge. *Religion, Deviance, and Social Control.* New York: Routledge, 1997. Does religion prevent crime, delinquency, suicide, or drug abuse? If so, under what circumstances? The authors answer questions such as these.

Wright, Stuart A., ed. *Armageddon in Waco: Critical Perspectives on the Branch Davidian Conflict.* Chicago: University of Chicago Press, 1996. These fifteen essays on the Mount Carmel tragedy help us understand why many scholars prefer to use the term *new religion* rather than *cult.*

Journals

The following three journals publish articles that focus on the sociology of religion: *Journal for the Scientific Study of Religion, Review of Religious Research,* and *Sociological Analysis: A Journal in the Sociology of Religion.*

Chapter 19 Medicine: Health and Illness

Bloor, Michael. *A Sociology of HIV Transmission*. Newbury Park, Calif.: Sage, 1995. An overview of the role of human behavior in the transmission of AIDS.

Bury, Michael, and Mary Ann Elston. *Health and Illness in a Changing Society*. New York: Routledge, 1997. The authors examine how social change affects the way we view and react to health and illness.

Fox, Renée C., and Judith P. Swazey. *Spare Parts: Organ Replacement in American Society*. New York: Oxford University Press, 1992. The authors explore moral and ethical aspects of organ replacement, a social issue destined to grow in importance as medical technology continues to advance.

Grob, Gerald N. *The Mad Among Us: A History of the Care of America's Mentally Ill*. New York: Free Press, 1994. From colonial to contemporary times, a detailed history of attitudes and approaches toward the mentally ill, some enlightened, most repressive.

Jones, James H. *Bad Blood*. New York: Free Press, 1993. An account of the syphilis experiments conducted by the U.S. Public Health Service at Tuskegee Institute, which were carried out on unwitting African Americans.

Karp, David A. *Speaking of Sickness: Depression, Disconnection, and the Meaning of Illness*. New York: Oxford University Press, 1996. Written by a sociologist who has suffered from depression for many years, this book provides deep insight into people's experience with this illness.

Lupton, Deborah. *Medicine as Culture: Illness, Disease, and the Body in Western Society*. Newbury Park, Calif.: Sage, 1994. In this exploration of the relationship between medicine, illness, and the body, the author stresses the role of power between patients and physicians.

Payer, Lynn. *Disease Mongers: How Doctors, Drug Companies, and Insurers Are Making You Feel Sick*. New York: Wiley, 1992. Since profits underlie the U.S. medical system, could it be that the U.S. medical establishment has a vested interest in keeping people ill? The author of this radical analysis thinks so.

Rodwin, Marc A. *Medicine, Money and Morals: Physicians' Conflicts of Interest*. New York: Oxford University Press, 1993. When you visit doctors, what is their top interest—your health or their bank accounts? The author's conclusion is disturbing.

Rushing, William A. *The AIDS Epidemic: Social Dimensions of an Infectious Disease*. Boulder, Colo.: Westview Press, 1995. A sociological overview of AIDS—from its origins and transmission to its control, with an emphasis on social reactions to the disease.

Smith, Barbara Ellen. *Digging Our Own Graves: Coal Miners and the Struggle over Black Lung Disease*. Philadelphia: Temple University Press, 1987. The author relates the coal miners' struggle to get black lung disease recognized by the medical community.

Journals

Health: An Interdisciplinary Journal for the Social Study of Health, Illness and Medicine, Journal of Health and Social Behavior, Research in the Sociology of Health Care, Social Science and Medicine, and *Sociological Practice: Health Sociology* publish research articles and essays in the field of medical sociology.

Chapter 20 Population and Urbanization

Anderson, Elijah. *StreetWise: Race, Class, and Change in an Urban Community*. Chicago: University of Chicago Press, 1992. A participant observation study that explores the relationships between those who are gentrifying an inner-city area and those who are being displaced.

Department of Agriculture. *Yearbook of Agriculture*. Washington, D.C.: Department of Agriculture, published annually. The yearbook focuses on specific aspects of U.S. agribusiness, especially international economies and trade.

Eade, John. *Living the Global City: Globalization as Local Process*. New York: Routledge, 1996. As he examines key debates and concepts, the author looks at how people's everyday lives are affected by globalization.

Flora, Cornelia Butler, Jan L. Flora, Jacqueline D. Spears, and Louis E. Swanson. *Rural Communities: Legacy and Change*. Boulder, Colo.: Westview Press, 1992. The authors examine profound changes that are transforming rural life.

Karp, David A., Gregory P. Stone, and William C. Yoels. *Being Urban: A Sociology of City Life*, 2nd ed. New York: Praeger, 1991. This overview of urban life stresses the everyday lives of city dwellers—what people *do* in cities, how they adjust and get along.

Liebow, Elliot. *Tally's Corner: A Study of Negro Streetcorner Men*. Boston: Little, Brown, 1967. This participant observation study of black street corner men and their families in Washington, D.C., has become a classic in sociology.

Mosher, Steven W. *A Mother's Ordeal: One Woman's Fight Against One-Child China*. New York: HarperCollins, 1994. This book puts a human face on China's coercive family planning policies.

Phillips, E. Barbara. *City Lights: Urban-Suburban Life in a Global Society*, 2nd ed. New York: Oxford University Press, 1995. What major challenges do U.S. cities face in our coming global society? That is the primary question examined by this author.

Sennett, Richard. *Flesh and Stone: The Body and the City in Western Civilization*. New York: Norton, 1994. This analysis of cities through history focuses on an interesting relationship, that of dominant ideas about the human body and the layout of cities.

Weeks, John R. *Population: An Introduction to Concepts and Issues*, 5th ed. Belmont, CA: Wadsworth, 1994. Focusing on both the United States and the world, the author analyzes major issues in population.

Whyte, William Foote. *Street Corner Society: The Social Structure of an Italian Slum*. Chicago: University of Chicago Press, 1993. First published in 1943. Still quoted and reprinted, this classic participant observation study provides insight into the social organization of an area of a U.S. city that, from an outsider's perspective, appeared socially disorganized.

Chapter 21 Collective Behavior and Social Movements

Brunvand, Jan Harold. *The Vanishing Hitchhiker: American Urban Legends and Their Meanings*. New York: Norton, 1981. This humorous analysis of urban legends helps us better understand how people adapt to social change. If you enjoy this book, you might try its 1984 sequel by the same author and publisher: *The Choking Doberman and Other "New" Urban Legends*.

d'Anjou, Leo. *Social Movements and Cultural Change: The First Abolition Campaign Revisited*. Hawthorne, N.Y.: Aldine de Gruyter, 1996. The author analyzes how the abolitionist movement succeeded in changing the public's definition of the slave trade—from a necessary evil to an evil to be eradicated.

Gitlin, Todd. *The Sixties: Years of Hope, Days of Rage*. New York: Bantam, 1987. The author, now a sociologist, was a leader in the peace movement that arose during the social unrest of the 1960s. He combines personal experience with a sociological perspective.

Goode, Erich, and Nachman Ben-Yehuda. *Moral Panics: The Social Construction of Deviance*. New York: Blackwell, 1994. An overview of moral panics, one of the forms of collective behavior discussed in this chapter, with an emphasis on the process by which something is determined to be a moral threat.

Jasper, James M. *The Art of Moral Protest: Culture, Biography, and Creativity in Social Movements*. Chicago: University of Chicago Press, 1998. A primary thrust of this book is how protest movements shape moral thinking.

Jasper, James M., and Dorothy Nelkin. *The Animal Rights Crusade: The Growth of a Moral Protest*. New York: Free Press, 1992. With an emphasis on philosophy, motivation, and tactics, the authors provide a kaleidoscopic overview of the animal rights movement, from its beginnings to its international participation.

Klee, Ernst, Willi Dressen, and Volker Riess. *"The Good Old Days": The Holocaust as Seen by Its Perpetrators and Bystanders*, Deborah Burnstone, trans. New York: Free Press, 1991. This chilling account of massacres by the SS is based on the photographs they took of their "work," their letters home, and their scrapbooks.

Lofland, John. *Social Movement Organizations: Guide to Research on Insurgent Realities*. Hawthorne, N.Y.: Aldine de Gruyter, 1996. An advanced analysis of social movement organizations.

McPhail, Clark. *The Myth of the Madding Crowd*. Hawthorne, N.Y.: Aldine de Gruyter, 1991. McPhail provides an overview of the history of research and theorizing about collective behavior.

Turner, Patricia. *I Heard It Through the Grapevine*. Berkeley: University of California Press, 1993. The author analyzes rumors among African Americans, including their effects on specific businesses.

Chapter 22 Social Change, Technology, and the Environment

Baber, Zaheer. *This Vulnerable Planet: A Short Economic History of the Environment*. New York: Monthly Review Press, 1994. An overview of how production is related to environmental degradation, from earlier times to capitalism and socialism, with too many apologies for environmental destruction in the former Soviet Union.

Brown, Lester R., ed. *State of the World*. New York: Norton, published annually. Experts on environmental issues analyze environmental problems throughout the world; a New Malthusian perspective.

Butel, Frederick H. *Forcing the Spring: The Transformation of the American Environmental Movement*. Washington, D.C.: Island Press, 1993. A history of the rise, decline, and resurgence of perhaps the most important global movement.

Colborn, Theo, Dianne Dumanoski, and John Peterson Myers. *Our Stolen Future: Are We Threatening Our Fertility, Intelligence, and Survival—A Scientific Detective Story*. New York: Dutton, 1996. Using a detective-style narrative, the authors argue that the bombardment of people and wildlife by chemicals commonly found in plastics, pesticides, and industrial pollutants are threatening our capacity to reproduce, fight off disease, and develop normal intelligence.

Council on Environmental Quality. *Environmental Quality*. Washington, D.C.: U.S. Government Printing Office, published annually. Each report evaluates the condition of some aspect of the environment.

Cross, Gary, S., and Rick Szostak. *Technology and American Society: A History*. Englewood Cliffs, N.J.: Prentice Hall, 1995. The authors analyze how technology, a driving force in social change, is having fundamental effects on our lives.

Feshbach, Murray, and Alfred Friendly. *Ecocide in the USSR*. New York: Basic Books, 1992. The authors analyze the political repression of environmentalists and the government's willing sacrifice of the environment for the sake of "building a brighter, industrial future."

Gates, Bill. *The Road Ahead*. New York: Viking, 1995. Will the new technology bring us a wallet PC that will dispense airline and concert tickets, function as a checkbook and a credit card, and communicate fax and e-mail messages? The chairman of Microsoft sees this—and many other surprises—as part of our trip down the information highway.

McCuen, Gary E., ed. *Ecocide and Genocide in the Vanishing Forest: The Rainforests and Native People*. Hudson, Wis.: GEM Publications, 1993. Eighteen brief readings examine why the rainforests are vanishing and explore possible solutions to this problem.

Stead, W. Edward, and Jean Garner Stead. *Management for a Small Planet*. Newbury Park, Calif.: Sage, 1992. The authors examine how we can reconcile our need for economic production with our need to protect the earth's ecosystem.

Journals

Earth First! Journal and *Sierra*, magazines published by Earth First! and the Sierra Club respectively, are excellent sources for keeping informed of major developments in the environmental movement.

References

Abdullah, Mohammed Nur. "Letter to the Editor." *Wall Street Journal*, November 2, 1995:A15.

Aberle, David. *The Peyote Religion Among the Navaho.* Chicago: Aldine, 1966.

Aberle, David F., A. K. Cohen, A. K. David, M. J. Leng, Jr., and F. N. Sutton. "The Functional Prerequisites of a Society." *Ethics, 60,* January 1950:100–111.

Abramson, Jill, and David Rogers. "The Keating 535." *Wall Street Journal*, January 10, 1991:A1, A8.

Ackernecht, Erwin H. "The Role of Medical History in Medical Education." *Bulletin of the History of Medicine, 21,* 1947:135–145.

Addams, Jane. *Twenty Years at Hull-House.* New York: Signet, 1981. First published in 1910.

Adler, Patricia A., Steven J. Kless, and Peter Adler. "Socialization to Gender Roles: Popularity Among Elementary School Boys and Girls." *Sociology of Education, 65,* July 1992:169–187.

Adorno, Theodor W., Else Frenkel-Brunswick, D. J. Levinson, and R. N. Sanford. *The Authoritarian Personality.* New York: Harper & Row, 1950.

Aeppel, Timothy. "More Amish Women Are Tending to Business." *Wall Street Journal*, February 8, 1996:B1, B2.

Aguirre, Benigno E., E. L. Quarantelli, and Jorge L. Mendoza. "The Collective Behavior of Fads: The Characteristics, Effects, and Career of Streaking." In *Collective Behavior and Social Movements,* Russell L. Curtis, Jr., and Benigno E. Aguirre, eds. Boston: Allyn and Bacon, 1993:168–182.

Ahlburg, Dennis A., and Carol J. De Vita. "New Realities of the American Family." *Population Bulletin, 47, 2,* August 1992:1–44.

Albert, Ethel M. "Women of Burundi: A Study of Social Values." In *Women of Tropical Africa,* Denise Paulme, ed. Berkeley: University of California Press, 1963:179–215.

Aldrich, Nelson W., Jr. *Old Money: The Mythology of America's Upper Class.* New York: Vintage Books, 1989.

Allen, Brandt. "Embezzler's Guide to the Computer." *Harvard Business Review, 53,* July-August 1975:79–89.

Allen, Katherine R., and David H. Demo. "The Families of Lesbians and Gay Men: A New Frontier in Family Research." *Journal of Marriage and the Family, 57,* February 1995:111–127.

Allport, Floyd. *Social Psychology.* Boston: Houghton Mifflin, 1954.

Alpert, Harry. *Emile Durkheim and His Sociology.* New York: Columbia University Press, 1939.

Amenta, Edwin, Bruce G. Carruthers, and Yvonne Zylan. "A Hero for the Aged? The Townsend Movement, the Political Mediation Model, and U.S. Old-Age Policy, 1934–1950." In *Social Movements: Readings on Their Emergence, Mobilization, and Dynamics,* Doug McAdam and David A. Snow, eds. Los Angeles: Roxbury Publishing, 1997:494–510.

American Sociological Association, "Section on Environment and Technology." Pamphlet, no date.

American Sociological Association. "Code of Ethics." Washington, D.C.: American Sociological Association, August 14, 1989; Spring 1997.

Amott, Teresa, and Julie Matthaei. *Race, Gender, and Work: A Multicultural Economic History of Women in the United States.* Boston: South End Press, 1991.

Amselle, Jorge. "HUD's Battle Against English Only." *Wall Street Journal*, August 21, 1995:A8.

Andersen, Margaret L. *Thinking About Women: Sociological Perspectives on Sex and Gender.* New York: Macmillan, 1988.

Anderson, Chris. "NORC Study Describes Homeless," *Chronicle,* 1986:5, 9.

Anderson, Elijah. *A Place on the Corner.* Chicago: University of Chicago Press, 1978.

Anderson, Elijah. *Streetwise.* Chicago: University of Chicago Press, 1990.

Anderson, Elijah. "Streetwise." In *Down to Earth Sociology: Introductory Readings,* 9th ed., James M. Henslin, ed. New York: Free Press, 1997:170–179.

Anderson, Nels. *The Hobo.* Chicago: University of Chicago Press, 1923.

Anderson, Nels. *Desert Saints: The Mormon Frontier in Utah.* Chicago: University of Chicago Press, 1966. First published in 1942.

Anderson, Philip. "God and the Swedish Immigrants." *Sweden and America,* Autumn 1995:17–20.

Anderson, Teresa A. "The Best Years of Their Lives," *Newsweek,* January 7, 1985:6.

Angell, Marcia. "Euthanasia in the Netherlands—Good News or Bad?" *New England Journal of Medicine, 335, 22,* November 28, 1996.

Angell, Robert C. "The Sociology of Human Conflict." In *The Nature of Human Conflict*, Elton B. McNeil, ed. Englewood Cliffs, N.J.: Prentice Hall, 1965.

Annin, Peter, and Kendall Hamilton. "Marriage or Rape?" *Newsweek*, December 16, 1996:78.

Ansberry, Clare. "Despite Federal Law, Hospitals Still Reject Sick Who Can't Pay." *Wall Street Journal*, November 29, 1988:A1, A4.

Ansberry, Clare. "Nannies and Mothers Struggle over Roles in Raising Children." *Wall Street Journal*, May 21, 1993:A1, A6.

"Anybody's Son Will Do." National Film Board of Canada, KCTS, and Films, Inc. 1983.

Aptheker, Herbert. "W.E.B. Du Bois: Struggle Not Despair." *Clinical Sociology Review*, 8, 1990:58–68.

Arías, Jesús. "La Junta rehabilita en Grenada casas que deberá tirar por ruina." *El Pais*, January 2, 1993:1.

Ariès, Philippe. *Centuries of Childhood: A Social History of Family Life.* Robert Baldick, trans. New York: Vintage, 1962.

Arlacchi, P. *Peasants and Great Estates: Society in Traditional Calabria.* Cambridge, England: Cambridge University Press, 1980.

Armitage, Richard L. "Red Army Retreat Doesn't Signal End of U.S. Obligation." *Wall Street Journal*, February 7, 1989:A20.

Arndt, William F., and F. Wilbur Gingrich. *A Greek-English Lexicon of the New Testament and Other Early Christian Literature.* Chicago: University of Chicago Press, 1957.

Asch, Solomon. "Effects of Group Pressure Upon the Modification and Distortion of Judgments." In *Readings in Social Psychology*, Guy Swanson, Theodore M. Newcomb, and Eugene L. Hartley, eds. New York: Holt, Rinehart and Winston, 1952.

Ashe, Arthur. "A Zero-Sum Game That Hurts Blacks." *Wall Street Journal*, February 27, 1992:A10.

Ashford, Lori S. "New Perspectives on Population: Lessons from Cairo." *Population Bulletin*, 50, 1, March 1995:1–44.

Ashley, Richard. *Cocaine: Its History, Uses, and Effects.* New York: St. Martin's, 1975.

Associated Press. "Future Medicine Looks Futuristic." December 2, 1995.

Atchley, Robert C. "Dimensions of Widowhood in Later Life," *Gerontologist*, 15, April 1975:176–178.

Auerbach, Judith D. "Employer-Supported Child Care as a Women-Responsive Policy." *Journal of Family Issues*, 11, 4, December 1990:384–400.

Baca Zinn, Maxine. "Adaptation and Continuity in Mexican-Origin Families." In *Minority Families in the United States: A Multicultural Perspective*, Ronald L. Taylor, ed. Englewood Cliffs, N.J.: Prentice Hall, 1994:64–81.

Bainbridge, William Sims. "Collective Behavior and Social Movements." In *Sociology*, Rodney Stark. Belmont, Calif.: Wadsworth, 1989:608–640.

Bales, Robert F. *Interaction Process Analysis.* Reading, Mass.: Addison-Wesley, 1950.

Bales, Robert F. "The Equilibrium Problem in Small Groups." In *Working Papers in the Theory of Action*, Talcott Parsons et al., eds. New York: Free Press, 1953:111–115.

Ballantine, Jeanne H. *The Sociology of Education: A Systematic Analysis.* Englewood Cliffs, N.J.: Prentice Hall, 1983.

Baltzell, E. Digby. *The Protestant Establishment: Aristocracy and Caste in America.* New York: Vintage, 1964.

Baltzell, E. Digby. *Puritan Boston and Quaker Philadelphia.* New York: Free Press, 1979.

Baltzell, E. Digby, and Howard G. Schneiderman. "Social Class in the Oval Office." *Society*, 25, Sept/Oct, 1988:42–49.

Bannon, Lisa. "How a Rumor Spread About Subliminal Sex in Disney's 'Aladdin'." *Wall Street Journal*, October 24, 1995:A1, A6.

Barbeau, Clayton, "The Man–Woman Crisis." In *Marriage and Family in a Changing Society*, 4th ed. James M. Henslin, ed. New York: Free Press, 1992:193–199.

Barberis, Mary. "Egypt." *Population Today*, 22, 6, June 1994:7.

Barkun, Michael. "Reflections After Waco: Millenialists and the State." *Christian Century*, June 2–9, 1993:596–600.

Barnes, Fred. "How to Rig a Poll." *Wall Street Journal*, June 14, 1995:A14.

Barnes, Harry Elmer. *The History of Western Civilization*, Vol. 1. New York: Harcourt, Brace, 1935.

Barnes, John A. "Canadians Cross Border to Save Their Lives." *Wall Street Journal*, December 12, 1990:A14.

Baron, Robert, and Gerald Greenberg. *Behavior in Organizations.* Boston: Allyn and Bacon, 1990.

Barrie, Marianna L. "Female Circumcision: Wounds That Never Heal." *Essence*, 26, 11, March 1996, 54.

Barry, Paul. "Strong Medicine: A Talk with Former Principal Henry Gradillas." *College Board Review*, Fall 1989:2–13.

Beals, Ralph L., and Harry Hoijer. *An Introduction to Anthropology*, 3rd ed. New York: Macmillan, 1965.

Beck, Allen J., Susan A. Kline, and Lawrence A. Greenfeld. "Survey of Youth in Custody, 1987." Washington, D.C.: U.S. Department of Justice, September 1988.

Beck, Scott H., and Joe W. Page. "Involvement in Activities and the Psychological Well-Being of Retired Men." *Activities, Adaptation, & Aging*, 11, 1, 1988:31–47.

Becker, Howard S. *Outsiders: Studies in the Sociology of Deviance.* New York: Free Press, 1966.

Beckett, Paul. "Even Piñatas Sold in Mexico Seem to Originate in Hollywood Now." *Wall Street Journal*, September 11, 1996:B1.

Beeghley, Leonard. *The Structure of Social Stratification in the United States*, 2nd ed. Boston: Allyn and Bacon, 1996.

Begley, Sharon. "Twins: Nazi and Jew." *Newsweek*, 94, December 3, 1979:139.

Belcher, John R. "Are Jails Replacing the Mental Health System for the Homeless Mentally Ill?" *Community Mental Health Journal*, 24, 3, Fall 1988:185–195.

Bell, Daniel. *The Coming of Post-Industrial Society: A Venture in Social Forecasting.* New York: Basic Books, 1973.

Bell, David A. "An American Success Story: The Triumph of Asian-Americans." In *Sociological Footprints: Introductory Readings in Sociology*, 5th ed., Leonard Cargan and Jeanne H. Ballantine, eds. Belmont, Calif.: Wadsworth, 1991:308–316.

Bellah, Robert N. *Beyond Belief.* New York: Harper & Row, 1970.

Benales, Carlos. "70 Days Battling Starvation and Freezing in the Andes: A Chronicle of Man's Unwillingness to Die." *New York Times*, January 1, 1973:3.

Bender, Sue, "Everyday Sacred: A Journey to the Amish." *Utne Reader*, September–October 1990:91–97.

Bender, William, and Margaret Smith. "Population, Food, and Nutrition." *Population Bulletin*, 51, 4, February 1997:1–47.

Benet, Sula. "Why They Live to Be 100, or Even Older, in Abkhasia." *New York Times Magazine*, 26, December 1971.

Bennett, Neil G., Ann Klimas Blanc, and David E. Bloo. "Commitment and the Modern Union: Assessing the Link between Premarital Cohabitation and Subsequent Marital Stability." *American Sociological Review*, *53*, 1988:127–138.

Benokraitis, Nijole V., and Joe R. Feagin. "Sex Discrimination—Subtle and Covert." In *Down to Earth Sociology: Introductory Readings*, 6th ed., James M. Henslin, ed. New York: Free Press, 1991:334–343.

Bergen, Raquel Kennedy. *Wife Rape: Understanding the Response of Survivors and Service Providers*. Newbury Park, Calif.: Sage, 1996.

Berger, Peter L. *Invitation to Sociology: A Humanistic Perspective*. New York: Doubleday, 1963.

Berger, Peter L. *The Sacred Canopy: Elements of a Sociological Theory of Religion*. Garden City, N.Y.: Doubleday, 1967.

Berger, Peter L. *The Capitalist Revolution: Fifty Propositions About Prosperity, Equality, and Liberty*. New York: Basic Books, 1991.

Berger, Peter L. *A Far Glory: The Quest for Faith in an Age of Credulity*. New York: Free Press, 1992.

Berger, Peter L. "Invitation to Sociology." In *Down to Earth Sociology: Introductory Readings*, 9th ed., James M. Henslin, ed. New York: Free Press, 1997:3–7.

Bergmann, Barbara R. "The Future of Child Care." Paper presented at the 1995 meetings of the American Sociological Association.

Bergström, Hans. "Pressures Behind the Swedish Health Reforms." *Viewpoint Sweden*, *12*, July 1992:1–5.

Berk, Laura E. *Child Development*, 3rd ed. Boston: Allyn and Bacon, 1994.

Berk, Richard A. *Collective Behavior*. Dubuque, Iowa: Brown, 1974.

Berle, Adolf, Jr., and Gardiner C. Means. *The Modern Corporation and Private Property*. New York: Harcourt, Brace and World, 1932. As cited in Useem 1980:44.

Bernard, Jessie. *The Future of Marriage*. New York: Bantam, 1972.

Bernard, Jessie. "The Good-Provider Role." In *Marriage and Family in a Changing Society*, 4th ed., James M. Henslin, ed. New York: Free Press, 1992:275–285.

Bernard, Viola W., Perry Ottenberg, and Fritz Redl. "Dehumanization: A Composite Psychological Defense in Relation to Modern War." In *The Triple Revolution Emerging: Social Problems in Depth*, Robert Perucci and Marc Pilisuk, eds. Boston: Little, Brown, 1971:17–34.

Bernstein, Jonas. "How the Russian Mafia Rules." *Wall Street Journal*, October 26, 1994:A20.

Bernstein, Richard. "Play Penn." *New Republic*, August 2, 1993.

Bessen, Jim. "No Need for More Unemployed." *New York Times*, August 4, 1993.

Besser, Terry L. "A Critical Approach to the Study of Japanese Management." *Humanity and Society*, *16*, 2, May 1992:176–195.

Bianchi, Suzanne M., and Daphne Spain. "Women Work, and Family in America." *Population Bulletin*, *51*, 3, December 1996:1–47.

Bijker, W. E., Hughes, T. and Pinch, T. *The Social Construction of Technological Systems*. Cambridge, Mass: MIT Press, 1987.

Bird, Chloe E. "Gender Differences in the Social and Economic Burdens of Parenting and Psychological Distress." *Journal of Marriage and the Family*, *59*, August 1997:1–16.

Bishop, Jerry E. "Study Finds Doctors Tend to Postpone Heart Surgery for Women, Raising Risk." *Wall Street Journal*, April 16, 1990:B4.

Blackwelder, Stephen P. "Duality of Structure in the Reproduction of Race, Class, and Gender Inequality." Paper presented at the 1993 meetings of the American Sociological Association.

Blau, Francine D., and Lawrence M. Kahn. "The Gender Earnings Gap: Some International Evidence." Working Paper No. 4224, National Bureau of Economic Research, December 1992.

Blau, Peter M. "Social Structure and Life Chances." *Current Perspectives in Social Theory*, *5*, Supplement 1, 1994:177–190.

Blau, Peter M. and Otis Dudley Duncan. *The American Occupational Structure*. New York: John Wiley, 1967.

Blauner, Robert. "Death and Social Structure." *Psychiatry*, *29*, 1966:378–394.

Blinick, Abraham. "Socialized Medicine Is No Cure-All." *Wall Street Journal*, January 17, 1992:A11.

Bloom, Dan, Veronica Fellerath, David Long, and Robert G. Wood. *LEAP: Interim Findings on a Welfare Initiative to Improve School Attendance Among Teenage Parents*. New York: Manpower Demonstration Research Corporation, May 1993.

Blumer, Herbert George. "Collective Behavior." In *Principles of Sociology*, Robert E. Park, ed. New York: Barnes and Noble, 1939:219–288.

Blumer, Herbert. "Sociological Implications of the Thought of George Herbert Mead." *American Journal of Sociology*, *71*, 1966:535–544.

Blumer, Herbert. *Industrialization as an Agent of Social Change: A Critical Analysis*, David R. Maines and Thomas J. Morrione, eds. Hawthorne, N.Y.: Aldine de Gruyter, 1990.

Blumstein, Alfred, and Jacqueline Cohen. "Characterizing Criminal Careers." *Science*, *237*, August 1987:985–991.

Blumstein, Philip, and Pepper Schwartz. *American Couples: Money, Work, Sex*. New York: Pocket Books, 1985.

Bobo, Lawrence, and James R. Kluegel. "Modern American Prejudice: Stereotypes, Social Distance, and Perceptions of Discrimination Toward Blacks, Hispanics, and Asians." Paper presented at the 1991 annual meetings of the American Sociological Association.

Bogardus, Emory S. *A History of Social Thought*, 2nd ed. Los Angeles: Jesse Ray Miller, 1929.

Bolgar, Robert, Hallie Zweig-Frank, and Joel Paris. "Childhood Antecedents of Interpersonal Problems in Young Adult Children of Divorce." *Journal of the American Academy of Child and Adolescent Psychiatry*, *34*, 2, February 1995:143–150.

Booth, Alan, and James M. Dabbs, Jr. "Testosterone and Men's Marriages." *Social Forces*, *72*, 2, December 1993:463–477.

Borrelli, Peter. "The Ecophilosophers." *Amicus Journal*, Spring 1988:30–39.

Boulding, Elise. *The Underside of History*. Boulder, Colo.: Westview Press, 1976.

Bourgois, Philippe. "Crack in Spanish Harlem." In *Haves and Have-Nots: An International Reader on Social Inequality*, James Curtis and Lorne Tepperman, eds. Englewood Cliffs, N.J.: Prentice Hall, 1994:131–136.

Bourque, L. B. *Defining Rape*. Durham, N.C.: Duke University Press, 1989.

Bowles, Samuel. "Unequal Education and the Reproduction of the Social Division of Labor." In *Power and Ideology in Education*. J. Karabel and A. H. Halsely, eds. New York: Oxford University Press, 1977.

Bowles, Samuel, and Herbert Gintis. *Schooling in Capitalist America*. New York: Basic Books, 1976.

Bradley, Martin B., Norman M. Green, Jr., Dale E. Jones, Mac Lynn, and Lou McNiel. *Churches and Church Membership in the United States 1990*. Atlanta: Glenmary Research Center, 1992.

Brajuha, Mario, and Lyle Hallowell. "Legal Intrusion and the Politics of Fieldwork: The Impact of the Brajuha Case." *Urban Life, 14,* 4, January 1986:454–478.

Brauchli, Marcus W. "China Cranks Up Propaganda Machine and Releases Dissident in Olympics Bid." *Wall Street Journal,* September 15, 1993a:A11.

Brauchli, Marcus W. "A Satellite TV System Is Quickly Moving Asia into the Global Village." *Wall Street Journal,* May 10, 1993b:A1, A8.

Brauchli, Marcus W. "Wary of Education But Needing Brains, China Faces a Dilemma." *Wall Street Journal,* November 15, 1994:A1, A10.

Bray, Rosemary L. "Rosa Parks: A Legendary Moment, a Lifetime of Activism. *Ms., 6,* 3, November–December 1995:45–47.

Brecher, Edward M., and the Editors of Consumer Reports. *Licit and Illicit Drugs.* Boston: Little, Brown, 1972.

Breen, Richard, and Christopher T. Whelan. "Gender and Class Mobility: Evidence from the Republic of Ireland." *Sociology, 29,* 1, February 1995:1–22.

Bretos, Miguel A. "Hispanics Face Institutional Exclusion." *Miami Herald,* May 22, 1994.

Bridgman, Ann. "Report from the Russian Front." *Education Week,* April 6, 1994:22–29.

Bridgwater, William, ed. *The Columbia Viking Desk Encyclopedia.* New York: Viking Press, 1953.

Brilliant, Ashleigh E. *Social Effects of the Automobile in Southern California During the 1920s.* Unpublished doctoral dissertation, University of California at Berkeley, 1964.

Brines, Julie. "Economic Dependency, Gender, and the Division of Labor at Home." *American Journal of Sociology, 100,* 3, November 1994:652–688.

Brink, Susan. "Elderly Empowerment." *U.S. News & World Report,* April 26, 1993:65–70.

Brinton, Crane. *The Anatomy of Revolution.* New York: Vintage Books, 1965.

Broad, William J. "The Shuttle Explodes." *New York Times,* January 29, 1986, A1, A5.

Bromley, David G. "The Satanic Cult Scare." *Culture and Society,* May–June 1991:55–56.

Bronfenbrenner, Urie. "Principles for the Healthy Growth and Development of Children." In *Marriage and Family in a Changing Society,* 4th ed., James M. Henslin, ed. New York: Free Press, 1992:243–249.

Brooke, James. "Amid U.S. Islam's Growth in the U.S., Muslims Face a Surge in Attacks." *New York Times,* August 28, 1995:A1, B7.

Brooks, Virginia R. "Sex Differences in Student Dominance Behavior in Female and Male Professors' Classrooms." *Sex Roles, 8,* 7, 1982:683–690.

Brown, Diane Robinson, and Lawrence E. Gary. "Unemployment and Psychological Distress Among Black American Women." *Sociological Focus, 21,* 1988:209–221.

Browne, Andrew. "Education Seen as the Solution." *Reuters On Line.* September 8, 1995.

Brownlee, Lisa. "On-Line Porn Sorely Tests Librarians' Free-Speech Principles." *Wall Street Journal,* April 23, 1997:B1. B11.

Brunvand, Jan Harold. *The Vanishing Hitchhiker: American Urban Legends and Their Meanings.* New York: Norton, 1981.

Brunvand, Jan Harold. *The Choking Doberman and Other "New" Urban Legends.* New York: Norton, 1984.

Brunvand, Jan Harold. *The Study of American Folklore.* New York: Norton, 1986.

Bryant, Clifton D. "Cockfighting: America's Invisible Sport." In *Down to Earth Sociology: Introductory Readings,* 7th ed., James M. Henslin, ed. New York: Free Press, 1993.

Brzezinksi, Matthew. "Where Cash Isn't King: Barter Lines Pockets in Ex-Soviet States." *Wall Street Journal,* May 1, 1997:A14.

Buckley, Stephen. "Shrugging Off the Burden of a Brainy Image." *Washington Post,* June 17, 1991:D1.

Budiansky, Stephen. "The Trees Fell—and So Did the People." *U.S. News and World Report,* February 9, 1987:75.

Buechler, Steven M. "Beyond Resource Mobilization: Emerging Trends in Social Movement Theory." *Sociological Quarterly, 34,* 2, 1993:217–235.

Bullard, Robert D., ed. *Unequal Protection: Environmental Justice and Communities of Color.* San Francisco: Sierra Club, 1994.

Bumiller, Elisabeth. "First Comes Marriage—Then, Maybe, Love." In *Marriage and Family in a Changing Society,* 4th ed., James M. Henslin, ed. New York: Free Press, 1992:120–125.

Bumpass, Larry. "Forum II. Patterns, Causes, and Consequences of Out-of-Wedlock Childbearing: What Can Government Do?" *Focus, 17,* 1, Summer 1995:41–45.

Bumpass, Larry L., James A. Sweet, and Andrew Cherlin. "The Role of Cohabitation in Declining Rates of Marriage." *Journal of Marriage and the Family, 53,* November 1991:913–927.

Bureau of the Census. "Income, Poverty, and Valuation of Noncash Benefits: 1994." Current Population Reports P60–189. Washington, D.C.: GPO, 1996.

Bureau of the Census. "Population Projections for States by Age, Sex, Race, and Hispanic Origin: 1995 to 2025." Washington, D.C.: October 1996.

Burgess, Ernest W. "The Growth of the City: An Introduction to a Research Project." In *The City,* Robert E. Park, Ernest W. Burgess, and Roderick D. McKenzie, eds. Chicago: University of Chicago Press, 1925:47–62.

Burgess, Ernest W., and Harvey J. Locke. *The Family: From Institution to Companionship.* New York: American Book, 1945.

Burnham, Walter Dean. *Democracy in the Making: American Government and Politics.* Englewood Cliffs, N.J.: Prentice Hall, 1983.

Bush, Diane Mitsch, and Robert G. Simmons. "Socialization Processes Over the Life Course." In *Social Psychology: Sociological Perspectives,* eds. Morris Rosenberger and Ralph H. Turner. New Brunswick, N.J.: Transaction, 1990:133–164.

Busby, Jim. "Hospices: Help for the Dying." *Current Health,* January 1993:30–31.

Butler, Robert N. *Why Survive? Being Old in America.* New York: Harper & Row, 1975.

Butler, Robert N. "Ageism: Another Form of Bigotry." *Gerontologist, 9,* Winter 1980:243–246.

Buttel, Frederick H. "New Directions in Environmental Sociology." *Annual Review of Sociology, 13,* W. Richard Scott and James F. Short, Jr., eds. Palo Alto, Calif.: Annual Reviews, 1987:465–488.

Butterworth, Katharine M. "The Story of a Nursing Home Refugee." In *Social Problems 92/93,* LeRoy W. Barnes, ed. Guilford, Conn.: Dushkin, 1992:90–93.

Caldwell, Cleopatra Howard, Angela Dungee Greene, and Andrew Billingsley. "The Black Church as a Family Support System: Instrumental and Expressive Functions." *National Journal of Sociology, 6,* 1, Summer 1992:21–40.

Callahan, Daniel. *Setting Limits: Medical Goals in an Aging Society.* New York: Simon & Schuster, 1987.

Canavan, Margaret M., Walter J. Meyer, III, and Deborah C. Higgs. "The Female Experience of Sibling Incest." *Journal of Marital and Family Therapy, 18,* 2, 1992:129–142.

Cannon, Lou. *Official Negligence: How Rodney King and the Riots Changed Los Angeles and the LAPD.* New York: Times Books, 1998.

Cantril, Hadley. *The Psychology of Social Movements.* New York: Wiley, 1941.

Caplow, Theodore. "The American Way of Celebrating Christmas." In *Down to Earth Sociology: Introductory Readings,* 6th ed., James M. Henslin, ed. New York: Free Press, 1991:88–97.

Cardoso, Fernando Henrique. "Dependent Capitalist Development in Latin America." *New Left Review, 74,* July–August 1972:83–95.

Carlson, Lewis H., and George A. Colburn. *In Their Place: White America Defines Her Minorities, 1850–1950.* New York: Wiley, 1972.

Carpenter, Betsy. "Redwood Radicals." *U.S. News & World Report, 109,* 11, September 17, 1990:50–51.

Carr, Deborah, Carol D. Ryff, Burton Singer, and William J. Magee. "Bringing the 'Life' Back into Life Course Research: A 'Person-Centered' Approach to Studying the Life Course." Paper presented at the 1995 meetings of the American Sociological Association.

Carrasquillo, Hector. "The Puerto Rican Family." In *Minority Families in the United States: A Multicultural Perspective,* Ronald L. Taylor, ed. Englewood Cliffs, N.J.: Prentice Hall, 1994:82–94.

Carrington, Tim. "Developed Nations Want Poor Countries to Succeed on Trade, But Not Too Much." *Wall Street Journal,* September 20, 1993:A10.

Carroll, Peter N., and David W. Noble. *The Free and the Unfree: A New History of the United States.* New York: Penguin, 1977.

Cartwright, Dorwin, and Alvin Zander, eds. *Group Dynamics,* 3rd ed. Evanston, Ill.: Peterson, 1968.

Casper, Lynne M., and Martin O'Connell, "State Estimates of Organized Child Care Facilities." Annual meetings of the Population Association of America, March 1997, as contained in *Population Today, 25,* 5, May 1997:6.

Cauthen, Nancy K., and James M. Jasper. "Culture, Politics, and Moral Panics." *Sociological Forum, 9,* 3, September 1994:495–503.

Centers for Disease Control. *HIV/AIDS Surveillance Report, 7,* 2, December 1995:1–39; *8,* 2, December 1966:1–39; *9,* 1, June 1997:1–37.

Cerulo, Karen A., and Janet M. Ruane. "Death Comes Alive: Technology and the Re-Conception of Death." In *Science as Culture,* forthcoming 1996.

Cerulo, Karen A., Janet M. Ruane, and Mary Chayko. "Technological Ties That Bind: Media-Generated Primary Groups." *Communication Research, 19,* 1, February 1992:109–129.

Chafetz, Janet Saltzman. *Masculine/Feminine or Human? An Overview of the Sociology of Sex Roles.* Itasca, Ill.: Peacock, 1974.

Chafetz, Janet Saltzman. *Gender Equity: An Integrated Theory of Stability and Change.* Newbury Park, Calif.: Sage, 1990.

Chafetz, Janet Saltzman, and Anthony Gary Dworkin. *Female Revolt: Women's Movements in World and Historical Perspective.* Totowa, N.J.: Rowman & Allanheld, 1986.

Chagnon, Napoleon A. *Yanomamo: The Fierce People,* 2nd ed. New York: Holt, Rinehart and Winston, 1977.

Chalfant, H. Paul. "Stepping to Redemption: Twelve-Step Groups as Implicit Religion." *Free Inquiry in Creative Sociology, 20,* 2, November 1992:115–120.

Chalkley, Kate. "Female Genital Mutilation: New Laws, Programs Try to End Practice." *Population Today, 25,* 10, October 1997:4–5.

Chambliss, William J. "A Sociological Analysis of the Law of Vagrancy." *Social Problems, 12,* Summer 1964:67–77.

Chambliss, William J. "The Saints and the Roughnecks." In *Down to Earth Sociology: Introductory Readings,* 9th ed., James M. Henslin, ed. New York: Free Press, 1997:246–260. First published in *Society, 11,* 1973.

Chandler, Daniel. "Technological or Media Determinism." Internet, "Media and Communication Studies Page," 1995. E-mail: dgc(a)aberystwyth.ac.

Chandler, Tertius, and Gerald Fox. *3000 Years of Urban Growth.* New York: Academic Press, 1974.

Chandra, Vibha P. "Fragmented Identities: The Social Construction of Ethnicity, 1885–1947." Unpublished paper, 1993a.

Chandra, Vibha P. "The Present Moment of the Past: The Metamorphosis." Unpublished paper, 1993b.

Charlier, Marj. "Little Bighorn from the Indian Point of View." *Wall Street Journal,* September 15, 1992:A12.

Chavez, Linda. "Rainbow Collision." *New Republic,* November 19, 1990:14–16.

Chen, Edwin. "Twins Reared Apart: A Living Lab." *New York Times Magazine.* December 9, 1979:112.

Chen, Kathy. "China's Women Face Obstacles in Workplace." *Wall Street Journal,* August 28, 1995:B1, B5.

Chen, Kathy. "Chinese Are Going to Town as Growth of Cities Takes Off." *Wall Street Journal,* January 4, 1996:A1, A12.

Cherlin, Andrew. "Remarriage as an Incomplete Institution." In *Marriage and Family in a Changing Society,* 3rd ed., James M. Henslin, ed. New York: Free Press, 1989:492–501.

Cherlin, Andrew, and Frank F. Furstenberg, Jr. "The American Family in the Year 2000." In *Down to Earth Sociology,* 5th ed., James M. Henslin, ed. New York: Free Press, 1988:325–331.

Chesnais, Jean-Claude. "The Demographic Sunset of the West?" *Population Today, 25,* 1, January 1997:4–5.

"Child Slave Trade in Africa Highlighted by Arrests." *New York Times,* August 9, 1997 (electronic version).

Chodorow, Nancy J. "What Is the Relation Between Psychoanalytic Feminism and the Psychoanalytic Psychology of Women?" In *Theoretical Perspectives on Sexual Difference,* Deborah L. Rhode, ed. New Haven, Conn.: Yale University Press, 1990:114–130.

Chua-Eoan, Howard. "Tripped Up by Lies." *Time,* October 11, 1993:39–40.

Chun, Ki-Taek, and Jadja Zalokar. *Civil Rights Issues Facing Asian Americans in the 1990s.* Washington, D.C.: U.S. Commission on Civil Rights, February 1992.

Clair, Jeffrey Michael., David A. Karp, and William C. Yoels. *Experiencing the Life Cycle: A Social Psychology of Aging,* 2nd ed. Springfield, Ill.: Thomas, 1993.

Clark, Candace. "Sympathy in Everyday Life." In *Down to Earth Sociology: Introductory Readings,* 6th ed., James M. Henslin, ed. New York: Free Press, 1991:193–203.

Clark, Lindley H., Jr. "How the Biggest Lobby Grew." *Wall Street Journal,* January 27, 1994:A14.

Clawson, Dan. "Editor's Note." *Contemporary Sociology, 26,* 4, July 1997:vii.

Clay, Jason W. "What's a Nation?" *Mother Jones,* November–December 1990:28, 30.

Clingempeel, W. Glenn, and N. Dickon Repucci. "Joint Custody After Divorce: Major Issues and Goals for Research." *Psychological Bulletin, 9,* 1982:102–127.

Cloward, Richard A., and Lloyd E. Ohlin. *Delinquency and Opportunity: A Theory of Delinquent Gangs.* New York: Free Press, 1960.

Cnaan, Ram A. "Neighborhood-representing Organizations: How Democratic Are They?" *Social Science Review,* December 1991:614–634.

Coburn, David, Carl D'Arcy, Peter New, and George Torrance. *Health and Canadian Society.* Toronto: Fitzhenry and Whiteside, 1981.

Cockerham, William. *Medical Sociology.* 4th ed. Englewood Cliffs, N.J.: Prentice Hall, 1989.

Cockerham, William C. "The Social Determinants of the Decline of Life Expectancy in Russia and Eastern Europe: A Lifestyle Explanation." *Journal of Health and Social Behavior, 38,* June 1997: 117–130.

Cohen, Adam. "The Great American Welfare Lab." *Time,* April 21, 1997:74–76, 78.

Cohen, Erik. "Lovelorn Farangs: The Correspondence Between Foreign Men and Thai Girls." *Anthropological Quarterly, 59,* 3, July 1986:115–127.

Cohen, Joel E. "How Many People Can the Earth Support?" *Population Today,* January 1996:4–5.

Cohen, Morris R. "Moral Aspects of the Criminal Law." *Yale Law Journal, 49,* April 1940:1009–1026.

Cohen, Steven M. "Hey NCR—We're the Shareholders, You Work for Us." *Wall Street Journal,* December 19, 1990:A16.

Cole, Jeff, and Sarah Lubman. "Weapons Merchants Are Going Great Guns in Post-Cold War Era." *Wall Street Journal,* January 28, 1994:A1, A4.

Coleman, James S., and Thomas Hoffer. *Public and Private Schools: The Impact of Communities.* New York: Basic Books, 1987.

Coleman, James William. *The Criminal Elite: The Sociology of White Collar Crime.* New York: St. Martin's Press, 1989.

Coleman, James William. "Politics and the Abuse of Power." In *Down to Earth Sociology: Introductory Readings,* 8th ed., James M. Henslin, ed. New York: Free Press, 1995:442–450.

Collins, Patricia Hill. "Learning from the Outsider Within: The Sociological Significance of Black Feminist Thought." *Social Problems, 33,* 6, December 1986:514–532.

Collins, Randall. *Conflict Sociology: Toward an Explanatory Science.* New York: Academic Press, 1974.

Collins, Randall. *The Credential Society: An Historical Sociology of Education.* New York: Academic Press, 1979.

Collins, Randall. *Theoretical Sociology.* San Diego, Calif.: Harcourt, Brace Jovanovich, 1988.

Collins, Randall, Janet Saltzman Chafetz, Rae Lesser Blumberg, Scott Coltrane, and Jonathan H. Turner. "Toward an Integrated Theory of Gender Stratification." *Sociological Perspectives, 36,* 3, 1993:185–216.

Common Cause. "Why the United States Does Not Have a National Health Program: The Medical-Industrial Complex and Its PAC Contributions to Congressional Candidates, January 1, 1981, through June 30, 1991." *International Journal of Health Services, 22,* 4, 1992:619–644.

Conahan, Frank C. "Human Experimentation: An Overview on Cold War Era Programs." Washington, D.C.: U.S. General Accounting Office, September 28, 1994:1–11.

Conrad, Peter. "Public Eyes and Private Genes: Historical Frames, New Constructions, and Social Problems." *Social Problems, 44,* 2, May 1997:139–154.

Cook, Philip W. *Abused Men: The Hidden Side of Domestic Violence.* New York: Praeger, 1997.

Cookson, Peter W., Jr. *School Choice: The Struggle for the Soul of American Education.* New Haven, Conn.: Yale University Press, 1994.

Cooley, Charles Horton. *Human Nature and the Social Order.* New York: Scribner's, 1902.

Cooley, Charles Horton. *Social Organization.* New York: Schocken, 1962. First published by Scribner's, 1909.

Coolidge, David Orgon. "At Last, Hawaiians Have Their Say on Gay Marriage." *Wall Street Journal,* April 23, 1997:A19.

Cooper, Helene. "Offering Aerobics, Karate, Aquatics, Hospitals Stress Business of 'Wellness.' " *Wall Street Journal,* August 9, 1993:B1, B3.

Cooper, Kenneth J. "New Focus Sought in National High School Exams: NEH Backs Approach Used in Europe and Japan to Assess Knowledge Rather Than Aptitude." *Washington Post,* May 20, 1991:A7.

Corbett, Thomas. "Welfare Reform in the 104th Congress: Goals, Options, and Tradeoffs." *Focus, 17,* 1, Summer 1995:29–31.

Corbin, Robert K. "The President's Column." *American Rifleman,* December 1993:56.

Cose, Ellis. *The Rage of the Privileged Class.* New York: HarperCollins, 1993.

Coser, Lewis A. *Masters of Sociological Thought: Ideas in Historical and Social Context,* 2nd ed. New York: Harcourt Brace Jovanovich, 1977.

Cottin, Lou. *Elders in Rebellion: A Guide to Senior Activism.* Garden City, N.Y.: Anchor Doubleday, 1979.

Couch, Carl J. *Social Processes and Relationships: A Formal Approach.* Dix Hills, N.Y.: General Hall, 1989.

Coughlin, Ellen K. "Studying Homelessness: The Difficulty of Tracking a Transient Population." *Chronicle of Higher Education,* October 19, 1988:A6–A12.

Courtney, Kelly. "Two Sides of the Environmental Movement: Radical Earth First! and the Sierra Club." Paper presented at the 1995 meetings of the American Sociological Association.

Cousins, Albert, and Hans Nagpaul. *Urban Man and Society.* New York: McGraw-Hill, 1970.

Cowen, Emory L., Judah Landes, and Donald E. Schaet. "The Effects of Mild Frustration on the Expression of Prejudiced Attitudes." *Journal of Abnormal and Social Psychology.* January 1959:33–38.

Cowgill, Donald. "The Aging of Populations and Societies." *Annals of the American Academy of Political and Social Science, 415,* 1974:1–18.

Cowley, Geoffrey. "Attention: Aging Men." *Newsweek,* November 16, 1996:66–75.

Cowley, Joyce. *Pioneers of Women's Liberation.* New York: Merit, 1969.

Cox, Paul. "Cyberdegrees." *Wall Street Journal,* November 17, 1997:R26.

Crispell, Diane. "People Patterns." *Wall Street Journal,* March 16, 1992:B1.

Croal, N'Gai, and Jane Hughes. "Lara Croft, the Bit Girl." *Newsweek,* November 10, 1997:82, 86.

Crosbie, Paul V., ed. *Interaction in Small Groups.* New York: Macmillan, 1975.

Crossen, Cynthia. *Wall Street Journal,* November 14, 1991:A1, A7.

Crossette, Barbara. "U.N. Documents Inequities for Women as World Forum Nears." *New York Times*, August 18, 1995a:A3.

Crossette, Barbara. "Worldwide Study Finds Decline in Election of Women Legislators." *New York Times*, August 27, 1995b.

Crossman, Donna K. "Global Structural Violence Against Women." Paper presented at the 1995 meetings of the American Sociological Association.

Cumming, Elaine. "Further Thoughts on the Theory of Disengagement." In *Aging in America: Readings in Social Gerontology*, Cary S. Kart and Barbara B. Manard, eds. Sherman Oaks, Calif.: Alfred Publishing, 1976:19–41.

Cumming, Elaine, and William E. Henry. *Growing Old: The Process of Disengagement*. New York: Basic Books, 1961.

Curtin, Sharon. "Nobody Ever Died of Old Age: In Praise of Old People." In *Growing Old in America*. Beth Hess, ed. New Brunswick, N.J.: Transaction, 1976:273–284.

Curwin, E. Cecil, and Gudmond Hart. *Plough and Pasture*. New York: Collier Books, 1961.

Cuzzort, Ray P. *Using Social Thought: The Nuclear Issue and Other Concerns*. Mountain View, Calif.: Mayfield, 1989.

"Cyberschool Makes Its Debut." *The American Schoolboard*, *183*, 1, January 1996:A11.

Dabbs, James M., Jr., and Robin Morris. "Testosterone, Social Class, and Antisocial Behavior in a Sample of 4,462 Men." *Psychological Science*, *1*, 3, May 1990:209–211.

Dahl, Robert A. *Who Governs?* New Haven, Conn.: Yale University Press, 1961.

Dahl, Robert A. *Dilemmas of Pluralist Democracy: Autonomy vs. Control*. New Haven, Conn.: Yale University Press, 1982.

Dahrendorf, Ralf. *Class and Class Conflict in Industrial Society*. Palo Alto, Calif.: Stanford University Press, 1959.

Daniels, Roger. *The Decision to Relocate the Japanese Americans*. Philadelphia: Lippincott, 1975.

Dannefer, Dale. "Adult Development and Social Theory: A Reappraisal." *American Sociological Review*, *49*, 1, February 1984:100–116.

Danzi, Angela D. "Savaria, The Midwife: Childbirth and Change in the Immigrant Community." In *Contemporary Readings in Sociology*. Judith N. DeSena, ed. Dubuque, Iowa: Kendall/Hunt, 1989:47–56.

Darley, John M., and Bibb Latané. "Bystander Intervention in Emergencies: Diffusion of Responsibility." *Journal of Personality and Social Psychology*, *8*, 4, 1968:377–383.

Darnell, Victor. "Qualitative-Quantitative Content Analysis of Graffiti in the Public Restrooms of St. Louis, Missouri, and Edwardsville, Illinois." Master's thesis, Southern Illinois University, Edwardsville, May 1971.

Darwin, Charles. *The Origin of Species*. Chicago: Conley, 1859.

Davis, Allison, Burleigh B. Gardner, and Mary R. Gardner. *Deep South: A Social-Anthropological Study of Caste and Class*. Chicago: University of Chicago Press, 1941.

Davis, Fred. "The Cabdriver and His Fare: Facets of a Fleeting Relationship." *American Journal of Sociology*, *65*, September 1959:158–165.

Davis, Kingsley. "Extreme Social Isolation of a Child." *American Journal of Sociology*, *45*, 4 Jan. 1940:554–565.

Davis, Kingsley. "Extreme Isolation." In *Down to Earth Sociology: Introductory Readings*, 9th ed., James M. Henslin, ed. New York: Free Press, 1997:121–129.

Davis, Kingsley, and Wilbert E. Moore. "Some Principles of Stratification." *American Sociological Review*, *10*, 1945:242–249.

Davis, Kingsley, and Wilbert E. Moore. "Reply to Tumin." *American Sociological Review*, *18*, 1953:394–396.

Davis, L. J. "Medscam." In *Deviant Behavior 96/97*, Lawrence M. Salinger, ed. Guilford, Conn.: Dushkin, 1996:93–97.

Davis, Nancy J., and Robert V. Robinson. "Class Identification of Men and Women in the 1970s and 1980s." *American Sociological Review*, *53*, February 1988:103–112.

Davis, Nanette J. "Prostitution: Identity, Career, and Legal-Economic Enterprise." In *The Sociology of Sex: An Introductory Reader*, rev. ed., James M. Henslin and Edward Sagarin, eds. New York: Schocken Books, 1978:195–222.

Deck, Leland P. "Buying Brains by the Inch." *Journal of the College and University Personnel Association*, *19*, 1968:33–37.

Deegan, Mary Jo. "W. E. B. Du Bois and the Women of Hull-House, 1895–1899." *American Sociologist*, Winter 1988:301–311.

Deevey, E. S., Don S. Rice, Prudence M. Rice, H. H. Vaughan, Mark Brenner, and M. S. Flannery. "Mayan Urbanism: Impact on a Tropical Karst Environment." *Science*, October 19, 1979:298–306.

De George, Richard T. *The New Marxism: Society and East European Marxism Since 1956*. New York: Pegasus 1968.

DeMartini, Joseph R. "Basic and Applied Sociological Work: Divergence, Convergence, or Peaceful Co-existence?" *The Journal of Applied Behavioral Science*, *18*, 2, 1982:203–215.

DeMause, Lloyd. "Our Forebears Made Childhood a Nightmare." *Psychology Today 8*, 11, April 1975:85–88.

"Democracy and Technology." *The Economist*, June 17, 1995:21–23.

Denney, Nancy W., and David Quadagno. *Human Sexuality*, 2nd ed. St. Louis: Mosby, 1992.

Dentzler, Susan. "The Vanishing Dream." *U.S. News and World Report*, April 22, 1991:39–43.

Denzin, Norman K. "The Suicide Machine." *Society*, July–August, 1992:7–10.

DePalma, Anthony. "Rare in Ivy League: Women Who Work as Full Professors." *New York Times*, January 24, 1993:1, 23.

DeParle, Jason. "Report to Clinton Sees Vast Extent of Homelessness." *New York Times*, February 17, 1994:A1, A10.

Derber, Charles, and William Schwartz. "Toward a Theory of Worker Participation." In *The Transformation of Industrial Organization: Management, Labor, and Society in the United States*. Frank Hearn, ed. Belmont, Calif.: Wadsworth, 1988:217–229.

De Vita, Carol J. "The United States at Mid-Decade." *Population Bulletin*, *50*, 4, March 1996:1–44.

deYoung, Mary. "The World According to NAMBLA: Accounting for Deviance." *Journal of Sociology and Social Welfare*, *16*, 1, March 1989:111–126.

Diamond, Edwin, and Robert A. Silverman. *White House to Your House: Media and Politics in Virtual America*. Cambridge, Mass.: MIT Press, 1995.

Diamond, Milton. "Sexual Identity: Monozygotic Twins Reared in Discordant Sex Roles and a BBC Follow-Up." *Archives of Sexual Behavior*, *11*, 2, 1982:181–186.

Diaz-Calderon, Joseph. "Letters to the Author." September 1996 and March 1997.

Dickey, Christopher. "The Death of Innocents." *Newsweek*, September 2, 1996:51.

Dickson, Tony, and Hugh V. McLachlan. "In Search of 'The Spirit of Capitalism': Weber's Misinterpretation of Franklin." *Sociology*, *23*, 1, 1989:81–89.

DiGiulio, Robert C. "Beyond Widowhood." In *Marriage and Family in a Changing Society*, 4th ed., James M. Henslin, ed. New York: Free Press, 1992:457–469.

Dillin, John. "Congress Begins Search for Answers in Waco Tragedy." *Christian Science Monitor,* April 22, 1993:1, 4.

Diver-Stamnes, Ann C., and R. Murray Thomas. *Prevent, Repent, Reform, Revenge: A Study in Adolescent Moral Development.* Westport, CT.: Greenwood Press, 1995.

Dixon, Celvia Stovall, and Kathryn D. Rettig. "An Examination of Income Adequacy for Single Women Two Years After Divorce." *Journal of Divorce and Remarriage,* 22, 1–2, 1994:55–71.

Doane, Ashley W., Jr. "Bringing the Majority Back In: Towards a Sociology of Dominant Group Ethnicity." Paper presented at the annual meetings of the Society for the Study of Social Problems, 1993.

Dobash, Russell P., and R. Emerson Dobash. "Community Response to Violence Against Wives: Charivari, Abstract Justice and Patriarchy." *Social Problems,* 28, June 1981:563–581.

Dobash, Russell P., R. Emerson Dobash, Margo Wilson, and Martin Daly. "The Myth of Sexual Symmetry in Marital Violence." *Social Problems,* 39, 1, February 1992:71–91.

Dobash, Russell P., R. Emerson Dobash, Margo Wilson, and Martin Daly. "Marital Violence Is Not Symmetrical: A Response to Campbell." *SSSP Newsletter,* 24, 3, Fall 1993:26–30.

Dobratz, Betty A., and Stephanie Shanks-Meile. "Conflict in the White Supremacist/Racialist Movement in the United States." *International Journal of Group Tensions,* 25, 1, 1995:57–75.

Dobriner, William M. "The Football Team as Social Structure and Social System." In *Social Structures and Systems: A Sociological Overview.* Pacific Palisades, Calif.: Goodyear, 1969a:116–120.

Dobriner, William M. *Social Structures and Systems.* Pacific Palisades, California: Goodyear, 1969b.

Dobyns, Henry F. *Their Numbers Became Thinned: Native American Population Dynamics in Eastern North America.* Knoxville: University of Tennessee Press, 1983.

Dollard, John, et al. *Frustration and Aggression.* New Haven, Conn.: Yale University Press, 1939.

Domhoff, G. William. *Who Rules America?* Englewood Cliffs, N.J.: Prentice Hall, 1967.

Domhoff, G. William. *Who Really Rules? New Haven and Community Power Reexamined.* New Brunswick, N.J.: Transaction, 1978.

Domhoff, G. William. *The Powers That Be.* New York: Random House, 1979.

Domhoff, G. William. *Who Rules America Now? A View of the '80s.* Englewood Cliffs, N.J.: Prentice Hall, 1983.

Domhoff, G. William. *The Power Elite and the State: How Policy Is Made in America.* Hawthorne, N.Y.: Aldine de Gruyter, 1990.

Domhoff, G. William. *State Autonomy or Class Dominance? Case Studies on Policy Making in America.* Hawthorne, N.Y.: Aldine de Gruyter, 1996.

Domhoff, G. William. "The Bohemian Grove and Other Retreats." In *Down to Earth Sociology: Introductory Readings,* 9th ed., James M. Henslin, ed. New York: Free Press, 1997:340–352.

Donelson, Samuel. "World News Tonight." Television broadcast. May 25, 1992.

Dove, Adrian. "Soul Folk 'Chitling' Test or the Dove Counterbalance Intelligence Test." no date. (Mimeo)

Drucker, Peter F. "The Rise and Fall of the Blue-Collar Worker." *Wall Street Journal,* April 22, 1987:36.

Drucker, Peter F. "There's More Than One Kind of Team." *Wall Street Journal,* February 11, 1992:A16.

Drucker, Peter F. "The Age of Social Transformation." *Atlantic Monthly,* 274, 5, November 1994:53+.

Du Bois, W.E.B. *The Souls of Black Folk: Essays and Sketches.* Chicago: McClurg, 1903.

Du Bois, W.E.B. *Black Reconstruction in America: An Essay Toward a History of the Part Which Black Folk Played in the Attempt to Reconstruct Democracy in America, 1860–1880.* New York: Frank Cass, 1966. First published 1935.

Du Bois, W.E.B. *The Philadelphia Negro: A Social Study.* New York: Schocken Books, 1967. First pubulished in 1899.

Du Bois, W.E.B. *The Autobiography of W. E. B. Du Bois: A Soliloquy on Viewing My Life from the Last Decade of Its First Century.* New York: International, 1968.

Du Bois, W.E.B. *Black Reconstruction in America, 1860–1889.* New York: Atheneum, 1992. First published in 1935.

Dudenhefer, Paul. "Poverty in the Rural United States." *Focus,* 15, 1, Spring 1993:37–46.

Duff, Christina. "Superrich's Share of After-Tax Income Stopped Rising in Early '90s, Data Show." *Wall Street Journal,* November 22, 1995:A2.

Duffy, Michael. "When Lobbyists Become Insiders." *Time,* November 9, 1992:40.

Dunlap, Riley E., and William R. Catton, Jr. "Environmental Sociology." *Annual Review of Sociology,* 5, 1979:243–273.

Dunlap, Riley E., and William R. Catton, Jr. "What Environmental Sociologists Have in Common Whether Concerned with 'Built' or 'Natural' Environments." *Sociological Inquiry,* 53, 2/3, 1983:113–135.

Dunleavey, M. P. "Reforming the 3 R's: Blueprints for the Schools of Tomorrow." *Publisher's Weekly,* February 21, 1994:33–35.

Dunn, Ashley. "Southeast Asians Highly Dependent on Welfare in U.S." *New York Times,* May 19, 1994:A1, A23.

Durbin, Stefanie. "Mexico." *Population Today,* July–August, 1995:7.

Durkheim, Emile. *The Division of Labor in Society.* George Simpson, trans. New York: Free Press, 1933. First published in 1893.

Durkheim, Emile. *The Rules of Sociological Method,* Sarah A. Solovay and John H. Mueller, trans. New York: Free Press, 1938, 1958, 1964. First published in 1895.

Durkheim, Emile. *Suicide: A Study in Sociology.* John A. Spaulding and George Simpson, trans. New York: Free Press, 1966. First published in 1897.

Durkheim, Emile. *The Elementary Forms of the Religious Life.* New York: Free Press, 1965. First published in 1912.

Durning, Alan. "Cradles of Life." In *Social Problems 90/91,* LeRoy W. Barnes, ed. Guilford, Conn.: Dushkin, 1990:231–241.

Dutton, D. G. and A. P. Aron, (1974). "Some Evidence for Heightened Sexual Attraction under Conditions of High Anxiety." *Journal of Personality and Social Psychology,* 30, 510–517.

Easterbrook, Gregg. "The Revolution in Modern Medicine." *Newsweek,* 109, Jan. 26, 1987:40–74.

Ebaugh, Helen Rose Fuchs. *Becoming an EX: The Process of Role Exit.* Chicago: The University of Chicago Press, 1988.

Ebomoyi, Ehigie. "The Prevalence of Female Circumcision in Two Nigerian Communities." *Sex Roles,* 17, 3/4, 1987:139–151.

Eder, Klaus. "The Rise of Counter-culture Movements Against Modernity: Nature as a New Field of Class Struggle." *Theory, Culture & Society,* 7, 1990:21–47.

Edgar, Gary. Author's interview with Gary Edgar of the Surveillance Branch of the CDC, March 28, 1994.

Edgerton, Robert B. *Deviance: A Cross-Cultural Perspective.* Menlo Park, Calif.: Benjamin/Cummings, 1976.

Edgerton, Robert B. *Sick Societies: Challenging the Myth of Primitive Harmony*. New York: Free Press, 1992.

Edwards, Richard. *Contested Terrain: The Transformation of the Workplace in the Twentieth Century*. New York: Basic Books, 1979.

Egan, Timothy. "Many Seek Security in Private Communities." *New York Times*, September 3, 1995:1, 22.

"Egipto prohibir la ablacion femenina y adoptar medidas contra infractores." *El Pais*, July 19, 1996:22.

Ehrenreich, Barbara, and Deidre English. *Witches, Midwives, and Nurses: A History of Women Healers*. Old Westbury, N.Y.: Feminist Press, 1973.

Ehrlich, Paul R., and Anne H. Ehrlich. *Population, Resources, and Environment: Issues in Human Ecology*, 2nd ed. San Francisco: Freeman, 1972.

Ehrlich, Paul R., and Anne H. Ehrlich. "Humanity at the Crossroads." *Stanford Magazine*, Spring–Summer 1978:20–23.

Erlich, Paul R., and Anne H. Ehrlich. *Betrayal of Science and Reason: How Anti-Environmental Rhetoric Threatens Our Future*. Washington, D.C.: Island Press, 1997.

Eibl-Eibesfeldt, Irenäus. *Ethology: The Biology of Behavior*. New York: Holt, Rinehart, and Winston, 1970.

Eisenhart, R. Wayne. "You Can't Hack It, Little Girl: A Discussion of the Covert Psychological Agenda of Modern Combat Training." *Journal of Social Issues*, *31*, Fall 1975:13–23.

Eisner, Robert. "No Need to Sacrifice Seniors or Children." *Wall Street Journal*, February 2, 1996:A10.

Ekman, Paul, Wallace V. Friesen, and John Bear. "The International Language of Gestures." *Psychology Today*, May 1984:64.

Elder, Glen H., Jr. "Age Differentiation and Life Course." *Annual Review of Sociology*, *1*, 1975:165–190.

Elkins, Stanley M. *Slavery: A Problem in American Institutional and Intellectual Life*, 2nd ed. Chicago: University of Chicago Press, 1968.

Ellis, Caroline. "Punish and Be Damned." *New Statesman and Society*, *17*, 1991:17.

Ellul, Jacques. *The Technological Society*. New York: Knopf, 1965.

El-Meligi, M. Helmy. "Egypt." In *Handbook of World Education: A Comparative Guide to Higher Education and Educational Systems of the World*, Walter Wickremasinghe, ed. Houston, Texas: American Collegiate Service, 1992:219–228.

Engelberg, Stephen, and Martin Tolchin. "Foreigners Find New Ally in U.S. Industry." *New York Times*, November 2, 1993:A1, B8.

Engels, Friedrich. *The Origin of the Family, Private Property, and the State*. New York: International Publishing, 1942. First published in 1884.

Epstein, Cynthia Fuchs. "Inevitabilities of Prejudice." *Society*, September–October 1986:7–15.

Epstein, Cynthia Fuchs. *Deceptive Distinctions: Sex, Gender, and the Social Order*. New Haven, Conn.: Yale University Press, 1988.

Epstein, Cynthia Fuchs. Letter to the author, January 26, 1989.

Erik, John. "China's Policy on Births." *New York Times*, January 3, 1982: IV, 19.

Ernst, Eldon G. "The Baptists." In *Encyclopedia of the American Religious Experience: Studies of Traditions and Movements*, Vol. 1, Charles H. Lippy and Peter W. Williams, eds. New York: Scribners, 1988:555–577.

Erturk, Yakin. "The Status of Moslem Women in Turkey and Saudi Arabia." In *Haves and Have-Nots: An International Reader on Social Inequality*, James Curtis and Lorne Tepperman, eds. Englewood Cliffs, N.J.: Prentice Hall, 1994:288–293.

Escalante, Jaime, and Jack Dirmann. "The Jaime Escalante Math Program." *Journal of Negro Education*, *59*, 3, Summer 1990:407–423.

Etzioni, Amitai, ed. *The Semi-Professions and Their Organization*. New York: Free Press, 1969.

"Executive Pay." *Issues and Controversies on File*, *2*, 8, 1997:314–321.

Ezekiel, Raphael S. *The Racist Mind: Portraits of American Neo-Nazis and Klansmen*. New York: Viking, 1995.

"Faddish Justice." *Wall Street Journal*, May 2, 1995:A19.

Famighetti, Robert, ed. *The World Almanac and Book of Facts 1995*. Mahwah, New Jersey, 1994.

Faris, Robert E. L., and Warren Dunham. *Mental Disorders in Urban Areas*. Chicago: University of Chicago Press, 1939.

Farkas, George. *Human Capital or Cultural Capital?: Ethnicity and Poverty Groups in an Urban School District*. New York: Walter DeGruyter, 1996.

Farkas, George, Robert P. Grobe, Daniel Sheehan, and Yuan Shuan. "Cultural Resources and School Success: Gender, Ethnicity, and Poverty Groups Within an Urban School District." *American Sociological Review*, *55*, February 1990a:127–142.

Farkas, George, Daniel Sheehan, and Robert P. Grobe. "Coursework Mastery and School Success: Gender, Ethnicity, and Poverty Groups Within an Urban School District." *American Educational Research Journal*, *27*, 4, Winter 1990b:807–827.

Farney, Dennis. "They Hold the Cards, But After All, They Do Own the Casino." *Wall Street Journal*, February 5, 1998: A1, A6.

Faunce, William A. *Problems of an Industrial Society*, 2nd ed. New York: McGraw-Hill, 1981.

FBI Uniform Crime Reports. Washington, D.C.: U.S. Government Printing Office, published annually.

Feagin, Joe R., "Death by Discrimination?" *SSSP Newsletter*, Winter 1997:15–16.

Featherman, David L. "Opportunities Are Expanding." *Society*, *13*, 1979:4–11.

Featherman, David L., and Robert M. Hauser. *Opportunity and Change*. New York: Academic Press, 1978.

Federal Trade Commission. *Federal Trade Commission Report to Congress for 1994 Pursuant to the Federal Cigarette Labeling and Advertising Act*. Washington, D.C.: U.S. Government Printing Office, October 9, 1996.

Feinglass, Joe. "Next, the McDRG." *The Progressive*, *51*, January 1987:28.

Feldman, Saul D. "The Presentation of Shortness in Everyday Life—Height and Heightism in American Society: Toward a Sociology of Stature." Paper presented at the 1972 meetings of the American Sociological Association.

Felsenthal, Edward. "Maine Limits Liability for Doctors Who Meet Treatment Guidelines." *Wall Street Journal*, May 3, 1993:A1, A9.

Fendrich, James Max, and Kenneth L. Lovoy. "Back to the Future: Adult Political Behavior of Former Student Activists." In *Collective Behavior and Social Movements*, Russell L. Curtis, Jr., and Benigno E. Aguirre, eds. Boston: Allyn and Bacon, 1993:429–434.

Ferguson, Thomas. *Golden Rule*. Chicago: University of Chicago, 1995.

Ferguson, Trudi, and Joan S. Dunphy. *Answers to the Mommy Track: How Wives and Mothers in Business Reach the Top and Balance Their Lives*. New York: New Horizon Press, 1991.

Feshbach, Murray. "Russia's Farms, Too Poisoned for the Plow." *Wall Street Journal*, May 14, 1992:A14.

Feshbach, Murray, and Alfred Friendly, Jr. *Ecocide in the USSR: Health and Nature Under Siege*. New York: Basic Books, 1992.

Fialka, John J. "Demands on New Orleans's 'Big Charity' Hospital Are Symptomatic of U.S. Health-Care Problem." *Wall Street Journal*, June 22, 1993:A18.

Finke, Roger, and Roger Stark. *The Churching of America, 1776–1990: Winners and Losers in Our Religious Economy*. New Brunswick, N.J.: Rutgers University Press, 1992.

Finkelhor, David, and Kersti Yllo. "Marital Rape: The Myth Versus the Reality." In *Marriage and Family in a Changing Society*, 3rd ed., James M. Henslin, ed. New York: Free Press, 1989:382–391.

Finkelhor, David, and Kersti Yllo. *License to Rape: Sexual Abuse of Wives*. New York: Henry Holt, 1985.

Fischer, Claude S. *The Urban Experience*. New York: Harcourt, 1976.

Fischer, Claude S. "Technology and Community: Historical Complexities." Paper presented at the 1995 meetings of the American Sociological Association.

Fish, Jefferson M. "Mixed Blood." *Psychology Today*, 28, 6, November–December 1995:55–58, 60, 61, 76, 80.

Fisher, Julie. "Is the Iron Law of Oligarchy Rusting Away in the Third World?" *World Development*, 22, 2, February 1994:129–143.

Fisher, Sue. *In the Patient's Best Interest: Women and the Politics of Medical Decisions*. New Brunswick, N.J.: Rutgers University Press, 1986.

Flanagan, William G. *Urban Sociology: Images and Structure*. Boston: Allyn and Bacon, 1990.

Flavel, J. H., et al. *The Development of Role-Taking and Communication Skills in Children*. New York: Wiley, 1968.

Fleming, Joyce Dudney. "The State of the Apes." *Psychology Today*, 7, 1974:31–38.

Fletcher, June. "Address Envy: Fudging to Get the Best." *Wall Street Journal*, April 25, 1997:B10.

Flexner, Abraham. *Medical Education in the United States and Canada: A Report to the Carnegie Foundation for the Advancement of Teaching*. Bulletin No. 4. Boston: Merrymount Press, 1910.

Flink, James J. *The Automobile Age*. Cambridge, Mass.: MIT Press, 1990.

Foley, Douglas E. "The Great American Football Ritual." In *Down to Earth Sociology: Introductory Readings*, 9th ed., James M. Henslin, ed. New York: Free Press, 1997:412–475.

Foley, Linda A., Christine Evancic, Karnik Karnik, Janet King, and Angela Parks. "Date Rape: Effects of Race of Assailant and Victim and Gender of Subjects on Perceptions." *Journal of Black Psychology*, 21, 1, February 1995:6–18.

Foote, Jennifer. "Trying to Take Back the Planet." *Newsweek*, 115, 6, February 5, 1990:24–25.

Ford, Constance Mitchell. "South Africa Is Drawing Enthusiasm from Wall Street." *Wall Street Journal*, December 23, 1993:C1, C21.

Form, William. "Comparative Industrial Sociology and the Convergence Hypothesis." In *Annual Review of Sociology*, 5, 1, 1979, Alex Inkeles, James Coleman, and Ralph H. Turner, eds.

Forsyth, Craig J., and Thomas A. Marckese. "Female Participation in Three Minor Crimes: A Note on the Relationship Between Opportunity and Crime." *International Journal of Sociology of the Family*, 25, 1, Spring 1995:127–132.

Fossedal, Gregory. "The American Dream Lives." *Wall Street Journal*, February 14, 1997:A12.

Fox, Elaine, and George E. Arquitt. "The VFW and the 'Iron Law of Oligarchy.' " In *Down to Earth Sociology*, 4th ed., James M. Henslin, ed. New York: Free Press, 1985:147–155.

Frank, Anthony. "Through the Open Door: What Is It Like to Be an Immigrant in America?" *Wall Street Journal*, July 3, 1990:A8.

Franklin, Clyde W., II. "Sex and Class Differences in the Socialization Experiences of African American Youth." *Western Journal of Black Studies*, 18, 2, 1994:104–111.

Freedman, Alix M. "Amid Ghetto Hunger, Many More Suffer Eating Wrong Foods." *Wall Street Journal*, Dec. 18, 1990:A1, A8.

Freudenburg, William R., and Robert Gramling. "The Emergence of Environmental Sociology: Contributions of Riley E. Dunlap and William R. Catton, Jr." *Sociological Inquiry*, 59, 4, November 1989:439–452.

Friedl, Ernestine. "Society and Sex Roles." In *Conformity and Conflict: Readings in Cultural Anthropology*. James P. Spradley and David W. McCurdy, eds. Glenview, Ill.: Scott, Foresman, 1990:229–238.

Frisbie, W. Parker & Kasarda, John D. "Spatial Processes." In *Handbook of Sociology*, Neil J. Smelser, ed. Newbury Park, CA: Sage, 1988:629–666.

Fritz, Jan M. "The History of Clinical Sociology." *Sociological Practice*, 7, 1989:72–95.

Froman, Ingmarie. "Sweden for Women." *Current Sweden*, 407, November 1994:1–4.

Frumkin, Robert M. "Early English and American Sex Customs." In *Encyclopedia of Sexual Behavior*, Vol. 1. New York: Hawthorne Books, 1967.

Fuchs, Victor R. "A Tale of Two States." In *The Sociology of Health and Illness: Critical Perspectives*, Peter Conrad and Rochelle Kern, eds. New York: St. Martin's Press, 1981:67–70.

Fuller, Rex, and Richard Schoenberger. "The Gender Salary Gap: Do Academic Achievement, Internship Experience, and College Major Make a Difference?" *Social Science Quarterly*, 72, 4, December 1991:715–726.

Furstenberg, Frank F., Jr., and Kathleen Mullan Harris. "The Disappearing American Father? Divorce and the Waning Significance of Biological Fatherhood." In *The Changing American Family: Sociological and Demographic Perspectives*, Scott J. South and Stewart E. Tolnay, eds. Boulder, Colo.: Westview Press, 1992:197–223.

Furtado, Celso. *The Economic Growth of Brazil: A Survey of Colonial to Modern Times*. Westport, Conn.: Greenwood Press, 1984.

Galanter, Marc. *Cults: Faith, Healing, and Coercion*. New York: Oxford University Press, 1989.

Galbraith, John Kenneth. *The Nature of Mass Poverty*. Cambridge Mass.: Harvard University Press, 1979.

Galinsky, Ellen, James T. Bond, and Dana E. Friedman. *The Changing Workforce: Highlights of the National Study*. New York: Families and Work Institute, 1993.

Galinsky, Ellen, and Peter J. Stein. "The Impact of Human Resource Policies on Employees: Balancing Work/Family Life." *Journal of Family Issues*, 11, 4 December 1990:368–383.

Galliher, John F. *Deviant Behavior and Human Rights*. Englewood Cliffs, N.J.: Prentice Hall, 1991.

Gallmeier, Charles P. "Methodological Issues in Qualitative Sport Research: Participant Observation among Hockey Players." *Sociological Spectrum*, 8, 1988:213–235.

Gallup Opinion Index. *Religion in America, 1987*. Report 259, April 1987.

Gallup, George, Jr. *The Gallup Poll: Public Opinion 1989*. Wilmington, Dela.: Scholarly Resources, 1990.

Gans, Herbert J. *The Urban Villagers*. New York: Free Press, 1962.

Gans, Herbert J. *People and Plans: Essays on Urban Problems and Solutions*. New York: Basic Books, 1968.

Gans, Herbert J. "Urbanism and Suburbanism." In *Urban Man and Society: A Reader in Urban Ecology*, Albert N. Cousins and Hans Nagpaul, eds. New York: Knopf, 1970:157–164.

Gans, Herbert J. *People, Plans, and Policies: Essays on Poverty, Racism, and Other National Urban Problems*. New York: Columbia University Press, 1991a.

Gans, Herbert J. "The Way We'll Live Soon." *Washington Post*, September 1, 1991b:BW3.

Garbarino, Merwin S. *American Indian Heritage*. Boston: Little, Brown, 1976.

Gardner, R. Allen, and Beatrice T. Gardner. "Teaching Sign Language to a Chimpanzee." *Science*, 165, 1969:664–672.

Garfinkel, Harold. "Conditions of Successful Degradation Ceremonies." *American Journal of Sociology*, 61, 2, March 1956:420–424.

Garfinkel, Harold. *Studies in Ethnomethodology*. Englewood Cliffs, N.J.: Prentice Hall, 1967.

Garreau, Joel. *Edge City: Life on the New Frontier*. New York: Doubleday, 1992.

Gatewood, Willard B. *Aristocrats of Color: The Black Elite, 1880–1920*. Bloomington, Ind.: Indiana University Press, 1990.

Gay, Jill. "The Patriotic Prostitute." *Progressive*, February 1985:34–36.

Gecas, Viktor. "Context of Soicalization." In *Social Psychology: Sociological Perspectives*, Morris Rosenberg and Ralph H. Turner, eds. New Brunswick, N.J.: Transaction, 1990:165–199.

Geis, Gilbert, Robert F. Meier, and Lawrence M. Salinger. *White-Collar Crime: Classic and Contemporary Views*, 3rd ed. New York: Free Press, 1995.

Gelles, Richard J. "The Myth of Battered Husbands and New Facts about Family Violence." In *Social Problems 80–81*, Robert L. David, ed. Guilford, Conn.: Dushkin, 1980.

Genetski, Robert. "Privatize Social Security." *Wall Street Journal*, May 21, 1993.

Gerson, Kathleen. *Hard Choices: How Women Decide about Work, Career, and Motherhood*. Berkeley: University of California Press, 1985.

Gerth, H. H., and C. Wright Mills. *From Max Weber: Essays in Sociology*. New York: Galaxy, 1958.

Giddens, Anthony. *Emile Durkheim*. New York: Penguin Books, 1978.

Giele, Janet Zollinger. *Women and the Future: Changing Sex Roles in Modern America*. New York: Free Press, 1978.

Gilbert, Dennis, and Joseph A. Kahl. *The American Class Structure: A New Synthesis*. Homewood, Ill.: Dorsey Press, 1982.

Gilbert, Dennis, and Joseph A. Kahl. *The American Class Structure: A New Synthesis*. 4th ed. Homewood, Ill.: Dorsey Press, 1993.

Gilham, Steven A. "The Marines Build Men: Resocialization in Recruit Training." In *The Sociological Outlook: A Text with Readings*, 2nd ed., Reid Luhman, ed. San Diego, Calif.: Collegiate Press, 1989:232–244.

Gillborn, David. "Citizenship, 'Race' and the Hidden Curriculum." *International Studies in the Sociology of Education*, 2, 1, 1992:57–73.

Gilligan, Carol. *In a Different Voice*. Cambridge, Mass: Harvard University Press, 1982.

Gilman, Charlotte Perkins. *The Man-Made World or, Our Androcentric Culture*. New York: 1971. First published 1911.

Gilmore, David D. *Manhood in the Making: Cultural Concepts of Masculinity*. New Haven, Conn.: Yale University Press, 1990.

Gitlin, Todd. *The Twilight of Common Dreams: Why America Is Wracked by Culture Wars*. New York: Metropolitan Books, 1997.

Glazer, Nathan. "In Defense of Multiculturalism." *New Republic*, September 2, 1991:18–22.

Glenn, Evelyn Nakano. "Chinese American Families." In *Minority Families in the United States: A Multicultural Perspective*, Ronald L. Taylor, ed. Englewood Cliffs, N.J.: Prentice Hall, 1994:115–145.

Glick, Paul C., and S. Lin. "More Young Adults Are Living with Their Parents: Who Are They?" *Journal of Marriage and Family*, 48, 1986:107–112.

"The Global Giants." *Wall Street Journal*, September 26, 1996: R26–R29.

Glueck, Sheldon, and Eleanor Glueck. *Physique and Delinquency*. New York: Harper & Row, 1956.

Goble, Paul. "Russia: Analysis from Washington—Organized Crime's Three Faces." Radio Free Europe, November 5, 1996.

Goffman, Erving. *The Presentation of Self in Everyday Life*. New York: Doubleday, 1959.

Goffman, Erving. *Asylums: Essays on the Social Situation of Mental Patients and Other Inmates*. Chicago: Aldine, 1961.

Goffman, Erving. *Stigma: Notes on the Management of Spoiled Identity*. Englewood Cliffs, N.J.: Prentice Hall, 1963.

Goffman, Erving. "The Presentation of Self in Everyday Life." In *Down to Earth Sociology: Introductory Readings*, 9th ed., James M. Henslin, ed. New York: Free Press, 1997:106–116.

Gold, Ray. "Janitors Versus Tenants: A Status–Income Dilemma." *American Journal of Sociology*, 58, 1952:486–493.

Goldberg, Steven. *The Inevitability of Patriarchy*, rev. ed. New York: Morrow, 1974.

Goldberg, Steven. "Reaffirming the Obvious." *Society*, September–October 1986:4–7.

Goldberg, Steven. *Why Men Rule: A Theory of Male Dominance*. Chicago: Open Court, 1993.

Goldberg, Susan, and Michael Lewis. "Play Behavior in the Year-Old Infant: Early Sex Differences." *Child Development*, 40, March 1969:21–31.

Goldman, Kevin. "Seniors Get Little Respect on Madison Avenue." *Wall Street Journal*, September 20, 1993:B6.

Goldscheider, Frances, and Calvin Goldscheider. "Leaving and Returning Home in 20th Century America." *Population Bulletin*, 48, 4, March 1994:2–33.

Goldstein, Mark L. "Time to Lock the Door." *Industry Week*, June 29, 1987:5859.

Goleman, Daniel. "Spacing of Siblings Strongly Linked to Success in Life." *New York Times*, May 28, 1985:C1, C4.

Goleman, Daniel. "Pollsters Enlist Psychologists in Quest for Unbiased Results." *New York Times*, September 7, 1993:C1, C11.

Gomez, Carlos F. *Regulating Death: Euthanasia and the Case of the Netherlands*. New York: Free Press, 1991.

Goode, Erich. *Drugs in American Society*, 3rd ed. New York: Knopf, 1989.

Goode, Erich. "The Ethics of Deception in Social Research: A Case Study." *Qualitative Sociology*, 19, 1, 1996:11–33.

Goode, Erich, and Nachman Ben-Yehuda. "Moral Panics: Culture, Politics, and Social Construction." *Annual Review of Sociology*, 20, 1994:149–171.

Goode, William J. "Encroachment, Charlatanism, and the Emerging Profession: Psychology, Sociology, and Medicine." *American Sociological Review*, 25, 6, December 1960:902–914.

Goodman, William E. "Why Canada's Doctors Flee South." *Wall Street Journal*, September 16, 1993:A25.

Goodwin, Glenn A., Irving Louis Horowitz, and Peter M. Nardi. "Laud Humphreys: A Pioneer in the Practice of Social Science" *Sociological Inquiry*, *61*, 2, May 1991:139–147.

Gordon, David M. "Class and the Economics of Crime." *The Review of Radical Political Economics*, *3*, Summer 1971:51–57.

Gorman, Christine. "A Boy Without a Penis." *Time*, March 24, 1997a:83.

Gorman, Christine. "The Disease Detective." *Time*, January 6, 1997b:56–65.

Gorman, Peter. "A People at Risk: Vanishing Tribes of South America." *The World & I.* December 1991:678–689.

Gotschall, Mary G. "A Marriage Made in Hell." *National Review, 46*, 6, April 4, 1994:57–60.

Gottfredson, Michael R., and Travis Hirschi. *A General Theory of Crime.* Stanford, Calif.: Stanford University Press, 1990.

Gottschalk, Peter, Sara McLanahan, and Gary Sandefur, "The Dynamics and Intergenerational Transmission of Poverty and Welfare Participation." In *Confronting Poverty: Prescriptions for Change*, Sheldon H. Danziger, Gary D. Sandefur, and Daniel H. Weinberg, eds. Cambridge, Mass.: Harvard University Press, 1994.

Gourevitch, Philip. "After the Genocide." *New Yorker*, December 18, 1995:78–94.

Gracey, Harry L. "Learning the Student Role: Kindergarten as Academic Boot Camp." In *Down to Earth Sociology: Introductory Readings*, 9th ed., James M. Henslin, ed. New York: Free Press, 1997:376–388.

Graham, Ellen. "Christian Bikers Are Holy Rollers of a Different Kind." *Wall Street Journal*, September 19, 1990:A1, A6.

Graham, Ellen. "Craving Closer Ties, Strangers Come Together as Family." *Wall Street Journal*, March 4, 1996:B1, B6.

Grant, Karen R. "The Inverse Care Law in the Context of Universal Free Health Insurance in Canada: Toward Meeting Health Needs Through Social Policy." *Sociological Focus*, *17*, 2, April 1984:137–155.

Grant, Nigel. *Soviet Education.* New York: Pelican Books, 1979.

Greeley, Andrew M. "The Protestant Ethic: Time for a Moratorium." *Sociological Analysis*, *25*, Spring 1964:20–33.

Greeley, Andrew. "A Religious Revival in Russia." *Journal for the Scientific Study of Religion*, *33*, 3, September 1994:253–272.

Greenberg, Larry M. "Take Two Tablespoons of Mustard and Call If You Don't Feel Better." *Wall Street Journal*, February 22, 1994:B1.

Greenhalgh, Susan, and Jiali Li. "Engendering Reproductive Policy and Practice in Peasant China: For a Feminist Demography of Reproduction." *Signs*, *20*, 3, Spring 1995:601–640.

Greenwood, Ernest. "Attributes of a Profession." In *Man, Work, and Society: A Reader in the Sociology of Occupations*, Sigmund Nosow and William H. Form, eds. New York: Basic Books, 1962:206–218.

Grossman, Lawrence K. *The Electronic Republic: Reshaping Democracy in the Information Age.* New York: Viking, 1995.

Guha, Ramachandra. "Radical American Environmentalism and Wilderness Preservation: A Third World Critique." *Environmental Ethics*, *11*, 1, Spring 1989:71–83.

Guidubaldi, John, Joseph D. Perry, and Bonnie K. Nastasi. "Growing Up in a Divorced Family: Initial and Long-Term Perspectives on Children's Adjustment." *Applied Social Psychology Annual*, *7*, 1987:202–237.

Gupta, Giri Raj. "Love, Arranged Marriage, and the Indian Social Structure." In *Cross-Cultural Perspectives of Mate Selection and Marriage*, George Kurian, ed. Westport, Conn.: Greenwood Press, 1979.

Haas, Jack. "Binging: Educational Control Among High-Steel Iron Workers." *American Behavioral Scientist*, *16*, 1972:27–34.

Haas, Jack and William Shaffir. "The Cloak of Competence." In *Down to Earth Sociology: Introductory Readings*, 7th ed. New York: Free Press, 1993:432–441. (orig. pub. 1978).

Hacker, Helen Mayer. "Women as a Minority Group." *Social Forces*, *30*, October 1951:60–69.

Hakansson, Stefan. "New Ways of Financing and Organizing Health Care in Sweden." *International Journal of Health Planning and Management*, *9*, 1, January 1994:103–124.

Hall, Edward T. *The Silent Language.* New York: Doubleday, 1959.

Hall, Edward T. *The Hidden Dimension.* Garden City, N.Y.: Anchor Books, 1969.

Hall, Edward T., and Mildred R. Hall. "The Sounds of Silence." In *Down to Earth Sociology: Introductory Readings*, 9th ed., James M. Henslin, ed. New York: Free Press, 1997:97–105.

Hall, G. Stanley. *Adolescence: Its Psychology and Its Relations to Physiology, Anthropology, Sociology, Sex, Crime, Religion, and Education.* New York: Appleton, 1904.

Hall, J. A. *Nonverbal Sex Differences: Communication Accuracy and Expressive Style.* Baltimore: Johns Hopkins University Press, 1984.

Hall, Richard H. "The Concept of Bureaucracy: An Empirical Assessment." *American Journal of Sociology*, *69*, July 1963:32–40.

Hamilton, Kendall, and Susan Miller. "Internet U—No Ivy, No Walls, No Keg Parties." *Newsweek*, March 10, 1997:12.

Hanke, Steve H. "Incarceration Is a Bargain." *Wall Street Journal*, September 23, 1996:A20.

Hanson, David J. "A Note on Sociology and Infrahuman Culture." *International Journal of Contemporary Sociology*, *10*, 2 & 3, April–July 1973:121–124.

Hardy, Dorcas. *Social Insecurity: The Crisis in America's Social Security and How to Plan Now for Your Own Financial Survival.* New York: Villard Books, 1991.

Hardy, Quentin. "Death at the Club Is Par for the Course in Golf-Crazed Japan." *Wall Street Journal*, June 16, 1993a:A1, A8.

Hardy, Quentin. "Fortunately, Many Japanese Have Training in the Art of Self-Defense." *Wall Street Journal*, June 29, 1993b:B1.

Harlow, Harry F., and Margaret K. Harlow. "Social Deprivation in Monkeys." *Scientific American*, *207*, 1962:137–147.

Harlow, Harry F., and Margaret K. Harlow. "The Affectional Systems." In *Behavior of Nonhuman Primates: Modern Research Trends*, Vol. 2, Allan M. Schrier, Harry F. Harlow, and Fred Stollnitz, eds. New York: Academic Press, 1965:287–334.

Harper, Mary S., ed. *Minority Aging: Essential Curricula Content for Selected Health and Allied Health Professions.* Washington, D.C.: U.S. Government Printing Office, 1990.

Harrington, Michael. *The Other America: Poverty in the United States.* New York: Macmillan, 1962.

Harrington, Michael. *The Vast Majority: A Journey to the World's Poor.* New York: Simon & Schuster, 1977.

Harris, Chauncey, and Edward Ullman. "The Nature of Cities." *Annals of the American Academy of Political and Social Science*, *242*, 1945:7–17.

Harris, Diana K. *The Sociology of Aging.* New York: Harper, 1990.

Harris, Marvin. "Why Men Dominate Women." *New York Times Magazine*, November 13, 1977:46, 115, 117–123.

Harrison, Paul. *Inside the Third World: The Anatomy of Poverty*, 3rd ed. London: Penguin Books, 1993.

Hart, Charles W. M., and Arnold R. Pilling. *The Tiwi of North Australia.* New York: Holt, Rinehart, and Winston, 1970.

Hart, Hornell. "Acceleration in Social Change." In *Technology and Social Change*, Francis R. Allen, Hornell Hart, Delbert C. Miller, William F. Ogburn, and Meyer F. Nimkoff. New York: Appleton, 1957:27–55.

Hart, Paul. "Groupthink, Risk-Taking and Recklessness: Quality of Process and Outcome in Policy Decision Making." *Politics and the Individual*, *1*, 1, 1991:67–90.

Hartley, Eugene. *Problems in Prejudice*. New York: King's Crown Press, 1946.

Harwood, John. "For California Senator, Fund Raising Becomes Overwhelming Burden." *Wall Street Journal*, March 2, 1994:A1, A13.

Harwood, John, and Geraldine Brooks. "Other Nations Elect Women to Lead Them, So Why Doesn't U.S.?" *Wall Street Journal*, December 14, 1993:A1, A9.

Haslick, Leonard. *Gerontologist*, *14*, 1974:37–45.

Haub, Carl. "New UN Projections Depict a Variety of Demographic Futures." *Population Today*, *25*, 4, April 1997:1–3.

Haub, Carl, and Diana Cornelius. "World Population Data Sheet." Washington, D.C.: Population Reference Bureau, 1997.

Haub, Carl, and Nancy Yinger. "The U.N. Long-Range Population Projections: What They Tell Us." Washington, D.C.: Population Reference Bureau, 1994.

Hauser, Philip, and Leo Schnore, eds. *The Study of Urbanization*. New York: Wiley, 1965.

Hawley, Amos H. *Urban Society: An Ecological Approach*. New York: Wiley, 1981.

Hayes, Arthur S. "Environmental Poverty Specialty Helps the Poor Fight Pollution." *Wall Street Journal*, October 9, 1992:B5.

Hayes, Donald P., and Loreen T. Wolfer. "Have Curriculum Changes Caused SAT Scores to Decline?" Paper presented at the annual meetings of the American Sociological Association, 1993a.

Hayes, Donald P., and Loreen T. Wolfer. "Was the Decline in SAT-Verbal Scores Caused by Simplified Schoolbooks?" Technical Report Series 93-8. Ithaca, N.Y.: Cornell University Press, 1993b.

Haynes, Richard M., and Donald M. Chalker. "World Class Schools." *American School Board Journal*, May 1997:20, 22–25.

Heckert, D. Alex, Thomas C. Nowak, and Kay A. Snyder. "The Impact of Husbands' and Wives' Relative Earnings on Marital Dissolution." Paper presented at the 1995 meetings of the American Sociological Association.

Heidemann, Elma. "The Canadian Health Care System: Cost and Quality." *Pan American Health Organization*, *28*, 2, June 1994:169–176.

Heilbrun, Alfred B. "Differentiation of Death-Row Murderers and Life-Sentence Murderers by Antisociality and Intelligence Measures." *Journal of Personality Assessment*, *64*, 1990:617–627.

Heller, Celia Stopnicka. "Social Stratification of the Jewish Community in a Small Polish Town." *American Journal of Sociology*, *59*, 1, July 1953:1–10.

Heller, Celia Stopnicka. Letter to the author. May 7, 1991.

Hellinger, Daniel, and Dennis R. Judd. *The Democratic Facade*. Pacific Grove, Calif.: Brooks/Cole, 1991.

Hendrix, Lewellyn. "What Is Sexual Inequality? On the Definition and Range of Variation." *Gender and Society*, *28*, 3, August 1994:287–307.

Henig, Jeffrey R. *Rethinking School Choice: Limits of the Market Metaphor*. Princeton, N.J.: Princeton University Press, 1994.

Henley, Nancy, Mykol Hamilton, and Barrie Thorne. "Womanspeak and Manspeak." In *Beyond Sex Roles*. Alice G. Sargent, ed. St. Paul, Minn.: West, 1985.

Henry, William A., III. "Beyond the Melting Pot." *Time*, April 9, 1990:28–31.

Henslin, James M. *The Cab Driver: An Interactional Analysis of an Occupational Culture.* Washington University Ph.D. dissertation, September 1967.

Henslin, James M. *Introducing Sociology: Toward Understanding Life in Society*. New York: Free Press, 1975.

Henslin, James M. "It's Not a Lovely Place to Visit, and I Wouldn't Want to Live There." In *Studies in Qualitative Methodology, A Research Annual: Reflections on Field Experiences*, Robert G. Burgess, ed. Greenwich, Conn: JAI Press, 1990a:51–76.

Henslin, James M. "When Life Seems Hopeless: Suicide in American Society." In *Social Problems Today: Coping with the Challenges of a Changing Society*. Englewood Cliffs, N.J.: Prentice Hall, 1990b:99–107.

Henslin, James M. "Centuries of Childhood." In *Marriage and Family in a Changing Society*, 4th ed., James M. Henslin, ed. New York: Free Press, 1992:214–225.

Henslin, James M. "Trust and Cabbies." In *Down to Earth Sociology: Introductory Readings*, 7th ed., James M. Henslin, ed. New York: Free Press, 1993:183–196.

Henslin, James M. *Social Problems*, 4th ed. Englewood Cliffs, N.J.: Prentice Hall, 1996.

Henslin, James M. "On Becoming Male: Reflections of a Sociologist on Childhood and Early Socialization." In *Down to Earth Sociology*, 9th ed., James M. Henslin, ed. New York: Free Press, 1997a:130–140.

Henslin, James M. "Sociology and the Social Sciences." In *Down to Earth Sociology: Introductory Readings*, 9th ed., James M. Henslin, ed. New York: Free Press, 1997b:8–18.

Henslin, James M. "The Survivors of the F-227." In *Down to Earth Sociology: Introductory Readings*, 9th ed., James M. Henslin, ed. New York: Free Press, 1997c:237–245.

Henslin, James M., and Mae A. Biggs. "Behavior in Pubic Places: The Sociology of the Vaginal Examination." In *Down to Earth Sociology: Introductory Readings*, 9th ed., James M. Henslin, ed. New York: Free Press, 1997:203–214. Original version published as "Dramaturgical Desexualization: The Sociology of the Vaginal Examination." In *Studies in the Sociology of Sex*, James M. Henslin ed. New York: Appleton-Century-Crofts, 1971:243–272.

Herbert, Bob. "The Real Jobless Rate." *New York Times*, August 4, 1993:A19.

Herring, George C. "Vietnam War." *World Book Encyclopedia*, *20*. Chicago: World Book, 1989:389–393.

Hertzler, Joyce O. *A Sociology of Language*. New York: Random House, 1965.

Hewa, Soma. "Sociology and Public Policy: The Debate on Value-Free Social Science." *International Journal of Sociology and Social Policy*, *13*, 1–2, 1993:64–82.

Hewitt Associates. *Summary of Work and Family Benefits Report*. Lincolnshire, IL: Hewitt Associates, 1995.

Hibbert, Christopher. *The Roots of Evil: A Social History of Crime and Punishment*. New York: Minerva, 1963.

Higginbotham, Elizabeth, and Lynn Weber. "Moving with Kin and Community: Upward Social Mobility for Black and White Women." *Gender and Society*, *6*, 3, September 1992:416–440.

Higley, John, Ursula Hoffmann-Lange, Charles Kadushin, and Gwen Moore. "Elite Integration in Stable Democracies: A Reconsideration." *European Sociological Review*, *7*, 1, May 1991:35–53.

Hilliard, Asa, III. "Do We Have the *Will* to Educate All Children?" *Educational Leadership*, *49*, September 1991:31–36.

Hilts, Philip J. "AIDS Death Rate Rising in 25–44 Age Group." *New York Times*, February 16, 1996.

Hiltz, Starr Roxanne. "Widowhood." In *Marriage and Family in a Changing Society*, 3rd ed., James M. Henslin, ed. New York: Free Press, 1989:521–531.

Hippler, Fritz. Interview in a television documentary with Bill Moyers in *Propaganda*, in the series "Walk Through the 20th Century," 1987.

Hirschi, Travis. *Causes of Delinquency*. Berkeley: University of California Press, 1969.

Hobson, John A. *Imperialism: A Study*. rev. ed. London: Allen, 1939. First published in 1902.

Hochschild, Arlie Russell. "The Sociology of Feeling and Emotion: Selected Possibilities." In *Another Voice: Feminist Perspectives on Social Life and Social Science*, Marcia Millman and Rosabeth Moss Kanter, eds. Garden City, N.Y.: Anchor Books, 1975.

Hochschild, Arlie. *The Second Shift: Working Parents and the Revolution at Home*. New York: Viking, 1989.

Hochschild, Arlie. "Note to the Author." 1991.

Hogan, Phyllis. "1990 Data on Interracial Households." Unpublished Paper, July 1994.

Holden, Benjamin A., and Frederick Rose. "Two Policemen Get 2 1/2-Year Jail Terms on U.S. Charges in Rodney King Case." *Wall Street Journal*, August 5, 1993:B2.

Holtzman, Abraham. *The Townsend Movement: A Political Study*. New York: Bookman, 1963.

Homblin, Dora Jane. *The First Cities*. Boston: Little, Brown, Time-Life Books, 1973.

Honeycutt, Karen. "Disgusting, Pathetic, Bizarrely Beautiful: Representations of Weight in Popular Culture." Paper presented at the 1995 meetings of the American Sociological Association.

Hornblower, Margot. "The Skin Trade." *Time*, June 21, 1993:45–51.

Horowitz, Irving Louis. *Three Worlds of Development: The Theory and Practice of International Stratification*. New York: Oxford University Press, 1966.

Horowitz, Ruth. *Honor and the American Dream: Culture and Identity in a Chicano Community*. New Brunswick, N.J.: Rutgers University Press, 1983.

Horowitz, Ruth. "Community Tolerance of Gang Violence." *Social Problems*, 34, 5, December 1987:437–450.

Horwitz, Tony. "Dinka Tribes Made Slaves in Sudan's Civil War." *Wall Street Journal*, April 11, 1989:A19.

Horwitz, Tony. "Toughing It Out in Kuwait Tested the 'Sultan' Family." *Wall Street Journal*, March 4, 1991:A1, A6.

Hostetler, John A. *Amish Society*, 3rd ed. Baltimore: Johns Hopkins University Press, 1980.

Houtman, Dick. "What Exactly Is a 'Social Class'?: On the Economic Liberalism and Cultural Conservatism of the 'Working Class'." Paper presented at the 1995 meetings of the American Sociological Association.

Howe, Henry, John Lyne, Alan Gross, Harro VanLente, Aire Rip, Richard Lewontin, Daniel McShea, Greg Myers, Ullica Segerstrale, Herbert W. Simons, and V. B. Smocovitis. "Gene Talk in Sociobiology." *Social Epistemology*, 6, 2, April–June 1992:109–163.

Howells, Lloyd T., and Selwyn W. Becker. "Seating Arrangement and Leadership Emergence." *Journal of Abnormal and Social Psychology*, 64, February 1962:148–150.

Hoyt, Homer. *The Structure and Growth of Residential Neighborhoods in American Cities*. Washington, D.C.: Federal Housing Administration, 1939.

Hoyt, Homer. "Recent Distortions of the Classical Models of Urban Structure." In *Internal Structure of the City: Readings on Space and Environment*, Larry S. Bourne, ed. New York: Oxford University Press, 1971:84–96.

Hsu, Francis L. K. *The Challenge of the American Dream: The Chinese in the United States*. Belmont, Calif.: Wadsworth, 1971.

Huber, Joan. "From Sugar and Spice to Professor." In *Down to Earth Sociology: Introductory Readings*, 5th ed., James M. Henslin, ed. New York: Free Press, 1988:92–101.

Huber, Joan. "Micro-Macro Links in Gender Stratification." *American Sociological Review*, 55, February 1990:1–10.

Huber, Joan, and William H. Form. *Income and Ideology*. New York: Free Press, 1973.

Huddle, Donald. "The Net National Cost of Immigration." Washington, D.C.: Carrying Capacity Network, 1993.

Hudson, Christopher G. "The Social Class and Mental Illness Correlation: Implications of the Research for Policy and Practice." *Journal of Sociology and Social Welfare*, 15, 1, March 1988:27–54.

Hudson, James R. "Professional Sports Franchise Locations and City, Metropolitan and Regional Identities." Paper presented at the annual meetings of the American Sociological Association, 1991.

Hudson, Robert B. "The 'Graying' of the Federal Budget and Its Consequences for Old-Age Policy." *Gerontologist*, 18, October 1978:428–440.

Huggins, Martha K. "Lost Childhoods: Assassinations of Youth in Democratizing Brazil." Paper presented at the annual meetings of the American Sociological Association, 1993.

Hughes, H. Stuart. *Oswald Spengler: A Critical Estimate*, rev. ed. New York: Scribner's, 1962.

Hughes, Jason. "A Legend Returns." *SF Bay Guardian*, November 7, 1995.

Hughes, Kathleen A. "Even Tiki Torches Don't Guarantee a Perfect Wedding." *Wall Street Journal*, February 20, 1990:A1, A16.

Humphreys, Laud. *Tearoom Trade: Impersonal Sex in Public Places*. Chicago: Aldine, 1970. Enlarged ed.

Humphreys, Laud. *Tearoom Trade: Impersonal Sex in Public Places*, enlarged ed. Chicago: Aldine, 1975.

Humphreys, Laud. "Impersonal Sex and Perceived Satisfaction." In *Studies in the Sociology of Sex*, James M. Henslin, ed. New York: Appleton-Century-Crofts, 1971:351–374.

Hunt, Albert R. "Democrats' Trade-Off: Kids or Seniors?" *Wall Street Journal*, May 25, 1995:A15.

Hurtado, Aída, David E. Hayes-Bautista, R. Burciaga Valdez, and Anthony C. R. Hernández. *Redefining California: Latino Social Engagement in a Multicultural Society*. Los Angeles: UCLA Chicano Studies Research Center, 1992.

Huth, Mary Jo. "China's Urbanization under Communist Rule, 1949–1982." *International Journal of Sociology and Social Policy*, 10, 7, 1990:17–57.

Hwang, Suein, L. "Letter from a Tobacco Company to an Art Professor, August 1970." *Wall Street Journal*, July 21, 1995:B1.

Ikels, Charlotte. *The Return of the God of Wealth: The Transition to a Market Economy in Urban China*. Stanford, Calif.: Stanford University Press, 1996.

"Immigration's Costs and Benefits Weighted." *Population Today*, 25, 7/8, July/August 1997:3.

Iori, Ron. "The Good, the Bad and the Useless." *Wall Street Journal*, June 10, 1988:18R.

Itard, Jean Marc Gospard. *The Wild Boy of Aveyron.* Translated by George and Muriel Humphrey. New York: Appleton-Century-Crofts, 1962.

Jacobs, Margaret A. "'New Girl' Network Is Boon for Women Lawyers." *Wall Street Journal*, March 4, 1997:B1, B7.

Jacobsen, Thorkild, and Robert M. Adams. "Salt and Silt in Ancient Mesopotamian Agriculture." *Science*, November 21, 1958:1251–1258.

Jaggar, Alison M. "Sexual Difference and Sexual Equality." In *Theoretical Perspectives on Sexual Difference*, Deborah L. Rhode, ed. New Haven, Conn.: Yale University Press, 1990:239–254.

James, Daniel. "To Cut Spending, Freeze Immigration." *Wall Street Journal*, June 24, 1993:A13.

Janis, Irving. *Victims of Groupthink.* Boston, Mass.: Houghton Mifflin, 1972.

Jankowiak, William R., and Edward F. Fischer. "A Cross-Cultural Perspective on Romantic Love." *Journal of Ethnology*, 31, 2, April 1992:149–155.

Jankowski, Martín Sánchez. *Islands in the Street: Gangs and American Urban Society.* Berkeley: University of California Press, 1991.

Jasper, James M. "Moral Dimensions of Social Movements." Paper presented at the annual meetings of the American Sociological Association, 1991.

Jasper, James M., and Dorothy Nelkin. *The Animal Rights Crusade: The Growth of a Moral Protest.* New York: Free Press, 1992.

Jasper, James M., and Dorothy Nelkin. *Animal Crusades.* New York: Free Press, 1993.

Jasper, James M., and Jane D. Poulsen. "Recruiting Strangers and Friends: Moral Shocks and Social Networks in Animal Rights and Anti-Nuclear Protests." *Social Problems*, 42, 4, November 1995:493–512.

Jáuregui, Gurutz. "El poder y la soberana en la aldea global." *El Pais.* July 19, 1996:11.

Jerrome, Dorothy. *Good Company: An Anthropological Study of Old People in Groups.* Edinburgh, England: Edinburgh University Press, 1992.

Johnson, Benton. "On Church and Sect." *American Sociological Review*, 28, 1963:539–549.

Johnson, Cathryn. "The Emergence of the Emotional Self: A Developmental Theory." *Symbolic Interaction*, 15, 2, Summer 1992:183–202.

Johnson, Colleen L., and Barbara M. Barer. "Patterns of Engagement and Disengagement Among the Oldest Old." *Journal of Aging Studies*, 6, 4, Winter 1992:351–364.

Johnson, Norris R. "Panic at 'The Who Concert Stampede': An Empirical Assessment." In *Collective Behavior and Social Movements*, Russell L. Curtis, Jr., and Benigno E. Aguirre, eds. Boston: Allyn and Bacon, 1993:113–122.

Johnston, Drue M., and Norris R. Johnson. "Role Extension in Disaster: Employee Behavior at the Beverly Hills Supper Club Fire." *Sociological Focus*, 22, 1, February 1989:39–51.

Johnston, Lloyd D., Patrick M. O'Malley, and Jerald G. Bachman. *National Survey Results on Drug Use from The Monitoring the Future Study, 1975–1994.* Rockville, Md.: U.S. Department of Health and Human Services, 1995.

Jones, James H. *Bad Blood: The Tuskegee Syphilis Experiment*, 2nd ed. New York: Free Press, 1993.

Jones, Lawrence N. "The New Black Church." *Ebony*, November 1992:192, 194–195.

Jordon, Mary. "College Dorms Reflect Trend of Self-Segregation." In *Ourselves and Others*, 2nd ed., The Washington Post Writer's Group, eds. Boston: Allyn and Bacon, 1996:85–87.

Josephson, Matthew. "The Robber Barons." In *John D. Rockefeller: Robber Baron or Industrial Statesman?* Earl Latham, ed. Boston: Heath, 1949:34–48.

Judis, John B. "The Japanese Megaphone." *New Republic, 202,* 4, January 22, 1990:20–25.

Kagan, Jerome. "The Idea of Emotions in Human Development." In *Emotions, Cognition, and Behavior*, Carroll E. Izard, Jerome Kagan, and Robert B. Zajonc, eds. New York: Cambridge University Press, 1984:38–72.

Kahn, Joseph. "P&G Viewed China as a National Market and Is Conquering It." *Wall Street Journal*, September 12, 1995:A1, A6.

Kalichman, Seth C. "MMPI Profiles of Women and Men Convicted of Domestic Homicide." *Journal of Clinical Psychology, 44,* 6, November 1988:847–853.

Kalish, Susan. "International Migration: New Findings on Magnitude, Importance." *Population Today, 22,* 3, March 1994:1–2.

Kalmijn, Matthijs. "Shifting Boundaries: Trends in Religious and Educational Homogamy." *American Sociological Review, 56,* December 1991:786–800.

Kamin, Leon J. *The Science and Politics of I.Q.* Hillsdale, N.J.: Erlbaum, 1975.

Kamin, Leon J. "Is Crime in the Genes? The Answer May Depend on Who Chooses What Evidence." *Scientific American*, February 1986:22–27.

Kaminski, Matthew, and Kim Palchikoff. "The Crisis to Come." *Newsweek*, April 14, 1997:44–46.

Kanabayashi, Masayoshi. "Work Week." *Wall Street Journal*, August 20, 1996:A1.

Kanter, Rosabeth Moss. *Men and Women of the Corporation.* New York: Basic Books, 1977.

Kanter, Rosabeth Moss. *The Change Masters: Innovation and Entrepreneurship in the American Corporation.* New York: Simon & Schuster, 1983.

Kanter, Rosabeth Moss, ed. *Innovation: Breakthrough Thinking at 3M, DuPont, GE, Pfizer, and Rubbermaid.* New York: HarperBusiness, 1997a.

Kanter, Rosabeth Moss. *World Class: Thriving Locally in the Global Economy.* New York: Touchstone Books, 1997b.

Kanter, Rosabeth Moss, Fred Wiersema, and John J. Kao, eds. *Innovation: Breakthrough Thinking at 3M, DuPont, GE, Pfizer, and Rubbermaid.* New York: Harper, 1997.

Karnow, Stanley, and Nancy Yoshihara. *Asian Americans in Transition.* New York: Asia Society, 1992.

Karp, David A., Gregory P. Stone, and William C. Yoels. *Being Urban: A Sociology of City Life*, 2nd ed. New York: Praeger, 1991.

Karp, David A., and William C. Yoels. "Sport and Urban Life." *Journal of Sport and Social Issues, 14,* 2, 1990:77–102.

Kart, Cary S. *The Realities of Aging: An Introduction to Gerontology*, 3rd ed. Boston: Allyn and Bacon, 1990.

Kasarda, John D., and Edward M. Crenshaw. "Third World Urbanization: Dimensions, Theories, and Determinants." *Annual Review of Sociology, 17,* 1991:467–501.

Katz, Michael B. *The Undeserving Poor: From the War on Poverty to the War on Welfare.* New York: Pantheon, 1989.

Katz, Sidney. "The Importance of Being Beautiful." In *Down to Earth Sociology: Introductory Readings*, 9th ed., James M. Henslin, ed. New York: Free Press, 1997:307–313.

Kaufman, Joanne. "Married Maidens and Dilatory Domiciles." *Wall Street Journal*, May 7, 1996:A16.

Kaufmann, Caroline. "Rights and the Provision of Health Care: A Comparison of Canada, Great Britain, and the United States." In *Dominant Issues in Medical Sociology*, 3rd ed., Howard D. Schwartz, ed. New York: McGraw-Hill, 1994:376–396.

Keith, Jennie. *Old People, New Lives: Community Creation in a Retirement Residence*, 2nd ed. Chicago: University of Chicago Press, 1982.

Kelley, Jonathan, and M. D. R. Evans. "Class and Class Conflict in Six Western Nations." *American Sociological Review, 60*, April 1995:157–178.

Kelly, Joan B. "How Adults React to Divorce." In *Marriage and Family in a Changing Society*, 4th ed., James M. Henslin, ed. New York: Free Press, 1992:410–423.

Kelman, Herbert, and V. Lee Hamilton. "The My Lai Massacre." In *Down to Earth Sociology: Introductory Readings*, 9th ed., James M. Henslin, ed. New York: Free Press, 1997:447–459.

Kelso, William A. *Poverty and the Underclass: Changing Perceptions of the Poor in America*. New York: New York University Press, 1995.

Kemp, Alice Abel. "Estimating Sex Discrimination in Professional Occupations with the *Dictionary of Occupational Titles*." *Sociological Spectrum, 10*, 3, 1990:387–411.

Keniston, Kenneth. *Youth and Dissent: The Rise of a New Opposition*. New York: Harcourt, Brace, Jovanovich, 1971.

Kennedy, Paul. *Preparing for the Twenty-First Century*. New York: Random House, 1993.

Kephart, William M., and William W. Zellner. *Extraordinary Groups: An Examination of Unconventional Life-Styles*, 5th ed. New York: St. Martin's Press, 1994.

Kerr, Clark. *The Future of Industrialized Societies*. Cambridge, Mass.: Harvard University Press, 1983.

Kerr, Clark, et al. *Industrialism and Industrial Man: The Problems of Labor and Management in Economic Growth*. Cambridge, Mass.: Harvard University Press, 1960.

Kershaw, Terry. "The Effects of Educational Tracking on the Social Mobility of African Americans." *Journal of Black Studies, 23*, 1, September 1992:152–169.

Kettl, Donald F. "The Savings-and-Loan Bailout: The Mismatch Between the Headlines and the Issues." *PS, 24*, 3, September 1991:441–447.

Kibria, Nazli. *Family Tightrope: The Changing Lives of Vietnamese Americans*. Princeton, N.J.: Princeton University Press, 1993.

"Kid's Count Data Sheet." Population Reference Bureau, 1996.

King, Martin Luther, Jr. *Stride Toward Freedom: The Montgomery Story*. New York: Harper & Brothers, 1958.

King, Ralph T., Jr. "Soon a Chip Will Test Blood for Diseases." *Wall Street Journal*, October 25, 1994:B1, B11.

Kinsella, Kevin, and Cynthia M. Taeuber. *An Aging World*. Washington, D.C.: U.S. Bureau of the Census, 1993.

Kirkpatrick, Melanie. "Gay Marriage: Who Should Decide?" *Wall Street Journal*, March 13, 1996:A21.

Kitsuse, John I. "Coming Out All Over: Deviants and the Politics of Social Problems." *Social Problems, 28*, 1, October 1980:1–13.

Klonoff, Elizabeth A., and Hope Landrine. "Sex Roles, Occupational Roles, and Symptom-Reporting: A Test of Competing Hypotheses on Sex Differences." *Journal of Behavioral Medicine, 15*, 4, August 1992:355–364.

Kluegel, James R., and Eliot R. Smith. *Beliefs About Inequality: America's Views of What Is and What Ought to Be*. Hawthorne, N.Y.: Aldine de Gruyter, 1986.

Knaus, William A. *Inside Russian Medicine: An American Doctor's First-Hand Report*. New York: Everest House, 1981.

Kohfeld, Carol W., and Leslie A. Leip. "Bans on Concurrent Sale of Beer and Gas: A California Case Study." *Sociological Practice Review, 2*, 2, April 1991:104–115.

Kohlberg, Lawrence, and Carol Gilligan. "The Adolescent as a Philosopher: The Discovery of the Self in a Postconventional World." *Daedalus, 100*, 1971:1051–1086.

Kohn, Alfie. "Make Love, Not War." *Psychology Today*, June 1988:35–38.

Kohn, Melvin L. "Social Class and Parental Values." *American Journal of Sociology, 64*, 1959:337–351.

Kohn, Melvin L. "Social Class and Parent–Child Relationships: An Interpretation." *American Journal of Sociology, 68*, 1963:471–480.

Kohn, Melvin L. "Occupational Structure and Alienation." *American Journal of Sociology, 82*, 1976:111–130.

Kohn, Melvin L. *Class and Conformity: A Study in Values*, 2nd ed. Homewood, Ill.: Dorsey Press, 1977.

Kohn, Melvin L., and Carmi Schooler. "Class, Occupation, and Orientation." *American Sociological Review, 34*, 1969:659–678.

Kohn, Melvin L., and Carmi Schooler. *Work and Personality: An Inquiry into the Impact of Social Stratification*. New York: Ablex Press, 1983.

Kohn, Melvin L., Kazimierz M. Slomczynski, and Carrie Schoenbach. "Social Stratification and the Transmission of Values in the Family: A Cross-National Assessment." *Sociological Forum, 1*, 1, 1986:73–102.

Komter, Aafke, "Hidden Power in Marriage." *Gender and Society, 3*, 2, June 1989:187–216.

Korbin, Jill E., Georgia Anetzberger, and J. Kevin Eckert. "Elder Abuse and Child Abuse: A Consideration of Similarities and Differences in Intergenerational Family Violence." In *Perspectives in Social Gerontology*, Robert B. Enright, Jr., ed. Boston: Allyn and Bacon, 1994:165–173.

Korda, Michael. *Male Chauvinism: How It Works*. New York: Random House, 1973.

Kornhauser, William. *The Politics of Mass Society*. New York: Free Press, 1959.

Kotkin, Joel. "The Emerging Latino Middle Class." *Wall Street Journal*, October 9, 1996:A18.

Kotlowitz, Alex. "A Businessman Turns His Skills to Aiding Inner-City Schools." *Wall Street Journal*, February 25, 1992:A1, A6.

Kramer, Josea B. "Serving American Indian Elderly in Cities: An Invisible Minority." *Aging Magazine*, Winter–Spring 1992:48–51.

Krattenmaker, Tom. "Single-Parent Families: Sara McLanahan Strikes a Balance in a Fierce Ideological Debate." *Princeton Alumni Weekly*, December 7, 1994:15. (As cited in Popenoe 1996)

Krause, Neal. "Race Differences in Life Satisfaction Among Aged Men and Women." *Journal of Gerontology, 48*, 5, 1993:235–244.

Kraybill, Donald B. *The Riddle of Amish Culture*. Baltimore: Johns Hopkins University Press, 1989.

Krupp, Helmar. "European Technology Policy and Global Schumpeter Dynamics: A Social Science Perspective." *Technological Forecasting and Social Change, 48*, 1995:7–26.

Kübler-Ross, Elisabeth. *On Death and Dying*. New York: Macmillan, 1969.

Kübler-Ross, Elisabeth. *Living with Death and Dying*. New York: Macmillan, 1981.

Kübler-Ross, Elisabeth. *Death: The Final Stage of Growth*. Englewood Cliffs, N.J.: Prentice Hall, 1989.

Kuhn, Margaret E. "The Gray Panthers." In *Social Problems*, 2nd ed., James M. Henslin, Englewood Cliffs, N.J.: Prentice Hall, 1990:56–57.

Krysan, Maria, and Reynolds Farley. "Racial Stereotypes: Are They Alive and Well? Do They Continue to Influence Race Relations?" Paper presented at the 1993 meeting of the American Sociological Association.

Kurian, George Thomas. *Encyclopedia of the First World*, Vols. 1, 2. New York: Facts on File, 1990.

Kurian, George Thomas. *Encyclopedia of the Second World*, New York: Facts on File, 1991.

Kurian, George Thomas. *Encyclopedia of the Third World*, Vols. 1, 2, 3. New York: Facts on File, 1992.

La Barre, Weston. *The Human Animal*. Chicago: University of Chicago Press, 1954.

Lacayo, Richard. "The 'Cultural' Defense." *Time*, Fall 1993a:61.

Lacayo, Richard. "In the Grip of a Psychopath." *Time*, May 3, 1993b:34–36, 39–43.

Lacayo, Richard. "The Lure of the Cult." *Time*, April 7, 1997:45–46.

Lachica, Eduardo. "Third World Told to Spend More on Environment." *Wall Street Journal*, May 18, 1992:A2.

LaDou, Joseph. "Deadly Migration: Hazardous Industries' Flight to the Third World." *Technology Review*, 94, 5, July 1991:46–53.

Lagaipa, Susan J. "Suffer the Little Children: The Ancient Practice of Infanticide as a Modern Moral Dilemma." *Issues in Comprehensive Pediatric Nursing*, 13, 1990:241–251.

Lagnado, Lucette. "Another Peril: Smoking Doubles Risk of Old-Age Blindness, Two Studies Say." *Wall Street Journal*, October 9, 1996:B8.

Lamb, Michael E. "The Effect of Divorce on Children's Personality Development." *Journal of Divorce*, 1, Winter 1977:163–174.

Lancaster, Hal. "Managing Your Career." *Wall Street Journal*, November 14, 1995:B1.

Landtman, Gunnar. *The Origin of the Inequality of the Social Classes*. New York: Greenwood Press, 1968. First published in 1938.

Lang, Kurt, and Gladys E. Lang. *Collective Dynamics*. New York: Crowell, 1961.

Langan, Patrick A., and Mark A. Cunniff. "Recidivism of Felons on Probation, 1986–89." Washington, D.C.: U.S. Department of Justice, February 1992.

Lannoy, Richard. *The Speaking Tree: A Study of Indian Culture and Society*. New York: Oxford University Press, 1975.

LaPiere, Richard T. "Attitudes Versus Action." *Social Forces*, 13, December 1934:230–237.

Larson, Jeffry H. "The Marriage Quiz: College Students' Beliefs in Selected Myths About Marriage." *Family Relations*, January 1988:3–11.

Lasch, Christopher. *Haven in a Heartless World: The Family Besieged*. New York: Basic, 1977.

Laska, Shirley Bradway. "Environmental Sociology and the State of the Discipline." *Social Forces*, 72, 1, September 1993:1–17.

Latané, Bibb, and John M. Darley. *The Unresponsive Bystander: Why Doesn't He Help?* New York: Appleton-Century-Crofts, 1970.

Latané, Bibb, and Steve Nida. "Ten Years of Research on Group Size and Helping." *Psychological Bulletin*, 89, 2, 1981:308–324.

Lauer, Jeanette, and Robert Lauer. "Marriages Made to Last." In *Marriage and Family in a Changing Society*, 4th ed., James M. Henslin, ed. New York: Free Press, 1992:481–486.

Lawlor, Julia. "Women Gain Power, Means to Abuse It." *USA Today*, January 12, 1994:1A, 2A.

Lazarsfeld, Paul F., and Jeffrey G. Reitz. "History of Applied Sociology." *Sociological Practice*, 7, 1989:43–52.

LeBon, Gustave. *Psychologie des Foules (The Psychology of the Crowd)*. Paris: Alcan, 1895. Various editions in English.

Leacock, Eleanor. *Teaching and Learning in City Schools*. New York: Basic Books, 1969.

Leacock, Eleanor. *Myths of Male Dominance*. New York: Monthly Review Press, 1981.

Lee, Alfred McClung, and Elizabeth Briant Lee. *The Fine Art of Propaganda: A Study of Father Coughlin's Speeches*. New York: Harcourt Brace, 1939.

Lee, Felicia R. "Infertile Couples Forge Ties Within Society of Their Own." *New York Times*, January 9, 1996:A1.

Lee, Sharon M., and Keiko Yamanaka. "Patterns of Asian American Intermarriage and Marital Assimilation." *Journal of Comparative Family Studies*, 21, 2, Summer 1990:287–305.

Leland, John, and Gregory Beals. "In Living Colors." *Newsweek*, May 5, 1997:58–60.

Lemann, Nicholas. *The Promised Land: The Great Black Migration and How It Changed America*. New York: Random House, 1991.

Lemann, Nicholas, "The Myth of Community Development." *New York Times Magazine*, January 9, 1994, p. 27.

Lemert, Charles. "A Classic from the Other Side of the Veil: Du Bois's *Souls of Black Folk*." *Sociological Quarterly*, 35, 3, 1994:383–396.

Lemert, Edwin M. *Human Deviance, Social Problems, and Social Control*, 2nd ed., Englewood Cliffs, N.J.: Prentice Hall, 1972.

Lenski, Gerhard. "Status Crystallization: A Nonvertical Dimension of Social Status." *American Sociological Review*, 19, 1954:405–413.

Lenski, Gerhard. *Power and Privilege: A Theory of Social Stratification*. New York: McGraw-Hill, 1966.

Lenski, Gerhard, and Jean Lenski. *Human Societies: An Introduction to Macrosociology*, 5th ed. New York: McGraw-Hill, 1987.

Lerner, Gerda. *Black Women in White America: A Documentary History*. New York: Pantheon Books, 1972.

Lerner, Gerda. *The Creation of Patriarchy*. New York: Oxford, 1986.

Lesser, Alexander. "War and the State." In *War: The Anthropology of Armed Conflict and Aggression*, Morton Fried, Marvin Harris, and Robert Murphy, eds. Garden City, N.Y.: Natural History, 1968:92–96.

Levinson, D. J. *The Seasons of a Man's Life*. New York: Knopf, 1978.

Levitt, Steven D. *The Quarterly Journal of Economics*, May 1996.

Levy, Judith A. "The Hospice in the Context of an Aging Society." In *Perspectives in Social Gerontology*, Robert B. Enright, Jr., ed. Boston: Allyn and Bacon, 1994:274–286.

Levy, Marion J., Jr. "Confucianism and Modernization." *Society*, 24, 4, May–June 1992:15–18.

Lewis, Dorothy Otnow, ed. *Vulnerabilities to Delinquency*. New York: Spectrum Medical and Scientific Books, 1981.

Lewis, Oscar. "The Culture of Poverty." *Scientific American*, 115, October 1966a:19–25.

Lewis, Oscar. *La Vida*. New York: Random House, 1966b.

Lewis, Richard S. *Challenger: The Final Voyage*. New York: Columbia University Press, 1988.

Liben, Paul. "Farrakhan Honors African Slavers." *Wall Street Journal*, October 20, 1995:A14.

Liebow, Elliot. "Tally's Corner." In *Down to Earth Sociology: Introductory Readings*, 9th ed., James M. Henslin, ed. New York: Free Press, 1997:330–339.

Liebow, Elliot. *Tally's Corner: A Study of Negro Streetcorner Men.* Boston: Little, Brown, 1967.

Light, Donald W. "Perestroika for Russian Health Care?" *Footnotes*, 20, 3, March 1992:7, 9.

Lightfoot-Klein, A. "Rites of Purification and Their Effects: Some Psychological Aspects of Female Genital Circumcision and Infibulation (Pharaonic Circumcision) in an Afro-Arab Society (Sudan)." *Journal of Psychological Human Sexuality*, 2, 1989:61–78.

Lind, Michael. *The Next American Nation: The New Nationalism and the Fourth American Revolution.* New York: Free Press, 1995.

Linden, Eugene. "Lost Tribes, Lost Knowledge." *Time*, September 23, 1991:46, 48, 50, 52, 54, 56.

Linton, Ralph. *The Study of Man.* New York: Appleton-Century-Crofts, 1936.

Lippitt, Ronald, and Ralph K. White. "An Experimental Study of Leadership and Group Life." In *Readings in Social Psychology*, 3rd ed., Eleanor E. Maccoby, Theodore M. Newcomb, and Eugene L. Hartley, eds. New York: Holt, Rinehart and Winston, 1958:340–365. (As summarized in Olmsted and Hare 1978:28–31.)

Lipset, Seymour Martin. "Democracy and Working-Class Authoritarianism." *American Sociological Review*, 24, 1959:482–502.

Lipset, Seymour Martin. "The Social Requisites of Democracy Revisited." Presidential address to the American Sociological Association, Boston, Massachusetts, 1993.

Lipton, Michael. *Why Poor People Stay Poor: Urban Bias in World Development.* Cambridge, Mass.: Harvard University Press, 1979.

Lofland, John F. *Protest: Studies of Collective Behavior and Social Movements.* New Brunswick, New Jersey: Transaction Books, 1985.

Lofland, John. "Collective Behavior: The Elementary Forms." In *Collective Behavior and Social Movements*, Russell L. Curtis, Jr., and Benigno E. Aguirre, eds. Boston: Allyn and Bacon, 1993:70–75.

Logan, John R., and Harvey L. Molotch. *Urban Fortunes: The Political Economy of Place.* Berkeley: University of California Press, 1987.

Lombroso, Cesare. *Crime: Its Causes and Remedies*, H. P. Horton, trans. Boston: Little, Brown, 1911.

Lopez, Julie Amparano. "Study Says Women Face Glass Walls as Well as Ceilings." *Wall Street Journal*, March 3, 1992:B1, B8.

Lorber, Judith. *Paradoxes of Gender.* New Haven, Conn.: Yale University Press, 1994.

Lublin, Joann S. "Trying to Increase Worker Productivity, More Employers Alter Management Style." *Wall Street Journal*, February 13, 1991:B1, B7.

Lublin, Joann S. "Women at Top Still Are Distant from CEO Jobs." *Wall Street Journal*, February 28, 1996:B1.

Luke, Timothy W. *Ideology and Soviet Industrialism.* Westport, Conn.: Greenwood Press, 1985.

Lundberg, Olle. "Causal Explanations for Class Inequality in Health—An Empirical Analysis." *Social Science and Medicine*, 32, 4, 1991:385–393.

Luoma, Jon R. "Acid Murder No Longer a Mystery." In *Taking Sides: Clashing Views on Controversial Environmental Issues*, 3rd ed., Theodore D. Goldfarb, ed. Guilford, Conn.: Dushkin, 1989:186–192.

Lurie, Nicole, Jonathan Slater, Paul McGovern, Jacqueline Ekstrum, Lois Quam, and Karen Margolis. "Preventive Care for Women: Does the Sex of the Physician Matter?" *New England Journal of Medicine*, 329, August 12, 1993:478–482.

MacDonald, Heather. "Law School Humbug." *Wall Street Journal*, November 8, 1995:A23.

MacDonald, William L., and Alfred DeMaris. "Remarriage, Stepchildren, and Marital Conflict: Challenges to the Incomplete Institutionalization Hypothesis." *Journal of Marriage and the Family*, 57, May 1995:387–398.

MacIver, Robert M. *Society.* New York: Holt, Rinehart and Winston, 1937.

Mack, Raymond W., and Calvin P. Bradford. *Transforming America: Patterns of Social Change*, 2nd ed. New York: Random House, 1979.

Mackay, Charles. *Memories of Extraordinary Popular Delusions and the Madness of Crowds.* London: Office of the National Illustrated Library, 1852.

Mackey, Richard A., and Bernard A. O'Brien. *Lasting Marriages: Men and Women Growing Together.* Westport, Conn.: 1995.

MacKinnon, Catharine A. *Sexual Harassment of Working Women: A Case of Sex Discrimination.* New Haven, Conn.: Yale University Press, 1979.

MacShane, Denis. "Lessons for Bosses and the Bossed." *New York Times*, July 19, 1993:A15.

Magnuson, E. "A Cold Soak, a Plume, a Fireball." *Time*, February 17, 1986:25.

Mahoney, John S., Jr., and Paul G. Kooistra. "Policing the Races: Structural Factors Enforcing Racial Purity in Virginia (1630–1930)." Paper presented at the 1995 meetings of the American Sociological Association.

Mahran, M. *Proceedings of the Third International Congress of Medical Sexology.* Littleton, Mass.: PSG Publishing, 1978.

Mahran, M. "Medical Dangers of Female Circumcision." *International Planned Parenthood Federation Medical Bulletin*, 2, 1981:1–2.

Maier, Mark. "Teaching from Tragedy: An Interdisciplinary Module on the Space Shuttle *Challenger*." *T.H.E. Journal*, September 1993:91–94.

Main, Jackson Turner. *The Social Structure of Revolutionary America.* Princeton, N.J.: Princeton University Press, 1965.

Malinowski, Bronislaw. *Sex and Repression in Savage Society.* Cleveland, Ohio: World, 1927.

Malinowski, Bronislaw. *The Dynamics of Culture Change.* New Haven, Conn.: Yale University Press, 1945.

Malmberg, Bo, and Gerdt Sundström. "Age Care Crisis in Sweden?" *Current Sweden*, 412, January 1996:1–6.

Malson, Lucien. *Wolf Children and the Problem of Human Nature.* New York: Monthly Review Press, 1972.

Malthus, Thomas Robert. *First Essay on Population 1798.* London: Macmillan, 1926. Originally published in 1798.

Mamdani, Mahmood. "The Myth of Population Control: Family, Caste, and Class in an Urban Village." New York: Monthly Review Press, 1973.

Mander, Jerry. *In the Absence of the Sacred: The Failure of Technology and the Survival of the Indian Nations.* San Francisco, Calif.: Sierra Club Books, 1992.

Manno, Bruno V. "The Real Score on the SATs." *Wall Street Journal*, September 13, 1995:A14.

Manski, Charles F. "Income and Higher Education." *Focus*, 14, 3, Winter 1992–1993:14–19.

Marcus, Amy Dockser. "Mideast Minorities: Kurds Aren't Alone." *Wall Street Journal*, September 5, 1996:A12.

Marger, Martin N. *Elites and Masses: An Introduction to Political Sociology*, 2nd ed. Belmont, Calif.: Wadsworth, 1987.

Markson, Elizabeth W. "Moral Dilemmas." *Society*, July–August, 1992:4–6.

Markusen, Eric. "Genocide in Cambodia." In *Down to Earth Sociology*, 8th ed., James M. Henslin, ed. New York: Free Press, 1995:355–364.

Marolla, Joseph, and Diana Scully. "Attitudes Toward Women, Violence, and Rape: A Comparison of Convicted Rapists and Other Felons." *Deviant Behavior*, 7, 4, 1986:337–355.

Marshall, Gordon. *In Search of the Spirit of Capitalism: An Essay on Max Weber's Protestant Ethic Thesis*. New York: Columbia University Press, 1982.

Marshall, Samantha. "It's So Simple: Just Lather Up, Watch the Fat Go Down the Drain." *Wall Street Journal*, November 2, 1995:B1.

Martin, Michael. "Ecosabotage and Civil Disobedience." *Environmental Ethics*, 12, 4, Winter 1990:291–310.

Martin, William G. "The World-Systems Perspective in Perspective: Assessing the Attempt to Move Beyond Nineteenth-Century Eurocentric Conceptions." *Review*, 17, 2, Spring 1994:145–185.

Martineau, Harriet. *Society in America*. Garden City, N.Y.: Doubleday 1962. First published in 1837.

Marvin, Carolyn. *When Old Technologies Were New: Thinking About Electronic Communication in the Late Nineteenth Century*. New York: Oxford University Press, 1988.

Marx, Gary T. "The New Surveillance." *Technology Review*, May–June 1985:43–48.

Marx, Gary T. "Monitoring on the Job: How to Protect Privacy as Well as Property." *Technology Review*, November–December 1986:63–72.

Marx, Gary T. "Thoughts On a Neglected Category of Social Movement Participant: The Agent Provocateur and the Informant." In *Collective Behavior and Social Movements*, Russell L. Curtis, Jr., and Benigno E. Aguirre, eds. Boston: Allyn and Bacon, 1993:242–258.

Marx, Gary T. "The Road to the Future." In *Triumph of Discovery: A Chronicle of Great Adventures in Science*. New York: Holt, 1995:63–65.

Marx, Karl. "Contribution to the Critique of Hegel's Philosophy of Right." In *Karl Marx: Early Writings*, T. B. Bottomore, ed. New York: McGraw-Hill, 1964:45. First published in 1844.

Marx, Karl, and Friedrich Engels. *Communist Manifesto*. New York: Pantheon, 1967. First published in 1848.

Masheter, Carol. "Postdivorce Relationships Between Ex-spouses: The Role of Attachment and Interpersonal Conflict." *Journal of Marriage and the Family*, 53, February 1991:103–110.

Massey, Douglas S., and Nancy A. Denton. *American Apartheid: Segregation and the Making of the Underclass*. Cambridge, Mass.: Harvard University Press, 1993.

Matthews, Marvyn. "Long Term Trends in Soviet Education." In *Soviet Education in the 1980s*, J. J. Tomiak, ed. London: Croom Helm, 1983:1–23.

Mauss, Armand. *Social Problems as Social Movements*. Philadelphia, Penn.: Lippincott, 1975.

Maybury-Lewis, David. "Tribal Wisdom." In *Sociology 95/96*, Kurt Finsterbusch, ed. Sluice Dock, Conn.: Dushkin, 1995:16–21.

Mayo, Elton. *Human Problems of an Industrial Civilization*. New York: Viking, 1966.

McAdam, Doug, John D. McCarthy, and Mayer N. Zald. "Social Movements." In *Handbook of Sociology*, Neil J. Smelser, ed. Newbury Park, Calif.: Sage, 1988:695–737.

McCabe, J. Terrence, and James E. Ellis. "Pastoralism: Beating the Odds in Arid Africa." In *Conformity and Conflict: Readings in Cultural Anthropology*, James P. Spradley and David W. McCurdy, eds. Glenview, Ill.: Scott, Foresman, 1990:150–156.

McCall, Michael. "Who and Where Are the Artists?" In *Fieldwork Experience: Qualitative Approaches to Social Research*, William B. Shaffir, Robert A. Stebbins, and Allan Turowetz, eds. New York: St. Martin's, 1980:145–158.

McCarthy, Colman. "America's Homeless: Three Days Down and Out in Chicago." *Nation*, 236, 9, March 5, 1983:1, 271.

McCarthy, John D., and Mark Wolfson. "Consensus Movements, Conflict Movements, and the Cooperation of Civic and State Infrastructures." In *Frontiers in Social Movement Theory*, Aldon D. Morris and Carol McClurg Mueller, eds. New Haven, Conn.: Yale University Press, 1992:273–297.

McCarthy, John D., and Mayer N. Zald. "Resource Mobilization and Social Movements: A Partial Theory." *American Journal of Sociology*, 82, 6, 1977:1212–1241.

McCarthy, Michael J. "James Bond Hits the Supermarket: Stores Snoop on Shoppers' Habits to Boost Sales." *Wall Street Journal*, August 25, 1993:B1, B8.

McCartney, Scott. "People Most Needing Transplantable Livers Now Often Miss Out." *Wall Street Journal*, April 1, 1993:A1, A7.

McCoy, Elin. "Childhood Through the Ages." In *Marriage and Family in a Changing Society*, 2nd ed., James M. Henslin, ed. New York: Free Press, 1985:386–394.

McCuen, Gary E., ed. *Ecocide and Genocide in the Vanishing Forest: The Rainforests and Native People*. Hudson, Wis.: GEM Publications, 1993.

McGinley, Laurie, and Christopher Georges. "Medicare Bill Passed by House Would End Egalitarian Approach." *Wall Street Journal*, October 20, 1995:A1, A8.

McGowan, Jo. "Little Girls Dying: An Ancient & Thriving Practice." *Commonweal*, August 9, 1991:481–482.

McGregor, James. "China's Aging Leader Seems Set to Carve Reformist Idea in Stone." *Wall Street Journal*, March 20, 1992:A9.

McGregor, James. "Running Bulls." *Wall Street Journal*, September 24, 1993:R16.

McIntyre, Jamie. "Army Rape Case Renews Debate on Coed Training." April 30, 1997: CNN Internet article.

McKenna, George. "On Abortion: A Lincolnian Position." *Atlantic Monthly*, September 1995:51–67.

McKeown, Thomas. *The Modern Rise of Population*. New York: Academic Press, 1977.

McLanahan, Sara, and Gary Sandefur. *Growing Up with a Single Parent: What Hurts, What Helps*. Cambridge, Mass.: Harvard University Press, 1994.

McLemore, S. Dale. *Racial and Ethnic Relations in America*. Boston: Allyn and Bacon, 1994.

McLuhan, Marshall. *Understanding Media: The Extensions of Man*. New York: Mentor, 1964.

McPhail, Clark. "Blumer's Theory of Collective Behavior: The Development of a Non-Symbolic Interaction Explanation." *Sociological Quarterly*, 30, 3, 1989:401–423.

McPhail, Clark. *The Myth of the Madding Crowd*. Hawthorne, N.Y.: Aldine de Gruyter, 1991.

Mead, George Herbert. *Mind, Self and Society*. Chicago: University of Chicago Press, 1934.

Mead, Margaret. *Sex and Temperament in Three Primitive Societies*. New York: New American Library, 1950. First published in 1935.

Meek, Anne. "On Creating 'Ganas': A Conversation with Jaime Escalante." *Educational Leadership*, 46, 5, February 1989:46–47.

Meier, Barry. "Health Studies Suggest Asbestos Substitutes Also Pose Cancer Risk." *Wall Street Journal*, May 12, 1987:1, 21.

Melloan, George. "Apartheid Is Dead—Now Comes the Hard Part." *Wall Street Journal*, November 22, 1993a:A15.

Melloan, George. "Italy 'Steps into the Tunnel' Toward Change." *Wall Street Journal*, April 26, 1993b:A15.

Meltzer, Bernard N., John W. Petras, and Larry T. Reynolds. *Symbolic Interactionism: Genesis, Varieties, and Criticism*. London: Routledge & Kegan Paul, 1975.

Menaghan, Elizabeth G., Lori Kowaleski-Jones, and Frank L. Mott. "The Intergenerational Costs of Parental Social Stressors: Academic and Social Difficulties in Early Adolescence for Children of Young Mothers." *Journal of Health and Social Behavior, 38*, March 1997:72–86.

Menzel, Peter. *Material World: A Global Family Portrait*. San Francisco: Sierra Club, 1994.

Merit Systems Protection Board. *Sexual Harassment in the Federal Workplace: Is It a Problem?* Washington, D.C.: Office of Merit Systems Review and Studies, 1981.

Merton, Robert K. *Social Theory and Social Structure*. Glencoe, Ill.: Free Press, 1949, Enlarged ed., 1968.

Merton, Robert K. "The Social-Cultural Environment and *Anomie*." In *New Perspectives for Research on Juvenile Delinquency*, Helen L. Witmer and Ruth Kotinsky, eds. Washington, D.C.: U.S. Department of Health, Education, and Welfare, 1956:24–50.

Merwine, Maynard H. "How Africa Understands Female Circumcision." *New York Times*, November 24, 1993.

Messner, Michael. "Boyhood, Organized Sports, and the Construction of Masculinities." *Journal of Contemporary Ethnography, 18*, 4, January 1990:416–444.

Meyrowitz, Joshua. "Shifting Worlds of Strangers: Medium Theory and Changes in 'Them' vs 'Us.'" Paper presented at the 1995 meetings of the American Sociological Association.

Michael, Robert T. "Measuring Poverty: A New Approach." *Focus, 17*, 1, Summer 1995:2–13.

Michalowski, Raymond J. *Order, Law, and Crime: An Introduction to Criminology*. New York: Random House, 1985.

Michels, Robert. *Political Parties*. Glencoe, Ill.: Free Press, 1949. First published in 1911.

Milbank, Dana. "Guarded by Greenbelts, Europe's Town Centers Thrive." *Wall Street Journal*, May 3, 1995a:B1, B4.

Milbank, Dana. "Working Poor Fear Welfare Cutbacks Aimed at the Idle Will Inevitably Strike Them, Too." *Wall Street Journal*, August 9, 1995b:A10.

Milbank, Dana. "No Fault Divorce Law Is Assailed in Michigan, and Debate Heats Up." *Wall Street Journal*, January 5, 1996:A1, A6.

Milgram, Stanley. "Behavioral Study of Obedience." *Journal of Abnormal and Social Psychology, 67*, 4, 1963:371–378.

Milgram, Stanley. "Some Conditions of Obedience and Disobedience to Authority." *Human Relations, 18*, February 1965:57–76.

Milgram, Stanley. "The Small World Problem." *Psychology Today, 1*, 1967:61–67.

Milkie, Melissa A. "Social World Approach to Cultural Studies." *Journal of Contemporary Ethnography, 23*, 3, October 1994:354–380.

Miller, Dan E. "Milgram Redux: Obedience and Disobedience in Authority Relations." In *Studies in Symbolic Interaction*, Norman K. Denzin, ed. Greenwich, Conn.: JAI Press, 1986:77–106.

Miller, John J. "Don't Close Our 'Golden Door.'" *Wall Street Journal*, May 25, 1995:A14.

Miller, Michael W. "Dark Days: The Staggering Cost of Depression." *Wall Street Journal*, December 2, 1993:B1, B6.

Miller, Walter B. "Lower Class Culture as a Generating Milieu of Gang Delinquency." *Journal of Social Issues, 14*, 3, 1958:5–19.

Miller-Loessi, Karen. "Toward Gender Integration in the Workplace: Issues at Multiple Levels." *Sociological Perspectives, 35*, 1, 1992:1–15.

Mills, C. Wright. *The Power Elite*. New York: Oxford University Press, 1956.

Mills, C. Wright. *The Sociological Imagination*. New York: Oxford University Press, 1959.

Mills, Karen M., and Thomas J. Palumbo. *A Statistical Portrait of Women in the United States: 1978*. U.S. Bureau of the Census, *Current Population Reports*, Series P-23, no. 100, 1980.

Miner, Horace. "Body Ritual among the Nacirema." In *Down to Earth Sociology: Introductory Readings*, 9th ed., James M. Henslin, ed. New York: Free Press, 1997:73–77.

Minkler, Meredith, and Ann Robertson. "The Ideology of 'Age/Race Wars': Deconstructing a Social Problem." *Ageing and Society, 11*, 1, March 1991:1–22.

Mintz, Beth A., and Michael Schwartz. *The Power Structure of American Business*. Chicago: University of Chicago Press, 1985.

Mitchell, G., Stephanie Obradovich, Fred Harring, Chris Tromborg, and Alyson L. Burns. "Reproducing Gender in Public Places: Adults' Attention to Toddlers in Three Public Locales." *Sex Roles, 26*, 7/8, 1992:323–330.

Mizruchi, Mark S., and Thomas Koenig. "Size, Concentration, and Corporate Networks: Determinants of Business Collective Action." *Social Science Quarterly, 72*, 2, June 1991:299–313.

Mohawk, John C. "Indian Economic Development: An Evolving Concept of Sovereignty." *Buffalo Law Review, 39*, 2, Spring 1991:495–503.

Money, John, and Anke A. Ehrhardt. *Man and Woman, Boy and Girl*. Baltimore: Johns Hopkins University Press, 1972.

Montagu, M. F. Ashley. *Introduction to Physical Anthropology*, 3rd ed. Springfield, Ill.: Thomas, 1960.

Montagu, M. F. Ashley. *The Concept of Race*. New York: Free Press, 1964.

Moore, Stephen D., and Ron Winslow. "Health-Care Systems in 12 Countries Near Crisis, Drug Maker Study Says." *Wall Street Journal*, September 15, 1993:B6.

Morgan, Lewis Henry. *Ancient Society*. 1877.

Morganthau, Tom. "Dr. Kevorkian's Death Wish." *Newsweek*, March 8, 1993:46–48.

Morris, Aldon. "Black Southern Student Sit-In Movement: An Analysis of Internal Organization." In *Collective Behavior and Social Movements*, Russell L. Curtis, Jr., and Benigno E. Aguirre, eds. Boston: Allyn and Bacon, 1993:361–380.

Morris, J. R. "Racial Attitudes of Undergraduates in Greek Housing." *College Student Journal, 25*, 1, March 1991:501–505.

Morrow, Betty Hearn. "Urban Families as Support after Disaster: The Case of Hurricane Andrew." Paper presented at the 1995 meetings of the American Sociological Association.

Moscos, Charles, C., and Sydney Butler. *All That We Can Be: Black Leadership and Racial Integration the Army Way*. New York: Basic Books, 1997.

Mosca, Gaetano. *The Ruling Class*. New York: McGraw-Hill, 1939. First published in 1896.

Mosher, Steven W. "Why Are Baby Girls Being Killed in China?" *Wall Street Journal*, July 25, 1983:9.

Mosher, Steven W. *A Mother's Ordeal: One Woman's Fight Against One-Child China.* New York: HarperCollins, 1994.

Mosher, Steven W. "Too Many People? Not by a Long Shot." *Wall Street Journal,* February 10, 1997:A18.

Mount, Ferdinand. *The Subversive Family: An Alternative History of Love and Marriage.* New York: Free Press, 1992.

Moyers, Bill. "Propaganda." In the series "A Walk Through the 20th Century." 1989. (video)

Moynihan, Daniel Patrick. "Social Justice in the *Next* Century." *America,* September 14, 1991:132–137.

Muehlenhard, Charlene L., and Melaney A. Linton. "Date Rape and Sexual Aggression in Dating Situations: Incidence and Risk Factors." *Journal of Counseling Psychology, 34,* 2, 1987:186–196.

Muir, Donal E. " 'White' Fraternity and Sorority Attitudes Toward 'Blacks' on a Deep-South Campus." *Sociological Spectrum, 11,* 1, January–March, 1991:93–103.

Murdock, George Peter. "Comparative Data on the Division of Labor by Sex." *Social Forces, 15,* 4, May 1937:551–553.

Murdock, George Peter. "The Common Denominator of Cultures." In *The Science of Man and the World Crisis,* Ralph Linton, ed. New York: Columbia University Press, 1945.

Murdock, George Peter. *Social Structure.* New York: Macmillan, 1949.

Murray, Charles. "The Coming White Underclass." *Wall Street Journal,* October 29, 1993:A16.

Murray, Charles, and R. J. Hernstein. "What's Really Behind the SAT-score Decline?" *Public Interest, 106,* Winter 1992:32–56.

Murray, G. W. *Sons of Ishmael.* London: Routledge, 1935.

Myers, Henry F. "Look for Jobless Rate to Stay High in '90s." *Wall Street Journal,* March 2, 1992:1.

Myrdal, Gunnar. *Challenge to Affluence.* New York: Pantheon Books, 1962.

Nachman, Sharon. "Elder Abuse and Neglect Substantiations: What They Tell Us About the Problem." *Journal of Elder Abuse and Neglect, 3,* 3, 1991:19–43.

Naj, Amal Kumar. "Some Manufacturers Drop Efforts to Adopt Japanese Techniques." *Wall Street Journal,* May 7, 1993:A1, A12.

Naj, Amal Kumar. "MIT Chemists Achieve Goal of Splitting Nitrogen Molecules in the Atmosphere." *Wall Street Journal,* May 12, 1995:B3.

Nakao, Keiko, and Judith Treas. "Occupational Prestige in the United States Revisited: Twenty-Five Years of Stability and Change." Paper presented at the annual meetings of the American Sociological Association, 1990. (As referenced in Kerbo, Harold R. *Social Stratification and Inequality: Class Conflict in Historical and Comparative Perspective.* 2nd ed. New York: McGraw-Hill, 1991:181.)

Narayan, Shoba. "A First in Child Care." *Boston Globe,* December 5, 1994:19–20.

Nash, Gary B. *Red, White, and Black.* Englewood Cliffs, N.J.: Prentice Hall, 1974.

National Center for Education Statistics. *Digest of Education Statistics.* Washington, D.C.: U.S. Government Printing Office, 1991.

National Women's Political Caucus. "Factsheet on Women's Political Progress." Washington, D.C., June 1995.

Nauta, André. "That They All May Be One: Can Denominationalism Die?" Paper presented at the annual meetings of the American Sociological Association, 1993.

Neikirk, William, and Glen Elsasser. "Ruling Weakens Abortion Right." *Chicago Tribune,* June 30, 1992:1, 8.

Nelson, Ruth K. "Letter to the Editor." *Wall Street Journal,* November 2, 1989:A23.

Neugarten, Bernice L. "Middle Age and Aging." In *Growing Old in America,* Beth B. Hess, ed. New Brunswick, N.J.: Transaction, 1976:180–197.

Neugarten, Bernice L. "Personality and Aging." In *Handbook of the Psychology of Aging,* James E. Birren and K. Warren Schaie, eds. New York: Van Nostrand Reinhold, 1977:626–649.

"The New Alchemy: How Science Is Molding Molecules into Miracle Materials." *Business Weekly,* July 29, 1991:48–55.

Newdorf, David. "Bailout Agencies Like to Do It in Secret." *Washington Journalism Review, 13,* 4, May 1991:15–16.

Niebuhr, H. Richard. *The Social Sources of Denominationalism.* New York: Holt, 1929.

Noah, Timothy. "White House Forms Panel to Investigate Cold War Radiation Tests on Humans." *Wall Street Journal,* January 4, 1994:A12.

Nsamenang, A. Bame. *Human Development in Cultural Context: A Third World Perspective.* Newbury Park, Calif.: Sage, 1992.

Oberschall, Anthony. *Social Conflict and Social Movements.* Englewood Cliffs, N.J.: Prentice Hall, 1973.

O'Brien, John E. "Violence in Divorce-Prone Families." In *Violence in the Family,* Suzanne K. Steinmetz and Murray A. Straus, eds. New York: Dodd, Mead, 1975:65–75.

O'Connell, Martin. "Where's Papa? Father's Role in Child Care." Population Trends and Public Policy no. 20. Washington, D.C.: Reference Bureau, September 1993.

Offen, Karen. "Feminism and Sexual Difference in Historical Perspective." In *Theoretical Perspectives on Sexual Difference,* Deborah L. Rhode, ed. New Haven, Conn.: Yale University Press, 1990:13–20.

Ogburn, William F. *Social Change with Respect to Culture and Human Nature.* New York: W. B. Huebsch, 1922. (Other editions by Viking in 1927, 1938, and 1950.)

Ogburn, William F. "The Hypothesis of Cultural Lag." In *Theories of Society: Foundations of Modern Sociological Theory,* Vol. 2, Talcott Parsons, Edward Shils, Kaspar D. Naegele, and Jesse R. Pitts, eds. New York: Free Press, 1961:1270–1273.

Ogburn, William F. *On Culture and Social Change: Selected Papers,* Otis Dudley Duncan, ed. Chicago: University of Chicago Press, 1964.

O'Hare, William P. "A New Look at Poverty in America." *Population Bulletin, 51,* 2, September 1996a:1–47.

O'Hare, William P. "U.S. Poverty Myths Explored: Many Poor Work Year-Round, Few Still Poor After Five Years." *Population Today: News, Numbers, and Analysis, 24,* 10, October 1996b:1–2.

Ohmae, Kenichi. *The End of the Nation State: The Rise of Regional Economies.* New York: Free Press, 1995.

Oliver, Pamela E., and Gerald Marwell. "Mobilizing Technologies for Collective Action." In *Frontiers in Social Movement Theory,* Aldon D. Morris and Carol McClurg Mueller, eds. New Haven, Conn.: Yale University Press, 1992:251–272.

Olmsted, Michael S., and A. Paul Hare. *The Small Group,* 2nd ed. New York: Random House, 1978.

Olneck, Michael R., and David B. Bills. "What Makes Sammy Run? An Empirical Assessment of the Bowles-Gintis Correspondence Theory." *American Journal of Education, 89,* 1980:27–61.

O'Malley, Jeff. "Sex Tourism and Women's Status in Thailand." *Society and Leisure, 11,* 1, Spring 1988:99–114.

O'Neill, Helen. "Strange, Strange Worlds." *Alton Telegraph,* April 6, 1997:A10.

Olshansky, S. Jay, Bruce Carnes, Richard G. Rogers, and Len Smith. "Infectious Diseases—New and Ancient Threats to World Health." *Population Bulletin*, 52, 2, July 1997:1–51.

Ono, Yumiko. "By Dint of Promotion Japanese Entrepreneur Ignites a Soccer Frenzy." *Wall Street Journal*, September 17, 1993:A1, A6.

Ono, Yumiko, and Jacob M. Schlesinger. "With Careful Planning, Japan Sets Out to Be 'Life Style Superpower.' " *Wall Street Journal*, October 10, 1992:A1, A11.

Ortega, Bob. "Portland, Ore., Shows Nation's City Planners How to Guide Growth." *Wall Street Journal*, December 26, 1995:A1, A8.

Ortega, Suzanne T., and Jay Corzine. "Socioeconomic Status and Mental Disorders." *Research in Community and Mental Health*, 6, 1990:149–182.

Orwell, George. *1984*. New York: Harcourt Brace, 1949.

Ouchi, William. *Theory Z: How American Business Can Meet the Japanese Challenge*. Reading, Mass.: Addison-Wesley, 1981.

Ouchi, William. "Decision-Making in Japanese Organizations." In *Down to Earth Sociology: Introductory Readings*, 7th ed., James M. Henslin, ed. New York: Free Press, 1993:503–507.

Overvold, Amy Zuckerman. *Surrogate Parenting*. New York: Pharos, 1988.

Pagelow, Mildred Daley. "Adult Victims of Domestic Violence: Battered Women." *Journal of Interpersonal Violence*, 7, 1, March 1992:87–120.

Palen, John J. *The Urban World*, 3rd ed., New York: McGraw-Hill, 1987.

Parfit, Michael, "Earth First!ers Wield a Mean Monkey Wrench." *Smithsonian*, 21, 1, April 1990:184–204.

Park, Robert Ezra. "Human Ecology." *American Journal of Sociology*, 42, 1, July 1936:1–15.

Park, Robert Ezra, and Ernest W. Burgess. *Human Ecology*. Chicago: University of Chicago Press, 1921a.

Park, Robert Ezra, and Ernest W. Burgess. *Introduction to the Science of Sociology*. Chicago: University of Chicago Press, 1921b. (As quoted in McPhail 1991:6)

Parkinson, C. Northcote. *Parkinson's Law and Other Studies in Administration*. New York: Ballantine Books, 1957.

Parsons, Talcott. "An Analytic Approach to the Theory of Social Stratification." *American Journal of Sociology*, 45, 1940:841–862.

Parsons, Talcott. *The Social System*. New York: Free Press, 1951.

Parsons, Talcott. "Illness and the Role of the Physician: A Sociological Perspective." In *Personality in Nature, Society, and Culture*, 2nd ed., Clyde Kluckhohn and Henry A. Murray, eds. New York: Knopf, 1953:609–617.

Parsons, Talcott. "The Professions and Social Structure." In *Essays in Sociological Theory*, rev. ed., Talcott Parsons, ed. New York: Free Press, 1954:34–49.

Parsons, Talcott. "The Sick Role and the Role of the Physician Reconsidered." *Milbank Memorial Fund Quarterly/Health and Society*, 53, 3, Summer 1975:257–278.

Passell, Peter. "Race, Mortgages and Statistics." *New York Times*, May 10, 1996:D1, D4.

Pasztor, Andy. "U.S., Grumman Reach Accord in Pentagon Case." *Wall Street Journal*, November 23, 1993:A3.

Paul, Ron. "Congressman Ron Paul." Newsletter issued April 1994.

Pearl, Daniel. "Futurist Schlock: Today's Cyberhype Has a Familiar Ring." *Wall Street Journal*, September 7, 1995a:A1, A6.

Pearl, Daniel. "Government Tackles a Surge of Smut on the Internet." *Wall Street Journal*, February 8, 1995b:B1, B8.

Pearlin, L. I., and Melvin L. Kohn. "Social Class, Occupation, and Parental Values: A Cross-National Study." *American Sociological Review*, 31, 1966:466–479.

Peart, Karen N. "Converts to the Faith." *Scholastic Update*, 126, 4, October 22, 1993:16–18.

Pennar, Karen, and Christopher Farrell. "Notes from the Underground Economy." *Business Week*, February 15, 1993:98–101.

Perrin, Kathleen. "Rationing Health Care: Should It Be Done?" In *Perspectives in Social Gerontology*, Robert B. Enright, Jr., ed. Boston: Allyn and Bacon, 1994:309–314.

Perrow, Charles. "A Society of Organizations." *Theory and Society*, 20, 6, December 1991:725–762.

Perry, James M. "Virginia's Wilder to Base Run for White House on Blend of Fiscal Conservatism and Compassion." *Wall Street Journal*, December 19, 1990:A18.

Persell, Caroline Hodges, Sophia Catsambis, and Peter W. Cookson, Jr. "Family Background, School Type, and College Attendance: A Conjoint System of Cultural Capital Transmission." *Journal of Research on Adolescence*, 2, 1, 1992:1–23.

Persell, Caroline Hodges, and Peter W. Cookson, Jr. "Where the Power Starts." *Signature*, August 1986:51–57.

Peter, Laurence J., and Raymond Hull. *The Peter Principle: Why Things Always Go Wrong*. New York: Morrow, 1969.

Peterson, James L., and Nicholas Zill. "Marital Disruption, Parent–Child Relationships, and Behavior Problems in Children." *Journal of Marriage and the Family*, 48, 1986:295–307.

Peterson, Paul E. "Vouching for a Religious Education." *Wall Street Journal*, December 28, 1995:A6.

Phillips, John L., Jr. *The Origins of Intellect: Piaget's Theory*. San Francisco: Freeman, 1969.

Piaget, Jean. *The Psychology of Intelligence*. London: Routledge & Kegan Paul, 1950.

Piaget, Jean. *The Construction of Reality in the Child*. New York: Basic Books, 1954.

Pillemer, Karl, and Beth Hudson. "A Model Abuse Prevention Program for Nursing Assistants." *Gerontologist*, 33, 1, 1993:128–131.

Pillemer, Karl, and J. Jill Suitor. "Violence and Violent Feelings: What Causes Them Among Family Caregivers?" *Journal of Gerontology*, 47, 4, 1992:165–172.

Pillemer, Karl, and Rosalie S. Wolf. *Elder Abuse: Conflict in the Family*. Dover, Mass.: Auburn House, 1987.

Pilling, D., and M. Kellmer Pringle. *Controversial Issues in Child Development*. London: Paul Elek, 1978.

Pines, Maya. "The Civilizing of Genie." *Psychology Today*, 15, September 1981:28–34.

Piotrow, Phylis Tilson. *World Population Crisis: The United States' Response*. New York: Praeger, 1973.

Piturro, Marlene. "Managing Diversity." *Executive Female*, May–June 1991:45–46, 48.

Piven, Frances Fox, and Richard A. Cloward. *Why Americans Don't Vote*. New York: Pantheon Books, 1988.

Platt, Tony. " 'Street' Crime—A View from the Left." *Crime and Social Justice: Issues in Criminology*, 9, 1978:26–34.

Polenberg, Richard. *One Nation Divisible: Class, Race, and Ethnicity in the United States Since 1938*. New York: Penguin, 1980.

Pollak, Lauren Harte, and Peggy A. Thoits. "Processes in Emotional Socialization." *Social Psychological Quarterly*, 52, 1, 1989:22–34.

Polsby, Nelson W. "Three Problems in the Analysis of Community Power." *American Sociological Review*, 24, 6, December 1959:796–803.

Polumbaum, Judy. "China: Confucian Tradition Meets the Market Economy." *Ms.*, September–October 1992:12–13.

Pope, Liston. *Millhands and Preachers: A Study of Gastonia*. New Haven, Conn.: Yale University Press, 1942.

Popenoe, David. *Life Without Father*. New York: Free Press, 1996.

"Population, Consumption, and the Earth's Future." *Population Today*, April 1996:4.

Population Reference Bureau. "World Information Data Sheet." Washington, D.C., May 1995.

"Population Update." *Population Today*, 25, 4, April 1997:6.

Portés, Alejandro, and Ruben G. Rumbaut. *Immigrant America*. Berkeley: University of California Press, 1990.

Postman, Neil. *Technopoly: The Surrender of Culture to Technology*. New York: Knopf, 1992.

Presley, Cheryl A., Philip W. Meilman, and Rob Lyerla. *Alcohol and Drugs on American College Campuses*. Carbondale, Ill.: Southern Illinois University, 1993.

Pressley, Sue Anne. "The Curious Continue Waco Siege." *Washington Post*, August 28, 1993:A1, A12.

Preston, Howard L. *Automobile Age Atlanta: The Making of a Southern Metropolis, 1900–1935*. Athens: University of Georgia Press, 1979.

Price, Daniel O., ed. *The 99th Hour*. Chapel Hill: University of North Carolina Press, 1967.

"Price of Entry into China Rises Sharply." *Wall Street Journal*, December 19, 1995:A12.

Prud'Homme, Alex. "Getting a Grip on Power." *Time*, July 29, 1991:15–16.

Public Information Bureau. "Information given by telephone." New York, March 24, 1994.

"Racial Balkanization at Cornell." *Wall Street Journal*, July 25, 1995:A10.

Ramo, Joshua Cooper. "Finding God on the Web." *Time*, December 16, 1996:60–67.

Rathus, Spencer, and Jeffrey Nevid. *Human Sexuality in a World of Diversity*. Boston: Allyn and Bacon, 1993.

Ray, J. J. "Authoritarianism Is a Dodo: Comment on Scheepers, Felling and Peters." *European Sociological Review*, 7, 1, May 1991:73–75.

Raymond, Chris. "New Studies by Anthropologists Indicate Amish Communities Are Much More Dynamic and Diverse Than Many Believed." *Chronicle of Higher Education*, December 19, 1990:A1, A9.

Raymond, Janice G. *Women as Wombs: Reproductive Technologies and the Battle over Women's Freedom*. New York: HarperCollins, 1993.

Read, Piers Paul. *Alive. The Story of the Andes Survivors*. Philadelphia: Lippincott, 1974.

Reckless, Walter C. *The Crime Problem*, 5th ed. New York: Appleton, 1973.

Reed, Susan, and Lorenzo Benet. "Ecowarrior Dave Foreman Will Do Whatever It Takes in His Fight to Save Mother Earth." *People Weekly*, 33, 15, April 16, 1990:113–116.

Reibstein, Larry. "Managing Diversity." *Newsweek*, November 25, 1996:50.

Reich, Michael. "The Economics of Racism." In *The Capitalist System*, Richard C. Edwards, Michael Reich, and Thomas E. Weiskopf, eds. Englewood Cliffs, N.J.: Prentice Hall, 1972:313–321.

Reich, Robert B. *Good for Business: Making Full Use of the Nation's Human Capital, The Environmental Scan*. Washington, D.C.: U.S. Department of Labor, March 1995.

Reitman, Valerie. "Japan's New Growth Industry: Schoolgirl Prostitution." *Wall Street Journal*, October 2, 1996:A8.

Reitman, Valerie, and Oscar Suris. "In a Cultural U-Turn, Mazda's Creditors Put Ford Behind the Wheel." *Wall Street Journal*, November 21, 1994:A1, A4.

Renteln, Alison Dundes. "Sex Selection and Reproductive Freedom." *Women's Studies International Forum*, 15, 3, 1992:405–426.

Renzetti, Claire M., and Daniel J. Curran. *Women, Men, and Society*, 2nd ed. Boston: Allyn and Bacon, 1992.

Rich, Spencer. "Number of Elected Hispanic Officials Doubled in a Decade, Study Shows." *Washington Post*, September 19, 1986:A6.

Richards, Bill. "Doctors Can Diagnose Illnesses Long Distance, to the Dismay of Some." *Wall Street Journal*, January 17, 1996:A1, A8.

Ricks, Thomas E. "Pentagon Considers Selling Overseas a Large Part of High-Tech Weaponry." *Wall Street Journal*, February 14, 1994:A16.

Ricks, Thomas E. "'New' Marines Illustrate Growing Gap Between Military and Society." *Wall Street Journal*, July 27, 1995:A1, A4.

Rieker, Patricia P., Chloe E. Bird, Susan Bell, Jenny Ruducha, Rima E. Rudd, and S. M. Miller, "Violence and Women's Health: Toward a Society and Health Perspective." Unpublished paper, 1997.

Riesman, David. *The Lonely Crowd*. New Haven, Conn.: Yale University Press, 1950.

Riesman, David. "The Suburban Dislocation." In *Urban Man and Society: A Reader in Urban Ecology*, Albert N. Cousins and Hans Nagpaul, eds. New York: Knopf, 1970:172–184.

Riessman, Catherine Kohler. "Women and Medicalization: A New Perspective." In *Dominant Issues in Medical Sociology*, 3rd ed., Howard D. Schwartz, ed. New York: McGraw-Hill, 1994:190–211.

Rifkin, Jeremy. *The End of Work: The Decline of the Global Labor Force and the Dawn of the Post-Market Era*. New York: Putnam, 1995.

Rigdon, Joan E., and Alecia Swasy. "Distractions of Modern Life at Key Ages Are Cited for Drop in Student Literacy." *Wall Street Journal*, October 1, 1990:B1, B3.

Riley, Nancy E. "Gender, Power, and Population Change." *Population Bulletin*, 52, 1, May 1997:1–47.

Rist, Ray C. "Student Social Class and Teacher Expectations: The Self-Fulfilling Prophecy in Ghetto Education." *Harvard Educational Review*, 40, 3, August 1970:411–451.

Ritzer, George. *Sociological Theory*, 3rd ed. New York: McGraw-Hill, 1992.

Ritzer, George. *The McDonaldization of Society: An Investigation into the Changing Character of Contemporary Life*. Thousand Oaks, Calif.: Pine Forge Press, 1993.

Ritzer, George. "The McDonaldization of Society." In *Down to Earth Sociology: Introductory Readings*, 9th ed., James M. Henslin, ed. New York: Free Press, 1997:492–504.

Robertson, Ian. "Social Stratification." In *The Study of Anthropology*, David E. Hunter and Phillip Whitten, eds. New York: Harper & Row, 1976.

Robertson, Ian. *Sociology*, 3rd ed. New York: Worth, 1987.

Robertson, Roland. *Globalization: Social Theory and Global Culture*. London: Sage, 1992.

Robinson, Arthur B., and Zachary W. Robinson. "Science Has Spoken: Global Warming is a Myth." *Wall Street Journal*, December 4, 1997:A22.

Rodash, Mary Flannery. "The College of Midwifery: A Sociological Study of the Decline of a Profession." Unpublished doctoral dissertation, Southern Illinois University at Carbondale, 1982.

Rodriguez, Richard. "The Education of Richard Rodriguez." *Saturday Review*, February 8, 1975:147–149.

Rodriguez, Richard. *Hunger of Memory: The Education of Richard Rodriguez*. Boston: Godine, 1982.

Rodriguez, Richard. "The Late Victorians: San Francisco, AIDS, and the Homosexual Stereotype." *Harper's Magazine*, October 1990:57–66.

Rodriguez, Richard. "Mixed Blood." *Harper's Magazine, 283,* November 1991:47–56.

Rodriguez, Richard. "Searching for Roots in a Changing Society." In *Down to Earth Sociology: Introductory Readings*, 8th ed., James M. Henslin, ed. New York: Free Press, 1995:486–491.

Rodríguez, Victor M. "Los Angeles, U.S.A. 1992: 'A House Divided Against Itself . . .'" *SSSP Newsletter,* Spring 1994:5–12.

Rodwin, Marc A. *Medicine, Money, and Morals: Physicians' Conflicts of Interest*. New York: Oxford University Press, 1993.

Roethlisberger, Fritz J., and William J. Dickson. *Management and the Worker*. Cambridge, Mass.: Harvard University Press, 1939.

Rogers, Joseph W. *Why Are You Not a Criminal?* Englewood Cliffs, N.J.: Prentice Hall, 1977.

Rohen, Thomas P. *Japan's High Schools*. Berkeley: University of California Press, 1983.

Rosaldo, Michelle Zimbalist. "Women, Culture and Society: A Theoretical Overview." In *Women, Culture, and Society*, Michelle Zimbalist Rosaldo and Louise Lamphere, eds. Stanford: Stanford University Press, 1974.

Rose, Frederick. "Los Angeles Tallies Losses; Curfew Is Lifted." *Wall Street Journal*, May 5, 1992:A3, A18.

Rose, Steven. "Stalking the Criminal Chromosome." *Nation 242* (20), 1986:732–736.

Rosenberg, Charles E. *The Care of Strangers: The Rise of America's Hospital System*. New York: Basic Books, 1987.

Rosenthal, Elisabeth. "From Lives Begun in Lab, Brave New Joy." *New York Times*, January 1, 1996:A1.

Rosenthal, Robert, and Lenore Jacobson. *Pygmalion in the Classroom: Teacher Expectation and Pupils' Intellectual Development*. New York: Holt, Rinehart, and Winston, 1968.

Ross, Catherine E., and Marieke van Willigen. "Education and the Subjective Quality of Life." *Journal of Health and Social Behavior, 38,* 3, September 1997:275–297.

Rossi, Alice S. "A Biosocial Perspective on Parenting." *Daedalus, 106,* 1977:1–31.

Rossi, Alice S. "Gender and Parenthood." *American Sociological Review, 49,* 1984:1–18.

Rossi, Peter H. *Down and Out in America: The Origins of Homelessness*. Chicago: University of Chicago Press, 1989.

Rossi, Peter H. "Going Along or Getting It Right?" *Journal of Applied Sociology, 8,* 1991:77–81.

Rossi, Peter H., Gene A. Fisher, and Georgianna Willis. *The Condition of the Homeless of Chicago*. Amherst: University of Massachusetts, September 1986.

Rossi, Peter H., James D. Wright, Gene A. Fisher, and Georgianna Willis. "The Urban Homeless: Estimating Composition and Size." *Science, 235,* March 13, 1987:1136–1140.

Rotello, Gabriel. "The Risk in a 'Cure' for AIDS." *New York Times*, July 14, 1996.

Rothman, Barbara Katz. *In Labor: Women and Power in the Birthplace*. New York: W. W. Norton, 1982.

Rothman, Barbara Katz. *Recreating Motherhood: Ideology and Technology in a Patriarchal Society*. New York: Norton, 1989.

Rothman, Barbara Katz. "Midwives in Transition: The Structure of a Clinical Revolution." In *Dominant Issues in Medical Sociology*, 3rd ed. Howard D. Schwartz, ed. New York: McGraw-Hill, 1994:104–112.

Rothschild, Joyce, and J. Allen Whitt. *The Cooperative Workplace: Potentials and Dilemmas of Organizational Democracy and Participation*. Cambridge, England: Cambridge University Press, 1986.

Rubenstein, Carin. "Is There Sex After Baby?" In *Marriage and Family in a Changing Society*, 4th ed., James M. Henslin, ed. New York: Free Press, 1992:235–242.

Rubin, Lillian Breslow. *Worlds of Pain: Life in the Working-Class Family*. New York: Basic Books, 1976.

Rubin, Lillian Breslow. "The Empty Nest." In *Marriage and Family in a Changing Society*, 4th ed., James M. Henslin, ed. New York: Free Press, 1992a:261–270.

Rubin, Lillian Breslow. "Worlds of Pain." In *Marriage and Family in a Changing Society*, 4th ed., James M. Henslin, ed. New York: Free Press, 1992b:44–50.

Rubin, Zick. "The Love Research." In *Marriage and Family in a Changing Society*, 2nd ed., James M. Henslin, ed. New York: Free Press, 1985.

Ruffenbach, Glenn. "Nursing-Home Care as a Work Benefit." *Wall Street Journal*, June 30, 1988:23.

Ruggles, Patricia. "Short and Long Term Poverty in the United States: Measuring the American 'Underclass.'" Washington, D.C.: Urban Institute, June 1989.

Rushing, William A. *The AIDS Epidemic: Social Dimensions of an Infectious Disease*. Boulder, Colo.: Westview Press, 1995.

Russell, Diana E. H. "Preliminary Report on Some Findings Relating to the Trauma and Long-Term Effects of Intrafamily Childhood Sexual Abuse." Unpublished paper.

Russell, Diana E. H. *Rape in Marriage*. Bloomington: Indiana University Press, 1990.

Russell, Dick. "The Monkeywrenchers." *Amicus Journal,* Fall 1987:28–42.

Sahlins, Marshall D. *Stone Age Economics*. Chicago: Aldine, 1972.

Sahlins, Marshall D., and Elman R. Service. *Evolution and Culture*. Ann Arbor: University of Michigan Press, 1960.

Salas, Rosalinda. Personal correspondence, May 1996.

Salholz, Eloise. "The Push for Power." *Newsweek*, April 9, 1990:19–20.

Sampson, Catherine. "Corrupt Care." *World Press Review, 39,* 5, May 1992:46.

Samuelson, Paul A., and William D. Nordhaus. *Economics*, 13th ed. New York: McGraw-Hill, 1989.

Samuelson, Robert J. "The Elderly Aren't Needy." *Newsweek*, March 21, 1988:68.

Sanchez, Laura. "Gender, Labor Allocations, and the Psychology of Entitlement Within the Home." *Social Forces, 13,* 2, December 1994:533–553.

Sandefur, Gary D. "Children in Single-Parent Families: The Roles of Time and Money." *Focus, 17,* 1, Summer 1995:44–45.

Sapir, Edward. "The Status of Linguistics as Science." In: *Culture, Language, and Personality*. David G. Mandelbaum, ed. Berkeley, Calif.: University of California Press, 1949.

Sapir, Edward. *Selected Writings of Edward Sapir in Language, Culture, and Personality.* David G. Mandelbaum, ed. Berkeley, Calif.: University of California Press, 1949.

Sayres, William. "What Is a Family Anyway?" In *Marriage and Family in a Changing Society*, 4th ed., James M. Henslin, ed. New York: Free Press, 1992:23–30.

Saxe, G. B. "Candy Selling and Math Learning." *Educational Researcher*, 17(6), 1988:14–21.

Scarce, Rik. "Rik Scarce Responds: A Clear-cut Case of Academic Freedom at Risk." *Daily News* (Moscow-Pullman), June 12–13, 1993a:1B.

Scarce, Rik. "Turnabout: Jailed for No Crime at All." *Morning Tribune* (Lewiston), June 15, 1993b.

Scarce, Rik. "(No) Trial (But) Tribulations." *Journal of Contemporary Ethnography*, 23, 2, July 1994:123–149.

Scarr, Sandra, and Marlene Eisenberg. "Child Care Research: Issues, Perspectives, and Results." *Annual Review of Psychology*, 44, 1993:613–644.

Schaefer, Richard T., *Racial and Ethnic Groups.* Boston: Little Brown, 1979.

Schaefer, Richard T. *Sociology*, 3rd ed. New York: McGraw-Hill, 1989.

Schafran, Lynn Hecht. "Rape Is Still Underreported." *New York Times*, August 29, 1995:19.

Schatz, Thomas A. "Medicare Fraud: Tales from the Gypped." *Wall Street Journal*, August 25, 1995:A8.

Schlesinger, Jacob M. "For What Ails Japan, Some Think the Cure Is a Good Hot Slogan." *Wall Street Journal*, January 31, 1994:A1, A7.

Schlesinger, Jacob M., and Jathon Sapsford. "Japan, Shaken by Plunging Stocks, Mulls Further Economic Measures." *Wall Street Journal*, December 1, 1993:A14.

Schlesinger, Jacob M., Michael Williams, and Craig Forman. "Japan Inc., Wracked by Recession, Takes Stock of Its Methods." *Wall Street Journal*, September 29, 1993:A1, A4.

Schlossberg, Nancy. *Overwhelmed: Coping with Life's Ups and Downs.* Boston: Lexington Books, 1990.

Schor, Juliet B. "Americans Work Too Hard." *New York Times*, July 25, 1991:A21.

Schottland, Charles I. *The Social Security Plan in the U.S.* New York: Appleton, 1963.

Schrieke, Bertram J. *Alien Americans.* New York: Viking, 1936.

Schur, Edwin M. *Labeling Women Deviant: Gender, Stigma, and Social Control.* New York: Random House, 1984.

Schwartz, Barry. "Waiting, Exchange, and Power: The Distribution of Time in Social Systems." In *Down to Earth Sociology: Introductory Readings*, 6th ed. New York: Free Press, 1991:217–224.

Schwartz, Felice N. "Management Women and the New Facts of Life." *Harvard Business Review*, 89, 1, January–February 1989:65–76.

Schwartz, Mildred A. *A Sociological Perspective on Politics.* Englewood Cliffs, N.J.: Prentice Hall, 1990.

Schwendinger, Julia R., and Herman Schwendinger. *Rape and Inequality.* Beverly Hills, Calif.: Sage, 1983.

Scommegna, Paola. "Teens' Risk of AIDS, Unintended Pregnancies Examined." *Population Today*, 24, 8, August 1996:1–2.

Scott, Ellen Kaye. "How to Stop the Rapists: A Question of Strategy in Two Rape Crisis Centers." *Social Problems*, 40, 3, August 1993:343–361.

Scully, Diana. *Understanding Sexual Violence: A Study of Convicted Rapists.* Boston: Unwin Hyman, 1990.

Scully, Diana. "Negotiating to Do Surgery." In *Dominant Issues in Medical Sociology*, 3rd ed., Howard D. Schwartz, ed. New York: McGraw-Hill, 1994:146–152.

Scully, Diana, and Joseph Marolla. "Convicted Rapists' Vocabulary of Motive: Excuses and Justifications." *Social Problems*, 31, 5, June 1984:530–544.

Scully, Diana, and Joseph Marolla. " 'Riding the Bull at Gilley's': Convicted Rapists Describe the Rewards of Rape." *Social Problems*, 32, 3, February 1985:251–263.

Searle, John R. *The Construction of Social Reality.* New York: Free Press, 1995.

Seaver, W. J. "Effects of Naturally Induced Teacher Expectancies." *Journal of Personality and Social Psychology*, 28, 1973:333–342.

Seib, Gerald F. "In Historic Numbers, Men and Women Split Over Presidential Race." *Wall Street Journal*, January 11, 1996:A1, A6.

Seltzer, Judith A. "Consequences of Marital Dissolution for Children." *Annual Review of Sociology*, 20, 1994:235–266.

Sennett, Richard, and Jonathan Cobb. *The Hidden Injuries of Class.* New York: Knopf, 1972.

Sennett, Richard, and Jonathan Cobb. "Some Hidden Injuries of Class." In *Down to Earth Sociology: Introductory Readings*, 5th ed., James M. Henslin, ed. New York: Free Press, 1988:278–288.

Seubert, Virginia R. "Sociology and Value Neutrality: Limiting Sociology to the Empirical Level." *American Sociologist*, Fall–Winter 1991:210–220.

"Sexual Identity Is Inborn Trait, According to Study." *Alton Telegraph*, March 16, 1997:A6.

Shanker, Albert. "Education Contract with America." *Wall Street Journal*, September 15, 1995:A10.

Shanks-Meile, Stephanie, and Betty A. Dobratz. " 'Sick' Feminists or Helpless Victims: Images of Women in Ku Klux Klan and American Nazi Party Literature." *Humanity and Society*, 15, 1, 1991:71–92.

Sharma, S. S. "Untouchables and Brahmins in an Indian Village." In *Haves and Have-Nots: An International Reader on Social Inequality*, James Curtis and Lorne Tepperman, eds. Englewood Cliffs, N.J.: Prentice Hall, 1994:299–303.

Sharp, Deborah. "Miami's Language Gap Widens." *USA Today*, April 3, 1992:A1, A3.

Sharp, Lauriston. "Steel Axes for Stone-Age Australians." In *Down to Earth Sociology: Introductory Readings*, 8th ed., James M. Henslin, ed. New York: Free Press, 1995:453–462.

Shaw, Sue. "Wretched of the Earth." *New Statesman*, 20, March 1987:19–20.

Sheldon, William. *Varieties of Delinquent Youth: An Introduction to Constitutional Psychiatry.* New York: Harper, 1949.

Shellenbarger, Sue. "The Aging of America Is Making 'Elder Care' a Big Workplace Issue." *Wall Street Journal*, February 16, 1994a:A1, A8.

Shellenbarger, Sue. "How Some Companies Help with Elder Care." *Wall Street Journal*, February 16, 1994b:A8.

Shellenbarger, Sue. "Child Care Is Worse Than Believed, with Safety Jeopardized, Study Suggests." *Wall Street Journal*, February 6, 1995a:A7.

Shellenbarger, Sue. "Work and Family." *Wall Street Journal*, May 3, 1995b:B1.

Shenon, Philip. "AIDS Epidemic, Late to Arrive, Now Explodes in Populous Asia." *New York Times*, January 2, 1995:A1, A12.

Shenon, Philip. "Arguments Conclude in Army Sex Hearing." *New York Times*, August 26, 1997 (electronic version).

Sherif, Muzafer, and Carolyn Sherif. *Groups in Harmony and Tension*. New York: Harper & Row, 1953.

Sherkat, Darren E., and John Wilson. "Status, Denomination, and Socialization: Effects on Religious Switching and Apostasy." Presented at the annual meetings of the American Sociological Association, 1991.

Sherman, Spencer. "The Hmong in America." *National Geographic*, October 1988:586–610.

Shibutani, Tamotsu. *Improvised News: A Sociological Study of Rumor*. Indianapolis, Ind.: Bobbs-Merrill, 1966.

Shibutani, Tamotsu. "On the Personification of Adversaries." In *Human Nature and Collective Behavior*, Tamotsu Shibutani, ed. Englewood Cliffs, N.J.: Prentice Hall, 1970.

Shill, Walt. "Lessons of the Japanese Mavericks." *Wall Street Journal*, November 1, 1993:A18.

Shirouzu, Norihiko. "Reconstruction Boom in Tokyo: Perfecting Imperfect Bellybuttons." *Wall Street Journal*, October 4, 1995.

Shirouzu, Norihiko, and Michael Williams. "Pummeled by Giants, Japan's Small Firms Struggle with Change." *Wall Street Journal*, July 25, 1995:A1, A5.

Shively, JoEllen. "Cultural Compensation: The Popularity of Westerns Among American Indians," Paper presented at the annual meetings of the American Sociological Association, 1991.

Shively, JoEllen. "Cowboys and Indians: Perceptions of Western Films Among American Indians and Anglos." *American Sociological Review*, 57, December 1992:725–734.

Shreve, Herbie. Personal communication, 1991.

Signorielli, Nancy. "Television and Conceptions About Sex Roles: Maintaining Conventionality and the Status Quo." *Sex Roles*, 21, 5/6, 1989:341–360.

Signorielli, Nancy. "Children, Television, and Gender Roles: Messages and Impact." *Journal of Adolescent Heath Care*, 11, 1990:50–58.

Sills, David L. *The Volunteers*. Glencoe, Ill.: Free Press, 1957.

Sills, David L. "Voluntary Associations: Sociological Aspects." In *International Encyclopedia of the Social Sciences*, 16, David L. Sills, ed. New York: Macmillan, 1968:362–379.

Silver, Isidore. "Crime and Conventional Wisdom." *Society*, 14, March–April, 1977:9, 15–19.

Simmel, Georg. *The Sociology of Georg Simmel*, Kurt H. Wolff, ed. and trans. Glencoe, Ill.: Free Press, 1950. First published between 1902 and 1917.

Simon, David R., and D. Stanley Eitzen. *Elite Deviance*, 4th ed. Boston: Allyn and Bacon, 1993.

Simon, Julian L. *The Ultimate Resource*. Princeton, N.J.: Princeton University Press, 1981.

Simon, Julian L. *Theory of Population and Economic Growth*. New York: Blackwell, 1986.

Simon, Julian L. "Population Growth Is Not Bad for Humanity." In *Taking Sides: Clashing Views on Controversial Social Issues*, Kurt Finsterbusch and George McKenna, eds. Guilford, Conn.: Dushkin, 1992:347–352.

Simon, Julian L. "The Nativists Are Wrong." *Wall Street Journal*, August 4, 1993:A10.

Simon, Julian L. *The Ultimate Resource 2*. Princeton, N.J.: Princeton University Press, 1996.

Simons, Marlise. "The Amazon's Savvy Indians." In *Down to Earth Sociology: Introductory Readings*, 8th ed. James M. Henslin, ed. New York: Free Press, 1995:463–470.

Simpson, George Eaton, and J. Milton Yinger. *Racial and Cultural Minorities: An Analysis of Prejudice and Discrimination*, 4th ed. New York: Harper & Row, 1972.

Singh, Ajit. "Urbanism, Poverty, and Employment: The Large Metropolis in the Third World." Unpublished monograph, Cambridge University, 1988. As quoted in Giddens, Anthony. *Introduction to Sociology*. New York: W. W. Norton, 1991:690.

Skeels, H. M. *Adult Status of Children with Contrasting Early Life Experiences: A Follow-up Study*. Monograph of the Society for Research in Child Development, *31*, 3, 1966.

Skeels, H. M., and H. B. Dye. "A Study of the Effects of Differential Stimulation on Mentally Retarded Children." *Proceedings and Addresses of the American Association on Mental Deficiency*, *44*, 1939:114–136.

Small, Albion W. *General Sociology*. Chicago: University of Chicago Press, 1905. As cited in Olmsted and Hare 1978:10.

Smart, Barry. "On the Disorder of Things: Sociology, Postmodernity and the 'End of the Social.'" *Sociology*, *24*, 3, August 1990:397–416.

Smith, Beverly A. "An Incest Case in an Early 20th-Century Rural Community." *Deviant Behavior*, *13*, 1992:127–153.

Smith, Clark. "Oral History as 'Therapy': Combatants' Account of Vietnam War." In *Strangers at Home: Vietnam Veterans Since the War*, Charles R. Figley and Seymore Leventman, eds. New York: Praeger, 1980:9–34.

Smith, Craig S. "China Becomes Industrial Nations' Most Favored Dump." *Wall Street Journal*, October 9, 1995:B1.

Smith, Daniel Scott, and Michael Hindus. "Premarital Pregnancy in America, 1640–1971: An Overview and Interpretation." *Journal of Interdisciplinary History*, *4*, Spring 1975:537–570.

Smith, Douglas A., and Robert Brame. "On the Initiation and Continuation of Delinquency." *Criminology*, *32*, 4, 1994:607–629.

Smith, Harold. "A Colossal Cover-Up." *Christianity Today*, December 12, 1986:16–17.

Smith, Joel B., and Dennis A. Tirpak. *The Potential Effects of Global Climate Change in the United States*. Washington, D.C.: U.S. Environmental Protection Agency, October 1988.

Smith, Kristen F., and Vern L. Bengston. "Positive Consequences of Institutionalization: Solidarity Between Elderly Parents and Their Middle-Aged Children." *Gerontologist*, *19*, October 1979:438–447.

Smith, Lee. "The War Between the Generations." *Fortune*, July 20, 1987:78–82.

Smith, Thomas M. *The Condition of Education 1996*. Washington, D.C.: U.S. Government Printing Office, 1996.

Smith-Lovin, Lynn, and Charles Brody. "Interruptions in Group Discussions: The Effects of Gender and Group Composition." *American Sociological Review*, *54*, 1989:424–435.

Snow, David A., Louis A. Zurcher, Jr., and Sheldon Ekland-Olson. "Social Networks and Social Movements: A Microstructural Approach to Differential Recruitment." In *Collective Behavior and Social Movements*, Russell L. Curtis, Jr., and Benigno E. Aguirre, eds. Boston: Allyn and Bacon, 1993:323–334.

Snow, David A., Louis A. Zurcher, and Robert Peters. "Victory Celebrations as Theater: A Dramaturgical Approach to Crowd Behavior." In *Collective Behavior and Social Movements*, Russell L. Curtis, Jr., and Benigno E. Aguirre, eds. Boston: Allyn and Bacon, 1993:194–208.

Snow, Margaret E., Carol Nagy Jacklin, and Eleanor E. Maccoby. "Birth-Order Differences in Peer Sociability at Thirty-Three Months." *Child Development*, *52*, 1981:589–595.

Snyder, Mark. "Self-Fulfilling Stereotypes." In *Down to Earth Sociology: Introductory Readings*, 7th ed., James M. Henslin, ed. New York: Free Press, 1993:153–160.

Solomon, Jolie. "Companies Try Measuring Cost Savings from New Types of Corporate Benefits." *Wall Street Journal*, December 29, 1988:B1.

Sontag, Susan. As quoted in Catherine Kohler Riessman, "Women and Medicalization: A New Perspective." In *Dominant Issues in Medical Sociology*, 3rd ed., Howard D. Schwartz, ed. New York: McGraw-Hill, 1994:190–211.

Sorokin, Pitirim A. *Social and Cultural Dynamics.* 4 vols. New York: American Book Company, 1937–1941.

Sorokin, Pitirim A. *The Crisis of Our Age.* New York: Dutton, 1941.

Sourcebook of Criminal Justice Statistics. Washington, D.C.: U.S. Government Printing Office, published annually.

South, Scott J. "Sociodemographic Differentials in Mate Selection Preferences." *Journal of Marriage and the Family, 53,* November 1991:928–940.

Sowell, Thomas. "Effrontery and Gall, Inc." *Forbes*, September 27, 1993a:52.

Sowell, Thomas. *Inside American Education: The Decline, the Deception, the Dogmas.* New York: Free Press, 1993b.

Specter, Michael. "Plunging Life Expectancy Puzzles Russians." *New York Times*, August 1, 1995:A1, A6.

Spector, Malcolm, and John Kitsuse. *Constructing Social Problems.* Menlo Park, Calif.: Cummings, 1977.

Spencer, Herbert. *Principles of Sociology.* 3 vols. New York: Appleton, 1884.

Spengler, Oswald. *The Decline of the West, 2* vols. Charles F. Atkinson, trans. New York: Knopf, 1926–1928. First published in 1919–1922.

Spitz, Renée. "Hospitalism." *Psychoanalytic Study of the Child, 1,* 1945:53–72.

Spitzer, Steven. "Toward a Marxian Theory of Deviance." *Social Problems, 22,* June 1975:608–619.

Spragins, Ellyn E. "To Sue or Not to Sue?" *Newsweek*, December 9, 1996:50.

Sprecher, Susan, and Rachita Chandak. "Attitudes About Arranged Marriages and Dating Among Men and Women from India." *Free Inquiry in Creative Sociology, 20,* 1, May 1992:59–69.

Srisang, Koson. "The Ecumenical Coalition on Third World Tourism." *Annals of Tourism Research, 16,* 1, 1989:119–121.

Srole, Leo, et al. *Mental Health in the Metropolis: The Midtown Manhattan Study.* New York: New York University Press, 1978.

Stack, Carol B. *All Our Kin: Strategies for Survival in a Black Community.* New York: Harper, 1974.

Stampp, Kenneth M. *The Peculiar Institution: Slavery in the Ante-Bellum South.* New York: Vintage Books, 1956.

Stark, Elizabeth. "Friends Through It All." In *Marriage and Family in a Changing Society*, 3rd ed., James M. Henslin, ed. New York: Free Press, 1989:441–449.

Stark, Rodney. *Sociology*, 3rd ed. Belmont, Calif.: Wadsworth, 1989.

Starna, William A., and Ralph Watkins. "Northern Iroquoian Slavery." *Ethnohistory, 38,* 1, Winter 1991:34–57.

Starr, Paul. *The Social Transformation of American Medicine.* New York: Basic Books, 1982.

Starrels, Marjorie. "The Evolution of Workplace Family Policy Research." *Journal of Family Issues, 13,* 3, September 1992:259–278.

Statham, Anne, Eleanor M. Miller, and Hans O. Mauksch. "The Integration of Work: Second-order Analysis of Qualitative Research." In *The Worth of Women's Work: A Qualitative Synthesis.* Statham, Anne, Eleanor M. Miller, and Hans O. Mauksch, eds. Albany, N.Y.: State University of New York Press, 1988:11–35.

Statistical Abstract of the United States. Washington D.C.: Bureau of the Census, published annually.

Stecklow, Steve. "Private Groups Compete for the Chance to Create New Schools with Public Funds." *Wall Street Journal*, January 24, 1994:B1, B4.

Stecklow, Steve. "SAT Scores Rise Strongly after Test Is Overhauled." *Wall Street Journal*, August 24, 1995:B1, B12.

Stein, Leonard I. "The Doctor–Nurse Game." In *Down to Earth Sociology: Introductory Readings*, 5th ed., James M. Henslin, ed. New York: Free Press, 1988:102–109.

Steinberg, Laurence, Stanford Dornbusch, and Bradford Brown. *Beyond the Classroom.* New York: Simon & Shuster, 1996.

Stengel, Richard. "South Africa's Mandela's First Year." America Online, May 4, 1995.

Stevens, Amy, and Sarah Lubman. "Deciding Moment of the Trial May Have Been Five Months Ago." *Wall Street Journal*, May 1, 1992:A6.

Stevenson, David Lee, and David P. Baker. "Shadow Education and Allocation in Formal Schooling in Japan." In *Haves and Have-Nots: An International Reader on Social Inequality*, James Curtis and Lorne Tepperman, eds. Englewood Cliffs, N.J.: Prentice Hall, 1994:352–359.

Stevenson, Richard W. "Catering to Consumers' Ethnic Needs." *New York Times*, January 23, 1992.

Stinnett, Nicholas. "Strong Families." In *Marriage and Family in a Changing Society*, 4th ed., James M. Henslin, ed. New York: Free Press, 1992:496–507.

Stipp, David. "Einstein Bird Has Scientists Atwitter over Mental Feats." *Wall Street Journal*, May 9, 1990:A1, A4.

Stipp, David. "Himalayan Tree Could Serve as Source of Anticancer Drug Taxol, Team Says." *Wall Street Journal*, April 20, 1992:B4.

Stockard, Jean, and Miriam M. Johnson. *Sex Roles: Sex Inequality and Sex Role Development.* Englewood Cliffs, N.J.: Prentice Hall, 1980.

Stockwell, John. "The Dark Side of U.S. Foreign Policy." *Zeta Magazine*, February 1989:36–48.

Stodgill, Ralph M. *Handbook of Leadership: A Survey of Theory and Research.* New York: Free Press, 1974.

Stone, Gregory P. "City Shoppers and Urban Identification: Observations on the Social Psychology of City Life." *American Journal of Sociology, 60,* November 1954:276–284.

Stone, Michael H. "Murder." *Psychiatric Clinics of North America, 12,* 3, September 1989:643–651.

Stouffer, Samuel A., Arthur A. Lumsdaine, Marion Harper Lumsdaine, Robin M. Williams, Jr., M. Brewster Smith, Irving L. Janis, Shirley A. Star, and Leonard S. Cottrell, Jr. *The American Soldier: Combat and Its Aftermath*, Vol. 2. New York: Wiley, 1949.

Stout, Hillary. "Harvard Team Says That AIDS Is Accelerating." *Wall Street Journal*, June 4, 1992:B10.

Straus, Murray A. "Victims and Aggressors in Marital Violence." *American Behavioral Scientist, 23,* May–June 1980:681–704.

Straus, Murray A. "Explaining Family Violence." In *Marriage and Family in a Changing Society*, 4th ed., James M. Henslin, ed. New York: Free Press, 1992:344–356.

Straus, Murray A., and Richard J. Gelles. "Violence in American Families: How Much Is There and Why Does It Occur?" In *Troubled Relationships*, Elam W. Nunnally, Catherine S. Chilman, and Fred M. Cox, eds. Newbury Park, Calif.: Sage, 1988:141–162.

Straus, Murray A., Richard J. Gelles, and Suzanne K. Steinmetz. *Behind Closed Doors: Violence in the American Family*. New York: Anchor/Doubleday, 1980.

Straus, Roger A. "The Sociologist as a Marketing Research Consultant." *Journal of Applied Sociology*, 8, 1991:65–75.

Stryker, Sheldon. "Symbolic Interactionism: Themes and Variations." In *Social Psychology: Sociological Perspectives*, Morris Rosenberg and Ralph H. Turner, eds. New Brunswick, N.J.: Transaction, 1990.

Sulloway, Frank J. *Born to Rebel: Birth Order, Family Dynamics, and Creative Lives*. New York: Vintage Books, 1997.

Sumner, William Graham. *Folkways: A Study in the Sociological Importance of Usages, Manners, Customs, Mores, and Morals*. New York: Ginn, 1906.

Sun, Lena H. "China Seeks Ways to Protect Elderly." *Washington Post*, October 23, 1990:A1.

Sun, Lena H. "A Great Leap Back: Chinese Women Losing Jobs, Status as Ancient Ways Subvert Socialist Ideal." *Washington Post*, February 16, 1993:A1.

Sutherland, Edwin H. *Criminology*. Philadelphia: Lippincott, 1924.

Sutherland, Edwin H. *Principles of Criminology*, 4th ed. Philadelphia: Lippincott, 1947.

Sutherland, Edwin H. *White Collar Crime*. New York: Dryden Press, 1949.

Sutherland, Edwin H., and Donald Cressey. *Criminology*, 9th ed. Philadelphia: Lippincott, 1974.

Sutherland, Edwin H., Donald R. Cressey, and David F. Luckenbill. *Principles of Criminology*, 11th ed. Dix Hills, N.Y.: General Hall, 1992.

Suzuki, Bob H. "Asian-American Families." In *Marriage and Family in a Changing Society*, 2nd ed., James M. Henslin, ed. New York: Free Press, 1985:104–119.

Swedish Institute, The. "Health and Medical Care in Sweden." July 1990:1–4.

Swedish Institute, The. "Fact Sheets on Sweden." February 1992.

Sweezy, Paul M., and Harry Magdoff. "Globalization—to What End? Part II." *Monthly Review*, 43, 10, March 1992:1–19.

Sykes, Gresham M., and David Matza. "Techniques of Neutralization." In *Down to Earth Sociology: Introductory Readings*, 5th ed., James M. Henslin, ed. New York: Free Press, 1988:225–231. First published in 1957.

Szasz, Thomas S. *The Myth of Mental Illness*, rev. ed. New York: Harper & Row, 1986.

Szasz, Thomas S. "Mental Illness Is Still a Myth." In *Deviant Behavior 96/97*, Lawrence M. Salinger, ed. Guilford, Conn.: Dushkin, 1996:200–205.

Szelenyi, Szonja. "Social Inequality and Party Membership: Patterns of Recruitment in the Hungarian Socialist Workers' Party." *American Sociological Review*, 52, 1987:559–573.

Tannen, Deborah. *You Just Don't Understand: Women and Men in Conversation*. New York: Morrow, 1990.

Tanouye, Elyse. "Researchers Say Chinese Medicine May Aid in Prevention of Liver Cancer." *Wall Street Journal*, September 6, 1995:B1.

Tanouye, Elyse. "SmithKline to Pay $325 Million to Settle Federal Claims of Lab-Billing Fraud." *Wall Street Journal*, February 25, 1997:B8.

Tapia, Andres. "Churches Wary of Inner-City Islamic Inroads." *Christianity Today*, 38, 1, January 10, 1994:36–38.

Taylor, Raymond G., and Alexander I. Mechitov. "Russian Schools and the Legacies of the Soviet Era." *Education*, 115, 2, Winter 1994:260–263.

Taylor, Verta. "Social Movement Continuity: The Women's Movement in Abeyance." In *Social Movements: Readings on Their Emergence, Mobilization, and Dynamics*, Doug McAdam and David A. Snow, eds. Los Angeles: Roxbury Publishing, 1997:409–420.

Thayer, Stephen. "Encounters." *Psychology Today*, March 1988: 31–36.

Thomas, Paulette. "EPA Predicts Global Impact from Warming." *Wall Street Journal*, October 21, 1988:B5.

Thomas, Paulette. "U.S. Examiners Will Scrutinize Banks with Poor Minority-Lending Histories." *Wall Street Journal*, October 22, 1991:A2.

Thomas, Paulette. "Boston Fed Finds Racial Discrimination in Mortgage Lending Is Still Widespread." *Wall Street Journal*, October 9, 1992:A3.

Thomas, R. Roosevelt, Jr. "From Affirmative Action to Affirming Diversity." *Harvard Business Review*, 90, 2, March–April, 1990:107–117.

Thomas, William I., and Florian Znaniecki. *The Polish Peasant in Europe and America*. Chicago: University of Chicago Press, 1918.

Thompson, William E. "Hanging Tongues: A Sociological Encounter with the Assembly Line." In *Down to Earth Sociology: Introductory Readings*, 9th ed., James M. Henslin, ed. New York: Free Press, 1995:193–202.

Thornburg, David. "Why Wait for Bandwidth? Schools Can Teleconference, Even with Ordinary Phone Lines." *Electronic Learning*, 14, 3, November–December 1994:20.

Thorne, Barrie. "Children and Gender: Constructions of Difference." In *Theoretical Perspectives on Sexual Difference*, Deborah L. Rhode, ed. New Haven, Conn.: Yale University Press, 1990:100–113.

Thorne, Barrie, and Zella Luria. "Sexuality and Gender in Children's Daily Worlds." In *Down to Earth Sociology: Introductory Readings*, 7th ed., James M. Henslin, ed. New York: Free Press, 1993:133–144.

Thornton, Russell. *American Indian Holocaust and Survival: A Population History Since 1492*. Norman: University of Oklahoma Press, 1987.

Thrasher, Frederic M. *The Gang*. Chicago: University of Chicago Press, 1927.

Tilly, Charles. *From Mobilization to Revolution*. Reading, Mass.: Addison-Wesley, 1978.

Timasheff, Nicholas S. *War and Revolution*. Joseph F. Scheuer, ed. New York: Sheed & Ward, 1965.

Timerman, Jacobo. *Prisoner Without a Name, Cell Without a Number*. New York: Knopf, 1981.

Tobias, Andrew. "The 'Don't Be Ridiculous' Law." *Wall Street Journal*, May 31, 1995:A14.

Toby, Jackson. "To Get Rid of Guns in Schools, Get Rid of Some Students." *Wall Street Journal*, March 23, 1992:A12.

Toch, Thomas. "Violence in Schools." *U.S. News & World Report*, 115, 18, November 8, 1993:31–36.

Tocqueville, Alexis de. *The Old Regime and the French Revolution*. Stuart Gilbert, trans. Garden City, N.Y.: Doubleday Anchor, 1955. First published in 1856.

Tocqueville, Alexis de. *Democracy in America*, J. P. Mayer and Max Lerner, eds. New York: Harper & Row, 1966. First published in 1835.

Tolchin, Martin. "Surgeon General Asserts Smoking Is an Addiction." *New York Times*, May 17, 1988:A1, C4.

Tolchin, Martin. "Mildest Possible Penalty Is Imposed on Neil Bush." *New York Times*, April 19, 1991:D2.

Tönnies, Ferdinand. *Community and Society (Gemeinschaft und Gesellschaft)*, with a new introduction by John Samples. New Brunswick, N.J.: Transaction, 1988. First published in 1887.

Tordoff, William. "The Impact of Ideology on Development in the Third World." *Journal of International Development*, 4, 1, 1992:41–53.

Toynbee, Arnold. *A Study of History*, D. C. Somervell, abridger and ed. New York: Oxford University Press, 1946.

Treas, Judith. "Older Americans in the 1990s and Beyond." *Population Bulletin*, 50, 2, May 1995:1–46.

Treiman, Donald J. *Occupational Prestige in Comparative Perspective.* New York: Academic Press, 1977.

Trice, Harrison M., and Janice M. Beyer. "Cultural Leadership in Organization." *Organization Science*, 2, 2, May 1991:149–169.

Troeltsch, Ernst. *The Social Teachings of the Christian Churches.* New York: Macmillan, 1931.

Tucker, Belinda M., and Claudia Mitchell-Kernan. "New Trends in Black American Interracial Marriage: The Social Structural Context." *Journal of Marriage and the Family*, 52, 1990:209–218.

Tumin, Melvin M. "Some Principles of Social Stratification: A Critical Analysis." *American Sociological Review 18*, August 1953:394.

Turnbull, Colin M. "The Mountain People." In *Sociology 95/96*, Kurt Finsterbusch, ed. Sluice Dock, Conn.: Dushkin, 1995:6–15. First published in 1972.

Turner, Bryan S. "Outline of a Theory of Citizenship." *Sociology*, 24, 2, May 1990:189–217.

Turner, Jonathan H. *American Society: Problems of Structure.* New York: Harper & Row, 1972.

Turner, Jonathan H. *The Structure of Sociological Theory.* Homewood, Ill.: Dorsey, 1978.

Turner, Ralph H. "Collective Behavior." In *Handbook of Modern Sociology*, Robert E. L. Faris, ed. Chicago: Rand McNally, 1964:382–425.

Turner, Ralph H. "Race Riots Past and Present: A Cultural-Collective Behavior Approach." Paper presented at the annual meetings of the American Sociological Association, 1993.

Turner, Ralph H., and Lewis M. Killian. *Collective Behavior*, 2nd ed. Englewood Cliffs, N.J.: Prentice Hall, 1987.

Tye, Larry. "After Waco, the Focus Shifts to Other Cults." *The Boston Globe*, April 30, 1993:1, 22.

Udy, Stanley H., Jr. "Bureaucracy and Rationality in Weber's Organizational Theory: An Empirical Study." *American Sociological Review*, 24, December 1959:791–795.

Ullman, Edward, and Chauncey Harris. "The Nature of Cities." In *Urban Man and Society: A Reader in Urban Ecology*, Albert N. Cousins and Hans Nagpaul, eds. New York: Knopf, 1970:91–100.

UNICEF. *The State of the World's Children.* New York: Oxford University Press, 1995.

Uniform Crime Reports. Washington D.C.: FBI, published annually. United Nations.

United Nations Statistical Yearbook 1995–1996. New York: The United Nations, 1997.

U.S. Bureau of the Census. *Statistical Abstract of the United States: The National Data Book.* Washington, D.C.: U.S. Government Printing Office. Published annually.

U.S. Department of Health and Human Services, Public Health Service. *Healthy People 2000.* Washington, D.C.: U.S. Government Printing Office, 1990.

Usdansky, Margaret L. "English a Problem for Half of Miami." *USA Today*, April 3, 1992:A1, A3, A30.

Useem, Michael. *The Inner Circle: Large Corporations and the Rise of Business Political Activity in the U.S. and U.K.* New York: Oxford University Press, 1984.

Vande Berg, Leah R., and Diane Streckfuss. "Prime-Time Television's Portrayal of Women and the World of Work: A Demographic Profile." *Journal of Broadcasting and Electronic Media*, Spring 1992:195–208.

Van Lawick-Goodall, Jane. *In the Shadow of Man.* Boston: Houghton Mifflin, 1971.

van den Haag, Ernest. *Punishing Criminals: Concerning a Very Old and Painful Question.* New York: Basic Books, 1975.

Vasil, Latika, and Hannelore Wass. "Portrayal of the Elderly in the Media: A Literature Review and Implications for Educational Gerontologists." *Educational Gerontology*, 19, 1, January–February 1993:71–85.

Vaughan, Diane. "Uncoupling: The Social Construction of Divorce." In *Marriage and Family in a Changing Society*, 2nd ed., James M. Henslin, ed. New York: Free Press, 1985:429–439.

Vayda, Eugene, and Ralsa B. Deber. "The Canadian Health Care System: An Overview." *Social Science and Medicine*, 18, 1984:191–197.

Veblen, Thorstein. *The Theory of the Leisure Class.* New York: Macmillan, 1912.

Vega, William A. "Hispanic Families in the 1980s: A Decade of Research." *Journal of Marriage and the Family*, 52, November 1990:1015–1024.

Vernon, JoEtta A., J. Allen Williams, Jr., Terri Phillips, and Janet Wilson. "Media Stereotyping: A Comparison of the Way Elderly Women and Men Are Portrayed on Prime-Time Television." *Journal of Women and Aging*, 2, 4, 1990:55–58.

Violas, P. C. *The Training of the Urban Working Class: A History of Twentieth Century American Education.* Chicago: Rand McNally, 1978.

Volti, Rudi. *Society and Technological Change.* 3rd ed. New York: St. Martin's Press, 1995.

Von Hoffman, Nicholas. "Sociological Snoopers." *Transaction* 7, May 1970:4, 6.

Vygotsky, Lev. "The Development of Language and Emotion." In *Inside Social Life: Readings in Sociological Psychology and Microsociology*, Spencer Cahill, ed. Los Angeles: Roxbury, 1995:36–41.

Waddington, Conrad H. *The Man-Made Future.* New York: St. Martin's, 1978.

Wagley, Charles, and Marvin Harris. *Minorities in the New World.* New York: Columbia University Press, 1958.

Waldholz, Michael. "Computer Brain' Outperforms Doctors in Diagnosing Heart Attack Patients." *Wall Street Journal*, December 2, 1991:7B.

Waldholz, Michael. "Three-Drug Therapy May Suppress HIV." *Wall Street Journal*, January 30, 1996:B1, B6.

Waldman, Peter. "Riots in Bahrain Arouse Ire of Feared Monarchy as the U.S. Stands By." *Wall Street Journal*, June 12, 1995a:A1, A8.

Waldman, Peter. "As Arab Rulers Age, the Succession Issue Isn't Raised in Public." *Wall Street Journal*, January 9, 1996:A1, A11.

Walker, Michael. "Canadian Health Care Is a Model for Disaster." *Wall Street Journal*, October 18, 1991:A15.

Walker, Tom. " 'Edge Cities' Represent a Quiet Social Revolution." *Atlanta Journal*, September 29, 1991:C1.

Wallace, Anthony F. C. *Religion: An Anthropological View.* New York: Random House, 1966.

Wallerstein, Immanuel. *The Modern World System: Capitalist Agriculture and the Origins of the European World-Economy in the Sixteenth Century.* New York: Academic Press, 1974.

Wallerstein, Immanuel. *The Capitalist World-Economy.* New York: Cambridge University Press, 1979.

Wallerstein, Immanuel. *The Politics of the World-Economy: The States, the Movements, and the Civilizations.* Cambridge, England: Cambridge University Press, 1984.

Wallerstein, Immanuel. "Culture as the Ideological Battleground of the Modern World-system." In *Global Culture: Nationalism, Globalization, and Modernity*, Mike Featherstone, ed. London: Sage, 1990:31–55.

Wallerstein, Judith S., and Joan B. Kelly. "How Children React to Parental Divorce." In *Marriage and Family in a Changing Society*, 4th ed., James M. Henslin, ed. New York: Free Press, 1992:397–409.

Walters, Alan. "Let More Earnings Go to Shareholders. *Wall Street Journal*, October 31, 1995:A23.

Walters, Jonathan. "Chimps in the Mist." *USA Weekend*, May 18–20, 1990:24.

Warner, W. Lloyd, and Paul S. Hunt. *The Social Life of a Modern Community.* New Haven, Conn.: Yale University Press, 1941.

Warner, W. Lloyd, Paul S. Hunt, Marchia Meeker, and Kenneth Eels. *Social Class in America.* New York: Harper, 1949.

Warr, Mark. "Age, Peers, and Delinquency." *Criminology*, 31, 1, 1993:17–40.

Watson, J. Mark. "Outlaw Motorcyclists." In *Down to Earth Sociology: Introductory Readings*, 5th ed., James M. Henslin, ed. New York: Free Press, 1988:203–213.

Webb, Eugene J., Donald T. Campbell, Richard D. Schwartz, and Lee Sechrest. *Unobtrusive Measures: Nonreactive Research in the Social Sciences.* Chicago: Rand McNally, 1966.

Weber, Max. *Economy and Society*, G. Roth and C. Wittich, eds. Berkeley: University of California Press, 1978. First published in 1922.

Weber, Max. *From Max Weber: Essays in Sociology.* Hans Gerth and C. Wright Mills, trans. and ed. New York: Oxford University Press, 1946a.

Weber, Max. *The Theory of Social and Economic Organization*, A. M. Henderson and Talcott Parsons, trans., Talcott Parsons, ed. Glencoe, Ill.: Free Press, 1947. First published in 1913.

Weber, Max. *The Protestant Ethic and the Spirit of Capitalism.* New York: Scribner's, 1958. First published in 1904–1905.

Weber, Max. *Economy and Society.* Ephraim Fischoff, trans. New York: Bedminster Press, 1968. First published in 1922.

Webster, Pamela S., and A. Regula Herzog. "Effects of Parental Divorce and Memories of Family Problems on Relationships Between Adult Children and Their Parents." *Journal of Gerontology*, 50B, 1, 1995:S24-S34.

Weeks, John R. *Population: An Introduction to Concepts and Issues*, 5th ed. Belmont, Calif.: Wadsworth, 1994.

Wei, William. *The Asian American Movement.* Philadelphia: Temple University Press, 1993.

Weintraub, Richard M. "A Bride in India." *Washington Post*, February 28, 1988.

Weisburd, David, Stanton Wheeler, and Elin Waring. *Crimes of the Middle Classes: White-Collar Offenders in the Federal Courts.* New Haven, Conn.: Yale University Press, 1991.

Weisskopf, Michael. "Scientist Says Greenhouse Effect Is Setting In." In *Ourselves and Others: The Washington Post Sociology Companion*, Washington Post Writers Group, eds. Boston: Allyn and Bacon, 1992:297–298.

Weitzman, Lenore J. *The Divorce Revolution.* New York: Free Press, 1985.

Wells, Ken. " 'Coloreds' Struggle to Find Their Place in a Free South Africa." *Wall Street Journal*, December 6, 1995:A1, A6.

Welsh, Stephanie. "A Dangerous Rite of Passage." *Nation*, May 7, 1995.

Wenneker, Mark B., and Arnold M. Epstein. "Racial Inequalities in the Use of Procedures for Patients with Ischemic Heart Disease in Massachusetts." *Journal of the American Medical Association*, 261, 2, January 13, 1989:253–257.

Wertz, Richard W., and Dorothy C. Wertz. "Notes on the Decline of Midwives and the Rise of Medical Obstetricians." In *The Sociology of Health and Illness: Critical Perspectives*, Peter Conrad and Rochelle Kern, eds. New York: St. Martin's Press, 1981:165–183.

West, Candace, and Angela Garcia. "Conversational Shift Work: A Study of Topical Transitions Between Women and Men." *Social Problems*, 35, 1988:551–575.

Whetstone, Muriel L. "What Black Men and Women Should Do Now (About Black Men and Women)." *Ebony*, February 1996:135–138, 140.

White, Jack E. "Forgive Us Our Sins." *Time*, July 3, 1995:29.

White, James A. "When Employees Own Big Stake, It's a Buy Signal for Investors." *Wall Street Journal*, February 13, 1991:C1, C19.

Whorf, Benjamin. *Language, Thought, and Reality*, J. B. Carroll, ed. Cambridge, MA: MIT Press, 1956.

Whyte, Martin King. "Choosing Mates—The American Way." *Society*, March–April 1992:71–77.

Whyte, William H. *The City: Rediscovering the Center.* New York: Doubleday, 1989.

Whyte, William H. "Street Corner Society." In *Down to Earth Sociology: Introductory Readings*, 9th ed., James M. Henslin, ed. New York: Free Press, 1997:59–67.

Willhelm, Sidney M. "Can Marxism Explain America's Racism?" *Social Problems*, 28, December 1980:98–112.

Williams, Christine L. *Still a Man's World: Men Who Do Women's Work.* Berkeley: University of California Press, 1995.

Williams, Robin M., Jr. *American Society: A Sociological Interpretation*, 2nd ed. New York: Knopf, 1965.

Willie, Charles V. "Caste, Class, and Family Life Experiences." *Research in Race and Ethnic Relations*, 6, 1991:65–84.

Wilson, Edward O. *Sociobiology: The New Synthesis.* Cambridge, Mass.: Harvard University Press, 1975.

Wilson, James Q. "Is Incapacitation the Answer to the Crime Problem?" In *Taking Sides: Clashing Views on Controversial Social Issues*, 7th ed., Kurt Finsterbusch and George McKenna, eds. Guilford, Conn.: Dushkin, 1992:318–324.

Wilson, James Q. "Lock 'Em Up and Other Thoughts on Crime." *New York Times Magazine*, March 9, 1975:11, 44–48.

Wilson, James Q., and Richard J. Hernstein. *Crime and Human Nature.* New York: Simon & Schuster, 1985.

Wilson, William Julius. *The Declining Significance of Race: Blacks and Changing American Institutions.* Chicago: University of Chicago Press, 1978.

Wilson, William Julius. *The Truly Disadvantaged: The Inner City, the Underclass, and Public Policy.* Chicago: University of Chicago Press, 1987.

Wilson, William Julius. *When Work Disappears: The World of the New Urban Poor.* Chicago: University of Chicago Press, 1996.

Winslow, Ron. "Study Finds Blacks Get Fewer Bypasses." *Wall Street Journal,* March 18, 1992:B1.

Winslow, Ron. "More Doctors Are Adding On-Line Tools to Their Kits." *Wall Street Journal,* October 7, 1994:B1, B4.

Winslow, Ron. "Smoking Increases Heart-Attack Risk Fivefold for People in Their 30s and 40s." *Wall Street Journal,* August 18, 1995:B5.

Wirth, Louis. "Urbanism as a Way of Life." *American Journal of Sociology, 44,* July 1938:1–24.

Wirth, Louis. "The Problem of Minority Groups." In *The Science of Man in the World Crisis,* Ralph Linton, ed. New York: Columbia University Press, 1945.

Wohl, R. Richard, and Anselm Strauss. "Symbolic Representation and the Urban Milieu." *American Journal of Sociology, 63,* March 1958:523–532.

Wolff, Michael, et al. *Where We Stand: Can America Make It in the Global Race for Wealth and Happiness?* New York: Bantam Books, 1992.

Wolfgang, Marvin E., and Franco Ferracuti. *The Subculture of Violence: Toward an Integrated Theory in Criminology.* London: Tavistock, 1967.

Womack, James P., Daniel T. Jones, and Daniel Roos. *The Machine That Changed the World: The Story of Lean Production.* New York: Harper Perrenial, 1991.

Woodward, Kenneth L. "Heaven." *Newsweek, 113,* 13, March 27, 1989:52–55.

World Health Organization. *Constitution of the World Health Organization.* New York: World Health Organization Interim Commission, 1946.

Worsley, Peter. *The Trumpet Shall Sound.* London: MacGibbon and Kee, 1957.

Wouters, Cas. "On Status Competition and Emotion Management: The Study of Emotions as a New Field." *Theory, Culture & Society, 9,* 1992:229–252.

Wray, Linda A. "Public Policy Implications of an Ethnically Diverse Elderly Population." *Journal of Cross-Cultural Gerontology, 6,* 1991:243–257.

Wright, Erik Olin. *Class.* London: Verso, 1985.

Wright, Lawrence. "One Drop of Blood." *New Yorker,* July 25, 1994:46–50, 52–55.

Wright, Lawrence. "Double Mystery." *New Yorker,* August 7, 1995:45–62.

Wrong, Dennis H. "The Over-Socialized Conception of Man in Modern Sociology." *American Sociological Review, 26,* April 1961:185–193.

Wysocki, Bernard, Jr. "Influx of Immigrants Adds New Vitality to Housing Market." *Wall Street Journal,* October 10, 1996:A1, A2.

Yearbook of American and Canadian Churches. Nashville, Tenn.: Abingdon. Various editions.

Yellowbird, Michael, and C. Matthew Snipp. "American Indian Families." In *Minority Families in the United States: A Multicultural Perspective,* Ronald L. Taylor, ed. Englewood Cliffs, N.J.: Prentice Hall, 1994:179–201.

Yinger, J. Milton. *Toward a Field Theory of Behavior: Personality and Social Structure.* New York: McGraw-Hill, 1965.

Yinger, J. Milton. *The Scientific Study of Religion.* New York: Macmillan, 1970.

Young, Laurie E. "The Overlooked Contributions of Women to the Development of American Sociology: An Examination of AJS Articles from 1895–1926." Paper presented at the 1995 meetings of the American Sociological Association.

Zachary, G. Pascal. "Behind Stocks' Surge Is an Economy in Which Big U.S. Firms Thrive." *Wall Street Journal,* November 22, 1995:A1, A5.

Zakuta, Leo. "Equality in North American Marriages." In *Marriage and Family in a Changing Society,* 3rd ed., ed. James M. Henslin. New York: Free Press, 1989:105–114.

Zald, Mayer N. "Looking Backward to Look Forward: Reflections on the Past and the Future of the Resource Mobilization Research Program." In *Frontiers in Social Movement Theory,* Aldon D. Morris and Carol McClurg Mueller, eds. New Haven, Conn.: Yale University Press, 1992:326–348.

Zald, Mayer N., and John D. McCarthy, eds. *Social Movements in an Organizational Society.* New Brunswick, N.J.: Transaction, 1987.

Zawitz, Marianne W. *Report to the Nation on Crime and Justice,* 2nd ed. Washington, D.C.: U.S. Department of Justice, Bureau of Justice Statistics, July 1988.

Zellner, William W. *Countercultures: A Sociological Analysis.* New York: St. Martin's, 1995.

Zerubavel, Eviatar. *The Fine Line: Making Distinctions in Everyday Life.* New York: Free Press, 1991.

Zey, Mary. *Banking on Fraud: Drexel, Junk Bonds, and Buyouts.* Hawthorne, N.Y.: Aldine de Gruyter, 1993.

Ziegler, Bart. "Banned by Comdex, Purveyors of Porn Put on Their Own Show." *Wall Street Journal,* November 14, 1995:B1, B8.

Zola, Irving K. *Socio-Medical Inquiries.* Philadelphia: Temple University Press, 1983.

Zorbaugh, Harvey W. *The Gold Coast and the Slum.* Chicago: University of Chicago Press, 1929.

Zou, Heng Fu. "'The Spirit of Capitalism' and Long-Run Growth." *European Journal of Political Economy, 10,* 2, July 1994:279–293.

Zuboff, Shoshana. "New Worlds of Computer-Mediated Work." In *Down to Earth Sociology: Introductory Readings,* 6th ed., James M. Henslin, ed. New York: Free Press, 1991:476–485.

Name Index

Subject Index

Emotional overload, 434–35
Emotions
    and gender, 71
    global aspects of, 71–72
    as social control, 73
    socialization into, 71–73
Employee stock ownership, 183
Empty nest, 442–43
Endogamy, 431–32
Energy shortage, 637
"English Only" movement, 334
Enterprise zones, 579
Environment, the. *See* Natural
    environment
Environmental movement, 638–40
Environmental racism, 637
Environmental sociology, 640–41
Episcopalians, 512
Equal Rights Amendment, 266, 292, 602
Equality
    and types of society, 146–50
    as a value, 46
Eskimos, 42, 193, 352–53, 421
Eta, 316
Ethics of social research, 136–38
Ethnic villagers, 581
Ethnic
    cleansing, 324, 325
    conflicts, 623
    groups, 314
    identity, 326–27
    work, 326–27
Ethnicity. *See* Race
Ethnocentrism, 36, 639
Ethnomethodology, 111–13
Euthanasia, 537–38
Evangelicals, 512
Evangelism, 508, 514
Everyday life, 104–15
    and emotions, 71–72
    and eye contact, 9, 10
    and gender inequality, 75, 296–97
    and kissing, 107
    sign-vehicles, 109–10
    as a stage, 108–11, 113–15
    symbolic interactionist perspective of,
        104–15
    symbols and, 21–22
    and touching, 9, 10, 107
Evolutionary theories of social change, 634
Exogamy, 431–32
Experiments, 130–33
Ex-spouses, 455–56
Extinction of species, 638, 640

Face-saving behavior, 111
Fads, 600–1
False class consciousness, 229
Family, 426–57. *See also* Marriage
    abuse in, 120–33, 456–58, 606
    African-American, 443–44
    Asian-American, 443, 445–46
    blended, 449
    conflict perspective of, 435–37
    defined, 430–31
    distance learning, 482
    education replacing functions of, 475
    emotional overload of, 434–35
    functionalist perspective on, 23–26,
        433–35

future of, 459
gay, 449
as harried group, 430
intentional, 450
Latino, 444–45
life cycle, 438–43
Native-American, 445, 446–47
and the new technology, 448
one-parent, 447
and social class, 442
as socializing agent, 77, 198
symbolic interactionist perspective of,
    437–38
without children, 447, 448
Family life
    and gender socialization, 73
    in the past, 25–26
    and social class, 265–66
Farming, 391
Fashions, 601
Fatherhood, serial, 455
Fathers, absent, 455, 603
FBI, 511, 603
Fears
    of loss of work, 269
Female circumcision, 228, 288, 289
Female infanticide, 569
Females. *See also* Gender, Women
    social stratification and 226, 228,
        282–83, 287–92
Femininity, 283–86, 293–95
Feminism, 292–93
Feminist interpretation of violence, 304
Feminization of poverty, 271–72
Feral children, 62
Fertilization, in vitro, 448
Fieldwork. *See* Participant observation
Final Exit, 537
Folkways, 43
Football, 95
Footbinding, 288, 291
Formal organizations. *See* Bureaucracies
Fossil fuels, 636–37
Fossils, 519
"Four noble truths," 504
France, 407, 452, 453, 478
Free will, 87, 199
Freedom, as a value, 46
French revolution, 10, 11
Full Gospel Motorcycle Association, 517
Functional equivalent, 494–95
Functional illiteracy, 484
Functionalist perspective
    on the aged, 355–57
    on deviance, 203–8
    on divorce, 24–25
    on education, 77–78, 471–75
    and explanation of divorce, 24–26
    on marriage and family, 433–35
    on medicine, 525–26
    overview of, 21, 23–26
    on politics, 418–19
    on pornography, 203
    on prejudice, 321–22
    on religion, 493–96
    on social class, 232–33, 473–74
    on social control, 194
    on social institutions, 100–102
    on social stratification, 230–32, 233
    on work, 387–88

Fundamentalist revival, 514

G7, 622, 635
Gangs, 206
Gated fortresses, 584
Gatekeeping, 473–74
Gemeinschaft, 102–4, 563, 619–21
Gender. *See also* Men, Women
    and abuse, 120–33, 303–4, 457–58, 606
    and age, 351–52
    and AIDS, 541
    and the Amish, 105
    automobile, effects on, 622–23
    and biology, 283–86
    and childbirth, 290, 291, 530
    and conversations, 297
    in the corporate world, 180, 181
    and discrimination, 287–306, 319, 346,
        352
    defined, 283
    doctorates and, 294–95
    and education, 293–95, 471
    and emotions, 71
    and eye contact, 9, 10
    and family life, 435–38
    and the future, 305–6
    in global perspective, 228
    and housework, 435–37, 453, 454
    and infanticide, 569
    and isolation, 362
    and marriage, 431, 435–38
    and medicine, 529, 530
    in the military, 303
    and murder, 304
    networking, 155
    and occupations, 287–88, 293–95
    and politics, 288, 304–5
    and population growth in Least
        Industrialized Nations, 560
    and poverty, 271–72, 361, 364–65
    and prestige, 286
    and religion, 499
    and sick role, 526
    and social control, 282–83
    and social mobility, 268
    socialization into, 73, 76–77, 78–80, 81,
        287, 293–95
    and stratification, 226, 228, 235, 236,
        268, 282–83, 287–90, 292–93
    and television images, 74, 75
    and touching, 9, 10, 107
    and traditional authority, 406
    and violence, 228, 286, 287, 288, 289,
        291, 303–4, 578, 580
    and work, 287–88, 296–302, 392–93
Gender gap
    in pay, 9, 10, 297–99
    in politics, 416
Gender messages, 73–76
Generalize, 8, 53, 129
Generalized other, 68
Genocide, 310, 324, 325
Gentrification, 576
Georgia Pacific Lumber Co., 640
Germany, 115, 170, 312, 314, 348, 386,
    396, 409, 411, 452, 453, 496
Gesellschaft, 102–4, 145, 619–21
Gestapo, 411
Gestures, 38–39
    in Italy, 39

Photo Credits